The Wiley Handbook
of Psychometric Testing

The Wiley Handbook of Psychometric Testing

A Multidisciplinary Reference on Survey, Scale and Test Development

Volume One

Edited by

Paul Irwing
Tom Booth
David J. Hughes

WILEY Blackwell

This paperback edition first published 2020
© 2018 John Wiley & Sons Ltd

All rights reserved. No part of this publication may be reproduced, stored in a retrieval system, or transmitted, in any form or by any means, electronic, mechanical, photocopying, recording or otherwise, except as permitted by law. Advice on how to obtain permission to reuse material from this title is available at http://www.wiley.com/go/permissions.

The right of Paul Irwing, Tom Booth, and David J. Hughes to be identified as the authors of the editorial material in this work has been asserted in accordance with law.

Registered Offices
John Wiley & Sons, Inc., 111 River Street, Hoboken, NJ 07030, USA
John Wiley & Sons Ltd, The Atrium, Southern Gate, Chichester, West Sussex, PO19 8SQ, UK

Editorial Office
The Atrium, Southern Gate, Chichester, West Sussex, PO19 8SQ, UK

For details of our global editorial offices, customer services, and more information about Wiley products visit us at www.wiley.com.

Wiley also publishes its books in a variety of electronic formats and by print-on-demand. Some content that appears in standard print versions of this book may not be available in other formats.

Limit of Liability/Disclaimer of Warranty
While the publisher and author have used their best efforts in preparing this book, they make no representations or warranties with respect to the accuracy or completeness of the contents of this book and specifically disclaim any implied warranties of merchantability or fitness for a particular purpose. It is sold on the understanding that the publisher is not engaged in rendering professional services and neither the publisher nor the authors shall be liable for damages arising herefrom. If professional advice or other expert assistance is required, the services of a competent professional should be sought.

Library of Congress Cataloging-in-Publication Data

Names: Irwing, Paul, editor.
Title: The Wiley handbook of psychometric testing : a multidisciplinary reference
  on survey, scale and test development / edited by Paul Irwing,
  Manchester University, UK, Tom Booth, The University of Edinburgh,
  Edinburgh, UK, David J. Hughes, Manchester Business School, Manchester, UK.
Description: First Edition. | Hoboken : Wiley, 2018. | Includes bibliographical
  references and index. |
Identifiers: LCCN 2017041032 (print) | LCCN 2017061203 (ebook) |
  ISBN 9781118489826 (pdf) | ISBN 9781118489703 (epub) |
  ISBN 9781118489833 (cloth : alk. paper) | ISBN 9781119121176 (pbk. : alk. paper)
Subjects: LCSH: Psychometrics. | Psychological tests.
Classification: LCC BF39 (ebook) | LCC BF39 .W545 2018 (print) |
  DDC 150.28/7–dc23
LC record available at https://lccn.loc.gov/2017041032

Cover image: Printed with permission from Anna Brown
Cover design by Wiley

Set in 10/12pt Galliard by SPi Global, Pondicherry, India

Contents

Notes on Contributors to Volume 1	vii
Preface	xi
Introduction	xiii

VOLUME I

Part I Practical Foundations — 1

1 Test Development — 3
   Paul Irwing and David J. Hughes

2 Classical Test Theory and Item Response Theory — 49
   Christine E. DeMars

3 Item Generation — 75
   Kristin M. Morrison and Susan Embretson

4 Survey Sampling and Propensity Score Matching — 95
   Bo Lu and Stanley Lemeshow

5 Sample Size Planning for Confirmatory Factor Models: Power and Accuracy for Effects of Interest — 113
   Ken Kelley and Keke Lai

6 Missing Data Handling Methods — 139
   Craig K. Enders and Amanda N. Baraldi

7 Causal Indicators in Psychometrics — 187
   Aja L. Murray and Tom Booth

Part II Identifying and Analyzing Scales — 209

8 Fundamentals of Common Factor Analysis — 211
   Stanley A. Mulaik

9	Estimation Methods in Latent Variable Models for Categorical Outcome Variables *Li Cai and Irini Moustaki*	253
10	Rotation *Robert I. Jennrich*	279
11	The Number of Factors Problem *Marieke E. Timmerman, Urbano Lorenzo-Seva, and Eva Ceulemans*	305
12	Bifactor Models in Psychometric Test Development *Fang Fang Chen and Zugui Zhang*	325
13	Nonnormality in Latent Trait Modelling *Dylan Molenaar and Conor V. Dolan*	347
14	Multidimensional Scaling: An Introduction *William G. Jacoby and David J. Ciuk*	375
15	Unidimensional Item Response Theory *Rob R. Meijer and Jorge N. Tendeiro*	413

Notes on Contributors to Volume 1

Amanda N. Baraldi is Assistant Professor of Psychology at Oklahoma State University. Dr. Baraldi received her doctorate in Quantitative Psychology from the Arizona State University in 2015. Dr. Baraldi's current research interests include missing data analyses, methods for assessing mediation, longitudinal growth modelling, and health and prevention research.

Tom Booth is Lecturer in Quantitative Research Methods in the Department of Psychology, University of Edinburgh. His primary methodological interests are in generalized latent variable modelling. His applied work covers individual differences, organizational, and health psychology.

Li Cai is Professor in the Advanced Quantitative Methodology program in the UCLA Graduate School of Education and Information Studies. He also serves as Director of the National Center for Research on Evaluation, Standards, and Student Testing (CRESST). In addition, he is affiliated with the UCLA Department of Psychology. His methodological research agenda involves the development of latent variable models that have wide-ranging applications in educational, psychological, and health-related domains of study.

Eva Ceulemans is Professor of Quantitative Data Analysis at the Faculty of Psychology and Educational Sciences, University of Leuven, Belgium. Her research focuses on the development of new techniques for modelling multivariate time series data and multi-group data, and exploring individual or group differences therein. To this end, she often combines general principles of cluster analysis with dimension reduction (principal component analysis, factor analysis) and/or regression.

Fang Fang Chen received her M.S. in psychology from Peking University, her doctoral training in Social and Quantitative Psychology from Arizona State University, and completed her post-doctoral training at the University of North Carolina at Chapel Hill. Her methodological work focuses on measurement invariance and the bifactor model. Dr. Chen was an assistant professor of psychology at the University of Delaware, and now is a senior research biostatistician at the Nemours Center for the HealthCare Delivery Science.

David J. Ciuk is an assistant professor in the Department of Government at the Franklin & Marshall College. His academic interests center on public opinion and political psychology. His research aims to build a better understanding of the attitude formation process in the mass public. More specifically, he looks at how morals and values, policy information, and political identity affect political attitudes. He is also interested in survey experimental designs, measurement, and various public health issues.

Christine E. DeMars serves at James Madison University as a professor in the department of graduate psychology and a senior assessment specialist in the Center for Assessment and Research Studies. She teaches courses in Item Response Theory, Classical Test Theory, and Generalizability Theory, and supervises Ph.D. students. Her research interests include applied and theoretical topics in item response theory, differential item functioning, test-taking motivation, and other issues in operational testing.

Conor V. Dolan is Professor at the VU University, Amsterdam. His research interests include: covariance structure modelling, mixture analyses, modelling of multivariate intelligence test scores, and modelling genotype-environment interplay.

Susan Embretson is Professor of Psychology at the Georgia Institute of Technology. She has been recognized nationally and internationally for her programmatic research on integrating cognitive theory into psychometric item response theory models and into the design of measurement tasks. She has received awards from the National Council on Measurement and Education; American Educational Research Association; and the American Psychological Association Division for research and theory on item generation from cognitive theory.

Craig K. Enders is a Professor in the Department of Psychology at UCLA where he is a member of the Quantitative program area. Professor Enders teaches graduate-level courses in missing data analyses, multilevel modelling, and longitudinal modelling. The majority of his research focuses on analytic issues related to missing data analyses and multilevel modelling. His book, *Applied Missing Data Analysis*, was published with Guilford Press in 2010.

David J. Hughes is an Organisational Psychologist at Manchester Business School. His research interests centre on individual differences and can be broken down into three main areas: the theory and measurement of individual differences, individual differences at work, and individual differences in financial behavior. He is interested in psychometric test evaluation and his statistical interests revolve around generalized latent variable models, in particular structural equation modelling, factor models, and other models appropriate for multivariate data with complex structures.

Paul Irwing is Professor of Psychometrics at the Manchester Business School. He chaired the Psychometrics at Work Research Group and is a director of the psychometric publishing company E-metrixx. He has authored two research and two commercial psychometric measures. He is known for research on sex differences and pioneering work on the general factor of personality. His current research concerns the 11+ Factor Model of Personality, and the newly proposed individual difference of Personality Adaptability.

William G. Jacoby is Professor of Political Science at Michigan State University and Editor of the *American Journal of Political Science*. He is the former Director of the Inter-university Consortium for Political and Social Research (ICPSR) Summer Program in Quantitative Methods of Social Research and former Editor of the Journal of Politics. Professor Jacoby's areas of professional interest include mass political behavior and quantitative methodology (especially scaling methods, measurement theory, and statistical graphics).

Robert I. Jennrich began his work with the development of the first internationally used statistical software package BMD. His main field is statistical computing. He contributed to the development of nearly half of the 25 programs in this package. Because of this, he was a member of the 1972 Soviet-American Scientific Exchange Delegation on Computing. Since these early days, he has published papers on stepwise linear and non-linear regression, stepwise discriminant analysis, goodness-of-fit testing for covariance structure analysis, and a number of papers in factor analysis, primarily on rotation. He has recently been nominated for a lifetime achievement award, which he unfortunately didn't get.

Ken Kelley is Professor of Information Technology, Analytics, and Operations (ITAO) and the Associate Dean for Faculty and Research in the Mendoza College of Business at the University of Notre Dame. Professor Kelley's work is on quantitative methodology, where he focuses on the development, improvement, and evaluation of statistical methods and measurement issues. Professor Kelley's specialties are in the areas of research design, effect size estimation and confidence interval formation, longitudinal data analysis, and statistical computing. In addition to his methodological work, Professor Kelley collaborates with colleagues on a variety of important topics applying methods. Professor Kelley is an Accredited Professional Statistician™ (PStat®) by the American Statistical Association, associate editor of *Psychological Methods*, and recipient of the Anne Anastasi early career award by the American Psychological Association's Division of Evaluation, Measurement, & Statistics, and a fellow of the American Psychological Association.

Keke Lai is Assistant Professor of Quantitative Psychology at University of California, Merced. His research interests include structural equation modelling and multilevel modelling.

Stanley Lemeshow earned his Ph.D. at UCLA, and his MSPH at UNC. He has coauthored three textbooks: Applied Logistic Regression; Applied Survival Analysis; and Sampling of Populations – Methods and Applications. His honors include: the Wiley Lifetime Award (2003); UCLA School of Public Health Alumni Hall of Fame (2006); Fellow of the AAAS (2003); Distinguished Graduate Alumnus (Biostatistics) – UNC Graduate School Centennial (2003); Fellow of the ASA (1995); and the Statistics Section Award of the APHA (1995).

Urbano Lorenzo-Seva is a professor in the Department of Psychology at Universitat Rovira i Virgili, Spain. He is the coauthor of FACTOR, a free-shared software to compute exploratory factor analysis, and has published numerous articles related to this subject. His research interests include the development of new methods for exploratory data analysis, and applied psychometric research. He has taught data analysis at university level and in short courses for many years.

Bo Lu earned his Ph.D. in Statistics from the University of Pennsylvania. He is an associate professor of Biostatistics at the Ohio State University. His research expertise includes causal inference with propensity score based adjustment for observational data, survey sampling design and analysis, statistical models for missing data. He has been PIs for multiple NIH and AHRQ grants and served as the lead statistician for the Ohio Medicaid Assessment Survey series since 2008.

Rob R. Meijer is Professor in Psychometrics and Statistics at the University of Groningen, the Netherlands. His work is in item response theory and applications of testing. He is also interested in educational assessment and educational and personnel selection.

Dylan Molenaar is Assistant Professor at the Department of Psychology, University of Amsterdam. His research interests include: item response theory, factor analysis, and response time modelling.

Kristin M. Morrison is an advanced Ph.D. student at the Georgia Institute of Technology. She has published and presented work on item generation at various conferences and meetings. Other research interests include computer adaptive testing, multistage testing, educational research, and cognitive complexity.

Irini Moustaki is Professor of Social Statistics at the London School of Economics and Political Science. Her research interests are in the areas of latent variable models and structural equation models. Her methodological work includes treatment of missing data, longitudinal data, detection of outliers, goodness-of-fit tests, and advanced estimation methods. Furthermore, she has made methodological and applied contributions in the areas of comparative cross-national studies and epidemiological studies on rare diseases. She has coauthored two books on latent variable models. She was elected Editor in Chief of the journal *Psychometrika* in November 2014.

Stanley A. Mulaik is Emeritus Professor in the School of Psychology, Georgia Institute of Technology. His work has broadly focussed on latent variable models and the underlying philosophy of causality. He is the author of the influential texts, *Foundations of Factor Analysis* and *Linear Causal Modeling with Structural Equations*.

Aja L. Murray is a Research Associate in the Violence Research Centre, Institute of Criminology, University of Cambridge. Her research interests include psychometrics and childhood and adolescent mental health developmental.

Jorge N. Tendeiro is Assistant Professor at the University of Groningen, the Netherlands. He has research interests within item response theory (IRT), with a large focus on person-fit analyses. Besides (co)authoring several papers on this topic, he is also the author of the PerFit R package. He is currently extending person-fit approaches to a broader type of IRT, which include the unfolding model.

Marieke E. Timmerman is a professor in multivariate data analysis at the Heymans Institute for Psychological Research at the University of Groningen, The Netherlands. Her research focuses on the development of models for multivariate data with complex structures, to achieve an understanding of the processes underlying these, mainly psychological, data. Her research interests are latent variable modelling, data reduction methods, including multiset models, and classification. She serves as an associate editor of *Psychometrika*.

Zugui Zhang obtained his Ph.D. in biostatistics from the University of Iowa. He is the lead Biostatistician of the Value Institute of Christiana Care Health System, Assistant Professor at Thomas Jefferson University, and Joint Professor at the University of Delaware. He has a broad background in biostatistics, health outcomes research, quality of life, public health, epidemiology, and health economics. He has worked extensively on large international and national, multicenter, randomized clinical trials, and observational studies.

Preface

The existence of this volume owes itself to both opportunity, and many hours of coffee fuelled conversation, the general form of which would run; "have you seen X's critique of Y…? Did you see the special issue on X…? Wouldn't it be great if we could do something to help improve methods knowledge within psychology?" Given our collective interest in individual difference psychology, our musings would often be triggered by a favourite conversation – the inappropriate application of principal components analysis. We all taught, and continue to teach, research methods and statistics at our institutions; we all develop and evaluate psychometrics in our research, but the idea of something larger – a conference, a journal special edition, a book – continued to surface. There are many excellent papers, books, and courses that cover research methods relevant for psychometrics but, we thought, not a single resource that brings cutting-edge knowledge from the journals in our fields together in an accessible manner.

So, imagine our delight and trepidation when Paul was invited to edit a handbook on psychometric testing. We could finally put our coffee-shop "wisdom" to the test! Although, "Who reads books anymore? Surely, it will be a ton of work editing such a volume? Come to think of it, we're not knowledgeable enough in half of the areas we need to cover… How will we ensure we get expert authors?" We had many questions and doubts and committing to producing this book was not a lightly taken decision. Nevertheless, we returned consistently to one question: how else can we do our small part in improving the availability of cutting-edge methodological knowledge within the field of psychometrics? We had decided (or at least Tom and David had, Paul took some convincing!) that together we would try to produce a book which covered the core topics in psychometrics, a book that harnessed the work of excellent authors, a book that we would like to have, a book that, if used, would see methodological awareness grow, and statistical practice improve.

At the outset of planning and preparing this book, all three of us were at the University of Manchester's Business School; Tom and David were Ph.D. students, and Paul, our supervisor, a Reader of Organisational Psychology. At the time of writing this preface, almost five years later, Ph.Ds are a distant memory, Tom and David have moved on several times (or moved on and then back to Manchester in David's case), and Paul is now a professor. This book, *The Handbook*, has been a labour of love and frustration throughout these five years, five years that have not only seen workplace changes but also a quite remarkable series of injuries and ill-health, several relegations for our relative football (soccer) teams, oh, and a wedding!

Now, here we are, a complete volume that looks remarkably close to our initial proposal and we are delighted with it. Our intention, succinctly described in the letters we sent to authors was to write chapters on key topics in psychometrics and that:

> Each chapter should cover the fundamentals. However, we favour a three-tiered approach, which covers: (1) historical and standard approaches, including all the core material, and then moves onto (2) a discussion of cutting-edge issues and techniques, together with a section on (3) how to do it, which should contain a worked example. These chapters should address real issues faced by both practitioners and researchers.

We hope with the help of our contributors that we have achieved our goal. We hope that a journey started with coffee-shop musings and reflections has led to the production of a useful resource for students, academics, and practitioners alike.

The biggest strength of *The Handbook* undoubtedly lies in the calibre of the authors who have contributed. Every chapter (modestly, with the exception of our own!) has been written by a field expert with specialist knowledge whose work we have admired and used to inform our own practice. Not only are our authors experts, they are also diverse with regard to nationality (e.g., Netherlands, U.K., U.S.A.), profession (e.g., academics, commercial test developers), and field (e.g., psychology, statistics, education, politics). This diversity was no accident. Approaching the topic of psychometrics from the perspective of one discipline would never showcase the range of theoretical and statistical advances that we hoped to convey to our readers. We wish to say a very large thank you to each and every author for sharing their expertise and for their patience throughout this process.

Beyond our excellent contributors, we would also like to acknowledge the help of our families, friends, and students, for their willingness to put up with constant references and sometimes play second fiddle to *The Handbook* over the last few years. Finally, we would also like to extend our deep gratitude to all the people at John Wiley & Sons who have helped us in this process (and there have been many).

Thank you all, and thank you to you as readers for picking this book up off the shelf. We hope it is useful.

David, Tom, and Paul.

Introduction

Aims and Scope

The principal aim of this Handbook was to provide researchers and practitioners from different academic and applied fields with a single practical resource covering the core aspects of psychometric testing. Psychometrics can be translated as mental measurement, however, the implication that psychometrics is confined to psychology is highly misleading. Virtually every conceivable discipline now uses questionnaires, scales, and tests developed from psychometric principles, and this book is therefore intended for a multidisciplinary audience. The field of psychometrics is vibrant with new and useful methods and approaches published frequently. Many of these new developments use increasingly sophisticated models and software packages that are easy to misunderstand. We have strived to make the chapters in this Handbook both intellectually stimulating, and practically useful, through the discussion of historical perspectives, cutting-edge developments, and providing practical illustrations with example code. Thus, each chapter provides an accessible account and example of the current state-of-the-art within the core elements of psychometric testing. We hope that this book is useful for those who develop, evaluate, and use psychometric tests.

Section and Chapter Structure

In structuring the chapters and sections of this Handbook, we attempted to approximate the process of test development. In Part I, the chapters cover core topics surrounding the foundations of test development. Here, we provide a macro view of the process of test development (Chapter 1); outline the broad differences in the classical and modern test theory approaches (Chapter 2); broach topics of the development and nature of item sets (Chapters 3 and 7); and address fundamental topics in study design (Chapters 4, 5, and 6). Chapter 1 is probably the most logical place to start, since this provides a context for most of the other chapters as to their role in test development.

In Part II, we consider the primary psychometric tools for analyzing item pools and identifying plausible scales. Here, we consider the fundamentals of both the common factor (Chapters 8, 10, 11, and 12) and item response (15 and 16) approaches. Chapter 9 sits somewhat at the intersection of the classic and modern test approaches in discussing estimation of categorical item factor models. Part II also provides introductory coverage of multidimensional scaling (MDS: Chapter 14), which has been a highly influential psychometric tool in fields such as political science (see Chapter 28), but is less commonly used in psychometric evaluations in fields such as psychology. The remaining chapters in Part II deal with a number of slightly more advanced, but highly important topics. These chapters address nonnormality (Chapter 13), Bayesian approaches to scaling (Chapter 17) and the modelling of forced choice item formats (Chapter 18). Each of these chapters covers something of an "up and coming" area of psychometrics based upon advancements in computation that now allow us to model more complex data appropriately (as opposed to forcing data into models which presuppose unmet assumptions). Chapter 18, which covers forced choice items, is also particularly valuable for those who test in high-stakes scenarios (i.e., employee selection).

Part III addresses the topic of test scores and also deals with the process of linking and equating test scores. The purpose of psychometric tools is more often than not to understand where someone stands on a given latent trait versus other individuals. Often, we desire scores to represent this standing. Here then, we deal with fundamental topics in score estimation and evaluation, from simple sum scores to advanced item response estimates (Chapters 19 and 20). But what happens when we develop a new version of a test? Or we attempt to develop parallel forms? Or we want to try and relate individuals who have taken different tests? These needs are very common in both applied and academic analyses in education, business, and psychology, and all are concerned with the topic of score linking and equating (Chapters 19 and 21).

Part IV is concerned with the evaluation of scales from a statistical and theoretical perspective. Chapters 23 and 24 provide state of the art treatments of the classic topics of reliability and validity, respectively. Chapter 22 concerns the evaluation of the strength of general and specific factors using bi-factor models. Chapter 25 uses multi-trait-multimethod analyses to explore the proportion of measured variance attributable to the construct and the measurement tool.

So, we have developed some items, collected some data, established our best set of measured constructs, and evaluated the quality of the scales. But does our test operate in the same way for all groups of people? This question is critically important for reasons of accuracy and fairness and can be approached through the application of the analytic methods discussed in Part V. Here, we deal with tools for modelling and understanding the measurement properties of psychometric tools across groups from a common factor (Chapter 26) and item response (Chapter 27) perspective.

Finally, in Part VI, we step away from topics related to the immediate development of tests, and we consider the role psychometrics has played, and may play in the future, in theoretical and practical arenas. In Chapters 28 and 29, we consider the substantial role psychometric tools and analyses have played in shaping the fields of political science and personality psychology. Lastly, we introduce recent work concerning the relationship between network and latent variable approaches to understanding behavior (Chapter 30). Both Chapters 29 and 30 provide critical appraisals of analytic tools common to the psychometrics world (i.e., factor analysis) and point the way to potential avenues of progress. Reviewing the contributions of psychometric testing and considering how future Handbooks of Psychometric Testing might look felt like a fitting way to close this volume.

Mathematical and Statistical Foundations

Our aim for this Handbook was to make the content as accessible as possible for as many individuals as possible, both practitioners and academics. You do not need to be a mathematician or statistician to read this book. Equations are kept to the minimum required to provide satisfactory explanations of the methods under discussion. Where equations are presented by authors, they are broken down and described verbally to add clarity.

However, it would be remiss of us as editors to try and claim that this handbook is going to be an easy read for all who pick it up. The topic under discussion is statistical and thus there is some technical content. The degree of technical content varies across chapters inline with the mathematical complexity of the topics discussed.

So, what statistical and mathematical knowledge is required? With regard to statistics, we have assumed certain background knowledge. Modern psychometrics depends, amongst other things, on knowledge of structural equation modelling (SEM), and in particular confirmatory factor analysis (CFA). However, both of these are already covered by many excellent texts. For example, the early chapters in Little (2013) provide an excellent introduction to both topics, while Brown (2015) provides arguably one of the most useful comprehensive treatments of CFA, and Bollen (1989) still represents the most definitive advanced treatment of both. SEM depends on an understanding of multiple regression. Probably one of the best and most neglected books on regression is Pedhazur (1997), which in fact provides a comprehensive coverage of everything you need to know about the basics of multivariate statistics.

With regards to mathematics knowledge, to understand the methods conceptually and use the practical examples as guides to analyze your own data, not very much is required. But to appreciate fully the topics under discussion here, a basic knowledge of calculus, algebra, and perhaps most importantly, matrix algebra (e.g., Fieller, 2015; Khuri & Searle, 2017) is required. It would also be valuable, as is true for any statistical topic, for readers to have some grounding in probability and significance testing. A number of chapters also extend into Bayesian statistics where a slightly deeper appreciation of probability theory may be necessary (DeGroot & Schervish, 2012). Chapter 17 contains a short introduction to concepts from Bayesian analysis, but this is intended more as a refresher than as a comprehensive treatment of the fundamental of Bayes. In terms of a comprehensive and accessible introduction to mathematical statistics Larsen and Marx (2011) is hard to better.

We have resisted the temptation to provide introductory chapters or appendices on these core statistical and mathematical topics for two reasons. First, there are a multitude of high quality introductory texts on these topics (see previously). It is also important to point out that there are now a huge number of excellent (and free) web resources on these topics, and the reader who feels they need a refresher is encouraged to explore this route (no need to spend money unnecessarily) whilst bearing in mind that finding the right mathematics or statistics text is often a personal thing. Second, the Handbook is intended to have a diverse target audience whose needs will vary greatly. To cover each of these topics, for a diverse audience, would have required us to turn what is already a large book, into a behemoth perfectly suited to act as doorstop for the *Black Gate of Mordor*.

Software

The contributors to the Handbook have made use of a variety of different statistical software packages, some freely available, others proprietary. The two most popular tools across chapters are the R statistical programming language and MPlus. R has a large number of advantages as a statistical tool, the details of which we will not get into here. However, perhaps the two most commonly cited and important are that it is free, and it is highly flexible. However, with this flexibility comes a requirement for some knowledge of programming and coding languages – with great power comes great responsibility.

In recent years, MPlus has established itself as one of the primary proprietary tools for conducting general latent variable analyses, quickly incorporating new methodologies, providing excellent help facilities and abundant online resources. MPlus is again a flexible tool that is very user-friendly. However, the program does come at a cost, with a full single user license for University affiliates costing approximately £720 ($895) at the time of writing.

Popular general-purpose statistical packages such as SPSS, SAS, or STATA, are used, but less frequently. This is not to say that these packages have no capability with respect to the types of analysis discussed in this Handbook but often they do lack some of the nuances needed to conduct state of the art analyses. This is perhaps the reason that authors have also made use of a variety of additional programs including, MIRT, *flex*MIRT, IRTPro, Factor, LISREL, EQS, MATLAB, WinBUGS, and more. What this shows is the huge variety and widespread availability of tools for empirical analysis.

So, which software should you use? In making this decision, one of the key things to consider is which models are best suited to which software. We hope the Handbook helps in this endeavor in two ways. First, our empirical examples show directly some of what can be done in certain packages. Second, we hope the level of presentation of the technical details of analyses will allow the readers to tackle the supporting documentation of software to gain a deeper understanding of what is going on "under the hood."

The available tools vary in a number of other ways, too. For example, the means by which analyses are conducted varies from coding languages (both program-specific and general) to graphical user interfaces with and without diagrammatical capabilities. Whilst drop-down menus are great, we would recommend writing code. Not only does this clarify understanding but it also allows you to specify all modelling options rather than resting on software defaults. Perhaps the most pragmatically relevant variation lies in monetary cost, and many readers will likely be limited to proprietary software available from their institutions or freely available software. Thankfully, for scientific progress, more tools than ever are now free! Indeed, more than a third of our chapters used free software and every analysis presented in this handbook could be conducted in this manner, which we will now discuss.

Chapter Code

For a majority of the chapters in this handbook, software code has been made available for the analyses, and some of the figures, presented in the chapters. In most cases, this is in the form of a Code Appendix at the end of the chapter. For a smaller subset of chapters, the code has been integrated into the body of the chapter. Chapter dependent, the detail of code provided varies, as does the level of annotation but in each case, it directly links to the practical examples presented.

Some chapters have made use of proprietary software, which if the reader does not have access to, obviously limits its usability. Here we wish to emphasize once again the abundance of freely available software for psychometric analyses. With very few exceptions, the analyses presented in this book can be conducted using a relatively limited number of R-packages. For those unfamiliar with R, we would strongly recommend investing some time to learn the basics of the program.

The packages *psych* (Revelle, 2016), *mirt* (Chalmers, 2012), *OpenMx* (Neale, et al. 2016; Pritikin, Hunter, & Boker, 2015; Boker et al., 2017), and *lavaan* (Rosseel, 2012), can be used to complete a vast majority of the common factor and IRT analyses presented in this Handbook. Other useful packages include *qgrpah* (Epskamp, Cramer, Waldorp, Schittmann, & Borsboom, 2012) for network models and plots, *smacof* (de Leeuw, & Mair, 2009) for multidimensional scaling, *rjags* (Plummer, 2016) for Bayesian analysis, and *mice* (van Buuren & Groothuis-Oudshoorn, 2011) for missing data analysis. Collectively, we hope that the code provided and access to the free R packages noted makes the Handbook a genuinely valuable practical tool.

How to Use the Book

As has been outlined here, this Handbook has been compiled with multiple audiences in mind and as such we anticipate the contents to be used in a variety of ways. Coarsely, our section structure can be seen as representing the process of developing and evaluating a psychometric test. Read from start to finish the chapters represent a comprehensive introduction to the process of test development, analysis, and revision. Readers interested in evaluating an extant scale for which they have collected some data will, dependent on their focus, find most value in the contents of sections two through four. Here we suggest that the readers treat the chapters and the associated reference lists as the start point for in depth consideration of a topic. Whilst we cover historical perspectives, state-of-the-art methods, and provide practical examples and code, the chapters of this handbook do not contain everything one might need to know.

In either case, whether a reader is interested in the start to finish process of scale development, or in methods for a specific purpose, the chapter content allows the reader to focus on either classical (common factor) or modern (IRT) approaches to most questions. For the reader unsure of which approach they wish to take, we would encourage them to read Chapter 2, and to consider their research focus in light of the type of information each approach has to offer. In some cases, this is overlapping, in others complementary, and so the choice is not always clear cut. Equally, whilst positioned towards the end of the book, Chapter 24, might be an interesting place to start because the treatment of "validity" aims to provide a coherent model to organize test development and evaluation procedures and references out to other chapters wherever relevant.

Practical hands on experience is a valuable part of the learning process. We hope that the code provided and the information on different software packages will provide a framework that will allow readers to apply analyses to their own data. The code is not a tutorial, and some knowledge of the different statistical packages will be needed.

We hope the Handbook is enjoyable and useful. Enjoy.

References

Boker, S. M., Neale, M. C., Maes, H. H., Wilde, M. J., Spiegel, M., Brick, T. R., …& Manjunath, B. G. (2017) *OpenMx 2.7.12 user guide*. Available at http://openmx.psyc.virginia.edu/docs/OpenMx/latest/OpenMxUserGuide.pdf (accessed October 2017).

Bollen, K. A. (1989). *Structural equations with latent variables*. New York: John Wiley & Sons, Inc.

Brown, T. A. (2015). *Confirmatory factor analysis for applied research* (2nd ed.). New York, NY: The Guilford Press.

Chalmers, P. R. (2012). mirt: A multidimensional item response theory package for the R environment. *Journal of Statistical Software*, 48, 1–29. URL http://www.jstatsoft.org/v48/i06/ (accessed October 2017).

DeGroot, M. H., & Schervish, M. J. (2012). *Probability and statistics*. Boston, MA: Pearson Education.

de Leeuw, J., & Mair, P. (2009). Multidimensional scaling using majorization: SMACOF in R. *Journal of Statistical Software*, 31, 1–30. URL http://www.jstatsoft.org/v31/i03/ (accessed October 2017).

Epskamp, S., Cramer, A. O. J., Waldorp, L. J., Schmittmann, V. D., & Borsboom, D. (2012). qgraph: Network visualizations of relationships in psychometric data. *Journal of Statistical Software*, 48, 1–18. URL http://www.jstatsoft.org/v48/i04/ (accessed October 2017).

Fieller, N. (2015). *Basics of matrix algebra for statistics with R*. Boca Raton, FL: Chapman Hall/CRC.

Khuri, A. I., & Searle, S. R. (2017). *Matrix algebra useful for statistics* (2nd ed.). Chichester, UK: Wiley-Blackwell.

Larsen, R. J., & Marx, M. L. (2011). *An introduction to mathematical statistics and its applications* (5th ed.). Boston, MA: Pearson Education.

Little, T. D. (2013). *Longitudinal structural equation modeling*. New York, NJ: The Guilford Press.

Neale, M. C., Hunter, M. D., Pritikin, J. N., Zahery, M., Brick, T. R., Kickpatrick, R. M… and Boker, S. M. (2016). OpenMx 2.0: Extended structural equation and statistical modeling. *Psychometrika*, 80, 535–549.

Pedhazur, E. J. (1997). *Multiple regression in behavioral research* (3rd ed.). Boston, MA: Wadsworth.

Plummer, M. (2016). *rjags: bayesian graphical models using MCMC. R package version 4-6*. https://CRAN.R-project.org/package=rjags (accessed October 2017).

Pritikin, J. N., Hunter, M. D., & Boker, S. M. (2015). Modular open-source software for Item Factor Analysis. *Educational and Psychological Measurement*, 75, 458–474.

Revelle, W. (2016) *psych: Procedures for personality and psychological research*, Northwestern University, Evanston, IL, USA, https://CRAN.R-project.org/package=psych Version = 1.6.12.

Rosseel, Y. (2012). lavaan: An R package for structural equation modeling. *Journal of Statistical Software*, 48, 1–36. URL http://www.jstatsoft.org/v48/i02/ (accessed October 2017).

van Buuren, S., & Groothuis-Oudshoorn, K. (2011). mice: Multivariate imputation by chained equations in R. *Journal of Statistical Software*, 45, 1–67. URL http://www.jstatsoft.org/v45/i03/ (accessed October 2017).

The Wiley Handbook of Psychometric Testing

Part I
Practical Foundations

1

Test Development

Paul Irwing and David J. Hughes

The purpose of this chapter is to explain how the psychometric principles outlined in the remaining chapters of this Handbook can be applied in order to develop a test. We take a broad definition both of what constitutes a test and what is understood by test development. This is because the principles of psychometric testing are very broad in their potential application. Among others, they can apply to attitude, personality, cognitive ability, interest, and diagnostic measures. For the purposes of this chapter all such measures will be referred to as **tests**. Psychometrics is broad in another sense: It applies to many more fields than psychology; indeed, biomedical science, education, economics, communications theory, marketing, sociology, politics, business, and epidemiology, among other disciplines, not only employ psychometric testing, but also have made important contributions to the subject. Our definition of a test is broad in another sense: It encompasses everything from a simple attitude scale, say to measure job satisfaction, to comprehensive test batteries such as the Woodcock–Johnson IV battery of cognitive tests (Schrank, Mather, & McGrew, 2014). Of course, not every aspect of test development applies to both, but the overlap is considerable.

It may be useful to distinguish the different levels of complexity involved in test development. In the simplest case, the test comprises just one scale, but more usually a test is comprised of multiple scales (**single scale versus test battery**). A second distinction is between tests comprised of similar as opposed mixed types of scales (**scale similarity**). For example, the European Social Survey measures multiple constructs but all are attitude scales. However, some instruments may combine assessments of mixed scale types; for example, cognitive ability, personality, and attitudes. A third dimension concerns whether the test is intended to sample the entire spectrum of a domain, or whether it is focused on specific aspects (**broad versus narrow spectrum**). For example, it would not be feasible for a selection test to reliably measure all facets of either personality or cognitive ability. The point being that some form of systematic choice procedure is required such as job analysis or meta-analysis (Hughes & Batey, 2017). Fourth, there is the issue of **team size**. There is a very big difference from the situation in which a single investigator takes responsibility for the major

---

The Wiley Handbook of Psychometric Testing: A Multidisciplinary Reference on Survey, Scale and Test Development, First Edition. Edited by Paul Irwing, Tom Booth, and David J. Hughes.
© 2018 John Wiley & Sons Ltd. Published 2020 by John Wiley & Sons Ltd.

portion of test development, and the situation in which there is a large team with diverse skill sets, which would be common when developing commercial tests. The MAT^{80} (Irwing, Phillips, & Walters, 2016), which we use later to demonstrate test development procedures, is a test battery with a mixed scale that combines personality and ability scales, involved a small test development team, and requires systematic selection of specific facets.

There are already many publications of relevance to the topic of test development. Probably the most useful single source is "The Standards for Educational and Psychological Testing" (American Educational Research Association [AERA], American Psychological Association [APA], National Council on Measurement in Education [NCME], 2014). However, as its name implies, this tells you what needs to be done, but not how to do it. There is now a very useful *Handbook of Test Development* (Downing & Haladyna, 2006), which largely specializes in the design of educational and ability tests. Of almost equal use are textbooks on questionnaire and survey design (Brace, 2005; De Vaus, 2014; Foddy, 1996; Oppenheim, 1992). Perhaps what none of these books quite do is link modern psychometrics to test development, which is the aim of this chapter and the whole Handbook.

We begin with a comprehensive model of the stages of test development, and then discuss the major considerations that apply at each stage. We will leave the reader to decide which of these stages apply to their own situation, depending on the type and purpose of the test. Table 1.1 outlines a 10-stage model of test development. There are a number of stage models of test development in existence (e.g., Althouse, n.d.; Downing, 2006) and, to a degree, such models are arbitrary in the sense that which tasks are grouped into a stage and the order of stages is probably more for explanatory convenience rather than a description of reality. In practice, tasks may actually be grouped and undertaken in many different combinations and orders, with many tasks undertaken iteratively. Nevertheless, a stage model provides a systematic framework in which to discuss the tasks that must be undertaken, although not all tasks are relevant to all types of test development.

Table 1.1 Stages of test development.

Stages and substages

1 Construct definition, specification of test need, test structure.
2 Overall planning.
3 Item development.
   a. Construct definition.
   b. Item generation: theory versus sampling.
   c. Item review.
   d. Piloting of items.
4 Scale construction – factor analysis and Item Response Theory (IRT).
5 Reliability.
6 Validation.
7 Test scoring and norming.
8 Test specification.
9 Implementation and testing.
10 Technical Manual.

Construct Definition, Specification of Test Need, and Structure

The motivation for test development often stems from a practical concern: can we help children learn, can we identify effective managers, can we identify those at risk of mental distress? However, while motivation may provide impetus, it is not the formal starting point of test development. The formal starting point for all test development is to generate a construct definition, which broadly is a definition of what is to be measured. An initial construct definition should be as clear as possible but will often be somewhat broad. For example, one might decide that a measure of cognitive ability, or leader potential, or anxiety is required (perhaps in order to address our previous practical concerns). From this point, one can define these constructs (using extant work or a newly generated definition as appropriate) and conduct a systematic literature review to identify existing tests and find out more about the nature of the target construct. This review should help the developer to refine their construct definition. For example, if you were interested in measuring cognitive ability an initial definition might be incomplete or very high level (e.g., ability to acquire and use knowledge or the speed and accuracy of information processing). However, based on a literature review, one could choose to devise sufficient tests to provide coverage of all second-order factors of cognitive ability contained within the Cattell–Horn–Carroll model (McGrew, 2009). This was broadly the strategy used in the development of the Woodcock–Johnson IV (McGrew, 2009).

However, relying solely on extant models might not always be the most useful strategy for at least two reasons, which we will explore using the Five Factor Model (FFM) of personality (Costa & McCrae, 1995). First, because the FFM is so widely accepted, there already exist a large number of tests based on this model and the question then arises as to what is the need for another identical test. Second, although the FFM is widely accepted, it seems unlikely that it is the final word on personality. Some argue that there are facets of personality out with the sphere of the FFM (Paunonen & Jackson, 2000), including some aspects of abnormal personality (Mathieu, Hare, Jones, Babiak, & Neumann, 2013). Of course, the NEO-PIR was not designed to measure abnormal personality, but there are strong arguments that broad-spectrum measures of personality should cover both the normal and abnormal (Markon, Krueger, & Watson, 2005). This may seem like a disadvantage but of course, from the point of view of a test developer, it is an opportunity. There is much more value in a new test that does something that an old test does not.

There may of course be many reasons for developing a test. There may be a need for research on a topic, but no extant measure suitable to carry out the research. For example, knowledge is a very important aspect of human behavior, but until about the year 2000 there were no standardized tests of knowledge (Irwing, Cammock, & Lynn, 2001; Rolfhus & Ackermann, 1999). Outside of research: diagnosis, assessment, and development, employee selection, market research, licensing and credentialing (e.g., the examinations that qualify one to practice as an accountant or lawyer) represent other broad categories of test needs. Broadly, there is a need for a test if your systematic literature review reveals that a test does not currently exist, current tests are judged to be inadequate, or there are tests, but not ones suitable for the particular population or use to which the test is to be put. Certainly, many instances of copycat tests exist, but I am not aware that this strategy has generally proven to be a recipe for a successful test.

Generally, successful tests are developed due to some combination of three circumstances:

1. Theoretical advances (NEO PI-R: Costa & McCrae, 1995; 16 PF: Conn & Rieke, 1994; VPI: Holland, Blakeney, Matteson, & Schnitzen, 1974; WAIS: Wechsler, 1981);
2. Empirical advances (MMPI: Butcher, Dahlstrom, Graham, Tellegen, & Kaemmer, 1989);
3. A practical (market) need (SAT: Coyle & Pillow, 2008; GMAT: Oh, Schmidt, Shaffer, & Le, 2008).

If the developer does not make a test based on theoretical advance, empirical advance, or a gap in the market and instead duplicates a test, or more realistically produces a test that shares a name with another but has subtle differences in content, then the result is construct proliferation and the well-documented problems commonly referred to as the Jingle-Jangle fallacy (Hughes, Chapter 24; Shaffer, DeGeest, & Li, 2016).

Theoretical and empirical advances

Theoretical advancements (often driven by prior empirical discoveries) undoubtedly provide the reason for the development of many tests. Briefly, the test developer must develop a theoretical framework, which is in some respect new and sounder than previous frameworks, or utilize existing theoretical frameworks that current tests have not exploited. A full discussion of the nature of theoretical advances is well beyond the practical bounds of this chapter because it will be unique for every construct. That said, the history of the development of the FFM is highly instructive as to the process whereby theory evolves from an interaction between theoretical and empirical developments (Block, 1995; John, & Srivastava, 1999, see later). Also, pivotal to test development is the evolution of tight construct definitions, which also emerges from the interaction between theory and empirical work.

Systematic domain mapping

Perhaps the most obvious example of an interaction between theoretical and empirical advance comes in the form of systematic domain mapping. Very simply, a systematic domain map consists of all construct-relevant content (e.g., every aspect of the domain of personality) mapped onto a theoretically supported structure. This serves as a precursor to developing a systematic taxonomy of the domain that ideally identifies all primary level and higher-level constructs and provides the basic material from which test items can be constructed.

The history of testing suggests ways in which this can be achieved. Although all attempts to map a domain suffer from practical and statistical limitations. For example, the total number of possible personality items is sizable and collecting data on so many items is difficult as is subsequent analysis. For instance, factor analysis cannot handle the size of data matrix that would be required, meaning that in practice the total domain needs to be divided into manageable chunks based on a subjective grouping (see Booth & Murray, Chapter 29). The process of grouping items inevitably means that some constructs which span the subjective groupings or sit at the interface between two are not sufficiently captured. Nevertheless, the development of the FFM, for example, is instructive both as to how domain mapping can be achieved and also the potential flaws in this process. Actually, the history of the development of the FFM is complex (Block, 1995; John, Angleiter, & Ostendorf, 1988), but a simplified account of the principles of its development will suffice for our purposes. Arguably, the development of the FFM stems from the lexical hypothesis, which is comprised of two major postulates. The first states that those personality characteristics that are most important in peoples' lives will eventually become a part of their language. The second follows from the first, stating that more important personality characteristics are more likely to be encoded into language as a single word (John et al., 1988). If true, then in principle, if all words that describe personality were incorporated into a questionnaire, and a large population were rated as to the extent these words apply to them, then a factor analysis of this data would provide the facet and higher-order structure of personality. In practice, despite claims to the contrary, for various practical reasons this has never been done, but something like it has (e.g., Ashton, Lee, & Goldberg, 2004). Personality research is now at a stage at which there are many respected measures of personality and the next step might be to administer all known measures of personality to a large population and, guided by theoretical developments, factor analyze the resultant data set in order to provide a new and more comprehensive taxonomy of personality (Booth, 2011; Woods & Anderson, 2016).

What this example illustrates is that successful test development often requires some form of systematic domain mapping, which is in at least some respects novel.

Practical (market) need

Of course, measures derived from a taxonomy or theory do not necessarily correspond to a practical need (beyond the need for measurement). Indeed, one difficulty with omnibus measures (such as the Woodcock–Johnson IV and the NEO PI-R) is that they rarely correspond to a direct market need. In the most part, this is because omnibus measures are often long and time-consuming to complete, resulting in equally long and detailed reports. Exhaustive reports concerned with all aspects of personality or cognitive ability can be difficult for laypersons to understand and use. Usually, the tests adopted by consumers are shorter and considered more user friendly. For example, despite being technically deficient (Hughes & Batey, 2017), the MBTI is among the most commonly used personality tests because it is relatively short, the results are easily communicated and understood, and therefore it can readily be used in a practical context. Probably therefore, marketable tests may be based on a systematic taxonomy but the actual constitution of the test will depend on additional considerations. In short, for a test to address a market need it should be both technically sound (in terms of theoretical grounding and psychometric properties) and practically useful.

The area of selection can help illustrate what some of these additional practical considerations might be. One starting point might be to identify the market for a selection test based on systematic market research. Let us imagine that the results of this research reveal there to be a large market for the recruitment of managers, not least because a large number of managers are employed, and secondly because their characteristics are often considered crucial to the success or failure of companies. How then could we devise a test for managers? Traditionally, most test developers for a selection instrument would begin with a job analysis (Smith & Smith, 2005). This is still an essential step in the development of selection tests, however, since the late 1970s psychometric meta-analysis has become an important source of information to guide the development of selection instruments.

Meta-analysis

The main purpose of psychometric meta-analysis is to obtain parameter estimates, which are unbiased and corrected for measurement artifacts. Hunter and Schmidt (2004) is probably the most useful introduction to meta-analysis, although some more recent developments are contained in Borenstein, Hedges, Higgins, and Rothstein (2009). Meta-analysis has many potential applications to test development. For example, with regard to the construction of test batteries for employee selection, findings of meta-analyses identify which constructs predict future job performance and, therefore, which should be included (e.g., Judge, Rodell, Kliner, Simon, & Crawford, 2013; Schmidt, Shaffer, & Oh, 2008).

Psychometric meta-analysis averages the value of an effect size across studies in order to obtain a reliable summary estimate. The most important effect size in a selection context is the predictive validity, which is measured by the correlation between the score on the selection measure and some measure of job performance. The biggest problem with most estimates of predictive validity from single studies arises from sampling error, which is more considerable than is generally imagined. As sample size tends to infinity, so sampling error tends to zero and thus by amalgamating findings across studies, large meta-analyses effectively reduce sampling error to miniscule proportions. Standardly, psychometric meta-analysis also corrects for artifacts due to error of measurement, range restriction, imperfect construct validity (e.g., different measures of purportedly the same personality construct typically correlate at 0.4–0.6, see Pace & Brannick, 2010), use of categorical measurement, study quality, and publication bias. However, once these corrections are made, the confidence interval around the effect size estimate may still be large. This may indicate that the effect size is dependent on a third variable, usually referred to as a moderator. For example, cognitive ability predicts more strongly for complex jobs (Schmidt & Hunter, 1998) and in the case of personality, traits predict more strongly when they are relevant (e.g., Extraversion and sales; Hughes & Batey, 2017).

The findings of meta-analysis with regard to which cognitive abilities and FFM personality factors predict job performance are, within limits, fairly definitive (Schmidt & Hunter, 1998, 1998; Schmidt, Shaffer, & Oh, 2008). Virtually every meta-analysis that has investigated the issue has concluded that, for most jobs, general cognitive ability is the best predictor and the level of prediction increases in proportion to the cognitive demands of the job (Schmidt & Hunter, 1998). Moreover, it is generally contended that second-order factors of cognitive ability such as spatial, verbal, and memory add little incremental prediction (e.g., Carretta & Ree, 2000; Ree, Earles, & Teachout, 1994). Although it is a hotly contested issue, meta-analyses of the predictive validity of personality show virtually the opposite; that is, that personality largely does not offer blanket prediction of job performance across roles. Some have argued from this data that personality tests should not be used in selection (Morgeson et al., 2007), but many have also argued otherwise (e.g., Ones, Dilchert,

Viswesvaran, & Judge, 2007; see Hughes & Batey, 2017, for a comprehensive review). So you would think that any selection program for a management position would incorporate a measure of cognitive ability. Actually, this is not so. In practice, it would seem that personality tests are more widely used in selection than cognitive ability tests; perhaps because of greater acceptability.

Of course, meta-analysis has its limits. Meta-analysis can only be applied where there is already a substantial body of research. For example, because of problems of acceptability there is a huge paucity of work on dark traits of personality, yet what work there is suggests that it is indeed important for organizational performance (Babiak, Craig, Neumann, & Hare, 2010; Boddy, 2011, 2014). To summarize, meta-analysis provides a very useful body of evidence about what works, but this needs to be balanced against what is acceptable. Whatever, decision is made, the findings of meta-analyses place the development of test batteries for selection on a sounder basis than has previously obtained.

We have considered some scenarios, and we will consider others in the context of item development, however, the range of possible scenarios for test development is large and you should consult other sources for aptitude and achievement tests, for example (Downing & Haladyna, 2006). Whatever the exact scenario, at the end of this stage you will have defined and refined your constructs, specified the test need (including the purpose of the test and the populations to which it will be administered), and identified the exact components to be included within your test.

Overall Planning

Once the purpose and test structure is defined, a process of planning is required that may be more or less extensive depending on whether the test involves just a single research scale or is designed to measure a large number of different constructs.

The planning phase involves answering a broad range of questions. For example:

1. How many items are needed to measure the constructs of interest?
2. Which response scale is to be used? A basic choice is between multiple choice formats, Likert type scales,[1] and constructed formats in which the test taker supplies a response to an open question.
3. How to score the test? For different purposes, it may be appropriate to use sum scores, standardized scores (e.g., t scores, Stanines, Stens, or IQ values), or some form of item response model for scoring.
4. Which psychometric model is most appropriate for modeling the test data? Usually the choice is posed as between a classical test theory approach and one based on IRT, however, we will suggest next that perhaps a combination of the two is to be preferred.
5. What item development process is most suitable? Item trialing and validation studies also have to be planned, together with the analyses of the resulting data. In addition, quality control systems need to be developed or adopted in order to ensure; for

---

[1] Strictly, a Likert scale is a summative scale in which the total score is the sum of the item scores. However, the term is commonly used to refer to a scale of a type with verbal anchors, most usually ranging from strongly agree to strong disagree. This is the sense intended here.

example, that the test specification is completely accurate and it is implemented precisely (see the later section on Test Specification).
6. How to administer the test? The modality of administration could be paper and pencil, interview, telephone interview, or computer based. There is no single format that is "best," but computer-based administration is becoming the preferred option since for many tests as it has the advantages of accessibility (anyone anywhere in the world who has a computer can take the test), automatic data capture, and instantaneously delivered feedback. The principal disadvantage of computer-based administration is that it may not provide access to segments of the population who do not have computer access. There is also the question of how to prevent cheating.

Once these decisions have been made a timeline is required that should include time for correction cycles, which will almost certainly be necessary. This should specify who is responsible for each major task together with completion dates (Roid, 2006). Lack of specificity of the plan will undoubtedly delay development and cost money.

Item Development

The nature of item development depends on the type of scale to be developed. The type of scale depends on what is to be measured, the response format, and scaling model employed. Broadly, there are attitude, trait, and ability scales. The most commonly employed response formats are Likert type, multiple choice, or forced-choice items. Scaling generally conforms to the types developed by Thurstone, Likert, or Guttman (Ghiselli, Campbell, & Zedeck, 1981). To a degree, the type of scale, response format, and approach to scaling has an effect on recommendations as to item writing and development.

Irrespective of the type of item to be developed, the first stage consists of the development of further refined construct definitions. This is an issue that is typically revisited several times. For some cognitive abilities, the construct is already extremely well defined. A good example is that of matrix reasoning tests. Carpenter, Just, and Shell (1990) have defined a set of rules that can be applied in order to develop such tests, and even suggest how different combinations of rules affect item difficulty. In order to apply these rules, all that is required is to define the tokens of which items are to be comprised and how these tokens are to be organized spatially. This clarity of construct definition underpins the development of automatic item generation described by Morrison and Embretson (Chapter 3). Alternatively, provided the construct definition is sufficiently clear, it is quite common practice to use professional item writers.

Achievement tests in contrast to pure measures of ability require mastery of a subject matter. Most tests of this type are developed in conjunction with subject matter experts. Recommendations for the development of such tests are contained in Downing and Haladyna (2006). Downing (2006) in particular specifies a 12-step procedure for the development of such tests.

Trait and attitude items are generally somewhat less well defined, with construct definitions normally arising either directly or indirectly from an exercise in domain mapping. Domain mapping at the test and item level involve similar processes. At the item level, domain mapping techniques can be focused on just those constructs to be measured. This process is so important that there is value in suggesting a number of additional strategies in order to accomplish this.

1. First, define the topic: political attitudes, car buying, environmental issues. Then ask a large and ideally population representative sample what they consider the key issues to be in relation to the topic. At a second stage, an equally large population representative sample can be asked to express what they consider to be commonly held opinions with respect to each issue. This should provide a very long list of statements from which items can be developed. These items should be grouped into scales, which measure just one dimension of the construct in question.
2. Use already extant systematic sources. Examples would include encyclopedias (knowledge tests), curriculum specification (educational tests), dictionaries (personality), diagnostic manuals (DSM-V), and web portals.
3. Use expert informants in order to aggregate comprehensive lists of attitudes, characteristics, successful traits, and critical incidents.

These processes should provide the raw materials for items. There are item writing guidelines for multiple choice items, and for Likert type items. Table 1.2 presents a distillation of rules concerning Likert type items. For equivalent sets of guidelines on multiple choice items you could consult Haladyna, Downing, and Rodriguez (2002).

Table 1.2 Item writing guidelines for Likert type items.

Guideline

1. Each item should tap a different aspect of the domain.
2. Simple language is preferred. There exist comprehensive lists of words in order of their frequency of usage, at least for the English language (e.g., *Corpus of Contemporary English*, 2016). In general, more commonly used words are more understandable.
3. Short items are preferable to long items. However, items should not be shortened so that specificity of meaning is lost. For example, short items comprised of several or more words rather than single words provide more reliable measures of personality.
4. Items should not be double-barreled. That is items should relate to one and not more than one subject.
5. Items should be positively phrased. Use of single or double negatives reduces comprehensibility.
6. Items should not be leading or elicit a prestige bias.
7. Items should use good grammar, punctuation, and spelling in a consistent manner.
8. Syntax and grammar should be of the simplest form consistent with conveying meaning.
9. The meaning of items should not be ambiguous.
10. In general, personalized phrasing is more involving and therefore preferable. However, this may not be appropriate when content is sensitive. In the latter case, an indirect strategy such as asking how you would advise a friend or how other people behave may be appropriate.
11. Items should not create attitudes, opinions, or responses that do not already exist. Equally, they should not require knowledge the respondent does not possess.
12. The frame of reference should be clear; e.g., one year, one week, one day.
13. Items should not overload working memory.
14. Answering should not require knowledge which is inaccessible, for instance, either because the respondent has never considered the issue, or because it is too taxing on memory.
15. Items should not be objectionable.
16. Items should be grammatically consistent with responses.
17. In general, items should hold the same meaning for all respondents. Following the above rules should help achieve this.

A further issue is that items should not produce response sets which either bias responses or produce response artifacts, although in general this is more a function of the organization and sequencing of items. There are many examples of response sets: yeah-saying, nay-saying, consistency and availability artifacts, halo, and social desirability artifacts. One of the most effective methods of countering response sets is to use forced-choice item formats, the subject of which is discussed extensively in Brown, Chapter 18.

Guideline 8 that, "syntax and grammar should be of the simplest form consistent with conveying the intended meaning," perhaps requires more comment. Many testees take tests in a second language. There is a large amount of research that shows that reducing the complexity of language also reduces the level of construct irrelevant variance in response to test items (Abedi, 2006). Although much of this research relates to educational and ability tests, it seems highly probable that it applies equally to other types of test. Abedi (2006) provides a useful list of features which reduce linguistic complexity, including: Using commonly occurring and familiar words; using shorter rather than longer words; using shorter sentences; adopting the active voice; using simple rather than compound subjects; reducing the use of comparative phrases, subordinate, conditional, and relative clauses; using concrete rather than abstract language; and using positive phrasing

Item review

Prior to piloting of items, it is common practice to subject items to a process of review. Probably the most common and arguably useful form of review is the use of expert groups (DeMaio & Landreth, 2004; Presser & Blair, 1994; Willis, Schechter, & Whitaker, 2000). Experts are typically subject matter experts, experts in test design, or representatives of participant samples. The function of different types of experts naturally varies to at least some degree, and of course, some individuals may embody more than one type of expertise. The major concern of subject matter experts is that of item accuracy (the extent to which a test measures what it is intended to measure), but they may also be asked to assess item bias. Very different types of subject matter experts would be required to evaluate items designed to assess personality, mathematics ability, business acumen, knowledge of accountancy, and so on. Experts in test design would be mainly concerned with assessing whether items conform to commonly accepted rules of good item design such as those listed in Table 1.2. In some circumstances, these experts may also be in a position to make accuracy judgments. Experts who are representative of participant samples are primarily used to assess the comprehensibility of the items to the particular population and to identify items that are potentially biased or objectionable. It has become standard practice to eliminate all items flagged as potentially biased or objectionable, unless this would clearly undermine the purpose of the test. Such practices may be misplaced in that there is the risk that informants confuse any form of difference with bias (Messick, 1989). Nevertheless, used well, and obviously dependent on just how expert panels actually are, there is evidence that review by expert groups can be highly effective and relatively inexpensive (DeMaio & Landreth, 2004; Presser & Blair, 1994; Willis et al., 2000).

There are broadly four other methods of item review that are commonly used. Field pretests represent the most commonly used traditional approach. Here the administration of the test is observed in a form as identical as possible to its final form. Debriefings with the observers may be used, the data may be coded to identify problem items, and even recordings of the test administration may be coded. Cognitive interviews use a combination of thinking aloud protocols and probes. In a thinking aloud protocol the test taker is instructed to verbalize their thought processes as they answer each test item. This may be followed by probes into any source of apparent difficulty in responding to the item. Randomized experiments are also used in which randomly chosen groups are administered different versions of the test in which the wording of items attempting to measure the same thing is varied. Focus groups represent a fourth method in which a semi-structured discussion with members of the target population is intended to explore their knowledge, common opinions, and terms used in relation to the test content. Groves et al. (2009) and Presser et al. (2004) are recommended for more in-depth treatments of these methods.

Piloting of test

To this point, the construction of the test depends on theory, previous empirical work, and subjective judgments based on prior experience and knowledge. The next stages involve administration of the test to an appropriate sample or samples. The sample should closely match the characteristics of the sample or samples in which the test will be used. That said, population representative samples are often useful irrespective of the population(s) at which the test is targeted.

Another consideration with respect to samples is sample size. Assuming that the sampling strategy is constant, bigger is always better in that the larger the sample the smaller the confidence intervals for all parameters. Much ad hoc advice is available on this. For example, 200 is a suggested minimum for factor analysis (Stevens, 2009). In my experience, samples need to be at least 500 to provide generalizable results, and my preference is a minimum sample of 1,000. Kelley and Lai (Chapter 5) describe a systematic procedure for calculating the required sample size for any given preferred confidence interval for factor loadings and other key parameters. This procedure is to be recommended, but ultimately there is a subjective judgment required as to what is an acceptable confidence interval.

Usually tests are administered, analyzed, revised, and readministered a number of times before their psychometric properties are acceptable.

Scale Construction

There is considerable debate about how test data should be analyzed. Here we will make recommendations on what we consider to represent best practice. The issues for initial analyses are whether proposed scales are unidimensional, whether scales actually measure the focal construct (accuracy), how well items measure the underlying construct (reliability), and whether the measure covers the full range of trait values (construct representativeness).

Which analytic techniques are to be recommended depends on the theoretical basis of the test constructs. Nevertheless, in terms of what is currently practicable we propose that in most cases a preferred strategy would involve some combination of confirmatory factor analysis (CFA) and IRT. There are many extensive sources detailing the theory and use of CFA and IRT, but as single sources probably most people would find Brown

(CFA: 2015), and Embretson and Reise (IRT: 2000) to be most useful, as are Chapters 8, 10, 15, and 16 in the current volume, each of which provides practical demonstrations of relevant analyses.

CFA is especially useful in terms of providing robust estimates of the number of dimensions underlying a dataset, addressing questions of convergent and discriminant validity, and providing generally optimal estimates of reliability (e.g., McDonald's Omega, see next). Whereas IRT provides precise information on item difficulty, reliability across the range of scale values, and can provide the basis for short tests with good reliability. For these reasons, we would generally recommend that test development should use a combination of both in order to fully explore the properties of scales and ensure that the final test is optimal in terms of its psychometric properties.

Many textbooks on statistics and articles on methods suggest the use of principal components analysis (e.g., Field, 2013; Hair, Anderson, Tatham, & Black, 2006; Johnson & Wichern, 2007). We suggest that in the majority of cases the disadvantages of using principal components analysis far outweigh the advantages. The choice in terms of theory is between principal components and the common factor model (Mulaik, 2005; Mulaik, Chapter 8). In the first case, principal components analysis is an observed variable model, whereas the common factor model assumes a latent variable model. The difference is very close to the distinction made between cause and effect indicator models (Murray & Booth, Chapter 7). Figure 1.1 shows the difference graphically. In the case of principal components, it is assumed that it is the items that give rise to the score, hence the direction of the arrows from the item to the observed score (see Figure 1.1a). A possible example might be overall health conceived of as the total number of health-related problems suffered in a specified period of time. There is no assumption of one underlying cause to these problems or that there should be a correlation between them, it is just that the sum score provides an indicator of overall health. While this may be an appropriate model for health indicators, for the vast majority of psychometric tests, it is not. Mostly, scientists conceive of their variables as underlying traits that manifest themselves in terms of observed behavior. For example, personality traits are normally conceived of as enduring characteristics of a person, which give rise to consistency in behavior across situations and time (Funder, 2001). They are in effect latent traits that cause manifest behavior. This conception corresponds to the common factor model, which assumes that it is the latent trait that

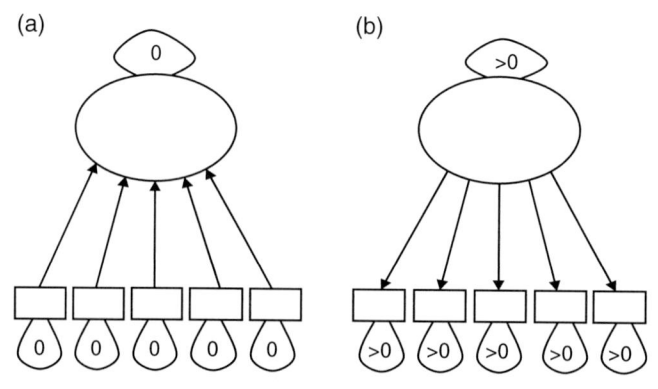

Figure 1.1 Principal component model (a) and common factor model (b) represented using structural equation models (SEM) diagram conventions.

causes the observed indicators. Hence, in Figure 1.1(b) the arrows point from the latent variable (not score) to the indicators.

It is often contended that, although the common factor model might be theoretically appropriate, the principal component model has mathematical advantages and that in practice solutions differ only to a minor degree and thus should be preferred. Among these advantages is that principal component is not subject to factor score indeterminacy (Mulaik, 2005) and also many scientists consider principal components to represent the most parsimonious representation of the data. We contend here that these advantages are outweighed by the disadvantages. In the first place, the circumstances in which principal component and common factor solutions are similar are more restrictive than is generally acknowledged; in many cases the differences are quite substantive (Widaman, 1993). To provide examples, it is very rare indeed that a principal component solution will fit a CFA model, whereas exploratory factor solutions using adequate samples and appropriate estimators more often result in good fitting confirmatory solutions (Gerbing & Hamilton, 1996; Hurley et al., 1997). Given the usefulness of CFA as an analytic technique, this is a serious disadvantage. Second, the methods used to estimate the number of factors underlying a data set that are available when using principal components rarely provide the most precise estimate (see Timmerman, Lorenzo-Siva, & Cuelemans, Chapter 11). Third, principal components analysis assumes perfect reliability of measurement, which is highly implausible with respect to most social science and many other types of data. Fourth, however small the difference, why would anyone prefer the theoretically incorrect solution? For these reasons, we suggest that the common factor model in exploratory, but preferably in confirmatory form is to be preferred in most instances.

Whether you can actually use CFA effectively depends on how well the scale is designed in the first instance. Sometimes an exploratory analysis is required because the items do not sufficiently precisely conform to your expected measurement model. The most common causes of this phenomenon are because the model was poorly specified (i.e., it has a poor theoretical underpinning) or because items were poorly constructed (e.g., Booth & Hughes, 2014). However, if it can be used, CFA has many advantages, including: it provides a relatively strong test of the number of factors, it provides relatively sound data on the behavior of items and, according to Joreskög (1969), avoids the problem of factor score indeterminacy. All of these advantages only accrue if the sampling procedures and sample size are adequate, and that sensible choices are made with respect to estimators and fit criteria.

From the perspective of developing scales with good psychometric properties, ideally a CFA model will conform to very simple structure. This is a structure in which items load on just one factor and loadings of items on all other factors are zero. This type of simple structure is different from Thurstone's original conception and for some purposes may not be strictly necessary (Mulaik, 2010). However, if all items provide effectively pure measures of a unidimensional construct this is highly desirable and would be the case if very simple structure holds (Hattie, 1985).

A key decision in CFA is the choice of estimator. Provided its assumptions are met maximum likelihood is a very attractive choice since asymptotically it provides consistent, efficient, and unbiased estimates, that is, estimates with small standard errors, and which tend toward the true population parameters (Bollen, 1989; Larsen & Marx, 1981). However, item-level data is almost never continuous or normally distributed, so in practice for scale development maximum likelihood is almost never the theoretically correct option. Nevertheless, many authors prefer maximum likelihood to the alternatives arguing that in practice it performs well with binary items and items with at least five response options (Dolan, 1994; Millsap & Kim, Chapter 26). However, at least theoretically, weighted least squares (Browne, 1984) and diagonally weighted least squares are preferable since they are designed for ordered-categorical data and make no assumptions about distribution (Flora & Curran, 2004). In practice, under most circumstances it is diagonally weighted least squares that recovers population parameters best (Flora & Curran, 2004). There is also clear evidence that maximum likelihood does not always perform well with ordered-categorical items (MacCallum, Browne, & Cai, 2012; Nye & Drasgow, 2011). Increasingly, therefore, diagonally weighted least squares is becoming a preferred option.

The issue of model fit is also important if the advantages of CFA are to be realized. There is an extensive literature on this subject much of it focusing on fit when using the maximum likelihood estimator (e.g., Bentler, 1990; Fan & Sivo, 2007; Hu & Bentler, 1999, 1998; Marsh, Hau, & Grayson, 2005; Schermelleh-Engel, Moosbrugger, & Muller, 2003). Classic studies by Hu and Bentler (1998, 1999) that used Monte Carlo simulations have provided empirically derived recommendations with respect both to which fit indices recover the correct solution most consistently and what cut-offs to employ. A somewhat simplified version of their recommendations is that multiple indices of fit should be employed, and that the following fit indices with associated cut-off values perform well; (Root Mean Square Error of Approximation (RMSEA) ≤ 0.06, Standardized Root Mean Square Residual (SRMSR) ≤ 0.08, Tucker–Lewis Index (TLI) ≥ 0.95, Comparative Fit Index (CFI) ≥ 0.95), and application of these golden rules more or less represents current practice. Actually, Hu and Bentler's recommendations were more nuanced, suggesting that different indices are particularly sensitive to different sources of misspecification. Moreover, many commentators have warned against slavishly following golden rules, and instead suggest that statistical judgment needs to be exercised (e.g., Marsh et al., 2010; Yuan, 2005).

One of the disadvantages of using the diagonally weighted least squares estimator is that there is less simulation data on which to base choices of fit indices and accompanying cut-off values. Nevertheless, Nye and Drasgow (2011) have shown that the golden rules do not work well with diagonally weighted least squares. They recommend that the RMSEA and SRMSR be used and warn that the TLI and CFI perform poorly. Their simulation shows that much more restrictive cut-offs are required, and that these are dependent on a number of factors including sample size. They offer an excel program to calculate the appropriate cut-off values. One limitation is that their simulation only applies to dichotomized data but, clearly, any data can be transformed into this form. Probably a similar approach could be adopted when using the maximum likelihood estimator given that the golden rules often perform poorly in this case too (Chen, Curran, Bollen, Kirby, & Paxton, 2008; Fan & Sivo, 2005, 2007; Yuan, 2005).

It has been recognized for many years than any statistical model is just an approximation and that it would rarely if ever hold exactly (MacCallum, Browne, & Cai, 2012). This is as true of CFA as any other model. However, there is a very general deficiency of CFA that would counsel against its sole use in scale development, which is that a CFA model can show excellent psychometric properties when in fact the scale provides unreliable measurement at some levels of the trait. For this reason alone, there is a strong argument for applying IRT as well as CFA for scale development. IRT has many other advantages, too (Embretson & Reise, 2000, p. 15). One principal advantage is that it can provide the statistical basis of computer adaptive testing. The latter can provide reliable tests with shorter testing times and is relatively robust to cheating when administered via the internet, without proctoring. In the modern era, these are considerable advantages. For these reasons, most widely used ability and achievement tests (e.g., the SAT, WAIS IV, Woodcock–Johnson IV) are actually based on IRT rather than CFA, although currently, IRT is not commonly used in personality or attitude testing. We will illustrate the uses of both CFA and IRT in our practical example.

Reliability

Psychometric tests are evaluated using three conceptually different estimates of reliability: internal consistency, test-retest, and coefficients of equivalence. Revelle and Condon (Chapter 23) provide an extensive treatment of reliability, here we will make some simplified recommendations. By some distance, the most commonly reported measure of reliability is Cronbach's alpha. What is not commonly realized is that under most conditions Cronbach's alpha is a Guttmann lower bound to reliability (Rae, 2007; Zinbarg, Revelle, Yovel, & Li, 2005). Under most circumstances, MacDonald's Omega provides the most accurate estimate of reliability. Code 2 in the Code Appendix provides example MPlus code to calculate Omega, and Revelle and Condon (Chapter 23) provide R code. Because Cronbach's alpha is so widely understood we recommend that both it and Omega are routinely reported in technical specifications of tests.

It can be shown that reliability is the ratio of true score variance to total observed variance, or the ratio of true score variance to the sum of true score and error variance. In reality, however, what is regarded as error depends on how a construct is theorized. Possible sources of error variance include the following:

1 Learning, growth, fatigue, forgetting, senescence, biorhythms, maturation, motivation, and historical events
2 Quality of items
3 Extent to which items conform to definition of trait
4 Situational factors: for example, noise, incorrect timing, ambiguous instructions
5 Effects due to (1) practice, (2) rehearsal, and (3) consistency

Schmidt and Hunter (1996) apply a somewhat different trichotomy to sources of error variance:

1 Random response errors that occur within occasions and include variations in attention, mental efficiency, momentary distractions, and so on.
2 Transient errors that vary across occasions and include errors due to mood, feeling, mental efficiency, and so on.
3 Specific errors that consist of variance specific to the tests but are unrelated to the defined trait; for example, item wording, instructions, and items unrelated to trait.

To a degree, internal consistency measures of reliability take account of random response errors and specific errors. However, they clearly do not take account of sources of error that vary over time. For this reason, test-retest or stability coefficients provide useful additional information on reliability. However, these are only appropriate if the focal construct is hypothesized to show stability over time. It is clearly unsuitable as a measure of the reliability of state measures, which are expected to change over time. Internal consistency measures also do not fully take account of the extent to which items correspond to the trait. For this reason, alternate form or equivalence coefficients are another important source of reliability information. In the case of personality, it is notorious that alternate forms providing measures of purportedly the same construct derived from different personality inventories show particularly poor reliability as measured by equivalence coefficients (Pace & Brannick, 2010). This suggests that different personality measures ostensibly measuring the same trait in fact do so only very approximately. This issue probably affects many other types of measure, although this issue is often not fully explored.

However, for traits used in selection: random response, transient, and specific effects should arguably all be treated as error. Traits used for selection are of little use if they vary much over time, measure irrelevant factors, or are subject to response artifacts. So, Schmidt and Hunter (1996) have argued that the measure of reliability appropriate to selection instruments is the coefficient of equivalence and stability (CES). The CES is estimated by correlating two parallel forms administered at two points in time. While the logic seems compelling, this is yet to become standard practice.

Which coefficients of reliability are actually appropriate to any given test depends on how the construct to be tested is theorized. However, APA, AERA, and NCME (2014) guidelines advise the reporting of internal consistency, stability, and, equivalence measures of reliability, so when developing a test all three should be measured or the technical specification should provide a clear rationale for the inappropriateness of those measures of reliability that are omitted.

Validation

Validation is also an important stage in test development and evaluation, many would argue the key stage (e.g., AERA, APA, NCME, 2014; Smith & Smith, 2005). Hughes (Chapter 24) provides a sophisticated treatment of this issue, while Bollen (1989) and Ghiselli, Campbell and Zedeck (1981) also provide invaluable treatments. Traditional views of validity have evolved over time (Newton & Shaw, 2014) with the current model suggesting that validity is a unitary construct examined using different sources of validity evidence. According to this conceptualization there are not different types of validity. Instead, validity is a summary construct based on varied categories of validity evidence (AERA, APA, NCME, 2014; Messick, 1989). There are broadly five such categories, namely evidence based on test content, response processes, test structure, relationships with other variables, and consequences of testing.

From a pragmatic perspective, it is useful to classify different sources of validity evidence, and as argued by Borsboom, Mellenberg, & van Heerden, (2004), Cizek (2012, 2016), and Hughes (Chapter 24) attempting to understand "validity" as a unitary concept is cumbersome, illogical, and perhaps even impossible. In this Handbook, Hughes (Chapter 24) argues that the types of validity evidence are best considered in response to two questions: Does the test measure what it purports to and is the test useful for some specified purpose. The first of these questions pertains to the accuracy of a psychometric test and the second refers to the appropriateness of a psychometric for a specified purpose. This distinction, though simple, is very useful and also bypasses one of the major problems often faced by test developers: Whether to maximize either accuracy of measurement or predictive utility. Under a unitary model of validity these two criteria contribute equally toward a single validity coefficient/argument despite the fact that they represent quite different goals that require quite different information and may be mutually exclusive (e.g., Borsboom et al., 2004). Using Hughes' accuracy and appropriateness model they represent separate goals and processes, so neither needs to be compromised in pursuit of the other (see also Borsboom et al., 2004; Cizek, 2016).

The accuracy of a psychometric test can be established by examining the response processes of the participant while taking the test, the content of the test, and the structure of the test.

Response processes: Psychometric tests are primarily designed to measure constructs (e.g., extraversion, school knowledge) with the underlying assumption that the construct in some way drives the test item response (e.g., those who are extraverted like parties and thus strongly agree with the statement "I like to go to parties"). Thus, if we are trying to measure the construct of extraversion we need to establish that the test item response is driven by extraversion (Borsboom et al., 2004; Embretson, 1984, 1994). There are several methods for investigating item responses: Perhaps the two most notable are cognitive models (e.g., Embretson, 1994, 1998, 2016) and think-aloud protocols (Ericsson & Simon, 1980). In brief, what the test developer needs to do is hypothesize the likely mental processes underlying the item response and then examine whether this is the case. If, in our example, participants strongly agree to the item "I like to go to parties," but only because they feel this is the appropriate response, then we are measuring social desirability and not extraversion. Thus, our test would be inaccurate.

Test content and structure: One of the most important elements of test construction is ensuring that the test content covers all relevant elements. Given that we are interested in examining test responses (e.g., rotating a shape, retrieving learned information) it is important that test content covers the whole domain of the response process. Thus, if a test is to measure human cognitive abilities then it should assess all known relevant elements of cognitive ability (e.g., Carroll, 1993; Jensen, 1998; Nyborg, 2003). It follows that the stronger the conceptual and empirical base that exists regarding the nature of a construct, the easier it is to apply in the process of test development. If the test systematically samples different and relevant domains of cognitive ability, carefully designs items in accordance with item design guidelines, controls response artifacts and construct irrelevant sources of variance, and makes use of empirical knowledge concerning item content and its relation to known measurement properties, then the test is likely to have content that accurately represents the construct. A related point pertains to the structure of the test content. In simple terms, the test content should match the theoretical model of the construct. If cognitive ability is theorized to consist of a general factor, three third-order factors, 16 second-order factors, and 120 primary factors (Johnson & Bouchard, 2005; McGrew, 2009), then these factors should be identifiable when analyzing test data. If they are identifiable then we can say that the structure accurately matches the theoretical framework posited. As discussed previously, forms of factor analysis provide the most common method for examining the structure of test data.

The second element of validation concerns the appropriateness of using a psychometric test for a given purpose. As with reliability, whether a particular source of validity evidence is relevant or not depends on the purpose to which the test score is put and there are many such purposes. In general, whether the use of a test for a specified purpose is appropriate or not is determined by examining the relation of test scores to other variables, the consequences of test use, and the feasibility of test use.

Criterion relations: This is most important in relation to selection tests, where the greatest weight is placed on criterion validity. The rationale is that if a test is to be used to select employees, then the test is useful to the extent that it predicts future performance. For selection tests, therefore, it is usual to measure the correlation between test scores and some measure of job performance, either at the same point in time (concurrent validity evidence) or at some future point in time (predictive validity evidence). The larger the correlation the more appropriate the use of the test for employee selection.

Relations with related and unrelated constructs: Convergent validity evidence refers to the extent to which purported measures of the same construct correlate together, while discriminant validity evidence is focused on the correlations that obtain between different constructs. To the extent that measures of the same trait correlate at one, so may they be said to demonstrate convergent validity evidence. In contrast, it is generally supposed that measures of different constructs should show a lesser degree of correlation. One of the most powerful approaches to the assessment of convergent and divergent validity derives from Campbell and Fiske's (1959) multitrait-multimethod approach. Koch, Eid, and Lochner, Chapter 25 in volume 2, describe how this initial insight has developed into a class of very sophisticated MTMM models based on SEM. One caution is required: However sophisticated and powerful the MTMM approach may be, it may not suit all types of data. As Koch et al. (Chapter 25) emphasize, which MTMM model is appropriate depends on the constructs of interest and how they are measured. In fact, it is conceivable that for certain purposes MTMM analyses may not be appropriate at all. It is frequently the case that the different methods in MTMM analyses are composed of different raters. Suppose for the sake of argument that the construct of interest is adaptability to different situations, and that each rater sees each participant in only one situation. One index of adaptability would be the extent of change from one situation to the other which would be a difference score. In this situation, the assumption that the extent to which ratings correlate provide convergent validity evidence, which is essentially the principle of MTMM models, would be entirely incorrect. Researchers should consider very carefully what model is appropriate to their data.

Consequences and fairness: One of the key elements of establishing whether test use is appropriate is a consideration of the consequences of test use. In short, tests should not be used if their use is likely to lead to unjustifiable discrimination or unfairness (consequential validity evidence). Both invariance testing and differential item functioning effectively serve the same purpose: To ensure that the test is fair across qualitatively different groups, examples of which might include groups that differ in terms of gender, age, ethnicity, religion, education, or occupation. The purpose of invariance testing is not to show that different groups obtain identical mean scores; there may be real mean score differences across groups (Del Giudice, Booth, & Irwing, 2012); but rather to show that the test scores are not biased. Two chapters in this volume provide a thorough treatment of both methods: Millsap and Kim (Chapter 26 in Volume 2) and Drasgow, Nye, Stark, and Chernyshenko (Chapter 27 in Volume 2).

With regard to invariance testing, it is generally contended that invariance has been demonstrated if the test has the same factor structure across groups (configural invariance), factor loadings are of identical magnitude (metric invariance), and the items show the same intercept values (scalar invariance: Meredith, 1993; Widaman & Reise, 1997). Appendix Code 3a–3c contains example MPlus code, for the main steps in invariance testing. Some authors also advocate that equality of error variances represents another necessary criterion for invariance to hold (Adolph, Schuurman, Borkenau, Borsboom, & Dolan, 2014). However, Little (2013) provides compelling arguments as to why this is not appropriate.

Differential item testing should, in principle, provide at least highly similar information concerning item and test bias. However, differential item testing is based on IRT modeling. First, a baseline model is estimated and Drasgow et al. (Chapter 27) suggest that the preferable approach is for the baseline model to allow all items to freely vary across groups, with one or more reference items constrained to equivalence. They then suggest that item parameters should be constrained one at a time, and the difference in fit examined. If, in the more constrained model, there is a marked decrement in fit then it is concluded that the constrained item evidences DIF. However, along with Millsap and Kim (Chapter 26), they also suggest that effect size measures of bias are examined. The question is not just whether bias exists but whether it is of practical significance, especially at the test rather than the item level.

Feasibility: One final consideration regarding the appropriateness of test use, not currently contained within standard validation guides (e.g., AERA, NCME, APA, 2014), pertains to the feasibility of test use (Cizek, 2016). This element of validation concerns the rather practical issue of whether or not test use is possible and whether it is sensible according to pragmatic boundaries (e.g., time, cost).

The many forms of validation evidence can be considered using Hughes' (Chapter 24) accuracy and appropriateness model to help test developers maximize the quality of their tests both in terms of measurement and utility. In sum, if responding to a test item requires the use of the target construct (and thus the item response is derivative of the construct), the test content accurately reflects the full domain of the construct and the structure of the data is as hypothesized then we can say we have an accurate test. If the use of a test for a given purpose is supported by criterion, consequential, and feasibility evidence then we can conclude that the use of a test is appropriate.

Test Scoring and Norming

The choice of which method to use in order to score a test is dealt with in more detail elsewhere in this volume (Brown, Chapter 20; Dorans, Chapter 19). IRT scoring is the norm for large commercial tests of cognitive ability, and it has considerable advantages, not least reduced testing time. However, in many situations this form of scoring is not practical. Here we describe unit weighted scoring schemes, which produce standardized scores using an appropriate standardization sample, variants of which include stanine, sten, and t scores (Smith & Smith, 2005). There are arguments for using either population representative samples or samples that are representative of the applicant pool. In many cases, test developers offer both. For many research scales, simple unit weighted sums of item scores without standardization are considered sufficient.

Scale scores are naturally based on the items that have been previously shown both to measure the focal construct and provide unidimensional, reliable, and unbiased measurement. Raw scale scores can either be based on a unit weighted sum of item scores or on factor scores. It is generally contended that unit weighting is more generalizable, although that should depend on the size of the standardization sample. Whichever form of scoring is used, the next step is usually to transform the raw scores so that they provide a good approximation to the normal distribution. Recently some sophisticated programs have been developed in order to achieve this, including the R package *fitdist*, which provides four different methods of fitting a variety of the most commonly used distributions to data (Delignette-Muller & Dutang, 2015). However, under most circumstances traditional Box–Cox procedures, which estimate the power to which the scale score should be raised in order to conform to a normal distribution, provide adequate approximations to normality (Box & Cox, 1964). A number of software packages will provide estimates of the power transformations required for scale scores to conform to normality, the "bcskew" algorithm in STATA being an example. Subsequently the scale score should be raised to the appropriate power previously estimated, and then standardized by subtracting the mean transformed score from the transformed scale scores and dividing by the standard deviation of the transformed scores. The resulting standardized scores (z scores) should then be multiplied by the standard deviation and added to the mean appropriate for the type of scale required: For stens (M = 5.5, SD = 2), stanines (M = 5, SD = 2), t scores (M = 50, SD = 10), and intelligence quotients (M = 100, SD = 15). Choice of scoring system is largely down to convention, although stens and stanines are preferred when measurement is more approximate as in the case of most personality scales, while t scores and intelligence quotients are preferred when measurement is highly reliable and a good approximation to continuous measurement (Smith & Smith, 2005).

Test Specification

The test specifications can only be prepared once all necessary trialing, validation, and standardization studies have been completed and analyzed, although intermediate specifications will likely be required. At one level, the requirement is fairly simple. You need a list of items and item codes (codes for each item are invaluable, e.g., in databases, when writing syntax, etc.) that comprise each version of the test, using an appropriate program and format for storage. Also required are demographic items and the response formats for each item (e.g., Strongly Agree, etc.). The scoring algorithm should be specified in detail and may take the form of lines of syntax in some high-level computer language. You also need to specify the exact design of the published form of the test, including features such as layout, text formatting, and question formatting, whether it appears in print form, or is administered via the internet.

However, the issue becomes complex because most test developers trial items both within the test and in separate pilot studies. Also, changes can be incremental, so what amounts to a new version of the test, and what is just a minor incremental change requires some consideration. What also complicates this issue is that many modern tests use procedures to preserve test usefulness in the circumstance that test taking is not proctored, and that therefore there is a potential for cheating. Measures to combat this may take the form of computer adaptive testing, or a procedure akin to what Morrison and Embretson (Chapter 3) describe as algorithmic item generation. In the case of computer adaptive testing the required item banks are large, whereas with algorithmic item generation large banks of alternative numerical values for each variable need to be pre-specified, Although ultimately designing test specifications is usually fairly simple, the most important lesson is that unless systematic attention is devoted to this issue, there can be a considerable cost in terms of confusion and wasted time.

Implementation and Testing

The sophistication of the implementation and testing will depend on the modality of administration and the four dimensions that affect test complexity defined before (e.g., single scale vs. battery, scale similarity, etc.). Whether the test is administered in paper and pencil form or using internet administration packages, some form of checking process is required to ensure that the test has been correctly implemented. In the case of some commercial tests using bespoke software and automatic scoring the testing process may be very thorough and extensive, which leaves many opportunities for test implementation errors to arise.

The MAT^{80}, described next, is a test battery that uses mixed scale types, narrow spectrum measures, and was developed using a small development team. It is implemented as an internet-based test, provides more or less instant scores which are incorporated into an extensive report, using static rather than dynamic text. For the MAT^{80}, the implementation checks were comprehensive and well defined. At a macro level the major objectives of the checks were to ensure that: (1) The test specification was entirely accurate, especially that it listed all items correctly, and that the scoring algorithm was error free; (2) the scoring algorithm had been correctly implemented on the server; (3) that the appearance and functionality of the interface conformed to the specification; (4) that the test worked on a variety of platforms and software; (5) that all reports were correctly generated within 40 seconds; and (6) that all faults were correctly logged and communicated to the appropriate person in order to be rectified. Probably the simplest example is the check on machine scoring of tests. First, a comprehensive list of test items with appropriate codes was compiled. Second, the scoring syntax was implemented in SPSS and repeatedly applied to test data until there were no faults in the scoring process and all resultant scores showed appropriate properties in terms of mean scores, standard deviations, range, kurtosis, and skewness. The repetition was required in order to eliminate errors from hundreds of lines of code. At this point the test specification was developed and checked. Next, the specification was presented to the team responsible for implementation on the server. This team translated the items and the scoring syntax into the appropriate machine language. In order to ensure that the scoring syntax had been correctly implemented on the server, a set of test data was then scored on the server. These scores were compared with scores based on the same data set, but this time scored on the original machine using the scoring syntax taken directly from the test specification. The scoring syntax was deemed to be correctly implemented on the server when both sets of scores were identical.

Subsequent steps involved directly inputting data by responding to all questions generated via the internet test interface. The simplest of these processes involved tapping in standard score patterns and ensuring that the resulting scores were correct. Many other checks were conducted, for example on the interface, and to ensure performance across different platforms (e.g., operating systems and web browsers), that different reports were all correctly produced. While the precise details will vary considerably, for tests to work to an appropriate standard some form of systematic checking procedure is required. Without a well-defined and systematic checking process, it is unlikely that the test interface or the test scores will be error free.

Technical Manual

The technical manual should describe the results of steps 1–9. No commercial test would be saleable without such a manual, and it is also invaluable for all other types of test. An extensive manual is also required for test administrators. The exact form of this manual will vary considerably depending on the nature of the test, but the most important information to be included concerns the interpretation of test scores.

Example analyses for the Technical Manual

The example analyses presented here are taken from the MAT^{80}, a test designed for recruitment to managerial positions or MBA programs. The full test is comprised of four sections: Section 1 measures Business Personality, Motivation, and Leadership; section 2 assesses Problem Solving, Creativity, and Innovation; section 3 tests Business Numeracy; and section 4 tests Business Reasoning. The subset of analyses presented do not represent a comprehensive account of the analyses conducted in the development of the MAT^{80}, but rather are chosen to be illustrative of the type of analyses required in test development.

Prior to the analyses presented here, each scale had been subject to a process of test development including initial construct definition, desk and empirical research designed to elucidate the dimensional structure of the items (Stage 1, Table 1.1), a process of item development and review (Stage 2, Table 1.1), followed by preliminary administration and analysis in two different data sets (Stage 3d, Table 1.1). Without this development, it is unlikely that scales would fit a confirmatory factor model.

The majority of analyses presented were based on a sample of 1,777 applicants to a Global MBA program, which provided the basis of version 1 of the MAT^{80}. Selected demographic characteristics of this sample are shown in Table 1.3. However, some of the analyses pertain to version 2 of the MAT^{80}. Of the 106 items that make up version 2 of the MAT^{80}, 74 items were new. The Business Numeracy items were also refined. This extensive program of item development was undertaken to increase diversity of item content, improve reliability, and minimize the already very low levels of bias.

We will use the accuracy and appropriateness model of test evaluation (Hughes, Chapter 24) to structure the presentation of the analysis. With respect to accuracy we conducted all of the recommended analyses, with the exception of examining response processes. Rather than examining response processes, the accuracy of the tests in representing each focal construct was assessed on the basis of expert review and structured interviews. Concretely based on an extensive knowledge of the literature, for example that contained in Carroll (1993), Booth (2011), the IPIP (Goldberg, 1999), and of course many other sources, we formulated tight construct definitions, and made an expert judgment as to whether scales conformed to these definitions. These evaluations were repeated on numerous occasions, both individually, in groups of two, and in expert panels. For all scales excepting those assessing cognitive ability, we also interviewed approximately 200 members of the public to explore their understanding of each construct, and the language used was incorporated into items. This process is

Table 1.3 Demographic characteristics of the norm sample for the MAT[80].

Demographic	Response	N
Gender	Male	1,256
	Female	497
	Missing	24
Ethnicity	White	326
	Asian	818
	Black	166
	Arab	268
	Hispanic	54
	Other	117
	Missing	28
Education	Secondary school to age 16 years	1
	Secondary school to age 18 years	13
	Non-university higher education	108
	Undergraduate university education	1,094
	Postgraduate university education	534
	Missing	27
Occupation	Professional/Senior Managerial	1,134
	Junior Professional/Managerial	522
	Administrative/Secretarial	32
	Skilled	15
	Semi-unskilled	28
	Service	8
	Missing	38
Age	Mean years	32.7

N = 1,777

not identical to the use of thinking aloud protocols, but arguably provides similar and some additional data, in that accuracy was engineered into the items. In addition, the structure of the test content was also examined using factor analysis.

With regard to appropriateness, we primarily investigated discriminant, predictive, and incremental predictive validity evidence as the ability to predict appropriate criteria is the key issue for a selection battery. We also examined the stability of the measure across groups to ensure that test use was fair.

Table 1.4 provides the definition together with an example item for each scale in the Business Personality, Motivation, and Leadership section of the test inventory. The 49 items comprising these eight scales were subject to CFA using the diagonally weighted least squares estimator as implemented in MPlus (Muthén & Muthén, 1998–2010). For example MPlus code, please see Appendix Code 1. The resulting pattern matrix is shown in Table 1.5. The corresponding indices of fit for this model were (χ^2 = 6,750.0, df = 1,099, CFI = 0.905, TLI = 0.899, RMSEA = 0.054). According to conventional cut-off values, the CFI and TLI are indicative of moderate fit, and the RMSEA indicates good fit. It is clear from a variety of simulations that simple rules of thumb with regard to fit do not work (Nye & Drasgow, 2011; Yuan, 2005). This model is also far more complex than CFA models typically used in Monte Carlo

Table 1.4 Definition and sample items for Business Personality Motivation and Leadership.

Construct	Definition	Example item
Leadership	The extent to which a person takes responsibility and leads others to success in pursuit of a common goal	People often look to me to make a decision
Assertiveness	The extent to which a person honestly and directly expresses their opinion without aggression	I prefer not to say anything if I disagree with people
Stress Resistance	The extent to which a person performs effectively when the situation pushes them to the limit of their energy, abilities, knowledge, and resources	I know that I can handle lots of stress at work
Achievement	The extent to which a person is hard-working and strives for excellence	I always aim to be the best
Optimism	The extent to which a person thinks good events happen due to stable, internal, global factors	I find the positive when others can only see negatives
Order	The extent to which a person is organized and plans things in advance	I am well organized
Curiosity	The extent to which a person engages with the external world and their own internal thoughts	I am always looking to learn about new things
Intrinsic Motivation	The extent to which a person has a tendency to derive pleasure from working on personal challenges	I prefer jobs that are challenging

simulations (Hu & Bentler, 1998, 1999; Nye & Drasgow, 2011). Strictly then, there is no definitive interpretation of these fit statistics. However, given the complexity of the model, the fit statistics suggest that the level of misspecification is not substantial.

The pattern matrix shows that all but three of the 49 loadings are greater than 0.5, 36 are greater than 0.6, and the highest loading is 0.907. That the loadings are substantial and that the pattern matrix matches the theorized structure suggests the items are accurate, that is, 46 of the 49 measure their respective constructs well, and they contain little construct irrelevant variance. The factor correlations range from 0.333 to 0.801 in magnitude. While the constructs are highly correlated, they are nevertheless distinct.

Reliability and scale characteristics For each of the eight scales, a unit weighted sum score was created. In order to reduce skewness and kurtosis, Box-Cox (1964) power transformations were first calculated in STATA and then applied to the sum scores. These transformed scores were then converted into stanines. The scale reliability (McDonald's Omega and Cronbach's Alpha), mean, standard deviation, skew, kurtosis, and standard error of measurement for each of the resultant Business, Personality, Motivation, and Leadership scales are presented in Table 1.6. McDonalds's Omega was chosen as the reliability statistic as it generally provides a good estimate of reliability (Revelle & Zinbarg, 2009; Zinbarg, et al., 2005). For example MPlus code, please

Table 1.5 Standardized factor loadings for the Business Personality, Motivation, and Leadership scales.

Item	1	2	3	4	5	6	7	8
1	0.669							
2	0.647							
3	0.658							
4	0.744							
5	0.563							
6	0.547							
7	0.616							
8	0.622							
9	0.559							
10	0.452							
11	0.573							
12	0.660							
13		0.448						
14		−0.595						
15		−0.688						
16		−0.731						
17			0.827					
18			−0.651					
19			0.767					
20			0.610					
21			0.783					
22			−0.657					
23				0.699				
24				0.686				
25				0.751				
26				0.375				
27				0.814				
28					0.755			
29					−0.722			
30					−0.695			
31					−0.614			
32						0.907		
33						−0.836		
34						0.698		
35						0.887		
36						−0.790		
37							0.631	
38							0.747	
39							0.525	
40							0.654	
41							0.539	
42							0.622	
43							0.530	
44								0.791

(*continued on p. 28*)

Table 1.5 (*Continued*)

				Factors				
Item	1	2	3	4	5	6	7	8
45								0.736
46								0.745
47								0.752
48								0.828
49								0.573

N = 1,771
Note: 1 = Strategic Leadership, 2 = Assertiveness, 3 = Stress Resistance, 4 = Achievement, 5 = Optimism, 6 = Order, 7 = Curiosity, 8 = Intrinsic Motivation

Table 1.6 Scale reliabilities, means, standard deviations, skew, kurtosis, and standard error of measurement for the Business, Personality, Motivation, and Leadership stanine scales.

Scale	Omega	Alpha	Omega-2	M	SD	Skew	Kurtosis	SEM
Leadership	0.86	0.70	0.90	5.00	2.00	0.00	−0.07	0.04
Assertiveness	0.59	0.64	0.83	5.00	2.00	0.00	−0.20	0.04
Stress Resistance	0.80	0.78	0.88	5.00	2.00	0.00	−0.38	0.04
Achievement	0.74	0.63	0.79	5.00	2.00	0.00	−0.28	0.04
Optimism	0.70	0.69	0.94	5.00	2.00	0.00	−0.49	0.04
Order	0.88	0.88	0.74	5.00	2.00	0.00	−0.72	0.04
Curiosity	0.74	0.65	0.84	5.00	2.00	0.00	0.38	0.04
Intrinsic Motivation	0.82	0.77	0.89	5.00	2.00	0.00	0.17	0.04

see Appendix Code 2. Perhaps it is to be expected that the stanine scores are correct, given that a simple numerical formula was applied to obtain them, however, it is also apparent that the Box-Cox transformations provide a good approximation to normality, and even the figures for kurtosis are acceptable. Without using power transformations, it is not possible to achieve all these properties simultaneously. Also provided are the reliabilities for version 2 of these scales (Omega-2), in which as described previously 77% of the items are new, excluding those measuring cognitive ability, which had just been refined. An extensive program of scale development has improved both the diversity of item content and the reliability of the scales, which are impressive.

Fairness and the Business Personality, Motivation, and Leadership Scales

The Business Personality, Motivation, and Leadership Scales were tested for fairness across gender and ethnicity using the method of assessing factorial invariance in ordered-categorical measures devised by Millsap and Yun-Tein (2004). All analyses were conducted using the diagonally weighted least squares estimator as implemented in MPlus (Muthén & Muthén, 2010). Testing for invariance provided a simultaneous test of the suitability of the MAT[80] for candidates for whom English is a second language. For example MPlus code, please see Appendix Code 3a–3c.

Various criteria have been suggested for the measurement of fairness. In a recent simulation study Chen (2007) suggested a two-step criterion, which differs depending on the magnitude of the sample and the evenness of sample sizes. For sample sizes of 300 or

Table 1.7 Tests of invariance across ethnicity and gender for the Business Personality, Motivation, and Leadership scales.

Model	X^2	df	CFI	ΔCFI	RMSEA	ΔRMSEA	TLI
White (N = 331) vs. E. Asian (Chinese, N = 382)							
Configural	3,806.1	2,295	.936		.043		.932
Metric	3,816.8	2,337	.938	.002	.042	−.001	.935
Scalar	4,017.8	2,465	.935	−.003	.042	.000	.935
White (N = 331) vs. S. E. Asian (Malaysian, N = 267)							
Configural	3,755.2	2,297	.921		.046		.916
Metric	3,775.8	2,339	.922	.001	.045	−.001	.919
Scalar	3,945.7	2,467	.920	−.002	.045	.000	.921
White (N = 331) vs. S. Asian (Indian/Pakistani, N = 169)							
Configural	3,488.1	2,296	.920		.046		.914
Metric	3,504.2	2,338	.921	.001	.045	−.001	.918
Scalar	3,659.0	2,466	.920	−.001	.044	−.001	.920
White (N = 331) vs. Arab (N = 282)							
Configural	3,604.4	2,297	.931		.043		.926
Metric	3,654.4	2,297	.931	.000	.043	.000	.927
Scalar	3,908.0	2,467	.924	−.007	.044	.001	.924
Male (N = 1,256) vs. Female (N = 497)							
Configural	7,475.8	2,298	.915		.051		.909
Metric	7,387.6	2,340	.917	.002	.050	−.001	.913
Scalar	6,830.3	2,562	.930	.013	.044	−.006	.933

less and uneven sample sizes Chen suggests that fairness requires that the CFI does not reduce by .005 or more and the RMSEA does not increase by more than .01 when: (1) comparing the metrically invariant to the configurally invariant model and (2) the scalar to the metrically invariant model. When sample sizes are 500 or more and are even in size then fairness requires that the CFI does not reduce by .010 or more and the RMSEA does not increase by more than .015.

The results of the invariance testing for ethnicity and gender for the Business Personality, Motivation, and Leadership scales are presented in Table 1.7. When considering the Business Personality, Motivation, and Leadership scales, the most stringent criterion only applies to the comparison of Whites with South Asians. Here the CFI increased by .001 (Metric vs. Configural), and then decreased by .001 (Scalar vs. Metric), and the RMSEA increased by .001 for both comparisons (see Table 1.7). These results are substantially within the stringent criteria specified by Chen and show convincingly that the Business Personality, Motivation, and Leadership scales are fair when comparing South Asians with Whites. Similarly, for the remaining comparisons across ethnicity and gender, the less stringent criteria for fairness were met in every case (see Table 1.7). In fact, considered as a whole in 6 out of 10 cases the CFI either increased in magnitude or showed no change and the RMSEA decreased; that is, the metrically and scalar invariant models showed a better fit than the configurally invariant model. Improvement in fit of more restrictive models is very unusual, and provides convincing evidence of the fairness of the Business Personality, Motivation, and Leadership Scales.

The MAT[80] was devised using an explicit language standard, including preferred use of the 850 most common English words wherever possible, explicit rules concerning the simplification of language, as well as highly explicit item writing guidelines. This approach to item development may explain why our test items do not appear to show bias across different ethnic groups residing in different countries.

Predictive validity evidence

In order to establish the predictive validity of the MAT^{80}, a number of analyses were undertaken. First, a series of SEM were estimated in order to determine the MAT^{80}'s ability to predict overall semester marks for MBA students. Second, these multiple Rs were combined using meta-analytic techniques to provide an overall estimate of the MAT^{80}'s predictive validity.

This approach to examining predictive validity differs from standard practice in two major respects. Firstly, the most common form of educational outcome data used to assess predictive validity of the Graduate Management Admission Test (GMAT), the most widely used selection test for MBA programs, is first-year grade point average, with graduate grade point average also used, but much less commonly. The disadvantage of both these outcome criteria is that the factor structure of these data is assumed rather than measured and there is no correction for unreliability of measurement. These difficulties with respect to standard practice reflect a subset of a complex range of problems with outcome criteria that have been collectively labeled the criterion problem (e.g., Austin & Villanova, 1992; Viswesvaran & Ones, 2000).

When we applied structural equation modeling to our outcome data we found that not all measures were reliable indicators, and that not all indicators loaded on a general factor. So, it may be concluded that the SEM models more accurately represent the criterion data. A disadvantage of this approach is that, because students take different courses, we cannot take a simple sum of grade scores in order to obtain an overall grade point average. Instead, we combined the estimates of multiple Rs using a weighted average, as is standard in psychometric meta-analysis (Hunter & Schmidt, 2004). However, here we are averaging across different outcomes and different subsets of students. While the overall point estimate is probably accurate, it is based on a missing data design with unknown missingness characteristics. Table 1.8 presents the results of this analysis.

Table 1.8 Prediction of semester grades from MAT^{80} scores, corrected for unreliability in the criterion, and with a further correction for range restriction.

Semester marks	N	RMSEA	SRMR	ρ	Prange res.
1st	734	.028	.024	.283	.355
2nd	608	.042	.026	.390	.470
3rd	368	.051	.038	.494	.630
4th	355	.040	.037	.377	.503
5th	294	.034	.021	.421	.553
All	1,599	NA	NA	.393	.507
Semesters 2–5	1,599	NA	NA	.420	.552

Note: Course marks for the semester are based on the courses taken in each semester. For Semesters 1–5 the courses are: 1st Semester: Marketing, Managerial Economics, Global Events and Leadership; 2nd Semester: Accounting in Business, Operations Management; 3rd Semester: Comparative and International Business, Corporate Finance, Business Simulation; 4th Semester: Strategic Management, Final Project Preparation; 5th Semester: People Management and Organisations. RMSEA = Root mean square residual; SRMR – SRMSR; ρ = multiple R corrected for unreliability in the criterion, Prange res. = Multiple R corrected for range restriction.

The RMSEA and SRMR estimates demonstrate that all models estimated were a close fit to the data (see Table 1.8) (for the RMSEA ≤ 0.06 = close fit, > 0.06–0.08 = good fit, 0.08–0.10 = acceptable fit; for the SRMR ≤ 0.05 = close fit, > 0.05–0.08 = good fit; Hu & Bentler, 1998, 1999; Schermelleh-Engel, Moosbrugger, & Muller, 2003).

Based on extensive experience of university examining, we suggest that Semester 1 marks are rarely a reliable indicator of future performance since the majority of students at this stage are going through a period of adjustment to the requirements of higher education. Examining the predictive validities in Table 1.8 also suggests that Semester 1 marks represent an outlier. Therefore, arguably the best estimate of the overall predictive validity of the MAT^{80} is based on the mean for Semesters 2–5. As can be seen in Table 1.8, the results of this analysis (e.g., MPlus code, please see Appendix Code 4) suggest that the overall predictive validity of the MAT^{80} in predicting MBA students' marks in Semesters 2–5 is 0.42 once unreliability in the criterion has been accounted for.

It is of note that the highest estimated predictive validity for the MAT^{80}, at 0.63, occurred when students undertook courses in Comparative and International Business, Corporate Finance, and Business Simulation (Semester 3). It appears that the MAT^{80} is most capable of predicting performance in those subjects most closely related to core business skills.

The predictive validity of the MAT^{80} can be understood further by considering it against the predictive validity of the GMAT, currently the most popular psychometric test utilized by business schools for admissions to graduate management programs. Table 1.9 presents comparison data for the GMAT taken from Kuncel, Credé, and Thomas' (2007) meta-analysis.

In order to determine the most appropriate grounds for comparison of the MAT^{80} and the GMAT, it is first necessary to consider that the MAT^{80} is primarily administered to applicants for whom English is a second language. This means that the most closely equivalent data for the GMAT is that for applicants who are non-native English speakers. The estimate of the overall predictive validity of the MAT^{80}, at 0.42, thus

Table 1.9 Meta-analysis of GMAT validities with corrections for unreliability in the criterion and range restriction.

Predictor	N	Corrected for unreliability	Corrected for unreliability and range restriction
		Native English-speaking	
Verbal	48,915	.253	.340
Quantitative	48,758	.325	.380
Total	28,624	.344	.470
		Non-native English-speaking	
Verbal	1,815	.157	.210
Quantitative	1,815	.299	.350
Total	1,815	.300*	.374*

* Estimate.
Note. Adapted from "A meta-analysis of the predictive validity of the Graduate Management Admission Test (GMAT) and undergraduate grade point average (UGPA) for graduate student academic performance." By Kuncel, N. R., Credé, M., Thomas, L. L. *Academy of Management Learning & Education*, 6, 60. Copyright 2007 by Academy of Management. Adapted with permission.

compares favorably to the equivalent GMAT estimate, which stands at 0.30. Importantly, however, the MAT^{80} also appears to enjoy a sizable advantage over the GMAT with respect to predictive validity in English-speaking samples.

It would be useful to know the true predictive validity of the MAT^{80} corrected for range restriction, and to compare that with the equivalent figure for the GMAT. One conservative approach is to use the same correction for direct range restriction as Table 1.9.

Applied by Kuncel et al. (2007). The correction for direct range restriction uses the ratio of the standard deviation (SD) from the unrestricted sample to that in the restricted sample. In the case of Kuncel et al. (2007), the unrestricted sample was the total applicant population to all business schools using the GMAT and the restricted sample was successful candidates to all business schools in the sample. Arguably, such a correction provides a lower bound correction for the MAT^{80}. Given the highly selective nature of the MBA program studied, it is likely that the successful applicants represent a more selected sample than is true for the full range of business schools. Thus, it is reasonable to assume that in such a sample the effects of range restriction would likely be greater than is true for the total GMAT sample, which includes the total range of business schools from top to bottom. If one applies corrections in this way then the best estimate of the mean predictive validity of the MAT^{80} is 0.55, whereas for the GMAT the estimate is 0.37 when administered to non-native English speakers, and 0.47 when administered to native English speakers.

The results of the predictive validity analyses thus suggest the following two conclusions. Firstly, on any reasonable comparison the MAT^{80} appears to have a higher predictive validity than the GMAT. Secondly, even at a conservative estimate of 0.55, the predictive validity of the MAT^{80} is strong by conventional criteria (Cohen, 1988). In 2008, Oh, Schmidt, Schaffer, and Lee applied a new indirect range restriction correction to the GMAT data of Kuncel et al. (2007) and concluded that the validities had been underestimated by 7%. Making this correction, the overall predictive validity of the GMAT in English-speaking samples is 0.50, and for the MAT^{80} the revised figure is 0.59, but for predominantly non-English-speaking samples, in which the GMAT performs poorly.

Illustrative IRT analysis of the Leadership scale

The MAT^{80} was not developed using IRT, with the sole exception of the Business Numeracy scale. This broadly follows convention in that until relatively recently IRT has not routinely been applied to the development of personality-type items. However, as argued previously, IRT has many advantages over classical test theory (see Brown, Chapter 21; Embretson & Reise, 2000).

Here we provide an illustrative analysis of the current measure of Strategic Leadership used in the MAT^{80}. Four of ten items are shown in Table 1.10. Notably the items are diverse in content with no repetition, something lacking in many scales of this type. Here we used responses from 2,360 applicants to a Global MBA program. The demographic characteristics of the sample are very similar to those shown in Table 1.3.

The fit of this data to a unidimensional factor model was reasonable, although we would have preferred a smaller value for the RMSEA (χ^2 = 813.2, df = 35, CFI = 0.951, TLI = 0.937, RMSEA = 0.097). We therefore, estimated the item parameters

Table 1.10 Example items from the Strategic Leadership scale.

Item
People often look to me to make a decision
I often see future developments before others
People always do their best work for me
I really understand people's strengths

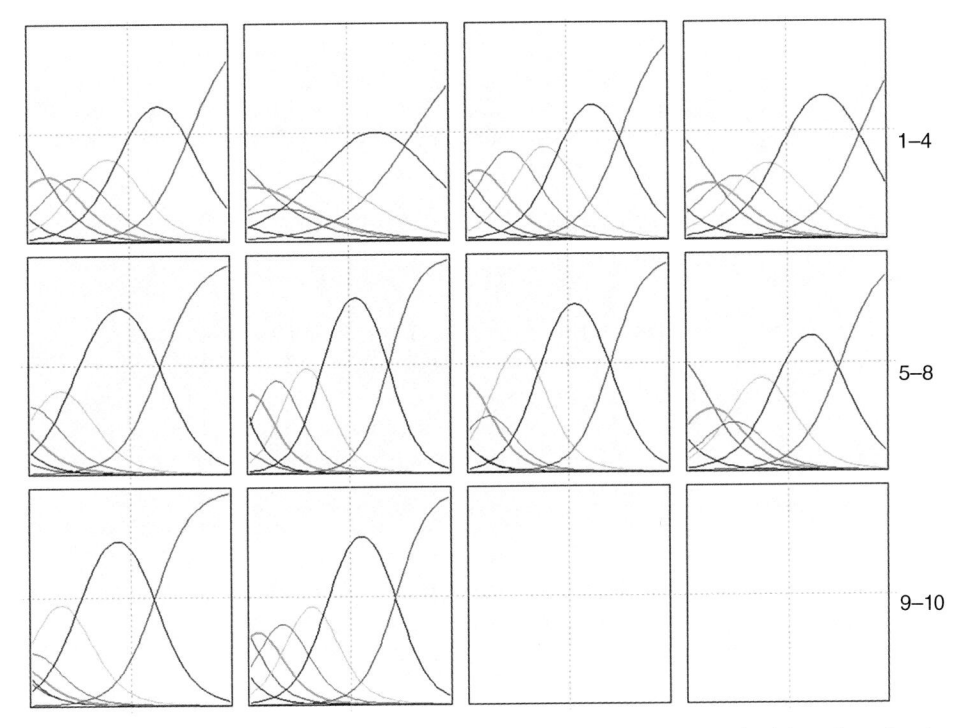

Figure 1.2 Item characteristic curves for the 10 items of the Strategic Leadership scale under the graded response model.

according to Samejima's Graded Response model, assuming unidimensionality, with the program Multilog version 7.0.1, using the Marginal Maximum Likelihood estimator. Figure 1.2 shows the item characteristic curves. It is apparent that the symmetrical pattern desired for these curves is not attained (see Chapters 15 and 16 for further IRT discussion). This is because the responses show a marked negative skew. Figure 1.3 shows the test information function and standard errors of measurement over the range $z = -3-+3$. Using this information and applying formula 20.19 from Brown (Chapter 20), the reliability of measurement at each trait level in the range $z = -3-1.6$, varies from a low of 0.93 to a high of 0.97. If candidates, in order to be selected, had to attain a z-score of 1.6, that would represent a selection ratio of 1:18.2. It would be unusual in practical selection contexts for the selection ratio to exceed 18.2. As Schmidt and Hunter (1998, p. 263) observe, "actual selection ratios are typically in the 0.30–0.70 range." In consequence, the reliability of the Strategic Leadership scale

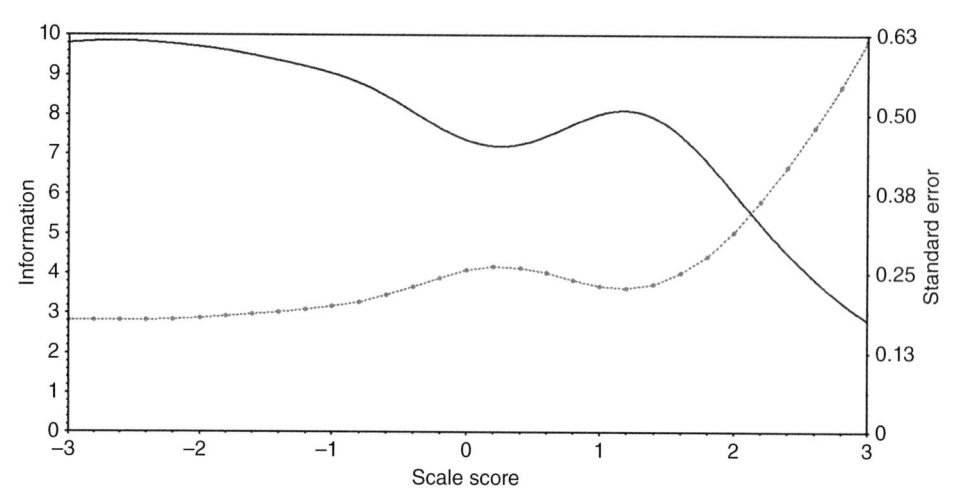

Figure 1.3 Test Information and Standard Errors of measurement for the Strategic Leadership scale under the graded response model.

would be regarded as excellent for most feasible selection decisions, according to conventional criteria. Although theoretically had we strengthened the wording of items we might have obtained a less skewed response distribution, in practice, skewing of responses in high stakes testing is universally obtained when using response options ranging from Strongly Agree to Strong Disagree as is the case here. So, we may conclude that although theoretically IRT should have advantages, in this specific instance little would have been gained by using IRT. For IRT to show an advantage we would have had to use a different testing strategy.

The major omissions from the analyses presented here, which should be included in any scale development, are tests of convergent validity together with tests of test-retest and equivalence reliability. Unfortunately, we are still in the process of gathering data in order to conduct such tests with the MAT[80].

References

Abedi, J. (2006). Language issues in item development. In S. M. Downing, & T. H. Haladyna (Eds.). *Handbook of test development*. Mahwah, NJ: Lawrence Erlbaum Associates.

Adolph, J., Schurrman, N. K., Borkenau, P., Borsboom, D., & Dolan, C. V. (2014). Measurement invariance within and between individuals: A distinct problem in testing the equivalence of intra- and inter- individual model structures. *Frontiers in Psychology, 5*, Article 883.

Althouse, L. A. (n.d.). *Test development: Ten steps to a valid and reliable certificate exam*. Cary, NC: SAS Institute Inc.

American Educational Research Association, American Psychological Association, & National Council on Measurement in Education (1999). Standards for Educational and Psychological Testing. Washington, DC: American Educational Research Association.

Ashton, M. C., Lee, K., & Goldberg, L. R. (2004). A hierarchical analysis of 1,710 English personality-descriptive adjectives. *Journal of Personality and Social Psychology, 87*, 707–721.

Austin, J. T., & Villanova, P. (1992). The criterion problem, 1917–1992. *Journal of Applied Psychology, 77*, 836–874.

Babiak, P., Craig, S., Neumann, Ph. D., & Hare, R. D. (2010). Corporate psychopathy: Talking the walk. *Behavioral Sciences and the Law, 28*, 174–193.

Bentler, P. M. (1990). Comparative fit indices in structural models. *Psychological Bulletin, 107*, 238–246.

Block, J. (1995). A contrarian view of the five-factor approach to personality description. *Psychological Bulletin, 117*, 187–215.

Boddy, C. R. (2011). The corporate psychopath's theory of the global financial crisis. *Journal of Business Ethics, 102*, 255–259.

Boddy, C. R. (2014). Corporate psychopaths, conflict, employee affective well-being and counterproductive work behaviour. *Journal of Business Ethics, 121*, 107–121.

Bollen, K. A. (1989). *Structural equations with latent variables.* New York: John Wiley & Sons, Inc.

Booth, T. (2011). *A review of the structure of normal range personality.* Unpublished doctoral dissertation, University of Manchester, UK.

Booth, T., & Hughes, D. J. (2014) Exploratory structural equation modelling of personality data. *Assessment, 21*, 260–271.

Borenstein, M., Hedges, L. V., Higgins, J. P. T., & Rothstein, H. R. (2009). *Introduction to meta-analysis.* Chichester, UK: John Wiley & Sons, Ltd.

Borsboom, D., Mellenbergh, G. J., & van Heerden, J. (2004). The concept of validity. *Psychological Review, 111*, 1061–1071.

Box, G. E. P., & Cox, D. R. (1964). An analysis of transformations. *Journal of the Royal Statistical Society. Series B (Methodological). 26*, 211–254.

Brace, I. (2005). *Questionnaire design: How to plan, structure and write survey material for effective market research.* London: Kogan Page.

Brown, T. A. (2015). *Confirmatory factor analysis for applied research* (2nd ed.). New York, NY: The Guilford Press.

Browne, M. W. (1984). Asymptotically distribution-free methods for the analysis of covariance structures. *British Journal of Mathematical and Statistical Psychology, 37*, 62–83.

Butcher, J. N., Dahlstrom, W. G., Graham, J. R., Tellegen, A., & Kaemmer, B. (1989). *Minnesota Multiphasic Personality Inventory–2 (MMPI-2). Manual for administration and scoring.* Minneapolis: University of Minnesota Press.

Campbell, D. T., & Fiske, D. W. (1959). Convergent and discriminant validation by the multitrait-multimethod matrix. *Psychological Bulletin, 56*, 81–105.

Carpenter, P. A., Just, M. A., & Shell, P. (1990). What one intelligence test measures: A theoretical account of the processing in the Raven progressive matrices test. *Psychological Review, 97*, 404–431.

Carretta, T. R., & Ree, M. J. (2000). General and specific cognitive and psychomotor abilities in personnel selection: The prediction of training and job performance. *International Journal of Selection and Assessment, 8*, 227–236.

Carroll, J. B. (1993). *Human cognitive abilities: A survey of factor analytic studies.* New York, NY; Cambridge University Press.

Chen, F. F. (2007). Sensitivity of goodness of fit indexes to lack of measurement invariance. *Structural Equation Modeling: A Multidisciplinary Journal, 14*, 464–504.

Chen, F., Curran, P. J., Bollen, K. A., Kirby, J., & Paxton, P. (2008). An empirical evaluation of the use of fixed cutoff points in RMSEA test statistic in structural equation models. *Sociological Methods and Research, 36*, 462–494.

Cizek, G. J. (2012). Defining and distinguishing validity: Interpretations of score meaning and justifications of test use. *Psychological Methods, 17*(1), 31–43.

Cizek, G. J. (2016). Validating test score meaning and defending test score use: different aims, different methods. *Assessment in Education: Principles, Policy & Practice, 23*(2), 212–225.

Cohen, J. (1988). *Statistical power analysis for the behavioral sciences* (2nd ed.). Hillsdale, NJ: Lawrence Erlbaum Associates.

Conn, S. R., & Rieke, M. L. (1994). (Eds.) *The 16PF fifth edition technical manual.* Champagne, IL: Institute for Personality and Ability Testing, Inc.

Corpus of Contemporary American English (2016). Word frequency data. Retrieved October 11, 2016, from, http://www.wordfrequency.info/free.asp.

Costa, P. T., & McCrae, R. R. (1995). Domains and facets: Hierarchical personality assessment using the revised NEO personality inventory. *Journal of Personality Assessment, 64,* 21–50.

Coyle, T. R., & Pillow, D. R. (2008). SAT and ACT predict college GPA after removing g. *Intelligence, 36,* 719–729.

De Vaus, D. (2014). *Surveys in social research* (6th ed.). London: Routledge.

Del Giudice, M., Booth, T., & Irwing, P. (2012). The distance between Mars and Venus: Measuring global sex differences in personality. *PloS ONE, 7*(1), e29265.

Delignette-Muller, M. L., & Dutang, C. (2015). Fitdistrplus: An R Package for Fitting Distributions. Journal of Statistical Software, *64,* 1–34.

Demaio, T., & Landreth, A. (2004). Do different cognitive interview methods produce different results. In S. Presser, J. Rothgeb, M. Couper, J. Lessler, E. Martin, J. Martin, and E. Singer (Eds.), *Questionnaire development and testing methods.* New York, NJ: John Wiley & Sons, Inc.

Dolan, C. V. (1994). Factor analysis of variables with 2-response, 3-response, 5-response and 7-response categories: A comparison of categorical variable estimators using simulated data. *British Journal of Mathematical and Statistical Psychology, 47,* 309–326.

Downing, S. M. (2006). Twelve steps for effective test development. In S. M. Downing & T. H. Haladyna (Eds.), *Handbook of test development.* Mahwah, NJ: Lawrence Erlbaum Associates.

Downing, S. M., & Haladyna, T. H. (Eds.) (2006). *Handbook of test development.* Mahwah, NJ: Lawrence Erlbaum Associates.

Embretson, S. (1984). A general latent trait model for response processes. *Psychometrika, 49*(2), 175–186.

Embretson, S. (1994). Applications of cognitive design systems to test development. In C. R. Reynolds (Ed.), *Cognitive assessment* (pp. 107–135). New York: Springer.

Embretson, S. E. (1998). A cognitive design system approach to generating valid tests: Application to abstract reasoning. *Psychological Methods, 3*(3), 380–396.

Embretson, S. E. (2016). Understanding examinees' responses to items: Implications for measurement. *Educational Measurement: Issues and Practice, 35*(3), 6–22.

Embretson, S. E., & Reise, S. P. (2000). *Item response theory for psychologists.* Mahwah, NJ: Lawrence Erlbaum Associates.

Ericsson, K. A., & Simon, H. A. (1980). Verbal reports as data. *Psychological Review, 87*(3), 215–251.

Fan, X., & Sivo, S. A. (2005). Sensitivity of fit indexes to misspecified structural or measurement model components: Rationale of two-index strategy revisited; *Structural Equation Modeling, 12,* 243–367.

Fan, X., & Sivo, S. A. (2007). Sensitivity of fit indexes to misspecification and model types. *Multivariate Behavioral Research, 42,* 509–529.

Field, A. (2013) *Discovering statistics using SPSS for Windows* (4th ed.). Sage Publications.

Flora, D. B., & Curran, P. J. (2004). An empirical evaluation of alternative methods of estimation for confirmatory factor analysis with ordinal data. *Psychological Methods, 4,* 466–491.

Foddy, W. (1996). *Constructing questions for interviews and questionnaires: Theory and practice in social research.* Cambridge, NY: Cambridge University Press.

Funder, D. C. (2001). Personality. *Annual Review of Psychology, 52,* 197–221.

Gerbing, D. W., & Hamilton, J. G. (1996). Viability of exploratory factor analysis as a precursor to confirmatory factor analysis. *Structural Equation Modeling, 3,* 62–72.

Ghiselli, E. E., Campbell, J. P., & Zedeck, S. (1981). *Measurement theory for the behavioural sciences.* San Francisco, CA: Freeman.

Goldberg, L. R. (1999). A broad-bandwidth, public domain, personality inventory measuring the lower-level facets of several five-factor models. In I. Mervielde, I. Deary, F. De Fruyt, & F.

Ostendorf (Eds.), *Personality psychology in Europe* (Vol. 7) (pp. 7–28). Tilburg, The Netherlands: Tilburg University Press.
Groves, R. M., Fowler, F. J. Jr., Couper, M. P., Lepkowski, J. M., Singer, E., & Tourangeau, R. (2009). *Survey methodology* (2nd ed.). Hoboken, NJ: John Wiley & Sons, Inc.
Hair, J. F., Jr., Anderson, R. E., Tatham, R. L. & Black, W. C. (2006). *Multivariate data analysis*. Upper Saddle River, NJ: Prentice-Hall.
Haladyna, T. M., Downing, S. M., & Rodriguez, M. C. (2002). a review of multiple-choice item writing guidelines for classroom assessment. *Applied Measurement in Education*, 15, 309–334.
Hattie, J. (1985). Methodology review: assessing unidimensionality of tests and items. *Applied Psychological Measurement*, 9, 139–164.
Holland, T. A., Blakeney, R. N., Matteson, M. T., & Schnizen, J. P. (1974). Empirical derivation of the SVIB-Holland scales and conversion scales. *Journal of Vocational Behavior*, 5, 23–29.
Hughes, D. J., & Batey, M. (2017). Using personality questionnaires for selection. In H. W. Goldstein, E. Pulakos, J. Passmore, & C. Semedo (Eds.), *The Wiley Blackwell handbook of the psychology of recruitment, selection & retention* (Ch. 8). Chichester, UK: Wiley-Blackwell.
Hunter, J. E., & Schmidt, F. L. (2004). *Methods of meta-analysis: Correcting error and bias in research findings*. Thousand Oaks, CA: Sage.
Hurley, A. E., Scandura, T. A., Schriesheim, C. A., Brannick, M. T., Seers, A., Vandenberg, R. J., & Williams, L. J. (1997). Exploratory and confirmatory factor analysis: Guidelines, issues, and alternatives. *Journal of Organizational Behavior*, 18, 667–683.
Hu, L.-T., & Bentler, P. M. (1998). Fit indices in covariance structure modeling: Sensitivity to underparameterized model misspecification. *Psychological Methods*, 3, 424–453.
Hu, L.-T., & Bentler, P. M. (1999). Cut-off criteria for fit indexes in covariance structure analysis: Conventional criteria versus new alternatives. *Structural Equation Modeling*, 6, 1–55.
Irwing, P., Cammock, T., & Lynn, R. (2001). Some evidence for the existence of a general factor of semantic memory and its components. *Personality and Individual Differences*, 30, 857–871.
Irwing, P., Phillips, A., & Walters, Z. (2016). *MAT-80: Technical manual*. Altrincham: E-Metrixx.
Jensen, A. R. (1998). *The g factor*. Westport, CT: Praeger.
John, O. P., Angleitner, A., & Ostendorf, F. (1988). The lexical approach to personality: A historical review of trait taxonomic research. *European Journal of Personality*, 2, 171–203.
John, O. P., & Srivastava, S. (1999). The Big Five Trait taxonomy: History, measurement and theoretical perspectives. In L. Pervin and O. P. Johns (Eds.) *Handbook of personality: Theory and research* (2nd ed.). New York: Guilford.
Johnson, W., & Bouchard, T. J. Jr. (2005). The structure of human intelligence: It is verbal, perceptual, and image rotation (VPR). Not fluid and crystallized. *Intelligence*, 33, 393–416.
Johnson, D. W., & Wichern, R. A. (2007). *Applied multivariate statistical analysis* (6th ed.). Harlow, Essex: Pearson.
Joreskög, K. G. (1969). A general approach to confirmatory maximum likelihood factor analysis. *Psychometrika*, 34, 183–202.
Judge, T. A., Rodell, J. B., Klinger, R., Simon, L. S., & Crawford, E. R. (2013). Hierarchical representation of personality in predicting job performance: Integrating three organizing frameworks with two theoretical perspectives. *Journal of Applied Psychology*, 98, 875–925.
Kuncel, N. R., Credé, M., & Thomas, L. L. (2007). A meta-analysis of the predictive validity of the Graduate Management Admission Test (GMAT) and undergraduate grade point average (UGPA) for graduate student academic performance. *Academy of Management Learning & Education*, 6, 51–68.
Larsen, R. J., & Marx, M. L. (1981). *An introduction to mathematical statistics and its applications*. Englewood Cliffs, NJ: Prentice-Hall Inc.
Little, T. D. (2013). *Longitudinal structural equation modeling*. New York, NY: Guilford Press.

MacCallum, R. C., Browne, M. W., & Cai, L. (2012). Factor analysis models as approximations. In R. Cudeck & R. C. MacCallum (Eds.), *Factor analysis at 100: Historical developments and future directions*. London: Taylor & Francis.

McGrew, K. S. (2009). CHC theory and the human cognitive abilities project: Standing on the shoulders of the giants of psychometric intelligence research. *Intelligence, 37*, 1–10.

Markon, K. E., Krueger, R. F., & Watson, D. (2005). Delineating the structure of normal and abnormal personality: An integrative hierarchical approach. *Journal of Personality and Social Psychology, 88*, 139–157.

Marsh, H. W., Hau, K.-T., & Grayson, D. (2005). Goodness of fit evaluation in structural equation modeling. In A. Maydeu-Olivares & J. McCardle (Eds.), *Psychometrics: A festschrift to Roderick P. McDonald* (pp. 225–340). Hillsdale, NJ: Erlbaum.

Marsh, H. W., Lüdtke, O., Muthén, B., Asparouhov, T., Morin, A. J. S., Trautwein, U., & Nagengast, B. (2010). A new look at the Big-Five factor structure through exploratory structural equation modeling. *Psychological Assessment, 22*, 471–491.

Mathieu, C., Hare, R. D., Jones, D. A., Babiak, P., & Neumann, C. S. (2013). Factor structure of the B-Scan 360: A measure of corporate psychopathy. *Psychological Assessment, 25*, 288–293.

Meredith, W. (1993). Measurement invariance, factor analysis and factorial invariance. *Psychometrika, 58*, 525–543.

Messick, S. (1989). Validity. In R. L. Linn (Ed.), *Educational measurement* (3rd ed.). (pp. 13–103). Washington, DC: The American Council on Education & The National Council on Measurement in Education.

Millsap, R. E., & Yun-Tein, J. (2004). Assessing factorial invariance in ordered-categorical measures. *Multivariate Behavioral Research, 39*, 479–515.

Morgeson, F. P., Campion, M. A., Dipboye, R. L., Hollenbeck, J. R, Murphy, K., & Schmitt, N. (2007). Reconsidering the use of personality tests in personnel selection contexts. *Personnel Psychology, 60*, 683–729.

Mulaik, S. E. (2005). Looking back on the indeterminacy controversies. In A. Maydeu-Olivares & J. J. McArdle (Eds.), *Contemporary psychometrics*. Mahwah, NJ: Lawrence Erlbaum Associates.

Mulaik, S. E. (2010). *Foundations of factor analysis* (2nd ed.). Boca Raton, FL: Chapman & Hall/CRC.

Muthén, L. K. & Muthén, B. O. (1998–2010) *MPlus user's guide* (6th ed.). Los Angeles, CA: Muthén & Muthén.

Newton, P., & Shaw, S. (2014). *Validity in educational and psychological assessment*. London: Sage.

Nyborg, H. (2003). *The scientific study of general intelligence*. Amsterdam: Elsevier.

Nye, C. D., & Drasgow, F. (2011). Assessing goodness of fit: Simple rules of thumb simply do not work. *Organizational Research Methods, 14*, 548–570.

Pace, V. L., & Brannick, M. T. (2010). How similar are personality scales of the "same" construct? A meta-analytic investigation. *Personality and Individual Differences, 49*, 669–676.

Presser, S., & Blair, J. (1994). Survey pretesting: Do different methods produce different results? In P. Marsden (Ed.), *Sociology methodology* (Vol. 24) (pp. 73–104). Washington, DC: American Sociological Association.

Presser, S., Rothgep, J., Couper, M., Lessler, J., Martin, E., Martin, J., & Singer, E. (Eds.) (2004). *Methods for testing and evaluating survey questionnaires*. New York, NJ: John Wiley & Sons, Inc.

Oh, I.-S., Schmidt, F. L., Shaffer, J. A., and Le, H. (2008). The graduate management admission test (GMAT) is even more valid than we thought: A new development in meta-analysis and its implications for the validity of the GMAT. *Academy of Management Learning and Education, 7*, 563–570.

Ones, D. S., Dilchert, S., Viswesvaran, C., & Judge, T. A. (2007). In support of personality assessment in organizational settings. *Personnel Psychology, 60*, 995–1027.

Oppenheim, A. N. (1992). *Questionnaire design, interviewing and attitude measurement*. New York, NY: Pinter Publishers.

Paunonen, S. V., & Jackson, D. N. (2000). What is beyond the Big Five? Plenty! *Journal of Personality, 68*, 821–835.

Rae, G. (2007). A note on using stratified alpha to estimate composite reliability of a test composed of interrelated nonhomogeneous items. *Psychological Methods, 12*, 177–184.

Ree, M. J., Earles, J. A., & Teachout, M. S. (1994). Predicting job performance: Not much more than G. *Journal of Applied Psychology, 79*, 518–524.

Revelle, W. & Zinbarg, R. E. (2009). Coefficients alpha, beta, omega and the glb: comments on Sijtsma. *Psychometrika, 74*, 145–154.

Roid, G. H. (2006). Designing ability tests. In S. M. Downing, & T. H. Haladyna (Eds.). *Handbook of test development*. Mahwah, NJ: Lawrence Erlbaum Associates.

Rolfhus, E. L., & Ackerman, P. L. (1999). Assessing individual differences in knowledge: Knowledge structures and traits. *Journal of Educational Psychology, 91*, 511–526.

Schermelleh-Engel, K., Moosbrugger, H., & Muller, H. (2003). Evaluating the fit of structural equation models: Tests of significance and descriptive goodness-of-fit measures. *Methods of Psychological Research, 8*, 23–74.

Schmidt, F. L., & Hunter, J. E. (1996). Measurement error in psychological research: Lessons from 26 research scenarios. *Psychological Methods, 1*, 199–223.

Schmidt, F. L., & Hunter, J. E. (1998). The validity and utility of selection methods in personnel psychology: Practical and theoretical implications of 85 years of research findings. *Psychological Bulletin, 124*(2), 262–274.

Schmidt, F. L., Shaffer, J. A., & Oh, I.-S. (2008). Increased accuracy for range restriction corrections: Implications for the role of personality and general mental ability in job and training performance. *Personnel Psychology, 61*, 827–868.

Shaffer, J. A., DeGeest, D., & Li, A. (2016). Tackling the problem of construct proliferation a guide to assessing the discriminant validity of conceptually related constructs. *Organizational Research Methods, 19*(1), 80–110.

Schrank, F. A., McGrew K. S., & Mather, N. (2014). *Woodcock-Johnson IV tests of cognitive abilities*. Rolling Meadows, IL: Riverside.

Smith, M., & Smith, P. (2005) *Testing people at work: competencies in psychometric testing*. London: Blackwell.

Stevens, J. P. (2009). *Applied multivariate statistics for the social sciences* (5th ed.). New York, NY: Routledge.

Viswesvaran, C., & Ones, D. S. (2000). Perspectives on models of job performance. *International Journal of Selection and Assessment, 8*, 216–226.

Wechsler, D. (1981). The psychometric tradition: Developing the Wechsler Adult Intelligence scale. *Contemporary Educational Psychology, 6*, 82–85.

Widaman, K. F. (1993). Common factor analysis versus principal component analysis: Differential bias in representing model parameters? *Multivariate Behavioral Research, 28*, 263–311.

Widaman, K. F., & Reise, K. F. (1997). Exploring the measurement invariance of psychological instruments: Applications in the substance use domain. In K. J. Bryant & M. Windle (Eds.), *The science of prevention: Methodological advances from alcohol and substance abuse research* (pp. 281–324). Washington, DC: American Psychological Association.

Willis, G, Schechter, S., & Whitaker, K. (2000). A comparison of cognitive interviewing, expert review and behavior coding: What do they tell us? In, *Proceedings of the Section on Survey Methods, American Statistical Association* (pp. 28–37). Alexandria, VA: American Statistical Association

Woods, S. A., & Anderson, N. R. (2016). Toward a periodic table of personality: Mapping personality scales between the Five Factor Model and the circumplex model. *Journal of Applied Psychology, 101*, 582–604.

Yuan, K.-H. (2005). Fit indices versus test statistics. *Multivariate Behavioral Research, 40*, 115–148.

Zinbarg, R. E., Revlle, W., Yovel, I., & Wen, L. (2005). Cronbach's α, Revelle's β, and McDonald's ωH: Their relationship with each other and two alternative conceptualizations of reliability. *Psychometrika, 74*, 145–154.

Code Appendix

Code 1 MPlus eight-factor CFA model using the WLSMV estimator.

```
TITLE:  CFA of Business Personality, Motivation and
Leadership scales

DATA:
  FILE IS "D:\Rdata\MAT-80.dat";

VARIABLE:
  NAMES ARE act1-act6 ass1-ass4 cuy1-cuy7 fly1-fly6
  iln1-iln6 img1-img6 imn1-imn6 inc1-inc6 lep1-lep7
  opm1 opm2 orr1-orr6 ory1-ory7 prg1-prg6 shg1-shg5
  stc1-stc3 sts1-sts6;
  USEVARIABLES ARE act1-act6 ass1-ass4 cuy1-cuy7
  inc1-inc6 lep1-lep7 stc1-stc3 orr1-orr6 sts1-sts6
  fly2 fly3 fly5 fly6 prg1 img4 img6
   iln6 opm1 opm2;
  CATEGORICAL ARE ALL;
  MISSING ARE ALL (-999);

MODEL:
   ACT BY act1-act6;
   ASS BY ass1-ass4;
   CUY BY cuy1-cuy7;
   INC BY inc1-inc6;
   LEAD BY lep1-lep7 stc1-stc3;
   ORDER By orr1-orr6;
   STRESSRS BY sts1-sts6;
   OPTIMISM By fly2 fly3 fly5 fly6 prg1 act1 img4 img6
   iln6 stc1 opm1 opm2;

ANALYSIS:
  TYPE IS GENERAL;
  ESTIMATOR IS WLSMV;
  PARAMETERIZATION = THETA;
  ITERATIONS = 1000;
  CONVERGENCE = 0.00005;

OUTPUT: SAMPSTAT MODINDICES STANDARDIZED (STDYX)RESIDUAL;
```

Code 2 McDonald's Omega for Optimism scale.

```
TITLE:    McDonald's Omega for Optimism

DATA:
  FILE IS "D:\Rdata\MAT-80-3.dat";
    FORMAT IS 89F5.2;

VARIABLE:
  NAMES ARE act1-act6 ass1-ass4 cuy1-cuy7 fly1-fly6
  iln1-iln6 img1-img6 imn1-imn6 inc1-inc6 lep1-lep7
  opm1 opm2 orr1-orr6 ory1-ory7 prg1-prg6 shg1-shg5
  stc1-stc3 sts1-sts6;
  USEVARIABLES ARE fly2 fly3 fly5 fly6 prg1 act1 img4 img6
     iln6 stc1 opm1 opm2;
  MISSING ARE ALL (-999);

ANALYSIS:
  TYPE IS GENERAL;
  ESTIMATOR IS ML;
  BOOTSTRAP = 2000;

MODEL:
     f1 BY fly2*(p1)
     fly3(p2)
     fly5(p3)
     fly6(p4)
     prg1(p5)
     act1 (p6)
     img4 (p7)
     img6(p8)
     iln6(p9)
     stc1(p10)
     opm1 (p11)
     opm2(p12);
     f1@1;
     fly2(r1)
     fly3(r2)
     fly5(r3)
     fly6(r4)
     prg1(r5)
     act1 (r6)
     img4 (r7)
     img6(r8)
     iln6(r9)
     stc1(r10)
     opm1 (r11)
```

```
    opm2(r12);

MODEL CONSTRAINT:

 NEW(omega);
  omega=
  (p1+p2+p3+p4+p5+p6+p7+p8+p9+p10+p11+p12)^2/

   ((p1+p2+p3+p4+p5+p6+p7+p8+p9+p10+p11+p12)^2+
   (r1+r2+r3+r4+r5+r6+r7+r8+r9+r10+r11+r12));

OUTPUT:   SAMPSTAT STANDARDIZED (STDYX) RESIDUAL;
```

Code 3   MPlus invariance tests for Business Personality, Motivation, and Leadership scales across gender.

(a) Configural invariance.

```
TITLE:  Test of Business Personality, Motivation and
Leadership scales for configural invariance across
Gender.

DATA:
  FILE IS "D:\Rdata\mat-80-gender.dat";
  FORMAT IS 90F5.2;


VARIABLE:
  NAMES ARE act1-act6 ass1-ass4 cuy1-cuy7 fly1-fly6
  iln1-iln6 img1-img6 imn1-imn6 inc1-inc6 lep1-lep7
  opm1 opm2 orr1-orr6 ory1-ory7 prg1-prg6 shg1-shg5
  stc1-stc3 sts1-sts6 gender;
USEVARIABLES ARE act1-act6 ass1-ass4 cuy1-cuy5 cuy7
  inc1-inc6 lep1-lep7 stc1-stc3 orr2-orr5 sts1-sts6
  fly2 fly3 fly5 fly6 prg1 img4 img6
   iln6 opm1 opm2;
CATEGORICAL ARE ALL;
MISSING ARE ALL (-999);
GROUPING IS gender(1 = male 2 = female);

MODEL:

   ACT BY act1-act6;
   ASS BY ass1-ass4;
```

```
   CUY BY cuy1-cuy7;
   INC BY inc1-inc6;
   LEAD BY lep1-lep7 stc1-stc3;
   ORDER By orr1-orr6;
   STRESSRS BY sts1-sts6;
   OPTIMISM By fly2 fly3 fly5 fly6 prg1 act1 img4 img6
   iln6 stc1 opm1 opm2;

MODEL female:

   ACT BY act1-act6;
   ASS BY ass1-ass4;
   CUY BY cuy1-cuy7;
   INC BY inc1-inc6;
   LEAD BY lep1-lep7 stc1-stc3;
   ORDER By orr1-orr6;
   STRESSRS BY sts1-sts6;
   OPTIMISM By fly2 fly3 fly5 fly6 prg1 act1 img4 img6
   iln6 stc1 opm1 opm2;

   [lep1$3 lep2$2 lep2$3];
   [lep3$2 lep3$3 lep4$2 lep4$3];
   [lep5$2 lep5$3 lep6$2 lep6$3];
   [lep7$2 lep7$3 stc1$2 stc1$3];
   [stc3$2 stc3$3];
   [ass1$3 ass2$2 ass2$3 ass3$2 ass3$3 ass4$2 ass4$3];
   [sts1$3 sts2$2 sts2$3 sts3$2 sts3$3];
   [sts4$2 sts4$3 sts5$2 sts5$3];
   [sts6$2 sts6$3 act1$3];
   [act2$2 act2$3 act3$2 act3$3 act4$2 act4$3 act5$2 act5
$3];
   [act6$2 act6$3 opm1$2 opm1$3 opm2$2 opm2$3];
   [fly2$3 fly3$2 fly3$3];
   [fly5$2 fly5$3 fly6$2 Fly6$3 prg1$2 prg1$3 img4$2 img4
$3];
   [img6$2 img6$3 iln6$2 iln6$3];
   [orr2$3 orr3$2 orr3$3];
   [orr4$2 orr4$3 orr5$2 orr5$3];
   [cuy1$3 cuy2$2 cuy2$3 cuy3$2 cuy3$3 cuy4$2 cuy4$3];
   [cuy5$2 cuy5$3];
   [cuy7$2 cuy7$3 inc1$3 inc2$2 inc2$3 inc3$2 inc3$2];
   [inc4$2 inc4$3 inc5$2 inc5$3 inc6$2 inc6$3];

ANALYSIS:
   TYPE IS GENERAL;
   ESTIMATOR IS WLSMV;
   PARAMETERIZATION = THETA;
```

```
    ITERATIONS = 1000;
    CONVERGENCE = 0.00005;

OUTPUT:  SAMPSTAT MODINDICES STANDARDIZED (STDYX)
RESIDUAL;
```

(b) Metric invariance.
```
TITLE:  Test of Business Personality, Motivation and
Leadership scales for configural invariance across
Gender.

DATA:
  FILE IS "D:\Rdata\mat-80-gender.dat";
  FORMAT IS 90F5.2;


VARIABLE:
  NAMES ARE act1-act6 ass1-ass4 cuy1-cuy7 fly1-fly6
  iln1-iln6 img1-img6 imn1-imn6 inc1-inc6 lep1-lep7
  opm1 opm2 orr1-orr6 ory1-ory7 prg1-prg6 shg1-shg5
  stc1-stc3 sts1-sts6 gender;
USEVARIABLES ARE act1-act6 ass1-ass4 cuy1-cuy5 cuy7
  inc1-inc6 lep1-lep7 stc1-stc3 orr2-orr5 sts1-sts6
  fly2 fly3 fly5 fly6 prg1 img4 img6
    iln6 opm1 opm2;
CATEGORICAL ARE ALL;
MISSING ARE ALL (-999);
GROUPING IS gender(1 = male 2 = female);

MODEL:

  ACT BY act1-act6;
  ASS BY ass1-ass4;
  CUY BY cuy1-cuy7;
  INC BY inc1-inc6;
  LEAD BY lep1-lep7 stc1-stc3;
  ORDER By orr1-orr6;
  STRESSRS BY sts1-sts6;
  OPTIMISM By fly2 fly3 fly5 fly6 prg1 act1 img4 img6
    iln6 stc1 opm1 opm2;

MODEL female:

  [lep1$3 lep2$2 lep2$3];
  [lep3$2 lep3$3 lep4$2 lep4$3];
  [lep5$2 lep5$3 lep6$2 lep6$3];
  [lep7$2 lep7$3 stc1$2 stc1$3];
```

```
    [stc3$2 stc3$3];
    [ass1$3 ass2$2 ass2$3 ass3$2 ass3$3 ass4$2 ass4$3];
    [sts1$3 sts2$2 sts2$3 sts3$2 sts3$3];
    [sts4$2 sts4$3 sts5$2 sts5$3];
    [sts6$2 sts6$3 act1$3];
    [act2$2 act2$3 act3$2 act3$3 act4$2 act4$3 act5$2 act5
$3];
    [act6$2 act6$3 opm1$2 opm1$3 opm2$2 opm2$3];
    [fly2$3 fly3$2 fly3$3];
    [fly5$2 fly5$3 fly6$2 Fly6$3 prg1$2 prg1$3 img4$2 img4
$3];
    [img6$2 img6$3 iln6$2 iln6$3];
    [orr2$3 orr3$2 orr3$3];
    [orr4$2 orr4$3 orr5$2 orr5$3];
    [cuy1$3 cuy2$2 cuy2$3 cuy3$2 cuy3$3 cuy4$2 cuy4$3];
    [cuy5$2 cuy5$3];
    [cuy7$2 cuy7$3 inc1$3 inc2$2 inc2$3 inc3$2 inc3$2];
    [inc4$2 inc4$3 inc5$2 inc5$3 inc6$2 inc6$3];

ANALYSIS:
  TYPE IS GENERAL;
  ESTIMATOR IS WLSMV;
  PARAMETERIZATION = THETA;
  ITERATIONS = 1000;
  CONVERGENCE = 0.00005;

OUTPUT:   SAMPSTAT MODINDICES STANDARDIZED (STDYX)
RESIDUAL;
```

(c) Scalar invariance.

```
TITLE:  Test of Business Personality, Motivation and
Leadership scales for configural invariance across
Gender.

DATA:
  FILE IS "D:\Rdata\mat-80-gender.dat";
  FORMAT IS 90F5.2;


VARIABLE:
  NAMES ARE act1-act6 ass1-ass4 cuy1-cuy7 fly1-fly6
  iln1-iln6 img1-img6 imn1-imn6 inc1-inc6 lep1-lep7
  opm1 opm2 orr1-orr6 ory1-ory7 prg1-prg6 shg1-shg5
  stc1-stc3 sts1-sts6 gender;
USEVARIABLES ARE act1-act6 ass1-ass4 cuy1-cuy5 cuy7
  inc1-inc6 lep1-lep7 stc1-stc3 orr2-orr5 sts1-sts6
  fly2 fly3 fly5 fly6 prg1 img4 img6
```

```
    iln6 opm1 opm2;
CATEGORICAL ARE ALL;
MISSING ARE ALL (-999);
GROUPING IS gender(1 = male 2 = female);

MODEL:

ACT BY act1-act6;
   ASS BY ass1-ass4;
   CUY BY cuy1-cuy7;
   INC BY inc1-inc6;
   LEAD BY lep1-lep7 stc1-stc3;
   ORDER By orr1-orr6;
   STRESSRS BY sts1-sts6;
   OPTIMISM By fly2 fly3 fly5 fly6 prg1 act1 img4 img6
   iln6 stc1 opm1 opm2;
MODEL female:

ANALYSIS:

  TYPE IS GENERAL;
  ESTIMATOR IS WLSMV;
  PARAMETERIZATION = THETA;
  ITERATIONS = 1000;
  CONVERGENCE = 0.00005;

OUTPUT:   SAMPSTAT MODINDICES STANDARDIZED (STDYX)
RESIDUAL;
```

Code 4 MPlus prediction of 3rd Semester grades using Mat^{80} scores.

```
TITLE:    Regression of semester grades on Mat⁸⁰ scores

DATA:
  FILE IS "D:\Rdata\mat10.DAT";
  FORMAT IS 52(F8.4);
  LISTWISE=ON;
VARIABLE:
  NAMES ARE lead opt order assert stress ach cur intrinsc
fluency
  orig ill prod shar implmnt math markass markwork markex
  aibass aibwork aibexam cfass cfwork cfexam cibass
cibwork      cibexam gelass gelwork meass mework meexam
nssass nsswork omanass omanwork omanexam pmass pmass2
pmexam pmoass pmowork pmoexam vcpeass vcpework smanass
smanwork smanexam bsimass bsimass2 ass1fpp ass2fpp;
```

```
USEVARIABLES ARE   cfass cfexam cibass
  cibexam opt assert intrinsc math;
  MISSING = ALL (101);

MODEL:
  F1 BY   cfass cfexam cibass
  cibexam;
  F1 ON   opt    assert   intrinsc   math;

ANALYSIS:
    TYPE IS GENERAL;
    ESTIMATOR IS MLR;
    ITERATIONS = 1000;
    CONVERGENCE = 0.00005;

OUTPUT:   SAMPSTAT STANDARDIZED (STDY) MOD(ALL 5);
```

2

Classical Test Theory and Item Response Theory

Christine E. DeMars

CTT

Classical Test Theory (CTT) is fundamentally a test-level theory, not an item-level theory. The **true score** (T) is the foundation of CTT. Each time we test an examinee, we obtain an **observed score** (X). Imagine that we could erase the examinee's memory and restore her physiological state to exactly what it was at the beginning of the test and then test her again, resulting in another X. Repeat this an infinite number of times. T is defined as the expected value (mean) of the examinee's Xs: $T = \varepsilon(X)$. Note that in CTT, the **true** in true score does not refer to some objective inner property of the person, which is sometimes termed the Platonic true score (Lord & Novick, 1968; Sutcliffe, 1965). The CTT true score simply indicates the expected value of the observed score over repeated testings under the same conditions. Conceptually, many people would think of true score as an examinee's score under ideal testing conditions – what the examinee could do if motivated and not anxious or distracted. But that is **not** what true score means in CTT.

Assumptions

Several mathematical assumptions (axioms[1]) are needed to define CTT. These assumptions can be found in many sources (e.g., Allen & Yen, 1979; Crocker & Algina, 1986; Lord & Novick, 1968). A selection of the key assumptions is described here. In the following, the subscript p will indicate the person (examinee). A dot in the subscript indicates the mean over the elements (in the immediate context, persons) represented by the subscript. Subscripts will be dropped for all variances, covariances, and correlations because those terms must refer to persons, not means across persons. These assumptions

---

[1] Raykov & Marcoulides (2011, p. 121) discourage the use of the word *assumption* in this context because these assumptions are not falsifiable. I am using the term to mean axiom or postulate. Also, Raykov & Marcoulides note that many of the assumptions I have listed do not necessarily follow from the definition of X = T + E. I have chosen the axioms used to derive the most common formulas used in CTT. Different axioms will lead to different formulas.

The Wiley Handbook of Psychometric Testing: A Multidisciplinary Reference on Survey, Scale and Test Development, First Edition. Edited by Paul Irwing, Tom Booth, and David J. Hughes.
© 2018 John Wiley & Sons Ltd. Published 2020 by John Wiley & Sons Ltd.

are defined in terms of the population values. Later in this chapter, sample estimates will be indicated by the symbol ^ over the appropriate index. Variance will be symbolized by σ^2, covariance by σ, and correlation by ρ, each followed by the variable in parentheses. Note that the symbol for correlation is the Greek rho (ρ), which unfortunately looks very similar to p.

1. $X_p = T_p + E_p$. X and T were defined previously as observed score and true score, respectively. E indicates random error. Errors are linearly uncorrelated with true score: $\rho(TE) = 0$.
2. The errors from two measurements are uncorrelated, or linearly independent. If E_1 and E_2 are the errors corresponding to two measurements for person p, $\rho(E_1 E_2) = 0$. It follows that $\rho(T_1 E_2) = 0$ and $\rho(T_2 E_1) = 0$.
3. $\varepsilon(X_p) = T_p$. It follows that $\varepsilon(E_p) = 0$. It also follows at the group level that $\varepsilon(E_\bullet) = 0$.
   Although $\sigma^2(E_p)$ may differ for individuals, the mean error variance within persons equals the error variance across persons. Because the group error variance can be estimated accurately with just two measurements (or two subdivisions of a single measurement), it is often substituted as an estimate for each examinee's error variance (Lord & Novick, 1968, p. 155). Within a person, $\sigma(E)$ is called the standard error of measurement (SEM).
4. Test reliability is defined as the squared correlation between the observed score and the true score: $\rho^2(XT)$. This is equivalent to the proportion of variance in the observed score due to true-score variance: $\rho^2(XT) = \dfrac{\sigma^2(T)}{\sigma^2(X)}$ (see Allen & Yen, 1979, Ch. 3, or Lord & Novick, 1968, Ch. 3, for derivations). Or equivalently $\rho^2(XT) = \dfrac{\sigma^2(X) - \sigma^2(E)}{\sigma^2(X)} = 1 - \dfrac{\sigma^2(E)}{\sigma^2(T) + \sigma^2(E)}$.
5. Parallel measurements are defined as measurements that have equal means, equal true-score variances, equal error variances, and equal correlations with the true-score. The observed score variances must also be equal because $\sigma^2(X) = \sigma^2(T) + \sigma^2(E)$. If X' is an observed score on a measurement parallel to X, $E(X_p) = E(X'_p)$, $\sigma^2(E) = \sigma^2(E')$, $\sigma^2(X) = \sigma^2(X')$, $\rho^2(XT) = \rho^2(X'T)$, and $\sigma(XX') = \sigma^2(T)$. It follows that $\rho(XX') = \rho^2(XT)$.

Tau-equivalent forms are defined as measurements that have equal true scores T_1 and T_2 for each examinee, but $\sigma^2(E_1)$ and $\sigma^2(E_2)$ may differ, where the subscripts 1 and 2 arbitrarily differentiate the two measurements. Essentially τ-equivalent forms are defined as $T_{2p} = T_{1p} + k$ for each examinee, where k is a constant. Thus, all parallel forms are necessarily τ-equivalent and all τ-equivalent forms are necessarily essentially τ-equivalent. The models are **nested**. The correlation between τ-equivalent scores is equal to the correlation between essentially τ-equivalent scores, because adding a constant to a score does not change the correlation. The covariance between essentially τ-equivalent scores equals the covariance between parallel scores; both equal $\sigma^2(T)$. But the correlation between parallel scores is not necessarily equal to the correlation between essentially τ-equivalent scores (unless the τ-equivalent scores happen to be parallel) because the denominator of the correlation coefficient includes $\sigma^2(E)$.

Congeneric forms may have different $\sigma^2(T)$ as well as different $\sigma^2(E)$ and different $E(X_p)$. $T_{2p} = cT_{1p} + k$, where c and k are constants. Essentially τ-equivalent scores are nested within congeneric scores. The assumption of linearly uncorrelated errors extends to τ-equivalent, essentially τ-equivalent, and congeneric scores.

Estimating reliability and the SEM

Hypothetically, the $\rho^2(XT)$ and $\sigma^2(E_p)$ could be known if we could test an infinite population, wipe out the memories of the participants and restore their psychological and physical states, and test them again and again. Then, we would know T_p for each person, as well as $\sigma^2(E)$, the mean $\sigma^2(E_p)$ and could calculate $\rho^2(XT) = 1 - \dfrac{\sigma^2(E)}{\sigma^2(T) + \sigma^2(E)}$. Or we could test each person in our infinite population just twice, as long as we did the memory erase and restore, and calculate reliability as the correlation between the two testings and then solve for $\sigma^2(E)$. In this hypothetical realm, the distinction between using the same test form or parallel forms is moot, because the properties of X and X' are identical.

Of course, this scenario is impossible. Instead, reliability is typically estimated either by administering the same test twice (test-retest reliability, coefficient of stability) or by administering two test forms that are as nearly parallel as possible (alternate forms reliability, coefficient of equivalence), or by treating parts within the test as separate measurements (internal consistency). With either of the first two designs, $\hat{\rho}^2(XT) = \hat{\rho}(XX')$ is the correlation between the two measurements. Then $\sigma^2(E)$ can be solved by substituting the empirical estimates $\hat{\sigma}^2(X)$ and $\hat{\rho}(XX')$ for $\sigma^2(X)$ and $\rho(XX')$ into a re-arranged form of the reliability definition:

$$\sigma^2(E) = \sigma(X)\sqrt{1-\rho(XX')} \qquad (2.1)$$

Or the error variance could be estimated as half the variance of the squared difference between the two scores: $\sigma^2(E) = \dfrac{\sum_p (d_p - d)^2}{2n}$, where $d_p = X_p - X'_p$. If we assume errors are normally and identically distributed, the SEM (square root of $\sigma^2(E)$) can be used to build confidence intervals around each X. Obviously conditional errors cannot be identically or normally distributed if X is the sum of the number of correct items (Lord & Novick, 1968, p. 502), but the approximation may be reasonable for scores away from the extremes of 0 and 100%. The assumption of normality is not necessary for the derivations in CTT; it only comes into play as one method of estimating confidence intervals.

Each of these methods is a lower-bound estimate of reliability if the assumption of linearly independent errors is met (Sitjsma, 2012; also see the discussion of these concepts in Lord & Novick, 1968, pp. 134–137). Alternate forms underestimates reliability to the extent that the forms are not truly parallel. Test-retest underestimates reliability to the extent that examinees' true scores change between measurements, possibly due to learning or even minor changes in mood or physical state. Some of the formulas based on subdividing the test, to be discussed in a later section, underestimate reliability to the extent that the parts are not essentially τ-equivalent. However, if the errors are correlated, reliability may be overestimated (Green & Yang, 2009; Komaroff, 1997; Zimmerman, Zumbo, & Lalonde, 1993), or underestimated less than it would otherwise be. In the test-retest design, for example, the assumption of uncorrelated errors may be violated because examinees may remember specific items. For internal consistency estimates, if the part tests are individual items, items linked to a common context may have correlated errors.

Subdividing the test Sometimes it is not practical to administer two full-length test forms, either alternate forms or the same test on two occasions. If both measurements are taken at the same time, examinees may not be able to maintain concentration and motivation. If the measurements are obtained at separate times, the testing conditions may vary too much to be considered parallel; learning may have taken place in between the testings, or the examinees' psychological states may have changed beyond what the researcher is willing to consider error. Additionally, researchers generally want to minimize testing time. Testing takes time that could be spent in other ways, such as learning if the testing takes place in school, or a myriad of personal activities if the testing takes place outside of school. Thus, very often, reliability is estimated from a single measurement.

To estimate reliability from a single test form, X must be subdivided into two or more scores. The resulting reliability estimate is sometimes called a measure of internal consistency, because it is an index of how consistent scores from the parts of the test are. For example, to calculate a split-halves reliability estimate, the items are divided into two scores, X_1 and X_2, that are as nearly parallel as possible. The Pearson correlation between X_1 and X_2 is corrected by the Spearman–Brown prophecy formula $\rho(XX') = \frac{2\rho(X_1 X_2)}{1+\rho(X_1 X_2)}$, which estimates what the correlation would be if X_1 and X_2 were both full length. Or reliability can be estimated by Rulon's formula: $\rho(XX') = 2\left[1 - \frac{\sigma^2(X_1) + \sigma^2(X_2)}{\sigma^2(X)}\right]$, where X is the full test score. If the test halves are parallel, these methods will be equivalent. Otherwise, the estimate from Rulon's formula will be slightly lower.

If X is subdivided into more than two parts, Rulon's formula generalizes to coefficient α (Cronbach, 1951), equivalent to Guttman's (1945) λ_3. This is often called Cronbach's alpha, although Cronbach discouraged this label and noted that the same result had been derived by others (Cronbach, 2004, p. 397). The computationally-simplest form of $\alpha = \frac{k}{k-1}\left(1 - \frac{\sum_{i=1}^{k} \sigma^2(x_i)}{\sigma^2(X)}\right)$, where k is the number of subtests and i indexes the subtest. Lowercase x is used here for the score on a subtest or item, to differentiate it from the total score X[2]. As with Rulon's formula for split-halves, coefficient α is a lower-bound estimate of reliability. If the subparts of the test are not at least essentially τ-equivalent, coefficient α will underestimate the correlation between parallel measurements, the classic definition of reliability. However, as will be discussed in a later section, Cronbach (1951) broadened the definition of parallel forms to include randomly parallel forms. I will use the term classically parallel to indicate the traditional meaning

---

[2] This departs from the statistical convention of uppercase for random variables and lowercase for the value of a random variable.

of parallel as measurements with exactly the same T_p for each person and the same $\sigma^2(E)$, and randomly equivalent to indicate Cronbach's randomly parallel measurements. When the part tests are not τ-equivalent and the assumption of uncorrelated errors is met, coefficient α is an underestimate of the correlation between classically parallel forms, but it is an accurate estimate of the correlation between randomly equivalent forms (Cronbach, 2004, p. 204). Cronbach derived coefficient α for randomly parallel test forms; others (Guttman, 1945; Kuder & Richardson, 1937; Lord & Novick, 1968, pp. 89–90; Novick & Lewis, 1967) derived the same results for classically parallel forms, showing that coefficient α is a lower bound for classical reliability if the assumption of linearly uncorrelated errors is met.[3] Unless all of the items within the domain are parallel to each other, the X scores based on different sets of items drawn from the domain are unlikely to be parallel. The correlation between random forms is necessarily a lower bound to the correlation between parallel forms. Thus, if one wishes to estimate the correlation between random forms, instead of the correlation between parallel test scores, coefficient α is not an underestimate[4] (Cronbach, 2004, p. 400). However, it does not meet the classical definition of reliability.

At the extreme, each item can be considered a separate part of the test and coefficient α can be calculated based on the item scores. This is the most frequent way coefficient alpha is calculated. If the items are dichotomously scored, this reduces to the Kuder–Richardson formula 20 (KR-20, Kuder & Richardson, 1937). $KR-20 = \frac{k}{k-1} \frac{\sigma^2(X) - \sum_{i=1}^{k} P_i(1-P_i)}{\sigma^2(X)}$, where P_i is the proportion correct for item i. If all items are of equal difficulty, KR-20 is equivalent to $KR-21 = \frac{k}{k-1} \frac{\sigma^2(X) - kP.(1-P.)}{\sigma^2(X)}$, where $P.$ is the mean proportion correct. If KR-21 is applied when the items are not of equal difficulty, the corresponding SEM will contain the variance in item difficulty. Thus $KR-21 \leq KR-20$.

Recall that coefficient alpha is a lower-bound estimate of reliability, equaling reliability only if the subdivisions of the test are at least essentially τ-equivalent. For long tests divided into just two or three parts, the scores may approach essential τ-equivalence. If there is a detailed test blueprint and the empirical characteristics of the items have been estimated, the test developer could split the items such that each subdivision of the test covers the blueprint proportionally and the parts have similar difficulty and variance. This seems far less plausible when the parts used in coefficient alpha are individual items. It becomes yet less plausible when the items are dichotomous. It is unlikely that dichotomous items could be essentially τ-equivalent unless they have the same mean, due to the relationship between mean and variance for dichotomous items. As Feldt (2002, p. 40) noted, if dichotomous items with different means were essentially τ-equivalent, all of the difference in variance would have to be due to differences in error variance. If this were the case, the covariances between items, which are not affected

---

[3] If the errors are correlated, such as would be likely when several items refer to the same scenario, coefficient α, and other estimates of reliability, may overestimate the correlation between parallel forms.
[4] Strictly speaking, the sample estimate of the covariance between random forms based on coefficient alpha, $\hat{\sigma}(X_1 X_2) = \alpha \hat{\sigma}^2(X)$, is an unbiased estimate, but $\alpha = \hat{\sigma}(X_1 X_2)/\hat{\sigma}^2(X)$ is biased for finite samples because the ratio of unbiased estimates is not in general unbiased except under select conditions. This bias is generally small.

by error variance, would be equal for all item pairs, which Feldt notes is contradicted by clear evidence of heterogeneity in item covariances within most tests.

Sometimes researchers explore whether dichotomous items are essentially τ-equivalent at the latent level instead of the observed level. Conceptually, this means that there is a latent continuous score x^* underlying the observed score x for an item. If x^* exceeds a threshold, which may vary by item, x = 1. Otherwise, x = 0. The non-linear relationship between x and x^* is typically modeled with either a probit or a logistic model. Because the x^*s are continuous, the squared correlation between x^* and T is not dependent on the mean of x^* and the latent x^*s may be essentially τ-equivalent without necessarily being parallel. This model can be tested through the methods of confirmatory factor analysis (CFA). But even if the latent x^*s are essentially τ-equivalent, it does not change the fact that the observed dichotomous item scores (the xs) cannot be essentially τ-equivalent unless they have the same mean. Coefficient α is estimated from the x's, not the x^*'s so it will be a lower-bound estimate of reliability unless the items are classically parallel. To provide an example of this concept, data were simulated for two test forms, each with 10 items (see Appendix, Code 1, for simulation details). On each test form, each x^* was correlated 0.6 with T and had a variance of 1, with means ranging from –1.35 to 1.35. Thus, the x^*s were τ-equivalent. For convenience, each x^* was normally distributed, although this is not an assumption of CTT. To approach the asymptotic true values, 10,000,000 examinees were simulated. The correlation between the parallel scores X_1^* and X_2^*, the sums of the 10 x^*s on each form, was 0.84909. Coefficient alpha was 0.849125 for X_1^*; the estimates differed at the fifth decimal because the samples were finite. The x^*s were τ-equivalent within each test form, so coefficient α was an accurate estimation of reliability.

Next, the x^*s were dichotomized. Any value of $x^* < -0.5$ was coded 0, and any value of $x^* >= -0.5$ was coded 1. Because the x^*s had different means (they were τ-equivalent, not parallel), this was equivalent to using a different threshold for each item. The resulting observed xs were no longer essentially τ-equivalent, even though the underlying x^*s were. The proportion correct on each item varied approximately from 0.20 to 0.97. The new X_1 and X_2, now integer values between 0 and 10, were still parallel. The correlation between the parallel measurements X_1 and X_2 was 0.68340. But coefficient α was slightly lower, at 0.665041 for X_1 and 0.665003 for X_2. Thus, if one is estimating the reliability of observed scores, it is the parallelness, or lack thereof, of the observed item scores, not the latent scores underlying the items, which determines whether coefficient alpha is an underestimate of reliability.

The extent to which coefficient α underestimates reliability due to using non-parallel items may be fairly small, as in the example before. For another example, Feldt (2002) estimated the bias in coefficient α, compared to a reliability formula derived for congeneric scores, for varying configurations of a test composed of 50 dichotomous items. Even the most extreme differences in true-score variance, not intended to be realistic, yielded a bias of –0.027. However, when the part tests were not items but subtests of different lengths, or raters using a rating scale, the bias was non-negligible. Similarly, very extreme violations of essential τ-equivalence for continuous item scores have demonstrated considerable negative bias on coefficient α (Komaroff, 1997; Zimmerman et al., 1993).

Another part-test estimate of reliability is McDonald's (1999) ω, estimated through CFA. For ω, the part tests are only assumed to be congeneric, not necessarily essentially τ-equivalent. For tests with a single factor, $\omega = \dfrac{\left(\sum_i \lambda_i\right)^2}{\left(\sum_i \lambda_i\right)^2 + \sum_i \Psi_i^2}$, where λ_i is the unstandardized loading of item i or subtest i and Ψ_i^2 is the error variance for item i. If the items are essentially τ-equivalent, ω will equal coefficient α; otherwise, α is a lower bound to ω (assuming errors are conditionally independent).

Returning to our simulated dataset with τ-equivalent continuous item, each item had a loading of .6 and an error variance of .64; thus $\omega = \dfrac{(10(.6))^2}{(10(.6))^2 + 10(.64)} = .849057$, which closely approximates both the empirical correlation between the parallel forms and the empirical estimate of coefficient α. For the dichotomized items, the CFA must be run using a linear model, ignoring the fact that the items are dichotomous (for example MPlus code, please see the Appendix, Code 2). If the nonlinear model, which would be correct for other purposes, is run, the resulting ω will be an estimate of the reliability of the x*s, not the observed item scores (see Appendix, Code 3, for example MPlus code). With the simulated data, using the nonlinear model resulted in loadings ranging from 0.599 to 0.601 and corresponding error variances from 0.359 to 0.361, producing the same ω as the continuous items, which is clearly an overestimate of the correlation of .683 between the parallel forms composed of dichotomous items. But for the linear model, the loadings ranged from .257 to .481 (unstandardized loadings ranged from .045 to .240). These loadings are smaller, reflecting the increased error due to dichotomizing the items, and more variable, reflecting the loss of essential τ-equivalence. The estimated ω = .676, slightly larger than coefficient α.

Permissible replications T_p was defined earlier as $\varepsilon(X_p)$, where each X is a parallel measurement, and reliability was defined as $\rho(XX')$, where X and X' are classically parallel. However, a researcher may actually be more interested in the correlation between test scores that are NOT strictly parallel.

> The correlation between truly parallel measurements taken in such a way that the person's true score does not change between them is often called the coefficient of precision... For this coefficient, the only source contributing to error variance is the unreliability or imprecision of the measurement procedure. This is the variance ratio that would apply if a measurement were taken twice and if no practice, fatigue, memory, or other factor affected repeated measurement. In most practical situations, other sources of error variation affect the reliability of measurement, and hence the coefficient of precision is not the appropriate measure of reliability. However, this coefficient can be thought of as representing the extent to which test unreliability is due solely to inadequacies of the test form and testing procedure, rather than the extent to which it is due to changes in people over time and lack of equivalence of nearly parallel forms. (Lord & Novick, 1968, p. 134)

Cronbach (1951) argued that "It is very doubtful if testers have any practical need for a coefficient of precision" (p. 307). Cronbach focused instead on test forms composed of randomly selected items drawn from a hypothetical domain of items; he termed measurements based on such test forms to be randomly parallel. Cronbach and colleagues (Cronbach, Rajaratnam, & Gleser, 1963) soon expanded this concept to include other random differences in the measurements, not just random selection of items. They developed generalizability theory methods to assess the contribution of different measurement facets, such as items, time, or observers.

Lord and Novick (1968, Ch. 8) termed the traditional true score the **specific** true score, and termed the expectation over randomly equivalent measurements the **generic** true score. They labeled the randomly equivalent measurements **nominally** parallel, and labeled the correlation between X and the generic true score the **generic** reliability. For the generic true score, one must define a **permissible replication**[5] (allowable observation). The definition of a replication of X defines how broad T is. For example, Thorndike (1951, p. 568) provided a table of factors that might impact score variance. He discussed how decisions about which factors contribute to true score and which to error variance impact data collection designs.

Consider the variable of human weight. To get truly parallel measurements, we would measure each person's weight on the same scale twice, without allowing restroom breaks or food/water ingestion; this would be a permissible replication. The correlation between these parallel measurements would be the classical reliability estimate, the coefficient of precision. This would be a useful summary of the consistency of the scale. But suppose a group of researchers wanted to get an estimate of each person's weight prior to a study of a weight-loss program. It would be more useful for this purpose to weigh each person several times throughout the day and average the results; the generic true score estimated here is the average weight across the day. Permissible replications are defined to require the same clothing and the same scale, but allow for fluctuations due to hydration and food intake. Each person would have a distribution of errors that would combine these fluctuations with inconsistency in the scale. The average error variance, together with the variance in weight over the group of study participants, could be used to estimate a reliability-like coefficient. This would clearly be a lower bound to the classical reliability because the error term is larger, just as coefficient alpha is a lower bound because of the additional error variance due to randomly sampling items. Permissible replications might also be broadened to include the use of different scales; this would again broaden the scope of the generic true score to include the mean across different scales as well as different weighing occasions. The error term expands to include the variance in the scales' accuracies as well as their consistencies and the humans' weight consistencies.

The strict definition of reliability in CTT defines X and X' as the same or parallel measures, which implies that nothing about the examinees or the tests changes between the measurements. Cronbach, as described, preferred to allow different test forms composed of random selections of items to be permissible replications. In many cases for achievement tests, we also want to generalize over occasions where the examinee's content knowledge has not changed, but concentration, motivation, and physical comfort may have changed slightly. These latter facets are allowed to vary randomly and the generic true score is the expected value of the measurements. For a psychological trait that is purported to be stable over lengthy time periods, observations many years apart would be permissible replications. The generic T would then be defined as the expected

---

[5] Lord & Novick reserved the use of replication for parallel measurements. I am using it more broadly here.

value over many years, perhaps a lifetime. Any time-related variances would become part of the error. Thus, in the generic conception of T, any facet that varies randomly is error. This broader definition of error yields lower reliability estimates – hence coefficient α as a lower bound to classical reliability.

Sometimes a characteristic may vary across measurements but consistently affect the scores of all examinees in the same way. This is sometimes called systematic error, a bit of a misnomer because CTT defines error as random. These types of errors are not detectable by correlational methods. If one test form is more difficult than the other for all examinees to the same extent, it will not change the correlation between the two scores. The variance in X is not changed by subtracting a constant from each score. If we were able to estimate each student's individual error variance from repeated testings, and some test forms were more difficult or easy, this error would be part of each student's error variance (called the absolute error variance in g theory). But when we estimate the error variance by substituting $\hat{\rho}(XX')$ and $\hat{\sigma}^2(X)$ into Equation 2.1, the systematic difficulty effect is not reflected in the error because it has no effect on either the correlation or the observed score variance. Similarly, any characteristics of the examinee that a researcher wishes to consider error must randomly vary across measurements or they become part of the true score. For example, if there is only one testing occasion and an examinee's motivation remains consistently low throughout the test, low motivation will be part of that examinee's true score, not error. As Thorndike (1951, p. 566) noted, all systematic factors are part of the true score.

In summary, before gathering data to estimate reliability, researchers must clarify which facets of the testing situation they consider part of the true score and which they consider error. The testing conditions must be designed so that facets considered error vary. The broader the pool of permissible replications, the more the generic reliability will underestimate the classical reliability. Thus, the generic reliability is a lower bound to the classical reliability. However, a broader definition of permissible replications may better match the score user's intentions than strictly parallel replications, even if achievable, would.

Additional considerations in reliability and the SEM

Increasing test length will generally increase the reliability of the test. Assuming that the additional test section will be parallel to the existing test, the error variance will increase linearly but the true-score variance will increase geometrically: $\sigma^2(E_X) = k\sigma^2(E_Y)$ and $\sigma^2(T_X) = k^2\sigma^2(T_Y)$, where Y is the original form, X is the lengthened or shortened form, and k is the multiplicative factor. Based on this relationship, the Spearman–Brown prophecy formula can be used to estimate the reliability of the lengthened test: $\rho(XX') = \frac{k\rho(YY')}{1 + (k-1)\rho(YY')}$. Notice how increasing the test length has diminishing returns. For example, if a test with 20 items has a reliability of .8, decreasing the test to 10 items decreases the reliability to .67, but adding 10 items to a test length of 20 only increases the reliability from .80 to .86.

When a test is administered to a group with more heterogeneous scores, the reliability should increase but the SEM should remain the same[6]. The reliability in the new group

---

[6] If the SEM varies with the true score, as it would if the test score were the sum of dichotomous item scores, the SEM will likely vary by group if one group has mostly extreme scores. CTT does not account for this.

can be estimated by setting the SEMs of the two groups equal, resulting in: $\rho_{NN'} = 1 - \frac{\sigma_X^2(1-\rho_{XX'})}{\sigma_N^2}$, where $\rho_{NN'}$ is the reliability in the new group, $\rho_{xx'}$ is the reliability in the existing group, and σ_N^2 and σ_X^2 are the variances in the new and old groups.

Validity (defined narrowly as the correlation between X and an external score Y) is limited by the reliability of the measures; the validity coefficient is attenuated by measurement error. The correction for attenuation can be used to estimate what the correlation between two measures would be if there were no measurement error, the latent correlation. $\rho(T_X T_Y) = \frac{\rho(XY)}{\sqrt{\rho(XX')\rho(YY')}}$. Note that for this formula, the reliability estimates should be the classical reliability estimate, the correlation between truly parallel measures. If one substitutes the correlation between randomly parallel measures, such as coefficient alpha or the correlation between alternate forms that are not perfectly parallel, one will likely overcorrect to the extent that the reliability is underestimated (Lord & Novick, 1968, p. 138).

Item-level indices

Even though CTT is fundamentally a theory about test scores, we have seen that item scores play a role in the most commonly used estimates of reliability, coefficient α, λ_2, and ω, if the part tests used in the computations are individual items. The item scores obviously play a role in the total score X and its mean, variance, and error variance. Indices of item discrimination and difficulty are typically used to decide which items are useful for measurement and which should be discarded and replaced. Item difficulty is typically indexed by the mean score on the item. For dichotomous items, this is P, the proportion of examinees who answered the item correctly or endorsed the item. Sometimes this is called the *P*-value, although that term is easily confused with the *p*-value from statistical significance testing and will be avoided here. P is thus an index of item easiness or item facility, but it is historically called item difficulty. P is obviously dependent on the ability distribution. Because P is limited to the range 0–1, estimates of P from samples of examinees with different ability distributions will have a nonlinear relationship. To make the relationship linear, sometimes a continuous latent score x^* is conceptualized as underlying the observed score x. The threshold above which x = 1 is used as the index of item difficulty. The classical method of estimating the threshold requires assuming that x^* is normally distributed and there is no correct guessing. Note that this is not generally an assumption of CTT, but is an additional assumption made specifically for the purpose of estimating the threshold. The threshold is defined as the z-score corresponding to P. Angoff and Ford (1973) multiplied this value by 4 and added 13, labeling the resulting index Δ.

Generically, item discrimination is any index of how well the item separates examinees with high values of X from examinees with low values of X. Items with high discrimination will add to the reliability of X. The most common index of item discrimination is the correlation between the item score x_i and the total score X. If the item is dichotomous, this is termed the **point-biserial** correlation. It can be calculated either with the usual Pearson correlation formula or equivalently through a shortcut formula specifically for dichotomous items. Usually, the point-biserial correlation for item *i* is computed without including x_i in X, termed the corrected item–total correlation.

The point-biserial correlation is impacted by P. Because the variance for a dichotomous item $= P(1 - P)$, items with P near 0.5 have the greatest potential for high point-biserial correlations. P depends on the ability distribution, so the point-biserial correlation varies across samples with differing ability distributions. In contrast, the biserial correlation does not depend on P: $\rho_{biserial} = \frac{\sigma(x_i)}{Y} \rho_{point-biserial}$, where Y is the Y ordinate of the standard normal function at the z-score corresponding to the proportion correct. The biserial correlation again invokes the concept of the latent item score x^*; it is an estimate of the correlation between x_i^* and X. It is greater than the point-biserial correlation between x_i and X, especially for items with very high or very low means. As was true of the estimate of the item threshold, the biserial correlation requires the additional assumption of normality of x_i^* and no correct guessing.

The biserial correlation is useful for comparing estimates from samples that differ in mean ability but not in variance. The point-biserial correlation is applicable for choosing test items if the mean ability of future testing samples will be roughly comparable to the current sample. If an item is very easy for a group of examinees, it cannot discriminate well in that group, regardless of how well the biserial indicates it would discriminate if it had not been dichotomized.

As an aside while discussing x^*, another related index is the tetrachoric correlation between pairs of dichotomous items. The tetrachoric correlation is the estimate of the correlation between the x^*'s for items i and j, as opposed to the phi correlation, which is the Pearson correlation between the observed xs. The tetrachoric correlation will be greater than the phi correlation, just as the biserial is greater than the point-biserial. There is no simple equation for estimating tetrachoric correlations (see Kirk, 1973 for one method). An additional note is that the models underlying the computation of thresholds and biserial and tetrachoric correlations generally do not take into account correct guessing (Lord & Novick, 1968, p. 153). Carroll (1945, 1987) developed methods of correcting Pearson, tetrachoric, and biserial correlations for guessing.

Another somewhat common index of item discrimination is the difference in P for the top 27% of examinees and the bottom 27% of examinees (Kelley, 1939). Although this index loses information through artificially categorizing X, it may be easier for teachers and content panels to understand.

Item discrimination can be calculated for each response option. It should be positive for the correct option, and negative for useful distractors. Negative values indicate that the probability of choosing the option decreases as X increases.

In summary, items that are more discriminating increase the reliability of the scores. Conditional on the latent relationship with the true score, middle-difficulty items will have higher observed discrimination indices, such as the point-biserial correlation.

Strong True-Score Theory

Strong true-score theory (STT) provides an alternative to CTT. The **strong** in STT refers to the assumptions, which are stronger than those of CTT. In STT, one has to assume a given distribution for the error variance, and often for the true-score variance as well. Here, we will limit the discussion of STT to contexts where X is the sum of the number of correct dichotomous items. STT, in some sense, is an item-level theory. In contrast, the score X in CTT is simply a score. It does not have to be the sum of item scores.

Following Lord and Novick's (1968, Ch. 23) notation, I will call the true score ζ instead of T. $\zeta_p = \varepsilon_i(x_{pi})$, where x_{pi} represents person p's score on item i. ζ may be estimated as X/I, where I is the number of items on a test form. In CTT, the hypothetical replications of X for person p are assumed to be parallel. In the discussion of coefficient α, the concept of randomly equivalent scores (Lord & Novick used the term nominally parallel scores) was briefly introduced. STT is applicable to randomly equivalent scores as well as classically parallel scores. The items for a test form are viewed as random draws from a hypothetical domain of items. If all of the items in the domain are equally difficult and have the same linear relationship with T, the resulting scores are classically parallel. In contrast to the T_p in CTT, ζ_p is person p's expected value over the domain, not just the set of items on one test form. ζ_p is often called the domain score, or the universe score in generalizability theory. Lord and Novick (1968) called ζ the generic true score, to contrast to the specific true score T.

ζ is continuous but limited to the range of 0–1. One of the strong assumptions in STT is that, across people, ζ follows a specific distribution, typically either the two-parameter beta or the four-parameter beta.[7] The errors are assumed to have a binomial distribution. $X_p = \zeta_p I + E_p$, so the observed scores are said to have a beta-binomial distribution.

Using the binomial distribution, the SEM is calculated as $\hat{\sigma}(E_p) = \sqrt{\frac{X_p(k-X_p)}{k-1}}$, where k is the number of items. The binomial distribution produces heteroscedastic error variance. The SEM will be smaller for more extreme scores, and higher for X/k near 0.5. Estimating binomial standard errors allows test developers to meet Standard 2.14 (AERA/APA/NCME, 1999), which suggests reporting the SEM at various levels on the score scale. The $\hat{\sigma}^2(E)$ could be averaged across examinees and is equivalent to the $\hat{\sigma}^2(E)$ based on KR-21. The average error variance can be combined with $\hat{\sigma}^2(X)$ for a reliability estimate. When all items are of equal difficulty, this index will be equivalent to the correlation between parallel forms. If the items are not equally difficult, the binomial error variance contains additional variance due to differences in item difficulty. The resulting reliability-like index is an estimate of $\rho^2(X\zeta)$ where each examinee is randomly assigned a different form and the scores are not equated. It will thus tend to underestimate the correlation that would be observed if all examinees took the same set of randomly selected items. For the purpose of estimating this index, $\sigma^2(X)$ should be estimated from a sample in which examinees did take different sets of items. If $\sigma^2(X)$ is estimated based on a sample that took the same set of items, and the items differ in difficulty, it will not contain variance due to item sampling (Feldt, 1984), further decreasing the estimated ratio of $\frac{\sigma^2(X) - \sigma^2(E)}{\sigma^2(X)}$ because $\sigma^2(E)$ **does** contain variance due to item sampling. Or equivalently, one could estimate what $\sigma^2(X)$ would be if each examinee took a different sample of items by adding the variance in item difficulty to $\sigma^2(X)$.

For the ζs, the two-parameter beta distribution ranges from 0 to 1. The four-parameter beta distribution has a lower limit > 0 and an upper limit < 1. The

---

[7] The beta distribution is typical for T when X is the sum of dichotomous scores. A Poisson distribution may be assumed for X when X is the number of words read correctly in a passage (Lord & Novick, 1968, Ch. 21; Rasch 1960/1980). Or for continuous scores, both errors and true scores might be assumed to be normally distributed.

four-parameter beta might better model scores where there is some correct guessing, such as multiple-choice item scores. However, estimating the parameters for the four-parameter beta from the observed data is considerably more complicated than estimating the parameters for the two-parameter beta (see Hanson, 1991; Lord, 1965 for details on the four-parameter beta). The parameters for the two-parameter beta distribution, often simply called the beta distribution without the qualifier **two-parameter**, can be estimated as:

$$\hat{\alpha} = \left(-1 + \frac{1}{KR_{21}}\right)\hat{\mu}_X, \quad \hat{\beta} = -\hat{\alpha} + \frac{I}{KR_{21}} - I,$$ where KR_{21} is the estimate of reliability using KR_{21}, $\hat{\mu}_X$ is the estimated mean score, and I is the number of items on the test form (Huyhn, 1979).

Combining the beta distribution for ζ and the binomial distribution for errors, one can estimate the X distribution. The resulting observed score distribution is applicable when either all items are of equal difficulty or each examinee responds to a different random subset of the items in the domain. To predict the X distribution for a specific test form with items of varying difficulty, a better estimate could be obtained from the compound binomial using subsets of items with similar difficulty (Lord & Novick, 1968, Ch. 23, section 10). Because the ζ distribution is continuous, it must be approximated at fixed points. At each point q on the ζ distribution, the distribution of X is binomial. The X distribution at q is then weighted by the density of ζ at q, then summed across the points. This approximates integrating the conditional X distribution over the ζ distribution. An example is shown in Figure 2.1. There were 10 items on the test, and alpha = 2.87, beta = 1.41 for the ζ distribution. Because the two-parameter beta-binomial distribution is equivalent to the negative hypergeometric distribution (Keats & Lord, 1962), the X distribution in this example could have been computed more directly, and without the need for approximating at discrete points on the ζ distribution, but the method described generalizes to any ζ distribution. This method could also be used to predict reliability for different populations by altering the density of ζ and re-weighting the distributions of X and E correspondingly.

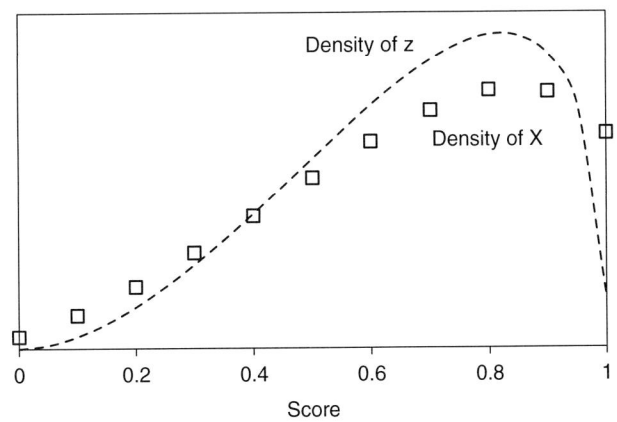

Note: z has a continuous beta distribution and X has a discrete (beta-binomial) distribution.

Figure 2.1 Density of latent (ζ) and observed (X) scores.

Generalizability Theory

Generalizability theory (g theory) is an extension of CTT that allows for multiple facets of measurement. G theory is based on randomly equivalent (nominally parallel) measurements, not classically parallel measurements. As discussed earlier, often researchers want to include variance due to random differences in test forms or random differences in examinee factors on different days as error. Although the classical definition of parallel measurements does not allow for these differences, Cronbach's randomly parallel measurements or Lord and Novick's generic true score do. In these conceptualizations, error variance due to test form can be estimated by administering two test forms, or error variance due to occasion test-retest can be estimated by administering the same test twice. The error variance could include both if the test-retest data were collected with alternate test forms, but the two sources of error would be confounded. G theory allows for the separation of different sources of error, called facets. For example, the design might include 20 test items given on two occasions. The SEM would include error due to items and error due to occasion, and would include a separate estimate of each. Similarly, a design might include two raters scoring three writing samples for each examinee, and the SEM would include separate estimates of the error due to each facet. As in STT, the unit of analysis is x_p (a score from one item on one occasion, for example) instead of the total score X_p, and the x_p are often assumed to be randomly drawn from a larger domain (called the universe in g theory) of items, occasions, raters, and so on. However, the mathematical assumptions are the same as for CTT and only a single SEM is estimated for all persons.

After the error variance is estimated in g theory, reliability-like coefficients can be calculated, although Cronbach (2004) noted that often the SEM is more informative. The reliability-like indices are denoted as the G-coefficient and Φ-coefficient. The G-coefficient is used for comparing examinees who were scored based on the same random sample of items, raters, or whatever facets were included in the study. Anything about the sample of items (or raters, etc.) that impacts all examinees equally is not part of the error variance. In g theory, these are the main effects of the facet. Only the interaction between the examinee and the facet are considered error, called **relative** error because it is used when comparing examinees to other examinees who were exposed to the same random levels of the facets. This is similar to estimating reliability by correlations between two measurements; factors that add a constant to all examinee's scores do not impact the correlation or the observed score variance and thus are missing from the error variance if it is estimated as a function of the correlation and observed score variance. If there is only one facet, the G-coefficient is equivalent to coefficient alpha and the interaction between examinee and item is equivalent to the SEM estimated from Equation 2.1. Thus, the G-coefficient would be a lower bound to the correlation between parallel forms.[8] The G-coefficient is considered a reliability-like index, not an estimate of classical reliability but on a similar metric.

The Φ-coefficient is an alternative reliability-like index. The Φ-coefficient is useful for comparing examinees who were given different random draws of items or raters. The error variance used in calculating phi is called the **absolute** error variance. This error

---

[8] More precisely, it is also a lower-bound to the correlation between random forms because the ratio of the estimates is a biased estimate of the ratio unless certain conditions hold (Cronbach et al., 1963). But this bias is generally quite small.

variance, unlike the error variance for the G-coefficient or the error variance calculated in CTT by Equation 2.1, includes error variance systematically due to the difficulty of the items or harshness of the raters (main effects of the facets). If everyone received the same random set of items and raters, as often happens because the universe of items and raters is hypothetical, these main effects would add a constant to everyone's score. But if different examinees receive different random sets, as would occur if items were drawn from an itembank or subsets of raters from a pool were assigned to different examinees, these main effects should be counted as error because they randomly affect examinee's scores differentially. They would also be considered error for an individual, assuming the goal is to estimate the sampling distribution of the examinee's scores across random sets of measurement conditions, not just parallel forms. If the only facet in the design is items, and those items are dichotomous, the absolute error variance is equal to the average binomial error variance calculated in STT. Despite this equivalency, g theory was not derived for dichotomous scores, not does it require any assumptions about the distributions of true scores or errors.

This brief description of g theory was only enough to place it in the perspective of CTT. For an introduction to g theory, readers should consider Meyer (2010), or Shavelson and Webb (1991), followed by more advanced topics in Brennan (2001).

IRT

In contrast to CTT, IRT is an item-level theory. In IRT, a latent trait or ability or proficiency, symbolized θ, is posited to underlie the observed responses. The term **latent**, like the term **true** in true score, is not meant to imply an inner ability that would be elicited under ideal conditions. Latent simply means that we cannot measure θ directly, the way we can count the number of correct responses. IRT models assume a specific relationship between θ and the observed responses. IRT requires stronger assumptions about the response process and the error distribution.

Assumptions

1. Correct dimensionality: The item responses are assumed to be a function of the dimensions specified in the model. The most commonly used IRT models are unidimensional, so this assumption is often referred to as unidimensionality. Conceptually, the trait measured by the test may be a combination of several abilities, motivation, concentration, anxiety, and so on. If the same combination applies to every item, unidimensionality will hold. Unidimensionality can be assessed by many methods (see Hattie, 1984; Tate, 2003, for an overview).
2. Local independence: After controlling for the θ (or θs if the test is multidimensional) measured by the test, item responses should be locally independent. **Local** denotes conditional on θ, or controlling for θ. Globally (not conditional on θ), the item responses should not be independent or they would not be measuring anything in common; it is only locally that we assume the responses are independent. Strict local independence holds for the entire response string. When checking the assumption, however, researchers often test for local independence between pairs of items. This is termed **weak** local independence. See Kim, De Ayala, Ferdous, and Nering (2011) or Chen and Thissen (1997) for descriptions of tests for local independence.

3 The form of the model is correctly specified. Sometimes this assumption is stated as multiple assumptions, depending on the model selected. For example, some of the models described next assume there is no correct guessing. The one-parameter model assumes that all items are equally discriminating. Most models assume that the probability of scoring in the highest category increases as theta increases. All models assume that the relationship between theta and the item response is a continuous, defined function, often with either a logistic form or normal ogive form, which implies the errors are logistically or normally distributed. Assumptions about model form are generally checked by estimating the item parameters and checking the fit of the data to the model. For discussions of item fit, see Glas and Suárez Falcón (2003); Li and Wells (2006); Liang and Wells (2009); Orlando and Thissen (2000; 2003); Sinharay and Lu (2008); Stone (2000; 2003); and Wells and Bolt (2008). For discussions of model fit, see Kang and Cohen (2007); Kang, Cohen, and Sung (2009); Maydeu-Olivares, Cai, and Hernández (2011); and Whittaker, Chang, and Dodd (2012). Also see Chapters 8 and 9 of this volume.

Models

IRT models can be distinguished by whether they are unidimensional/multidimensional or dichotomous/polytomous. Dichotomous models are for items with only two response categories, such as right/wrong or agree/disagree, and polytomous models are for items with more than two response categories, such as an item scored with partial credit or a Likert type item. Here I will only describe dichotomous unidimensional models. Additional models are covered in Chapters 15 of Volume 1 and 16 of Volume 2. IRT models can be specified in logistic or normal (probit) forms. Normal models are mathematically more difficult to work with because calculating the response probabilities requires integration over the normal distribution. Logistic models are thus more commonly used. Sometimes a constant of 1.7 is placed in the logistic model so that the parameters will be nearly equivalent to those of the normal model. This is called the logistic model on a normal metric, and is the form I will use here.

The three-parameter logistic (3PL) model uses three parameters to model item responses.

$$P(\theta) = c_i + (1-c_i)\frac{e^{1.7a_i(\theta-b_i)}}{1+e^{1.7a_i(\theta-b_i)}} \qquad (2.2)$$

where $P(\theta)$ is the probability of correct response or item endorsement for an examinee with ability of θ_j, a_i is the item discrimination, b_i is the item difficulty, and c_i is the lower asymptote. An example of two 3PL functions is shown in Figure 2.2. The higher the value of the a-parameter, the more rapidly response probabilities increase as a function of theta. Thus, the a-parameter describes how well the item discriminates among theta levels. The higher the b-parameter, the less likely a respondent is to score 1. Unlike the CTT item difficulty index, a higher b indicates a more difficult item. The c-parameter is a lower asymptote indicating the probability of correct response for an examinee with very low θ. It is sometimes called the guessing parameter because one way that examinees of very low θ may choose the correct response is by guessing. It is also possible that some

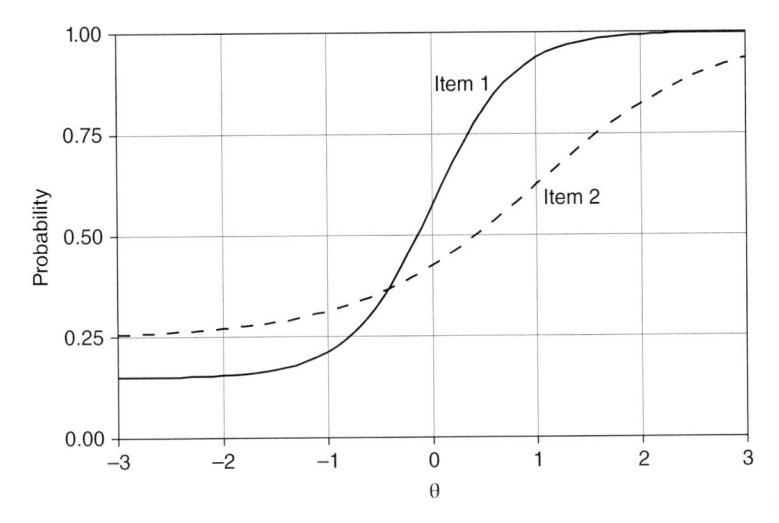

Figure 2.2 3PL items.

proportion of examinees know the information assessed by the item even if they are generally low on the θ measured by the test as a whole.

The phrase response probability, as used in this context, can be a bit ambiguous. Wainer, Bradlow, and Wang (2007, pp. 25–27) pointed out that, for most tests, it makes little sense to literally think about the response probability as the probability that examinee j will get item i correct. For example, based on the item parameters and θ_j, $P(x_{ij} = 1)$ might equal 0.5. But if we were to repeatedly test examinee j with this same item (with a memory erase, as in CTT), the examinee would likely select the same response very frequently, either because he knows the right answer or is consistently drawn to the same wrong answer. Instead, the response probability can be conceptualized in terms of a subpopulation of examinees with the same θ value. The response probability represents the probability that a randomly selected examinee from that subpopulation would answer the item correctly. Or it could be conceptualized in terms of a hypothetical population of items with the same parameters where the response probability represents the probability that the examinee would respond correctly to a randomly selected item with these parameters.

In the 2PL model, the c-parameter is fixed to zero and thus is removed from the model. In the 1PL model, a single a-parameter is estimated for all items and only the b-parameter differs. The 1PL model is equivalent to the Rasch model. The Rasch model was originally specified in terms of log-odds, not probabilities. It is now often specified similarly to the 1PL model, but without the 1.7 and using different symbols for the item difficulty and person ability/trait. The way the model is identified is also typically different in IRT and Rasch models. Two constraints need to be applied to fix the indeterminancy in the metric, one to center the scale and another to set the scale of the units. In IRT, the most common choice is to set the mean of the θs to 0 and the standard deviation of the θs to 1. Typically, Rasch modelers set the a-parameter to one, which frees the variance of θ, and the mean of the bs to 0, which frees the mean of θ. So the more discriminating the test, in terms of the IRT a-parameters, the greater the variance of the Rasch abilities. This illustrates that, like in CTT, the more heterogeneous the examinees' abilities are, the better we can discriminate among them.

If the model fits the data in all populations (an important caveat), the IRT item parameters are population invariant; they are the same in all populations. Aside from sampling error, the estimates of the parameters will vary by a linear transformation due to the indeterminacy in the metric. When the ability distributions of the populations differ, this cannot be true of the CTT item difficulty P; there is a nonlinear relationship between the item difficulty in different ability distributions. The point-biserial correlation, as discussed, depends on the item difficulty and also is not population invariant. However, if the ability distributions are not too discrepant, the relationships between estimates in different populations are often nearly linear (Fan, 1998). Additionally, if P is transformed to the threshold on the cumulative normal distribution corresponding to P, and the point-biserial correlation is transformed to the biserial correlation, invariance can be obtained if the additional assumptions of no correct guessing and normality of the underlying data are met.

The likelihood function

The likelihood function is an important concept in maximum-likelihood (ML) estimation. If the assumption of local independence is met, the likelihood of any observed response string, say 111101110011111000001000, is the product of the likelihoods of the individual item responses. For dichotomous items, the likelihood of an observed response of 1 is $P(\theta)$ and the probability of a response of 0 is $1 - P(\theta)$. If the item parameters are known, or treated as known, the likelihood is a function of θ. As long as there is at least one 0 and one 1 in the response string, the resulting function will have a maximum, and the value of θ where that maximum occurs is the ML estimate of θ. Figure 2.3 is an example of a likelihood function. Typically, the maximum is found using the Newton–Raphson method.

Sometimes information about the population distribution is used in estimating θ, employing Bayesian principles. The posterior distribution is the likelihood function multiplied by a prior distribution specifying the population density. The ML estimate

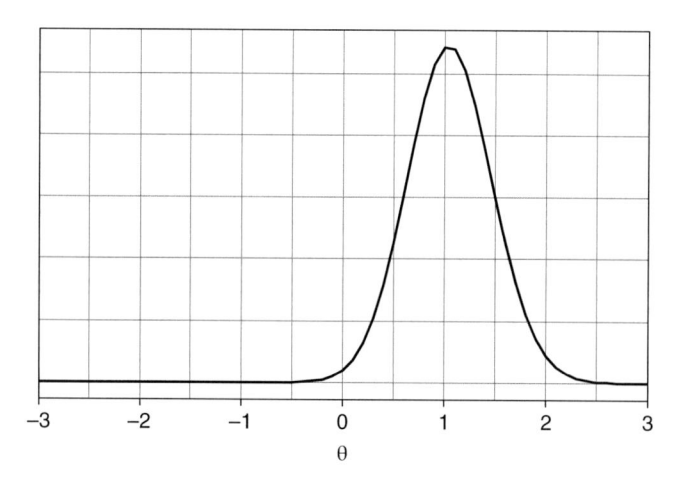

Figure 2.3 A likelihood function that reaches its maximum just above $\theta = 1$.

based on the posterior distribution is called the **modal-a-posterior** (MAP) estimate. $\hat{\theta}$ could instead be estimated as the mean, not the maximum of the posterior distribution, an estimate termed the **expected-a-posterior** (EAP, with the **expected** meaning **expected value**).

To estimate the item parameters, the $P(\theta)$ or $1 - P(\theta)$ in the likelihood is multiplied across people within an item. In most contexts, the individual θs are not known, and the likelihood is integrated across the θ distribution to reduce the dimensionality. This process is called maximum marginal likelihood (MML, also written as marginal maximum likelihood). The integration is approximated by the method of quadratures. The θ distribution may be assumed normal, or the shape of the distribution may be estimated as part of the MML process.

Item information and test information

Reliability and the SEM are major concepts in IRT, just as they are in CTT. Information underlies both concepts. Information is a statistical term, not unique to measurement. Information is the inverse of the asymptotic variance of a maximum-likelihood estimate. Thus, not only $\hat{\theta}$ but also each of the item parameters has an estimate of information and error variance. When the term **information** is used without a qualifier, it typically refers to the information for $\hat{\theta}$. The square root of the inverse of information ($\sqrt{\frac{1}{I(\theta)}}$) is the standard error of the parameter estimate. The standard error of $\hat{\theta}$ is the SEM, although some prefer to reserve the term SEM for observed scores. Because information is a function, not a single value, the standard error of $\hat{\theta}$ is also a function. An example is shown in Figure 2.4. In typical test forms, there is more information for middle values of θ, so the standard error is lower for these values. This contrasts with STT, where the standard errors are higher for those with observed scores nearer 50%. This difference can be explained by the difference in metrics. For examinees with very high or very low

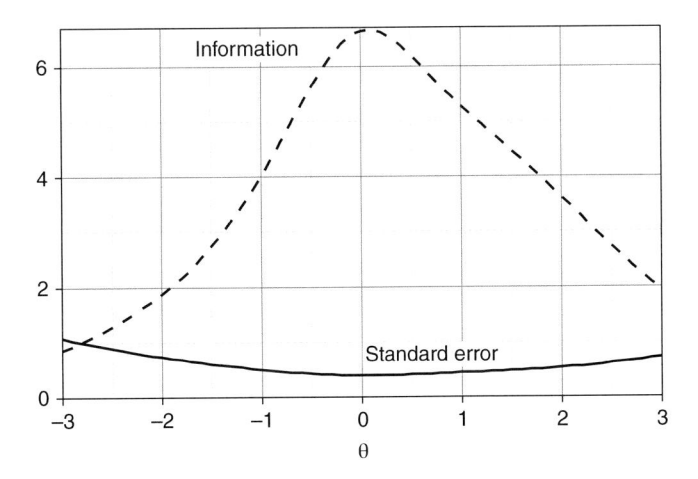

Figure 2.4 Information and standard error functions for θ.

θs, it can be difficult to estimate exactly how high or low θ is. But these examinees would consistently have observed scores near 100% or 0% on randomly selected test forms.

The information for θ can be decomposed into a series of item information functions. A useful property is that the item information functions sum to the test information function. Thus, the effect of adding or deleting an item or set of items can be easily calculated. In CTT, adding or deleting items changes T, so reliability and the SEM need to be re-calculated. If the IRT model fits, adding or deleting an item does not change the information function for any other items.[9] For dichotomous items, item information peaks at the difficulty value if the data follow a 1PL or 2PL model and somewhat above the difficulty value if the data follow a 3PL model. When item discrimination is high, the information is high at its peak but lower at other points. When item discrimination is low, information is spread over a broader theta range but is never very high. The higher the c-parameter, the lower the information, especially in the lower range of θ.

Items can be selected more precisely to provide information in specified ranges. Tests often are designed to have more information where the examinees are concentrated. If the intended examinee population matches the population used to center the metric, typically items would be chosen to provide the most information over a range between −2 and 2. If the test will be used on a more able group than the group used to center the metric, perhaps to select scholarship or award winners, more difficult items would be selected to provide more information in the top range. If the test has a passing standard, items might be selected to provide peak information at the cutscore, regardless of the θ distribution. Thus, the process of selecting items to fit an information function can be more systematic than the CTT method of selecting the more discriminating (usually middle-difficulty) items. Additionally, even if items have never been administered together on the same test form, once the items have been scaled to the same metric, possibly through a series of anchor items, the information for any set of items can be easily calculated, if the assumptions hold.

The information function is easier to work with than the standard error function because of its additive property. After the information function is calculated, the standard error function can be calculated. Due to the non-linear relationship between information and standard error, adding or deleting items has a non-linear effect on the standard error. Adding items has a decreasing impact on the standard error as the standard error gets smaller.

Information and the SEM are more useful than reliability because they are conditional on θ. But sometimes score users want a single summary of score precision. Reliability can be calculated from the CTT definition $\frac{\sigma^2(X) - \sigma^2(E)}{\sigma^2(X)}$, substituting the average standard error of θ for $\sigma^2(E)$ and the variance of the ML[10] $\hat{\theta}$s for the observed score variance, termed the empirical reliability (du Toit, 2003, p. 34). Or the theoretical reliability

---

[9] Of course, if the model does not fit, deleting a subset of items may change the estimation of $\hat{\theta}$ and all of the parameters of the other items.
[10] The formula is slightly different for Bayesian $\hat{\theta}$s because the variance of Bayesian estimates is the estimated true score variance.

can be estimated by integrating the information over the distribution of theta (either the hypothetical distribution or the distribution estimated along with the item parameters) and substituting the corresponding marginal standard error estimate. As in CTT, reliability must be in reference to a particular population. Reliability depends on the group variance.

One caveat regarding information: as noted in the introductory paragraph for this section, information is a property of ML estimates. In IRT, $\hat{\theta}$ is sometimes estimated by ML, with or without a Bayesian prior. The information function can be adjusted for the prior if the prior has a second derivative; for example, the second derivative of the normal distribution is the inverse of the standard deviation, so if a standard normal prior is used, a constant of 1 is added to the information across the θ range for the MAP estimates. EAP estimates are not ML estimates. The appropriate standard error for EAP estimates is the posterior standard deviation, which will be $< = \sqrt{\frac{1}{I(\theta)}}$ if $I(\theta)$ is based on the ML estimate without a prior but $> = \sqrt{\frac{1}{I(\theta)}}$ if $I(\theta)$ based on the ML estimates with a prior.

Chapter Summary

This chapter has provided an overview of CTT, STT as a variant of CTT with stronger assumptions and a focus on items instead of test scores, and g theory as an extension of CTT. With these theories, the true score or domain score or universe score is defined simply as the expected value of the observed score. Next, the focus moved to IRT. In IRT, a latent variable, θ, is posited to underlie the observed item responses. Although the observed responses are used in estimating $\hat{\theta}$, θ is not defined directly in terms of the responses the way T is defined in terms of X in CTT. Procedures for estimating the standard error and reliability of the scores were also discussed for the different score theories. In CTT and g theory, a single estimate of the SEM is obtained for all scores. In STT and IRT, the standard error is a function of ζ or θ. In STT, proportion-correct scores near 0 or 1 have the lowest standard errors. In IRT, $\hat{\theta}$s furthest from the item difficulties have the highest standard errors. In all test scoring theories, reliability, in contrast to the SEM, is group dependent.

References

Allen, M. J., & Yen, W. M. (1979). *Introduction to measurement theory*. Prospect Heights, IL: Waveland Press.
American Educational Research Association, American Psychological Association, and National Council on Measurement in Education. (1999). *Standards for Educational and Psychological Testing*. Washington, DC: American Educational Research Association.
Angoff, W. H., & Ford, S. F. (1973). Item-race interaction on a test of scholastic aptitude. *Journal of Educational Measurement, 10,* 95–105.
Brennan, R. L. (2001). *Generalizability theory*. New York, NY: Springer.
Carroll, J. B. (1945). The effect of difficulty and chance success on correlations between items or between tests. *Psychometrika, 10,* 1–19.

Carroll, J. B. (1987). Correcting point-biserial and biserial correlation coefficients for chance success. *Psychometrika, 47*, 359–360.

Chen, W. H., & Thissen, D. (1997). Local dependence indexes for item pairs using item response theory. *Journal of Educational and Behavioral Statistics, 22*, 265–289.

Crocker, L. C., & Algina, J. (1986). *Introduction to classical and modern test theory.* Belmont, CA: Wadsworth Group.

Cronbach, L. J. (1951). Coefficient alpha and the internal structure of tests. *Psychometrika, 16*, 297–334.

Cronbach, L. J. (2004). My current thoughts on coefficient alpha and successor procedures. *Educational and Psychological Measurement, 64*, 391–418.

Cronbach, L. J., Rajaratnam, N., & Gleser, G. C. (1963). Theory of generalizability: A liberalization of reliability theory. *The British Journal of Statistical Psychology, 16*, 137–163.

du Toit, M. (Ed.). (2003). *IRT from SSI: Bilog-MG, Multilog, Parscale, Testfact.* Lincolnwood, IL: Scientific Software International, Inc.

Fan, X. (1998). Item response theory and classical test theory: An empirical comparison of their item/person statistics. *Educational and Psychological Measurement, 58*, 357–381.

Feldt, L. S. (1984). Some relationships between the binomial error model and classical test theory. *Educational and Psychological Measurement, 44*, 883–891.

Feldt, L. S. (2002). Estimating the internal consistency reliability of tests composed of testlets varying in length. *Applied Measurement in Education, 15*, 33–48.

Glas, C. A. W., & Suárez Falcón, J. C. (2003). A comparison of item-fit statistics for the three-parameter logistic model. *Applied Psychological Measurement, 27*, 87–106.

Green, S. B., & Yang, Y. (2009). Commentary on coefficient alpha: A cautionary tale. *Psychometrika, 74*, 121–135.

Guttman, L. (1945). A basis for analyzing test-retest reliability. *Psychometrika, 10*, 255–282.

Hanson, B. A. (1991). *Method of moments estimates for the four-parameter beta compound binomial model and the calculation of classification consistency indexes.* (ACT Research Report Series 91-5). Iowa City, IA: ACT.

Hattie, J. (1984). An empirical study of various indices for determining unidimensionality. *Multivariate Behavioral Research, 19*, 49–78.

Huynh, H. (1979). Statistical inference for two reliability indices in mastery testing based on the beta-binomial model. *Journal of Educational Statistics, 4*, 231–246.

Kang, T., & Cohen, A. S. (2007). IRT model selection methods for dichotomous items. *Applied Psychological Measurement, 31*, 331–358.

Kang, T., Cohen, A. S., & Sung, H. J. (2009). IRT model selection methods for polytomous items. *Applied Psychological Measurement, 33*, 499–518.

Keats, J. A., & Lord, F. M. (1962). A theoretical distribution for mental test scores. *Psychometrika, 27*, 59–72.

Kelley, T. L. (1939). The selection of upper and lower grades for the validation of test items. *Journal of Educational Psychology, 30*, 17–24.

Kim, D., De Ayala, R. J., Ferdous, A. A., & Nering, M. L. (2011). The comparative performance of conditional independence indices. *Applied Psychological Measurement, 35*, 447–471.

Kirk, D. B. (1973). On the numerical approximation of the bivariate normal (tetrachoric) correlation coefficient. *Psychometrika, 38*, 259–268.

Komaroff, E. (1997). Effect of simultaneous violations of essential τ-equivalence and uncorrelated error on coefficient α. *Applied Psychological Measurement, 21*, 337–348.

Kuder, G. F., & Richardson, M. W. (1937). The theory of the estimation of test reliability. *Psychometrika, 2*, 151–160.

Li, S., & Wells, C. S. (2006). *A model fit statistic for Samejima's graded response model.* Paper presented at the annual meeting of the National Council on Measurement in Education, San Francisco, April 6–10.

Liang, T., & Wells, C. S. (2009). A model fit statistic for generalized partial credit model. *Educational and Psychological Measurement, 69*, 913–928.

Lord, F. M. (1965). A strong true-score theory, with applications. *Psychometrika, 30*, 239–270.

Lord, F. M., & Novick, M. R. (1968). *Statistical theories of mental test scores.* Reading, MA: Addison-Wesley.

Maydeu-Olivares, A., Cai, L., & Hernández, A. (2011). Comparing the fit of item response theory and factor analysis models. *Structural Equation Modeling, 18*, 333–356.

McDonald, R. P. (1999). *Test theory: A unified treatment.* Mahwah, NJ: Erlbaum.

Meyer, P. (2010). *Reliability.* New York, NY: Oxford University Press.

Novick, M. R., & Lewis, C. (1967). Coefficient alpha and the reliability of composite measurements. *Psychometrika, 32*, 1–13.

Orlando, M., & Thissen, D. (2000). Likelihood-based item-fit indices for dichotomous item response theory models. *Applied Psychological Measurement, 24*, 50–64.

Orlando, M., & Thissen, D. (2003). Further investigation of the performance of S-X2: An item fit index for use with dichotomous item response theory models. *Applied Psychological Measurement, 27*, 289–298.

Rasch, G. (1980). *Probabilistic models for some intelligence and attainment tests* (expanded ed.). Chicago, IL: University of Chicago Press. First published 1960, Copenhagen: Danish Institute for Educational Research.

Raykov, T., & Marcoulides, G. A. (2011). *Introduction to psychometric theory.* New York, NY: Routledge.

Shavelson, R. J., & Webb, N. M. (1991). *Generalizability theory: A primer.* Thousand Oaks, CA: Sage.

Sinharay, S., & Lu, Y. (2008). A further look at the correlation between item parameters and item fit statistics. *Journal of Educational Measurement, 45*, 1–15.

Sitjsma, K. (2012). Future of psychometrics: Ask what psychometric can do for psychology. *Psychometrika, 77*, 4–20.

Stone, C. A. (2000). Monte Carlo based null distribution for an alternative goodness-of-fit test statistic in IRT models. *Journal of Educational Measurement, 37*, 58–75.

Stone, C. A. (2003). Empirical power and type I error rates for an IRT fit statistic that considers the precision of ability estimates. *Educational and Psychological Measurement, 63*, 566–583.

Sutcliffe, J. P. (1965). A probability model for errors of classification. *Psychometrika, 30*, 73–96.

Tate, R. (2003). A comparison of selected empirical methods for assessing the structure of responses to test items. *Applied Psychological Measurement, 27*, 159–203.

Thorndike, R. L. (1951). Reliability. In E. F. Lindquist & F. Everet (Eds.), *Educational measurement* (pp. 560–620). Washington, DC: American Council on Education.

Wainer, H., Bradlow, E. T., & Wang, X. (2007). *Testlet response theory and its applications.* New York, NY: Cambridge University Press.

Wells, C. S., & Bolt, D. M. (2008). Investigation of a nonparametric procedure for assessing goodness-of-fit in item response theory. *Applied Measurement in Education, 21*, 22–40.

Whittaker, T. A., Chang, W., & Dodd, B. G. (2012). The performance of IRT model selection methods with mixed-format tests. *Applied Psychological Measurement, 36*, 159–180.

Zimmerman, D. W., Zumbo, B. D., & Lalonde, C. (1993). Coefficient alpha as an estimate of reliability under violation of two assumptions. *Educational and Psychological Measurement, 53*, 33–49.

Code Appendix

Code 1 SAS latent and observed tau-equivalence.

```
options nocenter;
*illustrates difference between latent and observed tau-
equivalence;
%let seed=552954; *so can recreate later;
libname lib1 "C:\Christine";
data lib1.tau;
seed=552954;
do id=1 to 100000000;
  array a[10]; *continuous items;
  array b[10]; *another set of continuous items;
  array c[10]; *di items;
  array d[10]; *another set of di items;
  T=rannor(&seed);
  do i=1 to 10;
    a[i]=.6*T + .8*rannor(&seed)+(i-1)*.3 -1.35;
      b[i]=.6*T + .8*rannor(&seed)+(i-1)*.3 -1.35;
      if a[i]<-.5 then c[i]=0; else c[i]=1;
    if b[i]<-.5 then d[i]=0; else d[i]=1;
  end;
  Xstar1=sum(of a1-a10);
  Xstar2=sum(of b1-b10);
  X1=sum(of c1-c10);
  X2=sum(of d1-d10);
  output;
 end;
 run;
data _null_; set lib1.tau;
file "C:\Christine\delta.dat";
put c1-c10 d1-d10;
run;

 proc corr; var Xstar1 Xstar2; run;
 proc corr alpha nocorr; var a1-a10; run;
 proc corr alpha nocorr; var b1-b10; run;
  proc corr; var X1 X2; run;
 proc corr alpha nocorr; var c1-c10; run;
 proc corr alpha nocorr; var d1-d10; run;
```

Code 2 MPlus delta linear model.

```
TITLE: dichotomous items linear model
DATA: FILE IS "C:\Christine\delta.dat";
FORMAT is (10F2);
NOBSERVATIONS=10000000;
VARIABLE: NAMES ARE I1-I10;
ANALYSIS: ESTIMATOR=ML;
MODEL: f1 by I1-I10*;
f1@1;
[f1@0];
OUTPUT: STDYX;
SAVEDATA:
RESULTS are "C:\Christine\deltaLin.res";
```

Code 3 MPlus delta probit model.

```
TITLE: dichotomous items probit link model
DATA: FILE IS 'C:\Christine\delta.dat';
 FORMAT is (10F2);
 NOBSERVATIONS=10000000;
VARIABLE: NAMES ARE I1-I10;
   CATEGORICAL ARE I1-I10;
ANALYSIS: ESTIMATOR=WLSMV;
MODEL: f1 by I1-I10*;
   f1@1;
  [f1@0];
OUTPUT: STDYX;
SAVEDATA:
 RESULTS are "C:\Christine\deltaProbit.res";
```

3

Item Generation

Kristin M. Morrison and Susan Embretson

Item generation is increasingly being considered as a solution to the huge demand for new items in testing (Embretson, 2002; Gierl & Lai, 2013). The demand for new items has increased substantially over the last few years. One source of item demand is the increased implementation of computerized adaptive testing (CAT). CAT requires large and diverse item banks to measure people at different levels with precision and efficiency. CAT is used on many personnel selection tests. For example, the Armed Services Vocational Aptitude Test (ASVAB) is a large-scale test implemented with CAT. Perhaps the biggest source of increased item demand arises from test security concerns resulting from item exposure. That is, items administered frequently may become available to examinees before the test with the effect of reducing item validity. Many high-stakes ability tests, such as the Graduate Record Examination (GRE) or SAT, require a plethora of items to counter the negative effects of item exposure. Items on these tests must be retired and new ones must continually be produced so that examinees do not have differential familiarity with item content. Similarly, item exposure issues arise with internet testing (Naglieri et al., 2004) particularly when testing time varies considerably between examinees. Other tests, such as end-of-the-year achievement tests that are administered for state school accountability, also require large item banks. As with the high-stakes aptitude tests, item exposure control is necessary to provide test security.

Unfortunately, traditional item development is a slow and painstaking process. The rate of item production from human item writers is relatively low and many items do not survive the subsequent evaluation processes. That is, the items that are produced must be reviewed for quality and appropriateness by test editors and, for some tests, by panels of experts. Then, item quality must be further established through empirical tryout for psychometric properties, preferably in the context of the operational test. Empirical tryout typically presents a significant roadblock to increasing item quantity. Only a limited number of items can be placed within an operational test for tryout. Then, many items do not obtain adequate psychometric properties and hence do not survive. Thus, the

---

[1] The research reported here was partially supported by the Institute of Education Sciences, U.S. Department of Education, through Grant R305A100234 to Georgia Institute of Technology. The opinions expressed are those of the authors and do not represent views of the Institute or the U.S. Department of Education.

The Wiley Handbook of Psychometric Testing: A Multidisciplinary Reference on Survey, Scale and Test Development, First Edition. Edited by Paul Irwing, Tom Booth, and David J. Hughes.
© 2018 John Wiley & Sons Ltd. Published 2020 by John Wiley & Sons Ltd.

traditional item development process provides only a limited number of new items that can be used for testing.

Item generation offers a potential solution to increase the number of items available for testing. Several automatic item generators have been developed. Items have been successfully generated for a range of abilities, including cognitive tasks that are used for military recruitment selection and classification (Collis, Tapsfield, Irvine, Dann, & Wright, 1995; Kyllonen, 2002), abstract reasoning (Arendasy, 2005; Embretson, 1999; Hornke, 2002; Primi, Zanarella-Cruz, Muniz-Nascimento, & Petrini, 2006), analytic reasoning (Newstead, Bradon, Handley, Dennis, & Evans, 2006), mathematical reasoning and achievement (Deane, Graf, Higgins, Futagi, & Lawless, 2006; Singley & Bennett, 2002), spatial ability (Bejar & Yocom, 1986; Embretson, 2010), and medical licensure examinations (Gierl & Lai, 2013). Since item generation is an active area, especially in the area of ability and achievement, many new examples of item generators can be expected soon.

This chapter will elaborate on the nature of item generation and research required to shorten the item development process. Various approaches to item generation will be considered and illustrated with examples. The importance of research to obtain the greatest advantages from item generation will be elaborated, followed by a description of research that provides support for item generation.

The Nature of Item Generation

Item generation has two basic components: (1) structures for items and (2) databases for substitution into the structures. Specifically, item generation requires a structure into which content can be substituted. The nature of these structures varies across item types and even across item generators for the same item type.

Item generation has two basic formats, algorithmic and automatic. Algorithmic item generation involves the production of items by item writers using defined substitution rules into tightly defined structures. Algorithmic item generation has been available for several decades and has been applied to a few tests. In these earlier examples of item generation, the substitution rules were based on conceptual/theoretical considerations, without empirical support.

For example, Hively, Patterson, and Page (1968) introduced the concept **item form**, an abstract representation of the item. They demonstrated item generation in the context of arithmetic. That is, a very simple problem (13 – 6 = ?) could be represented by a general form (A – B = ?) with item generation rules to define the permissible substitutions and constraints. For example, the database for permissible substitutions can be defined by lists of numbers (e.g., single digit numbers). Then, substitution rules, such that $A = a_1$ and $B = b_1$, are applied often with constraints (e.g., $a_1 > b_1$). More complex problems, with more digits or more complex operations (e.g., borrowing or zero) can be represented with different substitution rules and constraints or by other **item forms** (e.g., A – ? = B).

Algorithmic item generation has also been applied in the measurement of feelings and attitudes. Roskam and Broers (1996) used facet analysis to define templates for items that measured lonesomeness. For example, the item "Would you feel lonesome if it rarely occurs that a good friend of yours talks to you about his problems?" (p. 354) represents a specified combination of facets. That is, the statement about an interaction results from different combinations of partner, direction, mode, and area. Roskam and

Broers (1996) wrote items to fulfill the different combinations of elements within the facets.

Automatic item generation, in contrast, involves producing items by a computer program. As with algorithmic item generation, structures and databases with content substitution rules are required. Since item production is automated, complete databases and substitution rules must be explicitly specified. Automatic item generation can yield particularly impressive results in item production. Item generators for heterogeneous items with multiple generating structures can also produce large quantities of items quickly. Sometimes item generators with a single structure can have very impressive results. For example, Gierl and Alves (2011) recently demonstrated the production of 733 mathematical achievement items with relatively homogeneous content in a matter of seconds.

Advantages of item generation

Item generation has several advantages for test development. First, the sheer volume of items, particularly with automatic item generators, may help solve some practical problems in testing. Large numbers of available items can counter contemporary concerns about test security by substantially reducing item exposure across examinees. Second, CAT can benefit from the availability of large quantities of items generated from structures that target different difficulty levels to provide small measurement errors for each level. Third, when aligned with empirical support for the theoretical basis of item generation, the construct-relevancy of item content may be improved. Developing a computer program for item generation involves specification of all types of content that are to be sampled or fixed. Fourth, the length of the test development process may be substantially reduced. Item generators with supported quality of item properties and predictable item parameters can lead to item development with a greatly reduced item evaluation process. Fifth, construct validity can be enhanced with item generation. The necessary specifications for an item generation database define more precisely the nature of the construct domain with the consequence of increasing the content aspect of construct validity. Further, item generation with a supporting research foundation of cognitive modeling can provide evidence for the response process aspect of construct validity.

Approaches to item generation

A major difference in approaches to item generation is the level of abstraction of the item structures. The **item model approach** (Bejar et al., 2003) is the least abstract because existing items provide models for structures. The **template approach** is somewhat more abstract because structures result from a conceptually based framework that does not require existing items. The **cognitive design system** approach (Embretson, 1998) involves more abstract structures that are postulated to underlie existing items or items that have not been observed. Both of these latter approaches rely on initially having items with acceptable psychometric properties and content quality.

Item model approach In the **item model approach**, an existing test item with adequate psychometric properties becomes a structure (i.e., an item model) into which content can be substituted. Ideally, the item model approach creates isomorphic items; these are items that are comparable in content and psychometric parameters (Bejar et al., 2003).

Table 3.1 An example of the item model approach for a mathematics achievement test.

Item	Item Model
Sarah paid $6 for 4 pounds of apples. At this rate, how much will she pay for 7 pounds of apples? (A) $3.43 (B) $4.67 (C) X $10.50 (D) $12.00	Sarah s_1 paid $6 n_1 for 4 n_2 pounds of apples x_1. At this rate, how much will she s_1 pay for 7 n_3 pounds of apples x_1? (A) $3.43 n_4 $\left[\dfrac{n_1}{n_3} = \dfrac{x}{n_2}\right]$ (B) $4.67 n_5 $\left[\dfrac{n_3}{n_1} = \dfrac{x}{n_2}\right]$ (C) X $10.50 n_6 $\left[\dfrac{n_1}{n_2} = \dfrac{x}{n_3}\right]$ (D) $12.00 n_7 s = variable persons, x = variable objects, n = numbers
Structurally Variant Item I	*Structurally Variant Item Model I*
Sarah paid $6 for 4 pounds of apples and $4.00 for 3 pounds of pears. At this rate, how much will she pay for 7 pounds of apples? (A) $3.43 (B) $4.67 (C) X $10.50 (D) $12.00	Sarah s_1 paid $6 n_1 for 4 n_2 pounds of apples x_1 and $4.00 n_3 for 3 n_4 pounds of pears x_2. At this rate, how much will she s_1 pay for 7 n_5 pounds of apples x_1? (A) $3.43 n_6 $\left[\dfrac{n_1}{n_5} = \dfrac{x}{n_2}\right]$ (B) $4.67 n_7 $\left[\dfrac{n_5}{n_1} = \dfrac{x}{n_2}\right]$ (C) X $10.50 n_8 $\left[\dfrac{n_1}{n_2} = \dfrac{x}{n_5}\right]$ (D) $12.00 n_9 s = variable persons, x = variable objects, n = numbers
Structurally Variant Item II	*Structurally Variant Item Model II*
Sarah paid $6 for 4 pounds of apples, for a rate of $1.50 per pound. How much will she pay for 7 pounds of apples? (A) $3.43 (B) $4.67 (C) X $10.50 (D) $12.00	Sarah s_1 paid $6 n_1 for 4 n_2 pounds of apples x_1 for a rate of $1.50 n_3 per pound. How much will she s_1 pay for 7 n_4 pounds of apples x_1? (A) $3.43 n_5 $\left[\dfrac{n_1}{n_4} = \dfrac{x}{n_2}\right]$ (B) $4.67 n_6 $\left[\dfrac{n_4}{n_1} = \dfrac{x}{n_2}\right]$ (C) X $10.50 n_7 $\left[\dfrac{n_1}{n_2} = \dfrac{x}{n_4}\right]$ (D) $12.00 n_8 s = variable persons, x = variable objects, n = numbers

Table 3.1 presents an example of an existing mathematical problem-solving item that has become an item model for a mathematics item generator (Embretson, Walker, Wilson, & Lutz, 2012). The existing item is shown on the left side of Table 3.1. The specific content of the item is "variabilized" into an **item model**, as shown on the right side of Table 3.1. The symbols represent different types of content. Variable

subjects in the item are noted by s, where "Sarah" is s_1. Variable objects are represented by x, where x_1 is "fish." Finally, the numeral content is represented by n, where n_1 is $6. Notice that in this item, all response options have a numeral basis, hence providing for comparable distractors. Thus, for this item model, new items are generated by substituting s, x, and n according to content databases that are created for the item.

For the item model approach, it is assumed that all variants inherit the same psychometric properties as the item model itself. The validity of this assumption must be assessed empirically by estimating item parameters for the variants. However, items created through the use of the item model approach must be constructed so as not to create absurd items. To prevent these types of items, constraints or conditions, are placed on the databases to help ensure that sampled content does not impact item complexity, quality, or psychometric properties. For example, with the item in Table 3.1, if Sarah (s_1) is replaced with a male name (such as Peter), the subsequent pronoun she (also variablized as s_1) must be changed to reflect the appropriate gender. A constraint placed on the item is that the two variables defined as s_1 match in gender across databases (e.g., the name database and the pronoun database). Another constraint that would be imposed would be the plausibility of the numbers for the specific context. In the current item, a price of $1 would not be realistic for 4 pounds of fish. Therefore, ranges for price per pound should be specified for specific selected content.

The item model approach has some advantages (Bejar et al., 2003) over other item generation approaches. First, item models are often considered to be validity-enhancing since new items are based on current items with established psychometric properties. Second, this approach also automates the item production process once the item model has been created. Third, the item model approach requires less advanced theoretical/conceptual development than other approaches. Existing items that have survived the evaluation process provide the models. Finally, by using the item model approach, instance-specific feedback or tutoring can be built into item models (see Bejar et al., 2003, for an elaboration).

Template approach   The **template approach** is similar to the item model approach but the structure is not based on an existing item. That is, templates are developed specifically to allow for item generation; these templates include three components: stem, options, and auxiliary information (Luecht, 2013; Lai & Gierl, 2013). The stem of the item proposes the question or task to the examinee. The options include both the correct and incorrect responses to the item stem. Lastly, the auxiliary information consists of multimedia presentations (e.g., graphs, charts, tables) to facilitate an examinee's understanding.

To create item templates, task models (see Luecht, 2013) are developed first to provide a set of specifications for a particular template. For example, Lai and Gierl (2013, p. 82) illustrate a task model with the template shown in Table 3.2 that specifies

> 1) items must be worded in an applicative manner, 2) the verbal load of the items must contain a moderate level of distracting information, 3) items must involve a polynomial function, 4) applications of functions must contain one unknown variable, 5) the complexity of operations required in the items has to be at a moderate level for Grade 9 students, 6) only a few numerical operations are needed to get the correct answer.

Then, the template is developed to specify a general structure of the problem, including which elements are variables, along with a database of permissible substitutions.

Table 3.2 A template resulting from a task model (revised version of Luecht, 2013, p. 83).

Suppose at takeoff, the distance traveled by a passenger jet on the runway can be determined by the following equation in meters:

$D = n_1 S^2 + n_2 S$

Where S is the number of seconds the plane has traveled. How far would the airplane have traveled after $n3$ seconds?

Elements n_1 Value Range: 5–9 by 1
n_2 Value Range: 2–9 by 1
n_3 Value Range: 10–20 by 1

Once the item template is developed, the features of the task model are applied until all specifications and constraints are met. Further, noncognitive, nonmodel related effects on the item template (e.g., appropriateness of options) must be controlled (Lai & Gierl, 2013).

While the development process of item templates differs from item models, sometimes the generating forms of item models and templates are indistinguishable. The mathematical word problem in Table 3.1, while not written to provide an item generation structure, was actually written to fulfill a tightly specified indicator of mathematical achievement. That is, the test blueprint specified that an appropriate item would involve (1) use of algebraic concepts and procedures, (2) use of variables, symbols, rational numbers, and simple algebraic expressions in one variable to solve linear equations and inequalities in a variety of situations, and (3) knows the mathematical relationship between ratios, proportions, and percentages and how to solve for a missing term in a proportion with positive rational number solutions and monomials. This definition is intended to guide the item writers. With some additional structure and an elaboration of a database, it could lead to a precise generating template. The "variabilization" of the item, such as shown on Table 3.1, plus the database and constraints provide a structure similar to a template.

Typically, the template approach leads to greater variability between items from the same structure than the item model approach. Gierl, Lai, and Turner (2013) developed templates for medical licensure items that consist of several statements about a hypothetical patient and presenting symptoms. The information in the problem can be presented in a random order and, further, the distractors can be randomly sampled from a set of feasible distractors. Variation can also be optimized in the template approach by varying numerical variables or text-based variables (e.g., using a precompiled bank of possible texts). This increased variability in the content of generated items from item templates, as compared to item models, has both positive and negative effects. On the positive side, increased variability of content helps ensure that the item domain does not become excessively narrow. On the negative side, increased content variability can lead to increased item differences in item psychometric properties, thus requiring some additional method to equate items before test use.

Cognitive design system approach For this approach to item generation, many different structures are defined, based on cognitive complexity. That is, structures can be developed in the context of a cognitive model that has been applied to existing items with

Item Generation

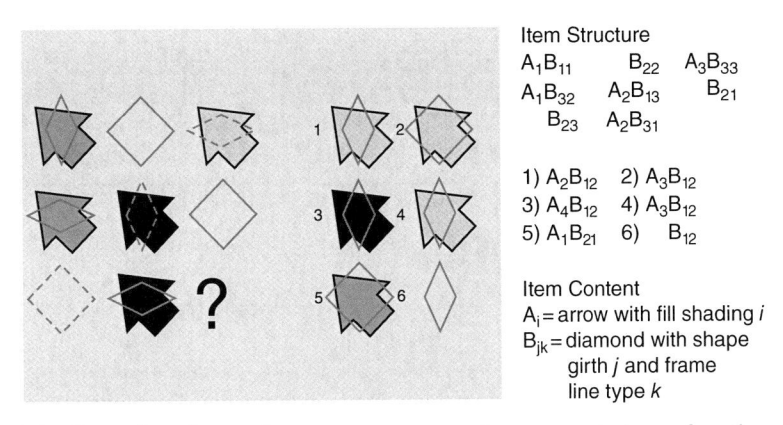

Item Structure
A_1B_{11} B_{22} A_3B_{33}
A_1B_{32} A_2B_{13} B_{21}
B_{23} A_2B_{31}

1) A_2B_{12} 2) A_3B_{12}
3) A_4B_{12} 4) A_3B_{12}
5) A_1B_{21} 6) B_{12}

Item Content
A_i = arrow with fill shading i
B_{jk} = diamond with shape girth j and frame line type k

Figure 3.1 Example of an abstract structure and generated item for the Abstract Reasoning Test.

adequate psychometric properties. Thus, existing items will be scored on variables that are hypothesized to impact complexity in the cognitive model. If research support is obtained for the cognitive model, structures can be defined as different combinations of the levels of the cognitive variables. To generate an item, databases of permissible content, along with constraints, are needed to fulfill the structures to specify an item.

Similar to the item model approach, it is assumed that items using the same structure have similar psychometric properties. Thus, the structures could be treated as item models and evaluated by the same type of psychometric models. However, unlike the item model approach, items can be generated from structures that have not previously been empirically studied. In this case, the cognitive model variables may be used to predict the difficulty of items derived from new structures.

To illustrate, consider the matrix completion item shown in Figure 3.1. In this example, a 3 × 3 matrix of figures must be completed by the examinee. Matrix problems have long been used to measure abstract reasoning and fluid intelligence (Raven, 1936). An empirically plausible theory of cognitive complexity, based on Carpenter, Just, and Shell's (1990) theory was developed and empirically supported as modeling item psychometric properties (Embretson, 1998). The most recent version of the theory (Embretson, 2008) consists of five variables. Two variables that relate directly to the item structure are working memory load (defined by the number and the level of the rules) and the number of unique elements. For the item in Figure 3.1, there are only two unique elements (the arrow and the diamond). Working memory load is high because there are four relationships defined by the changes in these objects. These relationships are (1) a pairwise progression relationship for the arrow shading (dark gray, black, light gray) across the columns, (2) a distribution of two relationship for the arrow presence because a null value exists in each row and column, (3) a distribution of three relationship for the diamond border (solid, small dash, large dash) such that each type appears once in each row and column, and (4) a distribution of three relationship for the diamond girth differences (thin, medium, wide) that appear once in each row and column.

This analysis of rules and objects results in scores for the item included in a cognitive complexity model to predict item psychometric properties. The score for number of

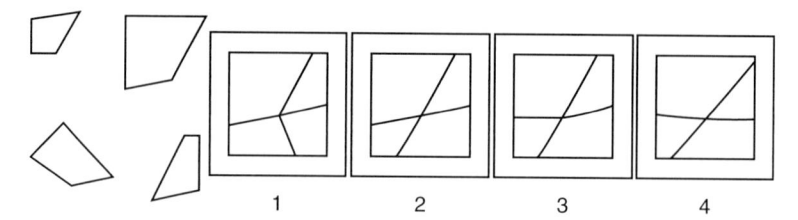

Figure 3.2 An Assembling Objects item from the item generator.

objects is 2 and the score for working memory load is 15, which is the sum of the rule levels.[2] There are also some display variables in the item generator that must be specified in a structure. The display variables perceptually impact the difficulty of finding relationships. These perceptual variables are the following: object overlay, where objects in a matrix are overlaid; object fusion, where multiple objects can be perceived as a larger object; and object distortion, where shapes of the objects are distorted (e.g., twisted; Embretson, 2002). For the item in Figure 3.2, the objects are overlaid but not fused or distorted.

Matrix problems can be represented by abstract structures, also shown in Figure 3.1. A formal abstract structure to represent these relationships was developed and implemented in the item generator program. Each entry in the matrix contains one or more objects, noted by the letters, A, B, and so on, with the properties noted by subscripts (e.g., 1, 2, 3). Thus, formally, for A_i, i varies across columns and the object A has a distributed null value (does not appear). For B_{jk}, both j and k are distributed in each row and column. Each symbol can be defined by a different set of properties or objects. The sampled objects are an arrow (A) and a diamond (B), while the sampled properties were frame fill shading for i (i = dark gray, black, and light gray), shape girth for j (j = thin, medium, wide), and frame line type for k (k = solid, small dash, large dash) as shown on Figure 3.1.

Similar to the item model approach, items from the same generating abstract structure would be predicted to have the same psychometric properties as the original item from which the structure is developed. However, the **cognitive design system approach** has some advantages beyond those in the item model approach, due to the development of a cognitive model. First, predictions can be extended to previously unobserved item structures. The cognitive model with the five predictors can be applied to predict the psychometric properties of newly generated items from any structure (see the prediction model section later). Second, evidence for the response process aspect of validity is obtained if the construct-relevant processes represented in the cognitive model are supported.

Other structures Although the three previously mentioned approaches to item generation are relatively standard, other structures do exist for item generation. One such structure is through the use of programming code (e.g., XML). Fairon and Williamson (2002) elaborate on the use of XML coding to create an automatic text generation

---

[2] The Carpenter et al. (1990) theory assumes that lower level rules are tried before higher-level rules; hence, the rule level is scored as follows: (1) constant in a row, (2) pairwise progression, (3) figure addition/subtraction, (4) distribution of three, and (5) distribution of two (null values).

system. The code in automatic test generation produces fundamental abstract representations of analytical reasoning items. Each abstract structure is composed of a set of item stems, restriction rules, and options for the item. Then, previously stored scenarios, which are stored in a digital library, are used to "clothe" the generated abstract structure. The process permits the generation of hundreds of items. On principle, it is assumed that items generated from the same structure have the same psychometric properties. Through the use of the automatic text generation system, item production is increased, generation controls on language can be implemented, a priori statistical characteristics of the items are known, and items can be generated in multiple languages (currently, English and French; Fairon & Williamson, 2002).

Another type of XML structure was developed for the Assembling Objects Test, which appears on the ASVAB. An example of a generated item is shown on Figure 3.2. The correct answer is that response option which can be assembled from the pieces in the stem (i.e., option 2 in Figure 3.2). The XML code defined item structures based on variables from a model of cognitive complexity differentiate between items. For example, two variables defining the item structures were number of pieces in the stem and number of pieces rotated from the stem to the correct answer. Database variables for the item generator included degrees of rotation of objects in stem as compared to the correct answer, shapes of assembled object and the position of the centerpoint of the rays.

Research Basis for Automatic Item Generation

In this section, some fundamental aspects of research on item generation are explicated. First, the relevance of a research foundation to item generation is described, followed by a consideration of different approaches to establish the prediction and explanation of item psychometric properties.

Relevance to item generation

Generated items can be submitted for empirical tryout using the same procedures used for items written by traditional methods. This approach would ensure that the psychometric properties of generated items are estimated and that tests based on variants of item structures can be equated. However, as described previously, empirical tryout can provide a substantial obstacle to item implementation due to the time and resources that must be devoted.

When items are generated from the same structures, it is sometimes assumed that the items have the same psychometric properties and therefore need not be submitted to further evaluation. This assumption may not be warranted. Thus, research on how varying content impacts item psychometric properties is required. Otherwise, individual scores from tests comprised of different generated items may not be comparable, even though the same structures were used in the generation of items. However, if research supports the prediction of item psychometric properties from the same generating structures, it may be possible to implement subsequently generated items with little or no empirical tryout, as note by Mislevy, Sheehan, and Wingersky (1993).

A basis in research is also required to understand the variability due to different generating structures. Not having appropriate prior research can be especially problematic if defining different structures requires knowledge about how item content differences impact item performance. For example, the underlying variable that produces items with different difficulties may be continuous. For the item in Figure 3.2, the differences in the centerpoint locations between the distractors and the key is a continuous variable that impacts the ease of falsifying the distractors. How can the sampling ranges for the centerpoint locations be set to yield items to be approximately equal in difficulty within structures but different between structures?

Also, for some item types, a basis in research can provide additional support for the response process aspect of construct validity. Evidence of construct validity would be obtained by modeling differences between item structures from a model of cognitive process complexity. For example, results from applying the cognitive model described previously for Abstract Reasoning Test items supported the items as measuring fluid intelligence because item working memory load had a very strong impact on item difficulty.

Finally, if research supports the prediction of item structures due to differences in the fixed aspects of item content, it may be possible to predict the psychometric properties of new item structures. This can be valuable in extending the difficulty levels of items or increasing the diversity of items.

Modeling psychometric properties

Prediction models for item variants Establishing a prediction model requires that items generated from the same structures be submitted for empirical tryout. That is, the psychometric properties (i.e., item difficulty, item discrimination) are estimated and examined for relationship to content and/or structural differences.

A multiple regression approach can be applied by regressing the estimated item difficulties and/or item discriminations of generated items on binary variables that represent the generating item structure. Suppose that item parameters are estimated with the two-parameter logistic (2PL) model, as follows:

$$P(X_{ij} = 1 | \theta_j, \beta_i, \alpha_i) = \frac{\exp(\alpha_i(\theta_j - \beta_i))}{1 + \exp(\alpha_i(\theta_j - \beta_i))} \quad (3.1)$$

where β_i is item difficulty, α_i is item discrimination and θ_j is examinee trait level. Then, regression modeling would involve β_i and α_i as dependent variables to be predicted from binary independent variables, q_{is}, that represent the mapping of item i to structure s. Thus, for example, the predicted item difficulty, β_i', for item i generated from structure s is as follows:

$$\beta_i' = \eta_0 + \sum \eta_s q_{is} \quad (3.2)$$

where η_s is the estimated weight for structure s and η_0 is an intercept. Likewise, item discrimination α_i can be modeled from the item structures. The squared multiple correlation would represent the strength of the relationship of the item models to predict the obtained parameter estimates. If prediction is sufficiently strong, the similarity of psychometric properties for items generated from the same structure is supported.

Another approach to building a prediction model is to apply an item response theory (IRT) model such as the linear logistic test model (LLTM; Fischer, 1973) that incorporates item content into the model. That is, the LLTM incorporates content through scored variables that are used in the modeling of item responses (i.e., those included in the generating item model). In the LLTM, item difficulty is predicted based on the weighted combination of variables, as in regression analysis, but the prediction is included directly in the IRT model, as follows:

$$P(X_{ij} = 1 | \theta_j, \mathbf{q}_i, \boldsymbol{\eta}) = \frac{\exp\left(\theta_j - \sum_{k=0}^{K} q_{is}\eta_s + \eta_0\right)}{1 + \exp\left(\theta_j - \sum_{k=0}^{K} q_{is}\eta_s + \eta_0\right)} \quad (3.3)$$

where q_{is}, η_s, and η_0 are defined as for Equation 3.2. Other IRT models, such as the 2PL constrained model (Embretson, 1999) include prediction models for both item discrimination and item difficulty. Advantages of the IRT-based approaches over the regression approach include appropriate standard errors since the target of modeling is the raw data rather than derived statistics and the parameters are readily equated to other calibrated items. A statistic similar to a multiple correlation can be obtained by comparing the fit of the LLTM with item model predictors to alternative IRT models with unique estimates for every item or the same estimate for every item (see Embretson, 1999).

For both approaches to estimating parameters for structures, strong relationships of structures to explain item differences support applying the predicted parameters for an item structure to new items. In some cases, covariates based on content differences between variants from the same structure can be added to increase levels of prediction.

Explanatory models for structures Explanatory models involve studying the basis for psychometric differences between generating item structures. Increased evidence for construct validity can result from developing explanatory models. One important aspect of construct validity evidence is based on the **response processes** of examinees (see AERA, APA, & NCME, 1999). If the items are measuring the intended construct, then examinees should respond in a fashion predicted by the construct. That is, construct-relevant aspects of items should be related to item difficulty. For example, the difficulty for mathematical reasoning items should be related to variables that impact mathematically relevant processes, such as number and level of operations or number of subgoals and unknown quantities. However, item responses may depend on processes that are not related to the intended construct. A highly contextualized mathematics word problem may depend also on verbal reasoning because the examinee must be able to read and understand the problem before mathematical operations can be involved. Thus, mathematical items that depend heavily on verbal-linguistic encoding would have construct-irrelevant processes contributing to their difficulty.

Explanatory models are implemented using the same statistical methods as prediction models except that the item scores represent variables from a theory or conceptual framework that is hypothesized to explain differences *between* generating item structures. Similar to studying differences between item variants, differences between item structures can be studied by regression modeling of item parameters or by estimation with appropriate IRT models. In this case, the independent variables of the prediction model would be features that are hypothesized to vary between item structures.

That is, q_{is} would represent scores on variable s that are hypothesized to impact item complexity according to the theoretical framework. Scores may be either continuous or binary. For example, the matrix structures for the Abstract Reasoning Test described previously are hypothesized to vary in working memory load. In turn, the working memory load of items is determined by the number of unique elements and relational complexity. These variables are construct-relevant because the Abstract Reasoning Test is intended to be a measure of fluid intelligence. Consequently, the number of unique elements and degree of relational complexity would be scored for each item and included as fixed predictors in the model. The other fixed predictors in the model concern the display properties of the generated items. Items would be scored for the nesting versus separation of elements in the matrix entries, and the distortion or fusion of elements that define relationships. These variables are a less construct-relevant source of item difficulty. The impact of the predictors, represented by their relative weights, provides information about construct validity across the whole test. If the variables that measure working memory demand in items has a strong weight in prediction, then the response process aspect of validity is supported. But also, the relative impact of the various features in difficulty or discrimination for specific items elucidates construct validity at the item level.

The weights for the predictors can also be used to predict the difficulty and discrimination parameters of structures that have not had empirical tryout and calibration of parameters. Further, the results can be useful for determining how to revise item structures to generate items with different psychometric properties. For example, item difficulty can be changed by increasing the level of the features with positive weights or removing features with negative weights in the prediction model.

Stages of Research

In this section, the various stages of research involved in building an item generator with predictable psychometric properties are described and illustrated with examples.

Development of theoretical/conceptual framework

Item development, whether automated or not, should begin with a clear definition of targeted measurement constructs (Embretson & Gorin, 2001). If item generation is applied to an existing test, as in the **item model approach**, this definition already exists. However, the development of a conceptual framework is an intrinsic aspect of some approaches to item generation, such as the template approach. Also, it should be noted that how precisely constructs are defined varies considerably between different types of tests. Achievement tests, for example, may have highly structured blueprints and item writer guidelines to represent the measurement construct. For example, test blueprints for measuring middle school mathematical achievement in the United States typically define four areas of mathematics (Number, Algebra, Geometry, and Data/Statistics) and then provide elaborated definitions of the specific skills within each area. The blueprint for a Grade 8 test that was used to build a mathematics item generator (Embretson et al., 2012) contained 33 skill definitions nested within four areas. Also, extensive

Item Generation

procedures to evaluate the adherence of items to the blueprint are typical for achievement tests.

Aptitude tests, in contrast, may not have a blueprint and only a few guidelines for item writing. Sometimes item writers are merely asked to develop items similar to items already in the test. New items may be evaluated by more minimal procedures, such as review by a test editor. In this case, it is typically assumed that empirical tryout will assess item quality.

Development of item structures and databases

The impact of research on developing item structures and databases varies across the various approaches. Thus, the role of research will be separately considered by approach.

Item model approach If the **item model approach** is applied to an existing test, item structures are developed directly by "variabilizing" content for items with adequate psychometric properties, as noted previously. Thus, research is not required to develop the item structures from existing items. However, if increased item diversity is desired by changing some aspects of the item model, a research foundation is needed. Further, research may be required to develop the databases in order to determine the sensitivity of the item psychometric properties to the range of substitutions being considered.

To illustrate, consider the **structural variants** of the item model shown on the bottom of Table 3.1. Additional text and numbers have been added. Cognitive model research on this item type (Embretson & Daniel, 2008) supports several stages of problem solving with different content features impacting the complexity of the various stages. Table 3.3 presents the five stages and a list of variables postulated to impact their complexity. For Structural Variant I, the translation stage of problem solving is increased in complexity by the addition of text and numerical content. For Structural Variant II, a subgoal is removed by stating the per pound rate. The LLTM has been previously applied to similar tests to obtain parameters to represent the impact of cognitive complexity on mathematical problem solving (Morrison & Embretson, 2012). Applying the parameter estimates for the cognitive model (shown on Table 3.3) to the changes in the structural variants indicated that item difficulty would be increased by .15 for Structural Variant I but would decrease by .40 for Structural Variant II.

That is, the change in the two variants, $\Delta\beta_I$ and $\Delta\beta_{II}$, would involve only those variables that were impacted by the change, as follows:

$$\Delta\beta_I = 2\eta_1 + 5\eta_2 + 2\eta_3 = .15$$
$$\Delta\beta_{II} = 5\eta_2 + 1\eta_3 - 1\eta_{15} - 1\eta_{19} = -.40$$

where η_1, η_2, η_3, η_{15}, and η_{19} refer to the variables in Table 3.3. While the changes in item difficulty for Structural Variant I are not drastic, Structural Variant II is predicted to be substantially easier. Thus, items generated from structurally variant item models can be expected to have somewhat different item difficulty parameters.

Similarly, a cognitive model can be useful to determine the impact of varying content in generated items on item psychometric parameters. In this case, prediction from a cognitive model could be used to anticipate differences in generated items from the same item model. For example, in the mathematics items, the types of numbers that are

Table 3.3 LLTM target model estimates using cognitive variables (Reprinted from Morrison & Embretson, 2012).

Parameter		Estimate	Standard error	t-value
Translation				
Mathematical	η_1	−0.0010	0.000519	−1.85
Contextual	η_2	0.0104	0.000433	24.04*
Number of Predicate Propositions	η_3	0.0494	0.00289	17.13*
Number of Modifier Propositions	η_4	−0.0884	0.002642	−33.47*
Number of Connective Propositions	η_5	0.0440	0.006645	6.62*
Total Argument Ratio	η_6	0.8156	0.01955	41.73*
Encode Diagram	η_7	0.0700	0.02374	2.95*
Integration				
Translate Word Equation	η_8	−0.1883	0.01549	−12.16*
Given Equation	η_9	−0.4661	0.01953	−23.86*
Generate Equation or Plausible Value	η_{10}	−0.2010	0.01428	−14.08*
Access Equation	η_{11}	−0.1330	0.02116	−6.29*
Translate Diagram Equations	η_{12}	0.6680	0.02598	25.72*
Visualization	η_{13}	0.4265	0.02171	19.65*
Semantic Memory	η_{14}	−0.0954	0.006723	−14.19*
Solution Planning				
Number of Subgoals	η_{15}	0.3175	0.009743	32.59*
Relative Def. of Variables	η_{16}	0.9854	0.03389	29.07*
Solution Execution				
Number Knowledge	η_{17}	0.0462	0.003563	12.96*
Procedural Knowledge	η_{18}	0.1096	0.003407	32.17*
Number of Operands	η_{19}	0.1629	0.007215	22.58*
Decision				
Decision Processing Confirmation	η_{20}	0.0738	0.01584	4.66*
σ		1.0914	0.0304	35.9*
Intercept		−2.4510	0.03371	−72.71*

*$p < .05$

substituted (fractions, decimals, integers) in the item models to generate items do impact item difficulty. To assure that generated items from the same item model have similar psychometric properties, the permissible values can be either constrained or controlled by covariates.

Cognitive design system and template approaches For these approaches, identification of the design features for structures requires a theoretical background or conceptual framework. To understand the impact of the design features on the complexity of construct-relevant and construct-irrelevant processes, however, involves a research foundation. Further, research on item design features is important in specifying fixed and variable content so that item differences are minimized within structures and maximized between structures.

An example of the **cognitive design system approach** is an item generator that was developed to produce spatial ability items as used on the Assembling Objects subtest on the ASVAB (see Embretson, 2010, 2012). A Puzzle item from the test is shown in Figure 3.2. The correct answer (Option 3) is the object that can be assembled from the pieces. Two sources of cognitive complexity were postulated: working memory load and spatial processing demand. Different features were specified to represent these sources of cognitive complexity. For working memory load, the number of pieces in the stem (pieces), number of total edges on the pieces (edges), expected number of stem pieces that must be compared to detect mismatches in the closest distractor (cycles), and number of distractors readily falsified for gross misfit (falsify) were postulated to impact complexity. The cycles variable depends on the number of wrong pieces in a distractor; if all pieces are mismatched, then number of cycles equals 1. Falsify is possible when the number of pieces is wrong in a distractor or when the pieces have shapes that obviously do not appear in the item stem. For spatial processing demand, number of rotated pieces from stem to key (rotate), displacement of pieces from stem to key (displace), distance of key from stem (target distance), and lack of verbal labels to describe pieces (labels) were postulated to impact complexity.

The features were scored for a large set of operationally used Puzzle items. Both item difficulty, β_i, and item discrimination, α_i, had been estimated for the items. The regression approach was applied to model α_i and β_i using the scored features as predictors. The following equations were obtained:

$$\beta_i' = -1.34 + .118 x_{pieces} + .005 x_{edges} + .002 x_{curves} - .067 x_{labels} - .111 x_{falsify}$$
$$+ .038 x_{rotated} + .101 x_{displaced} + .098 x_{targetdist} + .112 x_{angles} + .064 x_{cycles} \quad (3.4)$$

$$\alpha_i' = 1.210 + .067 x_{pieces} - .001 x_{edges} - .031 x_{curves} - .015 x_{labels} + .014 x_{falsify} - .013 x_{rotated}$$
$$- .021 x_{displaced} + .012 x_{targetdist} - .044 x_{angles} - .016 x_{cycles} \quad (3.5)$$

The strong relationship ($R = 0.69$) found for predicting item difficulty supported the cognitive model. Thus, item structures based on the predictors could be expected to yield a range of item difficulties, as required for the CAT method as used for the Assembling Objects Test. Item discrimination was uniformly high (i.e., the intercept value is 1.210) and varied little with the predictors, supporting the generation of items with similar discrimination levels. Thus, generating structures, specified as XML code, contained variables to impact each of the predictors in the equations previously. It was estimated that 540 unique structures resulted from various combinations of features that included the outer shape of the assembled object (i.e., square, hexagon, circle, etc.), the location of the centerpoint in the key and distractors, type of changes in distractors, and so on.

Abstract structures An elaborated version of the structures for the Abstract Reasoning Test items, as shown in Figure 3.1, was described previously. Similar to the Puzzle item example before, a cognitive model was developed by regression modeling (and also LLTM analysis) on existing items from other tests (see Embretson, 1998) using predictors for working memory load and spatial demand as described above. The abstract structures were developed and could be scored on the cognitive model variables directly to predict differences in item difficulty.

Item content evaluation An important issue in item generation is the extent to which an item generator produces items with acceptable content quality. The process of evaluating item quality differs substantially between different types of tests. The main distinction is between norm-referenced and standards-based tests, with the latter type involving the more stringent evaluation process for item quality.

Norm-referenced tests Score interpretations in norm-referenced tests depend on the position of the scores in an appropriate population of test-takers. Thus, it is crucial that different test forms, composed of different items, can be equated for psychometric properties. Item content, however, does not enter directly into score interpretation.

The evaluation of quality for generated items on norm-referenced tests ensures that the various combinations of content sampled from the databases do not lead to unexpected, inappropriate, or confusing item properties. Traditionally produced items by human item writers are always subjected to review. For high-stakes tests, traditionally produced items may be subjected to evaluation by a test editor and other item developers. For lower stakes tests, traditionally developed items may be evaluated only by a test editor. These processes can be applied also to generated items. However, if items from specific structures have reliable content quality, a reduced process is supported. An interesting issue is whether or not "on-the-fly" generation of items during testing without any content evaluation is supported.

Consider two item types used to illustrate item generation in the discussion previously. The Abstract Reasoning Test items and the Puzzle items are both used on norm-referenced tests. The current status of these generators supports a reduced evaluation process but not does not support an "on-the-fly" item generator. That is, for both item types, occasional combinations of sampling lead to items with confusing content. Thus, the minimal process of an item editor to view the items is required. Of course, future developments of database constraints or even an item evaluation computer program could lead to eliminating the process of content evaluation by test editors. If so, "on-the-fly" item generation could be supported.

Standards-based tests In standards-based tests, scores are interpreted by the content of the items that the examinee can solve rather than by norms. Content standards are established by panels of experts in advance of testing. Thus, the tests must represent the content faithfully for scores to be interpretable. Traditionally produced items are subjected to an extensive and expensive review process, including a test editor, a formal panel of content experts and a panel of educational policy administrators. An important issue is the extent to which this process can be reduced without sacrificing item quality.

The mathematics item generator (Embretson et al., 2012) was developed using the item model approach applied to standards-based tests for evaluating the achievement of middle school students at the end of the school year. Since the test is high stakes, for both students and teachers, all items on the test, including tryout items, are submitted to an extensive review process. Approximately 500 items from the mathematics item generator were evaluated over the course of two years. Items generated from both original item models and structurally variant item models were included. For the first set of items sent for evaluation, 81.3% of items survived the process. The most frequent concerns were that (1) items had unrealistic combinations of content sampling and (2) items from structural variant item models were below grade level expectations. The feedback received was used to update the item generator by setting constraints and linking various aspects of content substitutions. For example, lists of person names had to be linked to gender appropriate pronouns and the range of numbers had to be appropriate for the application (travel by bus could not be 100 mph.). During the second year, 92.3% of items survived the process.

Given that the test is high stakes, even the increased acceptability rate is not sufficient for items to be implemented with no review. However, it may be possible to substantially reduce the process, perhaps to a single test editor, once a particular item structure produces items reliably.

Item psychometric properties

For all types of tests, submitting items for empirical tryout is a sufficient bottleneck to obtaining usable items due to the limited capacity to embed items in operational tests. Successful application of item generation requires that the psychometric properties of items generated from the same structure have predictable psychometric properties. For all types of item structures, establishing predictable psychometric properties requires empirical tryout of items generated from the same structures. The central issue is the degree to which the item structure predicts item difficulty.

For generated Abstract Reasoning Test items (i.e., Figure 3.1), three variants of 30 generating item structures appeared on different test forms, which were randomly assigned to examinees. A multiple correlation of 0.91 of structures with estimated IRT item difficulty indicated high levels of predictability was obtained from membership in abstract structures. Further analysis indicated that person estimates using the estimated structural difficulties differed little from estimates based on the individual item parameters (Embretson, 2008). Thus, strong empirical support for the existing Abstract Reasoning Test structures was obtained.

For generated mathematical problem-solving items, similar results were obtained from the first generated set of 185 items. Items generated from both original item models and structurally variant item models were placed on different operational test forms that were randomly assigned to examinees. The estimated item difficulties from the 2PL IRT model were strongly predicted from item structural membership, yielding multiple correlations of 0.928 and 0.961 for original item models and structurally variant item models, respectively. Similarly, the prediction of item discrimination differences was also strong, 0.908 and 0.909, respectively. Interestingly, for reasons of test security, the operational test items appeared on three different forms that contained the same items but in different test positions. Predictability of item parameters estimated separately within test forms for the operational items was 0.978 and 0.963, respectively, of item difficulty and item discrimination. Thus, the predictability of item parameters for the same items appearing on different test forms was only slightly higher than the predictability of different items from the same item structure. Thus, applying item parameters estimated for structures to newly generated items is strongly supported by these results.

Finally, it should be noted that generated Puzzle items have not yet been evaluated by empirical tryout. Similar results are expected as for the other two item types.

Using generated items on tests

With the research foundation established as indicated previously, support can be obtained for using generated items with minimal evaluation procedures. Such support has been established for the mathematical item generator structures that have been evaluated. Similarly, support has been established for the Abstract Reasoning Test items. However, caveats should be mentioned. First, routine empirical auditing of the structures for generating items should be established. It is possible that changes in examinees or in the item generator could impact psychometric properties. Second, new item structures need to be studied in the same manner as the established structures. Although the cognitive models can be useful for anticipating item psychometric properties for new structures, and perhaps lead to reduced sample sizes, empirical tryout is nonetheless needed.

Summary and Conclusions

Automated item generation is becoming increasingly popular as a means to satiate the huge demand for test items. However, the full potential of automated item generation cannot be realized without a supporting foundation in research.

The goal of this paper was to present an overview of current item generation methods and the theoretical and empirical support that is needed to implement items. Item generators based on three different types of structures were used to illustrate the basic principles of item generation. Examples of generated items were presented to illustrate different types of structures that have been implemented in computerized algorithms. The research that is required to implement generated items with reduced requirements for content evaluation and empirical tryout was described and illustrated with examples. For the two examples for which empirical data has been obtained, support was obtained for using subsequently generated items with minimal content evaluation and empirical tryout.

Future developments will most likely not only include more item generators, but a consideration of additional guidelines for implementation. While some item generation methods lead to very similar items for a structure, other methods lead to more varied items. Variability in generated items typically leads to varied psychometric properties. Additional research would be required to yield the same level of predictability as for less varied items. This paper represents a first attempt to provide guidelines for item generation.

References

American Educational Research Association, American Psychological Association, & National Council on Measurement in Education (1999). *Standards for Educational and Psychological Testing*. Washington, D.C.: American Educational Research Association.

Arendasy, M. (2005). Automatic generation of Rasch-calibrated items: Figural Matrices Test GEOM and Endless-Loops Test EC. *International Journal of Testing*, 5(3), 197–224.

Bejar, I. I., & Yocom, P. (1986). *A generative approach to the development of hidden-figure items* (Research Report No. RR-86-20-ONR). Princeton, NJ: Educational Testing Service.

Bejar, I. I., Lawless, R. R., Morley, M. E., Wagner, M. E., Bennett, R. E., & Revuelta, J. (2003). A feasibility study of on-the-fly item generation in adaptive testing. *Journal of Technology, Learning, and Assessment*, 2(3). Available from www.jtla.org.

Carpenter, P. A., Just, M. A., & Shell, P. (1990). What one intelligence test measures: A theoretical account of processing in the Raven's Progressive Matrices Test. *Psychological Review*, 97, 404–431.

Collis, J. M., Tapsfield, P. G. C., Irvine, S. H., Dann, P. L., & Wright, D. (1995) The British Army Recruit Battery goes operational: From theory to practice in computer-based testing using item-generation techniques. *International Journal of Selection and Assessment, 3*(2), 96–104. DOI: 10.1111/j.1468-2389.1995.tb00014.x.

Deane, P., Graf, E. A., Higgins, D., Futagi, Y., & Lawless, R. (2006). *Model analysis and model creation: Capturing the task-model structure of quantitative domain items* (Research Report No. RR-06-01). Princeton, NJ: Educational Testing Service.

Embretson, S. E. (1998). A cognitive design system approach to generating valid tests: Application to abstract reasoning. *Psychological Methods, 3*(3), 380–396.

Embretson, S. E. (1999). Generating items during testing: Psychometric issues and models. *Psychometrika, 64*(4), 407–433.

Embretson, S. E. (2002). Generating abstract reasoning items with cognitive theory. In S. Irvine, & P. Kyllonen (Eds.), *Generating items for cognitive tests: Theory and practice*. Mahwah, NJ: Erlbaum.

Embretson, S. E. (2008). *Generated intelligence tests: Impact on scores and psychometric properties.* Paper presented at the annual conference of the International Society for Intelligence Research. Atlanta, GA: December.

Embretson, S. E. (2010). Cognitive design systems: A structural modeling approach to developing ability tests. In S. E. Embretson (Ed.). *Measuring psychological constructs with model-based approaches* (pp. 247–274). Washington, D.C.: American Psychological Association Books.

Embretson, S. E. (2012). *Functionality for generation of Assembling Objects items.* Defense Manpower Data Center, Report for GS09Q10F0506, 23. Seaside, California.

Embretson, S. E., & Daniel, R. C. (2008). Understanding and quantifying cognitive complexity level in mathematical problem solving items. *Psychology Science Quarterly, 50,* 328–344.

Embretson, S. E., & Gorin, J. (2001). Improving construct validity with cognitive psychology principles. Invited article for *Journal of Educational Measurement, 38,* 343–368.

Embretson, S. E., Walker, B., Wilson, J., & Lutz, M. (2012). *Generating complex items to assess mathematical achievement in middle school* (Report 1008A-2012 for Institute of Educational Sciences Grant R305A100234). *Cognitive Measurement Laboratory*, Georgia Institute of Technology: Atlanta, GA.

Fairon, C., & Williamson, D. M. (2002). Automatic item text generation in educational assessment. In Proceedings of *TALN*, 395–401.

Fischer, G. H. (1973). Linear logistic test model as an instrument in educational research. *Acta Psychologica, 37,* 359–374.

Gierl, M., & Alves, C. (2011). *Using item models for test development and item generation with IGOR.* Paper presented at the annual meeting of National Council on Measurement in Education. New Orleans, LA.

Gierl, M., & Lai, H. (2013). Using weak and strong theory to create item models for automatic item generation. In M. Gierl & T. Haladyna (Eds.), *Automatic item generation: Theory and practice,* New York, NY: Routledge.

Gierl, M. J., Lai, H., & Turner, S. (2013). Using automatic item generation to create multiple-choice items for assessments in medical education. *Medical Education, 46,* 757–765.

Hively, W., Patterson, H. L., & Page. S. H. (1968). A "Universe-Defined" system of arithmetic achievement tests. *Journal of Educational Measurement, 5*(4), 275–290.

Hornke, L. F. (2002). Item generation models for higher cognitive functions. In S. H. Irvine & P. C. Kyllonen (Eds.), *Item generation for test development* (pp. 159–178). Mahwah, NJ: Erlbaum.

Kyllonen, P. C. (2002). Item generation for repeated testing of human performance. In S. H. Irving & P. C. Kyllonen (Eds.), *Item generation for test development*. Mahwah, NJ: Lawrence Erlbaum Associates.

Lai, H., & Gierl, M. J. (2013). Generating items under the assessment engineering framework. In M. Gierl & T. Haladyna (Eds.), *Automatic item generation: Theory and practice*, New York, NY: Routledge.

Luecht, R. (2013). An introduction to assessment engineering for automatic item generation. In M. Gierl & T. Haladyna (Eds.), *Automatic item generation: Theory and practice*, New York, NY: Routledge.

Mislevy, R. J., Sheehan, K. M., & Wingersky, M. (1993). How to equate tests with little or no data. *Journal of Educational Measurement, 30*, 55–76.

Morrison, K. M., & Embretson, S. E. (2012). *A resource-based cognitive model for predicting mathematical item difficulty* (Report IES1004A-2012 for Institute of Educational Sciences Grant R305A100234). Cognitive Measurement Laboratory, Georgia Institute of Technology: Atlanta, GA.

Naglieri, J. A., Drasgow, F., Schmit, M., Handler, L., Prifitera, A., Margolis, A., & Velasquez, R. (2004). Psychological testing on the internet: New problems, old issues. *American Psychologist, 59*, 150–162.

Newstead, S. E., Bradon, P., Handley, S. J., Dennis, I., & Evans, J. (2006). Predicting the difficulty of complex logical reasoning problems. *Thinking & Reasoning, 12*(1), 62–90.

Primi, R., Zanarella-Cruz, M. B., Muniz-Nascimento, M., & Petrini, M. C. (2006). Validade de construto de um instrumento informatizado de avaliação dinâmica da inteligência fluida. *Psico, 37*(2), 109–122.

Raven, J. C. (1936). *Mental tests used in genetic studies: The performance of related individuals on tests mainly educative and mainly reproductive*. MSc Thesis, University of London.

Roskam, E., & Broers, N. (1996). Constructing questionnaires: An application of facet design and item response theory to the study of lonesomeness. In G. Engelhard & M. Wilson (Eds.), *Objective measurement: Theory into practice* (Vol. 3) (pp. 349–385). Norwood, NJ: Ablex Publishing.

Singley, M. K., & Bennett, R. E. (2002). Item generation and beyond: Applications of schema theory to mathematics assessment. In S. Irvine & P. Kyllonen (Eds.), *Item generation for test development*. Mahwah, NJ: Lawrence Erlbaum Associates, Inc.

4

Survey Sampling and Propensity Score Matching

Bo Lu and Stanley Lemeshow

Overview

Information on population characteristics is always needed for policy planning, evaluation of public program, development of marketing strategies, and research in health and social science. Such information includes demographics and measurements of knowledge, abilities, attitudes, and so on. For reasons relating to timeliness and cost, a complete census is not feasible and a subset of the population, known as sample, is often taken instead. Population characteristics are then inferred based on the sample and the validity of the conclusion depends largely on the representativeness of the sample. In psychometric research, a good sample leads to better generalizability of the testing instrument and measurement. Furthermore, psychometric measurements play a crucial role in evaluating the effect of an intervention, or an educational/training program. Survey data are usually observational, in which participants are not randomly allocated to the intervention groups. Due to the lack of randomization, treatment effect estimation is likely to be biased. For the past three decades, propensity score based adjustments have become a very popular approach in analyzing observational data. The propensity score, as a scalar summary of all relevant covariate information, can be utilized to create groups with comparable characteristics and hence reduce the bias in the effect estimation. Sample surveys provide good data sources for the application of the propensity score method given its relatively large size and rich covariate information. In this chapter, we provide a review of survey sampling concepts, designs, and analysis methods. We also introduce the framework and algorithms for propensity score matching, which does not depend on the specification of an outcome model and is widely used in inferring causal relationships in observational studies.

Survey Terminologies

Ideally, a prefect sample should be a miniature version of the population, mirroring every characteristic of the target population. Of course, such perfect samples rarely exist for complex populations. But a good sample should be representative in the sense that population characteristics of interest can be estimated from the sample with a reasonable degree of accuracy. Before we formally discuss the sampling methodology to obtain good samples, we first introduce terminologies used in survey sampling.

- **Population** (**universe** or **target** population). The entire set of individuals we intend to study.
- **Elementary unit** (**element**). The individual member of the population whose characteristics are to be measured.
- **Sample**. A subset of a population.
- **Sampling unit** (**listing unit**). A unit that can be selected for the purpose of sampling.
- **Sampled population**. The collection of all possible elementary units that might have been chosen in a sample; the collection of all sampling units.
- **Sampling frame**. A list of all sampling units in the sampled population.

For example, as the largest continuously conducted health survey system in the world, the Behavioral Risk Factor Surveillance System (BRFSS) collects data about U.S. residents regarding their health-related risk behaviors, chronic health conditions, and use of preventive services, with more than 400,000 adult interviews each year. In BRFSS, the population is the collection of all individuals living in U.S.; the elementary unit is an individual living in U.S.; the sample is the collection of adults interviewed at a given year; the sampled population is the collection of all adults with residential telephone numbers listed; the sampling unit is a household unit with a residential telephone number listed; the sampling frame is a list of all the residential telephone numbers in the U.S.

Survey sampling describes the process of selecting a sample of elements from a target population. Survey samples can be categorized into two very broad classes, namely **probability samples** and **nonprobability samples**. A probability sample has the feature that every element in the population has a known, nonzero, probability of being included in the sample. A nonprobability sample is one based on a sampling plan that does not have this feature.

Estimates from sample data are subject to two types of errors, sampling errors, and nonsampling errors. Sampling errors are those due to sample-to-sample variability. This occurs because we can only take a subset instead of examining the whole population. We can estimate the sampling error in probability sampling. Nonsampling errors are those not due to sample-to-sample variability, which includes selection bias, measurement bias, nonresponse bias, and so on. Selection bias occurs when some part of the target population is not in the sampled population. Convenience samples or samples consisting entirely of volunteers suffer from selection bias. Measurement bias occurs when the measuring instrument differs systematically from the true value. Nonresponse bias occurs when selected individuals do not respond to the survey. In general, nonsampling errors are difficult to deal with and thoughtful design and implementation are recommended to minimize the potential for nonsampling errors.

In probability sampling, because every unit has a known chance of being selected, unbiased estimates (free of selection bias) of population quantities can be constructed from the sample data. Also, the standard errors of these estimates can be obtained statistically, which measures the sampling error. In contrast, the nonprobability convenience sample is usually biased in the sense that people with certain characteristics might be more likely to participate and it is very difficult to eliminate such bias. In this chapter, we will consider only probability samples, since nonprobability sampling has no control over the sampling error and suffers a greater degree of nonsampling error.

Probability Sampling Designs

There are three major design components in probability sampling – simple random sampling, stratified sampling, and cluster sampling.

Simple random sampling

A simple random sample (SRS) is the simplest form of probability sampling. It obtains the representativeness of the sample by ensuring that each unit in the population has an equal chance of being selected. In finite population sampling, we usually select SRSs without replacement, in which all units in the sample are distinct. Suppose the population size is N and we want a SRS of size n. First, we create a list of all N sampling units indexed with numbers from 1 to N (the sampling frame). Then, using a random process, we generate n numbers between 1 and N. These n random numbers identify the n individuals in the sample. There are $\binom{N}{n}$ possible samples that can be selected from this population. For example, if $N = 25$ and a sample of size $n = 5$ is to be selected, there are $\binom{25}{5} = 53,130$ possible samples. A SRS is defined as a sample where each of the $\binom{N}{n}$ possible samples has the same probability of being selected and this is equal to $1/\binom{N}{n}$. Denoting the sample of n selected units as S, we use the sample mean

$$\bar{y} = \frac{1}{n}\sum_{i \in S} y_i$$

to estimate the population mean $\bar{y}_U$. An unbiased estimator of the variance of $\bar{y}$ is

$$\hat{V}(\bar{y}) = \left(1 - \frac{n}{N}\right)\frac{s^2}{n}$$

where $s^2 = \frac{1}{n-1}\sum_{i \in S}(y_i - \bar{y})^2$ is the sample variance and the factor $\left(1 - \frac{n}{N}\right)$ is known as the finite population correction factor. Intuitively, the greater the sampling fraction n/N, the more information we have about the population and thus the smaller the variance. Other population quantity estimates, such total or proportion, can be computed similarly. Levy and Lemeshow (2008) provide detailed illustrations for various population quantities (also for stratified and cluster sampling designs).

Systematic sampling is a sampling method in which the first case is selected at random from a list of population members and subsequent cases are selected at prescribed intervals. Sometimes, systematic sampling serves as a good proxy for simple random sampling, when the list of the population is roughly random. To obtain a systematic sample of size n from a population of size N, we first divide the population into n zones with $k = N/n$ units in each zone. Within the first zone, a random number between 1 and k is selected, say R. Then, this unit and every kth unit thereafter are chosen to be in the sample; that is, R, $R + k$, $R + 2k$, and so on. Systematic sampling may save much time and effort and is more efficient in some situations than simple random sampling. However, the major disadvantage of systematic sampling is that when the list is arranged in some periodic or cyclical order the resulting sample might not be representative. Therefore, caution needs to be taken in examining the list.

Stratified sampling

Stratified sampling is a probabilistic sampling method in which the population is initially divided into nonoverlapping subgroups or strata and then units are chosen randomly from each stratum. The strata are based on predetermined factors, such as geographic or demographic characteristics. It is typically used when there is a concern that certain subpopulations may be underrepresented if simple random sampling is used.

A stratum is defined as a subpopulation of the target population. The strata are formed on the basis of some known characteristics about the population that are believed to be related to the outcome of interest. The goal is to create strata containing elements that are homogeneous within each stratum, but heterogeneous between strata. With stratified random sampling, the population is broken into mutually exclusive and exhaustive strata. A random sample from each of the strata is taken and then the data from these within-stratum random samples are combined to form estimates of the population parameters. For example, suppose there are H strata in the population with N_h sampling units in stratum h. For stratified sampling to work, we must know the values of N_h's and have $N_1 + N_1 + \cdots + N_H = N$. If a SRS is taken independently from each stratum with size n_h, the total sample size is $n = n_1 + n_1 + \cdots + n_H$. Then we can calculate the sample mean for stratum h as

$$\bar{y}_h = \frac{1}{n_h}\sum_{i=1}^{n_h} y_{h,i}$$

and combine them to estimate the population mean as

$$\bar{y}_{str} = \frac{1}{N}\sum_{h=1}^{H} N_H \bar{y}_h$$

with variance

$$\hat{V}(\bar{y}_{str}) = \sum_{h=1}^{H}\left(1 - \frac{n_h}{N_h}\right)\left(\frac{N_h}{N}\right)^2 \frac{s_h^2}{n_h},$$

where s_h^2 is the sample variance from stratum h based on the SRS formula. Notice that the combined stratified sampling estimates are just weighted averages of the within-stratum estimates, with weights proportional to the size of the stratum. If the outcomes are more similar within strata and more different across strata, the variability will be much lower within strata. Therefore, the combined variance of the stratified sampling estimate will be smaller than that from a SRS. Other population quantity estimates, such as totals or proportions, can be computed similarly.

Prior to implementing stratified random sampling, a decision must be made with regards to how many units are to be selected from each stratum. This is known as sample allocation. The simplest allocation scheme just selects an equal number of units from each stratum. The most commonly used allocation scheme is proportional allocation in which the sampling fraction, n_h/N_h, is specified to be the same for each stratum. When proportional allocation is used estimates of the population quantities are self-weighting. This means that when estimating the population quantities each sample unit is multiplied by the same constant, $1/n$, irrespective of which stratum it comes from. A third allocation scheme is known as optimal allocation. This method results in estimates that have minimum variance because the sample units are allocated to strata in a manner that is proportional to the within-stratum variance (which is assumed to be known in advance). Thus, strata with larger variances will have more units sampled compared to strata with smaller variances. A modified optimal allocation may incorporate the sampling cost information. This is particularly useful if the cost associated with sampling units differs across strata, but the overall cost is fixed. Intuitively, you may decrease the variance by sampling more low-cost units.

There are several advantages to using stratified random sampling. First, a stratified random sample may provide increased precision over a SRS of the same size when the strata are chosen to be relatively homogeneous. Second, with stratified design, you can not only make inference to the entire population, but also to each stratum as well. Finally, for either administrative or logistical reasons, it may be easier to select a stratified sample than a SRS. The major disadvantage is, however, that it might be more expensive to select a stratified sample than a SRS since detailed frames must be constructed for each stratum prior to sampling. For this reason, in certain circumstances, cluster sampling is used more often.

Cluster sampling

In a cluster sample, observational units in the population are aggregated into larger sampling units, known as clusters or primary sampling units (PSU). Typically, the population is divided into M mutually exclusive and exhaustive clusters. The process by which a sample of observational units is selected is stepwise. For example, in a survey of high school students, schools are often treated as clusters and students are the observational units. The first step would involve selecting a sample of schools. At the second step, within each selected school, a sample of students would be selected. Individual students are allowed to be included in the sample only if they belong to a school (cluster) that is included in the sample

In sampling terminology, the steps are called stages, and sampling plans are often categorized in terms of the number of stages involved. For example, a single stage cluster sample is one in which the sampling is done at the cluster level. Following the selection of the clusters, every unit within each of the selected clusters is included in the sample. For simplicity, let's consider a special case of single stage cluster sample in which each cluster has the same number of units, N. The total population size is MN, provided that there are M clusters. If m clusters are randomly selected, the overall sample size is mN. Denote t_i, $i = 1, \cdots, m$, to be the total of all units in the selected cluster i. We can estimate the population mean with

$$\bar{y}_{clu} = \frac{\sum_{i=1}^{m} t_i}{mN}$$

and the variance with $\hat{V}(\bar{y}_{clu}) = \left(1 - \frac{m}{M}\right) \frac{s_t^2}{mN^2}$

Where $s_t^2 = \frac{1}{m-1} \sum_{i=1}^{m} \left(t_i - \frac{\sum_{j=1}^{m} t_j}{m} \right)^2$.

Formulas for single stage cluster sampling with unequal cluster size can be similarly derived. For more complex cluster sampling, such as two-stage and multi-stage cluster sampling, formulas can be found in standard sampling textbooks (Levy & Lemeshow, 2008; Lohr, 2010).

Cluster sampling is often used for two reasons. First, constructing a sampling frame of all units in the population may be difficult or impossible. Instead, it is easier to construct a list of clusters and the frames of units in selected clusters. Second, the population may occur in natural clusters such as households or schools. It is less expensive to take a sample of clusters rather than an SRS of all units. In practice, cluster sampling is often the most economical form of sampling since listing costs and travel costs are the lowest of any potential method.

Clusters resemble strata in the sense that both are groupings of the sampling units in the population. The selection process, however, is very different. In stratified sampling, a sample of units is taken from each and every stratum; in cluster sampling, on the other hand, samples are only taken from the selected clusters. Consequently, stratification usually increases precision when compared with simple random sampling and cluster sampling generally decreases it. Members of the same cluster tend to be more similar than units selected at random from the whole population. These similarities usually arise because of some underlying common factors – that is why they are clustered. Thus, we do not obtain as much information about the whole population by sampling two units in the same cluster as by sampling two units in different clusters. But, due to its convenience and low cost, cluster sampling is still a popular choice in practice. In addition, because the cost is lower, it may be possible to obtain a much larger sample size for a fixed cost with cluster sampling as opposed to other sampling methods. This increased sample size may result in increased precision with cluster sampling holding costs constant.

Survey Weights

In probability sampling, it is important to identify the probability that unit i is included in the sample, since these inclusion probabilities are used to calculate the estimates for population quantities. The sampling weight (survey weight) is defined as the reciprocal of the inclusion probability:

$$w_i = \frac{1}{\pi_i}$$

The sampling weight of unit i is interpreted as the number of population units represented by sampled unit i. Thus, the sum of sampling weights from all sampled units should be the population size, regardless of sampling design.

In a SRS, every sampled unit has the same probability of being included, $\pi_i = \frac{n}{N}$. Thus, the weights are identical too, with $w_i = \frac{1}{\pi_i} = \frac{N}{n}$. It implies that each sampled unit represents itself plus $\frac{N}{n} - 1$ of the unsampled units in the population.

It follows that $\sum_{i=1}^{n} w_i = \sum_{i=1}^{n} \frac{N}{n} = N$.

A sample in which every unit has the same sampling weight is also known as a self-weighting sample. The weight plays an important role in estimating population quantities. For example, the population mean is estimated by the weighted average of the sample, which turns out to be the sample mean in SRS:

$$\frac{\sum_{i=1}^{n} w_i y_i}{\sum_{i=1}^{n} w_i} = \frac{\sum_{i=1}^{n} \frac{N}{n} y_i}{\sum_{i=1}^{n} \frac{N}{n}} = \bar{y}$$

In a stratified random sample the sampling weights are usually different across different strata. If a SRS is taken within each stratum the sampling weight for unit j of stratum h is $w_{hj} = \frac{N_h}{n_h}$. For the simplest case of proportional allocation, the weights are the same for all units as $\frac{N}{n}$. In general, the population mean is estimated by

$$\bar{y}_{str} = \frac{\sum_{h=1}^{H} \sum_{j=1}^{n_h} w_{hj} y_{hj}}{\sum_{h=1}^{H} \sum_{j=1}^{n_h} w_{hj}}.$$

In a single stage cluster sample, since all units in the selected clustered are included in the sample, the sampling probabilities of units are the same as the sampling probabilities of clusters. If each cluster has the same number of units and we want to sample

m clusters out of M total clusters, the sampling probability for cluster i (and all units in cluster i) is:

$$w_i = \frac{1}{\pi_i} = \frac{M}{m}$$

Denote the value for unit j in cluster i as y_{ij}. The population mean is estimated by

$$\bar{y}_{clu} = \frac{\sum_{i=1}^{m}\sum_{j=1}^{N} w_{ij} y_{ij}}{\sum_{i=1}^{m}\sum_{j=1}^{N} w_{ij}}$$

The use of sampling weights can adjust the selection probability effectively to yield an unbiased population estimate. In addition to that, weighting is used widely in practice to adjust for bias due to nonresponse and to ensure the representativeness of the sample by matching to known population margins.

Nonresponse occurs in virtually all survey samples. There are two types of nonresponse: unit nonresponse, in which the entire observation unit is missing and item nonresponse, in which some measurements are collected but at least one item is missing. Usually, ignoring the missing unit or item tends to result in nonresponse bias in the estimates, especially when the nonresponse rate is extensive or the unmeasured units possess different characteristics than the measured ones. Weights can be used to adjust for nonresponse. Let S_i be the indicator for a unit being selected into the sample with probability $P(S_i = 1) = \pi_i$, and let R_i be the indicator for a unit to respond to the survey with probability $P(R_i = 1) = \psi_i$. If R_i is independent of S_i, the probability that unit i is sampled and measured is: P(unit i selected in sample and responds) = $\pi_i \psi_i$. The probability of responding, ψ_i, can be estimated for each unit in the sample using available auxiliary information and with the assumption that missingness only depends on observed covariates.

In large population surveys, such as the U.S. Centers for Disease Control and Prevention's Behavioral Risk Factors Surveillance Survey or the National Health Interview Survey, we would like to make sure our sample resembles the population in key characteristics. For example, the proportions of male and female in the sample should resemble those in the population and the distributions of age in the sample should be similar to those in the population. After the sample is taken, we may form poststrata based on key population characteristics. Since the population poststratum sizes are known (either through census data or administrative records), we may reweight each unit to make sure that the total weights in each poststratum match the true population count. This method is known as poststratification and is often used in large surveys to improve efficiency of the estimators or to correct for the effects of differential nonresponse in the poststrata. When poststrata are formed using multiple variables, but only the marginal population totals are known, the poststratification method is also referred as "raking."

Example: Random digit dialing (RDD) telephone survey

Telephone surveying began early in the twentieth century and has grown considerably since 1960. In 2010, about 98% of households in USA had telephone service, either through the traditional landline, cell phone, or internet-based telephone. Given the close-to-complete telephone coverage, data collection by telephone has become a popular and cost-effective method for obtaining reliable information from representative samples. Nowadays, telephone interviewing is done with the use of networked computers and computer-assisted telephone interviewing software. A popular method for sampling phone numbers is known as RDD. This method uses listed telephone numbers (usually compiled by a commercial vendor) to identify blocks of 100 telephone numbers, which is usually defined by area code, prefix, and the first two digits of the four-digit suffix. Numbers can then be sorted into those 100-blocks having one or more intended numbers and those with no intended numbers. For many surveys, the intended numbers are residential phone numbers. Samples are then drawn from blocks with one or more residential numbers or from both strata, with a higher proportion of numbers coming from blocks with residential numbers. This list-assisted RDD approach is shown to have small bias and improved precision.

A new trend in telephone surveys is to include cell phone sampling. According to 2010 National Health Interview Survey estimates, 29.7% of American homes are cell phone-only residences (Blumberg et al., 2011). To address the declining coverage of the traditional RDD sample, large-scale surveys often employ dual-frame designs, supplementing traditional RDD samples with cell phone samples. Statistical adjustment is also needed to account for the fact that people using both landline and cell phones have higher chances of being selected into the sample.

To illustrate how to analyze data from telephone surveys, we go through a recent large state health survey with a psychological measurement as the outcome. The 2012 Ohio Medicaid Assessment Survey (OMAS) is a population-based survey that measures the health status, health care experiences, and health insurance coverage of Ohio's Medicaid, Medicaid eligible, and non-Medicaid child and adult populations. A random stratified dual-frame telephone survey design was used to collect data from samples representative of all noninstitutionalized Ohio households and residents. This survey included both landline and cell phone frames. The landline sampling was based upon a list-assisted stratified RDD procedure and 88 counties in Ohio served as the strata. African-American and households with children were oversampled in landline sampling to boost their sample size because the Medicaid program is primarily designed for low-income people and households with children. The cell-phone sampling was a state-wide SRS.

From May to October 2012, trained telephone interviewers administered the OMAS to 22,929 Ohio residents. Households were randomly selected through a list-assisted RDD method. Upon reaching the household, the interviewer selected an eligible adult aged 19 years and older who had the most recent birthday to complete the adult version of the survey. When a respondent indicated that there were any children age 0–18 years in the household, the interviewer selected the child who had the most recent birthday. The adult who was most knowledgeable of the selected child completed the child version of OMAS on behalf of the child. There were 5,515 respondents to the child portion of the survey. The overall response rate for the survey was 29.4%, including a 30.2% response rate for the landline sample and 24.4% for the cell phone sample. A detailed description of the survey methodology can be found at www.grc.osu.edu/omas.

In 2012, the majority of the adult Ohioans with severe mental disability received at least one clinical service covered by Medicaid. Thus, it is very important to identify the characteristics of Ohioans with mental health conditions. The 2012 OMAS includes a

Table 4.1 Age distribution between MHI and non-MHI group, OMAS 2012.

	\[Age\]				
	19–24	25–34	35–44	45–54	55–64
MHI	10.9%	22.1%	28.2%	24.8%	13.9%
Non-MHI	22.7%	35.6%	20.0%	14.2%	7.6%

question concerning the number of days in the past 30 days when a mental health condition or emotional problem kept adults from doing their work or other usual activities. Adults who reported 14 or more days of functional impairment are identified as adults with mental health-related impairment (MHI). When analyzing the data, both weights and survey designs need to be incorporated. The 2012 OMAS is primarily a stratified design with adjustment for dual-frame sampling. There are 108 strata in total, including counties, oversampled African-American regions, and cell-phone strata. Statistical software packages capable of handling complex survey data are required. The popular choices include Stata, SAS, R with survey modules, and so on. In this example, we conduct our survey analysis using Stata. To use Stata to analyze OMAS data, we first need to set up the survey design as stratified and specify the weights. All Stata survey analysis commands start with prefix "svy." Interested readers may refer to the Stata manual for detailed explanations of available survey commands. MHI is treated as a binary variable and the survey weight adjusted prevalence of MHI in Ohio adults is 6.6% with a standard error of 0.23%. This implies that, in 2012, 6.6% of Ohioans (approximately 567,284 adults age 19 and older) reported MHI. To gauge the potential impact of MHI on Medicaid coverage, we can further restrict the analysis to adults between the age of 19 and 64. Table 4.1 compares the age distribution between people with and without MHI.

This suggests that a larger proportion of Ohio adults with MHI are in older age groups. Ohio adults without MHI tend to be much younger. This is consistent with other findings in the survey that Ohioans with MHI tend to have higher proportions of serious chronic physical health conditions. Combining all the findings regarding the characteristics of adults with and without MHI, health policy considerations were suggested to the Ohio Department of Mental Health, including prevention, early intervention, and wellness programs to mitigate the impact of costly, chronic physical health conditions (Cartens & Tam, 2013).

Propensity Score Matching

The aim of many studies in psychology and social science is to draw causal inferences about the effects of actions, treatments, or interventions. The ideal way to identify causal effects is through a randomized controlled experiment. Random assignment of subjects to treatment or control groups tends to balance all covariates, in the sense that the treated and control groups have similar distribution of covariates (e.g., similar age distributions). Random allocation, however, is not always feasible due to practical or ethical reasons and, as a result, observational studies are often employed. Observational studies attempt to estimate the effects of a treatment by comparing outcomes for subjects who are not randomly assigned to treatment or control groups. The data sources for observational studies are abundant, including administrative records, registry database, surveys, and so on. Due to the lack of randomization, in an observational study, some subjects are more likely than others to receive the treatment because of differences in covariates (e.g., age, personality, symptom severity). Therefore, differences in outcomes between treated and control groups could be due, in part, to differences in covariates prior to treatment rather than the treatments per se. Thus, careful statistical adjustments are needed to defend the causal interpretation based on the analysis of observational data. Propensity score-based statistical methodology in causal inference has grown in popularity in the past three decades. The propensity score, defined as the conditional probability of exposure to a treatment given observed covariates, is used to balance the observed covariates between treatment and nontreatment groups and thus approximate a randomization-like scenario in terms of treatment assignment. Thus, propensity score methods can reduce the covariate produced bias in treatment effect estimation (Rosenbaum & Rubin, 1983).

As shown in the literature, the propensity score has nice properties: (1) propensity scores balance observed covariates across treatment groups; (2) if it suffices to adjust for observed covariates, it suffices to adjust for their propensity scores; (3) the propensity score is a scalar summary of observed covariates, which greatly alleviates the potential problem of high dimensionality in analysis; (4) propensity score analysis usually does not need strong parametric assumptions regarding the function form of the response; and (5) estimated propensity scores are better at removing bias than the true propensity score, because they also remove some chance imbalance in observed covariates. The major limitation is that, unlike randomly assigned treatments, propensity scores cannot balance unobserved covariates. To overcome this limitation, the use of propensity scores often requires an assumption of strongly ignorable treatment assignment, which implies that no systematic, unobserved, pretreatment differences exist between treated and control groups that are related to the outcome under study. In practice, this might not be the case. To measure all covariates of relevance is often not possible. Sensitivity analysis may be conducted after the propensity score adjustment to gauge the impact of unmeasured confounding (Rosenbaum, 2009).

In practice, when the treatment group is dichotomous, propensity scores are usually estimated using a logistic regression model with a series of pretreatment covariates (Hosmer, Lemeshow, & Sturdivant, 2013). The use of propensity score adjustment may take many forms, including matching, stratification, weighting, or as a regression covariate. Matching creates sets of subjects from both treated and control groups with the same propensity score. Thus, within the matched set, the treatment assignment is regarded as random, unrelated to the observed covariates. The differences in outcome can be aggregated across matched sets to yield the average treatment effect. Stratification can be viewed as a crude way of matching, in which the dataset is divided into several strata based on the propensity score to reduce imbalance. Weighting adjustment tries to address the covariate imbalance by creating two balanced treated and control populations. Due to the nonrandom treatment assignment, the probabilities of receiving treatment are different for different subjects. This is just like sampling in the sense that subjects may have different probabilities of being selected in the sample. In the treated group, subjects are weighted by the inverse of the propensity score and in the control group, subjects are weighted by the inverse of one minus the propensity score. A Horvitz–Thompson type estimator is then used to obtain the average treatment effect. Propensity scores can also be included as a regression covariate for adjustment, but it would require more modeling assumptions to produce unbiased results. In general, the propensity score complements model-based analysis and is not a substitute for them. Often, propensity score adjustment is combined with further modeling to achieve the best results. In this section, we will focus on propensity score matching, which is considered to be more robust and less model dependent than other available methods. To properly implement the propensity score matching method, it usually involves following steps:

- Estimate the propensity score using treatment status and observed covariates
- Identify the matching structure based on the scientific problem and the dataset
- Choose an appropriate matching algorithm based on the distributions of covariates and the availability of the software
- Choose an appropriate matching design based on the distribution of covariates and the sample sizes in each group
- Conduct the propensity score matching using a software package and organize the matched sets
- Check the balance of covariates distribution after matching and with unsatisfactory balance results, consider redoing matching with different designs and algorithms, or readjusted propensity scores
- Perform postmatching analysis to estimate the treatment effect, accounting for matched sets

Propensity score matching structure and algorithm

In graph-theoretic terminology, a graph consists of nodes and edges between nodes. For applications, each individual unit of interest is a node (e.g., patients in treatment or control groups). A matching of a graph is a set of distinctive edges with no shared nodes. A matching can be classified as bipartite or nonbipartite depending on the number of disjoint groups in the graph. Matching producing pairs in a graph that involves only two disjoint groups is known as bipartite matching (left panel in Figure 4.1). When a graph has multiple disjoint groups, for example, a drug study involving more than two dose levels, say high dose, medium dose, low dose, and no dose (control), it is called a nonbipartite graph and the matching is referred to as nonbipartite matching. An extreme case of nonbipartite matching is one in which every single node is a group (right panel in Figure 4.1) and, as a result, any two nodes can be paired up in the matching.

Different algorithms are available for conducting matching. A traditional one is known as the nearest neighbor matching algorithm, which is popular for bipartite matching. Using this algorithm, we first randomly order units in one group, then pair the first unit with its nearest neighbor in the other group based on a predetermined distance measure. The process is repeated for the remaining units until no more pairs can be formed. It is very intuitive and easy to implement. However, in certain circumstances, it may produce a match with very large total distance, because the units in later pairs can be very "far away" from each other. The matching that minimizes the total distance among all the pairs is called an optimal matching. It requires some special algorithm with more

Survey Sampling and Propensity Score Matching 107

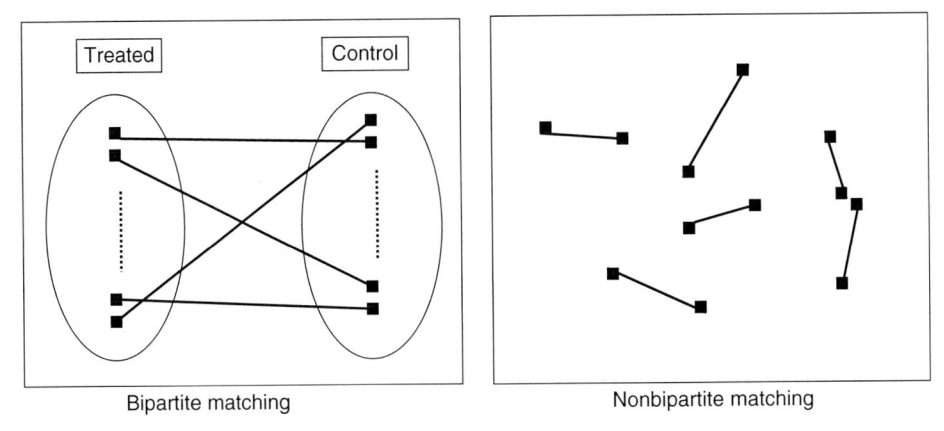

Figure 4.1 Bipartite matching and nonbipartite matching.

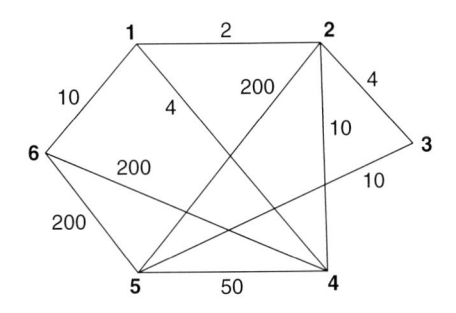

Figure 4.2 Optimal nonbipartite matching with six nodes.

complexity. For practitioners, computer codes are available for both algorithms. It is recommended to use the optimal algorithm since it usually produces better matching results.

Figure 4.2 presents a small example for optimal nonbipartite matching with six nodes. Each node is assumed to come from a different group, such as different dose levels. The lines between two nodes denoting existing edges, and the numbers besides the lines denote the associated distances. If a line is missing between two nodes, such as between nodes 3 and 4, it means that the two nodes cannot be matched (the distance between them is usually referred to as an infinite distance). The goal of optimal matching is to create a matching that has three disjoint pairs and achieves the smallest total distance. It is easy to show that the optimal matching for this figure is $\{[1, 6], [2, 4], [3, 5]\}$. The total distance is $10 + 10 + 10 = 30$. It is worth noting that node 1 is actually closer to node 2 than node 6, but if we matched node 1 with node 2 (which is the nearest neighbor algorithm), we would have to match node 6 with nodes 4 or 5 that incurs a very large distance. This illustrates a scenario when the optimal matching outperforms the nearest neighbor matching. Since the data cannot be clustered into two groups, the bipartite matching algorithm does not apply.

Propensity score matching design

Propensity score based matching can be used to create various designs, depending on the number and size of groups. Assuming a treatment group with sample size m_1 and a control group with sample size m_2, designs commonly seen in traditional bipartite matching include:

- One-to-one matching
  Each matched pair consists of one subject from the treatment group and one subject from the control group. If $m_1 = m_2$, complete matching is achieved. If $m_1 \neq m_2$, some subjects in the larger group are discarded to maintain a one-to-one ratio in matching.
- One-to-k matching
  This design is an extension of one-to-one matching, motived by the matched sampling scenario described in Rubin (1973), where a large pool of control subjects and only a limited number of treated subjects are available. To improve the efficiency of the estimation, each treated subject is matched with k controls, where $k > 1$ is a prespecified integer and $km_1 \leq m_2$ if $m_1 < m_2$. Some control subjects may be discarded.
- Variable matching
  This design further extends one-to-k matching by allowing each treated subject to be matched with different number of controls. To conduct variable matching, one needs to specify the lower and upper bounds of the number of control subjects matched to each treated subject. Usually, the lower bound is 1 and the upper bound is set based on the sample size ratio between treatment and control groups. It can reduce more bias in treatment effect estimation than the more conventional one-to-one matching (Ming & Rosenbaum, 2000). Again, some control subjects may be discarded if $m_1 < m_2$.
- Full matching
  This design further extends variable matching by allowing one control subject to be matched to several treated subjects. It partitions the sample into a collection of matched sets consisting either of a treated subject and any positive number of controls or a control subject and any positive number of treated subjects. Full matching is a general form of matching as it encompasses the above designs as special cases. If implemented properly, full matching is the optimal design for an observational study in the sense that it minimizes the weighted average distance between treated and control subjects among all possible matching designs (Rosenbaum, 2009). Also, unlike the other three matching designs, full matching uses all subjects from both treatment and control groups.

Matching designs involving multiple treatment groups are more complicated and, usually, need to be solved with nonbipartite matching algorithms. Interested readers may refer to Lu, Greevy, Xu, and Beck's work for more details (2011).

Propensity score matching software Matching routines for bipartite matching are widely available in many standard statistical software packages. In Stata, Leuven and Sianesi developed a package *PSMATCH2()* for conducting bipartite matching with either Mahalanobis distance or propensity score distance, based on the nearest neighbor algorithm (http://ideas.repec.org/c/boc/bocode/s432001.html). In SAS, Bergstralh and Kosanke developed a macro *vmatch()* for conducting optimal bipartite matching with one-to-one, one-to-*k* or variable matching designs (www.mayo.edu/research/departments-divisions/department-health-sciences-research/division-biomedical-statistics-informatics/software/locally-written-sas-macros). To conduct matching with more complex designs, such as full matching, more user-written packages can be found in R. For example, R package *optmatch()*, provided by Hansen, can handle all optimal bipartite matching including full matching (http://cran.r-project.org/web/packages/optmatch/). Another R package, *nbpMatch()* developed by Lu et al. (2011), implements Derig's algorithm to perform optimal nonbipartite matching (http://cran.r-project.org/web/packages/nbpMatching/index.html). The software appendix section in Stuart (2011) provides a more thorough review of the computer software packages for matching.

Propensity score matching example: Reevaluation of a job training program A famous example of applying propensity score matching in social science is the work on evaluating a labor training program using National Supported Work (NSW) demonstration data (Dehejia & Wahba, 1999). A central issue concerning many social scientists is the debate on experimental versus nonexperimental evaluation of a certain program. A randomized experiment has good internal validity, but can only be implemented in a restricted manner and for a restricted population. A nonexperimental study may have a good external validity by covering a much broader population, but it suffers confounding bias both observed and unobserved. Lalonde (1986) used data from a randomized experiment and examined the extent to which nonexperimental estimators can replicate the unbiased experimental estimate of the treatment effect when applied to a composite dataset of experimental treatment units and nonexperimental control units. The NSW demonstration was a job training program implemented in the mid-1970s and randomly selected participants to join the program. To compare the estimate with nonexperimental studies, Lalonde combined NSW data with two distinct comparison groups: The Panel Study of Income Dynamics (PSID) and Westat's Matched Current Population Survey – Social Security Administration File (CPS). Realizing the dramatic differences in preintervention covariates between treatment and comparison groups, Lalonde tried a series of regression methods, including linear regression, fixed-effects, and latent variable selection models, to estimate the intervention effect on posttraining earnings. Finally, Lalonde concluded that the regression models and comparison groups failed to replicate the treatment impact. Dehejia and Wahba reevaluated Lalonde's dataset by applying propensity score matching. They first estimated the propensity score of participating in the job training program using a logistic regression model. Different propensity score models were estimated when using different comparison groups. Then, each treatment unit was matched with a unit in the comparison group with the closest propensity score, which was essentially a one-to-one design using the nearest neighbor matching algorithm. The unmatched comparison units were discarded. Table 4.2 showed the estimated training effects for the NSW male participants using comparison groups from PSID and CPS. The reported figures were the NSW earnings in treatment group less comparison group earnings. Adjusted analyses were least square regression for raw comparison and weighted least square regression for propensity score matching (PSM) comparison. Both were adjusted for age, education, race/ethnicity, and previous earnings.

Table 4.2 Estimated earning effects for NSW versus comparison groups.

	Raw Comparison		PSM Comparison	
	Unadjusted	Adjusted	Unadjusted	Adjusted
NSW	1,794	1,672		
PSID	−15,205	731	1,691	1,473
CPS	−8,498	972	1,582	1,616

Table reproduced from Dehejia & Wahba (1999).

The row labeled with NSW showed the intervention effect from the original randomized study, which was used as the benchmark in the following comparisons. Adjusting for demographics and previous earnings reduced the effect slightly. Comparing with PSID group, effects from raw comparison were off the mark substantially regardless of adjustment or not, while effects from PSM comparison replicated the benchmark pretty well. Similar pattern was observed in CPS group. Those results demonstrated the ability of the propensity score to summarize all preintervention variables, and more importantly underlined the importance of using the propensity score in a sufficiently nonlinear functional form, where traditional regression models fell short. Interested readers may refer to Dehejia and Wahba (1999) for a detailed discussion.

As a cautionary note, practitioners need to be aware that adjusting for propensity score has no control over the potentially unmeasured confounders. A careful examination of unobserved confounding and implementation of sensitivity analysis to assess the potential impact are highly recommended (Rosenbaum, 2009).

References

Blumberg, S. J., Luke, J. V., Ganesh, N., Davern, M. E., Boudreaux, M. H., & Soderberg, K. (2011). *Wireless substitution: state-level estimates from the National Health Interview Survey, January 2007–June 2010*. (Rep. No. 39). Atlanta: United States Centers for Disease Control and Prevention.

Cartens C., & Tam, K. (2013). *Medicaid recipients with functional impairment due to a mental health condition or emotional problem*. Ohio Department of Mental Health report.

Dehejia, R. H., & Wahba, S. (1999). Causal effects in nonexperimental studies: Reevaluating the evaluation of training programs. *Journal of the American Statistical Association, 94*, 1053–1062.

Hosmer, D., Lemeshow, S., & Sturdivant, R. (2013). *Applied logistic regression* (3rd ed.). Hoboken, NJ: John Wiley & Sons, Inc.

Lalonde, R. (1986). Evaluating the econometric evaluations of training programs. *American Economic Review, 76*, 604–620.

Levy, P. S., & Lemeshow, S. (2008). *Sampling of populations: Methods and applications* (4th ed.). New York, NY: John Wiley & Sons, Inc.

Lohr, S. L. (2010) *Sampling: Design and analysis* (2nd ed.). Boston, MA: Brooks/Cole.

Lu B., Greevy R., Xu X., & Beck C. (2011). Optimal nonbipartite matching and its statistical applications. *The American Statistician, 65*(1), 21–30.

Ming, K., & Rosenbaum, P. R. (2000). Substantial gains in bias reduction from matching with a variable number of controls. *Biometrics, 56*, 118–124.

Rosenbaum, P. R. (2009). *Design of observational studies.* New York, NY: Springer.
Rosenbaum, P. R., & Rubin, D. B. (1983). The central role of the propensity score in observational studies for causal effects. *Biometrika, 70,* 41–55.
Rubin, D. B. (1973). The use of matched sampling and regression adjustment to remove bias in observational studies. *Biometrics, 29,* 185–203.
Stuart, E. (2011). Matching methods for causal inference: A review and a look forward. *Statistical Science, 25,* 1–21.

5

Sample Size Planning for Confirmatory Factor Models: Power and Accuracy for Effects of Interest

Ken Kelley and Keke Lai

Introduction

Confirmatory factor analysis (CFA) holds a special place in psychometrics because of the model's historical significance and widespread use when latent constructs are theorized and empirically evaluated. A special case of a CFA model is simply a composite measure.[1] Confirmatory factor models are themselves special cases of structural equation models. Within a structural equation model (SEM), the measurement model of a given construct is a confirmatory factor model. In an SEM, constructs are used to test a hypothesized structural relationship among latent variables. Thus, an SEM, the measurement model, itself a confirmatory factor model, is used in a larger framework of modeled constructs called the structural model. Although widely used in applied research, much of the writing on CFA is within an SEM framework treating CFA as a special case. In the introduction to Brown's book on CFA (2006), David Kenny says, "it is ironic that SEM has received so much more attention than CFA, because the social and behavioral sciences have learned much more from CFA than from SEM" (p. ix). With that strong endorsement of the importance of CFA, our focus in this chapter is sample size planning for CFA models. The ideas, however, are directly applicable to other related models, such as multiple regression, path analysis, and SEM among others. In fact, the ideas we discuss here are general and they are widely applicable to many contexts.

Consider the idea of sample size planning. First, in our experience, this is a topic that is often ignored by many researchers. We say this because so often the idea of planning an appropriate sample size is an afterthought to other aspects of a study. We believe one reason why sample size is sometimes an afterthought is because there are often a priori built-in limitations of a study, such as when there is only a short amount of time available to collect data, the number of potential participants is necessarily restricted (e.g., from a shared participant pool, from within an organization, from a special or limited

---

[1] For example, the sum of a set of items, with unit weights or unequal weights, can be conceptualized as a constrained CFA model.

The Wiley Handbook of Psychometric Testing: A Multidisciplinary Reference on Survey, Scale and Test Development, First Edition. Edited by Paul Irwing, Tom Booth, and David J. Hughes.
© 2018 John Wiley & Sons Ltd. Published 2020 by John Wiley & Sons Ltd.

population), or financial resources to collect data dictate only a small number of participants' data can be collected. Any of these limitations may be a very practical reason why, regardless of what a formal planning of sample size would suggest, researchers use the sample size that is available to them, at least conveniently. In these sorts of situations, the idea of doing an analysis to choose an appropriate sample size does not seem to be highly valued. However, as we explain momentarily, we believe that even in such constrained situations it is still important to plan sample size and the reason many studies fail to accomplish their original goals is often, but certainly not always, directly related to sample size.

An alternative scenario to the one just considered is one in which sample size planning is explicitly and carefully considered, such as in many proposals for funding (i.e., grant applications). Many funding agencies and reviewers will carefully consider the sample size justifications in proposals. The scrutiny of sample size considerations is widely known by authors of successful proposals. There is no technical reason of course why studies that are not being considered for funding should ignore sample size planning.

Although we realize that to some, perhaps many, researchers, planning sample size is not as exciting as planning other aspects of a study (e.g., selecting measures to use, theoretical model to evaluate, population from which to sample, hypothesis generation) or performing analyses on the collected data, sample size planning is itself a fundamentally important task to a well-designed study. We believe, in fact, that an appropriate sample size is a necessary, but certainly not a sufficient, requirement for a well-designed study. One reason why sample size should be explicitly considered before starting a study is to evaluate the potential success of a study with a specified sample size that the researcher wants, or is able, to use. That is to say, how likely is it that a study will be successful at the sample size that a researcher wants or is able to use? Alternatively, sample size should be explicitly considered in order to plan for a sample size that would have a sufficiently high likelihood of leading to a successful study.

A very practical reason why sample size should be considered is to avoid starting a study in which the a priori success rate is unacceptably low given the sample size that is available or that the researcher has the time or funds to collect. That is, if a researcher knows that he or she will only be able to have, say, 100 participants in the study, yet the sample size planning procedure suggests that 350 participants are needed, the researcher may elect not to start the study due to the less-than-desired probability of accomplishing the study's goals. For example, it could be the case that the goals of the study will only have a 10% chance of being successful. Is a 10% chance of success really worth putting in the substantial amount of time, effort, and resources required? Maybe it is still worth conducting a study that has a low chance of success, as there is often more than a single goal of a study. Either way, however, considering sample size before the start of the study allows the researcher to consider this information before conducting the study, rather than only learning of the likely reason why the failure after the study's completion.

We have said much about the "goals of a study" without identifying exactly what these "goals" are. First, consider an effect size, which we conceptualize along the lines of Kelley and Preacher (2012) as "a quantitative reflection of the magnitude of some phenomenon that is used for the purpose of addressing a question of interest" (p. 140). In this context, mean differences, regression coefficients, path coefficients, factor loadings, correlations, proportion of variance accounted for type measures (e.g., the squared multiple correlation, eta-squared), and measures of fit, among others, are effect sizes. When we say "the effect," we mean the effect size of interest.

When considering a study's goals, Maxwell, Kelley, and Rausch (2008) consider the idea of showing (1) the existence of an effect (and possibly its direction), (2) accurately estimating the magnitude of an effect, or (3) showing the existence of an effect **and** estimating an effect accurately. By "showing the existence of an effect," we mean that the specified null value of the effect is rejected with a null hypothesis significance test. By "accurately estimating the magnitude of the effect," we mean that the confidence interval for the parameter of interest is sufficiently narrow.

More formally, in the context of **showing the existence of an effect**, the study will often be considered a "success" if the p-value $< \alpha$, where the p-value is the probability of obtaining results as or more extreme than observed under the null hypothesis and α is the Type I error rate. That is to say, when the null hypothesis of the effect of interest can be rejected, support is shown for the alternative hypothesis, which is usually the research hypothesis of interest. When the goal of a study is to reject a false null hypothesis, a power analysis should be performed so that the sample size that leads to sufficient power, under the specified assumptions and study design, can be planned. This type of sample size planning is the traditional approach and is what Jacob Cohen spent considerable time positing should be done to improve research quality throughout much of his career (e.g., as is exemplified in his power analysis book, 1988).

In the context of **accurately estimating the magnitude of the effect**, such a conceptualization can be considered a success when the $(1-\alpha)100\%$ confidence interval for the corresponding population value is sufficiently narrow. That is to say, when sampling error is reduced (precision is improved) and the estimator is not more biased in the process of improving precision, the estimate is made more accurate. Accuracy of an estimate is a function of two quantities: precision and bias. If bias is zero, and thus the estimate is unbiased, improving precision improves accuracy: in the case of an unbiased estimate precision and accuracy are the same (e.g., Kelley & Maxwell, 2003). Thus, holding everything else constant, a narrower confidence interval equates to a more accurate estimate. Sample size planning in this framework has been termed accuracy in parameter estimation (AIPE; e.g., Kelley & Maxwell, 2003). Although, as noted, Cohen spent considerable time discussing the importance of appropriately powered studies, in the latter part of his career he shifted focus to the importance of effect sizes and their corresponding confidence intervals. A useful way of understanding the goal of AIPE is illustrated by solving the problem noted here with regards to why Cohen suspected, at that time, so few researchers reported confidence intervals: "I suspect that the main reason they [confidence intervals] are not reported is that they are so embarrassingly large!" (1994, p. 1002). The AIPE approach to sample size planning seeks to plan sample size so as to avoid "embarrassingly large" confidence intervals. All of these ideas are general and in no way limited to the CFA context.

Effect Size

When considering estimates in CFA, it is useful to frame them in the context of an effect size. In the context of CFA, factor loadings, correlations, and measures of fit are each effect sizes. There is an important distinction between two general types of effect sizes, namely omnibus and targeted. An omnibus effect size relates to the overall model, whereas a targeted effect size relates to a specific well-defined part of the model. In the context of CFA, a targeted effect size could be a factor loading or correlation coefficient among two constructs, whereas an omnibus effect size could be a fit index, such as the root mean square error of approximation (RMSEA), comparative fit index (CFI), or Tucker–Lewis index (TLI), for example.

In addition to the distinction between targeted and omnibus effect sizes, one can consider whether effect sizes are standardized or unstandardized. In general, unstandardized path coefficients in CFA (and SEM) models are preferred from a methodological perspective, as the sampling distribution of standardized coefficients has some technical issues associated with their standard errors (see Cudeck, 1989, for a discussion of issues associated with standardized coefficients in CFA and SEM models).[3] Fit indices are a different type of effect size that are standardized because they are not wedded to the particular measurement scales themselves. Unstandardized path coefficients, on the other hand, are wedded to the measurement scales of the variables used. Correspondingly, their interpretation is necessarily in the context of the variances and covariances of the manifest variables. This is no different than the interpretation of a regression coefficient. Consider the case of simple regression, where the regression coefficient of Y on X is estimated as $\frac{Covariance(X,Y)}{Variance(X)} = s_{xy}/s_x$, which clearly shows that the scaling depends on both the regressor (X) and the outcome variable (Y).

As we have illustrated, effect size can be considered in a two-by-two conceptualization comprised of scaling (standardized or unstandardized) and scope (targeted or omnibus). Coupling the type of effect size(s) with the goal of showing the existence of an effect or its magnitude is needed in order to plan an appropriate sample size. Kelley and Maxwell (2008) provide a two-by-two conceptualization for sample size planning. That conceptualization consists of one dimension in which the interest concerns whether the approach to planning sample size is statistical power or AIPE and another dimension in which interest concerns whether the effect of interest is omnibus or targeted. A modified version of that table was given in Kelley and Maxwell (2012) and is provided here in Table 5.1.

Table 5.1 shows that sample size can be considered in a two-by-two framework. Although the table does not make the distinction between standardized and unstandardized values, implicit is that the effect size of interest is either standardized or not.[4] Use of Table 5.1 is only a guide, as the table supposes that only a single effect size is of interest. Simultaneously considering multiple effect sizes (e.g., path coefficients and fit indices) or multiple goals (e.g., power and accuracy) is beyond the discussion of this chapter (but see Maxwell et al., 2008). However, a simple way to consider an appropriate sample size is to plan for effects of interest for the particular goal(s) and use as the necessary sample size the largest of the multiple sample sizes.

---

[3] The issue has to do with there being extra randomness in the model not explicitly accounted for due to the standardization process. Consider standardization in multiple regression in which an unstandardized regression coefficient is multiplied by a random variable that is the quotient of two estimated standard deviations, one for the dependent variable and one for the regressor of interest. In repeated samplings from the same population, the ratio of standard deviations (that is multiplied by the unstandardized regression coefficient) will vary. This extra variability is unaccounted for in the estimated standard errors of standard regression coefficients.

[4] It is also possible to consider partially standardized effect sizes. Consider, for example, a multiple regression model in which a regressor is standardized but the outcome variable is kept in its raw score form.

Table 5.1 Goals of statistical inference for a two-by-two conceptualization of possible scenarios when the approach (statistical power or AIPE) is crossed with the type of effect size (omnibus or targeted).

		Type of Effect Size	
		Omnibus	*Targeted*
Approach	Statistical Power	*Establish existence of an omnibus effect by rejecting the null hypothesis that the population value of the omnibus effect is consistent with the specified null hypothesis*	*Establish existence of a targeted effect by rejecting the null hypothesis that the population value of the targeted effect is consistent with the specified null hypothesis*
	Accuracy in Parameter Estimation	*Establish the magnitude of the omnibus effect by obtaining a narrow confidence interval for the population omnibus effect*	*Establish the magnitude of the targeted effect by obtaining a narrow confidence interval for the population targeted effect*

Table taken from Kelley & Maxwell (2012).

In the remainder of this chapter, we discuss how to plan sample size for the case of a single factor model and also for a bifactor model. We use R (R Core Team, 2014) and our R software package, MBESS (Kelley & Lai, 2014), both of which are open source and freely available. Many good introductions to R and their use in different fields are available, both online and in book form (and some online books, such as Venables, Smith, & the R Core Team, 2014). Some of the sample size planning methods discussed in this chapter are also available in other statistical packages. We use R because it is freely available, it is easy to use, and we have provided functions that can be used for each of the scenarios we discuss. We hope that our chapter is able to stimulate researchers to consider the multiple ways in which sample size planning can be conceptualized when interest concerns parameters from CFA or related models.

Empirical Demonstration 1

We provide two worked examples to illustrate the sample size planning theories discussed previously. The examples are in the context of studies in social and personality psychology, but they can be easily generalized to other psychometric problems. In particular, the first example is based on a one-factor CFA model, and the second example is a scenario in which a bifactor and a second-order CFA model are compared.

Suppose a researcher is interested in the cognition of a certain group of adults and selects five manifest variables to measure cognition. The proposed model is a one-factor CFA model and is depicted in Figure 5.1. Appropriate manifest variables in the present example can be (1) scores from questions such as "Have difficulty reasoning and solving problems?" or "Forget where you put things or appointments?"; (2) the summary scores of a group of items; or (3) scores from a standardized test. After selecting the five indicators for the model, the researcher plans the necessary sample size for the study. Recall that we previously explained four different methods to plan

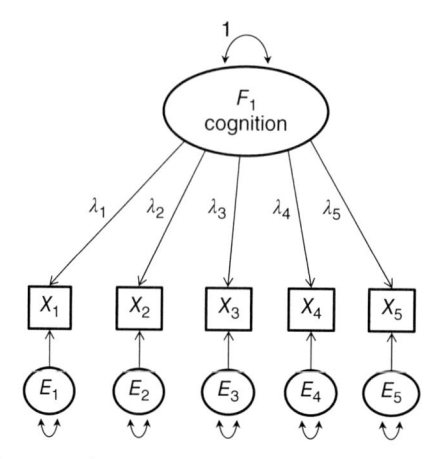

Figure 5.1 Confirmatory factor model for Cognition with five manifest variables.

the sample size in a factor analysis study, and in the present example sample size planning will be illustrated using all four of those methods. However, note that in practice the researcher may not be interested in all four questions, but only one or two of them and, accordingly, the sample size only needs to be large enough to address the one or two questions of interest.

Approach 1: Power analysis for the model's population RMSEA At least two types of null hypotheses can be stated with respect to the model's population RMSEA, denoted as ε: (1) the traditional null hypothesis in which $H_0 : \varepsilon = 0$ (often called the nil hypothesis because the hypothesized value is 0); (2) a more realistic null hypothesis that tests the minimum effect of interest, such as $H_0 : \varepsilon \geq .08$. Rejecting the first type of null hypothesis will lead to the conclusion that the model's fit is not perfect, but this conclusion is not informative because, even without carrying out the study, the researcher already knows that the proposed model is unlikely to have perfect fit. The second type of null hypothesis states that the proposed model's fit is worse than some value of interest and rejecting the null hypothesis will lead to the conclusion that the model's fit is better than the cutoff value. In the present example, we use .08 as the cutoff value of interest, and demonstrate how to test the null hypothesis $H_0 : \varepsilon \geq .08$. Depending on the researcher's interest and prior knowledge of the model's statistical adequacy, the second type of null hypothesis can use many other cutoff values to describe ε (e.g., $H_0 : \varepsilon \geq .05$, $H_0 : \varepsilon \geq .06$, $H_0 : \varepsilon \geq .10$, etc.). Regardless of which null hypothesis the researcher chooses to test, calculating the sample size in order to have adequate power to test either type of hypothesis with respect to the RMSEA requires the following input information: (1) the model's degrees of freedom (df), (2) the Type I error rate (α), (3) the desired power ($1-\beta$, with β being the Type II error rate), (4) the population RMSEA under the null hypothesis (ε_0), and (5) the true population RMSEA (ε). Based on the path diagram, $df = 5$. For this example, we use $\alpha = .05$ and $1-\beta = .80$. The value for ε_0 is the value H_0 states, and thus ε_0 is 0 or .08, depending on which null hypothesis is of interest. Then the last and most difficult piece of input information is the true population

Table 5.2 Covariance matrix (upper triangle) and correlation matrix (lower triangle) of a hypothetical previous study in Empirical Demonstration 1.

	X_1	X_2	X_3	X_4	X_5
X_1	$(1.1)^2$	.548	.320	.828	.343
X_2	.415	$(1.2)^2$	.430	1.024	.445
X_3	.364	.448	$(.80)^2$	.610	.326
X_4	.502	.569	.509	$(1.5)^2$	.619
X_5	.346	.412	.453	.459	$(.90)^2$

The principal diagonal is the standard deviation in parentheses squared (i.e., the variance)

RMSEA, which can be estimated by the researcher based on the literature, previously collected data, or even a pilot study.

Suppose a previous study using $N = 420$ reported a covariance matrix of X_1 through X_5 as Table 5.2 indicates. Fitting the proposed model to that sample covariance matrix will yield $\hat{\varepsilon} = .035$. Suppose, based on this previous study result and substantive theories, the researcher believes that the population RMSEA is likely to be around .045 and uses $\varepsilon = .045$ as the input information. To calculate the necessary sample size so as to reject $H_0 : \varepsilon = 0$, the researcher specifies the input information for the R function from the MBESS package ss.power.sem() as follows:

```
> ss.power.sem(RMSEA.null=0, RMSEA.true=.045, df=5,
alpha=.05, power=.80),
```

where RMSEA.null, RMSEA.true, df, alpha, and power refer to the RMSEA under the null hypothesis, the true population RMSEA, the model's degrees of freedom, the Type I error rate, and the desired power, respectively. The necessary sample size estimated based on this input information is 1,269.

Alternatively, if the researcher is interested in rejecting a more realistic null hypothesis, say $H_0 : \varepsilon \geq .08$, then the sample size can be calculated as follows:

```
> ss.power.sem(RMSEA.null=.08, RMSEA.true=.045, df=5,
alpha=.05, power=.80).
```

Note that in the present case RMSEA.null is .08 as it is the RMSEA value under H_0, and RMSEA.true remains 0.045 as the true population RMSEA does not change regardless of what the null hypothesis states. The necessary sample size estimate based on this input information is 1,113. Note also that in this case testing $H_0 : \varepsilon \geq .08$ requires a smaller sample size than does testing $H_0 : \varepsilon = 0$, but one should not over-generalize this result. Depending on the input information and how the null hypothesis is stated (e.g., $H_0 : \varepsilon \geq .05$ instead of $H_0 : \varepsilon \geq .08$), the minimum-effect hypothesis may require a larger or smaller sample size than does the nil hypothesis.

Approach 2: AIPE for the model's population RMSEA Consider again the covariance matrix in Table 5.2. Fitting the proposed model to this covariance matrix of $N = 420$ yields $\hat{\varepsilon} = .035$, as well as a 90% confidence interval for ε, namely [0, .082]. That is, if this CI indeed includes ε, then the population RMSEA may be very close to 0, meaning the model has nearly perfect fit, or may be as large as .082, meaning the model fit is just about "fair" according to common standards. Therefore, there is much uncertainty about the population RMSEA, although the sample data indicates that the fit is relatively "good." If the researcher is interested in estimating ε with a higher degree of accuracy, they can plan the sample size with the goal to achieve a sufficiently narrow CI. Planning the sample size for the RMSEA from the AIPE perspective requires the following input information: (1) model's degrees of freedom df, (2) confidence level $1-\alpha$, (3) the true population RMSEA ε, and (4) desired CI width ω. The first three pieces of input information are the same as before, so let us focus on the desired CI width ω. The width of the CI based on $N = 420$ is .082, and suppose for the future study the researcher desires a CI whose width is no larger than .060; that is, $\omega = .060$. Then the sample size can be calculated using the function `ss.aipe.rmsea()` as follows:

```
> ss.aipe.rmsea(RMSEA=.045, df=5, width=.060, conf.
level=0.90)
```

where `RMSEA`, `df`, `width`, and `conf.level` refer to the population RMSEA, model's degrees of freedom, desired CI width, and confidence level, respectively. The necessary sample size estimated based on this input information is 802.

Note there is no such thing as "the correct desired CI width" or "correct power," as the researcher sets either (or both) based on the goals he or she has for the study. In the present example, we selected $\omega = .060$ because we want to achieve a narrower width compared to the one observed in a previous study (i.e., .082). This estimated sample size, $N = 802$, means that, if the input information is correct and all the statistical assumptions are satisfied, the researcher can expect to obtain a CI whose width is no larger than .060. An implication of the expectation is that about half of the time the interval will be narrower than desired and about half of the time the interval will be wider than desired. The researcher could well use other values for ω, in a sensitivity analysis, so as to better understand the tradeoff between the increase in sample size and the reduction in CI width. That is, given ε, df, and α, a decrease in ω (i.e., narrower CI) will result in an increase in N, but the relationship between ω and N is usually nonlinear, and a small decrease in ω may require a small or large increase in N, depending on all factors. To illustrate, consider using $\omega = .050$ instead of $\omega = .060$ as input:

```
> ss.aipe.rmsea(RMSEA=.045, df=5, width=.050, conf.
level=0.90)
```

the estimated sample size would be 1,059. Therefore, in order to reduce the expected CI width from 0.060 to 0.050, it requires 257 additional participants. If one further reduces the desired expected CI width to $\omega = .040$, the necessary sample size would be 1,544. A 0.010 decrease from $\omega = .060$ to $\omega = .050$ requires an increase of 257 in N, whereas a 0.010 decrease from $\omega = .050$ to $\omega = .040$ requires an increase of 485 in N. By comparing the sample size estimates at various ω values, the researcher can better understand the interplay between resources (in the present context, N) and the estimation certainty (in the present context, expected CI width), and consider whether the gain in estimation certainty is worth the extra participants. Because there is no "correct" CI width, reasonable values for ω can be those that help achieve a balance between the sample size invested and the knowledge obtained about the population parameters. Lin and Weng (2014) provide a graphical approach to sample size planning for AIPE in the context of the RMSEA, where one can assess the effect sizes of desired width and the population RMSEA on the necessary sample size.

Approach 3: Power analysis for the population model parameter of interest In addition to the model's overall fit, some specific model parameters are frequently of interest. Suppose X_1 represents the scores on the item "Have difficulty reasoning and solving problems" and X_2 represents the scores on the item "React slowly to questions," and it is of interest to infer whether these two items have the same reliability in measuring the latent construct cognition. Put another way, it is of interest to know whether X_1 and X_2 have the same population factor loadings. The null hypothesis is $H_0: \lambda_1 = \lambda_2$, and rejecting this null hypothesis will lead to the conclusion that $H_a: \lambda_1 \neq \lambda_2$. To test this null hypothesis, one can carry out a chi-square likelihood ratio test that compares models with and without the constraint $\lambda_1 = \lambda_2$. To calculate the necessary sample size in order to have enough power to perform such a test, the input information is (1) the model, (2) Type I error rate, (3) desired power, and (4) the population covariance matrix of the manifest variables, Σ. Note this approach requires the complete specification of the statistical model, not just the model's degrees of freedom, and thus input item (1) in the present context is different from the input item (1) in the context of power analysis for the RMSEA.

Let us now consider input item (4), the population covariance matrix. Broadly speaking, there are two ways to specify Σ. The first way is to specify all the variances and covariances in Σ, and the second way is to specify the model parameter values first and then use the model-implied covariance matrix as Σ. Methods to facilitate specifying Σ are, for example, discussed in Lai and Kelley (2011). In the present example, we demonstrate how to specify Σ based on a previous study. Consider the sample covariance matrix in Table 5.2. Fitting the model to this covariance matrix will return the model parameter estimates shown in Table 5.3. Because the estimation is based on a covariance matrix, the resulting model parameter estimates are in the unstandardized metric and not straightforward to interpret. In Table 5.3 we have also provided model parameter estimates in the standardized metric, so let us focus on the standardized estimates for the moment. The researcher must then specify the input information Σ using the following

Table 5.3 Model parameter estimates based on the sample covariance matrix in Table 5.1.

	Unstandardized estimate	Standard error	Standardized estimates	Standardized input information
λ_1	.659	.054	.600	.550
λ_2	.839	.056	.700	.730
λ_3	.519	.038	.650	.680
λ_4	1.199	.068	.800	.750
λ_5	.539	.044	.600	.600
e_1	.773	.061	.640	.6636
e_2	.773	.065	.510	.4816
e_3	.369	.031	.577	.5376
e_4	.808	.093	.360	.4375
e_5	.517	.041	.640	.640

three steps. First, based on these standardized model parameter estimates, the researcher must make educated guesses as to the population model parameters in the standardized context. Second, using the population standardized model parameters, the model-implied correlation matrix $\mathbf{P}(\boldsymbol{\theta})$ is calculated. Third, the researcher specifies the standard deviations of the manifest variables, and using these transforms $\mathbf{P}(\boldsymbol{\theta})$ into the covariance matrix.

Suppose that, based on substantive theories, the researcher believes that X_1 should have lower reliability in measuring the latent factor and thus uses $\lambda_1 = .550$ as input. Similarly, substantive theory also suggests that the reliability of X_2 and X_3 should be higher than has been reported in the previous study, and accordingly the researcher uses $\lambda_2 = .730$ and $\lambda_3 = .680$ as input. To be conservative, the researcher uses a lower factor loading for X_4: $\lambda_4 = .750$. The input for λ_5 remains the same as reported in the previous study: $\lambda_5 = .600$. Because the model parameters are in the standardized metric, the error variance in the present model can be easily calculated as unity minus the square of the factor loading (i.e., $1 - \lambda^2$). Appendix Code 1 demonstrates how to obtain the model-implied correlation matrix using the MBESS package, and the resulting $\mathbf{P}(\boldsymbol{\theta})$ is included in Table 5.4. Based on the previous study, suppose the standard deviations of X_1 through X_5 are believed to be 1.20, 1.20, .70, 1.30, and 1.10, respectively. Now the input covariance matrix can be obtained and this is provided in Table 5.4. We use $\boldsymbol{\Sigma}_1$ to denote this input covariance matrix.

Now that all of the input information is complete, the researcher can calculate the necessary sample size using the method Satorra and Saris (1985) developed. In essence, Approach 3 is based on the sampling distributions of the model chi-square statistic under H$_0$ and H$_a$, and the Satorra–Saris (1985) method helps to obtain a key distribution parameter (namely the noncentrality parameter) for the sampling distribution under H$_a$ using the population covariance matrix of manifest variables. We will explain the underlying statistical theories in more detail in a later section, and for the moment let us continue to demonstrate how to use Approach 3 to plan the sample size. Recall the present task is after specifying the model, Type I error rate, desired power, and $\boldsymbol{\Sigma}_1$ as input information, how to calculate the sample size so as to reject H$_0$: $\lambda_1 = \lambda_2$ with a sufficiently high probability (i.e., desired power). Let the proposed model for the present study be referred to as the full model and the model that constrains $\lambda_1 = \lambda_2$ be referred to as the restricted model. The full model will fit the input covariance matrix $\boldsymbol{\Sigma}_1$ perfectly, but the restricted model will have some misfit to $\boldsymbol{\Sigma}_1$. In particular, fitting the restricted model to $\boldsymbol{\Sigma}_1$ will yield a maximum likelihood (ML) discrepancy value $F_{Res} = .02346$ and $\varepsilon_{Res} = .0625$, where F_{Res} is a shorthand for the F_{ML} value in the restricted model. The F_{ML} value in the full model is 0 ($F_{Full} = 0$). The difference in degrees of freedom between the full model and the restricted model is 1. Given this information the sample size can then be planned using the function ss.power.sem() as follows:

Table 5.4 Covariance matrix (upper triangle) and correlation matrix (lower triangle) of input information for sample size planning.

	X_1	X_2	X_3	X_4	X_5
X_1	$(1.20)^2$	.418	.394	.435	.348
X_2	.601	$(1.20)^2$	.490	.540	.432
X_3	.331	.411	$(.70)^2$	.510	.408
X_4	.679	.842	.464	$(1.30)^2$	.450
X_5	.459	.570	.314	.644	$(1.10)^2$

```
> ss.power.sem(F.full=0, F.res=.02346, df.full=5, df.res=6,
alpha=.05, power=.80)
```

where `F.full`, `F.res`, `df.full`, and `df.res` refer to the full model's F_{ML}, the restricted model's F_{ML}, the full model's degrees of freedom, and the restricted model's degrees of freedom, respectively. The necessary sample size is 336. Therefore, in order to have .80 power to demonstrate that X_1 and X_2 have different factor loadings, sample size needs to be $N = 336$.

Note the function `ss.power.sem()` asks for F_{ML} values as input only instead of the population covariance matrix of the manifest variables, and the Satorra–Saris method is sometimes difficult to employ because it usually requires a large amount of information to specify the population covariance matrix. Alternatively, MacCallum, Browne, and Cai (2006) proposed a method that utilizes the relationship between RMSEA and F_{ML}, so as to specify the F_{ML} values in terms of the RMSEA. The MacCallum et al. method has the same goal as does the Satorra–Saris method, namely to obtain a key distribution parameter for the sampling distribution under H_a, but it requires only the population RMSEA values under H_0 and H_a, and thus circumvents the task of specifying the population covariance matrix. We will explain this method's underlying theories in a later section, and for the moment continue to demonstrate the MacCallum et al. method. Recall we obtained the population RMSEA values earlier when fitting Σ_1 to the full and restricted models; that is, $\varepsilon_{Res} = .0625$ and $\varepsilon_{Full} = 0$. Accordingly, we can employ MacCallum et al. method and use the following call to the `ss.power.sem()`:

```
> ss.power.sem(RMSEA.full=0, RMSEA.res=.0625, df.full=5,
df.res=6, alpha=.05, power=.80),
```

which also returns $N = 336$, equivalent to the N obtained with the Satorra–Saris method using Σ_1 as input. In practice the MacCallum et al. method is easier to implement as compared to the Satorra–Saris method, because it is easier to obtain knowledge about the model's general adequacy (operationalized as the population RMSEA) as compared to the variances and covariances of all the manifest variables in the model.

The above example demonstrated that, if the input RMSEA equals the population RMSEA, the sample size estimate will equal the idealized sample size based on the population RMSEA. But if the input information is not exactly accurate, the sample size returned will be different from the idealized sample size. To illustrate, suppose the researcher does not have enough knowledge about the phenomenon under study to accurately specify Σ_1, but can only judge that the restricted model should have a "fair" to "good" statistical fit. Accordingly, the researcher chooses .07 as a proxy for ε_{Res} and plans the sample size as follows:

```
> ss.power.sem(RMSEA.full=0, RMSEA.res=.07, df.full=5,
df.res=6, alpha=.05, power=.80).
```

The resulting sample size estimate is $N = 268$, falling short of the theoretically optimal necessary sample size based on the correct population RMSEA (had it been known to the researcher). However, if the researcher uses .06 as the input RMSEA value, the resulting N will be 364, which is close to the idealized N. How much the sample size estimate differs from the idealized sample size hinges upon how close the input parameter is to the population parameters (e.g., population covariance matrix of manifest variables, population RMSEA of the restricted model), and therefore effort is required to ensure the quality of the input information.

Statistical theories for SEM power analysis In this subsection, we briefly explain the underlying statistical theories for the Satorra–Saris method and the MacCallum et al. method. Detailed explanations are available in Satorra and Saris (1985) and MacCallum et al. (2006). The present task is to assess the difference in statistical fit between a full model and a restricted model. Statistical fit in the current context is derived from the model estimation results using the following ML discrepancy function:

$$F_{ML} = \ln|\Sigma(\hat{\theta})| - \ln|S| + tr\left(S \cdot \Sigma^{-1}(\hat{\theta})\right) - p, \quad (5.1)$$

where $\ln(\cdot)$ is the natural logarithm, S is the sample covariance matrix, $\Sigma(\hat{\theta})$ is the model-implied covariance matrix given S, and p is the number of manifest variables. We use $\hat{F}$ and F^* to denote the sample and population discrepancy function value, respectively. If the data follow a multivariate normal distribution and the models are not badly misspecified, we have the following three approximate chi-square distributions:

$$n\hat{F}_{Full} \approx \chi^2(df_{Full}, \delta_{Full}); \quad (5.2)$$

$$n\hat{F}_{Res} \approx \chi^2(df_{Res}, \delta_{Res}); \quad (5.3)$$

$$n(\hat{F}_{Res} - \hat{F}_{Full}) \approx \chi^2(df_{Res} - df_{Full}, \delta_{Res} - \delta_{Full}); \quad (5.4)$$

where df_{Full} and df_{Res} refer to the degrees of freedom of the full and restricted models, respectively, δ_{Full} and δ_{Res} refer to the noncentrality parameter of their respective distributions, $n = N - 1$, and "$\approx$" signifies that the (random) quantity on the left approximately follows the distribution on the right. The noncentrality parameter is based on the population discrepancy function value:

$$\delta_{Full} = nF^*_{Full}; \quad (5.5)$$

$$\delta_{Res} = nF^*_{Res}. \quad (5.6)$$

Accordingly, the noncentrality parameter for the distribution in Equation 5.4 is simply $\delta_{Res} - \delta_{Full} = n(F^*_{Res} - F^*_{Full})$. Recall of interest is whether the full and restricted models have equal statistical fit, and we use the test statistic $n(\hat{F}_{Res} - \hat{F}_{Full})$ and its sampling distribution (i.e., Equation 5.4) to perform a hypothesis test and examine the question of interest. To simplify the exposition, let T_{Diff} denote this test statistic; accordingly, the sampling distribution can be expressed as $T_{Diff} \approx \chi^2(df_{Res} - df_{Full}, \delta_{Res} - \delta_{Full})$.

Now let us take these statistical theories back to Approach 3's example, where the interest is to infer whether the two factor loadings, λ_1 and λ_2, are equal in the population. If the null hypothesis $H_0 : \lambda_1 = \lambda_2$ is true, the full and restricted models fit equally well and are both correctly specified. Thus, under the null hypothesis, $F^*_{Res} = F^*_{Full} = 0$ and T_{Diff} approximately follows a chi-square distribution with degrees of freedom $(df_{Res} - df_{Full})$ and a noncentrality parameter of 0. That is,

$$T_{Diff} \approx \chi^2(df_{Res} - df_{Full}, 0) \quad (5.7)$$

under H_0. Under the alternative hypothesis $H_a : \lambda_1 \neq \lambda_2$, the full model is correctly specified but the restricted model is misspecified, and therefore $F^*_{Full} = 0$ and $F^*_{Res} > 0$, implying $\delta_{Full} = 0$ and $\delta_{Res} > 0$. The noncentrality parameter $\delta_{Res} - \delta_{Full}$ reduces to δ_{Res}, which is equivalent to nF^*_{Res}. That is,

$$T_{Diff} \approx \chi^2 \left(df_{Res} - df_{Full}, nF^*_{Res} \right) \tag{5.8}$$

under H_a. Given the distributions under H_0 and H_a, one can plan the sample size by finding the smallest value of n in Equation 5.8, such that there is $(1-\beta)100\%$ probability of rejecting H_0. But note F^*_{Res} in Equation 5.8 is a population parameter unknown to the researcher, and thus the specific form of the distribution is not determined and Equation 5.8 cannot be readily used for sample size planning. How to provide a value for F^*_{Res} (or equivalently speaking, the noncentrality parameter δ_{Res}) is where the Satorra–Saris method and the MacCallum–Browne–Cai method come into play.

In particular, Satorra and Saris proposed using the model-implied covariance matrix of the full model to obtain F^*_{Res}. That is, because the full model is specified correctly, $\Sigma = \Sigma_{Full}(\theta)$. If one supplies all the model parameter values to the full model, the model-implied covariance matrix $\Sigma_{Full}(\theta)$ will be equivalent to Σ. Next one fits the restricted model to Σ, and the resulting discrepancy function value will be F^*_{Res}. Alternatively, MacCallum et al. utilized the relationship between the discrepancy function value and RMSEA. Commonly, RMSEA is defined as

$$\varepsilon = \sqrt{\frac{F_{ML}}{df}} \tag{5.9}$$

in the population, and thus $F_{ML} = df \cdot \varepsilon^2$. If the population RMSEA of the restricted model is known, one can obtain F^*_{Res} using the identity $F^*_{Res} = df_{Res} \cdot \varepsilon^2_{Res}$. Therefore, the Satorra–Saris method and the MacCallum et al. method try to solve the same problem: namely how to obtain F^*_{Res} -- from two different perspectives, and they are independent approaches. After F^*_{Res} is obtained with either method, it is supplied to the sample size planning process along with other input information, such as the full and restricted models' degrees of freedom, Type I error rate, and desired power.

Approach 4: AIPE for the population model parameters of interest The fourth perspective on sample size planning concerns the case when it is desired to estimate a model parameter of interest with sufficient accuracy, as expressed by the width of the confidence interval. Consider again the model parameter estimates reported from the previous study as shown in Table 5.3. Suppose the researcher is interested in knowing the true value of λ_1 in the population. Based on the previous study $N = 420$, $se(\lambda_1) = .054$ and the 95% CI for λ_1 is $[.553, .765]$. The width of this CI is .212. If the researcher desires a narrower CI in the study being designed, the necessary sample size can be calculated with the following input information: (1) the model, (2) confidence level, (3) desired value of the CI width, and (4) the population covariance matrix of the manifest variables, Σ. Except for item (3), the required input information is the same as for Approach 3. The only difference in the input information between Approaches 3 and

4 is that the desired power is replaced with a desired CI width. In the present scenario, we continue to use all the input information we specified for Approach 3 except for item (3).

Recall that the 95% CI width for λ_1 reported in the previous study is .212 and that the researcher desires a narrower CI in the future study. If we used $\omega = .15$, the necessary sample size can be calculated using the function ss.aipe.sem.path() as follows:

```
> ss.aipe.sem.path(model=model.full, Sigma=Sigma.1, desired.
width=.15, which.path="l1", conf.level=0.95),
```

where model, Sigma, and which.path refer, respectively, to the model, the input population covariance matrix Σ_1 (i.e., the covariance matrix in Table 5.4), and the name of the model parameter of interest. Due to space limitations, this call to ss.aipe.sem.path() omits the intermediate steps that specify objects model.full and Sigma.1. These intermediate steps are included in Appendix Code 1. Given this input information, the function will return a necessary sample size estimate $N = 1007$.

Planning N using $\omega = .15$ only guarantees that the expectation of the (random) CI widths in the long run is no larger than .15, but in the particular study to be carried out, the CI width will be less than .15 with a probability of about 50%. That is, in practice one forms a confidence interval based on a sample covariance matrix, and because values in the sample covariance matrix vary over repeated sampling, the confidence interval obtained is necessarily random, varying over repeated sampling. Accordingly, the width of a CI varies from sample to sample as well and is a random variable. Let w, a random variable, denote the width of a CI. Using $N = 1007$ will only ensure $E[w] \le .15$, implying $w \le .15$ about half of the time and $w \ge .15$ about the other half of the time. Therefore, in the particular study the researcher is going to conduct, there is only about 50% probability that the CI width to be observed will be less than .15. If the researcher desires a higher probability for the event $w \le .15$ to appear in a particular study, the sample size can be planned with an extended procedure that ensures $\Pr(w \le .15) = \gamma$, where γ is referred to as the assurance parameter. For example, in order to achieve $\Pr(w \le .15) = .90$, we can calculate the sample size by specifying ss.aipe.sem.path() as follows:

```
> ss.aipe.sem.path(model=model.full, Sigma=Sigma.1, desired.
width=.15, which.path="l1", conf.level=0.95, assurance=.90),
```

where assurance is the assurance parameter. This call to the function will return $N = 1,064$. Thus, if the researcher increases the sample size from 1,007 to 1,064, there will be at least a 90% probability that $w \le .15$ in the particular study to be carried out.

Empirical Demonstration 2

The second empirical demonstration is for a bifactor model and a second-order model, both of which are important special cases of CFA models. Suppose, in addition to the latent construct cognition, there are two other latent constructs in the study, coping and social support, and they are measured by three and four indicators, respectively. Further suppose that the researcher hypothesizes that there is a more

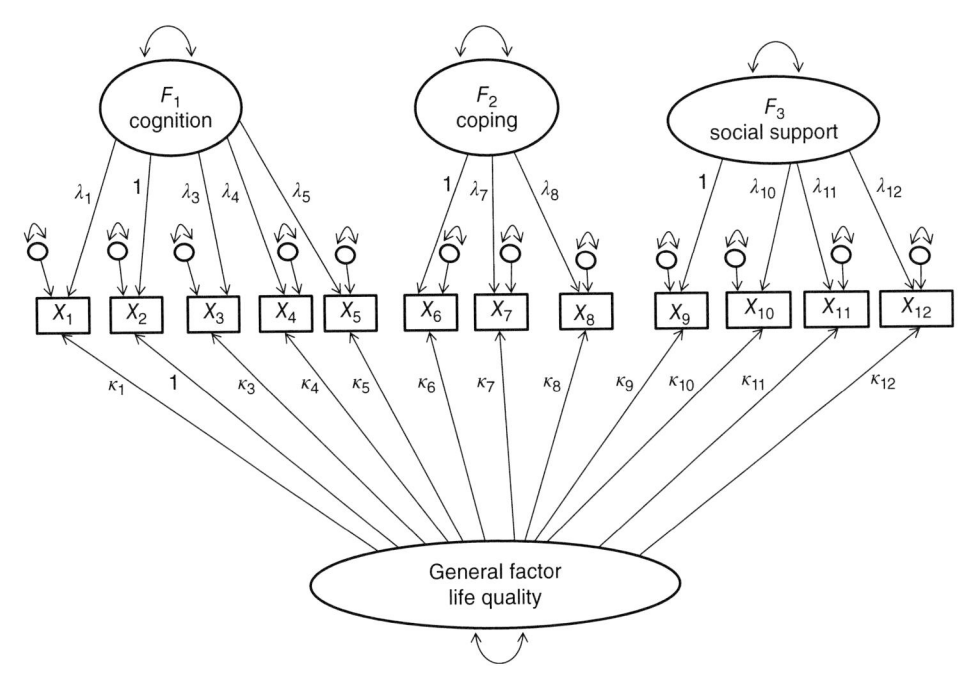

Figure 5.2 Bifactor model representation of items, where each item is measured from a specific factor (Cognition, Coping, or Social Support) and a general factor (Life Quality).

general factor than cognition, coping, and social support and terms this factor quality of life. Let cognition, coping, and social support be referred to as the specific factors, and let quality of life be referred to as the general factor. The dynamics among the general factor and specific factors can be conceptualized in terms of a bifactor model or a second-order CFA model. More specifically, the bifactor model hypothesizes that the general factor influences all of the 12 manifest variables directly, and the four latent factors are mutually independent. The second-order factor model hypothesizes that the general factor directly influences all the three specific factors, and thus the three specific factors are not independent of each other. The path diagrams for the bifactor model and the second-order factor model are included in Figures 5.2 and 5.3, respectively.

As we have discussed, and shown in Empirical Demonstration 1, the sample size for a bifactor model or second-order model can be planned from four different perspectives, and all the functions and methods we discussed previously are readily applicable in the present context. Therefore, in the present example we do not demonstrate sample size planning from all four perspectives, but rather focus on two interesting questions commonly raised in applications of bifactor and second-order models. First, the researcher often wants to understand whether the bifactor model or the second-order factor model can better explain the data. To address this question, we consider sample size calculations in the context of model comparisons. Second, after the researcher adopts one from these two competing models, some factor loadings within the model will likely be of interest. To address this question, we plan the sample size from the AIPE for model parameter perspective.

[Figure: Second-order factor model diagram showing General factor life quality at top connected to F₁ cognition, F₂ coping, and F₃ social support via γ₁, γ₂, γ₃; each factor connected to indicators X₁–X₁₂ via loadings λ.]

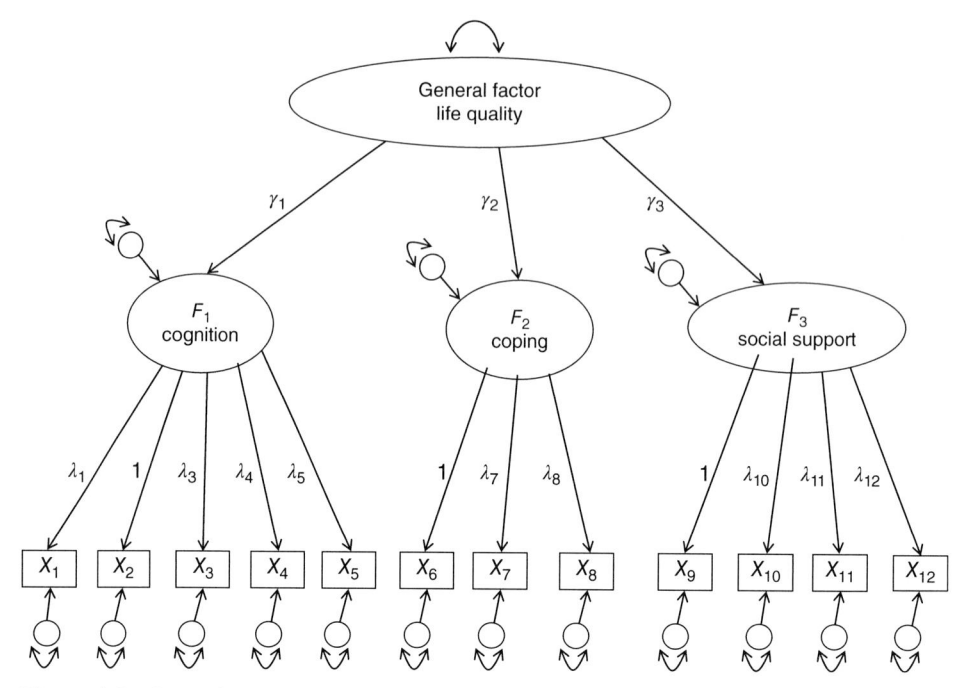

Figure 5.3 Second-order factor model representation of items, where the items are measured from specific factors (Cognition, Coping, or Social Support), and the specific factors are in turn measured from a second-order, higher level factor (Life Quality).

Approach 1: Power analysis comparing a bifactor model and a second-order factor model
Yung, Thissen, and McLeod (1999) proved that the second-order factor model is nested within the bifactor model, and thus will almost always fit less well compared to the bifactor model. Accordingly, one can test the null hypothesis that the second-order factor model fits equally as well as does the bifactor model. Rejecting this null hypothesis leads to the conclusion that the bifactor model has better fit. If one considers the bifactor model as the full model and the second-order factor model as the restricted model, sample size in the current study can be planned with Approach 3 in Empirical Demonstration 1. More specifically, it requires as input information the (1) full and restricted models, (2) Type I error rate, (3) desired power, and (4) population covariance matrix of the manifest variables, Σ. Again, all the input information except (d) can be specified easily. We obtain (4) by first specifying the model parameters in the full model (i.e., the bifactor model).

Following the scheme used in Approach 3 in Empirical Demonstration 1, we specify Σ by first specifying all the standardized model parameter values in the bifactor model (i.e., the full model). Compared to the previous one-factor CFA model with only five indicators, the present bifactor model has a large number of parameters to be specified. To simplify this task, we utilize an exchangeable pattern of factor loadings within the same measurement cluster; that is, indicators that measure the same latent factor have the same standardized factor loadings. The rationale for using the exchangeable pattern in the SEM context to simplify the input information specification is explained in greater detail in Lai and Kelley (2011). In essence, an exchangeable pattern is reasonable because the necessary sample size estimate usually does not differ from the idealized sample size by much. We maintain the input factor loadings for measuring cognition

Table 5.5 Specifying standardized model parameters for the bifactor model in Empirical Demonstration 2.

	General factor	Cognition	Coping	Social support	Error variance
X_1	.500	.550			.4475
X_2	.500	.730			.2171
X_3	.500	.680			.2876
X_4	.500	.750			.1875
X_5	.500	.600			.390
X_6	.600		.600		.280
X_7	.600		.600		.280
X_8	.600		.600		.280
X_9	.700			.450	.3075
X_{10}	.700			.450	.3075
X_{11}	.700			.450	.3075
X_{12}	.700			.450	.3075

in the previous example, and specify all the new factor loadings in an exchangeable manner. The resulting input information for the standardized model parameters are included in Table 5.5. Based on the input information in Table 5.5, the bifactor model will reproduce a correlation matrix of X_1 through X_{12}. Then the researcher should make educated guesses or informed from other studies about the standard deviation of the 12 manifest variables and thereby will obtain an input covariance matrix for sample size planning. We use Σ_2 to denote this input information. All of the syntax that leads to this input covariance matrix is included in Appendix Code 2.

Now that the input information is complete, one can plan the sample size. Note the bifactor model will fit Σ_2 perfectly, but the second-order factor model will have some misfit to Σ_2. More specifically, fitting the second-order factor model to Σ_2 will yield $F_{sec-order} = .01891$ and $\varepsilon_{sec-order} = .01926$. To calculate the necessary sample size so as to have .80 power to reject the null hypothesis that the second-order factor model has the same population fit as does bifactor model, one can use the function ss.power.sem() as follows:

> ss.power.sem(F.full=0, F.res=.01891, df.full=42, df.res=51, alpha=.05, power=.80).

The resulting necessary sample size estimate is $N = 829$. Note this is an application of the Satorra–Saris method to power analysis. Now suppose one does not have enough information to specify Σ_2 and chooses to plan the sample size in terms of RMSEA (an application of the MacCallum et al. method). If the researcher could correctly specify $\varepsilon_{sec-order} = .01926$ as the input information, the sample size returned will be equivalent to the method that uses Σ_2 as input information:

> ss.power.sem(RMSEA.full=0, RMSEA.res=.01926, df.full=42, df.res=51, alpha=.05, power=.80),

which also returns a sample size estimate $N = 829$. Therefore, to demonstrate that the bifactor model subsumes the second-order factor model and has better fit, it requires a sample of size 829, provided that the present input information is correct and all the assumptions are satisfied. Due to the complexity of bifactor and second-order factor models, it is usually not possible for the input RMSEA to exactly equal the population RMSEA. Suppose the researcher believes the difference in fit between the bifactor and second-order factor models is relatively small and uses .02 as the input value for RMSEA:

```
> ss.power.sem(RMSEA.full=0, RMSEA.res=.02, df.full=42,
df.res=51, alpha=.05, power=.80).
```

In this case, the function returns $N = 769$, slightly different from the idealized sample size 829.

Approach 2: AIPE for model parameters in the bifactor model In Approach 4 of Empirical Demonstration 1, the researcher was interested in the value of X_1's factor loading when measuring the latent factor cognition. Suppose in the present bifactor model, this factor loading is still of interest, but there is an extra parameter of interest, namely the loading of X_1 on the general factor, a loading denoted as κ_1. To plan sample size so as to achieve sufficient certainty (i.e., narrow enough CI) in estimating both λ_1 and κ_1, the process is exactly the same as was shown in Approach 4 of Empirical Demonstration 1, except that the researcher needs to perform the process twice, once for λ_1 and once for κ_1. The necessary sample size for the study is simply the larger of the two.

Recall that the input information for AIPE for model parameters is as follows: the (1) the model, (2) model parameter of interest, (3) confidence level, (4) desired expectation value of the CI width, and (5) population covariance matrix of the manifest variables. We continue to use Σ_2 as the input covariance matrix, and all of the other input information can be readily specified by this point. We plan the sample size with respect to λ_1 first. Suppose the desired CI width is still .15. Then the function ss.aipe.sem.path() can be specified as follows:

```
> ss.aipe.sem.path(model=AIPE.bifactor, Sigma=Sigma.2,
desired.width=.15, which.path="l1", conf.level=0.95),
```

where model refers to the model's specification, Sigma refers to the input population covariance matrix Σ_2, and which.path refers to the model parameter of interest. Due to space limit, we did not present the values of Σ_2 in the text, but have included the syntax that leads to Σ_2 in Appendix Code 2. All of the intermediate syntax that is used to specify the bifactor model AIPE.bifactor is included in Appendix Code 2 as well. Note that, although the factor loading of interest and the desired CI width remain the same as the example in Approach 4 of Empirical Demonstration 1, the model and input covariance matrix are different, and the resulting sample size estimate will likely be different as well. Executing this function ss.aipe.sem.path yields $N = 1011$. Next, we plan sample size with respect to κ_1 as follows and set the desired CI width to be .20:

```
> ss.aipe.sem.path(model=AIPE.bifactor, Sigma=Sigma.2,
desired.width=.20, which.path="k1", conf.level=0.95).
```

The necessary sample size estimate is $N = 1491$. Therefore, in order to obtain estimates of both λ_1 and for κ_1 with confidence intervals of desired width, the study needs a sample of size 1,491.

In addition to planning the sample size with respect to the expected CI width, one can include the assurance parameter in the process, so as to ensure a higher probability of observing a sufficiently narrow CI in a particular study. For example, we can use $\gamma = .90$ and plan the sample size again for for λ_1 and for κ_1:

```
> ss.aipe.sem.path(model=model.bifactor, Sigma=Sigma.2,
desired.width=.15, which.path="l1", conf.level=0.95,
assurance=.90)
> ss.aipe.sem.path(model=model.bifactor, Sigma=Sigma.2,
desired.width=.20, which.path="k1", conf.level=0.95,
assurance=.90).
```

The resulting sample size estimates are 1,068 and 1,560, respectively, and thus the study's planned sample size is 1,560.

Conclusion

In this chapter, we have discussed sample size planning in the context of CFA for omnibus and targeted effects from both the power analytic as well as the AIPE approaches. These ideas are general, but we illustrated our ideas specifically in the context of the CFA model, a model that is extremely important in psychometrics and in related fields that use psychometric principles.

We hope that our chapter will be useful for researchers considering a CFA (or even an SEM) study, because the chapter lays out a general framework for considering effect sizes and research goals. Our chapter shows that there is no simple answer to planning sample size for a CFA (or SEM) analysis, as the appropriate sample size necessarily depends on the effect size of interest (e.g., fit index or path coefficient), the goals of the study (to show the existence of an effect or its magnitude), the characteristics of the population under study (e.g., estimated/hypothesized values of covariance), and the desired likelihood of satisfying the goals (e.g., the degree of power or the level of assurance in AIPE). Taken together, we hope that the general framework to sample size planning we have discussed, and the software provided, will facilitate an understanding of the variety of issues involved in sample size planning for CFA.

References

Brown, T. A. (2006). *Confirmatory factor analysis for applied research*. New York, NY: Guilford.
Cohen, J. (1988). *Statistical power analysis for the behavioral sciences* (2nd ed.). Hillsdale, NJ: Erlbaum.
Cohen, J. (1994). The earth is round (p < .05). *American Psychologist, 49*, 997–1003.
Cudeck, R. (1989). Analysis of correlation matrices using covariance structure models. *Psychological Bulletin, 105*, 317–327.
Kelley, K., & Lai, K. (2014). MBESS (Version 3.0.0 and more recent) [computer software and manual], Accessible from http://cran.r-project.org/web/packages/MBESS/index.html.
Kelley, K., & Maxwell, S. E. (2003). Sample size for multiple regression: Obtaining regression coefficients that are accurate, not simply significant. *Psychological Methods, 8*, 305–321.

Kelley, K., & Maxwell, S. E. (2008). Power and accuracy for omnibus and targeted effects: Issues of sample size planning with applications to multiple regression. In P. Alasuuta, L. Bickman, & J. Brannen (Eds.), *Handbook of social research methods* (pp. 166–192). Newbury Park, CA: Sage.

Kelley, K., & Maxwell, S. E. (2012). Sample size planning. In H. Cooper (Ed.), *APA handbook of research methods in psychology* (pp. 181–202). Washington, DC: American Psychological Association.

Kelley, K., & Preacher, K. J. (2012). On effect size. *Psychological Methods, 17*, 137–152.

Lai, K., & Kelley, K. (2011). Accuracy in parameter estimation for targeted effects in structural equation modeling: Sample size planning for narrow confidence intervals. *Psychological Methods, 16*, 127–148.

Lin, T. Y., & Weng, L. J. (2014). Graphical extension of sample size planning with AIPE on RMSEA. *Structural Equation Modeling: A Multidisciplinary Journal, 21*, 482–490.

MacCallum, R. C., Browne, M. W., & Cai, L. (2006). Testing differences between nested covariance structure models: Power analysis and null hypotheses. *Psychological Methods, 11*, 19–35.

Maxwell, S. E., Kelley, K., & Rausch, J. R. (2008). Sample size planning for statistical power and accuracy in parameter estimation. *Annual Review of Psychology, 59*, 537–563.

R Core Team. (2014). *R: A language and environment for statistical computing*. Vienna, Austria: R Foundation for Statistical Computing.

Satorra, A., & Saris, W. E. (1985). Power of the likelihood ratio test in covariance structure analysis. *Psychometrika, 50*, 83–90.

Venables, W. N., Smith, D. M., & The R Core Team (2014). *An introduction to R.* Available at: https://cran.r-project.org/doc/manuals/R-intro.pdf (accessed September 6, 2017).

Yung. Y., Thissen, D., & McLeod, L. D. (1999). On the relationship between the higher-order factor model and the hierarchical factor model. *Psychometrika, 64*, 113–128.

Code Appendix

Code 1   R Code for Approaches 3 and 4 in Empirical Demonstration 1.

Step 1: Create the input covariance matrix.

We first load the packages MBESS and sem.

```
> library(MBESS)
> library(sem)
```

We start specifying the full model using the function `specifyModel()` in the sem package as follows. Each line of the model specification refers to one model parameter and consists of three parts, separated by comma: (1) to identify the model parameter, (2) parameter name, and (3) start value. For example, the argument "F1 -> X1, 11, .580" below means "the model parameter from F_1 to X_1; parameter name 11; start value .580." The argument "F1 <-> F1, NA, 1" below means "covariance between F_1 and F_1; not a free parameter; value fixed at 1." The argument "X1 <-> X1, e1, .6636" below means "covariance between error of X_1 and error of X_1 (i.e., error variance); parameter name e1; start value .6636."

```
> model.full <- specifyModel()
F1 -> X1, l1, .580
F1 -> X2, l2, 0.720
F1 -> X3, l3, 0.680
F1 -> X4, l4, 0.750
F1 -> X5, l5, .600
F1 <-> F1, NA, 1
X1 <-> X1, e1, .6636
X2 <-> X2, e2, .4816
X3 <-> X3, e3, .5376
X4 <-> X4, e4, .4375
X5 <-> X5, e5, .640
```

We then specify the vector of standardized model parameters θ as follows.

```
> theta <- c( .580, .720, .680, .750, .600,
.6636, .4816, .5376, .4375, .640)
> names(theta) <- c("l1","l2", "l3","l4","l5",
"e1", "e2","e3","e4", "e5")
```

We then obtain the model-implied correlation matrix $P(\theta)$ given θ and the full model as follows, using the theta.2.Sigma.theta() function in the MBESS package. The argument latent.vars indicates which variables in the model specification model.full are latent variables.

```
> res <- theta.2.Sigma.theta(model=model.full, theta=theta,
latent.vars=c("F1"))
> P.theta <- res$Sigma.theta
```

Given $P(\theta)$ and the standard deviations of manifest variables, we calculate the model-implied covariance matrix $\Sigma(\theta)$. The result Sigma.1 below is Σ_1 we referred to in the text.

```
> Sigma.1 <- cor2cov(P.theta, sd=c(1.2, 1.3, 0.7, 1.2, 1.1))
```

Step 2: Fit the input covariance matrix to the restricted model and obtain the ML discrepancy function value.

Note in the model specification below the factor loadings for X_1 and X_2 have the same name. This places the equality constraint on the two parameters, as the restricted model proposed.

```
> model.res <- specifyModel()
F1 -> X1, l1, .580
F1 -> X2, l1, 0.580
F1 -> X3, l3, 0.680
F1 -> X4, l4, 0.750
F1 -> X5, l5, .600
```

```
F1 <-> F1, NA,  1
X1 <-> X1, e1, .6636
X2 <-> X2, e2, .4816
X3 <-> X3, e3, .5376
X4 <-> X4, e4, .4375
X5 <-> X5, e5, .640
```

Next we fit the restricted model to $\Sigma(\theta)$ and obtain F^*_{Res} (see Equation 8). Because the model estimating function sem() within the sem package requires a sample size but we are interested in the population, we can simply assign an arbitrarily large value to the argument N as follows. The object F.res contains the value of F^*_{Res}.

```
> res2 <- sem(model=model.res, S=Sigma.1, N=1000001)
> F.res <- res2$criterion
```

Step 3a: Plan the sample size for sufficient statistical power.

Now that we have F^*_{Res}, we can plan the sample size from the power analytic perspective, using Approach 3 explained in Empirical Demonstration 1. We employ the ss.power.sem() function in the MBESS package as follows.

```
> ss.power.sem(F.full=0, F.res=F.res, df.full=5,
  df.res=6, alpha=.05, power=.80)
```

Step 3b: Plan the sample size for narrow confidence interval.

If the interest is in finding a necessary sample that ensures a sufficiently narrow confidence interval (i.e., Approach 4 in Empirical Demonstration 1), the function ss.aipe.sem.path in the MBESS package can be used. The model parameter of interest is λ_1 in the path diagram in Figure 1, or equivalently l1 in the previous specification of the full model in Step 1. The input covariance matrix Σ_1 (i.e., Sigma.1) was obtained previously in Step 1 as well.

```
> ss.aipe.sem.path(model=model.full, Sigma=Sigma.1,
  desired.width=.15, which.path="l1", conf.level=0.95)
```

Code 2 R Code for Approaches 1 and 2 in Empirical Demonstration 2.

This appendix code uses the same functions as does Code 1. Explanations for all the arguments and objects are available in Code 1, except for the ones newly introduced in the present code.

Step 1: Create the input covariance matrix.

```
> library(MBESS)
> library(sem)

> bifactor.std.coef <- specifyModel()
G -> X1, k1, 0.5
G -> X2, k2, 0.5
G -> X3, k3, 0.5
G -> X4, k4, 0.5
G -> X5, k5, 0.5
G -> X6, k6, 0.6
G -> X7, k7, 0.6
G -> X8, k8, 0.6
G -> X9, k9, 0.7
G -> X10, k10, 0.7
G -> X11, k11, 0.7
G -> X12, k12, 0.7
F1 -> X1, l1, .550
F1 -> X2, l2, 0.73
F1 -> X3, l3, 0.68
F1 -> X4, l4, 0.75
F1 -> X5, l5, .6
F2 -> X6, l6, 0.6
F2 -> X7, l7, 0.6
F2 -> X8, l8, 0.6
F3 -> X9, l9, .45
F3 -> X10, l10, 0.45
F3 -> X11, l11, 0.45
F3 -> X12, l12, 0.45
G <-> G, NA, 1
F1 <-> F1, NA, 1
F2 <-> F2, NA, 1
F3 <-> F3, NA, 1
X1 <-> X1, e1, .4475
X2 <-> X2, e2, .2171
X3 <-> X3, e3, .2876
X4 <-> X4, e4, .1875
X5 <-> X5, e5, .39
X6 <-> X6, e6, .28
X7 <-> X7, e7, .28
X8 <-> X8, e8, .28
X9 <-> X9, e9, .3075
```

```
X10 <-> X10, e10, .3075
X11 <-> X11, e11, .3075
X12 <-> X12, e12, .3075

> theta <- c(rep(0.5, 5), rep(.6, 3), rep(.7, 4),
.55, .73, .68, .75, .6, rep(.6,3), rep(.45,4),
.4475, .2171, .2876, .1875, .39, rep(.28,3), rep(.3075, 4))

> names(theta) <- c("k1", "k2", "k3", "k4", "k5", "k6", "k7",
"k8", "k9", "k10", "k11", "k12", "l1", "l2", "l3", "l4", "l5",
"l6", "l7", "l8", "l9", "l10", "l11", "l12", "e1", "e2", "e3",
"e4", "e5", "e6", "e7", "e8", "e9", "e10", "e11", "e12")

> res <- theta.2.Sigma.theta(model=bifactor.std.coef,
theta=theta, latent.vars=c("G", "F1","F2","F3"))

> P.theta.2 <- res$Sigma.theta

> Sigma.2 <- cor2cov(P.theta.2, sd=c(1.2, 1.2, 0.7, 1.3,
1.1, 1.5,1.6,1.7, 2.2,2.3,2.1,2.4))
```

Step 2: Fit the input covariance matrix to the second-order factor model and obtain the ML discrepancy function value.

```
> CFA.2order <- specifyModel()
G  -> F1, NA, 1
G  -> F2, g2, .4
G  -> F3, g3, .4
F1 -> X1, NA, 1
F1 -> X2, l2, 0.6
F1 -> X3, l3, 0.6
F1 -> X4, l4, 0.6
F1 -> X5, l5, .6
F2 -> X6, NA, 1
F2 -> X7, l7, 0.6
F2 -> X8, l8, 0.6
F3 -> X9, NA, 1
F3 -> X10, l10, 0.6
F3 -> X11, l11, 0.6
F3 -> X12, l12, 0.6
G  <-> G, r, 1
F1 <-> F1, p1, .5
F2 <-> F2, p2, .5
F3 <-> F3, p3, .5
X1 <-> X1, e1, .7
X2 <-> X2, e2, .7
X3 <-> X3, e3, .7
X4 <-> X4, e4, .7
```

```
X5  <-> X5,  e5,  .7
X6  <-> X6,  e6,  .7
X7  <-> X7,  e7,  .7
X8  <-> X8,  e8,  .7
X9  <-> X9,  e9,  .7
X10 <-> X10, e10, .7
X11 <-> X11, e11, .7
X12 <-> X12, e12, .7

> res2 <- sem(model=CFA.2order, S=Sigma.2, N=1000001)

> F.2order <- res2$criterion
```

Step 3a: Plan the sample size so as to obtain statistical power to demonstrate the bifactor model has better fit than the second-order model.

```
> ss.power.sem(F.full=0, F.res=F.2order, df.full=42,
df.res=51, alpha=.05, power=.80)
```

Step 3b: Plan the sample size so as to obtain narrow confidence intervals for bifactor model parameters.

The model specification `AIPE.bifactor` below implies the same model as does `bifactor.std.coef` in Step 1 previously, but uses a more common way to identify the model. The identification `bifactor.std.coef` makes it more convenient to specify model parameters in the standardized metric but is less common for analyzing covariance matrices.

```
> AIPE.bifactor <- specifyModel()
G  -> X1,  k1,  1
G  -> X2,  NA,  1
G  -> X3,  k3,  0.5
G  -> X4,  k4,  0.5
G  -> X5,  k5,  0.5
G  -> X6,  k6,  0.6
G  -> X7,  k7,  0.6
G  -> X8,  k8,  0.6
G  -> X9,  k9,  0.7
G  -> X10, k10, 0.7
G  -> X11, k11, 0.7
G  -> X12, k12, 0.7
F1 -> X1,  l1,  1
F1 -> X2,  NA,  1
F1 -> X3,  l3,  0.68
F1 -> X4,  l4,  0.75
F1 -> X5,  l5,  .6
F2 -> X6,  NA,  1
F2 -> X7,  l7,  0.6
F2 -> X8,  l8,  0.6
```

```
F3 -> X9, NA, 1
F3 -> X10, l10, 0.45
F3 -> X11, l11, 0.45
F3 -> X12, l12, 0.45
G <-> G, r, 1
F1 <-> F1, p1, 1
F2 <-> F2, p2, 1
F3 <-> F3, p3, 1
X1 <-> X1, e1, .4475
X2 <-> X2, e2, .2171
X3 <-> X3, e3, .2876
X4 <-> X4, e4, .1875
X5 <-> X5, e5, .39
X6 <-> X6, e6, .28
X7 <-> X7, e7, .28
X8 <-> X8, e8, .28
X9 <-> X9, e9, .3075
X10 <-> X10, e10, .3075
X11 <-> X11, e11, .3075
X12 <-> X12, e12, .3075

> ss.aipe.sem.path(model=AIPE.bifactor, Sigma=Sigma.2,
desired.width=.15, which.path="l1", conf.level=0.95)

> ss.aipe.sem.path(model=AIPE.bifactor, Sigma=Sigma.2,
desired.width=.20, which.path="k1", conf.level=0.95)
```

6
Missing Data Handling Methods
Craig K. Enders and Amanda N. Baraldi

Missing data are an exceedingly common problem for psychometricians and researchers employing psychometric methods. The missing data handling literature dates back several decades, with major developments occurring in the 1970s when methodologists developed the underpinnings of maximum likelihood estimation and multiple imputation (Beale & Little, 1975; Dempster, Laird, & Rubin, 1977; Rubin, 1978, 1987). Because they are computationally demanding, these approaches did not enjoy widespread use for many years. However, maximum likelihood and multiple imputation routines are now widely available in general-purpose and specialized software programs, and most methodologists regard these techniques as a gold standard (Schafer & Graham, 2002).

The goal of this chapter is to provide readers with a broad introduction to missing data handling issues, with a strong emphasis on maximum likelihood estimation and multiple imputation. The organization of the chapter is as follows. We begin with an overview of Rubin's (1976) theoretical work, as his missing data mechanisms describe the conditions under which these two methods achieve optimal statistical properties (and conversely, the conditions under which they fail). After a brief discussion of two older strategies – deletion and single imputation – we spend the majority of the chapter discussing maximum likelihood and multiple imputation. Next, we use an artificial data set to illustrate the application of these methods to some common psychometric analyses. Finally, we conclude with an overview of planned missing data designs.

We use an artificial data set to illustrate key ideas throughout the chapter. The data were patterned after a study that examined an online chronic pain management program (Ruehlman, Karoly, & Enders, 2012). At the start of the study, the researchers collected a number of background variables (e.g., age, frequency of exercise, gender) as well as psychological variables such as depression and pain catastrophizing (the tendency to believe that pain is far worse than it actually is). Individuals in the treatment group participated in the online pain management program for several weeks, whereas

---

The Wiley Handbook of Psychometric Testing: A Multidisciplinary Reference on Survey, Scale and Test Development, First Edition. Edited by Paul Irwing, Tom Booth, and David J. Hughes.
© 2018 John Wiley & Sons Ltd. Published 2020 by John Wiley & Sons Ltd.

Table 6.1 Variables in artificial data set.

Name	Description	Range	Missing
TXGROUP	Treatment condition (0 = control, 1 = treatment group)	0–1	0.0%
FEMALE	Respondent gender (0 = male, 1 = female)	0–1	0.0%
AGE	Respondent age	18–79	6.0%
EXERCISE	Frequency of exercise	1–20	8.0%
Pain Catastrophizing Scale			
CATAST1	When I'm in pain, I worry all the time.	1–6	10.0%
CATAST2	When I'm in pain, I feel I can't go on.	1–6	3.2%
CATAST3	When I'm in pain, it's awful and I feel overwhelmed.	1–6	0.0%
CATAST4	When I'm in pain, I feel I can't stand it anymore.	1–6	6.4%
Depression Scale			
DEPRESS1	I couldn't seem to experience any positive feeling.	1–4	0.0%
DEPRESS2	I just couldn't seem to get going.	1–4	4.2%
DEPRESS3	I felt that I had nothing to look forward to.	1–4	2.0%
DEPRESS4	I felt sad and depressed.	1–4	0.6%
DEPRESS5	I felt that I had lost interest in just about everything.	1–4	7.8%
DEPRESS6	I felt I wasn't worth much as a person.	1–4	0.0%
DEPRESS7	I felt that life wasn't worthwhile.	1–4	13.4%
Pain Interference Scale			
PAININT1	Pain interferes with enjoyable activities.	1–7	0.6%
PAININT2	Pain interferes with responsibilities at home.	1–7	9.6%
PAININT3	Pain interferes with relationships.	1–7	1.8%
PAININT4	Pain interferes with personal goals.	1–7	2.4%
PAININT5	Pain interferes with self-care.	1–7	0.0%
PAININT6	Pain interferes with thinking clearly or remembering.	1–7	0.0%
Pain Severity			
SEVERITY	Rate your average level of pain.	1–7	8.6%

individuals in the waitlist control group received no treatment. At the end of the intervention period, researchers administered scales that measured pain severity and pain interference with daily life.

To obtain an artificial data set that mimicked the one from the Ruehlman et al. (2012) study, we fit a multiple group structural equation model to the original data and used the resulting parameter estimates to generate a sample of $N = 500$ cases. The resulting artificial data set approximates the mean and covariance structure of the original and preserves the metrics of the variables (e.g., ordinal questionnaire items, continuous background measures such as age, etc.). For simplicity, we imposed a missing completely at random (MCAR) mechanism on a subset of the variables, with missing data rates ranging between approximately 1 and 34%. Table 6.1 gives a list of the variables in the data set along with their ranges and missing data rates. As seen in the table, the data include three scales comprised of multiple questionnaire items: a four-item pain catastrophizing scale, seven-item depression scale, and six-item pain interference scale. All questionnaire items, including pain severity ratings, have discrete response options. The data set and input files for subsequent analysis examples are available at www.appliedmissingdata.com.

Missing Data Mechanisms

Rubin and colleagues (Little & Rubin, 2002; Rubin, 1976) developed the modern theoretical framework for missing data problems. Rubin's theory defines the probability of missing data as a random variable that varies across respondents. His so-called missing data mechanisms – MCAR, missing at random, and not missing at random – describe different associations between these missingness probabilities and the data. In practical terms, missing data mechanisms function as assumptions for a missing data analysis, as they describe the conditions under which we can obtain accurate (consistent) parameter estimates.

To establish some notation for this section, we use Y_{com} to denote the hypothetical complete-data matrix. Y_{com} can be partitioned into observed and missing components, Y_{obs} and Y_{mis}, respectively. The would-be values in Y_{mis} exist in principle but are not observed in the sample data. As noted previously, Rubin views the probability of missing data as a random variable that varies across respondents. To capture this idea, each variable in Y_{com} has a corresponding missing data indicator that denotes whether scores are observed or missing (e.g., 0 = observed, 1 = missing). These missing data indicators are assembled in a matrix R that has the same dimension as Y_{com}. Defining R as a set of random variables implies that the missingness probabilities may depend on the data, and the missing data mechanisms describe different associations between R and Y_{com}.

To begin, the MCAR mechanism specifies that the probability of missingness is unrelated to both observed and unobserved scores. In formal terms, the MCAR mechanism is

$$p(R|Y_{com}) = p(R|Y_{obs}, Y_{mis}) = p(R) \tag{6.1}$$

where p is generic notation for a probability distribution. In words, Equation 6.1 says that the probability of missingness is the same for all respondents, such that the observed scores are a simple random sample of the hypothetical complete data. In the context of the pain study, MCAR could occur, for example, if a respondent inadvertently skips an item, or if researchers purposefully distribute the item pool across different test forms (e.g., a planned missing data design). In the context of educational testing, an MCAR mechanism would occur when an item pool is randomly distributed across different test forms (Mislevy, 2016). Note that MCAR can occur when unmeasured variables predict missingness, but these variables must be uncorrelated with the data in order for to Equation 6.1 to hold.

The missing at random (MAR) mechanism is less restrictive in the sense that the probability of missing data can depend on the observed scores in Y_{obs} but not on the would-be values in Y_{mis}. More formally, the MAR mechanism is

$$p(R|Y_{com}) = p(R|Y_{obs}, Y_{mis}) = p(R|Y_{obs}). \tag{6.2}$$

In words, Equation 6.2 says that the probability of missing data on a particular variable depends solely on the observed values of some other variable. In the pain study, MAR could occur, for example, if background variables such as gender or age predict nonresponse on certain questionnaire items. In a testing scenario, an MAR mechanism occurs with computer adaptive tests that select items from a pool, conditional on previous responses (Mislevy, 2016).

Importantly, MAR stipulates that missingness is conditionally independent of the unobserved item responses after controlling for these background variables. That is, for two respondents with identical demographic characteristics, the probability of missing data is purely random. MAR has been referred to as conditionally random for this reason (Graham, 2009). Finally, it is important to note that Equation 6.2 specifies a generic relation as opposed to a causal linkage. As such, MAR can occur because a measured variable directly influences missingness or because an unmeasured variable that predicts missingness is correlated with the data, thereby inducing a relation between R and Y_{obs}.

Finally, the not missing at random (NMAR) condition is the most general mechanism in the sense that it allows missingness probabilities to depend on both Y_{com} and Y_{mis}. More formally, the NMAR mechanism is

$$p(R|Y_{com}) = p(R|Y_{obs}, Y_{mis}). \tag{6.3}$$

In words, Equation 6.3 says that the probability of missing data on a particular variable depends on the would-be values of that variable, even after controlling for the observed values of other variables. In the pain study, NMAR could occur, for example, if participants with no depressive symptoms are more likely to skip the depression questions, perhaps because they perceive the items as not applicable to their situation. In a testing scenario, an NMAR mechanism could occur when an examinee intentionally skips an item because he does not possess sufficient knowledge to judge whether his intended response is correct (Mislevy, 2016).

From a practical perspective, missing data mechanisms are important because they describe the conditions under which we can obtain accurate (consistent) parameter estimates. Specifically, Rubin (1976) showed that excluding incomplete cases from an analysis requires MCAR and yields biased estimates with MAR and NMAR mechanisms. In contrast, he showed that maximum likelihood estimation with all available observed data produces consistent estimates under an MCAR or MAR mechanism. The same is true for multiple imputation. Finally, NMAR mechanisms require the researcher to incorporate (and correctly specify) an explicit model for the distribution of missingness probabilities. For example, the missingness model may consist of logistic regressions that predict a set of binary missing data indicators (e.g., a selection model), or it may involve estimating the parameters of interest within each missing data pattern (e.g., a pattern mixture model). Obtaining accurate estimates with an NMAR mechanism is usually very difficult because researchers do not have the necessary information to correctly specify the missingness model. NMAR analysis models are beyond the scope of this chapter, but detailed descriptions of these techniques are available in the literature (Enders, 2010, 2011; Little, 2009; Little & Rubin, 2002; Muthén, Asparouhov, Hunter, & Leuchter, 2011).

Illustrative Computer Simulation

In this section, we use illustrative computer simulations to demonstrate the impact of missing data mechanisms on the quality of the resulting parameter estimates. To keep things simple, we focus on coefficient alpha reliability estimates for a six-item scale. The population covariance matrix for the simulations derived from a single-factor model with a factor variance equal to unity, loadings equal to .70, and residual variances equal to .51. Collectively, these parameters imply a population reliability of .852. We used Mplus 7 (Muthén & Muthén, 1998–2012) to generate 1,000 samples of $N = 500$ and subsequently imposed a 20% missing data rate on three items. To simulate an MCAR mechanism where missingness is unrelated to the data, we randomly deleted scores. In the MAR simulation, the value of an auxiliary variable (a variable not in the factor model) determined missingness, such that higher scores were associated with higher rates of missingness on the three scale items. The scale items themselves influenced missingness in the NMAR simulation, with higher scores again producing a higher probability of missing data. We used maximum likelihood missing data handling and listwise deletion (i.e., excluding all cases with missing data) to estimate coefficient alpha in each artificial data set, and we evaluated the performance of these methods by comparing their average estimates to the true population value. For simplicity, we did not examine multiple imputation because it would produce estimates that are virtually identical to those of maximum likelihood. The Mplus input files for the simulation are available at www.appliedmissingdata.com.

Table 6.2 gives the average reliability estimates for each mechanism and missing data handling technique. To facilitate interpretation, we computed standardized bias by dividing the difference between the average estimates and population parameter by the standard deviation of the 1,000 complete-data estimates. Collins, Schafer, and Kam (2001) characterized standardized bias values greater than ± .40 as problematic. In the MCAR simulation, maximum likelihood and listwise deletion produced estimates that were effectively identical and free from bias. Although there appears to be no meaningful difference between the two methods, the listwise deletion estimates had considerably higher sampling variation; the standard deviation of the estimates was .0145 versus .0107 for maximum likelihood. To put this in perspective, the ratio of the squared standard deviations indicates that an 84% increase in the listwise deletion sample size would be necessary to achieve the sampling variance of maximum likelihood! Turning to the MAR simulation, maximum likelihood estimates exhibited virtually no bias, whereas deleting cases produced substantial bias. Finally, both methods produced bias under an NMAR mechanism, although the maximum likelihood estimates were considerably more accurate. The results in Table 6.2 are consistent with Rubin's (1976) theoretical work and dozens of empirical studies (Enders, 2010).

Table 6.2 Reliability estimates and bias values from the illustrative computer simulations.

Mechanism	Population value	Maximum likelihood Average estimate	Maximum likelihood Standardized bias	Listwise deletion Average estimate	Listwise deletion Standardized bias
MCAR	0.852	0.851	−0.046	0.851	−0.066
MAR	0.852	0.851	−0.055	0.839	−0.639
NMAR	0.852	0.841	−0.559	0.812	−1.995

Note. Standardized bias is the difference between the average reliability estimate and the population parameter divided by the standard deviation of the estimates from the complete data.

Older Missing Data Handling Methods

Methodologists have been interested in missing data issues for several decades, and the literature is replete with strategies for dealing with the problem, many of which have no theoretical rationale or are otherwise flawed. Unfortunately, reviews of published articles suggest that researchers still rely heavily on these flawed procedures (Jeličić, Phelps, & Lerner, 2009; Peugh & Enders, 2004; Wood, White, & Thompson, 2004). Older methods generally fall into one of two categories: deletion or single imputation. Perhaps because it is usually the default missing data handling strategy in general-purpose software packages, deletion is by far the most common of the older methods. Listwise deletion eliminates all cases with missing values from the data set, whereas pairwise deletion excludes cases on an analysis-by-analysis basis (e.g., a published correlation matrix where Ns vary across associations). The obvious downside to deletion is a reduction in power, but it also requires the restrictive MCAR mechanism where the probability of missingness is unrelated to measured variables. The previous simulations showed that deletion produces accurate (albeit noisy) estimates when MCAR holds, but the procedure is otherwise prone to substantial bias. The problems with deletion are well documented in the literature, leading the American Psychological Association Task Force on Statistical Inference to conclude that these approaches are "among the worst methods available for practical applications" (Wilkinson & the Task Force on Statistical Inference, 1999, p. 598).

Although they appear to be less common in substantive applications, the literature also describes a number of so-called single-imputation techniques that fill in the missing values with a single set of replacement values (this is in contrast to multiple imputation, which creates several copies of the data, each with different replacement values). This broad collection of methods includes imputing missing values with (1) the arithmetic mean (mean imputation), (2) predicted values from a regression equation (regression imputation), (3) observed scores from an individual with similar background characteristics (hot deck or similar response pattern imputation), (4) an individual's average score across a set of observed item responses (person mean imputation), and (5) scores from a previous wave in a longitudinal study (last observation carried forward), among others. Single-imputation techniques generally do not have a theoretical rationale and often produce biased estimates under any missing data mechanism. Because their shortcomings are widely documented in the literature, we do not discuss these methods here. A number of resources are available to readers who want additional information (Enders, 2010; Little & Rubin, 2002; Schafer & Graham, 2002; Widaman, 2006).

Maximum Likelihood Estimation

Maximum likelihood estimation identifies the population parameter values with the highest probability of producing the sample data. Notice that the goal is to estimate the parameters of a statistical model rather than impute missing values – this is in contrast to multiple imputation, where the goal is to fill in the data. From the user's perspective, maximum likelihood estimation with incomplete data is not much different from a complete-data analysis because missing data handling is integrated into the estimation routine; the analyst simply feeds an incomplete data set into a capable software package and estimates a model (e.g., means and covariances, a regression model, a confirmatory factor analysis model, etc.). The estimator uses an iterative optimization algorithm to "audition" different sets of parameter values, and it does so using all available data, including the incomplete records. Although estimation does not produce a filled-in data set, methodologists have described maximum likelihood as "implicit imputation" because it effectively generates temporary imputations at each iteration of the optimization routine (Widaman, 2006). We illustrate this idea later in the section.

The starting point for a maximum likelihood analysis is to specify a distribution for the population data (e.g., multivariate normal, multinomial, etc.). The population distribution is used as a basis for assessing model-data fit, but it also provides a mechanism for temporarily "imputing" missing values during estimation. We describe maximum likelihood in the context of multivariate normal data, but the logic of estimation is the same with other distributions. We previously stated that maximum likelihood identifies the population parameter values that are most likely to have produced the sample data. With multivariate normal data, the goal is to identify the mean vector and covariance matrix that maximizes fit to the observed data. The estimator uses a mathematical function called a log likelihood to quantify the discrepancy between the population parameters and the data. The log likelihood for multivariate normal data is

$$\log L_i = \log \left[\frac{1}{(2\pi)^{\frac{k}{2}} |\Sigma_i|^{.5}} e^{-\frac{1}{2}(Y_i - \mu_i)^T \Sigma_i^{-1}(Y_i - \mu_i)} \right] \quad (6.4)$$

$$= -\frac{k}{2}\log(2\pi) - \frac{1}{2}\log|\Sigma_i| - \frac{1}{2}(Y_i - \mu_i)^T \Sigma_i^{-1}(Y_i - \mu_i)$$

where the bracketed terms are the multivariate normal density function, k is the number of complete variables for case i, Y_i is the score vector for that individual, and μ_i and Σ_i are the mean vector and covariance matrix, respectively (the parameters being estimated). The sample log likelihood is obtained by computing Equation 6.4 for each case and summing the N values.

There are several ways to understand the log likelihood equation. In a general sense, the equation quantifies fit between one case's observed data and the population parameters in μ_i and Σ_i. The log likelihood yields a negative value, the magnitude of which captures the standardized difference between the scores and the means in Y_i and μ_i, respectively; scores close to the center of the distribution produce higher (i.e., less negative) log likelihood values, whereas scores far from the center of the distribution produce lower (i.e., more negative) log likelihood values. Equation 6.4 can also be viewed as the relative probability that the scores in Y_i originated from a multivariate normal distribution with the parameter values in μ_i and Σ_i. As noted previously, the collection of terms in square brackets is the multivariate normal distribution function. Substituting a score vector and parameter values into the expression yields a probability-like value that increases as scores get closer to the mean (the highest likelihood or relative probability corresponds to a score vector that is identical to mean vector). The log likelihood is natural logarithm of this probability. Finally, the equation also has a geometric interpretation. Substituting a score vector and parameter values into the normal distribution function yields a likelihood value that represents the "height" of the multivariate normal distribution at that score vector. The log likelihood is the natural logarithm of this height value.

Much of Equation 6.4 is simply a scaling factor that ensures that the area under the distribution sums (i.e., integrates) to one. The key kernel of the log likelihood equation is Mahalanobis distance, a collection of terms that represents the standardized difference between the scores and the means as a squared z score, as follows.

$$z_i^2 = (\mathbf{Y}_i - \boldsymbol{\mu}_i)^T \boldsymbol{\Sigma}_i^{-1} (\mathbf{Y}_i - \boldsymbol{\mu}_i) \tag{6.5}$$

The log likelihood value from Equation 6.4 is largely determined by Mahalanobis distance, such that small z scores produce larger (i.e., less negative) log likelihood values, and large z scores yield smaller (i.e., more negative) log likelihoods. The goal of estimation is to identify the parameter values that minimize the sum of the squared z values. In this sense, maximum likelihood is very similar to ordinary least squares regression.

Thus far, we have explained the log likelihood equation without raising the issue of missing data. We previously noted that missing data handling is integrated into the estimation routine and that estimation uses all available data, including the incomplete records. Returning to log likelihood in Equation 6.4, notice that the score vector and parameter matrices have an i subscript. This subscript allows the size and contents of the matrices to differ across missing data patterns, such the squared z score (and thus the log likelihood) depends only the observed scores for case i. To illustrate, consider a simple scenario with three incomplete variables, Y_1, Y_2, and Y_3. Further, suppose that data have three missing data patterns: (1) complete data on all variables, (2) missing values on Y_3, and (3) missing values on Y_1 and Y_2.

The Mahalanobis distance measure for cases with complete data is as follows.

$$z_i^2 = (\mathbf{Y}_i - \boldsymbol{\mu}_i)^T \boldsymbol{\Sigma}_i^{-1} (\mathbf{Y}_i - \boldsymbol{\mu}_i)$$

$$= \left(\begin{bmatrix} Y_1 \\ Y_2 \\ Y_3 \end{bmatrix} - \begin{bmatrix} \mu_1 \\ \mu_2 \\ \mu_3 \end{bmatrix} \right)^T \begin{bmatrix} \sigma_{Y_1}^2 & \sigma_{Y_1 Y_2} & \sigma_{Y_1 Y_3} \\ \sigma_{Y_2 Y_1} & \sigma_{Y_2}^2 & \sigma_{Y_2 Y_3} \\ \sigma_{Y_3 Y_1} & \sigma_{Y_3 Y_2} & \sigma_{Y_3}^2 \end{bmatrix}^{-1} \left(\begin{bmatrix} Y_1 \\ Y_2 \\ Y_3 \end{bmatrix} - \begin{bmatrix} \mu_1 \\ \mu_2 \\ \mu_3 \end{bmatrix} \right) \tag{6.6}$$

For cases with missing values on Y_3, standardized distance is computed using only Y_1 and Y_2 as follows.

$$z_i^2 = (\mathbf{Y}_i - \boldsymbol{\mu}_i)^T \boldsymbol{\Sigma}_i^{-1} (\mathbf{Y}_i - \boldsymbol{\mu}_i)$$

$$= \left(\begin{bmatrix} Y_1 \\ Y_2 \end{bmatrix} - \begin{bmatrix} \mu_1 \\ \mu_2 \end{bmatrix} \right)^T \begin{bmatrix} \sigma_{Y_1}^2 & \sigma_{Y_1 Y_2} \\ \sigma_{Y_2 Y_1} & \sigma_{Y_2}^2 \end{bmatrix}^{-1} \left(\begin{bmatrix} Y_1 \\ Y_2 \end{bmatrix} - \begin{bmatrix} \mu_1 \\ \mu_2 \end{bmatrix} \right) \tag{6.7}$$

Finally, Mahalanobis distance for the third missing data pattern is based only on Y_3.

$$z_i^2 = (\mathbf{Y}_i - \boldsymbol{\mu}_i)^T \boldsymbol{\Sigma}_i^{-1} (\mathbf{Y}_i - \boldsymbol{\mu}_i)$$
$$= (Y_3 - \mu_3)^T \left[\sigma_{Y_3}^2\right]^{-1} (Y_3 - \mu_3) \qquad (6.8)$$
$$= \frac{(Y_3 - \mu_3)^2}{\sigma_{Y_3}^2}$$

Equations 6.6 through 6.8 illustrate that maximum likelihood estimation uses all observed data to quantify the fit of a data to the parameter values, but it is not immediately obvious from the equations why including incomplete data records is beneficial. We previously noted that methodologists sometimes refer to maximum likelihood as "implicit imputation" because it temporarily fills in the missing values en route to estimating the parameters. The normal distribution is integral to this process because it defines a plausible score range for the missing data. To illustrate the implicit imputation idea, reconsider the pain study data. Further, suppose that it is of interest to estimate the association between the first two depression items, the second of which has missing data. Because the items are positively correlated, the observed values of the first item contain information about the missing scores of the second. Specifically, in a bivariate normal distribution with a positive correlation, a high score one on item is most likely to pair with a high score on the other item, and high scores are unlikely to pair with low scores. This pattern implies that we can use the observed values of the first item to infer plausible replacement values for the second item.

Figure 6.1 graphically illustrates the imputation process. The top panel of the figure depicts a bivariate normal distribution for the two questionnaire items (the items have discrete responses but estimation assumes a continuous scale). The height of the distribution represents the likelihood of different score pairs, given the parameter estimates at a particular iteration of the optimization routine. Maximum likelihood essentially uses the normal curve to infer plausible replacement values for the missing data. To illustrate, consider a pair of incomplete cases with scores of 2 and 3 on the first item, respectively. The middle panel of Figure 6.1 shows the slices of the bivariate normal distribution that correspond to these observed scores. These distributions show that, for a given score on the first questionnaire item, there is a distribution of plausible values on the second. The bottom panel of the figure rotates the conditional distributions to better highlight their differences. Notice that the peaks of the two curves are located at approximately 2.2 and 2.8, which implies that the distributions make different predictions about the missing values: 2.2 is the most likely value for the case with a score of 2 on the first item, and 2.8 is the most plausible replacement value for the case with a score of 3 on that item. The estimation algorithm effectively "imputes" the data with these values after which it updates the parameter values at the next iteration. This two-step process – update parameters, impute missing values – is repeated until the parameters no longer change (or change trivially) across successive iterations. A number of resources provide detailed descriptions of these algorithmic steps (Beale & Little, 1975; Enders, 2010; Little & Rubin, 2002).

Maximum likelihood estimation is not limited to estimating a mean vector and covariance matrix, as the $\boldsymbol{\mu}_i$ and $\boldsymbol{\Sigma}_i$ matrices in Equation 6.4 may be functions of model parameters. The individual log likelihood for this situation is

$$\log L_i = -\frac{k}{2}\log(2\pi) - \frac{1}{2}\log|\boldsymbol{\Sigma}_i(\boldsymbol{\theta})| - \frac{1}{2}(\mathbf{Y}_i - \boldsymbol{\mu}_i(\boldsymbol{\theta}))^T \boldsymbol{\Sigma}_i^{-1}(\boldsymbol{\theta})(\mathbf{Y}_i - \boldsymbol{\mu}_i(\boldsymbol{\theta})) \qquad (6.9)$$

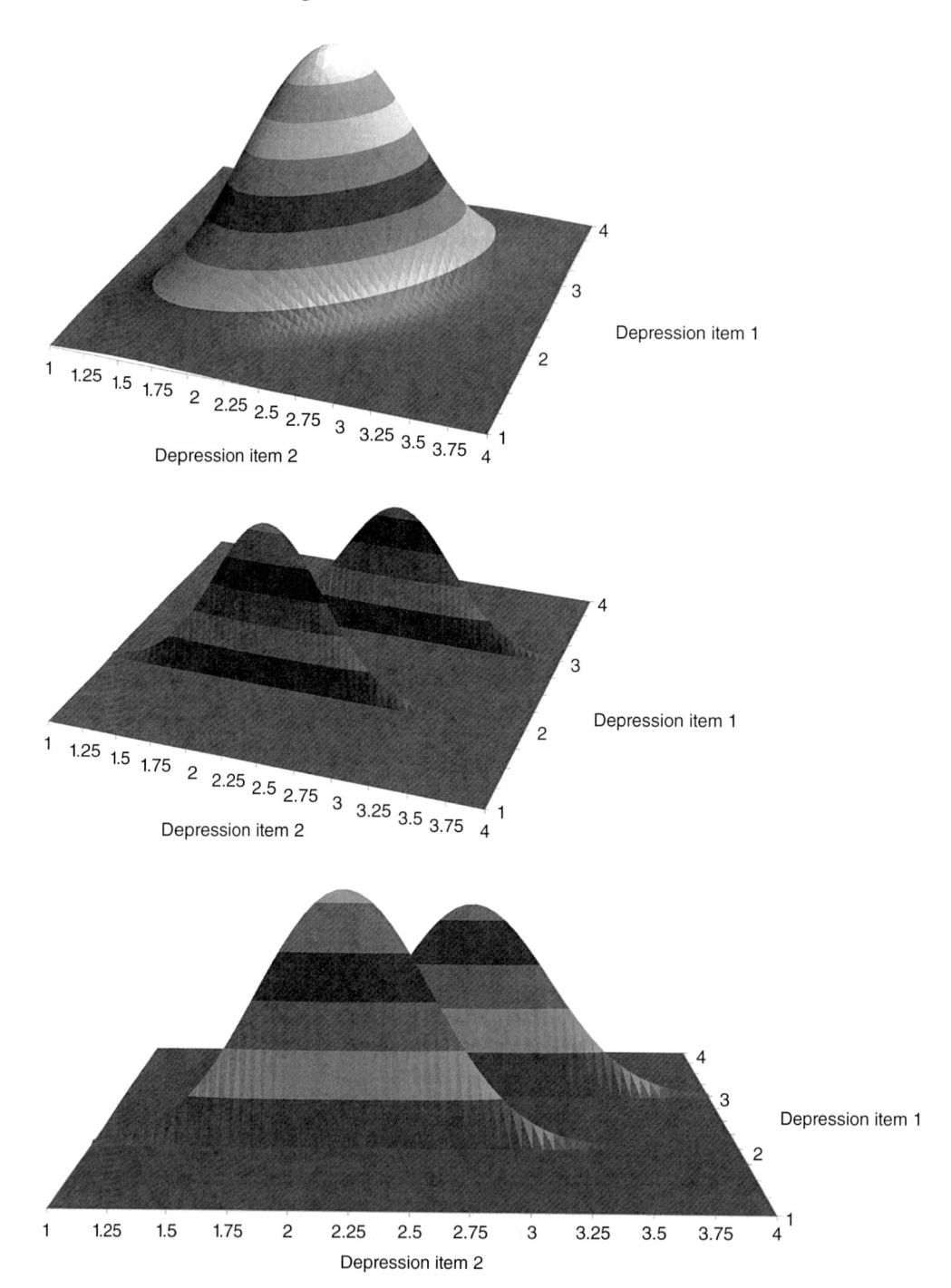

Figure 6.1 The top panel depicts a bivariate normal distribution for two positively correlated questionnaire items. The middle and bottom panels show the distribution of Item 2, conditional on Item 1 scores of 2 and 3.

where $\boldsymbol{\mu}_i(\boldsymbol{\theta})$ and $\boldsymbol{\Sigma}_i(\boldsymbol{\theta})$ are the model-implied mean vector and covariance matrix. For example, in a confirmatory factor analysis (CFA), the elements in $\boldsymbol{\mu}_i(\boldsymbol{\theta})$ and $\boldsymbol{\Sigma}_i(\boldsymbol{\theta})$ are a function of the factor model parameters, as follows

$$\boldsymbol{\mu}_i(\boldsymbol{\theta}) = \boldsymbol{\upsilon} + \boldsymbol{\Lambda}\boldsymbol{\kappa}$$

$$\boldsymbol{\Sigma}_i(\boldsymbol{\theta}) = \boldsymbol{\Lambda}\boldsymbol{\Phi}\boldsymbol{\Lambda}^T + \boldsymbol{\Theta}$$

where $\boldsymbol{\upsilon}$ is a vector of measurement intercepts, $\boldsymbol{\Lambda}$ is the matrix of factor loadings, $\boldsymbol{\kappa}$ is a vector of latent means, $\boldsymbol{\Phi}$ is the factor covariance matrix, and $\boldsymbol{\Theta}$ is the residual covariance matrix.

The log likelihood in Equation 6.9 is often referred to as direct maximum likelihood estimation because it yields parameter estimates and standard errors from a user-specified analysis model. This estimator (also referred to as full information maximum likelihood or FIML) is widely available in psychometric software packages (e.g., structural equation modelling and item response theory programs, numerous R packages). It is worth noting that maximum likelihood estimates of the mean vector and covariance matrix – estimates from the log likelihood in Equation 6.4 – can themselves be used as input data for further analyses (e.g., for a regression analysis, factor analysis, or other procedures that accept matrix input data). This so-called two-stage estimation approach is particularly useful for general-use software packages (e.g., SPSS, SAS) where maximum likelihood missing data handling is often limited to estimating summary statistics via the EM (expectation-maximization) algorithm. However, because no single sample size describes the precision of the covariance matrix, this procedure requires complicated corrective procedures to obtain accurate standard errors (Savalei & Bentler, 2009; Yuan & Bentler, 2000). Direct estimation is often a better option because implementing these correctives may be prohibitively difficult for many researchers.

Categorical variables

For simplicity, we have focused on maximum likelihood estimation for multivariate normal data, but the estimator is not limited to this situation. Maximum likelihood missing data handling is available for other population distributions, including logit and probit models; we encourage interested readers to consult Mislevy (2016) for a detailed treatment of missing data handling in item response theory (IRT) models. Estimation is relatively straightforward when missing values are restricted to outcome variables with a common scale (e.g., an IRT model with binary indicators), but maximum likelihood is arguably less adept at handling mixtures of categorical and continuous variables. Because the variables do not share a common joint distribution, estimation generally requires a software package that implements complex numerical integration techniques or Bayesian estimation. Even with a capable software package, estimating a model with mixtures of categorical and continuous variables may require simplifications that do not honor the original scaling (e.g., treating an incomplete binary covariate as normally distributed). As we will see in the next section, multiple imputation is typically a more flexible solution for handling mixtures of categorical and continuous variables.

Multiple Imputation

Multiple imputation is an alternative to maximum likelihood estimation that has enjoyed widespread use in published research. Multiple imputation consists of an imputation phase, analysis phase, and a pooling phase. The imputation phase yields several copies of the data set (e.g., 20 or more; Graham, Olchowski, & Gilreath, 2007), each of which contains different plausible replacement values. In the analysis phase, the researcher analyzes each filled-in data set, and the resulting estimates and standard errors are subsequently combined in the pooling phase. Notice that, unlike maximum likelihood estimation, multiple imputation separates missing data handling from the statistical analysis. Because the imputation phase typically employs a very general model (e.g., a regression model based on an unstructured covariance matrix), a single set of imputations can usually support a variety of statistical analyses.

Imputation phase

Methodologists have proposed a variety of algorithms for the imputation phase, most of which use some type of regression model to predict the incomplete variables from the complete variables. Although these iterative algorithms have different computational steps and functionality, they generally employ the same logic: treat the current regression model parameter values as known and draw imputations from a distribution of plausible replacement scores, then treat the imputations as real data and sample new parameter values from a probability (posterior) distribution. This section describes the two predominant algorithmic approaches to drawing imputations, joint imputation, and chained equations imputation.

Schafer's (1997) classic multiple imputation text popularized so-called joint imputation methods that assume a common distribution for the incomplete variables. The most common application of joint imputation treats variables as multivariate normal. The data augmentation algorithm alternates between an I-step (imputation step) and a P-step (posterior step). The I-step uses the current estimate of the mean vector and covariance matrix to construct linear regression equations that predict the incomplete variables from the complete variables. These linear regression parameters define a multivariate normal distribution from which imputations are drawn, as follows

$$Y_{\text{mis}} \sim MVN(\mathbf{X}\boldsymbol{\beta}, \Sigma_\varepsilon) \tag{6.10}$$

where Y_{mis} represents the incomplete variables for a particular missing data pattern, $\mathbf{X}$ includes the corresponding complete variables (including a unit vector), and Σ_ε is the residual covariance matrix from the regression. In words, Equation 6.10 says to draw the imputations for each case from a multivariate normal distribution with predicted values and a residual covariance matrix defining the center and spread of the distribution, respectively.

Having filled in the missing values, the P-step (posterior step) draws new parameter values from a posterior distribution. With multivariate normal data, the P-step requires two sampling steps: the first draws a new covariance matrix from an inverse Wishart distribution, and the second draws a new mean vector from a multivariate normal distribution. The parameters of both distributions derive from the filled-in data from the previous I-step. The updated mean vector and covariance matrix carry forward to the next I-step, where a new round of imputation begins. Because the P-step employs standard complete-data sampling steps, we direct interested readers to the literature for additional details on these probability distributions (Enders, 2010; Schafer, 1997; Gelman et al., 2013; Sinharay, Stern, & Russell, 2001).

To illustrate joint imputation, consider a simple scenario with three incomplete variables, Y_1, Y_2, and Y_3. Further, suppose that data have three missing data patterns: (1) complete data on all variables, (2) missing values on Y_3, and (3) missing values on Y_1 and Y_2. The imputation step uses the current estimate of the mean vector and covariance matrix to construct linear regression equations for each missing data pattern. Specifically, the following normal distribution generates imputations for cases where only Y_3 is incomplete.

$$Y_{3(mis)} \sim N\left(\beta_0 + \beta_1 Y_1 + \beta_2 Y_2,\ \sigma^2_{Y_3 \mid Y_1, Y_2}\right) \qquad (6.11)$$

As explained previously, a predicted score and residual variance define the mean and variance of the distribution, respectively. For cases with missing values on Y_1 and Y_2, the mean vector and covariance matrix elements are reconstituted to form the following distribution.

$$\begin{matrix} Y_{1(mis)} \\ Y_{2(mis)} \end{matrix} \sim MVN\left(\begin{bmatrix} \beta_0 + \beta_1 Y_3 \\ \gamma_0 + \gamma_1 Y_3 \end{bmatrix},\ \Sigma_{Y_1, Y_2 \mid Y_3}\right) \qquad (6.12)$$

After drawing replacement values from the appropriate distributions, the algorithm samples a new covariance matrix and mean vector, as described previously.

Whereas joint imputation generates imputations from a multivariate distribution, the chained equations approach (also known as fully conditional specification) cycles through the incomplete variables, using an appropriate univariate distribution to generate replacement values (Raghunathan, Lepkowski, van Hoewyk, & Solenberger, 2001; van Buuren, 2007, 2012; van Buuren, Brand, Groothuis-Oudshoorn, & Rubin, 2006). Consistent with the joint model approach, the chained equations algorithm repeatedly alternates between sampling imputations and parameter values, but it applies these steps to each incomplete variable, one at a time. The variable-by-variable imputation scheme is as follows

$$\begin{aligned} Y^{(t)}_{1(mis)} &\sim p\left(Y_1 \mid Y^{(t-1)}_2, \ldots, Y^{(t-1)}_k, \mathbf{X}, \boldsymbol{\theta}_1\right) \\ Y^{(t)}_{2(mis)} &\sim p\left(Y_2 \mid Y^{(t)}_1, Y^{(t)}_3, \ldots, Y^{(t-1)}_k, \mathbf{X}, \boldsymbol{\theta}_2\right) \\ &\ldots \\ Y^{(t)}_{k(mis)} &\sim p\left(Y_k \mid Y^{(t)}_1, Y^{(t)}_2, \ldots, Y^{(t)}_{k-1}, \mathbf{X}, \boldsymbol{\theta}_k\right) \end{aligned} \qquad (6.13)$$

where $Y^{(t)}_{k(mis)}$ denotes the variable being imputed at step k of iteration t, $\mathbf{X}$ contains the set of complete variables, and $\boldsymbol{\theta}_k$ represents a set of regression model parameters linking the incomplete variable to the complete (and imputed) variables. Each distribution in the previous equation requires supporting computational steps that draw the regression parameters in $\boldsymbol{\theta}_k$.

To illustrate chained equations imputation, reconsider the previous scenario with three incomplete variables, Y_1, Y_2, and Y_3. For simplicity, assume that the variables are normally distributed. A single iteration of the chained equations algorithm consists of three substeps, one for each incomplete variable. The imputation step for Y_1 uses linear regression parameters to define a univariate normal distribution from which imputations are drawn, as follows.

$$Y_{1(mis)}^{(t)} \sim N\left(\beta_0 + \beta_1 Y_2^{(t-1)} + \beta_2 Y_3^{(t-1)}, \sigma_{Y_1 \mid Y_2, Y_3}^2\right) \quad (6.14)$$

Notice that the filled-in values of Y_2 and Y_3 from the previous iteration serve as predictors in the imputation model (at the first iteration, the predictors are filled in with preliminary imputations, perhaps using mean imputation or some other ad hoc procedure). After drawing imputations, the algorithm samples new regression model parameters from posterior distributions that condition on the filled-in data. The sampling procedure first draws a residual variance from an inverse Wishart distribution, and it then draws a new coefficient vector form a multivariate normal distribution. The sampling steps are described elsewhere in the literature (Gelman et al., 2013; van Buuren, 2012).

The imputation models for Y_2 and Y_3 follow a similar logic and are as follows.

$$Y_{2(mis)}^{(t)} \sim N\left(\beta_0 + \beta_1 Y_1^{(t)} + \beta_2 Y_3^{(t-1)}, \sigma_{Y_2 \mid Y_1, Y_3}^2\right) \quad (6.15)$$

$$Y_{3(mis)}^{(t)} \sim N\left(\beta_0 + \beta_1 Y_1^{(t)} + \beta_2 Y_2^{(t)}, \sigma_{Y_3 \mid Y_1, Y_2}^2\right) \quad (6.16)$$

Again, notice that each imputed variable carries forward and serves as a predictor in all other imputation models. Although joint imputation and chained equations imputation appear quite different, the procedures are equivalent with multivariate normal data (Hughes, White, Seaman, Carpenter, & Sterne, 2014). However, it is important to note that chained equations imputation is capable of handling mixtures of categorical and continuous variables; the algorithm can apply a linear regression model to normal variables, a multinomial logistic model to nominal variables, an ordered logistic or probit model to ordinal variables, and so on. We return to this issue in the next section.

The imputation algorithms described in this section (and Markov chain Monte Carlo algorithms more generally; Fox, van den Berg, & Veldkamp, Chapter 17, Volume 2; Jackman, 2000; Levy, Mislevy, & Behrens, 2011) produce results that are highly correlated across steps (e.g., the imputations from one step depend on the parameter values from the previous step, the parameter values depend on the imputations, and so on). These strong autocorrelations produce filled-in values that are too similar across consecutive iterations, which ultimately yields negatively biased standard errors. To circumvent this problem, researchers usually allow the imputation algorithm to iterate for many computational cycles, saving a data set at specified intervals (the so-called between-imputation or thinning interval). For example, to generate 20 imputations, a researcher might specify a 4,000-iteration chain that saves a data set after every 200th computational cycle. Alternatively, the researcher could initiate 20 separate chains of 200 cycles each, saving a data set at the last iteration of each process. It is impossible provide general rules of thumb for determining the number of iterations because a number of data-specific factors impact this choice (e.g., the amount of missing data, correlations among the variables, number of variables). Imputation software packages generally provide graphical or numeric convergence diagnostics that can aid this decision (Gelman et al., 2013; Gelman & Rubin, 1992; Schafer, 1997).

Categorical variables

Thus far, we have focused on multiple imputation for multivariate normal data. Although researchers often apply this approach to categorical variables, perhaps in conjunction with a post-imputation rounding scheme (Allison, 2002; Horton, Lipsitz, & Parzen, 2003; Yucel, He, & Zaslavsky, 2008), it is no longer necessary to do so. Flexible imputation routines for categorical and continuous variables are now widely available software packages. Both joint imputation and chained equations imputation can accommodate categorical variables, but they do so in different ways.

Schafer (1997) outlined joint models for categorical variables, but these routines have not enjoyed widespread use, perhaps because they address a limited range of problems and are not widely available in software packages. The joint model for multivariate normal data can accommodate mixed response scales by recasting incomplete categorical variables as normally distributed latent variables (Albert & Chib, 1993; Carpenter & Kenward, 2013; Johnson & Albert, 1999). This formulation views discrete values as arising from one or more threshold parameters that divide an underlying normal distribution into sections. For example, consider a binary test item scored as 0 = incorrect and 1 = correct. The corresponding latent variable represents a normally distributed achievement continuum for the item (e.g., the propensity for a correct response), such that a single threshold parameter divides the underlying distribution into two segments: a correct response occurs when the measurement process yields a latent variable score above the threshold, and an incorrect response occurs when the latent variable falls below the threshold. Ordinal variables follow the same logic but require additional threshold parameters. The latent variable formulation is convenient because it accommodates the following imputation strategy: (1) for each categorical variable, sample latent variable scores from a normal distribution, (2) apply the joint imputation procedure for multivariate normal data, and (3) convert latent variable imputations to discrete score values. Latent variable imputation is available in Mplus, Blimp (Keller & Enders, 2014), and as a module for MLwiN and Stata (Carpenter, Goldstein, & Kenward, 2011). Interested readers can consult Carpenter and Kenward (2013) for additional details on this approach.

Chained equations imputation is naturally suited for mixed response scales because each imputation step in Equation 6.13 can be tailored to match the incomplete variable's scale (Raghunathan et al., 2001; van Buuren, 2007, 2012; van Buuren et al., 2006). For example, a linear regression can generate imputations for a normal variable, logistic regression can produce imputations for a nominal variable, a proportional odds model can generate ordered categorical imputations, and so on. Diagnosing convergence problems may be difficult when drawing imputations from disparate conditional distributions, but simulation studies suggest that chained equations imputation can produce accurate parameter estimates (Raghunathan et al., 2001; van Buuren et al., 2006). To date, limited research has compared joint imputation with latent variables to chained equations imputation, but it appears that the former may be preferable in smaller samples (e.g., less than $N = 1{,}000$; Wu, Jia, & Enders, 2015). Chained equations imputation for categorical and continuous variables is available in a variety of software packages, including the MICE package in R (van Buuren & Groothuis-Oudshoorn, 2011), SPSS, SAS, and Stata.

Analysis and pooling phases

As described previously, researchers analyze each imputed data set in the analysis phase, and they combine the estimates and standard errors into a single set of results in the pooling phase. Because the analysis phase is just a series of complete-data analyses, we focus on the pooling phase in this section. The data analysis examples later in the chapter demonstrate the process of analyzing imputed data sets and pooling their estimates.

Rubin's (1987) pooling equation for point estimates is simply the arithmetic average of the m parameter estimates

$$\hat{\theta}_{MI} = m^{-1} \sum_{t=1}^{m} \hat{\theta}_t \tag{6.17}$$

where $\hat{\theta}_t$ is the point estimate from data set t, and m is the number of data sets. The pooling process for standard errors is somewhat more complicated because it involves two sources of variation in the estimates. The so-called within-imputation variance is the arithmetic average of the m squared standard errors, as follows.

$$WIV = m^{-1} \sum_{t=1}^{m} SE_t^2 \tag{6.18}$$

Conceptually, the within-imputation variance estimates the sampling variation that would have resulted had the data been complete. The square root of Equation 6.18 underestimates the standard error because it fails to account for uncertainty due to missing data. The so-called between-imputation variance captures this additional source of variation by applying the usual formula for the sample variance to the m parameter estimates.

$$BIV = (m-1)^{-1} \sum_{t=1}^{m} \left(\hat{\theta}_t - \hat{\theta}_{MI} \right)^2 \tag{6.19}$$

Finally, the multiple imputation standard error combines the within- and between-imputation variance, as follows.

$$SE_{MI} = \sqrt{WIV + BIV + \frac{BIV}{m}} \tag{6.20}$$

The third term under the radical represents the sampling variance (i.e., squared standard error) of the average estimate from Equation 6.17 and effectively serves as a correction factor for a finite number of imputations. In line with a standard frequentist analysis, referencing the ratio of the point estimate to its standard error to a z or t distribution yields a probability value (Barnard & Rubin, 1999; Reiter, 2007).

An Inclusive Missing Data Handling Strategy

Maximum likelihood and multiple imputation require a MAR (or MCAR) mechanism and can produce biased estimates when the mechanism is NMAR. Unfortunately, it is usually impossible to infer anything about the missing data mechanism from the observed scores because the mechanisms make different propositions about the unobserved values in Y_{mis} – MCAR and MAR require that missingness is unrelated to the would-be values of the incomplete variable, whereas NMAR allows for this association. Researchers often try to evaluate the missing data mechanism by examining whether the missing data indicator for a particular variable is systematically related to other variables (e.g., examining mean differences between the complete and incomplete cases; Kim & Bentler, 2002; Little, 1998). While the presence of mean (or covariance) differences allows one to rule out an MCAR mechanism, the absence of such differences does not guarantee that MCAR is satisfied (Raykov, 2011). In a similar vein, finding an association between a missing data indicator and another variable is not diagnostic because either an MAR or NMAR mechanism could produce such an effect. As such, maximum likelihood and multiple imputation usually require researchers to adopt an MAR assumption that is fundamentally untestable.

It is important to clarify that MAR is not a property of an entire data set; rather, it is an assumption that applies to a particular analysis. Assuming that observed scores determine missingness, MAR is satisfied when the missing data handling procedure incorporates variables that predict the missingness probabilities of a particular set of analysis variables. Returning to the pain study, suppose that researchers use a factor analysis to examine the internal structure of the depression scale. Further, suppose that the missingness probabilities for the depression items are systematically related to age and gender. The MAR assumption is satisfied only if these background variables are included in the analysis model (maximum likelihood) or imputation phase (multiple imputation). Although age and gender would not have been part of the complete-data analysis, ignoring these variables results in an NMAR mechanism and can introduce nonresponse bias, particularly if the background variables are correlated with depression scores.

To maximize the chances of satisfying the MAR assumption, methodologists often recommend an inclusive missing data handling strategy that incorporates a number of so-called auxiliary variables (Collins, Schafer, & Kam, 2001; Graham, 2003; Rubin, 1996; Schafer & Graham, 2002). The ideal auxiliary variable has a strong correlation (e.g., greater than ± 0.40) with an incomplete analysis variable and its missingness probabilities, but auxiliary variables that correlate only with the analysis variables are also useful. Auxiliary variables can be identified by examining whether the missing data indicator for a particular variable is systematically related to other variables, but methodologists also recommend that researchers proactively add auxiliary variables to their data collection plans in anticipation of missing data (e.g., in a longitudinal study, add a survey question that asks how likely respondents are to participate in the next wave; Schafer & Graham, 2002).

In the context of multiple imputation, auxiliary variables are simply included in the imputation phase. The auxiliary variables need not be part of the subsequent analysis phase because their information is embedded in the imputations. However, because maximum likelihood integrates missing data handling and estimation, auxiliary variables must be included in the analysis model. This requirement is potentially problematic when the auxiliary variables would not have been part of the complete-data analysis (e.g., the age and gender variables from the previous depression example). Adding auxiliary variables as covariates is not an ideal solution because doing so alters the analysis model to accommodate the missing data. Rather, auxiliary variables should be incorporated into the analysis in a way that does not alter the substantive interpretation of the results.

Graham's (2003) saturated correlates model (sometimes called the spider model) uses a set of correlations to incorporate auxiliary variables into a maximum likelihood analysis. The specification rules for introducing auxiliary variables are as follows: an auxiliary variable must correlate with (1) manifest (as opposed to latent) predictor variables, (2) residual terms of manifest outcome variables (e.g., dependent variables or indicators of a latent construct), and (3) other auxiliary variables. Importantly, the previous rules do not specify correlations between auxiliary variables and latent variables. To illustrate the saturated correlates approach, consider a MIMIC model with a manifest covariate predicting a latent variable. The top panel of Figure 6.2 shows a path diagram for such a model, and the bottom panel shows the corresponding saturated correlates model with two auxiliary variables. Notice that the model implements all three of Graham's rules. The saturated correlates model is based on the idea that the analysis variables and their missingness probabilities are correlated when both quantities share a mutual association with an observed variable not in the analysis (a scenario consistent with the NMAR mechanism). Incorporating the auxiliary variable into the missing data handling procedure eliminates this spurious correlation, producing an MAR mechanism.

Importantly, the saturated correlates model yields parameter estimates with the same substantive interpretation as those from a complete-data analysis, and it does not alter the degrees of freedom or model fit because the auxiliary variable portion of the model estimates all possible correlations involving the auxiliary variables (i.e., the auxiliary part of the model is saturated). We illustrate this method later in the chapter.

Direct Estimation Versus Imputation

Although maximum likelihood and multiple imputation are quite different from a procedural standpoint, the methods tend to produce equivalent parameter estimates and standard errors, particularly when the imputation procedure and the maximum likelihood analysis utilize the same variables (Collins et al., 2001; Schafer, 2003). The analysis examples later in the chapter illustrate this point. Consequently, there is often no statistical reason to prefer maximum likelihood to imputation (or vice versa). All things being equal, maximum likelihood is often preferable because it is usually easier to implement – researchers need only estimate a model with a capable software package. However, a number of practical issues might lead one to prefer one method to the other. We briefly summarize a few of these considerations, and detailed discussions are available elsewhere in the literature (e.g., Enders, 2010, pp. 336–340; Widaman, 2006, pp. 60–63).

To begin, recall that the MAR mechanism occurs when the probability of missing data is conditionally independent of the missing values after controlling for the observed data. Assuming that the missing values themselves do not directly influence missingness, MAR is satisfied when the missing data handling procedure accounts for auxiliary variables that are mutually associated with the analysis variables and with the missingness

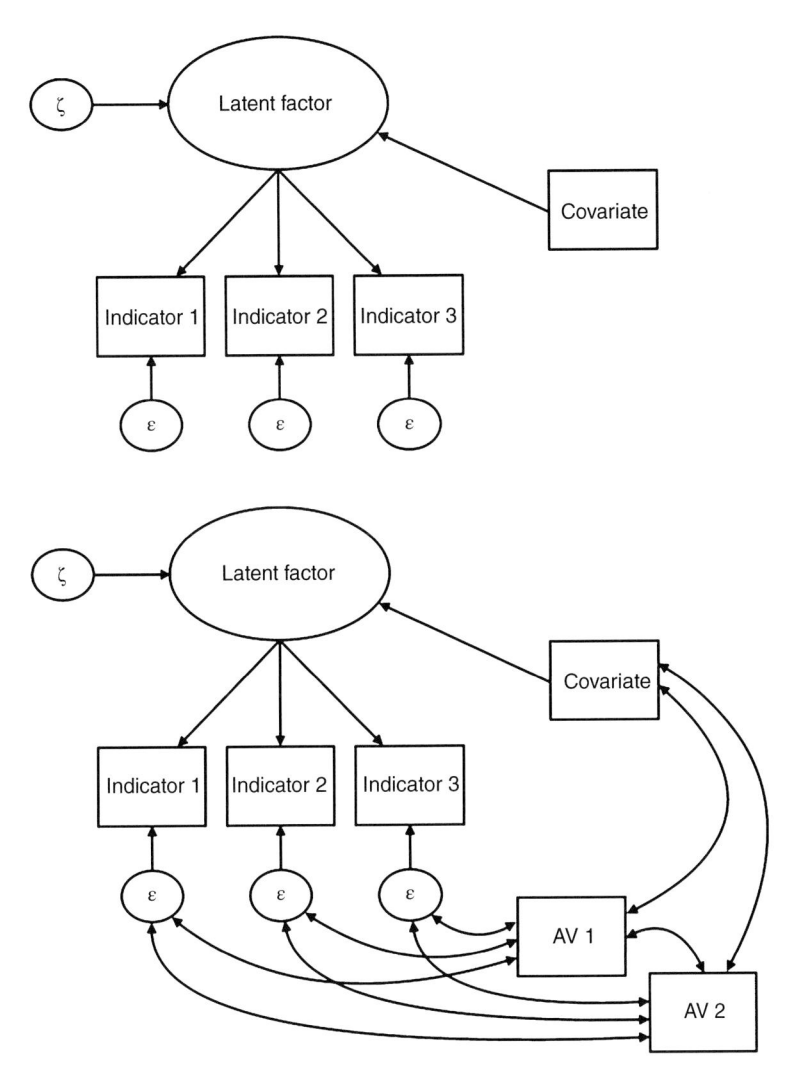

Figure 6.2 The top panel is a path diagram for a MIMIC model with a single manifest covariate. The bottom panel depicts the corresponding saturated correlates model with two auxiliary variables.

probabilities of those variables; excluding important auxiliary variables produces an NMAR mechanism that can introduce bias (Collins et al., 2001). Reconsider the earlier factor analysis example where age and gender (variables not in the model) were correlates of the depression questionnaire's missingness probabilities. Because maximum likelihood integrates missing data handling and estimation, MAR is satisfied only if age and gender are included in the analysis. This requirement is potentially problematic if the researcher has no substantive interest in these variables and would not have included them in the analysis had the data been complete. With multivariate normal data, structural equation modelling software programs can implement Graham's (2003) saturated correlates approach to auxiliary variables, but other modelling frameworks may not offer this functionality. Further, this approach is not applicable to logit models that cannot accommodate residual correlations between categorical outcomes and auxiliary variables. In contrast, multiple imputation can readily accommodate auxiliary variables, and mixed response scales do not pose a problem.

Models with categorical variables present tradeoffs when considering direct estimation and imputation. As noted previously, multiple imputation can readily accommodate categorical variables and mixtures of response types. Although researchers can use imputed data to estimate parameters and standard errors, evaluating model fit is usually difficult because pooling rules have not been developed for popular fit indices; global tests of model fit are available for multivariate normal data (e.g., the two-stage estimator, Lee & Li, 2012; pooled likelihood ratio tests, Meng & Rubin, 1992), but these procedures have not been extended to categorical data. Maximum likelihood estimation for logit and probit models (e.g., IRT models) can accommodate incomplete categorical outcomes, and the usual tests of model fit are typically available with incomplete data. However, estimation becomes complicated and may require numerical integration techniques with mixed response types (e.g., categorical outcomes and normally distributed covariates).

As an aside, researchers often use weighted least squares estimation when fitting measurement models to categorical data (e.g., the WLSMV estimator in Mplus; Finney & DiStefano, 2013; Muthén, du Toit, & Spisic, 1997). Briefly, this procedure uses bivariate probit regressions to estimate polychoric (or tetrachoric) associations among the variables, and it then uses the resulting correlation matrix as input data for weighted least squares estimation. Because each correlation is based on the available cases for a particular pair of variables (i.e., pairwise deletion), this estimator effectively assumes an MCAR missing data handling mechanism. As such, weighted least squares estimation for categorical variables will generally be prone to bias in situations where maximum likelihood and multiple imputation will not unless it is preceded by a categorical multiple imputation routine.

Next, maximum likelihood is usually preferable for latent class models. With multiple imputation, it is vital that the imputation model incorporates all variables and effects for a given analysis model (e.g., an analysis model that incorporates an interaction term requires an imputation model with an interaction term). Omitting an analysis variable biases that variable's effect toward zero, even when the mechanism is MCAR. Researchers typically employ imputation models based on an unstructured covariance matrix (i.e., a saturated model). This approach is flexible and very general because it does not assume a particular structure for the data. However, because latent class membership is not an observed variable, a saturated imputation model necessarily omits this important variable, generating filled-in values from a single-class model. Although some programs can generate imputations from a latent class model, maximum likelihood estimation is probably a more flexible solution.

Finally, multiple imputation is often preferable for multilevel data structures. Although it is the default estimator in virtually every multilevel software program, maximum likelihood missing data handling is best suited for incomplete repeated measures data (e.g., a growth model with attrition). Because they treat predictors as fixed (i.e., no distributional assumptions), most multilevel modelling programs necessarily exclude cases with missing predictors (for exceptions, see Shin & Raudenbush, 2007). Cases with missing outcome scores will also be excluded from cross-sectional analyses because these cases contribute no data to the likelihood. Deleting cases is particularly devastating with incomplete level-2 variables because entire clusters are excluded from analysis. In contrast, imputation is often an ideal solution for multilevel models because it treats missing data prior to the analysis and makes no distinction between independent and dependent variables. Specialized imputation routines for multilevel data are widely available in software packages, including Mplus (Muthén & Muthén, 1998–2012), Blimp (Keller & Enders, 2014), the PAN (Schafer, 2001; Zhao & Schafer, 2016), and MICE (van Buuren & Groothuis-Oudshoorn, 2011) packages in R, and MLwiN (Carpenter et al., 2011), among others.

Data Analysis Examples

Having described maximum likelihood estimation and multiple imputation, we now demonstrate the applications of these procedures to common psychometric analyses. Recall that we patterned the artificial data set after an online chronic pain management program where researchers collected a number of background and psychological variables at the start of the study and subsequently collected post-intervention measures of pain interference and severity. Table 6.1 gives a list of the variables along with their ranges and missing data rates.

We applied maximum likelihood estimation and multiple imputation to three common psychometric analyses: (1) an exploratory factor analysis (EFA) of the pain catastrophizing, depression, and pain interference items, (2) a reliability analysis of the three scale scores, and (3) a measurement invariance analysis that uses multiple group CFA to examine gender differences in the depression scale. We chose these procedures because they are common in published research articles and because they illustrate a number of nuances related to missing data handling. We used Mplus 7 (Muthén & Muthén, 1998–2012) for all analysis examples, primarily because it offers comprehensive set of missing data handling features, some of which are not available in other packages (e.g., some packages implement a wide array of maximum likelihood models but no imputation, other packages generate imputations but do not automate the pooling phase, etc.). Appendix Code 1 through 12 give the input files for the analyses, and the data set and input files are available for download at www.appliedmissingdata.com.

Maximum likelihood estimation

We began by factor analyzing the questionnaire items from the three scales and obtaining reliability estimates for the scale scores. There are two approaches to performing these analyses: two-stage and direct estimation. Recall that the two-stage approach obtains maximum likelihood estimates of the mean vector and covariance matrix, and it subsequently uses these quantities as input data for further analyses. The two-stage approach is particularly useful for general-purpose software packages where maximum likelihood missing data handling is often limited to estimating summary statistics via the EM algorithm. Although two-stage estimation requires complex standard error corrections, (Savalei & Bentler, 2009; Yuan & Bentler, 2000), it is readily applicable to psychometric analyses that do not require (or do not produce) standard error estimates (e.g., EFA and reliability analyses). In contrast, the direct estimation approach estimates model parameters and standard errors directly from the incomplete

Table 6.3 Rotated loadings from the EFA.

Item	Maximum likelihood			Multiple imputation		
	Factor 1	Factor 2	Factor 3	Factor 1	Factor 2	Factor 3
CATAST1	**0.895**	−0.015	−0.020	**0.904**	−0.017	−0.029
CATAST2	**0.484**	0.212	−0.003	**0.485**	0.203	−0.006
CATAST3	**0.584**	0.057	0.002	**0.578**	0.062	0.011
CATAST4	**0.630**	0.143	0.046	**0.619**	0.140	0.069
DEPRESS1	0.064	**0.693**	−0.019	0.062	**0.695**	−0.014
DEPRESS2	0.049	**0.668**	−0.044	0.056	**0.663**	−0.046
DEPRESS3	0.000	**0.889**	0.025	−0.003	**0.890**	0.028
DEPRESS4	0.106	**0.740**	−0.006	0.105	**0.740**	−0.001
DEPRESS5	0.011	**0.791**	0.075	0.014	**0.792**	0.080
DEPRESS6	0.017	**0.918**	−0.033	−0.023	**0.920**	−0.028
DEPRESS7	0.065	**0.879**	0.033	−0.043	**0.867**	0.025
PAININT1	0.023	0.003	**0.933**	0.022	0.005	**0.934**
PAININT2	0.014	0.008	**0.942**	−0.007	0.003	**0.943**
PAININT3	0.045	0.055	**0.881**	−0.056	0.058	**0.880**
PAININT4	0.009	−0.014	**0.862**	0.006	−0.015	**0.864**
PAININT5	0.040	−0.033	**0.655**	0.033	−0.028	**0.658**
PAININT6	0.019	−0.019	**0.700**	0.015	−0.022	**0.704**

data, with missing data handling built into the iterative optimization algorithm. As such, researchers need only feed a raw data set into a capable software package and estimate a model. As noted previously, direct estimation routines are widely available in dedicated psychometric and structural equation modelling software packages (e.g., the so-called FIML estimator).

We used direct estimation in Mplus to perform an EFA with a GEOMIN oblique rotation (the default), and we used a two-stage approach to estimate coefficient alpha. For the latter analysis, we estimated the mean vector and covariance matrix of the questionnaire items and used the Mplus MODEL CONSTRAINT command to compute coefficient alpha from these quantities. Enders (2003, 2004) illustrates a similar two-stage reliability analysis with general-purpose software. Appendix Code 1 and 2 give the Mplus inputs from the factor and reliability analyses, respectively.

The EFA produced three eigenvalues greater than one, and the three-factor solution produced a clear structure with adequate fit, $\chi^2(88) = 102.42$, $p = 0.14$. To illustrate, the left panel of Table 6.3 gives the rotated loadings from the analysis, with bold typeface highlighting values greater than .40. As seen in the table, the solution closely approximates simple structure, with all items producing strong positive loadings on one factor and trivially small cross-loadings on other factors. The internal consistency reliability estimates for the three scales were as follows: pain catastrophizing = .813, depression = .932, and pain interference = .927.

The final analysis examined the measurement invariance of the depression scale for males ($n = 300$) and females ($n = 200$). With discrete indicators, researchers might be inclined to use a weighted least squares estimator such as the WLSMV routine in Mplus. As noted previously, this estimator uses pairwise deletion to treat missing data and thus requires the stringent MCAR assumption. Instead, we used a maximum likelihood estimator that assumes multivariate normality along with robust standard errors and rescaled test statistics (Yuan & Bentler, 2000). For a true categorical variable model, researchers could implement maximum likelihood estimation with a probit link function, or they could first multiply impute the data and then apply weighted least squares estimation (the next section illustrates a categorical imputation routine).

We began by fitting a unidimensional model where all parameter estimates freely varied between groups, the syntax for which is in Appendix Code 3. The rescaled chi-square test from this model suggested adequate fit, $\chi^2(28) = 34.09$, $p = .20$, meaning that a one-factor model accurately reproduced the mean and covariance structure of both groups. Next, we fit a model with strict factorial invariance that imposed equality constraints on the measurement model parameters, the syntax for which is in Appendix Code 4. This model also produced adequate model fit, suggesting that males and females share common parameter values, $\chi^2(47) = 50.31$, $p = .34$. Other fit indices supported this conclusion (e.g., RMSEA = .017, CFI = .998). Because the invariant model fit the data, we did not perform additional analyses. The left panel of Table 6.4 gives the parameter estimates and standard errors from the invariant model.

Recall from a previous section that the MAR mechanism for maximum likelihood estimation allows the probability of missingness to depend on other variables but not on the would-be values of the incomplete variable itself. In the context of the multiple-group CFA model, MAR stipulates that the missingness probabilities for a given item are fully explained by gender and/or the observed scores of another item. MAR is not satisfied if variables outside of the model predict missingness, and excluding such

Table 6.4 Confirmatory factor analysis parameter estimates.

	Maximum likelihood		Multiple imputation	
Parameter	Est.	SE	Est.	SE
Factor Variance	0.457	0.050	0.458	0.050
Loading 1	1.000	N/A	1.000	N/A
Loading 2	0.963	0.063	0.958	0.062
Loading 3	1.392	0.064	1.391	0.064
Loading 4	1.249	0.064	1.249	0.064
Loading 5	1.146	0.060	1.147	0.060
Loading 6	1.366	0.066	1.368	0.066
Loading 7	1.161	0.065	1.164	0.064
Intercept 1	1.993	0.048	1.993	0.048
Intercept 2	2.579	0.051	2.582	0.051
Intercept 3	1.986	0.059	1.988	0.059
Intercept 4	2.265	0.057	2.267	0.058
Intercept 5	2.067	0.052	2.069	0.052
Intercept 6	1.821	0.057	1.822	0.058
Intercept 7	1.583	0.051	0.577	0.050
Residual 1	0.404	0.029	0.404	0.029
Residual 2	0.485	0.032	0.488	0.032
Residual 3	0.219	0.024	0.219	0.024
Residual 4	0.376	0.031	0.378	0.032
Residual 5	0.296	0.025	0.298	0.025
Residual 6	0.222	0.022	0.220	0.022
Residual 7	0.265	0.021	0.273	0.023

variables can introduce bias if the omitted variable is correlated with both the incomplete variable and its missingness probabilities. Although the mechanism is MCAR in this data set (which implies that MAR holds), researchers typically have no way of evaluating the missing data mechanism with any confidence. For this reason, methodologists often recommend an inclusive strategy that incorporates auxiliary variables. With an MCAR mechanism, auxiliary variables would not decrease bias, but they could improve power.

Because an excessive number of auxiliary variables can produce convergence problems (Enders, 2010; Savalei & Bentler, 2009), it is generally a good idea to select a small number of auxiliary variables that have strong correlations with the incomplete variables. The catastrophizing items would be good auxiliary variables because they have relatively strong correlations with the incomplete depression items (e.g., several correlations exceed .40 and .50). To illustrate Graham's (2003) saturated correlates approach to auxiliary variables, we reran the invariant model with the catastrophizing items as auxiliary variables. As seen in Appendix Code 5, adding the AUXILIARY command invokes saturated correlates model. Importantly, including auxiliary variables does not affect model fit or the degrees of freedom because the auxiliary portion of the model is saturated; the chi-square test of model fit for the auxiliary variable model was essentially unchanged, $\chi^2(47) = 54.33$, $p = .22$. Auxiliary variables can produce rather dramatic power gains (Baraldi & Enders, 2010), but the standard errors from this analysis were unaffected, most likely because the catastrophizing items did not correlate strongly with the residualized depression items. Nevertheless, the example is useful for demonstrating the procedure.

Multiple imputation

We now repeat the previous analyses with multiple imputation. Recall that multiple imputation consists of an imputation phase, analysis phase, and a pooling phase. The imputation phase yields several copies of the data set, each of which contains different plausible replacement values. Appendix Code 6 gives an Mplus imputation program that generates 50 data sets for the EFA and reliability analyses. The decision to use 50 data sets was somewhat arbitrary, but recent research suggests that 20 or more imputations are usually required to achieve comparable power to maximum likelihood (Graham et al., 2007). Although any number of programs can generate appropriate imputations for these examples, we chose Mplus because it offers a flexible set of imputation options. For example, the program can use a saturated model for imputation (the default method illustrated in Appendix Code 6), or it can generate imputations from a structured model (e.g., a three-factor CFA model). Imputing from a saturated model is usually a good idea because it does not assume a particular structure for the data, whereas imputing from a structured model assumes a known population model. Although the latter approach may yield a slight gain in precision, misspecifying the imputation model will generate replacement values that make the hypothesized model fit better than it should. Finally, Mplus can readily accommodate mixture of categorical and continuous metrics, including binary, ordinal, and normally distributed variables (Mplus uses the latent variable probit formulation described previously). We specified categorical imputation for the incomplete questionnaire items by listing "(c)" after each variable. Notice that we incorporated a number of variables that are not part of any analysis model, including age, exercise frequency, and pain severity. These additional variables effectively serve as auxiliary variables for the EFA and reliability analyses.

Evaluating the convergence behavior of the Markov chain Monte Carlo algorithm is an important part of the imputation phase, and Mplus offers both graphical and numeric diagnostics for this purpose. Based on the Gelman and Rubin (1992) potential scale reduction factor, we determined that the algorithm required approximately 3,000 iterations to converge. We subsequently used this information to specify a between-imputation (i.e., thinning) interval that saved an imputed data set after every 3,000th computational cycle. The slow convergence in this example owes to the relatively large number of threshold parameters required to impute the ordinal questionnaire items (Cowles, 1996). A number of resources are available for readers who want additional information on convergence diagnostics or the potential scale reduction factor (Enders, 2010; Gelman & Rubin, 1992; Gelman et al., 2013; Schafer, 1997).

Consistent with maximum likelihood analyses, we begin by factor analyzing the questionnaire items from the three scales and obtaining reliability estimates for the scale scores. Rotational indeterminacy poses problems for multiply imputed data because the factor order may differ across imputed data sets, making it difficult to automate the pooling process. The primary reason for analyzing multiple data sets is to properly estimate standard errors (the between-imputation variance in Equation 6.19 requires at least two data sets). However, if standard errors are not required, any single set of imputations will yield consistent parameter estimates (Schafer, 1997). Because researchers often employ extraction methods that do not produce standard errors, we arbitrarily selected a single filled-in data set for the EFA. To maintain consistency with the previous analyses, we used maximum likelihood estimation with a GEOMIN oblique rotation (the default). It is important to emphasize that the Mplus program in Appendix Code 7 produces standard errors and tests of model fit, but this information is invalid because it fails to account for missing data uncertainty.

The right panel of Table 6.3 gives the rotated loadings from the analysis, with bold typeface highlighting values greater than .40. As seen in the table, the solution closely approximates simple structure, with all items producing strong positive loadings on one factor and trivially small cross-loadings on other factors. Moreover, the multiple imputation estimates are virtually identical to those of maximum likelihood. As noted previously, the methods tend to produce equivalent parameter estimates and standard errors, particularly when the imputation procedure and the maximum likelihood analysis utilize the same variables (Collins et al., 2001; Schafer, 2003). In this example, the imputation phase used auxiliary variables that were not part of the maximum likelihood analysis (e.g., background variables such as age, gender, etc.), but including these additional variables appeared to have little impact on the results.

Appendix Code 8 gives the Mplus input for the two-stage reliability analysis based on 50 imputed data sets. With the exception of the DATA command, this program is virtually identical to the corresponding maximum likelihood analysis in Appendix Code 2. It is important to note that Mplus saves each data set to a separate text file (some programs stack the imputations in a single file). To automate the analysis and pooling phases, the researcher uses the FILE subcommand to specify a text file containing the names of the imputed files (Mplus automatically creates this file during the imputation process) and adds TYPE = IMPUTATION to the DATA command. Mplus then analyzes each data set separately and pools the resulting parameter estimates and standard errors. The coefficient alpha reliability estimates for the three scales were as follows: pain catastrophizing = .813, depression = .932, and pain interference = .927. These results are identical to those of maximum likelihood (to the third decimal).

The final analysis examined the measurement invariance of the depression scale for males and females. As before, we estimated two models, one with group-specific estimates and the other with invariant estimates. Importantly, the program in Appendix Code 6 generates imputations that are inappropriate for measurement invariance problems that posit group differences in the covariance structure. Although the imputation model includes gender as a predictor, the main effect of this variable preserves only the mean differences between males and females. Preserving group differences in the covariance structure additionally requires a set of gender-by-item product terms or a multiple-group imputation model (Enders & Gottschall, 2011). We adopted the latter approach, and Appendix Code 9 gives an Mplus program that specifies separate-group imputation for males and females. Importantly, invoking separate imputation models does not create group differences when none exist in the population. Rather, the procedure employs a model that is flexible enough to preserve group differences that may exist in the data. Finally, note that the multiple-group imputation program in Appendix Code 9 would have been appropriate for the EFA and reliability analyses because the imputation model is more general than either analysis model (i.e., it includes higher-order effects that are not present in or necessary for the EFA and reliability analyses). Normally, a single set of well-conceived imputations can serve as input data for many different analyses, but we used different imputation programs for didactic reasons.

We began by fitting a unidimensional model where all parameter estimates freely varied between groups, the syntax for which is in Appendix Code 10. The categorical imputations would be suitable for a weighted least squares estimator (e.g., the WLSMV routine in Mplus), but we used normal-theory estimation to facilitate comparisons with maximum likelihood. Note also that the imputation program in Appendix Code 9 rescales the ordinal questionnaire items to have a low score of 0 rather than 1, so we used the DEFINE command to add a point to each score, restoring the items to their original metric. To counteract normality violations, we implemented robust standard errors, but pooling rules for rescaled test statistics are not yet available for multiple imputation analyses. Consequently, we pooled normal-theory likelihood ratio tests (the so-called D_3 statistic; Meng & Rubin, 1992). The pooled chi-square test suggested adequate fit, $\chi^2(28) = 39.28$, $p = .08$, meaning that a one-factor model accurately reproduced the mean and covariance structure of both groups. Notice that, perhaps due to normality violations, the probability value is somewhat smaller than that from the maximum likelihood analysis ($p = .20$). Next, we fit a model with strict factorial invariance that imposed equality constraints on the measurement model parameters, the syntax for which is in Appendix Code 11. This model also produced adequate model fit, suggesting that males and females have identical parameter estimates, $\chi^2(47) = 55.24$, $p = .19$. Although formal pooling rules do not exist for fit indices such as the RMSEA and CFI, their average values across 50 data sets supported this conclusion (e.g., RMSEA = .026, CFI = .996). The right panel of Table 6.4 gives the parameter estimates and standard errors from the invariant model. Consistent with the EFA and reliability analyses, the estimates and standard errors are remarkably similar to those of the corresponding maximum likelihood analysis. Considered as a whole, the analysis examples underscore the proposition that personal preference is often the primary reason to prefer maximum likelihood to multiple imputation (or vice versa).

Planned Missing Data Designs

Having described and demonstrated maximum likelihood estimation and multiple imputation, we now turn to so-called planned missing data designs that produce MCAR or MAR missingness as a purposeful byproduct of data collection. Intentionally introducing missing data may seem like an odd idea at first, but this strategy has been around for some time. In fact, planned missing data applications are quite common in the psychometric literature (e.g., respondents or examinees are randomly administered different subsets of an item pool, computer adaptive tests). The idea behind these designs is to maximize precision while minimizing resources and respondent burden. Coupled with the missing data handling approaches from this chapter, planned missingness designs are a potentially powerful tool for researchers in a variety of disciplines.

Matrix sampling designs

In a multiple matrix sampling design, an item pool is divided into subsets that are then administered to different subgroups of respondents. The research on multiple matrix sampling largely originated from educational testing research (Gonzalez & Eltinge, 2007). According to Shoemaker (1973), researchers at Educational Testing Services (ETS) were considering these designs as early as the 1950s. Eventually, methodologists developed statistical procedures for estimating summary statistics from a multiple matrix sampling design (e.g., Hooke, 1956; Lord, 1960, 1962), and testing companies began to use this strategy to establish normative distributions for standardized tests. Subsequently, Shoemaker's (1973) seminal text subsequently provided procedural guidelines for implementing and analyzing data from matrix sampling designs.

Table 6.5 illustrates a simple matrix sampling design where 35 items are distributed across seven test forms. Notice that each test form is comprised of a unique block of five items, labeled A through G. This very basic design reduces test length while providing enough information to estimate student achievement (Gonzalez & Eltinge, 2007; Shoemaker, 1973). However, the design is not without limitations. In particular, items from different blocks never appear on the same test form, so researchers cannot estimate

Table 6.5 Multiple matrix design.

Form	Blocks	Items
1	A	1–5
2	B	6–10
3	C	11–15
4	D	16–20
5	E	21–25
6	F	26–30
7	G	31–35

Table 6.6 BIB spiral design with seven blocks.

Form	Blocks		
1	A	B	D
2	B	C	E
3	C	D	F
4	D	E	G
5	E	F	A
6	F	G	B
7	G	A	C

Table 6.7 Three-form design.

			Block					
	X		A		B		C	
Form	V_1	V_2	V_3	V_4	V_5	V_6	V_7	V_8
1	O	O	M	M	O	O	O	O
2	O	O	O	O	M	M	O	O
3	O	O	O	O	O	O	M	M

Note. O = observed, M = missing.

relationships between items from different blocks. To remedy this problem, psychometricians adapted the so-called Balanced Incomplete Block (BIB) design (Beaton, Johnson, & Ferris, 1987; Johnson, 1992; Kaplan, 1995). Like the design in Table 6.5, the item pool is distributed across blocks, but each block now appears on multiple test forms. To illustrate, Table 6.6 shows a BIB design that distributes the previous item blocks across seven forms. The design is balanced in three ways: (1) every pair of blocks appears together in at least one testing booklet, (2) the same number of participants responds to each item block, and (3) each block appears in each of the three positions. Importantly, the first feature allows researchers to estimate the association between any item pair because there is always a subset of respondents that answered both. The literature describes more complicated BIB designs that expand on the one from Table 6.6 (Beaton et al., 1987; van der Linden, Veldkamp, & Carlson, 2004).

Three-form design

Although BIB designs are well suited for large-scale testing applications, they have practical limitations for many research scenarios where a large number of test forms can pose logistical challenges. Graham and colleagues proposed a variation on multiple matrix sample designs known as the three-form design (Graham, Hofer, & MacKinnon, 1996; Graham et al., 2006). The e-form design is the close cousin of the BIB spiral design but is less cumbersome because it requires only three test forms. Table 6.7 shows a common variant of the three-form design that consists of four item blocks, labeled X, A, B, and C. Like the BIB design, each block consists of a set of variables (e.g., background variables, test questions, questionnaire items, etc.), and each test form is assigned to a different subsample of respondents. As seen in the table, the X block appears on every form, while the A, B, and C blocks appear on two of the three forms. Because each block appears with every other block, the three-form design allows researchers to estimate any zero-order association in the data, although it does require careful planning with higher-order (e.g., interactive) effects (Enders, 2010).

The three-form design is flexible and can be tailored to a variety of research goals, but a thoughtful approach is needed to achieve the best results. For example, variables with smaller effect sizes should be assigned to the X block in order to maximize power. Variables that are crucial to the research goals could also be assigned to the X block, and models with two-way interactions require at least one variable from X (Enders, 2010). Although the number of variables in each block can differ, Graham (2012) suggests that equal block sizes can optimize resources and power. Finally, researchers need to consider whether to distribute items from the same scale across blocks. For logistical reasons, Graham et al. (2006) recommended keeping all scale items together in the same block, but simulation studies suggest that distributing scale items across blocks can maximize power (Gottschall, West, & Enders, 2012). These are just a few issues that researchers must consider when implementing a three-form design, and detailed treatments are available elsewhere in the literature.

Designs for longitudinal data

Thus far, we have focused on planned missing data designs for cross-sectional research. Perhaps not surprisingly, methodologists have proposed a variety of planned missingness designs for longitudinal research. The idea of intentional missing data is a relatively old one in the developmental literature, where researchers are often interested in age-related change (Nesselroade & Baltes, 1979). These designs go by various names, including accelerated longitudinal designs, accelerated cohort designs, sequential cohort designs, and cross-sequential designs. The basic idea behind these designs is to combine a number of short-term longitudinal studies into a longer study. To illustrate, suppose that a researcher wants to examine age-related changes in student achievement across middle and high school. Table 6.8 illustrates a cross-sequential design with four years of data from 7th, 8th, and 9th grade students. Each age cohort essentially forms a four-year longitudinal study, and combining the cohorts into a single analysis allows researchers to examine change over a six-year age span, albeit with incomplete data (e.g., the 7th grade cohort has missing data at grades 11 and 12;

Table 6.8 Cross-sequential design for age-related change.

| | \multicolumn{6}{c}{Grade} |
Cohort	7	8	9	10	11	12
1 (7th)	O	O	O	O	M	M
2 (8th)	M	O	O	O	O	M
3 (9th)	M	M	O	O	O	O

Note. O = observed, M = missing.

Table 6.9 Wave missing design.

	Measurement Wave					
Pattern	1	2	3	4	5	6
1	O	O	O	O	O	O
2	M	O	O	O	O	O
3	O	M	O	O	O	O
4	O	O	M	O	O	O
5	O	O	O	M	O	O
6	O	O	O	O	M	O
7	O	O	O	O	O	M

Note. O = observed, M = missing.

the 8th grade cohort has missing data at grades 7 and 12). Other variations on this design are possible (Little, 2013).

In addition to age-related designs, methodologists have proposed a number of designs that apply the logic of matrix sampling to longitudinal data. In particular, the literature describes a number of "wave missing" designs where participants have missing data at one or more measurement occasions (Graham et al., 2001; Mistler & Enders, 2012). To illustrate, Table 6.9 shows a wave missing design with seven missingness patterns, each comprised of a different subsample of respondents (missing data patterns are analogous to test forms in the cross-sectional context). The design includes a group with complete data, but this is not a requirement. For example, Graham et al. (2001) proposed designs with all possible combinations of one or two missing waves, and many such designs are possible. Interestingly, Graham et al. (2001) reported that, holding the total number of observed data points constant, collecting complete data from N participants will yield less power than collecting incomplete data from a larger number of respondents. This feature makes planned missingness designs particularly attractive for longitudinal research.

Power in Planned Missing Data Designs

Planned missing data designs are incapable of introducing bias because they produce an MCAR or MAR mechanism. Consequently, when the overall sample size is fixed, the primary downside of these designs is a loss of statistical power. Fortunately, this reduction is often quite small. To illustrate the impact of planned missing data on power, we return to the three-form design in Table 6.7. Not surprisingly, power for the three-form design is largely determined by its missing data rates. To illustrate, Table 6.10 shows the percentage of missing data for each variable or pair of variables in the design. As seen in the table, variables in the X block are completely observed, whereas variables within the A, B, and C blocks have 33% missing data. Missingness rates are the highest between variables in the A and B, A and C, and B and C blocks, where 66% of the scores are incomplete. All things being equal, the values in Table 6.10 suggest that the three-form design yields three tiers of power. Power will be greatest for pairs of variables in the X set because the data are complete, while power will be somewhat lower for correlations between an X variable and a variable from block A, B, or C (e.g., V_1 and V_3) and

Table 6.10 Proportion of missing data from the three-form design.

		\multicolumn{8}{c}{Block}
		\multicolumn{2}{c}{X}	\multicolumn{2}{c}{A}	\multicolumn{2}{c}{B}	\multicolumn{2}{c}{C}
Block	Variable	V_1	V_2	V_3	V_4	V_5	V_6	V_7	V_8
X	V_1	0%							
	V_2	0%	0%						
A	V_3	33%	33%	33%					
	V_4	33%	33%	33%	33%				
B	V_5	33%	33%	66%	66%	33%			
	V_6	33%	33%	66%	66%	33%	33%		
C	V_7	33%	33%	66%	66%	66%	66%	33%	
	V_8	33%	33%	66%	66%	66%	66%	33%	33%

Table 6.11 Power estimates for correlations from the three-form design.

		\multicolumn{8}{c}{Block}
		\multicolumn{2}{c}{X}	\multicolumn{2}{c}{A}	\multicolumn{2}{c}{B}	\multicolumn{2}{c}{C}
Block	Variable	V_1	V_2	V_3	V_4	V_5	V_6	V_7	V_8
X	V_1								
	V_2	0.99							
A	V_3	0.95	0.95						
	V_4	0.95	0.95	0.94					
B	V_5	0.95	0.95	0.77	0.76				
	V_6	0.95	0.95	0.75	0.76	0.94			
C	V_7	0.94	0.95	0.76	0.77	0.76	0.76		
	V_8	0.95	0.95	0.75	0.76	0.76	0.77	0.94	

associations between variables within the A, B, or C blocks (e.g., V_3 and V_4). Finally, power will be lowest for correlations between the A, B, or C blocks (e.g., V_3 and V_5).

Computer simulations provide a straightforward tool for estimating power in planned missing data designs. To illustrate the process, we used Mplus to generate 5,000 artificial samples of $N = 200$, each with eight normally distributed variables. Appendix Code 12 gives the syntax for the simulation. To keep things simple, the correlations among the variables were uniformly fixed at .30, a value that corresponds to Cohen's (1988) benchmark for a moderate effect size. Missingness patterns followed the three-form design from Table 6.7 with an approximately equal distribution of cases across the three forms. Finally, we used maximum likelihood to estimate the correlations among the eight variables (multiple imputation would yield nearly identical results). Because we generated the samples from a population with nonzero correlations, the proportion of the 5,000 data sets that produced a statistically significant correlation is an estimate of power.

Table 6.11 gives power estimates for each correlation in the design. To establish a benchmark, note that that correlation between V_1 and V_2 (X block variables with complete data) produced power equal to .99. Given the large rates of missingness for other pairs of variables, it is reasonable to expect a rather dramatic reduction in power. However, this was not necessarily the case. For example, the 33% missing data rate for V_1 and V_3 reduced power from .99 to .95, a decrease of only 4%. Not surprisingly, the lowest power values were associated with correlations between A, B, and C block variables, where the missingness rate was 66%. Even then, the reductions were not as great as one might expect. For example, power for the correlation between V_3 and V_5 (A and B block variables, respectively) decreased from .99 to .77, a drop of approximately 23%. Considered as a whole, the relatively small reductions in power owe to the fact that maximum likelihood (or equivalently, multiple imputation) borrows from the observed data when estimating parameters from incomplete data. For example, power for the correlation between V_1 and V_3 is bolstered because V_1 is observed whenever V_3 is missing, and the observed scores carry information about the missing V_3 values.

Summary

Missing data are a common problem for psychometricians and researchers employing psychometric methods. A great deal of methodological research has focused on the development and evaluation of sophisticated missing data handling techniques, and two "gold standard" methods – maximum likelihood and multiple imputation – are now widely available in general-purpose and specialized software packages. Maximum likelihood estimation and multiple imputation are quite different from a procedural standpoint; the former estimates parameters and standard errors from the observed data, whereas the latter fills in missing values before the analysis. Despite their apparent differences, the techniques are often exchangeable, producing nearly identical results – such was the case with the data analysis examples we presented in the chapter. Aside from personal preference, there is often little reason to prefer one method to the other. However, statistical theory and empirical research studies tell us that there are strong reasons to prefer maximum likelihood and multiple imputation to older methods such as deletion and single imputation: relaxed assumptions about the missing data process, a reduction in nonresponse bias, and an improved statistical power. Maximum likelihood estimation and multiple imputation are ideally suited for a range of psychometric applications and, given their important advantages over older methods, researchers should decrease their reliance on older techniques in favor of these newer methods.

References

Albert, J. H., & Chib, S. (1993). Bayesian analysis of binary and polychotomous response data. *Journal of the American statistical Association, 88*, 669–679.

Allison, P. D. (2002). *Missing data*. Newbury Park, CA: Sage.

Baraldi, A. N., & Enders, C. K. (2010). An introduction to modern missing data analyses. *Journal of School Psychology, 48*, 5–37.

Barnard, J., & Rubin, D. B. (1999). Small-sample degrees of freedom with multiple imputation. *Biometrika, 86*, 948–955.

Beale, E. M. L., & Little, R. J. A. (1975). Missing values in multivariate analysis. *Journal of the Royal Statistical Society, Series B, 8*, 27–41.

Beaton, A. E., Johnson, E. G., & Ferris, J. J. (1987). The assignment of exercises to students. In A. E. Beaton (Ed.), *Implementing the new design: The NAEP 1983–84 technical report*. Princeton, NJ: Educational Testing Services.

Carpenter, J. R., Goldstein, H., & Kenward, M. G. (2011). REALCOM – IMPUTE software for multilevel multiple imputation with mixed response types. *Journal of Statistical Software*, 45, 1–14.

Carpenter, J. R., & Kenward, M. G. (2013). *Multiple imputation and its application.* Chichester, UK: John Wiley & Sons, Ltd.

Cohen, J. (1988). Statistical power analysis for the behavioral sciences (2nd ed.). Hillsdale, NJ: Erlbaum.

Collins, L. M., Schafer, J. L., & Kam, C. M. (2001). A comparison of inclusive and restrictive strategies in modern missing data procedures. *Psychological Methods*, 6, 330–351.

Cowles, K. (1996). Accelerating Monte Carlo Markov chain convergence for cumulative-link generalized linear models. *Statistics and Computing*, 6, 101–111.

Dempster, A. P., Laird, N. M., & Rubin, D. B. (1977). Maximum likelihood from incomplete data via the EM algorithm. *Journal of the Royal Statistical Society, Series B*, 39, 1–38.

Enders, C. K. (2003). Using the expectation maximization algorithm to estimate coefficient alpha for scales with item-level missing data. *Psychological Methods*, 8, 322–337.

Enders, C. K. (2004). The impact of missing data on sample reliability estimates: Implications for reliability reporting practices. *Educational and Psychological Measurement*, 64, 419–436.

Enders, C. K. (2010). *Applied missing data analysis.* New York: Guilford Press.

Enders, C. K. (2011). Missing not at random models for latent growth curve analyses. *Psychological Methods*, 16, 1–16.

Enders, C. K., & Gottschall, A. C. (2011). On the use of multiple imputation with multiple group latent variable models. *Structural Equation Modeling: A Multidisciplinary Journal*, 18, 35–54.

Finney, S. J., & DiStefano, C. (2013). Nonnormal and categorical data in structural equation models. In G. R. Hancock & R. O. Mueller (Eds.), *A second course in structural equation modeling* (2nd ed.) (pp. 439–492). Charlotte, NC: Information Age.

Gelman, A., & Rubin, D. B. (1992). Inference from iterative simulation using multiple sequences. *Statistical Science*, 7, 457–511.

Gelman, A., Carlin, J. B., Stern, H. S., Dunson, D. B., Vehtari, A., & Rubin, D. B. (2013). *Bayesian data analysis.* Boca Raton, FL: Chapman and Hall.

Gonzalez, J. M., & Eltinge, J. L. (2007). Multiple matrix sampling: A review. In *Proceedings of the Section on Survey Research Methods, American Statistical Association* (pp. 3069–3075).

Gottschall, A. C., West, S. G., & Enders, C. K. (2012). A comparison of item-level and scale-level multiple imputation for questionnaire batteries. *Multivariate Behavioral Research*, 47, 1–25.

Graham, J. W. (2003). Adding missing-data relevant variables to FIML-based structural equation models. *Structural Equation Modeling: A Multidisciplinary Journal*, 10, 80–100.

Graham, J. W. (2009). Missing data analysis: Making it work in the real world. *Annual Review of Psychology*, 60, 549–576.

Graham, J. W. (2012). *Missing data.* New York, NY: Springer New York.

Graham, J. W., Hofer, S. M., & MacKinnon, D. P. (1996). Maximizing the usefulness of data obtained with planned missing data patterns: An application of maximum likelihood procedures. *Multivariate Behavioral Research*, 31, 197–218.

Graham, J. W., Olchowski, A. E., & Gilreath, T. D. (2007). How many imputations are really needed? Some practical clarifications of multiple imputation theory. *Prevention Science*, 8, 206–213.

Graham, J. W., Taylor, B. J., & Cumsille, P. E. (2001). Planned missing-data designs in analysis of change. *In New Methods for the Analysis of Change* (pp. 335–353). Washington, D.C.: American Psychological Association.

Graham, J. W., Taylor, B. J., Olchowski, A. E., & Cumsille, P. E. (2006). Planned missing data designs in psychological research. *Psychological Methods*, 11, 323–343.

Hooke, R. (1956). Symmetric functions of a two-way array. *The Annals of Mathematical Statistics*, 27, 55–79.

Horton, N. J., Lipsitz, S. R., & Parzen, M. (2003). A potential for bias when rounding in multiple imputation. *The American Statistician*, 57, 229–232.

Hughes, R. A., White, I. R., Seaman, S. R., Carpenter, J. R., & Sterne, J. A. C. (2014). Joint modeling rationale for chained equations. *BMC Medical Research Methodology, 14*, 1–10.

Jackman, S. (2000). Estimation and inference via Bayesian simulation: An introduction to Markov chain Monte Carlo. *American Journal of Political Science, 44*, 375–404.

Jeličić, H., Phelps, E., & Lerner, R. M. (2009). Use of missing data methods in longitudinal studies: The persistence of bad practices in developmental psychology. *Developmental Psychology, 45*, 1195–1199.

Johnson, E. G. (1992). The design of the national assessment of educational progress. *Journal of Educational Measurement, 29*, 95–110.

Johnson, V. E., & Albert, J. H. (1999). *Ordinal data modeling*. New York: Springer.

Kaplan, D. (1995). The impact of BIB spiraling-induced missing data patterns on goodness-of-fit tests in factor analysis. *Journal of Educational and Behavioral Statistics, 20*, 69–82.

Keller, B. T., & Enders, C. K. (2014). *A latent variable chained equations approach for multilevel multiple imputation*. Paper presented at the Modern Modeling Methods Conference, Storrs, CN.

Kim, K. H., & Bentler, P. M. (2002). Homogeneity of means and covariance matrices for multivariate incomplete data. *Psychometrika, 67*, 609–624.

Lee, T., & Cai, L. (2012). Alternative multiple imputation inference for mean and covariance structure modeling. *Journal of Educational and Behavioral Statistics, 37*, 675–702.

Levy, R., Mislevy, R. J., & Behrens, J. T. (2011). MCMC in educational research. In S. Brooks, A. Gelman, G. L. Jones, & X. L. Meng (Eds.), *Handbook of Markov chain Monte Carlo: Methods and applications* (pp. 531–545). London: Chapman & Hall/CRC.

Little, R. J. A. (1988). A test of missing completely at random for multivariate data with missing values. *Journal of the American Statistical Association, 83*, 1198–1202.

Little, R. (2009). Selection and pattern mixture models. In G. Fitzmaurice, M. Davidian, G. Verbeke, & G. Molenberghs (Eds.), *Longitudinal data analysis* (pp. 409–431). Boca Raton, FL: Chapman & Hall.

Little, R. J. A., & Rubin, D. B. (2002). *Statistical analysis with missing data* (2nd ed.). Hoboken, NJ: John Wiley & Sons, Inc.

Little, T. D. (2013). *Longitudinal structural equation modeling*. New York, NY: Guilford Press.

Lord, F. M. (1960). Use of true-score theory to predict moments of univariate and bivariate observed-score distributions. *Psychometrika, 25*, 325–342.

Lord, F. (1962). Estimating norms by item-sampling. *Educational and Psychological Measurement, 22*, 259–267.

Meng, X. L., & Rubin, D. B. (1992). Performing likelihood ratio tests with multiply-imputed data sets. *Biometrika, 79*, 103–111.

Mislevy, R. J. (2016). Missing responses in item response theory. In W. J. van der Linden & R. K. Hambleton (Eds.), *Handbook of modern item response theory* (Vol. 2) (2nd ed.). Chapman & Hall/CRC Press.

Mistler, S. A., & Enders, C. K. (2012). Planned missing data designs for developmental research. In B. Laursen, T. Little, & N. Card (Eds.), *Handbook of developmental research methods* (pp. 742–754). New York: Guilford.

Muthén, B., Asparouhov, T., Hunter, A., & Leuchter, A. (2011). Growth modeling with nonignorable dropout: Alternative analyses of the STAR*D antidepressant trial. *Psychological Methods, 16*, 17–33.

Muthén, L. K., & Muthén, B. O. (1998–2012). *Mplus user's guide* (7th ed.). Los Angeles, CA: Muthén & Muthén.

Muthén, B., du Toit, S. H. C. & Spisic, D. (1997). *Robust inference using weighted least squares and quadratic estimating equations in latent variable modeling with categorical and continuous outcomes*. Unpublished technical report.

Nesselroade, J. R., & Baltes, P. B. (1979). *Longitudinal research in the study of behavior and development*. Academic Press.

Peugh, J. L., & Enders, C. K. (2004). Missing data in educational research: A review of reporting practices and suggestions for improvement. *Review of Educational Research, 74*, 525–556.

Raghunathan, T. E., Lepkowski, J. M., Van Hoewyk, J., & Solenberger, P. (2001). A multivariate technique for multiply imputing missing values using a sequence of regression models. *Survey Methodology, 27*, 85–95.

Raykov, T. (2011). On testability of missing data mechanisms in incomplete data sets. *Structural Equation Modeling: A Multidisciplinary Journal, 18*, 419–429.

Reiter, J. P. (2007). Small-sample degrees of freedom for multi-component significance tests with multiple imputation for missing data. *Biometrika, 92*, 502–508.

Rubin, D. B. (1976). Inference and missing data. *Biometrika, 63*, 581–592.

Rubin, D. B. (1978). Multiple imputations in sample surveys – a phenomenological Bayesian approach to nonresponse. *Proceedings of the Survey Research Methods Section of the American Statistical Association* (pp. 30–34).

Rubin, D. B. (1987). *Multiple imputation for nonresponse in surveys*. Hoboken, NJ: John Wiley & Sons, Inc.

Rubin, D. B. (1996). Multiple imputation after 18+ years. *Journal of the American Statistical Association, 91*, 473–489.

Ruehlman, L. S., Karoly, P., & Enders, C. (2012). A randomized controlled evaluation of an online chronic pain management program. *Pain, 153*, 319–330.

Savalei, V., & Bentler, P. M. (2009). A two-stage ML approach to missing data: theory and application to auxiliary variables. *Structural Equation Modeling, 16*, 477–497.

Schafer, J. L. (1997). *Analysis of incomplete multivariate data*. New York: Chapman & Hall.

Schafer, J. L. (2001). Multiple imputation with PAN. Chapter 12. In *New methods for the analysis of change*. L. M. Collins & A. G. Sayer (Eds.) (pp. 357–377), Washington D.C.: American Psychological Association.

Schafer, J. L. (2003). Multiple imputation in multivariate problems when the imputation and analysis models differ. *Statistica Neerlandica, 57*, 19–35.

Schafer, J. L., & Graham, J. W. (2002). Missing data: Our view of the state of the art. *Psychological Methods, 7*, 147–177.

Shin, Y., & Raudenbush, S.W. (2007). Just-identified versus overidentified two-level hierarchical linear models with missing data. *Biometrics, 63*, 1262–1268.

Shoemaker, D. M. (1973). Principles and procedures of multiple matrix sampling (Vol. xviii). Oxford: Ballinger.

Sinharay, S., Stern, H. S., & Russell, D. (2001). The use of multiple imputation for the analysis of missing data. *Psychological Methods, 6*, 317–329.

van Buuren, S. (2007). Multiple imputation of discrete and continuous data by fully conditional specification. *Statistical Methods in Medical Research, 16*, 219–242.

van Buuren, S. (2012). *Flexible imputation of missing data*. New York: Chapman & Hall.

van Burren, S., Brand, J. P. L., Groothuis-Oudshoorn, C. G. M., & Rubin, D. B. (2006). Fully conditional specification in multivariate imputation. *Journal of Statistical Computation and Simulation, 76*, 1049–1064.

van Buuren, S., & Groothuis-Oudshoorn, K. (2011). MICE: Multivariate imputation by chained equations in R. *Journal of Statistical Software, 45*, 1–67.

van der Linden, W. J., Veldkamp, B. P., & Carlson, J. E. (2004). Optimizing balanced incomplete block designs for educational assessment. *Applied Psychological Measurement, 28*, 317–331.

Widaman, K. F. (2006). Missing data: What to do with or without them. *Monographs of the Society for Research in Child Development, 71*, 42–64.

Wilkinson, L., & the Task Force on Statistical Inference (1999). Statistical methods in psychology journals: Guidelines and explanations. *American Psychologist, 54*, 594–604.

Wood, A. M., White, I. R., & Thompson, S. G. (2004). Are missing outcome data adequately handled? A review of published randomized controlled trials in major medical journals. *Clinical Trials, 1*, 368–376.

Wu, W., Jia, F., & Enders, C. K. (2015). *A comparison of imputation strategies to ordinal missing data for Likert scale variables. Multivariate Behavioral Research, 50,* 1–20, doi 10.1080/00273171.2015.1022644.

Yuan, K. H., & Bentler, P. M. (2000). Three likelihood-based methods for mean and covariance structure analysis with nonnormal missing data. *Sociological Methodology, 30,* 165–200.

Yucel, R. M., He, Y., & Zaslavsky, A. M. (2008). Using calibration to improve rounding in imputation. *The American Statistician, 62,* 1–5.

Zhao, J. H., & Schafer, J. L. (2016). PAN: Multiple imputation for multivariate panel or clustered data R package version 1.4.

Code Appendix

Code 1 Mplus EFA program (maximum likelihood).

```
DATA:

file = painexample.dat;

VARIABLE:

names = txgroup female age  exercise catast1 - catast4
   depress1 - depress7 painint1 - painint6 severity;

usevariables = catast1 - catast4
   depress1 - depress7 painint1 - painint6;
missing = all(-99);

ANALYSIS:

type = efa 1 4;
```

Code 2 Mplus two-stage reliability analysis program (maximum likelihood).

```
DATA:

file = painexample.dat;

VARIABLE:

names = txgroup female age  exercise catast1 - catast4
   depress1 - depress7 painint1 - painint6 severity;

usevariables = catast1 - catast4
   depress1 - depress7 painint1 - painint6;
```

```
missing = all(-99);

MODEL:

catast1 - catast4 with depress1 - depress7 painint1 -
painint6;
depress1 - depress7 with painint1 - painint6;

catast1 (cv1);
catast2 (cv2);
catast3 (cv3);
catast4 (cv4);
catast1 with catast2 (cc1);
catast1 with catast3 (cc2);
catast1 with catast4 (cc3);
catast2 with catast3 (cc4);
catast2 with catast4 (cc5);
catast3 with catast4 (cc6);

depress1 (dv1);
depress2 (dv2);
depress3 (dv3);
depress4 (dv4);
depress5 (dv5);
depress6 (dv6);
depress7 (dv7);
depress1 with depress2 (dc1);
depress1 with depress3 (dc2);
depress1 with depress4 (dc3);
depress1 with depress5 (dc4);
depress1 with depress6 (dc5);
depress1 with depress7 (dc6);
depress2 with depress3 (dc7);
depress2 with depress4 (dc8);
depress2 with depress5 (dc9);
depress2 with depress6 (dc10);
depress2 with depress7 (dc11);
depress3 with depress4 (dc12);
depress3 with depress5 (dc13);
depress3 with depress6 (dc14);
depress3 with depress7 (dc15);
depress4 with depress5 (dc16);
depress4 with depress6 (dc17);
depress4 with depress7 (dc18);
depress5 with depress6 (dc19);
depress5 with depress7 (dc20);
depress6 with depress7 (dc21);
```

```
painint1 (iv1);
painint2 (iv2);
painint3 (iv3);
painint4 (iv4);
painint5 (iv5);
painint6 (iv6);
painint1 with painint2 (ic1);
painint1 with painint3 (ic2);
painint1 with painint4 (ic3);
painint1 with painint5 (ic4);
painint1 with painint6 (ic5);
painint2 with painint3 (ic6);
painint2 with painint4 (ic7);
painint2 with painint5 (ic8);
painint2 with painint6 (ic9);
painint3 with painint4 (ic10);
painint3 with painint5 (ic11);
painint3 with painint6 (ic12);
painint4 with painint5 (ic13);
painint4 with painint6 (ic14);
painint5 with painint6 (ic15);

MODEL CONSTRAINT:

new(nitemc avgvarc avgcovc alphacat nitemd avgvard
avgcovd alphadep nitemi avgvari avgcovi alphaint);

nitemc = 4;
avgvarc = (cv1+cv2+cv3+cv4)/nitemc;
avgcovc = (cc1+cc2+cc3+cc4+cc5+cc6)/(nitemc*nitemc - 1)/2);
alphacat = (nitemc*avgcovc)/(avgvarc + (nitemc - 1)
*avgcovc);

nitemd = 7;
avgvard = (dv1+dv2+dv3+dv4+dv5+dv6+dv7)/nitemd;
avgcovd = (dc1+dc2+dc3+dc4+dc5+dc6+dc7+dc8+dc9+dc10+dc11
   +dc12+dc13+dc14+dc15+dc16+dc17+dc18+dc19
   +dc20+dc21)/(nitemd*(nitemd - 1)/2);
alphadep = (nitemd*avgcovd)/(avgvard + (nitemd - 1)
*avgcovd);

nitemi = 6;
avgvari = (iv1+iv2+iv3+iv4+iv5+iv6)/nitemi;
avgcovi = (ic1+ic2+ic3+ic4+ic5+ic6+ic7+ic8+ic9+ic10
   +ic11+ic12+ic13+ic14+ic15)/(nitemi*(nitemi - 1)/2);
alphaint = (nitemi*avgcovi)/(avgvari + (nitemi - 1)
*avgcovi);
```

Code 3 Mplus multiple group CFA with unconstrained parameters (maximum likelihood).

```
DATA:

file = painexample.dat;

VARIABLE:

names = txgroup female age  exercise catast1 - catast4
  depress1 - depress7 painint1 - painint6 severity;

usevariables = depress1 - depress7;
grouping = female (0 = male 1 = female);

missing = all(-99);

ANALYSIS:

estimator = mlr;

MODEL:

depress by depress1 - depress7;

model female:

[depress@0];
depress by depress2 - depress7;
[depress1 - depress7];
```

Code 4 Mplus multiple group CFA with constrained parameters (maximum likelihood).

```
DATA:

file = painexample.dat;

VARIABLE:

names = txgroup female age  exercise catast1 - catast4
  depress1 - depress7 painint1 - painint6 severity;
usevariables = depress1 - depress7;

grouping = female (0 = male 1 = female);

missing = all(-99);

ANALYSIS:

estimator = mlr;
```

```
MODEL:

depress by depress1 - depress7;
depress1 - depress7 (res1-res7);
[depress1 - depress7] (icept1-icept7);

MODEL FEMALE:

depress1 - depress7 (res1-res7);
[depress1 - depress7] (icept1-icept7);
```

Code 5 Mplus multiple group CFA with auxiliary variables (maximum likelihood).

```
DATA:

file = painexample.dat;

VARIABLE:

names = txgroup female age  exercise catast1 - catast4
   depress1 - depress7 painint1 - painint6 severity;
usevariables = depress1 - depress7;

grouping = female (0 = male 1 = female);

missing = all(-99);

auxiliary = (m) catast1 - catast4;

ANALYSIS:

estimator = mlr;

MODEL:

depress by depress1 - depress7;
depress1 - depress7 (res1-res7);
[depress1 - depress7] (icept1-icept7);

MODEL FEMALE:

depress1 - depress7 (res1-res7);
[depress1 - depress7] (icept1-icept7);
```

Code 6 Mplus imputation phase program (multiple imputation).

```
DATA:

file = painexample.dat;

VARIABLE:

names = txgroup female age  exercise catast1 - catast4
   depress1 - depress7 painint1 - painint6 severity;

usevariables = txgroup - severity;

missing = all(-99);

ANALYSIS:

type = basic;
bseed = 38291;

DATA IMPUTATION:

impute = age exercise catast1 (c) catast2 (c) catast4 (c)
   depress2 (c) depress3 (c) depress4 (c) depress5 (c)
   depress7 (c) painint1 - painint4 (c) severity (c);
ndatasets = 50;
save = painimp*.dat;
thin = 3000;

OUTPUT:

tech8;
```

Code 7 Mplus EFA program (multiple imputation).

```
DATA:

file = painimp1.dat;

VARIABLE:

names = txgroup female age exercise  catast1 - catast4
   depress1 - depress7 painint1 - painint6 severity;

usevariables = catast1 - catast4
   depress1 - depress7 painint1 - painint6;

ANALYSIS:

type = efa 1 4;
```

Code 6.8: Mplus two-stage reliability analysis and pooling program (multiple imputation).

```
DATA:

file = painimplist.dat;
type = imputation;

VARIABLE:

names = txgroup female age exercise  catast1 - catast4
  depress1 - depress7 painint1 - painint6 severity;

usevariables = catast1 - catast4
  depress1 - depress7 painint1 - painint6;

MODEL:

catast1 - catast4 with depress1 - depress7 painint1 -
painint6;

depress1 - depress7 with painint1 - painint6;

catast1 (cv1);
catast2 (cv2);
catast3 (cv3);
catast4 (cv4);
catast1 with catast2 (cc1);
catast1 with catast3 (cc2);
catast1 with catast4 (cc3);
catast2 with catast3 (cc4);
catast2 with catast4 (cc5);
catast3 with catast4 (cc6);

depress1 (dv1);
depress2 (dv2);
depress3 (dv3);
depress4 (dv4);
depress5 (dv5);
depress6 (dv6);
depress7 (dv7);
depress1 with depress2 (dc1);
depress1 with depress3 (dc2);
depress1 with depress4 (dc3);
depress1 with depress5 (dc4);
depress1 with depress6 (dc5);
depress1 with depress7 (dc6);
```

```
    depress2 with depress3 (dc7);
    depress2 with depress4 (dc8);
    depress2 with depress5 (dc9);
    depress2 with depress6 (dc10);
    depress2 with depress7 (dc11);
    depress3 with depress4 (dc12);
    depress3 with depress5 (dc13);
    depress3 with depress6 (dc14);
    depress3 with depress7 (dc15);
    depress4 with depress5 (dc16);
    depress4 with depress6 (dc17);
    depress4 with depress7 (dc18);
    depress5 with depress6 (dc19);
    depress5 with depress7 (dc20);
    depress6 with depress7 (dc21);

    painint1 (iv1);
    painint2 (iv2);
    painint3 (iv3);
    painint4 (iv4);
    painint5 (iv5);
    painint6 (iv6);
    painint1 with painint2 (ic1);
    painint1 with painint3 (ic2);
    painint1 with painint4 (ic3);
    painint1 with painint5 (ic4);
    painint1 with painint6 (ic5);
    painint2 with painint3 (ic6);
    painint2 with painint4 (ic7);
    painint2 with painint5 (ic8);
    painint2 with painint6 (ic9);
    painint3 with painint4 (ic10);
    painint3 with painint5 (ic11);
    painint3 with painint6 (ic12);
    painint4 with painint5 (ic13);
    painint4 with painint6 (ic14);
    painint5 with painint6 (ic15);

    MODEL CONSTRAINT:

    new(nitemc avgvarc avgcovc alphacat nitemd avgvard
    avgcovd
      alphadep nitemi avgvari avgcovi alphaint);

    nitemc = 4;
    avgvarc = (cv1+cv2+cv3+cv4)/nitemc;
    avgcovc = (cc1+cc2+cc3+cc4+cc5+cc6)/(nitemc*(nitemc - 1)/2);
    alphacat = (nitemc*avgcovc)/(avgvarc + (nitemc - 1)*avgcovc);
```

```
nitemd = 7;
avgvard = (dv1+dv2+dv3+dv4+dv5+dv6+dv7)/nitemd;
avgcovd =(dc1+dc2+dc3+dc4+dc5+dc6+dc7+dc8+dc9+dc10
   +dc11+dc12+dc13+dc14+dc15+dc16+dc17+dc18+dc19+dc20
   +dc21)/
   (nitemd*(nitemd - 1)/2);
alphadep = (nitemd*avgcovd)/(avgvard + (nitemd - 1)*avgcovd);

nitemi = 6;
avgvari = (iv1+iv2+iv3+iv4+iv5+iv6)/nitemi;
avgcovi =(ic1+ic2+ic3+ic4+ic5+ic6+ic7+ic8+ic9+ic10
   +ic11+ic12+ic13+ic14+ic15)/(nitemi*(nitemi - 1)/2);
alphaint = (nitemi*avgcovi)/(avgvari + (nitemi - 1)*avgcovi);
```

Code 9 Mplus multiple-group imputation phase program (multiple imputation).

```
DATA:

file = painexample.dat;

VARIABLE:

names = txgroup female age  exercise catast1 - catast4
   depress1 - depress7 painint1 - painint6 severity;
usevariables = txgroup age - severity;

categorical = txgroup catast1 - severity;

missing = all (-99);

classes = gender (2);

knownclass = gender (female = 0 female = 1);

ANALYSIS:

type = mixture;
estimator = bayes;
bseed = 394932;
model = allfree;
```

```
DATA IMPUTATION:

impute = age exercise catast1 (c) catast2 (c) catast4 (c)
   depress2 (c) depress3 (c) depress4 (c) depress5 (c)
   depress7 (c) painint1 - painint4 (c) severity (c);
ndatasets = 50;
save = painmfimp*.dat;
thin = 10000;

MODEL:

%overall%
txgroup age - severity with txgroup age - severity;

OUTPUT:

tech8;
```

Code 10 Mplus multiple group CFA with unconstrained parameters (multiple imputation).

```
DATA:

file = painmfimplist.dat;
type = imputation;

VARIABLE:

names = txgroup catast1 - catast4 depress1 - depress7
   painint1 - painint6 severity age exercise male female;

usevariables = depress1 - depress7;

grouping = female (0 = male 1 = female);

DEFINE:

depress1 = depress1 + 1;
depress2 = depress2 + 1;
depress3 = depress3 + 1;
depress4 = depress4 + 1;
depress5 = depress5 + 1;
depress6 = depress6 + 1;
depress7 = depress7 + 1;
```

```
ANALYSIS:

estimator = ml;

MODEL:

depress by depress1 - depress7;

model female:

[depress@0];
depress by depress2 - depress7;
[depress1 - depress7];
```

Code 11 Mplus multiple group CFA with constrained parameters (multiple imputation).

```
DATA:

file = painmfimplist.dat;
type = imputation;

VARIABLE:

names = txgroup catast1 - catast4 depress1 - depress7
  painint1 - painint6 severity age exercise male female;

usevariables = depress1 - depress7;

grouping = female (0 = male 1 = female);

DEFINE:

depress1 = depress1 + 1;
depress2 = depress2 + 1;
depress3 = depress3 + 1;
depress4 = depress4 + 1;
depress5 = depress5 + 1;
depress6 = depress6 + 1;
depress7 = depress7 + 1;

ANALYSIS:

! specify ml for pooled chi-square test;
estimator = mlr;
```

```
MODEL:

depress by depress1 - depress7;
depress1 - depress7 (res1-res7);
[depress1 - depress7] (icept1-icept7);

MODEL FEMALE:

depress1 - depress7 (res1-res7);
[depress1 - depress7] (icept1-icept7);
```

Code 12 Mplus power simulation for a three-form design (maximum likelihood).

```
MONTECARLO:

names = q1 - q8;
nobservations = 200;
nreps = 5000;
seed = 56798;

patmiss =
  q1(0) q2(0) q3(0) q4(0) q5(0) q6(0) q7(1) q8(1)|
  q1(0) q2(0) q3(0) q4(0) q5(1) q6(1) q7(0) q8(0)|
  q1(0) q2(0) q3(1) q4(1) q5(0) q6(0) q7(0) q8(0);

patprobs = .333 | .333 | .334;

MODEL POPULATION:

[q1-q8*0];
q1-q8*1;
q1-q8 with q1-q8*.30;

ANALYSIS:

MODEL:

[q1-q8*0];
q1-q8*1;
q1-q8 with q1-q8*.30;
```

7

Causal Indicators in Psychometrics

Aja L. Murray and Tom Booth

Introduction

Effect indicator models are models in which some latent attribute is assumed to underlie and determine responses to observed indicators. Effect indicator models have been the bread and butter of psychometrics, representing the basis for latent variable models including item response theory and factor models and being central to definitions of reliability and validity. However, there are regions of psychometric territory that effect indicator models do not cover. In particular, effect indicator models do not provide a basis for operationalizing a construct that cannot feasibly be considered a common cause of a set of item responses, but, rather represents the outcome of their combined influence. These kinds of models have been termed "causal indicator" models. The prototypical example of such a construct is socioeconomic status (SES) (Bollen, 1989; Hagger-Johnson, Batty, Deary, & von Stumm, 2011) but in recent years there has been a growing interest in the wider application of causal indicators. In this chapter, we lay out the conceptual basis of causal indicator models, highlight the challenges and controversies associated with their use, and review common practices relating to their application in empirical research.

Defining "Causal Indicators"

Causal indicators are associated with considerable controversy; an important reason for which – we believe – is an almost complete lack of undergirding psychometric theory. In lieu of a guiding theory, conceptual definitions of causal indicators tend to rely on contrasting them with effect indicators, which have a better-developed theoretical basis. Following in this tradition, we will first define effect indicators before proceeding to introduce causal indicators and the features that distinguish them from effect indicators.

Effect indicators

Effect indicator responses are assumed to reflect a latent dimension that is the common cause of all those responses. From this concept, it follows that a measurement model is one in which the latent variable is considered to be the antecedent of all observed indicators. This is depicted in the top of Figure 7.1 (see Wang, Engelhard Jr., & Lu, 2015 for an extended diagram of this type). Diagrammatically, the connection between effect indicators and the latent dimension of interest is represented as a single headed arrow being emitted from the construct, to the indicator (top, Figure 7.1). In the model, effect indicators (y_i), can be modelled as a function of the latent variable, with the magnitude of its causal impact measured by the factor loading (λ_i). The latent variable does not necessarily completely determine responses to items, therefore, residual terms for indicators (δ_i) are also included. Lower factor loadings are taken to imply a smaller causal effect of the latent dimension on the indicator.

An important feature of the idealized effect indicators model is **local independence conditional on the conceptual variable**. Here, because the conceptual variable is assumed to be the sole common cause of all the effect indicators in the set, the effect indicators are locally independent conditional on the latent variable. In the diagram, this feature is indicated by an absence of double-headed arrows between the indicator residuals. In practice, conditional local independence is often violated; in an effects indicator model framework, this would be attributed to a failure to attain an ideal set of indicators, or that a given pair of indicators is multi-dimensional in that multiple common cause latent variables may be related to the indicators. Importantly, within the effects indicator framework, the necessity to model these effects are not taken to not imply any fundamental mis-specification of the direction of causality between indicators and the latent dimension but attributed to imperfect measurement.

Another feature of the idealized effect indicators model is **conceptual parallelism**; that is, that all indicators are conceptually interchangeable with one another and that swapping one indicator for another would not change the meaning of the latent dimension being measured (Borsboom, Mellenbergh, & van Heerden, 2004). For example, substituting a measure of verbal ability for a measure of spatial ability when attempting to capture general intellectual ability would not, in theory, alter the fact that general intellectual ability was being measured. Again, in an effects indicator framework any failure to maintain the (empirical) meaning of a latent dimension following indicator changes would commonly be attributed to imperfection of the indicators rather than the underlying theoretical assumption, that the latent dimension causes the indicators, is incorrect.

Causal indicators

In the case of **causal indicators** (middle, Figure 7.1), the direction of causation is theorized as opposite to that in an effects indicator model. Individual arrows show the regression paths from the x_is to the conceptual variable, depicting the proposed flow of causality. The regression or structural paths (γ_i) indicate the magnitude of causal impact of the observed variables on the variable of interest. The model for the conceptual variable is also usually depicted as including a disturbance term (ζ). The x_is in the causal indicator model are allowed to correlate as indicated by the

Causal Indicators in Psychometrics 189

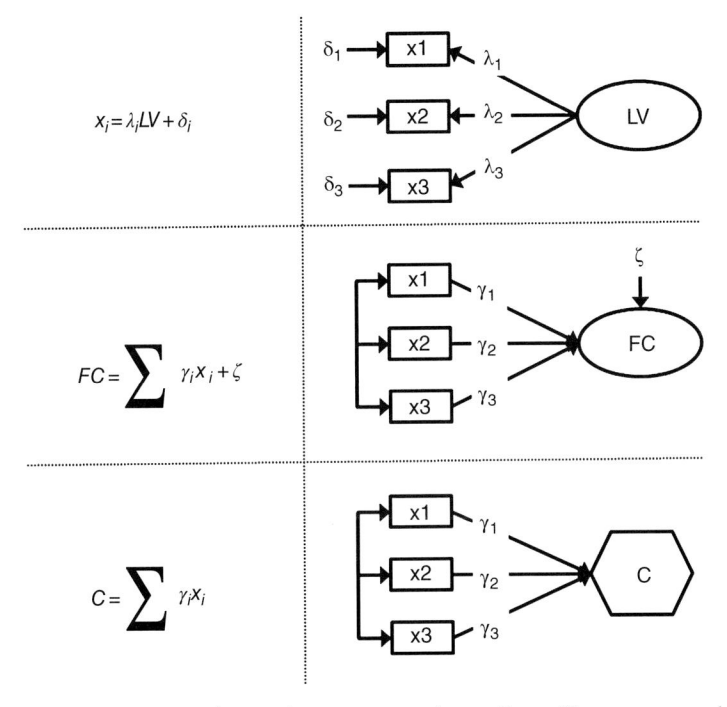

$x_i = \lambda_i LV + \delta_i$

$FC = \sum \gamma_i x_i + \zeta$

$C = \sum \gamma_i x_i$

Figure 7.1 Diagrammatic and equation representations of an effect, cause, and composite indicator model.

double-headed arrows between the x_is. This is because the indicators are assumed to be entirely exogenously determined and their covariance is in no part due to the causal influence of a latent variable; only to unmeasured external influences and/or local interactions.

The change in the conceptualization of the causal relation means that the latent variable is the common effect rather than the common cause of its indicators. However, while the direction of relation has changed, it has been argued that causal indicators should possess **conceptual unity** (Bollen & Diamantopoulos, 2017). That is, the causal indicators represent observed measures that all match the theoretical definition of the concept of interest.

Causal indicators are not assumed to be interchangeable with one another because they do not all reflect the same common cause. Therefore, to omit, change, or add an indicator would be to change the nature of the variable being measured.

Lastly, the inclusion of a disturbance term captures the fact that there may exist further indicators of the variable of interest that have not been measured. The presence of a disturbance term and the theoretical conceptual unity are the key features that differentiate causal indicators from another type of indicator, composite indicators (Bollen & Diamantopoulos, 2017; Figure 7.1, bottom panel). Composites (the variable measured by a set of composite indicators) need not correspond to any single definition of a concept; that is, they do not require conceptual unity. Further, composite indicators come together to define a composite variable in its entirety; there is no residual, as there are no additional unmeasured indicators of that composite.

Issues with traditional definitions of causal indicators

While this definition of causal indicators has proven useful for highlighting when effect indicator models may not be appropriate, it has not proven sufficiently unambiguous to allow clear and consistent interpretations of causal indicator models. For example, causal indicators have been variously interpreted as (1) **indicators** or **measures** of an underlying conceptual variable; (2) measures **of the causes** of a conceptual variable; and (3) **causes** of a conceptual variable (e.g., Hardin & Marcoulides, 2011). While a number of helpful expositions have clarified these differences in definition (see Bollen & Bauldry, 2011; Bollen & Diamantopoulos, 2017), there remains much debate. The debate primarily revolves around researchers' desire to apply interpretation (1) to models such as that depicted in the middle panel of Figure 7.1. However, a structural model such as that presented in Figure 7.1 (middle panel) does not define causal indicators as measures (1), but defines them as standing for causes (i.e., as measures of causes) of the relevant conceptual variable (2). Therefore, the main confusions in the literature tend to represent a conflation of the first two definitions.

A further set of critiques has focused on the two features that differentiate causal and composite indicators. Firstly, it has been argued that the definition of conceptual unity is vague and does not contain sufficient constraints to make the criterion one that can reasonably be used to differentiate between the nature of types of indicators (Markus, 2015; see also Widaman, 2015). Markus notes that under current definitions, post-hoc arguments for conceptual unity could be made about almost any set of indicator variables. Second, issues have been raised with the definition of and practical distinction between causal and composite indicators by the presence or not of a disturbance term. Widaman (2015) notes that the variance of the disturbance term is unbounded, and thus it is impossible to tell if it is large or near zero. If it is near zero, then what differentiates the operationalization of a construct with cause or composite indicators? Further, Widaman points out that in any given study we do not know what the "other sources" captured by the residual are and whether their omission has introduced bias in parameter estimates.

It is beyond the scope of the current chapter to resolve these issues but they are important to note here to give a reader a sense of the very active debate surrounding the modelling of causal indicators. Instead, this chapter provides suggestions for how to decide when to use causal indicators, how to develop and select causal indicators, and how to combine them is the subject of the sections that follow. For the remainder of the chapter we adopt the definition of a causal indicator as "an indicator that measures the cause of a conceptual variable that is not directly observed but which can be represented by the combined effect of a set of indicators measuring a set of its causes."

Determining when Indicators Should be Viewed as Causal Indicators

There are two broad cases in which the decision as to whether to use causal indicators or not is important. First, when beginning the process of scale construction; and second, when considering how to model an existing set of indicators. The latter issue most commonly confronts researchers; therefore, we will address this question first before presenting recommendations for the development of causal indicators.

The issue of when to model a set of indicators as causal rather than effect indicators is highly contentious. Some researchers have been critical of studies that use latent variable

Table 7.1 Example items from the job contents questionnaire.

Dimension	Example item
Skill Discretion	Concerns the level of skill required and the freedom to exercise those skills in completing tasks.
Decision Authority	Concerns the degree to which the organization constrains and impacts the freedom of individuals to make decisions concerning work tasks.
Psychological Job Demands	Concerns how hard workers work, constraints placed on task completion and conflicting demands.
Co-worker Support	Concerns how social relations with co-workers can influence strain through their competence and quality of social interaction.
Supervisor Support	Concerns how social relations with supervisors can influence strain through socio-emotional support and interest.

Note. Brief definitions taken from Karasek et al. (1998) and Karasek and Theorell (1990).

modelling for indicators that they argue are in fact causal indicators, while others have suggested that attempting to use causal indicator "measurement models" is meaningless (e.g., Rhemtulla, van Bork & Borsboom, 2015). These debates center, in part, around the use and results from the empirical and conceptual decision criteria used to determine whether a set of indicators represent causal indicators or effect indicators. As we review these techniques next, the challenges inherent in using causal indicators will become apparent.

Example: Iso-strain

For the remainder of this chapter we will use an example construct called iso-strain. Iso-strain is defined by Karasek et al. (1998; see also Karasek & Thorell, 1990) as **the psychological strain resulting from the joint effects of the demands of the workplace**. Iso-strain is commonly operationalized based on the Job Contents Questionnaire (JCQ; see Karasek et al., 1998). The JCQ is based on the theoretical demand/control model of occupational stress, which focuses on how the objective features of work environments may be related to strain and stress. In its most general form, this theoretical model states that when demand is high and control is low, individuals will feel a greater level of strain. This model was subsequently extended to include aspects of social support. The JCQ assesses five core demands, namely Skill Discretion, Decision Authority, Psychological Job Demands, Co-Worker Support, and Supervisor Support. Brief definitions of these demands are provided in Table 7.1.

Our data come from a sample of 372 participants (Female = 222, 59.7%) who were at the time of testing employed in a variety of organizations in the public and private sector. Further details on this sample can be found in Booth, Murray, Marples, and Batey (2013).

Conceptual criteria for choosing a causal indicators approach

Several conceptual criteria have been proposed to aid in determining whether indicators are best conceived as cause or effect indicators of a construct (e.g., Bollen, 1989; Jarvis, MacKenzie, & Podsakoff, 2003). These assume that a set of indicators has been developed and data collected on these indicators for some empirical study. The issue at hand is how to operationalize the construct statistically. In particular, whether an effect

Table 7.2 Conceptual criteria to aid in differentiating causal and effect indicators.

Criterion	Explanation
1. Does the direction of causality flow from construct to indicators or vice versa according to the theoretical definition of the construct?	In a causal indicator model, the indicators define the construct and so the direction of causality runs from indicator to construct. In an effect indicator model, the construct determines indicator responses and thus the direction of causality runs from construct to indicator.
2. Would a change in the indicator produce a change in the construct?	In a causal indicator model, manipulating the values of the indicators should affect the value of the construct, e.g., increasing a person's occupational prestige should increase their socioeconomic status. In an effect indicator model changes in an indicator do not affect changes in the construct, e.g., increasing a person's test score would not increase their intellectual ability.
3. Is the construct the common cause of all the indicators?	In a causal indicator model, the construct is not the common cause of indicators, it is their common effect, e.g., the "work environment" is the emergent effect of all the aspects of a work environment that contribute to its global valence. For this reason, causal indicators need not be positively correlated.
4. Do the indicators have the same antecedents and consequences?	In a causal indicator model, there is no requirement that indicators have the same causes and effects (with the exception that they all affect the construct). In an effect indicator model, all indicators are expected to have the same causes and effects.
5. Are the indicators interchangeable?	In a causal indicator model, the indicators are not thought to be interchangeable because they measure unique aspects of a construct. This means that omitting an indicator would result in a change in the construct, e.g., if an item referring to "physical space" was removed from a scale measuring a residential environment, then the nature of the construct measured by the scale would be affected. In an effect indicator model, all items are assumed to "reflect" the same thing and can, therefore, be interchanged in principle.

indicators measurement model such as a factor model is appropriate, or whether it will be necessary to consider the indicators to be causal indicators.

These conceptual criteria are summarized in Table 7.2. They correspond to the conceptual definitions of cause and effect indicator models outlined previously, and can be used as a heuristic device for deciding whether a preexisting set of indicators should be modelled as causal or effect indicators.

To consider the direction of causation (criterion 1), we pose the question: is the questionnaire intended to capture an overall strain (iso-strain) variable that **causally**

influences aspects of their workplace? Here, it seems that although there are likely to be some bidirectional influences in practice (e.g., Jonge et al., 2001; Taris, Bok, & Caljé, 1998), the items measure features of jobs that would **cause** strain, rather than arise from strain. In fact, the authors' definitions of the indicators are based on how the features **influence** strain, and that strain **results from** these features. In a similar vein, we may ask whether manipulating the value of any of the indicators is likely to cause an increase in iso-strain (criterion 2). So, for example, if there were a sudden increase in the demands placed on an individual or the level of support in the workplace decreased, would we expect an increase in strain? The answer seems likely to be, yes, and this is indeed a central premise of the demand/control model of work stress (Karasek et al., 1998). On the other hand, increasing levels of iso-strain would not be expected to have a direct impact on skill discretion, decision authority, psychological job demands, coworker support, and supervisor support all in tandem.

The antecedents of the five JCQ indicators also seem relatively distinct (criterion 3). For example, the degree of support provided by a supervisor is likely a function of that supervisors' own characteristics, experiences, and the line-management structures and policies of the organization whereas the degree of skill discretion one can exercise in a given job will be influenced by factors such as the job description and content, organizational size, training provision, and individual ability. Thus, the antecedents of the five JCQ indicators seem to overlap very little and the idea that iso-strain is their major or common antecedent seems implausible (criterion 4).

Next, we may ask if the indicators can be considered interchangeable in the sense of reflecting the same underlying construct (criterion 5). Put another way, can they be considered akin to a random sample from a hypothetical universe of indicators reflecting iso-strain or do they come together from different domains? Karasek et al. (1998) discuss how the construction of the JCQ and the theory of the demand/control model of work stress are at odds with classical concept of reliability as it assumes the presence of a single underlying construct (p. 328). Indeed, the observed measures appear to be assessing largely distinct aspects of the workplace that contribute to strain.

On balance, conceptual consideration of the JCQ would appear to suggest that the causal indicator model is more appropriate than an effect indicator model.

Statistical criteria for choosing a causal indicators approach

Confirmatory factor analysis and confirmatory tetrad analysis As is exemplified in the previous section, application of conceptual criteria is subjective and relies heavily on subject matter expertise (Bollen & Bauldry, 2011). A number of authors have proposed empirical tests to complement these conceptual judgments. First, a simple test of whether an effect indicator model is defensible is to fit a confirmatory factor analysis (CFA) model (e.g., see Bollen, 1989). A poor fitting model evidencing violations of local independence suggests that an effects indicator model should be rejected. However, this does not imply that a causal indicator model is superior, it merely highlights that **either** the construction of the indicators has been suboptimal (i.e., many established effect indicator models fail to fit in CFA), or that assumptions about the nature of their connection to the latent trait should be re-evaluated (Cramer et al., 2012).

A disadvantage of the CFA framework is that it is not possible to make nested model comparisons between causal and effect indicator models, and therefore, there is no way within the CFA to empirically test competing models. Bollen and Ting (2000) proposed a confirmatory tetrad analysis (CTA) as an alternative means of comparing models involving either causal indicators, effect indicators, or both. CTA is based on a test of vanishing tetrads. A tetrad is the difference between the products of two covariances formed from four variables. A tetrad is said to vanish when this product is not significantly different from zero. Any model assuming causal and/or effect indicators will imply a certain set of vanishing tetrads based on its specification. In models containing all true effect indicators, all tetrads vanish. In a model with all true causal indicators, none will vanish. It is for this reason that the two models are "tetrad-nested": the set of vanishing tetrads implied by one model is a subset of those implied by the other model (Bollen & Ting, 2000). Models may also be compared, which comprise a mix of cause and effect indicators.

The first step in the CTA procedure involves defining the set of models to be tested. Then, for each of the models in the set, the model-implied vanishing tetrads need to be determined. For example, to compare an effect indicator model and a causal indicator model with the same four observed indicators (g, h, i, j), six covariances are formed implying three population tetrads (τ):

$$\tau_{ghij} = \sigma_{gh} - \sigma_{ij}$$
$$\tau_{gijh} = \sigma_{gi} - \sigma_{jh} \qquad (7.1)$$
$$\tau_{gjhi} = \sigma_{gj} - \sigma_{hi}$$

where σ is the population covariance between two variables indexed. For a model with n indicators, there will be $n!/(n-4)!4!$ sets of tetrads like this. So, for an effect indicator model for JCQ in which we have five observed variables, there are 10 covariances and 15 population tetrads (see Bollen & Ting, 2000). Bollen and Ting (1993) note that model-implied vanishing tetrads can be identified analytically, however, it may be more practical to identify them using empirical means based on the model-implied covariance matrix for the specified model covariance structure (see Hipp & Bollen, 2003, for an example using covariance algebra).

Once the model-implied vanishing tetrads have been identified, redundant tetrads need to be removed. Redundancy arises because some vanishing tetrads are implied by others. For example, in an effect indicator model with four indicators, the first two vanishing tetrads imply the third. In general, whenever the same pair of covariances appears in two vanishing tetrads, a redundant pair of vanishing tetrads is implied.

The next step is to establish whether the vanishing tetrads implied by the model vanish in the sample data. This is done using a test statistic for vanishing tetrads that compares the model-implied vanishing tetrads to the sample tetrads given a sample covariance matrix. Bollen (1990) derived the T statistic for this purpose, which asymptotically approximates a chi-square distribution with df equal to the number of vanishing tetrads in the test. A comparison of the test statistics for tetrad-nested models differing in their composition of causal and effect indicators provides the empirical test of causal versus effect indicators.

Bollen and Ting (1998) noted that for a range of small to moderate sample sizes and/or larger models that were realistic in empirical research, the approximation of the distribution of T to the relevant chi-square distribution was relatively poor. Bollen and Ting (1998) initially proposed a bootstrap test for the p-value for the observed

T statistic, which has been subsequently developed by Johnson and Bodner (2007). Johnson and Bodner's bootstrap test demonstrated improved statistical power in small samples, with statistical power increasing with model size and reduced computational demands substantially.

When using CTA in real data, Bollen and Ting (2000) caution that if an effect indicator model is supported, additional checks may be needed. This is because it is possible that a tetrad could vanish in a causal indicators model if it so happens that there is no linear relation between some of the causal indicators. One useful check is to estimate a confirmatory factor model and examine the factor loadings and variance. If any factor loadings or the variance of the latent variable is not significantly different from zero, this suggests that in spite of the CTA result, a causal indicator model may be more appropriate.

While CTA has a number of appealing features, it also has a number of limitations. First, CTA does not prove that one has a causal indicator model; it simply shows that the data are inconsistent with an effect indicator model. Bollen and Bauldry (2011) note there is no definitive statistical test of cause versus effect indicators. Second, CTA is complicated by situations in which both cause and effect indicators are hypothesized; for example, as in the multiple indicator multiple cause (MIMIC) model. Third, it is not possible to construct tetrads with fewer than four observed variables. Common practice in factor analysis and structural equation models is to use a minimum of three indicators (i.e., the minimum required for identification) and in such a model it is not possible to apply CTA. Fourth, the presence of correlated residuals complicates CTA as it impacts the vanishing tetrads implied by the model (Bollen & Ting, 2000).

Procedures for computing CTA are available for SAS (Bollen, Lennox, & Dahly, 2009; Hipp, Bauer, & Bollen, 2005), and Stata (Bauldry & Bollen, 2015). Interested readers are referred, for example, to Glanville and Paxton (2007) who used the method to compare two theoretical models of generalized trust (see also Bollen et al., 2009; Wilson et al., 2007).

CFA and CTA of JCQ Continuing our examination of the JCQ, we here apply CTA analysis using TetradSEM (Chen & Bollen, 2014) to the data described previously. All analyses were conducted in R version 3.0.2 (R Core Team, 2013).

In this analysis, we first test a simple CFA of the JCQ data and consider model fit, factor loadings, and evidence of violations of local independence from modification indices. Next, we conduct CTA analysis comparing the effect indicator to the causal indicator model. As the causal indicator model has no implied vanishing tetrads, the p-value for the test statistic for the effect indicator model provides the test of whether this model should be accepted or not. To demonstrate the comparison of tetrad-nested models, we also compare the complete effect indicator model to a model that includes three effect and two causal indicators. For the CTA analysis, we apply the modified bootstrap procedure suggested by Johnson and Bodner (2007).

Results of the CFA for the JCQ suggested poor fit to the data (χ^2 = 403.57 (10), p < .001, CFI = 0.75, TLI = 0.50; RMSEA = 0.23; SRMR = 0.11). Factor loadings for the five indicators differed markedly. The loadings for Skill Discretion (0.73), Decision Authority (0.90), Co-Worker Support (0.33), and Supervisor Support (0.39) were all statistically significant (p < .001). However, the loading for Psychological Demands (0.01, p = .90) was not. Inspection of the modification indices, which provide an estimate of the improvement in the chi-square statistic if the parameter were included in the model, suggested the presence of correlated residuals between Co-Worker and Supervisor Support (MI = 40.18), Skill Discretion and Decision Authority (MI = 38.38), and between Skill Discretion and Psychological Demands (MI = 44.81).

Next, we conducted an individual CTA on the effect indicator model. As noted before, the all causal indicator model has no implied tetrads and so the nested tetrad test can be conducted simply by examining the p-value for the all effect indicator model. In the case of the JCQ, this was significant ($p < .001$), suggesting the effect indicator model was an inferior description of the data to the causal indicator model. Finally, and to demonstrate the nested test procedure, we compared a model with all effect indicators to one with three effect and two causal indicators (see Appendix Code 1). For these models, the effect indicator model implies 120 vanishing tetrads, whereas our mixed indicators model implies 72. The modified bootstrap test yielded a significant effect (Δimplied tetrads = 48, $p < .001$), indicating that the mixed indicators model resulted in significantly better model fit than the effect indicator model.

The results of the empirical tests appear to support the conclusion that the five scores of the JCQ are not effect indicators and may be better thought of as causal indicators of iso-strain.

Mediation tests One further suggestion for testing whether causal or effect indicators are present is based on a test of mediation. That is, it is proposed that if the effect of some external variable on the indicators is entirely mediated by the latent variable, then it is defensible to treat those indicators as effect indicators. For example, in behavior genetic models it is possible to address this question by comparing a "common pathway model" with an "independent pathway mode" (see Franić et al., 2013). The former posits that the genetic and environmental influences on a set of indicators is completely mediated by a latent variable in an effects indicator measurement model, while the latter allows the genetic and environmental influences on the indicators to be direct (unmediated). The external variable need not be latent genetic and environmental influences but could be some other variable hypothesized to affect the latent variable of the effects indicator model such as an experimental manipulation or treatment. However, this method relies on a priori knowledge that the external variable should only affect the putative latent variable measured by the indicators and not aspects that are item specific. For example, this would be undermined if a treatment for a psychological disorder acted disproportionately on specific symptoms measured by items in an inventory used to measure pre- and posttreatment levels of the disorder even if the symptoms first arose from the disorder as a common underlying cause (Murray, McKenzie, Murray, & Richelieu, 2014).

Mediation test on the JCQ In the context of our JCQ example, we can explore the mediation test by fitting a CFA model to the five indicators, and predicting the latent iso-strain variable from a relevant criterion variable. In this model, the direct paths from the criterion variable to each indicator can be fixed to zero, and the modification indices (MIs) explored to evaluate whether the effect of the criterion is entirely mediated through the latent variable. This model is depicted in Figure 7.2.

The critical value for chi-square with an alpha level of .05 on one degree of freedom is 3.841. Therefore, if all MIs fall below this value, then we can consider that the effect of the criterion variable is empirically mediated by the latent variable. Here we ran this model (see Appendix Code 2) using Anxiety as measured by the General Health Questionnaire as our criterion. The MIs ranged from 0.517 to 3.135, suggesting the effect of

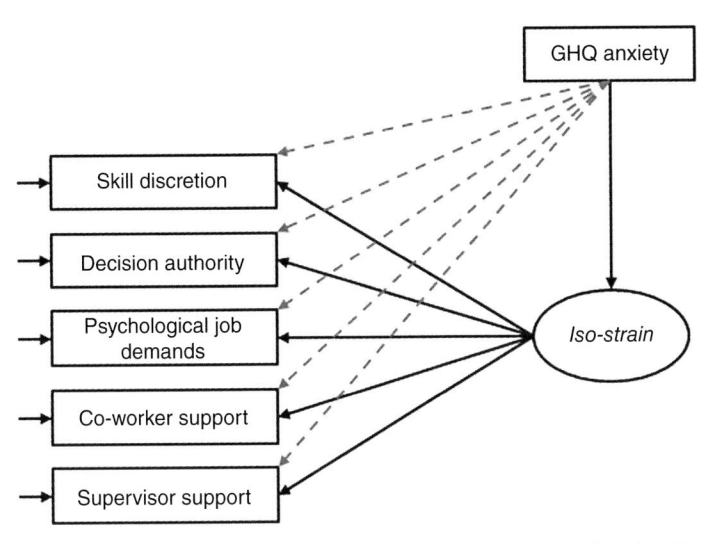

Figure 7.2 Mediation test for iso-strain and anxiety as measured by the General Health Questionnaire.

Anxiety was mediated by the latent construct, thus supporting the effect indicator model for iso-strain. Note this is to some degree contrasting with the theoretical and empirical findings noted previously, emphasizing the difficulty in establishing the nature of indicators for extant inventories.

Developing Scales with Causal Indicators

Much of the literature on causal indicators has been concerned with reconceptualizing and respecifying models based on existing scales developed under an explicit or implicit "effect indicators" assumption which has subsequently been suspected to be false (e.g., Jarvis et al., 2003). Taking a causal indicator approach to the development of a measure of a conceptual variable from the outset leads to the emergence of markedly different measures from those developed without this explicit focus (Juniper, Guyatt, Streiner, & King, 1997; Diamantopoulos & Siguaw, 2006). In fact, many of the procedures recommended for the development and evaluation of effect indicator scales are inappropriate for causal indicators and their misapplication to causal indicator scales is expected to damage their quality as measures (e.g., MacKenzie, Podsakoff, & Jarvis, 2005). These methods, which include cornerstone psychometric methods such as common factor analysis and item response theory models, evaluate items with respect to the extent to which they conform to effect indicator measurement models. Causal indicators would be liable to fail these tests not necessarily because they are poor causal indicators, but because there is no expectation that they should possess the same measurement properties as effect indicators (e.g., Juniper et al., 1997; MacKenzie, Podsakoff, & Jarvis, 2005).

Whether one approaches the construction of a scale from a cause or effect indicator approach, a first step is to define theoretically the construct of interest (Bagozzi, 2011). A given theoretical definition for a construct does not necessarily completely determine whether its indicators should be cause or effect. For example, one could score a person's level of SES based on a combination of indicators such as occupational level, education, and income (causal indicators) or one could ask an individual to complete several items assessing the extent to which they perceive themselves to be of high or low SES. The method described by Adler, Epel, Castellazzo, and Ickovics (2000), for example, asks individuals to indicate how high up on a depiction of a ladder representing social standing they would place themselves (Adler et al., 2000). These kinds of subjective measures can easily be extended to multi-item scales to which an effect indicators model can be applied on the assumption that the item responses are caused by a person's general impression of their standing on the conceptual variable (e.g., Bagozzi, 2011). The decision as to whether to pursue a causal indicators approach to constructing a scale is not necessarily straightforward in that it is not possible to simply classify some phenomena as requiring cause and others effect indicators.

Assuming that a causal indicators approach is preferred, developing and evaluating new scales is challenging. This is, in part, due to the fact that methods for scale evaluation with causal indicators and universal guidelines are difficult to determine owing to a lack of measurement theory for causal indicators (Howell, Breivik, & Wilcox, 2007; Markus & Borsboom, 2013). If we take the ultimate goal of test development to be the production of a valid scale, a major challenge is in defining exactly what is meant by the validity of causal indicators. Traditional notions of validity – for example, that a test measures what it purports to measure – are not applicable to causal indicators in a straightforward way and may not be applicable at all (Borsboom et al., 2004; Markus & Borsboom, 2013; Rhemtulla, van Bork & Borsboom, 2015). To get around these issues many authors take a pragmatic approach to validity and contribute suggestions on how to assess the psychometric properties of causal indicators on the assumption that certain favorable psychometric properties support the use of particular sets of causal indicators (e.g., Bollen, 2011). Here, we largely leave aside the theoretical question of what constitutes validity in the context of causal indicators, noting that it will be an important area for future discussion, and instead we review some practical recommendations for developing scales with causal indicators.

Construct definition and item generation

As has been noted previously, a key difference in cause and effect indicator models is whether the indicators themselves are in theory interchangeable (effect) or not (cause). In the effect indicator model, although indicators may vary in the extent to which they relate to the construct (e.g., factor loading), they are generally conceived of as being a random sample from a universe of items that could have been selected for the construct. In this view, the item selection should not fundamentally change the nature of the construct. For causal indicators, this does not hold. The omission of a given indicator will potentially change the meaning of the construct (Howell et al., 2007; Widaman, 2015). Approaches to developing effect indicator scales emphasize comprehensiveness and over-inclusiveness in the item generation stage. It could be argued that the need for over-inclusiveness in the item generation stage for scales with causal indicators is even greater (Roberts & Thatcher, 2009).

Scale refinement

The process of scale refinement involves the removal of the "poorest" indicators of the conceptual variable, leaving behind the best indicators for the construct of interest. While there are many ways in which a given indicator could be considered good or bad, alignment to the theoretical nature of the proposed construct (classically referred to as content validity) is of the utmost importance in causal indicator models.

To ensure correspondence between the definition of the conceptual variable and the causal indicators, content validity should be assessed by carefully comparing indicators to the definition of the construct (Bollen, 2011). Checks of content validity such as these weigh more heavily in the indicator elimination stage of causal indicator than in effect indicator scales because causal indicators play such a key definitional role in shaping the empirical meaning of constructs. As previously mentioned, lack of indicator interchangeability in causal indicators complicates the process of item elimination because removing an indicator removes a noncompensable piece of the overall scale (e.g., see Fayers & Hand, 2002). It is equally important to avoid including items that would fall outside the previously defined boundaries of the conceptual variables definition.

Petter, Straub, and Rai (2007) recommend assessing content validity of causal indicators prior to data collection and the assessment of other forms of validity (e.g., see Fayers & Hand, 2002). Content validity checks may employ methods such as Q-sorting (see Petter et al., 2007) and consultation of experts or the target population (Fayers & Hand, 2002). For example, Juniper et al. (1997) used the impact method to determine which indicators to retain in a scale measuring quality of life in asthma sufferers. Patients were asked which of the events described in the indicators they had experienced and how important they rated the event. They used an "impact" metric which was the frequency with which an event was experienced across patients and how important it was rated on average to select items for the final scale. In our job contents example, asking respondents to rate each item with respect to its salience in their personal work environment could provide information on whether items generally capture relevant job characteristics.

Another suggestion is to correlate each of the items with a "global" item that captures the essence of the construct, possibly excluding items with low correlations on the assumption that this indicates that they are not central to the construct (Diamantopoulos & Winklhofer, 2001). For example, for a measure of the psychological characteristics of job roles, one could correlate candidate indicators with a global prototypical item such as "Please rate the extent to which your job has negative characteristics." This would provide a gauge of which items contribute to a person's subjective impression of their job contents that presumably corresponds broadly to the intended construct. Diamantopoulos and Siguaw (2006) used this method to inform the construction of a causal indicators scale measuring the construct of intra-organizational export coordination. Finally, the scale and constituent items can be evaluated with respect to other validity criteria in the scale refinement stage where appropriate. This may include obtaining indices of external validity, interrater reliability, test-retest stability, face validity, or clinical validity (Fayers & Hand, 2002).

Using Causal Indicators in Research

In applied studies utilizing effect indicators, researchers will often fit a measurement model, such as a confirmatory factor model, within a broader structural equation modelling framework. Assuming that the global model specification is correct, such measurement models also yield information that is useful for scale refinement of effect indicator models (e.g., Bollen, 2011). However, there remains much debate as to how best to operationalize causal indicators in the context of broader empirical models. The primary issue with the application of causal indicator models is that statistically, they are not, and cannot, be identified (Rhemtulla, van Bork, & Borsboom, 2015). Here we outline a number of commonly used methodologies and the difficulties in their applications.

Multiple indicator multiple cause (MIMIC) models

One of the most widely discussed models to operationalize causal indicators is the MIMIC model (see Figure 7.3; Appendix Code 3). A primary reason for this popularity is the fact that the MIMIC model overcomes the inherent identification problem in operationalizing a causal indicator latent variable. Here, a number of effect indicators, usually the minimum for identification (see Bollen & Davis, 2009 for discussion) are included in the model.

It has been suggested that the coefficients relating the causal indicators to the latent variable in a MIMIC model can be interpreted as "validity coefficients," that is, the magnitude of the structural relation between the indicator and latent variable (e.g., see Bollen, 2011). However, a number of authors have questioned the use of the MIMIC model for causal indicators (Howell et al., 2007; Lee, Cadogan, & Chamberlain, 2013; Rhemtulla, van Bork & Borsboom, 2015; Treiblmaier, Bentler, & Mair, 2011). The main point made by these authors is that within the MIMIC model, the supposed causal indicators are simply covariates or predictors of a reflective latent variable defined by the effect indicators included in the model. Given this interpretation, it has been argued that if the effect indicators are changed, so too will the coefficients of the causal indicators, and thus it cannot be the causal indicators that are providing meaning to the construct.

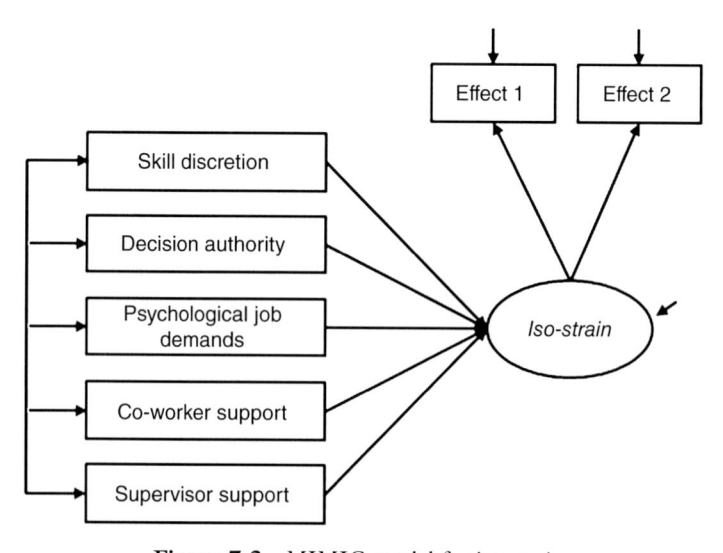

Figure 7.3 MIMIC model for iso-strain.

However, this interpretation of the latent variable in the MIMIC model is not shared by all in the field. Bollen and Diamantopoulos (2017), among others, have argued that this line of reasoning only follows from an incorrectly specified model. In an effect indicator model, indicators should be interchangeable with one another, without the meaning of the latent variable changing. Therefore, if I have a correctly specified effect indicator model with six indicators, I should be able to select any subset of three indicators, and the nature of the latent variable should not change. Subsequently, the relations of the causal indicators to the latent variable should not change. If, then, when I change a subset of effect indicators within a MIMIC model, the relations between my causal indicators and the latent variable change, this is not evidence against the causal indicators, but an indication that my effect indicators were misspecified.

At the point of writing, and to the authors' knowledge, there remains no consensus regarding the interpretation of the MIMIC latent variable within causal models.

Canonical correlation analysis

Treiblmaier, Bentler, and Mair (2011) proposed a measurement model that implements causal indicators via a common factor methodology based on canonical correlations. The proposed method has the advantage of producing an operationalization of the construct of interest that can be embedded and analyzed within a broader structural equation modelling framework in the same way as an effect indicator model. The method has two stages. In the first, the causal indicators are split into two weighted composite variables that are formed from the observed indicators. Treblmaier et al. (2011) suggest using canonical correlation analysis to obtain weights that result in maximally correlated composites. In the second stage of the analysis, these two composites are used as effect indicators of a common factor latent variable. The drawback of this approach is that while it allows constructs otherwise not easily operationalizable to be included in SEMs, there is a danger that the resulting latent factor no longer aligns with the intended theoretical definition of the construct because the weight that each indicator is given is defined on empirical grounds.

Indicator weight determination

An alternative approach to the use of SEM-based operationalizations of causal indicator models is to specify a rule for combining causal indicators into a single composite variable. In principle, this could be any logical rule, such as multiplicative or compensatory combinations of indicators (e.g., Busemeyer & Jones, 1983; Fayers & Hand, 2002; Mackenzie, Podsakoff, & Podsakoff, 2011). In practice, however, it will usually involve specifying or estimating indicator weights for a linear combination of the indicators, therefore, we will limit our discussion to this latter specification.

Weights may be specified using multiple schemes. For example, weights may be prespecified and fixed based on the construct definition and on theoretical grounds (Fayers & Hand, 2002). Researchers may disagree on the theories that underpin a measure or on the weights implied by these theories and fix the weights in their composite according to their own particular stance. A variant on this approach would be to specify indicator combination rules adaptively for different empirical applications but fix the relevant parameters according to those rules; that is, **adaptively specified and fixed**

weights. An example of this would be using different weighted composites for different empirical applications, but the researcher specifies these weights rather than estimating them from the data. This may arise if two researchers utilizing the same causal indicators have different theories regarding the nature of the construct, or, alternatively, if the construct is thought to have different meanings in different contexts or groups.

A disadvantage of using theoretically driven or respondent defined weights is that it ignores pragmatic but potentially important features of the indicators such as variations in psychometric quality or indicator collinearity. For example, an indicator with low reliability will receive a high weight if theoretically important even if this means a higher contribution of error to the final composite. Therefore, there is also some argument for pragmatic weighting approaches that take into account factors such as redundancy among indicators or unreliability. Markus and Borsboom (2013) outlined several methods of estimating weights according to different criteria. Principal components analysis provides weights that maximize explained variance in the indicators; regression can be used to estimate weights that maximize the variance explained in some construct-relevant criterion; and latent regression can be used to estimate weights that maximize the variance explained in a reflectively measured criterion. Correlation weights (weights defined by the zero order correlations of the items with some criterion) could also be used as an alternative to regression weights (Rigdon, 2013).

A broader issue with respect to the use of weights also arises when we consider the presence or absence of a disturbance term. If we believe the indicators should be causal indicators on theoretical grounds, and that we have not measured all indicators of the construct of interest, then we would be required to specify a disturbance term (or define a reliability) for the score or variable we have estimated. Without the inclusion of a disturbance term, then the score or variable and the indicators that comprise it are more consistently interpreted as composite indicators (e.g., as specified in Bollen & Diamantopoulos, 2017, Table 2, model D). Bollen and Diamantopoulos (2017) note that a score with prespecified weights and no disturbance term may be seen as a special case of a causal indicator model (Table 2, Model C), where the distinguishing feature is conceptual unity.

Summary

The primary purpose of this chapter was to summarize the current literature on the use of causal indicators in psychometrics. While there is largely an acceptance that effect indicators and associated models cannot meet all the psychometric needs of empirical research, there remains much debate and work to be done in developing and reaching consensus on appropriate methods for handling their (to date) main alternative; namely, causal indicators.

References

Adler, N. E., Epel, E. S., Castellazzo, G., & Ickovics, J. R. (2000). Relationship of subjective and objective social status with psychological and physiological functioning: Preliminary data in healthy, white women. *Health Psychology, 19*, 586–592.

Bagozzi, R. P. (2011). Measurement and meaning in information systems and organizational research: methodological and philosophical foundations. *MIS Quarterly, 35*, 261–292.

Bollen, K. A. (1989). *Structural equations with latent variables*. New York: John Wiley & Sons, Inc.

Bollen, K. A. (1990). Outlier screening and a distribution-free test for vanishing tetrads. *Sociological Methodology and Research*, 19, 80–92.

Bollen, K. A. (2011). Evaluating effect, composite, and causal indicators in structural equation models. *MIS Quarterly*, 35, 359–372.

Bollen, K. A., & Bauldry, S. (2011). Three Cs in measurement models: causal indicators, composite indicators, and covariates. *Psychological Methods*, 16, 265.

Bollen, K. A., & Davis, W. R. (2009). Causal indicator models: Identification, estimation, and testing. *Structural Equation Modeling: A Multidisciplinary Journal*, 16(3), 498–522.

Bollen, K. A., & Diamantopoulos, A. (2017, September 21). In defense of causal-formative indicators: A minority report. *Psychological Methods*, 22, 581–596, DOI: 10.1037/met0000056.

Bollen, K. A., Lennox, R. D., & Dahly, D. L. (2009). Practical application of the vanishing tetrad test for causal indicator measurement models: An example from health-related quality of life. *Statistics in Medicine*, 28, 1524–1536.

Bollen, K., & Ting. K-F. (1993). Confirmatory tetrad analysis. In P. Marsden (Ed.), *Sociological methodology* (pp. 147–1750). Washington, D.C.: American Sociological Society.

Bollen, K. A., & Ting, K.-F. (1998). Bootstrapping a test statistic for vanishing tetrads. *Sociological Methods & Research*, 27, 77–102.

Bollen, K. A., & Ting, K-F. (2000). A tetrad test for causal indicators. *Psychological Methods*, 5, 3–22.

Booth, T., Murray, A. L., Marples, K., & Batey, M. (2013). What role does neuroticism play in the association between negative job characteristics and anxiety and depression? *Personality and Individual Differences*, 55, 422–427.

Borsboom, D., Mellenbergh, G. J., & van Heerden, J. (2004). The concept of validity. *Psychological Review*, 111, 1061–1071.

Busemeyer, J. R., & Jones, L. E. (1983). Analysis of multiplicative combination rules when the causal variables are measured with error. *Psychological Bulletin*, 93, 549–562.

Cramer, A. O., Sluis, S., Noordhof, A., Wichers, M., Geschwind, N., Aggen, S. H.,... & Borsboom, D. (2012). Dimensions of normal personality as networks in search of equilibrium: You can't like parties if you don't like people. *European Journal of Personality*, 26, 414–431.

Diamantopoulos, A., & Siguaw, J. A. (2006). Formative versus reflective indicators in organizational measure development: a comparison and empirical illustration. *British Journal of Management*, 17, 263–282.

Diamantopoulos, A., & Winklhofer, H. M. (2001). Index construction with formative indicators: an alternative to scale development. *Journal of Marketing Research*, 38, 269–277.

Fayers, P. M., & Hand, D. J. (2002). Causal variables, indicator variables and measurement scales: an example from quality of life. *Journal of the Royal Statistical Society: Series A (Statistics in Society)*, 233–253.

Franić, S., Dolan, C. V., Borsboom, D., Hudziak, J. J., van Beijsterveldt, C. E., & Boomsma, D. I. (2013). Can genetics help psychometrics? Improving dimensionality assessment through genetic factor modeling. *Psychological Methods*, 18, 406–433.

Glanville, J. L., & Paxton, P. (2007). How do we learn to trust? A confirmatory tetrad analysis of the sources of generalized trust. *Social Psychology Quarterly*, 70, 230–242.

Hagger-Johnson, G., Batty, G. D., Deary, I. J., & von Stumm, S. (2011). Childhood socioeconomic status and adult health: comparing formative and reflective models in the Aberdeen Children of the 1950s Study (prospective cohort study). *Journal of Epidemiology and Community Health*, 65, 1024–1029.

Hardin, A., & Marcoulides, G. A. (2011). A commentary on the use of formative measurement. *Educational and Psychological Measurement*, 71, 753–764.

Hipp, J. R., Bauer, D. J., & Bollen, K. A. (2005). Conducting tetrad tests of model fit and contrasts of tetrad-nested models: a new SAS macro. *Structural Equation Modeling*, 12, 76–93.

Hipp, J. R., & Bollen, K. A. (2003). Model fit in structural equation models with censored, ordinal, and dichotomous variables: Testing vanishing tetrads. *Sociological Methodology, 33*, 267–305.

Howell, R. D., Breivik, E., & Wilcox, J. B. (2007). Reconsidering formative measurement. *Psychological Methods, 12*, 205.

Jarvis, C. B., MacKenzie, S. B., & Podsakoff, P. M. (2003). A critical review of construct indicators and measurement model misspecification in marketing and consumer research. *Journal of Consumer Research, 30*, 199–218.

Johnson, T. R., & Bodner, T. E. (2007). A note on the use of bootstrap tetrad tests for covariance structures. *Structural Equation Modeling, 14*, 113–124.

Jonge, J., Dormann, C., Janssen, P. P., Dollard, M. F., Landeweerd, J. A., & Nijhuis, F. J. (2001). Testing reciprocal relationships between job characteristics and psychological well-being: A cross-lagged structural equation model. *Journal of Occupational and Organizational Psychology, 74*(1), 29–46.

Juniper, E. F., Guyatt, G. H., Streiner, D. L., & King, D. R. (1997). Clinical impact versus factor analysis for quality of life questionnaire construction. *Journal of Clinical Epidemiology, 50*, 233–238.

Karasek, R., Brisson, C., Kawakami, N., Houtman, I., Bongers, P., & Amick, B. (1998). The Job Content Questionnaire (JCQ): an instrument for internationally comparative assessments of psychosocial job characteristics. *Journal of Occupational Health Psychology, 3*, 322–355.

Karasek, R. A., & Theorell, T. (1990). *Health, work, stress, productivity and the reconstruction of working life*. New York: Basic Books.

Lee, N., Cadogan, J. W., & Chamberlain, L. (2013). The MIMIC model and formative variables: problems and solutions. *AMS Review, 3*, 3–17.

MacKenzie, S. B., Podsakoff, P. M., & Jarvis, C. B. (2005). The problem of measurement model misspecification in behavioral and organizational research and some recommended solutions. *Journal of Applied Psychology, 90*, 710–730.

MacKenzie, S. B., Podsakoff, P. M., & Podsakoff, N. P. (2011). Construct measurement and validation procedures in MIS and behavioral research: integrating new and existing techniques. *MIS Quarterly, 35*, 293–334.

Markus, K. (2015). Unfinished business in clarifying causal measurement: Commentary on Bainter and Bollen. *Measurement: Interdisciplinary Research and Perspectives, 12*, 146–150.

Markus, K. A., & Borsboom, D. (2013). *Frontiers of test validity theory: Measurement, causation, and meaning*. Routledge.

Murray, A. L., McKenzie, K., Murray, K. R., & Richelieu, M. (2014). Mokken scales for testing both pre-and postintervention: An analysis of the Clinical Outcomes in Routine Evaluation – Outcome Measure (CORE–OM) before and after counseling. *Psychological Assessment, 26*, 1196–1204.

Petter, S., Straub, D., & Rai, A. (2007). Specifying formative constructs in information systems research. *MIS Quarterly, 31*, 623–656.

R Core Team (2013). R: A language and environment for statistical computing. R Foundation for Statistical Computing, Vienna, Austria. URL www.R-project.org/.

Rhemtulla, M., van Bork, R., & Borsboom, D. (2015). Calling models with causal indicators "measurement models" implies more than they can deliver. *Measurement: Interdisciplinary Research and Perspectives, 13*, 59–62.

Rigdon, E. E. (2013), Lee, Cadogan, and Chamberlain: An excellent point…but what about that iceberg? *AMS Review, 3*, 24–29.

Roberts, N., & Thatcher, J. (2009). Conceptualizing and testing formative constructs: tutorial and annotated example. *ACM SIGMIS Database, 40*, 9–39.

Taris, T. W., Bok, I. A., & Caljé, D. G. (1998). On the relation between job characteristics and depression: a longitudinal study. *International Journal of Stress Management, 5*(3), 157–167.

Treiblmaier, H., Bentler, P. M., & Mair, P. (2011). Formative constructs implemented via common factors. *Structural Equation Modeling, 18*, 1–17.

Wang, J., Engelhard Jr., G., & Lu, Z. (2015). Clarifying the conceptualization of indicators within different models. *Measurement: Interdisciplinary Research and Perspectives, 12*, 155–159.

Widaman, K. (2015). Much Ado About Nothing – Or at best, very little. *Measurement: Interdisciplinary Research and Perspectives, 12*, 165–168.

Wilson, B., Callaghan, W., & Stainforth, G. (2007). An application of vanishing tetrad analysis to a brand model. *International Review of Business Research Papers, 3*, 456–485.

Code Appendix

Code 1 R Code for the empirical examples.

Text following # are author annotations.

```
##################################################
# Packages
library(TetradSEM)
library(psych)
library(lavaan)

# The data used throughout is called CTA.data

##################################################
# Using lavaan code, describe the models to be tested

# Pure effect indicator model

effect ='JCQeffect =~ SkD + DA + PD + CS + SS'

# Mix of effect (3) and cause (2) indicators

mix = ' JCQmix =~ SkD + DA + PD
JCQmix ~ CS + SS
CS ~~ SS '

##################################################
# Fit a CFA model in lavaan
JCQcfa = cfa(effect, CTA.data, std.lv=T)

# Ask for model output including model fit
summary(JCQcfa, standardized=T, fit.measures=T)
```

```
# Ask for modification indices for violations of independence
modindices(JCQcfa)

####################################################
# Run CTA on effect indicator model
ZeroTetradTest(model.formulas = list(effect),
               data = CTA.data,
               mbootsrap.test=F,
               individual.test=T,
               simultaneous.test=T,
               nested.test=F,
               Latent_var_list = list("JCQeffect"),
               Num_equations_list = list("1"))

####################################################
# Run nested CTA on mix versus effect indicator model
ZeroTetradTest(model.formulas = list(effect, mix),
               data = CTA.data,
               mbootsrap.test=T,
               individual.test=T,
               simultaneous.test=F,
               nested.test=T,
              Latent_var_list = list("JCQeffect", "JCQmix"),
               Num_equations_list = list("1", "3"))
```

Code 2   R Code for mediation test.

Text following # denotes author annotations.

```
## Read in the data
med <- read.csv("D:/JCQ data2.csv", header=T)

## Create a new variable to Anx to act as predictor
med$Anx <- (med$ANX_P1 + med$ANX_P2)/2

# required package
library(lavaan)

# Specify the model with paths from Anx to latent Iso
# And paths fixed to zero to each indicator
jcq <- '
Iso =~ SkD + DA + PD + CS + SS
SkD ~~ DA + PD
```

```
DA  ~~ PD
Iso ~  Anx
SkD ~  0*Anx
DA  ~  0*Anx
PD  ~  0*Anx
CS  ~  0*Anx
SS  ~  0*Anx
'

# Run the model of the data
model <- sem(jcq, med)

# Look at summary output including MIs (mod)
summary(model, fit=T, mod=T)
```

Code 3   Example R Code for MIMIC models.

Text following # denotes author annotations.

```
# Example MIMIC model code following variable names in
Figure 7.3

# SkD = Skill Discretion
# DA  = Decision Authority
# PD  = Psychological Job Demands
# CS  = Co-worker Support
# SS  = Supervisor Support

# Specify the model
mimic1 = '
iso-strain =~ a*Effect1 + a*Effect2
iso-strain ~ SkD + DA + PD + CS + SS
SkD ~~ DA
SkD ~~ PD
SkD ~~ CS
SkD ~~ SS
DA  ~~ PD
DA  ~~ CS
DA  ~~ SS
PD  ~~ CS
PD  ~~ SS
CS  ~~ SS'

# Fit to the data using lavaan sem() function
mim1 = sem(mimic1, data=CTA.data, std.lv=T, fixed.x=F)
summary(mim1, standardized=T, fit.measures=T)
```

Part II
Identifying and Analyzing Scales

8
Fundamentals of Common Factor Analysis

Stanley A. Mulaik

Exploratory Factor Analysis

Single Common Factor of intellectual tasks

At the turn of the twentieth century, the concepts of correlation and linear regression developed by Francis Galton, Karl Pearson, and G. Udny Yule (Galton, 1886, 1888, 1889; Pearson, 1896; Yule, 1897) were new. As psychological and educational researchers began to calculate correlations between numerous psychological and anthropometric variables (Spearman, 1897, 1904a; Yule, 1900), they became interested in why variables were correlated. Frequently this occurred in studies of intellectual abilities. Spearman (1904b) is credited with formulating the first factor analytic model to account for the correlations between six variables representing scores on five tests of academic achievement and one of pitch discrimination in 33 school children. Spearman argued that a correlation between two "series of things" (variables), if "beyond the range of chance coincidence," could be assumed "to indicate and measure something common to both series in question," (Spearman, 1904b, p. 258). The correlations between his six variables were all significantly different from zero in all cases. Furthermore the correlations were generally moderate to large. Given a collection of variables measuring intellectual activity, he held that "Whenever branches of intellectual activity are at all dissimilar, then their correlations with one another appear wholly due to their being all variously saturated with some common fundamental Function (or group of Functions)" (Spearman, 1904b, p. 273). So, the issue was how to determine if indeed a collection of variables had just a single common "factor." See the correlation matrix in Table 8.1.

Spearman concluded on the basis of procedures not regularly used in factor analysis today that his six tests had a single general factor and consequently generalized "that all branches of intellectual activity have in common one fundamental function (or group of functions), whereas the remaining or specific elements of the activity seem in every case to be wholly different from that in all the others" (Spearman, 1904b, p. 284).

This leads us to the model equations of his model. Let $Y_1, \cdots, Y_n$ denote n "observed" variables, like test scores, grades, trait ratings. Spearman designated the general common factor by g and by ζ_i, the *ith* specific or "unique" factor, a "specific" component

Table 8.1 Correlation matrix for Spearman's six variables (N = 33).

	Classics	French	English	Mathem.	Discrim.	Music
Classics	1.00	0.83	0.78	0.70	0.66	0.63
French	0.83	1.00	0.67	0.67	0.65	0.57
English	0.78	0.67	1.00	0.64	0.54	0.51
Mathem.	0.70	0.67	0.64	1.00	0.45	0.51
Discrim.	0.66	0.65	0.54	0.45	1.00	0.40
Music	0.63	0.57	0.51	0.51	0.40	1.00

found only in variable Y_i. Often this is referred to as the "Two-Factor Model," which refers to two kinds of factors, found in each observed variable; the common factor and the unique factor. Then the model equations are:

$$\begin{aligned} Y_1 &= \lambda_{1g}g + \psi_1\zeta_1 \\ Y_2 &= \lambda_{2g}g + \psi_2\zeta_2 \\ Y_3 &= \lambda_{3g}g + \psi_3\zeta_3 \\ Y_4 &= \lambda_{4g}g + \psi_4\zeta_4 \\ Y_5 &= \lambda_{5g}g + \psi_5\zeta_1 \\ Y_6 &= \lambda_{6g}g + \psi_6\zeta_6 \end{aligned} \quad (8.1)$$

λ_{ig} denotes a numerical weight multiplied times the g factor variable to indicate how much a unit change of g was contributed to Y_i. Usually g (and common and unique factors generally) are assumed to have unit variances, for convenience. Working with correlations, we also assume the variance of the observed variables is unity. Whatever was in the *ith* variable not due to the common factor g was the *ith* specific or unique factor. ψ_i denotes the numerical weight to be multiplied times ζ_i representing how much a unit change of the *ith* unique factor contributes to the variable Y_i. Spearman assumed that the variables had been selected to be so diverse as to have only in common the general factor g. This assumption is not always recognized because it was thought that Spearman's model had been refuted by the discovery of other common factors. He recognized their possibility, but just wanted to focus on "general intelligence," g, and to do that, he had to select intellectual variables that did not share anything with other variables, so that whatever was not g was unique to the variable. The general factor and the specific factors are "latent" variables, meaning they are not directly observed. They are hypothetical variables invoked to account for whatever is common and whatever is unique to each observed variable. We'll deal with the question of interpreting the common factor later.

There are two major assumptions made with this model. (1) The correlations between the common factor and the unique factors are zero, $\rho(g,\zeta_i) = 0$. (2) The correlations among the pairs of unique factors are zero, $\rho(\zeta_i,\zeta_j) = 0$. This makes the general factor unrelated to any of the unique factors, and the unique factors are mutually unrelated. Generalizations of these assumptions to when there is more than one common factor, keep common factors uncorrelated with unique factors and the unique factors still mutually uncorrelated. But common factors may be correlated. Also by convention usually the common factor and unique factor variances are set to unity because they are not observed and their variances can be set arbitrarily to whatever is convenient.

Table 8.2 Factor loadings, communalities, unique variances, and unique pattern coefficients.

Variable	λ loading	Communality	Unique variance	ψ loading
Classics	.95613	.91418	.08582	.29295
French	.87078	.75827	.24173	.49166
English	.80712	.65144	.34856	.59039
Math	.74343	.55269	.44731	.66881
Discrim	.68878	.47442	.52558	.72496
Music	.65322	.42670	.57330	.75716

From the model equations in Equation 8.1 and the additional assumptions about correlations and variances between and among the common g and the n unique factors ζ_i, we can derive the correlations between distinct observed variables as

$$\rho(i,j) = \lambda_{ig}\lambda_{jg} \quad i \neq j \tag{8.2}$$

where $\rho(i,j)$ denotes the correlation between variables i and j. The correlation between variables is simply the product of the respective λ_{ig}s. The common variance in variable i, known as the *communality*, h_i^2, of variable i, is denoted by convention as

$$h_i^2 = \lambda_{ig}^2 \tag{8.3}$$

We now need to obtain estimates for the λs and ψs in the model equation. Rather than try to do this Spearman's way, I'm going to use the modern way and obtain a maximum likelihood factor analysis solution using SPSS. I indicate that the number of observations (subjects) is 33. I set the number of factors to extract to one.

The common factor analysis yielded Table 8.2 for the values of the λs and the ψs and the communalities and unique variances.

The λ_{ig} loading is often called the factor loading or **factor-pattern** loading. It represents how much a unit change of the factor variable g will produce a change in the normalized observed variable i. In this case the loadings are substantial. The communality is the proportion of variance in the data due to the common factor. In this case, with only one factor, it is equal to the square of the factor loading of the variable. The unique variance is one minus the communality. It is the proportion of the total variance of the variable (here it is unity) due to the unique factor. And the ψ loading is the square root of the unique variance.

Assessing fit

At this point after formulating a model, collecting data, and estimating its parameters (the λ_{ig} and ψ_i), we need to determine how well the model fits the data. Here we wish to see to what extent we can accurately reproduce the correlation matrix from the estimated parameters. This we will do by comparing the original correlation matrix to a matrix of correlations reproduced by the λ_{ig} as in Equation 8.2. In Table 8.3 we show a 6 × 6 matrix. Because a correlation matrix is symmetric on either side of its principal diagonal from the left upper corner to the right lower corner, we will show the model's reproduced correlation matrix below the principal diagonal, the communalities in the

Table 8.3 Reproduced correlations below diagonal, communalities designated with* down the principal diagonal, and residuals above the diagonal.

	Classic	French	English	Math	Discrim	Music
Classic	.91418*	−.00258	.00829	−.0108	.00144	.00544
French	.83258	.75827*	−.0328	.02263	.05022	.00118
English	.77171	.70283	.65144*	.03996	−.0159	−.0172
Math	.71082	.64737	.60004	.55269*	−.0621	.02437
Discrim	.65856	.59978	.55593	.51206	.47442*	−.0499
Music	.62456	.56882	.52723	.48563	.44993	.42670*

principal diagonal with ∗ to distinguish them, and the difference between the corresponding elements of the original correlations in Table 8.1 with those in Table 8.3, called the **residuals**, placed above the principal diagonal. The residuals are all near zero, which indicates good fit. But a statistical test of the fit of this one-common-factor model is given by a chi-square statistic, which has the value of 2.5157 for 9 degrees of freedom, which is **not** significant with $p = .9805$, indicating **support** for the model. The degrees of freedom are computed by the formula $df = n(n + 1)/2 - m$, where df are the degrees of freedom, n the number of observed variables, $n(n+1)/2$ the number of distinct observed elements in the symmetric correlation matrix – the elements on the principal diagonal and on one side of the diagonal – and m the number of estimated parameters. Here, with n equal to 6, the number of distinct elements is 21 and the number of estimated parameters (the λ_{ig} and ψ_i) is $6 + 6 = 12$. Hence $21 - 12 = 9$. Degrees of freedom represent the number of dimensions in which the data is free to differ from the model (Mulaik, 2001).

Any possibility of difference between the reproduced and the observed correlations is due to the constraints on the model: the number of common factors, the zero correlations between and among the common and unique factors. The estimated parameters are estimated conditional on the assumed constraints of the model. Because of the small sample size of $N = 33$, there is very little power to reject the hypothesis of a single common factor. So, one needs to take this good fit with a grain of salt.

Interpretation

At this point the issue of interpretation of the results arises. This concerns relating the numerical quantities to something in the world. It must be understood that Spearman's British colleagues were operating under the influence of the philosophical school known as British empiricism: In that school all knowledge begins with sense data and gets formulated by repeated associations in space and time of similar sensory experiences. So, the researcher seeks to make **inductive generalizations** from experience. What that boiled down to was that British scientists (other than their physicists) tended to look at data and seek what was common to them. In effect their method was "exploratory." Spearman may have instead held a belief in the preexistent reality of general intelligence in the kinds of tasks that seem to call it forth and thought to demonstrate that in a confirmatory manner in his 1904 study. But exploratory factor analysis is how his British colleagues interpreted the method and began to use it to discover what is common to various intellectual performances by examining their content. Cautiously, Spearman really doesn't come up with a definitive interpretation of g in this study. It is enough for him to establish that there is a single common factor among the variables he studied and a few other facts about how men and women do not differ in its capacity, how children seem to increase in their capacity until about 9 years of age, how it controls the relative position of children in school, and is to a large part responsible for success in pitch discrimination. It is important to understand that factor analysis does not yield its interpretation. Interpretation is a somewhat subjective process for the researcher to perform. It involves comparing what you have from the analysis and what you know about what occurs when a person solves problems given in tests. And the more experience you have had with things like those in the variables studied the better you will be at successfully interpreting a factor. In a way, what you are doing in interpreting a factor is formulating hypotheses that you will want to test in the future. Spearman already was testing his hypothesis.

Multiple Factors of the Intellect

Other researchers built on what Spearman had shown in his 1904 paper. They extended his methods to other tests of intellectual functioning and in doing so they discovered more than one common factor among these tests. Their reflecting on the many factors they were revealing led them to seek how to arrange them with respect to one another. By 1930 the British psychologists had developed a hierarchical theory of the intellect, with g at the pinnacle common to all intellective functioning, and other abilities beginning with those not as broad as g in their applications like verbal ability, spatial and mechanical ability, numerical ability, then descending down to more and more specific abilities confined to small groups of intellectual tasks, and finally to individual tasks (Vernon, 1961). It was like roots branching out from the trunk in large roots, to be followed by further branching into smaller roots, and eventually into small fiberous roots.

The British school of factor analysis also developed new methods for extracting many factors, which led to a growing recognition that their method was heavily based on the mathematics of linear algebra and the use of matrices. They extended the idea of an average of scores on a single variable to an average variable by adding all variables in a study together in seeking a general factor and other factors distinct from it. This came to be known as the "centroid method."

But the prominence of the British school of factor analysis was to be displaced in the 1930s and afterwards by developments in the United States. In the late 1930s L. L. Thurstone at the University of Chicago disagreed with the hierarchical structure of the intellect with general intelligence at the peak. He was suspicious of the general factor because it was usually the first factor in a centroid or principal axes solution, which he thought was just an artifact of the method of extraction. He was influenced by the theory of color vision that regarded the various hues as combinations of primary colors. Thus, by analogy, he sought to discover the "primary mental abilities" that occur in various combinations in individual tasks. He also was not satisfied with the factors produced by the summation of variables due to Burt, which came to be known as the centroid method. They simply helped us find the number of common factors by discovering at any point the additive combination of the variables that extracted the next most variance among the observed variables, after preceding factors, regarded now as additive combinations of the common parts of the variables, had been extracted. But the resulting factors were not the primary mental abilities.

There is an indeterminacy known as **rotational indeterminacy** in the common factor model. This holds that factor solutions are not unique. Different sets of factors having the same number of factors may be found that are linear transformations of one another and these could be used to reproduce the same correlation matrix. The problem was which, if any of these should be preferred? Thurstone's solution to this problem was **rotation to simple structure**. We will discuss this further later in the paper.

Thurstone's **simple structure** solutions allowed the common factors to be correlated. The factors tended to be linked to sets of quasi-homogeneous variables with large loadings on one factor and only minimal or zero loading on other factors. That made it easier to interpret the meaning of the factors by whatever was common to just those variables having high loadings on a factor. But because the common factors ended up correlated, the question arose as to what was the basis for their correlation? The obvious answer was that there were "second-order common factors" common this time to the first-order factors as opposed to individual observed variables. Here a factor analysis was performed on the correlations among the first-order factors, resulting in second-order factors. And the second-order common factors, though fewer now in number, were also correlated. So the correlations among the second-order factors were factor analyzed to find the third-order factors. This process continued to ever higher-order factors until there resulted just one factor, the g factor found in all the factors and variables below it, or none.

World War II, which began in 1939, led to the need by the military for tests of mental abilities that were crucial for selecting personnel with different aptitudes for training as officers, noncommision officers, and enlisted men in specialized areas. While a number of factor analytic studies were conducted during the war, they were limited by the computational burden required. After World War II, in the late 1950s computers were developed, and psychologists began to take advantage of this. Prior to computers, a factor analysis might take more than a month to complete. Today they can be calculated in seconds. Factor analysis was used to create general tests for both military and civilian use of multiple aptitudes where a number of test items, respectively, would contribute to testing each of certain intellectual abilities. Initially items thought relevant to certain intellectual abilities were assembled and subjected to factor analysis to discover the common factors that differentiated between the items. Items that did not relate with other items to a given factor were either discarded or new items were created to measure suspected new common factors.

J. P. Guilford (1967) reported on a number of studies done during World War II with the Air Force that produced 120 common factors from several studies. This led to a need to organize these factors in a meaningful manner. Guilford classified each intellectual test according to three facets. These facets were (1) mental operation (evaluation, convergent production, divergent production, memory, cognition), (2) content operated on (visual, auditory, symbolic, semantic, behavioral), and (3) the product of the operation on the content (units, classes, relations, systems, transformations, implications). Each facet contained a number of abilities, kinds of content, or kinds of products, respectively. So a distinct factor could be identified by the ability it measured, the kind of content operated on, and the result produced.

Raymond B. Cattell (1905–1998) was an English psychologist who studied under Spearman, with influences from Cyril Burt and R. A. Fisher, at the University of

London, where he obtained his Ph.D. in 1929. He emigrated to the United States in the late 1930s and after several academic appointments ended up at the University of Illinois. He conducted a profusion of factor analytic studies of the intellect, temperament, and personality. In the area of intellect, influenced by Spearman's theories of g and Thurstone's primary mental abilities, his major contribution, with his student John Horn (Cattell & Horn, 1978), was a factor analytic theory of intelligence with two major general factors, **fluid intelligence** and **crystalized intelligence** and a number of other factors of more restricted application. These originally were a division by Cattell of Spearman's g into two broad general factors. **Fluid intelligence** involves "…skills of perceiving relationships among stimulus patterns, drawing inferences from relationships, and comprehending implications" (Horn, 1988, p. 660). This factor is initially identified by a second-order factor analysis of first-order factor correlations, and it is interpreted by the nature of the test items subsumed under the common factors that have high second-order factor loadings on this factor. It has affinities to Spearman's **eduction of relations**, which Spearman defined as the power a person has when given to consider two things "to bring to mind any relations that essentially hold between them" (Spearman, 1927). It also has affinities to Louis Guttman's **analytic ability** or **rule-inferring ability** (Guttman, 1965). Both Spearman and Guttman derived these, not from factor analysis, but from examining test-item tasks as to what is shown the subject and what they require a subject to do. In items of eduction of relations or rule inferring, the subject is shown two or several pairs of things and is supposed to infer a **relation** between pairs of them. Guttman (1965) regarded intelligence as about correct perceptions of logical aspects of relations. He drew upon the concept of a relation in mathematics as a subset of a Cartesian product of two sets. The Cartesian product generates ordered pairs of elements from the two sets. A subset of these pairs is a relation between the sets. In the present case, where the subject had to demonstrate a correct perception of the relation, the subject might be required to fill in the blank for another pair in the relation where only the first member is shown. For example, "**This** is to **That**, as "**Now** is to **?**" (Answer: **Then**). Or "Dog is to puppy as Cat is to **?**." (Answer: **Kitten**, for the relation of **names of offspring of animals**). To some extent the variation in ability to answer these questions correctly depends on being able to grasp the rule of what is required by the instructions, which takes general intelligence, which may be part of the basis for correlations across different tests.

Crystallized intelligence is the general ability to correctly apply a broad range of widely applicable learned concepts, rules, terms, vocabulary, logic, arithmetic, mathematics, general knowledge, and/or practical judgment to the solution of well-defined problems. Again it is a second-order factor interpreted by what is common to tests under first-order factors that define the second-order factor. It has affinities to what Spearman called the **eduction of correlates**: "when a person has in mind any idea together with a [specified] relation, he has more or less power to bring up into the mind the correlative ideas" (Spearman, 1927, p. 166). For Guttman (1965) this is **achievement** or **rule-applying ability**. Shown a rule or given the name of its relation and a member of a pair in the relation, give the name or show correctly the other member of the pair in that relation. For example, "Who is the first President of the United States?" The relation is between the set of first presidents (of countries) and countries. Given "United States" as a member of a pair in the relation of first presidents to countries what is its counterpart? (Answer: Washington). "What is the area of a circle with a two-unit radius?" The relation shown in the instructions to the item is **areas of circles as functions of their**

radii. The subject needs to have learned that $A = \pi r^2$ and applies this rule to this problem, $A = 3.14159 \times (2)^2 = 12.5664$. So, now we can tell whether our interpretation of the g factor as **rule inferring** is correct if we can examine the instructions of all the the tasks of the variables under this factor and determine that they require rule inferring, but other tasks under Crystalized Intelligence do not involve rule inferring, but, instead, rule applying. Showing what does not indicate the factor helps as much as showing what indicates the factor. This is an objective method for verifying the objective validity of an interpretation of factors.

More recently, John B. Carroll (1993) conducted a massive survey involving factor analytic reanalyzes of 460 data sets of cognitive abilities in nine domains of cognition, from language, reasoning, memory and learning, visual perception, auditory reception, idea production, cognitive speed, knowledge and achievement, and psychomotor abilities. These analyses were conducted on the main-frame computers at the University of North Carolina in Chapel Hill. At the conclusion of his book he attempted a synthesis of the findings that resulted in a hierarchical theory of cognition in three strata. He described it as

> ...an expansion and elaboration of factor models proposed by Spearman, Holzinger, Thurstone, P. E. Vernon, R. B. Cattell, Horn, and others. It is fundamentally different from taxonomic theories such as those proposed by Guilford and Guttman, but can be accommodated within, or show correspondences with, radex theories that assume hierarchical structures. (Carroll, 1993, p. 654)

Subsequently, this has come to be known as the CHC theory, named after Cattell, Horn, and Carroll. The three strata are roughly first-order factors of test items, second-order factors of analyses of correlations among first-order factors, and the general factor g at the third stratum.

My own view on these factor analytic studies of cognition is that Carroll has brought coherence to the realm of factor analytic cognitive abilities by a uniformity of methods of factor extraction and rotation followed by what is known as a Schmid–Leiman procedure (Schmid & Leiman, 1957; see also Humphreys, Tucker, & Dachler, 1970) that orthogonalizes a set of higher-order factors into orthogonal factors at a first-order level. This makes it possible to show what degree of contribution a higher-order factor has on the individual raw variables. But I think when he called Guttman's method merely a taxonomic theory, he failed to grasp the full import of Guttman's faceted theory of intelligence as a method for external validation of interpretations of factors.

Interpretation of the factors is best when there is a close coordination between the factor analytic results and external (nonfactor analytic) analyses of test items according to classification schemas based on the task analyses of what the subject is required to do and produce. Guttman's approach to developing such schemas, called **facet analysis** (Guttman, 1994) is much more systematic and comprehensive than Guilford's. I recommend the use of facet analysis in gaining an understanding of the task requirements of items to provide a better and more objective, differentiated understanding of the nature of the processes to be associated with the various factors at different levels or strata. Combined with the Schmid–Leiman results, the facet analysis may provide a more objective and reproducible understanding of the factors. Hopefully the classification schemas may be able to reproduce the hierarchy of the common factors.

Personality

The concept of a general factor was extended beyond intelligence into the realm of personality. Webb (1915), Rushton and Irwing (2011) described a general common factor he called "will power" and designated as w. He based his analyses on ratings by peers and teachers on seven-point rating scales of 200 college students they knew well. This was the first application of factor analysis outside of the area of the intellect.

The area of personality is different from that of cognition and the intellect. Cognitive and/or intellectual abilities are studied by tests on which subjects perform. Their performance is evaluated by objective criteria of correctness given by the tester. That subjects respond similarly to different tasks may be because of the similarity those tasks have in invoking similar responses. In contrast, personality traits and characteristics are frequently judged by external raters, or by the subject of him or herself, on verbally defined scales. The judgments are formed sometimes from fleeting observations of a subject or at other times from long-time, close, intimate relations with the subject. The external perspective of others may produce different reports than from the internal perspective of the self-rater. So the accuracy of the rating as an objective description of the person can at times be questioned. One may also question whether correlations between rating scales are due to causal sources of variation within the subject, neurophysiological processes, or in external appearances of the subject to the raters that provoke similar ratings on trait scales having similar meanings.

An analogy here is with color versus hues in color vision. Color concerns the objective wavelength of light, while hue is a subjective response to light. A given hue like "yellow" may be produced by either a specific wavelength or by a mixture of two distinct wavelengths ("red" and "green"). Similarly, some traits rated may be determined by more than one distinct kind of behavior exhibited by the subject. "Friendliness" may be apparent for different reasons. In one person "friendliness" is a spontaneous trait. In another it is cultivated for deceptive purposes.

Lexical similarity between trait scales can also produce the correlations. For example to describe someone as "very friendly" is similar to saying that he is "somewhat loving." Also because many distinct traits, like "friendly," "incapable," "sociable," "domineering," "conscientious," and "self-centered" provoke implicit value judgments ("this is a good/bad person"), then a broad second-order general factor across many trait scales with diverse meanings may be an "evaluative factor," which is a subjective value judgment of the rater. Thus because some of the raters' judgments concern the conceptual dimensions on which they are able to describe or characterize persons and the artifact of similarity of lexic meaning between trait scales, these lexic rater dimensions will be confounded with dimensions on which the subjects objectively vary within themselves under the skin. In other words there is a confounding of rater dimensions with ratee dimensions (Mulaik, 1964).

Hans J. Eysenck, a German immigrant to England in the 1930s, received his Ph.D. from the University of London under Sir Cyril Burt, one of the prominent English factor analysts. Eysenck worked in hospitals during World War II and there began developing self-rating personality tests for diagnostic purposes. In 1947 his book *Dimensions of Personality* described two major dimensions, **Extraversion** and **Neuroticism** derived by factor analysis from his questionnaires. In the 1970s he added a third dimension **Psychoticism** to his theory. Eysenck interpreted extraversion as due neurophysiologically to a condition of "higher cortical arousal." Neuroticism is shown in anxiety, guilt, depression, envy, and jealousy and interpreted as a condition of a more reactive sympathetic nervous system that is more sensitive to environmental stimulation. Psychoticism is believed associated with levels of dopamine in the brain. It has been criticized as not being a unitary trait.

In the 1940s, Raymond B. Cattell also produced a famous personality inventory, the 16PF using factor analysis. The test has gone through several revisions, with the last, Fifth Edition, in 1993. It has 185 multiple-choice questions about the individual's behavior, interests, and opinions in daily life situations. It does not ask the individual to rate him or herself on certain personality traits, which some personality inventories do. Factor analysis of the questions has yielded 16 personality factors (hence "16PF").

A series of research studies by several researchers have converged to what they regard as the five major factor dimensions underlying correlations among numerous terms and phrases descriptive of personality used in self-ratings. These have become known as "The Big Five" factors, and are now in clinical use. The Big Five factors are based on self-report responses to multi-item questionnaires. The factors are (1) extraversion versus introversion, (2) agreeableness versus antagonism, (3) conscientiousness versus undirectedness, (4) neuroticism versus emotional stability, and (5) openness to experience versus not open to experience. These are each defined by about 10 items to which subjects indicate whether they agree or disagree on five-point rating scales, from Strongly Disagree through to Strongly Agree.

The author, Mulaik (1963), however, has developed a theory of personality concepts representing an expansion of Osgood, Suci, and Tannenbaum's (1957) finding of three major concepts in factor analyses of the similarity in meaning of words: **evaluation**, **potency**, and **activity**. Evaluation concerns good-bad judgments; potency judgments of power, strength, forcefulness, and bigness; active-inactive judgments of fast-slow, moving-unmoving, varying-unvarying, changing-unchanging, lively-lifeless. These same judgments occur in reactive concepts, where someone reacts to something else.

The author's theory developed a three-facet model of personality concepts based on an expansion of Osgood, Suci, and Tannenbaum's (1957) "Big Three" factors of meaning. The Big Three used here are **Good-Bad, Strong-Weak**, and **Active-Inactive**. Corresponding words implying a reaction to something can be formed from these, and so we have two forms of action in a facet called "Mode of Action." The Big Three are basic concepts. A third facet represents different domains of the person:

$$\begin{Bmatrix} action \\ reaction \end{Bmatrix} \times \begin{Bmatrix} good-bad \\ strong-weak \\ active-inactive \end{Bmatrix} \times \begin{Bmatrix} affect \\ intellect \\ psychomotor \\ self\text{-}interest \\ interpersonal \\ work \\ \vdots \end{Bmatrix}$$

Mode of Action   Concept   Domain

The first two facets generate a Cartesian product of six basic concepts, which are **Good-Bad, Strong-Weak, Active-Inactive, Resistance to Internal Change, Resistance to External Change**, and **Evaluation with an External Standard**. A third facet is the Domain of Personality, and in Table 8.4 I have indicated six domains, but potentially more may be identified. In each domain there are six corresponding variants of the six basic concepts. These domains tend to be independent of one another. But metaphors from one domain to another are possible and make the domains not totally independent. The Cartesian product of the Cartesian product of Mode of Action and Concept with Domain of Person produces 36 distinct concepts of personality. Many of the factors found in Table 8.4 were found in other studies in the literature.

In a factor analytic study each of these potentially could correspond to a common factor, if at least three or more synonymous traits were included for each of the 36 hypothesized factors. We will illustrate farther on a factor analytic study of the six hypothesized factors in the row of the Interpersonal Domain of the table.

Factor analysis has also been used to study attitudes, organizational behavior, personality of apes and zebra finches, word meanings, beliefs, political opinions, anthropological artifacts, and nations, to name a few of many topics, and reference to these may be found in searches in the Webb using "factor analysis," and the respective topic.

Multiple Factor Analysis

We are now going to consider in greater detail the common factor model with more than one common factor. Usually the factor analytic model is expressed in matrix algebra, because this is a more compact notation, and there is a well-developed mathematical theory for this algebra. However, to make this chapter useful for those without a background in matrix algebra, we will use equations from ordinary algebra.

As in the single common factor model, we will have an algebraic equation for each observed variable. We will use Greek letters for parameters and latent variables. Capital Roman letters will stand for observed variables:

$$\begin{aligned} Y_1 &= \lambda_{11}\xi_1 + \lambda_{12}\xi_2 + \cdots + \lambda_{1k}\xi_k + \cdots + \lambda_{1r}\xi_r + \psi_1\zeta_1 \\ Y_2 &= \lambda_{21}\xi_1 + \lambda_{22}\xi_2 + \cdots + \lambda_{2k}\xi_k + \cdots + \lambda_{2r}\xi_r + \psi_2\zeta_2 \\ Y_3 &= \lambda_{31}\xi_1 + \lambda_{32}\xi_2 + \cdots + \lambda_{3k}\xi_k + \cdots + \lambda_{3r}\xi_r + \psi_3\zeta_3 \\ &\cdots\cdots\cdots\cdots\cdots\cdots\cdots\cdots\cdots\cdots\cdots \\ Y_n &= \lambda_{n1}\xi_1 + \lambda_{n2}\xi_2 + \cdots + \lambda_{nk}\xi_k + \cdots + \lambda_{nr}\xi_r + \psi_n\zeta_n \end{aligned} \quad (8.4)$$

$Y_1, Y_2, \cdots, Y_i, \cdots Y_n$ are n observed variables. $\lambda_{i1}, \lambda_{i2}, \cdots, \lambda_{ik}, \cdots \lambda_{ir}$ (lambda) are factor-pattern loadings representing how much a unit change in a specified common factor ξ_k (xi) will produce a change in the ith observed variable. $\xi_1, \xi_2, \cdots, \xi_k, \cdots \xi_r$ denote the r common factors (variables). $\psi_1, \psi_2, \cdots, \psi_i, \cdots \psi_n$ (psi) denote n unique factor loadings (one for each unique factor variable). And $\zeta_1, \zeta_2, \cdots, \zeta_i, \cdots \zeta_n$ (zeta) denote n unique factor variables (one for each observed variable). Each equation states that an observed variable is a distinct linear (additive) combination of the r latent common factors and the latent unique factor associated with that observed variable.

Again the additional assumptions made in the single common factor model apply: The correlation $\rho(\xi_k, \zeta_i)$ between any common factor ξ_k and any unique factor variable ζ_i is zero; that is, $\rho(\xi_k, \zeta_i) = 0$. The correlation $\rho(\zeta_i, \zeta_j)$, $i \neq j$ between any two distinct unique factors is zero. However, we do not make the assumption that the correlation

Table 8.4 Mulaik's Table of Personality Dimensions.

		Action		Reaction	
	Good vs. Bad	Strong vs. Weak	Active vs. Inactive	Resistance to Internal Change	Resistance to External Standard	Evaluation by External Standard
DOMAIN *Affect*	Euphoria vs. Melancholy	Strength of Affect	Spontaneity of Affect	Repressed Affect	Labile Affect	Appropriate Affect
Intellect	Evaluation	Intelligence	Creativity	Memory	Field Independence	Convergent Thinking
Psychomotor	Gracefulness	Physical Strength	Impulsion	Static Poise	Physical Flexibility	Dynamic Poise
Self-Interest	Narcissistic	Domineering	Frivolous	Suppressed vs. Impulsive	Stubborn vs. Compliant	Subjective vs. Objective
Interpersonal	Positive Regard	Dominance	Sociability	Prohibitive	Nonconformity	Fair vs. Unfair
Work	Conscientious vs. Careless	Skillful vs. Inept	Ambitious vs. Lazy	Steady Worker	Persistent	Has Business Sense

$\rho(\xi_k, \xi_h)$ between any two distinct common factors is zero. It might be zero, but it also could be nonzero. But we can show mathematically that the correlation between any two observed variables Y_i and Y_j is due only to their loadings on the common factors and the correlations among the common factors, that is,

$$\rho(Y_i, Y_j) = \sum_{h=1}^{r}\sum_{k=1}^{r} \lambda_{ik}\lambda_{jh}\rho(\xi_h, \xi_k).$$

The correlations between common and unique factors and between any two unique factors all being zero, the unique factor terms do not enter into this equation. When the common factors are all mutually uncorrelated, that is

$$\rho(\xi_h, \xi_k) = \begin{cases} 1 \text{ if } h = k \\ 0 \text{ if } h \neq k \end{cases} h, k = 1, \cdots, r \text{ then } \rho(Y_i, Y_j) = \sum_{k=1}^{r} \lambda_{ik}\lambda_{jk}.$$

In the case of uncorrelated common factors the correlations are just due to the sum of products of the factor loadings of the two variables on the r common factors. Uncorrelated factors can be mathematically convenient to work with in some cases because of this simplification. But generally, in the world, common factors can be correlated.

The common factor model separates the total variance of an observed variable into two components: common variance, or communality, and unique variance. In contrast, the theory of true and error scores separates the total variance of a variable into the sum of true and error variance. Combining these two ways of composing the total variance into a single equation, we may write

$$\text{Total variance} = \underbrace{\overbrace{\text{common variance} + \text{specific variance}}^{\text{True variance}} + \text{error variance}}_{\text{Unique variance}}$$

Unique variance consists of both specific-true variance and error variance. True variance consists of common variance plus specific-true variance. Common variance is thus always a lower bound to true variance. Dividing true variance by total variance yields reliability. Dividing common variance by total variance yields the communality of a variable. The communality of a variable represents the portion of the total variance in the observed variable due to the common factors, or common variance. Communality is a close lower bound to reliability, surpassing the squared multiple correlation for predicting a variable from all the other variables as a lower bound estimate of reliability. If the common factors are correlated, then the communality is given as

$$h_i^2 = \sum_{h=1}^{r}\sum_{k=1}^{r} \lambda_{ik}\lambda_{ih}\rho(\xi_h, \xi_k).$$ In the uncorrelated-factors case it is given as $h_i^2 = \sum_{k=1}^{r} \lambda_{ik}^2$.

Note: these formulas are exact only when the common factor model is appropriate for a given set of variables and the parameters are regarded as population parameters.

Illustration of An Exploratory Common Factor Analysis

There are a series of stages at each of which certain things must be done in conducting a factor analysis. The first stage involves choosing the variables you will analyze. Keep in mind that your data will be scores of each subject on each variable you have chosen in a large sample. That will be essential for computing correlations between each variable with every other variable in your study. Factor analysis begins with the matrix of pair-wise correlations between every distinct pair of your your variables. So, avoid whenever possible missing data where some subjects do not have scores on some of your variables.

There are work-arounds for cases of missing data, but they degrade to some extent the quality of your study. Tossing out cases having missing data loses the excluded cases' information on pairs of variables for which there is no missing data. That may work if you are sure the missing data is completely at random and in only a very small percentage of your cases. Computing correlations between each pair of variables for just cases in which there is no missing data, will make the correlation matrix be what mathematicians say is "not positive definite" because it will not be a "gramian matrix" obtained by multiplying a score matrix times its transpose, which is what is involved in getting a proper correlation matrix. So it is better to find some value to impute in place of the missing values.

Generally, the theory of imputation is that one tries to use information that is available in other variables and cases to determine the missing scores on a given variable in a given case. But there are numerous such methods and they often involve advanced statistical theory that is beyond the level of this article. So I will simply recommend that if you have missing data, do a search of the Web for "missing data" and "missing data factor analysis." Also consult the manual for the computer program you use for how it handles missing data for computing a correlation matrix and pick the method that seems most appropriate for your data.

In some cases you may simply be interested in determining the common factors among items in, say, an existing attitude inventory. So you will have little freedom in what variables you will study. You might be interested in finding the common factors among course grades and aptitude inventories available in student records. Each item in the inventory and each course grade and aptitude test score in a student's record will be a variable in your analysis.

Simply collecting an arbitrary collection of observed variables and getting measurements on numerous cases of them to compute their intercorrelations will usually not produce easily interpreted factors. The better situation to be in is where you are designing an inventory or developing a theory of the common factors in some domain of interest. There you will have the freedom to create variables you think are needed. It helps to have a clear idea of the domain of variables you wish to study and even hypotheses about what and how many common factors span this domain. If you are studying cognitive, personality, or attitude variables, then you need to review the literature to determine what factors may have been found by others and consult examples of items measuring these factors. You may need to create new items to add to those already in the literature for measuring a given factor or replace some with new ones you think better reveal the factor. Or if the factor is new, you need to work out rules for how to construct items to represent that factor and create at least three and preferably four or more of such items.

Thurstone (1937) set the standard for how to do an exploratory factor analysis. He put forth five conditions basic to common factor theory a factor analytic study should meet:

1 The number of basic factors should be less than the number of (observed) tests.
2 The diagonals of the correlation matrix (the communalities) must be regarded as unknown (and estimated).

3   The axes (factors) must be rotated into a simple (structure) configuration.
4   Each factor must be overdetermined by appearance in several (three or more) tests.
5   Tests (observed variables) should have simple factorial composition.

Let us focus here on (4) and (5). Condition (4) states that a common factor will only be determined if three or more variables in the study have strong loadings on the factor. Thurstone held that science requires evidence of objectivity for a latent construct to be obtained from different but coherent observations. So, you must already be anticipating the factors to result even as you select or create variables. And you make a special effort to include variables that measure these factors. Furthermore this is essential if you are to avoid ambiguity in interpreting the psychological content of the factor. Condition (5) requires that you include in your study variables that are relatively "pure" in measuring just one common factor, respectively, and exclude variables that measure more than one. Furthermore the assumption that unique factors are uncorrelated means that you should try not to have two indicators of a common factor that also have additional common sources of variation just between them. In my view excluding variables that depend on more than one common factor is not absolutely essential if you have at least three or four other variables that are relatively pure and strong in measuring each common factor, respectively. Simple structure will allow for variables being dependent on more than one common factor since they will fall in the hyperplanes spanned by the factors at their intersections. But in early studies it is better to have only pure representatives of the common factors. In later studies, where you are interested in how other tests depend on the basic common factors, you can include variables that depend on more than one common factor.

I will now illustrate a factor analysis using an unpublished study conducted under my supervision by Dan Griffith, for a student senior thesis at the School of Psychology at the Georgia Institute of Technology in 1998. A Power Point presentation of this study was given by Griffith and Mulaik (1998) at the Society for Multivariate Experimental Psychology (SMEP). The original study was intended to test my theory of personality trait factors described earlier in this article. It was not a complete test. We used four synonomous trait items respectively to represent each of the six potential factors, respectively, from just two personality domains – Interpersonal and Work – plus the Anxiety factor from the Affect domain. That involved 13 potential common factors. A group of 175 Georgia Tech introductory psychology students of both sexes each rated, respectively, three stereotypical persons selected at random from a large list of stereotypes on 52 bipolar seven-point trait-adjective scales, for example:

$$\text{loving} : 1 : 2 : 3 : 4 : 5 : 6 : 7 : \text{unloving}$$

That produced ratings on 525 cases. Inspection of the ratings led to the ratings of two cases being discarded because obviously the raters did not take the task seriously. In the end the number of cases analyzed was 523. We obtained 13 simple structure factors as expected, which gave tentative support for the theory.

Because of space limitations I will use 24 variables from this study representing just the six hypothetical factors from the Interpersonal domain. The correlations among these 24 variables are shown in Table 8.5.

Because we will do a **common** factor analysis, we will need to estimate communalities. This leads to the question of how to estimate them and extract the factors. Generally, you must first begin with provisional starting estimates of the communalities. From

Table 8.5 Correlations among 24 trait scales (corresponding elements above diagonal not shown).

ALLOWING																							
.12	OUTGOING																						
-.01	-.59	NONTALKATIVE																					
.63	.09	.00	PERMISSIVE																				
.24	.26	-.08	.22	FAIR																			
-.34	-.45	.35	-.30	-.47	UNFRIENDLY																		
.53	-.19	.24	.44	.13	-.16	FORCELESS																	
-.20	-.13	.20	-.14	.04	.07	-.06	RESTRAINING																
.47	-.21	.25	.43	.12	-.12	.72	-.07	NONDOMINANT															
-.33	-.32	.24	-.24	-.47	.57	-.22	.05	-.19	UNLOVING														
-.14	-.02	-.04	-.15	-.04	.14	-.17	-.01	-.13	.08	NONCONFORMING													
.13	.07	.02	.14	.23	-.20	.15	.01	.15	-.20	-.34	COMPLIANT												
.17	-.07	.11	.10	.24	-.12	.15	.04	.18	-.09	-.01	.18	IMPARTIAL											
-.24	.36	-.31	-.17	.20	-.15	-.46	.08	-.51	-.14	.09	.04	-.06	LEADER										
-.37	-.38	.25	-.31	-.52	.59	-.21	.08	-.23	.67	.11	-.27	-.16	-.16	UNKIND									
.04	-.07	-.01	.01	-.22	.09	-.01	-.10	-.04	.12	.38	-.30	-.04	-.13	.21	UNCONVENTIONAL								
-.38	.26	-.19	-.29	.06	.00	-.56	.19	-.58	.04	.14	-.03	-.11	.64	.06	-.05	DIRECTING							
-.40	-.09	.06	-.32	-.14	.24	-.32	.21	-.26	.22	-.01	-.02	-.17	.14	.24	-.08	.22	PROHIBITIVE						
.02	-.27	.24	.05	-.04	.18	.13	.11	.15	.11	.01	-.01	.15	-.21	.13	.10	-.15	.03	UNGREGAIOUS					
.22	.26	-.09	.23	.69	-.45	.17	.07	.14	-.45	-.11	.30	.24	.21	-.59	-.27	.02	-.16	-.15	JUST				
.29	.00	.07	.28	.34	-.23	.28	.07	.28	-.29	-.14	.24	.32	-.04	-.34	-.15	.13	-.20	-.22	.03	NEUTRAL			
.17	.58	-.47	.16	.30	-.50	-.06	-.08	-.05	-.37	-.05	.13	.00	.34	-.40	-.15	.21	-.11	-.26	.31	.15	SOCIABLE		
-.33	-.36	.25	-.28	-.40	.51	-.20	.09	-.22	.62	.07	-.20	-.12	-.09	.59	.11	.04	.23	.13	-.41	-.27	-.46	UNAFFECTIONATE	
-.11	-.04	-.11	-.08	-.31	.24	-.18	-.19	-.18	.30	.31	-.38	-.12	-.06	.34	.47	.07	.04	.00	-.33	-.28	-.11	.25	REBELLIOUS

those you will determine the number of common factors to retain, and the iterative analysis will obtain a solution for the common factor model, including new estimates of communalities based on that number. There are many methods of factor extraction. The SPSS FACTOR program I use lists seven extraction methods: **PC** principal components (not a true common factor analysis); **PAF** principal axes factoring (least squares with squared multiple correlations for predicting each variable from the rest as initial communality estimates); **ML** (maximum likelihood); **ALPHA** (alpha factoring); **IMAGE** (image analysis); **ULS** (unweighted least squares); and **GLS** (generalized least squares). A detailed description of the mathematical theory behind these methods is given in Mulaik (2010). I will use the **ML** estimation (Jöreskog, 1967). This method usually assumes the observed variables are distributed according to a multivariate normal distribution with means of zero and variances of unity. Obviously the rating scales are not continuous variables, being "polytomous" seven-point scales. Still the ML method is robust and may be justified here by the equivalence of the equations for this model with another model that makes no distributional assumptions. Howe (1953) developed a model that sought to maximize the determinant of the matrix of partial covariances among the residual variables after r common factors were partialled from the original covariance matrix. (A matrix is a rectangular array of numbers arranged in rows and columns.) This determinant tends to a maximum when the matrix is diagonal and is near a maximum when off-diagonals are near zero. This is an algebraic criterion and not a statistical criterion. Optimizing this criterion produces the same equations to optimize as in ML, and hence produces the same solution as the ML method (see Mulaik, 1972, pp. 169–172).

ML estimation involves an iterative procedure. It usually begins with estimates of the squared multiple correlations $\hat{R}_i^2$ for predicting each variable from the rest of the variables in the correlation matrix as provisional initial estimates of the communalities. (These squared multiple correlation coefficients are given by a matrix equation we do not need to discuss here.) That is, $\hat{h}_i^2 = \hat{R}_i^2$. The squared multiple correlation is a strong lower bound to the communality of a variable (Guttman, 1956). The procedure then subtracts each of these squared multiple correlations $\hat{R}_i^2$ from 1, $\hat{\psi}_i^2 = 1 - \hat{R}_i^2$, to get the initial estimate of the unique variance $\hat{\psi}_i^2$ of the ith variable. Next it takes the reciprocals of the square roots of the unique variances $\hat{\psi}_i^{-1}$ of each observed variable and multiplies every element in the ith row and column of the correlation matrix by the respective $\hat{\psi}_i^{-1}$. Now, the rows and columns of the correlation matrix represent variables. So, these coefficients act as weights that have the effect of converting the correlation matrix to a variance/covariance matrix. Variables having small unique variances (hence large communalities) thus have larger variances, giving greater weight in the analysis to variables with high communalities.

Next the computer program computes the eigenvectors and eigenvalues of the resulting weighted correlation matrix. The eigenvectors are the columns of a matrix known as the **eigenvector matrix**. The eigenvalues constitute the elements of the principal diagonal of a $n \times n$ square diagonal matrix with zero off-diagonals, known as the **eigenvalue matrix**. The process of how this computation is done is too technical to discuss here. But there are n eigenvectors eigenvalues that can be obtained from any square symmetric matrix, like a correlation matrix. Each **eigenvector** is a column array of n numbers, $\mathbf{a}_j = [a_{1j}, a_{2j}, \cdots, a_{nj}]$, $j = 1, \cdots, n$ represented in text by elements within brackets. The sum of the squares of these numbers in each eigenvector add up to unity, $\sum_{i=1}^{n} a_{ik}^2 = 1$.

The sum of cross products of corresponding elements in two distinct eigenvectors k and h is equal to zero. That is, $\sum_{i=1}^{n} a_{ik} a_{ih} = 0$, $k \neq h$. Thus we say that two distinct eigenvectors are mutually **orthogonal**.

The coefficients in the eigenvector arrays will be used as weights to get linear (additive) combinations $X_k = \sum_{i=1}^{n} a_{ik} \tilde{Y}_i$ of the observed variables after the unique factor parts of them have been partialled out, that is, $\tilde{Y}_i = Y_i - \psi_i \zeta_i$. (Actually we never know what the unique factor scores are; but to aid understanding we act as if we do.) Here, X_k is derived by using the coefficients from the kth eigenvector as weights in adding together the n modified observed variables $\tilde{Y}_i$. So there can be potentially n such linear combinations, each a new variable. The covariance between any two linear combinations so obtained is $\sigma(X_k, X_h) = 0$, $k \neq h$. The variance $\gamma_k = \sigma_k^2(X_k)$ of the variable that is the linear combination of the observed variables using coefficients of the kth eigenvector as weights respectively to additively combine the respective observed variables is known as the kth **eigenvalue**.

The column eigenvectors are by convention ordered in the eigenvector matrix in descending order of magnitude of their corresponding eigenvalues. The eigenvalues on the principal diagonal of the eigenvalue matrix begin with the largest in the upper left corner, and procede in descending magnitude down the principal diagonal to the smallest in the lower right corner. So, assuming we have ordered the eigenvectors according to the descending order of their eigenvalues, the first linear combination X_1 has variance $\gamma_1 = \sigma_1^2(X_1)$, which is the maximum variance of any of the linear combinations. So, X_1 determines a dimension in which there is the greatest common variance in common factor space. X_2 determines a dimension orthogonal to (independent of, uncorrelated with) X_1 that has the next largest variance in common factor space. Each successive linear combination X_k determines a dimension orthogonal to the preceding dimensions with the next largest variance. At some point, if the modified observed variables $\tilde{Y}_i$ contain only effects of the common factors, the remaining linear combinations will have zero variances or zero eigenvalues.

The magnitudes and number of positive eigenvalues determines the number of common factors to retain. That's the theory anyway. In practice, with sampling error, population zero variances become nonzero, though small. Usually a number of the smaller positive eigenvalues are still near zero, while with random overestimates of the unique factor variances the smaller eigenvalues frequently are negative, and these might be joined with the zero eigenvalues to be discarded because, usually, they correspond to unanticipated minor sources of covariance between the variables that are uninterpretable. They may even correspond to residual covariation between pairs only of variables, which are not uniquely determined. The common factor model does not prescribe anything about covariation due only to two variables, since such factors in principle could equal $n(n-1)/2$ in number, which is greater than the number of observed variables and unique factors. These are known as **doublet factors** in the literature. Thurstone (1947, p. 442) thought these were produced by two variables measuring the same performance and one should be discarded because they were uninterpretable together in any unique way. Attempts to identify and eliminate doublets from the analysis are described in Mulaik (2010, pp. 253–262). Image analysis explicitly models doublets in an approximation to common factor analysis and could be used.

In practice the eigenvectors and eigenvalues are calculated directly from the correlation matrix among the observed variables with communality estimates replacing 1 s in the principal diagonal, beginning with lower bound estimates like the squared multiple correlations. Often the correlation matrix is rescaled by multiplying respective rows and columns by the reciprocals, respectively, of the square roots of the corresponding initial estimates of unique factor variances, given by $\hat{\psi}_i^{-1} = 1/\sqrt{1-R_i^2}$, where R_i^2 is the squared multiple correlation for predicting the ith observed variable from the $n - 1$ other observed variables. An initial iteration is used to determine the number of factors to retain and this number made a fixed value. Then subsequent iterations are used iteratively to recalculate improved values until some criterion of good fit is achieved.

How many factors?

If one knew exactly the true values for the communalities and placed these in their corresponding places in the principal diagonal of the correlation matrix, then the number of common factors would equal the number of positive, nonzero eigenvalues of this "reduced" correlation matrix. There are a number of heuristic criteria for the number of factors to retain based on the magnitude of the eigenvalues. A common but criticized criterion is to save the factors with eigenvalues greater than 1.00 of the unmodified correlation matrix. This happens to be the weakest lowest bound for the number of common factors according to Guttman (1956), corresponding to the number of positive eigenvalues of the correlation matrix with 0 s replacing the 1 s in the principal diagonal of the raw correlation matrix. Zero is the worst possible estimate for a communality. So, this criterion may discard valid common factors with small nonzero eigenvalues. Even Henry Kaiser (1960, 1961) who first proposed this criterion recognized it as the weakest lower bound to the number of common factors (personal communication).

Another popular criterion is to plot the magnitudes of the eigenvalues, arranged in descending magnitude, against the ordinal numbers of the eigenvalues. (This should be done with eigenvalues of either the reduced or the weighted correlation matrix $S^{-1}RS^{-1}$ (see Appendix I) and not the raw correlation matrix. Unfortunately, SPSS only plots the eigenvalues of the raw correlation matrix, which is not appropriate for ML.) If you connect the dots in the plot, the resulting curve through the dots begins with a very large eigenvalue followed by rapidly descending values as the curve advances. At some point the curve may suddenly change from a steep downward slope to a more gentle straight-line drop of the curve with subsequent eigenvalues. R. B. Cattell called this the "scree point," because it reminded him of the place at the base of a steep cliff where falling rocks have rolled away in a gentle straight-line descent from the base of the cliff. Sometimes there is no clear sharp break in the slope, but a gradual curve, and this criterion is ambiguous.

Another related method the author uses is the "ruler method" (Mulaik, 2010, p. 187; Figure 8.1). This is inspired by the observation that if samples are obtained from multivariate normal populations in which the variables are all uncorrelated, the sample eigenvalues, when plotted against their ordinal value, fall on a gently-downward-sloping straight line from left to right. By symmetry, the population line passes through the average eigenvalue of $1 = n/n$ at $m = n/2$. The slope seems to be a function of sample size, the number of variables, and the multivariate normal distribution. The smaller the

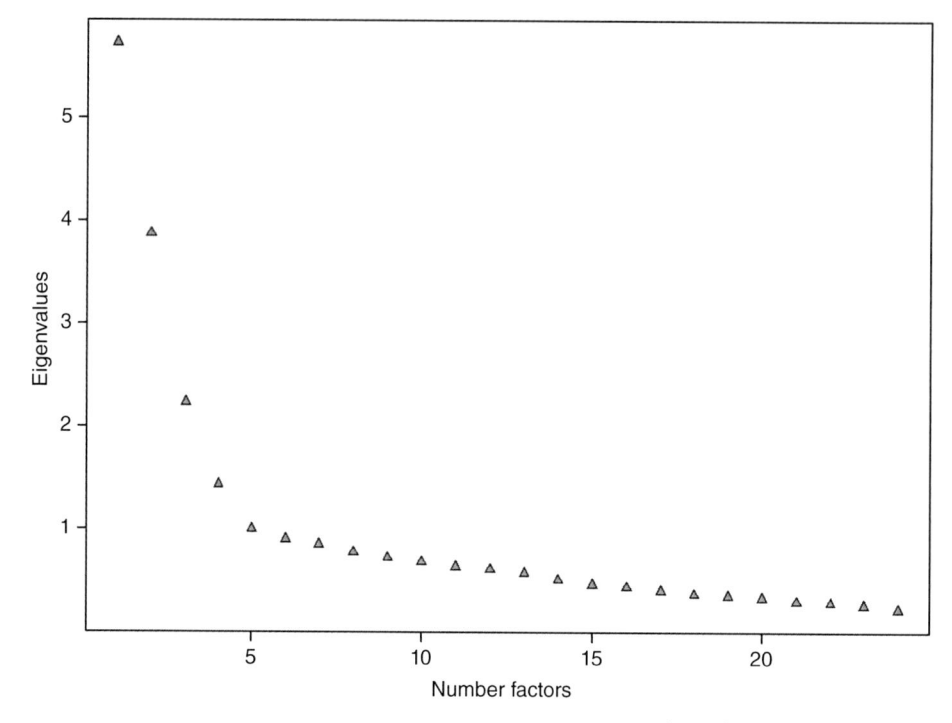

Figure 8.1 Plot of eigenvalues of matrix $S^{-1}RS^{-1}$.

sample the steeper the slope. The sum of the eigenvalues always equals the sum of the diagonal elements of the correlation matrix. In this case the average eigenvalue is $1 = n/n$. Presuming that the first r population eigenvalues of a correlation matrix with communalities in the principal diagonal should be nonzero and represent common variance, and the remainder all be zero, then after the number r of factors has been identified, the remaining sample eigenvalues should fall on a gentle downward sloping straight line to the right. So, if we fit a straight line through as many of the last eigenvalues on the right as we can, and we extend the line to the left, any eigenvalue clearly above the line should represent common variance. What is "clearly" above the line will be a subjective choice. This is an eye-ball heuristic.

A related method to the ruler method is the Parallel Analysis (PA) method for determining the number of common factors (Horn, 1965). Researchers have assembled tables of the averaged eigenvalues for numerous samples of specified size N from sample correlation matrices sampled from a population of uncorrelated variables of size n in number. If you have plotted the eigenvalues from your sample correlation matrix with communalities in the principal diagonal, you next superimpose on the plot values of the averaged eigenvalues from the tables for a similar size sample and the same number of observed variables. Where the lines cross is the number of factors to be retained. But the method seems to be biased to take too few factors. Turner (1998) noted that a very large size for the first eigenvalue of the real data would force the remaining eigenvalues to sum to a smaller number because the sum of the eigenvalues always equals the sum of the diagonal elements respectively of the correlation or the modified correlation matrix. That would lower the last several eigenvalues. Perhaps it would be better to note the difference between the smallest eigenvalues of the real data and that of the tables, which would correspond to zero eigenvalues in the real population. The curves through the smallest eigenvalues in both plots seem to be almost parallel, straight lines. The slopes seem to be a function of sample size. The difference in level between them seems to be due to the common factor variance in the real data curve If this difference is subtracted from each of the table eigenvalues and these points plotted, you get effectively the same line as the ruler method.

There is also a series of **chi-square tests** that you can perform to test whether the number of factors is as specified. This involves a series of analyses done for each hypothesized number for the common factors. You can begin with the null hypothesis that the number of factors is one and test that. If the chi-square test yields a significant chi-square, you reject that hypothesis and go to the next, there are two common factors and reanalyze accordingly. You keep going with these tests until you just accept the null hypothesis that the number of common factors is whatever number you have arrived at.

Experience with the chi-square tests is that usually they reject the null hypothesis for any but a quite large number of common factors. And the larger the sample, the more factors must be taken until chi-square is not significant. When applied to polytomous data like the seven-point rating scale data of the present study, in a large sample the test may reject the model because the data is not distributed as a continuous multivariate normal distribution with that number of factors. Other possibilities of failure are the presence of other common factors or even doublet factors not anticipated and controlled for in variable selection and/or construction. Most exploratory factor analysts prefer the heuristic tests to the chi-square test.

Nevertheless for the current factor analysis of the 24 variables with six factors retained, the chi-square statistic was 275.5282 with 147 degrees of freedom and a p value less than .001, which is significant. This means that the exploratory common factor model with six factors did not fit the data to within sampling error. But remember that the sample size is 523, which means that the power to detect small deviations beyond chance is quite high. With large samples, degree of approximation becomes more important in exploratory studies.

There are other indices of degree of approximation of the model to the data, such as the CFI (Bentler, 1990; McDonald, 1990) and the RMSEA (Steiger & Lind, 1980), which are built from the chi-square statistic values. Mulaik (2009) discusses these and several other approximate fit indices. These have been developed in structural equation modelling and current commercial computer programs should be including these indices in current upgrades.

Simple structure rotation

At this point in the analysis the program will have computed the "unrotated factor matrix," which is formed from the first r eigenvectors, with elements in each column respectively multiplied by the square root of the eigenvalues. The correlations between the corresponding distinct factors are necessarily zero. Because ML estimation analyzes the data after rescaling the data by multiplying elements in each row and corresponding column of the correlation matrix by the reciprocals of the respective unique factor loadings $\hat{\psi}_i^{-1}$, the elements in each row of the modified eigenvector matrix is rescaled to its original metric by multiplying each element in a row by $\hat{\psi}$. I will not show this here because of space limitations, and it is not the final result we want. We may note, however, that the first column of the unrotated matrix usually has mostly larger loadings. From early on the first factor was often confused with the general factor, because almost every variable had a large loading on the first factor. But this is an artifact of the method. The general factor has to be a higher-order factor obtained by factor analyzing correlations among simple structure factors. But the unrotated factor matrix is the basis for the next step, which is rotating this initial factor loading matrix to a factor-pattern matrix having **oblique simple structure**. Technically, this involves what mathematicians call a **linear transformation** of the unrotated factor matrix.

The idea for simple structure was first proposed in the late 1930s and described in detail later by L. L. Thurstone (1947). Until computers were applied to this problem, rotations were conducted graphically, by hand, by rotating two factors at a time. It took well over a month to rotate a factor matrix by hand to oblique simple structure. We will not discuss the details of the procedures but will describe the why and the what for simple structure. These details are discussed in Mulaik (2010). But the concept of simple structure is still not well understood and many misconceptions about it still abound in the literature.

The problem is that the unrotated factor matrix is not unique. In fact, there are an unlimited number of distinct linear transformations or rotations of the unrotated factor matrix that might be obtained. All of them will generate the same reproduced correlation matrix. So, which rotation should we obtain? Thurstone saw the problem as finding an objective solution because he believed the common factors were real and should be found with different sets of variables from the same factor domain (i.e., variables that were all linear combinations of the same common factors).

Thurstone (1947) devised an ingenous method for finding the simple structure factors and their loadings. He first regarded that all variables could be represented by vectors radiating from a common origin in what he called common factor space (see Figure 8.2). Vectors in this case are just arrows. The cosines of angles between vectors would equal correlations between the corresponding variables, which constrains their positioning with respect to one another in multidimensional space. There would be arrows for observed variables, arrows for the common factor variables and arrows for what he called the "reference structure axes." The reference structure axes were to be used to determine planes or "hyperplanes" (a subspace of $r-1$ dimensions in r-dimensional space). A hyperplane would contain all variables that were linear combinations of at most $r-1$ of the common factors in those hyperplanes. And each of the r common factors would be common to $r-1$ hyperplanes, so they would be at the intersections of r hyperplanes.

So, how would we discover these hyperplanes? The reference structure axes were the solution. They would be vectors at right angles to every vector in a given hyperplane. So, if you plotted, say, two factors all the variables in the plane passing through these two factors would be orthogonal to a reference axis at right angles to these two factors, and to every variable that was a linear combination of just these two factors. We can see that in Figure 8.2, which shows a three-factor simple structure solution in three dimensions. A hyperplane in this figure is a subspace of $3-1=2$ dimensions, a plane, spanned by the two common factors. Every other variable that is just a linear combination of these two factors would fall in the plane common to the two factors. To find this plane we would use the reference axes like handles rigidly attached at right angles to the plane of two

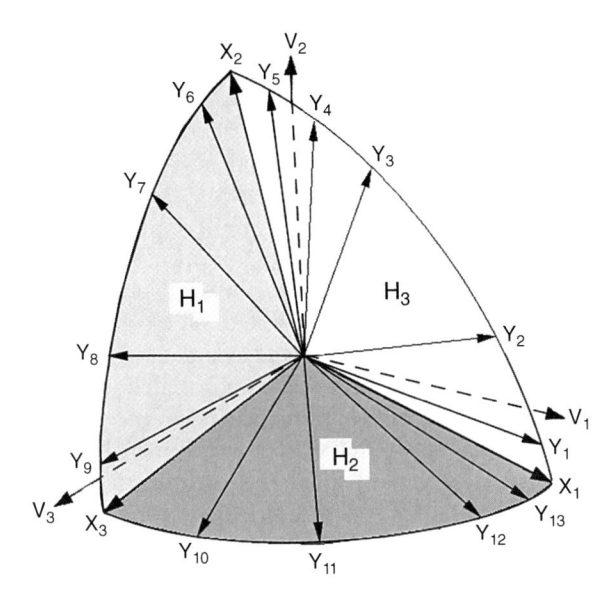

Figure 8.2 A simple structure factor solution in three dimensions showing the three hyperplanes H_1, H_2, and H_3 at the intersection of which are the factors X_1, X_2, and X_3. The reference axes are the vectors V_1, V_2, and V_3, orthogonal to their respective hyperplanes. Y-vectors are observed variables in the hyperplanes that are linear combinations of pairs of factors.

dimensions, and we would move it around in three-dimensional space and in doing so move the plane around in space until we had identified a group of observed variables that were at right angles to the reference axis in the hyperplane. We would do the same thing for each reference axis, making sure it identified distinct sets of observed variables that were at right angles to the respective reference axis and containing very few variables from any other hyperplanes. Once the hyperplanes are found, we can use the reference axes to determine the common factors at the intersections of these hyperplanes.

This may be difficult to grasp at first, but the important point made by Thurstone (1947) was that the determination of the simple structure common factors did not depend on the particular set of observed variables in the analysis. A common factor exists independently in the world and more than one set of variables is dependent on it. As long as we can select several variables for study that are linear combinations of less than all of the same factor variables, these will fall in the same hyperplanes and determine the same factors at their intersections. He also showed that mathematically you could determine the factor-pattern loadings on the common factors using the correlations or cosines of the observed variables with the reference axes.

This approach worked well with graphical rotation, but it was slow going to do it. The arrival of computers made it possible to consider analytic methods of rotation, but the problem was how to represent what a simple structure solution was like in a form a computer program could use to do the rotations. First it was essential to find a **reference structure matrix** representing correlations of observed variables with the hypothetical reference axes. By identifying variables that had zero correlations with the provisional reference axes, we could determine the reference axes. These zeros would be located in key places in the resulting reference structure matrix. Thurstone (1947) developed five rules of what the reference structure matrix would look like once we had a simple structure solution (I paraphrase):

1. So that each variable will not be dependent on all r of the common factors it must be in a subspace of at most $r - 1$ dimensions, so, each row of the reference structure matrix should have at least one zero in it.
2. To overdetermine the reference axes each column of the reference structure matrix should have r zeros with the corresponding reference axis.
3. To ensure distinctness of the reference axes, for every pair of columns of the reference structure matrix there should be a number of zero entries in one column corresponding to nonzero entries in the other column.
4. To further separate and overdetermine the reference axes, when there are more than four common factors, each pair of columns of the reference structure matrix should have a large proportion of corresponding zero entries, which forces separation of the observed variables into distinct clusters. So that each variable depends on, at most, a small number of common factors; in every pair of columns of the reference structure matrix there should be only a small number of corresponding nonzero entries. Once a reference structure matrix was found with these properties, the factor-pattern matrix could be immediately derived by a specific linear transformation.

Some of the first successful computer programs for rotating factors found "simple structure solutions" with orthogonal factors. The most popular of these is Kaiser's (1958) VARIMAX method. Generally, however, I do not recommend orthogonal factor solutions in common factor analysis. Orthogonality, or factors that are mutually uncorrelated, imposed a priori by the researcher, is an artifact and does not represent a condition in the world. So, calling an orthogonal solution a simple structure solution is a contradiction. To identify the hyperplanes and the factors at their intersection we must allow for correlated factors.

Of many programs that were developed to obtain correlated or "oblique" simple structure solutions, the most successful, in my opinion, until very recently was Jennrich and Sampson's (1966) **direct oblimin method**. This method originally rotated two factors at a time (known as **planar rotations**). They realized further that to each zero entry in the reference structure matrix there would be a corresponding zero in the factor-pattern matrix. So, rather than using a reference structure matrix as an intermediate solution, they made transformations directly to produce a factor-pattern matrix by producing zeros (or near zeros) appropriately in the matrix. The factor-pattern matrix contains the coefficients indicating how much a unit change of a common factor produces a change in an observed variable.

Jennrich (2002) made furthermore a major breakthrough in factor rotation methods by the use of an easily implemented algorithm known as the **gradient projection algorithm**. This method further transforms the whole factor-pattern matrix at a time rather than using planar rotations. That has made it possible to provide programs for numerous rotation algorithms, including some newer ones that slightly improve over the direct oblimin method in yielding simple structure solutions (Bernaards & Jennrich, 2005). Jennrich streamlines the criterion by seeking to minimize

$$\text{Quartimin} = \sum_{j=1}^{r}\sum_{k=1}^{r}\sum_{i=1}^{n} \lambda_{ij}^2 \lambda_{ik}^2 / 4 \; j \neq k \tag{8.5}$$

This criterion is minimized when squared loadings in one column correspond to zeros or near-zero loadings in the other, and when some columns have corresponding zeros or near zeros in both columns.

Among the new methods are Geomin (Yates, 1987), Infomax (McKeon, 1968; Browne, 2001), Promin (Lorenzo-Seva, 1999), Simplimax (Kiers, 1994), several based on **component loss functions** (CLF) like Katz and Rolf's (1974) Functionplane, Rozeboom's (1991a, 1991b) HYBALL, and several simple CLF algorithms by Jennrich (2006), and Absolmin and Epsolmin (Mulaik, 2010).

Absolmin is a simple CLF criterion recommended by Jenrich and named by Mulaik (2010), which contains details of these newer methods based on the gradient projection algorithm. A component loss function seeks to minimize each element in the pattern matrix irrespective of other elements, under constraints of a linear transformation.

$$\text{Absolmin} = \sum_{i=1}^{n} \sum_{j=1}^{r} |\lambda_{ij}| \qquad (8.6)$$

This simple CLF criterion seeks to minimize the sum of the absolute values of the elements of the rotated matrix. Unfortunately the solution has many local minima, and numerous randomly generated orthogonal transformation matrices should be used as starting values, and the converged solution from these that has the smallest Absolmin criterion value should be retained.

Also accompanying the factor-pattern matrix, there should be a matrix of correlations among the factors. This suggests the possible existence of "higher-order" factors common to the "first-order" factors. To save space, I have not computed a factor analysis of these correlations. Jennrich has made his programs available in several programming languages for the gradient projection algorithm (gpa) at www.stat.ucla.edu/research/gpa/.

In Table 8.6, I show the factor-pattern matrices and correlations among factors respectively for the Direct Oblimin solution and the Absolmin solution. These are the principal data for interpretation of the factors. Both solutions are quite similar. I have placed in **bold type** the largest elements, and with few exceptions they correspond to the first decimal place between the two solutions. The remaining loadings are zero or near zero. Furthermore, the large loadings determine factors that correspond to factors expected under the hypothesized model for the interpersonal domain. Factor 1 can be called **Permissiveness**, Factor 2 **Introversion**, Factor 3 **Unjustness**, Factor 4 **Negative regard for others**, Factor 5 **Nondirecting**, and Factor 6 **Nonconformity**.

One thing you may notice is that in columns for Factor 3, the loadings for the Direct Oblimin solution are generally negative of those, respectively, in the Absolmin solution. Furthermore Factor 5 in both solutions is predominantly negative, when we expected positive loadings. This occurs commonly in factor rotation solutions and is an artifact of the rotation algorithm. What this suggests is that the solution for the third factor under Direct Oblimin is the opposite of that under Absolmin. But both identify nearly the same dimension; one solution for the factor just points along the same line but in the opposite direction from the other. It is easy to make everything the same or predominantly positive by simply reversing the signs in the column in question and making corresponding adjustments for the signs of the correlations among the factors. Or you can interpret the factor according to the predominant negative loadings, if they occur.

Table 8.6 Simple structure factor-pattern matrices and correlations among factors for Direct Oblimin and Absolmin.

Simple Structure Factor-Pattern Matrices

Variable	Direct oblimin							Absolmin						
	1	2	3	4	5	6	1	2	3	4	5	6
ALLOW	**.746**	.000	-.007	.099	.060	-.024	**.727**	-.021	-.049	-.039	**.244**	.047
OUTGO	.103	**-.649**	-.045	.126	-.211	-.045	.174	**-.600**	.079	-.061	**-.263**	-.070
NONTALK	.067	**.692**	-.079	-.158	.048	-.050	.007	**.684**	.019	.084	**.167**	-.021
PERMISS	**.773**	.009	-.061	-.046	-.054	-.063	**.756**	.019	.000	.097	**.154**	.000
FAIR	.022	-.079	**-.675**	.144	-.098	.005	.090	.051	**.604**	-.247	-.032	.000
UNFRIEND	-.142	**.289**	.138	**-.450**	.030	.047	**-.201**	**.275**	-.127	**.423**	.040	.038
FORCELSS	**.323**	**.200**	-.063	.155	**.473**	-.092	**.322**	.147	-.009	-.170	**.579**	-.019
RESTRAIN	**-.128**	**.319**	-.079	.016	**-.206**	-.105	-.133	**.347**	.064	-.061	**-.191**	-.120
NONDOMIN	**.235**	.183	-.070	.166	**.547**	-.102	**.242**	.126	.000	**-.191**	**.629**	-.032
UNLOVING	.030	-.026	-.001	**-.875**	-.010	-.035	.000	.028	.000	**.847**	.052	-.048
NONCNFRM	-.112	.067	-.107	.082	-.089	**.632**	-.192	.059	.143	-.096	-.117	**.615**
COMPLINT	.068	.021	-.105	.057	-.022	**-.458**	.139	.060	.058	-.079	.017	**-.449**
IMPARTL	.079	.119	**-.334**	-.026	.047	.022	.090	.171	**.281**	-.039	.122	.036
LEADER	.043	-.086	-.060	.068	**-.770**	-.002	.051	.000	.096	-.038	**-.768**	-.057
UNKIND	-.037	.138	**.247**	**-.582**	-.029	.064	-.103	.121	**-.217**	**.594**	-.015	.053
UNCNVENT	.137	.060	.098	.039	.021	**.670**	.024	.000	-.057	.000	.032	**.681**
DIRECTNG	.028	.043	.059	-.014	**-.850**	.059	.000	.112	-.008	.055	**-.848**	.000
PROHIBTV	**-.335**	.062	.083	-.111	-.120	-.113	**-.325**	.073	-.055	.091	**-.198**	-.150
UNGREGAR	.070	**.348**	.061	-.005	.061	.055	.022	**.312**	-.079	-.009	.111	.076
JUST	-.070	-.191	**-.851**	.031	.011	-.063	.033	-.023	**.762**	-.174	.071	-.073

NEUTRAL	.161	.105	-.298	.128	.068	-.130
SOCIABLE	.185	-.465	-.021	.222	-.234	-.111
UNAFFECT	-.080	.108	.021	-.651	-.015	.015
REBELLOS	.084	-.186	.034	-.301	-.002	.567

NEUTRAL	.195	.146	.234	-.178	.151	-.105
SOCIABLE	.246	-.429	.038	-.159	-.252	-.122
UNAFFECT	-.118	.140	-.017	.617	.017	.000
REBELLOS	.002	-.196	.012	.331	.000	.559

Factor Correlations

Direct oblimin

	1	2	3	4	5	6
Permissiveness 1	1.00	-.093	-.291	.388	.491	-.054
Introversion 2	-.093	1.00	-.048	-.314	.280	-.051
Unjustness 3	-.291	-.048	1.00	-.549	.050	.334
Negative Regard 4	.388	-.314	-.549	1.00	-.028	-.270
Nondirecting 5	.491	.280	.050	-.028	1.00	.025
Nonconformity 6	-.054	-.051	.334	-.270	.025	1.00

Absolmin

	1	2	3	4	5	6
Permissiveness 1	1.00	-.169	.308	-.530	.200	-.046
Introversion 2	-.169	1.00	-.055	.241	.281	-.059
Unjustness 3	.308	-.055	1.00	-.436	-.204	-.297
Negative Regard 4	-.530	.241	-.436	1.00	-.011	.243
Nondirecting 5	.200	.281	-.204	-.011	1.00	.021
Nonconformity 6	-.046	-.059	-.297	.243	.021	1.00

Appendix II contains the MATRIX – END MATRIX program from SPSS to obtain the Absolmin solutions. The program requires that you begin with an orthogonal solution for a factor-pattern matrix. It could be the initial unrotated principal axes factor-pattern matrix, or it could be an orthogonal rotation of that matrix. In this case we begin with the VARIMAX solution. The iterations begin with a random orthogonal transformation matrix and the gradient projection algorithm is used to find a solution that minimizes the absolute value of each element of the rotated factor-pattern matrix. The Absolmin algorithm yields numerous "local minima." So the way to use it is to begin the iterations many (e.g., 100) times with different random transformation matrices and compare the criterion values of each solution. Pick the solution with the smallest criterion value.

Factor scores and factor indeterminacy

Having examined the factor-pattern and factor-correlation matrix to determine interpretations for the factors, the next question that may arise is "How can we get scores on the common factors?" My personal preference is to avoid factor scores unless the squared multiple correlation for predicting the common factors is in the high .90s. My reason for this opinion is **factor indeterminacy**. Factor scores are generally obtained by regression. Regression estimates give the least squares estimates of the factor scores by predicting them from the observed variables using the correlations among the observed variables and the correlations of the variables with the factors given in what is known as the factor structure matrix to compute the regression weights for the prediction of the scores. Other methods cannot get better least-squares fit than the regression method. The concept of factor indeterminacy has received an extensive treatment in the literature, and I and R. P. McDonald have been major contributors (Mulaik, 1972, 1996a,b, 2005; Mulaik & McDonald, 1978). But briefly the problem is this: The common factor model has n observed variables and $n + r$ latent common and unique factor variables. The observed variables are thus determined by what is not observable. There is no way to turn around to get unique determinations of the more numerous common and unique factors from the smaller number that is observed. We can get the factor structure matrix of correlations between the observed variables and the common factors, for these are derived from the factor-pattern matrix multiplied times the factor correlation matrix, which are determinable. And the correlation matrix among the observed variables is observed (we based our factor analysis on it). So, we can get regression weights for predicting the common factors from the observed variables. But these predictions frequently have multiple correlations less than .7071. Now, let me illustrate a simple analogy.

Suppose I have a variable X and I say that it is correlated .7071 with some unknown variable Y. Can you tell me from this what variable Y is? You are smart and say "No!" Why? Because, you say, there are an unlimited number of other variables that might be correlated .7071 with X. But, I ask, haven't we narrowed down the problem of what Y is from knowing it is correlated .7071 with X? "Well, yes," you say. "Suppose we represent variables by vectors emanating from a common origin, with cosines of the angles between them positioning them with respect to one another in space. Correlation = cosine of angle. Then the set of all variables Y having the correlation of .7071 correspond to vectors in a cone surrounding X as the central axis of the cone with cosine of .7071 for the angle between the X vector and any vector Y in the cone." The number of vectors in the cone is infinite. And you can't tell which it is.

But suppose you are Louis Guttman (1954). He says, suppose you chose one of these Y vectors as your guess. How possibly wrong could you be? He then shows you that you could be the most wrong if the correct Y is 180° directly opposite from the vector you chose. And the angle between them is twice the angle between X and your Y. Well, what would be the cosine of the angle between your guess and the correct Y? It's the cosine of twice this angle. And by a double angle formula in trignonometry we know this is equal to $\cos 2\theta = 2\cos^2\theta - 1$. So, if we convert correlations to cosines and vice versa, this means the correlation between your guess and the correct Y could be as little as $2 \times (.7071)^2 - 1 \approx 2 \times .5 - 1 = 0$. And if the correlation between X and Y is less than .7071, the correlation between your guess and the correct Y could be negative. So, your interpretation of the factor could be possibly the opposite of what it is when R is less than .7071. That gives one pause for thought.

Well, if we replace X by the regression estimate $\hat{\xi}$ of the common factor ξ, the correlation between X and Y by the multiple correlation R between the regression estimate and the unknown ξ, then the variable ξ can be any variable in the cone surrounding $\hat{\xi}$ with cosine equal to R. If the multiple correlation between $\hat{\xi}$ and ξ is $R = .95$ and the correlation between the factor estimator $\hat{\xi}$ and a variable Z is .60, what is the range of possible correlations between Z and ξ? The solution requires inverse trigonometric functions, which are available on any mathematical calculator. Let $\cos\alpha = .60$ and $\cos\rho = .95$. The minimum possible correlation is $\min r = \cos(\cos^{-1}\alpha + \cos^{-1}\rho) = \cos[\cos^{-1}(.60) + \cos^{-1}(.95)] = .3202$ and the maximum possible correlation is $\max r = \cos(\cos^{-1}\alpha - \cos^{-1}\rho) = \cos[\cos^{-1}(.60) - \cos^{-1}(.95)] = .8198$. So, our uncertainty as to what the true correlation between the latent factor and an external variable is that it is between .3202 and .8198. Furthermore, in many cases with R less than .7071 the true common factor variable could be negatively related to your interpretation of it. So, working with factor scores in common factor analysis has too much indeterminacy to be generally useful.

Factorial invariance

There are three cases of factorial invariance. (1) Invariance of the reproduced correlation matrix under rotation of factors. (2) Invariance of factors under selection of variables for analysis, and (3) invariance of model parameters under restriction of range.

Rotational invariance meant that it didn't matter what rotation for the factors took place, you would always get the same reproduced correlation matrix. Thurstone showed that there was an objective reason for picking one kind of rotation out of all, and this was the simple structure solution. Not only was it usually simpler to interpret because it disentangled the variables into clusters around certain factors, but the simple structure solution for the factors would be invariant across studies with different variables selected from the factor domain for analysis. But there is a little recognized stipulation behind that assertion. You must use care in selecting the variables to be close to the hyperplanes defining the primary axes (the factors). And this will only occur if you have a clear idea of how to define the factor domain to select from in the first place. Every variable in the factor domain is some linear combination of the same common factors of the domain, and preferably of at most $r-1$ of them. This also solves the problem of the second case, of getting the same factors with different selections of variables from the domain.

Many factor analytic studies are done with selections of subjects from restricted populations. For example, many studies use college students as subjects and these are more intelligent, more educated than many persons in the general population. It can be shown that correlations among variables become attenuated (made smaller) when computed from highly selected populations. But to make this explanation short, factor-pattern coefficients will be unaffected by restriction of range, while correlations, variances, and covariances are affected. This means factor structure coefficients are not invariant under restriction of range and difficult to meaningfully compare across studies. With comparative studies, it is important to study raw covariances rather than standardized variables with correlation coefficients within a given sample. Standardizing changes the metric of the measurments and this can become a confound with restriction of range, especially when comparing results across studies. See Mulaik (2010) for further details.

Common factor analysis versus component analysis

Common factor analysis models treat observed variables as linear functions of latent, unobserved variables. A closely related set of models are component analysis models, among which the most known is **principal components analysis**. These models find observable linear combinations of the original observed variables and treat these linear combinations as independent variables which determine the observed variables.

The model equations of a component analysis model would be

$$Y_1 = a_{11}X_1 + a_{12}X_2 + \cdots + a_{1n}X_n$$
$$Y_2 = a_{21}X_1 + a_{22}X_2 + \cdots + a_{2n}X_n$$
$$\vdots$$
$$Y_1 = a_{n1}X_1 + a_{n2}X_2 + \cdots + a_{nn}X_n$$
(8.7)

There are no unique factor or error variables. Furthermore the independent variables $X_1, \cdots, X_n$ are themselves functions of the observed variables

$$X_1 = b_{11}Y_1 + b_{12}Y_2 + \cdots + b_{1n}Y_n$$
$$X_2 = b_{21}Y_1 + b_{22}Y_2 + \cdots + b_{2n}Y_n$$
$$\vdots$$
$$X_n = b_{n1}Y_1 + b_{n2}Y_2 + \cdots + b_{nn}Y_n$$
(8.8)

Furthermore, there can be as many X variables as observed variables, but frequently there are fewer as these component analysis models seek to imitate common factor analysis models.

Mulaik (2010) describes three component analysis models: principal components (Pearson, 1901), weighted principal components (Mulaik, 1972), and image analysis (Guttman, 1953; Kaiser, 1963).

Component analysis models at first glance seem to have all the advantages and none of the disadvantages of the common factor models. They have observed independent variables constructable from the observed variables. They can have rotated factors. There is no "factor indeterminacy." Factor scores are indeed observable since they are perfectly determined by the observable variables.

One important thing that component analysis models lack is the ability to represent objective reality. Empiricists liked component analysis models because they regarded what appeared to the senses was reality. But they provided no general criterion for differentiating an illusion from reality. But science abandoned that simplistic view in favor of regarding what is real is given by a concept independent of the particular actions and means of observation of a particular observer. This concept should be coherent and invariant with diverse appearances from different points of view, to many observers, perspectives, methods of observation, from many locations, and invariant across many occasions. A dinner plate is seen as a circular, flat, and enduring object, distinct from the observer as the observer moves around and views it from different positions and even on different occasions. Some of the time its appearance is as an ellipse but it is still conceived as a round circular object.

Physicists regard certain subatomic particles as real, but no one can see them directly. One sees their effects on what is observed in a cloud chamber from different angles, as for example, the condensing of droplets of vapor in the chamber in a certain curved path typical of the particle produced by the ionizing effects on the vapor of the particle as it moves through the vapor. These particles are seen to have the same path forms in different cloud chambers, with different vapor media, different laboratories, by different researchers under similar conditions.

In common factor analysis the common and unique factors model variables exist independently of each of the observed variables in the analysis. Three or more observed variables could indicate a single common factor. Four would allow you to test for its existence, with each indicator an independent point of view of the latent variable. But Thurstone (1937, 1947) argued that unless you had a simple structure solution in a common factor analysis, you still would not have anything better than a principal components solution with a rotation to "simple structure," (like orthogonal varimax). In the latter case, the rotation would be limited to the space of just the observed variables and would differ from an analysis with communalities and unique variances. Communalities make the difference by isolating what is common to the tests and by hypothesis to other tests not in the battery. Then, using simple structure solutions, you could use different test items and still recover the same underlying abilities as common factors. Thus Thurstone held that,

> The factorial description of a test must remain invariant when the test is moved from one battery to another. This simply means that if a test calls for a certain amount of one ability and a certain amount of another ability, then that test should be so described irrespective of the other tests in the battery. (Thurstone, 1937, p. 75)

That would be a further test of the objective independence of the ability. In contrast, he said,

> If we ask the subjects to take some more tests at a later time and if we add these tests to the battery, then the principal components and centroid axes will be altered, and the factorial description of each test will also be altered. (p. 75)

The principal components maximize the variance of a linear combination of the variables. That is based on just the variables in the battery. And you cannot determine what the psychological content is of a factor without having at least three, four, or more tests or indicators of it. A single indicator may have many things within it. Having multiple indicators of it allows us to isolate what in them is common to them. And the indicators' loadings must be invariant across batteries of other tests.

But principal components and other component analysis models do produce factor-pattern matrices that are very similar in many cases to the factor-pattern matrix of a common factor analysis derived from the same data. Principal components solutions with rotations tend to overestimate the factor-pattern loadings relative to the common factor solutions. But Widaman (1993) showed that the difference in loadings between principal components analysis and common factor analysis decreased as the ratio of the number of observed variables to the number of common factors increased, when the magnitudes of the pattern loadings of the common factor model increased, and when the communalities increased. Otherwise, principal components models do not model accurately data generated by a common factor model.

Principal components models are still useful as data reduction procedures. Factor scores for a smaller number of component factors rotated to orthogonal simple structure from a principal components analysis of a given set of predictor variables are determinate and can be used to reduce the number of highly correlated predictor variables for a regression analysis and avoid effects of multicollinearity (Jolliffe, 1986).

Confirmatory Factor Analysis

Confirmatory research versus exploratory research

The philosopher of science Charles Saunders Peirce (1931–1938) was the first to expressly articulate a modern theory of scientific method that involved cycling over and over through three stages: **abduction**, **deduction**, and **induction**. In **abduction** the scientist encounters phenomena that require an explanation. He/she then considers a number of explanations that account for them and then chooses the one that best fits all of the phenomena to serve as the basis for a hypothesis. But that does not prove the validity of the hypothesis. Any number of distinct explanations might be imagined to account for the same phenomena. There is a need to test the explanation. This leads to the next stage in which **deduction** from the hypothesis together with prior knowledge and assumptions leads to an observable consequence that can be tested. The deduced consequence must not be logically possible from prior knowledge and assumptions without the hypothesis to combine with them to yield the consequence. The deduced consequence yields a specific set of quantities that should be observed if the hypothesis is true. In the third stage an appropriate set of data are collected to test the hypothesis. The data could never be all the logically possible observations one might have. And so there may be sampling error making the observed quantities deviate from the theoretical quantitities if the hypothesis were true. So, the new data should constitute a random sample from a population with a known probability distribution: then a test statistic measuring the degree of difference between the observed and hypothetical quantities should be chosen and have a known probability distribution for deviations from the hypothesized values. The hypothesis is provisionally accepted if the test statistic indicates that the deviations are not so large as to be so improbable and so deviant as to cast doubt on the truth of the hypothesis. This is an inductive inference, because the smaller and more probable the actual deviations conditional on the hypothesis, the more likely the data is consistent with the hypothesis.

If the hypothesis is accepted, other deductions leading to other new studies may be conducted to further test the hypothesis. If rejected, that starts over the abduction, deduction, and induction cycle, to discover a model that fits both previous and current data and in turn new data derived by deduction.

This represents a different way of testing substantive hypotheses in confirmatory studies. You are likely most familiar from basic statistics with nil hypothesis statistical testing. In nil hypothesis testing you begin with a substantive hypothesis that there is a difference between means or a correlation between two variables. But you have no specific value for the difference or the correlation. You just test the nil hypothesis as the null hypothesis that the difference or correlation is zero. If the result is significant, you then declare the substantive hypothesis is supported because the difference or correlation is not zero. But this is very weak support, because any number of different nonzero quantities might be hypothesized under distinct theories and be consistent with a nonzero result. In inductive inference from a deduced specific hypothesis, the null hypothesis is the pre-specified theoretical quantities of a substantive hypothesis, which may be nonzero. One hopes to accept rather than reject the null hypothesis. We will now see how this applies to confirmatory factor analysis.

I need to point out here that the same kinds of procedures used by L. L. Thurstone in selecting and constructing items for his inventories to be factor analyzed also apply in confirmatory factor analysis. In many ways Thurstone tried to test theories of underlying human cognitive abilities, but all he had was the exploratory factor analysis method to do it. He would have welcomed the methods of confirmatory factor analysis developed after his death.

Model equations

Basically the model equations of confirmatory factor analysis are the same as in exploratory factor analysis as given in Equation (8.4). The difference lies in more parameters (coefficients) being constrained by hypothesis in the confirmatory factor analysis model than in the exploratory factor analysis model. Confirmatory factor analyses (Jöreskog, 1969) are done with structural equation modelling programs, because confirmatory factor analyses are special cases of more general structural equation models.

The programs for structural equations modelling (Jöreskog, 1969, 1973) indicate constraints on model parameters usually in three ways: (1) as unknown free or estimated parameters, indicated often by a *; (2) as fixed parameters having specific numerical values respectively; or (3) by constraining a group of parameters to be equal to one another. It is important to understand that free or estimated parameters are not specified and are not really what is hypothesized about the model. Not shown are the fixed zero correlations between common and unique factors and among the unique factors. These are assumed given by the model.

The free parameters are unknowns to be estimated iteratively in such a way that their values make the model fit the data as well as possible **conditional on the constraints**, which are fixed during the iterations. The estimated parameters are needed to fill out the model so that a reproduced correlation matrix among the observed variables can be generated from the model. Lack of fit will concern differences between the original, observed correlation matrix, and the reproduced correlation matrix. Any lack of fit is to be attributed to the constraints. Computer programs designed to estimate these parameters systematically adjust values for the free parameters iteratively over and over to improve fit until the reproduced model correlation matrix fits the observed correlation matrix as well as possible subject to unchanging constraints. There are no eigenvalues and eigenvectors in confirmatory factor analysis.

In the model we are testing here, we have relied on our sense of word meanings to determine what words are **not** related to what factors. We indicate this by fixed zero coefficients shown in bold type (see Table 8.7). This is usual at the outset of research.

Table 8.7 Hypothesized factor-pattern loadings are indicated by specified quantities (in this case **0**). Estimated parameters are indicated by *.

| | \multicolumn{7}{c}{*Hypothesis*} |
| | \multicolumn{7}{c}{*factor-pattern loadings*} |
Variable	1	2	3	4	5	6	ψ_i
ALLOW	*	0	0	0	*	0	*
OUTGO	*	*	0	0	*	0	*
NONTALK	0	*	0	0	*	0	*
PERMISS	*	0	0	0	0	0	*
FAIR	0	0	*	*	0	0	*
UNFRIEND	*	*	*	*	0	0	*
FORCELESS	*	*	0	*	*	0	*
RESTRAIN	*	*	0	0	*	0	*
NONDOMIN	*	*	0	*	*	0	*
UNLOVING	0	0	0	*	0	0	*
NONCNFRM	0	0	0	0	0	*	*
COMPLINT	*	0	0	0	0	*	*
IMPARTIAL	0	*	*	0	*	0	*
LEADER	0	0	0	0	*	0	*
UNKIND	0	*	*	*	0	0	*
UNCNVENT	0	0	0	0	0	*	*
DIRECTNG	0	0	0	*	*	0	*
PROHIBTV	*	0	0	0	*	*	*
UNGREGAR	0	*	0	0	0	0	*
JUST	0	0	*	*	0	0	*
NEUTRAL	*	*	*	*	*	0	*
SOCIABLE	*	*	0	*	*	*	*
UNAFFECT	0	*	0	*	0	0	*
REBELLOS	0	*	0	*	0	*	*

| | \multicolumn{6}{c}{*Correlations among factors*} |
	1	2	3	4	5	6
Permissive 1	1.00					
Introversion 2	*	1.00				
Fair, Just 3	*	*	1.00			
Unloving 4	*	*	*	1.00		
Nondirecting 5	*	*	*	*	1.00	
Unconventional 6	*	*	*	*	*	1.00

We do not know what the loadings are of certain variables on certain factors, so we leave them as estimated free parameters. We may believe they have a nonzero loading, but by not knowing what these specifically are, we are compelled to leave them as estimated unknowns. If a factor is to be determined by the hypothesized model it must be in terms of what variables are not related to the factor. Thus the hypothesis tested is about the particular pattern of zero coefficients in the factor loading matrix in the context of the fixed zero correlations between common and unique factors and among the unique factors.

In later research, after we have found specific nonzero loadings for certain variables on certain factors, we may in addition to zero loadings, specify these nonzero values as fixed parameters, while leaving the common factor variances to be free parameters, which will fix the metric for the factors as the same as in an initial study. In such later studies we should also use raw covariances instead of correlations for the observed variables. "Fixing the metric" means specifying the units of measurement in terms of how much a unit change of one variable yields a given change in another variable. One parameter needs to be fixed for each common factor, either its variance or the loading of a selected indicator on it to determine the metric. Because in this study both common factors and observed variables are standardized to have unit variances, we would have to rely on the fixed value of a factor loading to establish the metric in later studies while letting observed variables and common factors have whatever variances the data allows.

In Table 8.8, I show the results of a confirmatory factor analysis. We show the common factor-pattern loadings and the unique factor loading for each variable, indicated by name on the left. The correlation matrix among the six factors is also shown. The largest nonzero loadings in each column correspond to items thought by hypothesis to best represent a corresponding factor. While that may be thought of as a test of the model, the test is really about the fixed zero coefficients, and that includes the zero coefficients representing zero correlations between common and unique factor variables, and among the unique factor variables as well.

Tests of fit

What we need to consider now is an overall test of the fit of the model to the data, which is the chi-square test. The chi-square value was 406.672 with 201 degrees of freedom. For a sample size of N = 523, the p value is less than .001, which indicates a statistical lack of fit. The sample size allows for high power to detect small discrepancies. But the model still has a close approximation to the data in the fit of the reproduced model correlation matrix to the observed correlation matrix, indicated by a CFI index of .958, where 1.00 would indicate perfect fit. The close approximation means just that. It does not mean the model is necessarily exactly correct. The significant chi-square indicates a need to discover possible reasons for the failure to get fit to within sampling error. There are numerous possibilities to consider. To begin with, the correlations of the observed variables were assumed to be among continuous variables distributed as the multivariate normal distribution. But we know they were **discrete** polytomous variables. That alone could produce some lack of fit in the discrepancy between distributional assumptions and reality.

Table 8.8 Results of confirmatory factor analysis of the 24 trait words based on six hypothesized concepts.

Results

factor-pattern loadings

Variable	1	2	3	4	5	6	ψ_i
ALLOW	.805	0	0	0	−.049†	0	.570
OUTGO	.225	−.660	0	0	.183	0	.183
NONTALK	0	.814	0	0	.081†	0	.631
PERMISS	.724	0	0	0	0	0	.689
FAIR	0	0	.756	−.064	0	0	.601
UNFRIEND	−.163	.271	−.165	.395	0	0	.665
FORCELESS	.353	.276	0	−.304	−.399	0	.589
RESTRAIN	−.071†	.412	0	0	.355	0	.914
NONDOMIN	.231	.264	0	−.381	−.495	0	.587
UNLOVING	0	0	0	.804	0	0	.595
NONCNFRM	0	0	0	0	0	.495	.869
COMPLINT	.174	0	0	0	0	−.508	.839
IMPARTIAL	0	.167	.362	0	−.095	0	.925
LEADER	0	0	0	0	.799	0	.601
UNKIND	0	.031†	−.216	.662	0	0	.556
UNCNVENT	0	0	0	0	0	.707	.707
DIRECTNG	0	0	0	.261	.834	0	.573
PROHIBTV	−.491	0	0	0	−.001†	−.103	.868
UNGREGAR	0	.357	0	0	0	0	.934
JUST	0	0	.836	−.033†	0	0	.514
NEUTRAL	.144	.212	.317	.183	−.044†	0	.844
SOCIABLE	.241	−.465	0	−.135	.193	−.101	.696
UNAFFECT	0	.060†	0	.721	0	0	.665
REBELLOS	0	−.206	0	.301	0	.575	.696

Correlations among factors

	1	2	3	4	5	6
Permissive 1	1.00					
Introversion 2	†	1.00				
Fair, Just 3	−.377	−.176	1.00			
Unloving 4	−.535	.392	−.650	1.00		
Nondirecting 5	−.319	−.525	.291	−.213	1.00	
Unconventional 6	−.046†	−.015†	−.398	.282	−.138	1.00

Note. **Bold type** indicates parameters prespecified and fixed by hypothesis. Numbers not in bold type are estimated values. † indicates an estimated value that does not differ significantly from zero. Zero correlations between common and unique factors and among unique factors are not shown.

But substantively each one of the fixed zero coefficients in the hypothesized model could be responsible for lack of fit. There are individual single degree-of-freedom tests for each of these fixed parameters separately known as Lagrange multiplier tests. Associated with each is a p value. These tests are not statistically independent, so after the first test of the largest chi-square value, the p values may be off the mark. I will not show those here, other than to mention that the largest significant discrepancy with a chi-square of 4.889 and 1 degree of freedom was on a correlation between the unique factors of the FORCELESS and the NONDOMINATING variables. Both share (negatively) the common factor of DIRECTING with LEADER, DIRECTING, and RESTRAINING. All of these concern some aspect of applying force in the interpersonal realm. But people who are forceless and nondominating may have other characteristics in common which would come out with these variables on what is now a possible doublet factor. But that is only the basis for a hypothesis that might be tested in the future by including other variables such as indicators of anxiety, timidity, inadequacy, physical strength, and size to see if these also contribute to the common variance of these two variables.

In any case, a careful examination of the results is essential to discover possible explanations of the discrepancy needing further testing in future research.

Tests are also possible for the free parameters. The standard errors are usually given for these in structural equation modelling programs used to do confirmatory factor analyses. So, it is possible to test prior nonzero hypotheses as to their values. But ordinarily, you might simply test the hypothesis that these values differ significantly from zero. In that case the programs usually provide the z-statistic based on the standardized normal distribution for the test of the difference from zero. A z value greater than 2.00 would indicate significance. In Table 8.8 I have used the symbol † to show that a loading treated as a free parameter, was estimated to be not significantly different from zero.

It is also important to learn that degrees of freedom respresent the degree to which the model is disconfirmable by lack of fit. Mulaik (2001, 2009) showed that the number of degrees of freedom equaled the number of dimensions in which the model of the data was free to differ from the data and thus fail to fit. It is given in factor analysis and structural equation modelling by the formula

$$df = n(n+1)/2 - m \qquad (8.9)$$

where df are the degrees of freedom of the model, $n(n+1)/2$ is the number of distinct elements of the observed symmetric correlation/covariance matrix to be fitted, and m the number of estimated parameters. Thus for the present data we have $24(24+1)/2 - [24 + 6(5)/2 + 60] = 201$. There are 300 elements to fit to. There are 24 unique variances, 15 correlations among 6 factors, and 60 factor-pattern coefficients to estimate. Hence there are 201 degrees of freedom. The more degrees of freedom, the more disconfirmable is the model. Given the number of elements to fit, you lose a degree of freedom for each parameter estimated. Hence ideally you should estimate as few parameters as possible. And models with more estimated parameters are able to better fit the data just as a mathematical artifact. So, estimating lots of parameters is not desirable. A scientific model is more desirable the more ways by which it can be disconfirmed by data. If it passes the fit test, the more degrees of freedom indicate the stronger the evidence for the model. An exploratory factor analysis model usually has fewer degrees of freedom than a corresponding confirmatory factor analysis model because it estimates more parameters.

Some Remaining Problems.

Factorial homogeneity

The common factor model, being the oldest multivariate technique used by psychologists, has achieved widespread use. But an almost universally unrecognized assumption of its use is that every subject should behave according to the same common factor model in responding to tests or questionaires. I call this the implicit assumption of **factorial homogeneity of the observations**. This assumes that one subject or observation can be substituted for another without changing the factor analytic results. This does not assume that they will get scores at the same level on each variable, but that their scores will be the same linear functions of the same common factors, regardless of the level of their scores on the factors.

How might this assumption be compromised? In the case of personality trait ratings and attitude questionnaires, subjects might vary in their understanding and use of the words. As a result the combined ratings of all raters in computing the variances and correlations may yield factor loadings and correlations that represent no single individual rater exactly. The model may then fail to fit precisely and yield significant chi-square goodness of fit indices. On performance tests, subjects may vary in the manner in which they perform a task or solve a problem. Those at different levels of the spectrum of ability may use different abilities to try to solve the same problem implying different factor analytic models are needed at different levels of ability. Unlike physical objects, humans are highly variable and complex in their behavior.

Factorial heterogeneity

The opposite case I call **factorial heterogeneity of the observations**. How can we determine whether this is the case with a given sample of responders to our rating scales and performance tests? Can we isolate individuals in a sample into subgroups that are factorially homogeneous? That I leave as a problem for some doctoral dissertation in the future to resolve. But it is an important problem yet unresolved.

Nonlinearity

Another problem concerns the possible nonlinearity of functional relations between variables. Factor analysis assumes linear functional relations between factors and observed variables. But suppose, in fact, the relations between factors and observed variables are monotonically increasing (or decreasing). A monotonically increasing (decreasing) function is one in which, as the independent variable increases (decreases), the dependent variable never decreases (increases) but always increases (decreases). But the increase (decrease) may not be by constant sized increments. Monotonic functions can be approximated in many cases with straight line (linear) functional relations. But at some point there will be lack of fit. More serious is the case in which nonlinear nonmonotonic functional relations exist between observed dependent variables and the independent common factor variables wherein the dependent variables are increasing and decreasing throughout the range of the independent variables. Factor analysis with linear relations cannot model this behavior, even approximately. Factor analysis fitted to such data may require many more common factors than actually are driving the behavior of the observed variables.

Causal structure

Another problem is that factor analysis only assumes that any relations between two observed variables are due to a third variable common to them: $Y_1 \leftarrow \xi_j \rightarrow Y_2$. But other possibilities are that one variable is the cause of the other, $Y_1 \rightarrow Y_2$ or $Y_1 \leftarrow Y_2$. Two observed variables may be correlated because there is an unobserved chain of latent variables linking them, $Y_1 \rightarrow \xi_j \rightarrow \xi_j \rightarrow Y_2$. Factor analysis is not able to reveal such relationships. Since the 1970s new models with latent and observed variables have developed to handle such relationships, known as structural equations models. But there are many textbooks now available on that subject.

In the twenty-first century, factor analysis will still have a place in some studies where the data conforms to a common factor model. But the rapid development of linear and nonlinear models of complex causal relations between variables will mean these will be increasingly the focus of researchers in this century.

References

Bentler, P. M. (1990). Comparative fit indexes in structural models. *Psychological Bulletin, 107,* 238–246.

Bernaards, C. A., & Jennrich, R. I. (2005). Gradient projection algorithms and software for arbitrary rotation criteria in factor analysis. *Educational and Psychological Measurement, 65,* 676–696.

Browne, M. W. (2001). An overview of analytic rotation in exploratory factor analysis. *Multivariate Behavioral Research, 36,* 111–115.

Carroll, J. B. (1993). *Human cognitive abilities. A survey of factor-analytic studies.* Cambridge: Cambridge University Press.

Cattell, R. B., & Horn, J. L. (1978). A check on the theory of fluid and crystallized intelligence with description of new subtest designs. *Journal of Educational Measurment, 15,* 139–164. DOI: 10.1111/j.1745-3984.1978.tb00065.x.

Galton, F. (1886). Family likeness in stature. *Proceedings of the Royal Society, 40,* 42–73.

Galton, F. (1888). Co-relations and their measurement, chiefly from anthropometric data. *Proceedings Royal Society of London, 45,* 135–145.

Galton, F. (1889). *Natural Inheritance.* London: Macmillan.

Guilford, J. P. (1967). *The nature of human intelligence.* New York: McGraw-Hill.

Guttman, L. (1953). Image theory for the structure of quantitative variates. *Psychometrika, 18,* 277–296.

Guttman, L. (1954). Some necessary conditions for common-factor analysis. *Psychometrika, 19,* 149–161.

Guttman, L. (1956). "Best Possible" systematic estimates of communalities. *Psychometrika, 21,* 273–285.

Guttman, L. (1965). A faceted definition of intelligence. In R. R. Eiferman (Ed.), *Studies in psychology, Scripta hierosolymitana* (Vol. 14). Jerusalem, Israel: The Hebrew University.

Guttman, L. (1994). *Louis Guttman on theory and methodology: Selected writings.* S. Levy (Ed.). Aldershot, UK: Darthmouth Publishing Co.

Horn, J. L. (1965). A rationale and test for the number of factors in factor analysis. *Psychometrika, 30*, 179–185.

Horn, J. (1988). Thinking about human abilities. In J. R. Nesselroade & R. B. Cattel (Eds.), *Handbook of multivariate experimental psychology* (2nd ed.) (pp. 645–665). New York: Plenum Press.

Howe, W. G. (1955). Some contributions to factor analysis. Report No. ONRL-1919. Oak Ridge, TN: Oak Ridge National Laboratory.

Humphreys, L. G., Tucker, L. R., & Dachler. P. (1970). Evaluating the importance of factors in any given order of factoring. *Multivariate Behavioral Research, 5*, 209–215.

Jennrich, R. I. (2002). A simple general method for oblique rotation. *Psychometrika, 67*, 7–20.

Jennrich, R. I. (2006). Rotation to simple loadings using component loss functions: The oblique case. *Psychometrika, 71*, 173–191.

Jennrich, R. I., & Sampson, P. F. (1966). Rotation to simple loadings. *Psychometrika, 31*, 313–323.

Jolliffe, I. T. (1986). *Principal component analysis.* New York: Springer-Verlag.

Jöreskog, K. G. (1967). Some contributions to maximum likelihood factor analysis. *Psychometrika, 32*, 443–482.

Jöreskog, K. G. (1969). A general approach to confirmatory maximum likelihood factor analysis. *Psychometrika, 34*, 183–202.

Jöreskog, K. G. (1973). A general method for estimating a linear structural equation system. In A. S. Goldberger & O. D. Duncan (Eds.), *Structural equation models in the social sciences* (pp. 86–223). New York: Seminar Press.

Kaiser, H. F. (1958). The varimax criterion for analytic rotation in factor analysis. *Psychometrika, 23*, 187–200.

Kaiser, H. F. (1961). A note on Guttman's lower bound for the number of common factors. *British Journal of Statistical Psychology, 14*, 1–2.

Kaiser, H. F. (1963). Image Analysis. In C. W. Harris (Ed.), *Problems in measuring change* (pp. 156–166). Madison, WI: University of Wisconsin Press.

Katz, J. O., & Rohlf, F. J. (1974). Functionplane – A new approach to simple strucure rotation. *Psychometrika, 39*, 37–51.

Kiers, H. A. L. (1994). SIMPLIMAX: Oblique rotation to an optimal target with simple structure. *Psychometrika, 59*, 567–579.

Lorenzo-Seva, U. (1999). Promin: A method for oblique factor rotation. *Multivariate Behavioral Research, 34*, 347–365.

McDonald, R. P., & Marsh, H. W. (1990). Choosing a multivariate model: Noncentrality and goodness-of-fit. *Psychological Bulletin, 107*, 247–255.

McKeon, J. J. (1968). *Rotation for maximum association between factors and tests* (Unpublished manuscript). Biometric Laboratory, George Washington University.

Mulaik, S. A. (1963). *A factor analytic investigation of the equivalence of personality factors with semantic factors* (Unpublished doctoral dissertation). University of Utah, Salt Lake City, UT.

Mulaik, S. A. (1964). Are personality factors raters' conceptual factors? *Journal of Consulting Psychology, 28*, 506–511.

Mulaik, S. A. (1996a). On Maraun's deconstructing of factor indeterminacy with constructed factors. *Multivariate Behavioral Research, 31*, 579–592.

Mulaik, S. A. (1996b). Factor analysis is not just a model in pure-mathematics. *Multivariate Behavioral Research, 31*, 655–661.

Mulaik, S. A. (1972). *The foundations of factor analysis.* New York: McGraw Hill.

Mulaik, S. A. (2001). The curve-fitting problem: An objectivist view. *Philosophy of Science, 68*, 218–241.

Mulaik, S. A. (2005). Looking back on the factor indeterminacy controversies in factor analysis. In A. Maydeu-Olivares & J. J. McArdle (Eds.), *Contemporary psychometrics: A festschrift for Roderick P. McDonald* (pp. 173–206). Mahwah, NJ: Lawrence Erlbaum Associates.

Mulaik, S. A. (2009). *Linear causal modeling with structural equations.* Boca Raton, FL: Chapman and Hall/CRC Press, Taylor & Francis Group.

Mulaik, S. A. (2010). *Foundations of factor analysis* (2nd ed.). Boca Raton, FL: Chapman and Hall/CRC Press, Taylor & Francis Group.

Mulaik, S. A., & McDonald, R. P. (1978). The effect of additional variables on factor indeterminacy in models with a single common factor. *Psychometrika, 43,* 177–192.

Osgood, C. E., Suci, G. J., & Tannenbaum, P. H. (1957). *The measurement of meaning.* Champaign, IL: University of Illinois Press.

Pearson, K. (1896). Mathematical contributions to the theory of evolution, III: regression, heredity and panmixia. *Philosophical Transactions of the Royal Society of London (A), 18,* 253–318.

Pearson, K. (1901). On lines and planes of closest fit to systems of points in space. *Philosophical Magazine, 2,* 559–572.

Peirce, C. S. (1931–1958). *Collected papers of Charles Sanders Peirce.* (Vol. 1–8); C. Hartshorne & P. Weiss (Eds.) (Vol. 1–6), and A. W. Burks (Ed.) (Vols. 7–8). Cambridge, MA: Harvard University Press.

Rozeboom, W. W. (1991a). Hyball: A method for subspace constrained factor rotation. *Multivariate Behavioral Research, 26,* 163–177.

Rozeboom, W. W. (1991b). Theory and practice of hyperplane optimization. *Multivariate Behavioral Research, 26,* 179–197.

Rushton, J. P., & Irwing, P. (2011). The general factor of personality: normal and abnormal. In T. Chamorro-Premuzic, S. von Stumm, & A. Furnham (Eds.), *The Wiley-Blackwell handbook of individual differences.* New York: Wiley-Blackwell.

Schmid, J., & Leiman, J. M. (1957). The development of hierarchical factor solutions. *Psychometrika, 22,* 53–61.

Spearman, C. (1904a). The proof and measurement of association between two things. *American Journal of Psychology, 15,* 72–101.

Spearman C. (1904b). General intelligence, objectively determined and measured. *American Journal of Psychology, 15,* 201–293.

Spearman, C. (1927). *The abilities of man.* New York: Macmillan.

Steiger, J. H., & Lind, J. C. (1980). *Statistically based tests for the number of common factors.* Paper presented at the Annual Meeting of the Psychometric Society, Iowa City, IO.

Thurstone, L. L. (1937). Current misuse of the factorial methods. *Psychometrika, 2,* 73–76.

Thurstone, L. L. (1947). *Multiple factor analysis.* Chicago, IL: University of Chicago Press.

Turner, N. E. (1998). The effect of common variance and structure pattern on random data eigenvalues: Implications for the accuracy of parallel analysis. *Educational and Psychological Measurement, 58,* 541–568.

Vernon, P. E. (1961). *The structure of human abilities* (2nd ed.). London: Methuen.

Webb, E. (1915). *Character and intelligence: an attempt at an exact study of character.* Cambridge: Cambridge University Press.

Widaman, K. F. (1993). Common factor analysis versus principal component analysis: Differential bias in representing model parameters? *Multivariate Behavioral Research, 28,* 263–311.

Yates, A. (1987). *Multivariate exploratory data analysis: A perspective on exploratory factor analysis.* Albany: State University of New York Press.

Yule, G. U. (1897). On the theory of correlation. *Journal of the Royal Statistical Society, 60,* 812–854.

Yule, G. U. (1900). On the association of attributes in statistics: with illustrations from the material of the Childhood Society, &c. *Philosophical Transactions of the Royal Society of London (A), 194,* 257–319.

9

Estimation Methods in Latent Variable Models for Categorical Outcome Variables

Li Cai and Irini Moustaki

Introduction

The data usually encountered in social sciences and social surveys in particular are categorical in nature (ordinal or nominal, including the dichotomous case), such as responses to educational achievement tests marked as right or wrong; responses to attitudinal items on sexual attitudes rated as strongly agree, agree, disagree, and strongly disagree; or responses in a consumer preference survey on which flavor of ice cream one prefers most.

In this chapter, we present the most widely known factor analysis models for handling categorical responses, and provide references for other models that the reader might find more applicable or useful for his/her applications. The models specify the probability of response in each category as a function of parameters attributed to items (difficulty and discrimination) and of a latent value attributed to the respondent.

Models with discrete latent variables such as the latent class model (Lazarsfeld & Henry, 1968; McCutcheon, 1987) or the HYBRID model (Gitomer & Yamamoto, 1991; Von Davier, 1996) that combines continuous with discrete latent variables can be equally useful and in some cases more appropriate for modeling data and provide answers to specific research questions. But they remain out of the scope of our chapter and therefore will not be included here.

Latent Variable Models for Categorical Responses

Let $\mathbf{y}' = (y_1, y_2, \ldots, y_p)$ denote a vector of p categorical observed variables/items/indicators, where y_i has m_i categories, $i = 1, \ldots, p$. Thus, there are $R = \prod_{i=1}^{p} m_i$ possible response patterns of the form $\mathbf{y}'_r = (c_1, c_2, \ldots, c_p)$, where $r = 1, \ldots, R$ and $c_i = 1, \ldots, m_i$. Let us denote with $\boldsymbol{\xi}' = (\xi_1, \xi_2, \ldots, \xi_q)$ the vector of q latent variables or factors. We will focus here on models with continuous latent variables. The interest lies in specifying the probability of each response pattern as a function of $\xi_1, \xi_2, \ldots, \xi_q$:

The Wiley Handbook of Psychometric Testing: A Multidisciplinary Reference on Survey, Scale and Test Development, First Edition. Edited by Paul Irwing, Tom Booth, and David J. Hughes.
© 2018 John Wiley & Sons Ltd. Published 2020 by John Wiley & Sons Ltd.

$$\Pr(y_1 = c_1, y_2 = c_2, \ldots, y_p = c_p \mid \xi_1, \ldots, \xi_q) = f(\xi_1, \xi_2, \ldots, \xi_q), \tag{9.1}$$

where $c_1, c_2, \ldots, c_p$ represent the different response categories of $y_1, y_2, \ldots, y_p$, respectively.

There are two main approaches for the analysis of categorical variables with factor models. The underlying variable (UV) approach (Jöreskog, 1990, 1994; Lee, Poon, & Bentler, 1990a, 1990b, 1992; Muthén, 1984), and the item response theory (IRT) approach (Bartholomew, Knott, & Moustaki, 2011; Bock & Moustaki, 2007; van der Linden & Hambleton, 1997). In the UV approach, the categorical variables are assumed to be generated by underlying continuous variables, which are partially observed through their categorical counterparts. Correlations for pairs of the underlying continuous variables are estimated (known as tetrachoric for binary items and polychoric for ordinal items) and the classical normal factor analysis model is fitted to the estimated correlation matrix. In the IRT approach, categorical indicators are treated as they are by making distributional assumptions for the observed items conditional on the latent variables. The UV and IRT approaches differ in the way they parameterize and model Equation 9.1. We will discuss the two approaches in detail below.

Underlying variable approach

Under the UV approach, the categorical variables are assumed to be generated by underlying continuous variables. For example, the connection between an observed ordinal variable y_i and the underlying continuous variable y_i^* is

$$y_i = c_i \Leftrightarrow \tau_{c_i-1}^{(y_i)} < y_i^* < \tau_{c_i}^{(y_i)}, \tag{9.2}$$

where $\tau_{c_i}^{(y_i)}$ is the c_ith threshold of variable y_i and $-\infty = \tau_0^{(y_i)} < \tau_1^{(y_i)} < \cdots < \tau_{m_i-1}^{(y_i)} < \tau_{m_i}^{(y_i)} = +\infty$. Since only ordinal information is available, the distribution of y_i^* is determined only up to a monotonic transformation. In practice it is convenient to assume a standard normal distribution. In the case that the mean and the variance of y_i^* are of interest, Jöreskog (2002) discusses an alternative parametrization.

Since the observed items **y** have now been transformed to unobserved continuous variables **y***, the classical common factor analysis model (e.g., Jöreskog, 1967) can be used, giving:

$$\mathbf{y}^* = \mathbf{\Lambda}\boldsymbol{\xi} + \boldsymbol{\epsilon}, \tag{9.3}$$

where **y*** is the p-dimensional vector of the underlying variables, $\mathbf{\Lambda}$ is the $p \times q$ matrix of factor loadings, and $\boldsymbol{\epsilon}$ is the p-dimensional vector of unique factors. In addition, it is assumed that $\boldsymbol{\xi} \sim N_q(\mathbf{0}, \mathbf{\Phi})$, where $\mathbf{\Phi}$ is the factor correlation matrix with unit diagonals. The unique factors $\boldsymbol{\epsilon}$ follow an $N_p(\mathbf{0}, \mathbf{\Psi})$ distribution, with $\mathbf{\Psi} = \mathbf{I} - \text{diag}(\mathbf{\Lambda}\mathbf{\Phi}\mathbf{\Lambda}')$ a diagonal matrix containing the unique variances on the diagonal. Furthermore, the common factors in $\boldsymbol{\xi}$ and the unique factors are orthogonal: $\text{Cov}(\boldsymbol{\xi}, \boldsymbol{\epsilon}) = \mathbf{0}$. The vector of free parameters can be written as $\boldsymbol{\theta}' = (\boldsymbol{\lambda}, \boldsymbol{\varphi}, \boldsymbol{\tau})$. $\boldsymbol{\lambda}$ and $\boldsymbol{\varphi}$ are the vectors of the free/unconstrained nonredundant parameters in matrices $\mathbf{\Lambda}$ and $\mathbf{\Phi}$, respectively, and $\boldsymbol{\tau}$ is the vector of all free thresholds.

Under the model, the unconditional probability of response pattern r is

$$f_r(\mathbf{y};\boldsymbol{\theta}) = P(y_1 = c_1, y_2 = c_2, \ldots, y_p = c_p;\boldsymbol{\theta})$$
$$= \int_{\tau_{c_1-1}^{(y_1)}}^{\tau_{c_1}^{(y_1)}} \cdots \int_{\tau_{c_p-1}^{(y_p)}}^{\tau_{c_p}^{(y_p)}} \phi_p(\mathbf{y}^\star;\boldsymbol{\Sigma}_\star)\mathrm{d}\mathbf{y}^\star, \qquad (9.4)$$

where $\phi_p(\mathbf{y}^\star;\boldsymbol{\Sigma}_\star)$ is a p-dimensional normal density with zero mean, and correlation matrix $\boldsymbol{\Sigma}_\star = \boldsymbol{\Lambda}\boldsymbol{\Phi}\boldsymbol{\Lambda}' + \boldsymbol{\Psi}$ under the model defined in Equation 9.3.

Item response theory approach

In the IRT approach, we do not make explicit assumptions about underlying continuous variables but instead categorical variables are treated as they are. We now define the probability $f(\mathbf{y};\boldsymbol{\theta})$ as:

$$f(\mathbf{y};\boldsymbol{\theta}) = \int g(\mathbf{y};\boldsymbol{\theta}\mid\boldsymbol{\xi})\phi(\boldsymbol{\xi})\mathrm{d}\boldsymbol{\xi}, \qquad (9.5)$$

where $\phi(\boldsymbol{\xi})$ is the joint distribution of latent variables and the integral is over the domain of $\phi(\boldsymbol{\xi})$. The latent variables are usually assumed to be independent standard normal variables, but a correlation matrix $\boldsymbol{\Phi}$ can also be assumed as in the UV approach, giving $\phi(\boldsymbol{\xi};\boldsymbol{\phi})$. Assuming that the associations among the observed variables can be solely explained by the latent variables (assumption of conditional independence), the conditional response pattern probability factors into a product of item-specific conditional response probabilities:

$$g(\mathbf{y};\boldsymbol{\theta}\mid\boldsymbol{\xi}) = \prod_{i=1}^{p} g(y_i;\boldsymbol{\theta}\mid\boldsymbol{\xi}),$$

where $g(y_i;\boldsymbol{\theta}\mid\boldsymbol{\xi})$ is the density of item y_i conditional on the vector of latent variables $\boldsymbol{\xi}$.

Various models have been developed within the IRT approach for binary, ordinal, and nominal variables. Notable models include the one-parameter logistic model (1PL: Rasch:1960, 1961) that estimates one ability parameter for each individual and an item intercept parameter known in educational testing as the item difficulty parameter, the two-parameter logistic model (2PL: Birnbaum, 1968a, 1968b) that allows each item to be characterized by an intercept (difficulty parameter) and a factor loading for ability (discrimination parameter), and the three-parameter logistic model (3PL: Birnbaum, 1968a), which defines the probability of a correct response as a function of item difficulty and the ability of the examinee, as well as proclivity to guess. The 2PL model has been generalized to more than one latent variable, leading to a multidimensional model. Many more models have been developed within the IRT framework for allowing for partial credit scoring, analysis of nominal data and ranked data. For a review see Embretson and Reise (2000), van der Linden and Hambleton (1997), and Bock and Moustaki (2007).

We will provide results for the general case of q factors. In the case of binary items, the response probability of giving a positive or correct response is modeled as follows:

$$\text{link } P(y_i = 1; \boldsymbol{\theta} \mid \boldsymbol{\xi}) = \alpha_{0i} + \sum_{j=1}^{q} \alpha_{ij}\xi_j, \quad i = 1,\ldots,p, \qquad (9.6)$$

where the link can be the probit (inverse normal) function as in Bock & Aitkin (1981) or the logit as in Bartholomew et al. (2011). In the case of ordinal items, the response category probability is written:

$$P(y_i = c_i; \boldsymbol{\theta} \mid \boldsymbol{\xi}) = \gamma(y_i \leq c_i; \boldsymbol{\theta} \mid \boldsymbol{\xi}) - \gamma(y_i \leq c_i - 1; \boldsymbol{\theta} \mid \boldsymbol{\xi}), \qquad (9.7)$$

where $\gamma(y_i \leq c_i; \boldsymbol{\theta}|\boldsymbol{\xi})$ is the cumulative probability of a response in category c_i, or below, for variable y_i. The cumulative probability is modeled as follows:

$$\text{link}(\gamma(y_i \leq c_i; \boldsymbol{\theta} \mid \boldsymbol{\xi})) = \alpha_{c_i}^{(y_i)} - \sum_{j=1}^{q} \alpha_{ij}\xi_j, \qquad (9.8)$$

where the $\alpha_{0c_i}^{(y_i)}$ are thresholds ($-\infty = \alpha_0^{(y_i)} < \alpha_1^{(y_i)} < \cdots < \alpha_{m_i-1}^{(y_i)} < \alpha_{m_i}^{(y_i)} = +\infty$), and the α_{ij} are factor loadings. The link function can be any monotonically increasing function mapping $(0, 1)$ onto $(-\infty, \infty)$, such as the logit (Samejima, 1969) or the probit. Alternatively, the multinomial logit link function can be used, resulting in the nominal categories model and its variants (see Bock, 1972; Thissen, Cai, & Bock, 2010).

Overview of Estimation Methods

In this section, we will review estimation methods that have been widely used in estimating latent variable and structural equation models. We will also outline recent estimation advances. Before we apply these methods to our specific models we will describe each method and discuss their merits. Estimation methods such as maximum likelihood (ML), unweighted least squares (ULS), weighted least squares (WLS), and generalized least squares (GLS) have been the main estimation methods in structural equation modeling and psychometrics. Those estimation methods in some cases utilize all the information from the sampled data (whole response pattern) leading to full information estimation methods where in other instances they only utilize information from lower-order margins such as univariate and/or bivariate margins, leading to limited information methods. Multivariate categorical data can be represented by an $(m_1 \times m_2 \times \cdots \times m_p)$ contingency table, where m_i denotes the number of categories of the ith item. Each cell of that table represents a response pattern and comes with a corresponding observed frequency. Full information maximum likelihood estimation methods use that contingency table as the unit of analysis. However, one could instead write down all the possible $m_i \times m_j$ two-way tables and perform the estimation on those bivariate tables. Those estimation methods that utilize information from the bivariate or in general from the lower-order tables are known as limited information estimation methods. There will be a lengthy discussion on that topic in a later section.

Maximum likelihood estimation (MLE) methods are widely used for parameter estimation and inference in statistics. The reason is that ML estimators have desirable large-sample asymptotic properties, under suitable regularity conditions. These properties include consistency and asymptotic unbiasedness (for sufficiently large samples the estimated values tend to go close to the true parameter values generated by the data, but in finite/small samples there might be some bias), asymptotic efficiency (asymptotically it will produce estimators with the lowest possible variance / standard error among unbiased estimators), asymptotic normality, and invariance (the ML method will provide the same solution under parameter transformation). Note that all these desirable and useful properties for ML estimates are only true for large samples, and therefore in small samples alternative estimation methods might be preferred. Furthermore, ML estimation requires one to make fully specified distributional assumptions (e.g. normal, binomial, Poisson, etc.) about the data, where methods such as least squares (LS) do not.

We will briefly describe MLE for a simple random sample of n independent data points written as $\mathbf{y}' = (y_1, y_2, \ldots, y_n)$ from an unknown population. In statistical modeling, we assume that some probability distribution $f(\mathbf{y};\boldsymbol{\theta})$ with population/unknown parameters $\boldsymbol{\theta}$ is responsible for generating the data. The probability of the data expressed in $f(\mathbf{y};\boldsymbol{\theta})$ as a function of the parameter vector $\boldsymbol{\theta}$ for fixed data is called the likelihood function. We are now faced with the following question: What are the parameter values that maximize the likelihood that the selected model has generated the observed data? To answer that question we write down the likelihood function:

$$L(\boldsymbol{\theta}\,|\,\mathbf{y}) = f(\mathbf{y};\boldsymbol{\theta}),$$

treating observed data $\mathbf{y}$ as fixed. Therefore the likelihood function is a function of the parameter vector $\boldsymbol{\theta}$. In the case of a single parameter θ the shape of the likelihood is a curve. Since the observations are taken to be independent and identically distributed, the likelihood function for a random sample of size n is written as the product of the probability distributions evaluated for each of the data points:

$$L(\boldsymbol{\theta}\,|\,\mathbf{y}) = \prod_{h=1}^{n} f(y_h;\boldsymbol{\theta}). \tag{9.9}$$

To obtain the ML estimates we need to maximize Equation 9.9. It is often easier to maximize instead the log-likelihood that replaces the product of densities with the sum of the log densities given by:

$$l(\boldsymbol{\theta}) = \ln L(\boldsymbol{\theta}\,|\,\mathbf{y}) = \sum_{h=1}^{n} \ln f(y_h;\boldsymbol{\theta}). \tag{9.10}$$

The value of $\boldsymbol{\theta}$ that leads to a maximum of $l(\boldsymbol{\theta})$ is the maximum likelihood estimate, and is often denoted as $\hat{\boldsymbol{\theta}}$. Often the maximization of the log-likelihood (Equation 9.10) is an application of standard calculus related to solving the ML equations obtained from the first derivative of the log-likelihood with respect to the unknown parameters $\boldsymbol{\theta}$, written as $\dfrac{\partial l(\boldsymbol{\theta})}{\partial \boldsymbol{\theta}} = 0$. For some models, the ML equations are linear in the parameters and therefore produce explicit solutions for $\hat{\boldsymbol{\theta}}$. The ML equations of latent variable models for categorical items are not linear and therefore iterative algorithms are required for solving the ML equations with respect to $\hat{\theta}$. There will be some further explanations on the topic of iterative algorithms in a later section.

On the other hand, estimation methods such as ULS, WLS, and GLS aim to estimate parameters that minimize a discrepancy measure between statistics from the observed data and their model-implied counterparts, e.g., squared differences between observed correlations vs. model-implied correlations. The quantities being minimized are known as fit functions or discrepancy functions. For example, in unweighted least squares factor analysis, the aim is to find estimates of Λ and Ψ that minimize the squared difference between the $(p \times p)$ sample covariance matrix $\mathbf{S}$ and the covariance matrix implied by the model, Σ. We will discuss these estimation methods in the sections to follow.

A review of estimation methods for continuous variables

We will briefly review here estimation methods for the factor analysis model for continuous variables, since these can also be used for noncontinuous variables under the UV approach and adjusted to produce correct standard errors and goodness-of-fit test statistics (see Muthén, 1984).

Assuming that we have independently and identically distributed observations on a $p \times 1$ vector of $\mathbf{y}$ variables, and assuming multivariate normality for $\mathbf{y}$, the sample covariance matrix $\mathbf{S}$ contains the estimates of variances and covariances between the ys and all the required sufficient statistics for estimating the factor analysis model parameters, say θ. If nothing is assumed about the distributions of $\mathbf{y}$, it remains true that the covariance matrix predicted by the factor analysis model is given by $\Sigma = \Lambda \Phi \Lambda' + \Psi$. We could then aim to estimate Λ, Φ, and Ψ in such a way that Σ becomes as close to $\mathbf{S}$ as possible. For this we need some scalar measure of difference between Σ and $\mathbf{S}$, which must then be minimized with respect to $\theta' = (\Lambda, \Phi, \Psi)$.

Under multivariate normality, two fit functions are natural candidates. The first is the ML fit function given by

$$F_{\mathrm{ML}} = \ln|\Sigma| + \mathrm{tr}(\Sigma^{-1}\mathbf{S}) - \ln|\mathbf{S}| - p, \qquad (9.11)$$

and the second fit function is based on generalized least squares and is given by

$$F_{\mathrm{GLS}} = \mathrm{tr}\left[(\Sigma - \mathbf{S})\mathbf{S}^{-1}\right]^2, \qquad (9.12)$$

where Equations 9.11 and 9.12 are functions of all the independent and distinct parameters in Λ, Φ, and Ψ, and will be minimized with respect to those parameters taking into account any constraints imposed by the model (i.e. equality constraints or fixed parameters). An iterative algorithm is needed for the minimization. We sketch here the Fletcher–Powell algorithm, which is also the main minimization algorithm in commercial structural equation modeling (SEM) software such as LISREL (Jöreskog, 1970a, 1970b). The algorithm requires the gradient vector (first derivative) and the second derivative of the fit function with respect to the parameter vector θ given by $\frac{\partial F}{\partial \theta}$ and $\frac{\partial F^2}{\partial \theta \partial \theta'}$ respectively. The Fletcher–Powell method makes use of a matrix A, which is evaluated in each iteration. Initially, A is any positive definite matrix approximating the inverse of $\frac{\partial F^2}{\partial \theta \theta'}$. In every iteration, the computation of that matrix is improved so that finally the A matrix converges to an approximation of the inverse of $\frac{\partial F^2}{\partial \theta \theta'}$ at the minimum. Good starting values for all the model parameters and a good approximation of the A matrix will speed the convergence of the minimization algorithm.

Furthermore, n times the minimum value of F_{ML} gives the likelihood ratio test statistic of goodness of fit. F_{GLS} weights the distance between the model-implied covariance matrix Σ and S with S^{-1}. The fit function for GLS and ML are scale free, and therefore the covariance matrix can be used to fit the model. Under the assumption that the **y** variables follow a multivariate normal distribution, GLS has the same asymptotic properties as ML (see jöreskog, 1972).

There are many other possible measures of discrepancy that could be used that do not necessarily require the normality assumption of the **y**s. An example is the unweighted least squares fit function:

$$F_{ULS} = \text{tr}(S - \Sigma)^2. \tag{9.13}$$

Unlike F_{ML}, the ULS fit function is not scale free. More generally, the weighted least squares discrepancy function can be used (Browne, 1984):

$$F_{WLS} = (s - \sigma)' W^{-1}(s - \sigma), \tag{9.14}$$

where $s = \text{vech}(S)$ and $\sigma = \text{vech}(\Sigma)$ are vectors of dimension $p(p+1)/2 \times 1$, and vech denotes the half-vectorization operator that stacks the distinct elements of S and Σ into vectors. In practice, W must chosen to be a symmetric positive definite matrix. Note that Equation 9.12 is a special case of Equation 9.14 derived under the assumption of multivariate normality for **y**, in which case W is replaced by a consistent estimate of the asymptotic covariance matrix of S (Browne and Shapiro, 1986; Neudecker and Wesselman, 1990). Note also that under nonnormality of **y**, the asymptotic covariance matrix of S has as a typical element

$$\sigma_{ijkl} - \sigma_{ij}\sigma_{kl},$$

for variable pairs ij and kl, where σ_{ijkl} is a fourth-order central moment. If one uses a consistent estimator of the asymptotic covariance matrix in Equation 9.14, F_{WLS} becomes the asymptotic distribution-free (ADF) fit function proposed by Browne (1982) for nonnormal continuous variables. This consistent estimator of the covariance matrix is also used for obtaining correct standard errors and goodness-of-fit tests under nonnormality. Furthermore, Browne (1984) provided a general corrected chi-square test to be used under nonnormality. The above estimation methods for continuous data are well presented and discussed in Bollen (1989).

Similar ideas to the ones explained above have been used for tetrachoric and polychoric correlations for estimation and computation of standard errors and test statistics that take into account the categorical nature of the data (skewed distributions produced by binary or ordinal items). Those will be explored in a later section.

Estimation of the Latent Variable Model with Categorical Items

Since our data are categorical, it is common to assume that they have been generated by a multinomial distribution. Therefore, for a random sample of size n the log-likelihood is

$$l(\boldsymbol{\theta};\mathbf{y}) = \ln L(\boldsymbol{\theta};\mathbf{y}) = \sum_{r=1}^{R} n_r \ln f_r(\mathbf{y};\boldsymbol{\theta}), \qquad (9.15)$$

where $\boldsymbol{\theta}$ is a parameter vector, n_r and $f_r(\mathbf{y};\boldsymbol{\theta})$ are the observed frequency and the probability under the model, respectively, for the response pattern r, $f_r(\mathbf{y};\boldsymbol{\theta}) > 0$, $\sum_{r=1}^{R} n_r = n$, and $\sum_{r=1}^{R} f_r(\mathbf{y};\boldsymbol{\theta}) = 1$. Each approach imposes a different model on the probability $f_r(\mathbf{y};\boldsymbol{\theta})$, but both UV (Equation 9.4) and IRT (Equation 9.5) approaches assume the presence of a q-dimensional vector of continuous latent variables $\boldsymbol{\xi} = (\xi_1, \ldots, \xi_q)$, where $q < p$.

Limited-information estimation methods

Under the UV approach, the maximization of log-likelihood defined in Equation 9.15 over the parameter vector $\boldsymbol{\theta}$ requires the evaluation of the p-dimensional integral given in Equation 9.4, which cannot be written in a closed form. Lee et al. (1990a, 1990b) discuss full-information maximum likelihood (FIML) estimation in the case of the UV approach, but restrict their example to the case of four ordinal observed variables. Full-information maximum likelihood involves high-dimensional integrations, the dimensions of which increase with the number of observed variables. As a consequence, limited-information estimation methods have been proposed instead.

Limited-information methods utilize information from lower-order margins such as univariate and bivariate margins rather than from the p-way margins that define the whole response pattern. We will discuss here the standard limited-information estimation methods widely used in latent variable modeling. These methods have been incorporated into commercial structural equation modeling software such as LISREL, Mplus, and EQS. They are also known as three-stage estimation methods. We will also discuss limited information methods along the lines of composite likelihood estimation that have recently been applied in many areas in statistics (for a review, see Varin, Reid, & Firth, 2011). Pairwise likelihood estimation has been implemented in the R package Lavaan (Rosseel, 2012).

Three-stage estimation methods The three-stage estimation methods (Jöreskog, 1990, Muthén 1984) work as follows. First, thresholds are estimated by maximizing the univariate marginal likelihoods separately for each item. Then, given the estimated thresholds, tetrachoric/polychoric correlations are estimated by maximizing the bivariate marginal likelihoods separately for each item pair. In the third stage, the factor analysis model given in Equation 9.3 is fitted to the estimated tetrachoric/polychoric correlation matrix using a version of generalized least squares such as ULS, diagonally weighted least squares (DWLS), or full weighted least squares (e.g., Jöreskog, 1990, 1994; Jöreskog & Sörbom, 1996, Muthén, 1984; Muthén, du Toit, & Spisic, 1997) In WLS, the weight matrix is an estimate of the inverse of the asymptotic covariance matrix of tetrachoric/polychoric correlations, while DWLS involves only the diagonal elements of that weight matrix. While WLS is asymptotically optimal among the class of generalized least squares estimators, Forero et al. (2009) and Yang-Wallentin et al. (2010) compared WLS with DWLS and ULS and concluded that the WLS estimator requires substantial n before its asymptotic properties start to emerge and therefore does not perform well in the typically small sample sizes encountered in social science research. Diagonally weighted least squares and ULS are preferable due to not requiring the full weight matrix during estimation, and they seem to perform similarly well for finite samples. However, in order to compute correct standard errors, the full weight matrix is needed nonetheless.

The advantages of the three-stage DWLS and ULS estimators are that they are computationally less demanding than FIML. However, the estimate of the weight matrix is relatively unstable for small sample sizes. Under the UV approach, robust maximum likelihood (RML) estimation can also be used. This is the standard maximum likelihood estimation employed with continuous observed variables but with standard errors and chi-square tests corrected against nonnormality (Browne, 1984; Satorra, 1989). For other recent extensions one is referred to the work by Bollen and Maydeu-Olivares (2007) on the polychoric instrumental variable estimator (PIV) for structural equation models with categorical data, which is developed to be robust against structural misspecifications.

Composite likelihood estimation   It has already been stated that computing the asymptotic covariance matrix of the tetrachoric/polychoric correlations can be unstable in small sizes. That, together with an attempt to propose a single-stage approach to avoid the intricacies of the three-stage method, led to further research within the area of composite maximum likelihood estimation (CML).

Such methods offer a reduction in estimation complexity. Varin and Vidoni (2005) divide the composite likelihood approaches into two categories: the first represents the "subsetting methods" (Cox and Reid 2004) that are based upon likelihoods that use lower-order densities (see the Overview section)—marginal likelihoods or conditional likelihoods (Lindsay, 1988; Varin, 2008); the second, formed by the "omission methods" (see Azzalini, 1983; Besag, 1974; Cox, 1975), omits elements of the likelihood that contain less important information about the model parameters. Varin et al. (2011) provide an excellent review of the recent developments in composite likelihood methods.

Composite maximum likelihood estimators have the desired properties of being asymptotically unbiased, consistent, and normally distributed, but are not the most efficient (with the smallest possible standard errors / variances). Jöreskog and Moustaki (2001) proposed an underlying bivariate normal (UBN) method within the UV approach, which is found to yield estimates close to those of the FIML approach. This can be seen as a composite maximum likelihood method, involving maximizing the sum of both univariate and bivariate marginal distributions. Katsikatsou, Moustaki, Yang-Wallentin, and Jöreskog (2012) developed a pairwise maximum likelihood

(PML) estimation method for the factor model with ordinal variables, and Katsikatsou (2013) extended it to the full SEM framework. Pairwise maximum likelihood has been implemented and is available in the R package Lavaan for structural equation modeling (Rosseel, 2012). Liu (2007) proposed a multistage estimation method for structural equation models, an alternative to the commonly used three-stage methods. In particular, in the first stage, thresholds, polychoric, and polyserial correlations are estimated simultaneously by using the PML approach. Given these estimates, structural parameters, such as loadings and factor correlations, are estimated in a second stage using GLS. His simulation studies show that the proposed methodology performs equally as well as the conventional three-stage methods.

We will briefly explain composite likelihood estimation and then apply the principles to estimate factor models. Cox and Reid (2004) proposed a pseudo log-likelihood written as

$$l(\boldsymbol{\theta};\mathbf{y}) = \sum_{i<j} \ln L(\boldsymbol{\theta};(y_i,y_j)) - ap\sum_i \ln L(\boldsymbol{\theta};y_i),$$

where a is a constant to be chosen for optimal efficiency, p is the number of observed variables, $\ln L(\boldsymbol{\theta};(y_i,y_j))$ is the bivariate marginal log-likelihood of variables y_i and y_j, and $\ln L(\boldsymbol{\theta};y_i)$ is the univariate marginal log-likelihood of variable y_i. Cox and Reid (2004) point out that if the univariate likelihoods are independent of $\boldsymbol{\theta}$ then the choice of $a = 0$ is appropriate; taking $a = \frac{1}{2}$ corresponds to the situation where all possible conditional distributions of one variable, given another, are considered. In general, they suggest that a nonnegative value of a is appropriate.

Katsikatsou et al. (2012) conducted a small-scale simulation study with different values of a that indicated that the sum of univariate log-likelihoods affects neither the accuracy nor the efficiency of estimation. They suggested that one should consider the composite pairwise log-likelihood, $pl(\boldsymbol{\theta};\mathbf{x})$, to estimate the UV parameter $\boldsymbol{\theta}' = (\lambda, \varphi, \tau)$. This is of the form

$$pl(\boldsymbol{\theta};\mathbf{x}) = \sum_{i<j} \ln L(\boldsymbol{\theta};(y_i,y_j)) = \sum_{i<j}\sum_{c_i=1}^{m_i}\sum_{c_j=1}^{m_j} n_{c_i c_j}^{(y_i,y_j)} \ln \pi_{c_i c_j}^{(y_i,y_j)}(\boldsymbol{\theta}), \qquad (9.16)$$

where $n_{c_i c_j}^{(y_i,y_j)}$ is the observed frequency of a response in category c_i and c_j for variables y_i and y_j, respectively, and $\pi_{c_i c_j}^{(y_i,y_j)}(\boldsymbol{\theta})$ is the corresponding probability under the model. Based on Equation 9.4, the latter is of the form

$$\begin{aligned}\pi_{c_i c_j}^{(y_i,y_j)}(\boldsymbol{\theta}) &= \pi(y_i = c_i, y_j = c_j; \boldsymbol{\theta}) \\ &= \Phi_2\left(\tau_{c_i}^{(y_i)}, \tau_{c_j}^{(y_j)}; \rho_{y_i y_j}\right) - \Phi_2\left(\tau_{c_i}^{(y_i)}, \tau_{c_j-1}^{(y_j)}; \rho_{y_i y_j}\right) \\ &\quad - \Phi_2\left(\tau_{c_i-1}^{(y_i)}, \tau_{c_j}^{(y_j)}; \rho_{y_i y_j}\right) + \Phi_2\left(\tau_{c_i-1}^{(y_i)}, \tau_{c_j-1}^{(y_j)}; \rho_{y_i y_j}\right),\end{aligned} \qquad (9.17)$$

where $\Phi_2(a, b; \rho)$ is the bivariate cumulative normal distribution with correlation ρ evaluated at the point (a, b), and

$$\rho_{y_i y_j}(\boldsymbol{\theta}) = \boldsymbol{\lambda}_{i\cdot} \boldsymbol{\Phi} \boldsymbol{\lambda}_{j\cdot}',$$

where $\boldsymbol{\lambda}_{i\cdot}$ is a $1 \times q$ row vector containing the elements of the ith row of the factor-loading matrix $\boldsymbol{\Lambda}$, $i = 1, \ldots, p-1$, $j = i+1, \ldots, p$.

Maximization of the log-likelihood function in Equation 9.16 over the parameter vector $\boldsymbol{\theta}$ leads to the composite pairwise maximum likelihood estimator $\hat{\boldsymbol{\theta}}_{\text{PML}}$. The gradient (first derivative) of the pairwise log-likelihood $\nabla pl(\boldsymbol{\theta}; \mathbf{x})$ is equal to the sum of the gradients of the bivariate log-likelihood components $\nabla \ln L(\boldsymbol{\theta}; (y_i, y_j))$. Details can be found in Katsikatsou et al. (2012).

Under regularity conditions on the component likelihoods, the central limit theorem for the composite likelihood score statistic can be applied, leading to the asymptotic distribution result

$$\sqrt{n}\left(\hat{\boldsymbol{\theta}}_{\text{PML}} - \boldsymbol{\theta}\right) \xrightarrow{d} N_q\left(0, G^{-1}(\boldsymbol{\theta})\right),$$

where q is the dimension of $\boldsymbol{\theta}$, and $G(\boldsymbol{\theta})$ is the Godambe information (also known as sandwich information) matrix of a single observation (Varin, 2008; Varin et al., 2011). The Godambe information matrix provides standard errors under misspecified models. When the model is correctly specified the Godambe information matrix equals the Fisher information matrix.

The obvious advantage of PML over FIML estimation is that it only requires the evaluation of up to two-dimensional normal probabilities, regardless of the number of observed or latent variables. In this way, it is always computationally feasible. The advantage of the PML approach when compared with the three-stage limited-information estimation methods is that the estimation of all parameters is carried out simultaneously. Moreover, the standard errors of the estimates can be obtained without using any weight matrix. Likelihood ratio tests for comparing nested models and for overall goodness of fit, as well as model selection criteria (AIC and BIC) that are not available in the three-stage methods, have been developed for pairwise likelihood estimation (Katsikatsou & Moustaki, 2016).

Full-information maximum likelihood estimation

Under the IRT model framework, we replace equation $f_r(\mathbf{y}; \boldsymbol{\theta})$ in the log-likelihood Equation 9.15 with Equation 9.5. In the IRT model specification, this is known as the marginal or observed log-likelihood, since the latent variables have been integrated out. Marginal maximum likelihood, also known as full-information maximum likelihood, is often used to estimate model parameters under the IRT framework. We have two options for maximizing the log-likelihood given in Equation 9.15. We can either employ the expectation–maximization (E–M) algorithm (Bartholomew et al., 2011; Bock & Moustaki 2007; Dempster, Laird, & Rubin, 1977) or the Newton–Raphson algorithm (N–R: Skrondal & Rabe-Hesketh, 2004).

In the E–M algorithm, the latent variables are considered to be missing data. The basic idea of the E–M algorithm is that rather than maximizing the observed likelihood given in Equation 9.15, E–M maximizes the expected conditional complete data likelihood conditional on the observed data and the parameter estimates obtained from the more recent iteration. In the E step of the algorithm the expected complete log-likelihood is computed, where the expectation is taken with respect to the posterior distribution of the missing data given everything that is observed, and it is maximized with respect to all the elements in the parameter vector θ in the M step of the algorithm. The new estimate of θ is obtained and used in the E step, and this new conditional expectation function is maximized again to obtain the new estimate for θ. The two steps continue until a convergence criterion is satisfied. Usually, the convergence criterion is related to how close the new estimated θ is from the one obtained from the previous iteration, or with the closeness of the value of the log-likelihood from one iteration to the other. The estimate of θ in the final iteration is proven to be the ML estimator that maximized the marginal or observed log-likelihood. The steps of the E–M algorithm will be further explained in a section below.

Alternatively, one can consider a direct maximization of the log-likelihood in Equation 9.15 by using a Newton–Raphson-type maximization algorithm. This requires the integrals to be numerically approximated. As will be shown later, FIML requires the evaluation of q-dimensional integrals, whether E–M or N–R is chosen. The integrals in general cannot be written in a closed form, but there are several numerical methods that can be used to approximate them (Schilling & Bock, 2005). However, for all these methods, the computational burden increases rapidly with the number of factors q, rendering FIML with quadrature impractical or even infeasible beyond a certain number of factors.

Later we will discuss two alternatives to standard quadrature-based numerical methods for FIML estimation. The first alternative is based on analytical dimension reduction (e.g., Cai, Yang, & Hansen, 2011; Gibbons & Hedeker, 1992) for models with specific and frequently encountered factor structures (e.g., of bi-factor, testlet, or two-tier type; Cai, 2010c). When implemented effectively, the actual dimension of integration can be substantially lower than the manifest dimensionality q. However, if the factor pattern and latent correlation structure do not lend themselves to dimension reduction, one can still efficiently optimize the marginal log-likelihood via stochastic variants of E–M. We focus on one recently developed algorithm, the Metropolis–Hastings Robbins–Monro (MH-RM) algorithm (Cai, 2010a, 2010b), that juxtaposes elements of Markov chain Monte Carlo with stochastic approximation.

Newton–Raphson with numerical integration and E–M algorithms Both the N–R and E–M algorithms can be used to estimate the model parameters of IRT models. We outline below how the two algorithms work. Details for the estimation of various IRT models can be found in Bock and Moustaki (2007), Skrondal and Rabe-Hesketh (2004), and Bartholomew et al. (2011).

Newton–Raphson The integration for obtaining the marginal log-likelihood given in Equation 9.15 under the IRT framework is performed numerically by fixed-point quadrature rules or by variable-point adaptive quadrature. These methods have the advantage of not requiring a functional form for the latent distribution: with a sufficient number of equally distant points in an open interval, normalized point masses on those points are a suitable representation of the distribution. However, if the latent distribution is assumed normal, Gauss–Hermite quadrature is appropriate. For example, the marginal response pattern probability in Equation 9.5 can be approximated to an arbitrary degree of precision with a Q-point quadrature rule

$$f_r(\mathbf{y};\boldsymbol{\theta}) \approx \sum_{i_q=1}^{Q} \cdots \sum_{i_1=1}^{Q} g(\mathbf{y};\boldsymbol{\theta} \mid X_{i_1}, \ldots X_{i_q}) w_{i_1} \cdots w_{i_q},$$

where X_{i_q} denotes quadrature point (node) i for latent variable q, and w_{i_q} is the corresponding quadrature weight.

Maximization of the numerically integrated likelihood of Equation 9.15 requires the gradient vector (first-order partial derivatives of the log-likelihood with respect to the parameter vector $\boldsymbol{\theta}$) and the Hessian matrix (a square matrix of second-order partial derivatives of the log-likelihood function). The Hessian describes the local curvature of the log-likelihood function of many variables. The gradient vector is

$$\frac{\partial l(\boldsymbol{\theta};\mathbf{y})}{\partial \boldsymbol{\theta}} = \sum_{r=1}^{R} \frac{n_r}{f_r(\mathbf{y};\boldsymbol{\theta})} \frac{\partial f_r(\mathbf{y};\boldsymbol{\theta})}{\partial \boldsymbol{\theta}}. \tag{9.18}$$

Minus one times the Hessian matrix is

$$-\frac{\partial^2 l(\boldsymbol{\theta};\mathbf{y})}{\partial \boldsymbol{\theta} \partial \boldsymbol{\theta}'} = \sum_{r=1}^{R} \left[\frac{n_r}{f_r(\mathbf{y};\boldsymbol{\theta})^2} \frac{\partial f_r(\mathbf{y};\boldsymbol{\theta})}{\partial \boldsymbol{\theta}} \frac{\partial f_r(\mathbf{y};\boldsymbol{\theta})}{\partial \boldsymbol{\theta}'} - \frac{n_r}{f_r(\mathbf{y};\boldsymbol{\theta})} \frac{\partial^2 f_r(\mathbf{y};\boldsymbol{\theta})}{\partial \boldsymbol{\theta} \partial \boldsymbol{\theta}'} \right]. \tag{9.19}$$

Note that the gradient and Hessian expressions above directly utilize the multinomial log-likelihood presented in Equation 9.15, and the summation is nominally over the R possible response patterns. In practice, only response patterns with nonzero observed counts ($n_r > 0$) will contribute to the log-likelihood, gradient vector, and Hessian matrix.

Taking the expected value of minus one times the Hessian matrix, and under certain regularity conditions, one obtains the expected (Fisher) information matrix $\mathcal{I}(\boldsymbol{\theta})$ (see Rao, 1973). The expected Fisher information is a way of measuring the amount of information that the observable random variables $\mathbf{y}$ carry about the unknown parameter vector $\boldsymbol{\theta}$:

$$E\left[-\frac{\partial^2 l(\boldsymbol{\theta};\mathbf{y})}{\partial \boldsymbol{\theta} \partial \boldsymbol{\theta}'}\right] = n \sum_{r=1}^{R} \frac{\partial f_r(\mathbf{y};\boldsymbol{\theta})}{\partial \boldsymbol{\theta}} \frac{1}{f_r(\mathbf{y};\boldsymbol{\theta})} \frac{\partial f_r(\mathbf{y};\boldsymbol{\theta})}{\partial \boldsymbol{\theta}'} = n\mathcal{I}. \tag{9.20}$$

An empirical information matrix (a positively weighted sum of cross-products of the first derivatives of the response functions) is also frequently computed:

$$\mathcal{J} = \sum_{r=1}^{R} \frac{n_r}{f_r(\mathbf{y};\boldsymbol{\theta})^2} \frac{\partial f_r(\mathbf{y};\boldsymbol{\theta})}{\partial \boldsymbol{\theta}} \frac{\partial f_r(\mathbf{y};\boldsymbol{\theta})}{\partial \boldsymbol{\theta}'}. \tag{9.21}$$

The empirical information matrix can be recognized as a sample approximation to the alternative expression of the Fisher information matrix as the expectation of the cross-product of log-likelihood gradients:

$$E\left[\frac{\partial l(\boldsymbol{\theta};\mathbf{y})}{\partial \boldsymbol{\theta}}\frac{\partial l(\boldsymbol{\theta};\mathbf{y})}{\partial \boldsymbol{\theta}'}\right].$$

If the number of distinct response patterns in the sample exceeds the number of free parameters and the model is identified, the empirical information matrix will be positive definite. The empirical information matrix $\mathcal{J}$ is to be distinguished from the Fisher information matrix $\mathcal{I}$, which is an expectation over all possible response patterns and is not readily calculable with large numbers of items.

Let $\boldsymbol{\theta}^{(0)}$ represent a set of starting values. A Fisher scoring type minimization algorithm generates successive points $\boldsymbol{\theta}^{(1)}, \boldsymbol{\theta}^{(2)}, \ldots$ in the parameter such that

$$l\left[\boldsymbol{\theta}^{(t+1)}\right] > l\left[\boldsymbol{\theta}^{(t)}\right].$$

For $t = 0, 1, 2, \ldots$ let $\mathbf{d}^{(t)}$ be the gradient vector and let $\mathbf{B}^{(t)}$ be the inverse of the information matrix at $\boldsymbol{\theta} = \boldsymbol{\theta}^{(t)}$. Then the algorithm is

$$\boldsymbol{\theta}^{(t+1)} = \boldsymbol{\theta}^{(t)} + \mathbf{B}^{(t)}\mathbf{d}^{(t)}. \tag{9.22}$$

The Newton–Raphson algorithm uses the inverse of the observed information matrix, whereas the Fisher scoring algorithm uses the inverse of the empirical information matrix.

E–M algorithm The E–M algorithm (Dempster et al., 1977) consists of an expectation and a maximization step. To maximize the log-likelihood given in Equation 9.15 with the E–M algorithm we need to write down the complete data log-likelihood, which consists of the observed data, the variables $\mathbf{y}' = (y_1, \ldots, y_p)$, and the missing or unobserved data, the latent variables $\boldsymbol{\xi}' = (\xi_1, \ldots, \xi_q)$. More specifically, the complete data density for an individual h is

$$l_c(\boldsymbol{\theta};\mathbf{y}_h,\boldsymbol{\xi}_h) = f(\mathbf{y}_h,\boldsymbol{\xi}_h;\boldsymbol{\theta}) = g(\mathbf{y}_h \mid \boldsymbol{\xi}_h;\boldsymbol{\theta})\phi(\boldsymbol{\xi}_h). \tag{9.23}$$

Taking into account the conditional independence assumption, the complete data log-likelihood for a random sample of size n is

$$l_c(\boldsymbol{\theta};\mathbf{y},\boldsymbol{\xi}) = \sum_{h=1}^{n} \ln f(\mathbf{y}_h,\boldsymbol{\xi}_h;\boldsymbol{\theta}) = \sum_{h=1}^{n}\left[\ln \prod_{i=1}^{p} g_i(y_{ih} \mid \boldsymbol{\xi}_h;\boldsymbol{\theta}) + \ln \phi(\boldsymbol{\xi}_h)\right]. \tag{9.24}$$

The form of $g_i(y_{ih}|\boldsymbol{\xi}_h;\boldsymbol{\theta})$ can be different for different types of items. For example, in the binary case it is taken to be the Bernoulli:

$$g_i(y_{ih} \mid \boldsymbol{\xi}_h;\boldsymbol{\theta}) = [P_i(y_i = 1 \mid \boldsymbol{\xi};\boldsymbol{\theta})]^{y_{ih}}[1 - P_i(y_i = 1 \mid \boldsymbol{\xi};\boldsymbol{\theta})]^{1-y_{ih}}, \tag{9.25}$$

where $P_i(y_i = 1|\boldsymbol{\xi};\boldsymbol{\theta})$ is obtained from Equation 9.6.

In the expectation step of the algorithm (E step), we calculate the expected complete-data log-likelihood with respect to the conditional distribution of $\boldsymbol{\xi}$ given $\mathbf{y}$ under the current parameter estimates $\boldsymbol{\theta}^{(t)}$:

$$Q\left(\boldsymbol{\theta} \mid \boldsymbol{\theta}^{(t)}\right) = E_{\boldsymbol{\xi}}\left[l(\boldsymbol{\theta};\mathbf{y},\boldsymbol{\xi}) \mid \mathbf{y},\boldsymbol{\theta}^{(t)}\right]. \tag{9.26}$$

In the maximization step of the algorithm (M step), we find the parameters that maximize

$$\boldsymbol{\theta}^{(t+1)} = \arg\max Q\left(\boldsymbol{\theta} \mid \boldsymbol{\theta}^{(t)}\right). \tag{9.27}$$

If the M step does not admit closed-form optimization, such as in the case of IRT estimation, Newton or Fisher scoring may be used to solve the nonlinear ML equations. The algorithm alternates between E and M steps until the sequence of parameter estimates converge. The E–M steps for a large class of IRT models can be found in Bock and Moustaki (2007) and Bartholomew et al. (2011).

The E step requires integrating against the posterior distribution of the latent variables, $f(\boldsymbol{\xi}|\mathbf{y};\boldsymbol{\theta}^{(t)})$, which in general does not have closed-form solutions. There are different methods of approximating that integral, such as Gauss–Hermite fixed quadrature points (Bock & Aitkin, 1981), adaptive quadrature (Schilling & Bock, 2005), Monte Carlo methods (Sammel, Ryan, & Legler, 1997), and Laplace approximations (Huber, Ronchetti, & Victoria-Feser, 2004). To ease the exponentially increasing computational burden as the number of factors increases, it is often necessary to use a small number of points for each dimension, resulting in degraded precision of approximation and biased and unstable parameter estimates. Methods to alleviate the challenge of high dimensionality are discussed next.

The rate of convergence of E–M is linear in the neighborhood of the maximum, but it performs well when the estimates are far from the mode. On the other hand, Newton methods converge at a super-linear rate but require starting values not too far from the solution point. For this reason, it is often advisable to start with the E–M algorithm to obtain improved starting values of the parameters before switching to N–R. This is the hybrid approach combining E–M and Newton steps already implemented in R packages such as ltm (Rizopoulos, 2006).

A diversion: analytical dimension reduction

As mentioned earlier, high dimensionality in latent variable modeling frequently presents obstacles to maximum likelihood estimation because the marginal log-likelihood and its derivatives contain intractable integrals that must be approximated when E–M or N–R algorithms are applied. As shown by numerous authors (e.g., Cai, 2010c; Gibbons & Hedeker, 1992; Rijmen, Vansteelandt, & De Boeck, 2008), when the factor structure and the latent variable correlation structure satisfy certain conditions, the high-dimensional integrals can be re-expressed as a series of substantially lower-dimensional integrals. The most prominent example is the item bifactor model (see Cai et al., 2011; Gibbons & Hedeker, 1992).

In a bifactor model, there exists a general factor on which all items are permitted to load. In addition, there may be several group/specific dimensions that influence non-overlapping subsets of items. For instance, the following is a potential bifactor pattern for six items and three dimensions:

$$\begin{pmatrix} \alpha_{11} & \alpha_{12} & 0 \\ \alpha_{21} & \alpha_{22} & 0 \\ \alpha_{31} & \alpha_{32} & 0 \\ \alpha_{41} & 0 & \alpha_{43} \\ \alpha_{51} & 0 & \alpha_{53} \\ \alpha_{61} & 0 & \alpha_{63} \end{pmatrix}.$$

The first column corresponds to the general dimension, and the two group/specific dimensions are each defined by items 1–3 and 4–6, respectively. Furthermore, the group/specific dimensions are restricted to be independent conditionally on the general dimension. In this case, the marginal probability associated with response pattern r can be expressed as

$$f_r(y;\theta) = \int \int \int \prod_{i=1}^{6} g(y_i;\theta \mid \xi_1,\xi_2,\xi_3) \phi(\xi_1,\xi_2,\xi_3) d\xi_1 d\xi_2 d\xi_3)$$

$$= \int \left[\int \prod_{i=1}^{3} g(y_i;\theta \mid \xi_1,\xi_2) \phi(x_2 \mid \xi_1) d\xi_2 \right]$$

$$\times \left[\int \prod_{i=4}^{6} g(y_i;\theta \mid \xi_1,\xi_3) \phi(x_2 \mid \xi_1) d\xi_3 \right] \varphi(\xi_1) d\xi_1.$$

Note that the first line shows that the marginal probability requires a dimensional integral, consistent with the manifest dimensionality of the model, $q = 3$. On the second line, the factor pattern and the conditional independence of the group/specific dimensions are utilized to reduce the dimensionality of integration to two. In fact, as long as the bifactor restrictions hold, the actual dimensionality of integration can always be reduced to two, irrespective of the number of factors in the model. We refer to this general approach as analytical dimension reduction. Expectation–maximization or N–R algorithms can then be used in conjunction with analytical dimension reduction. The computational shortcut, in addition to the significant theoretical appeal of the bifactor structure in applied measurement situations (see Reise, 2012), makes analytical dimension reduction a highly practical approach for IRT parameter estimation. Analytical dimension reduction is implemented in new IRT software packages such as IRTPRO (Cai, Thissen, & du Toit, 2011) and flexMIRT (Cai, 2013).

Metropolis–Hastings Robbins–Monro

While highly efficient when appropriate, analytical dimension reduction is not without its own problems. For example, if the factors are correlated, the actual dimensionality of integration frequently cannot be reduced much beyond the manifest dimensionality of integration. In this case, a completely different optimization method is needed, one that eschews numerical integration in favor of stochastic optimization. The MH-RM algorithm is one such approach that has been successfully applied to multidimensional IRT estimation (Cai, 2010a, 2010b).

In brief, the MH-RM algorithm is a data-augmented Robbins–Monro-type (RM; Robbins & Monro, 1951) stochastic approximation (SA) algorithm. Stochastic approximation algorithms have been well studied in engineering (see, e.g., Benveniste, Métivier, & Priouret, 1990; Borkar, 2008; Kushner & Yin, 1997) since the pioneering work of Robbins and Monro (1951). Instead of numerical integration, the MH-RM algorithm draws random samples from a Metropolis–Hastings sampler (MH; Hastings, 1970; Metropolis, Rosenbluth, Rosenbluth, Teller, & Teller, 1953) that has as its target the posterior predictive distribution of the latent variables.

The MH-RM algorithm is motivated by Titterington's (1984) recursive algorithm for incomplete data estimation. It is closely related to Gu and Kong's (1998) SA algorithm, which is analogous to a stochastic Newton–Raphson algorithm. For application to IRT, it can also be viewed as an extension of the stochastic approximation EM algorithm (SAEM; Celeux and Diebolt, 1991; Celeux, Chauveau, & Diebolt, 1995; Delyon, Lavielle, & Moulines, 1999) to the case of nonlinear complete data models. Probability one convergence of the sequence of estimates to a local maximum of the likelihood surface has been established (Cai, 2010a).

Robbins and Monro's (1951) algorithm is a root-finding algorithm under observational noise. In the simplest case, let $g(\cdot)$ be a real-valued function of a real variable θ. Suppose that $g(\theta)$ can only be measured imprecisely as $g(\theta) + \zeta$, where ζ is a zero-mean random variable representing the noise process. The RM method iteratively updates the approximation to the root according to the following recursive scheme:

$$\theta^{(t+1)} = \theta^{(t)} + \gamma_t R_{t+1}, \tag{9.28}$$

where $R_{t+1} = g(\theta^{(t)}) + \zeta_{t+1}$ is an estimate of $g(\theta^{(t)})$ and $\{\gamma_t; t \geq 1\}$ is a sequence of *gain constants* such that $\gamma_t \in (0, 1]$, $\sum_{t=1}^{\infty} \gamma_t = \infty$, and $\sum_{t=1}^{\infty} \gamma_t^2 < \infty$. Taken together, these conditions ensure that the gain constants decrease *slowly* to zero. The intuitive appeal of this algorithm is that R_{t+1} does not have to be highly accurate. This can be understood from the following: if $\theta^{(t)}$ is still far away from the root, taking a large number of observations to compute a good estimate of $g(\theta^{(t)})$ is inefficient because R_{t+1} is useful insofar as it provides the right direction for the next move. The decreasing gain constants eventually eliminate the noise effect so that $\theta^{(t)}$ converges to the root in a pointwise fashion.

Just as in the E–M algorithm, the MH-RM algorithm takes a missing data formulation of the latent variable model. It regards the gradient of the observed data log-likelihood as the true function $g(\theta)$. Maximum likelihood estimation amounts to finding the zeros of the gradient equations. In a latent variable model, one's ability to directly evaluate the gradient of the observed data log-likelihood is limited by the presence of latent variables that must be integrated out. However, Fisher's identity (Fisher, 1925) suggests that the conditional expectation of the gradient of the complete data log-likelihood is the same as the gradient of the observed data log-likelihood. The expectation is taken against the posterior predictive distribution of the latent variables (the missing data). If one were to draw from the posterior predictive distribution of the latent variables, say, with an MH sampler, one can form a Monte Carlo estimate of the observed data gradient with complete data quantities. This estimate is corrupted by intentionally introduced observational noise due to the random imputations. Just as with the classical RM method, it is not necessary that the estimate of the observed data ascent directions be highly accurate as the sequence of gain constants serve to eliminate the Monte Carlo noise and the sequence of iterations converge to the maximum likelihood estimate.

Let

$$\mathbf{H}(\boldsymbol{\theta};\mathbf{y},\boldsymbol{\xi}) = -\frac{\partial^2 l_c(\boldsymbol{\theta};\mathbf{y},\boldsymbol{\xi})}{\partial \boldsymbol{\theta} \partial \boldsymbol{\theta}'}$$

be the complete data information matrix. Let starting values be $(\boldsymbol{\theta}^{(0)}, \boldsymbol{\Gamma}_0)$, where $\boldsymbol{\Gamma}_0$ is a symmetric positive definite matrix. Let $\boldsymbol{\theta}^{(t)}$ be the estimate at the end of iteration t. The $(t+1)$th iteration of the MH-RM algorithm consists of three steps:

1. *Stochastic imputation*: Draw m_k sets of missing data from an MH sampler that has as its target the posterior predictive distribution of the latent variables, i.e., $\phi(\boldsymbol{\xi}|\mathbf{y},\boldsymbol{\theta}^{(t)})$, to form m_t sets of complete data $\left\{\mathbf{y},\boldsymbol{\xi}_j^{(t+1)}; j=1,\ldots,m_t\right\}$.

2. *Stochastic approximation*: Compute a Monte Carlo estimate of the gradient of the observed data log-likelihood $\nabla_{\boldsymbol{\theta}} l(\boldsymbol{\theta}^{(t)}|\mathbf{y})$ by the sample average of complete data gradients

$$\widetilde{\mathbf{s}}_{t+1} = \frac{1}{m_t} \sum_{j=1}^{m_t} \mathbf{s}\left(\boldsymbol{\theta}^{(t)};\mathbf{y},\boldsymbol{\xi}_j^{(t+1)}\right), \qquad (9.29)$$

as well as a recursive approximation of the complete data information matrix

$$\boldsymbol{\Gamma}_{t+1} = \boldsymbol{\Gamma}_t + \gamma_t \left[\frac{1}{m_t}\sum_{j=1}^{m_t} \mathbf{H}\left(\boldsymbol{\theta}^{(t)};\mathbf{y},\boldsymbol{\xi}_j^{(t+1)}\right) - \boldsymbol{\Gamma}_t\right].$$

3. *Robbins–Monro update*: Set the new parameter estimate to

$$\boldsymbol{\theta}^{(t+1)} = \boldsymbol{\theta}^{(t)} + \gamma_t \left(\boldsymbol{\Gamma}_{t+1}^{-1} \widetilde{\mathbf{s}}_{t+1}\right).$$

The iterations are terminated when the estimates converge. In practice, γ_t may be taken as $1/k$, in which case the choice of $\boldsymbol{\Gamma}_0$ becomes arbitrary. One can show that under certain regularity conditions the MH-RM algorithm converges to a local maximum of $l(\boldsymbol{\theta}; \mathbf{y})$ with probability one (Cai, 2010a). Though the simulation size m_t is allowed to depend on the iteration number t, it is by no means required. The convergence result applies even with a small and fixed simulation size, i.e., $m_t \equiv 1$. The MH-RM method is implemented in new IRT software packages such as IRTPRO (Cai et al., 2011) and flexMIRT (Cai, 2013).

Applications

We use the Quality of Life (QoL) data to illustrate the foregoing theoretical discussions. This data set has been analyzed by Gibbons et al. (2007) and Cai (2010c), among others; it consists of responses from $n = 586$ psychiatric patients to 34 items about 7 specific aspects of their quality of life such as social, financial, health, family interactions, etc., in addition to a single item about their overall quality of life, making the total number of items $p = 35$. The specific aspects are covered by four to six items each. The patients are asked to respond to the items on a seven-point ordinal rating scale. Gibbons et al. (2007) found that an eight-factor bifactor model with a general quality of life

Table 9.1 Item bifactor model logistic slope estimates (E–M with dimension reduction).

Item	QoL	Family	Money	Health	Leisure	Living	Safety	Social
1	2.39							
2	1.70	1.93						
3	1.58	1.45						
4	2.79	3.27						
5	2.83	2.84						
6	1.73		2.49					
7	1.09		1.38					
8	2.15		2.74					
9	1.95		2.52					
10	1.25			0.37				
11	1.61			1.55				
12	1.40			1.49				
13	1.66			1.68				
14	1.68			0.54				
15	1.83			0.27				
16	1.94				0.83			
17	1.45				0.97			
18	1.72				1.13			
19	2.25				1.93			
20	1.50				1.23			
21	0.93				0.29			
22	1.46					1.46		
23	1.11					1.15		
24	1.51					2.11		
25	1.64					2.31		
26	1.24					1.43		
27	1.93						1.96	
28	1.86						1.70	
29	1.18						0.79	
30	1.64						1.49	
31	1.76						1.31	
32	2.25							2.48
33	1.93							1.56
34	1.42							1.18
35	0.93							0.53

Note. Fixed (zero) slopes are shown as blanks.

dimension plus seven group/specific dimensions fits the QoL data well. The overall quality of life item loads on the general dimension only.

A rather large number of software programs could have been used to estimate the parameters of the latent variable models reviewed in this chapter. For example, structural equation modeling software programs such as LISREL, EQS, and Mplus can all fit the Gibbons et al. (2007) bifactor model using the limited-information estimators reviewed earlier. In addition, recent versions of LISREL and Mplus also implement full-information estimation approaches (E–M algorithm or Newton-type algorithms) with numerical integration. Here, we use IRT software.

Table 9.1 presents the item slope estimates from fitting a logistic version of the item bifactor model as described in Cai et al. (2011) to the QoL data. The software program

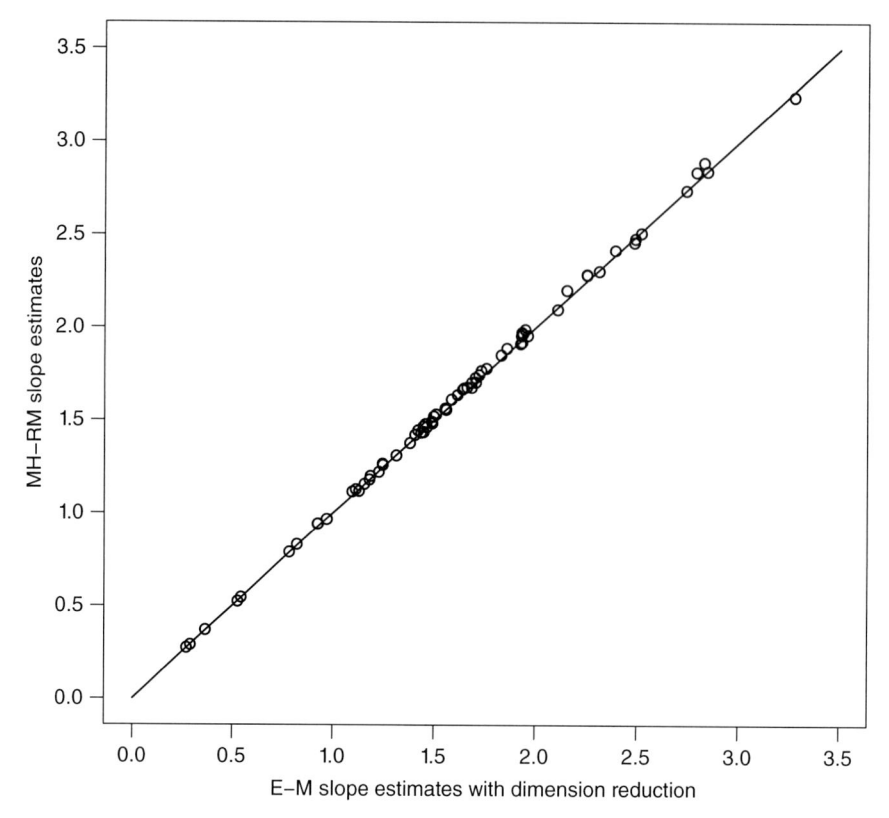

Figure 9.1 Comparison of slope estimates from E–M and MH-RM.

flexMIRT 2.0 (Cai, 2013) is used to obtain the marginal maximum likelihood solution with analytical dimension reduction in conjunction with the E–M algorithm. Rectangular quadrature is used to approximate the integrals in the E step with 49 points equally spaced between −6.0 and 6.0. The total computing time, excluding computation of fit statistics but including standard error computations, is around 90 seconds.

Indeed, the bifactor model fits the data reasonably well. While the M_2^* overall goodness-of-fit statistic (Cai & Hansen, 2013) is equal to 566.6 on 351 degrees of freedom, $p < 0.001$, the M_2^*-based approximate fit index root mean square error of approximation (RMSEA) is equal to 0.03, indicating an acceptable degree of remaining model error. Notably, the unidimensional graded IRT model for these 35 items is nested within the eight-dimensional bifactor model, with a highly significant likelihood ratio chi-square difference equal to 3313 on 34 degrees of freedom (reflecting implausibility of the fixed zero constraints on the 34 group/specific slopes). Furthermore, analogous to the case in linear factor analysis, a Tucker–Lewis-type index (Cai & Monroe, 2013) based on incremental fit comparisons between the fitted model and the zero-factor independence model also shows marked improvement in model fit from unidimensional model to bifactor model. The Tucker–Lewis index for the unidimensional model is equal to 0.63, which is in the typically unacceptable range, while that of the bifactor model is 0.96, solidly in the range of well-fitting models.

Using the MH-RM algorithm implemented in flexMIRT 2.0, we fitted the bifactor model again. Figure 9.1 presents a scatterplot of the estimated item slopes from MH-RM against the estimates from E–M. It is clear that the two sets of estimates are virtually identical. The MH-RM algorithm does not utilize dimension reduction, and it took a total of 250 seconds to converge to the solution.

Conclusions

This chapter is concerned primarily with the estimation methods for latent variable models where the outcome (observed) variables in the model are categorical. While historically predominant methods of estimation rely on the correlation matrices (e.g., using tetrachoric or polychoric correlations) and least squares estimation (e.g., weighted least squares) that are the mainstay of parameter estimation in structural equation modeling, newer approaches based on full-information maximum marginal likelihood or composite likelihood tend to be more flexible. A wider range of measurement and latent structural models may be specified with more modern approaches, albeit at the expense of heavier computational burden. We review likelihood-based estimation methods that are based on either Newton–Raphson or Expectation–Maximization principles. Central to these algorithms are numerical integration (with quadrature) and stochastic approximation methods. With the former, a special class of models (e.g., the item bifactor model) permit the implementation of analytic dimension reduction algorithms to facilitate more efficient numerical integration. In the latter, Monte Carlo methods are favored in lieu of numerical integration, thus lifting the computational challenge of high-dimensional latent variable models. With the increasing importance of general latent variable models, we believe that more modern estimation approaches will improve the application of these models in the social and behavioral sciences.

References

Azzalini, A. (1983). Maximum likelihood estimation of order m for stationary stochastic processes. *Biometrika*, 70, 381–387.

Bartholomew, D. J., Knott, M., and Moustaki, I. (2011). *Latent variable models and factor analysis: A unified approach* (3rd ed.). London: John Wiley & Sons Ltd.

Benveniste, A., Métivier, M., and Priouret, P. (1990). *Adaptive algorithms and stochastic approximations*. Berlin: Springer-Verlag.

Besag, J. E. (1974). Spatial interaction and the statistical analysis of lattice systems (with discussion). *Journal of the Royal Statistical Society, Series B*, 36, 192–236.

Birnbaum, A. (1968a). Some latent trait models and their use in inferring an examinee's ability. In F. M. Lord and M. R. Novick (Eds.), *Statistical theories of mental test scores* (pp. 425–435). Reading, MA: Addison-Wesley. Chapter 18.

Birnbaum, A. (1968b). Test scores, sufficient statistics, and the information structures of tests. In F. M. Lord and M. R. Novick (Eds.), *Statistical theories of mental test scores*. Reading, MA: Addison-Wesley.

Bock, D. and Moustaki, I. (2007). Item response theory in a general framework. In C. Rao and S. Sinharay (Eds.), *Handbook of statistics on psychometrics*. New York, NY: Elsevier.

Bock, R. D. (1972). Estimating item parameters and latent ability when responses are scored in two or more nominal categories. *Psychometrika*, 37(1), 29–51.

Bock, R. D. and Aitkin, M. (1981). Marginal maximum likelihood estimation of item parameters: application of an EM algorithm. *Psychometrika, 46*(4), 443–459.

Bollen, K. and Maydeu-Olivares, A. (2007). A polychoric instrumental variable (PIV) estimator for structural equation models with categorical variables. *Psychometrika, 72*, 309–326.

Bollen, K. A. (1989). *Structural equations with latent variables.* New York: Wiley and Sons.

Borkar, V. S. (2008). *Stochastic approximation: A dynamical systems viewpoint.* Cambridge, UK: Cambridge University Press.

Browne, M. W. (1982). Covariance structures. In D. M. Hawkins (Ed.), *Topics in applied multivariate analysis* (pp. 72–141). Cambridge, UK: Cambridge University Press.

Browne, M. W. (1984). Asymptotically distribution-free methods for the analysis of covariance structures. *British Journal of Mathematical and Statistical Psychology, 37*, 62–83.

Browne, M. W. and Shapiro, A. (1986). The asymptotic covariance matrix of sample correlation coefficients under general conditions. *Journal of Linear Algebra and its Applications, 82*, 169–176.

Cai, L. (2010a). High-dimensional exploratory item factor analysis by a Metropolis–Hastings Robbins–Monro algorithm. *Psychometrika, 75*, 33–57.

Cai, L. (2010b). Metropolis–Hastings Robbins–Monro algorithm for confirmatory item factor analysis. *Journal of Educational and Behavioral Statistics, 35*, 307–335.

Cai, L. (2010c). A two-tier full-information item factor analysis model with applications. *Psychometrika, 75*, 581–612.

Cai, L. (2013). flexMIRT®2.0: Flexible multilevel multidimensional item analysis and test scoring [Computer software]. Chapel Hill, NC: Vector Psychometric Group.

Cai, L. and Hansen, M. (2013). Limited-information goodness-of-fit testing of hierarchical item factor models. *British Journal of Mathematical and Statistical Psychology, 66*, 245–276.

Cai, L. and Monroe, S. (2013). IRT model fit evaluation from theory to practice: Progress and some unanswered questions. *Measurement: Interdisciplinary Research and Perspectives, 11*(3), 102–106.

Cai, L., Thissen, D. and du Toit, S. H. C. (2011). IRTPRO 2.1: Flexible, multidimensional, multiple categorical IRT modeling [Computer software]. Chicago, IL: Scientific Software International.

Cai, L., Yang, J. S., and Hansen, M. (2011). Generalized full-information item bifactor analysis. *Psychological Methods, 16*, 221–248.

Celeux, G., Chauveau, D., and Diebolt, J. (1995). On stochastic versions of the EM algorithm. Technical Report 2514, The French National Institute for Research in Computer Science and Control.

Celeux, G. and Diebolt, J. (1991). A stochastic approximation type EM algorithm for the mixture problem. Technical Report 1383, The French National Institute for Research in Computer Science and Control.

Cox, D. R. (1975). Partial likelihood. *Biometrika, 62*, 269–274.

Cox, D. R. and Reid, N. (2004). A note on pseudolikelihood constructed from marginal densities. *Biometrika, 91*, 729–737.

Delyon, B., Lavielle, M., and Moulines, E. (1999). Convergence of a stochastic approximation version of the EM algorithm. *The Annals of Statistics, 27*, 94–128.

Dempster, A. P., Laird, N. M., and Rubin, D. B. (1977). Maximum likelihood from incomplete data via the EM algorithm. *Journal of The Royal Statistical Society, Series B, 39*, 1–38.

Embretson, S. E. and Reise, S. P. (2000). *Item response theory for psychologists.* Mahwah, NJ: Lawrence Erlbaum Associates.

Fisher, R. A. (1925). Theory of statistical estimation. *Proceedings of the Cambridge Philosophical Society, 22*, 700–725.

Forero, C. G., Maydeu-Olivares, A., and Gallardo-Pujol, D. (2009). Factor analysis with ordinal indicators: a Monte Carlo study comparing DWLS and ULS estimation. *Structural Equation Modeling: A Multidisciplinary Journal, 16*, 625–641.

Gibbons, R. D., Bock, R. D., Hedeker, D., Weiss, D. J., Segawa, E., Bhaumik, D. K., Kupfer, D. J., Frank, E., and Grochocinski, V. J. (2007). Full-information item bifactor analysis of graded response data. *Applied Psychological Measurement, 31*, 4–19.

Gibbons, R. D. and Hedeker, D. (1992). Full-information item bifactor analysis. *Psychometrika, 57*, 423–436.

Gitomer, D. H. and Yamamoto, K. (1991). Performance modeling that integrates latent trait and class theory. *Journal of Educational Measurement, 28*, 173–189.

Gu, M. G. and Kong, F. H. (1998). A stochastic approximation algorithm with Markov chain Monte Carlo method for incomplete data estimation problems. *The Proceedings of the National Academy of Sciences, 95*, 7270–7274.

Hastings, W. K. (1970). Monte Carlo simulation methods using Markov chains and their applications. *Biometrika, 57*, 97–109.

Huber, P., Ronchetti, E., and Victoria-Feser, M.-P. (2004). Estimation of generalized linear latent variable models. *Journal of the Royal Statistical Society, Series B, 66*, 893–908.

Jöreskog, K. G. (1967). Some contributions to maximum likelihood factor analysis. *Psychometrika, 32*, 443–482.

Jöreskog, K. G. (1970a). A general method for analysis of covariance structures. *Biometrika, 57*, 239–251.

Jöreskog, K. G. (1970b). A general method for estimating a linear structural equation system. Technical Report RB-70-54, Educational Testing Service, New Jersey.

Jöreskog, K. G. (1972). Factor analysis by generalized least squares. *Psychometrika, 37*, 243–260.

Jöreskog, K. G. (1990). New developments in LISREL: Analysis of ordinal variables using polychoric correlations and weighted least squares. *Quality and Quantity, 24*, 387–404.

Jöreskog, K. G. (1994). On the estimation of polychoric correlations and their asymptotic covariance matrix. *Psychometrika, 59*, 381–389.

Jöreskog, K. G. (2002). Structural equation modeling with ordinal variables using LISREL. Retrieved from http://www.ssicentral.com/lisrel/ordinal.htm.

Jöreskog, K. G. and Moustaki, I. (2001). Factor analysis of ordinal variables: A comparison of three approaches. *Multivariate Behavioral Research, 36*, 347–387.

Jöreskog, K. G. and Sörbom, D. (1996). *LISREL 8 user's reference guide*. Chicago, IL: Scientific Software International.

Katsikatsou, M. (2013). *Composite likelihood estimation for latent variable models with ordinal and continuous or ranking variables*. Ph.D. thesis, Uppsala Universitet.

Katsikatsou, M. and Moustaki, I. (2014). *Pairwise likelihood estimation and testing in structural equation modeling with ordinal and continuous variables*. Manuscript submitted for publication.

Katsikatsou, M. and Moustaki, I. (2016) Pairwise likelihood ratio tests and model selection criteria for structural equation model with ordinal variables. *Psychometrika, 81*(4), 1046–1068.

Katsikatsou, M., Moustaki, I., Yang-Wallentin, F., and Jöreskog, K. G. (2012). Pairwise likelihood estimation for factor analysis models with ordinal data. *Computational Statistics and Data Analysis, 56*, 4243–4258.

Kushner, H. J. and Yin, G. G. (1997). *Stochastic approximation algorithms and applications*. New York: Springer.

Lazarsfeld, P. F. and Henry, N. W. (1968). *Latent structure analysis*. New York, NY: Houghton-Mifflin.

Lee, S. Y., Poon, W. Y., and Bentler, P. M. (1990a). Full maximum likelihood analysis of structural equation models with polytomous variables. *Statistics and Probability Letters, 9*, 91–97.

Lee, S. Y., Poon, W. Y., and Bentler, P. M. (1990b). A three-stage estimation procedure for structural equation models with polytomous variables. *Psychometrika, 55*, 45–51.

Lee, S. Y., Poon, W. Y., and Bentler, P. M. (1992). Structural equation models with continuous and polytomous variables. *Psychometrika, 57*, 89–105.

Lindsay, B. (1988). Composite likelihood methods. In N. U. Prabhu (Ed.), *Statistical inference from stochastic processes* (pp. 221–239). Providence, RI: Americal Mathematical Society.

Liu, J. (2007). *Multivariate ordinal data analysis with pairwise likelihood and its extension to SEM.* Ph.D. thesis, University of California.

McCutcheon, A. L. (1987). Latent class analysis, *Volume 64 of* Quantitative applications in the social sciences. Beverly Hills: Sage Publications.

Metropolis, N., Rosenbluth, A. W., Rosenbluth, M. N., Teller, A. H., and Teller, E. (1953). Equations of state space calculations by fast computing machines. *Journal of Chemical Physics, 21,* 1087–1092.

Muthén, B. (1984). A general structural model with dichotomous, ordered categorical and continuous latent variable indicators. *Psychometrika, 49*(1), 115–132.

Muthén, B., du Toit, S., and Spisic, D. (1997). Robust inference using weighted least squares and quadratic estimating equations in latent variable modeling with categorical and continuous outcomes. Technical report, UCLA. Retrieved from http://gseis.ucla.edu/faculty/muthen/articles/Article_075.pdf.

Neudecker, H. and Wesselman, A. M. (1990). The asymptotic covariance matrix of the sample correlation matrix. *Journal of Linear Algebra and its Applications, 127,* 589–599.

Rao, C. R. (1973). *Linear statistical inference and its applications* (3rd ed.). New York, NY: John Wiley & Sons.

Rasch, G. (1960). *Probabilistic models for some intelligence and attainment tests.* Copenhagen, Denmark: Paedagogiske Institut.

Rasch, G. (1961). On general laws and the meaning of measurement in psychology. In J. Neyman (Ed.), *Proceedings of the fourth Berkeley symposium on mathematical statistics and probability* (Vol. 4, pp. 321–334). Berkeley, CA: University of California Press.

Reise, S. P. (2012). The rediscovery of bifactor measurement models. *Multivariate Behavioral Research, 47,* 667–696.

Rijmen, F., Vansteelandt, K., and De Boeck, P. (2008). Latent class models for diary method data: Parameter estimation by local computations. *Psychometrika, 73,* 167–182.

Rizopoulos, D. (2006). ltm: An R package for latent variable modeling and item response analysis. *Journal of Statistical Software, 17,* 1–25.

Robbins, H. and Monro, S. (1951). A stochastic approximation method. *The Annals of Mathematical Statistics, 22,* 400–407.

Rosseel, Y. (2012). lavaan: An R package for structural equation modeling. *Journal of Statistical Software, 48,* 1–36.

Samejima, F. (1969). Estimation of latent ability using a response pattern of graded scores. *Psychometrika, Monograph Supplement No. 17, 34.*

Sammel, R. D., Ryan, L. M., and Legler, J. M. (1997). Latent variable models for mixed discrete and continuous outcomes. *Journal of the Royal Statistical Society, B, 59,* 667–678.

Satorra, A. (1989). Alternative test criteria in covariance structure analysis: A unified approach. *Psychometrica, 54,* 131–151.

Schilling, S. and Bock, R. (2005). High-dimensional maximum marginal likelihood item factor analysis by adaptive quadrature. *Psychometrika, 70*(3), 533–555.

Skrondal, A. and Rabe-Hesketh, S. (2004). *Generalized latent variable modeling: Multilevel, longitudinal and structural equation models.* Boca Raton, FL: Chapman & Hall/CRC.

Thissen, D., Cai, L., and Bock, R. D. (2010). The nominal categories item response model. In M. Nering and R. Ostini (Eds.), *Handbook of polytomous item response theory models: Developments and applications* (pp. 43–75). New York, NY: Taylor & Francis.

Titterington, D. M. (1984). Recursive parameter estimation using incomplete data. *Journal of the Royal Statistical Society – Series B, 46,* 257–267.

van der Linden, W. and Hambleton, R. K. (Eds.) (1997). *Handbook of modern item response theory.* New York, NY: Springer.

Varin, C. (2008). On composite marginal likelihoods. *Advances in Statistical Analysis, 92,* 1–28.

Varin, C., Reid, N., and Firth, D. (2011). An overview of composite likelihood methods. *Statistica Sinica*, *21*, 5–42.

Varin, C. and Vidoni, P. (2005). A note on composite likelihood inference and model selection. *Biometrika*, *92*, 519–528.

Von Davier, M. (1996). Mixtures of polytomous Rasch models and latent class models for ordinal variables. In F. Faulbaum and W. Bandilla (Eds.), *Softstat 95-Advances in Statistical Software 5*. Stuttgart, Germany: Lucius and Lucius.

Yang-Wallentin, F., Jöreskog, K. G., and Luo, H. (2010). Confirmatory factor analysis of ordinal variables with misspecified models. *Structural Equation Modeling: A Multidisciplinary Journal*, *17*, 392–423.

10
Rotation
Robert I. Jennrich

Introduction

Rotation arises in exploratory factor analysis and represents the primary distinction between exploratory and confirmatory factor analysis. This chapter attempts to provide an overview of the main components of rotation, from the work of Thurstone to the present. These components are rotation methods, rotation algorithms, and standard errors for rotated factor loadings.

Because it was simpler, early rotation methods used orthogonal rotation, and in particular varimax rotation. Today, because it is more general, oblique rotation is becoming the standard. At first quartimin was the most popular form of oblique rotation, but now qeomin seems to be replacing quartimin because geomin seems to work better for more complex structures.

At first, every rotation method came with a rotation algorithm designed specifically for the method, or more precisely for the criterion that defined the method. Today we have algorithms designed to optimize arbitrary criteria. A new method is proposed by defining its criterion, and a general algorithm is used to optimize it. This makes it much easier to investigate new methods.

A number of rotation algorithms including general closed-form pairwise algorithms for quartic criteria and general pairwise and gradient projection algorithms for arbitrary criteria, are discussed below.

Standard errors for rotated loadings using linear approximation methods are also reviewed. These include methods using the asymptotic distribution of the initial loadings, constrained maximum likelihood methods, nonparametric constrained minimum deviance methods, and nonparametric pseudo-value methods.

The chapter concludes with a comparison of some popular rotation methods, the difficulties that arise when doing this, some advice on choosing a method, and some real data examples.

Exploratory Factor Analysis

The exploratory factor analysis (EFA) model has the form

$$x = \Lambda f + u, \qquad (10.1)$$

where x is a vector of observed responses, f is a vector of common factors, u is a vector of unique factors, and Λ is a $p \times k$ matrix of factor loadings. It is assumed that the vectors f and u have mean zero and are uncorrelated, and that the components of u are uncorrelated.

Let Φ and Ψ be the covariance matrices of f and u. Then the covariance matrix of x is

$$\Sigma = \Lambda \Phi \Lambda' + \Psi.$$

Extraction

An EFA begins with an extraction step. Assume $\Phi = I$. Under this assumption an EFA model is called an orthogonal model because the factors are uncorrelated. With this assumption, $\Sigma = \Lambda \Lambda' + \Psi$. Let S be a sample covariance matrix and $D(S, \Sigma)$ be a deviance function that measures how close Σ is to S. Two popular deviance functions are the least squares deviance function,

$$D(S, \Sigma) = \|S - \Sigma\|^2,$$

and the maximum likelihood deviance function,

$$D(S, \Sigma) = \log(|\Sigma|) + \operatorname{tr}(S\Sigma^{-1}) - \log(|S|) - p.$$

The extraction step minimizes

$$D(S, \Lambda\Lambda' + \Psi)$$

with respect to Λ and Ψ. Let A and $\hat{\Psi}$ be the minimizing values of Λ and Ψ produced by the algorithm used for minimization. The matrix A is called an initial loading matrix. Note that A is a function of the data, but by convention it does not carry a hat. Finally, let

$$\hat{\Sigma} = AA' + \hat{\Psi}$$

be the estimate of Σ defined by A and $\hat{\Psi}$.

Oblique rotation

Our interest is primarily in oblique rotation. Let

$$\hat{\Lambda} = AT^{-1},$$

where A is an initial loading matrix and T is an arbitrary $k \times k$ nonsingular matrix with rows of length one. For reasons that will become clear shortly this is called an oblique rotation of the initial loading matrix A.

Let $\hat{\Phi} = TT'$, and note that

$$\hat{\Lambda}\hat{\Phi}\hat{\Lambda}' + \hat{\Psi} = AT^{-1}TT'(T')^{-1}A' + \hat{\Psi} = AA' + \hat{\Psi} = \hat{\Sigma}.$$

Thus, $\hat{\Sigma}$ is determined only up to an oblique rotation of A. This is called the rotation problem.

Among all oblique rotations of A, we seek one that looks nice—which more often than not means looks simple.

Orthogonal rotation

Let

$$\hat{\Lambda} = AT',$$

where A is an initial loading matrix and T is an arbitrary $k \times k$ orthogonal matrix. Since T' is an orthogonal matrix, the rows of $\hat{\Lambda}$ are rotations of the rows of A. This motivates calling $\hat{\Lambda}$ an orthogonal rotation of A.

Note that an orthogonal rotation is a restricted form of an oblique rotation, because an oblique rotation

$$\hat{\Lambda} = AT^{-1}$$

becomes an orthogonal rotation when T is an orthogonal matrix. An oblique rotation does not rotate the rows of A. Nevertheless, it is called a rotation because it is a generalization of an orthogonal rotation.

Because oblique rotation is more general than orthogonal rotation current practice favors oblique rotation, and our discussion will be oriented toward the oblique case.

Dealing with the Rotation Problem

There are many orthogonal and oblique rotations of the initial loading matrix A produced by the extraction step. The real rotation problem is choosing a rotation that may be of interest. This is usually done by using a rotation criterion $Q(\Lambda)$ that measures the complexity of Λ and minimizing this over all Λ that are rotations of A.

The main problem is, what does the vague statement "of interest" mean? One case is clear. If each row of Λ has at most one nonzero element, Λ is said to have perfect simple structure, an example of which is displayed in Table 10.1. However, there may not be a rotation of A with perfect simple structure, and this is the usual case. Thurstone (1935) proposed a less demanding definition of simple structure. The second loading matrix in Table 10.1 has Thurstone simple structure, which requires a fair number of zeros, but far fewer than perfect simple structure. The complexity of a row of Λ is the number of

Table 10.1 Examples of perfect and Thurstone simple structure.

Perfect			Thurstone		
1	0	0	1	0	0
1	0	0	0	1	0
1	0	0	0	0	1
0	1	0	.89	.45	0
0	1	0	.89	0	.45
0	0	1	0	.71	.71

nonzero elements in the row. Thurstone simple structure can have row complexities greater than one. As with perfect simple structure there may be no rotation of A that has Thurstone simple structure, and this is the usual case. It may, however, be possible to find a rotation of A that approximates Thurstone simple structure, or even perfect simple structure. The phrase "simple structure" is sometimes used to denote "perfect simple structure," and sometimes used to denote "approximate perfect simple structure". Here, "simple structure" will mean "approximate perfect simple structure."

Graphical Methods

The original rotation methods were graphical. The first term $c = \Lambda f$ in the factor analysis model of Equation 10.1 is called the common part of x. The ith component of c has the form

$$c_i = \lambda_{i1} f_1 + \cdots + \lambda_{ik} f_k.$$

This is plotted in Figure 10.1 for the case of two factors. Plotting all c_i gives the representation shown in Figure 10.2. The two-factor solution is obtained by choosing new factors $\tilde{f}_1$ and $\tilde{f}_2$ through the clusters of c_i and updating the λ_{ir}.

For more than two factors one cycles through pairs of factors making similar plots. Because it is better to actually do it than simply talk about doing it, the author attempted to graphically rotate the well-known Thurstone 26-variable box data (Thurstone, 1947, p. 371). Table 10.2 shows Thurstone's results and those of the author.

To aid in comparing these solutions their sorted absolute loading (SAL) plots (Jennrich, 2004) are given in Figure 10.3. The author did not do as well as Thurstone. A proper solution is known to have 27 small values. Thurstone got 27 small values. The author also got 27 small values, but clearly not as small. It is also known that a proper solution has three pure indicators, and these should produce three distinctly larger values. Thurstone found three distinctly larger values. The author failed to find these. The only conclusion one can draw from Figure 10.3 is that Thurstone is much better at graphical rotation than Jennrich.

While this may be the case, with the reader's indulgence the author would like a rematch. Thurstone's 26-variable box problem is known as a hard problem. Many rotation methods fail on this problem. Thurstone's 20-variable box problem, on the other hand, is much simpler. It was used to train students. Figure 10.4 shows the author's and

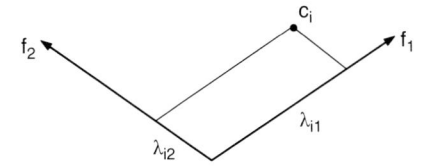

Figure 10.1 Components of the common part of x for two factors.

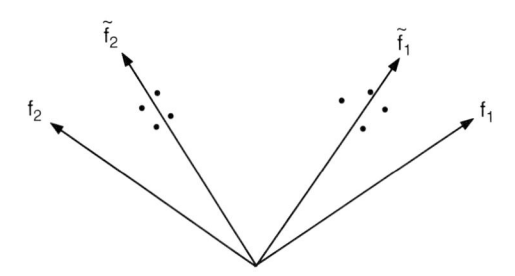

Figure 10.2 All the common part components.

Table 10.2 Graphical solutions to Thurstone's 26-variable box problem. The formulas on the left were used to generate values for the 26 variables from the dimensions x_1, x_2, and x_3 of Thurstone's boxes.

Formula	Thurstone			Jennrich		
x_1	.95	.01	.01	.98	.02	.02
x_2	.02	.92	.01	.04	.97	−.02
x_3	.02	.05	.91	−.02	−.07	1.02
$x_1 x_2$	.59	.64	−.03	.62	.69	−.05
$x_1 x_3$	.60	.00	.62	.58	−.07	.70
$x_2 x_3$	−.04	.60	.58	−.05	.55	.63
$x_1^2 x_2$	.81	.38	.01	.81	.43	−.00
$x_1 x_2^2$	.35	.79	.01	.36	.85	−.02
$x_1^2 x_3$	.79	−.01	.41	.77	−.05	.46
$x_1 x_3^2$	.40	−.02	.79	.42	−.07	.92
$x_2^2 x_3$	−.04	.74	.40	−.04	.73	.42
$x_2 x_3^2$	−.02	.41	.74	−.05	.35	.80
x_1/x_2	.74	−.77	−.06	.75	−.83	.09
x_2/x_1	−.74	.66	.06	−.75	.83	−.09
x_1/x_3	.74	.02	−.73	.82	.15	−.85
x_3/x_1	−.74	−.02	.73	−.82	−.15	.85
x_2/x_3	−.07	.80	−.76	−.01	.99	−.91
x_3/x_2	.07	−.80	.76	.01	−.99	.91
$2x_1 + 2x_2$	.51	.70	−.03	.53	.76	−.06
$2x_1 + 2x_3$	.56	−.04	.69	.54	−.10	.74
$2x_2 + 2x_3$	−.02	.60	.58	−.03	.55	.62
$(x_1^2 + x_2^2)^{1/2}$	.50	.69	−.03	.52	.74	−.05
$(x_1^2 + x_3^2)^{1/2}$	.52	−.01	.68	.51	−.08	.74
$(x_2^2 + x_3^2)^{1/2}$	−.01	.60	.55	−.01	.56	.59
$x_1 x_2 x_3$	.43	.46	.45	.43	.45	.47
$(x_1^2 + x_2^2 + x_3^2)^{1/2}$	.31	.51	.46	.32	.49	.48

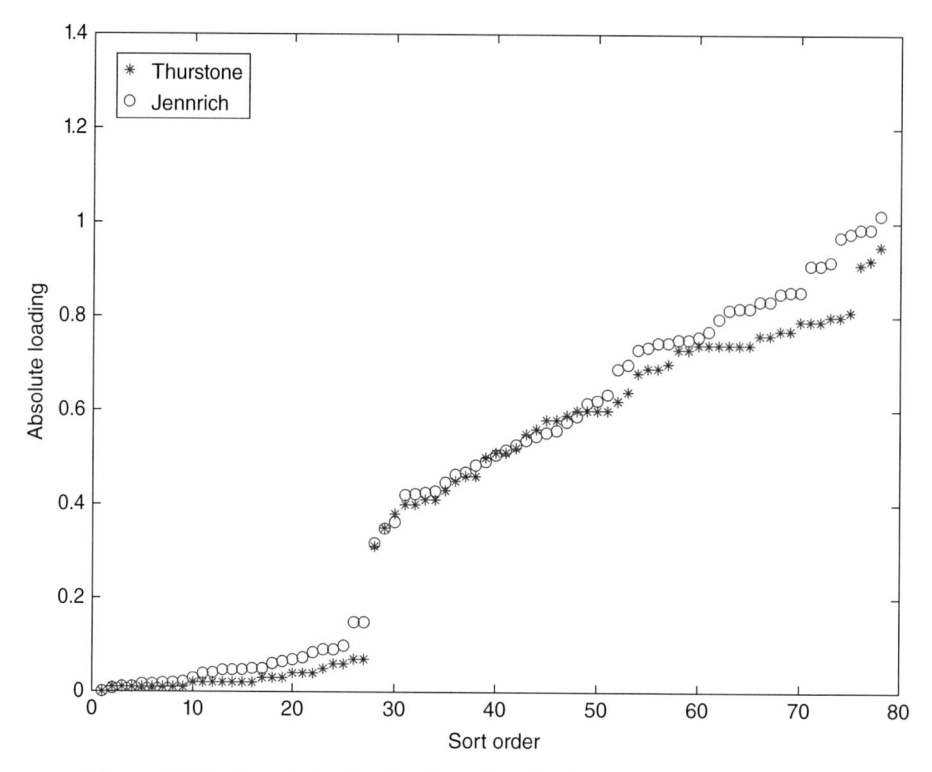

Figure 10.3 Sorted absolute loading plots for the 26-variable box problem.

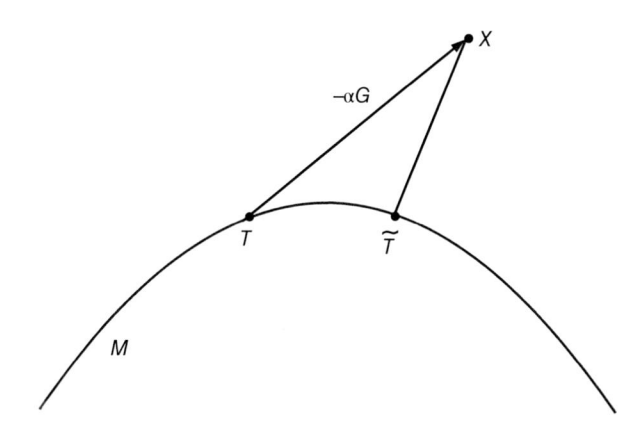

Figure 10.4 Graphical representation of the gradient projection algorithm.

Thurstone's results on this problem. Again, a proper solution should have 27 small values. The author found these almost as well as Thurstone. A proper solution to this problem is known to have nine pure indicators. The author found nine large values, as did Thurstone, but the author's are a little more distinct. The author would like to declare this contest a tie.

Analytic Methods

Analytic methods begin by choosing a rotation criterion Q defined on all $p \times k$ loading matrices Λ. $Q(\Lambda)$ is a measure of the complexity of Λ. An analytic method proceeds by minimizing

$$f(T) = Q(AT^{-1})$$

over all nonsingular T with rows of length one. Using the minimizing value $\hat{T}$,

$$\hat{\Lambda} = A\hat{T}^{-1} \tag{10.2}$$

is the oblique rotation of A corresponding to Q. Some authors replace T by T' and write $f(T) = Q(A(T')^{-1})$, but this seems unnecessarily complicated. Many rotation criteria have been proposed. Some of the more popular are identified in the following subsections.

Quartic criteria

By quartic criteria we mean criteria Q such that $Q(\Lambda)$ is a quartic function of the components of Λ. The earliest of these was the quartimin criterion,

$$Q(\Lambda) = \sum_{r \neq s}\sum_i \lambda_{ir}^2 \lambda_{is}^2.$$

The quartimin criterion has a nice theoretical property. Quartimin rotation will produce perfect simple structure whenever it exists. If A can be rotated to a loading matrix with close to perfect simple structure, continuity suggests that quartimin rotation will do this as well.

A generalization of the quartimin criterion is the Crawford–Ferguson (Crawford & Ferguson, 1970) family (CF) of criteria. Let $0 \leq \kappa \leq 1$. The CF criterion corresponding to κ is given by

$$Q(\Lambda) = (1-\kappa)\sum_{r \neq s}\sum_i \lambda_{ir}^2 \lambda_{is}^2 + \kappa \sum_{i \neq j}\sum_r \lambda_{ir}^2 \lambda_{jr}^2.$$

The first term of this criterion is a multiple of the quartimin criterion and can be viewed as a measure of row complexity. The second term is a similar measure of column complexity. The parameter κ weights the two complexities. When $\kappa = 0$ the CF criterion is the quartimin criterion, and when $\kappa = 1/p$ it is the CF-varimax criterion.

The geomin criterion

The best known of the non-quadratic criteria is Yates' (1987) geomin criterion,

$$Q(\Lambda) = \sum_i \left(\prod_r \lambda_{ir}^2\right)^{1/k},$$

where k is the number of columns of Λ. Yates called this a geomin criterion because it is the sum of the geometric mean of each row of Λ^2, the element-wise square of Λ.

The geomin criterion Q has a nice theoretical property. If a loading matrix Λ has at least one zero in each row then $Q(\Lambda)$ is zero, which is the smallest value it can have. If there is a rotation Λ of an initial loading matrix A with at least one zero in each row, a geomin rotation of A will have this property.

If there is a rotation of A with perfect simple structure, some geomin rotation of A will have perfect simple structure. Unfortunately this is not true for all geomin rotations of A, but this seems to happen often in practice.

A problem with the geomin criterion is that it is not differentiable at Λ if Λ has one or more components that are zero. This can make it difficult to minimize by analytic methods. Browne (2001) suggested dealing with this problem by replacing λ_{ir} in Yates' formula by $\lambda_{ir} + \epsilon$, where ϵ is a small positive value. This makes the resulting Q differentiable at all Λ. Browne suggested using $\epsilon = .01$. When used here, the geomin criterion will have this modified form.

Bifactor criteria

Bifactor analysis is a form of confirmatory factor analysis using a factor loading matrix of the form

$$\Lambda = \begin{pmatrix} * & * & 0 \\ * & * & 0 \\ * & * & 0 \\ * & 0 & * \\ * & 0 & * \\ * & 0 & * \end{pmatrix}.$$

More precisely, the loadings in the first column are free parameters and after the first column the loading matrix has at most one free parameter in each row. Loading matrices of this form are said to have bifactor structure. In bifactor analysis the first factor is called a general factor and the remaining factors are called group factors. Bifactor analysis is a fairly extensively used form of confirmatory factor analysis.

Recently, Jennrich and Bentler (2011) introduced an exploratory form of bifactor analysis. This was done by using orthogonal EFA with a rotation criterion that does not involve the loadings on the first factor and encourages perfect simple structure for the loadings on the remaining factors. To avoid confusion, they call this confirmatory bifactor analysis to differentiate it from exploratory bifactor analysis.

$B(\Lambda)$ is called a bifactor rotation criterion if Λ minimizes $B(\Lambda)$ if and only if Λ has bifactor structure. The following theorem identifies a specific bifactor rotation criterion.

Theorem 10.1: If Λ is an arbitrary $p \times k$ loading matrix and

$$B_q(\Lambda) = q\min(\Lambda_2),$$

where Λ_2 is the submatrix of Λ containing its last $k - 1$ columns and qmin() is the quartimin rotation criterion, then B_q is a bifactor rotation criterion.

The criterion B_q in Theorem 10.1 is called the biquartimin criterion. Although $B_q(\Lambda)$ does not depend on the first column of Λ, when $B_q(\Lambda)$ is used for rotation, it is all columns of Λ, including its first, that are rotated.

Some care must be used in defining bifactor rotation criteria. One might be tempted to use

$$B_v(\Lambda) = -v\max(\Lambda_2),$$

where vmax( ) is the varimax rotation criterion. The authors show that B_v is not a bifactor rotation criterion and that its use can lead to very poor results.

Other criteria

There are many other rotation criteria, including Bentler's (1977) invariant pattern simplicity criterion, McCammon's (1966) minimum entropy criterion, and McKeon's (1968) infomax criterion. There is a cottage industry of numerous papers proposing new criteria.

Reference structure and early analytic methods

Analytic oblique rotation was not originally formulated as described by Equation 10.2 because the required optimization, which involves T^{-1}, seemed too difficult. Using T^{-1} can be avoided by using reference structures. Following Thurstone (1947) and Harman (1976), let the rows of a nonsingular matrix U be biorthogonal to the rows of T and have length one. Biorthogonal means the rth row of U is orthogonal to the sth row of T whenever $r \neq s$. Let

$$R = AU'.$$

This is called the reference structure corresponding to U. Note that

$$R = AT^{-1}TU' = \hat{\Lambda}D,$$

where D is diagonal because the rows of T and U are biorthogonal. This result is of interest because it means the columns of R are rescaled versions of the columns of $\hat{\Lambda}$, and this suggests that R is simple when $\hat{\Lambda}$ is simple, and conversely. Rather than apply a complexity criterion to Λ one can apply it to R. The analytic rotation problem is then to minimize

$$Q(R) = Q(AU')$$

over all nonsingular U with rows of length one. Here, U' has replaced the T^{-1} in the definition of an oblique rotation. Harman (1976) calls making R simple an indirect method and making Λ simple a direct method because it simplifies the loadings directly.

Carroll (1953) has shown that when Q is the quartimin criterion, $Q(AU')$ viewed as a function of a single row of U is a constant plus a homogeneous quadratic function of the row. Because the row must have length one, an optimal value is the eigenvector of the matrix defining the quadratic function that corresponds to its smallest eigenvalue. Cycling through the rows of U gives a relatively simple algorithm for minimizing $Q(R)$. Actually, this can be generalized to Carroll's (1960) oblimin family of criteria. It does not, however, seem to generalize to other criteria. For some time, indirect oblimin was the standard method of oblique analytic rotation.

Direct methods

Indirect methods based on criteria applied to reference structures were eventually replaced by methods based on criteria applied to loading matrices directly. The first such method was introduced by Jennrich and Sampson (1966) for direct quartimin rotation. Today, direct methods are standard. Algorithms for these will be discussed in the next section.

Analytic Oblique Rotation Algorithms

In the beginning, all proposed rotation criteria came with a rotation algorithm designed to optimize the specific proposed criterion. These algorithms were sometimes quite complex. Later, algorithms were developed that worked for entire classes of criteria, and later still algorithms that worked for essentially all criteria. Some of these will be discussed here.

Closed-form pairwise algorithms for quartic criteria

Let f_1 and f_2 be a pair of factors and consider rotating f_1 in the plane of f_1 and f_2. More precisely, the new f_1 factor has the form

$$\tilde{f}_1 = \alpha_1 f_1 + \alpha_2 f_2$$

and has variance one. Jennrich and Sampson (1966) showed that the values of the quartimin criterion under such rotations can be expressed as a fourth-degree polynomial $Q'(\delta)$ in $\delta = \alpha_1/\alpha_2$. This may be minimized in closed form without iteration by solving the cubic equation $Q'(\delta) = 0$. Cycling through all ordered pairs of factors gives a pairwise algorithm for minimizing the criterion. This method generalized to the oblimin family of criteria is used in a number of major software systems.

Although to date no formal proof has been given, this approach also works when the quartimin criterion is replaced by any quartic criterion $Q(\Lambda)$ that is invariant under sign changes in the columns of Λ. These include essentially all quartic criteria, and in particular the oblimin and CF families of criteria. Because five values determine a quartic polynomial, $Q(\delta)$ can be found by evaluating Q at five loading matrices corresponding to five values of δ. As a consequence, the only specific information required to implement these methods is a formula for $Q(\Lambda)$.

General pairwise line search algorithms

Browne and Cudeck have developed a pairwise line search algorithm for minimizing arbitrary rotation criteria. Let $Q(\Lambda)$ be any rotation criterion that is invariant under sign changes in the columns of Λ. These include all criteria known to the author. As was done by Jennrich and Sampson, Browne and Cudeck let f_1 and f_2 be an arbitrary pair of factors and consider rotating f_1 in the plane of f_1 and f_2. For pairwise rotations of this form they have shown that the values of the criterion Q can be expressed as a function $Q(\delta)$ of the parameter δ used by Jennrich and Sampson. In general $Q(\delta)$ will not be quartic, but it can be minimized using a general line search algorithm. This forms a basis for a pairwise algorithm for minimizing Q. This is a remarkable algorithm:

- it works for almost any rotation criterion $Q(\Lambda)$;
- all that is required is a formula for $Q(\Lambda)$;
- it is remarkably simple;
- it has been used successfully for many different criteria.

Unfortunately, Browne and Cudeck have not published an account of their method or observations on its performance. Their method is used, however, by Browne, Cudeck, Tateneni, and Mels (2002) in the CEFA (comprehensive exploratory factor analysis) software. This free software deals with almost every aspect of EFA, including a broad variety of methods for extraction and rotation, factoring correlation matrices, and providing standard errors for the estimates produced. It has a graphical user interface and a nice manual. The software and manual may be downloaded.[1]

Gradient projection algorithms

Jennrich (2002) gave a general gradient method that does not require cycling through pairs of factors. The oblique rotation problem is to minimize

$$f(T) = Q(AT^{-1})$$

over all T in the manifold M of nonsingular T with rows of length one. This is a slightly more precise expression of the problem than that given earlier. The gradient projection (GP) algorithm proceeds as follows.

Given a $T \in M$ and an arbitrary scalar $\alpha > 0$, compute the gradient G of f at T and project $X = T - \alpha G$ onto M—see Figure 10.4. The algorithm moves T in a negative gradient direction and then projects the result back onto M. At first it seems like the required projection may be difficult to find because projecting onto a nonlinear manifold is a nonlinear regression problem and these generally require complex iterative procedures. For the manifold M, however, projection is very easy and this is what motivates the method. The projection $\tilde{T}$ of X onto M is simply X scaled to have rows of length one.

Theorem 10.2: If T is not a stationary point of f restricted to M, then

$$f(\tilde{T}) < f(T)$$

for all $\alpha > 0$ and sufficiently small.

---

[1] http:/quantrm2.psy.ohio-state.edu/browne/

Using Theorem 10.2, the GP algorithm halves an initial value of α until $f(\tilde{T}) < f(T)$. Replacing T by $\tilde{T}$ gives a strictly monotone iterative algorithm for minimizing f over M, and hence Q over all rotations of the initial loading matrix A. Strictly monotone algorithms are desirable because they must converge to stationary points. Moreover, since the only points of attraction of a strictly monotone algorithm are local minima, strictly monotone algorithms are almost guaranteed to converge to a local minimum.

This approach requires a formula for the gradient of Q in addition to a formula for Q. Jennrich (2004) has shown that this problem-specific requirement can be removed with almost no loss of precision by using numerical gradients. Using these, the gradient projection algorithm has the same nice properties as the Browne and Cudeck line search algorithm without the need to cycle through pairs of factors.

Free SAS, SPSS, R/S, and Matlab code for GP rotation can be downloaded.[2] Thus, for almost any computing environment one is working in, one can find code written specifically for that environment and hence code that may be used immediately without any need for translation. There is code for both orthogonal and oblique rotation using analytic and numerical gradients. The analytic gradients tend to be quite simple. They are given for the most popular, and some less popular but promising, criteria.

Advantages and disadvantages

The pairwise quartic algorithms have the advantage that no line search is required, and they are probably the fastest of the algorithms discussed. Their main disadvantage is that they are restricted to quartic criteria.

The main advantage of the general pairwise line search algorithm is that it applies to arbitrary criteria and the only method-specific code required is that for evaluating the criterion. Also, it is a very simple algorithm. Disadvantages are that it requires cycling through pairs and requires a line search subalgorithm.

The main advantage of the GP algorithm is that it applies to arbitrary rotation criteria, it does not require stepping through pairs of factors, and when using numerical gradients, it is very simple. When using analytic gradients, it appears to be significantly faster than the general pairwise line search algorithm, at least in the limited experience of the author. Its main disadvantage is that when used with analytic gradients it requires method-specific code to produce these. Fortunately, gradient formulas for popular rotation criteria are given at the URL cited above. While gradient formulas can be avoided with almost no loss of precision by using numerical gradients, their use slows the algorithm.

Choosing a Rotation Method

Up to this point we have not discussed the problem of choosing a rotation method. Unfortunately, there is no right or wrong choice. Exploratory factor analysis is an exploratory method. It is used to suggest a relation between observed variables and latent factors. A rotation method suggests what such a relation may look like, but there are many rotation methods and they can suggest different relations. It is the user who

---

[2] http://www.stat.ucla.edu/research/gpa

must ultimately decide which if any of these may be of interest. The data can identify an initial loading matrix, but it cannot determine what rotation, if any, is of interest in a specific context.

There is some theoretical guidance:

- If an initial loading matrix can be rotated to a loading matrix with perfect simple structure, the quartimin method will do this. Continuity suggests the quartimin method will do this at least approximately when the initial loading matrix can be rotated to a loading matrix that approximates perfect simple structure.
- If an initial loading matrix A can be rotated to a loading matrix with at least one zero loading in each row, a geomin rotation of A will have this property. When A can be rotated to a loading matrix with at least one nearly zero loading in each row one expects a geomin rotation of A will have at least one nearly zero loading in each row.

There is a cottage industry devoted to proposing new rotation methods. Every time a new method is introduced its performance on one or two examples is given and compared with one or two natural alternatives. The purpose is to show that the new method works at least in appropriate circumstances. There are only a limited number of papers that compare a number of popular methods on a number of examples from an unbiased point of view. These include Browne (2001) and Schmitt and Sass (2011).

Browne looked at two classical examples, the 24 psychological tests problem (Harman, 1976) and Thurstone's (1947) 26-variable box problem. In the case of the 24 psychological tests problem Browne found that an initial loading matrix can be rotated to a loading matrix with simple structure using a number of methods, including quartimin, CF-varimax, geomin, and infomax.

To investigate a more complex case Browne considered Thurstone's 26-variable box problem. Here there is a rotation that suggests the way the data were generated, and Browne considered the ability of various methods to obtain this.

Among the methods considered, only geomin and infomax identified the way the data were generated. Browne goes on to show how one can use Cureton and Mulaik (1975) standardization to obtain satisfactory results for other methods as well. We will not attempt to discuss this here.

Using a somewhat different approach, Schmitt and Sass (2011) began with the population loading matrix Λ displayed in the first three columns of Table 10.3 above the horizontal line. This has very a complex structure because it is far from perfect simple structure. They used a population factor correlation matrix Φ given by the 3×3 matrix below the population loading matrix and for Ψ a diagonal matrix of unique variances:

.3188 .3425 .3315 .1845 .1518 .3215 .3315 .0235 .0713 .3695 .4303 .2845

.2123 .0235 .2535 .3915 .2563 .3695

Rather than using Λ, Φ, and Ψ to generate a sample and analyzing its correlation matrix R, Schmitt and Sass constructed the population correlation matrix P and analyzed this rather than R. This avoids random results and the problem of choosing the sample size n. What Schmitt and Sass did was to let $n = \infty$. Their analysis should give results that approximate large-n results. This seems like a good place to start when comparing rotation methods.

Table 10.3 Comparing rotations for a model with complex structure.

Population			Quartimin			Geomin			CFvarimax		
0.75	0.25	0.15	0.79	0.07	0.03	0.74	0.11	0.07	0.72	0.13	0.09
0.75	0.10	0.25	0.78	−0.10	0.17	0.73	−0.06	0.21	0.72	−0.02	0.21
0.75	0.30	0.05	0.82	0.13	−0.09	0.76	0.18	−0.06	0.74	0.19	−0.02
0.75	0.45	0.10	0.77	0.27	−0.05	0.71	0.32	−0.03	0.70	0.32	0.01
0.75	0.15	0.45	0.70	−0.07	0.36	0.65	−0.04	0.40	0.65	0.01	0.38
0.75	0.20	0.20	0.78	0.01	0.09	0.73	0.05	0.13	0.72	0.08	0.14
0.05	0.75	0.30	−0.04	0.72	0.23	−0.04	0.75	0.18	−0.02	0.72	0.21
0.30	0.75	0.45	0.19	0.59	0.33	0.17	0.62	0.31	0.20	0.62	0.13
0.45	0.75	0.25	0.39	0.59	0.11	0.36	0.63	0.09	0.37	0.62	0.13
0.10	0.75	0.20	0.04	0.73	0.11	0.03	0.76	0.06	0.05	0.73	0.11
0.05	0.75	0.05	0.01	0.80	−0.06	0.01	0.84	−0.11	0.02	0.78	−0.04
0.30	0.75	0.15	0.27	0.66	0.02	0.25	0.71	−0.01	0.25	0.68	0.05
0.05	0.45	0.75	−0.13	0.34	0.75	−0.12	0.34	0.73	−0.06	0.38	0.68
0.45	0.30	0.75	0.29	0.10	0.68	0.28	0.12	0.69	0.32	0.17	0.65
0.30	0.20	0.75	0.15	0.04	0.76	0.14	0.04	0.76	0.19	0.10	0.70
0.15	0.10	0.75	−0.01	−0.03	0.84	−0.00	−0.04	0.84	0.05	0.03	0.76
0.25	0.25	0.75	0.09	0.10	0.76	0.09	0.10	0.75	0.14	0.16	0.70
0.20	0.10	0.75	0.05	−0.04	0.82	0.05	−0.04	0.83	0.10	0.02	0.75
1.00	0.40	0.40	1.00	0.66	0.72	1.00	0.64	0.67	1.00	0.59	0.60
0.40	1.00	0.40	0.66	1.00	0.66	0.64	1.00	0.70	0.59	1.00	0.59
0.40	0.40	1.00	0.72	0.66	1.00	0.67	0.70	1.00	0.60	0.59	1.00

Schmitt and Sass considered a number of popular rotation methods, but the primary contenders were geomin, quartmin, and CF-varimax. They used a maximum likelihood factor analysis program applied to P to produce an initial loading matrix A and rotated this.

There is a way to obtain an initial loading matrix A corresponding to P that does not require the use of an EFA program. One can simply unrotate Λ and Φ by using a Cholesky factorization to write Φ in the form $\Phi = TT'$. Then,

$$\Sigma = \Lambda\Phi\Lambda' + \Psi = \Lambda TT'\Lambda' + \Psi.$$

Let $D = \text{diag}(\Sigma)^{-1/2}$. Then

$$P = D\Lambda\Phi\Lambda'D + D\Psi D = (D\Lambda T)(D\Lambda T)' + D\Phi D = AA' + \tilde{\Psi},$$

where

$$A = D\Lambda T.$$

This A is an initial loading matrix that generates P. This is much simpler and more accurate than running an iterative factor analysis extraction program to produce an initial loading matrix.

Using the method just described, the results for quartimin, geomin, and CF-varimax are given in Table 10.3. To the precision displayed, the quartimin and CF-varimax

Table 10.4 Example 1 rotations

Canonical					Orthogonal					Oblique				
54	42	-13	-0	-7	29	63	4	9	-5	66	0	11	-1	-7
44	27	-8	6	-1	26	45	8	0	-2	47	8	-0	4	-3
59	42	-15	5	8	33	66	4	-4	5	74	1	-6	3	6
48	46	-16	5	6	22	65	2	-3	2	73	-2	-6	-4	1
59	40	-13	-0	-0	33	64	4	6	1	68	1	7	2	-1
50	3	33	22	-5	38	18	48	6	3	3	62	4	-4	1
50	-5	26	18	-5	42	13	39	5	1	-2	52	5	9	0
53	2	28	27	-11	41	20	48	4	-6	4	65	1	4	-9
53	-3	34	14	11	44	14	43	3	20	1	53	1	1	21
54	-5	16	-21	25	48	16	7	12	38	9	0	19	10	44
62	-6	15	-24	-4	56	18	9	31	16	2	4	46	15	16
51	-7	24	-13	20	45	12	18	12	34	2	15	17	5	39
62	9	2	-13	-4	50	34	6	19	7	26	3	29	16	8
63	4	21	-28	-20	51	25	14	47	7	5	9	66	1	3
74	-35	-26	1	-7	84	9	-10	-4	-12	1	-5	8	86	-6
70	-26	-7	8	1	74	11	9	-5	-2	1	17	1	61	4
68	-34	-20	7	8	78	6	-5	-14	-1	1	2	-9	79	8

results in Table 10.3 are the same as those in Table 10.4 of Schmitt and Sass. The geomin results, however, differ significantly.

The value of the geomin criterion for the geomin result in Table 10.3 is 1.3231. Schmitt and Sass do not report the value of the geomin **criterion** for their result, but when it is computed from the rounded numbers in their Table 10.4 the value is 1.3491. Because this value is larger, this suggests that the Schmitt and Sass result may be incorrect.

Schmitt and Sass don't seem to have a favorite method. Instead, they show how the methods they consider compare to one another, and in particular how the CF methods change with increasing values of κ. They consider a variety of values of κ and observe that as κ increases the factor correlations decrease, but the complexity of the rotations increases.

As noted above, the quartimin method is the Crawford–Ferguson method with $\kappa = 0$ and the CF-varimax method corresponds to $\kappa = 1/p$. The factor correlations in Table 10.3 decrease as κ increases, in agreement with their observation. To consider the change in complexity this author constructed SAL plots for the rotations in Table 10.3. These are displayed in Figure 10.5. Schmitt and Sass call a loading λ_{ir} a primary loading if its absolute value is the largest among the loadings in the same row, and call it a cross loading otherwise. There are a total of 18 primary loadings in each loading matrix. These are displayed in the upper left-hand corner of the plot.

The cross loadings for CF-varimax tend to be a bit larger than those for quartimin and geomin. This is in agreement with Schmitt and Sass' observation that complexity increases with κ. Overall, however, the methods displayed are more similar than different. One might seek an example where differences are more dramatic. For the box data considered by Browne, there was a substantial difference between quartimin and geomin.

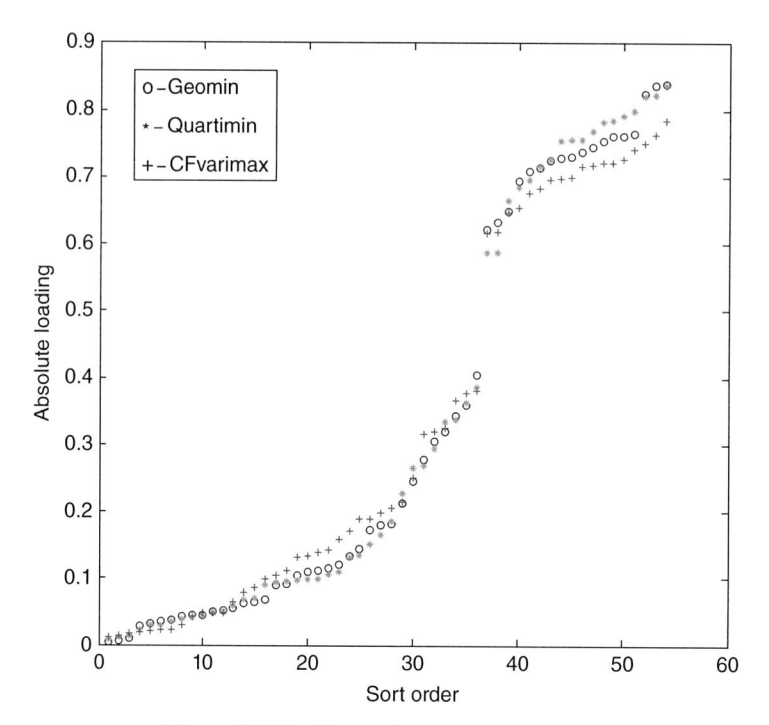

Figure 10.5 Comparison using SAL plots.

At present, the only simple thing one can say about comparing rotation methods in the complex case is that it is complex. Clearly, more work on this case is needed.

Where to start

The first problem faced by a factor analyst is where to start. For this, one can give fairly reasonable advice.

- A number of popular EFA programs use a normal deviance function to extract an initial loading matrix. This seems to work well and is probably a reasonable way to begin. The normal deviance function is a proper deviance function and a reasonable choice even when one is not sampling from a normal distribution.
- Because it is more general it seems reasonable to begin with oblique rotation and reserve orthogonal rotation for applications where orthogonal rotation is required or desired.
- Theory suggests that quartimin rotation works well when one is seeking simple structure and some limited computer experience suggests that geomin may work well when seeking rotations with simple and more complex structure.

A number of EFA programs use oblique quartimin or oblique geomin as default choices for a rotation method, and presently at least these seem appropriate first choices.

Standard Errors for Rotated Loadings

Measured in terms of actual computer usage, EFA is one of the most frequently used methods of statistical analysis. Among statistical methods it is somewhat unique in that standard computer implementations fail to produce standard errors for the parameter estimates. For many forms of statistical analysis standard errors are a by-product of the fitting procedure. This is true, for example, for regression analysis and the many forms of analysis related to it. It is also true for confirmatory factor analysis, but because of the rotation problem it is not true for EFA. Other methods for producing standard errors are required. Here we outline a number of methods that may be used to produce standard errors for rotated loadings. For the most part these are asymptotic methods based on linear approximations. As discussed below, little progress seems to have been made using less linear methods such as the jackknife, the bootstrap, and Markov chain Monte Carlo (MCMC) methods. Cudeck and O'Dell (1994) discuss a variety of uses for standard errors in EFA.

Historical note

An analytic rotation of an initial loading matrix A has the form

$$\hat{A} = AT^{-1}.$$

Because both A and T are random, Lawley and Maxwell (1971) believed that:

> It would be almost impossible to take sampling errors in the elements of T into account. The only course is, therefore, to ignore them in the hope they are relatively small.

Wexler (1968) provided some evidence that one cannot always ignore sampling errors in T. Archer and Jennrich (1973) and Jennrich (1973) showed that the Lawley and Maxwell approximation is not needed. This is discussed in the next subsection.

Methods using the asymptotic distribution of the initial loadings

Under appropriate assumptions an initial loading matrix A is asymptotically normally distributed. More precisely, if n is the sample size used to compute A, then as $n \to \infty$,

$$\sqrt{n}(a - a_0) \to N(0, \mathrm{acov}(a)),$$

where a is A written in vector form, a_0 is a constant vector, and $\mathrm{acov}(a)$ is the asymptotic covariance matrix for a.

Results of this form have been given by

- Anderson and Rubin (1956) for principal component EFA and normal sampling;
- Lawley (1967) for canonical loadings and normal sampling;
- Jöreskog (1969) for confirmatory factor analysis and normal sampling;
- Browne (1984) for confirmatory factor analysis and non-normal sampling;
- Girshick (1939) for principal component analysis and normal sampling.

Actually, Lawley's formula for acov($\hat{a}$) has an error that was corrected by Jennrich and Thayer (1973).

The confirmatory factor analysis approach is particularly attractive. It assumes that the upper diagonal part of A is zero. A standard confirmatory factor analysis then produces an estimate for acov($\hat{a}$) as a by-product of the analysis.

Consider any analytic rotation. Let A be the initial loading matrix and let $\hat{\Lambda}$ be the corresponding rotated loading matrix, which is a function of A. In vector form let

$$\hat{\lambda} = h(a).$$

Assuming that a is asymptotically normally distributed, it follows from the delta method that $\hat{\lambda}$ is also, and that

$$\text{acov}\hat{\lambda} = \frac{dh}{da}\text{acov}(a)\frac{dh'}{da},$$

where dh/da is the Jacobian of h at a. Thus, the problem of finding the asymptotic distribution for rotated loadings given that this is known for the corresponding initial loadings reduces to finding the Jacobian of the function that defines the rotation. Jennrich (1973) has shown how to compute dh/da using implicit differentiation.

Constrained maximum likelihood methods

For the case when the observed responses are a normal sample Jennrich (1974) used a result of Silvey (1971) on constrained maximum likelihood estimation to find the asymptotic distribution of the rotated loadings $\hat{\Lambda}$.

Let λ be Λ written as a vector, ϕ be the upper-diagonal part of Φ written as a vector, ψ be the diagonal of Ψ written as a vector, $\theta = (\lambda', \phi', \psi')'$ be the complete parameter vector, and $\ell(\theta)$ be the likelihood of θ given the observed responses.

This likelihood is over-parameterized. Jennrich (1973) has shown, however, that for oblique rotation, Λ and Φ must satisfy the stationary condition

$$\text{ndg}\left(\Lambda'\frac{dQ}{d\Lambda}\Phi^{-1}\right) = 0.$$

Write this as

$$\varphi(\theta) = 0.$$

Let $\dot{\varphi}$ be the Jacobian of φ at θ and $\mathcal{I}$ be the information matrix at θ. Using Silvey's result on constrained maximum likelihood estimation,

$$\begin{pmatrix} \mathcal{I} & \varphi' \\ \varphi & 0 \end{pmatrix}^{-1} = \begin{pmatrix} \text{acov}(\hat{\theta}) & * \\ * & * \end{pmatrix}.$$

That is, when the augmented information matrix on the left is inverted, what is in the upper left-hand corner of the inverse is the asymptotic covariance matrix for the constrained maximum likelihood estimate $\hat{\theta}$. If $\mathcal{I}$ and $\dot{\varphi}$ are replaced by sample estimates, what is in the upper left-hand corner of the inverse is a consistent estimate of the asymptotic covariance matrix of $\hat{\theta}$. This can be used to assign standard errors to the factor loading estimates λ_{ir}. If $\dot{\varphi}$ is computed numerically, this is a very simple approach when using maximum likelihood factor analysis.

A method based on the asymptotic distribution of $s = \text{vech}(S)$

A difficulty with the previous approach is the assumption that one is sampling from a normal distribution. In practice this is at best only approximately true. To relax this assumption, consider the use of a method based on the asymptotic distribution of $s = \text{vech}(S)$, where $\text{vech}(S)$ is a column vector containing the diagonal and upper diagonal components of the sample co-variance matrix S.

More specifically, let θ be the parameter vector defined in the previous subsection. An EFA estimate $\hat{\theta}$ of these parameters is a function of s. That is,

$$\hat{\theta} = h(s).$$

Let Γ be the asymptotic covariance matrix for s. By the delta method, the asymptotic covariance matrix for $\hat{\theta}$ is given by

$$\widehat{\text{acov}}(\hat{\theta}) = \dot{h}(\sigma)\Gamma\dot{h}(\sigma)',$$

where $\sigma = \text{vech}(\Sigma)$ and $\dot{h}(\sigma)$ is the Jacobian of h at σ. This can be consistently estimated using

$$\widehat{\text{cov}}(\hat{\theta}) = \dot{h}(s)\hat{\Gamma}\dot{h}(s)',$$

where $\hat{\Gamma}$ is a consistent estimator of Γ. The diagonal elements of $\widehat{\text{acov}}(\hat{\theta})$ can be used to assign standard errors to the components of $\hat{\theta}$, including the factor loadings $\hat{\lambda}_{ij}$.

To use this apparently very simple method one needs a formula for $\dot{h}(s)$ and $\hat{\Gamma}$. In EFA there is no formula for $h(s)$. The estimate $\hat{\theta}$ is implicitly defined as a vector that minimizes

$$f(\theta, s) = D(S, \Lambda\Phi\Lambda' + \Psi)$$

and satisfies $\varphi(\theta) = 0$, where

$$\varphi(\theta) = \text{ndg}\left(\Lambda'\frac{dQ}{d\Lambda}\Phi^{-1}\right)$$

and Q is the criterion used to define the rotation. Let

$$g(\theta, s) = \begin{pmatrix} \dot{f}_1(\theta, s) \\ \varphi(\theta) \end{pmatrix},$$

where $\dot{f}(\theta, s)$ is the Jacobian of $f(\theta, s)$ viewed as a function of its first argument. It follows that

$$g(\hat{\theta}, s) = 0.$$

One can use this and implicit differentiation to find a formula for $\dot{h}(s)$. Since $\hat{\theta} = h(s)$,

$$g(h(s), s) = 0.$$

Differentiating this with respect to s gives

$$\dot{g}_1(h(s), s)\dot{h}(s) + \dot{g}_2(h(s), s) = 0.$$

Solving for $\dot{h}(s)$ gives

$$\dot{h}(s) = -\dot{g}_1(h(s), s)^{-1} \dot{g}_2(h(s), s).$$

When using a least squares or normal deviance function the derivatives $\dot{g}_1(\theta, s)$ and $\dot{g}_2(\theta, s)$ can be computed easily using numerical differentiation and, with some effort, analytically as well.

A convenient estimator for Γ is the sample covariance matrix of the n vectors

$$d_i = \text{vech}\big((x_i - \bar{x})(x_i - \bar{x})'\big);$$

see, for example, Satorra and Bentler (1990, Formula 2.4).

One trouble with the method of this subsection is that it has not been published. The author suspects, however, it is the method used in CEFA.

Pseudo-value methods

In practice researchers analyze sample covariance matrices S that probably were not generated by a factor analysis model. In fact, this is probably the usual case. These analyses violate the assumptions made by the standard error methods discussed above. One might wonder if it is nevertheless possible to provide standard errors for the estimates $\hat{\Lambda}, \hat{\Phi}$, and $\hat{\Psi}$ produced by these analyses. This can in fact be done using the infinitesimal jackknife (IJK).

Jennrich (2008) showed how to use the IJK to produce standard errors for a covariance structure analysis of nonnormal data. This proceeds as follows.

Let S be a sample covariance matrix for a sample $x_1, \ldots, x_n$ and let

$$\hat{\theta} = h(S),$$

where h is an arbitrary function. For each x_i the IJK produces a pseudo-value

$$\theta_i^+ = dh_S((x_i - \bar{x})(x_i - \bar{x})'),$$

where dh_S is the differential of h at S. The sample covariance matrix of these values is a consistent estimate of the asymptotic covariance matrix for $\hat{\theta}$.

The IJK method has several advantages.

- It is a non-parametric method. One can sample from any distribution.
- The covariance structure $\Sigma(\theta)$ need not be correctly specified. That is, there may be no θ such that $\Sigma(\theta)$ is equal to the covariance matrix for the population sampled. This is important because in practice it almost never is.
- The third and fourth sample moments of the sample values x_t are not required.
- The only real difficulty when using this method is finding the derivatives of D and Σ, which is simple if numerical derivatives are used, but can be a bit messy otherwise.

In the context of EFA, Zhang, Preacher, and Jennrich (2012) have shown how to use the IJK methods of Jennrich (2008) to produce standard errors for an EFA of a sample correlation matrix obtained from a nonnormal sample. This is important because in practice one often analyzes sample correlation matrices rather than sample covariance matrices.

The authors give explicit formulas for ordinary least squares and maximum likelihood extraction and for arbitrary CF rotation. They indicate the modifications required for the analysis of a sample covariance matrix rather than a sample correlation matrix.

Because these IJK methods are nonparametric and do not require data generated by a correctly specified factor analysis model they may provide an attractive option for general purpose factor analysis software such as SAS, SPSS, Stata, CEFA, and Mplus.

Less linear methods

By less linear methods we mean things like the jackknife, the bootstrap, and for Bayesian estimation MCMC methods. Pennell (1972) and Clarkson (1979) have used the jackknife to produce standard errors for rotated loadings. The basic jackknife uses n jackknife values each of which requires carrying out a factor analysis extraction and rotation. Doing this n times makes this an expensive procedure. Jackknifing by groups helps to reduce this expense, but the main problem with using the jackknife concerns alignment. In EFA the rotated loading matrix Λ is determined only up to column permutation and column sign change. To make the jackknife work the generated loading matrices must be aligned. Doing this in an automated way that is good enough for jackknifing is pretty much an unsolved problem. Alignment failures can have devastating effects on jackknife standard error estimates.

There is also considerable expense when using bootstrap methods, and again alignment is the main problem. MCMC methods face these problems as well, and require a parametric form for the sampling distribution of x. At present the only feasible estimates for standard errors of rotated loadings seem to be linearization methods like those in the previous subsections.

Some Examples Using Real Data

Chen, West, and Sousa (2006) used a 17-variable quality of life data set to compare two methods of analysis. The covariance matrix for their investigation is given in their paper and will be used here.

Example 1: Comparing orthogonal and oblique rotation

Using the covariance matrix of Chen et al., maximum likelihood EFA was used to extract initial loadings A and unique variances $\hat{\Psi}$. The initial loadings are given on the left-hand side of Table 10.4. To simplify comparisons the loadings have been rounded to two decimal places and the decimal points removed. These loadings are canonical loadings, which means $A'\hat{\Psi}^{-1}A$ is diagonal. They are the loadings initially produced by standard maximum likelihood EFA programs. It is these loadings that are rotated to produce various forms of rotated loadings.

Many EFA programs do not display the initial loadings they produce. We obtained these by requesting "no rotation." To compare orthogonal and oblique rotation we have used the quartimin criterion because it can be used for either orthogonal or oblique rotation. The orthogonal and oblique quartimin rotations of A are also given in Table 10.4. Clearly the oblique rotation is much closer to simple structure than the orthogonal rotation. This is also displayed by the SAL plots given in Figure 10.6. Clearly the oblique loadings are much closer to simple structure than the orthogonal loadings. One expects this in general, because there are many more oblique rotations of A than orthogonal rotations.

Example 2: Comparing quartimax and varimax rotation

The earliest analytic rotations were orthogonal and based on the quartimax criterion. Varimax rotation was introduced to reduce the tendency of quartimax to weight too heavily on the first factor.

Table 10.5 contains quartimax and varimax rotations of the initial loading matrix A from the previous subsection.

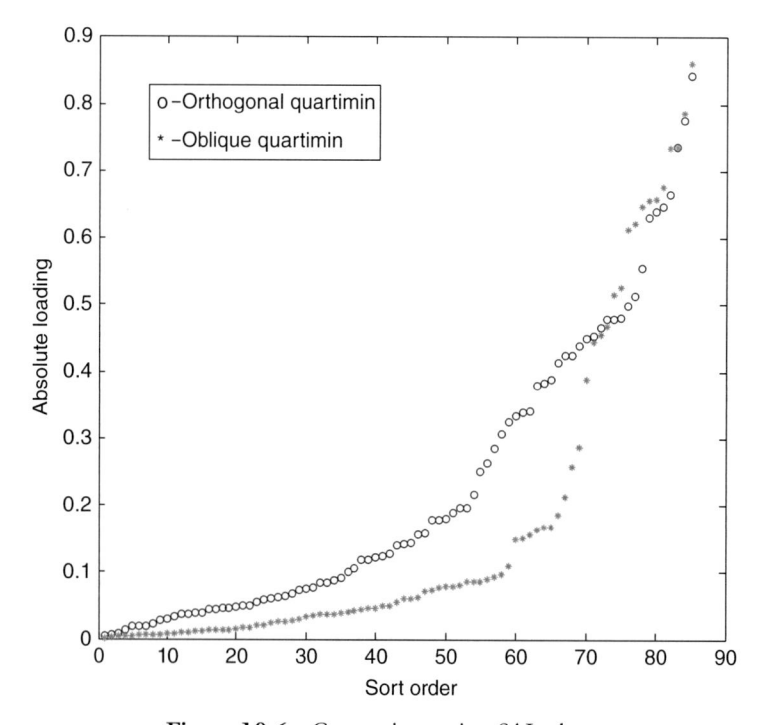

Figure 10.6 Comparison using SAL plots.

Table 10.5 Example 2 rotations

Quartimax					Varimax				
29	63	4	9	−5	17	65	12	18	−0
26	45	8	0	−2	17	47	15	9	3
33	66	4	−4	5	21	69	13	8	11
22	65	2	−3	2	12	66	9	5	6
33	64	4	6	1	21	66	13	17	6
38	18	48	6	3	20	18	55	17	9
42	13	39	5	1	27	14	47	16	8
41	20	48	4	−6	25	21	56	15	1
44	14	43	3	20	25	15	50	16	26
48	16	7	12	38	31	18	16	27	44
56	18	9	31	16	38	20	19	45	21
45	12	18	12	34	28	13	25	26	40
50	34	6	19	7	35	36	17	33	13
51	25	14	47	7	30	25	23	59	10
84	9	−10	−4	−12	82	18	10	17	2
74	11	9	−5	−2	66	17	25	14	11
78	6	−5	−14	−1	75	14	14	6	13

Varimax does seem to load the first factor more lightly and spread the loadings across factors more than quartimax does, which is as expected. The differences in this example, however, are not great, and neither is close to simple structure.

Quartimax rotation is the same as orthogonal quartimin rotation (Harman, 1976, p. 284). Thus the orthogonal quartimin rotation in Table 10.4 is the same as the quartimax rotation in Table 10.5.

Example 3: Exploratory bifactor rotation

Chen et al. used their data to compare confirmatory bifactor and two-stage factor analysis models for their quality of life data.

Building a bifactor model is a bit of a project. Chen et al. used a standard bifactor model for quality of life data based on a number of earlier studies and goodness of fit testing to help identify structural zeros. We will use exploratory bifactor analysis to see what bifactor model their data might suggest without any prior knowledge about the quality of life data.

An exploratory bifactor analysis of their data using the biquartimin criterion defined in Theorem 10.1 gave the loading matrix in Table 10.6. One can use Table 10.6 to suggest a bifactor model by setting all loadings with absolute value less than 0.02 equal to zero. This gives the loading matrix in Table 10.7.

The bifactor model suggested by Table 10.7 agrees exactly with Chen et al.'s standard model except for the three loadings on the third factor denoted by an "x." These were free loadings in Chen et al.'s model. In Chen et al.'s confirmatory analysis the loading estimates in these three positions were "insignificant." This motivated Chen et al. to suggest that the third group factor might be absorbed by the general factor and dropped. A less extreme alternative suggested by Table 10.7 would be to retain the third group factor, but add structural zeros in the positions containing an x. In any event, exploratory bifactor analysis has effortlessly discovered a bifactor model that is at least close to that found

Table 10.6 Exploratory bifactor rotation loading matrix.

0.46	0.52	0.02	0.09	0.00
0.38	0.36	0.05	0.00	0.02
0.51	0.53	−0.02	−0.06	0.00
0.41	0.55	−0.01	−0.05	−0.03
0.51	0.51	−0.00	0.04	0.01
0.53	−0.01	0.35	−0.01	−0.07
0.51	−0.04	0.29	0.00	0.02
0.53	0.03	0.41	0.00	0.01
0.60	−0.09	0.22	−0.09	−0.08
0.61	−0.08	−0.19	−0.03	−0.04
0.64	−0.03	−0.07	0.23	0.06
0.60	−0.12	−0.08	−0.03	−0.07
0.59	0.17	−0.03	0.15	0.08
0.64	0.04	0.00	0.39	−0.01
0.62	0.02	−0.02	0.06	0.60
0.63	−0.02	0.07	−0.02	0.39
0.60	−0.04	−0.02	−0.09	0.51

Table 10.7 Adjusted exploratory bifactor rotation loading matrix.

0.46	0.52	0	0	0
0.38	0.36	0	0	0
0.51	0.53	0	0	0
0.41	0.55	0	0	0
0.51	0.51	0	0	0
0.53	0	0.35	0	0
0.51	0	0.29	0	0
0.53	0	0.41	0	0
0.60	0	0.22	0	0
0.61	0	0	x	0
0.64	0	0	0.23	0
0.60	0	0	x	0
0.59	0	0	x	0
0.64	0	0	0.39	0
0.62	0	0	0	0.60
0.63	0	0	0	0.39
0.60	0	0	0	0.51

by Chen et al., and this suggests that exploratory bifactor analysis, which is a form of EFA, may be a valuable tool for constructing confirmatory bifactor models.

Discussion

We have given a primarily historical overview of rotation methods in EFA. This included a discussion of rotation, rotation criteria, rotation algorithms, choosing a rotation method, producing standard errors for rotated loadings, and some real data applications.

The problem of extracting initial loadings is fairly well resolved. Least squares and maximum likelihood extraction seem to work well.

We seem to have done very well on the algorithm problem. In a sense the problem is solved. The very general and simple pairwise line search algorithm of Browne and Cudeck and the faster gradient projection algorithm of Jennrich allow one to optimize almost any rotationcriterion. There is always room for improvement, but the need at present is not pressing.

The problem of assigning standard errors to factor loading estimates is also fairly well resolved using the linearization methods discussed, and in particular the infinitesimal jackknife method.

Choosing a good rotation method is a difficult problem. EFA is an exploratory method that suggests a relation between observed variables and unobserved factors. But different rotation methods suggest different relations. A rotation method that makes sense in one application may not be satisfactory in another. It is ultimately the user who must decide which rotation, if any, is best in a particular application.

For those seeking loading matrices with simple structure, quartimin and geomin seem to work well when it is possible to have such rotations.

When it is not possible to obtain rotations with simple structure, or structures with greater complexities are desired, little progress has been made to recommend a specific choice. The best we have at present are a few examples for which desirable rotation methods have been identified, for example geomin on Thurstone's box problem. In the complex case the problem of comparing rotation methods or choosing a good rotation method appears to be stalled. Some new ideas are needed.

We have recommended the use of numerical derivatives in several places. Psychometricians and more generally statisticians seem to fear numerical derivatives. What they should fear are the consequences of failing to try new methods because the derivatives required are too complex. The work described here suggests that numerical derivatives can produce accurate results and can greatly simplify what would otherwise be very complicated methods.

References

Anderson, T. W. & Rubin, H. (1956). Statistical inference in factor analysis. *Proc. Third Berkeley Symp. Math. Statist. Probability*, 5, 111–150.

Archer, C. O. & Jennrich, R. I. (1973). Standard errors for rotated factor loadings. *Psychometrika*, 38, 581–592.

Bentler, P. M. (1977). Factor simplicity index and transformations. *Psychometrika*, 42, 277–295.

Browne, M. W. (1984). Asymptotically distribution-free methods for the analysis of covariance structures. *British Journal of Mathematical and Statistical Psychology*, 37, 62–83.

Browne, M. W. (2001). An overview of analytic rotation in exploratory factor analysis. *Multivariate Behavioral Research*, 36, 111–150.

Browne, M. W., Cudeck, R., Tateneni, K. & Mels, G. (2002). CEFA: Comprehensive Exploratory Factor Analysis, Version 1.10 [Computer software and manual]. Retrieved from http://quantrm2.psy.ohio-state.edu/browne/

Carroll, J. B. (1953). An analytical solution for approximating simple structure in factor analysis. *Psychometrika*, 18, 23–28.

Carroll, J. B. (1960). IBM 704 program for generalized analytic rotation solution in factor analysis. Harvard University, unpublished.

Chen F. F., West S. G. & Sousa K. H. (2006). A comparison of bifactor and second-order models of the quality of life. *Multivariate Behavioral Research, 41*, 189–225.

Clarkson, D. B. (1979). Estimating the standard errors of rotated factor loadings by jackknifing. *Psychometrika, 44*, 297–314.

Crawford, C. B. & Ferguson, G. A. (1970). A general rotation criterion and its use in orthogonal rotation. *Psychometrika, 35*, 321–332.

Cudeck, R. & O'Dell, L. L. (1994). Application of standard error estimates in unrestricted factor analysis: Significance tests for factor loadings and correlations. *Psychological Bulletin, 115*, 475–487.

Cureton, E. E. & Mulaik, S. A. (1975). The weighted varimax rotation and the promax rotation. *Psychometrika, 40*, 183–195.

Girshick, M. A. (1939). On the sampling theory of roots of determinantal equations. *Annals of Mathematical Statistics, 10*, 203–224.

Harman, H. H. (1976). *Modern factor analysis* (3rd ed.). Chicago, IL: University of Chicago Press.

Jennrich, R. I. (1973). Standard errors for obliquely rotated factor loadings. *Psychometrika, 38*, 593–604.

Jennrich, R. I. (1974). Simplified formulae for standard errors in maximum likelihood factor analysis. *British Journal of Mathematical and Statistical Psychology, 27*, 122–131.

Jennrich, R. I. (2002). A simple general procedure for oblique rotation. *Psychometrika, 66*, 289–306.

Jennrich, R. I. (2004). Derivative free gradient projection algorithms for rotation. *Psychometrika, 69*, 475–480.

Jennrich, R. I. (2008). Nonparametric estimation of standard errors in covariance analysis using the infinitesimal jackknife. *Psychometrika, 73*, 579–594.

Jennrich, R. I. & Bentler, P. M. (2011). Exploratory bifactor analysis. *Psychometrika, 76*, 537–549.

Jennrich, R. I. & Sampson, P. F. (1966). Rotation for simple loadings. *Psychometrika, 31*, 313–323.

Jennrich, R. I. & Thayer, D. T. (1973). A note on Lawley's formulas for standard errors in maximum likelihood factor analysis. *Psychometrika, 38*, 571–580.

Jöreskog, K. G. (1969). A general approach to confirmatory maximum likelihood factor analysis. *Psychometrika, 34*, 183–202.

Lawley, D. N. (1967). Some new results on maximum likelihood factor analysis. *Proceedings of the Royal Society of Edinburgh, A67*, 256–264.

Lawley, D. N. & Maxwell, A. E. (1971). *Factor analysis as a statistical method*. New York, NY: Elsevier.

McCammon, R. B. (1966). Principal component analysis and its application in large-scale correlation studies. *Journal of Geology, 74*, 721–733.

McKeon, J. J. (1968). *Rotation for maximum association between factors and tests*. Unpublished manuscript, Biometric Laboratory, George Washington University.

Pennell, R. (1972). Routinely computable confidence intervals for factor loadings using the "jackknife." *British Journal of Mathematical and Statistical Psychology, 25*, 107–114.

Satorra, A. & Bentler, P. M. (1990). Model conditions for asymptotic robustness in the analysis of linear relations. *Computational Statistics and Data Analysis, 10*, 235–249.

Schmitt, T. A. & Sass, D. A. (2011). Rotation criteria and hypothesis testing for exploratory factor analysis: Implications for factor pattern loadings and interfactor correlations. *Educational and Psychological Measurement, 71910*, 95–113.

Silvey, D. S. (1971). *Statistical inference*. Baltimore, MD: Penguin Books.

Thurstone, L. L. (1935) *Vectors of the mind*. Chicago, IL: University of Chicago Press.

Thurstone, L. L. (1947) *Multiple factor analysis*. Chicago, IL: University of Chicago Press.

Wexler, N. (1968). *An evaluation of an asymptotic formula for factor loading variance by random methods*. Unpublished doctoral dissertation. Rutgers University.

Yates, A. (1987). *Multivariate exploratory data analysis: A perspective on exploratory factor analysis*. Albany, NY: State University of New York Press.

Zhang, G., Preacher, K. J. & Jennrich, R. I. (2012). The infinitesimal jackknife with exploratory factor analysis. *Psychometrika, 77*, 634–648.

11

The Number of Factors Problem

Marieke E. Timmerman, Urbano Lorenzo-Seva, and Eva Ceulemans

Introduction

Psychological assessment relies heavily on the use of measurement instruments. Those instruments commonly take the form of questionnaires or scales. Typically, such a scale is designed to measure one or more psychological constructs. In the process of scale evaluation, a common step is to collect item responses in a sample of respondents, and model them using factor analysis or item response analysis. The key idea in both modelling approaches is that the model captures the dimensional structure underlying the observed item scores, and that the dimensional structure can be meaningfully interpreted in terms of the psychological constructs to be measured. The dimensions are generally denoted as factors in factor analysis, and as latent traits in item response analysis. Both approaches assume that individuals' scores on the factors (or the latent traits in item response analysis) are due to individuals' scores on the corresponding latent variables.

The dimensional structure involves two aspects, namely the number of dimensions needed to adequately model the item responses, and the mathematical relationship between the individual position on the dimension(s) and the item scores. The form of the mathematical relationship depends on the model considered. For example, the factor model specifies a linear relationship. Furthermore, it is important to note that the number of dimensions needed for a given set of item responses may depend on the specific model considered, as will become clear next.

To assess the dimensional structure underlying a set of item responses, one could proceed in an exploratory or a confirmatory way. In both ways, the target model to consider, like a common factor model, is typically selected beforehand. The exploratory approach is taken when clear hypotheses about the structure are lacking. Also, in the presence of a hypothesized structure, the exploratory approach is sometimes used as a strong test of the hypothesized structure. However, this interpretation warrants some caution, because the results of an exploratory analysis fully depend on the criterion underlying the analysis. If this criterion does not match the hypothesized structure, the latter will not be retrieved, regardless whether it is present or not in the data. Taking

---

The Wiley Handbook of Psychometric Testing: A Multidisciplinary Reference on Survey, Scale and Test Development, First Edition. Edited by Paul Irwing, Tom Booth, and David J. Hughes.
© 2018 John Wiley & Sons Ltd. Published 2020 by John Wiley & Sons Ltd.

the confirmatory approach boils down to testing a specific model, in which each item is only associated with a particular (and often a single) dimension.

The exploratory approach typically involves a multiple step procedure, in which both formal criteria and substantive considerations play a role. First, using some formal criterion, one obtains an indication of the dimensionality; that is, the number of dimensions needed. Some criteria require a series of target models with increasing dimensionality to be fitted, whereas others are based on measures derived from the observed data. Second, the target model with the indicated dimensionality is fitted to the data. Obviously, when the selected model is among the fitted target models in the first step, one can select it from the fitted models. Third, the interpretability of the fitted model is judged. In case of difficulties in interpretation, it is common to consider alternative models with a different number of dimensions as well.

In this chapter, we focus on formal criteria to assess the dimensionality for exploratory factor modelling with the aim to facilitate the selection of a proper criterion in empirical practice. We first introduce the different foundations that underlie the various criteria. Then, we elaborate on the meaning of an indicated dimensionality. Subsequently, we provide an overview of currently available formal criteria, which we selected on the basis of their popularity in empirical practice and/ or proven effectiveness. Further, we provide guidance in selecting a dimensionality assessment method in empirical practice. We illustrate the use of the methods with an empirical example.

Categorizing Criteria to Indicate the Number of Factors

To understand the properties of the criteria to indicate the number of factors, and hence to make a well-founded choice in empirical practice, it is useful to categorize the criteria. A first categorization is that the criteria to indicate the number of factors are associated with either principal component analysis (PCA), common factor analysis (CFA), or CFA for ordinal variables (CFA-ord) (see e.g., Mislevy, 1986). In case of PCA, it would be more appropriate to use the term **component** rather than **factor**, but for ease of presentation, we use the term "factor" in the context of PCA as well. PCA and CFA are suitable for modelling continuous item responses, and CFA-ord for polytomous, ordered item responses.

From a theoretical point of view, it is best to have a match between the type of criterion to assess the number of factors and the specific model subsequently used to fit the data. However, in empirical practice, one often finds a discrepancy; most often when the number of common factors (for a CFA or CFA-ord) is being indicated using a PCA-based criterion. This practice is not necessarily problematic, because the number of factors indicated by a nonmatching method often equals that of a matching method. The reason for the equality in dimensionality suggested is that performing PCA, CFA, and CFA-ord on the same empirical data set can yield similar results, especially with respect to the statistic (e.g., fit value) used in the number of factors criterion. However, differences in the indicated number of factors may occur. They are to be expected particularly when the PCA, CFA, and CFA-ord would reveal substantially different results. This may occur when a PCA- or CFA-based method rather than a CFA-ord based method is applied to ordinal items of which (1) the number of categories is five or smaller (e.g., Dolan, 1994), (2) the univariate distributions of items are asymmetric or with excess of kurtosis (Muthén & Kaplan, 1985, 1992), or (3) when a PCA-based method is used to indicate the number of common factors when the loadings are low (and hence the unique variances high) (e.g., Widaman, 1993) and there are few variables per factor (e.g., Velicer & Jackson, 1990).

A second categorization is according to the definition underlying the criterion. We distinguish statistical test and major factors criteria. Statistical test criteria are based on a strict definition of dimensionality, as the minimum number of latent variables needed to completely describe the scores in a population (Zhang & Stout, 1999). Though this definition is well-founded from a mathematical point of view, a strict adherence to this definition appears of limited use in empirical practice.

Indeed, when applied to empirical data, a statistical test criterion may yield as many latent variables as there are items in the scale. The reason is that such criteria presume the model considered to hold exactly at the population level, implying that no model error is involved (see MacCallum & Tucker, 1991). This contrasts to the view that a model is an approximation to reality (Browne & Cudeck, 1992), a view that appears to be generally accepted nowadays.

In the current context, the absence of model error would imply that the relationship between the latent variables and the items (e.g., linear in the case of a CFA) holds exactly. Even if this would be the case, one would expect the need for many latent variables. The reason is that items within a scale typically show diversity in item content. This diversity can only be captured fully by a model with a large dimensionality. To solve for this, it might seem attractive to limit the diversity in item content. However, the price to be paid is that it results in a measure of conceptually narrow constructs (Cattell & Tsujioka, 1964). This has led to the view that any scale with a reasonable degree of substantive breadth has item diversity (Reise, Waller, & Comrey, 2000). Typically, all items in such a scale share a single (or a few) major dimension(s), whereas small subsets of items share minor parts that are independent of the remaining observed items. Within a factor analysis, the associated major factors are thought to account for a large part, and the minor factors for a small part of the observed variance. This property enables major factors to be identified, and it forms the basis of major factor based criteria.

In empirical practice, statistical test criteria are useful to identify the maximal number of factor to use. Depending on the research aims and the data characteristics, it can be appropriate to consider the major factors only, or the major and a few minor factors. In the latter case, one would end up with a number of factors that are in between the numbers of major and total factors.

The Meaning of Dimensionality

Being the number of dimensions needed to adequately model the item responses, the dimensionality defines the number of axes that span the space in which the subjects are projected. In this low-dimensional space, each subject and each item in the data set can be depicted. Their specific positions are estimated in the analysis. In an exploratory analysis, the low-dimensional space is typically estimated such that the variability in the subject positions in the low-dimensional space is as large as possible. This implies that the dimensionality for a given data set crucially depends on both the subjects and the items involved (see Reckase, 2009). That is, it depends on the number of dimensions on which the subjects differ, and on the number of dimensions to which the items are sensitive. Typically, the subjects are considered to be a sample from a population. This leads to the important notion that the dimensionality may be population dependent. Furthermore, to detect the dimensions on which the subjects differ, the items included should be sensitive to those dimensions, whereas the sensitivity to the various dimensions should vary across items (Reckase, 2009). Ideally, the dimensions have a substantive meaning, and thus can be interpreted from an explanatory-theory perspective.

For example, suppose that we are interested in levels of anxiety and depression, and that we use a set of items to measure the degrees of anxiety and depression in a sample. We can sensibly distinguish between the two if and only if (1) the subjects in our sample show variability in the degrees of both anxiety and depression, (2) the degrees of anxiety and depression are at most moderately related, and (3) the items are sensitive to anxiety and depression to varying degrees. In empirical practice, the latter requirement is usually satisfied when the items are designed with the aim to tap only a single substantive dimension of interest (i.e., anxiety or depression in this example). It is important to recognize that the other two requirements may not be satisfied; for example, because subjects under study differ considerably in their degree of anxiety, but are all similar in their degree of depression, or because in the sample under study the degrees of anxiety and depression are highly correlated. This would typically yield a single indicated major dimension, which does not match the substantive dimensions of depression and anxiety.

To interpret the dimensional structure, one considers the position of the items in the low-dimensional space. Items in a similar direction (i.e., when depicted as vectors from the origin) are interpreted as being sensitive to the same dimension. The position is expressed in a factor model via the loadings. To ease the interpretation, the axes are typically rotated to so-called simple structure, implying that the axes are positioned such that the direction of each item is as close as possible to only a single axis. Kaiser (1974) denoted this as factor simplicity. The meaning of each rotated axis is derived from the common content of the items associated with that axis. Ideally, each rotated axis matches a substantive dimension.

For example, reconsidering the set of items indicative of the degrees of anxiety and depression, the items may be designed so that two subsets of items are relatively pure indicators of anxiety and depression, respectively, and the remaining items indicate a combination of both. Then, it is useful to position the two axes such that their directions coincide as much as possible with the two subsets of "pure" anxiety and depression items. In this approach, the construct of interest is defined beforehand, and the causal relationship between the levels of depression and anxiety of a given person and his/her responses to the items is reasonable to assume.

In some applications, the dimensions are identified on the basis of items solely, rather than that constructs of interest are defined beforehand. Then, one strictly needs an exploratory analysis approach. A typical example is found in personality research, since the theories on distinguishing personality traits have not been settled yet. For example, the Big Five personality traits have found large adherence, but claims for traits beyond the Big Five have been made (De Raad & Bareldts, 2008). In such cases, the dimensional structure of the items under study is the key issue to settle.

Dimensionality Assessment Methods

We now successively review PCA-based methods and CFA-based methods to assess the number of common factors. For each method, we outline the rationale behind the method. We summarize the findings on its quality to indicate the number of (total and/or major) common factors. An overview of the different methods, categorized according to the associated model and the type of criterion, is provided in Table 11.1.

Though from a theoretical point of view PCA-based methods are inappropriate in a CFA context, their fundamental differences are often hidden in empirical practice, because they may yield very similar results. Furthermore, PCA-based methods appear to be even more popular than their CFA-based counterparts to indicate the number of factors in empirical practice (ten Holt, van Duijn, & Boomsma, 2010).

Kaiser Criterion

The Kaiser criterion (Kaiser, 1960) aims at indicating the number of principal components (PCs) of a correlation matrix, and can be viewed as a statistical criterion. The basic idea originates from the observation that if all items involved would be independent, the number of PCs should equal the number of items, and each PC has a variance of one at the population level. Because PCs should reflect dependencies among variables, the Kaiser criterion is to retain PCs with a variance larger than one only. Because the variance of a PC equals the associated eigenvalue of a correlation matrix, the Kaiser criterion is also known as the eigenvalue-over-one criterion.

A fundamental problem with the Kaiser criterion is that it is based on properties at the population level only. It is known that the eigenvalues of the correlation matrix resulting from samples of limited size, even if the variables are uncorrelated in the population, are larger than one (Buja & Eyuboglu, 1992; Horn, 1965). This observation explains the finding in many studies that the Kaiser criterion clearly yields inaccurate indications of the number of PCs and common factors, mostly indicating too many factors (e.g., Revelle & Rocklin, 1979; Zwick & Velicer, 1982, 1986). In spite of its poor performance, the Kaiser criterion appears very popular in empirical practice (Costello &

Table 11.1 Overview of the dimensionality assessment methods discussed, categorized according to the associated model and the type of criterion; q is the true number of common factors.

	Model associated with criterion	
	PCA	CFA/CFA-ord
Major factor criterion	Scree test	PA-MRFA and variants (for $q > 1$)
	Horn's PA (for $q > 1$)	Goodness-of-fit measures (as RMSEA, CFI)
		Hull
Statistical criterion	Kaiser criterion	PA-MRFA and variants (for $q = 1$)
	MAP	LRT: Chi-square test
	Horn's PA (for $q = 1$)	LRT: Chi-square difference test

Osborne, 2005), probably simply because it is the default criterion to select the number of factors in popular statistical packages.

Scree test

The scree test (Cattell, 1966) involves the visual inspection of a so-called scree-plot. The scree-plot is a plot of the successive eigenvalues ($m = 1,\ldots,n$, with n the number of items) of the observed correlation or covariance matrix versus the number of the associated eigenvalue. Note that the successive eigenvalues are linearly related to the percentage of explained variance of the successive PCs. Cattell proposed to locate an "elbow," which is the point beyond which the scree-plot follows an approximately straight line, and take the first point on that line as the indicated number of factors. In practice, researchers often take the number of factors before the elbow. This makes sense because the PC associated with the elbow itself already explains relatively little variance. Because the scree test is based on variances explained of PCs, it is PCA-based method, though Cattell explicitly aimed at finding the number of common factors. Furthermore, the scree test optimally balances the fit and number of parameters involved, and can therefore viewed as a major factor criterion.

The scree test has been criticized for its subjectivity. One may expect this to be problematic when a clear elbow is missing in the scree-plot. This may particularly occur when the scree-plot shows a gradual slope, or when multiple elbows can be indicated (Jolliffe, 2002). Based on simulated data, the scree test has been found to be reasonably accurate to indicate the number of major factors. Its performance deteriorated with increasing unique variances, making the method less suitable for items with large unique variances (Zwick & Velicer, 1986).

Minimum Average Partial (MAP)

Based on partial correlations, the MAP (Velicer, 1976) is a statistical criterion for indicating the number of PCs. For a sequence of numbers of PCs, $m = 1,\ldots,n$ (with n the number of items), the partial correlations first decrease, and then increase. The partial correlation for a solution with m PCs is computed as the average squared partial correlations between all pairs of items involved, with each of m components partialled out. The MAP indicates the number of components associated with the minimum partial correlation.

Though MAP was proposed in a PC context, it is noteworthy that it employs the concept of common factors. This is so because the solution with the minimum partial correlations is associated with a residual matrix that closely resembles an identity matrix, and for which at least two variables load high on each component involved.

MAP has been examined in comparative simulation studies based on a common factor model (CFM) including both major and minor factors (Tucker, Koopman, & Linn, 1969). MAP performances in indicating the number of major factors deteriorated when the unique variances increased, with no clear tendency to over- or underindicate the number of factors (Lorenzo-Seva, Timmerman, & Kiers, 2011; Zwick & Velicer, 1986). Because MAP performed poorly in empirically relevant conditions (i.e., certain levels of unique variances), Lorenzo-Seva et al. (2011) discourage the use of MAP to indicate the number of common factors.

Horn's Parallel Analysis (Horn's PA)

In its original form, PA (Horn, 1965) is a method to indicate the number of PCs. It is based on the same principle as the Kaiser criterion, with PA also taking sampling fluctuations into account. The central idea that components to retain must be associated with eigenvalues larger than the eigenvalues of components derived from random data, where the random data involve the same sample size as the sample data.

The procedure followed in Horn's PA can be summarized as follows. First, one obtains the sampling distributions of the random eigenvalues; these are the sampling distributions of the successive eigenvalues ($m = 1,...,n$, with n the number of items) of sample correlation matrices for independent items. Second, one obtains the empirical eigenvalues, which are the eigenvalues of the correlation matrix of the observed data. Third, one successively compares each empirical eigenvalue to the sampling distribution of the random eigenvalues at the same position (i.e., the first empirical eigenvalue is compared to the distribution of the first random eigenvalue, the second empirical eigenvalue to the distribution of the second random eigenvalue, etc.). PA indicates to retain all components of which the empirical eigenvalues are larger than a given threshold in the distribution of random eigenvalues. Horn (1965) proposed using the average as the threshold. Because this threshold appeared to yield a tendency to overestimate the dimensionality, the use of a more stringent threshold was advocated, like the 95% quantile (Buja & Eyuboglu, 1992; Glorfeld, 1995). Nowadays, the 95% threshold appears to be most popular.

Though Horn's PA has been interpreted as an inferential method (i.e., a method to assess the significance of each dimension), this interpretation is appropriate only for the first eigenvalue (Buja & Eyuboglu, 1992). The reason is that one faces inherent dependencies between successive eigenvalues, which results in a loss of statistical power for increasing number of components. The size of the power loss is data dependent and cannot be generally predicted. Because successive eigenvalues of a correlation matrix are directly related to the explained variance of successive PCs, the preceding implies that Horn's PA is a statistical method when it comes to indicating the first principal component. For the remaining successive PCs, Horn's PA suffers from loss of statistical power, and can be expected to function as a major factor criterion.

Horn's PA has been extensively studied, on the basis of empirical data (Cota, Longman, Holden, & Fekken, 1993; Hubbard & Allen, 1987) and simulated data (Glorfeld, 1995; Peres-Neto, Jackson, & Somers, 2005; Turner, 1998; Velicer, Eaton, & Fava, 2000; Zwick & Velicer, 1986). The performance of Horn's PA appeared to be generally good, resulting in strong recommendations for PA in empirical practice (Fabrigar, Wegener, MacCallum, & Strahan, 1999; Hayton, Allen, & Scarpello, 2004; Thompson, 2004).

PA-MRFA and other variants, for common factors, and for ordinal items

Noting that Horn's PA is not well-founded to assess the number of common factors (CFs), Humphreys and Ilgen (1969) proposed a variant of Horn's PA to assess the number of CFs. In this procedure, the eigenvalues are obtained from the reduced correlation matrix, with estimates of the communalities on its diagonal. This approach suffers from fundamental problems (Buja & Eyuboglu, 1992; Steger, 2006), among which the fact that the empirical eigenvalue and the random eigenvalues lack a common interpretation (e.g., in terms of explained variances, as in Horn's PA), and therefore cannot be sensibly compared (Timmerman & Lorenzo-Seva, 2011). A better alternative to indicate the number of CFs is found in PA-MRFA (Timmerman & Lorenzo-Seva, 2011), in which the proportions of explained common variance of empirical and random data are compared, rather than the eigenvalues.

Typically, PA is performed on Pearson correlation matrices, making the approach suitable for modelling continuous item responses. In case of polytomous, ordered item responses, it has been proposed to use polychoric correlations (e.g., Olsson, 1979) as a basis for PA (Cho, Li, & Bandalos, 2009; Weng & Cheng, 2005).

The different PA variants have been compared in simulation studies. On the basis of those results, for polytomous, ordered item responses the use of polychoric correlations rather than Pearson correlations seems indicated (Timmerman & Lorenzo-Seva, 2011). Furthermore, PA-MRFA with 95% threshold is the preferred variant for indicating the number of major CFs (Timmerman & Lorenzo-Seva, 2011), with Horn's PA with 95% threshold as a second best, with still acceptable performance. In empirical practice, one may encounter convergence problems for the polychoric correlations. Then, one could resort to Pearson correlations, where PA-MRFA performed best with mean threshold (Timmerman & Lorenzo-Seva, 2011).

Model Selection Methods in SEM: CFM as a Special Case of SEM

The issue of the number of CFs to retain can be viewed as a model selection problem. That is, one aims at selecting the most appropriate model from a series of CFMs, with different numbers of factors. By noting that an exploratory CFM is a special case of a structural equation model, the methods used for model selection in structural equation modelling (SEM) can be readily applied in selecting the number of CFs (Fabrigar et al., 1999). In the course of years, statistical tests and a vast number of goodness-fit-measures have been proposed. In selecting the number of CFs, the general procedure is to fit a sequence of CFMs, with zero up to some maximal number. For each model, one performs the statistical test, or computes the selected goodness-of-fit measure(s), and applies, implicitly or explicitly, a certain criterion involving those measures to indicate the number of factors. To understand why the tests and goodness-of-fit criteria may indicate different number of factors, it is essential to understand the theoretical underpinnings of the statistical tests and the goodness-of-fit measures.

The statistical tests and most goodness-of-fit measures considered in SEM are based on the chi-square measure. The chi-square measure can be obtained using various estimation methods, of which their suitability depends on the nature of the data at hand. For multivariate normally distributed items, maximum likelihood (ML) estimation is appropriate. For continuous items that are not multivariate normally distributed, robust ML (Yuan & Bentler, 2000), which adjusts standard errors and fit indices, is indicated. For ordered polytomous items, different estimation methods, like unweighted least squares (ULS), weighted least squares (WLS) (Browne, 1984) and robust WLS (Muthén, du Toit, & Spisic, 1997), are available (see Wirth & Edwards, 2007, for a nice review). Though from a theoretical point of view the use of those variants is justified only for the type of items indicated, the story is more shaded in empirical practice. First, the consequences of taking an "inappropriate" estimation method depend on the severity and type of violation and on the parameter of interest. For example, ML estimates, which are suitable for multivariate normally distributed items, appeared to yield reasonable estimates for ordered polytomous items with five or more categories (Dolan, 1994). Second, the applicability of estimation methods depends on the sample size available. WLS requires extremely large sample sizes, whereas ULS and robust WLS (Muthén et al., 1997) work better in a smaller sample (say, minimally 250 (e.g., Beauducel & Herzberg, 2006)). Comparative simulation studies show ULS and robust WLS performing similarly (Yang-Wallentin, Joreskog, & Luo, 2010).

The statistical tests and the many available goodness-of-fit measures share the purpose of expressing the degree to which the model at hand approximates the population correlation or covariance matrix of the items concerned. They differ in their foundations and the specific aspects of lack of model fit stressed. We limit our discussion on goodness-of-fit measures to the currently popular variants. For a review of the goodness-of-fit measures in SEM, we refer to Hu and Bentler (1999) and Hooper, Coughlan, and Mullen (2008). Now, we will specifically discuss various approaches used in SEM for model selection, and examine their usefulness in indicating the number of CFs. We start with statistical tests, followed by fit measures.

Likelihood ratio tests: the chi-square test and the chi-square difference test

Likelihood ratio tests (LRTs) are statistical tests. Those tests involve the population covariance matrix Σ (i.e., the covariance matrix in the population from which the sample at hand has been randomly drawn) and the model implied covariance matrix Σ_m (i.e., here, the covariance matrix associated with the CFM with at most m CFs). To assess the number of factors, two LRT tests (see e.g., Hayashi, Bentler, & Yuan, 2007) have been put forward. Both tests have the null-hypothesis that the population covariance matrix $\Sigma = \Sigma_m$. The chi-square test tests against the saturated model, that is, has the alternative hypothesis that Σ is any positive definite matrix. The chi-square difference test tests against the model with at least $m + 1$ factors, that is, has the alternative hypothesis that $\Sigma = \Sigma_{m+1}$. The chi-square test statistic involved is based on the discrepancy between Σ_m and the observed sample covariance matrix. For both LRTs, rejecting the null-hypothesis for a model with m factors indicates that more than m factors are needed.

A fundamental problem with the LRTs is that they are only appropriate for applying to CFMs with m factors if the number of factors in the population does not exceed m. The reason is that the chi-square statistic of a model with more than the number of population factors no longer follows a chi-square distribution, with as a consequence a tendency to indicate too many factors (Hayashi et al., 2007). Therefore, the chi-square difference test to test for the number of factors in the population appears inappropriate, because it involves computing the chi-square statistics for models with both m and $m + 1$ factors. This problem does not hold for the chi-square test itself, because it only uses the chi-square statistic of the model with m factors.

To assess the number of CFs, one may apply a stepwise forward procedure. That is, one starts with a one-factor model and applies the chi-square test. If this test is rejected, one fits a two-factor model, and uses the chi-square test. If this test is rejected, one fits a three-factor model. One proceeds until the m-factor model is not rejected, and selects the model with m factors.

This stepwise forward procedure implies that one uses a significance test to confirm a null-hypothesis. Therefore, any nonreject should be considered with caution, since a nonreject can be due to either a true null-hypothesis or a lack of power to detect differences. Obviously, the latter is more likely to occur in small sample sizes. Thus, in empirical practice, when considering samples from the same population, one would expect the number of indicated factors to decrease with decreasing sample sizes. This dependency on the sample size is indeed a major problem of the use of LRT in empirical practice.

A further objection that has been raised with respect to LRTs (e.g., Bentler & Bonett, 1980) is that in large sample sizes even tiny deviations from the null-hypothesis are likely to result in a reject. "Tiny deviations" can occur for many different reasons, including distributional misspecification (e.g., assuming a normal distribution of the items scores in case of ordered polytomous items) and the presence of minor factors (e.g., factors on which the individuals show little variance). From a theoretical point of view, the sensitivity of the LRT to misspecifications is appropriate. In fact, it is exactly what would be expected from a method founded on the strict definition of dimensionality. From an empirical point of view, some authors considered the behavior of the LRT to be problematic. They argued that the LRT is also sensitive to model misspecifications that pertain to characteristics that are trivial from an explanatory-theory perspective (Barrett, 2007), that is, characteristics that do not match any substantive dimension. To alleviate the problems with the LRT in evaluating models, various goodness-of-fit measures were developed. The use of those measures to indicate the dimensionality can be viewed as a major factor criterion.

Goodness-of-fit measures

The Root Mean Square Error of Approximation (RMSEA) (Steiger, 1990) appears among the most popular goodness-of-fit measures used in SEM. The RMSEA expresses the discrepancy between the population covariance matrix Σ and the model implied covariance matrix Σ_m per degree of freedom of the model. Thus, the RMSEA expresses the fit of the model relative to its complexity, implying that simpler models are favored over more complex models. Furthermore, the RMSEA is a property defined at the population level.

An RMSEA value of zero indicates a perfect model fit at the population level. Recognizing that any model is an approximation to reality (Browne & Cudeck, 1992), models with an RMSEA larger than zero can be acceptable. RMSEA values smaller than .05 (Browne & Cudeck, 1992) or .06 (Hu & Bentler, 1999) are considered to indicate close fit, and values in the range of .05 to .08 fair fit (e.g., MacCallum, Browne, & Sugawara, 1996). By noting that in empirical practice the RMSEA is estimated on the basis of sample data, and hence is influenced by sampling fluctuations, it is useful to consider a (say, 95%-) confidence interval for the RMSEA (Browne & Cudeck, 1992), rather than its point estimate.

Another popular fit index is the Standardized Root Mean square Residual (SRMR), which summarizes the differences between the sample covariances and the model implied covariances. Unlike the RMSEA, model complexity does not play a role in the SRMR. Furthermore, the SRMR only expresses the fit to the current sample data (rather than to the population, as the RMSEA). An SRMR value of zero indicates perfect fit. SRMR values of .05 (Sivo, Fan, Witta, & Willse, 2006) or .08 (Hu & Bentler, 1999) are recommended as cut-off values for model selection.

The comparative fit index (CFI) is a measure of improvement of fit, where the model at hand is compared to a nested baseline model. Typically, one uses as a baseline model a model specifying completely uncorrelated items. CFI values are in the range from 0 to 1, with 1 indicating a perfect fit. A value > .95 is considered to indicate good fit (Hu & Bentler, 1999).

Model selection on the basis of goodness-of-fit criteria typically takes place by selecting those models with associated goodness-of-fit criteria below the recommended cut-off values, which were determined on the basis of extensive simulation studies in a SEM context. However, a strict adherence to cut-off values appears inappropriate. On the one hand, strictly applying the cut-off values may yield the selection of unacceptably misspecified models, depending on the specific characteristics of the data (e.g., Marsh, Hau, & Wen, 2004). This is so because also small degrees of misspecification may pertain to aspects that are important from an explanatory-theory perspective, that is, match a substantive dimension. On the other hand, strictly applying the cut-off values may also result in including minor factors, which are unimportant from an explanatory-theory perspective.

As an alternative to strict cut-off values, one may apply the goodness-of-fit values as relative measures (Yuan, 2005). In the exploratory common factor context, this would imply considering goodness-of-fit measures for a series of CFMs with sequentially increasing numbers of factors. Fabrigar et al. (1999, p. 279) suggested to select the model "…which constitutes a substantial improvement in fit over a model with one fewer factor but for which a model with one more factor provides little if any improvement in fit." This suggestion, which is based on the same principle as the scree test, requires a subjective decision on what constitutes a substantial improvement in fit. A method that formalizes this step is the Hull method.

Hull method

The Hull method (Lorenzo-Seva et al., 2011) aims at indicating the number of major, CFs. The Hull method is based on the same principle as the scree test, namely to optimally balance the fit and number of parameters involved. The optimal balance is found using a numerical convex hull-based heuristic (Ceulemans & Kiers, 2006). This heuristic makes a visual inspection, as in the scree test, superfluous. Further, the Hull method limits the possible maximum number of factors to the number of factors indicated by Horn's PA, to guard against overfactoring. The fit of a CFA model can, depending on the estimation method, be expressed in different ways. Based on the results of a comparative simulation study (Lorenzo-Seva et al., 2011), including the CFI, RMSEA, and SRMR as fit measures, it is advised to use the CFI (Bentler, 1990) as a fit measure when chi-square statistics are available, yielding Hull-CFI. When chi-square statistics are unavailable, such as when Principal Axis Factoring is used as an estimation method, it is advised to use as a fit measure the Common part Accounted For (CAF), which expresses the amount of variance of the common part explained by the factor model at hand.

In a comparative simulation study, Hull-CFI and Hull-CAF performed generally very well in indicating the number of major factors, and on average outperformed alternatives as PA and MAP. The performance of the Hull variants seems to improve as the sample size increases, and the number of observed variables per factor increases. As a consequence, Hull is a suitable approach when large datasets are analyzed: with this kind of dataset, it outperforms such classical methods as PA. However, PA outperformed both Hull variants in case of small sample sizes ($N = 100$) and small numbers of items (i.e., 5) per factor.

Assessment of the Number of Factors in Empirical Practice

To assess the number of factors underlying an empirical data set, we suggest the following strategy. First, one should decide about the most appropriate model for the data at hand. In this chapter, we considered the models associated with PCA, CFA, and CFA-ord. In the evaluation of measurement instruments, typically CFA and CFA-ord are more appropriate than PCA. CFA-ord is generally preferred for ordinal polytomous items, and CFA for continuous items.

Second, one should select the estimation procedure, taking into account the distribution of item scores and the sample size available. Note that the minimally required sample sizes to achieve a reasonable estimate of an exploratory CFM crucially depend on the size of the communalities and the level of overdetermination (i.e., number of items per factor) (e.g., MacCallum, Widaman, Preacher, & Hong, 2001). In general, identifying a large number of factors (relative to the overall number of items) and/or small factors (i.e., factors related to a low number of items per factor) require large sample sizes. For "easy" cases, a sample size of 100 may suffice, whereas for "complicated" cases one may need up to 20 cases per item observed.

Third, one should decide whether the aim of the research requires assessing the number of major factors, the number of major factors and (some) minor factors. To assess the maximum number of factors to possibly consider, thus including minor factors, one can use the chi-square test in a stepwise manner, as explained in the section Likelihood ratio test. To assess the number of major factors, we suggest considering various criteria. In particular, we recommend HULL and PA, both in a variant that is in line with the model and estimation procedure selected. Further, we recommend considering various goodness-of-fit measures, as RMSEA, CFI, and SRMR. This implies examining the minimal number of factors required (associated with the model selected) to meet the recommend cut-off values for acceptable model fit. In our view, those cut-off values should be applied with some lenience. Then, the model(s) with the indicated number(s) of factor should be examined carefully, to judge the interpretability and theoretical plausibility.

Empirical example

To illustrate our strategy, we re-analyze data collected to evaluate the Dutch translation (van Dijk, Timmerman, Martel, & Ramsay, 2011) of the **Montreal Children's Hospital Feeding Scale** (MCH-FS) (Ramsay, Martel, Porporino, & Zygmuntowicz, 2011). This scale is a screening instrument for the detection of feeding problems in young children. Such problems are rather common, with 10–33% of the caregivers reporting feeding problems. The negative consequences range from increased parental difficulties to hampered physical growth and mental development. Food problems are described by various types of symptoms, as food refusal, irregular eating, noncompliance during mealtime, and "mealtime negativity".

The MCH-FS was developed to provide clinicians with a valid and reliable screening instrument. The primary aim is to quickly identify the severity of feeding problems as reported by primary caregivers during a short consultation session, so that caregivers having severe problems can be referred to specialists. This implies that it is unnecessary to obtain a detailed picture of the nature of the feeding problems, as long as those parents having severe problems will be identified correctly. Because the scale is used in clinical practice, the scale should be as brief and easy to administer as possible. This implies that in this case, both the numbers of items and subscales should be as small as possible, as long as the instrument is sufficiently reliable in identifying severity of feeding problems. Note that for other purposes, like scientific research or a more detailed diagnosis, an instrument that disentangles several symptoms of feeding problems, and hence consists of various subscales, may be more appropriate.

The MCH-FS consists of 14 items on symptoms of feeding problems in the following domains: oral sensory/motor symptoms, appetite, parental concerns, mealtime behaviors, compensatory strategies, and family reactions. The primary feeder is asked to rate each of the 14 items on a seven-point Likert scale.

The Dutch translation of the MCH-FS is the SEP (*Screeningslijst Eetgedrag Peuters*). A normative sample of caretakers filled in the SEP when visiting their local Child Health Center. For details about the sampling procedure, we refer to van Dijk et al. (2011). We consider the scores of a sample of 1,386 caretakers, who completed all items of the SEP for their child, who was in the range from 6 to 208 months of age.

To illustrate the various methods to identify the number of factors underlying a data set, we estimated a series of CFMs, with one up to eight factors. Given that the number of domains covered equals six, the maximum of eight factors appeared to be large enough. All item distributions were right skewed (skewness range .32–2.30). Given the ordinal polytomous nature of the items and their skewness, we estimated CFA-ord models with robust weighted least squares (WLSMV) of polychoric correlations. We used the ESEM procedure of the computer program MPlus (Muthén & Muthén, 1998–2011), which provides both estimates of the CFA-ord models with the requested number of factors, and their associated measures of the chi-square, RMSEA, CFI, and SRMR.

In Table 11.2, the various fit measures associated with the estimated CFA-ord models are presented. The chi-square test result is significant (at $\alpha = .05$) for the CFA-ord models with seven and eight factors, suggesting that the total number of factors underlying the data set equals seven.

When considering the fit measures RMSEA, CFI, and SRMR and applying the recommended cut-off values for good fit, it is salient that mixed results appear. On the basis of the 95% CIs of the RMSEA (with recommended cut-off values of .05–.06 for close fit and .05–.08 for fair fit), two to three factors appear to be indicated. On the basis of the CFI value, with a commonly used cut-off value of .95, two factors are indicated. The SRMR value suggests either two (applying the stringent cut-off value of .05), or one (applying the more lenient cut-off value .08).

On the CFI values, we applied the Hull procedure (using own code). In Figure 11.1 (a), the CFI values versus degrees of freedom taken by the CFM concerned, are

Table 11.2 Fit measures for the CFA-ord model with m = 1 up to eight common factors. VAF is percentage explained variance.

m	χ^2	Df	p-value χ^2-test	RMSEA [95% CI]	CFI	SRMR
1	1,255.64	77	.00	.11 [.10; .11]	.92	.07
2	498.55	64	.00	.07 [.06; .08]	.97	.05
3	241.76	52	.00	.05 [.05; .06]	.99	.03
4	125.79	41	.00	.04 [.03; .05]	.99	.02
5	72.36	31	.00	.03 [.02; .04]	1.00	.01
6	34.52	22	.04	.02 [.00; .03]	1.00	.01
7	16.25	14	.30	.01 [.00; .03	1.00	.01
8	4.44	7	.73	.00 [.00; .02]	1.00	.00

presented. The thus obtained Hull-CFI indicated one factor. Hull-CFI based on a ULS estimation procedure on polychoric correlation matrices with the program Factor (Lorenzo-Seva & Ferrando, 2006) revealed the same result.

Finally, we applied PA-MRFA with polychoric correlation matrices, again using the program Factor. In Figure 11.1(b), the proportion of variance explained by the CFs and the 95th percentile of the variances explained of random data versus the number of factors estimated with MRFA are presented. As can be seen, the percentage of explained variance of the observed data exceeds that of random data only at a number of factors equal to one. Thus, PA-MRFA with a 95% threshold indicates a single factor to retain.

Given the aim of the MCH-FS as a screening instrument, the number of major factors is of primary interest, whereby possibly a few minor factors could be interesting to reveal the structure of the items. The major factor criteria considered suggest one or two factors, with only the RMSEA possibly indicating three. The solutions with one and two factors are well-interpretable. The solution with three factors is more difficult to interpret, because of substantial cross-loadings.

In Table 11.3, the loadings of the one-factor and two-factor models, after Geomin rotation, are presented. In the two-factor solution, Factor 1 clusters behavior that can be labeled as Negative mealtime behavior (e.g., poor appetite, start refusing food). The second factor pertains to a broader range of symptoms that can be labeled as Negative causes and consequences (e.g., holding food in mouth, poor growth). Item 5, involving the duration of mealtimes, has low loadings on both factors. The ordered categories of item 5 pertain to increasing duration of meals (in minutes), and those ordered categories do not necessarily indicate increasing feeding problems, because both very long and very brief mealtimes can be indicative of problematic behavior. This implies that in its current form item 5 is a weak item in the scale. The correlation between the two factors is .64, indicating that there is a rather strong positive relation between the two types of Negative symptoms in the normative population.

In the one-factor solution, the factor can be interpreted as Feeding Problems. Apart from item 5, which was already identified as a weak item, item 11 occurs as an item with a low loading. Given the interpretable relationships shown in the two-factor solution, we conclude that to represent in detail the various types of feeding problems, one needs a two-factor solution. To represent Feeding Problems in general, the one-factor solution suffices.

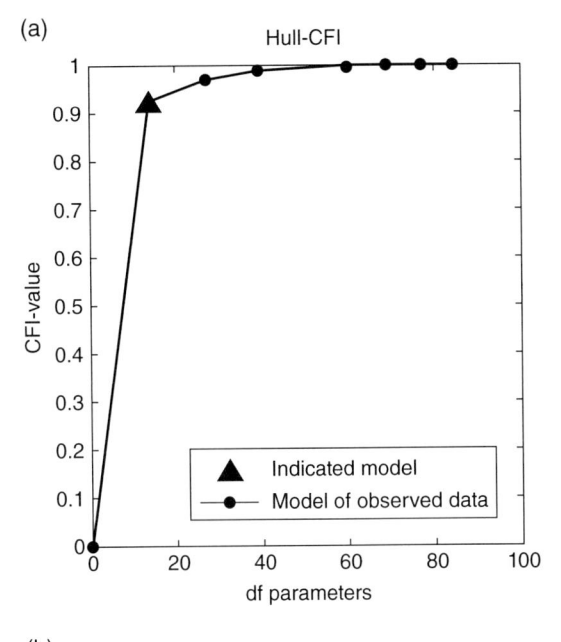

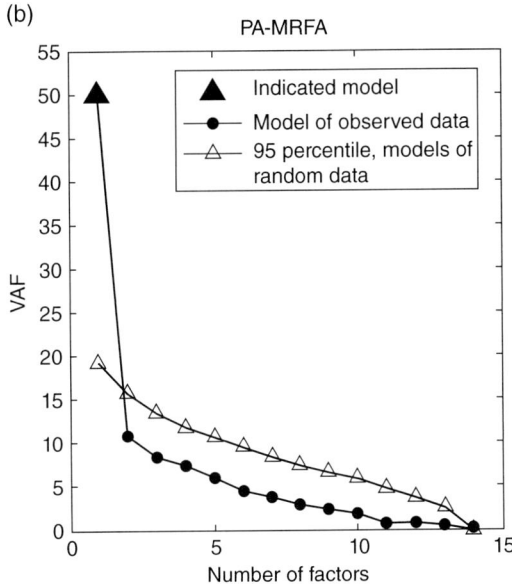

Figure 11.1 (a) Hull-CFI: CFI values versus number of parameters in CFM; (b) PA-MRFA: VAF for models of observed data and 95th percentile of VAF for models of random data versus the number of CFs in the model. VAF is percentage explained variance.

Those results suggest that to meet the goal of a screening instrument, it is sufficient to compute the score on a single total scale, for example by summing the item scores. The reliability of the total scale including all items (estimated on the basis of the one-factor solution (omega) (McDonald, 1999, p. 89)) appears to be rather high, namely 0.88. One may consider removing items 11 and 5, because they add relatively little to the

Table 11.3 Estimated loadings of the CFA-ord, two factors, after Geomin rotation. Items indicated with* are mirrored before analysis. Loadings >0.3 in absolute value are printed in bold type.

	One-factor solution		Two-factor solution		
Item number (brief description)	Loading	Unique variance	Loading Factor 1	Loading Factor 2	Unique variance
7 (gags/spits/vomits)	.30	.91	−.15	**.51**	.81
8 (holding food in mouth)*	**.44**	.80	.06	**.44**	.77
11 (poor chewing abilities)	.20	.96	−.28	**.54**	.83
3 (poor appetite)*	**.52**	.73	**.55**	−.01	.70
4 (start refusing food)*	**.69**	.52	**.79**	−.07	.44
1 (difficult mealtimes)*	**.86**	.26	**.90**	.01	.17
2 (worries about feeding)	**.64**	.59	.28	**.45**	.56
12 (poor growth)*	**.52**	.73	.15	**.43**	.71
6 (bad behavior at table)	**.78**	.40	**.71**	.13	.37
5 (long mealtimes)	.27	.93	**.30**	−.01	.92
9 (follow around/distract)	**.60**	.64	**.37**	**.30**	.63
10 (force to eat)*	**.74**	.46	**.50**	**.31**	.45
13 (influence relation)*	**.78**	.40	−.02	**.87**	.24
14 (influence family relations)	**.73**	.46	.10	**.73**	.36

reliability of the total scale. In future developments of the scale, one may consider to change item 5.

If the goal would have been to offer a more detailed diagnosis, the use of two sub-scales would be indicated, on the basis of the factor analysis results. Note that those results could be population dependent. In particular, it might be that even more than two subscales could be sensibly distinguished when a clinical sample, suffering from a varied range of feeding problems, would be considered.

Concluding Remark

In this chapter, we considered various approaches to arrive at the number of factors to use in an exploratory CFA. We included the standard linear CFA, suitable for continuous items, and CFA-ord for ordered polytomous items. As an alternative for polytomous items, exploratory item response theory (IRT) based models could be used. For two-parameter (normal ogive and logistic) IRT models, or constrained versions thereof, the approaches discussed here can be readily applied. This is so because CFA-ord is intimately related to the two-parameter IRT models (Takane & de Leeuw, 1987). For less constrained versions, the models differ, and hence the usefulness of the current approaches cannot be guaranteed.

Acknowledgments

We would like to thank Marijn van Dijk for sharing her data.

References

Barrett, P. (2007). Structural equation modelling: Adjudging model fit. *Personality and Individual Differences, 42*(5), 815–824.

Beauducel, A., & Herzberg, P. Y. (2006). On the performance of maximum likelihood versus means and variance adjusted weighted least squares estimation in CFA. *Structural Equation Modeling: A Multidisciplinary Journal, 2*, 186–203.

Bentler, P. M. (1990). Comparative fit indexes in structural models. *Psychological Bulletin, 107*(2), 238–246.

Bentler, P. M., & Bonett, D. G. (1980). Significance tests and goodness of fit in the analysis of covariance structures. *Psychological Bulletin, 88*(3), 588–606.

Browne, M. W. (1984). Asymptotically distribution-free methods for the analysis of covariance structures. *British Journal of Mathematical and Statistical Psychology, 37*(1), 62–83.

Browne, M. W., & Cudeck, R. (1992). Alternative ways of assessing model fit. *Sociological Methods & Research, 21*(2), 230–258.

Buja, A., & Eyuboglu, N. (1992). Remarks on parallel analysis. *Multivariate Behavioral Research, 27*(4), 509–540.

Cattell, R. B. (1966). The scree test for the number of factors. *Multivariate Behavioral Research, 1*(2), 245–276.

Cattell, R. B., & Tsujioka, B. (1964). The importance of factor-trueness and validity, versus homogeneity and orthogonality, in test scales 1. *Educational and Psychological Measurement, 24*(1), 3–30.

Ceulemans, E., & Kiers, H. A. L. (2006). Selecting among three-mode principal component models of different types and complexities: A numerical convex hull based method. *British Journal of Mathematical and Statistical Psychology, 59*(1), 133–150.

Cho, S., Li, F., & Bandalos, D. (2009). Accuracy of the parallel analysis procedure with polychoric correlations. *Educational and Psychological Measurement, 69*(5), 748–759.

Costello, A. B., & Osborne, J. W. (2005). Best practices in exploratory factor analysis: Four recommendations for getting the most from your analysis. *Practical Assessment, Research & Evaluation, 10*(7), Retrieved from: http://pareonline.net/pdf/v10n7.pdf.

Cota, A. A., Longman, R. S., Holden, R. R., & Fekken, G. C. (1993). Comparing different methods for implementing parallel analysis: A practical index of accuracy. *Educational and Psychological Measurement, 53*(4), 865–876.

De Raad, B., & Barelds, D. P. H. (2008). A new taxonomy of Dutch personality traits based on a comprehensive and unrestricted list of descriptors. *Journal of Personality and Social Psychology, 94*(2), 347–364.

Dolan, C. V. (1994). Factor analysis of variables with 2, 3, 5 and 7 response categories: A comparison of categorical variable estimators using simulated data. *British Journal of Mathematical and Statistical Psychology, 47*(2), 309–326.

Fabrigar, L. R., Wegener, D. T., MacCallum, R. C., & Strahan, E. J. (1999). Evaluating the use of exploratory factor analysis in psychological research. *Psychological Methods, 4*(3), 272–299.

Glorfeld, L. W. (1995). An improvement on Horn's parallel analysis methodology for selecting the correct number of factors to retain. *Educational and Psychological Measurement, 55*(3), 377–393.

Hayashi, K., Bentler, P. M., & Yuan, K. (2007). On the likelihood ratio test for the number of factors in exploratory factor analysis. *Structural Equation Modeling: A Multidisciplinary Journal, 14*(3), 505–526.

Hayton, J. C., Allen, D. G., & Scarpello, V. (2004). Factor retention decisions in exploratory factor analysis: A tutorial on parallel analysis. *Organizational Research Methods, 7*(2), 191–205.

Hooper, D., Coughlan, J., & Mullen, M. (2008). Structural equation modelling: Guidelines for determining model fit. *Electronic Journal of Business Research Methods, 6*(1), 53–60.

Horn, J. L. (1965). A rationale and test for the number of factors in factor analysis. *Psychometrika*, *30*(2), 179–185.

Hu, L., & Bentler, P. M. (1999). Cutoff criteria for fit indexes in covariance structure analysis: Conventional criteria versus new alternatives. *Structural Equation Modeling: A Multidisciplinary Journal*, *6*, 1–55.

Hubbard, R., & Allen, S. (1987). An empirical comparison of alternative methods for principal component extraction. *Journal of Business Research*, *15*(2), 173–190.

Humphreys, L. G., & Ilgen, D. R. (1969). Note on a criterion for the number of common factors. *Educational and Psychological Measurement*, *29*(3), 571–578.

Jolliffe, I. T. (2002). *Principal component analysis* (2nd ed.). New York: Springer-Verlag.

Kaiser, H. F. (1960). The application of electronic computers to factor analysis. *Educational and Psychological Measurement*, *20*, 141–151.

Kaiser, H. F. (1974). An index of factorial simplicity. *Psychometrika*, *39*(1), 31–36.

Lorenzo-Seva, U., & Ferrando, P. J. (2006). FACTOR: a computer program to fit the exploratory factor analysis model. *Behavior Research Methods, Instruments & Computers*, *38*, 88–91.

Lorenzo-Seva, U., Timmerman, M. E., & Kiers, H. A. L. (2011). The Hull method for selecting the number of common factors. *Multivariate Behavioral Research*, *46*(2), 340–364.

MacCallum, R. C., Browne, M. W., & Sugawara, H. M. (1996). Power analysis and determination of sample size for covariance structure modeling. *Psychological Methods*, *1*(2), 130–149.

MacCallum, R. C., & Tucker, L. R. (1991). Representing sources of error in the common-factor model: Implications for theory and practice. *Psychological Bulletin*, *109*(3), 502–511.

MacCallum, R. C., Widaman, K. F., Preacher, K. J., & Hong, S. (2001). Sample size in factor analysis: The role of model error. *Multivariate Behavioral Research*, *36*(4), 611–637.

Marsh, H. W., Hau, K., & Wen, Z. (2004). In search of golden rules: Comment on hypothesis-testing approaches to setting cutoff values for fit indexes and dangers in overgeneralizing Hu and Bentler's (1999) findings. *Structural Equation Modeling: A Multidisciplinary Journal*, *11*(3), 320–341.

McDonald, R. P. (1999). *Test theory: A unified treatment*. Mahwah, NJ: Lawrence Erlbaum Associates.

Mislevy, R. J. (1986). Recent developments in the factor analysis of categorical variables. *Journal of Educational and Behavioral Statistics*, *11*(1), 3–31.

Muthén, B. O., du Toit, S. H. C., & Spisic, D. (1997). Robust inference using weighted least squares and quadratic estimating equations in latent variable modeling with categorical and continuous outcomes. *Unpublished technical report.*, Retrieved from: http://pages.gseis.ucla.edu/faculty/muthen/articles/Article_075.pdf (accessed October 2017).

Muthén, B., & Kaplan, D. (1985). A comparison of some methodologies for the factor analysis of non-normal Likert variables. *British Journal of Mathematical and Statistical Psychology*, *38*(2), 171–189.

Muthén, B., & Kaplan, D. (1992). A comparison of some methodologies for the factor analysis of non-normal Likert variables: A note on the size of the model. *British Journal of Mathematical and Statistical Psychology*, *45*(1), 19–30.

Muthén, L. K., & Muthén, B. O. (1998–2011). *MPlus user's guide* (6th ed.). Los Angeles, CA: Muthén & Muthén.

Olsson, U. (1979). Maximum likelihood estimation of the polychoric correlation coefficient. *Psychometrika*, *44*(4), 443–460.

Peres-Neto, P. R., Jackson, D. A., & Somers, K. M. (2005). How many principal components? stopping rules for determining the number of non-trivial axes revisited. *Computational Statistics & Data Analysis*, *49*(4), 974–997.

Ramsay, M., Martel, C., Porporino, M., & Zygmuntowicz, C. (2011). The Montreal Children's Hospital Feeding Scale: A brief bilingual screening tool for identifying feeding problems. *Paediatrics & Child Health*, *16*(3), 147.

Reckase, M. D. (2009). *Multidimensional item response theory.* New York, NY: Springer-Verlag.

Reise, S. P., Waller, N. G., & Comrey, A. L. (2000). Factor analysis and scale revision. *Psychological Assessment, 12*(3), 287–297.

Revelle, W., & Rocklin, T. (1979). Very simple structure: An alternative procedure for estimating the optimal number of interpretable factors. *Multivariate Behavioral Research, 14*(4), 403–414.

Sivo, S. A., Fan, X., Witta, E. L., & Willse, J. T. (2006). The search for "optimal" cutoff properties: Fit index criteria in structural equation modeling. *The Journal of Experimental Education, 74*(3), 267–288.

Steger, M. F. (2006). An illustration of issues in factor extraction and identification of dimensionality in psychological assessment data. *Journal of Personality Assessment, 86*(3), 263–272.

Steiger, J. H. (1990). Structural model evaluation and modification: An interval estimation approach. *Multivariate Behavioral Research, 25*(2), 173–180.

Takane, Y., & de Leeuw, J. (1987). On the relationship between item response theory and factor analysis of discretized variables. *Psychometrika, 52*(3), 393–408.

ten Holt, J. C., van Duijn, M. A. J., & Boomsma, A. (2010). Scale construction and evaluation in practice: A review of factor analysis versus item response theory applications. *Psychological Test and Assessment Modeling, 52*(3), 272–297.

Thompson, B. (2004). *Exploratory and confirmatory factor analysis: Understanding concepts and applications.* Washington, D.C.: American Psychological Association.

Timmerman, M. E., & Lorenzo-Seva, U. (2011). Dimensionality assessment of ordered polytomous items with parallel analysis. *Psychological Methods, 16*(2), 209–220.

Tucker, L. R., Koopman, R. F., & Linn, R. L. (1969). Evaluation of factor analytic research procedures by means of simulated correlation matrices. *Psychometrika, 34*(4), 421–459.

Turner, N. E. (1998). The effect of common variance and structure pattern on random data eigenvalues: Implications for the accuracy of parallel analysis. *Educational and Psychological Measurement, 58*(4), 541–568.

van Dijk, M., Timmerman, M. E., Martel, C., & Ramsay, M. (2011). Towards the development of a Dutch screening instrument for the detection of feeding problems in young children. *Netherlands Journal of Psychology, 66*(4), 112–119.

Velicer, W. F. (1976). Determining the number of components from the matrix of partial correlations. *Psychometrika, 41,* 321–327.

Velicer, W. F., Eaton, C. A., & Fava, J. L. (2000). Construct explication through factor or component analysis: A review and evaluation of alternative procedures for determining the number of factors or components. In E. Helmes (Ed.), *Problems and solutions in human assessment: Honoring Douglas N. Jackson at seventy* (pp. 41–71). New York, NY: Kluwer Academic/Plenum Publishers.

Velicer, W. F., & Jackson, D. N. (1990). Component analysis versus common factor analysis: Some issues in selecting an appropriate procedure. *Multivariate Behavioral Research, 25*(1), 1–28.

Weng, L., & Cheng, C. (2005). Parallel analysis with unidimensional binary data. *Educational and Psychological Measurement, 65*(5), 697–716.

Widaman, K. F. (1993). Common factor analysis versus principal component analysis: differential bias in representing model parameters? *Multivariate Behavioral Research, 28*(3), 263–311.

Wirth, R. J., & Edwards, M. C. (2007). Item factor analysis: Current approaches and future directions. *Psychological Methods, 12*(1), 58–79.

Yang-Wallentin, F., Joreskog, K. G., & Luo, H. (2010). Confirmatory factor analysis of ordinal variables with misspecified models. *Structural Equation Modeling: A Multidisciplinary Journal, 17*(3), 392–423.

Yuan, K. (2005). Fit indices versus test statistics. *Multivariate Behavioral Research, 40*(1), 115–148.

Yuan, K., & Bentler, P. M. (2000). Three likelihood-based methods for mean and covariance structure analysis with nonnormal missing data. *Sociological Methodology, 30*(1), 165–200.

Zhang, J., & Stout, W. (1999). The theoretical detect index of dimensionality and its application to approximate simple structure. *Psychometrika, 64*(2), 213–249.

Zwick, W. R., & Velicer, W. F. (1982). Factors influencing four rules for determining the number of components to retain. *Multivariate Behavioral Research, 17*(2), 253–269.

Zwick, W. R., & Velicer, W. F. (1986). Comparison of five rules for determining the number of components to retain. *Psychological Bulletin, 99*(3), 432–442.

12

Bifactor Models in Psychometric Test Development

Fang Fang Chen and Zugui Zhang

Bifactor Models in Psychometric Test Development

Bifactor models have been used increasingly in recent years as an alternative yet more advantageous approach to testing multifaceted constructs and for addressing the critical issue of dimensionality in psychological research. Many psychological constructs are comprised of multiply related yet distinct subdomains. Such constructs can be found in most areas of psychology, including personality traits, affect, achievement motivation, depression, psychopathology, well-being, primary and secondary control, cognitive functioning, and health behaviors. For example, extraversion is one of the major five personality factors and is associated with important psychological processes. Extraversion is conceptualized as a multifaceted construct. In the Revised NEO Personality Inventory (NEO-PI-R; Costa & McCrae, 1992), the general construct of extraversion incorporates six related facets: warmth, gregariousness, assertiveness, activity, excitement seeking, and positive emotions. Ryff and colleagues (Ryff, 1989; Ryff & Keyes, 1995; Ryff & Singer, 2008) proposed a general structure of psychological well-being that was comprised of six closely related domains. Diener (1984) hypothesized a general structure of subjective well-being that consisted of three related domains. In these multifaceted structures, the central scientific interest lies in the general construct as well as in the subdomains. That is, whether a more focused domain may make a unique contribution, over and above the general factor, to the prediction of external criteria.

Bifactor models are potentially applicable when (1) there is a general factor that is accounts for the commonality among the items related domains; (2) there are multiple domain or group factors, each of which accounts for the unique influence of the specific domain over and above the general factor; and (3) researchers are interested in the domain factors as well as the common factor. Figure 12.1 illustrates a bifactor model of subjective well-being derived from Diener's conceptual framework (1984). In this case there is a general factor of subjective well-being that underlies all the domains. Separately, there are domain factors of positive affect, negative affect, and life satisfaction, each of which accounts for the unique variance in its own separate set of domain-related items.

We first review bifactor models within the framework of confirmatory factor analysis (CFA) and examine the conceptual differences between bifactor models and

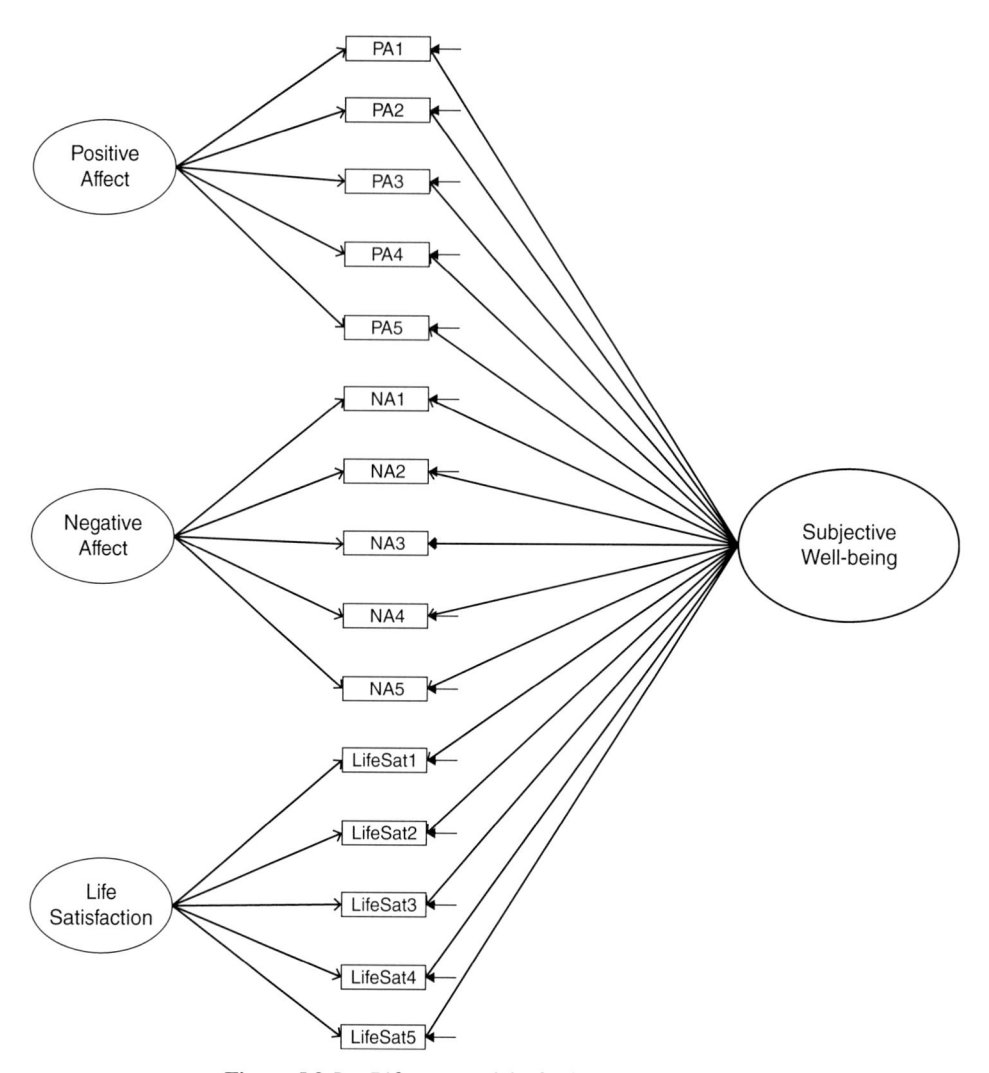

Figure 12.1 Bifactor model of subjective well-being.

higher-order factor models, along with other commonly used CFA models. We then present the bifactor models within the framework of exploratory factor analysis (EFA) and examine the conceptual differences among three EFA estimation methods: bifactor rotations, target rotations, and Schmid–Leiman Transformations. Finally, we introduce the potential applicability of bifactor models in psychological research.[1]

---

[1] The focus of this chapter is on confirmatory and exploratory bifactor analysis within the framework of structural equation modeling. However, it is important to note that bifactor models have also become a valuable tool in the field of item response theory (IRT). Bifactor models have been used to examine several critical issues related to the unidimensionality nature of multifaceted constructs and the possible biases related to treating multifaceted constructs as unidimensional within the IRT conceptual framework (Reise, 2012; Reise, Moore, & Haviland, 2010; Reise, Moore, & Maydeu-Olivares, 2011; Reise, Morizot, & Hays, 2007; Reise, Scheines, Widaman, & Haviland, 2013). Generalized full-information item bifactor analysis has been developed to conduct flexible multiple group analysis for psychological constructs that are measured with a mixture of dichotomous, ordinal and nominal items (Cai, Yan, & Hansen, 2011).

Confirmatory Bifactor Models

Within CFA, two alternative models, bifactor models and second-order model, have been proposed to represent the factor structure of items that assess several related domains that are hypothesized to comprise a general construct. Bifactor models, also known as general-specific or nested models, is a form of CFA originally introduced by Holzinger and Swineford (1937). It is less familiar because they have been used primarily in the area of intelligence research (e.g., Gustafsson & Balke, 1993; Luo, Petrill, & Thompson, 1994). Second-order models are more familiar as they have been applied in a wider variety of substantive areas, such as personality (DeYoung, Peterson, & Higgins, 2002; Judge, Erez, Bono, & Thoresen, 2002), and self-concept (Marsh, Ellis, & Craven, 2002). It is only recently that the bifactor models have been used more frequently in the study of personality (e.g., Bludworth, Tracey, & Glidden-Tracey; 2010; Brouwer, Meijer, Weekers, & Baneke, 2008; Chen, Hayes, Carver, Laurenceau, & Zhang, 2012), depression and anxiety (Simms, Grös, Watson, & O'Hara, 2008), psychopathology (Patrick, Hicks, Nichol, & Krueger, 2007), affect (Chen, Bai, Lee, & Jing, 2016), and well-being (Chen, West, & Sousa, 2006; Chen, Jing, Hayes, & Lee, 2014). Our first goal in this section is to compare the similarities and differences between the two models and to propose the potential advantages of bifactor models over second-order models when researchers have an interest in the predictive power of the general construct as well as the specific domains.

Comparing bifactor models and second-order models

A bifactor model hypothesizes that: (1) there is a general factor that accounts for the commonality shared by the related domains, and (2) there are multiple group factors, each of which accounts for the unique influence of the specific domains over and above the general factor. We use the construct of subjective well-being to illustrate how the bifactor model can be applied to a multifaceted construct. Diener (1984) proposed that subjective well-being is comprised of three related domains: the presence of positive affect, absence of negative affect, and cognitive evaluation of life satisfaction. The three domains contribute to an overarching factor of subjective well-being. Each of the three domains also accounts for unique variance, stemming from its own separate set of facet-related items. We consider the canonical bifactor model in which the relations between the general and group specific factors are assumed to be orthogonal, given that the group factors account for the variance over and above the general factor.

The bifactor model is constructed with the following features: (1) each item has a nonzero loading on both the general factor and the group factor that it is designed to measure, but zero loadings on the other group factors; (2) the group factors are uncorrelated with each other and with the general factor; and (3) all error terms associated with the items were uncorrelated. In other words, each item is allowed to load on the general factor and the intended group factor. All other loadings are fixed to zero. All factors are specified to be orthogonal, including the relations between the general factor and group factors, and the relations among the group factors.

For the model in Figure 12.1, let vector Y represent observed variables; matrix Λy represent the factor loadings of the general and group factors; vector η represent the general and group factors; and vector ε represent residual variance (uniquenesses). A factor loading matrix is expressed in the following form.

$$Y = \begin{bmatrix} y_1 \\ y_2 \\ y_3 \\ y_4 \\ y_5 \\ y_6 \\ y_7 \\ y_8 \\ y_9 \\ y_{10} \\ y_{11} \\ y_{12} \\ y_{13} \\ y_{14} \\ y_{15} \end{bmatrix} \quad \Lambda_y = \begin{bmatrix} \lambda_{g1,1} & \lambda_{s1,1} & 0 & 0 & 0 \\ \lambda_{g2,1} & \lambda_{s2,1} & 0 & 0 & 0 \\ \lambda_{g3,1} & \lambda_{s3,1} & 0 & 0 & 0 \\ \lambda_{g4,1} & \lambda_{s4,1} & 0 & 0 & 0 \\ \lambda_{g5,1} & \lambda_{s5,1} & 0 & 0 & 0 \\ \lambda_{g6,1} & 0 & \lambda_{s6,2} & 0 & 0 \\ \lambda_{g7,1} & 0 & \lambda_{s7,2} & 0 & 0 \\ \lambda_{g8,1} & 0 & \lambda_{s8,2} & 0 & 0 \\ \lambda_{g9,1} & 0 & \lambda_{s9,2} & 0 & 0 \\ \lambda_{g10,1} & 0 & \lambda_{s10,2} & 0 & 0 \\ \lambda_{g11,1} & 0 & 0 & \lambda_{s11,3} & 0 \\ \lambda_{g12,1} & 0 & 0 & \lambda_{s12,3} & 0 \\ \lambda_{g13,1} & 0 & 0 & \lambda_{s13,3} & 0 \\ \lambda_{g14,1} & 0 & 0 & \lambda_{s14,3} & 0 \\ \lambda_{g15,1} & 0 & 0 & \lambda_{s15,3} & 0 \end{bmatrix} \quad \eta = \begin{bmatrix} \eta_{g1} \\ \eta_{s1} \\ \eta_{s2} \\ \eta_{s3} \end{bmatrix} \quad \varepsilon = \begin{bmatrix} \varepsilon_1 \\ \varepsilon_2 \\ \varepsilon_3 \\ \varepsilon_4 \\ \varepsilon_5 \\ \varepsilon_6 \\ \varepsilon_7 \\ \varepsilon_8 \\ \varepsilon_9 \\ \varepsilon_{10} \\ \varepsilon_{11} \\ \varepsilon_{12} \\ \varepsilon_{13} \\ \varepsilon_{14} \\ \varepsilon_{15} \end{bmatrix}$$

Specifically, the loadings in the first column are free parameters. For the remaining columns, the loading matrix has only one free parameter across each row. In the bifactor model, the first factor is called a general factor and the remaining factors are called group factors.

The observed variables can be expressed in the following equation:

$$Y = \Lambda_y \eta + \varepsilon \qquad (12.1)$$

The first term represents the contribution of the general and group factors, the second term represents the contribution of the residual variance.[2]

Similar to bifactor models, second-order models are also used when it is hypothesized that measurement instruments assess several related domains. Second-order models are potentially applicable when (1) the lower-order factors are correlated with each other, and (2) there is a higher-order factor that accounts for the relations among the lower-

---

[2] The residual variance is composed of measurement error and variance that is not captured by the general and group factors.

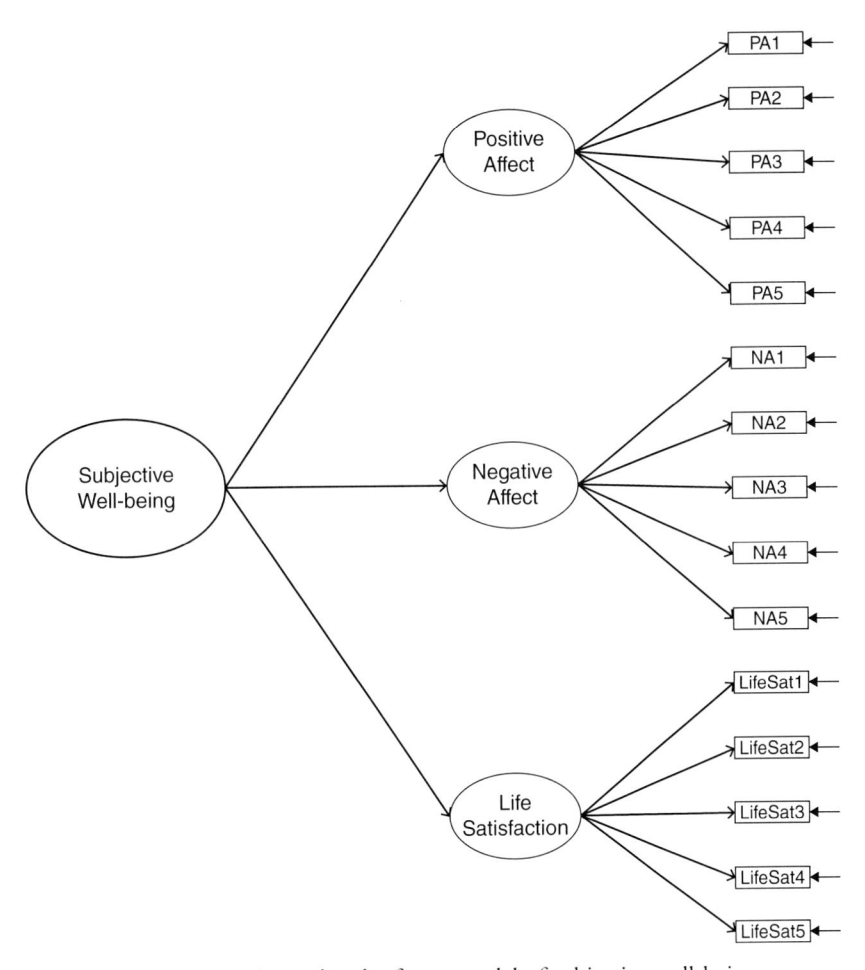

Figure 12.2 Second-order factor model of subjective well-being.

order factors. Figure 12.2 illustrates the second-order model of subjective well-being. In this hierarchical structure, subjective well-being is a second-order factor that accounts for the commonality among lower-order factors representing the three domains: positive affect, negative affect, and life satisfaction. Multiple items on the measure, in turn, represent each of the lower-order factors. Such second-order models can be estimated and the fit of the second-order structure can be statistically tested so long as three or more first-order factors are hypothesized. In other words, the second-order model places a measurement structure on the correlations between the lower-order factors in an attempt to explain the correlations among the lower-order factors.

The second-order model is specified in the following way: (1) each item has a nonzero loading on the first-order factors that it is designed to measure and a zero loading on the other first-order factors; (2) error terms associated with each item are uncorrelated; and (3) all covariance among first-order factors is explained by a higher-order factor, such as – subjective well-being.

For the model in Figure 12.2, let the Y vector represent observed variables; Λy represent the loadings of the measured variables on the first-order factors; the η vector represent the lower-order factors; the Γ vector represent the loadings of the lower-order factors on the higher-order factor; the ξ vector represent the higher-order factor; the ζ vector represent the disturbances of the lower-order factors (unique variance that is not shared with the common higher-order factor); and the ε vector represents the residuals. The equations for the second-order model are:

$$\eta = \Gamma\xi + \zeta \qquad (12.2)$$

$$Y = \Lambda_y \eta + \varepsilon \qquad (12.3)$$

The first equation 12.2 represents the structure for each of the lower-order factors; the second equation 12.3 represents the measurement model for the observed variables.

$$Y = \begin{bmatrix} Y_1 \\ Y_2 \\ Y_3 \\ Y_4 \\ Y_5 \\ Y_6 \\ Y_7 \\ Y_8 \\ Y_9 \\ Y_{10} \\ Y_{11} \\ Y_{12} \\ Y_{13} \\ Y_{14} \\ Y_{15} \end{bmatrix} \Lambda_y = \begin{bmatrix} \lambda_{1,1} & 0 & 0 \\ \lambda_{2,1} & 0 & 0 \\ \lambda_{3,1} & 0 & 0 \\ \lambda_{4,1} & 0 & 0 \\ \lambda_{5,1} & 0 & 0 \\ 0 & \lambda_{6,2} & 0 \\ 0 & \lambda_{7,2} & 0 \\ 0 & \lambda_{8,2} & 0 \\ 0 & \lambda_{9,2} & 0 \\ 0 & \lambda_{10,2} & 0 \\ 0 & 0 & \lambda_{11,3} \\ 0 & 0 & \lambda_{12,3} \\ 0 & 0 & \lambda_{13,3} \\ 0 & 0 & \lambda_{14,3} \\ 0 & 0 & \lambda_{15,3} \end{bmatrix} \Gamma = \begin{bmatrix} \Gamma_{1,1} \\ \Gamma_{2,1} \\ \Gamma_{3,1} \end{bmatrix} \xi = [\xi] \zeta = \begin{bmatrix} \zeta_1 \\ \zeta_2 \\ \zeta_3 \end{bmatrix} \varepsilon = \begin{bmatrix} \varepsilon_1 \\ \varepsilon_2 \\ \varepsilon_3 \\ \varepsilon_4 \\ \varepsilon_5 \\ \varepsilon_6 \\ \varepsilon_7 \\ \varepsilon_8 \\ \varepsilon_9 \\ \varepsilon_{10} \\ \varepsilon_{11} \\ \varepsilon_{12} \\ \varepsilon_{13} \\ \varepsilon_{14} \\ \varepsilon_{15} \end{bmatrix}$$

Early work suggested that the bifactor model and second-order models are mathematically equivalent (Wherry, 1959). However, recent work by several researchers (Gustafsson & Balke, 1993; McDonald, 1999; Mulaik & Quartetti, 1997; Yung, Thissen, & McLeod, 1999) has independently pointed out that these two models are not generally equivalent. A bifactor model and a second-order model are mathematically equivalent only when proportionality constraints are imposed by using the Schmid–Leiman transformation method (Schmid & Leiman, 1957). The Schmid–Leiman transformation imposes two specific constraints: (1) the factor loadings of the general factor in the bifactor model must be the product of the corresponding lower-order factor loadings and the second-order factor loadings in the second-order model

(Mulaik & Quartetti, 1997); and (2) the ratio of the general factor loading to its corresponding domain factor loading is the same within each domain factor (Yung, et al., 1999).

Yung et al. (1999) have used the **generalized** Schmidt–Leiman transformation, in which no proportionality constraints are imposed, to demonstrate that second-order model is in fact nested within the bifactor model (see also Rindskopf & Rose, 1988). For every bifactor model (see Figure 12.1), there is an equivalent full second-order model with direct effects (factor loadings) from the second-order factor to every observed variable, over and above the second-order effect on the lower-order factors. A standard second-order model (see Figure 12.2) is a special case (constrained version) of the full second-order model with the direct effects from the second-order factor to the observed variables eliminated. In other words, the "reduced" second-order model is more restricted than the full second-order model, which is equivalent to the bifactor model. Consequently, the "reduced" second-order model is more restricted than the bifactor model (A is nested in B, B is equal to C, so that A is nested in C).

Although the second-order model is not mathematically equivalent to the bifactor model, these two models have similar interpretations (Chen et al., 2006; Gustafsson & Balke, 1993). First, the second-order factor corresponds to the general factor in the bifactor model; second, the disturbances of the first-order factors in the second-order model resemble the domain factors in the bifactor model; and third, in the bifactor model the general factor and the domain factors are assumed to be orthogonal paralleling the representation in the second-order model in which the second-order factor and the disturbances are defined to be orthogonal. However, the differences between the two models become more pronounced when researchers are also interested in the contribution of the domain factors over and above the general/second-order factor.

Conventional alternative models

In addition to using the bifactor or second-order models, multifaceted constructs can be represented by other conventional models, such as the one-factor model and the correlated-factor model.

One-factor model As the bifactor model, the one-factor model hypothesizes that there is a general factor that accounts for the commonality shared by the facets. However, different from the bifactor model, the group factors, each of which accounts for the unique influence of the specific component over and above the general factor, are not taken into consideration in the model. Specifically, in the one-factor model, each item is allowed to load on the single latent general factor. This model is nested within the bifactor as it can be derived by setting all group factor loadings in the bifactor to zero.

Correlated-factor model The correlated-factor model hypothesizes that there are multiple related factors that account for the relations among the items. Different from the bifactor model, it does not incorporate a general factor that accounts for the commonality shared by the facets, nor does it estimate the unique variance of the specific facets over and above the general factor. The correlated-factor model can be derived from the bifactor model by fixing the loadings in the general factor to zero and relaxing the orthogonality constraint on the group factors.

Advantages of bifactor models

Compared to the widely used second-order models,[3] bifactor models have several potential advantages, particularly when researchers are interested in the predictive relations between group factors and external criteria, over and above the general/second-order factor. First, a bifactor model can be used as a less restricted baseline model to which a second-order model can be compared, given that the second-order model is nested within the bifactor model (Yung, et al., 1999). A likelihood ratio test (chi-square difference test) can be used to distinguish the two models.

Second, the bifactor model can be used to study the role of domain factors that are independent of the general factor. For example, drawing on Spearman's (1927) conception of general and domain factors, suppose there is factor of general intelligence of focal interest as well as domain factors of intelligence-related abilities such as verbal, spatial, mathematical, and analytic. However, suppose that verbal ability reflects only general intelligence, whereas spatial, mathematical, and analytic abilities still exist as specific domains, after partialling out general intelligence. In this example, verbal ability will no longer exist as a domain factor in the bifactor model. If verbal ability is included as a domain factor in the bifactor model, problems in estimation will occur because of identification problems due to factor overextraction (Rindskopf, 1984). These identification problems will be manifested in three primary ways: (1) factor loadings of the verbal domain factor will be small and non-significant; (2) the variance of the verbal domain factor will not be significant; and/or (3) the model will not converge. In this example, the common variance in the verbal ability items is entirely explained by the general intelligence factor. However, such problems will typically not be easily discovered in the second-order model, as verbal ability will legitimately exist as a lower-order factor.

The second-order factor model will manifest the nonexistence of the domain factor as nonsignificant disturbance of the lower-order factor. The lack of significance in the variance of the disturbance will typically not cause any problem in a model, and, therefore, the possibility that one or more of the domain factors may not exist can be easily glossed over by researchers examining the output from the second-order models.

Third, in the bifactor model, we can directly examine the strength of the relationship between the domain factors and their associated items, as the relationships are reflected in the factor loadings, whereas such relationships cannot be directly tested in the second-order factor model as the domain factors are represented by disturbances of the first-order factors.

Fourth, the bifactor model can be particularly useful in testing whether a subset of the domain factors predict external variables, over and above the general factor, as the

---

[3] Here we focus on the comparisons between the bifactor model and second-order models. The advantages of the bifactor model over the one-factor and correlated-factor models will be addressed in the application section, where total score and individual score approached are discussed.

domain factors are directly represented as independent factors (Gustafsson & Balke, 1993). Domain factors may also be used to predict external criteria, over and above the second-order factor, in second-order models, but such tests require the use of non-standard structural equation models. That is, the disturbances of the first-order factors must be used as predictors (Gustafsson & Balke, 1993). However, such non-standard models are not easily implementable in many of the standard structural equation modeling software packages and the results may be difficult to explain to substantive researchers.

Fifth, in the bifactor model, we can test measurement invariance of the domain factors, in addition to the general factor in different groups (e.g., males vs. females). In contrast, in the second-order model, only the second-order factor can be directly tested for invariance between groups, as the domain factors are represented by disturbances. Measurement invariance involves testing the equivalence of measured constructs in two or more independent groups to assure that the same constructs are being assessed in each group (Chen, 2007).

Finally, in the bifactor model, latent mean differences in both the general and domain factors can be compared across different groups, given an adequate level of measurement invariance. In contrast, in the second-order model only the second-order latent means can be directly compared. For example, using a bifactor model, Gustafsson (1992) was able to compare latent mean differences between white and black participants in general intelligence as well as three domain specific abilities: "broad" verbal ability, "broad" spatial-figure ability, and "narrow" memory span ability. In their Swedish sample, it was found that the white participants scored higher than black participants on all abilities except for memory span.

We do not wish to imply that bifactor model is more applicable than second-order models under all conditions, however. If the general factor is the main focus of the research, the second-order factor model may be more parsimonious. Moreover, the bifactor and second-order representations are not mutually exclusive, and they can coexist in different parts of the same complex model. Eid, Litschetzke, Nussbeck, and Trierweiler (2003) provide some examples in their representations of second-order multi-trait multi-method models.

Exploratory Bifactor Model Analysis

As the conventional confirmatory factor analysis, the bifactor CFA requires that an a priori factor structure in which each item loads on the general factor as well as on its intended group factor (Chen et al., 2006). However, if items cross-load on more than one factor it can be problematic for the CFA bifactor model in which the cross-loadings are forced to be zero.

One way to detect the issue of cross-loadings is to conduct exploratory bifactor analysis. There are three estimation methods within the framework of exploratory bifactor analysis: Schmid–Leiman transformations, target rotations, and bifactor rotations. These exploratory models are in fact functionally equivalent, even though they seem to offer different representations of the factor structure. In other words, they provide different types of reparameterization for a multidimensional data set with correlated factors.

Schmid–Leiman transformations

The history of exploratory bifactor analysis can be dated back in Holzinger and Swineford's early work (Holzinger & Swineford, 1937). Twenty years later, a simple bifactor estimation method, the Schmid–Leiman transformation (SL; Schmid & Leiman, 1957), was introduced, and it has become the primary approach in exploratory bifactor modeling. Specifically, it follows a four-step approach: Step 1: a specified number of primary factors were extracted from a covariance matrix based on an estimation method (e.g., Maximum Likelihood). Step 2: an oblique factor rotation is performed. Step 3: a second-order factor is extracted from the primary factor covariance matrix. Step 4: an SL orthogonalization of the second-order factor solution is performed to obtain the loadings for each item on the orthogonal general factor and group factors.

As in the confirmatory bifactor model, each item is expected to load on two primary factors: the general factor and its intended group factor. However, as in the conventional EFA, each item is also allowed to load on more than one group factor. Importantly, as noted earlier, the Schmid–Leiman transformation imposes two specific proportion constraints in its factor structure (Yung, et al., 1999). When the assumption of proportionality constraints is violated, which is not unusual in real data, the parameter estimation of the SL transformation will be biased. For example, in the presence of non-negligible cross-loadings, loadings on the general factor tend to be overestimated and loadings on the group factor tend to be underestimated. The larger the cross-loadings of items on multiple group factors, the larger the degree of this distortion (Reise et al., 2010, 2011). On the other hand, these proportionality constraints can be relaxed for broader application of the SL transformation. For example, Yung et al. (1999) have used the generalized Schmidt–Leiman transformation, in which no proportionality constraints are imposed, to demonstrate that second-order models are in fact nested within the bifactor models (see also Rindskopf & Rose, 1988).

Target rotations

The target bifactor rotation estimation represents an alternative approach for the estimation of the parameters in exploratory bifactor models in which no proportionality constraints are imposed (Reise et al., 2011). It allows a researcher to specify a target pattern matrix in which each element in the target factor pattern is either specified or unspecified. Extracted factors are then rotated to this target matrix. Specifically, it involves three steps: Step 1, a priori factor pattern matrix is specified based on theory or preliminary data analyses. Step 2, regular EFA is conducted. Step 3, the extracted factor matrix is rotated to minimize the difference between the estimated factor pattern obtained in Step 2 and the specified elements of the target factor pattern specified in Step 1 (Browne, 2001).

The major challenge that faces the use of targeted bifactor rotations is that a researcher must correctly specify the initial target matrix. One can rely on theory to determine the number of factors and the domain factors that items intend to measure. A researcher can also conduct preliminary factor analyses to guide the development of a bifactor target structure. The target matrix in a targeted rotation thus represents partial knowledge with regard to the structure of the factor pattern. It forms the foundation for a rotation that minimizes the sum of squared differences between the target and the rotated factor pattern. When the target matrix is not correctly specified, the results can be misleading.

Given a correctly specified target pattern, Monte Carlo simulation work suggests that the target bifactor rotations could recover the known true population parameters successfully, even when there were cross-loadings on group factors (Reise et al., 2011). To judge the adequacy of the resulting solution, the root mean square standard deviation can be computed based on the difference between the estimated pattern and the target pattern (Cai, 2010).

Bifactor rotations

The bifactor rotation estimation provides another alternative for exploratory bifactor analysis (Jennrich & Bentler, 2011). As in the confirmatory bifactor model, each item is expected to load on two primary factors: the general factor and its intended group factor. However, as in the conventional EFA, each item is also allowed to load on all other factors. Therefore, the only different between the exploratory bifactor rotations and the confirmatory bifactor analysis is that each item can load on its primary factors as well as other factors. Researchers have applied the bifactor rotations to data sets that had been previously analyzed using confirmatory bifactor methods. It was found that results from the exploratory bifactor rotation estimation and those from the confirmatory bifactor analyses were rather consistent (Jennrich & Bentler, 2011).

The readers are reminded that EFA can only inform us the approximate nature of the factor structure, but it can never solve the problem of cross-loadings or correlated domain factors in the bifactor model. Even though the model can be now correctly specified, the issue of interpretation remains. One major attraction of the bifactor model is its conceptual clarity, in that the general factor captures the commonality shared by all domains and the group factors represent the unique contribution of individual domains, over the beyond the general factor. However, with cross-loaded items on multiple group factors or correlated group factors, the bifactor model loses its major attraction. The fundamental solution would have to come from researchers who develop and actively use these multifaceted scales. We need to develop new scales or modify existing ones so that clear a factor structures can emerge and be used subsequently in psychological research.

Applications of Bifactor Models

The main purpose of this section is to introduce the potential applicability of bifactor models in psychometric test development. Bifactor models can be applied over a wide range of domains, and we will focus on two areas: its suitability for testing and measurement of multidimensional constructs and its potential for addressing conceptual debates in psychological research.

Testing and measurement of multifaceted constructs

Psychological constructs are often characterized by several related facets. There is, however, a long-standing and unresolved debate in psychological research on how to measure and test such multifaceted constructs (e.g., Briggs & Cheek, 1988; Carver,

1989; Finch & West, 1997; Hull, Lehn, & Tedlie, 1991; Neuberg, Judice, & West, 1997; Smith, McCarthy, & Zapolski, 2009). There is also a related debate in industrial and organizational psychology on the bandwidth-fidelity dilemma. It concerns the use of broad versus narrow personality measures to predict job performance for personnel selection (e.g., Ones & Viswesvaran, 1996; Paunonen, Rothstein, & Jackson, 1999; Tett, Steele, & Beauregard, 2003).

Researchers working with multifaceted constructs often have to choose between two problematic approaches that can yield very different results. The multifaceted constructs are often measured with several subscales, each of which intends to tap one facet of the construct. For example, in the motivational example of this paper, subjective well-being is comprised of three related facets: positive affect, negative affect, and life satisfaction. The total score approach involves creating a composite score from the individual facets. The individual score approach involves analyzing separately each facet of the construct.[4] The challenge that researchers face is that each approach sacrifices some useful information. A composite score mostly captures the shared effects but does not separate the unique effects from the shared variance. On the other hand, analyzing the facets separately appears to capture their unique contributions, but the specific effects of the facets are often entangled with the effects of the shared general construct. Both approaches can result in conceptual ambiguity.

Which method is preferable? Researchers have debated this issue for some time (e.g., Carver, 1989; Hull et al., 1991), and it is still a dilemma today (e.g., Smith et al., 2009). This article proposes that the bifactor model can offer the best of both worlds (Chen et al., 2012). This approach can have broad applicability across areas of psychology, as it combines the advantages, but avoids the drawbacks, of the two existing methods.

We first review the strengths and weaknesses of the total score and individual score approaches. We then introduce the bifactor model, which simultaneously assesses the general effect shared by the facets and the specific effects associated with the facets.

Total score approach The total score approach forms a composite by taking the sum or mean of the facets of a multifaceted construct, giving each component equal weight. The composite score is then correlated with predictors or outcome variables of interest. The total score approach has three primary advantages: (1) It is simple both conceptually and data-analytically; (2) it incorporates more items than any of the facets, and as the number of items increases, the reliability of a scale also tends to increase; and (3) it tends to provide greater content validity than its individual facets. That is, the conceptual coverage of the total score is broader than any of its facets, and thus more adequately captures the complexity of the underlying construct (Carmines & Zeller, 1979).

A significant drawback of the total score approach, however, is that it does not provide information on the relations between the individual facets and the outcome variables. When a total score is used to predict an outcome variable, it is unclear whether the outcome is equally associated with all of the facets, associated with a single facet in all settings, or associated with different facets in different settings. This ambiguity could have important implications. If only some facets of a multifaceted construct predict an observed effect, the total score will yield weaker research findings relative to the individual components because nonpredictive facets are included in the total score.

---

[4] The distinction between the total score and individual score approaches to analyzing multifaceted constructs is similar to the distinction between subscale and item-level analyses.

More than a decade ago, researchers have warned that inclusion of nonpredictive facets can lead to the development of inappropriate theories, wasted research efforts, and inappropriate prevention and therapy programs aimed at modifying irrelevant facets (Carver, 1989; Hull et al., 1991). In principle, it is even possible that the facets are related to an external variable in opposite directions, resulting in a misleading null effect. The total score approach is still commonly used, yet the drawbacks of this approach are rarely mentioned in the discussion of research findings.

Individual score approach The individual score approach tests the facets of a construct individually by associating each facet with external variables.[5] This strategy appears to compensate for the disadvantages of the total score approach by considering the role of each facet in the prediction of the outcome variable. However, this apparent advantage also contains disadvantages. The individual score approach is conceptually ambiguous because it cannot separate the unique contributions of a facet from the effect of the overall construct shared by all interrelated facets. Conceptually, two sources are contributing to a significant correlation between a facet and an outcome variable: unique variance associated with the facet and common variance shared by all facets. For some facets, both the unique and common variances are related to the outcome variable. For others, only the common variance is related to the outcome variable. The two sources of contribution can be distinguished only when the unique aspect of a facet is separated from the common aspect shared by all facets. In addition, the individual score approach tests multiple correlations (of each component) with an external variable, thus making it difficult to interpret the results. In an attempt to overcome the shortcomings of the individual approach, some researchers have related the residual of each facet (i.e., partialling out all other facets) to external measures (Jang, McCrae, Angleitner, Riemann, & Livesley, 1998; McCrae & Costa, 1992, 2008; McCrae et al., 1999). We term this approach the residual regression method. However, this approach does not have the modeling advantages that the bifactor model and second-order model offer, and it cannot be used to study mean differences in the facets.

Bifactor model approach We argue that the bifactor model is a viable solution for the test of multifaceted constructs in that it provides richer and conceptually less ambiguous information than either the total or individual score approach. As with the total score approach, the bifactor model estimates a general factor with greater content validity than any of its facets. As with the individual score approach, the bifactor model tests the unique contributions of the facets. It also overcomes the major drawback of the individual score approach in that it partials out the commonality among the facets when testing the unique association between each facet and an external variable. More specifically, this approach has several advantages. (1) It can simultaneously examine the general factor shared by the facets and group factors unique to the facets, and thus provide a conceptually unambiguous picture of the factor structure for the multifaceted construct. (2) It can simultaneously test the association of an outcome variable with the general factor as well as the unique contributions of the group factors that are distinct from the general construct, which can be important when researchers are interested in the unique contribution of the specific factors. (3) It can compare mean differences on

---

[5] The individual facets can also be entered simultaneously as predictors of an outcome variable in a multiple regression analysis. This type of analysis, often referred to as the regression approach (e.g., Hull et al., 1991), is often combined with the individual score approach.

variables, such as gender and ethnicity, on both the general and group factors. (4) It can be used to identify a facet that may no longer remain a unique contributor, after taking into account the common variance shared with other facets. Together, the advantages of the bifactor model can lead to greater conceptual clarity than the total and/or individual score approaches. The bifactor model clearly distinguishes the variances explained by the common factor and the group factors, whereas the other two approaches do not make such distinctions (Chen et al., 2006; Chen et al., 2012).

Addressing conceptual debates: Psychological Well-Being versus Subjective Well-Being

Bifactor models can also be used to address conceptual debates in psychological research. For example, one major controversy concerns whether there is a meaningful differentiation between psychological well-being (PWB) and subjective well-being (SWB). Understanding the structure of well-being has both theoretical and practical implications, as well-being plays a central role in the key psychological processes.

Theories of well-being The SWB perspective emphases the hedonic aspect of well-being (i.e., happiness and the pleasant life), which involves global evaluations of affect and quality of life (Diener, 1984). Hedonic theories of well-being have been the most extensively studied models of well-being. Exemplifying the hedonic tradition, researchers such as Flugel (1925) and Bradburn (1969) examined how people feel as they go about their daily lives. Diener's (1984) review of research on SWB culminated in a model composed of a person's cognitive and affective evaluations of life as a whole. Specifically, Diener considers SWB to be the experience of high levels of pleasant emotions and moods, low levels of negative emotions and moods, and high levels of life satisfaction.

The PWB perspective focuses on the eudaimonic aspect of well-being (i.e., human potential and the meaningful life), which involves perceived thriving in meeting the existing challenges of life (e.g., pursuing meaningful goals, growing and developing as a person, establishing quality ties to others) (Ryff, 1989; Ryff & Keyes, 1995; Ryff & Singer, 2008). In the eudaimonic tradition (Waterman, 1993), well-being is considered the outcome of positive goal pursuits (Ryan, Huta, & Deci, 2008). Ryff (1989) reviewed work from developmental, humanistic, and clinical psychology and presented a model of psychological (eudaimonic) well-being that includes six components: autonomy, environmental mastery, personal growth, positive relations with others, purpose in life, and self-acceptance. This model of eudaimonic well-being rests on the assumption that individuals strive to function fully and realize their unique talents. The six dimensions of eudaimonic well-being encompass that includes positive evaluation of oneself and one's past life, a sense of continued growth and development as a person, the belief that one's life is purposeful and meaningful, quality relations with others, the capacity to effectively manage one's life and surrounding world, and a sense of self-determination (Ryff & Keyes, 1995; Ryff & Singer, 2008).

The conceptual distinction between these two types of well-being is under debate. One camp argues that SWB and PWB address distinct aspects of well-being, although both are fundamentally concerned with the subjective nature of well-being (Keyes, Shmotkin, & Ryff, 2002). The other camp proposes that SWB and PWB reflect two traditions rather than two separate concepts of well-being, as they are more similar than different from each other (Kashdan, Biswas-Diener, & King, 2008).

Testing the debate: Bifactor modeling of well-being Are SWB and PWB two separate constructs or simply two approaches to the study of well-being? One direct way to address this issue is to examine the joint factor structure of SWB and PWB and their differential predictive power. However, the existing studies did not separate the unique variance associated with SWB and PWB from the common variance shared by both types of well-being, which is crucial for clarifying the debate regarding the nature of well-being. Given that SWB and PWB are both concerned with the positive aspect of psychological functioning, it is expected that the two types of well-being would share some common ground. Given that SWB and PWB tend to address different aspect of well-being, it is expected that they would demonstrate distinctive nature of their own.

The bifactor model provides an ideal tool for examining the commonality between the two types of well-being as well as the unique aspect of each. Specifically, the bifactor model can estimate a general well-being factor shared by the two types of well-being, as well as the unique contribution of SWB and PWB in predicting outcome measures.

If SWB and PWB are indeed different constructs (Keyes et al., 2002), the two types of well-being would form a general factor, given that both are related to the positive nature of well-being, but their components would also form strong specific domain with unique predictive power, over and above the general well-being factor. On the other hand, if SWB and PWB reflect two theoretical perspectives rather than two distinct constructs (Kashdan, et al., 2008), they would form a strong general factor, and the residual variance of SWB and PWB would not form strong domain factors, as their variances would be largely explained by the general factor. Conceptually, the bifactor model can provide a synthetic understanding of the relations between SWB and PWB and their associations with important external variables.

The bifactor model was used to test these hypotheses in a college sample and a large nationally representative community sample (Chen et al., 2013). Findings from the bifactor model suggest that, on the one hand, the overall constructs of PWB and SWB are strongly related to each other. This is because PWB and SWB form a strong general factor of global well-being, which captures the common ground shared by the two types of well-being. This finding provides reasonable support for the notion that PWB and SWB are conceptually related to each other. On the other hand, after controlling for the general factor of global well-being, the components of PWB and of SWB formed group factors, which capture the unique variances of the domains. These group factors were related to a wide range of external variables, independent of the general well-being factor. This finding provides support for the view that PWB and SWB are distinct constructs, even though they are closely related.

Together, results from the bifactor model provide reasonable support for both views regarding the relations between PWB and SWB – the two constructs perspective and the two approaches perspective. When well-being is tested at general level, the two constructs are more similar than different. However, when well-being is examined with the specific components of PWB and SWB after partialling out the common variance shared with the general construct of global well-being, the two constructs are distinct with unique explanatory power of their own. The findings suggest that there might be merit to both perspectives on the relations between PWB and SWB and that it is more fruitful to study both types of well-being. Therefore, the bifactor model enables us to reconcile the two competing hypotheses and clarify the debate about the relations between PWB and SWB.

Testing convergent and discriminant validity of constructs: Depression and anxiety

Bifactor models can be used to test the convergent and divergent validity of psychological constructs that are closely related to each other. For example, there is substantial comorbidity among depression and anxiety disorders, which has resulted in an urgent need for developing new models to describe and explain the complex relations in these domains (see Simms et al., 2008). Ideally, the new models are expected to serve two major purposes. On the one hand, it can cover the general domain of these disorders that is broad enough to encompass the full range of features observed clinically. On the other hand, it can identify parsimonious and distinct dimensions of anxious and depressive symptomatology, independent of the general domain.

In an attempt to capture the common and distinct features of anxiety and depression, a number of complex dimensional models have been proposed, and there is some consensus among these models. First, the central role that general distress plays in the mood and anxiety disorder is emphasized. Second, the importance of the unique features of these disorders is acknowledged. That is, the general distress factor is not sufficient enough to capture the heterogeneity in mood or anxiety disorder. Rather, the existence of the unique components will help differentiate diverse symptom groups (e.g., panic vs. generalized anxiety), independent of the shared general distress.

Once again, the bifactor model represents an ideal tool for answering these questions. Simms et al. (2008) examined the bifactor structure of depression and anxiety symptoms in samples of psychiatric patients, community adults, and college students. The findings were generally consistent across the three samples: (1) The general factor represented a general distress dimension that was shared by depression and anxiety disorders, as it was strongly associated with depressive and anxious symptomatology as well as trait negative emotionality. The general distress dimension also differentiated psychiatric from nonpsychiatric patients. (2) Certain symptom groups (e.g., dysphoria, generalized anxiety, and irritability) shared more variance with the general factor, whereas others (e.g., appetite gain, appetite loss, and low well-being) were more distinct from rest of the disorders, as they formed strong group factors. (c) Finally, some symptom groups (e.g., suicidality, panic, appetite loss, and ill temper) showed higher severity levels than other symptom groups. These findings have important implications for how psychopathological disorders should be described, assessed, and studied.

Scale construction

Bifactor models can also be useful in scale construction and evaluation. When developing a new multifaceted scale or evaluating an existing instrument that intends to measure a multifaceted construct, the strength of the factor loadings on the general and group factors can be used to guide item selection or re-evaluation of an existing scales. Ideally, items should load stronger on the general construct than on the facets. If certain items primarily load on the general construct with weak loadings on their facets, those facets should be eliminated. If certain items load primarily on the group factor, they should be omitted from the multifaceted scale, as they do not contribute substantially to the general construct.

Limitations

There are several limitations to consider with the bifactor models.

First, as in the test of any CFA models, the bifactor model requires sufficiently large sample sizes, given that more parameters are estimated than in total score or individual score approaches. Minimum sample size depends on several aspects of a given study, including the level of communality of the variables and the level of overdetermination of the factors (MacCallum, Widaman, Zhang, & Hong, 1999). Compared to regular CFA models, the bifactor model may require the provision of start values for the model to converge, and thus it may take more effort to run the model, given the unique nature of the bifactor models. In addition, as in other CFA models, the bifactor model is not appropriate given weak loadings, nonconvergence, and poor fit.

Second, the bifactor model that we have considered here is the canonical version in which the general factor and each of the domain factors are assumed to be orthogonal. An attractive feature of this version is that the results are easy to interpret and it can wide applicability in applied research. However, the orthogonality constraints, which are imposed on the relations between the general and group factors as well as on the relations among the group factors, may be too stringent under certain circumstances. In cases where some group factors are in fact correlated, such orthogonality constraints will not be appropriate, which in turn can lead to model misspecification.

However, as we move away from the orthogonal version of the model and allow covariances between group factors, problems of identification can occur. For example, Mulaik and Quartetti (1997) found that when the general factor is allowed to covary with group factors, the model will not converge. Similarly, Rindskopf and Rose (1988) found evidence of identification problems when they allowed group factors to covary.[6] In addition to the identification problem, it becomes difficult to interpret a bifactor model when group factors are allowed to correlate with each other (Chen et al., 2006; Rindskopf & Rose, 1988).

When two or more group factors are substantially correlated with each other, independent of the general factor, it suggests that there are additional unmodeled general factors. In this case, the solution is simple: to create a second layer of a general factor among the correlated group factors. For example, the bifactor model has recently been used to test the fundamental structure of affect (Chen et al., 2016). Positive affect and negative affect were measured with respect to high, moderate, and low levels of activation. It was found that independent of the general affect factor across positive affect and negative affect, the three levels of negative affect across activation (i.e., high, moderate, and low) were still correlated substantially. The original bifactor model was then modified by collapsing the three levels of negative affect into a second layer of general factor, termed negative affect, independent of the general factor that represents the commonality shared by all levels of positive affect and negative affect.

Finally, not all multifaceted constructs can be subjected to a bifactor structure. Only when the multidimensional facets are moderately or strongly correlated with each other,

---

[6] Similar identification issues also affect second-order models in which assumptions of orthogonality are relaxed.

can a bifactor model apply. In other words, when the facets are connected by a common underlying factor, the bifactor model provides an ideal tool for representing such multifaceted constructs.

Conclusions

Bifactor models can be applied to a wide range of psychological constructs and help researchers address both conceptual and methodological issues. Psychological constructs are often characterized by several related facets and bifactor models are particularly useful for representing such constructs. Bifactor models are also well-suited for testing the unique predictive power of group factors, independent of the general factor. Similarly, bifactor models can be used to test group differences such as gender and culture on group factors after partialling out the general factor. Bifactor models also represent an ideal tool for assessing the dimensionality of constructs. Importantly, bifactor models can be used to address debates regarding conceptual differences among several related constructs and test the convergent and divergent validity of these constructs. Finally, bifactor models can be useful in scale construction and evaluation.

References

Bentler, P. M. (1990). Latent variable structural models for separating specific from general effects. In L. Sechrest, E. Perrin, & J. Bunker (Eds.), *Research methodology: Strengthening causal interpretations of nonexperimental data* (pp. 61–80). U.S. Department of Health and Human Services, Public Health Service, Agency for Health Care Policy and Research.

Bludworth, J. L., Tracey, T. J. G., & Glidden-Tracey, C. (2010). The bi-level structure of the outcome questionnaire-45. *Psychological Assessment, 22,* 350–355.

Bradburn, N. M. (1969). *The structure of psychological well-being.* Chicago: Aldine.

Briggs, S. R., & Cheek, J. M. (1988). On the nature of self-monitoring: Problems with assessment, problems with validity. *Journal of Personality and Social Psychology, 54,* 663–678.

Brouwer, D., Meijer, R. R., Weekers, A. M., & Baneke, J. J. (2008). On the dimensionality of the dispositional hope scale. *Psychological Assessment, 20,* 310–315.

Browne, M. W. (2001). An overview of analytic rotation in exploratory factor analysis. *Multivariate Behavioral Research, 36,* 111–150.

Cai, L. (2010). A two-tier full-information item factor analysis model with applications. *Psychometrika, 4,* 581–612.

Cai, L., Yang, J. S., & Hansen, M. (2011). Generalized full-information item bifactor analysis. *Psychological Methods, 16,* 221–248.

Carmines, E. G., & Zeller, R. A. (1979). *Reliability and validity assessment.* Beverly Hills, CA: Sage.

Carver, C. S. (1989). How should multifaceted personality constructs be tested? Issues illustrated by self-monitoring, attributional style, and hardiness. *Journal of Personality and Social Psychology, 56,* 577–585.

Chen, F. F. (2007). Sensitivity of goodness of fit indices to lack of measurement invariance. *Structural Equation Modeling, 14,* 464–504.

Chen, F. F., Hayes, A., Carver, C. S., Laurenceau, J. P., & Zhang, Z. (2012). Modeling general and specific variance in multifaceted constructs: A comparison of the bifactor model to other approaches. *Journal of Personality, 80,* 219–251.

Chen, F. F., Jing, Y., Hayes, A., & Lee, J. (2013). Two concepts or two approaches? A bifactor analysis of psychological and subjective well-being. *Journal of Happiness Studies*, *14*, 1033–1068.

Chen, F. F., Bai, L., Lee, J. M., & Jing, Y. (2016). Culture and the structure of affect: A bifactor modeling approach. *Journal of Happiness Studies*, *17*, 1801–1824. DOI: 10.1007/s10902-015-9671-3.

Chen, F. F., West, S. G., & Sousa, K. H. (2006). A comparison of bifactor and second-order models of quality of life. *Multivariate Behavioral Research*, *41*, 189–225.

Costa, P. T., & McCrae, R. R. (1992). *Revised NEO Personality Inventory (NEO-PI-R) and NEO Five-Factor Inventory (NEO-FFI) professional manual*. Odessa, FL: Psychological Assessment Resources.

DeYoung, C. G., Peterson, J. B., & Higgins, D. M. (2002). Higher-order factors of the Big Five predict conformity: Are there neuroses of health? *Personality and Individual Differencesi 33*, 533–552.

Diener, E. (1984). Subjective well-being. *Psychological Bulletin*, *95*, 542–575.

Eid, M., Lischetzke, T., Nussbeck, F., & Trierweiler, L. (2003). Separating trait effects from trait-specific method effects in multitrait-multimethod models: A multiple-indicator CT-C(M-1) Model. *Psychological Methods*, *8*, 38–60.

Finch, J. F. & West, S. G. (1997). The investigation of personality structure: Statistical models. *Journal of Research in Personality*, *31*, 439–485.

Flugel, J. (1925). A quantitative study of feeling and emotion in everyday life. *British Journal of Psychology*, *15*, 318–355.

Gustafsson, J. (1992). The relevance of factor analysis for the study of group differences. *Multivariate Behavioral Research*, *27*, 239–247.

Gustafsson, J., & Balke, G. (1993). General and specific abilities as predictors of school achievement. *Multivariate Behavioral Research*, *28*, 407–434.

Holzinger, K. J., & Swineford, S. (1937). The bi-factor method. *Psychometrika*, *47*, 41–54.

Hull, J. G., Lehn, D. A., & Tedlie, J. C. (1991). A general approach to testing multifaceted personality constructs. *Journal of Personality and Social Psychology*, *61*, 932–945.

Jang, K. L., McCrae, R. R., Angleitner, A., Riemann, R., & Livesley, W. J. (1998). Heritability of facet-level traits in a cross-cultural twin sample: Support for a hierarchical model of personality. *Journal of Personality and Social Psychology*, *74*, 1556–1565.

Jennrich, R. I., & Bentler, P. M. (2011). Exploratory bi-factor analysis. *Psychometrika*, *76*, 537–549.

Judge, T. A., Erez, A., Bono, J. E., & Thoresen, C. J. (2002). Are measures of self-esteem, neuroticism, locus of control, and generalized self-efficacy indicators of a common core construct? *Journal of Personality and Social Psychology*, *83*, 693–710.

Kashdan, T. B., Biswas-Diener, R., & King, L. A. (2008). Reconsidering happiness: The costs of distinguishing between hedonics and eudaimonia. *The Journal of Positive Psychology*, *3*, 219–233.

Keyes, C. L. M., Shmotkin, D., & Ryff, C. D. (2002). Optimizing well-being: The empirical encounter of two traditions. *Journal of Personality and Social Psychology*, *82*, 1007–1022.

Luo, D., Petrill, S. A., & Thompson, L. A. (1994). An exploration of genetic g: Hierarchical factor analysis of cognitive data from the western reserve twin project. *Intelligence*, *18*, 335–347.

MacCallum, R. C., Widaman, K. F., Zhang, S., & Hong, S. (1999). Sample size in factor analysis. *Psychological Methods*, *4*, 84–99.

Marsh, H. W., Ellis, L. A., & Craven, R. G. (2002). How do preschool children feel about themselves? Unraveling measurement and multidimensional self-concept structure. *Developmental Psychology*, *38*, 376–393.

McCrae, R. R., & Costa, P. T. (1992). Discriminant validity of NEO-PIR facet scales. *Educational and Psychological Measurement*, *52*, 229–237.

McCrae, R. R., & Costa, P. T., Jr. (2008). Empirical and theoretical status of the five-factor model of personality traits. In G. J. Boyle, G. Matthews, & D. H. Saklofske (Eds.), *The SAGE handbook of personality theory and assessment, Vol 1: Personality theories and models* (pp. 273–294). Thousand Oaks, CA, US: Sage Publications, Inc.

McCrae, R. R., Costa, P. T., de Lima, M. P., Simões, A., Ostendorf, F., Angleitner, A., Marušić, I., Bratko, D., Caprara, G. V., Barbaranelli, C., Chae, J., & Piedmont, R. L. (1999). Age differences in personality across the adult life span: Parallels in five cultures. *Developmental Psychology, 35,* 466–477.

McDonald, R. P. (1999). *Test theory: A unified treatment.* Mahwah, NJ: Lawrence Erlbaum Associates.

Mulaik, S. A., & Quartetti, D. A. (1997). First order or higher order general factor? *Structural Equation Modeling, 4,* 193–211.

Neuberg, S. L., Judice, T. N., & West, S. G. (1997). What the need for closure scale measures and what it does not: Toward conceptually and operationally differentiating among related epistemic motives. *Journal of Personality and Social Psychology, 72,* 1396–1412.

Ones, D. S., & Viswesvaran, C. (1996). Bandwidth-fidelity dilemma in personality measurement for personnel selection. *Journal of Organizational Behavior, 17,* 609–626.

Patrick, C. J., Hicks, B. M., Nichol, P. E., & Krueger, R. F. (2007). A bi-factor approach to modeling the structure of the Psychopathy checklist-revisited. *Journal of Personality Disorders, 21,* 118–141.

Paunonen, S. V., Rothstein, M. G., & Jackson, D. N. (1999). Narrow reasoning about the use of broad personality measures for personnel selection. *Journal of Organizational Behavior, 20,* 389–405.

Reise, S. P. (2012). The rediscovery of bifactor measurement models. *Multivariate Behavioral Research, 47,* 667–696.

Reise, S. P., Moore, T. M., & Haviland, M. G. (2010). Bi-factor models and rotations: Exploring the extent to which multidimensional data yield univocal scale scores. *Journal of Personality Assessment, 92,* 544–559.

Reise, S. P., Moore, T. M., & Maydeu-Olivares, A. (2011). Targeted bifactor rotations and assessing the impact of model violations on the parameters of unidimensional and bifactor models. *Educational and Psychological Measurement, 71,* 684–711.

Reise, S. P., Morizot, J., & Hays, R. D. (2007). The role of the bifactor model in resolving dimensionality issues in health outcomes measures. *Quality of Life Research, 16,* 19–31.

Reise, S. P., Scheines, R., Widaman, K. F., & Haviland, M. G. (2013). Multidimensionality and structural coefficient bias in structural equation modeling: A bifactor perspective. *Educational and Psychological Measurement, 73,* 5–26.

Rindskopf, D. (1984). Structural equation models: Empirical identification, Heywood cases, and related problems. *Sociological Methods and Research, 13,* 109–119.

Rindskopf, D., & Rose, T. (1988). Some theory and applications of confirmatory second-order factor analysis. *Multivariate Behavioral Research, 23,* 51–67.

Ryan, R. M., Huta, V., & Deci, E. L. (2008). Living well: A self-determination theory perspective on eudaimonia. *Journal of Happiness Studies, 9,* 139–170.

Ryff, C. D. (1989). Happiness is everything, or is it? Explorations on the meaning of psychological well-being. *Journal of Personality and Social Psychology, 57,* 1069–1081.

Ryff, C. D., & Keyes, C. L. M. (1995). The structure of psychological well-being revisited. *Journal of Personality and Social Psychology, 69,* 719–727.

Ryff, C. D., & Singer, B. H. (2008). Know thyself and become what you are: A eudaimonic approach to psychological well-being. *Journal of Happiness Studies, 9,* 13–39.

Schmid, J., & Leiman, J. M. (1957). The development of hierarchical factor solutions. *Psychometrika, 22,* 53–61.

Simms, L. J., Grös, D. F., Watson, D., & O'Hara, M. W. (2008). Parsing the general and specific components of depression and anxiety with bifactor modeling. *Depression and Anxiety, 25,* E34–E46.

Smith, G. T., McCarthy, D. M., & Zapolski, T. C. B. (2009). On the value of homogeneous constructs for construct validation, theory testing, and the description of psychopathology. *Psychological Assessment, 21,* 272–284.

Tett, R. P., Steele, J. R., & Beauregard, R. S. (2003). Broad and narrow measures on both sides of the personality-job performance relationship. *Journal of Organizational Behavior, 24,* 335–356.

Waterman, A. S. (1993). Two conceptions of happiness: Contrasts of personal expressiveness (eudaimonia) and hedonic enjoyment. *Journal of Personality and Social Psychology, 64,* 678–691.

Wherry, R. J. (1959). Hierarchical factor solutions without rotation. *Psychometrika, 24,* 45–51.

Yung, Y.-F., Thissen, D., & McLeod, L. D. (1999). On the relation between the higher-order factor model and the hierarchical factor model. *Psychometrika, 64,* 113–128.

13

Nonnormality in Latent Trait Modelling

Dylan Molenaar and Conor V. Dolan

"Since its inception a century ago (Spearman, 1904, 1927), factor analysis has become one of the most widely used multivariate statistical procedures [...]" (Brown, 2006; p. 12).

In his influential 1927 book on intelligence that led to the development of linear factor analysis, Charles Spearman presented two correlation matrices of ability tests. One matrix was obtained in a sample of healthy individuals and the other matrix was obtained in a sample of individuals with low IQ who today might be diagnosed with an intellectual disability. Spearman noted that the correlations were much larger in the latter sample. From this observation, he formulated what is now often referred to by **Spearman's Law of Diminishing Returns**, or ability differentiation. These refer to the hypothesis that the general factor of intelligence factor, that is, the predominant source of individual differences commonly found in intelligence test scores, is a stronger source of variance at its lower end as compared to its upper end. If this hypothesis it true, it has interesting implications for the expected distribution of scores on intelligence tests, specifically, that they will be nonnormal in the population.

Although Spearman hinted at the possibility of nonnormally distributed variables in his classic 1927 book, the normal distribution has played a central role in modern factor analysis. In many of the developments that followed Spearman's work (e.g., multidimensional factor analysis, Thurstone, 1947; multigroup factor analysis, Jöreskog, 1971; item factor analysis, Christoffersson, 1975), the observed data are assumed to originate from a normal distribution. This is assumed either directly (i.e., in the use of normal theory maximum likelihood estimation on the subtest scores; Lawley, 1947) or indirectly (in the use of polychoric correlations that are based on a normally distributed latent response variate underlying the discrete variables; Olsson, 1979).

The use of the normal distribution in factor analysis is largely pragmatic. That is, the probability density, being reasonably simple, results in tractable likelihood functions. In addition, under a normal distribution, the (polychoric) means and covariances are sufficient statistics for the model parameters. In the case of item scores, assuming a normal distribution for the latent response variates has the additional practical advantage that the well-established methodology for linear factor analysis (e.g., absolute model fit assessment by the RMSEA) can be applied to the item models.

The use of a normal distribution can be justified by the central limit theorem. For instance, in the case of subtest scores, the observed distribution will approach a normal distribution if many items are summed. In addition, for item scores, the latent response variates will approach a normal distribution if many independent processes underlie these variables. This idea is consistent with the findings of genome wide association studies that very many genetic variants contribute to the variance of psychological variables (such as intelligence; Davies et al., 2011). However, even though a normal distribution can serve as a reasonable approximation of the true distribution of the subtest scores and latent response variates in some areas of application, nonnormality is not exceptional. For instance, Micceri (1989) collected 440 datasets containing psychometric and achievement measures, and found all measures to be nonnormally distributed. Fortunately, numerous approaches are available to handle such data. For instance, models could be fitted using asymptotic distribution free theory (Browne, 1984) or unweighted least squares (Bollen, 1989), and the model could be evaluated using the rescaled χ^2 procedure (Satorra & Bentler, 1988). For item scores, nonparametric models exist such as the Mokken model (Mokken, 1970) and models that use splines to approximate the distribution function of the latent response variates (Ramsay & Abrahamowicz, 1989).

In these nonparametric approaches, possible violations of normality are accommodated, but the nonnormality is not explicitly tested. That is, it is unclear whether a nonparametric approach is needed at all. As the nonparametric approaches come with a cost (e.g., they are numerically demanding and require large sample sizes), an explicit statistical test on nonnormality is desirable to establish whether one can rely on the standard, less demanding parametric approaches (e.g., normal theory maximum likelihood estimation). For subtest scores, testing for nonnormality is possible using the test developed by Mardia (1970) for multivariate skewness and kurtosis of the observed data. In addition, the well-known test on univariate normality by Shapiro and Wilks (1965) could be used to test each variable separately. For tests on the normality of the latent response variate underlying item scores in item factor analysis, tests have been proposed by Jöreskog (2002, p. 13) and by Muthén and Hofacker (1988). However, all these tests are omnibus tests in the sense that they do not consider the exact source of nonnormality in the factor model (e.g., floor/ceiling effects or nonlinearity). As we show in this chapter, more specific tests are possible. That is, within the (item) factor model, nonnormality may arise because of a nonnormal latent trait, nonnormal or heteroscedastic residuals, and level-dependent factor loadings (i.e., the values of the factor loadings depend on the value or level of the latent trait).

Testing for the specific source of nonnormality has a number of advantages. First, it constitutes a test on the assumptions per se. That is, results of statistical models can only be trusted if the underlying assumptions are met. So, testing these assumptions is important in its own right. Bauer (2005), for instance, illustrates how applying a linear factor model to nonlinear data can result in wrong conclusions concerning group differences in subtest scores.

A second advantage is that tests on specific sources of nonnormality provide more powerful tests than marginal tests (i.e., tests that do not distinguish between the different sources of variability in the data). As shown by Molenaar, Dolan, and Verhelst

(2010), tests on heteroscedastic residuals, nonlinear factor loadings, and/or a nonnormal latent trait distribution are associated with larger statistical power as compared to the marginal test by Shapiro and Wilks (1965). Thus, if the normality assumptions need to be tested to justify application of a factor model, it is advisable to test for specific sources of nonnormality, as nonnormality due to – for instance – heteroscedastic residuals can be missed by the Shapiro–Wilks test.

Third, models for nonnormality within the (item) factor model facilitate investigation of parameter bias. A straightforward and common procedure to investigate the effect of unmodelled nonnormality within the (item) factor model would involve (1) simulating data according to a factor model in which a specific source of nonnormality is incorporated (e.g., heteroscedasticity) and (2) apply the standard model assuming normality. If conducted within a larger simulation study, bias on the parameter estimates (if any) will be noticeable by comparing the true parameter values to the average parameter estimates. However, as mentioned an explicit model is needed to enable data simulation. Thus, development of such an explicit model advances the investigation of parameter bias.

Finally, explicit (item) factor models for nonnormality enable tests of various substantive hypotheses that imply nonnormality. For instance, Spearman's Law of Diminishing Returns as discussed above implies that nonnormality in intelligence variables is caused by level-dependent factor loadings (Molenaar et al., 2010; see also Tucker-Drob, 2009), or a skewed latent trait distribution (Molenaar et al., 2010). However, if the nonnormality is due to heteroscedastic residuals, this implies that Spearman's postulation is based on a measurement problem, and not on a true (substantive) phenomenon. Thus, such heteroscedasticity should also be taken into account. Other examples of substantive applications in which specific departures from normality play a role include schematicity (Markus, 1977) in personality research, and genotype by environment interaction (Jinks & Fulker, 1970; van der Sluis, et al., 2006; Molenaar, van der Sluis, Boomsma, & Dolan, 2012) in behavior genetics.

In this chapter, we present tools to facilitate specific tests on three sources of nonnormality in subtest scores or latent response variates: nonnormality of the latent trait, heteroscedasticity of the manifest variable residuals, and level dependency of the factor loadings. The outline is as follows. First, the (item) factor model is outlined and existing approaches to test for each of the three sources of nonnormality are discussed. Then, a unified approach is outlined in which the different sources of nonnormality are tested simultaneously. Next, two examples are discussed in which the models are applied to intelligence subtest scores, and to affective analyzing item scores.

The Factor Model and Existing Approaches to Test for Sources of Nonnormality

Let z_{pi} denote the normally distributed score of subject p on variable i. A collection of these variables ($i = 1, ..., n$) can be submitted to a linear model as follows

$$z_{pi} = \nu_i + \lambda_i \eta_p + \varepsilon_{pi}, \qquad (13.1)$$

where ν_i is the intercept, λ_i is the factor loading, η_p is the latent trait, and ε_{pi} is a residual term with variance $\sigma_{\varepsilon i}^2$. Note that z_{pi} is not necessarily observable. Now let y_{pi} denote the observed score of subject p on variable i which is a realization of z_{pi}. If the realization y_{pi} is continuous (e.g., in the case of subtest scores or continuous item scores), the linear factor model is obtained from Equation 13.1 by

$$z_{pi} = y_{pi} \tag{13.2}$$

that is, there is a one-to-one mapping of the normally distributed z_{pi} variable and the observed continuous scores.[1] In the case that the realization y_{pi} is discrete (e.g., in the case of binary or polytomous item scores), the mapping between z_{pi} and y_{pi} is given by

$$y_{pi} = c \quad \text{if } \tau_{ic} < z_{pi} < \tau_{i(c+1)} \quad \text{for } c = 0, \ldots, C-1 \tag{13.3}$$

where C is the number of possible responses, τ_{ic} are the thresholds, and $\tau_{i0} = -\infty$ and $\tau_{iC} = \infty$. That is, it is assumed that the item responses in y_{pi} have arisen because of categorization of the normally distributed z_{pi} variable at thresholds τ_{ic}. The model given by Equation 13.1 and 13.3 is commonly referred to as the item factor model (Wirth & Edwards, 2007), and it can be shown to be equivalent to a two-parameter item response theory model for dichotomous data (Birnbaum, 1986), or a graded response model for polytomous data (Samejima, 1969; see Takane & De Leeuw, 1987).

In Equation 13.1, the assumed normality of z_{pi} implies that (1) the latent trait η_p has a normal distribution; (2) the residuals ε_{pi} are homoscedastic and normally distributed; and (3) the size of the factor loadings λ_i does not depend on the level of η_p (level independent factor loadings). In the next section, we review models that can be employed to tests these assumptions.

Distribution of the trait

Various nonnormal latent trait distributions have been proposed, including a lognormal distribution (van der Maas, et al., 2011), a generalized log-normal distribution (Verhelst, 2009), a skew-normal distribution (Azevedo, Bolfarine, & Andrade, 2011), and a distribution based on Johnson curves (van den Oord, 2005). Both the generalized log-normal distribution and the skew-normal distribution include one extra skewness parameter in addition to the common location and scale parameters in the normal distribution. If this skewness parameter equals zero, both distributions simplify to the normal distribution. That is, a normal trait model is nested in the generalized log-normal trait model and in the skew-normal trait model. Thus, a test on nonnormality in these models involves estimating the model parameters and testing the estimate of the skewness parameter on redundancy using one of the model selection tools discussed later. Testing for nonnormality using the Johnson curve approach proceeds in the same way except that there are two additional parameters, a skewness and a kurtosis parameter that need to be tested. As a log-normal trait model does not include the normal trait

---

[1] Truly continuous observed scores are rare. Pragmatically, one can consider a seven-point Likert scale to be continuous (Dolan, 1994).

model as a special case, nonnormality is investigated by comparing a log-normal trait model to normal trait model using fit indices that do not require nesting.

In addition to the parametric approaches here, nonnormal latent trait distributions have been accommodated by finite mixtures (Muthén & Muthén, 2007; Vermunt, 2004; Vermunt & Hagenaars, 2004), histograms (Schmitt, Mehta, Aggen, Kubarych, & Neale, 2006), or splines (Woods, 2007). In contrast to the methods previously, these approaches approximate the distribution instead of specifying an explicit distribution. As a result, a test on nonnormality involves comparison of the model to a normal baseline model as there are no explicit parameters that can be tested.

Heteroscedastic residuals

Approaches have been developed to incorporate heteroscedastic residuals in the linear factor model. These differ in the information that they use. Meijer and Mooijaart (1996), and Lewin-Koh and Amemiya (2003) presented heteroscedastic linear factor models that make use of the first three sample moments. Hessen and Dolan (2009), on the contrary, presented a full information test of heteroscedastic residuals. All these methods have in common that the residual variance is made a deterministic function of the latent trait, resulting in additional parameters (one in Meijer & Mooijaart, 1996; and one or more in Hessen & Dolan, 2009; and Lewin-Koh & Amemiya, 2003). If these additional parameters are constrained to equal zero, the standard homoscedastic model arises. Therefore, testing heteroscedasticity involves tests on these parameters similarly as in the nested model case discussed previously. Interestingly, with respect to the item factor model, heteroscedastic residuals have not previously been studied. This is remarkable as heteroscedasticity is well studied in probit and logit regression models (see Agresti, 2002, p. 15); that is, models that are closely related to the item factor model.

Level-dependent factor loadings

We employ the term level-dependent factor loadings if the magnitude of the factor loadings depends on the level of the latent trait. Note that models with quadratic factor loadings are an instance of level-dependent factor loadings. Factor models with quadratic terms have been well studied (e.g., Etezadi-Amoli & McDonald, 1983; Jaccard & Wan, 1995; Kenny & Judd, 1984; Klein & Moosbrugger, 2000; Lee & Zhu, 2002; McDonald, 1962; Yalcin & Amemiya, 2001). The level-dependent factor model extends this class of models by considering other functional forms for the factor loadings. For instance, in intelligence research, the positive manifold is a well-established phenomenon that implies strictly positive factor loadings. Quadratic factor loadings are potentially unsuitable because they can be negative given negative values of the latent trait. A more suitable form is the exponential function, which implies strictly positive factor loadings. In the item factor model, level-dependent factor loadings have yet to be considered. Notwithstanding the exact functional form of the relation between the factor loadings and the latent trait, tests on level dependency are conducted similarly as before. That is, the standard linear model is extended by incorporating level dependency parameters, which can be tested for redundancy using the model selection tools discussed later.

A Unified Approach to Test for Nonnormality

We present a unified full information approach that includes all three effects in a single model. The approach is applicable both to the item factor model (discrete scores) and to the linear factor model (continuous scores).

Nonnormal factor distribution

In principle, any distribution can be chosen for the latent trait. Here, we opt for the skew-normal distribution (Azzalini, 1986, 2005), because it includes the normal distribution as a special case, which facilitates the test of normality. Specifically, the skew-normal distribution includes a shape parameter that quantifies the degree of nonnormality in the trait distribution, and that is amenable to a direct statistical test. The density function of the skew-normal distribution is given by

$$g(\eta_p) = \frac{2}{\omega}\Phi\left(\zeta\frac{\eta_p - \kappa}{\omega}\right)\varphi\left(\frac{\eta_p - \kappa}{\omega}\right), \quad (13.4)$$

where $\Phi(.)$ denotes the normal distribution function, $\varphi(.)$ denotes the normal density function, ζ is the shape or nonnormality parameter, and κ and ω are location and scale parameters, respectively. These determine the latent trait mean and variance as follows (see Azzalini & Capatanio, 1999):

$$E(\eta_p) = \kappa + \omega\sqrt{\frac{2}{\pi}}\frac{\zeta}{\sqrt{1+\zeta^2}}, \quad (13.5)$$

and

$$VAR(\eta_p) = \omega\sqrt{1 - \frac{2}{\pi}\left(\frac{\zeta^2}{1+\zeta^2}\right)}. \quad (13.6)$$

In this distribution, the shape parameter ζ is of main interest. If this parameter equals 0, the skew-normal distribution simplifies to a normal distribution. This implies that a test of normality can be based on testing whether ζ differs significantly from 0. In addition, ζ can be used to quantify the departure from normality, and the direction of this departure. That is, if $\zeta < 0$, the distribution is negatively skewed or "skewed to the left" (i.e., the distribution has a disproportionally long left tail, see Figure 13.1, left). If $\zeta > 0$, the distribution if positively skewed or "skewed to the right" (i.e., the distribution has a disproportionally long right tail, see Figure 13.1, right).

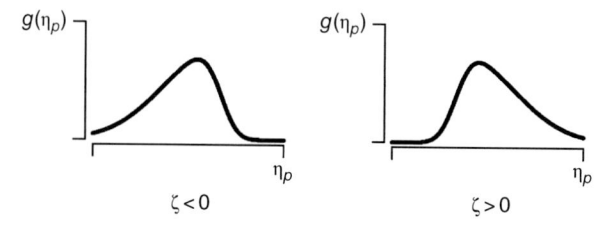

Figure 13.1 The skew-normal distribution for $\zeta < 0$ and $\zeta > 0$. The parameters values are $\kappa = 1$, $\omega = 1.7$, $\zeta = -4$ (left), and $\kappa = -1$, $\omega = 1.7$, $\zeta = 4$ (right).

Heteroscedastic residuals

Residuals are heteroscedastic if the residual variance varies with the value of latent trait. Hessen and Dolan (2009) incorporated heteroscedasticity in the linear factor model by making the residual variance an exponential function of the latent trait (i.e., they assume systematic heteroscedasticity). Here, their approach is adopted in the linear factor model. That is, in the case of subtest scores or continuous item scores, the residual variance $\sigma_{\varepsilon i}^2$ is modeled as

$$\sigma_{\varepsilon i}^2 | \eta_p = \exp\left(\beta_{0i} + \beta_{1i}\eta_p\right) \qquad (13.7)$$

where "$|\eta_p$" denotes conditioning on η_p (the latent trait). The exponential function is used as it has a lower asymptote of 0 (see Harvey, 1976; Hessen & Dolan, 2009), thus avoiding negative residual variance (i.e., a Heywood case). In the Equation (13.7), β_0 is a baseline parameter, and β_1 is a so-called heteroscedasticity parameter. If β_1 is equal to 0, the residuals are homoscedastic and equal to $\exp(\beta_0)$. A test on heteroscedasticity thus involves testing whether β_1 departs significantly from 0. If $\beta_1 < 0$, the residual variance is decreasing for increasing levels of the trait, see Figure 13.2 (left). If $\beta_1 > 0$, the residual variance is increasing for increasing levels of the trait, see Figure 13.2 (right). The function in Equation 13.7 includes only the linear term $\beta_1\eta$. Hessen and Dolan (2009) refer to this model as the minimal heteroscedasticity model. The function between $\sigma_{\varepsilon i}^2$ and η_p can be extended to include higher order terms (e.g., $\beta_2\eta^2, \beta_3\eta^3$, etc.) For this, see van der Sluis et al. (2006), and Molenaar et al. (2013).

For the item factor model, the function in Equation 13.7 to model heteroscedasticity will generally not work, as discussed by Molenaar, Dolan, and De Boeck (2012) and Molenaar (2015). Specifically, this function will cause the probability of choosing the first and last response option (i.e., 0 and C-1) to approach 0.5 for increasing values of η_p. This is undesirable, as the response probability in these answer categories should approach 0 or 1 for extreme values of the trait. Therefore, the following function to relate $\sigma_{\varepsilon i}^2$ to η_p is used for the item factor model,

$$\sigma_{\varepsilon i}^2 | \eta_p = \frac{2\beta_{0i}}{1 + \exp\left(-\beta_{1i}\eta_p\right)}. \qquad (13.8)$$

The key difference with Equation 13.8 is that in addition to the lower asymptote, the function has an upper asymptote of $2\beta_0$ that, for reasonable effect sizes, prevents the undesirable behavior, as discussed in Molenaar et al. (2012) and Molenaar (2015).

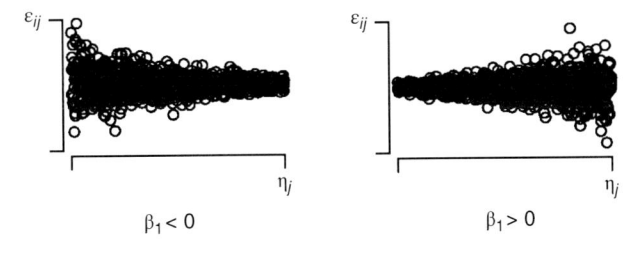

Figure 13.2 Heteroscedasticity according to the exponential function in Equation 13.7 for $\beta_{1i} < 0$ and $\beta_{1i} > 0$. Parameter values are $\beta_{0i} = -2, \beta_{1i} = -0.6$ (left), and $\beta_{0i} = -2, \beta_{1i} = 0.6$ (right).

Interpretation of the β_1 parameter is the same as in the case of the linear factor model in Equation 13.7. That is, for $\beta_1 = 0$ the residual variance is homoscedastic and equal to β_0. For $\beta_1 < 0$ residual variance is decreasing for increasing levels of the trait. For $\beta_1 > 0$ residual variance is increasing for increasing levels of the trait.

Level-dependent factor loadings

In the standard (item) factor model, the factor loadings are constant across the latent trait. To make the factor loadings level dependent, one needs to make the factor loadings a function of the latent trait (Molenaar et al., 2010). For instance, a simple option is the linear function, that is

$$\lambda_i(\eta_p) = \gamma_{0i} + \gamma_{1i}\eta_p, \tag{13.9}$$

where $\lambda_i(\eta_p)$ indicates that the factor loading is a function of η_p.[2] Substituting the linear function 13.9 into the factor model in Equation 13.1, the quadratic factor model arises (see Molenaar et al., 2010). In this model, parameter γ_{0i} is a baseline parameter, and parameter γ_{1i} is a level dependency parameter. If γ_{1i} is equal to 0, the factor loading is level independent and equal to λ_{0i}. A test on level dependency thus involves testing whether γ_{1i} departs significantly from 0. If $\gamma_{1i} < 0 (\gamma_{1i} > 0)$, the factor loading decreases (increases) with increasing levels of the trait. Note that the resulting relation between y_{pi} and η_p is quadratic. There could be reasons to consider a different function for $\lambda_i(\eta_p)$. For instance, if the data is standardized in the case of continuous scores, factor loadings will be bounded by –1 and 1. In such a case, a logistic function seems more appropriate. In addition, as discussed before, there may be substantive reasons to choose a different function for $\lambda_i(\eta_p)$. For instance, an exponential function might be considered to prevent negative factor loadings (as could be desirable in intelligence research to retain the positive manifold; i.e., strictly positive subtest correlations). As with the heteroscedastic model, higher order terms can be added to the $\lambda_i(\eta_p)$ function.

Molenaar et al. (2010) and Smits, Timmerman, and Stegeman (2016) show that quadratic factor loadings and the skew-normal trait distribution cannot be estimated simultaneously. Therefore, one has to choose which one of the two effects to include in the model. The skew-normal trait model is more parsimonious, but the level-dependent factor loading model can capture nonnormality, better if it varies greatly across subtests. Molenaar et al. (2012, 2014) favored the skew-normal model for item scores, as it turned out to work well. It is an open question whether level-dependent factor loadings can be estimated in the item factor model, and if so, whether this can be combined with heteroscedastic residual variances.

Identification

In the case of the linear factor model, only the standard location and scale identification constraints (Bollen, 1989, p. 238) are necessary. These can be imposed in different ways. Usually, the mean of the trait is fixed to equal 0, and the variance of the trait or a factor loading is fixed to 1. For item level data, additionally two adjacent thresholds, τ_{ic}, need

---

[2] As the factor loadings are not random, one cannot condition on η_p as with the residual variances.

to be fixed to arbitrary increasing values for each item (in the case of polytomous data; see Mehta, Neale, & Flay, 2004; Molenaar et al., 2012), or β_{0i} is fixed to 1 for each item (in the case of dichotomous or polytomous data; see Molenaar, 2015). For dichotomous data, additionally β_{1i} should be fixed to 0 for one item (the reference item).

Parameter estimation

As the level-dependent factor loadings and the skew-normal latent trait distribution cannot be combined in the same model, two "full" models are possible: A model with heteroscedastic residuals and a skew-normal trait, or a model with heteroscedastic residuals and level-dependent factor loadings. As discussed previously, in the case of the item factor model, only the former is considered. Parameters of these models can be estimated using marginal maximum likelihood (MML; Bock & Aitkin, 1981), which is a full information procedure and relatively easy to implement. Limited information procedures like least squares estimation are more cumbersome to implement – if possible at all – as the model-implied higher order moments need to be derived. Adopting a Bayesian approach to model fitting is straightforward and feasible, but numerically more demanding. We will therefore rely on MML. Models can be implemented in OpenMx (Boker et al., 2010), Mx (Neale, Boker, Xie, & Maes, 2002), SAS (SAS Institute, 2011), and MPlus (Muthén & Muthén, 2007). See Molenaar et al. (2010) for details of implementation in the case of approximately continuous data, and see Molenaar et al. (2012) for details of implementation in case of discrete data.

Model selection

To make inferences about the possible source(s) of nonnormality, various approaches are possible. As discussed previously, our main interest is to test whether parameters β_1, γ_1, and/or ζ are of importance to the model. This can be tested by (1) conducting a Wald test on the parameter(s) of interest (i.e., dividing the parameter by its standard error to obtain a t-value); (2) by comparing models with and without the parameter(s) of interest using a likelihood ratio test, or comparative fit indices like the Akaike's Information Criterion (AIC; Akaike, 1987) and the Bayesian Information Criterion (BIC; Schwarz, 1978); or (3) calculating confidence intervals for the parameter(s) of interest. For the models discussed here, we do not advocate the use of #1 as the Wald test assumes the asymptotic sampling distribution of the parameters to be symmetrical. As the models discussed here include nonlinear and nonnormal effects, it is doubtful whether this assumption is tenable. Therefore, we advocate the use of #2. In addition, we recommend in the case of #3 that confidence intervals are calculated based on the likelihood profile (Neale & Miller, 1997). The main difference between confidence intervals based on the likelihood profile and traditional confidence intervals is that in the profile based approach, the lower and upper bounds of the interval are estimated separately, allowing for asymmetry in the asymptotic sampling distribution of the parameter. We will illustrate the use of profile likelihood based confidence intervals in Example I and the use of fit indices in Example II.

356 Dylan Molenaar and Conor V. Dolan

Examples

The examples that follow concern two applications of the models discussed in this chapter. In Example I, we analyze intelligence subtest scores that will be treated as approximately continuous variables, that is, we assume that $z_{pi} = y_{pi}$. In this application, we illustrate how confidence intervals can be used to make inferences about the source of nonnormality in the data. For example Mx code, please see Appendix Code 1. In Example II we analyze ordinal item level data from a personality questionnaire. In this application, we illustrate how competing models can be compared using various fit statistics to come to an inference about the source of nonnormality of z_{pi}. For example Mx code, please see Appendix Code 2.

Example I: Intelligence Subtest Scores. The following illustration is taken from Molenaar et al. (2010). The data comprise scores of 500 subjects on five subtests of the Armed Services Vocational Aptitude Battery (ASVAB) as completed within the National Longitudinal Survey of Youth 1997. The subtests are Arithmetic Reasoning (AR), Paragraph Comprehension (PC), Auto Information (AI), Mathematics Knowledge (MK), and Assembling Objects (AO). The ASVAB was administered adaptively, thus the scores comprise estimated scale scores. Using standard linear factor analysis, it was established that the one-factor model fits acceptably (RMSEA equaled 0.06, where commonly a 0.08 cut-off is used between acceptable and poor model fit, see Schermelleh-Engel, Moosbrugger, & Müller, 2003). We fit the following models to these data:

1 "FM": A Factor Model without any effects (baseline model);
2 "het-FM": A Factor Model with heteroscedastic residuals;
3 "het-FM(lin)": A Factor Model with heteroscedastic residuals and linear dependency between the factor loadings and the latent trait (which is equal to quadratic factor loadings as discussed previously);
4 "het-FM(exp)": A Factor Model with heteroscedastic residuals and an exponential function between the factor loadings and the latent trait;
5 "het-FM(log)": A Factor Model with heteroscedastic residuals and an logistic function between the factor loadings and the latent trait;
6 "het-FM-skew": A Factor Model with heteroscedastic residuals and a skew-normal latent trait.

The models are identified by fixing the mean of the latent trait to 0, and the baseline parameter of the factor loading of the test AR to equal 1.[3]

Parameter estimates and 99% confidence intervals based on the univariate likelihood profile (see Neale & Miller, 1997) are in Table 13.1. Results for the het-FM show that the residuals of AR and AO display significant heteroscedasticity. That is, according to the parameter estimates of β_{1i} for these subtests, the residual variance of AR significantly decrease for increasing levels of the trait, while the residual variance of AO significantly increase for increasing levels of the trait. Results in obtained with models het-FM(lin), het-FM(exp), and het-FM(log) show that there is no level dependency in the factor loadings, that is, all relevant parameters (γ_{1i}) are nonsignificant, as judged by their confidence intervals. In the final model, het-FM-skew, it can be seen that the

---

[3] In the case of the model het-FM(exp) the baseline factor loading parameter of AR is fixed to 0 (as exp(0) = 1).

Table 13.1 Parameter estimates and 99% confidence intervals for the various models in Example I.

		Model				
Parameter	Subtest	het-FM	het-FM(lin)	het-FM(exp)	het-FM(log)	het-FM-skew
γ_{1i}	AR	–	-0.02 (-0.10;0.06)	-0.03 (-0.11;0.06)	-0.19 (-0.45;0.29)	–
	PC	–	-0.02 (-0.11;0.07)	-0.02 (-0.10;0.07)	-0.11 (-0.48;0.32)	–
	AI	–	-0.03 (-0.09;0.04)	-0.07 (-0.25;0.09)	-0.12 (-0.42;0.19)	–
	MK	–	0.00 (-0.09;0.10)	0.00 (-0.07;0.08)	0.01 (-0.37;0.49)	–
	AO	–	0.04 (-0.05;0.13)	0.05 (-0.07;0.17)	0.17 (-0.25;0.68)	–
β_{1i}	AR	-0.43 (-0.71;-0.17)	-0.35 (-0.74;-0.02)	-0.35 (-0.73;-0.02)	-0.28 (-0.71;0.01)	-0.42 (-0.72;-0.16)
	PC	0.00 (-0.23; 0.24)	-0.02 (-0.25;0.22)	-0.02 (-0.25;0.22)	-0.02 (-0.23;0.21)	0.00 (-0.23;0.23)
	AI	0.06 (-0.11;0.25)	0.08 (-0.10;0.27)	0.08 (-0.10;0.28)	0.07 (-0.09;0.25)	0.07 (-0.11;0.25)
	MK	-0.16 (-0.39;0.06)	-0.19 (-0.46;0.05)	-0.19 (-0.46;0.05)	-0.18 (-0.42;0.04)	0.16 (-0.39;0.06)
	AO	0.23 (0.03;0.44)	0.22 (0.01;0.42)	0.22 (0.01;0.42)	0.19 (0.00;0.40)	0.23 (0.03;0.44)
ζ		–	–	–	–	-0.71 (-2.32;1.30)

distribution of the trait does not depart significantly from a normal distribution. That is, the estimate of the scale parameter ζ suggests a negatively skewed trait distribution; however, it is nonsignificant in the light of its confidence interval. In conclusion, some nonnormality underlies the scores on the tests AR and OA. This nonnormality can be attributed to heteroscedasticity in the residuals. However, the trait distribution is found to be normal, and the factor loadings are not level-dependent. Therefore, in these data, there seems no evidence for Spearman's postulation that the general intelligence factor gets a weaker source of individual differences toward the upper end of its range.

Example II: Self-reported Affective Analyzing Item Scores. The following illustration is taken from Molenaar et al. (2012). The data comprise scores of 816 Dutch citizens on the eight items of the "Affective Analyzing" subtest of the Bermond–Vorst alexithymia questionnaire (Vorst & Bermond, 2001). Alexithymia is a personality trait that reflects the inability to understand, process, or describe emotions. The subjects completed the items at home on a computer. The items were administered using a five-point Likert scale. An example of an item in the affective analyzing scale is: "There is little use to examine your feelings." A standard item factor model fitted acceptably (RMSEA = 0.064). We fitted the following models to these data:

1. "IFM": An Item Factor Model without any effects (baseline model);
2. "het-IFM": An Item Factor Model with heteroscedastic residuals;

3 "IFM-skew": An Item Factor Model with a skew-normal latent trait distribution;
4 "het-IFM-skew": An Item Factor Model with heteroscedastic residuals and a skew-normal latent trait distribution.

The models are identified by fixing the mean and the variance of the latent trait to 0 and 1, respectively, and by fixing τ_{1i} and τ_{2i} to −2 and −0.75, respectively (for all items). To determine which model fits best, the following fit indices were used: the AIC, the BIC, the sample size adjusted BIC (sBIC; Sclove, 1987), and the Deviance Information Criterion (DIC; Spiegelhalter, Best, Carlin, & van Der Linde, 2002). In all cases, smaller values indicate a better model fit.

Model fit indices for the different models are shown in Table 13.2. The best fitting model, according to all indices, is the het-IFM-skew, the model with both effects. We therefore conclude that the latent trait distribution departs from a normal distribution and that the residuals are heteroscedastic. The parameter estimates of this model are shown in Table 13.3. Factor loadings of the even items have negative signs because these items are reverse scored. The negative estimate of the scale parameter ζ indicates that a negatively skewed latent trait distribution underlies the item scores. See Figure 13.3 for the model-implied distribution of the latent trait. The heteroscedasticity parameters β_{1i} are quite consistent across items. That is, all heteroscedasticity parameters are estimated to be negative, except for item 8. This indicates that responses of subjects higher on the affective analyzing trait are more consistent in their answers compared to subjects with lower levels on the affective analyzing trait. In Molenaar et al. (2012) it is concluded that high alexithymia individuals are less ambiguous about their psychological functioning.

Table 13.2 Model fit indices for the different models in Example II.

Model	AIC	BIC	sBIC	DIC
IFM	279.17	−15121.54	−4819.87	−9159.47
het-IFM	105.91	−15189.35	−4900.39	−9234.63
IFM-skew	260.91	−15128.31	−4828.23	−9167.16
het-IFM-skew	**49.15**	**−15215.38**	**−4928.00**	**−9261.57**

Note. Best values are in bold face

Table 13.3 Parameter estimates for the affective analyzing items in Example II.

Parameter	item 1	item 2	item 3	item 4	item 5	item 6	item 7	item 8
v_i	−1.00	1.13	−1.15	0.82	−1.03	2.99	−1.27	1.54
τ_{i2}	−0.28	0.60	−0.31	0.60	−0.21	1.23	−0.33	0.60
τ_{i3}	0.30	3.81	0.10	3.27	0.38	6.55	0.11	2.97
λ_i	0.47	−1.12	0.55	−0.81	0.52	−1.96	0.53	−1.00
β_{0i}	0.35	1.60	0.24	1.23	0.28	3.00	0.34	0.67
β_{1i}	−1.43	−1.45	−1.72	−0.87	−0.91	−1.47	−1.68	0.42

Note. ζ was estimated to be −2.05

$g(\eta_p)$

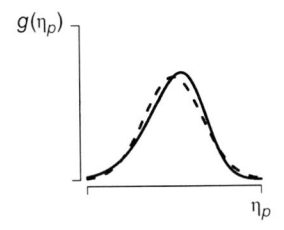

η_p

Figure 13.3 Model-implied distribution of the affective analyzing trait under het-IFM-skew model (solid line) and under the standard IFM model (dashed line).

Discussion

Testing and modeling nonnormality is of potential interest, as various authors have shown that parameter bias can arise due to distributional misspecification (i.e., assuming normality, where normality does not hold). Specifically, in the item factor model, authors have reported bias in the factor loadings (Azevedo, Bolfarine, & Andrade, 2011; Molenaar et al., 2012), the threshold parameters (Molenaar et al., 2012; Zwinderman & van der Wollenberg, 1990), and the trait estimates (Ree, 1979; Seong, 1990; Swaminathan & Gifford, 1983). In addition, some instances of nonnormality may result in trait estimates that are inconsistent in subjects with higher values on the latent trait (see for details Samejima, 1997, 2000). For the linear factor model, Curran, West, and Finch (1996) show that wrongfully assuming a normal distribution results in biased parameter estimates and biased goodness-of-fit measures. However, in some studies of the item factor model, no bias has been found (Flora & Curran, 2004; Stone, 1992), which suggests that the occurrence of bias depends on conditions such as test length and sample size (as discussed in Kirisci, Hsu, & Yu, 2001).

Besides parameter bias, the models discussed in this chapter have interesting substantive applications. For instance, in the field of behavior genetics, a genotype by environment interaction can be defined as heteroscedastic environmental influences across the genetic influences on a given phenotypic variable (Jinks & Fulker, 1970). In an (item) factor model this can be accommodated by making the variance of a latent environmental variable (a latent variable that is uncorrelated within the same members of a twin pair) a function of the scores on a latent genetic variable (a latent variable that is correlated 1 across twin members who share 100% of their genes, and 0.5 across twin members who share on average 50% of their alleles). The present methodology is used to this end by van der Sluis et al. (2006) and Molenaar, van der Sluis, et al. (2012) in the linear factor model, and by Molenaar and Dolan (2014) in the item factor model.

Another substantive application of the models in this chapter concerns the law of diminishing returns. As discussed previously, the hypothesis implies nonnormal intelligence variables, which should be due to level-dependent factor loadings or a skew-normal trait distribution. This hypothesis is tested using present methodology in Molenaar, Dolan, and van der Maas (2011) using Spanish standardization data of the WAIS. It was found that the general intelligence factor is negatively skewed, a finding that is in line with Spearman's 1924 claim. However, these results should be interpreted with caution. Specifically, finding an effect using the methodology outlined is this chapter identifies statistical effects in the data. However, to ensure that the effects could also be interpreted in terms of substantive predictions from theory, alternative explanations of the nonnormality should be ruled out. In case of the linear factor model, it is possible that the statistical effects arise due to the use of poorly constructed composite scores (e.g., summed item scores). If, for instance, disproportionally easy or difficult items are summed, the resulting variable will be nonnormal by definition. But this source of nonnormality is of little theoretical value (see Tucker-Drob, 2009). For the item factor model, this does not pose a threat as the difficulty of the items is explicitly taken into account (see for an illustration Molenaar & Dolan, 2014). Another complication in the interpretation of statistical effects in terms of substantive phenomenon is that nonnormality may be due to the use of an unrepresentative sample. For instance, if in a given intelligence dataset the brighter subjects are overrepresented (because they are possibly more willing to participate in intelligence research), the dataset will contain a disproportionate number of observations in the upper tail of the trait. This could be detected as level-dependent factor loadings or nonnormal trait distribution.

Future research into the nonnormal latent trait model can possibly focus on the extensions of present methodology into multidimensional models for continuous and categorical data. Currently, the only model available is a multidimensional factor model for continuous data with a nonnormal second-order latent variable and residual variances that are heteroscedastic across this second-order variable (Molenaar et al., 2012). This model could be extended to incorporate multiple second-order latent variables, a nonnormal distribution for the first-order traits, and residual variances that are allowed to be heteroscedastic across all first- and/or second-order latent variables. This can be accomplished by implementation of the multivariate skew-normal distribution, which is statistically well documented (Azzalini & Capatanio, 1999). In addition, item level versions of this model can be considered.

Throughout this chapter, we have used specific functional forms for the relation between the latent trait on the one side and the residuals variances and the factor loadings on the other side. The choices for these functions are mainly pragmatic. Therefore, another line of possible future research could involve the development of nonparametric approaches to the specification of these functions between the trait and the parameters in the model. These developments could ideally be combined in to a single model with existing nonparametric approaches to modeling the latent trait distribution (e.g., Schmitt, et al., 2006; Vermunt, 2004).

Acknowledgments

Conor V. Dolan is supported by the European Research Council (Genetics of Mental Illness; Grant number: ERC-230374).

References

Agresti, A. (2002). *Categorical data analysis* (2nd ed.). New York: John Wiley & Sons, Inc.
Akaike, H. (1974). A new look at the statistical model identification. *Automatic Control, IEEE Transactions on, 19,* 716–723.
Azzalini, A. (2005). The skew-normal distribution and related multivariate families. *Scandinavian Journal of Statistics, 32,* 159–188. DOI: 10.1111/j.1467-9469.2005.00426.x
Azzalini, A., & Capatanio, A. (1999). Statistical applications of the multivariate skew normal distribution. *Journal of the Royal Statistical Society. Series B, 61,* 579–602.

Azevedo, C. L. N., Bolfarine, H., & Andrade, D. F. (2011). Bayesian inference for a skew-normal IRT model under the centred parameterization. *Computational Statistics and Data Analysis, 55*, 353–365.

Bauer, D. J. (2005). The role of nonlinear factor-to-indicator relationships in tests of measurement equivalence. *Psychological Methods, 10*, 305.

Birnbaum, A. (1968). Some latent trait models and their use in inferring an examinee's ability. In F. M. Lord & M. R. Novick (Eds.), *Statistical theories of mental test scores* (Ch. 17–20). Reading, MA: Addison Wesley.

Boker, S., Neale. M. C., Maes, H. H., Wilde, M., Spiegel, M., Brick, T., et al. (2010). OpenMx: An open source extended structural equation modeling framework. *Psychometrika, 76*, 306–317.

Bollen, K. A. (1989). *Structural equations with latent variables*. New York: John Wiley & Sons, Inc.

Bollen, K. A. (1996). A limited-information estimator for LISREL models with or without heteroscedastic errors. In G. A. Marcoulides & R. E. Schumacker (Eds.), *Advanced structural equation modeling: Issues and techniques* (pp. 227–241). Mahwah, NJ: Erlbaum.

Brown, T. A. (2006). *Confirmatory factor analysis for applied research*. New York: Guilford Press

Browne, M. W. (1984). Asymptotically distribution-free methods for the analysis of covariance structures. *British Journal of Mathematical and Statistical Psychology, 37*, 62–83.

Christoffersson, A. (1975). Factor analysis of dichotomized variables. *Psychometrika, 40*, 5–32.

Curran, P. J., West, S. G., & Finch, J. F. (1996). The robustness of test statistics to nonnormality and specification error in confirmatory factor analysis. *Psychological Methods, 1*, 16.

Davies, G., Tenesa, A., Payton, A., Yang, J., Harris, S. E., Liewald, D., et al. (2011). Genome-wide association studies establish that human intelligence is highly heritable and polygenic. *Molecular Psychiatry, 16*, 996–1005.

Dolan, C. V. (1994). Factor analysis of variables with 2, 3, 5 and 7 response categories: A comparison of categorical variable estimators using simulated data. *British Journal of Mathematical and Statistical Psychology, 47*, 309–326.

Etezadi-Amoli, J., & McDonald, R. P. (1983). A second generation nonlinear factor analysis. *Psychometrika, 48*, 315–342.

Harvey, A. C. (1976). Estimating regression models with multiplicative heteroscedasticity. *Econometrica: Journal of the Econometric Society, 44*, 461–465.

Hessen, D. J., & Dolan, C. V. (2009). Heteroscedastic one-factor models and marginal maximum likelihood estimation. *British Journal of Mathematical and Statistical Psychology, 62*, 57–77.

Jaccard, J., & Wan, C. K. (1995). Measurement error in the analysis of interaction effects between continuous predictors using multiple regression: Multiple indicator and structural equation approaches. *Psychological Bulletin, 117*, 348–357.

Jinks, J. L., & Fulker, D. W. (1970). Comparison of the biometrical genetical, mava, and classical approaches to the analysis of human behavior. *Psychological Bulletin, 73*, 311–349.

Jöreskog, K. G. (1971). Simultaneous factor analysis in several populations. *Psychometrika, 36(4)*, 409–426.

Jöreskog, K. G. (2002). Structural equation modeling with ordinal variables using LISREL. *Scientific Software International Inc*. Retrieved January 16, 2014, from: www.ssicentral.com/lisrel/techdocs/ordinal.pdf (accessed September 2017).

Kenny, D. A., & Judd, C. M. (1984). Estimating the nonlinear and interactive effects of latent variables. *Psychological Bulletin, 96*, 201–210.

Kirisci, L., Hsu, T., & Yu, L. (2001). Robustness of item parameter estimation programs to assumptions of unidimensionality and normality. *Applied Psychological Measurement, 25*, 146–162.

Klein, A., & Moosbrugger, H. (2000). Maximum likelihood estimation of latent interaction effects with the LMS method. *Psychometrika, 65*, 457–474.

Lawley, D. N. (1943). The application of the maximum likelihood method to factor analysis. *British Journal of Psychology, 33*, 172–175.

Lee, S. Y., & Zhu, H. T. (2002). Maximum likelihood estimation of nonlinear structural equation models, *Psychometrika, 67*, 189–210.

Lewin-Koh, S., & Amemiya, Y. (2003). Heteroscedastic factor analysis. *Biometrika*, *90*, 85–97.

Mardia, K. V. (1970). Measures of multivariate skewness and kurtosis with applications. *Biometrika*, *57*, 519–530.

Markus, H. (1977). Self-schemata and processing information about the self. *Journal of Personality and Social Psychology*, *35*, 63–78.

McDonald, R. P. (1962). A general approach to nonlinear factor analysis. *Psychometrika*, *27*, 392–415.

Mehta, P. D., Neale, M. C., & Flay, B. R. (2004). Squeezing interval change from ordinal panel data: Latent growth curves with ordinal outcomes. *Psychological Methods*, *9*, 301–333.

Meijer, E., & Mooijaart, A. (1996). Factor analysis with heteroscedastic errors. *British Journal of Mathematical and Statistical Psychology*, *49*, 189–202.

Micceri, T. (1989). The unicorn, the normal curve and other improbable creatures. *Psychological Bulletin*, *105*, 156–166.

Mokken, R. J. (1970). *A theory and procedure of scale analysis*. Gravenhage: Mouton.

Molenaar, D. (2015). Heteroscedastic latent trait models for dichotomous data. *Psychometrika*, *80*(3), 625–644.

Molenaar, D., & Dolan, C. V. (2014). Testing systematic genotype by environment interactions using item level data. *Behavior Genetics*, *44*, 212–231.

Molenaar, D., Dolan, C. V., & de Boeck, P. (2012). The heteroscedastic graded response model with a skewed latent trait: Testing statistical and substantive hypotheses related to skewed item category functions. *Psychometrika*, *77*, 455–478.

Molenaar, D., Dolan, C. V., & van der Maas, H. L. J. (2011). Modeling ability differentiation in the second-order factor model. *Structural Equation Modeling*, *18*, 578–594.

Molenaar, D., Dolan, C. V., & Verhelst, N. D. (2010). Testing and modeling nonnormality within the one factor model. *British Journal of Mathematical and Statistical Psychology*, *63*, 293–317.

Molenaar, D., van der Sluis, S., Boomsma, D. I., & Dolan, C. V. (2012). detecting specific genotype by environment interactions using marginal maximum likelihood estimation in the classical twin design. *Behavior Genetics*, *42*, 483–499.

Molenaar, D., van der Sluis, S., Boomsma, D. I., Haworth, C. M., Hewitt, J. K., Martin, N. G., et al. (2013). Genotype by environment interactions in cognitive ability: a survey of 14 studies from four countries covering four age groups. *Behavior Genetics*, *43*, 208–219.

Muthén, B., & Hofacker, C. (1988). Testing the assumptions underlying tetrachoric correlations. *Psychometrika*, *53*, 563–578.

Muthén, L. K., & Muthén, B. O. (2007). *MPlus user's guide* (5th ed.). Los Angeles, CA: Muthén & Muthén.

Neale, M. C., Boker, S. M., Xie, G., & Maes, H. H. (2002). *Mx: Statistical modeling* (6th ed.). VCU, Richmond, VA: Author.

Neale, M. C., & Miller, M. (1997). The use of likelihood-based confidence intervals in genetic models. *Behavior Genetics*, *27*, 113–120.

Olsson, U. (1979). Maximum likelihood estimation of the polychoric correlation coefficient. *Psychometrika*, *44*, 443–460.

Ramsay, J. O., & Abrahamowicz, M. (1989). Binomial regression with monotone splines: A psychometric application. *Journal of the American Statistical Association*, *84*, 906–915.

Ree, M. J. (1979). Estimating item characteristic curves. *Applied Psychological Measurement*, *3*, 371–385.

Samejima, F. (1969). *Estimation of ability using a response pattern of graded scores* (Psychometric Monograph No. 17). Richmond, VA: The Psychometric Society.

Samejima, F. (1997). Departure from normal assumptions: A promise for future psychometrics with substantive mathematical modeling. *Psychometrika*, *62*, 471–493.

Samejima, F. (2000). Logistic positive exponent family of models: Virtue of asymmetric item characteristic curves. *Psychometrika*, *65*, 319–335.

SAS Institute. (2011). *SAS/STAT 9.3 user's guide*. SAS Institute.

Satorra, A., & Bentler, P. M. (1988). Scaling corrections for chi-square statistics in covariance structure analysis. *ASA Proceedings of the Business and Economic Section*, 308–313.

Schermelleh-Engel, K., Moosbrugger, H., & Müller, H. (2003). Evaluating the fit of structural equation models: Tests of significance and descriptive goodness-of fit measures. *Methods of Psychological Research*, 8, 23–74.

Schmitt, J. E., Mehta, P. D., Aggen, S. H., Kubarych, T. S., & Neale, M. C. (2006). Semi nonparametric methods for detecting latent nonnormality: A fusion of latent trait and ordered latent class modeling. *Multivariate Behaviour Research*, 41, 427–443.

Schwarz, G. (1978). Estimating the dimension of a model. *The Annals of Statistics*, 6, 461–464.

Sclove, L. (1987). Application of model-selection criteria to some problems in multivariate analysis. *Psychometrika*, 52, 333–343.

Seong, T. J. (1990). Sensitivity of marginal maximum likelihood estimation of item and ability parameters to the characteristics of the prior ability distributions. *Applied Psychological Measurement*, 14, 299–311.

Smits, I. A. M., Timmerman, M. E., & Stegeman, A. (2016). Modelling nonnormal data: The relationship between the skew-normal factor model and the quadratic factor model. *British Journal of Mathematical and Statistical Psychology*, 69, 105–121. DOI: 10.1111/bmsp.12062

Shapiro, S. S., & Wilks, M. B. (1965). An analysis of variance test for normality (complete samples). *Biometrika*, 52, 591–611.

Spearman, C. (1904). General intelligence, objectively determined and measured. *American Journal of Psychology*, 15, 201–293.

Spearman, C. (1927). *The abilities of man*. New York: Macmillan.

Spiegelhalter, D. J., Best, N. G., Carlin, B. P., & van der Linde, A. (2002). Bayesian measures of model complexity and fit. *Journal of the Royal Statistical Society Series B*, 64, 583–639.

Stone, C. A. (1992). Recovery of marginal maximum likelihood estimates in the two-parameter logistic response model: An evaluation of MULTILOG. *Applied Psychological Measurement*, 16, 1–16.

Swaminathan, H., & Gifford, J. (1983). Estimation of parameters in the three- parameter latent trait model. In D. J. Weiss (Ed.), *New horizons in testing: Latent trait test theory and computerized adaptive testing* (pp. 13–30). New York: Academic Press.

Takane, Y., & de Leeuw, J. (1987). On the relationship between item response theory and factor analysis of discretized variables. *Psychometrika*, 52, 393–408.

Thurstone, L. L. (1947). *Multiple-factor analysis*. Chicago: University of Chicago Press.

Tucker-Drob, E. M. (2009). Differentiation of cognitive abilities across the life span. *Developmental Psychology*, 45, 1097–1118.

van den Oord, E. J. (2005). Estimating Johnson curve population distributions in MULTILOG. *Applied Psychological Measurement*, 29, 45–64.

van der Maas, H. L., Molenaar, D., Maris, G., Kievit, R. A., & Borsboom, D. (2011). Cognitive psychology meets psychometric theory: On the relation between process models for decision making and latent variable models for individual differences. *Psychological Review*, 118, 339.

van der Sluis, S., Dolan, C. V., Neale, M. C., Boomsma, D. I., & Posthuma, D. (2006). Detecting genotype–environment interaction in monozygotic twin data: Comparing the Jinks and Fulker Test and a new test based on marginal maximum likelihood estimation. *Twin Research and Human Genetics*, 9, 377–392.

Verhelst, N. D. (2009). *Latent variable analysis with skew distributions*. Technical Rapport. Cito: Arnhem, The Netherlands.

Vermunt, J. K. (2004). An EM algorithm for the estimation of parametric and nonparametric hierarchical nonlinear models. *Statistica Neerlandica*, 58, 220–233.

Vermunt, J. K., & Hagenaars, J. A. (2004). Ordinal longitudinal data analysis. In R. C. Hauspie, N. Cameron, & L. Molinari (Eds.), *Methods in human growth research* (pp. 374–393). Cambridge: Cambridge University Press.

Vorst, H. C. M., & Bermond, B. (2001). Validity and reliability of the Bermond–Vorst alexithymia questionnaire. *Personality and Individual Differences*, 30, 413–434.

Wirth, R. J., & Edwards, M. C. (2007). Item factor analysis: Current approaches and future directions. *Psychological Methods, 12,* 58–79.
Woods, C. M. (2007). Ramsay-curve IRT for Likert type data. *Applied Psychological Measurement, 31,* 195–212.
Yalcin, I., & Amemiya, Y. (2001). Non linear factor analysis as a statistical method. *Statistical Science, 16,* 275–294.
Zwinderman, A. H., & van den Wollenberg, A. L. (1990). Robustness of marginal maximum likelihood estimation in the Rasch model. *Applied Psychological Measurement, 14,* 73–81.

Code Appendix

Code 1 Mx Code for Example I.

Note code following ! is author annotation.

```
#define nv 5       ! number of variables
#define nq 100     ! number of nodes and weights
#ngroups 2         ! number of groups in run

G1: Calculate stacked cov. and means

Calculation

BEGIN MATRICES;
E full 1 1 fi    ! Shape parameter, ζη
F diag nv nv fr  ! residual variances, baseline parameters βj0
G diag nv nv fi  ! residual variances, heteroscedasticity
                   parameters βj1
U full nv 1 fi   ! factor loadings, baseline parameters γj0
V full nv 1 fi   ! factor loadings, level dependency
                   parameters γj1
T full nv 1 fr   ! intercepts, νj
K full 1 1 fi    ! factor variance, ση2
N full 1 1 fi    ! factor mean, μη
A full nq 1      ! Gauss Hermite Quadrature, Nodes
H unit 1 1       ! matrix containing '1'
I unit nq 1      ! (nq by 1) row vector containing 1's
J iden nv nv fi  ! identity matrix
P full 1 1       ! pi
Y unit nv 1      ! (nv by 1) row vector containing 1's,
END MATRICES;

ma P
3.141593
```

```
ma A                 ! specify the Nodes
-18.9596362 -18.1355915 -17.4555874 -16.8504422
-16.2937419 -15.7718815
-15.2767037 -14.8028356 -14.3465035 -13.9049293
-13.4759927 -13.0580291
-12.6497008 -12.2499125 -11.8577521 -11.4724502
-11.0933491 -10.7198814
-10.3515523 -9.9879272 -9.6286212 -9.2732911 -8.9216290
-8.5733569
-8.2282228 -7.8859966 -7.5464675 -7.2094417 -6.8747397
-6.5421953
-6.2116532 -5.8829684 -5.5560048 -5.2306341 -4.9067351
-4.5841926
-4.2628973 -3.9427446 -3.6236343 -3.3054703 -2.9881597
-2.6716128
-2.3557425 -2.0404641 -1.7256947 -1.4113532 -1.0973601
-0.7836367
-0.4701054 -0.1566890 0.1566890 0.4701054 0.7836367
1.0973601
1.4113532 1.7256947 2.0404641 2.3557425 2.6716128
2.9881597
3.3054703 3.6236343 3.9427446 4.2628973 4.5841926
4.9067351
5.2306341 5.5560048 5.8829684 6.2116532 6.5421953
6.8747397
7.2094417 7.5464675 7.8859966 8.2282228 8.5733569
8.9216290
9.2732911 9.6286212 9.9879272 10.3515523 10.7198814
11.0933491
11.4724502 11.8577521 12.2499125 12.6497008 13.0580291
13.4759927
13.9049293 14.3465035 14.8028356 15.2767037 15.7718815
16.2937419
16.8504422 17.4555874 18.1355915 18.9596362

pa E                 !the shape parameter $\zeta\eta$ is estimated
1

Ma E                 ! the starting value for the shape
                       parameter is set to 2
2

pa U                 ! the model is identified by fixed $\gamma 10$ to
                       equal 1
0 1 1 1 1

ma U
1 1 1 1

pa V                 ! the $\gamma j1$'s are not estimated
0 0 0 0 0
```

```
pa F
1 1 1 1 1

pa G                    ! the heteroskedastic parameters, βj1, are
                          estimated
1 1 1 1 1

pa K                    ! ση² is estimated
1

ma K
1

ma N                    ! μη is fixed to 0
0

BEGIN ALGEBRA;
R=\sqrt(\sqrt(K*K)%(H-(H+H)*E*E%(H+E*E)*H%P));

B=N-R*\sqrt((H+H)%P)*E%\sqrt(H+E*E);

C= A@R+B@I;

L=I@U'+C@V';        !linear function between λ and η

!L=(I@U').(\exp(C@V'));              !exponential function
                                       between λ and η
!L=I@U'+V'@(\exp(C)%(I+\exp(C))); !logistic function
                                       between λ and η

M = L.(C@Y') + T'@I; ! conditional means

S = \exp(I@F + C@G).(I@J); ! stacked 40 conditional cov.
matrices
END ALGEBRA;

END;


G2: data group
da ni=5 Nmodel=100    ! Nmodel=100 corresponds to 100
                        quadrature points
mi=-999
Rec File =data.dat    ! 'data.dat' is the data file
la
y1 y2 y3 y4 y5

BEGIN MATRICES;
C comp = C1
M comp = M1
```

```
  S comp = S1
  B comp = B1
  R comp = R1
  F diag nv nv = F(1)
  G diag nv nv = G(1)
  T full nv 1 = T(1)
  U full nv 1 = U(1)
  V full nv 1 = V(1)
  K full 1 1 = K(1)
  N full 1 1= N(1)
  E full 1 1 = E(1)
  H unit 1 1 fi
  I unit nq 1
  W full nq 1              ! Gauss Hermite Quadrature, Weights
  END MATRICES;

  Matrix W ! Specify the Weights
  3.333270e-79 0.000000e+00 0.000000e+00 0.000000e+00
  0.000000e+00
  0.000000e+00 0.000000e+00 0.000000e+00 0.000000e+00
  0.000000e+00
  0.000000e+00 0.000000e+00 2.886525e-36 4.104238e-34
  4.551562e-32
  4.006768e-30 2.842269e-28 1.645939e-26 7.869551e-25
  3.137473e-23
  1.052212e-21 2.991512e-20 7.260177e-19 1.513434e-17
  2.724943e-16
  4.259009e-15 5.804805e-14 6.927563e-13 7.266219e-12
  6.721194e-11
  5.499676e-10 3.992125e-09 2.577290e-08 1.483309e-07
  7.626699e-07
  3.510119e-06 1.448622e-05 5.369484e-05 1.790128e-04
  5.374990e-04
  1.455199e-03 3.556087e-03 7.851073e-03 1.567269e-02
  2.830867e-02
  4.629279e-02 6.857047e-02 9.203626e-02 1.119707e-01
  1.234969e-01
  1.234969e-01 1.119707e-01 9.203626e-02 6.857047e-02
  4.629279e-02
  2.830867e-02 1.567269e-02 7.851073e-03 3.556087e-03
  1.455199e-03
  5.374990e-04 1.790128e-04 5.369484e-05 1.448622e-05
  3.510119e-06
  7.626699e-07 1.483309e-07 2.577290e-08 3.992125e-09
  5.499676e-10
  6.721194e-11 7.266219e-12 6.927563e-13 5.804805e-14
  4.259009e-15
  2.724943e-16 1.513434e-17 7.260177e-19 2.991512e-20
```

```
1.052212e-21
3.137473e-23  7.869551e-25  1.645939e-26  2.842269e-28
4.006768e-30
4.551562e-32  4.104238e-34  2.886525e-36  0.000000e+00
0.000000e+00
0.000000e+00  0.000000e+00  0.000000e+00  0.000000e+00
0.000000e+00
0.000000e+00  0.000000e+00  0.000000e+00  0.000000e+00
3.333270e-79

Begin algebra;
Z=(H+H)@\cumnor((E%R)@(C-B@I));
D=(Z.W);
end algebra;

Mean M;
Covariance S;
Weight D;
Option
END;
```

Code 2   Mx Code for Example II.

Note code following ! is author annotation.

```
#define nfac 1            ! number of factors
#define nv 8              ! number of variables in model
#define maxcat 4          ! Maximum score of any item (e.g.,
                            0,1,2)
#define nq 50 ! quadrature points

!-----------------------------------------------------
#ngroups    2             ! number of groups in run

G1: Calculation group
Calculation
Begin Matrices;

A Full nq 1               ! quadrature points

K full 1 1 fi             ! factor variance
N full 1 1 fi             ! factor mean

F fu nv 1                 ! residual baseline par
G fu nv 1                 ! heteroscedasticity par
```

```
H unit 1 1 fi           ! 1

I Unit nq 1             ! numabs 1
J unit maxcat 1         ! identity

E full 1 1              ! skew par

L Full nv nfac   FRee   ! Factor loadings
P full 1 1 fi           ! pi

U Full maxcat nv        ! Item thresholds
V full nv 1             ! underlying variable (Z in the
                          paper) mean
Z unit nv 1

  End Matrices;

ma A ! specify the Nodes
-12.9858845 -12.0530184 -11.2792333 -10.5873817 -9.9480357
-9.3460396
-8.7722996    -8.2208159  -7.6873624  -7.1688148  -6.6627754
-6.1673474
-5.6809923    -5.2024350  -4.7305986  -4.2645578  -3.8035057
-3.3467278
-2.8935827    -2.4434875  -1.9959047  -1.5503332  -1.1062993
-0.6633497
-0.2210452     0.2210452   0.6633497   1.1062993   1.5503332
 1.9959047
 2.4434875     2.8935827   3.3467278   3.8035057   4.2645578
 4.7305986
 5.2024350     5.6809923   6.1673474   6.6627754   7.1688148
 7.6873624
 8.2208159     8.7722996   9.3460396   9.9480357  10.5873817
11.2792333
12.0530184    12.9858845

ma P
3.141593

pa E
0

ma E            ! skewness parameter (zeta)
0               ! fit the model using multiple starting values
                ! for E (e.g., -3, 0, and 3) to ensure
                  that the final solution is not a local
                ! minimum

!thresholds (tau) do not estimate the first two threshold
for each item
```

```
pa U

0 0 0 0 0 0 0 0
0 0 0 0 0 0 0 0
1 1 1 1 1 1 1 1
1 1 1 1 1 1 1 1

! fix the first two threshold to -2 and -1 respectively
for each item
MA U
-2 -2 -2 -2 -2 -2 -2 -2
-1 -1 -1 -1 -1 -1 -1 -1
 0  0  0  0  0  0  0  0
 1  1  1  1  1  1  1  1

pa V
1 1 1 1 1 1 1 1

ma V
0 0 0 0 0 0 0 0

pa L
1 1 1 1 1 1 1 1

MA L
1 1 1 1 1 1 1 1

pa F
1 1 1 1 1 1 1 1

ma F
0 0 0 0 0 0 0 0

pa G
0 0 0 0 0 0 0 0

ma G
0 0 0 0 0 0 0 0

pa K            ! latent trait variance
0

ma K
1

ma N            ! latent trait mean
0

BEgin ALgebra;
```

```
R=\sqrt(\sqrt(K*K)%(H-(H+H)*E*E%(H+E*E)*H%P));
B=N-R*\sqrt((H+H)%P)*E%\sqrt(H+E*E);
C= A@R+B@I;

M = C@(J@L')+I@(J@V');        ! Conditional mean of z_{pi}

Y= I@(J@Z') + \exp(-C@(J@G'));

S = (I@(J@Z')+I@(J@Z')).(I@(J@F') % Y ); ! conditional
    variance of z_{pi}

O = I@\v2d(Z);

! standardize thresholds using mean conditional and
  conditional variance
T = (I@U-M) % \sqrt(\sqrt(S.S));

ENd ALgebra;

option

ENd
!-------------------------------------------
 G 2: data group
 Data Ninput=nv  Nmodel=50
 mi=9
 ORdinal File=data

 Begin matrices;

  M COMP = M1
  T comp = T1
  W FULL nq 1
  H unit 1 1 = H(1)
  E full 1 1 = E(1)

  L Full nv nfac = L(1)
  U Full maxcat nv = U(1)
  V full nv 1 = V(1)
  F diag nv nv = F(1)
  G diag nv nv = G(1)
  O comp = O1
  C comp = C1
  B comp = B1
  I Unit nq 1 = I(1)
  R comp = R1

 End Matrices;

 Matrix W ! Specify the Weights
```

```
1.034608e-37  9.443415e-33  6.856281e-29  1.206045e-25
7.995094e-23
2.522483e-20  4.368172e-18  4.566698e-16  3.083829e-14
1.414229e-12
4.576637e-11  1.077061e-09  1.888226e-08  2.514610e-07
2.584938e-06
2.078485e-05  1.321726e-04  6.708281e-04  2.738161e-03
9.045054e-03
2.430481e-02  5.334352e-02  9.593054e-02  1.416854e-01
1.721259e-01
1.721259e-01  1.416854e-01  9.593054e-02  5.334352e-02
2.430481e-02
9.045054e-03  2.738161e-03  6.708281e-04  1.321726e-04
2.078485e-05
2.584938e-06  2.514610e-07  1.888226e-08  1.077061e-09
4.576637e-11
1.414229e-12  3.083829e-14  4.566698e-16  4.368172e-18
2.522483e-20
7.995094e-23  1.206045e-25  6.856281e-29  9.443415e-33
1.034608e-37

Begin algebra;

Z=(H+H)@\cumnor((E%R)@(C-B@I));
D=(Z.W);

end algebra;

Thresholds T;
Covariance O;
Weight D;

option mu
end



!!!!!!!!!!!!!!!!!!!!!!!!!!!!!!!!!!!!!!!!!!!!!!!!!!!
Above code specifies the full model, but only fits the
baseline model (the skewness and heteroscedasticity
parameters are still fixed). Below we will free the
relevant parameters. Doing so is advisable as the
baseline estimates will be good starting values for the
heteroscedastic model. The models could be compared using
fit statistics as discussed in the chapter.
!!!!!!!!!!!!!!!!!!!!!!!!!!!!!!!!!!!!!!!!!!!!!!!!!!!!
```

```
!!!!!!!!!!!!!!!!!!!!!!!!!!!!!!!!
!! SKEW NORMAL ONLY   !!
!!!!!!!!!!!!!!!!!!!!!!!!!!!!!!!!

fr E 1 1 1
va -3 E 1 1 1

op
end

!!!!!!!!!!!!!!!!!!!!!!!!!!!!!!!!!!!!!!!!!!!!!!!!
!! SKEWNESS & HETEROSCEDASTICITY  !!
!!!!!!!!!!!!!!!!!!!!!!!!!!!!!!!!!!!!!!!!!!!!!!!!

fr G 1 1 1 G 1 2 1 G 1 3 1 G 1 4 1 G 1 5 1 G 1 6 1 G 1 7 1
G 1 8 1
st .2 G 1 1 1 G 1 2 1 G 1 3 1 G 1 4 1 G 1 5 1 G 1 6 1 G 1 7
1 G 1 8 1

op
end

!!!!!!!!!!!!!!!!!!!!!!!!!!!!!!!!!!!!!!!!
!! HETEROSCEDASTICITY ONLY  !!
!!!!!!!!!!!!!!!!!!!!!!!!!!!!!!!!!!!!!!!!

drop E 1 1 1

op
end
```

14

Multidimensional Scaling: An Introduction

William G. Jacoby and David J. Ciuk

Introduction

The term *multidimensional scaling* (often abbreviated MDS) refers to a family of procedures used to construct geometric models of sets of objects, using information on proximities between these objects. The term *objects*, in this context, refers to whatever the researcher is examining. For a psychologist, the objects might be individual test questions drawn from an item pool. For a market researcher, the objects might be consumer products (e.g., brands of cereal). For a sociologist, the objects might be different occupations. For a political scientist, the objects might be candidates for public office. Of course, the list of possible object sets goes on endlessly.

The term *proximities* refers to any kind of symmetric relationship defined for pairs of the objects. Among the most comprehensible of these symmetric relationships is similarity— information about how similar or dissimilar each pair of objects are to each other. For the moment, we will assume that this information is available for every distinct pair of objects that can be created from the full set of objects.

In the *geometric model* each object is represented as a point within a space, and the proximities between the objects are shown as distances between the points. Specifically, more similar pairs of objects are shown as points separated by smaller distances. Conversely, more dissimilar pairs of objects are shown in the model as points separated by larger distances. Thus, the results from a multidimensional scaling analysis consist of a spatial array of points, where the distances between the points correspond (as closely as possible) to the proximities between the objects. The results from the MDS analysis are most useful when the dimensionality of the space containing the scaled points is small (no more than two or, at most, three) such that the researcher can look directly at the "cloud" of points produced in the solution.

In sum, multidimensional scaling generates a fairly intuitive and readily comprehensible representation of proximities information. But, why would a researcher want to create such a model? The typical answer is that he or she is trying to determine whether there is any underlying systematic structure that exists across the object set. Do the

---

The Wiley Handbook of Psychometric Testing: A Multidisciplinary Reference on Survey, Scale and Test Development, First Edition. Edited by Paul Irwing, Tom Booth, and David J. Hughes.
© 2018 John Wiley & Sons Ltd. Published 2020 by John Wiley & Sons Ltd.

points that lie close to each other within the scaled space represent objects that share common characteristics? Do points that are widely separated from each other correspond to objects that differ from each other in some identifiable way? Answering these kinds of question provides insights about the nature of variability across the objects. That is, it helps the researcher understand *why* some objects are more similar, and others are less similar, to other objects. Multidimensional scaling facilitates this process because the spatial configuration of points generated by the scaling analysis is usually easier to comprehend than the original, numeric, information about the inter-object proximities.

Multidimensional scaling possesses several important strengths that make it a very useful tool for social and behavioral research:

- Multidimensional scaling is an important data reduction strategy. This can be useful for exploring large datasets, but it is also very relevant for testing substantive theories whose elements can be represented in spatial form.
- In several fields, MDS can be useful for modeling the perceptual structures that underlie survey respondents' or experimental subjects' preference responses toward interesting stimuli. This was probably the main motivation behind the original development of MDS methods. The general idea is that better understanding of the ways people think about a set of objects will provide important insights about their reasons for liking or disliking the respective objects.
- Multidimensional scaling methods are extremely flexible with respect to the input data. Many different types of information can be used to create proximities data. At the same time, MDS methods exist for varying levels of measurement, from ratio through interval and ordinal, down even to nominal-level data (although the latter can be extremely tricky). MDS can also be used to combine proximities information from multiple sources, in several different ways.
- Because MDS output provides at least interval-level information about the distances between objects, it can be used as a tool to improve measurement. While this may not be surprising if the input data are measured at the interval or ratio level, it is also the case when ordinal-level proximities are analyzed. The general idea is that a successful MDS provides insights about how objects differ from each other; it is a relatively small additional step to quantify those differences from the MDS output. But, once this is done, the resultant numeric values "measure" the scaled objects with respect to each other.
- The main output from an MDS analysis is graphical in nature. This is relevant because it provides a convenient way to represent complex information in a relatively comprehensible manner. While parsimony is valued in scientific communities, this feature of MDS is especially valuable when analytic results must be presented to lay audiences.

Multidimensional Scaling: A General Formulation

In order to understand multidimensional scaling, it is useful to think in terms of a map. All of us who travel are familiar with using a map. But, the map itself is a geometric model of the *proximities* (i.e., physical distances) between points representing a set of objects (i.e., we will assume they are cities, but they could represent other geographic features). By measuring the size of the interval between two points on the map, and comparing that to the map's scale, we can determine the distances between the two cities represented by the points.

Multidimensional scaling "reverses" the preceding task. We start with the intercity distances, perhaps conveniently arrayed into a triangular table. These comprise our numeric proximities data. We use the information in these proximities to produce the map, or the geometric model in which the actual distances between cities are represented as (much smaller) distances between points on a two-dimensional surface. That is, basically, all there is to it!

Let us next move to a slightly more formal representation of multidimensional scaling. Begin with a $k \times k$ square matrix, Δ, of *proximities* among k objects. The proximity between the object represented by the ith row and the object represented by the jth column is shown by the cell entry, δ_{ij}. In the vast majority of situations, Δ is a symmetric matrix, implying that $\delta_{ij} = \delta_{ji}$.[1]

Greater proximity between objects i and j corresponds to a *smaller* value of Δ_{ij}, and vice versa. Therefore, the proximities are often called *dissimilarities*. Admittedly, this terminology is a bit confusing! But, it leads to a more straightforward characterization of the scaling problem.

Multidimensional scaling tries to find a set of k points in m-dimensional space such that the distances between pairs of points approximate the dissimilarities between pairs of objects. More specifically, MDS uses the information in Δ to find a $k \times m$ matrix of point coordinates, $\mathbf{X}$. The distance between the points representing objects i and j, d_{ij}, is calculated from the entries in the ith and jth rows of $\mathbf{X}$, usually using the familiar Pythagorean formula:

$$d_{ij} = \left[(x_{i1} - x_{j1})^2 + (x_{i2} - x_{j2})^2 + \cdots + (x_{im} - x_{jm})^2 \right]^{1/2}. \quad (14.1)$$

We want MDS to find $\mathbf{X}$ such that $d_{ij} \approx \delta_{ij}$ for all pairs of objects, i and j. Stated a bit differently, multidimensional scaling uses the proximities contained in Δ to find the point coordinates (contained in $\mathbf{X}$) such that the interpoint distances are functionally related to the pairwise dissimilarities. So, for all pairs composed of objects i and j, with $i \neq j$:

$$d_{ij} = f(\delta_{ij}) + e_{ij}. \quad (14.2)$$

In Equation 14.2, the f represents a function, or a specific rule for transforming dissimilarities into distances. The nature of the function (i.e., the actual contents of the transformation rule) is determined by the type of MDS that is performed on the dissimilarities data. The e_{ij} term represents an *error* that also contributes to the distance;

---

[1] A square matrix can be subdivided into two triangular arrays. One such triangle consists of the cells below and to the left of the main diagonal (which, itself, consists of the cells running from the upper-left corner to the lower-right corner) and the other triangle consists of the cells above and to the right of the main diagonal. If the matrix is symmetric, then the two triangles contain the same information; one is a transposed version of the other. Strictly speaking, MDS only requires one of these triangles (since the other is redundant). But, the metric MDS procedure discussed below requires the full, square, matrix form with both triangles, as well as the main diagonal.

its presence in this functional relationship implies that the scaled distances do not need to be a deterministic function of the input dissimilarities. For the moment, let us assume that the number of dimensions, m, is known prior to the analysis.

In a multidimensional scaling analysis, the researcher begins by specifying the nature of the function, f, that maps from dissimilarities to distances. This is tantamount to selecting a specific type of MDS, as we will see. Once the type of analysis is selected, the scaling procedure, itself, calculates the values of the parameters associated with f. That, in turn, enables us to move from the numeric information in the Δ matrix of dissimilarities to the X matrix of point coordinates. Finally, we use the information in X to plot the points, and generate a graphical representation of the model. If we were to calculate the distances between all pairs of points in the graphical display, they could be placed into a square matrix of order k that we could designate as D. There is a one-to-one correspondence between the elements in Δ and the elements in D. And, MDS always includes a fit measure which summarizes in a single numeric value how close the correspondence is between the elements of these two matrices. Alternatively, the fit measure shows how close the transformation from dissimilarities to distances comes to being a deterministic function, in which the error terms are all equal to zero.

So-called *classical multidimensional scaling* (or CMDS) uses information from a single set of pairwise dissimilarities among objects to generate a spatial configuration of points representing those objects. This general category actually subsumes a number of specific scaling methods that mainly vary according to the assumptions they make about the nature of the input data. The major distinction is between *metric* MDS and *nonmetric* MDS. The former, metric MDS, assumes that the input data are measured at the interval or ratio level. Nonmetric MDS only assumes that the input data provide an ordering of the dissimilarities between the objects; hence they are only measured at the ordinal level. There are two very important caveats that must be raised about the distinction between metric and nonmetric MDS. First, the output from the MDS is *always* metric, in the sense that it produces a map in which the distances between the object points are measured at the interval or ratio levels, regardless of the assumptions about the metric or nonmetric nature of the input data. Second, it is always the researcher that decides whether the input data are measured at the ordinal, interval, or ratio level; there is nothing intrinsic to any dataset that determines the measurement level.

Metric Multidimensional Scaling

Metric MDS requires that the distances in the scaling solution are related to the dissimilarities by a parametric function, usually linear in form. For example:

$$d_{ij} = a + b\delta_{ij} + e_{ij}. \tag{14.3}$$

To reiterate, δ_{ij} is the dissimilarity between the ith and jth objects, while d_{ij} is the distance between the points representing objects i and j in the multidimensional scaling solution. The a and b terms are coefficients to be estimated, and e_{ij} is an error term that is associated with objects i and j. If the a coefficient is constrained to be zero, then the input data are assumed to be ratio level. If a is permitted to be a nonzero value, then the input data are interval level.[2]

A well-known scaling procedure, developed by Warren S. Torgerson (1958), begins with the $k \times k$ dissimilarities matrix, $\mathbf{\Delta}$. We assume that the dissimilarities are *equal to* the distances between the points for the k objects in m-dimensional space, except for random error. The $k \times k$ matrix of interpoint distances is $\mathbf{D}$, and the $k \times k$ matrix $\mathbf{E}$ contains random errors. The main hypothesis of MDS analysis is that $\mathbf{\Delta} = \mathbf{D} + \mathbf{E}$. Stated informally, the objective of the analysis is to find the $k \times m$ coordinate matrix, $\mathbf{X}$, such that the entries in $\mathbf{E}$ are as close to zero as possible.

Torgerson's procedure creates a *double-centered* version of $\mathbf{\Delta}$, designated $\mathbf{\Delta}^*$. It does so by squaring all the entries in the original $\mathbf{\Delta}$, and then transforming the resultant squared matrix so that the row sums, the column sums, and the overall sum of the cell entries in the final double-centered matrix are all zero. For dissimilarity δ_{ij}, Torgerson proved that the corresponding entry in the double-centered matrix can be calculated as follows:

$$\delta_{ij}^* = -0.5\left(\delta_{ij}^2 - \delta_{i.}^2 - \delta_{.j}^2 + \delta_{..}^2\right), \tag{14.4}$$

where $\delta_{i.}^2$ is the mean of the entries in the ith row of the squared dissimilarities matrix, $\delta_{.j}^2$ is the mean of the entries in the jth column of the squared dissimilarities matrix, and $\delta_{..}^2$ is the mean of all entries in the squared dissimilarities matrix. The double-centered matrix, $\mathbf{\Delta}^*$, can be factored to obtained the point coordinates for the scaling solution. The factoring process is carried out by performing an eigendecomposition on $\mathbf{\Delta}^*$:

$$\mathbf{\Delta}^* = \mathbf{V}\mathbf{\Lambda}^2\mathbf{V}'. \tag{14.5}$$

In Equation 14.5, $\mathbf{V}$ is the $k \times q$ matrix of eigenvectors, $\mathbf{\Lambda}^2$ is the $q \times q$ diagonal matrix of eigenvalues, and q is the rank of $\mathbf{\Delta}^*$ (usually equal to k). Next, we create $\mathbf{X}$ from the first m eigenvectors ($\mathbf{V}_m$) and the first m eigenvalues ($\mathbf{\Lambda}_m^2$):

$$\mathbf{X} = \mathbf{V}_m\mathbf{\Lambda}_m. \tag{14.6}$$

The matrix of interpoint distances is created from $\mathbf{X}$ as follows:

$$\mathbf{D} = \mathbf{X}\mathbf{X}'. \tag{14.7}$$

Torgerson proved that the $\mathbf{X}$ matrix contains point coordinates such that the distances between the points (i.e., the entries in $\mathbf{D}$) have a least-squares fit to the entries in $\mathbf{\Delta}$. In this sense, the metric MDS procedure produces the best-fitting set of points for the dissimilarities within the specified dimensionality of the scaling solution.

---

[2] This distinction about the value of the a coefficient stems from the definitions of the respective levels of measurement. With interval-level measurement, the numeric values reflect the amount of difference between the objects being measured (this is shown by the value of the b coefficient). But, the zero point is arbitrary. And, the latter feature is represented by a nonzero value for the a coefficient. At the ratio level of measurement, the numeric values still reflect differences between the objects, but now the origin of the scale is fixed (usually at the position that represents complete absence of the property being measured); hence, the a coefficient must be constrained to zero.

Table 14.1 Driving distances between ten U.S. cities (in thousands of miles).

Atlanta	Chicago	Denver	Houston	Los Angeles	Miami	New York	San Francisco	Seattle	Washington D.C.	
0	0.587	1.212	0.701	1.936	0.604	0.748	2.139	2.182	0.543	Atlanta
0.587	0	0.920	0.940	1.745	1.188	0.713	1.858	1.737	0.597	Chicago
1.212	0.920	0	0.879	0.831	1.726	1.631	0.949	1.021	1.494	Denver
0.701	0.940	0.879	0	1.374	0.968	1.420	1.645	1.891	1.220	Houston
1.936	1.745	0.831	1.374	0	2.339	2.451	0.347	0.959	2.300	Los Angeles
0.604	1.188	1.726	0.968	2.339	0	1.092	2.594	2.734	0.923	Miami
0.748	0.713	1.631	1.420	2.451	1.092	0	2.571	2.408	0.205	New York
2.139	1.858	0.949	1.645	0.347	2.594	2.571	0	0.678	2.442	San Francisco
2.182	1.737	1.021	1.891	0.959	2.734	2.408	0.678	0	2.329	Seattle
0.543	0.597	1.494	1.220	2.300	0.923	0.205	2.442	2.329	0	Washington D.C.

Substantive example of metric MDS: Constructing a map

As the first substantive example of MDS, we will build upon the map analogy described earlier. Table 14.1 shows the driving distances (in thousands of miles) between ten North American cities. Thus, the table can be interpreted as a dissimilarities matrix for the cities, in which "dissimilarity" is operationalized as physical distance. We will apply metric MDS to this information in order to generate a map in which cities are shown as points and the distances between the points are, to the greatest extent possible, exactly proportional to the dissimilarities. Of course, this task is a bit trivial in terms of its substantive importance (after all, perfectly adequate maps of the U.S. are already available). But, it provides an excellent example for metric multidimensional scaling because: (1) we already know the dimensionality of the solution; and (2) we already know the true "shape" of the point configuration. Thus, we are in a good position to evaluate how well the metric MDS routine actually works.

As a preliminary caveat, note that Table 14.1 contains 100 cells, but there are really only 45 interesting pieces of information, or entries in the input data for the MDS. First, the entries in the main diagonal are all zero (because an object is not at all dissimilar to itself, by definition). Second, the matrix is perfectly symmetric, so the upper-right triangle contains the same entries as the lower-left triangle. With 10 objects (cities, in this case), there are 45 distinct pairs, each of which is associated with a dissimilarity. Those 45 dissimilarities comprise the actual data that are analyzed in the metric MDS.

Since this is the first example, we will show the results from all of the steps. Table 14.2 shows the double-centered version of the dissimilarities matrix—this is obtained by squaring the entries from Table 14.1, calculating the row, column, and grand means of the new matrix, and applying the transformation from Equation 14.4 to all of the cells. We will obtain a two-dimensional MDS solution (thus ignoring any potential effects due to the curvature of the Earth). So, Table 14.3 gives the first two eigenvectors and eigenvalues for the double-centered dissimilarities matrix. Each eigenvector is multiplied by the square root of the corresponding eigenvalue to produce the "rescaled" eigenvectors shown in Table 14.4. These are also the point coordinates for the cities, so each row of this last matrix is labeled accordingly.

The point coordinates can be plotted in two-dimensional space, and the results are shown in the first panel of Figure 14.1. Obviously, we can see that the relative positions of the points approximate those of cities in the U.S. But the horizontal direction looks odd, because eastern cities fall to the left, and western cities fall to the right. While there is nothing intrinsically wrong with this depiction, it contradicts common practice. Fortunately, an eigendecomposition is invariant under a reflection of the eigenvalues. So, we can multiply the elements in the first eigenvalue by -1, thereby reversing the positions of the points on the first (i.e., horizontal) coordinate axis. This reflected set of points is shown in the second panel of Figure 14.1, and the similarity to a typical map of the U.S. should be obvious.

Here, the MDS solution *seems* to reproduce a regular map very well. But, "eyeballing" the scaling results is not enough to provide a rigorous assessment of how well the geometric model represents the numeric data in the dissimilarities matrix. One way of evaluating the correspondence between the input data and the output scaled

Table 14.2 Double-centered version of driving distances between ten U.S. cities.

Atlanta	Chicago	Denver	Houston	Los Angeles	Miami	New York	San Francisco	Seattle	Washington D.C.	
0.537	0.228	-0.348	0.199	-0.808	0.895	0.697	-1.005	-1.050	0.656	Atlanta
0.228	0.263	-0.174	-0.134	-0.594	0.234	0.585	-0.581	-0.315	0.488	Chicago
-0.348	-0.174	0.236	-0.092	0.570	-0.563	-0.504	0.681	0.658	-0.463	Denver
0.199	-0.134	-0.092	0.352	0.029	0.516	-0.124	-0.163	-0.550	-0.033	Houston
-0.808	-0.594	0.570	0.029	1.594	-1.130	-1.499	1.751	1.399	-1.313	Los Angeles
0.895	0.234	-0.563	0.516	-1.130	1.617	0.920	-1.542	-1.867	0.918	Miami
0.697	0.585	-0.504	-0.124	-1.499	0.920	1.416	-1.583	-1.130	1.222	New York
-1.005	-0.581	0.681	-0.163	1.751	-1.542	-1.583	2.028	1.846	-1.432	San Francisco
-1.050	-0.315	0.658	-0.550	1.399	-1.867	-1.130	1.846	2.124	-1.115	Seattle
0.656	0.488	-0.463	-0.033	-1.313	0.918	1.222	-1.432	-1.115	1.071	Washington D.C.

Table 14.3 First two eigenvectors and eigenvalues from the double-centered matrix of driving distances between ten U.S. cities.

First two eigenvectors of double-centered data matrix, Δ^*		First two eigenvalues of double-centered data matrix, Δ^*	
−0.23217	−0.11011	9.58217	1.68664
−0.12340	0.26253		
0.15554	0.01929		
−0.05216	−0.44079		
0.38889	−0.30037		
−0.36618	−0.44802		
−0.34640	0.39964		
0.45892	−0.08658		
0.43346	0.44649		
−0.31645	0.25843		

Table 14.4 Point coordinates for metric MDS of driving distances between ten U.S. cities. Columns in table are obtained by multiplying each eigenvector from Table 14.3 by the square root of its associated eigenvalue.

First MDS point coordinate	Second MDS point coordinate	
−0.71867	−0.14300	Atlanta
−0.38197	0.34095	Chicago
0.48149	0.02505	Denver
−0.16147	−0.57246	Houston
1.20382	−0.39009	Los Angeles
−1.13352	−0.58185	Miami
−1.07228	0.51901	New York
1.42058	−0.11244	San Francisco
1.34179	0.57986	Seattle
−0.97958	0.33562	Washington D.C.

interpoint distances is to construct a scatterplot showing the relationship between the two. Since we are conducting a metric MDS, a good scaling solution would be indicated by a linear array of points. Since we are assuming ratio-level data, the linear trend should pass through the origin, and if the coordinate axes are scaled to equal the input data values (as they are in this example) the slope of the linear trend should be 1.0. Figure 14.2 shows such a scatterplot for the metric MDS of the intercity distances. There are 45 points in the graph, one for each unique pair of cities. The horizontal axis corresponds to the intercity driving distances (the input data), and the vertical axis shows the interpoint distances in the scaling solution. The gray line shown behind the array of points is a line with slope of one and a zero intercept. So, this diagram confirms

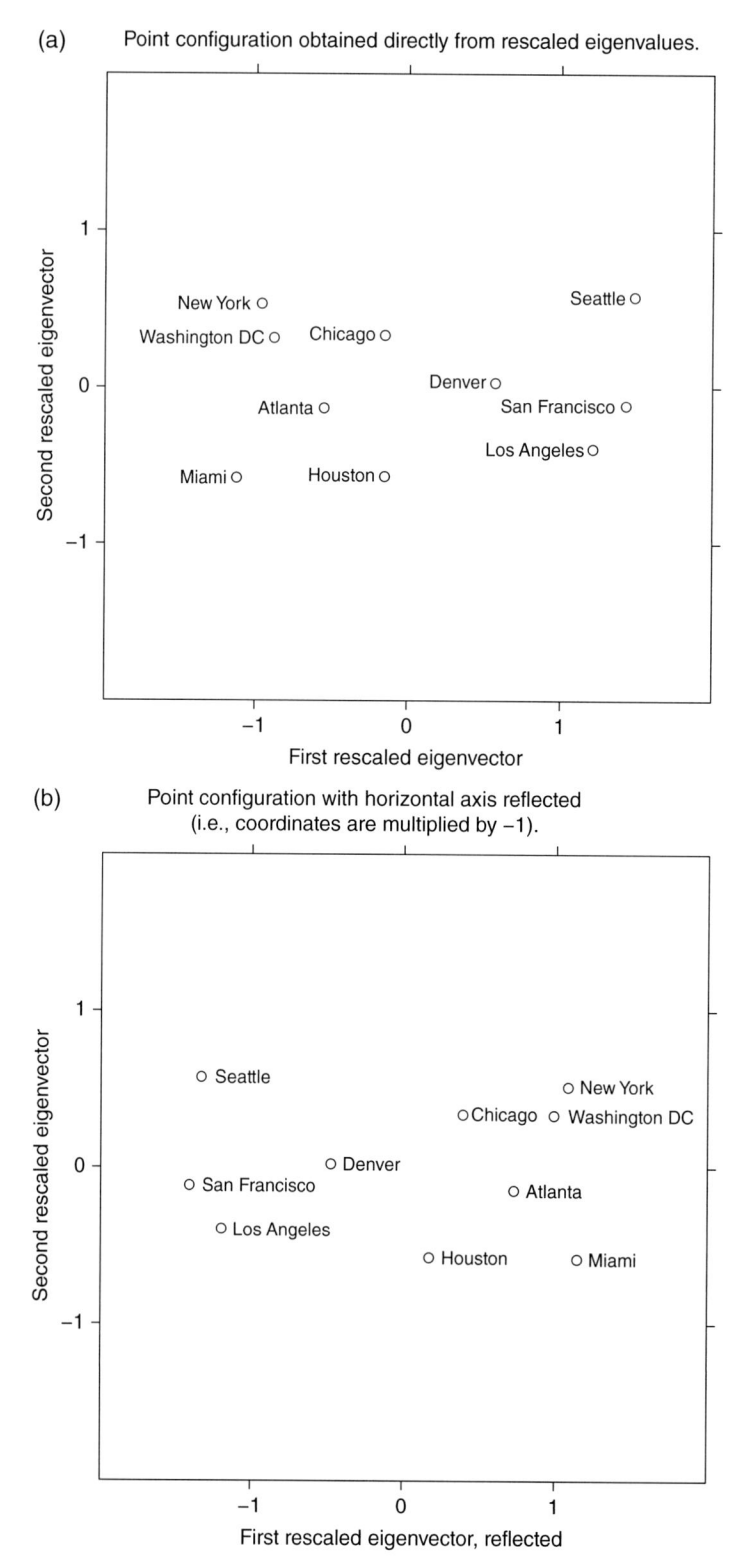

Figure 14.1 Point configuration obtained from metric multidimensional scaling of intercity driving distances.

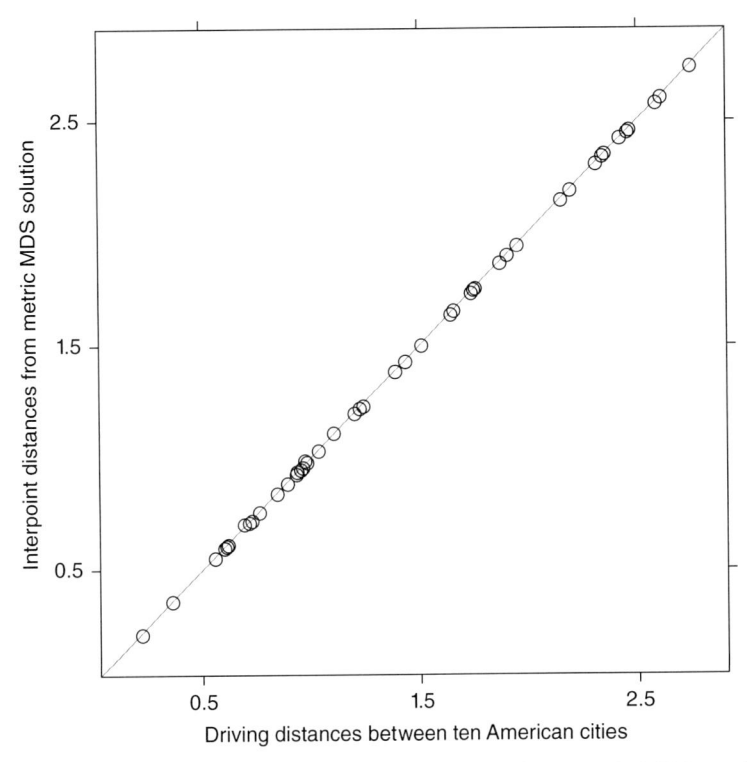

Figure 14.2 Shepard diagram showing interpoint distances from metric MDS as a function of input dissimilarities (intercity driving distances). The gray reference line has a slope of one and an intercept of zero.

that the scaling solution represents the input data *very* well. Note that a graphical display plotting the scaled distances against the input dissimilarities data is called a *Shepard diagram* after one of the early pioneers of multidimensional scaling, Roger N. Shepard.

The Shepard diagram provides a visual representation of the scaling solution's adequacy as a representation of the input data. But, it is also useful to have a numeric measure of fit. In order to obtain such a measure, we will use the eigenvalues that were produced during the process of calculating the coordinate matrix, **X**. The sum of all the eigenvalues is equal to the sum of squares in the dissimilarities matrix. And, each eigenvalue gives the sum of squares associated with the corresponding eigenvector (i.e., the first eigenvalue is associated with the first eigenvector, the second eigenvalue is associated with the second eigenvector, and so on). We used the first two eigenvectors to form the scaling solution, so the sum of the first two eigenvalues gives the sum of squares associated with (or "explained by") that solution. Here, the sum of all ten eigenvalues is 11.32; the first two eigenvalues are 9.58 and 1.69, respectively. So, the fit measure is $(9.58 + 1.69)/11.32 = 0.996$. From this value, we can see that the two-dimensional MDS solution accounts for 99.6% of the total variance in the dissimilarities matrix.[3] Obviously, the geometric model produced by the metric MDS strategy fits the data extremely well—almost perfectly. Thus, metric MDS works!

Data for Multidimensional Scaling

In the previous example of metric MDS, we used physical distances as the input data. So, perhaps it is not so surprising that the output distances in the scaling solution worked so well. But, if multidimensional scaling works for physical distances, then it may also work for data that can be interpreted as "conceptual distances." And, there are many types of data that can be interpreted this way.

Even though we usually call the input data "dissimilarities," MDS can actually handle any kind of data that can be interpreted as a distance function.[4] And, many kinds of information can be interpreted as distances. This leads to one of the strongest features of MDS—its ability to analyze many substantively different kinds of data.

One obvious type of data for MDS consists of direct dissimilarity judgments. For example, a single individual might indicate his or her perceptions of the similarities of k objects. Or, a researcher might have a set of subjects sort pairs of objects according to their perceived pairwise similarities. Alternatively, the analyst could have subjects or respondents rate the similarity of object pairs on some predefined scale and then take the mean of the individual similarity ratings. In any case, the *similarity* judgments are easily converted to dissimilarities by subtracting the "raw" values from some constant, thereby reflecting the data values.

Profile dissimilarity measures assume that each of the k objects to be scaled possesses scores on a common set of characteristics; let v represent the number of these characteristics. The profile dissimilarity between any pair of objects is obtained by taking the sum of the squared differences in the scores of the two objects, across the full set of

---

[3] This use of eigenvalues to measure the "variance explained" in the MDS solution is an exact parallel to the use of summed eigenvalues to represent the amount of variance explained in a multivariate dataset by a subset of components in principal components analysis. And, just as we do here, the summed eigenvalues for the subset of components can be divided by the sum of all the eigenvalues (which is equal to the sum of the variances of the observed variables) to provide the proportion of variance explained by those components. Similarly, in some variants of common factor analysis, the sum of the eigenvalues for the retained set of factors gives the amount of variance in the observed variables that is "explained by" the retained factors. But, the interpretation as a proportion of variance explained can be tricky. If the summed eigenvalues for the retained factors are divided by the summed eigenvalues for the full set of variables, then the resulting numeric value gives the proportion of *common* variance in the observed variables that is explained by the factors. In order to obtain the proportion of *total* variance in the observed variables that is explained by the factors, the summed eigenvalues for the retained factors must be divided by the summed variances for the full set of observed variables.

[4] Assume that D is some function that takes two arguments (say, a and b). D is a distance function if the following four properties hold for all possible subsets of objects, a, b, and c, in a given set of objects:

$D(a, b) \geq 0$ (Nonnegativity)
$D(a, a) = 0$ (Identity)
$D(a, b) = D(b, a)$ (Symmetry)
$D(a, b) + D(a, c) \geq D(b, c)$ (Triangle inequality)

Any type of data that possesses the preceding four characteristics (or can be transformed to possess them) can be treated as a distance, and used as input to an MDS analysis.

characteristics. Often, the square root of the sum of squared differences is used; in that case, the profile dissimilarities are the distances between the objects in the v-dimensional space defined by the characteristics. Profile dissimilarities are particularly useful because they convert multivariate data (i.e., a rectangular matrix in which each object is characterized by a vector of scores) to dissimilarities (i.e., a square matrix summarizing the differences of each pair of objects across their respective vectors of scores). Of course, the profiles themselves could be constructed from an arbitrarily large number (say, v) of scores for the respective objects. An MDS of these data could thus be employed as a strategy to summarize hypervariate v-dimensional data in a space of m dimensions, where m is assumed to be quite small, perhaps only 2 or 3.

Still another kind of information that might be interpreted as dissimilarities are *confusions data*. So, if the researcher has information on the degree to which one stimulus is mistaken for another stimulus, it might be interpreted as a representation of the similarity between those stimuli—the assumption, of course, is that objects that are more similar are more easily confused for each other. Following the same kind of logic, measures of temporal stability could also be interpreted as dissimilarities. For example, assume that a set of objects are sorted into k different categories at each of two time points. The proportion of objects that move from one category to the other over the time interval could be interpreted as the similarity of the two categories. Note that in this latter case, it is the *categories* that are scaled, not the objects that are sorted into the respective categories.

There are a variety of theory-based measures of spatial separation that can be used as input dissimilarities for MDS. For example, the number of times two objects display the same behaviors can be interpreted as the similarity between the objects. The degree to which a pair of objects share common characteristics can be viewed the same way. And, the line-of-sight dissimilarity measure developed by Rabinowitz (1976) creates a pairwise dissimilarity measure among a set of k objects using n subjects rating scale scores for those objects.

Finally, correlation coefficients are sometimes used as similarity measures and inputs for MDS. In fact, this is usually problematic, because the geometric interpretation of a correlation coefficient consists of the angular separation between two variable vectors, and not the spatial distance between two points. By imposing certain assumptions, the correlation coefficient can be transformed into a dissimilarity measure. But, those assumptions are fairly stringent, so it is generally best to seek an alternative, more appropriate, type of dissimilarity to use as input for multidimensional scaling.

So, the flexibility in the kinds of input data that can be used constitutes an important strength of MDS as an analytic strategy. But, it also raises a new concern: In many such cases, we would be hesitant to assume that our dissimilarities comprise interval- or ratio-level data. Instead, we may only have ordinal-level dissimilarities among the objects we seek to scale. In that case, we cannot talk about a specific parametric function (e.g., linear) relating the input dissimilarity values to the scaled interpoint distances. Instead, we could try the following:

$$d_{ij} = f^m(\delta_{ij}) + e_{ij}. \tag{14.8}$$

In Equation 14.8, f^m means a *monotonic function* and e_{ij} is an error term. A monotonic relationship exists if, for all subsets of three objects (say, i, j, and l), the following holds:

$$\delta_{ij} < \delta_{il} \Rightarrow d_{ij} \leq d_{il}. \tag{14.9}$$

Here we are making a far less stringent assumption about the "translation" from dissimilarity to distance. Now, it is only the *ordering* of the distances that needs to be consistent with the values of the input dissimilarities.[5]

Do we really need to worry about this? Why not simply treat ordinal data as if it were interval or ratio level? This strategy is used often for other statistical analyses in the social and behavioral sciences (e.g., ordinal dependent variables in regression equations). And, it is often the case that metric MDS analysis of ordinal dissimilarities seems to generate interpretable results. Nevertheless, doing so remains a highly problematic strategy. For one thing, it is "cheating" with respect to the data characteristics. Treating ordinal data as if they were interval-level (or higher) imposes an implicit but extremely stringent assumption about the relative sizes of the differences between the dissimilarities. In addition, the concept of *variance* is undefined for ordinal data. Therefore, it is inappropriate to use the eigendecomposition, which maximizes the variance explained by successive dimensions in the scaling solution. For these reasons, it is better to use an entirely different strategy for MDS with ordinal dissimilarities data.

Nonmetric Multidimensional Scaling

Nonmetric MDS is used to construct a geometric model of dissimilarities data relying strictly on the ordinal properties, rather than the actual numeric values, of the data values. The general strategy is different from that used to obtain the solution in metric MDS. With the latter, one estimates each dimension of the scaling solution successively; that is, new dimensions are added to the previously estimated dimensions until adequate goodness of fit is achieved. With nonmetric MDS, a complete scaling solution is obtained in a given dimensionality; that is, all of the dimensions are estimated simultaneously rather one at a time, successively. If the goodness of fit for the resultant point configuration is adequate, there is no need to go any further; simply stop and report the results of the analysis. But, if the fit of the scaled interpoint distances to the input ordinal dissimilarities is poor, then discard the results and try a solution in the next higher dimensionality (again, estimating all of the dimensions in the new solution at the same time). Continue this process until an adequate fit is obtained.

---

[5] The monotonic relationship between scaled distances and input dissimilarities is analogous to the monotonic item response functions that are used in Mokken scaling (Sijtsma & Molenaar, 2002; van Schuur, 2011), a form of nonmetric item response theory (IRT). In metric IRT, the analyst specifies a particular parametric function (usually a sigmoid or "S-shaped" function such as the logistic or the cumulative normal) that relates a subject's position along an unobserved dimension to the probability that that person will give a positive response on a given test item. This enables estimation of interval-level values for the items and for the subjects. In nonmetric IRT, the researcher only specifies that the item response functions for the items are monotonic with respect to the underlying dimension (i.e., the exact shape is not known or assumed) and that the functions for separate items never overlap each other. The cost associated with the weaker assumptions about the item response functions used in nonmetric IRT is that Mokken scaling only produces an ordinal-level depiction of the items and the subjects (although, in practice, good-fitting Mokken scales can often be treated as interval-level data with few harmful consequences). Nonmetric MDS does not suffer from a similar limitation: If the analysis is successful, then the scaling solution produces interval-level estimates of the distances between the scaled points, despite the fact that the input data are only assumed to be ordinal-level (and, therefore, monotonically related to the distances). The reason for the difference is that a properly conducted nonmetric MDS results in a very sizable number of metric constraints on the relative locations of the points. Therefore, it is impossible to move the points in a nonmetric MDS solution very much without violating the monotonicity assumption and degrading the fit of the scaling solution.

Within a specific dimensionality, the scaling procedure relies on an iterative process. We start with some initial configuration of k points representing the objects to be scaled. The interpoint distances in this initial configuration are not expected to reflect the dissimilarities between the objects very accurately. So we move the points around within the space, as necessary, in order to make the interpoint distances monotonic with the order of the dissimilarities. This usually takes several (and often many) sets of point movements. We (or, more realistically, the scaling software) keep moving the points until one of two things occurs: (1) the interpoint distances are perfectly monotonic with respect to the dissimilarities; or (2) the movements stop enhancing the consistency between the dissimilarities and the distances. In real MDS applications, the second condition is more common than the first. In other words, the scaled configuration of points does not produce distances that are a *perfectly* monotonic function of the dissimilarities. But, hopefully, they are nearly so.

In order to illustrate the general idea underlying (if not the exact procedure used in) nonmetric MDS, we will once again scale the ten U.S. cities we used in the previous metric MDS example. Table 14.5 shows a new dissimilarities matrix for the ten cities. But now, the dissimilarities are created from the respective cities' economic, social, and cultural characteristics.[6] And, the matrix only rank-orders the pairs of cities in terms of their dissimilarities with respect to these characteristics. Thus, there is no question that this information comprises strictly ordinal data. Again, the objective is to find a configuration of points in m-dimensional space such that the ordering of the interpoint distances matches as closely as possible the ordering of the pairs of cities in Table 14.5.

We start by specifying m, the dimensionality in which we will seek a scaling solution. For now, we will set $m = 2$. If we can produce a set of points in two-dimensional space such that the relative sizes of the interpoint distances are consistent with the rank-ordered dissimilarities, then we will be able to show the results easily in a graphical display. We will only move to a higher dimensionality if the two-dimensional solution fails to produce an adequate fit to the data.

We next need to generate a configuration of points, so we have the "raw material" for the point-moving process that will produce the scaling solution. This initial configuration is just to get us started; we do not expect that the interpoint distances will reflect accurately the ordered dissimilarities. The starting configuration is obtained by randomly positioning ten points in two-dimensional space. Figure 14.3 shows such a starting configuration for the ten cities. Clearly, this configuration is *not* an accurate representation of the dissimilarities. For example, the least dissimilar pair of cities is Denver and Atlanta, scored 1 in Table 14.5. Yet, the points representing these cities are widely separated in the space, with Atlanta near the bottom of the point configuration and Denver near the top. At the opposite extreme, the third most dissimilar pair is New York City and Atlanta, scored 43 in Table 14.5. But, the points for these cities are adjacent to each other at the bottom of the point configuration.

The inadequacy of the scaling solution is illustrated in Figure 14.4, where interpoint distances from Figure 14.3 are plotted against the corresponding ordinal dissimilarity values; again, this type of graph is usually called a Shepard diagram. If the distances were consistent with the dissimilarities, then the plotted points would form a monotonic array

---

[6] The values in the matrix are created by calculating the profile dissimilarities between the cities across the nine measures of social, economic, and cultural characteristics presented in the *Places Rated Almanac* (Savageau & D'Agostino, 2000). The table just gives the rank-order of the actual profile dissimilarity values.

Table 14.5 Rank-ordered dissimilarities of ten U.S. cities, based upon their social, economic, and cultural characteristics.

Atlanta	Chicago	Denver	Houston	Los Angeles	Miami	New York	San Francisco	Seattle	Washington D.C.	
0	12	1	10	32	19	43	31	8	6	Atlanta
12	0	15	28	21	33	27	24	26	2	Chicago
1	15	0	3	36	16	44	25	13	5	Denver
10	28	3	0	39	20	45	41	30	18	Houston
32	21	36	39	0	9	23	7	14	22	Los Angeles
19	33	16	20	9	0	40	29	4	37	Miami
43	27	44	45	23	40	0	38	42	35	New York
31	24	25	41	7	29	38	0	17	11	San Francisco
8	26	13	30	14	4	42	17	0	34	Seattle
6	2	5	18	22	37	35	11	34	0	Washington D.C.

Note. Table entries are rank-ordered versions of profile dissimilarities calculated across the nine social, economic, and cultural scores assigned to the cities in the *Places Rated Almanac*, by Richard Boyer and David Savageau. The data are used here with the kind permission of the publisher, Rand McNally.

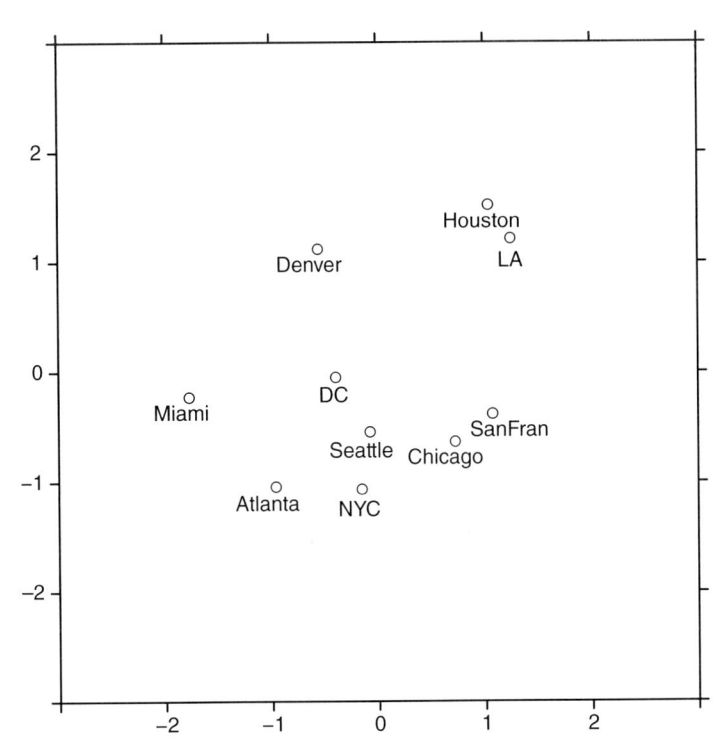

Figure 14.3 Randomly located points for ten American cities, to be used as starting configuration for nonmetric MDS of cities' social, economic, and cultural characteristics.

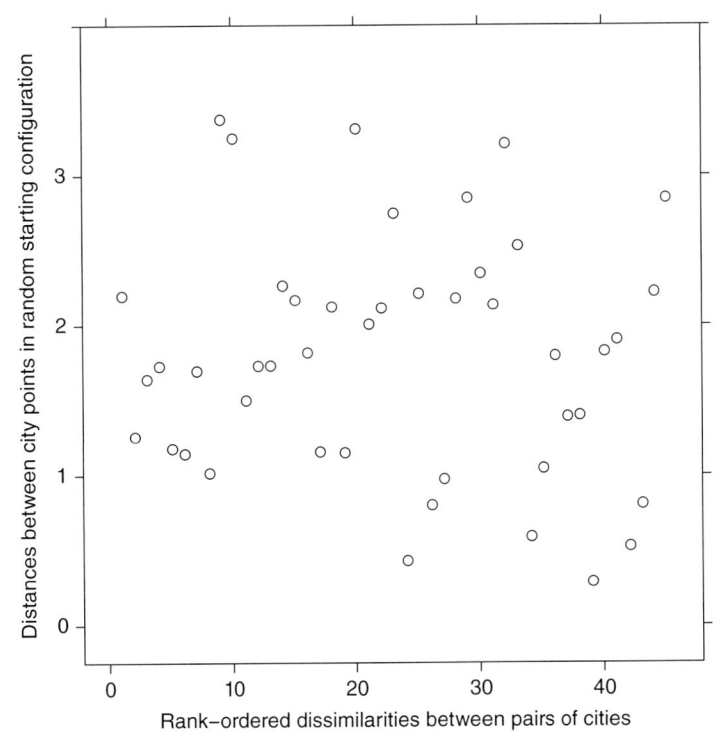

Figure 14.4 Shepard diagram showing distances between pairs of city points (from random starting configuration) versus input ordinal dissimilarities between pairs of cities.

from lower-left to upper-right. Obviously, that is not the case here. So, it is definitely necessary to move the points from their current randomly determined locations to make the distances more consistent with the dissimilarities. In order to do this, we will generate a new set of 45 values—one for each interpoint distance—called *disparities*. The disparity for objects i and j is designated $\hat{d}_{ij}$. The disparities have two properties:

- The disparities are as similar as possible to the distances, in the least-squares sense.
- The disparities are weakly monotonic to the rank-ordered dissimilarities; that is, as the rank of the distances increases, the values of the disparities cannot decrease (though they need not increase).

Stated differently, the disparities comprise a set of values that is maximally correlated with the distances, but still monotonic to the original ordinal input data for the MDS. A simple procedure for calculating the disparities was developed by Joseph Kruskal (1964b).

The first panel of Figure 14.5 shows the Shepard diagram from Figure 14.4, with the disparities (plotted as x's) superimposed over the points determined by the distances and dissimilarities (plotted as open circles). Notice that, unlike the distances, the disparity points *do* form a weak monotonic array: As we move from left to right along the horizontal axis, the array of x's always moves upward or to the right; it never reverses direction on itself. The second panel of Figure 14.5 connects each disparity to its corresponding distance with a gray line segment. This emphasizes how the former are *targets* for the latter. If the disparity point falls below the distance point, then the points in the MDS solution for that object pair need to be moved closer to each other. Conversely, if the disparity point falls above the distance point, then the points in the MDS solution for that object pair need to be moved farther apart. The relative size of the point movement is indicated by the length of the line segment; shorter segments represent point pairs in the MDS configuration that do not need to be moved very much, while longer segments indicate that a larger movement is necessary.

The separation between the distances and the disparities also enables us to construct a fit measure for the MDS solution. If the configuration of points in the MDS solution *were* monotonic to the dissimilarities, then the disparities would be equal to the distances themselves. The greater the departure from monotonicity in the MDS solution, the greater the discrepancy between the distances and disparities. Thus, the sum of squared differences between the two summarizes the degree to which the scaling solution departs from the stated objective of distances that are monotonic with the dissimilarities. We also need to normalize our fit measure, to remove its dependence on the measurement units in the scaling solution (which are arbitrary). There are several ways to do this, but one simple method is to divide the sum of squares by the sum of the squared distances. This leads to a fit measure called *Kruskal's Stress* (an acronym for *standardized residual sum of squares*), defined as follows:

$$\text{Stress}_1 = \left[\frac{\sum^{\#\text{pairs}} \left(d_{ij} - \hat{d}_{ij} \right)^2}{\sum^{\#\text{pairs}} d_{ij}^2} \right]^{0.5}. \tag{14.10}$$

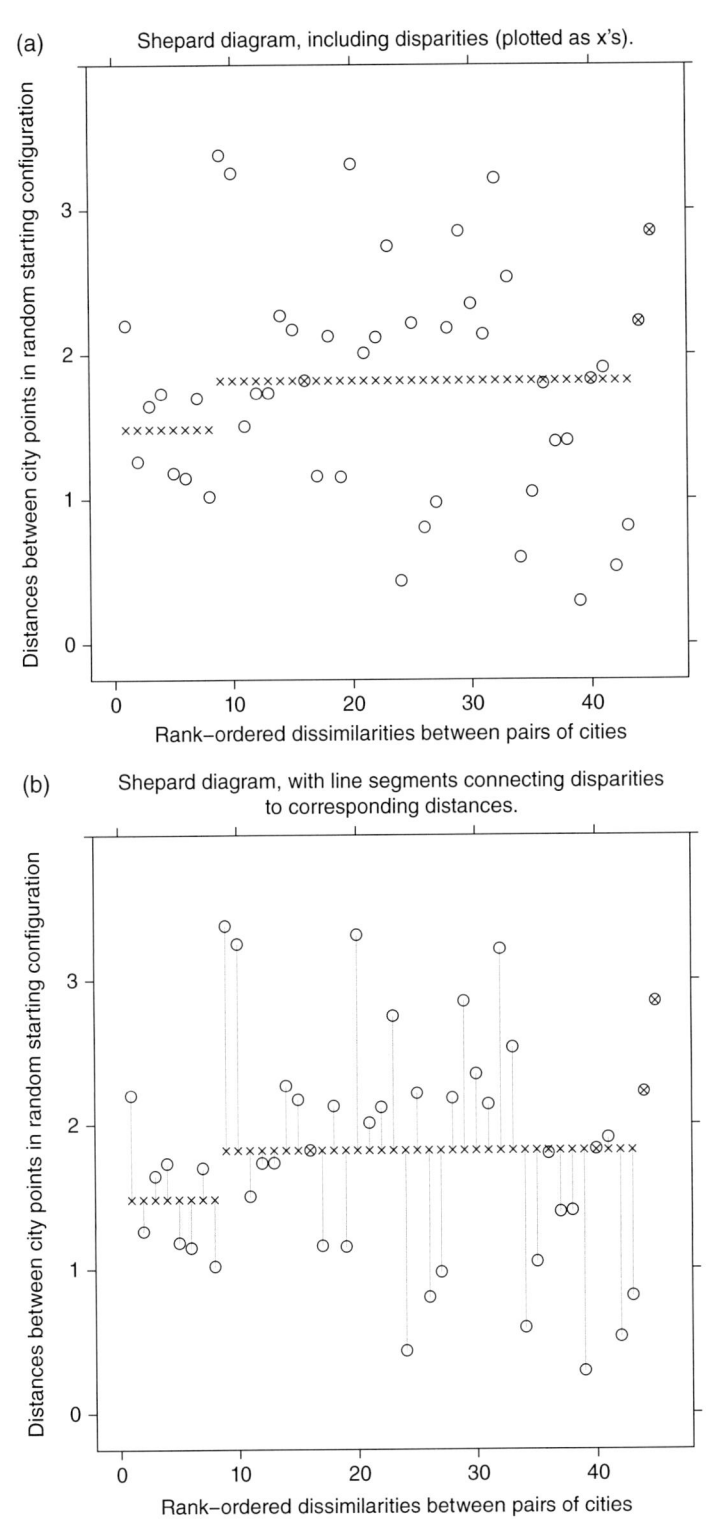

Figure 14.5 Shepard diagram for random starting configuration in nonmetric MDS of dissimilarities between cities, showing disparities for the scaled distances.

The subscript indicates that this is the first of two Stress formulas Kruskal developed. The other, Stress$_2$, is identical except that the denominator contains the corrected sum of squares for the distances. In some widely quoted guidelines, Kruskal (1964a) suggests that a Stress$_1$ value of .1 is "fair," while .05 is "good," and anything .025 or below is "excellent." Kruskal's Stress is a *badness-of-fit* measure, in that values closer to zero are better. The Stress value for the bad point configuration from Figure 14.3 is quite a bit larger than zero, at .148.

While we want Stress values closer to zero, it is a bit difficult to interpret the specific values for any given scaling solution. Therefore, many analysts rely on an alternative fit measure, the squared correlation between the distances and the disparities. Here, the idea is that the disparities are monotonic to the dissimilarities. The higher the correlation between the distances and the disparities, the greater the extent to which the current point configuration meets the scaling objective (i.e., distances which are monotonic to the dissimilarities). The squared correlation of the distances and disparities for the MDS solution in Figure 14.3 is very small, at .076. Of course, this is not surprising, since the points are randomly located.

Getting back to the scaling procedure, we use the disparities to move the points. We do this by creating a new *dissimilarities* matrix, in which the δ_{ij}'s are replaced by the $\hat{d}_{ij}$'s. Then, we carry out a metric MDS on the new matrix, generating a new configuration of ten city-points in two-dimensional space. This latter MDS effectively moves the points from their initial random locations to a new configuration in which (hopefully) the interpoint distances are more nearly monotonic to the original rank-ordered dissimilarities. In order to save space, we do not show the new point configuration. But, the two panels of Figure 14.6 show the Shepard diagram for this new MDS solution—though it is important to emphasize that the values on the horizontal axis are the original rank-ordered profile dissimilarities, and *not* the disparities that were actually used as the input to the metric MDS that was just carried out. From the first panel, we can see that the point cloud is more clearly oriented from lower-left to upper-right in the plotting region, suggesting that the interpoint distances in the MDS solution are coming closer to monotonicity with the input dissimilarities. The second panel adds the disparities for the latest MDS point configuration. From the vertical gray line segments, we can see that the discrepancies between the MDS interpoint distances and the disparities tend to be quite a bit smaller than they were in the initial, random, configuration of city-points. This is confirmed by the two fit measures. The second point configuration produces a Stress value of .079, and a squared correlation of .624; clearly, we are moving toward a better-fitting model.

We now create a new matrix containing the latest set of disparities (i.e., from Figure 14.6), and repeat the process. Each time we carry out an MDS on the disparities constitutes an iteration. We will not show the intervening steps, to save space. But, on each iteration, the fit improves, the point cloud in the Shepard diagram provides a closer approximation to monotonicity, and the discrepancies between the disparities and the distances get smaller. After eight such iterations, the movements of the points in the MDS solution become extremely tiny, and the fit of the point configuration to the data barely changes from the last iteration. Figure 14.7 shows the two versions of the Shepard diagram for the MDS solution after the eighth iteration. At this stage, the MDS configuration provides an excellent fit to the ordinal dissimilarities: Stress is very close to zero, at .014, and the squared correlation is very large, at .922.

Multidimensional Scaling: An Introduction 395

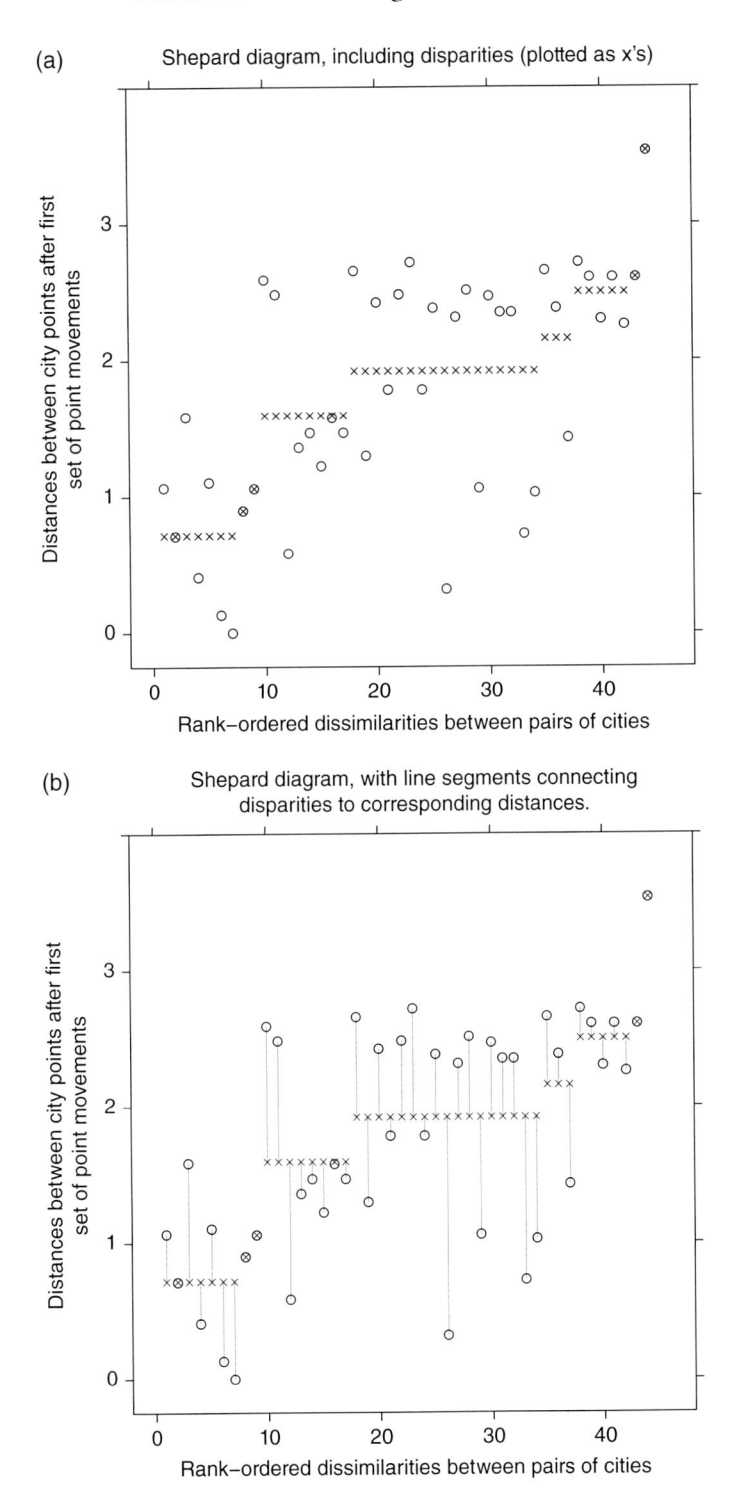

(a) Shepard diagram, including disparities (plotted as x's)

(b) Shepard diagram, with line segments connecting disparities to corresponding distances.

Figure 14.6 Shepard diagram for interpoint distances after the first set of point movements (obtained by performing metric MDS on the disparities from the random starting configuration).

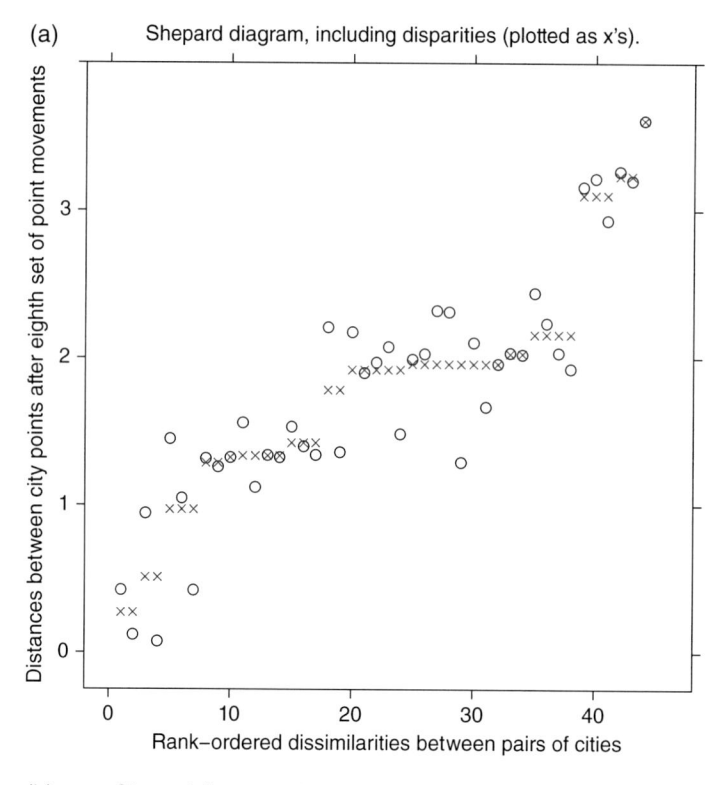

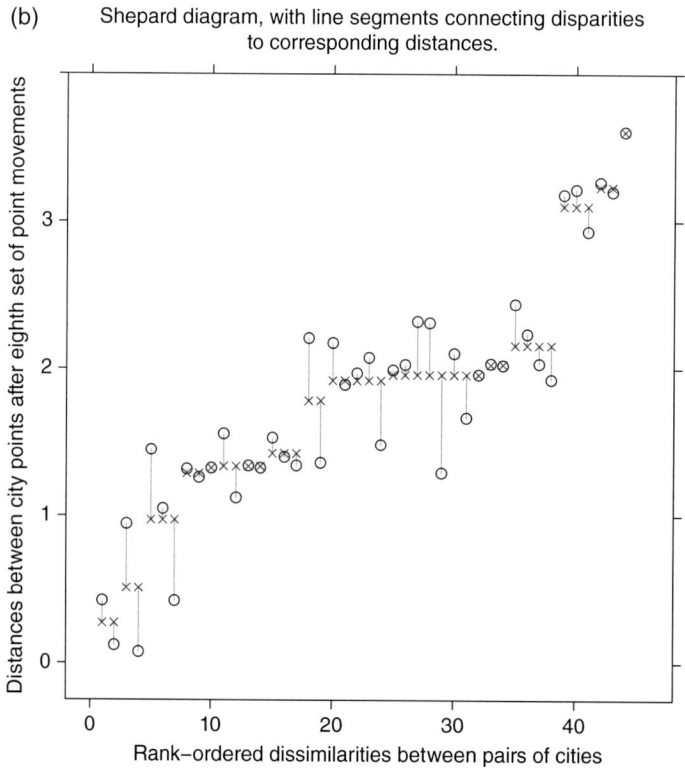

Figure 14.7 Shepard diagram for interpoint distances after the eighth set of point movements.

Multidimensional Scaling: An Introduction 397

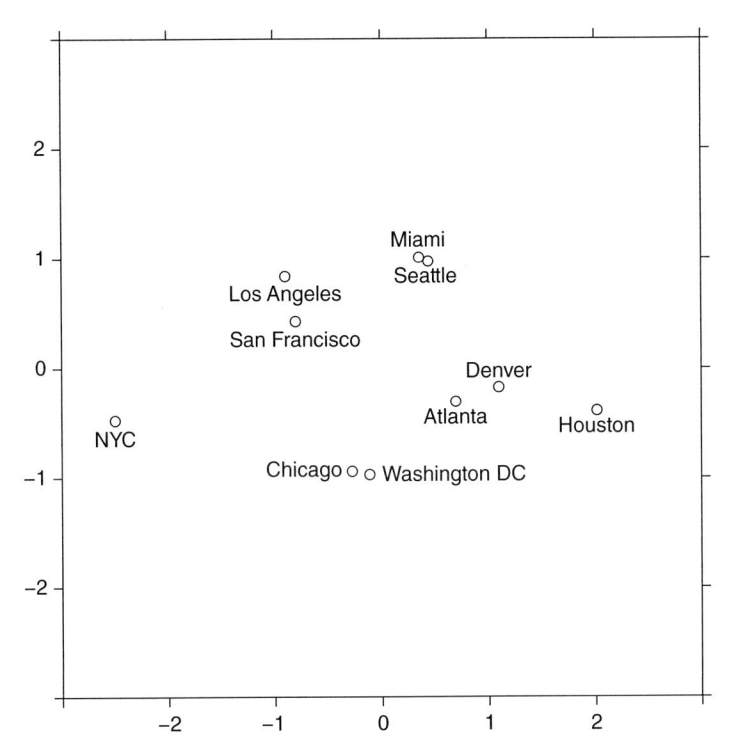

Figure 14.8 Point configuration obtained from nonmetric multidimensional scaling of social, economic, and cultural dissimilarities among ten American cities.

Figure 14.8 shows the nonmetric MDS solution, itself. Without going into a great deal of detail, this scaling solution does seem to make sense in substantive terms. Consider the cities that fall into the various groupings or clusters of points. On the right side of the plot, the points for three sun-belt cities (Houston, Denver, and Atlanta) are relatively close to each other. Near the bottom, two large metropolitan areas that are well known for their cosmopolitan environments (Chicago and Washington D.C.) form another cluster. The two California cities are separated from the other points in the upper-left part of the plotting region. At the top of the region, two coastal cities at opposite corners of the country (Miami and Seattle) fall close to each other. And, finally, New York City is off by itself in the lower-left part of the space; the isolation of this point is not at all unreasonable, given the unique aspects of that particular city.

The preceding example gives an intuitive sense of the general strategy underlying nonmetric multidimensional scaling. But, even though it works quite well, this approach is not the way most "real" nonmetric MDS software works. Instead, they capitalize on the fact that the Stress coefficient is a function of the point coordinates in the current MDS configuration (which are used to calculate the distances and, indirectly, the disparities). Accordingly, the partial derivatives of Stress, relative to the coordinates, can be calculated. The partial derivatives show how Stress changes when the point coordinates are changed by an infinitesimal amount. Therefore, they help us achieve a scaling solution by showing how to change the point coordinates in the ways that make the partial derivatives the smallest possible negative values (thereby decreasing the discrepancy between distances and disparities). After the points are moved, the scaling software recalculates the disparities, evaluates the fit of the new configuration, and repeats the process as necessary. So, it is an iterative process, as in the preceding intuitive example. But, the MDS software focuses more directly on the process of changing the point coordinates and, hence, moving the points, rather than carrying out a complete metric MDS on each iteration.

The steps in a typical nonmetric MDS routine proceed as follows:

1. Generate a starting configuration of object points. The points could be located randomly, as in the previous example, but most modern MDS software uses a "rational" starting configuration obtained by performing a metric MDS on the ordinal data.
2. Calculate the disparities for the starting configuration.

    Use the distances from the starting configuration and the disparities to calculate Stress.

    If Stress is zero (unlikely with a random start, but possible with a rational start), then terminate the routine.

    Otherwise, proceed to the next step.
3. Calculate the partial derivatives of Stress relative to the coordinates, and move the points in order to produce the largest possible decrease in the Stress value.
4. Use the new distances between the just-moved points to calculate disparities and Stress for the new object point configuration.

    If Stress is zero, then the distances are monotonic to the dissimilarities so terminate the routine.

    If Stress has not changed since the last iteration, or it has gotten larger, indicating a worse fit than on the previous iteration (unlikely with modern software), then terminate the routine.

    If Stress is smaller than it was on the previous iteration, the MDS solution is improving, so go back to step 3 and repeat.
5. Terminate the MDS routine and print out the results:

    An iteration history, showing how Stress has changed as the object points are moved from the starting configuration to the final configuration.

    The coordinates for the object points in the final MDS solution.

    The fit statistics for the final MDS solution (usually Stress and the squared correlation between the interpoint distances and the disparities).

Substantive example of nonmetric multidimensional scaling

In order to illustrate the utility of multidimensional scaling for dealing with substantive research problems, let us move on to a more realistic substantive example. The problem is drawn from the field of political psychology, and the specific research question is, what do citizens "see" when they think about a field of candidates for public office? Stated a bit differently, what is the nature of the cognitive structure that the electorate brings to bear on a set of electoral stimuli?

Assume that we have information about the American electorate's perceptions of 13 prominent political figures from the period of the 2004 American presidential election. The figures are: George W. Bush; John Kerry; Ralph Nader; Richard Cheney; John Edwards; Laura Bush; Hillary Clinton; Bill Clinton; Colin Powell; John Ashcroft; John McCain; the Democratic Party; and the Republican Party. The information comes from a high-quality public opinion survey (the 2004 American National Election Study), and it is the perceived dissimilarities between all pairs of these political figures. With 13 figures, there will be 78 distinct pairs of figures. And, the perceptions of the individual survey respondents are aggregated to form one summary dissimilarity score for each pair of political figures. With such perceptual information, we probably would be hesitant to attribute metric properties to the specific dissimilarity scores; instead, we will only assume that the latter represent ordinal-level measurement. Therefore, we rank-order the pairs of political figures according to their perceived dissimilarity, assigning integer values from one (for the least dissimilar or most similar pair) to 78 (for the most dissimilar or least similar pair).[7]

As with the previous smaller examples, we arrange the rank-ordered dissimilarity values into the square, symmetric matrix shown in Table 14.6. The zeroes in the main diagonal indicate that each figure is not at all dissimilar to him/her/itself. In the off-diagonal cells, the value 1 appears in the fifth row, second column (and the second row, fifth column, since the matrix is symmetric), indicating that Kerry and Edwards are the most similar pair of figures. At the opposite extreme, the 78 in the cell at the fourth row and second column shows that Kerry and Cheney are the most dissimilar pair. Noninteger values, such as the 74.5 in the cell at the fifth row, fourth column, and also in the cell at the thirteenth row and second column, indicate tied degrees of dissimilarity.

The results from a nonmetric MDS analysis of the data in Table 14.6 are shown in Figure 14.9. The point configuration in this figure is a nearly perfect representation of the information that was contained in Table 14.6. The Stress value is tiny, at .04, and the squared correlation between the disparities and the scaled interpoint distances is very high, at .993. Thus, the rank-order of the distances between pairs of points corresponds extremely closely to the rank-ordered dissimilarities between pairs of political figures. Of course, Figure 14.9 is not the *only* point configuration that would provide such an excellent depiction of the data. But, any other sets of points that provide equally good representation of the dissimilarities would be almost identical to this one. For example, the orientation of the points could differ (e.g., what is now the horizontal axis could be vertical, and vice versa), the points could be reflected in one or both of the axes, and the overall size of the point cloud could be magnified or shrunk. But, these kinds of differences do not affect the *relative* distances between the points. If we were to hold the overall orientation and size of the point cloud fixed, then it is impossible to move any of the points very much at all without degrading the exact correspondence between pairwise dissimilarities and pairwise distances.

The contents of this point configuration should make a great deal of sense to anyone familiar with American electoral politics. Looking first at the lower half of the plotting region, the points representing Democratic figures are grouped near the left side of the space (i.e., Kerry, Edwards, the Clintons, and the Democratic Party). In contrast, the points closer to the right side represent Republicans (Ashcroft, Cheney, George Bush,

---

[7] The dissimilarities are obtained by applying the line-of-sight procedure (Rabinowitz, 1976) to survey data on respondents' feeling thermometer ratings of the 13 political figures from the Center for Political Studies' 2004 American National Election Study. A more complete analysis of these data is provided in Jacoby (2009).

Table 14.6 Perceptual dissimilarities between political figures from the 2004 U.S. presidential election.

G.W. Bush	John Kerry	Ralph Nader	Dick Cheney	John Edwards	Laura Bush	Hillary Clinton	Bill Clinton	Colin Powell	John Ashcroft	John McCain	Democ. Party	Repub. Party	
0.0	73.0	62	8.0	68.0	20.0	51.5	41.0	24.0	7	25.5	50	5.0	G.W. Bush
73.0	0.0	56	78.0	1.0	54.0	15.0	17.0	47.0	77	37.0	2	74.5	Kerry
62.0	56.0	0	72.0	59.0	53.0	60.0	49.0	58.0	70	39.0	57	71.0	Nader
8.0	78.0	72	0.0	74.5	25.5	65.0	51.5	29.0	12	30.0	66	4.0	Cheney
68.0	1.0	59	74.5	0.0	44.0	14.0	16.0	46.0	76	38.0	3	69.0	Edwards
20.0	54.0	53	25.5	44.0	0.0	42.0	34.0	9.5	23	22.0	45	18.0	L. Bush
51.5	15.0	60	65.0	14.0	42.0	0.0	19.0	32.0	67	40.0	13	55.0	H. Clinton
41.0	17.0	49	51.5	16.0	34.0	19.0	0.0	31.0	61	36.0	11	48.0	B. Clinton
24.0	47.0	58	29.0	46.0	9.5	32.0	31.0	0.0	28	9.5	35	21.0	Powell
7.0	77.0	70	12.0	76.0	23.0	67.0	61.0	28.0	0	33.0	63	6.0	Ashcroft
25.5	37.0	39	30.0	38.0	22.0	40.0	36.0	9.5	33	0.0	43	27.0	McCain
50.0	2.0	57	66.0	3.0	45.0	13.0	11.0	35.0	63	43.0	0	64.0	Dem. Pty.
5.0	74.5	71	4.0	69.0	18.0	55.0	48.0	21.0	6	27.0	64	0.0	Rep. Pty.

Note. Table entries are line-of-sight dissimilarities (Rabinowitz, 1976) calculated from feeling thermometer ratings in the 2004 CPS American National Election Study.

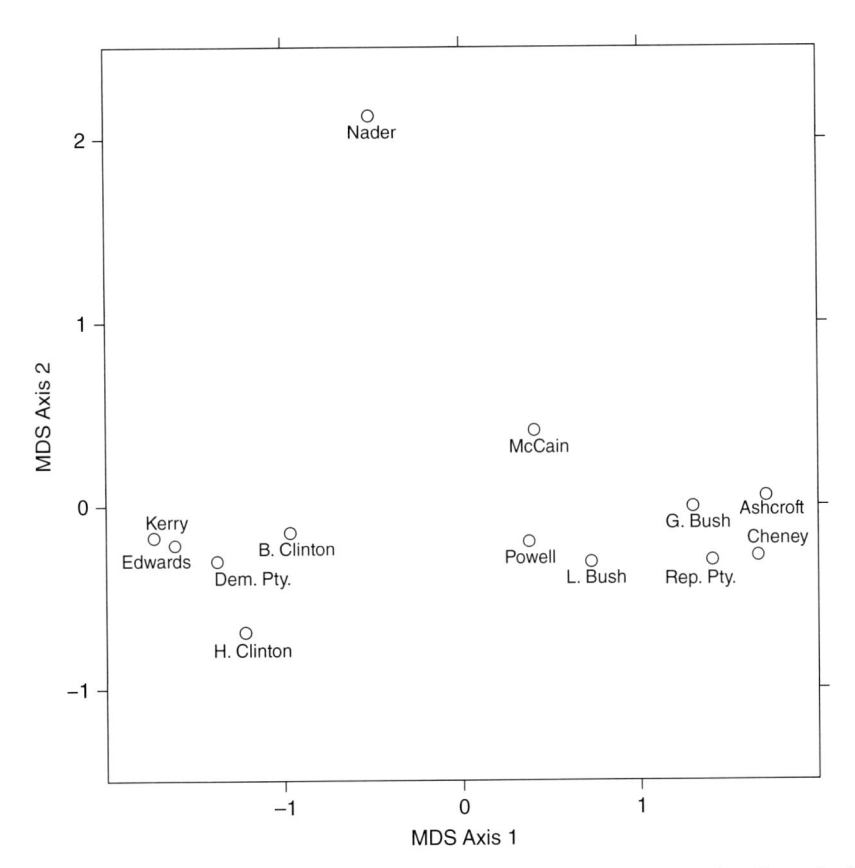

Figure 14.9 Point configuration obtained from nonmetric multidimensional scaling of political figures from the 2004 U.S. presidential election.

and so on). The point representing Nader, an independent candidate in 2004, lies separated by a great distance from both of the two partisan sets of points. So, these groupings correspond to partisan differences between the political figures. But, there is more: Looking at the array of points from left to right (i.e., ignoring their differences in the vertical direction), the ordering corresponds closely to common understandings of ideology, with the clearest left-leaning figures (Kerry and Edwards) positioned fittingly enough at the left side of the space, the most extreme right-wing figures (Ashcroft and Cheney) over at the opposite extreme, and relatively moderate figures (e.g., Colin Powell) located near the center. For now, it is sufficient to emphasize that interesting substantive features are immediately obvious in the scaled points, but they would have been much more difficult to discern in the original 13 × 13 matrix of dissimilarity scores. This, in itself, demonstrates the power of a successful multidimensional scaling analysis.

Interpretation Strategies for Multidimensional Scaling

Of course, MDS (like any other data analysis strategy) is usually used to provide substantive insights about the objects contained in the data being analyzed. One important interpretational aspect of MDS involves the dimensionality of the scaling solution.

Specifically, how many dimensions should be used in any given analysis? It is impossible to provide a general answer to this question. There is always a trade-off between two considerations: First, the scaling solution needs enough dimensions to provide an accurate representation of the dissimilarities (i.e., a low Stress value and a high correlation between the distances and the input dissimilarities or disparities). Second, the scaling solution needs a relatively small number of dimensions to facilitate interpretation. In practical terms, the latter criterion usually wins out—MDS solutions with more than two, or at most three, dimensions are quite rare.

Once the MDS solution is obtained, it is important to emphasize that the analysis only determines the relative distances between the points in the scaling solution. The locations of the coordinate axes, and their orientation relative to the scaled points, are completely arbitrary. Regardless of the software used to perform the analysis, the final MDS solution is usually rotated to a varimax orientation. That is, the location of the point "cloud" relative to the coordinate axes is set in a way that maximizes the variance of the point coordinates along each of the rectangular axes. The numeric values of the point coordinates themselves are usually standardized in some way. For example, they may be set so the mean coordinate on each axis is zero, and the variance of the point coordinates across all of the axes is equal to one (or to some other arbitrary value, such as the sum of squares for the entries in the dissimilarities matrix). Regardless of the rotation or numeric values, the coordinate axes in the MDS solution are simply a device to "hang" the points within the m-dimensional space. They have no intrinsic substantive importance or interpretation!

The simplicity of the underlying geometric model and the graphical nature of the main output constitute big advantages for interpreting MDS solutions. Typically, the analyst would look for two kinds of features: (1) interesting "directions" within the space, which may correspond to the substantive dimensions underlying the processes that produced the dissimilarities in the first place; and (2) distinct groups or clusters of points, which may reveal how the data source differentiates the objects being scaled. Simply "eyeballing" the MDS results is often sufficient for identifying these kinds of features. In fact, that is exactly what we did with the configuration of 2004 political figures in the preceding example. Similarly, the first metric MDS example (reproducing the map from the intercity distances) implicitly emphasized directions (i.e. north–south and east–west) while interpreting the solution. And, the second substantive example (the metric and nonmetric analyses of the profile dissimilarities between the cities) emphasized groupings of the city-points. So, visual inspection is often enough in itself. But, the subjectivity inherent in simple visual interpretation of MDS results makes it desirable to use more systematic (and hopefully, "objective") interpretation strategies.

Embedding external information

One interpretation strategy uses regression analysis to *embed* additional information into the MDS point configuration. The researcher often has prior hypotheses about the substantive dimensions that differentiate the stimulus objects in an MDS analysis. If so, then it is useful to obtain external measures of these dimensions; that is, variables that are obtained separately from the dissimilarities used to create the MDS solution. Each object in the MDS analysis is assumed to have a score on this external dimension. Then, it is easy to incorporate the external information into the scaling solution by regressing

Table 14.7 Nonmetric MDS point coordinates and ideology scores for political figures from the 2004 U.S. presidential election.

	First MDS Coordinate	Second MDS Coordinate	Ideology Score
George W. Bush	0.615	−0.022	36.359
John Kerry	−0.830	−0.079	−21.135
Ralph Nader	−0.234	1.030	−0.010
Dick Cheney	0.778	−0.157	28.010
John Edwards	−0.785	−0.087	−20.614
Laura Bush	0.356	−0.132	20.288
Hillary Clinton	−0.600	−0.311	−26.450
Bill Clinton	−0.484	−0.075	−24.178
Colin Powell	0.190	−0.086	12.810
John Ashcroft	0.809	−0.005	24.423
John McCain	0.198	0.200	4.499
Dem. Pty.	−0.673	−0.135	−16.563
Rep. Pty.	0.661	−0.140	28.985

Note. MDS coordinates are obtained from nonmetric multidimensional scaling analysis of data in Table 14.6. Ideology variable consists of mean scores assigned by experts on a scale from −100 for maximally liberal to +100 for maximally conservative.

the external measure on the point coordinates. If the point coordinates are highly correlated with the external variable, then the estimated regression coefficients can be used to draw a new axis within the space, corresponding to the external measure. This strategy is useful for determining whether the MDS results conform to prior substantive expectations.

We can illustrate the use of an external measure with the MDS of 2004 political figures. Table 14.7 shows the point coordinates for the MDS configuration from Figure 14.9, along with a third variable, a measure of each figure's liberal–conservative ideology. The latter was obtained by having a panel of experts locate each of the 13 figures along a numeric continuum ranging from −100 for "maximally liberal" or left-leaning, to +100 for "maximally conservative" or right-leaning. The 13 political figures' scores on this ideology variable are regressed on their MDS point coordinates, and the ordinary least squares estimates are as follows:

$$\text{Ideol}_i = -3.574 + 16.963 \text{Dim}_{1i} + -2.130 \text{Dim}_{2i} + e_i. \tag{14.11}$$

The R^2 for Equation 14.11 is .918; this excellent fit confirms that the spatial configuration of points is highly consistent with the ideological positions of the political figures. Hence, that may well be one of the substantive criteria that the survey respondents used when they evaluated the dissimilarities among the figures to produce the input data for the MDS.

In order to locate an ideology axis within the MDS configuration itself, we take the ratio of the regression coefficients for the second MDS axis relative to the first MDS axis. Thus, −2.130/16.963 = −0.126. Now just insert a line with slope −0.126 into the MDS configuration. The perpendicular projections from the scaled points onto this line correspond to the ideology scores for the respective figures. The exact location of the

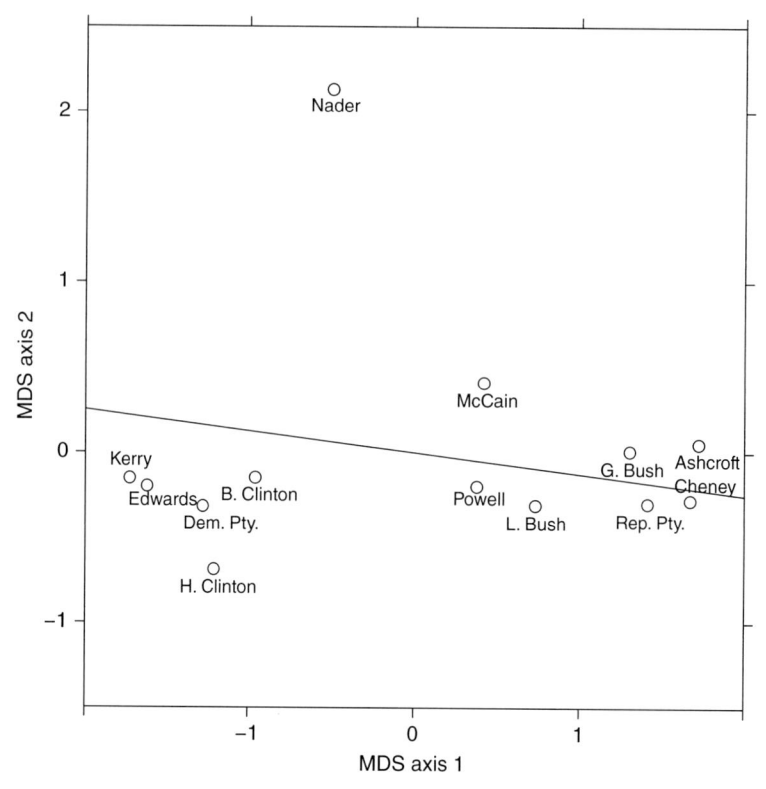

Figure 14.10 Nonmetric MDS solution for 2004 political figures, with ideological dimension embedded within the point configuration.

line does not really matter (since the projections are invariant, as long as the line's slope remains at −0.126), but it is convenient to have this line pass through the origin.[8]

Figure 14.10 shows the nonmetric MDS solution with the ideology axis drawn in. The nearly horizontal orientation of this objectively determined line confirms the more informal interpretation based on simple visual inspection. That is, the left–right positioning of the points corresponds to ideological distinctions among the political figures, with more liberal candidates toward the left side of the space, and more conservative figures toward the right. But, the MDS solution really goes beyond simple intuition because the metric distances between the points along the fitted dimension provide

---

[8] This strategy for embedding external information generalizes very easily for MDS solutions in higher dimensionalities. For example, in a three-dimensional solution the external variable is regressed on the point coordinates for the three coordinate axes in order to define a two-dimensional plane within the threedimensional space. In still higher dimensionalities, the regression would produce a hypersurface of one fewer dimensions than the dimensionality of the MDS space. From a practical perspective, higher-dimensioned MDS solutions are rarely a problem for fitted external criteria. In most cases, the user looks "into" the dimensional space by looking at two-dimensional subsets of the space (e.g., in a three-dimensional solution, we would inspect plots of dimension 1 versus dimension 2, dimension 1 versus dimension 3, and dimension 2 versus dimension 3). And, in each such subspace, we could simply locate a line for the external variable by taking the ratio of the regression coefficients associated with those two coordinate axes.

an interval-level estimate of the respective figures' liberal–conservative ideology. And, since the MDS solution was, itself, produced without any reference to ideology at all, we can take these results as empirical evidence supporting the hypothesis that the American public has ideology in mind when it looked at the "political field" in the 2004 presidential election.

Cluster analysis

Cluster analysis provides an objective strategy for identifying groups of stimulus points within the MDS solution. The analyst can then determine whether the clusters correspond to substantively interesting groups of stimulus objects. There are *many* varieties of cluster analysis. They all work by joining closer objects together into groups or *clusters*. Here, the "objects" are the points in the MDS solution, and "closeness" is based upon the interpoint distances in the scaled space.

Hierarchical clustering methods are probably the most common variant of this general methodology. The analysis begins by regarding each object point as a separate "cluster." In the first step, the routine joins together the two closest clusters to form a new cluster; from that step on, the constituent objects are no longer regarded as separate. The location of this new cluster is some summary of the locations of the original two stimulus points (e.g., perhaps the mean of their coordinates along each axis of the space). The routine proceeds through k such steps, on each one joining together the two most similar (i.e., closest) clusters to form a new cluster. It continues until all k objects are together in a single cluster. A tree diagram called a *dendrogram* traces out the process of joining clusters, and is usually considered the main output from a cluster analysis.

Figure 14.11 shows the dendrogram from a cluster analysis of the MDS configuration for the 2004 political figures. The diagram starts at the bottom of the display, where the figures form 13 distinct clusters. Then, it is easy to see the two partisan groupings develop as we move upward through the diagram. And, it is interesting to observe the intra-party distinctions—for example, Laura Bush, Colin Powell, and John McCain are relatively distinct from the other Republican figures, forming a separate cluster of their own within the overall Republican group. Similarly, Bill and Hillary Clinton are separate from the 2004 Democratic candidates (Kerry and Edwards) and the Democratic party itself. Such subgroups actually make quite a bit of sense from a substantive perspective. Cluster analysis helps accentuate these kinds of distinctions and, in so doing, helps the analyst understand the variability within the scaled point locations.

A caveat regarding MDS interpretation

It is important to be aware that most MDS solutions are amenable to several different substantive interpretations. So, for example, does the horizontal direction in Figures 14.10 and 14.11 correspond to partisanship or ideology? In fact, the positions of the points are fairly consistent with either of these two interpretations. Objective strategies like those discussed in the previous two sections can be used to show that the scaling results are consistent with some particular interpretation of the space. But, objective methods can never be used to find the single "true" meaning of the MDS-produced point configuration. While this uncertainty bothers some researchers, it is really no different from the general scientific approach of theory construction and revision through empirical hypothesis-testing.

Cluster dendrogram

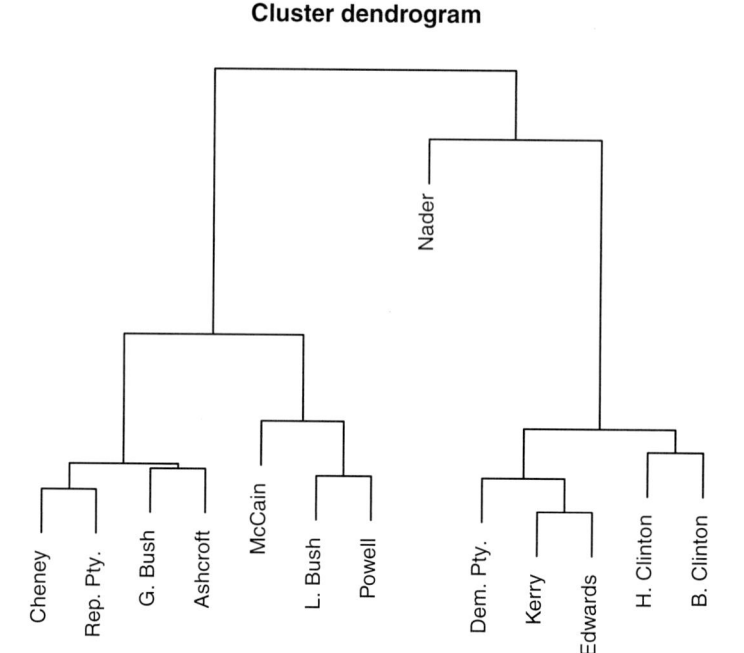

Figure 14.11 Dendrogram from cluster analysis of point configuration from nonmetric MDS of 2004 political figures.

A Variety of Multidimensional Scaling Models

Up to this point, the discussion has focused on classical multidimensional scaling, or CMDS, in which one square matrix of proximities data is used to produce a single geometric map of points representing the objects. This is both the simplest MDS model and the most common type of MDS used in actual research settings. But, there are a variety of additional MDS variants and models that adapt the general methodology to specific data analysis contexts.

First, there are several models that generalize MDS to situations where there is more than one square matrix of proximities among the k objects. For example, the researcher may have perceived dissimilarities among a set of stimuli for several (say, n) different experimental subjects. Or, there may be several matrices of profile dissimilarities for a common set of objects, collected at n different time points. In any case, there are n distinct square, symmetric, matrices of dissimilarities among the same set of k objects. So, the question is how can the information from the n different data sources be combined in an MDS analysis?

The answer to the preceding question depends upon how the researcher wants to treat the multiple data sources. If the differences between the data sources are uninteresting, so that the n matrices are regarded as simple repeated measurements of the same dissimilarity structure, then replicated MDS (or RMDS) may be appropriate. In the RMDS model, the differences across the n dissimilarity matrices are "smoothed out" to still produce a single configuration of k points in m-dimensional space. In technical terms, the function relating each of the n sets of input dissimilarities to the single set of output distances between the k scaled points is allowed to vary across the n data sources. If the analysis is a metric RMDS, then each data source's dissimilarities are related to the distances by a linear function; but, the slope and intercept of the linear relationship between dissimilarities and distances differs across the n data sources. Similarly, a nonmetric RMDS would have a different monotonic function connecting each of the n data sources' dissimilarities to the final set of interpoint distances. Note that the goodness of fit for the scaling solution can vary across the data sources depending upon how well the common MDS point configuration represents the dissimilarities data associated with each source. Typically, the individual fit measures for the respective data sources are averaged to produce a global fit measure for the entire scaling solution. Note that RMDS can be useful for handling a problem known as *differential item functioning*, where a common measurement instrument is used in different ways by different individuals (or other data sources). But it is usually still the case that the differences across the matrices are treated as errors that are not interesting from a substantive perspective.

If the differences across the n matrices *are* substantively important, then the weighted multidimensional scaling (or WMDS) model may be appropriate. This model still generates a single m-dimensional point configuration for the k objects. But, each data source is associated with its own set of m weights (one for each dimension). A larger weight value for a given dimension "stretches out" the corresponding coordinate axis relative to the other axes in the scaling solution. And, a smaller weight "shrinks in" an axis, relative to the others. Thus, each data sources is associated with a "distorted" version of the common point configuration, obtained by stretching and shrinking the m coordinate axes according to its own set of weights. Note that WMDS differs from CMDS in that the axes of the space should be interpretable in substantive terms—they cannot be rotated without degrading the model fit.

To give some sense about substantive examples of RMDS and WMDS, we will return to the context of the American electorate's perceived dissimilarities between political candidates and other figures. But now, let us assume that we have stratified a random sample of the electorate into subgroups based upon their levels of political knowledge (presumably measured through answers to factual questions on the survey used to obtain the information about the dissimilarities). WMDS analyses of such data from the 1980s and 1990s typically revealed systematic differences in the salience or importance of the ideological dimension; that is, higher levels of political knowledge corresponded to larger weights on the dimension that separates liberal from conservative figures, and vice versa (e.g., Jacoby, 1986). Interestingly, however, similar analyses of data from 2000 and 2004 produce minuscule differences in the weights; more and less knowledgeable citizens seem to show relatively equal reliance on the liberal–conservative continuum in their judgments about candidates and political figures. In the latter case, a single point configuration generated by RMDS is sufficient to represent the perceived dissimilarities of all the knowledge strata in the electorate.

The WMDS model actually has some variants of its own. For example, *general Euclidean model MDS* (sometimes called GEMSCAL) allows for differential rotations, as well as stretching and shrinking of coordinates, across the data sources. Using this approach allows for even greater idiosyncrasies across the data sources than the simpler WMDS, which only allows for differential importance of a common set of dimensions. For example, assume we have dissimilarities in the voting records for members of a legislative body (e.g., the percentage of times each pair of members votes differently from each other on bills), across several legislative sessions. Partisan voting coalitions are usually stable over long periods of time, but punctuated by brief intense periods of realignment when old voting blocs break down and new coalitions form. If this is the case, applying the GEMSCAL model to the legislative dissimilarities data across sessions could show how the underlying dimensions of legislative voting exhibit stability and change over time (e.g., Easterling, 1987).

Finally, *asymmetric MDS* (sometimes called ASYMSCAL) uses a single matrix of proximities data but it allows for asymmetric data values; that is, it anticipates the situation where $\delta_{ij} \neq \delta_{ji}$. For example, such a model might be useful for analyzing sociometric data on interpersonal interactions (Collins, 1987). Basically, the ASYMSCAL approach generates a single point configuration for the k objects, but also estimates two $k \times m$ weight matrices—one for the rows of the matrix and one for the columns. Thus, there is quite a bit of flexibility in the kind of geometric representation that can be constructed using MDS. But, it should be noted that actual empirical applications of the GEMSCAL and ASYMSCAL models are quite rare.

A second generalization of MDS applies to nonsquare data matrices. The unfolding model is useful for preferential choice data, in which n *subjects* each give their preference orders for k objects. An unfolding analysis seeks to recover an m-dimensional space containing n points for the respective subjects and k points for the objects. The relative point locations are determined by the preferential choices expressed by the subjects for the objects. Speaking very informally, if a subject indicates greater preference for an object, then the distance between the subject's point and the object point is smaller, and vice versa. The dimensions of the space recovered by the unfolding analysis should provide insights about the judgmental criteria that the subjects used to make their choices among the objects. And, as in CMDS, the relative positions of the points within the two sets contained in the space depict the variability across the subjects and objects, respectively. Unfolding models are particularly useful for market research, in which the objective is to explicate consumers' preferential choices across a set of products. A variant of the unfolding model is sometimes called MDPREF, for *multidimensional analysis of preferences*. Here, the k objects are still shown as points within a space, located so that objects that receive similar patterns of preferences from the subjects are represented by points that are close together within the space, and vice versa. But, unlike the unfolding model (which represents subjects as points), the MDPREF model shows each subject as a unit-length vector emanating from the origin of the space. Each subject's vector is positioned so that the ordering of the perpendicular projections from the object points onto that vector correspond to the subject's preference ordering for the objects. In this manner, variability across the subjects is represented by the angular separation between the vectors. The MDPREF model has been used recently to study individual choices across a set of core values (Jacoby, 2014).

Finally, *correspondence analysis* (abbreviated CA) is usually regarded as a different methodology than MDS. But, CA can be viewed as a strategy for scaling the rows and columns of a crosstabulation table. Basically, each row and column from a table is shown as a point in a low-dimensional space. Rows that have similar distributions of observations across their cells (i.e., across the columns of the table) have points that are located closer together in the space, and similarly for the columns. The relationships between the rows and columns are depicted in a slightly more complicated manner: For a given row, the point for that row can be regarded as a vector emanating from the origin. And, the perpendicular projections from the column points onto that row's vector will correspond to the distribution of observations across the cells in that row (i.e., more heavily populated cells for that row project onto the vector at a point farther away from the origin). In this manner, CA can be used to produce a geometric representation of the numeric information from a crosstabulation, which may prove very useful for interpreting large or complex tables.

Software for Multidimensional Scaling

Until fairly recently, multidimensional scaling required standalone, special-purpose software. But, a tangible indicator of MDS's increasing popularity is the fact that all of the major statistical software packages now contain routines to estimate these models. For example, SPSS has two MDS routines, ALSCAL and PROXSCAL. Both of these procedures are very flexible and capable of performing many different varieties of MDS (e.g., metric and nonmetric CMDS, RMDS, WMDS). They can also calculate profile dissimilarities from multivariate data prior to also performing the scaling analysis. The SAS system has long included PROC MDS, a very flexible procedure that can perform many varieties of MDS. PROC MDS is generally modeled after ALSCAL, although its estimation algorithm is a bit different. Although less well known than the preceding two packages, SYSTAT is a venerable and very powerful statistical software package. SYSTAT contains a very flexible and easy-to-use MDS routine that can perform most varieties of MDS. SYSTAT also contains an excellent graphics system which integrates well with the output from its MDS routine.

For many years, STATA did not include multidimensional scaling among its formidable array of statistical procedures. That changed with Version 9.0, when STATA introduced the mds and mdsmat procedures. The two procedures carry out identical analyses but make different assumptions about the nature of the input data. mds assumes multivariate input data that must be converted to profile dissimilarities prior to the scaling analysis; mds carries out this conversion. mdsmat assumes that the data are already contained in a dissimilarities matrix. The mds and mdsmat procedures can perform metric and nonmetric CMDS. Users will find that both of these procedures are well integrated with STATA's overall system of model estimation and postestimation commands, and its extensive graphics system.

The R statistical computing environment contains several options for MDS. The Base R installation only includes the function cmdscale, which performs metric MDS. The MASS package (distributed with all R installations) includes the functions isoMDS, sammon, and Shepard, all of which perform nonmetric CMDS. But, most researchers using R will probably prefer to use the smacof package, which provides functions for estimating metric and nonmetric CMDS, WMDS, RMDS, and GEMSCAL models, using a unified analytic approach. The smacof package includes generic plotting methods for the MDS models it estimates, but users will often find it more useful to take the smacof model estimates and use them as input to R's unparalleled graphics functions and packages to produce geometric representations of MDS models.

Finally, ggvis is an MDS module within the ggobi software package. ggobi is a program for visualizing high-dimensional data. It is freely available on the web, at http://ggobi.org. The ggobi system (including ggvis) can be integrated with the R statistical computing environment, via the rggobi package. ggvis itself can estimate metric and nonmetric CMDS models. It is an interactive MDS program in that the user can directly manipulate the scaled configuration of points. This can be very useful for evaluating the robustness of an MDS solution.

Conclusion

In conclusion, multidimensional scaling is a relatively new methodological approach, having been in existence for less than 70 years. As such, it is fairly straightforward to specify a set of useful references for this methodological strategy. Recent general texts on MDS include Cox and Cox (2001), Borg and Groenen (2005), and Armstrong, Bakker, Carroll, Hare, Poole, and Rosenthal (2014). Seminal contributions to the field include Torgerson (1958) for metric MDS, Shepard (1962a, 1962b) and Kruskal (1964a, 1964b) for nonmetric MDS, and Carroll and Chang (1970) for weighted MDS. Young and Hamer (1987) give a theoretical overview of MDS that integrates a wide variety of specific models. Work aimed at developing the statistical properties of MDS includes Ramsay (1977), Takane and Carroll (1981), Brady (1985), Oh and Raftery (2001), Bakker and Poole (2013), and Jacoby and Armstrong (2014). Coombs (1964) provides the original development of unfolding, while Carroll (1972) provides further discussion of its relationship to MDS. Greenacre (1984) is a standard reference for correspondence analysis.

MDS is not necessarily viewed as a "mainstream" analytic strategy for most social and behavioral scientists. It is certainly not encountered as frequently as several other scaling or data reduction techniques, such as principal components or factor analysis. Nevertheless, there are signs that the use of MDS is becoming more widespread. For one thing, MDS applications are appearing across a widening variety of academic disciplines. The methodology was originally developed by psychologists who were interested in constructing empirical representations of human cognitive structures. That application has receded somewhat, but MDS has proven invaluable in a variety of other contexts. For example, anthropologists have used it to compare characteristics across cultures (Herrmann & Raybeck, 1981), and archaeologists have employed MDS for seriation of artifacts (Drennan, 1976) and also to develop classification schemes for objects recovered from site excavations (Hodson, Sneath, & Doran, 1966). Market researchers have long employed MDS to assess consumers' perceptions of products (Carroll & Green, 1997). And, political scientists have found the methodology useful to operationalize the formal spatial model of voting (Enelow & Hinich, 1984) and to represent legislative roll-call votes (Hoadley, 1980; Poole, 2005). More recently, MDS has been used in conjunction with network analysis as a tool for laying out graph models of interacting units (Di Battista, Eades, Tamassia, & Tollis, 1998). And, statisticians have found MDS to be a useful tool for overcoming the "curse of dimensionality" that is encountered when one attempts to visualize hypervariate data (Buja & Swayne, 2002). Moving on into the future, researchers should routinely consider MDS whenever they find it useful to produce geometric representations of dissimilarities data.

References

Armstrong II, D. A., Bakker, R., Carroll, R., Hare, C., Poole, K. T., and Rosenthal, H. (2014). *Analyzing spatial models of choice and judgment with R*. Boca Raton, FL: CRC Press.

Bakker, R. and Poole, K. T. (2013). Bayesian metric multidimensional scaling. *Political Analysis*, 21, 125–140.

Borg, I. and Groenen, P. (2005). *Modern multidimensional scaling: Theory and applications* (2nd ed.). Berlin, Germany: Springer-Verlag.

Brady, H. E. (1985). Statistical consistency and hypothesis testing for nonmetric multidimensional scaling. *Psychometrika, 50,* 509–537.

Buja, A. and Swayne, D. F. (2002). Visualization methodology for multidimensional scaling. *Journal of Classification, 19,* 7–43.

Carroll, J. D. (1972). Individual differences and multidimensional scaling. In R. N. Shepard, A. Kimball Romney, & S. B. Nerlove (Eds.), *Multidimensional scaling: Theory and applications in the behavioral sciences* (Vol. *I*, pp. 105–155). New York, NY: Seminar Press.

Carroll, J. D. and Chang, J. J. (1970). An analysis of individual differences in multidimensional scaling via an *N*-way generalization of "Eckart–Young" decomposition. *Psychometrika, 35,* 283–319.

Carroll, J. D. and Green, P. E. (1997). Psychometric methods in marketing research: Part II, multidimensional scaling. *Journal of Marketing Research, 34,* 193–204.

Collins, L. M. (1987). Sociometry: Deriving sociograms via asymmetric multidimensional scaling. In F. W. Young & R. M. Hamer (Eds.), *Multidimensional scaling: History, theory, and applications.* Mahwah, NJ: Lawrence Erlbaum.

Coombs, C. H. (1964). *A theory of data.* Chichester, UK: John Wiley & Sons (Reprinted 1976, Mathesis Press).

Cox, T. F. and Cox, M. A. A. (2001). *Multidimensional scaling* (2nd ed.). London, UK: Chapman and Hall.

Di Battista, G., Eades, P., Tamassia, R., and Tollis, I. G. (1998) *Graph drawing: Algorithms for the visualization of graphs.* Indianapolis, IN: Prentice-Hall.

Drennan, R. D. (1976). A refinement of chronological seriation using nonmetric multidimensional scaling. *American Antiquity, 41,* 290–302.

Easterling, D. V. (1987). Political science: Using the generalized Euclidean model to study ideological shifts in the U.S. Senate. In F. W. Young & R. M. Hamer (Eds.), *Multidimensional scaling: History, theory, and applications.* Mahwah, NJ: Lawrence Erlbaum.

Enelow, J. M. and Hinich, M. (1984). *The spatial theory of voting.* Cambridge, UK: Cambridge University Press.

Greenacre, M. J. (1984). *Theory and applications of correspondence analysis.* London, UK: Academic Press.

Herrmann, D. J. and Raybeck, D. (1981). Similarities and differences in meaning in six cultures. *Journal of Cross-Cultural Psychology, 12,* 194–206.

Hoadley, J. F. (1980). The emergence of political parties in Congress, 1789–1803. *American Political Science Review, 74,* 757–779.

Hodson, F. R., Sneath, P. H. A, and Doran, J. E. (1966). Some experiments in the numerical analysis of archaeological data. *Biometrika, 53,* 311–324.

Jacoby, W. G. (1986). Levels of conceptualization and reliance on the liberal–conservative continuum. *Journal of Politics, 48,* 423–432.

Jacoby, W. G. (2009). Ideology and vote choice in the 2004 election. *Electoral Studies, 28*: 584–594.

Jacoby, W. G. (2014). Is there a culture war? Conflicting value structures in American public opinion. *American Political Science Review, 108*(4), 754–771. doi: 10.1017/S0003055414000380

Jacoby, W. G. and Armstrong II, D. A. (2014). Bootstrap confidence regions for multidimensional scaling solutions. *American Journal of Political Science, 58*(1), 264–278.

Kruskal, J. B. (1964a). Multidimensional scaling by optimizing goodness of fit to a non-metric hypothesis. *Psychometrika, 29,* 1–27.

Kruskal, J. B. (1964b). Non-metric multidimensional scaling: A numerical method. *Psychometrika, 29,* 115–129.

Oh, M.-S. and Raftery, A. E. (2001). Bayesian multidimensional scaling and choice of dimension. *Journal of the American Statistical Association, 96,* 1031–1044.

Poole, K. T. (2005). *Spatial models of parliamentary voting.* Cambridge, UK: Cambridge University Press.

Rabinowitz, G. B. (1976). A procedure for ordering object pairs consistent with the multidimensional unfolding model. *Psychometrika, 41,* 349–373.

Ramsay, J. O. (1977). Maximum likelihood estimation in multidimensional scaling. *Psychometrika, 42,* 241–266.

Savageau, D. and D'Agostino, R. (2000). *Places rated almanac.* Foster City, CA: IDG Books.

Shepard, R. N. (1962a). The analysis of proximities: Multidimensional scaling with an unknown distance function, I. *Psychometrika, 27,* 125–140.

Shepard, R. N. (1962b). The analysis of proximities: Multidimensional scaling with an unknown distance function, II. *Psychometrika, 27*: 219–246.

Sijtsma, K. and Molenaar, I. W. (2002). *Introduction to nonparametric item response theory.* Thousand Oaks, CA: Sage.

Takane, Y. and Carroll, J. D. (1981). Nonmetric maximum likelihood multidimensional scaling from directional rankings of similarities. *Psychometrika, 46,* 389–405.

Torgerson, W. S. (1958). *Theory and methods of scaling.* Chichester, UK: John Wiley & Sons.

van Schuur, W. H. (2011). *Ordinal item response theory: Mokken scale analysis.* Thousand Oaks, CA: Sage.

Young, F. W. and Hamer, R. M. (1987). *Multidimensional scaling: History, theory, and applications.* Mahwah, NJ: Lawrence Erlbaum.

15

Unidimensional Item Response Theory

Rob R. Meijer and Jorge N. Tendeiro

Unidimensional item response theory (IRT) models have become important tools to evaluate the quality of psychological and educational measurement instruments. Strictly unidimensional data are unlikely to be observed in practice because data often originate from complex multifaceted psychological traits. Still, unidimensional models may provide a reasonable description of these data in many cases. In large-scale educational testing IRT is now the standard. Also for the construction and evaluation of psychological measurement instruments, IRT is starting to replace classical test theory (CTT). To illustrate this: When we recently obtained reviews of a paper from *Psychological Assessment*, one of the leading journals with respect to measurement and empirical evaluation of clinical instruments, it was stated that we did not have to explain in detail our IRT models because those models "are well-known to the audience of the journal." We would not have received this message, say, 10 years ago.

In this chapter, we distinguish parametric and nonparametric IRT models, and IRT models for dichotomous and polytomous item scores. We describe model assumptions, and we discuss model-data fit procedures and model choice.

Standard unidimensional IRT models do not take test content into account, that is, IRT models are formulated without specific reference to maximum performance testing (intelligence, achievement) and typical performance testing (personality, mood, vocational interest). Yet, when these models are applied to different types of data, there are interesting differences that will be discussed in this chapter and that may guide the use of these models in different areas of psychology.

Item Response Theory

Although CTT contributed to test and questionnaire construction for many years, in the papers by Lord (1952, 1953) and Birnbaum (1968) the foundation of modern test theory, or what was later called item response theory, was formulated. In these models the responses to items are explicitly modeled as the result of the interaction between characteristics of the items (e.g., difficulty, discrimination) and a person's latent variable (often denoted by the Greek letter θ). This variable may be intelligence, a personality trait, mood disorder, or any other variable of interest. Another important contribution in the development of, in particular, nonparametric IRT (NIRT) was made by Guttman (1944, 1950). His deterministic approach was based on the idea that, in the case of maximum performance testing, when a person p knows more than person q, then p responds positively to the same items as q plus one or more additional items. Furthermore, the items answered positively by a larger proportion of respondents are always the easiest or most popular items in the test. Because empirical data almost never satisfied these very strong model assumptions, stochastic nonparametric IRT versions of his deterministic model were formulated that were more suited to describe both typical and maximum performance data.

Researchers started with formulating models for dichotomous data, which were later extended for polytomous data. Because conceptually it is also easier to first explain the principles of dichotomous IRT models we first describe these types of models.

Dichotomous parametric item response models

All unidimensional IRT models (dichotomous and polytomous) are based on a number of assumptions with respect to the data. The data in this chapter are the answers of k persons to n items. In the case of dichotomous items these answers are almost always scored as 0 (incorrect, disagree) and 1 (correct, agree). In the case of polytomous items there are more than two categories. For example, in maximum performance testing these scores may be 0 (incorrect), 1 (partly correct), or 2 (correct), or in typical performance testing the scores may be 0 (agree), 1 (do not agree nor disagree), or 2 (disagree).

Assumptions and basic ideas The assumption of unidimensionality (UD) states that between-persons' differences in item responses are mainly caused by differences in one variable. Although all tests and questionnaires require more than one variable (or trait) to explain response behavior, some of these variables do not cause important differences in response behavior of respondents of a given population. Because items may generate different response behavior in different populations, dimensionality also depends on the population of persons. Instead of total (sum) scores as in CTT, scores are expressed on a θ scale (representing the assumed unique dimension of interest). This scale has a mean of zero and a standard deviation of 1, and can be interpreted as a z-score scale. Thus, someone with $\theta = 1$ has a θ-score that is 1SD above the mean score in the population of interest.

Another important assumption in IRT modeling is local independence (LI), which states that the responses in a test are statistically independent conditional on θ. Finally, it is assumed that the probability of giving a positive or correct response to an item is *monotonically* nondecreasing in θ (M assumption). This conditional probability is also called the item response function (IRF) and is denoted $P_i(\theta)$, where i indexes the item. The UD, LI, and M assumptions form the basis of the most widely used nonparametric and parametric IRT models in practice. All NIRT and IRT models presented in this chapter are based on these assumptions.

Parametric dichotomous item response models are further constrained by imposing well-defined mathematical models on the IRF. These models typically differ with respect to the number of parameters used. In the one-parameter logistic model (1PLM) or the Rasch (1960) model, only an item location parameter (denoted b_i) is used to define an IRF, in the two-parameter Birnbaum model (2PLM) a discrimination parameter is added (denoted a_i), and in the three-parameter model (3PLM) an additional guessing parameter (denoted c_i) is used to describe the data. In Figure 15.1 we depict IRFs that comply with the 1, 2, and 3 PLM. Note that for the Rasch model the IRFs do not intersect because it is assumed that all IRFs have the same discrimination parameter (this parameter is not in the equation and thus it does not vary between items), whereas for the 2PLM different items may have different discrimination parameters and as a result the IRFs can cross; for the 3PLM the additional guessing parameter may result in IRFs that also have different lower asymptotes. Some authors also explore the use of a four-parameter logistic model with an additional parameter for the upper asymptote, but there are few published research examples of this model and we will not discuss it any further.

The IRF of the 3PLM for item i is given by

$$P_i(\theta) = P(X_i = 1|\theta) = c_i + (1-c_i)\frac{\exp(a_i(\theta - b_i))}{1 + \exp(a_i(\theta - b_i))},$$

where X_i is the random variable representing the score of item i. The 2PLM can be obtained from the 3PLM by setting the guessing parameter (c_i) equal to zero and the Rasch model can be obtained from the 2PLM by setting the discrimination parameter (a_i) to 1. As an example, consider the IRF of item 3 displayed in Figure 15.1(c). The probability that a person 1SD below the mean ($\theta = -1$) gives a positive answer to this item is equal to $.25 + (1-.25) \times \exp(.5(-1-1))/(1 + \exp(.5(-1-1))) = .45$, whereas for a person 1SD above the mean ($\theta = 1$) the probability is $.25 + (1-.25)/2 = .63$.

The item location parameter, b_i, is defined as the point at the θ scale where the probability of giving a positive answer to an item equals $(1 + c_i)/2$ (i.e., halfway between c_i and 1). When $c_i = 0$ (in the 1PLM and 2PLM) the item location is defined as the point at the θ scale where the probability of endorsing this item equals .5. Thus, when we would move the IRF to the right side of the scale, the IRF would pertain to a more difficult item in the case of maximum performance testing; when we would move the IRF to the left side of the scale it would pertain to an easier item. For this reason, parameter b_i is also known as the *difficulty* parameter. Item location parameters usually range from –2.5 through +2.5. Furthermore, in parametric IRT models the item difficulties and the θ values are placed on the same scale. This is not the case in CTT where a total score has a different metric than the item difficulty, which in CTT is the proportion-correct score. The advantage of a common scale for the item difficulty and θ is that they can be very easily interpreted in relation to each other.

The steepness of the IRF is expressed in the discrimination parameter a_i. This parameter is a function of the tangent to the IRF at the point $\theta = b_i$. For most questionnaires and tests a_i parameters fluctuate between $a_i = .5$ and $a_i = 2.5$. The M assumption prevents negative values for this parameter. Moreover, values close to zero are related to items that discriminate poorly between persons close together in the θ scale (i.e., the associated IRFs are "flat"). The magnitude of the discrimination parameters depends on the type of questionnaire or test. Our experience is that for typical performance questionnaires (especially for clinical scales) *a*s are in general somewhat higher than for maximum performance questionnaires. This has to do with the broadness of the construct. Many clinical scales consist of relatively homogeneous constructs, where questions are very similar, whereas maximum performance measures tap into broader constructs. When scales consist of items that are similar, all items have a strong relation

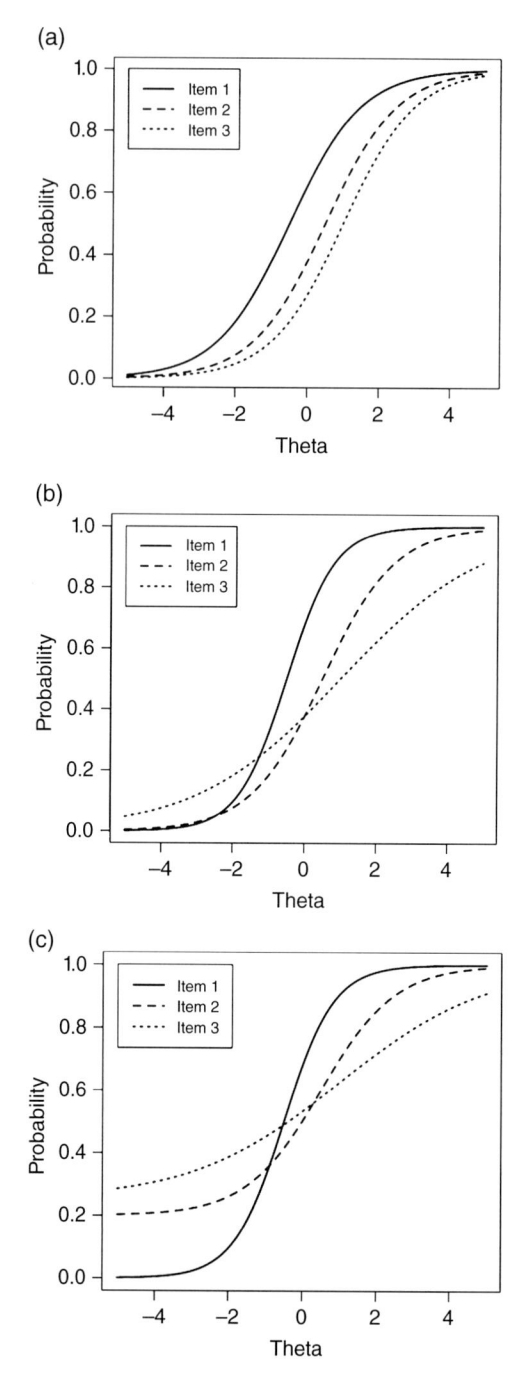

Figure 15.1 (a) Three IRFs from the 1PLM (Item 1: $b_1=-.5$; Item 2: $b_2=.5$; Item 3: $b_3=1.0$). (b) Three IRFs from the 2PLM (Item 1: $a_1=1.5$, $b_1=-.5$; Item 2: $a_2=1.0$, $b_2=.5$; Item 3: $a_3=.5$, $b_3=1.0$). (c) Three IRFs from the 3PLM (Item 1: $a_1=1.5$, $b_1=-.5$, $c_1=0$; Item 2: $a_2=1.0$, $b_2=.5$, $c_2=.2$; Item 3: $a_3=.5$, $b_3=1.0$, $c_3=.25$).

to the underlying trait and as a result the IRFs will be relatively steep. When the trait being measured is more heterogeneous in content IRFs will be, in general, less steep.

Although test constructors will, in general, strive for tests with items that have high discrimination parameters, there is a trade-off between tests measuring relatively narrow constructs with high discrimination parameters and tests measuring relatively broad constructs with lower discrimination parameters.

The guessing parameter of the 3PLM, c_i, specifies the lower asymptote of the IRF. For example, a value of $c_i = .20$ (Figure 15.1(c), item 2) implies that any person, regardless of his or her ability, has at least a 20% probability of answering the item correctly. This assumption is adequate for a multiple-choice item with five possible answer options, because a person may just try to *guess* the correct answer. The guessing parameter of item 3 in Figure 15.1(c) is .25, which is adequate for a multiple-choice item with four possible answer options. Of the three models presented, the Rasch model is most restrictive to the data because it has only one parameter, whereas the 3PLM is the least restrictive (more flexible).

Figure 15.2 further illustrates the use of IRFs. Two IRFs are shown from a Social Inhibition (SI) Scale with answer categories true/false (see Meijer & Tendeiro, 2012). We used the 2PLM to describe these data. Note that the probability of giving a positive answer is an increasing function of θ. First consider item SI23, "I find it difficult to meet strangers" ($a = 2.21$, $b = 0.22$). It is clear that someone with a trait value $\theta = 0$ has a probability of about .4 to endorse this item, whereas someone with, for example, $\theta = 1$ has a probability of about .8. The IRF of item SI23 is steep between $\theta = -1$ and $\theta = +1$, which means that this item discriminates well between persons that are relatively close on this region of the θ scale. Furthermore, persons with θ values smaller than $\theta = -1$ have a probability of endorsing this item of almost 0, whereas persons with θ at or above $+1.5$ have a probability of almost 1. Now consider item SI105, "I find it difficult to make new friends" ($a = 1.5$, $b = 1.65$). This item is less popular than item SI23: The difficulty parameter is larger, so the IRF is more to the right than the IRF of

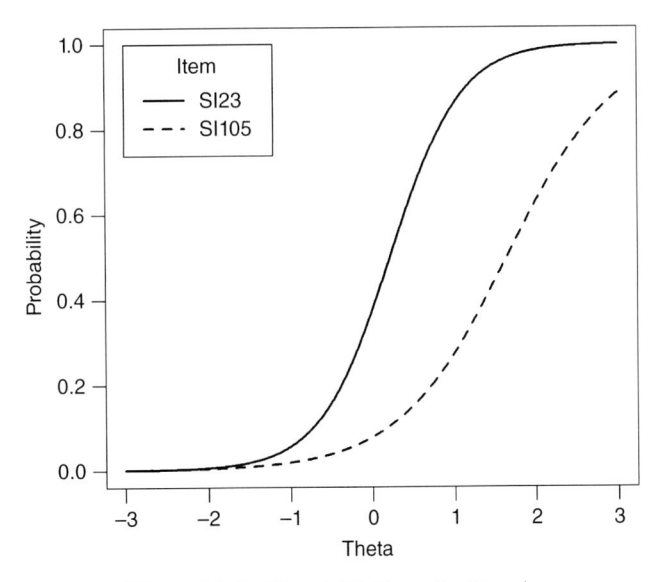

Figure 15.2 Two IRFs from the SI scale.

item SI23. Thus, a person should have a higher level of social inhibition to endorse item SI105 than to endorse item SI23. Moreover, item SI105 is less steep (smaller discrimination parameter).

Polytomous models

There are different types of polytomous IRT models and the theoretical foundations of the models are sometimes different (Embretson & Reise, 2000). However, the practical implications of the different models are often negligible. For example, Dumenci and Achenbach (2008) showed that differences between trait estimates obtained under the partial credit model and the graded response model were trivial. We will not discuss the different theoretical foundations of the models, see for example Embretson and Reise (2000) for more details, but instead emphasize their practical usefulness.

Polytomous item response models can be used to describe answers to items with more than two categories. In psychological assessment polytomous item scores are mostly used in combination with typical performance data like personality and mood questionnaires. Often five-point Likert scales are used where the score categories are ordered from "not indicative" to "indicative." An example is the question "I like to go to parties" from an Extraversion scale. Answer categories may be "Agree strongly" (scored 0), "Agree" (1), "Do not agree or disagree" (2), "Disagree" (3), and "Disagree strongly" (4). To model the response behavior for these types of items several models have been proposed.

In contrast to dichotomous IRT models, the unit of analysis is not the item but the answer categories. Each answer category has an associated response function (CRF). In polytomous IRT various models have been formulated to describe these CRFs. In van der Linden and Hambleton (1997), Embretson and Reise (2000), and Nering and Ostini (2010) a detailed overview is given of the nature and statistical foundations of the different polytomous IRT models. Next, we discuss the most often-used polytomous models for which easy-to-use software is available. We discuss the nominal response model, the partial credit model, the generalized partial credit model, and the graded response model.

Nominal response model The most general and most flexible polytomous model is the nominal response model (NRM) proposed by Bock (1972; see Thissen, Cai, & Bock, 2010 for a recent discussion). For example IRTPRO code, please see Appendix Code 1. Originally the NRM was proposed to model item responses to nominal data, such as the responses to multiple-choice items. Hence, and in contrast to other polytomous IRT models discussed next, in the NRM it is not assumed that the responses are ordered along the θ continuum. Assume that item i has $m+1$ response categories $k = 0, 1, \ldots, m$. The CRF $P_{ik}(\theta) = P(X_i = k|\theta)$ is the probability that a person with latent variable θ responds in category k on item i. Thus, an item has as many CRFs as response categories. In the NRM the probability of answering in category k depends on slope (a_{ik}) and intercept (c_{ik}) parameters, one pair per category response $k = 0, 1, \ldots, m$. The CRF for category k on item i is given by

$$P_{ik}(\theta) = \frac{\exp(a_{ik}\theta + c_{ik})}{\sum_{j=0}^{m} \exp(a_{ij}\theta + c_{ij})} \tag{15.1}$$

Parameter a_{ik} is related to the slope and parameter c_{ik} to the intercept of the k-th CRF. Because the model is not identified, Bock (1972) used the following constraint:

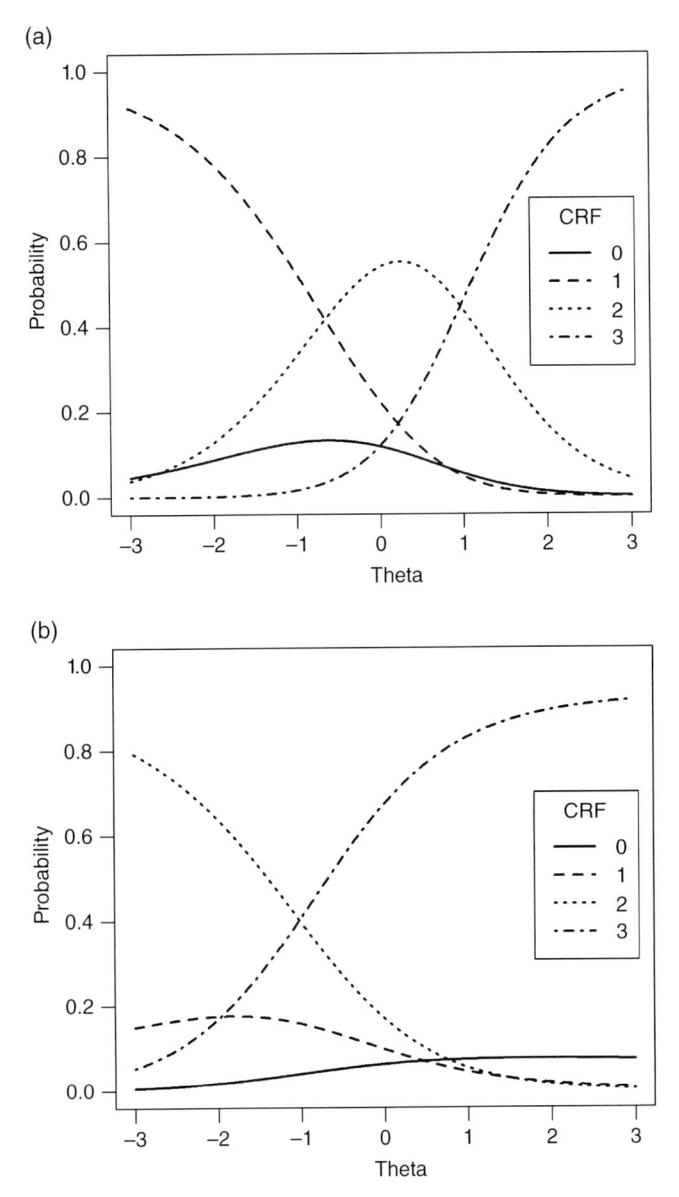

Figure 15.3 (a) CRFs for item 4 of the SPPC estimated using the NRM. (b) CRFs for item 5 of the SPPC estimated using the NRM.

$\Sigma a_{ik} = \Sigma c_{ik} = 0$. Alternatively, the parameters of the lowest CRF can be constrained to zero (e.g., the default in IRTPRO): $a_{i0} = c_{i0} = 0$.

In contrast to the graded response model and the generalized partial credit model (both discussed next), the NRM allows for different discrimination parameters within one item. This makes it a very interesting model to explore the quality of individual items. For example, Preston, Reise, Cai, and Hays (2011) argued that the NRM is very useful to check that presumed ordered responses indeed elicit ordered response behavior. Furthermore, the NRM can be used to check whether all item categories discriminate equally well between different θ values.

Table 15.1 Estimated item parameters of items 4 and 5 from the subscale Athletic Competence of Harter's SPPC.

Item (SPPC)	Parameter	CRF 0	CRF 1	CRF 2	CRF 3
Item 4	a_{ik}	0.00	−.78	.57	2.11
	c_{ik}	0.00	.64	1.52	.02
Item 5	a_{ik}	0.00	−.94	−1.31	.05
	c_{ik}	0.00	.44	1.00	2.38

Note. a_{ik} is the slope parameter and c_{ik} the intercept parameter; CRF is the category response function.

In Figure 15.3 we depicted the CRFs of the NRM for two items of the subscale Athletic Competence of Harter's Self Perception Profile for Children (SPPC, see Meijer et al. 2008 for a further description of this questionnaire and data). When a child fills out the SPPC, first he or she has to choose which of two statements applies to him or her and then indicates if the chosen statement is "sort of true for me" or "really true for me." Parameters were estimated using the IRTPRO software; estimates are shown in Table 15.1 In this example the actual ordinal nature of the answer categories of both items was disregarded by the NRM. Figure 15.3(a) shows an item that performs relatively well ("*Some children think they are better in sports than other children*"). It can be seen that category 1 is the most popular for low-θ children (for θ less than about −1.0). Note that θ here represents the amount of self-perceived Athletic Competence. Category 2 is preferred for children with θ between about −1.0 and +1.0, and for children with θ larger than about 1.0 category 3 is preferred. Category 0 was relatively unpopular across the entire θ scale. Now consider Figure 15.3(b). For this item ("*I am usually joining other children while playing in the schoolyard*") most children (with θ larger than about −1.0) chose category 3 independently of their position on the Athletic Competence scale. Category 2 was the most preferred category for children with ability below about −1.0. Furthermore, two out of the four category response functions are relatively flat. This item might be a badly functioning item: Half of its answer categories are seldom chosen. This item might need to be rephrased, or some answer options might need to be dropped.

Partial credit model, generalized partial credit model The partial credit model (PCM; Masters 1982) is suitable for items that involve a multistep procedure to find the item's correct answer. Partial credit is assigned to each step. Hence the item's score reflects the extent to which a person approached the correct answer. The PCM defining the CRF for category $k(k=0,\ldots,m)$ of item i involves parameters $b_{ij}(j=1,\ldots,m)$, which are often described as item-step difficulties. Item-step difficulties are the imaginary thresholds to take the step from one item score to the next. So, for a three-category item there are two item steps. b_{ij} is the point on the θ-axis where two consecutive CRFs intersect (more precisely, b_{ij} is the value of θ for which the probability of endorsing category j is the same as endorsing category $(j-1)$, $P_{ij}(\theta) = P_{i,j-1}(\theta)$) with $j = 1,\ldots,m$. The CRF for category k on item i is given by

$$P_{ik}(\theta) = \frac{\exp \Sigma_{j=0}^{k}(\theta - b_{ij})}{\Sigma_{h=0}^{m} \exp \Sigma_{j=0}^{h}(\theta - b_{ij})}, \text{ with } \Sigma_{j=0}^{0}(\theta - b_{ij}) \equiv 0 \qquad (15.2)$$

As an example, consider an item "I am good at sports" with three score categories, scored 0 (*not characteristic for me*), 1 (*a bit characteristic for me*), and 2 (*very characteristic for me*). In this case, we have two item-step difficulties, say $b_1 = -.5$ and $b_2 = 1.5$. What is the probability that a person that is very sport-minded and performs at a national level in soccer, say with $\theta = 2$, will choose the answer category 2? To obtain this probability we fill out the numerator in Equation 15.2 noting that in this case $k = 2$, and thus: $\exp(2.5 + .5) = \exp(3) = 20.09$. The denominator in Equation 15.2 equals $\exp(0) + \exp(2.5) + \exp(2.5 + .5) = 33.27$, and thus the required probability equals $20.09/33.27 = 0.60$. Thus, there is a probability of 60% that this good athlete will choose option 2. Figure 15.4 displays the three CRFs for this item. Observe how b_1 and b_2 correspond to the intersection points of consecutive CRFs, as previously explained. It can be seen that persons with θ below $-.5$ have a high probability of not passing the first step (i.e., not collecting any credit for the item), persons with θ between $-.5$ and 1.5 have high probability of passing the first step, and persons with θ above 1.5 have a high probability of passing the second step.

An important observation is that in the PCM there is no discrimination parameter specified, so that the probability of endorsing a category only depends on the item-step locations and the person parameter. Like for the dichotomous Rasch model this may be a strong assumption, too strong for many data. Therefore, in the *generalized* partial credit model (Muraki, 1992) a slope parameter is added to the model. The CRF for category k on item i under the generalized PCM is given by

$$P_{ik}(\theta) = \frac{\exp \sum_{j=0}^{k} a_i(\theta - b_{ij})}{\sum_{h=0}^{m} \exp \sum_{j=0}^{h} a_i(\theta - b_{ij})}, \text{ with } \sum_{j=0}^{0} a_i(\theta - b_{ij}) \equiv 0 \quad (15.3)$$

Important is that the item discrimination depends on a combination of the slope parameter and the category intersections. Large slope parameters indicate steep category response functions and low slope parameters indicate flat response functions. The rating scale model (RSM; Andrich, 1978a, 1978b) can be derived from the PCM, but in the RSM each item has its own location parameter and the item-step difficulties are the same across items.

Graded response model The graded response model (GRM; Samejima, 1969, see Appendix Code 2 for example IRTPRO code) is suitable when answer categories are ordered (e.g., in Likert scales). Each item i is defined by a slope parameter, a_i, and by several threshold parameters, $b_{ij} (j = 1, \ldots, m)$. To define the CRFs, we first define the item-step response function (ISRF) given by

$$P^*_{ik}(\theta) = P(X_i \geq k|\theta) = \frac{\exp[a_i(\theta - b_{ik})]}{1 + \exp[a_i(\theta - b_{ik})]} \quad (15.4)$$

that is, the probability of responding in category k or higher ($k = 1, \ldots, m$) computed using the 2PLM. Because the probability of responding in or above the lowest category equals one and because responding above the highest category equals 0, the CRF for category k is given by $P_{ik}(\theta) = P^*_{ik}(\theta) - P^*_{i(k+1)}(\theta)$, with $P^*_{i0}(\theta) = 1$ and $P^*_{i(m+1)}(\theta) = 0$. More specifically, for an item with three item score categories ($k = 0, 1, 2$), the item's CRFs are given by $P_{i0}(\theta) = 1.0 - P^*_{i1}(\theta)$, $P_{i1}(\theta) = P^*_{i1}(\theta) - P^*_{i2}(\theta)$, and $P_{i2}(\theta) = P^*_{i2}(\theta) - 0$. In Figure 15.5 we depicted the CRFs for the two items of the SPPC Athletic Competence subscale discussed previously, parameters were estimated using IRTPRO. For

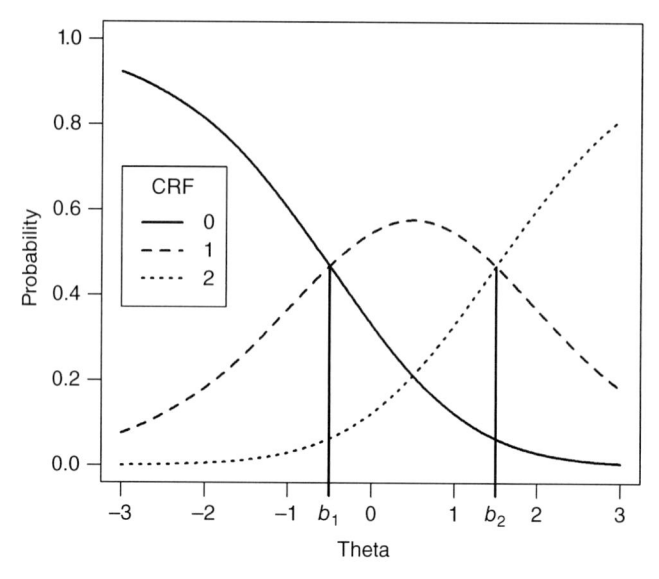

Figure 15.4 CRF of a polytomous item (three answer categories) using the PCM ($b_1 = -.5$, $b_2 = 1.5$).

good performing items, CRFs should be relatively steep (reflecting larger discrimination values) and separate (reflecting spread of the threshold parameters). The model shown in Figure 15.5a performs relatively well. It can be seen that category 0 is the most popular for low-ability children (for θ less than about −2.0). For children with θ between about −2.0 and −0.5 category 1 is preferred, for children with θ between about −0.5 and 1.0 category 2 is preferred, and for children with θ larger than about 1.0 category 3 is preferred. On the other hand, for the item shown in Figure 15.5b most children (with θ larger than about −1.0) chose category 3 independently of their position on this part of the θ scale. Furthermore, three out of the four category response functions are relatively flat. This item should be reviewed, for instance perhaps response categories 0, 1, 2 may be collapsed.

Item parameters estimation

Because parameter estimation is a relatively technical topic, we restrict ourselves here to some basic ideas and refer the reader to Baker and Kim (2004) and van der Linden and Hambleton (1997) for further details. There are essentially two types of methods to estimate the parameters of an IRT model: Maximum likelihood estimation (MLE) and Bayesian estimation. There are three types of MLE procedures: Joint maximum likelihood estimation (JML; Birnbaum, 1968), conditional maximum likelihood (CML; Rasch, 1960, Andersen, 1972), and marginal maximum likelihood (MML; Bock & Lieberman, 1970). Although JML allows estimating both item and person parameters jointly, an important drawback is that item parameter estimates are not necessarily consistent. CML solves this problem for the 1PLM by using a sufficiency property of this model that states that the likelihood function (a function with both item and person parameters as variables) of a person's response vector, conditional on his/her total score, does not depend on θ. This property allows estimating the 1PLM's item

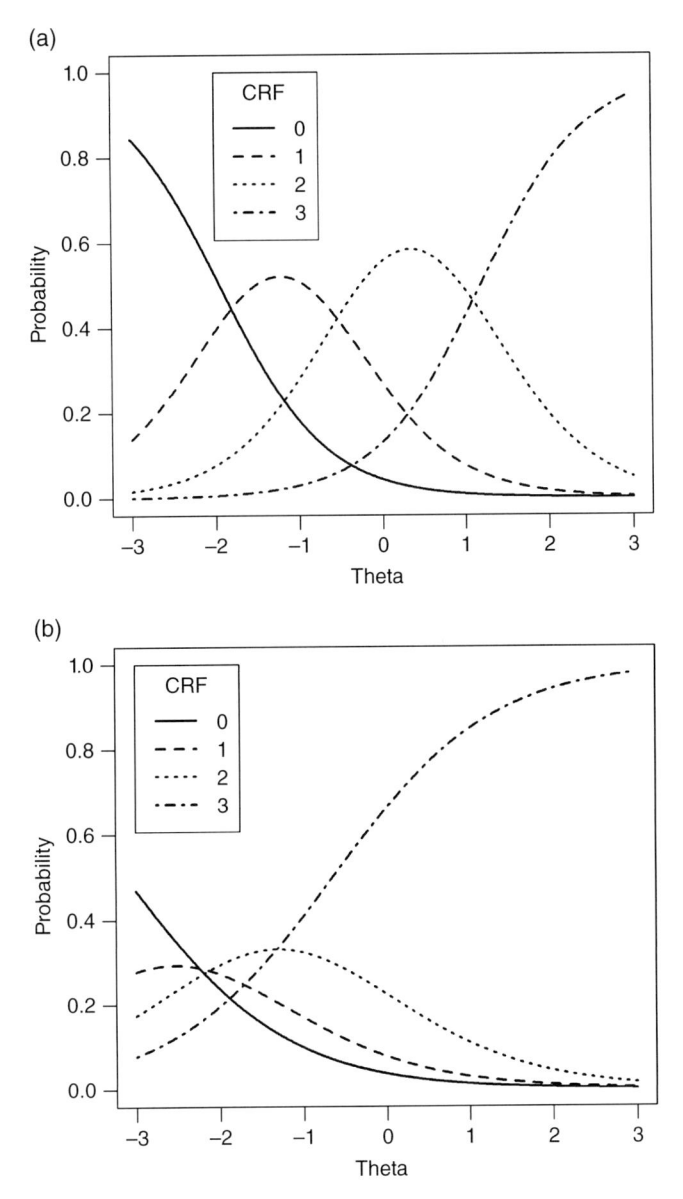

Figure 15.5 (a) CRFs for item 4 of the SPPC estimated using the GRM ($a_i = 1.59$, $b_1 = -1.94$, $b_2 = -.49$, $b_3 = 1.19$). (b) CRFs for item 5 of the SPPC estimated using the GRM ($a_i = 1.04$, $b_1 = -3.12$, $b_2 = -1.96$, $b_3 = -0.64$).

difficulty parameters independently from θ. Unfortunately, the CML only applies to the 1PLM, since there are no sufficient estimators for θ under the 2PLM or 3PLM. As an alternative, MML can be used. For MML it is assumed that the θ values have some known distribution (the normal distribution is typically used). This allows integrating the likelihood function over the ability distribution, thus estimation of item parameters can be freed from the person parameters. In conclusion, for the Rasch model both CML and MML can be chosen, whereas for the 2PLM and the 3PLM only the MML applies.

As an alternative to these procedures, one may use a Bayesian approach. Bayesian approaches have the advantage that they can be used in cases for which MLE methods lead to unreasonable estimated values or even fail to provide parameter estimates (e.g., for all 0's or all 1's response vectors). Bayesian methods based on marginal distributions (Mislevy, 1986) are currently the most widely used.

Bayesian methods are also used in Markov chain Monte Carlo (MCMC) methods that are applied in more advanced IRT models to solve complex dependency structures.

Test scoring and information

Once item parameters have been estimated using any of the methods explained in the previous section, it is possible to estimate the person parameters. A person parameter describes the person's position on the latent trait variable (θ). Both MLE and Bayesian estimation approaches are available. In MLE, the value of θ that maximizes the likelihood function for a particular response pattern is used as the estimate for θ. Advantages of MLE are that they tend to be consistent and efficient. The main disadvantages of MLE are that the peak of the likelihood function does not exist for perfect score patterns and patterns with all items incorrect. As a consequence, MLE can over- or under-estimate θ for nearly perfect response vectors. Warm (1989) proposed a weighted maximum likelihood estimation procedure (WML) that takes this problem into consideration.

As an alternative to MLE, two Bayesian approaches can be used. Both the expected a posteriori (EAP) and the modal or maximum a posteriori (MAP) methods rely on the person's response vector and on a prior distribution for θ. The likelihood (estimated from the response vector) is combined with the prior distribution for θ, which results in a posterior distribution for θ. The EAP estimate consists of the expected value of the posterior distribution, whereas the MAP consists of the mode of the same distribution. An advantage of Bayesian estimation is that the extra information obtained using the prior can improve the estimation of θ. A limitation of this type of procedure is that if the distance between a parameter and the mean of the prior distribution is large, the resulting estimated parameter will tend to regress to the mean of the prior (shrinkage).

Model-data fit

Item and model fit Several statistical methods are available to check whether an IRT model is in agreement with the data. There are global methods that can be used to investigate the fit of the IRT model to the complete test and there are methods to investigate item fit. For fit tests for the Rasch model we refer to Suárez-Falcón and Glas (2003) and Maydeu-Olivares and Montaño (2013). Next, we concentrate on a number of fit statistics that can be obtained when running the program IRTPRO and that are relatively easy to understand. Traditional approaches concern Pearson (Bock, 1972; Yen, 1981) and likelihood ratio (McKinley & Mills, 1985) χ^2 procedures. We will focus on dichotomous items unless stated otherwise because the procedures underlying fit for polytomous items do not fundamentally differ from the fit procedures for dichotomous items.

The Pearson approach is based on a statistic which assesses the distance between observed and expected scores. Large differences between observed and expected scores indicate misfit. Originally it was required to divide the latent scale in a number of disjoint intervals (say, *u*) such that roughly the same number of persons was placed in each interval, according to their estimated ability. Yen's (1981) Q_1 statistic, for example, prespecified $u = 10$ such intervals. Next, observed and predicted scores were computed for each ability interval and each item score. Bock (1972) suggested using the median of the ability estimates in each interval to compute the predicted scores, whereas Yen (1981) suggested using the sample ability mean in each interval (Yen's statistic). The test statistic is given by

$$X_i^2 = \Sigma_{v=1}^{u} N_v \frac{(O_{iv} - E_{iv})^2}{E_{iv}(1 - E_{iv})}, \quad (15.5)$$

where i indexes the item, v indexes the group defined on the ability latent scale (Bock, 1972; Yen, 1981) u is the number of groups, N_v is the number of persons in group v, and O_{iv} and E_{iv} are the observed and expected proportion-correct responses for item i in group v, respectively. This test statistic follows approximately a χ^2 distribution with $u - g$ degrees of freedom, where g is the number of item parameters estimated by the IRT model. However, because groupings are based on an estimate of θ, which is both sample- and model-based and violates the assumption of the χ^2 statistic, Orlando and Thissen (2000) proposed instead to use NC scores on the test to create the groups of persons; their item fit statistic is denoted by $S - X_i^2$. For dichotomous items the summation in Equation 15.5 runs through NC scores 1 and $n - 1$ (n = number of items), since the proportion of persons answering item i correctly when NC = 0 is always 0 and the proportion of persons answering item i correctly when NC = n is always 1. The $S - X_i^2$ statistic is approximately χ^2 distributed with $(n - 1 - g)$ degrees of freedom. An extension of the $S - X_i^2$ statistic to polytomous items is readily available (Kang & Chen, 2008). The $S - X_i^2$ statistic is available in the IRTPRO software.

The likelihood ratio approach (McKinley & Mills, 1985) uses a different test statistic denoted G_i,

$$G_i^2 = 2\Sigma_{v=1}^{u} N_v \left[O_{iv} \log \frac{O_{iv}}{E_{iv}} + (1 - O_{iv}) \log \frac{1 - O_{iv}}{1 - E_{iv}} \right], \quad (15.6)$$

with the same notation as Equation 15.5. This statistic is also based on groups defined on the θ scale and follows approximately a χ^2 distribution with $(u - g)$ degrees of freedom. Orlando and Thissen (2000; see also Orlando & Thissen, 2003) proposed $S - G_i^2$, which is based on NC-groups.

Model-fit tests other than the χ^2 procedures just discussed have been proposed. Limited information fit tests (Bartholomew & Leung, 2002; Cai, Maydeu-Olivares, Coffman, & Thissen, 2006; Maydeu-Olivares & Joe, 2005) use observed and expected frequencies based on classifications of all possible response patterns. Specifically, low-order margins of contingency tables are used. Such approaches arose because it was verified that the traditional χ^2 (i.e., full information) statistics, when applied to contingency tables, led to empirical type I errors larger than the nominal errors of their asymptotic distributions (due to the sparseness of the tables for even realistic test lengths and/or number of response categories). An example of the limited information approach is the M_2 (Maydeu-Olivares & Joe, 2006) statistic, which is also available in the program IRTPRO.

There are item fit approaches that evaluate violations of LI. Yen (1984) proposed a statistic, Q_3, which was one of the first statistics used to investigate LI between item responses conditional on θ. Q_3 statistic is the correlation between the scores of a pair of items from which the model's expected score has been partialled out. There are two problems associated to Q_3. On the one hand, Q_3 relies on estimated θ values for each response pattern. Such estimates are not always available because the likelihood function is sometimes not well defined, as explained previously. On the other hand, the reference distribution of Q_3 suggested by Yen (a normal distribution after a Fisher's transformation) does not seem to work well (Chen & Thissen, 1997). Chen and Thissen (1997) proposed instead a Pearson's χ^2 statistic to test LI between any pair of items. This statistic is given in IRTPRO as the LD $X2$ statistic. According to the software manual these statistics are standardized χ^2 scores that are approximately z-scores. However, the LD $X2$ LI statistics given in IRTPRO are difficult to interpret. As discussed in the IRTPRO manual, because these statistics are only approximately standardized, values of 2 or 3 should not be considered large. Instead, only values of 10 or larger should be taken as a serious violation. Our own experience with using these statistics to identify locally dependent item pairs is that it is often advisable to take item content into account. Moreover, very high a parameters (say, larger than $a = 3$) are sometimes a better indication of redundant items than local independence statistics like the LD $X2$.

Another model-fit approach is based on the Lagrange multiplier (LM) test (Glas, 1999). The idea of a LM test is to consider a model where an additional parameter is added to the IRT model of interest. Under the null hypothesis of LI this additional parameter equals zero. The LM test statistics are asymptotically χ^2 distributed with a number of degrees of freedom equal to the number of parameters fixed under the null hypothesis. This approach can also be used to test deviations between theoretical and empirical IRFs. Glas and Suárez-Falcón (2003) compared the detection performances between LM and other tests and concluded that the LM tests work relatively well. Extensions to polytomous models exist (Glas, 1999).

Recently, Ranger and Kuhn (2012) proposed fit statistics based on the information matrix and compared these statistics with other fit statistics. More details, and comparisons to other methods, can be found in their article.

Person fit Although an IRT model may give a reasonable description of the data, the item score patterns of some persons may be very unlikely under the assumed IRT model. For these persons, it is questionable whether the estimated θ score gives an adequate description of θ. Several statistical methods have been proposed to investigate whether an item score pattern is unlikely given the assumed IRT model. Meijer and Sijtsma (2001) give an overview of the different approaches and statistics that are available. The most often-used statistic is the standardized log-likelihood statistic l_z (Dragow, Levine, & Williams, 1985). This statistic is based on the likelihood of a score pattern given the estimated trait value. To classify an item score pattern as fitting or misfitting a researcher needs a distribution of person-fit scores. One major problem with the l_z statistic is that its asymptotic standard normal distribution is only valid when true (not estimated) θs are used. This is a severe limitation in practice, since true abilities are typically unknown. Snijders (2001) proposed an extension of l_z, denoted l_z^*, which takes this problem into account. Magis, Raîche, and Béland (2012; see also Meijer & Tendeiro, 2012 for some important additional remarks) wrote a very readable tutorial and also provided R code to calculate the l_z^*.

Alternative approaches to calculating likelihood statistics were proposed by van Krimpen-Stoop and Meijer (2001) and recently by Tendeiro, Meijer, Schakel, and Maij-de

Meij (2013). They used the so-called cumulative sum statistics that are sensitive to strings of item scores that may indicate aberrant behavior, like cheating behavior or random responding.

How serious is misfit and what does it mean? As some authors have mentioned, fit research is not unproblematic. Because IRT models are simple stochastic models that will never perfectly describe the data, fit always is a matter of degree. Also, for large datasets a model will always be rejected because of high power, even if model violations are small and have no practical consequences.

Furthermore, as we discussed before, the numerical values of many fit indices are sensitive to particular characteristics of the data. For example, the LD $X2$ local independence statistics given in IRTPRO are difficult to interpret because the associated standardization has limitations. Thus, there is always an important subjective element in deciding when an item or item score pattern does not fit the model. Therefore, some authors argue for more research that investigates the effects of model misfit on the estimation of structural parameters.

When practically applying IRT models, it is often difficult to decide on the basis of fit research which items to remove from a scale. Some researchers only use some general indicators of misfit, others conclude after some detailed fit research that "despite the model misfit for the scale, we used the full scale, because the effects on the outcome measures were small." Perhaps removing items from a scale because of flat IRFs or violations of monotonicity is easiest because it is clear that such items do not contribute to any meaningful measurement. For example, Meijer, Tendeiro, and Wanders (2015) showed that an item from the aggression scale "I tell my friends openly when I disagree with them" did not discriminate between different trait levels and as such does not contribute to meaningful measurement.

With respect to person-fit research a sometimes-heard criticism is that although it is technically possible to identify misfitting item score patterns, the practical usefulness has not yet been shown. That is, it is often unclear what the misfit of an item score pattern really means in psychological terms. Is misfit due to random response behavior because of unmotivated test behavior? Or is it due to misunderstanding the questions? One of the few studies that tried to explain person misfit is Meijer et al. (2008). They combined person-fit results with qualitative information from interviews with teachers and other background variables to obtain information why children produced unlikely response patterns on a self-evaluation scale. Another interesting application was given in Conijn (2013) who conducted several studies to explain person misfit. For example, Conijn (2013) found that patients were more likely to show misfit on clinical scales when they experienced higher levels of psychological distress. What is clearly needed here are studies that address the psychological meaning of misfitting response patterns: We are very curious to see more empirical studies that explain *why* a score pattern is misfitting.

Nonparametric IRT

Nonparametric IRT (NIRT) models are based on the same set of assumptions as parametric IRT models (UD, LI, and M). However, unlike parametric IRT models, in NIRT the IRFs (dichotomous case) or CRFs (polytomous case) do not need to have a logistic or any other functional form. In other words, no parameterized models of θ involving item and person parameters are defined. As a consequence, it is not possible to estimate person parameters even though a θ-latent scale is still assumed to exist. Instead of estimating θ, in NIRT the ordering of respondents on the observable sum score (total score) X_+ is used to stochastically order persons on the latent θ scale (Sijtsma & Molenaar, 2002). Hence, only the *ordinal* nature of the latent scale is of interest in NIRT. Under the UD, LI, and M assumptions the stochastic ordering of persons on the θ scale by X_+ holds for dichotomous items. Although for polytomous items this stochastic ordering does not hold in all cases (in theory; Hemker, Sijtsma, Molenaar, & Junker, 1997), van der Ark (2005) showed that this is not problematic in practical settings. However, this ordering holds for the *rest score* (total score minus score on an item) and therefore the rest-score is used instead of the total score. Also, item difficulty parameters are not estimated in NIRT. Instead, item proportion-correct scores similar to the ones in CTT are used. However, unlike CTT, in NIRT explicit models have been formulated and methods have been proposed to check these models.

The most popular nonparametric models are the Mokken (1971) models. Sijtsma and Molenaar (2002) devoted a complete monograph to these models and there are many papers that discuss measurement properties of these models and/or show how these models can be used to investigate the psychometric quality of tests and questionnaires (e.g., Meijer & Baneke, 2004).

Mokken (1971) proposed two models: The monotone homogeneity model (MHM) and the double monotonicity model (DMM). Both models have been formulated for dichotomous and polytomous item scores.

Monotone homogeneity model The MHM applies to both dichotomously and polytomously scored items. Both the dichotomous and polytomous MHMs are based on the UD and LI assumptions. Furthermore, monotonicity is assumed for the nonparametric IRFs (in the dichotomous case) or ISRFs (in the polytomous case). To check these assumptions several methods have been proposed that are incorporated in the R package *mokken* (van der Ark, 2007, 2012). We will discuss some of these methods in this chapter.

The MHM can be considered a nonparametric version of the GRM (for model selection, see next). In Figure 15.6 we plotted the nonparametric ISRFs for the SPPC Athletic Competence items 4 and 5. In Figure 15.5 we already showed the associated CRFs for the GRM; it is now interesting to compare the corresponding Figures 15.5 and 15.6. Persons were grouped according to their rest score; proportions of positive response per item step were then computed for each rest-score group of persons. Focusing first on item 5, it can be observed that item steps $P(X_i > 1)$ and $P(X_i > 2)$ are close together (Figure 15.6b). This shows that there is little difference between the first two answer options: Persons passing the first item step had a high probability of also passing the second step. In other words, item 5 does not discriminate well among persons, which confirms what we found via the GRM's CRFs (see Figure 15.5b). Figure 15.6a, on the other hand, shows ISRFs that are well separated from each other, highlighting item 4 as a good, discriminating item (supporting our previous findings using the GRM, see Figure 15.5a).

Double monotonicity model In his book in 1971 Mokken proposed the double monotonicity model for dichotomous items, later adapted for polytomous items (Molenaar, 1997). The DMM also assumes UD, LI, and M. Moreover, for *dichotomous* items, this

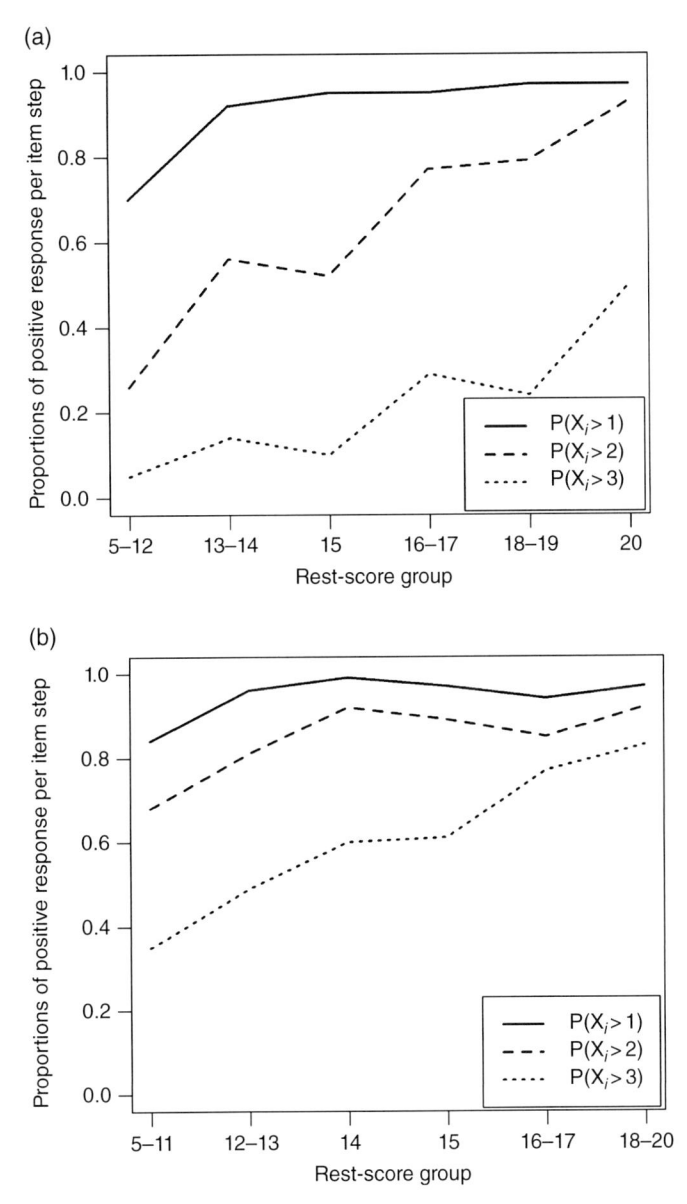

Figure 15.6 (a) Nonparametric ISRFs for item 4 of the Athletic Competence scale of the SPPC. (b) Nonparametric ISRFs for item 5 of the Athletic Competence scale of the SPPC.

model implies that the ordering of the items according to the proportion-correct score is the same for any value of θ. This invariant item ordering (IIO) property may be an interesting property for several applications. For example, it is often assumed but seldom checked that items have the same difficulty ordering for different levels of the latent trait. For example, for many psychological tests for children items are ordered from easy to difficult. When a child does not give the correct answer to, say, three or four subsequent items the test administration is stopped. Here it is assumed that for every child the item difficulty order is the same independently of the trait value. Another example can be found in all kinds of scales that measure physical functioning. Egberink and Meijer (2011) showed that items from the Physical Functioning of the SF-36 complied with this model. For *polytomous* items the DMM does not imply IIO, but there are several methods proposed to check IIO for polytomous items. The interested reader is referred to Ligtvoet, van der Ark, te Marvelde, and Sijtsma (2010) and Meijer and Egberink (2012); we shall briefly refer to some options later in the chapter. Sijtsma, Meijer, and van der Ark (2011) provide an overview for conducting several steps for a Mokken scale analysis that incorporate both MHM and DMM, and IIO. Next, we briefly discuss some of these methods.

Dimensionality Assessing the dimensionality of the data to be analyzed is an important step in IRT model fitting. Basically, dimensionality of the data concerns the number of different latent variables that determine the scores of each item. Since the IRT models previously discussed are all unidimensional, it is important that relatively homogeneous sets of items are selected prior to attempt fitting an IRT model, whether parametric or not. We next discuss two different approaches to analyze dimensionality.

As mentioned in Sijtsma and Meijer (2007), nonparametric unidimensionality analysis is based on so-called conditional association (CA). For a general definition of CA see Holland and Rosenbaum (1986). One practical implication of CA is that all inter-item covariances within a test should be nonnegative in the sample. Strictly speaking, one negative covariance between a pair of items indicates misfit of the MHM (and of the DMM, since the latter implies the former). However, it is important to observe that all nonnegative inter-item covariances in the data do not imply that the MHM fits. Hence, having nonnegative inter-item covariances is a necessary, but not sufficient, condition for MHM fit.

To investigate Mokken scalability the automated item selection algorithm (AISP) is often used. The AISP is a popular method, although it is sensitive to specific item characteristics (see discussion that follows). The AISP uses the so-called *scalability* coefficient H. H is defined at the item level (H_i) and at the scale level (H). All H coefficients can be expressed as ratios of (sums of) observed covariances and maximum possible covariances. The scalability coefficients play a similar role in the MHM as the slopes of IRFs do in logistic IRT models: The steeper the nonparametric IRF, the larger the scalability indices. The AISP is an iterative algorithm that selects, in each step, the item that maximizes H given the already selected items up to that iteration. Thus, items that have relatively steep IRFs are successively added by the AISP. The procedure continues until the largest item scalability H_i is below a prespecified lowerbound, c. If there are unselected items, the AISP can be run again to create a second item cluster, and so on, until all items have been assigned to some cluster.

For the interpretation of scalability coefficients, Sijtsma and Molenaar (2002, p. 60) give the following guidelines. Item scalability coefficients H_i should be larger than a lowerbound c to be specified ($c = 0.3$ is often used in practice). Also, a scale H coefficient of at least equal to 0.3 is required to ensure that the ordering of persons according to their total score does provide a fair image of the true ordering of the persons on the latent scale (which cannot be directly assessed). More precisely, a scale can be classified as weak ($0.3 \leq H < 0.4$), medium ($0.4 \leq H < 0.5$), and strong ($H \geq 0.5$) according to the value of H.

Recently, Straat, van der Ark, and Sijtsma (2013) proposed alternatives to this procedure. They tackled the problem that when using the AISP procedure scales may be

Table 15.2 Estimated item parameters and H_i values.

Item	True parameters a	True parameters b	a (SE)	b (SE)	H_i (SE)
1	1.0	−1.0	1.07 (.14)	−0.88 (.11)	0.27 (.03)
2	1.0	−0.5	1.11 (.14)	−0.45 (.08)	0.25 (.02)
3	1.0	0.0	0.98 (.13)	−0.05 (.08)	0.22 (.02)
4	1.0	0.5	1.10 (.14)	0.53 (.09)	0.25 (.02)
5	1.0	1.0	1.03 (.14)	0.98 (.12)	0.27 (.03)

selected that satisfy scaling conditions at the moment the items are selected but may fail to do so when the scale is completed. They proposed a genetic algorithm that tries to find the most optimal division of a set of items into different scales. Although they found that this procedure performed better in some cases, a drawback of this procedure is that a user only gets information about the final result and cannot see which items are being selected during the selection process. So, we recommend using both the AISP and this genetic algorithm when selecting Mokken scales.

Although Mokken scaling has been quite popular to evaluate the quality of empirical datasets, two caveats are important to mention. A first caveat, as explained before, is that Mokken scaling procedures are especially sensitive to forming subscales with items that have high discriminating power and thus are especially sensitive to select items with steep IRFs. This is so, because H_i can be considered a nonparametric equivalent of the discrimination parameter in parametric IRT models. Although one may argue that these types of scales are very useful to discriminate persons with different total scores, compared to parametric models a Mokken scale analysis using the AISP procedure may reject items that may fit a 3PLM or 2PLM but have low discriminating power. In Table 15.2 we show numerical values of H_i under the 1PLM in a five-item test with item location parameters ranging from $(−1,1)$. These values were calculated on the basis of simulated data with θ drawn from $N(0,1)$. As can be seen, estimated item discrimination parameters around 1.0 resulted in H_i values lower than $H_i = 0.30$. Thus, although these six items perfectly fit the Rasch model, all of them will be rejected from the scale in case a researcher uses $c = 0.3$ as the lower bound in the AISP, which is the common choice in practice.

As an alternative, a second procedure to assess dimensionality is the nonparametric DETECT (Dimensionality Evaluation To Enumerate Contributing Traits; Kim, 1994; Stout, Habing, Douglas, & Kim, 1996; Zhang & Stout, 1999) approach. In contrast to the AISP algorithm in Mokken analysis, DETECT is based on covariances between any pair of items, conditional on θ. The LI assumption implies that all these conditional covariances are equal to zero; this condition is known as weak LI. To check weak LI, Stout and coworkers based their method on the observable property that the covariance between any pair of items, say items i and j, must be nonnegative for subgroups of persons that have the same rest score $R_{(-i,-j)}(R_{(-i,-j)} = X_+ - (X_i + X_j))$. Assuming that the items measure Q latent variables to a different degree (i.e., multidimensionality), we may assume that θ_q is a linear combination of these variables. The performance on the Q latent variables is estimated by means of total score, X_+, or rest scores, $R_{(-i,-j)}$. Both scores summarize test performance but ignore multidimensionality. Zhang and Stout (1999), however, showed that the sign of $\text{Cov}(X_i, X_j|\theta_q)$ provides useful information about the dimensionality of the data. The covariance is positive when the two items measure the same latent variable and negative when they clearly measure different latent variables. This observation forms the basis of DETECT, allowing a set of items to be divided into clusters that together approach weak LI as well as is possible given all potential item clusters.

Several studies suggested rules-of-thumb that can be used to decide whether a dataset is unidimensional or multidimensional. Stout et al. (1996) considered DETECT values smaller than 0.1 indicating unidimensionality and DETECT values larger than 1 indicating multidimensionality (Stout et al., 1996). Roussos and Ozbek (1996) suggested to use the following rules-of-thumb: $DETECT < 0.2$ displays weak multidimensionality/approximate unidimensionality; $0.2 < DETECT < 0.4$: weak to moderate multidimensionality; $0.4 < DETECT < 1.0$ = moderate to large multidimensionality; $DETECT > 1.0$: strong multidimensionality. Recently, however, Bonifay et al. (2015) discussed that these values are sensitive to the factor structure of the dataset and the relation between general and group factors in the test. They investigated the effect of multidimensionality item parameter bias. The underlying idea was that every dataset is multidimensional to some extent and that it is more important to investigate what the effect is of using a unidimensional IRT model on particular outcome variables (such as item parameter bias) than to investigate whether or not a test is unidimensional. Perhaps, the most important conclusion of their study was that (Bonifay et al., 2015, p. 515);

> when the concern is with parameter bias caused by model misspecification, measuring the degree of multidimensionality does not provide the full picture. For example, in a long test with a reasonably strong general factor and many small group factors, parameter bias is expected to be relatively small regardless of the degree of multidimensionality. Thus, we recommend that *DETECT* values always be considered interactively with indices of factor strength (*ECV*) and factor structure (*PUC*).

Several studies compared the AISP algorithm with *DETECT*. van Abswoude, van der Ark, and Sijtsma (2004), and Mroch and Bolt (2006) showed that *DETECT* was better able to identify unidimensionality than the AISP. van Abswoude et al. (2004) suggested that unidimensionality can best be investigated using *DETECT* and that the best discriminating items can be selected through the AISP. Thus, the reader should be aware of the fact that both methods investigate different characteristics of the data. AISP is in particular sensitive to selecting items with high discriminating power.

Checking monotonicity and invariant item ordering In our discussion on assessing the dimensionality of the data, UD and LI assumptions were already considered. We next discuss how to check the M and IIO assumptions.

The assumption of monotonicity can be fairly easily investigated using graphical methods and eye-ball inspection (as we showed in Figure 15.6), since Junker (1993) proved that UD, LI, and M imply that $P(X_i = 1|R_{(-i)})$ is nondecreasing in $R_{(-i)}$, where $R_{(-i)} = X_+ - X_i$. This property is known as *manifest* monotonicity (MM). A simple statistical test exists to test the statistical significance to violations of MM; violations of MM imply violations of M, but the reverse is not necessarily valid. Both MSP and the R package *mokken* allow performing these analyses. R package *KernSmoothIRT* (Mazza,

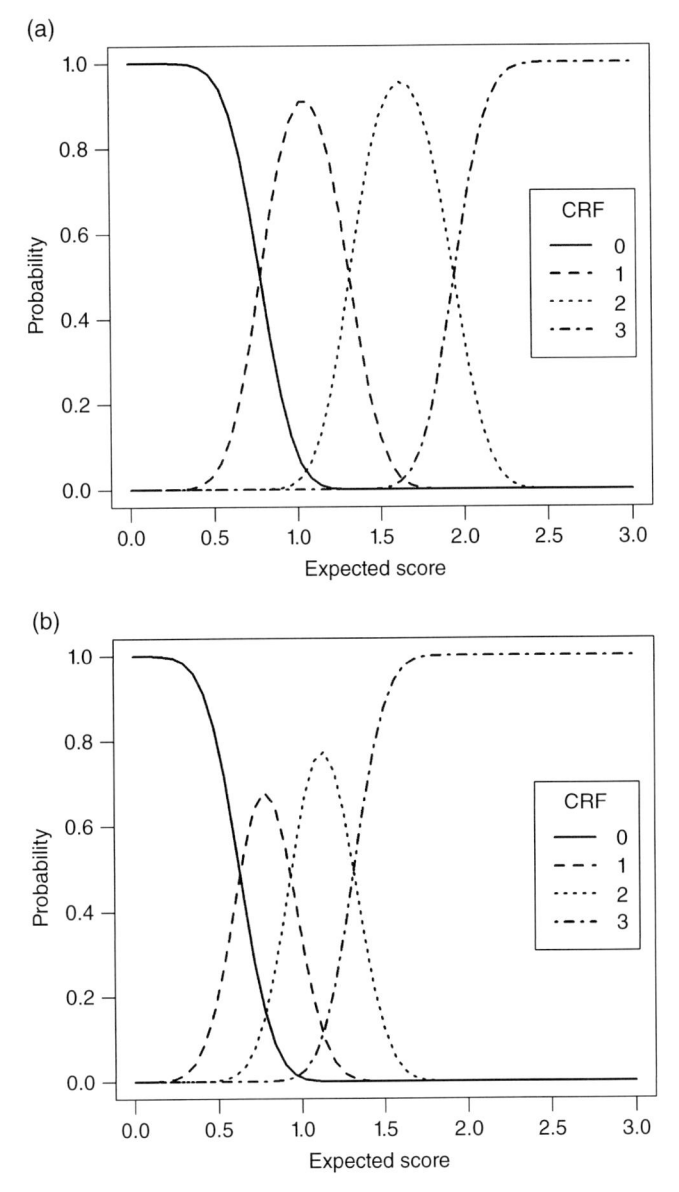

Figure 15.7 (a) Nonparametric CRFs for item 4 of the SPPC estimated using the R KernSmoothIRT package. (b) Nonparametric CRFs for item 5 of the SPPC estimated using the KernSmoothIRT package.

Punzo, & McGuire, 2012) provides an alternative to assess the M assumption which is based on kernel smoothing, a nonparametric regression technique. Figures 15.7(a) and (b) show CRFs estimated using this package for the same items of the SPCC considered previously. It is interesting to compare these CRFs with the parametric CRFs estimated using the GRM (see Figures 15.5a and b). Note that Figure 15.7(a) is very similar to Figure 15.5(a). In Figure 15.7(a) we use expected scores instead of latent trait values.

Figure 15.5(b) seems different than Figure 15.7(b), but note that options 1 and 2 only discriminate in a small area of the expected score. An alternative is to use the program TestGraf (Ramsay, 2000). In TestGraf continuous functions are provided that are based on kernel smoothing and that can be used to investigate the form of the IRFs or CRFs.

Several methods are available to check whether IIO can be safely assumed in the DMM framework. Technical details can be found in Sijtsma and Junker (1996), Sijtsma and Molenaar (2002), and van der Ark (2012). Here we outline the methods that are easily available for practitioners to use. The *mokken* package in R offers the *pmatrix* and *restscore* methods, which are two different variants of the same procedure to inspect IIO for *dichotomous* items. Given items i and j with $\bar{X}_i < \bar{X}_j$, and given an unweighed sum score S that does not depend on items i and j, the idea is to verify whether $P(X_i = 1 | S = s) \leq P(X_j = 1 | S = s)$ for all admissible realizations of S. That is, it is checked whether for every total score s, the probability of answering the easiest item correctly (thus, the proportion-correct score) is larger than answering the more difficult item correctly. Violations of the inequality are tested for their statistical significance. The *pmatrix* and *restscore* methods are not suitable for polytomous items since DMM does not imply IIO in this case. Ligtvoet et al. (2010) introduced a method (*check.iio* command in R) that is suitable for both dichotomous and polytomous items. In MSP5.0, the p-matrix and rest-score methods are available for dichotomous items; for polytomous items the *mokken* package in R should be used.

Model selection

There are basically two strategies for IRT model selection. In the first strategy, a researcher tries to find the best fitting model with the least number of item parameters. Thus, when the Rasch model can describe the data, a researcher will use the Rasch model and not the 3PLM, and when the 3PLM shows the best fit, this model will be used. A second strategy is to select items for which the responses are in agreement with a prespecified model. For example, the Rasch model may be preferred because the total scores are sufficient statistics for the trait score (i.e., the trait scores can be estimated using the item parameters and the total scores only, no pattern of responses is required). Another argument to use the Rasch model has to do with sample size. As Lord (1980) discussed, if there is only a small group of persons, the a parameter cannot be determined accurately for some items. Lord (1980) conducted a small empirical study and he concluded that "for the 10- and 15-item tests, the Rasch estimator x may be slightly superior to the two-parameter estimator (...) when the number of cases available for estimating the item parameters is less than 100 or 200." Alternatively, the DMM model may be preferred because the ordering of the items according to their difficulty is the same for each person independent of the θ level. In such cases the model can be selected first and then items are selected that can be best described through this model.

For dichotomous data, the 2PLM and the 3PLM are often used because they give an adequate description of many types of data. The 2PLM model may be chosen when there is no guessing involved. Thus, the 2PLM seems to be a suitable model to describe answering behavior on noncognitive questionnaires (personality, mood disorders). The 3PLM can be used when any guessing is involved, as it may happen with cognitive measures (intelligence and educational testing). For polytomous items, as we discussed previously, the NRM is a valid option for cases in which score categories cannot be necessarily ordered, whereas the (generalized) PCM and the GRM can be considered when the score categories are ordered.

Then there is the question of whether to use a parametric or a nonparametric model. One reason for using nonparametric IRT models is that they are more flexible than parametric models. For example, an IRF may be increasing but not have a logistic structure. A second reason may be sample size. An often-used argument is that when the sample size is relatively modest nonparametric approaches can be used as alternatives to parametric models that, in general, require more persons to estimate parameters. However, recent research showed that researchers should be careful when using small samples. For example, Kappenberg-ten Holt (2014) cautioned that the use of samples of $n = 200$ results in positive bias of the H coefficient, which reduces with increasing sample sizes. In relation to this, a researcher can use standard errors for the H coefficient to obtain an idea about the variability of the coefficient. Also, DETECT input specification file requires a minimum size of 400 persons. Therefore, perhaps the biggest advantage of the nonparametric approach is that it provides some alternative techniques to explore data quality without forcing the data in a structure they may not have.

There are also limitations to the use of nonparametric IRT models. The models are less suited to the construction of computer adaptive tests or when using change scores. Several authors have discussed that change scores are more difficult to interpret using total scores than when using parametric IRT scoring (Brouwer, Meijer, & Zevalkink, 2013; Embretson & Reise, 2000; Reise & Haviland, 2005). A general guide in deciding which model to apply is that nonparametric IRT is an interesting tool to explore data quality, however when trait estimates are needed parametric models must be used.

Alternative approaches: Ideal point models

To analyze polytomous scale data we discussed several models that assume a dominance response process where an individual high on θ is assumed to answer positively with high probability. This approach dates back from Likert's approach to the development and analysis of rating scales. In a recent issue of *Industrial and Organizational Psychology-Perspectives on Science and Practice*, Drasgow, Chernyshenko, and Stark (2010; see also Weekers & Meijer, 2008) published a discussion paper in which they argued that for personality assessment ideal point test models based on Thurstone scaling procedure are superior over dominance models because the former models provide a better representation of the choice process underlying rating scale judgments. They also discussed that model misspecification can have important consequences in practical test use, such as in personnel selection. In ideal point models the probability of endorsement is assumed to be directly related to the proximity of the statement to the person's standing on the assessed trait. In a series of response papers to this article, several authors criticized or endorsed the claims made by Drasgow et al. (2010) and made suggestions for further research. From these papers, it is clear that still much is unknown about (1) the underlying response process to rating scale data, (2) which test model should be used to describe responses to noncognitive measures, and (3) what the consequences are of model misspecification in practice. We think that future research may shed light on these issues.

Concluding Remarks

In this chapter, we presented an overview of unidimensional IRT modeling. At the start of this chapter we discussed that in scientific journals devoted to test construction and evaluation, IRT is the state-of-the-art technique. In test and questionnaire construction of commercial test batteries our experience is that IRT is not the standard. Evers, Sijtsma, Lucassen, and Meijer (2010) described in the 2009 revision of the Dutch Rating System for Test Quality for the first time IRT criteria to judge whether IRT techniques were in agreement with professional standards. We think there is much to be gained through the application of IRT in test construction. Our experience is that IRT analyses on existing scales show that many scales consist of items and subtests that can be improved through a more rigorous analysis of the quality of individual items. Although IRT is a stronger measurement theory than CTT and estimation of item and person parameters is not easy, for a practitioner there is (sometimes free) software available (see Box 15.1). Hopefully, this chapter contributes to the more wide-spread use of IRT analyses in test construction and evaluation.

Box 15.1: Computer Programs

X Calibre (www.assess.com). One, two, three PL, graded response model, rating scale model, partial credit model.

BILOG-MG (www.ssicentral.com) one, two, three parameter logistic model, differential item functioning.

WINSTEPS and FACETS (www.winsteps.com) Rasch model.

PARSCALE (www.ssicentral.com). Graded response model, partial credit model, generalized partial credit model, generalized partial credit model,

IRTPRO (www.ssicentral.com) One, two, three parameter logistic model, graded, generalized partial credit model, differential functioning

MSP5.0 Mokken models

R package Mokken Mokken models

R package KernSmothIRT Kernel smoothing

TESTGRAF

References

Andersen, E. B. (1972). The numerical solution of a set of conditional estimation equations. *Journal of the Royal Statistical Society, Series B, 34,* 42–54.

Andrich, D. (1978a). Application of a psychometric rating model to ordered categories which are scored with successive integers. *Applied Psychological Measurement, 2*(4), 581–594.

Andrich, D. (1978b). A rating formulation for ordered response categories. *Psychometrika, 43*(4), 561–573.

Baker, F. B., & Kim, S. H. (2004). *Item response theory: Parameter estimation techniques.* New York, NY: Marcel Dekker, Inc.

Bartholomew, D. J., & Leung, S. O. (2002). A goodness of fit test for sparse 2^P contingency tables. *British Journal of Mathematical and Statistical Psychology, 55*(1), 1–16.

Birnbaum, A. (1968). *Some latent trait models and their use in inferring an examinee's ability.* In F. M. Lord & M. R. Novic (Eds), Statistical theories of mental test scores *(Ch. 17–20).* Reading, MA: Addison-Wesley.

Bock, R. D. (1972). Estimating item parameters and latent ability when responses are scored in two or more nominal categories. *Psychometrika*, *37*, 29–51.

Bock, R. D., & Lieberman, M. (1970). Fitting a response model for n dichotomously scored items. *Psychometrika*, *35*(2), 179–197.

Bonifay, W. E., Reise, S. P., Scheines, R., & Meijer, R. R. (2015). When are multidimensional data unidimensional enough for structural equation modeling? An evaluation of the DETECT multidimensionality index. *Structural Equation Modeling*, *22*, 504–516. DOI: 10.1080/10705511.2014.938596.

Brouwer, D., Meijer, R. R., & Zevalkink, J. (2013). Measuring individual significant change on the BDI-II through IRT-based statistics. *Psychotherapy Research*, *23*(5), 489–501.

Cai, L., Maydeu-Olivares, A., Coffman, D. L., & Thissen, D. (2006). Limited-information goodness-of-fit testing of item response theory models for sparse 2^P tables. *British Journal of Mathematical and Statistical Psychology*, *59*(1), 173–194.

Chen, W. H., & Thissen, D. (1997). Local dependence indexes for item pairs using item response theory. *Journal of Educational and Behavioral Statistics*, *22*(3), 265–289.

Conijn, J. M. (2013). *Detecting and explaining person misfit in non-cognitive measurement* (Unpublished Doctoral Dissertation). University of Tilburg, the Netherlands.

Drasgow, F., Chernyshenko, O. S., & Stark, S. (2010). 75 years after Likert: Thurstone was right! *Industrial and Organizational Psychology: Perspectives on Science and Practice*, *3*(4), 465–476.

Drasgow, F., Levine, M. V., & Williams, E. A. (1985). Appropriateness measurement with polychotomous item response models and standardized indices. *British Journal of Mathematical and Statistical Psychology*, *38*(1), 67–86.

Dumenci, L., & Achenbach, T. M. (2008). Effects of estimation methods on making trait-level inferences from ordered categorical items for assessing psychopathology. *Psychological Assessment*, *20*(1), 55–62.

Egberink, I. J. L., & Meijer, R. R. (2011). An item response theory analysis of Harter's Self-Perception Profile for Children or why strong clinical scales should be distrusted. *Assessment*, *18*(2), 201–212.

Embretson, S. E., & Reise, S. P. (2000). *Item response theory for psychologists*. Mahwah, NJ US: Lawrence Erlbaum Associates Publishers.

Evers, A., Sijtsma, K., Lucassen, W., & Meijer, R. R. (2010). The Dutch review process for evaluating the quality of psychological tests: History, procedure, and results. *International Journal of Testing*, *10*(4), 295–317.

Glas, C. A. W. (1999). Modification indices for the 2-PL and the nominal response model. *Psychometrika*, *64*(3), 273–294.

Glas, C. A. W., & Suárez-Falcón, J. C. (2003). A comparison of item-fit statistics for the three-parameter logistic model. *Applied Psychological Measurement*, *27*(2), 87–106.

Guttman, L. (1944). A basis for scaling qualitative data. *American Sociological Review*, *9*, 139–150.

Guttman, L. (1950). The basis for scalogram analysis. In S. A. Stouffer, L. Guttman, E. A. Suchman, P. F. Lazersfeld, S. A. Star, & J. A. Clausen (Eds.), *Measurement and prediction*. Princeton, NJ: Princeton University Press.

Hemker, B. T., Sijtsma, K., Molenaar, I. W., & Junker, B. W. (1997). Stochastic ordering using the latent trait and the sum score in polytomous IRT models. *Psychometrika*, *62*(3), 331–347.

Holland, P. W., & Rosenbaum, P. R. (1986). Conditional association and unidimensionality in monotone latent variable models. *The Annals of Statistics*, *14*(4), 1523–1543.

IRTPRO 2.1, Scientific Software International, Lincolnwood, IL.

Junker, B. W. (1993). Conditional association, essential independence and monotone unidimensional item response models. *The Annals of Statistics*, *21*(3), 1359–1378.

Kang, T., & Chen, T. T. (2008). Performance of the generalized S-X^2 item fit index for polytomous IRT models. *Journal of Educational Measurement*, *45*(4), 391–406.

Kim, H. R. (1994). *New techniques for the dimensionality assessment of standardized test data* (Unpublished Doctoral dissertation). University of Illinois at Urbana-Champaign.

Ligtvoet, R., van der Ark, L. A., te Marvelde, J. M., & Sijtsma, K. (2010). Investigating an invariant item ordering for polytomously scored items. *Educational and Psychological Measurement, 70*(4), 578–595.

Lord, F. M. (1952). A theory of test scores. *Psychometric Monographs, 7*.

Lord, F. M. (1953). The relation of test score to the trait underlying the test. *Educational and Psychological Measurement, 13*, 517–549.

Lord, F. M. (1980). *Applications of item response theory to practical testing problems*. Hillsdale, NJ: Erlbaum.

Magis, D., Raîche, G., & Béland, S. (2012). A didactic presentation of Snijders's l_z* index of person fit with emphasis on response model selection and ability estimation. *Journal of Educational and Behavioral Statistics, 37*(1), 57–81.

Masters, G. N. (1982). A Rasch model for partial credit scoring. *Psychometrika, 47*(2), 149–174.

Maydeu-Olivares, A., & Joe, H. (2005). Limited- and full-information estimation and goodness-of-fit testing in 2^n contingency tables: A unified framework. *Journal of the American Statistical Association, 100*(471), 1009–1020.

Maydeu-Olivares, A., & Joe, H. (2006). Limited information goodness-of-fit testing in multidimensional contingency tables. *Psychometrika, 71*(4), 713–732.

Maydeu-Olivares, A., & Montaño, R. (2013). How should we assess the fit of Rasch-type models? Approximating the power of goodness-of-fit statistics in categorical data analysis. *Psychometrika, 78*(1), 116–133.

Mazza, A., Punzo, A., & McGuire, B. (2012). *KernSmoothIRT: An R package for kernel smoothing in item response theory*. Accessed 09 April 2012. http://arxiv.org/pdf/1211.1183v1.pdf.

McKinley, R. L., & Mills, C. N. (1985). A comparison of several goodness-of-fit statistics. *Applied Psychological Measurement, 9*(1), 49–57.

Meijer, R. R., & Baneke, J. J. (2004). Analyzing psychopathology items: A case for nonparametric item response theory modeling. *Psychological Methods, 9*(3), 354–368.

Meijer, R. R., & Egberink, I. J. L. (2012). Investigating invariant item ordering in personality and clinical scales: Some empirical findings and a discussion. *Educational and Psychological Measurement, 72*(4), 589–607.

Meijer, R. R., Egberink, I. J. L., Emons, W. H. M., & Sijtsma, K. (2008). Detection and validation of unscalable item score patterns using item response theory: An illustration with Harter's Self-Perception Profile for Children. *Journal of Personality Assessment, 90*(3), 227–238.

Meijer, R. R., & Sijtsma, K. 2001. Methodology review: Evaluating person fit. *Applied Psychological Measurement, 25*(2), 107–135.

Meijer, R. R., & Tendeiro, J. J. (2012). The use of the l_z and the l_z* person-fit statistics and problems derived from model misspecification. *Journal of Educational and Behavioral Statistics, 37*(6), 758–766.

Meijer, R. R., Tendeiro, J. N., & Wanders, R. B. K. (2015). The use of nonparametric item response theory to explore data quality. In S. P. Reise & D. Revicki (Eds.), *Handbook of item response theory modeling: Applications to typical performance assessment*. (pp. 85–110). London: Routledge.

Mislevy, R. J. (1986). Bayes modal estimation in item response models. *Psychometrika, 51*(2), 177–195.

Mokken, R. J. (1971). *A theory and procedure of scale analysis*. The Hague: Mouton/Berlin: De Gruyter.

Molenaar, I. W. (1997). Nonparametric model for polytomous responses. In W. J. van der Linden & R. K. Hambleton (Eds.), *Handbook of modern item response theory* (pp. 369–380). New York: Springer-Verlag.

Mroch, A. A., & Bolt, D. D. (2006). A simulation comparison of parametric and nonparametric dimensionality detection procedures. *Applied Measurement in Education, 19*(1), 67–91.

Muraki, E. (1992). A generalized partial credit model: Application of an EM algorithm. *Applied Psychological Measurement, 16*(2), 159–176.

Nering, M. L., & Ostini, R. (2010). *Handbook of polytomous item response theory models.* New York, NY: Routledge/Taylor & Francis Group.

Orlando, M., & Thissen, D. (2000). Likelihood-based item-fit indices for dichotomous item response theory models. *Applied Psychological Measurement, 24*(1), 50–64.

Orlando, M., & Thissen, D. (2003). Further investigation of the performance of S-X^2: An item fit index for use with dichotomous item response theory models. *Applied Psychological Measurement, 27*(4), 289–298.

Preston, K., Reise, S., Cai, L., & Hays R. D. (2011). Using the nominal response model to evaluate response category discrimination in the PROMIS emotional distress item pools. *Educational and Psychological Measurement, 71*(3), 523–550.

Ramsay, J. O. (2000). *TestGraf: A program for the graphical analysis of multiple choice test and questionnaire data.* www.psych.mcgill.ca/faculty/ramsay/ramsay.html.

Ranger, J., & Kuhn, J. T. (2012). Assessing fit of item response models using the information matrix test. *Journal of Educational Measurement, 49*(3), 247–268.

Rasch, G. (1960). *Studies in mathematical psychology: I. Probabilistic models for some intelligence and attainment tests.* Oxford: Nielsen & Lydiche.

Reise, S. P., & Haviland, M. G. (2005). Item response theory and the measurement of clinical change. *Journal of Personality Assessment, 84*(3), 228–238.

Roussos, L. A., & Ozbek, O. Y. (2006). Formulation of the DETECT population parameter and evaluation of DETECT estimator bias. *Journal of Educational Measurement, 43*(3), 215–243.

Samejima, F. (1969). Estimation of latent ability using a response pattern of graded scores. *Psychometrika Monograph, 17*.

Sijtsma, K., & Junker, B. W. (1996). A survey of theory and methods of invariant item ordering. *British Journal of Mathematical and Statistical Psychology, 49*(1), 79–105.

Sijtsma, K., & Meijer, R. R. (2007). Nonparametric item response theory and special topics. In C. C. Rao & S. Sinharay (Eds.), *Handbook of statistics* (Vol. 26) (pp. 719–746). Amsterdam: Elsevier.

Sijtsma, K., Meijer, R.R., & van der Ark, L. A. (2011). Mokken scale analysis as time goes by: An update for scaling practitioners. *Personality and Individual Differences, 50*(1), 31–37.

Sijtsma, K., & Molenaar, I. W. (2002). *Introduction to nonparametric item response theory.* Thousand Oaks, CA: Sage Publications, Inc.

Snijders, T. A. B. (2001). Asymptotic null distribution of person fit statistics with estimated person parameter. *Psychometrika, 66*(3), 331–342.

Stout, W., Habing, B., Douglas, J., & Kim, H. R. (1996). Conditional covariance-based nonparametric multidimensionality assessment. *Applied Psychological Measurement, 20*(4), 331–354.

Straat, J. H., van der Ark, L. A., & Sijtsma, K. (2013). Methodological artifacts in dimensionality assessment of the hospital anxiety and depression scale (HADS). *Journal of Psychosomatic Research, 71*(2), 116–121.

Suárez-Falcón, J. C., & Glas, C. A. W. (2003). Evaluation of global testing procedures for item fit to the Rasch model. *British Journal of Mathematical and Statistical Psychology, 56*(1), 127–143.

Tendeiro, J. N., Meijer, R. R., Schakel, L., & Maij-de Meij, A. M. (2013). Using cumulative sum statistics to detect inconsistencies in unproctored internet testing. *Educational and Psychological Measurement, 73*(1), 143–161.

Thissen, D., Cai, L., & Bock, R. D. (2010). The nominal categories item response model. In *Handbook of polytomous item response theory models* (pp. 43–75). New York, NY: Routledge/Taylor & Francis Group.

van Abswoude, A. A. H., van der Ark, L. A., & Sijtsma K. (2004). A comparative study of test data dimensionality assessment procedures under nonparametric IRT models. *Applied Psychological Measurement, 28*(1), 3–24.

van der Ark, L. A. (2005). Stochastic Ordering of the latent trait by the sum score under various polytomous IRT models. *Psychometrika, 70*(2), 283–304.

van der Ark, L. A. (2007). Mokken scale analysis in R. *Journal of Statistical Software, 20*(11), 1–19.

van der Ark, L. A. (2012). New developments in Mokken scale analysis in R. *Journal of Statistical Software, 48*(5), 1–27.

van der Linden, W. J., & Hambleton, R. K. (Eds.). (1997). *Handbook of modern item response theory.* New York: Springer-Verlag.

van Krimpen-Stoop, E. M. L. A., & Meijer, R. R. (2001). CUSUM-based person-fit statistics for adaptive testing. *Journal of Educational and Behavioral Statistics, 26*(2), 199–218.

Warm, T. A. (1989). Weighted likelihood estimation of ability in item response theory. *Psychometrika, 54*(3), 427–450.

Weekers, A. M., & Meijer, R. R. (2008). Scaling response processes on personality items using unfolding and dominance models: An illustration with a Dutch dominance and unfolding personality inventory. *European Journal of Psychological Assessment, 24*(1), 65–77.

Yen, W. M. (1981). Using simulation results to choose a latent trait model. *Applied Psychological Measurement, 5*(2), 245–262.

Yen, W. M. (1984). Effects of local item dependence on the fit and equating performance of the three-parameter logistic model. *Applied Psychological Measurement, 8*(2), 125–145.

Zhang, J., & Stout, W. (1999). The theoretical DETECT index of dimensionality and its application to approximate simple structure. *Psychometrika, 64*(2), 213–249.

Code Appendix

Code 1 IRTPRO code for nominal response model of athletic competence.

```
Project:
    Name = SPPC Athletic Competence;

Data:
    File = .\SPPC Athletic Competence.ssig;

Analysis:
    Name = Test1;
    Mode = Calibration;
```

```
Title:
Comments:
Estimation:
    Method = BAEM;
    E-Step = 500, 1e-005;
    SE = S-EM;
    M-Step = 50, 1e-006;
    Quadrature = 49, 6;
    SEM = 0.001;
    SS = 1e-005;

Scoring:
    Mean = 0;
    SD = 1;

Miscellaneous:
    Decimal = 2;
    Processors = 4;
    Print CTLD, P-Nums, Diagnostic;
    Min Exp = 1;

Groups:

Group :
    Dimension = 1;
    Items = sp1, sp2, sp3, sp4, sp5, sp6;
    Codes(sp1) = 1(0), 2(1), 3(2), 4(3);
    Codes(sp2) = 1(0), 2(1), 3(2), 4(3);
    Codes(sp3) = 1(0), 2(1), 3(2), 4(3);
    Codes(sp4) = 1(0), 2(1), 3(2), 4(3);
    Codes(sp5) = 1(0), 2(1), 3(2), 4(3);
    Codes(sp6) = 1(0), 2(1), 3(2), 4(3);
    Model(sp1) = Nominal;
    AlphaMatrix(sp1) = Trend;
    GammaMatrix(sp1) = Trend;
    Model(sp2) = Nominal;
    AlphaMatrix(sp2) = Trend;
    GammaMatrix(sp2) = Trend;
    Model(sp3) = Nominal;
    AlphaMatrix(sp3) = Trend;
    GammaMatrix(sp3) = Trend;
    Model(sp4) = Nominal;
    AlphaMatrix(sp4) = Trend;
```

Code 2 IRTPRO code for graded response model of athletic competence.

```
Project:
    Name = SPPC Athletic Competence;

Data:
    File = .\SPPC Athletic Competence.ssig;

Analysis:
    Name = Test1;
    Mode = Calibration;

Title:
Comments:
Estimation:
    Method = BAEM;
    E-Step = 500, 1e-005;
    SE = S-EM;
    M-Step = 50, 1e-006;
    Quadrature = 49, 6;
    SEM = 0.001;
    SS = 1e-005;

Scoring:
    Mean = 0;
    SD = 1;

Miscellaneous:
    Decimal = 2;
    Processors = 4;
    Print CTLD, P-Nums, Diagnostic;
    Min Exp = 1;

Groups:

Group :
    Dimension = 1;
    Items = sp1, sp2, sp3, sp4, sp5, sp6;
    Codes(sp1) = 1(0), 2(1), 3(2), 4(3);
    Codes(sp2) = 1(0), 2(1), 3(2), 4(3);
    Codes(sp3) = 1(0), 2(1), 3(2), 4(3);
    Codes(sp4) = 1(0), 2(1), 3(2), 4(3);
    Codes(sp5) = 1(0), 2(1), 3(2), 4(3);
    Codes(sp6) = 1(0), 2(1), 3(2), 4(3);
    Model(sp1) = Graded;
    Model(sp2) = Graded;
```

```
    Model(sp3) = Graded;
    Model(sp4) = Graded;
    Model(sp5) = Graded;
    Model(sp6) = Graded;
    Mean = 0.0;
    Covariance = 1.0;

Constraints:
```

Printed in the USA/Agawam, MA
February 27, 2023

The Wiley Handbook of Psychometric Testing

The Wiley Handbook of Psychometric Testing

A Multidisciplinary Reference on Survey, Scale and Test Development

Volume Two

Edited by

Paul Irwing
Tom Booth
David J. Hughes

WILEY Blackwell

This paperback edition first published 2020
© 2018 John Wiley & Sons Ltd

All rights reserved. No part of this publication may be reproduced, stored in a retrieval system, or transmitted, in any form or by any means, electronic, mechanical, photocopying, recording or otherwise, except as permitted by law. Advice on how to obtain permission to reuse material from this title is available at http://www.wiley.com/go/permissions.

The right of Paul Irwing, Tom Booth and David J. Hughes to be identified as the authors of the editorial material in this work has been asserted in accordance with law.

Registered Offices
John Wiley & Sons, Inc., 111 River Street, Hoboken, NJ 07030, USA
John Wiley & Sons Ltd, The Atrium, Southern Gate, Chichester, West Sussex, PO19 8SQ, UK

Editorial Office
The Atrium, Southern Gate, Chichester, West Sussex, PO19 8SQ, UK

For details of our global editorial offices, customer services, and more information about Wiley products visit us at www.wiley.com.

Wiley also publishes its books in a variety of electronic formats and by print-on-demand. Some content that appears in standard print versions of this book may not be available in other formats.

Limit of Liability/Disclaimer of Warranty
While the publisher and author have used their best efforts in preparing this book, they make no representations or warranties with respect to the accuracy or completeness of the contents of this book and specifically disclaim any implied warranties of merchantability or fitness for a particular purpose. It is sold on the understanding that the publisher is not engaged in rendering professional services and neither the publisher nor the authors shall be liable for damages arising herefrom. If professional advice or other expert assistance is required, the services of a competent professional should be sought.

Library of Congress Cataloging-in-Publication Data
Names: Irwing, Paul, editor.
Title: The Wiley handbook of psychometric testing : a multidisciplinary reference
   on survey, scale and test development / edited by Paul Irwing,
   Manchester University, UK, Tom Booth, The University of Edinburgh,
   Edinburgh, UK, David J. Hughes, Manchester Business School, Manchester, UK.
Description: First Edition. | Hoboken : Wiley, 2018. | Includes bibliographical
   references and index. |
Identifiers: LCCN 2017041032 (print) | LCCN 2017061203 (ebook) |
   ISBN 9781118489826 (pdf) | ISBN 9781118489703 (epub) |
   ISBN 9781118489833 (cloth : alk. paper) | ISBN 9781119121176 (pbk. : alk. paper)
Subjects: LCSH: Psychometrics. | Psychological tests.
Classification: LCC BF39 (ebook) | LCC BF39 .W545 2018 (print) |
   DDC 150.28/7–dc23
LC record available at https://lccn.loc.gov/2017041032

Cover image: Printed with permission from Anna Brown
Cover design by Wiley

Set in 10/12pt Galliard by SPi Global, Pondicherry, India

10 9 8 7 6 5 4 3 2 1

Contents

Notes on Contributors to Volume 2   vii
Preface   xiii
Introduction   xv

VOLUME II

Part II   Identifying and Analyzing Scales (cont.)

16   Multidimensional Item Response Theory   445
     Yang Liu, Brooke Magnus, Hally O'Connor, and David Thissen

17   Bayesian Psychometric Scaling   495
     Jean-Paul Fox, Stéphanie van den Berg, and Bernard Veldkamp

18   Modelling Forced-Choice Response Formats   523
     Anna Brown and Albert Maydeu-Olivares

Part III   Scale Scoring   571

19   Scores, Scales, and Score Linking   573
     Neil J. Dorans

20   Item Response Theory Approaches to Test Scoring and Evaluating the Score Accuracy   607
     Anna Brown

21   IRT Linking and Equating   639
     Won-Chan Lee and Guemin Lee

Part IV   Evaluating Scales   675

22   Bifactor Modelling and the Evaluation of Scale Scores   677
     Steven P. Reise, Wes Bonifay, and Mark G. Haviland

23   Reliability   709
     William Revelle and David M. Condon

24	Psychometric Validity: Establishing the Accuracy and Appropriateness of Psychometric Measures *David J. Hughes*	751
25	Multitrait-Multimethod-Analysis: The Psychometric Foundation of CFA-MTMM Models *Tobias Koch, Michael Eid, and Katharina Lochner*	781

Part V Modelling Groups   847

26	Factorial Invariance Across Multiple Populations in Discrete and Continuous Data *Roger E. Millsap and Hanjoe Kim*	849
27	Differential Item and Test Functioning *Fritz Drasgow, Christopher D. Nye, Stephen Stark, and Oleksandr S. Chernyshenko*	885

Part VI Applications   901

28	Psychometric Methods in Political Science *Christopher Hare and Keith T. Poole*	903
29	How Factor Analysis Has Shaped Personality Trait Psychology *Tom Booth and Aja L. Murray*	933
30	Network Psychometrics *Sacha Epskamp, Gunter Maris, Lourens J. Waldorp, and Denny Borsboom*	953
Index		987

Notes on Contributors to Volume 2

Wes Bonifay received his Ph.D. in Quantitative Psychology in 2015 from the University of California, Los Angeles. Presently, he is an Assistant Professor in Statistics, Measurement, and Evaluation in Education at the University of Missouri. His psychometric research emphases are model evaluation and novel applications of item response theory and diagnostic classification models.

Denny Borsboom is Professor of Psychological Methods at the University of Amsterdam. His work has focused on (1) the conceptual analyses of existing psychometric models, such as the latent variable model, (2) the construction of novel psychometric theories and models, such as the network model, and (3) general methodological topics, such as promoting standards for open and reproducible research in psychology. He has published on these topics in psychological, philosophical, and psychometric journals.

Tom Booth is Lecturer in Quantitative Research Methods in the Department of Psychology, University of Edinburgh. His primary methodological interests are in generalized latent variable modelling. His applied work covers individual differences, organizational, and health psychology.

Anna Brown is Lecturer in Psychological Methods and Statistics at the University of Kent. Anna's research focuses on modelling response processes to non-cognitive assessments using multidimensional Item Response Theory (IRT). She is particularly interested in modelling preference decisions, and modelling processes contributing to response biases. Anna's key publications introduce the Thurstonian IRT model (*Item Response Modeling of Forced-Choice Questionnaires*, 2011; and *How IRT can Solve Problems of Ipsative Data in Forced-Choice Questionnaires*, 2013).

Oleksandr S. Chernyshenko received his Ph.D. in psychology from the University of Illinois at Urbana-Champaign in 2002. He is currently an Associate Professor at the Nanyang Business School in Singapore where he is conducting research and teaching courses related to talent management and personnel selection. He is an Academic Director of the Nanyang Executive MBA program and serves as an Associate Editor of *Personnel Assessment and Decisions* and *International Journal of Testing*.

David M. Condon is Assistant Professor in the Department of Medical Social Sciences at Northwestern University. His research focuses on the hierarchical structure of individual differences (including traits, interests, and cognitive abilities), psychometrics, and the application of personality in healthcare settings (especially in areas such as health literacy and patient engagement). This includes the development of tools for use in clinical settings as well as the identification of targeted intervention strategies.

Neil J. Dorans is in the Research & Development division at Educational Testing Service. Dorans was the architect for the recentered SAT scales, was involved with equating the SAT for over a quarter of a century, and performed linking studies relating the SAT to the ACT and the PAA. Editor of a book on score linking and scale aligning, he authored several articles and chapters on scaling and linking. Dorans received the NCME Career Contributions Award in 2010.

Fritz Drasgow is Dean of the School of Labor and Employment Relations and Professor of Psychology at the University of Illinois at Urbana-Champaign. His research focuses on psychological measurement, computerized testing, and personality assessment. He is a former President of the Society for Industrial and Organizational Psychology (SIOP), received the SIOP Distinguished Scientific Contributions Award in 2008, and received the 2016 Distinguished Career Award from the Academy of Management Research Method Division.

Michael Eid is Professor of Psychology at the Freie Universität Berlin. His research focuses on the development of psychometric models for multimethod and longitudinal data analysis. Moreover, he has published several articles and books on subjective well-being, emotion regulation, and health psychology.

Sacha Epskamp is an assistant professor of Psychological Methods at the University of Amsterdam. His work focuses on the estimation of network models in psychological datasets and the application of such models in psychometrics; network psychometrics. Sacha Epskamp publishes both technical advances and introductory tutorials to network psychometrics in addition to developing and maintaining several free to use software packages.

Jean-Paul Fox is Professor at the Department of Research Methodology, Measurement and Data Analysis, at the University of Twente, the Netherlands. He is a researcher in the area of Bayesian item response modelling and author of the monograph Bayesian Item Response Modeling published in 2010. He is known for his work on multilevel IRT modelling, where a multilevel survey design is integrated in the psychometric model. He received the 2001 Psychometric Association Dissertation award for his work on multilevel IRT modelling. He received two personal grants from the Netherlands Organisation for Scientific Research to develop psychometric models for large-scale survey research.

Christopher Hare is an assistant professor of political science at the University of California, Davis. His research focuses on the use of measurement and machine learning techniques to analyze ideology and mass political behavior. He is the coauthor of *Analyzing Spatial Models of Choice and Judgment in R*, and has published work in the *American Journal of Political Science*, *Politics and Religion*, and *Social Science Quarterly*.

Mark G. Haviland is a professor of psychiatry and basic sciences at the Loma Linda University School of Medicine and director of research in the department of psychiatry. His research interests include the consequences of traumatic stress; notably, emotion regulation deficits. He has developed and evaluated observer measures with both Q and R methodology and published theoretical and psychometric chapters and articles with Dr. Steven Reise on item response theory and bifactor model applications.

David J. Hughes is an Organisational Psychologist at Manchester Business School. His research interests center on individual differences and can be broken down into three main areas: The theory and measurement of individual differences, individual differences at work, and individual differences in financial behavior. He is interested in psychometric test evaluation and his statistical interests revolve around generalized latent variable models, in particular structural equation modelling, factor models, and other models appropriate for multivariate data with complex structures.

Hanjoe Kim is a Ph.D. candidate at Arizona State University expected to defend his dissertation in Spring 2017. His interest is in quantitative methods including survival analysis, mediation analysis, measurement invariance, and causal inference (causal mediation and propensity score analysis). He is also interested in applying these methods to prevention-intervention research. Hanjoe Kim was one of Roger Millsap's last students.

Tobias Koch is currently Assistant Professor in the Center for Methods at the Leuphana University Lüneburg, Lüneburg, Germany. He received his Ph.D. at the Freie University Berlin in 2013. The title of his dissertation is "Multilevel-structural equation modeling of multitrait-multimethod-multioccasion data." His research interests include measurement theory and psychometrics, multitrait-multimethod analysis, structural equation modeling, multilevel analysis, longitudinal data analysis, and simulation studies.

Guemin Lee is a professor in the Department of Education in the College of Education at Yonsei University. He received his bachelor's and master's degrees from Yonsei University and his doctorate from the University of Iowa. He worked as a Research Associate at Iowa Testing Programs from 1998–1999, as a Research Scientist at CTB/McGraw-Hill from 1999–2002, and as a professor at Keimyung University from 2002–2006. Dr. Lee's research interests include scaling, equating, college admission testing, generalizability, and item response theories.

Won-Chan Lee is a professor of Psychological and Quantitative Foundations in the College of Education at the University of Iowa. He is also the Director of the Center for Advanced Studies in Measurement and Assessment. Dr. Lee received his doctorate from the University of Iowa in 1998. He worked as a Research Associate at ACT from 1999–2003. Dr. Lee's research addresses scaling, linking, equating, and test theories.

Yang Liu is a is a graduate in quantitative psychology from the Department of Psychology and Neuroscience at the University of North Carolina and the L. L. Thurstone Psychometric Laboratory, where he was when this chapter was written. He is now an assistant professor in the Department of Psychology at the University of California, Merced, CA, USA; e-mail: yliu85@ucmerced.edu. His research interests include psychometrics, item response theory, and categorical data analysis.

Katharina Lochner is the Head of Research and Development for the *cut-e* Group. She has a degree in work and organizational psychology from RWTH Aachen University, a doctorate in psychology from the Freie Universität Berlin and over 10 years' experience working with clients in Europe and Asia Pacific. Within *cut-e*, she connects research with the practice of work and organizational psychology.

Brooke Magnus is a graduate in quantitative psychology from the Department of Psychology and Neuroscience at the University of North Carolina and the L. L. Thurstone Psychometric Laboratory, where she was when this chapter was written. She is now an assistant professor in the Department of Psychology at Marquette University, Milwaukee, W, USAI; e-mail: brooke.magnus@marquette.edu. Her research interests include the development of statistical methods for the analysis of item response data from tests, surveys, and questionnaires, and the use of tests and questionnaires in practice.

Gunter Maris is Professor of Psychological Methods at the University of Amsterdam, and Principal Research Scientist at CITO. His research focuses on psychometric models of and for learning and education. The research ranges from topics such as formal characterization and equivalent representation, to the development of statistical tools for doing inference on such models. Gunter Maris publishes on these topics in general science, psychology, and psychometric journals.

Albert Maydeu-Olivares is Professor of Psychology at the University of South Carolina and former president of the Psychometric Society. He has received the American Psychological Association (Division 5) dissertation award, the Catalan Young Investigator award, and the Society of Multivariate Experimental Psychology Young Investigator (Cattell) award. He is currently an editor of Psychometrika. He has edited the volumes *Contemporary Psychometrics* (Lawrence Erlbaum, 2005), and the H*andbook of Quantitative Methods in Psychology* (Sage, 2009).

Roger E. Millsap (1954–2014) was a professor at Arizona State University and a distinguished scholar in psychometrics especially known for his work in measurement invariance. His work in measurement invariance is compiled into a book entitled *Statistical Approaches to Measurement Invariance* (Millsap, 2011). Roger Millsap still lives in the hearts of his beloved wife Michelle and four children, Mason, Laura, Simone, and Aiden.

Aja L. Murray is Research Associate in the Violence Research Centre, Institute of Criminology, University of Cambridge. Her research interests include psychometrics and childhood and adolescent mental health developmental.

Christopher D. Nye received his Ph.D. from the University of Illinois in Urbana-Champaign and is currently an Assistant Professor of Organizational Psychology at Michigan State University. His research primarily involves personnel selection and assessment, individual differences, and organizational research methods. He has published a number of scholarly articles and/or chapters on these topics and has received awards from the Society for Industrial and Organizational Psychology and the International Personnel Assessment Council for his work.

Hally O'Connor is a is a graduate in quantitative psychology from the Department of Psychology and Neuroscience at the University of North Carolina and the L. L.

Thurstone Psychometric Laboratory, where she was when this chapter was written. She is now a psychometrician at the Camber Corporation, Orlando, FL, USA; e-mail: hallyoconnor@gmail.com. Her research interests include psychological testing, measurement, and item response theory.

Keith T. Poole holds the Philip H. Alston Jr. Distinguished Chair as a professor of political science at the University of Georgia. His research interests include methodology, political-economic history of American institutions, and the political-economic history of railroads. He was a Fellow of the Center for Advanced Study in Behavioral Sciences 2003–2004 and was elected to the American Academy of Arts and Sciences in 2006. Poole received the Political Methodology Career Achievement Award in 2016.

Steven P. Reise received his Ph.D. in Psychology in 1990 from the University of Minnesota and is presently a professor in the Department of Psychology at the University of California, Los Angeles. Dr. Reise's interests include the application of item response theory and structural equation modelling, as well as the development and application of person-fit indices. Dr. Reise has a long-standing research interest in the role bifactor models play in the psychometric analysis of psychological measures.

William Revelle is a professor of psychology at Northwestern University. As a personality psychologist, his interests range from the biological bases to computational models of personality as means to understand the sources and consequences of individual differences in temperament, cognitive ability, and interests. He is particularly interested in applying quantitative methods to studying psychological phenomena and is the author of the psych package in R.

Stephen Stark is Professor of Psychology at the University of South Florida. He teaches courses on measurement and personnel selection, and his research focuses on differential item functioning, computerized adaptive testing, and multidimensional forced-choice models for noncognitive assessment. He is a Fellow of the Society of Industrial and Organizational Psychology and the American Psychological Association, a member of the editorial board for *Applied Psychological measurement*, and Editor of the *International Journal of Testing*.

David Thissen is a professor of quantitative psychology in the Department of Psychology and Neuroscience at the University of North Carolina and the L. L. Thurstone Psychometric Laboratory, The University of North Carolina, Chapel Hill, NC, USA; e-mail: dthissen@email.unc.edu. His research interests include psychological testing, measurement, and item response theory.

Lourens J. Waldorp works at the Psychological Department of the University of Amsterdam. His interests include networks and their properties, especially in the area of percolation, dynamics, and phase transitions. He has also developed non-asymptotic techniques to determine properties of networks in estimation and dynamics. In terms of applications, he has developed analysis techniques for model selection and algorithms for estimation in model misspecification in the areas of signal analysis (EEG/MEG), brain imaging data (fMRI), and psychopathology.

Stéphanie van den Berg is an international expert on psychometric models specially tailored to twin research and genetics. The models, most of them either multilevel or mega-level item-response models, are usually estimated using Gibbs sampling and are particularly suited to distinguish between measurement error variance and environmental (nongenetic) variance. She also specializes on data harmonization (test linking) in large research consortia.

Bernard Veldkamp is Head of the Department of Research Methodology, Measurement and Data Analysis at University of Twente. He specializes in research methodology and data analytics. His interests focus on optimization, text mining, and computer-based assessment. His work spans a range of issues, from the development of new methods/models for the design and construction of (adaptive) psychological and educational tests, to the development of data mining models for application in social analytics.

Preface

The existence of this volume owes itself to both opportunity, and many hours of coffee fuelled conversation, the general form of which would run; "have you seen X's critique of Y…? Did you see the special issue on X…? Wouldn't it be great if we could do something to help improve methods knowledge within psychology?" Given our collective interest in individual difference psychology, our musings would often be triggered by a favourite conversation – the inappropriate application of principal components analysis. We all taught, and continue to teach, research methods and statistics at our institutions; we all develop and evaluate psychometrics in our research, but the idea of something larger – a conference, a journal special edition, a book – continued to surface. There are many excellent papers, books, and courses that cover research methods relevant for psychometrics but, we thought, not a single resource that brings cutting-edge knowledge from the journals in our fields together in an accessible manner.

So, imagine our delight and trepidation when Paul was invited to edit a handbook on psychometric testing. We could finally put our coffee-shop "wisdom" to the test! Although, "Who reads books anymore? Surely, it will be a ton of work editing such a volume? Come to think of it, we're not knowledgeable enough in half of the areas we need to cover… How will we ensure we get expert authors?" We had many questions and doubts and committing to producing this book was not a lightly taken decision. Nevertheless, we returned consistently to one question: how else can we do our small part in improving the availability of cutting-edge methodological knowledge within the field of psychometrics? We had decided (or at least Tom and David had, Paul took some convincing!) that together we would try to produce a book which covered the core topics in psychometrics, a book that harnessed the work of excellent authors, a book that we would like to have, a book that, if used, would see methodological awareness grow, and statistical practice improve.

At the outset of planning and preparing this book, all three of us were at the University of Manchester's Business School; Tom and David were Ph.D. students, and Paul, our supervisor, a Reader of Organisational Psychology. At the time of writing this preface, almost five years later, Ph.Ds are a distant memory, Tom and David have moved on several times (or moved on and then back to Manchester in David's case), and Paul is now a professor. This book, *The Handbook*, has been a labour of love and frustration throughout these five years, five years that have not only seen workplace changes but also a quite remarkable series of injuries and ill-health, several relegations for our relative football (soccer) teams, oh, and a wedding!

Now, here we are, a complete volume that looks remarkably close to our initial proposal and we are delighted with it. Our intention, succinctly described in the letters we sent to authors was to write chapters on key topics in psychometrics and that:

> Each chapter should cover the fundamentals. However, we favour a three-tiered approach, which covers: (1) historical and standard approaches, including all the core material, and then moves onto (2) a discussion of cutting-edge issues and techniques, together with a section on (3) how to do it, which should contain a worked example. These chapters should address real issues faced by both practitioners and researchers.

We hope with the help of our contributors that we have achieved our goal. We hope that a journey started with coffee-shop musings and reflections has led to the production of a useful resource for students, academics, and practitioners alike.

The biggest strength of *The Handbook* undoubtedly lies in the calibre of the authors who have contributed. Every chapter (modestly, with the exception of our own!) has been written by a field expert with specialist knowledge whose work we have admired and used to inform our own practice. Not only are our authors experts, they are also diverse with regard to nationality (e.g., Netherlands, U.K., U.S.A.), profession (e.g., academics, commercial test developers), and field (e.g., psychology, statistics, education, politics). This diversity was no accident. Approaching the topic of psychometrics from the perspective of one discipline would never showcase the range of theoretical and statistical advances that we hoped to convey to our readers. We wish to say a very large thank you to each and every author for sharing their expertise and for their patience throughout this process.

Beyond our excellent contributors, we would also like to acknowledge the help of our families, friends, and students, for their willingness to put up with constant references and sometimes play second fiddle to *The Handbook* over the last few years. Finally, we would also like to extend our deep gratitude to all the people at John Wiley & Sons who have helped us in this process (and there have been many).

Thank you all, and thank you to you as readers for picking this book up off the shelf. We hope it is useful.

David, Tom, and Paul.

Introduction

Aims and Scope

The principal aim of this Handbook was to provide researchers and practitioners from different academic and applied fields with a single practical resource covering the core aspects of psychometric testing. Psychometrics can be translated as mental measurement, however, the implication that psychometrics is confined to psychology is highly misleading. Virtually every conceivable discipline now uses questionnaires, scales, and tests developed from psychometric principles, and this book is therefore intended for a multidisciplinary audience. The field of psychometrics is vibrant with new and useful methods and approaches published frequently. Many of these new developments use increasingly sophisticated models and software packages that are easy to misunderstand. We have strived to make the chapters in this Handbook both intellectually stimulating, and practically useful, through the discussion of historical perspectives, cutting-edge developments, and providing practical illustrations with example code. Thus, each chapter provides an accessible account and example of the current state-of-the-art within the core elements of psychometric testing. We hope that this book is useful for those who develop, evaluate, and use psychometric tests.

Section and Chapter Structure

In structuring the chapters and sections of this Handbook, we attempted to approximate the process of test development. In Part I, the chapters cover core topics surrounding the foundations of test development. Here, we provide a macro view of the process of test development (Chapter 1); outline the broad differences in the classical and modern test theory approaches (Chapter 2); broach topics of the development and nature of item sets (Chapters 3 and 7); and address fundamental topics in study design (Chapters 4, 5, and 6). Chapter 1 is probably the most logical place to start, since this provides a context for most of the other chapters as to their role in test development.

In Part II, we consider the primary psychometric tools for analyzing item pools and identifying plausible scales. Here, we consider the fundamentals of both the common factor (Chapters 8, 10, 11, and 12) and item response (15 and 16) approaches. Chapter 9 sits somewhat at the intersection of the classic and modern test approaches in discussing estimation of categorical item factor models. Part II also provides introductory coverage of multidimensional scaling (MDS: Chapter 14), which has been a highly influential psychometric tool in fields such as political science (see Chapter 28), but is less commonly used in psychometric evaluations in fields such as psychology. The remaining chapters in Part II deal with a number of slightly more advanced, but highly important topics. These chapters address nonnormality (Chapter 13), Bayesian approaches to scaling (Chapter 17) and the modelling of forced choice item formats (Chapter 18). Each of these chapters covers something of an "up and coming" area of psychometrics based upon advancements in computation that now allow us to model more complex data appropriately (as opposed to forcing data into models which presuppose unmet assumptions). Chapter 18, which covers forced choice items, is also particularly valuable for those who test in high-stakes scenarios (i.e., employee selection).

Part III addresses the topic of test scores and also deals with the process of linking and equating test scores. The purpose of psychometric tools is more often than not to understand where someone stands on a given latent trait versus other individuals. Often, we desire scores to represent this standing. Here then, we deal with fundamental topics in score estimation and evaluation, from simple sum scores to advanced item response estimates (Chapters 19 and 20). But what happens when we develop a new version of a test? Or we attempt to develop parallel forms? Or we want to try and relate individuals who have taken different tests? These needs are very common in both applied and academic analyses in education, business, and psychology, and all are concerned with the topic of score linking and equating (Chapters 19 and 21).

Part IV is concerned with the evaluation of scales from a statistical and theoretical perspective. Chapters 23 and 24 provide state of the art treatments of the classic topics of reliability and validity, respectively. Chapter 22 concerns the evaluation of the strength of general and specific factors using bi-factor models. Chapter 25 uses multi-trait-multimethod analyses to explore the proportion of measured variance attributable to the construct and the measurement tool.

So, we have developed some items, collected some data, established our best set of measured constructs, and evaluated the quality of the scales. But does our test operate in the same way for all groups of people? This question is critically important for reasons of accuracy and fairness and can be approached through the application of the analytic methods discussed in Part V. Here, we deal with tools for modelling and understanding the measurement properties of psychometric tools across groups from a common factor (Chapter 26) and item response (Chapter 27) perspective.

Finally, in Part VI, we step away from topics related to the immediate development of tests, and we consider the role psychometrics has played, and may play in the future, in theoretical and practical arenas. In Chapters 28 and 29, we consider the substantial role psychometric tools and analyses have played in shaping the fields of political science and personality psychology. Lastly, we introduce recent work concerning the relationship between network and latent variable approaches to understanding behavior (Chapter 30). Both Chapters 29 and 30 provide critical appraisals of analytic tools common to the psychometrics world (i.e., factor analysis) and point the way to potential avenues of progress. Reviewing the contributions of psychometric testing and considering how future Handbooks of Psychometric Testing might look felt like a fitting way to close this volume.

Mathematical and Statistical Foundations

Our aim for this Handbook was to make the content as accessible as possible for as many individuals as possible, both practitioners and academics. You do not need to be a mathematician or statistician to read this book. Equations are kept to the minimum required to provide satisfactory explanations of the methods under discussion. Where equations are presented by authors, they are broken down and described verbally to add clarity.

However, it would be remiss of us as editors to try and claim that this handbook is going to be an easy read for all who pick it up. The topic under discussion is statistical and thus there is some technical content. The degree of technical content varies across chapters inline with the mathematical complexity of the topics discussed.

So, what statistical and mathematical knowledge is required? With regard to statistics, we have assumed certain background knowledge. Modern psychometrics depends, amongst other things, on knowledge of structural equation modelling (SEM), and in particular confirmatory factor analysis (CFA). However, both of these are already covered by many excellent texts. For example, the early chapters in Little (2013) provide an excellent introduction to both topics, while Brown (2015) provides arguably one of the most useful comprehensive treatments of CFA, and Bollen (1989) still represents the most definitive advanced treatment of both. SEM depends on an understanding of multiple regression. Probably one of the best and most neglected books on regression is Pedhazur (1997), which in fact provides a comprehensive coverage of everything you need to know about the basics of multivariate statistics.

With regards to mathematics knowledge, to understand the methods conceptually and use the practical examples as guides to analyze your own data, not very much is required. But to appreciate fully the topics under discussion here, a basic knowledge of calculus, algebra, and perhaps most importantly, matrix algebra (e.g., Fieller, 2015; Khuri & Searle, 2017) is required. It would also be valuable, as is true for any statistical topic, for readers to have some grounding in probability and significance testing. A number of chapters also extend into Bayesian statistics where a slightly deeper appreciation of probability theory may be necessary (DeGroot & Schervish, 2012). Chapter 17 contains a short introduction to concepts from Bayesian analysis, but this is intended more as a refresher than as a comprehensive treatment of the fundamental of Bayes. In terms of a comprehensive and accessible introduction to mathematical statistics Larsen and Marx (2011) is hard to better.

We have resisted the temptation to provide introductory chapters or appendices on these core statistical and mathematical topics for two reasons. First, there are a multitude of high quality introductory texts on these topics (see previously). It is also important to point out that there are now a huge number of excellent (and free) web resources on these topics, and the reader who feels they need a refresher is encouraged to explore this route (no need to spend money unnecessarily) whilst bearing in mind that finding the right mathematics or statistics text is often a personal thing. Second, the Handbook is intended to have a diverse target audience whose needs will vary greatly. To cover each of these topics, for a diverse audience, would have required us to turn what is already a large book, into a behemoth perfectly suited to act as doorstop for the *Black Gate of Mordor*.

Software

The contributors to the Handbook have made use of a variety of different statistical software packages, some freely available, others proprietary. The two most popular tools across chapters are the R statistical programming language and MPlus. R has a large number of advantages as a statistical tool, the details of which we will not get into here. However, perhaps the two most commonly cited and important are that it is free, and it is highly flexible. However, with this flexibility comes a requirement for some knowledge of programming and coding languages – with great power comes great responsibility.

In recent years, MPlus has established itself as one of the primary proprietary tools for conducting general latent variable analyses, quickly incorporating new methodologies, providing excellent help facilities and abundant online resources. MPlus is again a flexible tool that is very user-friendly. However, the program does come at a cost, with a full single user license for University affiliates costing approximately £720 ($895) at the time of writing.

Popular general-purpose statistical packages such as SPSS, SAS, or STATA, are used, but less frequently. This is not to say that these packages have no capability with respect to the types of analysis discussed in this Handbook but often they do lack some of the nuances needed to conduct state of the art analyses. This is perhaps the reason that authors have also made use of a variety of additional programs including, MIRT, *flex*MIRT, IRTPro, Factor, LISREL, EQS, MATLAB, WinBUGS, and more. What this shows is the huge variety and widespread availability of tools for empirical analysis.

So, which software should you use? In making this decision, one of the key things to consider is which models are best suited to which software. We hope the Handbook helps in this endeavor in two ways. First, our empirical examples show directly some of what can be done in certain packages. Second, we hope the level of presentation of the technical details of analyses will allow the readers to tackle the supporting documentation of software to gain a deeper understanding of what is going on "under the hood."

The available tools vary in a number of other ways, too. For example, the means by which analyses are conducted varies from coding languages (both program-specific and general) to graphical user interfaces with and without diagrammatical capabilities. Whilst drop-down menus are great, we would recommend writing code. Not only does this clarify understanding but it also allows you to specify all modelling options rather than resting on software defaults. Perhaps the most pragmatically relevant variation lies in monetary cost, and many readers will likely be limited to proprietary software available from their institutions or freely available software. Thankfully, for scientific progress, more tools than ever are now free! Indeed, more than a third of our chapters used free software and every analysis presented in this handbook could be conducted in this manner, which we will now discuss.

Chapter Code

For a majority of the chapters in this handbook, software code has been made available for the analyses, and some of the figures, presented in the chapters. In most cases, this is in the form of a Code Appendix at the end of the chapter. For a smaller subset of chapters, the code has been integrated into the body of the chapter. Chapter dependent, the detail of code provided varies, as does the level of annotation but in each case, it directly links to the practical examples presented.

Some chapters have made use of proprietary software, which if the reader does not have access to, obviously limits its usability. Here we wish to emphasize once again the abundance of freely available software for psychometric analyses. With very few exceptions, the analyses presented in this book can be conducted using a relatively limited number of R-packages. For those unfamiliar with R, we would strongly recommend investing some time to learn the basics of the program.

The packages *psych* (Revelle, 2016), *mirt* (Chalmers, 2012), *OpenMx* (Neale, et al. 2016; Pritikin, Hunter, & Boker, 2015; Boker et al., 2017), and *lavaan* (Rosseel, 2012), can be used to complete a vast majority of the common factor and IRT analyses presented in this Handbook. Other useful packages include *qgrpah* (Epskamp, Cramer, Waldorp, Schittmann, & Borsboom, 2012) for network models and plots, *smacof* (de Leeuw, & Mair, 2009) for multidimensional scaling, *rjags* (Plummer, 2016) for Bayesian analysis, and *mice* (van Buuren & Groothuis-Oudshoorn, 2011) for missing data analysis. Collectively, we hope that the code provided and access to the free R packages noted makes the Handbook a genuinely valuable practical tool.

How to Use the Book

As has been outlined here, this Handbook has been compiled with multiple audiences in mind and as such we anticipate the contents to be used in a variety of ways. Coarsely, our section structure can be seen as representing the process of developing and evaluating a psychometric test. Read from start to finish the chapters represent a comprehensive introduction to the process of test development, analysis, and revision. Readers interested in evaluating an extant scale for which they have collected some data will, dependent on their focus, find most value in the contents of sections two through four. Here we suggest that the readers treat the chapters and the associated reference lists as the start point for in depth consideration of a topic. Whilst we cover historical perspectives, state-of-the-art methods, and provide practical examples and code, the chapters of this handbook do not contain everything one might need to know.

In either case, whether a reader is interested in the start to finish process of scale development, or in methods for a specific purpose, the chapter content allows the reader to focus on either classical (common factor) or modern (IRT) approaches to most questions. For the reader unsure of which approach they wish to take, we would encourage them to read Chapter 2, and to consider their research focus in light of the type of information each approach has to offer. In some cases, this is overlapping, in others complementary, and so the choice is not always clear cut. Equally, whilst positioned towards the end of the book, Chapter 24, might be an interesting place to start because the treatment of "validity" aims to provide a coherent model to organize test development and evaluation procedures and references out to other chapters wherever relevant.

Practical hands on experience is a valuable part of the learning process. We hope that the code provided and the information on different software packages will provide a framework that will allow readers to apply analyses to their own data. The code is not a tutorial, and some knowledge of the different statistical packages will be needed.

We hope the Handbook is enjoyable and useful. Enjoy.

References

Boker, S. M., Neale, M. C., Maes, H. H., Wilde, M. J., Spiegel, M., Brick, T. R., ...& Manjunath, B. G. (2017) *OpenMx 2.7.12 user guide*. Available at http://openmx.psyc.virginia.edu/docs/OpenMx/latest/OpenMxUserGuide.pdf (accessed October 2017).

Bollen, K. A. (1989). *Structural equations with latent variables*. New York: John Wiley & Sons, Inc.

Brown, T. A. (2015). *Confirmatory factor analysis for applied research* (2nd ed.). New York, NY: The Guilford Press.

Chalmers, P. R. (2012). mirt: A multidimensional item response theory package for the R environment. *Journal of Statistical Software*, 48, 1–29. URL http://www.jstatsoft.org/v48/i06/ (accessed October 2017).

DeGroot, M. H., & Schervish, M. J. (2012). *Probability and statistics*. Boston, MA: Pearson Education.

de Leeuw, J., & Mair, P. (2009). Multidimensional scaling using majorization: SMACOF in R. *Journal of Statistical Software*, 31, 1–30. URL http://www.jstatsoft.org/v31/i03/ (accessed October 2017).

Epskamp, S., Cramer, A. O. J., Waldorp, L. J., Schmittmann, V. D., & Borsboom, D. (2012). qgraph: Network visualizations of relationships in psychometric data. *Journal of Statistical Software*, 48, 1–18. URL http://www.jstatsoft.org/v48/i04/ (accessed October 2017).

Fieller, N. (2015). *Basics of matrix algebra for statistics with R*. Boca Raton, FL: Chapman Hall/CRC.

Khuri, A. I., & Searle, S. R. (2017). *Matrix algebra useful for statistics* (2nd ed.). Chichester, UK: Wiley-Blackwell.

Larsen, R. J., & Marx, M. L. (2011). *An introduction to mathematical statistics and its applications* (5th ed.). Boston, MA: Pearson Education.

Little, T. D. (2013). *Longitudinal structural equation modeling*. New York, NJ: The Guilford Press.

Neale, M. C., Hunter, M. D., Pritikin, J. N., Zahery, M., Brick, T. R., Kickpatrick, R. M... and Boker, S. M. (2016). OpenMx 2.0: Extended structural equation and statistical modeling. *Psychometrika*, 80, 535–549.

Pedhazur, E. J. (1997). *Multiple regression in behavioral research* (3rd ed.). Boston, MA: Wadsworth.

Plummer, M. (2016). rjags: bayesian graphical models using MCMC. R package version 4-6. https://CRAN.R-project.org/package=rjags (accessed October 2017).

Pritikin, J. N., Hunter, M. D., & Boker, S. M. (2015). Modular open-source software for Item Factor Analysis. *Educational and Psychological Measurement*, 75, 458–474.

Revelle, W. (2016) *psych: Procedures for personality and psychological research*, Northwestern University, Evanston, IL, USA, https://CRAN.R-project.org/package=psych Version = 1.6.12.

Rosseel, Y. (2012). lavaan: An R package for structural equation modeling. *Journal of Statistical Software*, 48, 1–36. URL http://www.jstatsoft.org/v48/i02/ (accessed October 2017).

van Buuren, S., & Groothuis-Oudshoorn, K. (2011). mice: Multivariate imputation by chained equations in R. *Journal of Statistical Software*, 45, 1–67. URL http://www.jstatsoft.org/v45/i03/ (accessed October 2017).

The Wiley Handbook of Psychometric Testing

16

Multidimensional Item Response Theory

Yang Liu, Brooke Magnus, Hally O'Connor, and David Thissen[1]

Multidimensional Item Response Theory

The discussion of item response theory (IRT) in previous chapters assumes unidimensionality among test items, which means that a single latent variable underlies the probability of item responses. Researchers interested in elucidating thought processes and investigating cognitive abilities often use IRT models to measure multiple unobserved variables (i.e., attitudes, abilities, proficiencies, etc.). Unidimensional IRT is not able to model the full complexity of these phenomena. In addition, it has been argued that "every test and every set of responses by real individuals is multidimensional to some degree" (Harrison, 1986, p. 91). Some have gone so far as to state that "the assumption that a single common latent variable explains item response data (unidimensionality) is a convenient fiction" (Reise, Bonifay, & Haviland, 2013, p. 136). Such observations have motivated the development of multidimensional item response theory (MIRT) models, which may provide more informative solutions than can be obtained using unidimensional IRT methods.

Contemporary MIRT is a convergence of developments from two psychometric traditions, test theory and factor analysis. In early descriptions of item response models for test theory, Lord and Novick (1978, pp. 359–360) and Samejima (1974, p. 111) defined IRT models on the "complete latent space," with a multidimensional latent variable. However, at that time, no use was made of the multidimensional idea except in Lord and Novick's (1968, pp. 371–373) algebraic description of the relation between the normal ogive model and a unidimensional factor analysis of tetrachoric correlations among dichotomous item responses. In the factor-analytic tradition, McDonald (1967, 1982), Christoffersson (1975), and Muthén (1978) described alternative methods for the factor analysis of dichotomous variables, which they observed is the same as fitting a (potentially) multidimensional normal ogive item response model. Those factor-analytic approaches are referred to as **limited information** methods because they only make use of bivariate relations among the items, summarized in item i by item j two-by-two tables of response frequencies, or a matrix of tetrachoric correlations. During the

---

[1] The order of authors is alphabetical. We are grateful to Alberto Maydeu-Olivares for providing the data used in the example.

same period, in the test theory literature, Bock and Aitkin (1981) provided the first practical, general method to obtain **full-information** maximum likelihood estimates of the parameters of item response models, using all of the information available in the item response data. Bock and Aitkin's illustrations included both unidimensional and multidimensional examples; soon thereafter, Bock, Gibbons, and Muraki (1988) described a general purpose algorithm for exploratory item factor analysis using full-information parameter estimation.

In the 1980s and 1990s, Reckase and his collaborators provided extensive theoretical analysis of the meanings and uses of the parameters of MIRT models; Reckase (1997, 2007, 2009) summarizes this work. In the past two decades, application of MIRT models has become practical due to a combination of the inexorable increase in electronic computing speed and power, new extensions of IRT parameter estimation algorithms to bifactor models and two-tier models (Cai, 2010c; Cai, Yang, & Hansen, 2011; Gibbons & Hedeker, 1992; Gibbons et al., 2007), and estimation algorithms for increasing numbers of underlying dimensions (Cai, 2010a, 2010b; Edwards, 2010; Schilling & Bock, 2005). Assembly of all of these developments into contemporary software makes it practical to analyze data based on MIRT. Modern software packages for parameter estimation for MIRT models include IRTPRO (Cai, Thissen, & du Toit, 2011), flexMIRT (Cai, 2013), and EQSIRT (Multivariate Software, 2010); MPlus (Muthén & Muthén, 2012) also implements some full-information estimation methods for some models in addition to its procedures for structural equation modeling.

Compensatory and noncompensatory models

The previously described historical development of multidimensional item response models yields **compensatory** item response models. Similar to the factor analysis of continuous variables, the observed response depends on a linear combination of the values of the latent variables through some link function, so the model is compensatory in the sense that an increase in any of the factor scores is related to an increase in the response, and many combinations of underlying scores are associated with high responses. For items that are indicators of more than one factor, the combination rule for a positive response is that the respondent may be high on one factor **or** another factor.

Sympson (1978) suggested an alternative model formulation based on the idea that an item response may depend on two or more latent variables, and both (or all) must be high to observe a positive response. As a hypothetical example, Sympson (1978) described a word problem on a mathematics test, for which both verbal and mathematics proficiency must be high to produce a correct response: sufficient verbal proficiency to read the item **and** sufficient mathematics proficiency to do the required computation. Sympson's (1978) model involves the multiplication of probabilities in place of the linear combination of compensatory models; such multiplicative models have been called **noncompensatory** models, although Reckase (2009, p. 79) uses the term **partially compensatory**.

Among noncompensatory models, Embretson (1997) summarizes research on the General Component Latent Trait Model (GLTM; Embretson, 1984), a generalization of the Multicomponent Latent Trait Model (MLTM; Whitely, 1980); these models are designed for cognitive items with **components** or **subtasks**, all of which must be completed for a correct response. Thissen-Roe and Thissen (2013) describe a **two-decision model** for Likert-type responses in contexts in which individual differences in a tendency to select extreme alternatives may be one of the factors underlying the response; that model is also multiplicative in form, and noncompensatory in nature.

Noncompensatory models are mentioned for completeness; the remainder of this chapter describes compensatory MIRT models, because they are in widespread general use. Noncompensatory (or partially compensatory) models have generally been developed for some very specific item types in some equally specific testing context. While such specialized models may often be more useful in their context, they are not intended for general purpose item analysis.

Factors and local dependence – Constructs at different levels of generality

Between- versus within-item multidimensionality Two types of multidimensionality, between-item and within-item multidimensionality, have different consequences for test assembly and scoring; the distinction is based on the number of constructs an item measures. If each item measures a single construct, but multiple constructs are measured by the set of items as a whole, there is between-item multidimensionality. Between-item multidimensionality may be illustrated with two questions on the Eysenck's Personality Questionnaire-Revised (EPQ-R; Eysenck, et al., 1985), "Are you a talkative person?" and "Are you a worrier?" The first question is about sociability and measures extraversion whereas the second question is about anxiety and measures neuroticism; each question assesses a single latent variable. If a single item reflects variation on more than one underlying construct, it exhibits within-item multidimensionality. An example of within-item multidimensionality can also be found on the EPQ-R: "Do you enjoy co-operating with others?" Cooperation involves both being considerate and interacting with another person, so that item measures both psychoticism (reverse scored) and extraversion. Mathematical word problems may be another instance of within-item multidimensionality. Both reading and quantitative abilities are necessary for such questions.[2]

Planned versus unintentional factor structure The conceptual prototype for a multidimensional test or questionnaire is one that is planned or intended to measure individual differences on more than one dimension. An example that provides the basis for the empirical illustration described later in this chapter is the EPQ-R, with scales intended to measure extraversion, neuroticism, and psychoticism. Other examples include health outcomes measures intended to measure depression, anxiety, and anger as distinct, but correlated, factors of emotional distress; or, in educational settings, measures of verbal and mathematical proficiency on an admissions test; or the subscales of an intelligence test. Using the kinds of contemporary technology discussed in this chapter, planned multidimensionality is relatively easy to analyze using MIRT models. There tend to be few planned factors, each represented by many items, and the way in which the items

---

[2] Although mathematical word problems were the original inspiration for noncompensatory models, compensatory models have often been used to analyze data arising from tests comprising such items. It may be the case that the distinction between reading ability and mathematical proficiency is somewhat blurry, and in fact the two can compensate over some range of problems.

are matched with each of the several dimensions is known a priori; those features combine to make MIRT models easy to fit.

However, a test or questionnaire intended to measure one dimension, or just a few, may have item clusters that are indicators for other factors that are not the intended targets of measurement. Thissen and Steinberg (2010, p. 123) observed that "Psychological constructs, or latent variables ... may have different scopes or levels of generality"; unintentionally-measured factors may have low levels of generality. The idea of levels of generality is illustrated by a reading comprehension test comprising blocks of questions following passages; the passages must each have some topic – in an example discussed by Thissen and Steinberg (2010), that originated with Thissen, Steinberg, and Mooney (1989), four passages were from the fields of history, biology, literature, and earth science. To varying degrees, MIRT analysis reveals four somewhat distinct dimensions of individual differences for reading proficiency for the four passages; those factors may be associated with differential competence in the disciplines. However, it is unlikely that one wants several distinct reading comprehension scores, by discipline, from an admissions test; a single, more general, aggregate measure of reading proficiency is desired. Thus, although latent variables measuring discipline-specific reading skills may be needed to fit the data, they are not the dimensions of interest. The influence of undesired dimensions of individual differences on test items is referred to as **local dependence** (LD), because it represents a violation of the assumption of conditional independence of item responses that is the basis of any (M)IRT model. The dependence is **local** because it appears even within a narrow ("local") range on the primary factor(s).

Passage factors on reading comprehension tests, or more generally, factors associated with stimuli that are the basis for clusters of items on any test, are examples of content-based LD. Content-based LD may also arise when pairs or small clusters of items on social, personality, or health outcomes questionnaires use very similar wording to ask questions that are only slightly different. Indeed, Thissen, Reeve, Bjorner, and Chang (2007, p. 113) remarked that "a casual definition of perfect LD ... is 'asking the same question twice'." Method effects may also appear as factors, or LD: For example, Thissen and Steinberg (2010) discuss two pairs of items measuring preschool mathematics that were used as examples by Thissen and Steinberg (1988) and Hoskens and De Boeck (1997); one pair of items was based on identifying numerals, while the other pair involved matching numerals to a corresponding number of blocks. Using these two methods to determine whether the children knew the numbers produced a degree of LD within the item pairs. Such method-based "factors" are another class of dimensions that are not the intended target of measurement.

We note in passing that there are conceptual and statistical models for LD that do not involve additional factors; Hoskens and De Boeck (1997) describe a flexible class of models with added interaction terms for LD, and Glas and Suárez Falcón (2003) proposed statistical tests for a model for LD in which the response to one item somehow induces a change in the difficulty or endorsability of some subsequent item. However, in many contexts LD is probably most straightforwardly attributed to the effect of too-specific factors.

Response sets Cronbach (1946) described a number of response sets, which are individual differences variables that may affect item response selection separately from the intended item content. A tendency to select socially desirable responses is likely the most widely discussed among these, but a tendency to select extreme responses on

Likert-type response scales has elicited more development of special purpose MIRT models; among them, those of Bolt and Johnson (2009) and Thissen-Roe and Thissen (2013) are multidimensional, the first a kind of compensatory model and the second noncompensatory.

Complete modeling It is a well-known general principle of statistical estimation that model parameters may be poorly estimated if the model omits features that are important to fit the data. For that reason, it is useful to include all relevant factors, even when some of the factors represent LD, and for which no measurement is desired. In many test development contexts, during the process of test assembly, it is desirable to remove items that are locally dependent on others in order to reduce redundancy in the item set and simplify the IRT model that is ultimately used for scoring. For these reasons, it is useful to have an MIRT model that includes enough factors to fit the data well, whether they represent dimensions that are the intentional targets of measurement or unintentionally included.

MIRT Models

In this section, we describe the most widely used MIRT models in more detail.

Dichotomous MIRT

The 2PL MIRT Model The two-parameter logistic (2PL) MIRT model is a straightforward extension of the unidimensional 2PL model. The multiple traits being measured are represented by a vector of thetas ($\boldsymbol{\theta}$), rather than the scalar theta (θ) in the unidimensional model. The probability of endorsing item i is

$$T_i(u_i = 1) = \frac{1}{1 + \exp\left[-\left(\boldsymbol{a}_i'\boldsymbol{\theta} + c_i\right)\right]} \qquad (16.1)$$

in which u_i is the item response (1 for endorsement, 0 otherwise), $\boldsymbol{\theta}$ is the vector of latent variables being measured, and $\boldsymbol{a}_i$ and c_i are the two item parameters of the 2PL model. In the multidimensional case, this function represents a (hyper) surface in the space of latent traits.

In the unidimensional case, the a parameter is referred to as the slope or discrimination parameter; in MIRT, there is a vector of slope parameters, $\boldsymbol{a}_i$. The magnitude of each slope parameter indicates the degree of the relationship between each θ and the item responses. Higher values of the slope indicate a stronger relationship. An item measuring multiple traits may be more discriminating for one of the traits than the other(s); a vector of slope parameters reflects such differences.

The trace surface represented in Equation 16.1 is referred to as slope-intercept form. The intercept parameter c_i represents the level of endorsement of the item; larger values indicate greater endorsement. Computationally, estimating item parameters in slope-intercept form is efficient; however, some prefer the MIRT model written in slope-threshold form:

$$T_i(u_i = 1) = \frac{1}{1 + \exp\left[-\boldsymbol{a}_i\left(\boldsymbol{\theta}' - b_i\right)\right]}. \qquad (16.2)$$

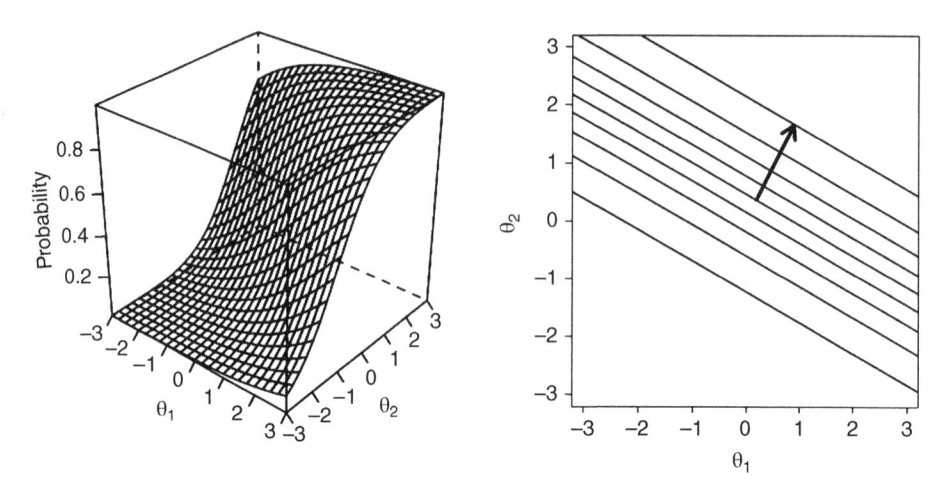

Figure 16.1 Alternative representations of the trace surface for a two-dimensional MIRT model with parameters $a_i = [0.7, 1.3]$ and $c_i = -0.6$, which implies $b_i = 0.41$. The left panel shows a wireframe or mesh plot of the surface; the right panel shows shaded contours of the same surface, dark for probabilities near zero and light for probabilities near one. In the right panel, an arrow extends from the point of maximum discrimination along a line from the origin in the direction of the item's measurement.

The parameter $b_i = -c_i/\sqrt{a_i a_i'} = -c_i/\sqrt{\sum_{k=1}^{m} a_{ik}^2}$, where m is the number of latent variables being measured (Reckase, 2009). When expressed in slope-threshold form, the intercept c_i is replaced by b_i, which represents the distance from the origin in the direction of highest discrimination of the item, to a point at which the trace surface rises most steeply. In the context of educational measurement, b_i represents the relative difficulty of the item (Ackerman, 1994; Reckase, 2009). In the unidimensional case, difficulty is interpreted as the level of θ at which someone has a 0.5 probability of endorsing the item. To extend this interpretation to the multidimensional case, note that the probability of endorsing an item is 0.5 when $-(a'_i \theta + c_i) = 0$: this is a line or (hyper)plane along which a respondent has a 0.5 probability of endorsing the item (Reckase, 2009).

Understanding the meaning of these parameters is assisted by graphical display for the case of two latent dimensions. Figure 16.1 shows two alternative representations of the trace surface for a two-latent variable model with MIRT parameters $a_i = [0.7, 1.3]$ and $c_i = -0.6$, which implies $b_i = 0.41$. The left panel shows a **wireframe** or **mesh** plot of the surface; the right panel shows the contours of the same surface.

The meaning of the model parameters can be seen in both plots. The probability of endorsing the item increases at a faster rate along the θ_2-axis than it does along the θ_1-axis. The compensatory nature of this model is clear in the contour plot: high values on θ_1 can compensate for low values on θ_2, and vice versa, for the probability of endorsing the item. The difficulty parameter, 0.41, gives the distance from the origin to the $p = .5$ point in the direction in which the item is most discriminating; the arrow on the contour plot has its base at this point. Reckase (1997, 2007) plots arrows like that for all items on a test on the same axes, as indicators of the directions measured by the items in a two-dimensional space. Each arrow has length proportional to $\sqrt{aa'}$, a summary of multidimensional discrimination.

Similar extensions from unidimensional to multidimensional IRT exist for other models for dichotomous data, including the Rasch and 3PL models.

Polytomous MIRT

The Graded Response MIRT Model The multidimensional graded response model (GRM) is a generalization of the unidimensional GRM (Samejima, 1969, 1997) and is used when data are ordinal, such as with item responses on a rating scale. Consider an item with $m + 1$ response categories; the probability that an individual i will endorse category $k(k = 0, ..., m)$ on item j is

$$T(u_{ij} = k|\theta_i) = T^*(u_{ij} = k|\theta_i) - T^*(u_{ij} = k+1|\theta_i) \quad (16.3)$$

where T^* is the probability of endorsing category k **or higher** (Reckase, 2009). $T(u_{ij} = k|\theta_i)$, the probability of endorsing category k, can be computed as a difference in probabilities: the probability of endorsing category k or higher minus the probability of endorsing category $k + 1$ **or higher**. In logistic form,

$$T(u_{ij} = k|\theta_i) = \frac{1}{1+\exp[-(a_i'\theta + c_{ik})]} - \frac{1}{1+\exp[-(a_i'\theta + c_{i(k+1)})]} \quad (16.4)$$

in which a_i is a vector of slopes and c_{ik} and $c_{i(k+1)}$ are intercepts. The two most extreme response categories, $k = 0$ and $k = m$ have corresponding probabilities of 0 and 1, respectively. Consequently, for these two special cases,

$$T(u_{ij} = 0|\theta_j) = 1 - \frac{1}{1+\exp[-(a_i'\theta + c_{i1})]} \quad (16.5)$$

and

$$T(u_{ij} = m|\theta_j) = \frac{1}{1+\exp[-(a_i'\theta + c_{im})]} \quad (16.6)$$

The parameters are interpreted similarly to the multidimensional 2PL case, except there are m intercept parameters for each item. The intercept parameters are ordered, reflecting the ordinal nature of the scale.

Figure 16.2 depicts the trace surfaces for a four-category graded response MIRT model with the following parameters: $a_i = [0.7, 1.3]$ and $c_i = [1.5, 0.5, -1.5]$. These graphics are made like the right panel of Figure 16.1: The rightmost graphic, for response 3, is similar to the right panel of Figure 16.1; both represent a surface that rises in the direction of the upper right-hand corner. The leftmost contour plot, for response 0, represents a surface that decreases from the lower left-hand corner, and the two center graphics, for response 1 and 2, represent ridges.

MIRT models for nominal responses Bock's (1972) model for nominal responses has been used for the responses to **testlets** that are the concatenation of two or more test items (Steinberg & Thissen, 1996), as well as for items with response categories that are

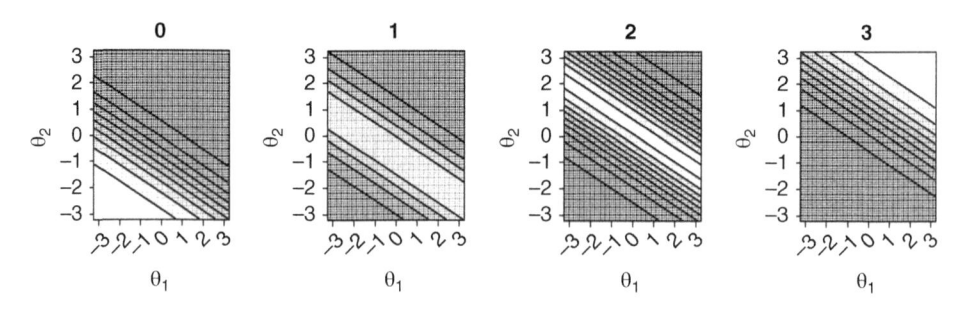

Figure 16.2 Shaded contour representations for the four trace surfaces for a four-category graded response MIRT model with the following parameters: $a_i = [0.7, 1.3]$ and $c_i = [1.5, 0.5, -1.5]$.

not evenly or uniformly graded (see e.g., Revicki et al., 2009) and for presence-severity items (Liu & Verkuilen, 2013). Thissen, Cai, and Bock (2010) developed a multidimensional generalization of this model for items with nominal responses. With nominal responses, the order of the response alternatives as a function of the latent variable(s) is a result of the data analysis, as opposed to an a priori specification as it is for models for graded responses. In keeping with the compensatory nature of general purpose MIRT models, the generalization proposed by Thissen et al. (2010) imposed the constraint that the order of the response alternatives is the same for all latent variables, or in all directions of the parameter space.

Bolt and Johnson (2009) described the completely unconstrained multidimensional nominal response model (MNRM), capable of modeling multiple traits with differential influence on each of several response options. This MNRM is flexible; indeed, it is so flexible its parameters may not be well identified with many sets of data: It has separate slope parameters for each response category in the direction of each latent dimension, so alternative solutions that interchange the relations between responses and dimensions may be common. However, when the model is treated as a template, more-identified versions of the model may be used for data with specific properties. Under different constraints, constrained versions of the MNRM have been demonstrated to model response sets in a survey (Bolt & Newton, 2011; Johnson & Bolt, 2010) or multiple sequential skill components in educational items (Bolt & Newton, 2010).

MIRT is Item Factor Analysis

Compensatory MIRT models and factor analysis

Item factor analysis models (models used to factor analyze categorical item response data) are compensatory MIRT models (Bock, Gibbons, & Muraki, 1988; Wirth & Edwards, 2007). Factor analysis models are usually expressed with factor loadings and underlying thresholds. For ordinal data, the loadings are regression parameters for an item-specific latent response value (e.g., x^*_{ij} in equation 1 of Wirth & Edwards, 2007) on the latent variable being measured. The thresholds are the values that divide the item-specific latent values into those that yield ordered categorical responses. There is a direct relationship between MIRT parameters and factor-analytic factor loadings, λ, and thresholds, τ (McLeod, Swygert, & Thissen, 2001, p. 199); for orthogonal factors, the relations are:

$$\lambda = \frac{a/D}{\sqrt{1+\Sigma\left(\frac{a}{D}\right)^2}} \qquad \tau = \frac{b(a/D)}{\sqrt{1+\Sigma\left(\frac{a}{D}\right)^2}} \qquad (16.7)$$

and

$$a = D\left(\frac{\lambda}{\sqrt{1-\Sigma\lambda^2}}\right) \qquad b = \frac{\tau}{\lambda} \qquad (16.8)$$

Equations 16.7 show the transformation of the unstandardized slopes into the standardized factor loading (λ) metric, and the transformation of the IRT b parameter into the threshold (τ) on the scale of the underlying response process variable. Equations 16.8 reverse those transformations from the notation of factor analysis back to IRT. $D = 1.7$ is the scaling constant that must be included in the equation when the IRT parameter estimates are in logistic form. If the IRT parameters are already in the normal ogive metric, $D = 1.0$, and therefore, drops out of the equations.

Exploratory item factor analysis

Exploratory factor analysis (EFA) is a two-stage procedure that can be used to investigate the structure of data. A priori model specification is not necessary with EFA; instead, nearly all of the slopes (or loadings) on each factor are estimated. Although EFA can be an effective tool to find unexpected structure in data, it has two main shortcomings: (1) A large number of factors are usually needed to fit item response data, and (2) there are an infinite number of alternative solutions that fit the data equally well – this is the classic problem of indeterminacy in factor analysis, discussed in more detail in the chapters on factor analysis, estimation, and rotation.

Pairs or triples of items that are locally dependent (doublets or triplets) are often found in item response data. In EFA, each doublet or triplet may be modeled by a new, separate factor, which yields an excessive number of parameters because almost all of the slopes are estimated for each factor, not constrained to be zero. With each additional factor (and consequently many more parameters), the EFA parameter estimates generally become less accurate.

In order for the parameter estimates from the first stage of EFA to be computed, a minimum number of restrictions must be placed on the model so that it is identified. For an orthogonal model with m factors, $m(m-1)/2$ slopes (or loadings) must be fixed. The resulting uninterpretable item parameter estimates need to be rotated in the second stage of EFA for the solution to be interpreted. Oblique CF-Quartimax rotation (Crawford & Ferguson, 1970) can be a useful method of rotation to obtain a solution that is the most similar to a correlated simple structure model (Browne, 2001), at least for the most commonly-encountered contexts for exploratory item factor analysis, which involve relatively few factors that are likely correlated.

Confirmatory item factor analysis

Jöreskog (1966) proposed that the problem of rotational indeterminacy could be avoided by fitting a multidimensional model with parameter constraints – usually fixing a large number of parameters at zero. Jöreskog (1969) called the procedure **confirmatory factor analysis** (CFA) to emphasize its use for hypothesis testing, and that is what it is called now, even when the data analytic context is exploratory. There are as many ways to specify CFA models as there are potential theoretical descriptions of the latent variables underlying the item responses for a test; two widely used general purpose classes of CFA models are **simple structure** and **bifactor** models.

Simple structure models The most obvious CFA models in many item analysis contexts are variously called **correlated simple structure** or **independent clusters** or **perfect clusters** models; they express an extreme form of Thurstone's (1947) **simple structure**. The idea behind these models is that the test measures more than one latent variable, but each item is an indicator for only one of the constructs. The constructs may be correlated. As MIRT models, simple structure models are essentially several unidimensional IRT models bolted together by the correlations among the latent variables; indeed, if those correlations are zero, the model is simply multiple unidimensional models.

As an example, consider the EPQ-R (Eysenck et al., 1985). Again, this measure involves three substantive scales: extraversion, neuroticism, and psychoticism. The data analyst knows in advance which items are intended to measure each of the three constructs, and would restrict the a parameters for each item on the other two θs to be zero. Such restrictions over-identify the model, even when the correlations among the three constructs are also nonzero estimated values.

Bifactor models An alternative conceptual model for a test is that all of the items indicate variation on some **general** factor to some extent; however, in addition, each item reflects one of a small number of more narrowly specified latent variables. Factor-analytic models reflecting this conceptualization are called **bifactor** (Holzinger & Swinford, 1937) or **hierarchical** models. As MIRT models, they are constructed with estimated slopes (a parameters) for all items on the first, or general, factor; then there are several more specific, or second-tier factors, and each item has a nonzero slope on one (or none) of those. In its most common form, a bifactor model looks like a simple structure model with a unidimensional IRT model for the general factor prepended, and the further constraint that the specific or second-tier factors are orthogonal (uncorrelated).

As an example, consider an emotional distress scale with items measuring depression, anxiety, and anger. The first factor would be generalized emotional distress. The second and subsequent factors are the specific parts of component constructs of emotional distress. They reflect individual differences in the degree to which the respondent is relatively higher or lower specifically on items measuring depression, or anxiety, or anger.

Gibbons and Hedeker (1992) provided a practical, efficient estimation algorithm for dichotomous bifactor models; Gibbons et al. (2007) extended this algorithm to polytomous models. Because these special algorithms are available, bifactor models provide an easy way to test the hypothesis that clusters of items on a scale exhibit LD, and/or to measure the relative degree to which items measure cluster constructs versus a general construct. Recently, Cai, Yang, and Hansen (2011) discussed a flexible multiple-group item bifactor modeling framework and illustrated its usefulness.

Wainer, Bradlow, and Wang (2007) described a **testlet response model** that looks somewhat different from a CFA model: Each item has only one slope parameter, and a set of variance parameters are estimated – those are the variances associated with the second-tier factors, relative to 1.0 as the variance of the general factor. However, Li, Bolt, and Fu (2006) showed that the testlet response model is a constrained bifactor model: A bifactor model becomes a testlet response model if the slope parameters on the general and second-tier factors for each item are equal and the variances of the second-tier factors are estimated.

The bifactor/testlet response model and the correlated independent clusters model are, further, very closely related. For traditional factor analysis, results by Schmid and Leiman (1957) and Yung, Thissen, and McLeod (1999) show that a second-order factor model is equivalent to a constrained bifactor model; the constraints are the same as those that give rise to the testlet response model. A second-order factor model is a simple structure model in which one second-order factor explains the correlations among the factors. Rijmen (2010) has shown that these results apply to MIRT models for categorical item response data. This set of relations explains the common alternative use of simple structure or bifactor MIRT models with the same, or similar, data.

Elaborated or generalized simple structure and bifactor models When used for data analysis, simple structure and bifactor models are usually starting points for elaboration as additional features of the data are revealed. A simple structure model may almost, but not quite, fit data; diagnostic statistics may indicate that one or more items have nonzero cross-loadings on a factor other than their designated one. Or there may be LD between a pair of items, or among three or four, that suggests the addition of one or more factors that are not conceptually important, but are needed to fit the data, and provide good parameter estimates overall. While diagnostic statistics may suggest model modification, we would emphasize that in item analysis the content of the questions and the interpretability of any additional parameters should be the final basis for the decision to add components to the model. Even so, it is possible that some parameters that appear to be significant after data-driven model modification may represent Type I errors. The use of a cross-validation sample is typically recommended to address this concern in general. However, during scale construction, the consequence of erroneously declaring an item cross-loaded or locally dependent is probably to set the item aside and use others in the assembly of a final scale. Because there are usually more items than are ultimately needed, it is usually safer to err on the side of modeling all relevant aspects of the data.

Generalizing bifactor models, Cai (2010c) extended Gibbons and Hedeker's computational results to cases in which the **general** part of the model contains more than one factor. This multi-factor **first-tier** section of the model can be a (potentially modified) simple structure model and second-tier factors may be appended to account for various kinds of LD. The empirical illustration provided later in this chapter makes use of such a model.

Parameter Estimation

Parameter estimation for unidimensional IRT models, and low-dimensional MIRT models, usually uses the method of maximum likelihood; the Bock–Aitkin EM algorithm (Bock & Aitkin, 1981) is highly effective (and very fast) for unidimensional models, and for MIRT models with two, or perhaps three dimensions. However, the Bock–Aitkin algorithm suffers from the **curse of dimensionality** in that it requires computation across a grid of quadrature points that increase in number exponentially with the number of dimensions, so alternative solutions are often used for three or more dimensions. Gibbons and Hedeker (1992) pointed out that for bifactor models for dichotomous items the Bock–Aitkin algorithm could be modified in such a way that the numerical integration using quadrature grids could be reduced to a series of two-dimensional problems regardless of the number of factors. Gibbons et al. (2007) extended this result to apply to bifactor models for polytomous items. Cai and his colleagues (Cai, 2010c; Cai, Yang, & Hansen, 2011) further expanded this strategy with the two-tier algorithm that permits a multidimensional first tier in place of the single general factor of a bifactor model, followed by a series of independent group-specific second-tier factors. Bifactor and two-tier models provide all the multidimensionality necessary for many applied problems.

For more general MIRT models, other solutions to the curse of dimensionality may be useful. Adaptive quadrature (Schilling & Bock, 2005), that uses a quadrature grid with many fewer points per dimension, can be useful for as many as (about) five dimensions, at some cost in computational complexity. Beyond that, some kinds of stochastic methods are used to replace numerical integration using quadrature: Cai's (2010a, 2010b) **Metropolis–Hastings Robbins–Monro** (MH-RM) algorithm yields maximum likelihood estimates of the parameters for any number of dimensions without a steep increase in computational time as a function of the number of dimensions. For researchers willing to embrace the statistical complexity of Bayesian inference, **Markov chain Monte Carlo** (MCMC) methods have also been used (see, e.g., Edwards, 2010).

Goodness of Fit

Overall fit assessment

Either unidimensional or multidimensional item response data can be conceptualized as a multivariate contingency table, in which each dimension corresponds to the response categories of an item and each cell of the table corresponds to a response pattern. Therefore, it is natural to assess MIRT model fit by means of asymptotic goodness of fit (GOF) tests for contingency table data, testing whether the multinomial probabilities of the full table are identical to the MIRT model-implied response pattern probabilities.

The number of cells in the contingency table increases exponentially with the number of items on an assessment, so sparseness (i.e., many cells with counts of zero or one and their corresponding small expected cell probabilities) determines the performance of asymptotic GOF tests. For short tests (e.g., less than 8 binary items or 4 four-category items), the commonly-used Pearson's X^2 and the likelihood ratio G^2 (Agresti, 2002) can be applied given large samples; however, for more realistic sample sizes common in MIRT applications, the contingency table is so sparse that both X^2 and G^2 tend to deviate substantially from their asymptotic reference distribution.

For long tests, GOF can be assessed using a limited information approach (Maydeu-Olivares and Joe, 2005, 2006; Reiser, 1996). The M_2 statistic (Maydeu-Olivares & Joe, 2005, 2006) is the most widely used and studied GOF statistic; it is a quadratic form in residuals (i.e., the discrepancy between the observed and expected) of the first two moments, with a weight matrix that leads to a chi-square asymptotic distribution. The degrees of freedom are the number of first and second moments minus the number of item parameters minus one. The first two moments can be transformed into cell probabilities of bivariate marginal tables, so this limited information approach reduces sparseness by collapsing cells in a systematic way.

More recently, Maydeu-Olivares (2012) proposed an RMSEA statistic based on M_2 (denoted $RMSEA_2$) to assess the approximate fit of IRT models. It is common to reject the exact fit of IRT models because they often involve many degrees of freedom; in most applications, researchers only want a useful approximation of the data, not an exact fit. Based on simulation results, Maydeu-Olivares suggested that $RMSEA_2 \leq 0.05$ provides a close approximation to the true model, and that $RMSEA_2 \leq 0.05 / (K-1)$ provides an excellent approximation (where K is the number of response categories).

To improve the fit of MIRT models, researchers need to identify the source of model misfit, make model modifications (e.g., changing the factor structure) or item-level decisions (e.g., removing some items), and re-assess fit. In practice, this procedure may be repeated several times until the desirable fit is achieved. As we noted earlier, in the process of scale construction, the consequences of Type I errors arising from data-driven model modification may be acceptable. On the other hand, when the intention is to interpret the parameters of the model in some meaningful scientific way, only cross-validation can provide assurance that the final MIRT model is generalizable.

Source of model misfit

A parametric MIRT model is based on a series of assumptions:

- The most important, statistically-defining assumption is **conditional**, or **local**, **independence** of the responses given the model.
- A closely related assumption is that the number of factors is specified correctly (where **correctly** means that local independence is obtained).
- It is assumed that the parametric forms of the model's parametric functions are correct, both for the population distribution of the latent variable(s), usually (multivariate) normal, and the trace lines or surfaces, usually logistic.

Any violation of MIRT model assumptions, such as LD, too few factors, a nonmonotone trace surface, nonnormally distributed latent variables, and so on, may lead to model misfit. If there is a priori information about a potential violation of an assumption, researchers may parameterize an alternative model that has the original model as a special case by incorporating a less stringent version of the focal assumption. Then a nested model comparison can be performed to determine whether this source of misfit is a cause for concern. If no a priori information is available, the misfit can be investigated in a piecewise manner, such as testing GOF in marginal subtables, to facilitate model modifications or item-level decisions to improve the fit.

Nested model comparisons Two statistical models are nested if it is possible to obtain one model by imposing constraints on the parameter space of the other. The less restricted model always fits the data better, provided some minimum discrepancy function estimator is used (e.g., maximum likelihood estimator: MLE). A nested model comparison approach can be useful for model modification when it is possible to reparameterize the original misfitting hypothesized model as a restricted version of an alternative model. When comparing the two models, if the unrestricted model fits significantly better than the restricted one, that suggests that the unrestricted model serves as a better approximation to the data; as a result, the constraints of the original model should be removed. The choice of an alternative model is the key to the success of this method; it requires researchers to be aware of potential causes of misfit.

For example, suppose we have a single-group MIRT model that fits poorly, and we suspect one item might have different parameters across genders. To examine this, we set up a two-group analysis that constrains the two groups to have identical parameters except for the item in question, which has parameters estimated for both groups. The resulting two-group MIRT model is less restricted compared to the original single-group model; one could revert back to the original model by fixing all item parameters to be equal across the two groups. If the two-group model fits significantly better than the one-group model, then we may conclude that this focal item exhibits differential item functioning (DIF). The same idea can be applied to testing the assumption of conditional independence, the functional form of trace surface, and so on.

The comparative fit of nested models can be assessed formally with asymptotic tests. If the MLE is used, one can choose among three widely used alternative tests: the Wald test, the likelihood ratio test, and the score (or Lagrange multiplier) test (Buse, 1982). For applications in IRT literature, interested readers are referred to Glas (1998, 1999), Glas and Suárez Falcón (2003), and Liu and Thissen (2012, 2013).

Piecewise fit assessment When a priori information of model misfit is absent, marginal subtable GOF tests are used to detect the source of misfit. A marginal subtable is the contingency table formed by responses to a subset of items (e.g., pairs, triplets, etc.). For instance, if we are interested in testing how well the model fits to pairs of items, GOF tests are applied to the bivariate marginal subtables. Model modification for item subsets with large test statistics may improve the overall fit substantially. We can remove the items that are frequently involved in poorly fitting subsets if simple model modification is not applicable or if it is not necessary to retain all items.

Various statistics have been proposed for this purpose; however, many of them have only a heuristic reference distribution, and others may suffer from either computational instability or lack of power. Liu and Maydeu-Olivares (2012) suggest the use of a mean and variance adjusted Pearson's X^2, which outperforms other candidates in terms of both Type I error rate and power.

An Example, Using Data from the Eysenck Personality Questionnaire

We illustrate various aspects of the application of MIRT with analyses of the male UK normative sample data ($N = 610$) for the EPQ-R (Eysenck, et al., 1985). This measure involves three substantive scales: extraversion (E), neuroticism (N), and psychoticism

(P). All items are dichotomous; the responses are "yes" and "no." In these analyses, we used data from the short form, which includes 12 items for each scale. Items are labeled with the first letter of the scale on which they are scored, followed by the original item number in the full EPQ-R scale. For all analyses, the maximum likelihood estimates of the item parameters were obtained using the Bock–Aitkin EM algorithm (Bock & Aitken, 1981) as implemented in IRTPRO (Cai, Thissen, & du Toit, 2011). For example, IRTPRO code for the models presented, please see Appendix Codes 1–6. To compute the Fisher information matrix, which is required in computing pairwise fit statistics and standard errors, we used the supplemented EM (SEM) estimator (Cai, 2008) for the unidimensional and three-dimensional models, and the cross-product approximation for the ultimate eight-dimensional model.

Unidimensional model

We began the analysis by fitting a (unidimensional) 2PL model. Theory indicates that the EPQ-R is not unidimensional; however, it is often good practice to begin by fitting a unidimensional model for data analyses in a more exploratory mode. As expected, the model fit poorly: $M_2 = 5,448.84$ on 594 degrees of freedom, $p < .01$, and the associated $RMSEA_2 = 0.12$. This implies that it is unlikely that these data reflect a single factor. The bivariate Pearson's X^2 statistics (Chen & Thissen, 1997), which indicate locally dependent items, are tabulated in Figure 16.3; their asymptotic p-values are computed using an inversion method (Imhof, 1961; Liu & Maydeu-Olivares, 2012). The upper triangle of the graphical table contains the values of the X^2 statistics for each item pair; the lower triangle is a tableplot (Kwan, Lu, & Friendly, 2009), with the circle size proportional to the X^2 statistics. This figure displays only those X^2 statistics that are significant at the $\alpha = .05$-level after a Benjamini-Hochberg adjustment for multiplicity, which controls the false discovery rate (Benjamini & Hochberg, 1995; Thissen, Steinberg, & Kuang, 2002; Williams, Jones, & Tukey, 1999).

The pairwise fit statistics suggest that the unidimensional model fails to fit pairs mostly within the psychoticism and neuroticism dimensions; there are a few significantly misfitting pairs within extraversion and across the three dimensions, but the magnitude of those statistics is much smaller. These results suggest that the fitted single latent variable may be a good representation of the extraversion scale; however, because the scales were designed to be orthogonal (which will be checked later), this latent variable alone does not suffice to explain the association among items on the other two scales. This pattern of pairwise fit statistics leads us to conduct a three-dimensional exploratory item factor analysis.

Three-dimensional exploratory item factor analysis Fitting a three-dimensional EFA is a reasonable next step because the theory used to develop the EPQ-R is that personality is measured by three factors. We use Oblique Quartimax rotation, so that any correlation that may exist among the scales is visible in the analysis. Figure 16.4 displays a tableplot of the rotated factor loading estimates. The original theory of the EPQ-R suggests that the three factors are orthogonal with items exhibiting simple structure. Results of the EFA indicate that the factors are nearly orthogonal ($r = 0.09$ for psychoticism-extraversion, $r = -0.09$ for psychoticism-neuroticism, and $r = 0.13$ for extraversion-neuroticism). Examination of the factor loadings reveals that two items may exhibit within-item

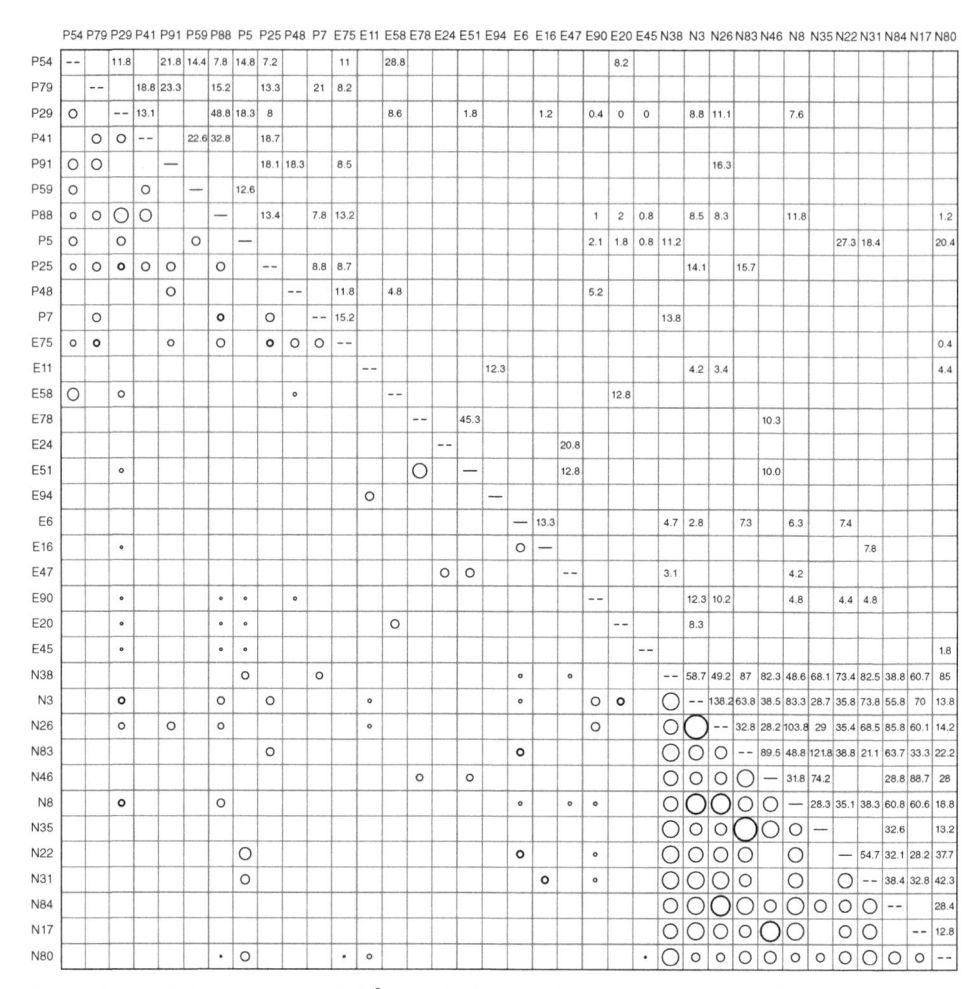

Figure 16.3 Bivariate Pearson's X^2 statistics for a unidimensional 2PL model fitted to the EPQ-R male data. The upper triangle of the graphical table contains the values of the X^2 statistics for each item pair; the lower triangle is a tableplot, with the circle size proportional to the X^2 statistics. Only significant entries after a Benjamini–Hochberg adjustment of α-levels are shown, and the order of the items corresponds to the size of their factor loadings within the three-factor EFA (see Figure 16.4).

multidimensionality. The item "Do you enjoy cooperating with others" (P54) loads on both the psychoticism and extraversion factors. While this item was originally intended to measure psychoticism, it may be that someone who dislikes cooperating with others will also have low levels of extraversion. Another item, "Would you take drugs which may have strange or dangerous effects?" (P25) has loadings on both psychoticism and neuroticism. Therefore, in subsequent analyses we investigate possible within-item multidimensionality for those two items.

Three-dimensional confirmatory MIRT model To further examine the factor structure of the EPQ-R, a confirmatory MIRT model was fitted in which two items with potential within-item multidimensionality (P54 and P25) have cross-loadings (i.e., load onto

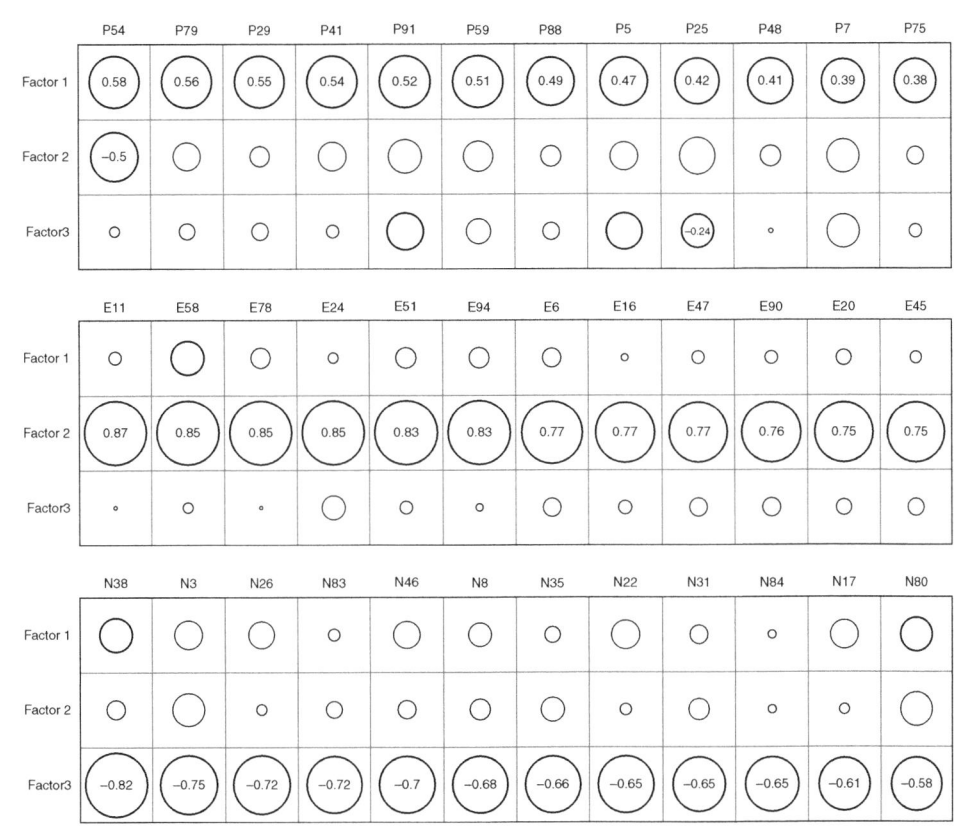

Figure 16.4 Tableplot of the rotated factor loading estimates from three-factor EFA; circle size is proportional to the factor loading (interpreted loadings their have numeric values in the circle).

more than one factor). Of the three models considered thus far, this model exhibits the best overall fit: $M_2 = 1{,}566.19$ on 589 degrees of freedom, $p < .01$; $RMSEA_2 = 0.05$, which indicates close fit. The three factors were only weakly correlated: $r = 0.28$ ($s.e. = 0.06$) for psychoticism-extraversion, $r = 0.07$ ($s.e. = 0.06$) for psychoticism-neuroticism, and $r = -0.16$ ($s.e. = 0.05$) for extraversion-neuroticism. The CFA model makes the psychoticism-extraversion correlation (0.28) appear slightly higher than it was with the EFA model (0.09); that is probably because some correlation between the psychoticism and extraversion factors is probably absorbed in nonzero cross-loadings in the EFA solution whereas it appears only in the correlation in the CFA model in which those cross-loadings are restricted to zero.

Examination of residual pairwise relations for this model suggested that there may be pairs or small groups of items that exhibit LD, specifically four pairs and a quadruplet:

Rules: P29, "Do you prefer to go your own way rather than act by the rules?" and P88, "Is it better to follow society's rules than go your own way?".

Worry: N38, "Are you a worrier?", N80, "Do you worry too long after an embarrassing experience?", P7, "Would being in debt worry you?", and P59, "Does it worry you if you know there are mistakes in your work?".

Life of the Party: E51, "Can you easily get some life into a rather dull party?" and E78, "Can you get a party going?".
Wallflower: E24, "Do you tend to keep in the background on social occasions?" and E47, "Are you mostly quiet when you are with other people?".
Nerves: N35, "Would you call yourself a nervous person?" and N83, "Do you suffer from 'nerves'?".

Eight-dimensional confirmatory MIRT model To test the significance of these potential sources of LD, an eight-dimensional confirmatory MIRT model was fitted using the two-tier algorithm (Cai, 2010c; Cai, Yang, & Hansen, 2011). The first tier of this model comprised three correlated factors for the P, E, and N scales with the two cross-loadings included in the three-factor model; the second tier included four additional factors for the four doublets listed before, as well as a factor for the quadruplet about **worry**. The two slope parameters within each of the doublet factors are constrained to be equal for model identification; the single (equal) value of those two slopes has the same model functionality as an error correlation or covariance term in a structural equation model.

While none of the second-tier factors merits substantive interpretation, to the extent that they are sources of covariation in the data, omitting them from the model could affect the factor loadings and correlations for the important first-tier factors. Table 16.1 contains the MIRT parameter estimates for this model. All of the estimated (nonzero) item slope parameters in this model are reasonably large. The three factors are still only weakly correlated: $r = 0.28$ $(s.e. = 0.06)$ for psychoticism-extraversion, $r = 0.13$ $(s.e. = 0.07)$ for psychoticism-neuroticism, and $r = -0.13$ $(s.e. = 0.05)$ for extraversion-neuroticism.

Conclusion of the illustration Modern factor-analytic technique confirms that the three substantive subscales of the short form of the EPQ-R measure three nearly orthogonal dimensions of personality, as designed. We also found a small number of items that appear to exhibit LD – four pairs and a quadruplet. It is not likely that this degree of LD could have been detected with any technology that was available in the 1980s when this questionnaire was assembled. However, if this had been a contemporary test-construction project, it may well be that one of the items from each item pair might have been set aside in favor of some other, less locally dependent, replacement. And the test developers might have considered carefully how many of the items would be about **worry**.

More germane to this chapter, this example illustrates the feasibility of both exploratory and relatively high-dimensional confirmatory item factor analysis using modern statistical methods for parameter estimation.

Conclusion and Future Directions

Up until the first decade of this century, MIRT was a relatively obscure area of primarily theoretical interest for quantitative psychologists. Now, parallel advances in computational speed and algorithms for statistical parameter estimation have made the application of MIRT practical for real-world research problems, as illustrated by the example in

Table 16.1 MIRT parameter estimates for the three-factor model with cross-loadings, plus four doublets and a quadruplet.

Item	a_1	s.e.	a_2	s.e.	a_3	s.e.	a_4	s.e.	a_5	s.e.	a_6	s.e.	a_7	s.e.	a_8	s.e.	c	s.e.
P91	1.46	0.30	0	—	0	—	0	—	0	—	0	—	0	—	0	—	−2.31	0.26
P54	1.41	0.35	−1.53	0.27	0	—	0	—	0	—	0	—	0	—	0	—	−2.87	0.33
P79	1.37	0.24	0	—	0	—	0	—	0	—	0	—	0	—	0	—	−2.27	0.21
P25	1.20	0.22	0	—	0.30	0.15	0	—	0	—	0	—	0	—	0	—	−1.77	0.18
P88	1.17	0.20	0	—	0	—	1.13	0.24	0	—	0	—	0	—	0	—	0.02	0.13
P29	1.06	0.19	0	—	0	—	1.13	0.24	0	—	0	—	0	—	0	—	1.39	0.16
P59	0.96	0.21	0	—	0	—	0	—	0	—	−0.91	0.28	0	—	0	—	−1.83	0.20
P41	0.91	0.21	0	—	0	—	0	—	0	—	0	—	0	—	0	—	−1.83	0.17
P75	0.82	0.16	0	—	0	—	0	—	0	—	0	—	0	—	0	—	−0.56	0.10
P7	0.80	0.19	0	—	0	—	0	—	0	—	−0.69	0.21	0	—	0	—	−1.30	0.15
P48	0.59	0.17	0	—	0	—	0	—	0	—	0	—	0	—	0	—	−1.63	0.13
P5	0.47	0.14	0	—	0	—	0	—	0	—	0	—	0	—	0	—	−0.68	0.10
E78	0	—	5.39	0.81	0	—	0	—	0	—	0	—	3.56	0.52	0	—	−1.04	0.40
E51	0	—	4.76	0.69	0	—	0	—	0	—	0	—	3.56	0.52	0	—	−2.36	0.44
E24	0	—	4.40	0.61	0	—	0	—	0	—	0	—	0	—	2.34	0.34	0.16	0.3
E11	0	—	3.36	0.42	0	—	0	—	0	—	0	—	0	—	0	—	1.16	0.24
E47	0	—	3.30	0.45	0	—	0	—	0	—	0	—	0	—	2.34	0.34	1.20	0.27
E94	0	—	2.87	0.34	0	—	0	—	0	—	0	—	0	—	0	—	−0.08	0.19
E58	0	—	2.60	0.36	0	—	0	—	0	—	0	—	0	—	0	—	2.47	0.30
E16	0	—	2.06	0.24	0	—	0	—	0	—	0	—	0	—	0	—	1.32	0.18
E6	0	—	2.03	0.24	0	—	0	—	0	—	0	—	0	—	0	—	0.21	0.15
E90	0	—	1.98	0.23	0	—	0	—	0	—	0	—	0	—	0	—	0.48	0.15
E45	0	—	1.93	0.21	0	—	0	—	0	—	0	—	0	—	0	—	0.32	0.15
E20	0	—	1.91	0.24	0	—	0	—	0	—	0	—	0	—	0	—	2.34	0.23
N38	0	—	0	—	2.92	0.91	0	—	0	—	2.20	1.01	0	—	0	—	−0.16	0.23
N83	0	—	0	—	2.34	0.33	0	—	1.75	0.28	0	—	0	—	0	—	−1.58	0.24
N26	0	—	0	—	2.08	0.25	0	—	0	—	0	—	0	—	0	—	−0.26	0.15
N35	0	—	0	—	1.97	0.27	0	—	1.75	0.28	0	—	0	—	0	—	−2.03	0.25

(*continued on p. 464*)

Table 16.1 (*Continued*)

Item	a_1	s.e.	a_2	s.e.	a_3	s.e.	a_4	s.e.	a_5	s.e.	a_6	s.e.	a_7	s.e.	a_8	s.e.	c	s.e.
N3	0	—	0	—	1.96	0.24	0	—	0	—	0	—	0	—	0	—	0.56	0.16
N8	0	—	0	—	1.80	0.21	0	—	0	—	0	—	0	—	0	—	-0.34	0.14
N46	0	—	0	—	1.69	0.23	0	—	0	—	0	—	0	—	0	—	-1.71	0.19
N84	0	—	0	—	1.48	0.19	0	—	0	—	0	—	0	—	0	—	-1.01	0.14
N17	0	—	0	—	1.40	0.18	0	—	0	—	0	—	0	—	0	—	-0.79	0.13
N31	0	—	0	—	1.34	0.17	0	—	0	—	0	—	0	—	0	—	-0.47	0.13
N22	0	—	0	—	1.26	0.17	0	—	0	—	0	—	0	—	0	—	0.23	0.12
N80	0	—	0	—	1.11	0.18	0	—	0	—	0.95	0.27	0	—	0	—	0.04	0.13

Note. – as *s.e.* indicates parameter (and associated *s.e.*) fixed at 0.

this chapter, fitting three- and then eight-dimensional models. In this chapter, we have briefly summarized the intellectual history of MIRT, with its roots in both test theory and factor analysis. We have discussed some sources of multidimensionality in item response data, and described in some detail the most commonly used MIRT models and methods to check their goodness of fit. Finally, we have concluded with an example that illustrates many of the concepts in the preceding sections.

We have emphasized the use of MIRT models for item analysis, concentrating on the description and the example on model specification, fit, and interpretation. That emphasis reflects the current use of MIRT models. Unidimensional IRT models are also used for test scoring, and in theory MIRT models may similarly be used to compute scores. However, multidimensional test scores present challenges to interpretation: They have different meanings for different models – for example, scores on the specific or second-tier factors of bifactor or two-tier models are estimates of residuals or deviations around the general factor(s), while scores on simple structure multiple factors are more intuitive. And MIRT scores may not always behave in ways untutored intuition might expect (Hooker, Finkelman, & Schwartzman, 2009; van der Linden, 2012). Given the recently increased computational practicality of application of MIRT, we expect that in the near future additional pedagogical materials will appear to aid practitioners in the use of multidimensional scores. After that happens, we expect an increase in the use of MIRT for scoring, to take advantage of its potentially greater precision of measurement for multiple correlated scores. Then MIRT will be coequal with unidimensional IRT, and any distinction between the two will gradually be dropped.

References

Ackerman, T. A. (1994). Using multidimensional item response theory to understand what items and tests are measuring. *Applied Measurement in Education, 7*, 255–278.

Agresti, A. (2002). *Categorical data analysis*. Hoboken, NJ: John Wiley & Sons, Inc.

Benjamini, Y., & Hochberg, Y. (1995). Controlling the false discovery rate: A practical and powerful approach to multiple testing. *Journal of the Royal Statistical Society Series B, 57*, 289–300.

Bock, R. D. (1972). Estimating item parameters and latent ability when responses are scored in two or more latent categories. *Psychometrika, 37*, 29–51.

Bock, R. D., & Aitkin, M. (1981). Marginal maximum likelihood estimation of item parameters: an application of the EM algorithm. *Psychometrika, 46*, 443–459.

Bock, R. D., Gibbons, R., & Muraki, E. (1988). Full-information item factor analysis. *Applied Psychological Measurement, 12*, 261–280.

Bolt, D. M., & Johnson, T. R. (2009). Applications of a MIRT model to self-report measures: Addressing score bias and DIF due to individual differences in response style. *Applied Psychological Measurement, 33*, 335–352.

Bolt, D., & Newton, J. (2010). *Application of a multidimensional partial credit model allowing within-item slope heterogeneity*. Paper presented at the Annual Meeting of the National Conference on Measurement in Education (NCME), Denver, CO, May 3, 2010.

Bolt, D. M., & Newton, J. R. (2011). Multiscale measurement of extreme response style. *Educational and Psychological Measurement, 71*, 814–833.

Browne, M. W. (2001). An overview of analytic rotation in exploratory factor analysis. *Multivariate Behavioral Research, 36*, 111–150.

Buse, A. (1982). The likelihood ratio, Wald, and Lagrange multiplier tests: An expository note. *The American Statistician, 36*, 153–157.

Cai, L. (2008). SEM of another flavour: Two new applications of the supplemented EM algorithm. *British Journal of Mathematical and Statistical Psychology, 61,* 309–329.

Cai, L. (2010a). High-dimensional exploratory item factor analysis by a Metropolis-Hastings Robbins-Monro algorithm. *Psychometrika, 75,* 33–57.

Cai, L. (2010b). Metropolis-Hastings Robbins–Monro algorithm for confirmatory item factor analysis. *Journal of Educational and Behavioral Statistics, 35,* 307–335.

Cai, L. (2010c). A two-tier full-information item factor analysis model with applications. *Psychometrika, 75,* 581–612.

Cai, L. (2013). *flexMIRT® version 2: Flexible multilevel multidimensional item analysis and test scoring* [Computer software]. Chapel Hill, NC: Vector Psychometric Group.

Cai, L., Thissen, D., & du Toit, S. H. C. (2011). *IRTPRO for Windows* [Computer software]. Lincolnwood, IL: Scientific Software International, Inc.

Cai, L., Yang, J. S., & Hansen, M. (2011). Generalized full- information item bifactor analysis. *Psychological Methods, 16,* 221–248.

Chen, W. H., & Thissen, D. (1997). Local dependence indices for item pairs using item response theory. *Journal of Educational and Behavioral Statistics, 22,* 265–289.

Christoffersson, A. (1975). Factor analysis of dichotomized variables. *Psychometrika, 40,* 5–32.

Crawford, C. B., & Ferguson, G. A. (1970). A general rotation criterion and its use in orthogonal rotation. *Psychometrika, 35,* 321–332.

Cronbach, L. J. (1946). Response sets and test validity. *Educational and Psychological Measurement, 6,* 475–494.

Edwards, M. C. (2010). A Markov chain Monte Carlo approach to confirmatory item factor analysis. *Psychometrika, 75,* 474–497.

Embretson, S. E. (1984). A general multicomponent latent trait model for response processes. *Psychometrika, 49,* 175–186.

Embretson, S. E. (1997). Multicomponent latent trait models. In W. van der Linden & R. Hambleton (Eds.), *Handbook of modern item response theory* (pp. 305–322). New York: Springer-Verlag.

Eysenck, S. B. G., Eysenck, H. J., & Barrett, P. (1985). A revised version of the psychoticism scale. *Personality and Individual Differences, 6,* 21–29.

Gibbons, R. D., & Hedeker, D. (1992). Full-information item bi-factor analysis. *Psychometrika, 57,* 423–436.

Gibbons, R. D., Bock, R. D., Hedeker, D., Weiss, D. J., Segawa, E., Bhaumik, D. K., Kupfer, D. J., Frank, E., Grochocinski, V. J., & Stover, A. (2007). Full-information item bifactor analysis of graded response data. *Applied Psychological Measurement, 31,* 4–19.

Glas, C. A. W. (1998). Detection of differential item functioning using Lagrange multiplier tests. *StatisticaSinica, 8,* 647–667.

Glas, C. A. W. (1999). Modification indices for the 2-pl and the nominal response model. *Psychometrika, 64,* 273–294.

Glas, C. A. W., & Suárez Falcón, J. C. (2003). A comparison of item-fit statistics for the three-parameter logistic model. *Applied Psychological Measurement, 27,* 81–100.

Harrison, D. A. (1986). Robustness of IRT parameter estimation to violations of the unidimensionality assumption. *Journal of Educational Statistics, 11,* 91–115.

Holzinger, K. J., & Swineford, F. (1937). The bi-factor method. *Psychometrika, 2,* 41–54.

Hooker, G., Finkelman, M., & Schwartzman, A. (2009). Paradoxical results in multidimensional item response theory. *Psychometrika, 74,* 419–442.

Hoskens, M., & De Boeck, P. (1997). A parametric model for local dependence among test items. *Psychological Methods, 2,* 261–277.

Imhof, J. P. (1961). Computing the distribution of quadratic forms in normal variables. *Biometrika, 48,* 419–426.

Johnson, T. R., & Bolt, D. M. (2010). On the use of factor-analytic multinomial logit item response models, to account for individual differences in response style. *Journal of Educational and Behavioral Statistics, 35,* 92–114.

Jöreskog, K. G. (1966). Testing a simple structure hypothesis in factor analysis. *Psychometrika, 31,* 165–178.

Jöreskog, K. G. (1969). A general approach to confirmatory maximum likelihood factor analysis. *Psychometrika, 34,* 183–202.

Kwan, E., Lu, I. R. R., & Friendly, M. (2009). Tableplot: A new tool for assessing precise predictions. *ZeitschriftfürPsychologie/Journal of Psychology, 217,* 38–48.

Li, Y., Bolt, D. M., & Fu, J. (2006). A comparison of alternative models for testlets. *Applied Psychological Measurement, 30,* 3–21.

Liu, Y., & Maydeu-Olivares, A. (2012). The use of quadratic form statistics of residuals to identify IRT model misfit in marginal subtables. *Presentation at the 77th Annual Meeting of the Psychometric Society,* Lincoln, NE.

Liu, Y., & Thissen, D. (2012). Identifying local dependence with a score test statistic based on the bifactor logistic model. *Applied Psychological Measurement, 36,* 670–688.

Liu, Y., & Thissen, D. (2013). Comparing score tests and other local dependence diagnostics for the graded response model. *British Journal of Mathematical and Statistical Psychology.* doi: 10.1111/bmsp.12030.

Liu, Y., & Verkuilen, J. (2013). Item response modeling of presence-severity items: application to measurement of patient-reported outcomes. *Applied Psychological Measurement, 37,* 58–75.

Lord, F. M., & Novick, M. R. (1968). *Statistical theories of mental test scores.* Reading, MA: Addison-Wesley.

Maydeu-Olivares, A. (2012). Testing for approximate fit in categorical data analysis. *Presentation at the 77th Annual Meeting of the Psychometric Society,* Lincoln, NE.

Maydeu-Olivares, A., & Joe, H. (2005). Limited and full information estimation and testing in 2^n contingency tables: A unified framework. *Journal of the American Statistical Association, 100,* 1009–1020.

Maydeu-Olivares, A., & Joe, H. (2006). Limited information goodness-of-fit testing in multidimensional contingency tables. *Psychometrika, 71,* 713–732.

McDonald, R. P. (1967). Nonlinear factor analysis. *Psychometric Monograph,* Whole No. 15.

McDonald, R. P. (1982). Linear versus nonlinear models in latent trait theory. *Applied Psychological Measurement, 6,* 379–396.

McLeod, L. D., Swygert, K., & Thissen, D. (2001). Factor analysis for items scored in two categories. In D. Thissen & H. Wainer (Eds.), *Test scoring* (pp. 189–216). Mahwah, NJ: Lawrence Erlbaum Associates.

Multivariate Software. (2010). *EQSIRT: Item response theory software* [Computer software]. Encino, CA: Author

Muthén, B. (1978). Contributions to factor analysis of dichotomous variables. *Psychometrika, 43,* 551–560.

Muthén, L. K., & Muthén, B. O. (2012). *MPlus user's guide* (7th ed.). Los Angeles, CA: Muthén & Muthén.

Reckase, M. D. (1997). A linear logistic multidimensional model for dichotomous item response data. In W. van der Linden & R. K. Hambleton (Eds.), *Handbook of modern item response theory* (pp. 271–286). New York: Springer.

Reckase, M. D. (2007). Multidimensional item response theory. In C. R. Rao & S. Sinharay (Eds.), *Handbook of statistics: Volume 26. Psychometrics* (pp. 607–642). Amsterdam: North-Holland.

Reckase, M. D. (2009). *Multidimensional item response theory.* New York, NY: Springer.

Reise, S. P., Bonifay, W. E., & Haviland, M. G. (2013). Scoring and modeling psychological measures in the presence of multidimensionality. *Journal of Personality Assessment, 95,* 129–140.

Reiser, M. (1996). Analysis of residuals for the multinomial item response model. *Psychometrika, 61,* 509–528.

Revicki, D., Chen, W., Harnam, N., Cook, K., Amtmann, D., Callahan, L., et al. (2009). Development and psychometric analysis of the PROMIS pain behavior item bank. *Pain, 146,* 158–169.

Rijmen, F. (2010). Formal relations and an empirical comparison between the bi-factor, the testlet, and a second-order multidimensional IRT model. *Journal of Educational Measurement*, 47, 361–372.

Samejima, F. (1969). Estimation of latent ability using a response pattern of graded scores. *Psychometric Monograph*, Whole No. 17, 34, Part 2.

Samejima, F. (1974). Normal ogive model on the continuous response level in the multidimensional space. *Psychometrika*, 39, 111–121

Samejima, F. (1997). Graded response model. In W. van der Linden & R. K. Hambleton (Eds.), *Handbook of modern item response theory* (pp. 85–100). New York: Springer.

Schilling, S., & Bock, R. D. (2005). High-dimensional maximum marginal likelihood item factor analysis by adaptive quadrature. *Psychometrika*, 70, 533–555

Schmid, J., & Leiman, J. M. (1957). The development of hierarchical factor solutions. *Psychometrika*, 22, 53–61.

Steinberg, L., & Thissen, D. (1996). Uses of item response theory and the testlet concept in the measurement of psychopathology. *Psychological Methods*, 1, 81–97.

Sympson, J. B. (1978). A model for testing multidimensional items. In D. J. Weiss (Ed.), *Proceedings of the 1977 computerized adaptive testing conference* (pp. 82–98). Minneapolis, MN: University of Minnesota, Department of Psychology, Psychometric Methods Program.

Thissen, D., Cai, L., & Bock, R. D. (2010). The nominal categories item response model. In M. L. Nering & R. Ostini (Eds.), *Handbook of polytomous item response theory models* (pp. 43–75). New York: Routledge.

Thissen, D., Reeve, B. B., Bjorner, J. B., & Chang, C. H. (2007). Methodological issues for building item banks and computerized adaptive scales. *Quality of Life Research*, 16, 109–116.

Thissen, D., & Steinberg, L. (1988). Data analysis using item response theory. *Psychological Bulletin*, 104, 385–395.

Thissen, D., & Steinberg, L. (2010). Using item response theory to disentangle constructs at different levels of generality. In S. Embretson (Ed.), *Measuring psychological constructs: Advances in model-based approaches* (pp. 123–144). Washington, DC: American Psychological Association.

Thissen, D., Steinberg, L., & Kuang, D. (2002). Quick and easy implementation of the Benjamini-Hochberg procedure for controlling the false positive rate in multiple comparisons. *Journal of Educational and Behavioral Statistics*, 27, 77–83.

Thissen, D., Steinberg, L., & Mooney, J. A. (1989). Trace lines for testlets: A use of multiple-categorical-response models. *Journal of Educational Measurement*, 26, 247–260.

Thissen-Roe, A., & Thissen, D. (2013). A two-decision model for responses to Likert-type items. *Journal of Educational and Behavioral Statistics*, 38, 522–547.

Thurstone, L. L. (1947). *Multiple factor analysis*. Chicago: University of Chicago Press.

van der Linden. (2012). On compensation in multidimensional response modeling. *Psychometrika*, 77, 21–30.

Wainer, H., Bradlow, E. T., & Wang, X. (2007). *Testlet response theory and its applications*. New York: Cambridge University Press.

Whitely, S. E. (1980). Multicomponent latent trait models for ability tests. *Psychometrika*, 45, 479–494.

Williams, V., Jones, L. V., & Tukey, J. W. (1999). Controlling error in multiple comparisons, with examples from state-to-state differences in educational achievement. *Journal of Educational and Behavioral Statistics*, 24, 42–69.

Wirth, R. J., & Edwards, M. C. (2007). Item factor analysis: Current approaches and future directions. *Psychological Methods*, 12, 58–79.

Yung, Y. F., McLeod, L. D., & Thissen, D. (1999). On the relationship between the higher-order factor model and the hierarchical factor model. *Psychometrika*, 64, 113–128.

Code Appendix

Code 1 Example IRTPRO code for the unidimensional 2PL model of the EPQ.

```
Project:
    Name = males_labeledSF;

Data:
    File = .\males_labeledSF.ssig;

Analysis:
    Name = UniD;
    Mode = Calibration;

Title:
EPQ male data, short form, Unidimensinal 2PL fit
Comments:
Estimation:
    Method = BAEM;
    E-Step = 500, 1e-005;
    SE = S-EM;
    M-Step = 50, 1e-006;
    Quadrature = 49, 6;
    SEM = 0.001;
    SS = 1e-005;

Scoring:
    Mean = 0;
    SD = 1;

Miscellaneous:
    Decimal = 2;
    Processors = 2;
    Print M2, CTLD, P-Nums, Diagnostic;
    Min Exp = 1;

Groups:

Group:
    Dimension = 1;
    Items = p_25, p_29, p_48, p_75, p_91, p_5, p_7, p_41,
    p_54, p_59, p_79,
    p_88, e_6, e_11, e_16, e_20, e_45, e_51, e_58, e_78,
    e_90, e_94, e_24,
    e_47, n_3, n_8, n_17, n_22, n_26, n_31, n_35, n_38,
    n_46, n_80, n_83,
```

```
n_84;
Codes(p_25) = 0(0), 1(1);
Codes(p_29) = 0(0), 1(1);
Codes(p_48) = 0(0), 1(1);
Codes(p_75) = 0(0), 1(1);
Codes(p_91) = 0(0), 1(1);
Codes(p_5) = 0(0), 1(1);
Codes(p_7) = 0(0), 1(1);
Codes(p_41) = 0(0), 1(1);
Codes(p_54) = 0(0), 1(1);
Codes(p_59) = 0(0), 1(1);
Codes(p_79) = 0(0), 1(1);
Codes(p_88) = 0(0), 1(1);
Codes(e_6) = 0(0), 1(1);
Codes(e_11) = 0(0), 1(1);
Codes(e_16) = 0(0), 1(1);
Codes(e_20) = 0(0), 1(1);
Codes(e_45) = 0(0), 1(1);
Codes(e_51) = 0(0), 1(1);
Codes(e_58) = 0(0), 1(1);
Codes(e_78) = 0(0), 1(1);
Codes(e_90) = 0(0), 1(1);
Codes(e_94) = 0(0), 1(1);
Codes(e_24) = 0(0), 1(1);
Codes(e_47) = 0(0), 1(1);
Codes(n_3) = 0(0), 1(1);
Codes(n_8) = 0(0), 1(1);
Codes(n_17) = 0(0), 1(1);
Codes(n_22) = 0(0), 1(1);
Codes(n_26) = 0(0), 1(1);
Codes(n_31) = 0(0), 1(1);
Codes(n_35) = 0(0), 1(1);
Codes(n_38) = 0(0), 1(1);
Codes(n_46) = 0(0), 1(1);
Codes(n_80) = 0(0), 1(1);
Codes(n_83) = 0(0), 1(1);
Codes(n_84) = 0(0), 1(1);
Model(p_25) = 2PL;
Model(p_29) = 2PL;
Model(p_48) = 2PL;
Model(p_75) = 2PL;
Model(p_91) = 2PL;
Model(p_5) = 2PL;
Model(p_7) = 2PL;
Model(p_41) = 2PL;
Model(p_54) = 2PL;
Model(p_59) = 2PL;
```

```
    Model(p_79) = 2PL;
    Model(p_88) = 2PL;
    Model(e_6)  = 2PL;
    Model(e_11) = 2PL;
    Model(e_16) = 2PL;
    Model(e_20) = 2PL;
    Model(e_45) = 2PL;
    Model(e_51) = 2PL;
    Model(e_58) = 2PL;
    Model(e_78) = 2PL;
    Model(e_90) = 2PL;
    Model(e_94) = 2PL;
    Model(e_24) = 2PL;
    Model(e_47) = 2PL;
    Model(n_3)  = 2PL;
    Model(n_8)  = 2PL;
    Model(n_17) = 2PL;
    Model(n_22) = 2PL;
    Model(n_26) = 2PL;
    Model(n_31) = 2PL;
    Model(n_35) = 2PL;
    Model(n_38) = 2PL;
    Model(n_46) = 2PL;
    Model(n_80) = 2PL;
    Model(n_83) = 2PL;
    Model(n_84) = 2PL;
    Mean = 0.0;
    Covariance = 1.0;

Constraints:
```

Code 2 Example IRTPRO code for the three-factor EFA model of the EPQ.

```
Project:
    Name = males_labeledSF;

Data:
    File = .\males_labeledSF.ssig;

Analysis:
    Name = 3F EFA;
    Mode = Calibration;
```

```
Title:
3F EFA
Comments:
Estimation:
    Method = BAEM;
    E-Step = 500, 1e-005;
    SE = S-EM;
    M-Step = 50, 1e-006;
    Quadrature = 21, 6;
    SEM = 0.001;
    SS = 1e-005;

Scoring:
    Mean = 0;
    SD = 1;

Miscellaneous:
    Decimal = 2;
    Processors = 4;
    Print M2, CTLD, Loadings, P-Nums, Diagnostic;
    Min Exp = 1;

Groups:
    EFA = ObDQ;

Group:
    Dimension = 3;
    Items = p_25, p_29, p_48, p_75, p_91, p_5, p_7, p_41, p_54, p_59, p_79,
        p_88, e_6, e_11, e_16, e_20, e_45, e_51, e_58, e_78, e_90, e_94, e_24,
        e_47, n_3, n_8, n_17, n_22, n_26, n_31, n_35, n_38, n_46, n_80, n_83,
        n_84;
    Codes(p_25) = 0(0), 1(1);
    Codes(p_29) = 0(0), 1(1);
    Codes(p_48) = 0(0), 1(1);
    Codes(p_75) = 0(0), 1(1);
    Codes(p_91) = 0(0), 1(1);
    Codes(p_5)  = 0(0), 1(1);
    Codes(p_7)  = 0(0), 1(1);
    Codes(p_41) = 0(0), 1(1);
    Codes(p_54) = 0(0), 1(1);
    Codes(p_59) = 0(0), 1(1);
    Codes(p_79) = 0(0), 1(1);
    Codes(p_88) = 0(0), 1(1);
    Codes(e_6)  = 0(0), 1(1);
```

```
Codes(e_11)  =  0(0),  1(1);
Codes(e_16)  =  0(0),  1(1);
Codes(e_20)  =  0(0),  1(1);
Codes(e_45)  =  0(0),  1(1);
Codes(e_51)  =  0(0),  1(1);
Codes(e_58)  =  0(0),  1(1);
Codes(e_78)  =  0(0),  1(1);
Codes(e_90)  =  0(0),  1(1);
Codes(e_94)  =  0(0),  1(1);
Codes(e_24)  =  0(0),  1(1);
Codes(e_47)  =  0(0),  1(1);
Codes(n_3)   =  0(0),  1(1);
Codes(n_8)   =  0(0),  1(1);
Codes(n_17)  =  0(0),  1(1);
Codes(n_22)  =  0(0),  1(1);
Codes(n_26)  =  0(0),  1(1);
Codes(n_31)  =  0(0),  1(1);
Codes(n_35)  =  0(0),  1(1);
Codes(n_38)  =  0(0),  1(1);
Codes(n_46)  =  0(0),  1(1);
Codes(n_80)  =  0(0),  1(1);
Codes(n_83)  =  0(0),  1(1);
Codes(n_84)  =  0(0),  1(1);
Model(p_25)  =  2PL;
Model(p_29)  =  2PL;
Model(p_48)  =  2PL;
Model(p_75)  =  2PL;
Model(p_91)  =  2PL;
Model(p_5)   =  2PL;
Model(p_7)   =  2PL;
Model(p_41)  =  2PL;
Model(p_54)  =  2PL;
Model(p_59)  =  2PL;
Model(p_79)  =  2PL;
Model(p_88)  =  2PL;
Model(e_6)   =  2PL;
Model(e_11)  =  2PL;
Model(e_16)  =  2PL;
Model(e_20)  =  2PL;
Model(e_45)  =  2PL;
Model(e_51)  =  2PL;
Model(e_58)  =  2PL;
Model(e_78)  =  2PL;
Model(e_90)  =  2PL;
Model(e_94)  =  2PL;
Model(e_24)  =  2PL;
Model(e_47)  =  2PL;
```

```
Model(n_3)  = 2PL;
Model(n_8)  = 2PL;
Model(n_17) = 2PL;
Model(n_22) = 2PL;
Model(n_26) = 2PL;
Model(n_31) = 2PL;
Model(n_35) = 2PL;
Model(n_38) = 2PL;
Model(n_46) = 2PL;
Model(n_80) = 2PL;
Model(n_83) = 2PL;
Model(n_84) = 2PL;
```

Code 3 Example IRTPRO code for the three-factor confirmatory MIRT of the EPQ.

```
Project:
    Name = males_labeledSF;
Data:
    File = .\males_labeledSF.ssig;
Analysis:
    Name = 3F CFA;
    Mode = Calibration;
Title:
3F CFA simple structure
Comments:
Estimation:
    Method = BAEM;
    E-Step = 500, 1e-005;
    SE = S-EM;
    M-Step = 500, 1e-006;
    Quadrature = 21, 6;
    SEM = 0.001;
    SS = 1e-005;
Scoring:
    Mean = 0;
    SD = 1;
Miscellaneous:
    Decimal = 2;
    Processors = 4;
    Print M2, CTLD, Loadings, P-Nums, Diagnostic;
    Min Exp = 1;
```

```
Groups:
Group:
    Dimension = 3;
    Items = p_25, p_29, p_48, p_75, p_91, p_5, p_7, p_41,
p_54, p_59, p_79,
    p_88, e_6, e_11, e_16, e_20, e_45, e_51, e_58, e_78,
e_90, e_94, e_24,
    e_47, n_3, n_8, n_17, n_22, n_26, n_31, n_35, n_38,
n_46, n_80, n_83,
    n_84;
    Codes(p_25) = 0(0), 1(1);
    Codes(p_29) = 0(0), 1(1);
    Codes(p_48) = 0(0), 1(1);
    Codes(p_75) = 0(0), 1(1);
    Codes(p_91) = 0(0), 1(1);
    Codes(p_5) = 0(0), 1(1);
    Codes(p_7) = 0(0), 1(1);
    Codes(p_41) = 0(0), 1(1);
    Codes(p_54) = 0(0), 1(1);
    Codes(p_59) = 0(0), 1(1);
    Codes(p_79) = 0(0), 1(1);
    Codes(p_88) = 0(0), 1(1);
    Codes(e_6) = 0(0), 1(1);
    Codes(e_11) = 0(0), 1(1);
    Codes(e_16) = 0(0), 1(1);
    Codes(e_20) = 0(0), 1(1);
    Codes(e_45) = 0(0), 1(1);
    Codes(e_51) = 0(0), 1(1);
    Codes(e_58) = 0(0), 1(1);
    Codes(e_78) = 0(0), 1(1);
    Codes(e_90) = 0(0), 1(1);
    Codes(e_94) = 0(0), 1(1);
    Codes(e_24) = 0(0), 1(1);
    Codes(e_47) = 0(0), 1(1);
    Codes(n_3) = 0(0), 1(1);
    Codes(n_8) = 0(0), 1(1);
    Codes(n_17) = 0(0), 1(1);
    Codes(n_22) = 0(0), 1(1);
    Codes(n_26) = 0(0), 1(1);
    Codes(n_31) = 0(0), 1(1);
    Codes(n_35) = 0(0), 1(1);
    Codes(n_38) = 0(0), 1(1);
    Codes(n_46) = 0(0), 1(1);
    Codes(n_80) = 0(0), 1(1);
    Codes(n_83) = 0(0), 1(1);
    Codes(n_84) = 0(0), 1(1);
    Model(p_25) = 2PL;
```

```
    Model(p_29) = 2PL;
    Model(p_48) = 2PL;
    Model(p_75) = 2PL;
    Model(p_91) = 2PL;
    Model(p_5)  = 2PL;
    Model(p_7)  = 2PL;
    Model(p_41) = 2PL;
    Model(p_54) = 2PL;
    Model(p_59) = 2PL;
    Model(p_79) = 2PL;
    Model(p_88) = 2PL;
    Model(e_6)  = 2PL;
    Model(e_11) = 2PL;
    Model(e_16) = 2PL;
    Model(e_20) = 2PL;
    Model(e_45) = 2PL;
    Model(e_51) = 2PL;
    Model(e_58) = 2PL;
    Model(e_78) = 2PL;
    Model(e_90) = 2PL;
    Model(e_94) = 2PL;
    Model(e_24) = 2PL;
    Model(e_47) = 2PL;
    Model(n_3)  = 2PL;
    Model(n_8)  = 2PL;
    Model(n_17) = 2PL;
    Model(n_22) = 2PL;
    Model(n_26) = 2PL;
    Model(n_31) = 2PL;
    Model(n_35) = 2PL;
    Model(n_38) = 2PL;
    Model(n_46) = 2PL;
    Model(n_80) = 2PL;
    Model(n_83) = 2PL;
    Model(n_84) = 2PL;
    Means = 0.0, 0.0, 0.0;
    Covariances = 1.0,
                  Free, 1.0,
                  Free, Free, 1.0;

Constraints:
    (p_25, Slope[1]) = 0.0;
    (p_25, Slope[2]) = 0.0;
    (p_29, Slope[1]) = 0.0;
    (p_29, Slope[2]) = 0.0;
    (p_48, Slope[1]) = 0.0;
    (p_48, Slope[2]) = 0.0;
```

```
(p_75, Slope[1]) = 0.0;
(p_75, Slope[2]) = 0.0;
(p_91, Slope[1]) = 0.0;
(p_91, Slope[2]) = 0.0;
(p_5, Slope[1]) = 0.0;
(p_5, Slope[2]) = 0.0;
(p_7, Slope[1]) = 0.0;
(p_7, Slope[2]) = 0.0;
(p_41, Slope[1]) = 0.0;
(p_41, Slope[2]) = 0.0;
(p_54, Slope[1]) = 0.0;
(p_54, Slope[2]) = 0.0;
(p_59, Slope[1]) = 0.0;
(p_59, Slope[2]) = 0.0;
(p_79, Slope[1]) = 0.0;
(p_79, Slope[2]) = 0.0;
(p_88, Slope[1]) = 0.0;
(p_88, Slope[2]) = 0.0;
(e_6, Slope[0]) = 0.0;
(e_6, Slope[2]) = 0.0;
(e_11, Slope[0]) = 0.0;
(e_11, Slope[2]) = 0.0;
(e_16, Slope[0]) = 0.0;
(e_16, Slope[2]) = 0.0;
(e_20, Slope[0]) = 0.0;
(e_20, Slope[2]) = 0.0;
(e_45, Slope[0]) = 0.0;
(e_45, Slope[2]) = 0.0;
(e_51, Slope[0]) = 0.0;
(e_51, Slope[2]) = 0.0;
(e_58, Slope[0]) = 0.0;
(e_58, Slope[2]) = 0.0;
(e_78, Slope[0]) = 0.0;
(e_78, Slope[2]) = 0.0;
(e_90, Slope[0]) = 0.0;
(e_90, Slope[2]) = 0.0;
(e_94, Slope[0]) = 0.0;
(e_94, Slope[2]) = 0.0;
(e_24, Slope[0]) = 0.0;
(e_24, Slope[2]) = 0.0;
(e_47, Slope[0]) = 0.0;
(e_47, Slope[2]) = 0.0;
(n_3, Slope[0]) = 0.0;
(n_3, Slope[1]) = 0.0;
(n_8, Slope[0]) = 0.0;
(n_8, Slope[1]) = 0.0;
(n_17, Slope[0]) = 0.0;
```

```
   (n_17, Slope[1]) = 0.0;
   (n_22, Slope[0]) = 0.0;
   (n_22, Slope[1]) = 0.0;
   (n_26, Slope[0]) = 0.0;
   (n_26, Slope[1]) = 0.0;
   (n_31, Slope[0]) = 0.0;
   (n_31, Slope[1]) = 0.0;
   (n_35, Slope[0]) = 0.0;
   (n_35, Slope[1]) = 0.0;
   (n_38, Slope[0]) = 0.0;
   (n_38, Slope[1]) = 0.0;
   (n_46, Slope[0]) = 0.0;
   (n_46, Slope[1]) = 0.0;
   (n_80, Slope[0]) = 0.0;
   (n_80, Slope[1]) = 0.0;
   (n_83, Slope[0]) = 0.0;
   (n_83, Slope[1]) = 0.0;
   (n_84, Slope[0]) = 0.0;
   (n_84, Slope[1]) = 0.0;
```

Code 4 Example IRTPRO code for the eight-factor confirmatory MIRT model of the EPQ.

```
Project:
    Name = males_labeledSF;

Data:
    File = .\males_labeledSF.ssig;

Analysis:
    Name = new CLs;
    Mode = Calibration;

Title:
Comments:
Estimation:
    Method = BAEM;
    E-Step = 500, 1e-005;
    SE = S-EM;
    M-Step = 500, 1e-006;
    Quadrature = 21, 6;
    SEM = 0.001;
    SS = 1e-005;
```

```
Saves:
    PRM, COV, DBG

Scoring:
    Mean = 0;
    SD = 1;

Miscellaneous:
    Decimal = 3;
    Processor = 1;
    Print M2, CTLD, Loadings, P-Nums, Diagnostic;
    Min Exp = 1;

Groups:

Group:
    Dimension = 3;
    Items = p_25, p_29, p_48, p_75, p_91, p_5, p_7, p_41,
    p_54, p_59, p_79,
    p_88, e_6, e_11, e_16, e_20, e_45, e_51, e_58, e_78,
    e_90, e_94, e_24,
    e_47, n_3, n_8, n_17, n_22, n_26, n_31, n_35, n_38,
    n_46, n_80, n_83,
    n_84;
    Codes(p_25) = 0(0), 1(1);
    Codes(p_29) = 0(0), 1(1);
    Codes(p_48) = 0(0), 1(1);
    Codes(p_75) = 0(0), 1(1);
    Codes(p_91) = 0(0), 1(1);
    Codes(p_5)  = 0(0), 1(1);
    Codes(p_7)  = 0(0), 1(1);
    Codes(p_41) = 0(0), 1(1);
    Codes(p_54) = 0(0), 1(1);
    Codes(p_59) = 0(0), 1(1);
    Codes(p_79) = 0(0), 1(1);
    Codes(p_88) = 0(0), 1(1);
    Codes(e_6)  = 0(0), 1(1);
    Codes(e_11) = 0(0), 1(1);
    Codes(e_16) = 0(0), 1(1);
    Codes(e_20) = 0(0), 1(1);
    Codes(e_45) = 0(0), 1(1);
    Codes(e_51) = 0(0), 1(1);
    Codes(e_58) = 0(0), 1(1);
    Codes(e_78) = 0(0), 1(1);
    Codes(e_90) = 0(0), 1(1);
    Codes(e_94) = 0(0), 1(1);
    Codes(e_24) = 0(0), 1(1);
    Codes(e_47) = 0(0), 1(1);
```

```
Codes(n_3)  = 0(0), 1(1);
Codes(n_8)  = 0(0), 1(1);
Codes(n_17) = 0(0), 1(1);
Codes(n_22) = 0(0), 1(1);
Codes(n_26) = 0(0), 1(1);
Codes(n_31) = 0(0), 1(1);
Codes(n_35) = 0(0), 1(1);
Codes(n_38) = 0(0), 1(1);
Codes(n_46) = 0(0), 1(1);
Codes(n_80) = 0(0), 1(1);
Codes(n_83) = 0(0), 1(1);
Codes(n_84) = 0(0), 1(1);
Model(p_25) = 2PL;
Model(p_29) = 2PL;
Model(p_48) = 2PL;
Model(p_75) = 2PL;
Model(p_91) = 2PL;
Model(p_5)  = 2PL;
Model(p_7)  = 2PL;
Model(p_41) = 2PL;
Model(p_54) = 2PL;
Model(p_59) = 2PL;
Model(p_79) = 2PL;
Model(p_88) = 2PL;
Model(e_6)  = 2PL;
Model(e_11) = 2PL;
Model(e_16) = 2PL;
Model(e_20) = 2PL;
Model(e_45) = 2PL;
Model(e_51) = 2PL;
Model(e_58) = 2PL;
Model(e_78) = 2PL;
Model(e_90) = 2PL;
Model(e_94) = 2PL;
Model(e_24) = 2PL;
Model(e_47) = 2PL;
Model(n_3)  = 2PL;
Model(n_8)  = 2PL;
Model(n_17) = 2PL;
Model(n_22) = 2PL;
Model(n_26) = 2PL;
Model(n_31) = 2PL;
Model(n_35) = 2PL;
Model(n_38) = 2PL;
Model(n_46) = 2PL;
Model(n_80) = 2PL;
Model(n_83) = 2PL;
Model(n_84) = 2PL;
```

```
    Means = 0.0, 0.0, 0.0;
    Covariances = 1.0,
                  Free, 1.0,
                  Free, Free, 1.0;

Constraints:
    Equal = (p_88, Slope[2]), (p_29, Slope[1]), (p_48, Slope
    [1]), (p_75,
    Slope[1]), (p_91, Slope[1]), (p_5, Slope[1]), (p_7,
    Slope[1]), (p_41,
    Slope[1]), (p_59, Slope[1]), (p_79, Slope[1]), (p_88,
    Slope[1]), (p_29,
    Slope[2]), (p_48, Slope[2]), (p_75, Slope[2]), (p_91,
    Slope[2]), (p_5,
    Slope[2]), (p_7, Slope[2]), (p_41, Slope[2]), (p_54,
    Slope[2]), (p_59,
    Slope[2]), (p_79, Slope[2]);
    (p_25, Slope[1]) = 0.0;
    (p_29, Slope[1]) = 0.0;
    (p_29, Slope[2]) = 0.0;
    (p_48, Slope[1]) = 0.0;
    (p_48, Slope[2]) = 0.0;
    (p_75, Slope[1]) = 0.0;
    (p_75, Slope[2]) = 0.0;
    (p_91, Slope[1]) = 0.0;
    (p_91, Slope[2]) = 0.0;
    (p_5, Slope[1]) = 0.0;
    (p_5, Slope[2]) = 0.0;
    (p_7, Slope[1]) = 0.0;
    (p_7, Slope[2]) = 0.0;
    (p_41, Slope[1]) = 0.0;
    (p_41, Slope[2]) = 0.0;
    (p_54, Slope[2]) = 0.0;
    (p_59, Slope[1]) = 0.0;
    (p_59, Slope[2]) = 0.0;
    (p_79, Slope[1]) = 0.0;
    (p_79, Slope[2]) = 0.0;
    (p_88, Slope[1]) = 0.0;
    (p_88, Slope[2]) = 0.0;
    (e_6, Slope[0]) = 0.0;
    (e_6, Slope[2]) = 0.0;
    (e_11, Slope[0]) = 0.0;
    (e_11, Slope[2]) = 0.0;
    (e_16, Slope[0]) = 0.0;
    (e_16, Slope[2]) = 0.0;
    (e_20, Slope[0]) = 0.0;
    (e_20, Slope[2]) = 0.0;
    (e_45, Slope[0]) = 0.0;
```

```
        (e_45, Slope[2]) = 0.0;
        (e_51, Slope[0]) = 0.0;
        (e_51, Slope[2]) = 0.0;
        (e_58, Slope[0]) = 0.0;
        (e_58, Slope[2]) = 0.0;
        (e_78, Slope[0]) = 0.0;
        (e_78, Slope[2]) = 0.0;
        (e_90, Slope[0]) = 0.0;
        (e_90, Slope[2]) = 0.0;
        (e_94, Slope[0]) = 0.0;
        (e_94, Slope[2]) = 0.0;
        (e_24, Slope[0]) = 0.0;
        (e_24, Slope[2]) = 0.0;
        (e_47, Slope[0]) = 0.0;
        (e_47, Slope[2]) = 0.0;
        (n_3,  Slope[0]) = 0.0;
        (n_3,  Slope[1]) = 0.0;
        (n_8,  Slope[0]) = 0.0;
        (n_8,  Slope[1]) = 0.0;
        (n_17, Slope[0]) = 0.0;
        (n_17, Slope[1]) = 0.0;
        (n_22, Slope[0]) = 0.0;
        (n_22, Slope[1]) = 0.0;
        (n_26, Slope[0]) = 0.0;
        (n_26, Slope[1]) = 0.0;
        (n_31, Slope[0]) = 0.0;
        (n_31, Slope[1]) = 0.0;
        (n_35, Slope[0]) = 0.0;
        (n_35, Slope[1]) = 0.0;
        (n_38, Slope[0]) = 0.0;
        (n_38, Slope[1]) = 0.0;
        (n_46, Slope[0]) = 0.0;
        (n_46, Slope[1]) = 0.0;
        (n_80, Slope[0]) = 0.0;
        (n_80, Slope[1]) = 0.0;
        (n_83, Slope[0]) = 0.0;
        (n_83, Slope[1]) = 0.0;
        (n_84, Slope[0]) = 0.0;
        (n_84, Slope[1]) = 0.0;

Analysis:
    Name = newCLs+bifactor;
    Mode = Calibration;

Title:
cross loading items + LD subsets
```

```
Comments:
"social rule pair": P29, P88
"nerves pair": N35, N83
"worrying" 4-tuples: N38, N80, P7, P59
"party" pair: E51, E78
"hiding" pair: E47, E24

Estimation:
    Method = BAEM;
    E-Step = 5000, 1e-005;
    SE = Xpd;
    M-Step = 50, 1e-006;
    Quadrature = 21, 5;
    SEM = 0.001;
    SS = 1e-005;

Saves:
    PRM, COV, DBG

Scoring:
    Mean = 0;
    SD = 1;

Miscellaneous:
    Decimal = 2;
    Processor = 1;
    Print CTLD, Loadings, P-Nums, Diagnostic;
    Min Exp = 1;

Groups:

Group:
    Dimension = 8;
    GenDim = 3;
    Items = p_25, p_29, p_48, p_75, p_91, p_5, p_7, p_41,
    p_54, p_59, p_79,
    p_88, e_6, e_11, e_16, e_20, e_45, e_51, e_58, e_78,
    e_90, e_94, e_24,
    e_47, n_3, n_8, n_17, n_22, n_26, n_31, n_35, n_38,
    n_46, n_80, n_83,
    n_84;
    Codes(p_25) = 0(0), 1(1);
    Codes(p_29) = 0(0), 1(1);
    Codes(p_48) = 0(0), 1(1);
    Codes(p_75) = 0(0), 1(1);
    Codes(p_91) = 0(0), 1(1);
    Codes(p_5) = 0(0), 1(1);
    Codes(p_7) = 0(0), 1(1);
```

```
Codes(p_41) = 0(0), 1(1);
Codes(p_54) = 0(0), 1(1);
Codes(p_59) = 0(0), 1(1);
Codes(p_79) = 0(0), 1(1);
Codes(p_88) = 0(0), 1(1);
Codes(e_6)  = 0(0), 1(1);
Codes(e_11) = 0(0), 1(1);
Codes(e_16) = 0(0), 1(1);
Codes(e_20) = 0(0), 1(1);
Codes(e_45) = 0(0), 1(1);
Codes(e_51) = 0(0), 1(1);
Codes(e_58) = 0(0), 1(1);
Codes(e_78) = 0(0), 1(1);
Codes(e_90) = 0(0), 1(1);
Codes(e_94) = 0(0), 1(1);
Codes(e_24) = 0(0), 1(1);
Codes(e_47) = 0(0), 1(1);
Codes(n_3)  = 0(0), 1(1);
Codes(n_8)  = 0(0), 1(1);
Codes(n_17) = 0(0), 1(1);
Codes(n_22) = 0(0), 1(1);
Codes(n_26) = 0(0), 1(1);
Codes(n_31) = 0(0), 1(1);
Codes(n_35) = 0(0), 1(1);
Codes(n_38) = 0(0), 1(1);
Codes(n_46) = 0(0), 1(1);
Codes(n_80) = 0(0), 1(1);
Codes(n_83) = 0(0), 1(1);
Codes(n_84) = 0(0), 1(1);
Model(p_25) = 2PL;
Model(p_29) = 2PL;
Model(p_48) = 2PL;
Model(p_75) = 2PL;
Model(p_91) = 2PL;
Model(p_5)  = 2PL;
Model(p_7)  = 2PL;
Model(p_41) = 2PL;
Model(p_54) = 2PL;
Model(p_59) = 2PL;
Model(p_79) = 2PL;
Model(p_88) = 2PL;
Model(e_6)  = 2PL;
Model(e_11) = 2PL;
Model(e_16) = 2PL;
Model(e_20) = 2PL;
Model(e_45) = 2PL;
Model(e_51) = 2PL;
Model(e_58) = 2PL;
```

```
    Model(e_78) = 2PL;
    Model(e_90) = 2PL;
    Model(e_94) = 2PL;
    Model(e_24) = 2PL;
    Model(e_47) = 2PL;
    Model(n_3)  = 2PL;
    Model(n_8)  = 2PL;
    Model(n_17) = 2PL;
    Model(n_22) = 2PL;
    Model(n_26) = 2PL;
    Model(n_31) = 2PL;
    Model(n_35) = 2PL;
    Model(n_38) = 2PL;
    Model(n_46) = 2PL;
    Model(n_80) = 2PL;
    Model(n_83) = 2PL;
    Model(n_84) = 2PL;
    Means = 0.0, 0.0, 0.0, 0.0, 0.0, 0.0, 0.0, 0.0;
    Covariances = 1.0,
                  Free, 1.0,
                  Free, Free, 1.0,
                  0.0, 0.0, 0.0, 1.0,
                  0.0, 0.0, 0.0, 0.0, 1.0,
                  0.0, 0.0, 0.0, 0.0, 0.0, 1.0,
                  0.0, 0.0, 0.0, 0.0, 0.0, 0.0, 1.0,
                  0.0, 0.0, 0.0, 0.0, 0.0, 0.0, 0.0, 1.0;

Constraints:
    Equal = (p_29, Slope[3]), (p_88, Slope[3]);
    Equal = (n_83, Slope[4]), (n_35, Slope[4]);
    Equal = (e_78, Slope[6]), (e_51, Slope[6]);
    Equal = (e_47, Slope[7]), (e_24, Slope[7]);
    (p_25, Slope[1]) = 0.0;
    (p_25, Slope[3]) = 0.0;
    (p_25, Slope[4]) = 0.0;
    (p_25, Slope[5]) = 0.0;
    (p_25, Slope[6]) = 0.0;
    (p_25, Slope[7]) = 0.0;
    (p_29, Slope[1]) = 0.0;
    (p_29, Slope[2]) = 0.0;
    (p_29, Slope[4]) = 0.0;
    (p_29, Slope[5]) = 0.0;
    (p_29, Slope[6]) = 0.0;
    (p_29, Slope[7]) = 0.0;
    (p_48, Slope[1]) = 0.0;
    (p_48, Slope[2]) = 0.0;
    (p_48, Slope[3]) = 0.0;
    (p_48, Slope[4]) = 0.0;
```

```
(p_48, Slope[5]) = 0.0;
(p_48, Slope[6]) = 0.0;
(p_48, Slope[7]) = 0.0;
(p_75, Slope[1]) = 0.0;
(p_75, Slope[2]) = 0.0;
(p_75, Slope[3]) = 0.0;
(p_75, Slope[4]) = 0.0;
(p_75, Slope[5]) = 0.0;
(p_75, Slope[6]) = 0.0;
(p_75, Slope[7]) = 0.0;
(p_91, Slope[1]) = 0.0;
(p_91, Slope[2]) = 0.0;
(p_91, Slope[3]) = 0.0;
(p_91, Slope[4]) = 0.0;
(p_91, Slope[5]) = 0.0;
(p_91, Slope[6]) = 0.0;
(p_91, Slope[7]) = 0.0;
(p_5, Slope[1]) = 0.0;
(p_5, Slope[2]) = 0.0;
(p_5, Slope[3]) = 0.0;
(p_5, Slope[4]) = 0.0;
(p_5, Slope[5]) = 0.0;
(p_5, Slope[6]) = 0.0;
(p_5, Slope[7]) = 0.0;
(p_7, Slope[1]) = 0.0;
(p_7, Slope[2]) = 0.0;
(p_7, Slope[3]) = 0.0;
(p_7, Slope[4]) = 0.0;
(p_7, Slope[6]) = 0.0;
(p_7, Slope[7]) = 0.0;
(p_41, Slope[1]) = 0.0;
(p_41, Slope[2]) = 0.0;
(p_41, Slope[3]) = 0.0;
(p_41, Slope[4]) = 0.0;
(p_41, Slope[5]) = 0.0;
(p_41, Slope[6]) = 0.0;
(p_41, Slope[7]) = 0.0;
(p_54, Slope[2]) = 0.0;
(p_54, Slope[3]) = 0.0;
(p_54, Slope[4]) = 0.0;
(p_54, Slope[5]) = 0.0;
(p_54, Slope[6]) = 0.0;
(p_54, Slope[7]) = 0.0;
(p_59, Slope[1]) = 0.0;
(p_59, Slope[2]) = 0.0;
(p_59, Slope[3]) = 0.0;
(p_59, Slope[4]) = 0.0;
(p_59, Slope[6]) = 0.0;
```

```
(p_59, Slope[7]) = 0.0;
(p_79, Slope[1]) = 0.0;
(p_79, Slope[2]) = 0.0;
(p_79, Slope[3]) = 0.0;
(p_79, Slope[4]) = 0.0;
(p_79, Slope[5]) = 0.0;
(p_79, Slope[6]) = 0.0;
(p_79, Slope[7]) = 0.0;
(p_88, Slope[1]) = 0.0;
(p_88, Slope[2]) = 0.0;
(p_88, Slope[4]) = 0.0;
(p_88, Slope[5]) = 0.0;
(p_88, Slope[6]) = 0.0;
(p_88, Slope[7]) = 0.0;
(e_6, Slope[0]) = 0.0;
(e_6, Slope[2]) = 0.0;
(e_6, Slope[3]) = 0.0;
(e_6, Slope[4]) = 0.0;
(e_6, Slope[5]) = 0.0;
(e_6, Slope[6]) = 0.0;
(e_6, Slope[7]) = 0.0;
(e_11, Slope[0]) = 0.0;
(e_11, Slope[2]) = 0.0;
(e_11, Slope[3]) = 0.0;
(e_11, Slope[4]) = 0.0;
(e_11, Slope[5]) = 0.0;
(e_11, Slope[6]) = 0.0;
(e_11, Slope[7]) = 0.0;
(e_16, Slope[0]) = 0.0;
(e_16, Slope[2]) = 0.0;
(e_16, Slope[3]) = 0.0;
(e_16, Slope[4]) = 0.0;
(e_16, Slope[5]) = 0.0;
(e_16, Slope[6]) = 0.0;
(e_16, Slope[7]) = 0.0;
(e_20, Slope[0]) = 0.0;
(e_20, Slope[2]) = 0.0;
(e_20, Slope[3]) = 0.0;
(e_20, Slope[4]) = 0.0;
(e_20, Slope[5]) = 0.0;
(e_20, Slope[6]) = 0.0;
(e_20, Slope[7]) = 0.0;
(e_45, Slope[0]) = 0.0;
(e_45, Slope[2]) = 0.0;
(e_45, Slope[3]) = 0.0;
(e_45, Slope[4]) = 0.0;
(e_45, Slope[5]) = 0.0;
(e_45, Slope[6]) = 0.0;
```

```
(e_45, Slope[7]) = 0.0;
(e_51, Slope[0]) = 0.0;
(e_51, Slope[2]) = 0.0;
(e_51, Slope[3]) = 0.0;
(e_51, Slope[4]) = 0.0;
(e_51, Slope[5]) = 0.0;
(e_51, Slope[7]) = 0.0;
(e_58, Slope[0]) = 0.0;
(e_58, Slope[2]) = 0.0;
(e_58, Slope[3]) = 0.0;
(e_58, Slope[4]) = 0.0;
(e_58, Slope[5]) = 0.0;
(e_58, Slope[6]) = 0.0;
(e_58, Slope[7]) = 0.0;
(e_78, Slope[0]) = 0.0;
(e_78, Slope[2]) = 0.0;
(e_78, Slope[3]) = 0.0;
(e_78, Slope[4]) = 0.0;
(e_78, Slope[5]) = 0.0;
(e_78, Slope[7]) = 0.0;
(e_90, Slope[0]) = 0.0;
(e_90, Slope[2]) = 0.0;
(e_90, Slope[3]) = 0.0;
(e_90, Slope[4]) = 0.0;
(e_90, Slope[5]) = 0.0;
(e_90, Slope[6]) = 0.0;
(e_90, Slope[7]) = 0.0;
(e_94, Slope[0]) = 0.0;
(e_94, Slope[2]) = 0.0;
(e_94, Slope[3]) = 0.0;
(e_94, Slope[4]) = 0.0;
(e_94, Slope[5]) = 0.0;
(e_94, Slope[6]) = 0.0;
(e_94, Slope[7]) = 0.0;
(e_24, Slope[0]) = 0.0;
(e_24, Slope[2]) = 0.0;
(e_24, Slope[3]) = 0.0;
(e_24, Slope[4]) = 0.0;
(e_24, Slope[5]) = 0.0;
(e_24, Slope[6]) = 0.0;
(e_47, Slope[0]) = 0.0;
(e_47, Slope[2]) = 0.0;
(e_47, Slope[3]) = 0.0;
(e_47, Slope[4]) = 0.0;
(e_47, Slope[5]) = 0.0;
(e_47, Slope[6]) = 0.0;
(n_3, Slope[0]) = 0.0;
(n_3, Slope[1]) = 0.0;
```

```
(n_3,  Slope[3]) = 0.0;
(n_3,  Slope[4]) = 0.0;
(n_3,  Slope[5]) = 0.0;
(n_3,  Slope[6]) = 0.0;
(n_3,  Slope[7]) = 0.0;
(n_8,  Slope[0]) = 0.0;
(n_8,  Slope[1]) = 0.0;
(n_8,  Slope[3]) = 0.0;
(n_8,  Slope[4]) = 0.0;
(n_8,  Slope[5]) = 0.0;
(n_8,  Slope[6]) = 0.0;
(n_8,  Slope[7]) = 0.0;
(n_17, Slope[0]) = 0.0;
(n_17, Slope[1]) = 0.0;
(n_17, Slope[3]) = 0.0;
(n_17, Slope[4]) = 0.0;
(n_17, Slope[5]) = 0.0;
(n_17, Slope[6]) = 0.0;
(n_17, Slope[7]) = 0.0;
(n_22, Slope[0]) = 0.0;
(n_22, Slope[1]) = 0.0;
(n_22, Slope[3]) = 0.0;
(n_22, Slope[4]) = 0.0;
(n_22, Slope[5]) = 0.0;
(n_22, Slope[6]) = 0.0;
(n_22, Slope[7]) = 0.0;
(n_26, Slope[0]) = 0.0;
(n_26, Slope[1]) = 0.0;
(n_26, Slope[3]) = 0.0;
(n_26, Slope[4]) = 0.0;
(n_26, Slope[5]) = 0.0;
(n_26, Slope[6]) = 0.0;
(n_26, Slope[7]) = 0.0;
(n_31, Slope[0]) = 0.0;
(n_31, Slope[1]) = 0.0;
(n_31, Slope[3]) = 0.0;
(n_31, Slope[4]) = 0.0;
(n_31, Slope[5]) = 0.0;
(n_31, Slope[6]) = 0.0;
(n_31, Slope[7]) = 0.0;
(n_35, Slope[0]) = 0.0;
(n_35, Slope[1]) = 0.0;
(n_35, Slope[3]) = 0.0;
(n_35, Slope[5]) = 0.0;
(n_35, Slope[6]) = 0.0;
(n_35, Slope[7]) = 0.0;
(n_38, Slope[0]) = 0.0;
(n_38, Slope[1]) = 0.0;
```

```
(n_38, Slope[3]) = 0.0;
(n_38, Slope[4]) = 0.0;
(n_38, Slope[6]) = 0.0;
(n_38, Slope[7]) = 0.0;
(n_46, Slope[0]) = 0.0;
(n_46, Slope[1]) = 0.0;
(n_46, Slope[3]) = 0.0;
(n_46, Slope[4]) = 0.0;
(n_46, Slope[5]) = 0.0;
(n_46, Slope[6]) = 0.0;
(n_46, Slope[7]) = 0.0;
(n_80, Slope[0]) = 0.0;
(n_80, Slope[1]) = 0.0;
(n_80, Slope[3]) = 0.0;
(n_80, Slope[4]) = 0.0;
(n_80, Slope[6]) = 0.0;
(n_80, Slope[7]) = 0.0;
(n_83, Slope[0]) = 0.0;
(n_83, Slope[1]) = 0.0;
(n_83, Slope[3]) = 0.0;
(n_83, Slope[5]) = 0.0;
(n_83, Slope[6]) = 0.0;
(n_83, Slope[7]) = 0.0;
(n_84, Slope[0]) = 0.0;
(n_84, Slope[1]) = 0.0;
(n_84, Slope[3]) = 0.0;
(n_84, Slope[4]) = 0.0;
(n_84, Slope[5]) = 0.0;
(n_84, Slope[6]) = 0.0;
(n_84, Slope[7]) = 0.0;
```

Code 5 Example R code for the production of Figure 16.3.

```
## "correlation" plot for display statistics
x2.tab <- as.matrix(read.table("x2tab.txt"));
bh.tab <- as.matrix(read.table("bhsig.txt"));
sf_names <- scan("sf_names.txt", what=character());
colnames(x2.tab) <- rownames(x2.tab) <- sf_names;
colnames(bh.tab) <- rownames(bh.tab) <- sf_names;

x2.tabP <- permute(x2.tab,
                   ser_permutation(c(9,11,2,8,5,10,12,6,1,
                                     3,7,4,14,19,20,23,18,
                                     22,13,15,24,21,16,17,
                                     32,25,29,35,33,26,31,
                                     28,30,36,27,34),
```

```
                              c(9,11,2,8,5,10,12,6,1,
                                3,7,4,14,19,20,23,18,
                                22,13,15,24,21,16,17,
                                32,25,29,35,33,26,31,
                                28,30,36,27,34)))
bh.tabP <- permute(bh.tab,
               ser_permutation(c(9,11,2,8,5,10,12,6,1,
                                 3,7,4,14,19,20,23,18,
                                 22,13,15,24,21,16,17,
                                 32,25,29,35,33,26,31,
                                 28,30,36,27,34),
                               c(9,11,2,8,5,10,12,6,1,
                                 3,7,4,14,19,20,23,18,
                                 22,13,15,24,21,16,17,
                                 32,25,29,35,33,26,31,
                                 28,30,36,27,34)))
sf_namesP <- permute(sf_names,
               ser_permutation(c(9,11,2,8,5,10,12,6,1,
                                 3,7,4,14,19,20,23,18,
                                 22,13,15,24,21,16,17,
                                 32,25,29,35,33,26,31,
                                 28,30,36,27,34)))

require(corrplot);
pdf("x2P.pdf", width=16, height=15);

corrplot(round(x2.tabP, digits=1), diag=T, type="full",
         tl.pos="lt", tl.srt=0, tl.offset=0.6, is.corr=F,
         bg="white", addgrid.col="white", col="white",
         cl.pos="n", addshade="all", shade.col="black",
         p.mat=1 - bh.tabP, insig="blank", tl.
col="black");

colnames(x2.tabP) <- rownames(x2.tabP) <- rep("-", 36);

corrplot(round(x2.tabP, digits=1), add=T, diag=T,
type="full",
         tl.pos="d", tl.srt=0, tl.offset=0.6, is.corr=F,
         bg="white", addgrid.col="grey", col="white",
         cl.pos="n", addshade="all", shade.col="black",
         p.mat=1 - bh.tabP, insig="blank", tl.
         col="black");

corrplot(round(x2.tabP, digits=1), add=T, diag=F,
         type="lower",
         tl.pos="n", is.corr=F, bg="white", addgrid.
         col="grey",
```

```
              outline=T, col="white", cl.pos="n",
              addshade="all",
              shade.col="black", p.mat=1 - bh.tabP,
              insig="blank",
              tl.col="black");

corrplot(round(x2.tabP, digits=1), add=T, diag=F, tl.
      pos="n",
      type="upper", method="number", is.corr=F,
      bg="white",
      addgrid.col="grey", outline=T, col="black", cl.
      pos="n",
      addshade="all", shade.col="black", p.mat=1 - bh.
      tabP,
      insig="blank", tl.col="black");

dev.off();
colnames(x2.tabP) <- rownames(x2.tabP) <- sf_namesP;
```

Code 6 Example R code for the production of Figure 16.4.

```
require(corrplot);
require(seriation)

efa_lmbd <- as.matrix(read.table("male_efa3_loadings.
txt"));
efa_se <- as.matrix(read.table("male_efa3_se.txt"));
sfnames <- scan("sf_names.txt", what=character(),
quiet=T);
colnames(efa_lmbd) <- c("Factor 1", "Factor 2", "Factor 3");
rownames(efa_lmbd) <- sfnames;

efa_lmbdP <- permute(efa_lmbd,
                ser_permutation(c(9,11,2,8,5,10,12,6,
                        1,3,7,4,14,19,20,23,
                        18,22,13,15,24,21,16,
                        17,32,25,29,35,33,26,
                        31,28,30,36,27,34),
                        1:3))
efa_seP <- permute(efa_se,
                ser_permutation(c(9,11,2,8,5,10,12,6,1,
                        3,7,4,14,19,20,23,18,
```

```
                                  22,13,15,24,21,16,17,
                                  32,25,29,35,33,26,31,
                                  28,30,36,27,34),
                                  1:3))

pdf("efalmbdP.pdf", width=8.5, height=8.5);
par(mfrow=c(3, 1), mar=c(0, 0, 0, 0));

title <- c("Psychoticism", "Extraversion", "Neuroticism");
for (i in 1:3) {
    lmbd_block <- efa_lmbdP[(i - 1) * 12 + 1:12, ]; ## block of
    lambda matrix
    se_block <- efa_seP[(i - 1) * 12 + 1:12, ];   ## block
of se matrix
    sig <- matrix(NA, NROW(lmbd_block), NCOL
(lmbd_block));   ## significant matrix
    for (i in 1:NROW(lmbd_block)) {
        for (j in 1:NCOL(lmbd_block)) {
            if (abs(lmbd_block[i, j]) / se_block[i, j] >=
            qnorm(0.975))
                sig[i, j] <- lmbd_block[i, j]
            else sig[i, j] <- -999;
        }
    }
    corrplot(t(lmbd_block), col="white", outline=T, cl.
    pos="n",
             tl.srt=0, tl.offset=0.6, tl.col="black", p.
             mat=t(sig),
             insig="p-value", sig.level=-998);
}
dev.off()
```

17

Bayesian Psychometric Scaling

Jean-Paul Fox, Stéphanie van den Berg, and Bernard Veldkamp

Introduction

Within the scope of psychometrics, measurement models are used to assess student proficiency levels and test characteristics given assessment results. The assessment results are most often response data, which are usually categorical observations. Therefore, a nonlinear or a generalized linear modelling approach is necessary to define a relation between the item response observations and the test and student characteristics.

Such item–based response models have received much attention, especially in the area of academic assessment where student proficiency is considered to be a latent variable of interest. Multiple items are used to measure the latent variable, and a scale measurement is derived using an item response (measurement) model. Within the framework of item response theory, response models are defined that describe the probabilistic relationship between a student's response and the student's latent variable level being measured.

Recently, Bayesian item response models have been developed to analyze test data and to measure latent variables. In Bayesian psychometric modelling, it is possible to include genuine prior information about the assessment in addition to information available in the observed response data. Inferences can be made based on the observed data and additional information, which can be important in nonstandardized settings, complex experimental designs, or complex surveys, where common modelling assumptions do not hold. As prior information, uncertainties can be explicitly quantified that might relate to different models, parameters, or hypotheses.

The Bayesian modelling approach is very flexible and provides direct estimates of student proficiencies. In addition, by modelling the raw observations, a direct interpretation can be given of the model parameters and their priors. Furthermore, for small sample sizes, the flexible Bayesian approach depends less on asymptotic results and is therefore very useful for small samples (e.g., Lee & Song, 2004).

In this chapter, Bayesian psychometric modelling is introduced. It is shown that an item response modelling framework can be defined that can adapt to real case scenarios. Prior information can be incorporated in the analysis, which adds to the data information, with Bayesian inferences based on the total information available. The Bayesian response modelling framework comes with powerful simulation-based estimation methods, which supports the joint estimation of all model parameters given the observed data. The work of Albert (1992), Albert and Chib (1993), Bradlow, Wainer, and Wang (1999), Fox (2010), Fox and Glas (2001), Patz and Junker (1999a, 1999b), and Patz, Junker, Johnson, and Mariano (2002), among others, advocated simulation-based estimation methods for psychometric models and stimulated their use.

Bayesian item response models are discussed to provide insight into the various measurement models and the Bayesian way of making psychometric inferences. A hierarchical item response modelling approach is discussed, where observations are nested in subjects and items (e.g., Johnson, Sinharay, & Bradlow, 2007). Priors are used to define the nested structure of the data by modelling item and student parameters in a hierarchical way. Dependencies between observations within the same cluster are taken into account by modelling the nested structure of the response data. The development of Bayesian item response models started with the work of Mislevy (1986), Novick, Lewis, and Jackson (1973), Swaminathan and Gifford (1982, 1985), Tsutakawa and Lin (1986). In the 1990s, this approach was further developed by Kim, Cohen, Baker, Subkoviak, and Leonard (1994) and Bradlow et al. (1999), among others.

After introducing unidimensional item response models for dichotomous responses, it is shown how to make inferences from posterior distributions. Then, specific attention will be given to the influence of priors on the statistical inferences. It is shown that informative priors will influence the posterior results more than uninformative priors, where the influence is estimated by considering the amount of shrinkage of the posterior estimate to the prior estimate. In estimating student proficiencies, different simulation studies are done to illustrate the prior influence.

Then, an additional clustering of students is discussed, where performances from students in the same cluster are more alike than from different clusters. This leads to an extension of the Bayesian item response model to more than two levels (i.e., item response defines level 1, and student level 2), thus a multilevel item response theory (IRT) model is discussed. A classic example is educational survey data collected through multistage sampling, where the primary sampling units are schools, and students are sampled conditional on the school unit. Following Fox (2010), Fox and Glas (2001), and Aitkin and Aitkin (2011), among others, a complete hierarchical modelling framework is defined by integrating the item response model with the survey population distribution. Besides item-specific differences, this multilevel item response model takes the survey design into account, the backgrounds of the respondents, and clusters in which respondents are located.

Finally, advantages of Bayesian item response models in computer based testing are discussed. The introduction of empirical prior information in item parameter estimation reduces the costs of item bank development. Besides, in Bayesian computerized (adaptive) testing, test length can be reduced considerably when prior information about the ability level of the candidates is available. Methods to elicit empirical priors are presented, and an overview of Bayesian item selection is given.

Bayesian Methods

Here, a brief introduction is given to the Bayesian methodology. A thorough discussion of Bayesian methods can be found in Gelman et al. (2014). Our emphasis here will be how to model item response data and to make inferences from the Bayesian perspective.

The software package WinBUGS makes such an analysis relatively straightforward, and in this chapter the use of WinBUGS is illustrated. The Bayesian methodology is attractive since it allows one to incorporate other sources of information to improve, for example, the estimation of parameters that are poorly identified by the data. Another advantage is that more information can be obtained about the parameter estimates and the fit of the model, and new types of models can be evaluated. A disadvantage is that the computation of Bayesian estimates can be intensive.

The Bayesian modelling approach starts with defining a likelihood function, which constitutes a parametric model for the data observations. The parameters of the likelihood model are treated as random variables, and they need to be given distributions, referred to as prior distributions. Notice that the frequentist approach differs from this perspective, since it treats parameters as constants and not as random variables. The prior distributions define knowledge about the parameters before seeing the data, and the priors can be diffuse (noninformative) or informative.

In a hierarchical modelling approach, the parameters of the prior distributions are also treated as random variables. These parameters are referred to as hyperparameters. The distributions for the hyperparameters are known as hyper priors, and they are used to specify uncertainty about the prior parameters. Often the priors and hyper priors are used to define modelling assumptions or hypotheses about the nature of the parameters. It will be shown in the context of Bayesian IRT that the (hyper)prior distributions can be used to define an assumption of conditional independence or to define a sampling design underlying the data collection.

The statistical inferences are based on the likelihood and prior information. When the parameter of interest is denoted as θ, the likelihood of the observed data is given by $p(\mathbf{y}|\theta)$ and the prior distribution by $p(\theta)$. The joint distribution of parameters and data can be defined from standard probability theory, it follows that

$$p(\mathbf{y},\theta) = p(\mathbf{y}|\theta)p(\theta) = p(\theta|\mathbf{y})p(\mathbf{y}).$$

The conditional distribution of the parameter given the data can be derived from this expression. By rearranging terms, it follows that

$$p(\theta|\mathbf{y}) = \frac{p(\mathbf{y}|\theta)p(\theta)}{p(\mathbf{y})},$$

where the denominator on the right-hand side is also known as the marginal likelihood of the data. The distribution on the left-hand side is known as the posterior distribution of the parameter and contains the information from the data and prior. The expression for the posterior is also known as Bayes' theorem.

Bayesian inference is based on the posterior distribution. When the prior and likelihood are conjugate (i.e., the prior and posterior are of the same type), the prior is referred to as conjugate, and analytic results can often be obtained from the posterior. However, in many cases the analytical form of the posterior distribution is unknown, and it is not possible to compute directly the posterior distribution. Especially when more parameters are involved, computational methods are required to make inferences from the posterior distribution. Most of computational methods are based on sampling, and inferences can be made using samples retrieved from the posterior. This includes Markov chain Monte Carlo (MCMC) methods, which receive a lot of attention in the literature. An MCMC method can be used to generate simulated values in such a way that the values are distributed according to the posterior distribution, when the chain is run long enough. A key feature of MCMC is that the chain can be simulated using only the prior distributions and likelihood and the data, and not the unknown posterior distribution. Once the sampled values are obtained, posterior moments, such as the mean and variance, can be computed to make inferences about the unknown parameters given the data and prior information. An introduction to MCMC can be found in Gelman et al. (2014) and Gilks, Richardson, and Spiegelhalter (1996).

Bayesian Item Response Models Using Latent Variables

In educational measurement, student proficiency cannot be measured directly with one observed variable. More observations are necessary to measure the construct. Usually a range of items are required to assess the construct. In IRT and structural equation modelling, constructs are represented by latent variables, which are defined by observations from multiple test items.

IRT models are very popular for modelling relationships among latent variables and observed variables. Basic IRT models can be found in van der Linden and Hambleton (1997), which provide a wide range of models for different standard test situations. In common assessments, students are assessed and their performances are observed using a test. Each response observation is considered to be an outcome of a random response variable, denoted as Y_{ik}, where index i refers to the student and k to the item. The observations are influenced by item k's characteristics and student i's proficiency level. The psychometric measurement of student proficiencies is usually done using an IRT model. This model is based on a probabilistic relationship between the performance and the proficiency. A probabilistic relationship is defined to reflect uncertainty about the observed responses.

Several factors (e.g., subject, group, and item characteristics) influence the observed response. Student observations cannot be interpreted as fixed entities, since a high-proficiency student can make a mistake once in a while and a low-proficiency student may guess an item correctly. Furthermore, given the limited number of assessment items, students' proficiencies can only be measured up to some level of accuracy. The uncertainty due to the limited number of items will be captured by the stochastic modelling of the item responses. The limited number of students in the assessment will provide information about the test characteristics but up to some level of accuracy. The uncertainty induced by the sampling of students is modelled through a population distribution. This population distribution characterizes the distribution of students in the population from which students are sampled. In a straightforward way, students are sampled through simple random sampling, such students are assumed to be independently selected, where each member of the population has equal probability of being selected.

Although students are commonly assumed to be sampled through simple random sampling, observations are said to be nested within students. In practice, observations from one student are more alike than observations from different students. The response observations of each student are correlated but given the proficiency level, they are assumed to be conditionally independently distributed. The proficiency is explicitly modelled as a latent variable since it is the primary object of measurement and/or to model the within-student dependencies. The latent variable representing student performance is measured using multiple items.

Let θ_i define the proficiency level of student i. When considering items with two response options, each item has specific item characteristics, for item k denoted as a_k and b_k, representing the level of discrimination and difficulty. Then, the success probability of student i for item k, or the probability of endorsing item k, according to the two-parameter IRT model is given by,

$$P(Y_{ik} = 1 | \theta_i, a_k, b_k) = \begin{cases} \dfrac{\exp(Da_k(\theta_i - b_k))}{1 + \exp(Da_k(\theta_i - b_k))} & \text{Logistic Model} \\ \Phi(a_k(\theta_i - b_k)) & \text{Probit Model} \end{cases} \quad (17.1)$$

The observed value for random variable Y_{ik} is one and coded a success. A zero observed value would indicate a failure, which is modelled by one minus the success probability. The function $\Phi(.)$ denotes the cumulative normal distribution function. For the logistic model, when $D = 1.7$, a metric close to the normal-ogive (Probit) model is specified. As a result, the parameters of the Logistic and the Probit model are defined on the same scale. A typical special case is the Rasch model or one-parameter model, where all item discriminations are equal to one.

Prior specification of Bayesian IRT models

The observed responses are modelled at the lowest level (i.e., observational level, level 1). At this level, a likelihood function can quantify how well the model fits the data, given values for the student and item parameters. This likelihood component describes the distribution of the data given the lower level model parameters. In Bayesian modelling, the lower level model parameters are modelled using so-called prior distributions.

The prior distributions are used to specify information about the student and item parameters. This information is not based on the data modelled at level one, but typically include information about the parameter region, the survey design, relationships with other model parameters, and so forth. Any information about the assessment can be included and it can lead to more accurate inferences since the prior information simply adds to the data information.

Assume a simple random sampling design for the students, and let students be sampled from a normal distribution such that

$$\theta_i \sim N(\mu_\theta, \sigma_\theta^2), \quad (17.2)$$

where the population mean (μ_θ) represents the average level and the population variance (σ_θ^2) the variability between students. The normal distribution is a symmetric distribution, which means that students of above- and below-average performance are expected to be selected with equal probability. The normal distribution does not have wide tails, which means that students with extreme proficiency levels are rare and unlikely to be sampled.

The test items are assumed to measure a single construct. A variety of item difficulties are necessary to measure accurately construct levels at different positions of the latent scale. The items are nested in the test and they reflect the subject matter of the test. Depending on the content of the test, items can show strong interitem correlations. The test is supposed to cover the content of the domain to be assessed. Subsequently, test scores are generalized to the test domain by assuming that test items are a random sample from an item bank. The item bank is supposed to contain many items which cover a specific test domain. Therefore, a prior for the item parameters can be interpreted from a sampling perspective, where items are sampled from an item population. The correlation among items in the test can be modelled by a hierarchical prior, where the item characteristics are assumed to vary from the general test characteristics. In that case, item difficulty parameters are assumed to be normally distributed,

$$b_k \sim N(\mu_b, \sigma_b^2), \tag{17.3}$$

where μ_b and σ_b^2 are the average test difficulty and the variability in item difficulties in the test. A comparable prior can be defined for discrimination parameters, except that they are assumed to be positive such that a log-normal prior distribution is defined,

$$\log(a_k) \sim N(\mu_a, \sigma_a^2). \tag{17.4}$$

On the logarithmic scale, the average level of discrimination and the between-item variability in test discrimination is given by μ_a and σ_a^2, respectively.

The prior distributions in Equation 17.3 and 17.4 no longer assumed to be fixed as in traditional (frequentist) IRT modelling. However, this sampling interpretation does not always hold, since it may not always be possible to sample items that cover a specific test domain. Only when the test domain is specifically defined, can a representative sample be drawn. For example, to design a spelling test, a dictionary would cover the domain to sample from. The sampling perspective can be generalized to include item generation or item cloning, where each item generated is a draw (e.g., Geerlings, Glas, & van der Linden, 2011). In this case, each item can be generated or cloned and will show some variation in characteristics compared to the original test item.

Besides the sampling argument, random item parameters can also be defined from an uncertainty perspective, since the prior expresses the uncertainty in item characteristics before seeing the data. Variation in item difficulties is expected with respect to the general test difficulty, and this variation in item difficulties is specified through the variance term. Furthermore, the prior mean and variance parameter can be modelled themselves to express uncertainty about the specific test difficulty and the between-item variability. The modelling of prior parameters is done using hyper priors. More thorough discussion about random item parameters can be found in Glas and van der Linden (2003), Fox (2010), and De Boeck (2008).

Bayesian parameter estimation

Inferences are based on posterior distributions, which are constructed from the data (i.e., sampling distribution) and prior information (i.e., prior distribution). The posterior distribution contains all relevant information. To introduce this approach, consider the latent variable θ_i, representing the proficiency level of student i. Assume that the item characteristics are known. The posterior distribution is derived from the data information according to an IRT model M, denoted as $p(\mathbf{Y}_i|\theta_i, M)$, and the prior distribution, denoted as $p(\theta_i; \mu_\theta, \sigma_\theta^2)$. According to Bayes' theorem, it follows that

$$p(\theta_i|\mathbf{Y}_i, M) = \frac{p(\mathbf{Y}_i|\theta_i, M) p(\theta_i; \mu_\theta, \sigma_\theta^2)}{p(\mathbf{Y}_i|M)}$$

$$\propto \underbrace{p(\mathbf{Y}_i|\theta_i, M)}_{\text{Likelihood}} \underbrace{p(\theta_i; \mu_\theta, \sigma_\theta^2)}_{\text{Prior}}, \qquad (17.5)$$

where the term $p(\mathbf{Y}_i|M)$ does not depend on the proficiency variable and can be treated as a constant. The posterior is proportional to the likelihood function times the prior distribution. The semicolon notation in the prior distribution states that the remaining parameters are fixed and known, instead of treating them as random and conditioning on some specific values. It follows that the sample information enters the posterior information through the likelihood, which only depends on the sample size.

When increasing the number of assessed items, the sample information will dominate the prior information, and the prior information will play a less important role in the estimation of the student proficiency. When the number of assessed items is small or moderate, the prior distribution becomes more important, and the sample information will play a less important role. In this case, the posterior distribution depends less on asymptotic theory and given accurate prior information reliable results can be obtained given small samples. Informative priors are required for moderate to small sample sizes, while noninformative priors are often used when there is sufficient data information. In practical settings, good prior information might be available from experts, similar analyses, or past data samples.

Posterior-Based Measurement of Student Proficiency

To give a simple example, consider a test, where all items have equal difficulty and discrimination characteristics, which are zero and one respectively. Interest is focused on the ability measurement of a student.

Let the probability of a correct response be specified by the Probit model for a student with ability parameter θ; that is, the success probability is modelled by $\Phi(\theta)$. When a response pattern of 10 items is observed with first six successes and then four failures, the posterior distribution of θ is given by,

$$p(\theta|\mathbf{Y}) \propto \underbrace{(\Phi(\theta))^6 (1-\Phi(\theta))^4}_{\text{Likelihood}} \underbrace{p(\theta)}_{\text{Prior}}, \qquad (17.6)$$

where $p(\theta)$ is the prior. The maximum likelihood estimate is the parameter value that maximizes the likelihood,[1] which is $\Phi(\hat{\theta}) = 6/10, \hat{\theta} \approx .25$.

---

[1] When maximizing the log-likelihood, $\underset{\theta}{\text{Max}} \ 6\log\Phi(\theta) + 4\log(1-\Phi(\theta))$, set the first derivative equal to zero, $\frac{6}{\Phi(\hat{\theta})} - \frac{4}{1-\Phi(\hat{\theta})} = 0$. It follows that $\Phi(\hat{\theta}) = \frac{6}{10}$.

Often a conjugate prior is used such that the posterior and prior distribution are of the same parametric form. In this example, consider the beta distribution, with hyperparameters α and β, as a prior for the success rate. The hyperparameters α and β represent the number of successes and failures in a sample of $\alpha + \beta - 2$ independent Bernoulli trials, respectively. Then, the posterior distribution in Equation 17.6 can be expressed as can be expressed as

$$p(\theta|Y) \propto (\Phi(\theta))^6 (1-\Phi(\theta))^4 (\Phi(\theta))^{\alpha-1} (1-\Phi(\theta))^{\beta-1}$$
$$\propto (\Phi(\theta))^{6+\alpha-1} (1-\Phi(\theta))^{4+\beta-1} \qquad (17.7)$$

The posterior distribution of the success rate is also a beta distribution. When maximizing the posterior, it follows in the same way that $\Phi(\hat{\theta}) = \dfrac{6+\alpha-1}{10+\alpha+\beta-2}$.

The hyperparameters are assumed to be equal ($\alpha = \beta$) when there is no reason to assume that a priori successes are more likely than failures. Furthermore, assume that this prior belief is as strong as the total data information (i.e., $2\alpha - 2 = 10$). This means that the precision of the prior mode is equal to the precision of the maximum likelihood estimate. Then, $\Phi(\hat{\theta}) = 11/20$, and $\hat{\theta} \approx .13$, which is much lower than the maximum likelihood estimate. The prior mode of parameter θ is zero, which corresponds with a prior success rate of .50. As a result, the posterior mode is shrunk toward the prior mode of zero. Since the amount of prior information is equal to the amount of data information, the posterior mode is located almost exactly between the prior mode of zero and the maximum likelihood estimate of .25. The posterior mode is simply the weighted average of two point estimates, and both estimates have equal precision.

A less informative prior can still assume that successes and failures are equally likely, but its prior mode has simply a lower precision compared to the data precision. The minimum informative beta prior consists of one success and one failure out of two independent Bernoulli trials such $\alpha = \beta = 2$, which is one fifth of the total amount of data. Subsequently, the posterior mode is $\Phi(\hat{\theta}) = 7/12$, $\hat{\theta} \approx .21$, and this posterior mode is shrunk toward zero with almost one fifth of the maximum likelihood estimate.

In most situations, the posterior distribution is not easily maximized and more parameters are involved. Integration is required to compute the posterior mode, but the integration does not have a closed form. When it is possible to draw samples from the posterior distribution, the posterior mean and variance can be approximated using the simulated values.

In simulation-based methods, latent variables are handled as missing data. By drawing values for the latent variables, a complete data set is constructed, which is used to draw samples from the other posterior distributions. In particularly, Markov chain Monte Carlo (MCMC) methods can be used to obtain samples from the posterior distributions by drawing samples in iterative way from the full conditional posterior distributions.

For most Bayesian IRT models, directly simulating observations from the posterior distributions is difficult. The posterior distributions of the model parameters have an unknown complicated form and/or it is difficult to simulate from them. Tanner and Wong (1987) introduced the idea of the data augmentation method, which greatly stimulated the use of posterior simulation methods.

This idea is illustrated using the example previously. Assume that the student is sampled from a standard normal population distribution. This normal prior for the student's proficiency level is a nonconjugate prior, given the likelihood specified in Equation 17.6 simulating directly from the posterior distribution is difficult, since this distribution has an unknown form. However, augmented data can be defined, which are assumed to be underlying normally distributed latent responses with a mean of θ and a variance of one, and restricted to be positive (negative) when the response is correct (incorrect).

The normal prior is a conjugate prior for the normally distributed latent responses, and subsequently, the posterior distribution of θ is normal. The mean and variance of the posterior distribution can be derived from properties of the normal distribution (e.g., Albert, 1992; Fox, 2010), and the posterior mean equals,

$$E(\theta|Z,\Upsilon) = \frac{10\bar{Z}}{11} + \frac{\mu_\theta}{11}, \qquad (17.8)$$

where $\bar{Z}$ is the average augmented latent response. In Code 1 (see Code Appendix), R code is given to draw samples from the posterior distribution of the student proficiency parameter. The mean value of the sampled values will approximate the posterior mean of the posterior distribution, which can be used as an estimate of the student proficiency. The posterior mean in Equation 17.8 has a precision-weighted form, where the precision of the maximum likelihood estimate is 10 and the prior precision is 1. The posterior precision is the sum of the prior and the data precision. has a precision-weighted form, where the precision of the maximum likelihood estimate is 10 and the prior precision is 1. The posterior precision is the sum of the prior and the data precision.

In Figure 17.1 the posterior distribution of the student proficiency is plotted using simulated draws according to the R Code 1 in the Code Appendix. It can be seen that the posterior is shrunk toward the prior mean of zero, but the amount of shrinkage is small since the data precision is 10 times higher than the prior precision. The posterior is slightly higher peaked than the likelihood since the precision of the posterior mean is the sum of the data and the prior precision.

A simulation study using WinBUGS

For those who do not want to derive all full conditional posterior distributions and implement an MCMC method to sample from them, various statistical software programs facilitate simulation-based estimation techniques. A popular program is WinBUGS (Lunn, Thomas, Best, & Spiegelhalter, 2000), which supports the estimation of Bayesian models using MCMC techniques. The program can handle a wide variety of Bayesian IRT models. The program will generate simulated samples from the joint posterior, which can be used to estimate parameters, latent variables, and functions of them.

When dealing with multiple students and items with different item difficulties and discriminations, a more complex MCMC method is needed to draw samples from all posteriors. Code 2 (see Code Appendix) gives the WinBUGS code for the Bayesian two-parameter IRT model as described in Equations 17.1–17.4.

Responses were generated, for 1,000 students and 10 items, according to a two-parameter logistic IRT model. For prior specification I, the precision of the prior

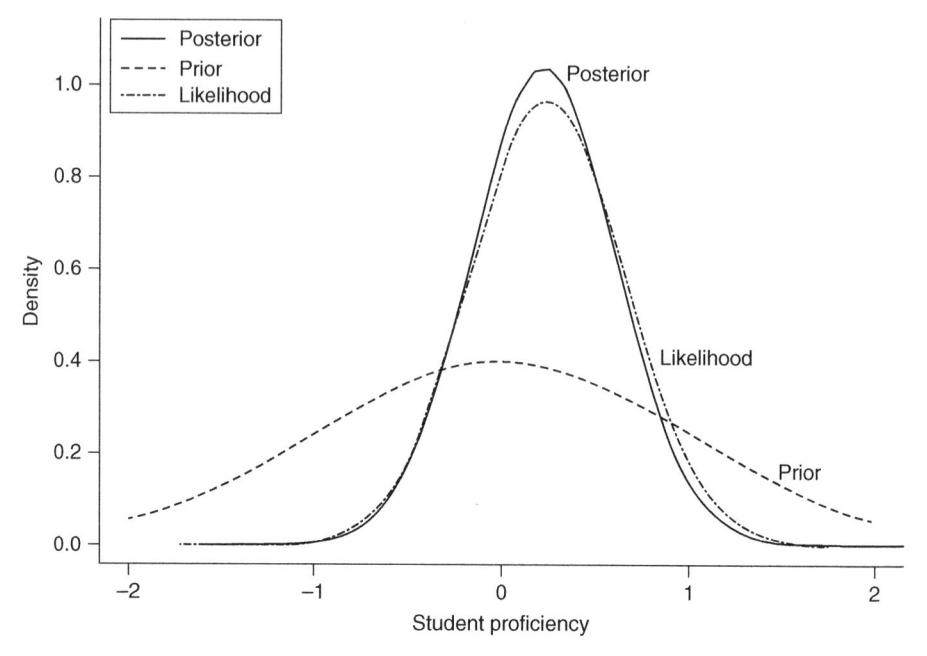

Figure 17.1 Prior, likelihood, and posterior distribution of student proficiency.

distributions was not a priori specified but modelled using hyperpriors. As discussed in the example before, the prior precision influenced the amount of shrinkage of the posterior mean to the prior mean. By modelling the precision parameters of the prior distributions, these parameters are estimated using the data. For prior specification II, the parameters of the prior distributions were a priori fixed.

In Table 17.1, posterior estimates of hyperparameters under different item priors are given. It follows that the average discriminating level of the items is around .121 (on the logarithmic scale) and the between-item variability in discrimination is around .265. The average item difficulty is .200, and the variability in difficulty across items is estimated to be .438. For Prior II, the hyperprior parameters were fixed at specific values, as given in Table 17.1. As a result, the model with Prior II does not provide information about the posterior population item characteristics, since they are restricted by the prior to specific values.

To compare the fit of both models, Akaike's information criterion (AIC) and the Bayesian information criterion (BIC) were computed (Fox, 2010, pp. 57–61). The AIC and the BIC are given in Table 17.1. The model with Prior I fits the data better. Under Prior II, the parameters are shrunk toward the average discriminations and difficulty values due to their relatively high precision values. Prior II allows less variation in item characteristic across items. This leads to a less optimal fit of the model, since the AIC and BIC are both higher for the model with Prior II. Note that the AIC and BIC model selection indices usually perform well when data were generated using the one-parameter or two-parameter model (e.g., Whittaker, Chang, & Dodd, 2012).

The relevance of modelling the prior parameters becomes even more important when assuming that students might guess answers correctly. To account for randomly guessing, the three-parameter IRT model extends the two-parameter model by introducing a guessing or pseudo-chance parameter, which represents the probability that a student guesses the item correctly.

Table 17.1 Posterior estimates of hyperparameters under different item priors

	Prior I Mean	SD	Prior II Mean
Discrimination			
μ_a	.121	.165	.50
σ_a^2	.265	.142	.10
Difficulty			
μ_b	.200	.206	.00
σ_b^2	.438	.228	.10
Information Criterion			
BIC	9,192	47	9,283
AIC	9,094	47	9,185

Let the three-parameter model be defined as

$$P(Y_{ik}=1|\theta_i,a_k,b_k,c_k) = \begin{cases} c_k + (1-c_k)\dfrac{\exp(Da_k(\theta_i-b_k))}{1+\exp(Da_k(\theta_i-b_k))} & \text{Logistic Model} \\ c_k + (1-c_k)\Phi(a_k(\theta_i-b_k)) & \text{Probit Model} \end{cases}$$

where c_k denotes the probability of guessing the item correctly.

In the Bayesian modelling approach, a prior distribution is required to define the prior information about random guessing behavior in the test. For a multiple-choice item, it is reasonable to assume that the probability of guessing an item correctly is one divided by the number of response categories. This will not control for educated guesses, when one or more incorrect response options are easily identified. Other response formats can lead to more discussion about the appropriateness of the prior, since it will influence the estimate of the guessing parameter and the student's ability parameter. When overestimating the pseudo-chance parameter, student's abilities are underestimated since they obtain less credit for correctly scored items. In fact, the weighted estimator for ability under the three-parameter model, includes a component to adjust for guessing. However, Chiu and Camilli (2013) showed that according to the three-parameter scoring rule, better performing students, as opposed to poorer performing students, obtained more credit for a correct response. This difference in scores become larger when the guessing probability increases.

Furthermore, in the three-parameter IRT model, the prior distribution for the guessing parameter influences the posterior estimates, where the prior parameters define the amount of shrinkage of the posterior mean to the prior mean. The amount of shrinkage can be severe, when the response data do not contain much information about the random guessing behavior. Consequently, student scores can be highly influenced by the prior information.

To illustrate this, consider an artificial data set, generated using the three-parameter logistic model (3PL), of 500 students responding to 10 items. The uncommented code of the 3PL in Code 2 (see Code Appendix), was used to estimate the parameters of the 3PL, using the same priors for the discrimination and difficulty parameters. For the guessing parameter, a beta distribution was defined with parameters α and β (i.e., b11 and b12 in Listing 1). The beta distribution restricts the guessing parameter to take

Table 17.2 Posterior mean estimates of the hyperparameters for different guessing priors.

	Prior I		Prior II	
	Mean	SD	Mean	SD
Discrimination				
μ_a	.63	.26	.66	.23
σ_a^2	.39	.25	.33	.18
Difficulty				
μ_b	.17	.32	.19	.33
σ_b^2	1.07	.60	1.11	.65
Guessing				
α	3.30	.89	122.20	42.91
β	8.23	1.37	336.30	97.24
Information Criterion				
BIC	5,315	38	5,317	37
AIC	5,231	38	5,233	37

values between zero and one. As in the example of modelling success rates, hyperparameters α and β define the number of successes (correctly guesses) and failures (incorrectly guesses), respectively, in a sample of $\alpha + \beta - 2$ independent Bernoulli trials.

At a third level, the hyperparameters α and β were modelled according to a uniform distribution. Different boundary values of the uniform distribution were used to explore the effects of the hyperprior specification. For prior I, the hyperparameters were uniformly distributed between two and 10. The estimated average guessing probability was around .29 $(3.30/(3.30 + 8.23))$. The posterior mean estimates are given in Table 17.2. There was a moderate variation in guessing probability between items with a posterior standard deviation of .13. For Prior II, the hyperparameters were uniformly distributed between 2 and 500, which allowed the estimation of a much tighter prior for the guessing parameters compared to the restriction in Prior I. Using this prior, the average guessing probability was around .27 $(122.20/(122.20 + 336.30))$, and the variability in guessing across items almost zero.

It follows that the estimated beta prior parameters are very high under Prior II. As a result, the posterior information is highly peaked around .27. The more flexible uniform Prior II leads to much higher hyperparameter estimates. Under Prior II, the posterior information about guessing is much more centered than under Prior I. The data do not support between-item variability in guessing. The beta prior accumulates the evidence for guessing by shrinking all item guessing estimates to a general level of guessing. The AIC and BIC are based on the same likelihood and do not indicate that one model fits the data better.

Following the scoring rule of the 3PL model as stated in Chiu and Camilli (2013),

$$T_i = \sum_{k=1}^{K} y_{ik} a_k \left(1 + \lambda_{ik}^{-1}\right)$$

$$\lambda_{ik} = c_k \exp(-D a_k (\theta_i - b_k)),$$
(17.9)

student ability-scores were estimated for the different priors. The sum of the logarithmic scores of students was computed under both prior specifications, since otherwise small sampled values of λ_{ik} led to numerical problems. In Figure 17.2, the sum scores are

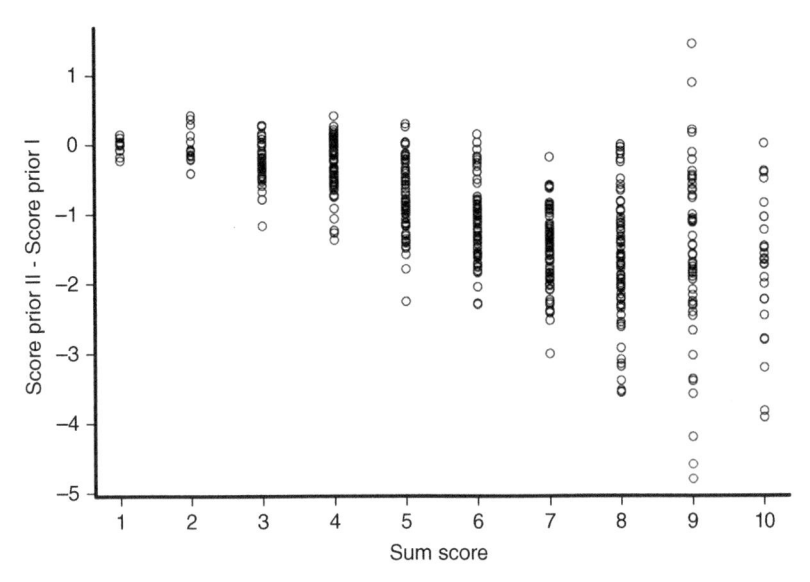

Figure 17.2 Differences between scores under different guessing priors versus the sum scores.

plotted against the difference in scores for all students. It follows that score differences become larger for higher scoring students. This difference can be around four points when making just one item incorrect. The differences are mostly negative, which means that under the more flexible Prior II, students obtained relatively lower scores. In that situation guessing seemed to be more prominent, which led to an underestimate of student's performances.

Multistage Sampling Design: Clustering Students

In many data collection designs, individuals are sampled from different subgroups, for instance sampled from different schools. Such a multistage design leads to correlated observations, since students from the same school are more similar in their performances than students from different schools. A multilevel modelling approach is required to account for the (intraclass) correlation induced by the clustering of students in schools, where for example students from the same school have the same education program (Fox & Glas, 2001).

The clustering of students can be modelled as an extension of Equation 17.2: a simple random sampling design, a multistage sampling design applies. Therefore, consider J schools randomly sampled from a population of schools, after which students are randomly sampled within each school. Let $\theta_{ij}i$ in school j, and $Y_{ijk}k$. The two-parameter IRT model defines the relationship between the observation and the latent variable. The two-parameter IRT model defines the relationship between the observation and the latent variable,

$$P(Y_{ijk} = 1 | \theta_{ij}, a_k, b_k) = \frac{\exp(Da_k(\theta_{ij} - b_k))}{1 + \exp(Da_k(\theta_{ij} - b_k))}. \quad (17.10)$$

The population distribution of students is generalized by assuming that students are sampled at random given the school average,

$$\theta_{ij} \sim N\left(\mu_j, \sigma_j^2\right), \qquad (17.11)$$

where μ_j represents the school mean and σ_j^2 the school-specific variance of the latent variable. Schools are sampled at random from a population with μ_θ the overall expected proficiency in the population, and σ_θ^2 the variability across school means; that is,

$$\mu_j \sim N\left(\mu_\theta, \sigma_\theta^2\right) \qquad (17.12)$$

Equations 17.3 and 17.4 be used as prior distributions for the item parameters. In order to identify the model parameters, it is sufficient to constrain and μ_θ to 0 and 1, respectively. σ_θ^2 means that the residual variance is the same for each school, thus for all $\sigma_j^2 = \sigma^2 j$, the intraclass correlation is given by $\sigma_\theta^2/(\sigma_\theta^2 + \sigma^2)$, which represents the proportion of variance in the latent variable explained by the clustering of students in schools.

When the intraclass correlation is substantial, the question arises where this similarity comes from. Are teaching methods different across schools and can this explain the homogeneity in performances within a school? Or are certain background variables such as socioeconomic status of the parents very similar within schools and can this explain the similarity?

To study these questions, this multilevel structure is extended to include predictor variables that might explain the similarity within schools. Two types of predictors can be recognized, a variable that says something about the individual i in school j, like for example the gross income of the parents or the sex of the student, or that says something about the school j, for example the number of students or the teaching methods. Assume that both types of predictors are available, where X contains student and Z school explanatory information. Then, the previous population model for students and schools, Equations 17.11 and 17.12 at the student and school level, respectively, such that,

$$\begin{aligned}\theta_{ij} &\sim N\left(\mu_j + \mathbf{X}_{ij}^t \boldsymbol{\beta}, \sigma^2\right) \\ \mu_j &\sim N\left(\mu_\theta + \mathbf{Z}_j^t \boldsymbol{\gamma}, \sigma_\theta^2\right),\end{aligned} \qquad (17.13)$$

where $\boldsymbol{\beta}$ is a vector with the regression coefficients at the individual level, and $\boldsymbol{\gamma}$ is a vector of regression coefficients at the school level. Both vectors of regression coefficients can be given multivariate normal prior distributions, or alternatively, independent identical normal priors.

An additional clustering of schools in countries leads to a three-level model. Following the multistage sampling design of large international educational surveys; item data are nested in students, which are nested in schools, which are in turn nested in countries. Next, this will be illustrated in an example concerning an international comparison of reading performances.

Plausible values

In large-scale international educational surveys, three-level IRT models can be used to compare student proficiency across countries, where item response data is clustered within individuals, individuals within schools, and schools within countries. Such nonlinear multilevel models are difficult to estimate, given the large amount of data, the large number of model parameters, the often-complicated design of the individual tests where not all students are administered the exact same questions, and the nonrandom nature of sampling of schools and individuals. In that case, it is often more convenient to work with plausible values using multiple imputation, rather than working with the raw item data (Rubin, 1987).

The plausible values are draws from the posterior distribution of proficiency scores that are based on the response data but also on covariate information of individuals. Instead of using single proficiency estimates in the statistical analysis, multiple draws are used to take the uncertainty in the estimate of the proficiency into account. For each individual, multiple draws are taken from the individual's posterior distribution of proficiency and they are included in the dataset. Then, subsequent analyses can be carried out where the plausible values are treated as imputed data for the missing proficiency scores.

For example, for a large-scale PISA study (OECD, 2009) concerning reading proficiency, a multilevel model is specified with the latent reading proficiencies as outcomes. Plausible values for reading proficiency are defined as posterior samples, conditioning on the student's observed item data and a large number of covariates. The general idea is to take at least three different plausible values for each student. The multilevel analysis can be carried out for each set of plausible values, and then results are summarized. The formulas for multiple imputation in Rubin (1987) can be used to summarize results.

Multilevel IRT using plausible values

For this example, a three-level IRT model was applied to the 2009 PISA data on reading proficiency taking plausible values as provided by PISA (http://pisa2009.acer.edu.au). The data set consists of 13 countries, with a varying number of schools for each country, and in turn a varying number of students for each school. The model of interest had two predictors at the country level (age of first selection and number of school types), two predictors at the school level (autonomy regarding resources and autonomy regarding curriculum), and one predictor at the individual level (socioeconomic status). These data were reported by Scheerens, Luyten, van den Berg, and Glas (2015). Consider one plausible value for reading proficiency, called PV1, it follows that

$$PV1_{ijc} \sim N\left(E(PV1_{ijc}), \sigma^2\right), \tag{17.14}$$

with

$$E(PV1_{ijc}) = \mu + z_c^t \gamma + x_{jc}^t \beta + SES_{ijc}\alpha + r_c + e_{jc}$$

$$r_c \sim N\left(0, \sigma^2_{res.country}\right)$$

$$e_{jc} \sim N\left(0, \sigma^2_{res.school}\right),$$

where $PV1_{ijc}$ is a standardized plausible value for individual i in school j in country c, z_c is the vector of standardized country covariates, multiplied by regression coefficients γ, x_{jc} is the vector of standardized school covariates, multiplied by school-level regression parameters β, and α is the regression coefficient for standardized socioeconomic status (SES). Parameter r_c is the residual at the country level (i.e., a country effect that is not explained by covariates, be it at country, school or individual level) with variance $\sigma^2_{res.country}$, and e_{jc} the residual at the school level (i.e., a school effect not accounted for by the covariates in the model) with variance $\sigma^2_{res.school}$. As priors for the individual, school, and country level residual variances, inverse gamma priors can be specified,

$$\sigma^2_{res.country} \sim InvGamma(.1,.1)$$
$$\sigma^2_{res.school} \sim InvGamma(.1,.1)$$
$$\sigma^2 \sim InvGamma(.1,.1)$$

For the remaining regression parameters, a normal prior was specified with mean zero and variance 10, which seems reasonable since most predictor variables are standardized. The model was run using the WinBUGS script in Code 3 (see Code Appendix). Table 17.3 presents the means and standard deviations of the posterior distributions for each model parameter.

Given that the posterior mean for α is more than two standard deviations away from zero, it is concluded that there is a clear effect of SES on individual proficiency in reading. The regression parameters β are not clearly different from zero, it is concluded that autonomy in resources and curriculum do not explain variation in reading proficiency across schools. Also, the country level predictors do not explain much variance. Furthermore, school effects are clearly present within countries but there is a lot of unexplained variance at the individual level (PV1 was standardized, so 52% of the variance in individual differences is left unexplained). Note however, that these conclusions are based on only one set of plausible values.

Possible model extensions include the possibility of different regression coefficients across countries, for example different effects of SES across countries, and different school-level and individual-level variances across countries, for example more variation in school quality within a particular country. Note that in all such models all students belong to only one school, and all schools belong to only one country.

Table 17.3 Posterior mean estimates of multilevel IRT model parameters using plausible values.

	Mean	SD
μ	0.09	0.03
σ^2	0.52	0.00
$\sigma^2_{res.school}$	0.43	0.01
$\sigma^2_{res.country}$	0.08	0.04
α	0.15	0.00
β_1	−0.07	0.09
β_2	0.02	0.05
γ_1	−0.07	0.06
γ_2	−0.03	0.03

A further possible extension is to allow individuals to belong to multiple groups. For example, in genetic models, individuals can be correlated because they either share two parents (siblings) or only one parent (half-siblings): half-siblings are correlated because they belong to the same group of people that are the offspring of one particular parent (sharing on average 25% of the genetic variance, see Falconer & MacKay, 1996), and full siblings are correlated because they belong to two such separate groups (thus sharing on average 50% of the genetic variance). Such genetic IRT models for item data are available for twin data (van den Berg, Glas, & Boomsma, 2007) and for pedigree data (van den Berg, et al., 2010).

Bayesian Scale Construction

In Bayesian scale construction (BSC), a Bayesian IRT model is applied in the process of constructing a scale, also referred to as a test. The starting point in BSC is a collection of items that have been pretested and for which posterior-based measurement has been applied to estimate the item parameters. All of these items and their item parameters are stored in an item bank. Especially in the area of educational measurement, large item banks have been developed. Item selection algorithms can be applied to construct a scale based on specifications like, for example, specifications related to measurement properties of the scale, to the content, or to the time available.

In a typical BSC problem, the goal is to select those items that maximize measurement precision, while a list of constraints related to various specifications of the scale have to be met. Various classes of BSC problems can be distinguished based on the formats of the scales. The first class of BSC problems is related to the paper-and-pencil (P&P) scales. Scales in this class have a fixed format. All respondents answer the same set of questions. Nowadays, these scales could be administered on a computer as well, but the basic format is still comparable to a P&P scale.

A second class, mainly used in the area of educational measurement, is related to multistage scales or tests. These tests consist of a number of stages. After completing a stage, the ability level of the respondent is estimated and the respondent is directed to an easier module, a more difficult module, or a module of comparable difficulty. Both the number of stages, and the number of modules might vary.

The third class of BSC problems are related to Computerized Adaptive Tests (CATs). The general procedure of CAT is the following. After administering an item, the ability of the respondent is estimated and the subsequent item is selected that is most informative at the estimated ability level. Respondents with high ability estimates get more difficult items, while respondents with low ability estimates get easier ones. The CAT stops after a fixed number of items or when a certain level of measurement precision for the ability estimate has been obtained. The main advantage of BSC is that collateral information about the respondents can be taken into account during test assembly. This advantage holds for all classes of BSC problems, but is most prominent in CAT.

Item selection in BSC

Van der Linden (2005) describes how BSC problems can be formulated as mathematical programming models. Mathematical programming models are general models for solving optimization problems. They have been applied in business and economics, but also for some engineering problems. Areas that use mathematical programming models include transportation, energy, telecommunications, and manufacturing. These models have proved to be useful in modelling diverse types of problems in planning, routing, scheduling, assignment, and design.

Theunissen (1985) was among the first to apply these models to scale construction (SC). Decision variables x_i can be introduced that denote whether an item is selected ($x_i = 1$) or not ($x_i = 0$). Test specifications can be modelled as either categorical, quantitative, or logical constraints, where categorical constraints are related to item attributes that classify items in various categories, quantitative constraints are about numerical attributes of items, and logical constraints are related to interitem relationships. A generic model for SC can be formulated as:

$$\max \sum_{i=1}^{I} J_i(\theta) x_i$$
$$\sum_{i \in c} x_i \leq n_c \quad c = 1, \ldots, C,$$
$$\sum_{i=1}^{I} q_i x_i \leq b_q \quad q = 1, \ldots, Q, \quad (17.15)$$
$$\sum_{i \in l} x_i \leq 1 \quad l = 1, \ldots, L,$$
$$\sum_{i=1}^{I} x_i = n,$$
$$x_i \in \{0,1\}.$$

where $J_i(\theta)$ denotes the contribution of item $i = 1, \ldots, I$, to the measurement precision of the test, c denotes a category, n_c the number of items for category c, q_i a numerical attribute of item i, b_q the bound of a numerical constraint q, l is an index for the various logical constraints, and n denotes the test length.

Computer programs, like CPLEX or LPSolve, can be used to generate tests that perform optimally with respect to the objective function and meet all the constraints. For the classes of P&P and the multistage SC problems, a single SC model has to be solved. For CAT problems, the shadow test approach (van der Linden & Reese, 1998) can be applied, where an SC model is solved iteratively. One by one the items are added to the test. Instead of finding the item that provides most information at the current ability estimate, in every iteration of CAT a full-length test that contains all the items already administered and that meets all the test specifications is selected. From this shadow test, the optimal next item is selected. Since items are selected from a shadow test that meets all the constraints, it is guaranteed that each CAT meets all the test specifications.

When Bayesian IRT is used to measure the ability parameters, the measurement precision is related to the posterior distribution of the ability parameter. In BSC, those items have to be selected that contribute most to the measurement precision. There are several ways to deal with the relationship between the posterior and the measurement precision. Therefore, several item selection criteria have been proposed.

Owen (1975) proposed to select items with a difficulty level closest to the estimated ability. Van der Linden (1998) introduced Maximum Posterior Weighted Information, Maximum Expected Information, Minimum Expected Posterior Variance, and Maximum Expected Posterior Weighed Information as item selection criteria. Chang and Ying (1996) introduced the Maximum Posterior Weighted Kullback–Leibler

Information criterion. This is not an exhaustive list, but all of these criteria have in common that they are posterior-based, where some of them employ Fisher Information and others are based on Kullback–Leibler information. Fisher information is a local information measure about how much information a response pattern carries about at a certain ability level. Kullback–Leibler information, a divergence measure for comparing the information at any ability level relative to the true ability level, can be seen as a global information measure about a broad spectrum of ability levels. Fisher Information is most popular, since it is easier to implement, and the difference in performance between various item selection criteria is very small for tests of reasonable length. Veldkamp (2010) describes how all of these criteria can be implemented in the shadow test approach. For example, for Owen's criterion, the model for the selection of the gth item is given by

$$\min \sum_{i=1}^{I} |b_i x_i - \hat{\theta}|$$
$$\sum_{i \in V_{g-1}} x_i = g - 1,$$
$$\sum_{i=1}^{I} x_i = n,$$
$$x_i \in \{0,1\}.$$
(17.16)

where the set V_{g-1} denotes the items that have been selected in the previous $(g-1)$ steps of CAT.

The posterior distribution of the latent variable contains information from the prior and the response data. When an uninformative prior distribution is used, the measurement precision solely depends on the response data. When an informative prior is used, the information from the response data is combined with prior beliefs. For some applications, like licensure exams, relying on prior beliefs might be undesirable. In other cases, there might be quite a strong argument in favor of incorporating prior beliefs. Imagine the case were a lot of collateral information (i.e., information about the respondent coming from different sources) is available. Collateral information could come from earlier tests of the same topic (as in progress testing), or from other subtests that correlate highly with the test at hand. Following Mislevy (1987) and Zwinderman (1991), Matteucci and Veldkamp (2012) elaborated the framework for dealing with collateral information.

Bayesian Dutch intelligence scale construction

The methodology of BSC was applied to a computerized adaptive Dutch intelligence scale (Maij-de Meij, et al., 2008). The scale consisted of three subscales (Number Series, Figure Series, and Matrices). First, the Matrices subtest is administered, after that the Number Series subtest. The correlation between the scores on the Number Series subtest and the Matrices subtest is equal to $\rho = 0.394$. This information was used to elicit an empirical prior for the number series ability, based on the estimated ability for the Matrices subtest:

$$\theta_{NS} \sim N(-.243 + .394\hat{\theta}_M, .414)$$
(17.17)

where θ_{NS} and θ_M represent the latent scores on the Number Series and the Matrices subscales, respectively.

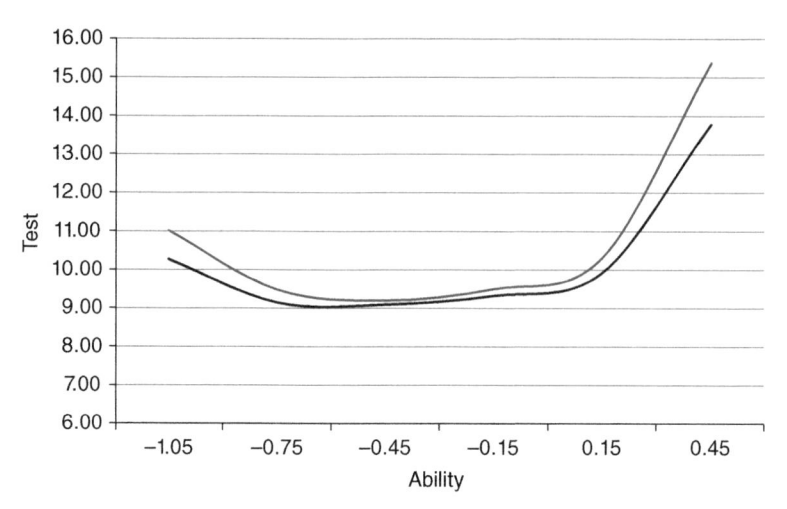

[figure]

Figure 17.3 Test length; BSC with an informative empirical prior (darker gray) and with an uninformative prior.

In order to demonstrate the attributed value of BSC, the use of this empirical prior was compared to the standard normal prior $\theta_{NS} \sim N(0,1)$. For this computerized adaptive scale, an item bank was available that consisted of 499 items calibrated with the Probit model described in Equation 17.1. The intelligence test is a variable length CAT where a stopping rule is formulated based on the measurement precision.

Based on the estimated abilities of 660 real candidates, more or less evenly distributed over the ability range, answer patterns to the variable length CAT were simulated and the person parameters were re-estimated using the Bayesian framework described previously (Equation 1.1–1.4). The WinBUGS codes described in this chapter could be applied for the analyses, although we wrote our own code for MCMC in MATLAB (The MathWorks Inc., 2005). The test length for various levels of the estimated ability is shown in Figure 17.3. For a more elaborate description of this example, see also Matteucci and Veldkamp (2012).

For those candidates with an ability level in the middle of the population, the informative prior resulted in slightly shorter tests, but the effect of adding collateral information was only small. For the candidates with the lowest and highest ability values, however, considerable reduction in test length was obtained. In other words, empirical priors can be used successfully to reduce test length for respondents in the tails of the distribution, without any loss of measurement precision.

Here, the use of BSC was illustrated for ability estimation. Another application of BSC is related to the estimation of item parameters, see, for example, Matteucci, Mignani, and Veldkamp (2012).

Discussion

Bayesian psychometric modelling has received much attention with the introduction of simulation-based computational methods. With the introduction of these powerful computational methods, Bayesian IRT modelling became feasible, which made it possible to analyze much more complex models and to include prior information in the statistical analysis. Prior information can be used to quantify uncertainties concerning model parameters or hypotheses. Furthermore, especially in educational measurement, prior information can be useful when dealing with a nonstandardized test setting, a complex experimental design, a complex survey, or any other measurement situation where common modelling assumptions do not hold.

The Bayesian approach in combination with sampling based estimation techniques is particularly powerful for hierarchically organized item response data. A multilevel modelling approach for item response data has been described, where item response observations are nested in items and students. Prior distributions are defined for the parameters of the distribution of the data. Subsequently, the parameters of these prior distributions can be described by hyperpriors. Extending this multilevel modelling approach even further, the survey population distribution of students and/or items can be integrated into the item response model. Such a multilevel modelling framework takes the survey design into account, the backgrounds of the respondents, and clusters in which respondents are located. A classic example is discussed, where educational survey data are collected through multistage sampling (PISA, 2009), where the primary sampling units are schools, and students are sampled conditional on the school unit.

Advantages of Bayesian item response models have also been discussed in Bayesian scale construction. The use of empirical prior information in student and item parameter estimation can reduce the costs of item bank development. Furthermore, it is shown that the test length can be reduced considerably when prior information about the ability level of the candidates is available.

References

Aitkin, M., & Aitkin, I. (2011). *Statistical modeling of the national assessment of educational progress*. Springer Science & Business Media.

Albert, J. H. (1992). Bayesian estimation of normal ogive item response curves using Gibbs sampling. *Journal of Educational Statistics, 17,* 251–269.

Albert, J. H., & Chib, S. (1993). Bayesian analysis of binary and polychotomous response data. *Journal of the American Statistical Association, 88,* 669–679.

Bradlow, E. T., Wainer, H. H., & Wang, X. (1999). A Bayesian random effects model for testlets. *Psychometrika, 64,* 153–168.

Chang, H. H., & Ying, Z. (1996). Global information approach to computerized adaptive testing. *Applied Psychological Measurement, 20,* 213–229.

Chiu, T. W., & Camilli, G. (2013). Comment on 3PL IRT adjustment for guessing. *Applied Psychological Measurement, 37,* 76–86.

De Boeck, P. (2008). Random item IRT models. *Psychometrika, 73,* 533–559.

Falconer, D. S., & MacKay, T. F. C. (1996). *Introduction to quantitative genetics* (4th ed.). Harlow, Essex, UK: Longman.

Fox, J. P. (2010). *Bayesian item response modeling: Theory and methods*. New York: Springer.

Fox, J. P., & Glas, C. A. W. (2001). Bayesian estimation of a multilevel IRT model using Gibbs sampling. *Psychometrika, 66,* 271–288.

Geerlings, H., Glas, C. A. W., & van der Linden, W. J. (2011). Modeling rule-based item generation. *Psychometrika, 76,* 337–359.

Gelman, A., Carlin, J. B., Stern, H. S., Dunson, D. D., Vehtari, A., & Rubin, D. B. (2014). *Bayesian data analysis* (3rd ed.). New York: Chapman & Hall.

Gilks, W. R., Richardson, S., & Spiegelhalter, D. (1996). *Markov chain Monte Carlo in practice*, New York: Chapman & Hall.

Glas, C. A. W., & van der Linden, W. J. (2003). Computerized adaptive testing with item cloning. *Applied Psychological Measurement, 27,* 247–261.

Johnson, M. S., Sinharay, S., & Bradlow, E. P. (2007). Hierarchical item response theory models. In C. R. Rao, & S. Sinharay (Eds.), *Handbook of statistics, Volume 26: Psychometrics* (pp. 587–605). Amsterdam: Elsevier.

Kim, S. H., Cohen, A. S., Baker, F. B., Subkoviak, M. J., & Leonard, T. (1994). An investigation of hierarchical Bayes procedures in item response theory. *Psychometrika, 59*, 405–421.

Lee, S. Y., & Song, X. Y. (2004). Evaluation of the Bayesian and maximum likelihood approaches in analyzing structural equation models with small sample sizes. *Multivariate Behavioral Research, 39*, 653–686.

Lunn, D. J., Thomas, A., Best, N., & Spiegelhalter, D. (2000). WinBUGS – a Bayesian modelling framework: Concepts, structure, and extensibility. *Statistics and Computing, 10*, 325–337.

Matteucci, M., Mignani, S., & Veldkamp, B. P. (2012). Prior distributions for item parameters in IRT models. *Communications in Statistics, Theory and Methods, 41*, 2944–2958.

Matteucci, M., & Veldkamp, B. P. (2012). The use of MCMC CAT with empirical prior information to improve the efficiency of CAT. *Statistical Methods and Applications, 22*, 243–267. DOI: 10.1007/s10260-012-0216-1.

Maij-de Meij, A. M., Schakel, L., Smid, N., Verstappen, N., & Jaganjac, A. (2008). *Connector ability; Professional manual.* Utrecht, The Netherlands: PiCompany B.V.

Mislevy, R. J. (1986). Bayes model estimation in item response models, *Psychometrika, 51*, 177–195.

Mislevy, R. J. (1987). Exploiting auxiliary information about examinees in the estimation of item parameters. *Applied Psychological Measurement, 11*, 81–91.

Novick, M. R., Lewis, C., & Jackson, P. H. (1973). The estimation of proportions in m groups. *Psychometrika, 38*, 19–46.

OECD (2009). *PISA 2009 assessment framework: Key competencies in reading, mathematics and science.* Paris: OECD Publishing.

Owen, R. J. (1975). A Bayesian sequential procedure for quantal response in the context of adaptive testing. *Journal of the American Statistical Association, 70*, 351–356.

Patz, R. J., & Junker, B. W. (1999a). A straightforward approach to Markov chain Monte Carlo methods for item response models. *Journal of Educational and Behavioral Statistics, 24*, 146–178.

Patz, R. J., & Junker, B. W. (1999b). Applications and extensions of MCMC in IRT: Multiple item types, missing data, and rated responses. *Journal of Educational and Behavioral Statistics, 24*, 342–366.

Patz, R. J., Junker, B. W., Johnson, M. S., & Mariano, L. T. (2002). The hierarchical rater model for rated test items and its application to large-scale educational assessment data. *Journal of Educational and Behavioral Statistics, 27*, 341–384.

Rubin, D. B. (1987). *Multiple imputation for nonresponse in surveys.* New York: John Wiley & Sons, Inc.

Scheerens, J., Luyten, H., van den Berg, S. M., & Glas, C. A. W. (2015). Exploration of direct and indirect associations of system-level policy-amenable variables with reading literacy performance. *Educational Research and Evaluation, 21*, 15–39.

Swaminathan, H., & Gifford, J. A. (1982). Bayesian estimation in the Rasch model. *Journal of Educational Statistics, 7*, 175–192.

Swaminathan, H., & Gifford, J. A. (1985). Bayesian estimation in the two-parameter logistic model. *Psychometrika, 50*, 349–364.

Tanner, M. A., & Wong, W. H. (1987). The calculation of posterior distributions by data augmentation (with discussion). *Journal of the American Statistical Association, 82*, 528–550.

The MathWorks Inc. (2005). *MATLAB [computer program].* The MathWorks Inc., Natick, MA

Theunissen, T. J. J. M. (1985). Binary programming and test design. *Psychometrika, 50*, 411–420.

Tsutakawa, R. K., & Lin, H. Y. (1986). Bayesian estimation of item response curves. *Psychometrika, 51*, 251–267.

van den Berg, S. M., Fikse, F., Arvelius, P., Glas, C. A. W., & Strandberg, E. (2010). Integrating phenotypic measurement models with animal models. *Proceedings of the 9th World Congress on Genetics applied to Livestock Production.* Leipzig, Germany.

van den Berg, S. M., Glas, C. A. W., & Boomsma, D. I. (2007). Variance decomposition using an IRT measurement model, *Behavior Genetics, 37,* 604–616.

van der Linden, W. J. (1998). Bayesian item selection criteria for adaptive testing. *Psychometrika, 63,* 201–216.

van der Linden, W. J. (2005). *Linear models for optimal test design.* New York: Springer.

van der Linden, W. J., & Hambleton, R. K. (Eds.). (1997). *Handbook of modern item response theory.* New York: Springer.

van der Linden, W. J., & Reese, L. M. (1998). A model for optimal constrained adaptive testing. *Applied Psychological Measurement, 22,* 259–270.

Veldkamp, B. P. (2010). Bayesian item selection in constrained adaptive testing using shadow tests. *Psicologica, 31,* 149–169.

Whittaker, T. A., Chang, W., & Dodd, B. G. (2012). The performance of IRT model selection methods with mixed-format tests. *Applied Psychological Measurement, 36,* 159–180.

Zwinderman, A. H. (1991). A generalized Rasch model for manifest predictors. *Psychometrika, 56,* 589–600.

Code Appendix

Code 1   Data augmentation scheme in R.

Note text following # is author annotation.

```
# Sample size
N <- 10

# simulate response pattern
Y <- sample(c(0,1), N, replace = T, prob = c(.5,.5))

#initialize vector of latent response data
Z <- Y

#prior mean value
mutheta <- 0

# number iterations
XG <- 1000

# Store output
Mtheta <- matrix(0,ncol=2,nrow=XG)

# use function rtnorm to sample from truncated normal
distribution
library(msm)
        for(ii in 1:XG){
 Z[Y==1] <-    rtnorm(sum(Y), mean=theta, sd=1, lower=0,
 upper=Inf)
```

```
            #sample Z>0 when Y=1
    Z[Y==0] <- rtnorm(sum(1-Y), mean=theta, sd=1, lower=-
    Inf, upper=0)
            #sample Z<0 when Y=0
            #sample posterior values for θ given normal prior
            with mean mutheta
    theta1<-rnorm(1,mean = sum(Z)/(N+1)+mutheta/(N+1),sd=sqrt
    (1/(N+1)))
            #sample posterior values for θ given uniform prior
            theta2 <- rnorm(1,mean = mean(Z),sd=sqrt(1/N))

    Mtheta[ii,1] <-theta1 # Average approximates posterior
    mean
    Mtheta[ii,2] <-theta2 # Average approximates posterior
    mean (and maximum likelihood estimate)
    }
```

Code 2   WinBUGS code Bayesian IRT for binary response data.

```
  model{
      for (i in 1:N) { #Students
        for (k in 1:K) { #Items
           p[i,k] <- (exp(1.7*(a[k]*theta[i]-
b[k]))/(1+exp(1.7*(a[k]*theta[i]-b[k]))))  #Logistic 2PL
IRT Model
           #p[i,k]<-c[k]+(1-c[k])*(exp(1.7*(a[k]*theta[i]-
b[k]))/(1+exp(1.7*(a[k]*theta[i]-b[k]))))  #Logistic 3PL IRT
Model
           Y[i,k] ~ dbern(p[i,k])
        }
           theta[i] ~ dnorm(0,1) #Standard Normal Population
Distribution for Students
      }

  for (k in 1:K) {
    adummy[k] ~ dnorm(mu[2],prec[2]) #Lognormal
distribution for Item Discriminations
    a[k] <- exp(adummy[k])
    b[k] ~ dnorm(mu[1],prec[1]) #Normal Distribution for
    Item Difficulties
    #c[k] ~ dbeta(b11,b12) #Beta distribution for Guessing
    parameters
  }
```

```
  #Hyperprior specifications
   mu[1] ~ dnorm(0,1)
   mu[2] ~ dnorm(1,1)
   prec[1] ~ dgamma(1,1)
   prec[2] ~ dgamma(1,1)
   sigma[1] <- 1/prec[1]
   sigma[2] <- 1/prec[2]
  ##guessing hyperprior specification
  #b11~dunif(2,10)
  #b12~dunif(2,10)
  #ec <- b11/(b11+b12)    # posterior mean of average guessing in
  the test
  #varc <- (b11*b12)/(pow(b11+b12,2)*(b11+b12+1)) #
posterior variance of average guessing in the test
   }
```

Code 3   WinBUGS code multilevel model for IRT-based plausible values.

```
model

{

#############################
##### description of variables
#############################

# school covariates
#x variables: x[country number, school number, variable number]
#1. Autonomy resources  (simple ratio) school level variable
#2. Autonomy curriculum (simple ratio) school level variable

# country covariates (z variables)
#     1 = Standardized(normal): Age of first selection
      (system level)
#     2 = Standardized(normal): Number of school types
      (system level)

# student SES: SES.student[country, school, student]
# plausible value 1: PV1[country, school, student]

# K: number of countries with complete data on country
covariates
# M: number of schools within country
```

```
# N: number of students  per [country,school]
# which.countries: a vector describing the countries with
complete data on all country covariates.
# R: number of country covariates
# Q: number of school covariates


###########################################################
### the actual modelling of the plausible values,
ie the likelihood
###########################################################

for (k in 1:K) # for every country
        {
z.gamma[which.countries[k]] <- inprod(z[which.countries
[k],], gamma[])
        v[which.countries[k]] ~ dnorm(0,tau.country)
        for (j in 1:M[which.countries[k]]) # for every school in
        each country
                {
                x.beta[which.countries[k],j]    <- inprod
(x[which.countries[k], j, ], beta[])
                u[which.countries[k],j] ~ dnorm(0, tau.school)
                for (i in 1:N[which.countries[k],j]) # for every
individual in each school in each country
                        {
                        PV1[which.countries[k],j,i]  ~ dnorm
(expTheta[which.countries[k],j,i], tau.individual)
                        expTheta[which.countries[k],j,i] <- mu +
alpha*SES.student[which.countries[k],j,i] +    x.beta
[which.countries[k],j] + z.gamma[which.countries[k]]  +
u[which.countries[k],j]+ v[which.countries[k]]
                        }
                }
        }




###########################################################
## Priors for population mean and variances
###########################################################

mu ~ dnorm(0,.1) # normal prior for the population mean

tau.individual ~ dgamma(.1, .1)  # inverse gamma prior
for residual variance at student level
var.individual <- 1/tau.individual
```

```
tau.school ~ dgamma(.1, .1)  # inverse gamma prior for
residual variance at school level
var.school <- 1/tau.school

tau.country~ dgamma(.1,.1) # inverse gamma prior for
residual variance at country level
var.country<- 1/tau.country


#####################################################
####priors for regression coefficients alpha, beta and
gamma
#####################################################

# effect of individual covariate SES:
alpha ~dnorm(0,.1)

# effects of school covariates:
beta[1] ~ dnorm(0, .1)
beta[2] ~ dnorm(0, .1)

# effects of country covariates
gamma[1] ~ dnorm(0,.1)
gamma[2] ~ dnorm(0,.1)


}
```

18

Modelling Forced-Choice Response Formats

Anna Brown and Albert Maydeu-Olivares

What are Forced-Choice Response Formats?

When thinking of a "typical" questionnaire, we imagine a series of stimuli (statements, questions, words, phrases, pictures, etc.) that our subjects respond to, usually by selecting one of several response options. For example, we may ask respondents to indicate the extent to which the following statements are true of them:

	very untrue of me	*somewhat untrue of me*	*somewhat true of me*	*very true of me*
I am relaxed most of the time		X		
I start conversations				X

The common characteristic of this type of questionnaire format is that the stimuli (we will refer to them as questionnaire **items**) are responded to **one at a time**. Regardless of the exact type and number of response options used, respondents are supposed to consider one single stimulus at a time, and provide a response to it independently of other stimuli. This response format is called the **single-stimulus format**. The single-stimulus format is by far the most popular in psychometric practice. In his Theory of Data (1964), Clyde Coombs devoted a whole class (Type II) to single-stimulus data.

There is, however, an alternative way to gather responses to the same stimuli. Instead of presenting them one by one, we can present two stimuli together and ask the respondents to express their **preference** with respect to the stimuli presented. For instance, for the two statements from the example before, we can ask them to indicate which statement is **most** true:

	most true of me
I am relaxed most of the time	
I start conversations	X

The Wiley Handbook of Psychometric Testing: A Multidisciplinary Reference on Survey, Scale and Test Development, First Edition. Edited by Paul Irwing, Tom Booth, and David J. Hughes.
© 2018 John Wiley & Sons Ltd. Published 2020 by John Wiley & Sons Ltd.

In this task, the respondent is forced to make a choice (hence the name – **forced-choice format**). Regardless of whether both statements are true or untrue of the respondent, he/she will have to select one that is most true. This will unambiguously imply that the remaining statement is less true; therefore, a full rank order of the two statements is obtained. Examples of tests using forced-choice pairs are the Tailored Adaptive Personality Assessment System (TAPAS; Drasgow, Chernyshenko, & Stark 2010b), and the Navy Computerized Adaptive Personality Scales (NCAPS; Schneider et al., 2007).

We can add another statement to the forced-choice pair, and ask respondents to rank order three statements according to the extent to which they are true of them, for example:

	rank order
I am relaxed most of the time	3
I start conversations	1
I catch on to things quickly	2

Another variation of rank ordering is to ask respondents to select only the top and bottom ranks, as follows:

	most/least true of me
I am relaxed most of the time	least
I start conversations	most
I catch on to things quickly	

In the example scenario with three statements, making the "most–least" choices will unambiguously place the remaining statement in between the two selected statements, and therefore this format is equivalent to complete rank ordering. If, however, we add another statement to make a block of four forced-choice items, selecting the top and bottom ranks would yield an incomplete ranking:

	most/least true of me	rank order
I am relaxed most of the time	least	4
I start conversations		
I catch on to things quickly		
I sympathize with others' feelings	most	1

In the above example, the ranking is **incomplete** because we do not know which of the two remaining statements would receive rank "2," and which one would receive rank "3." There are more examples of forced-choice formats producing incomplete rankings, for instance this would occur if the respondent were asked to select only the top-ranking item from a block of three or more items (as we already know, this format would yield a complete ranking if only two items were involved).

All these examples conform to an **ordinal** forced-choice format (Chan, 2003), since only the order of the items is obtained. Examples of tests using ordinal forced-choice formats are the Occupational Personality Questionnaire (OPQ32i; SHL 2006), the Personality and Preference Inventory (PAPI; Cubiks, 2010), the Customer Contact Styles Questionnaire (CCSQ 7.2; SHL 1997), the Gordon's Personal Profile Inventory (GPP-I; Gordon, 1993), the Survey of Interpersonal Values (SIV; Gordon, 1976), and the Kolb Learning Style Inventory (Kolb & Kolb, 2005).

Another, more complicated type of ranking is the so-called Q-sort (Block, 1961), whereby respondents perform ranking with ties. In this format, respondents have to assign a number of items to several categories, complying with a predefined distribution, (i.e., the number of items to be assigned to each category is fixed). For example, respondents are asked to sort 45 items into five piles, according to the extent to which the items are characteristic of them, and to make sure that every pile contains the precise number of items specified:

		Pile Number				
most uncharacteristic	1	2	3	4	5	most characteristic
	5	10	15	10	5	
		Number of items in pile				

Although seemingly a rating task, the Q-sort is in fact a pure forced-choice format, because rating decisions have to consider assignments to categories both below and above, thus necessitating direct comparisons between items. Examples of tests using this format are the California Adult Q-Set (Block, 2008), the Riverside Behavioral Q-sort (Funder, Furr, & Colvin, 2000) and the Riverside Situational Q-sort (Wagerman & Funder, 2009).

Some forced-choice formats go beyond simple rank ordering and involve judgments of **the extent** of preference for one item over another. In our example with two items, respondents may be asked to indicate to what extent one statement is more (or less) true of them:

	much more true of me	*slightly more true of me*	*slightly more true of me*	*much more true of me*	
I am relaxed most of the time				X	I start conversations

Now we not only have the preferential ordering of the items; we also have some quantitative information about the relative merits of the two items. We can also collect quantitative information by asking the respondents to distribute a fixed number of points between several items. For instance, we may ask respondents to distribute 10 points between three statements according to the extent to which the statements are true of them:

	Points (10 in total)
I am relaxed most of the time	1
I start conversations	5
I catch on to things quickly	4

Comparing this format with the most-least selections using the same items, it is clear that although the preference for the statement "I start conversations" remains, the latter format captures more information about the extent of that preference. From the example responses, it can be seen that the respondent judged "I start conversations" is only slightly more true of the self than "I catch on to things quickly"; however, he/she judged it to be much more true of the self than "I am relaxed most of the time." Another typical example of this format is asking respondents to distribute 100 points between several items; in this case, the points awarded to each item can be interpreted as percentages of a total amount. This type of forced-choice is referred to as **multiplicative** or compositional (Chan, 2003).

Having considered several examples of forced-choice formats, the reader will see that they are fundamentally different from single-stimulus formats. When using single-stimulus formats, the respondents make **absolute judgments** about every individual item. When using forced-choice formats, the respondents engage in **comparative judgments**. The Theory of Data (Coombs, 1964) devotes two whole classes (Type I – Preferential Choice, and Type III – Stimulus Comparison) to data obtained by using forced-choice formats.[1]

The Advantages of Presenting Questionnaire Items Using the Forced-Choice Format

While it is clear that forced-choice formats are different from single-stimulus formats, we have not yet discussed why we might want to present questionnaire items in this fashion. Do comparative judgments have any advantages over absolute judgments? Indeed, the forced-choice format does have its own merits.

Firstly, comparative judgments eliminate any systematic response sets that apply uniformly across items (Cheung & Chan, 2002). For instance, having to make a choice between items will make it impossible to endorse them all indiscriminately (so-called **acquiescence** bias). It will also make it impossible to produce uniformly elevated or decreased judgments across all items, therefore eliminating rater effects such as **leniency/severity**. Indeed, if instead of rating several employees on the same performance indicator, a rater simply rank-orders the employees according to their performance, any effects associated with leniency (or severity) of this particular rater are removed. Another example of uniform response sets is the individual tendency to provide extreme versus middle-ground ratings (**extremity/central tendency** responding). These tendencies are also overcome by the use of the forced-choice formats.

---

[1] Type I (Preferential Choice) and Type III (Stimulus Comparison) can use exactly the same response formats, but differ in whether the data capture information on the respondents themselves (and whether this information is of interest). In Type I comparisons, the participant indicates own relationship with the stimuli (preference, applicability to self, etc.), and therefore can be placed on the same psychological continuum as the stimuli. On contrary, Type III data captures comparisons between stimuli regarding a certain property (brightness, sweetness, competence, fairness, etc.). In such comparisons, the respondents act merely as judges, they do not indicate own relation to the psychological continuum of interest and therefore cannot be placed on this continuum (Coombs, 1964). The Type III data is very common in marketing; it is also popular in psychometric applications where judgements about other individuals are collected.

Secondly, simple rank ordering removes the need for any rating scale. This is an important and perhaps overlooked advantage of **ordinal** forced-choice formats. In addition to the problem of extremity/central tendency, and biases caused by the order of response options and whether they have numerical or verbal anchors (e.g., Schwarz, et al., 1991), there are further complex and difficult to classify issues which concern the idiosyncratic interpretation and use of rating scales. Respondents may interpret the response options or any other verbal and nonverbal anchors provided with the rating scale differently, resulting in a violation of the main assumption of rating scales – that their effects are fixed across respondents (Friedman & Amoo, 1998). Some argue that performing direct comparisons between items may be simpler for respondents than arriving at ratings for each item – a process that requires discrimination between various response options (Maydeu-Olivares & Böckenholt, 2008). This might be particularly true when rating scales contain many response options and provide few verbal anchors, or when the response options are ambiguous or inappropriate for the items. This argument, however, can be turned on its head when we consider extremely complex forced-choice tasks such as Q-sorts. Clearly, the cognitive complexity of such forced-choice designs is by far greater than that of almost any rating scale.

Thirdly, forced-choice formats may be useful in research involving personal or sensitive information. Chan (2003) provides an example whereby respondents are asked to indicate the proportion of their household income spent on several commodity groups (food, clothes, electricity, etc.). In such a survey, the respondents may not want to disclose their spending patterns in monetary value, but they may be happy to provide a percentage breakdown. Taking issues of privacy into account is important in many research topics; and ensuring that the respondents' privacy is protected may be essential for guaranteeing valid responses.

Fourthly, imposing forced choices directly tackles the problem with lack of differentiation in ratings. This problem, reported almost 100 years ago by Thorndike (1920) and still widespread in ratings of individuals, organizations, and services, is known as the *halo* effect. The halo effect is characterized by overgeneralized assessments of all characteristics of the rated object based on one important dimension. Unlike uniform rater biases such as leniency/severity, the halo effect might not act uniformly across all items, and instead might influence some of them more than others. Forced-choice makes raters differentiate between various characteristics of the rated object, and thus this reduces halo effects. Bartram (2007) showed that the use of forced-choice formats in line manager assessments of employees' job competencies could increase correlations with external measures by as much as 50% compared to single-stimulus competency ratings.

Finally, and perhaps most controversially, forced-choice formats have been used in personality and similar assessments when responses were thought to be subject to **socially desirable responding**, whether due to self-deception or motivated **impression management** (Zerbe & Paulhus, 1987). The latter types of distortion often referred to as **faking good** are of particular concern in high stakes assessments, such as assessments in recruitment or selection of employees. It has been argued that because it is impossible to endorse all items, when combining equally desirable items in the same forced-choice block that this would prevent respondents from endorsing the desirable items and rejecting the undesirable ones. Over the years, some authors have reported positive evidence for the use of forced-choice formats in these contexts (Christiansen, Burns, & Montgomery, 2005; Jackson, Wroblewski, & Ashton, 2000; Martin, Bowen, & Hunt, 2002; Vasilopoulos, et al., 2006), while others have found the forced-choice format to be as susceptible to faking as the single-stimulus format (Heggestad, Morrison, Reeve, & McCloy, 2006). While inarguably dependent on particular questionnaire designs and specific contexts, these disparate findings highlight problems in using the forced-choice format for eliminating motivated response distortions. Matching items on social desirability levels is one such problem. Research shows that respondents have different perceptions of item desirability (Kuncel, Goldberg, & Kiger 2011). Coupled with the fact that item desirability depends on the testing context (e.g., the job for which respondents are being assessed), it follows that even the most careful matching cannot make all respondents in all contexts perceive all items in one block as equally desirable. Another problem was summarized by Feldman and Corah (1960), who argued that direct comparisons between items might actually invite finer distinctions between their desirability levels than rating each item independently, therefore potentially heightening the social desirability effects. The jury is still out on the question of the effectiveness of forced-choice formats in reducing socially desirable responding. We believe that to answer this question conclusively, a better understanding of the psychological process behind socially desirable responding is required, and of how this process may interact with comparative judgments.

Having discussed the potential advantages of forced-choice formats, the reader might wonder why their use is not more widespread. It turns out that the forced-choice formats also have major disadvantages, which are concerned with scaling. We turn to the scaling of forced-choice data next.

Scaling of Forced-Choice Responses

The purpose of gathering responses on questionnaire items in psychometric applications is to scale the objects of assessment on the psychological attributes measured by the questionnaire. Typically, we are interested in absolute scaling so that every object is associated with a number on a psychological continuum, and objects can be assessed relative to the scale origin. How do we derive absolute scale scores (e.g., personality trait scores,) from relative information provided by forced-choice formats (e.g., relative preferences for personality test items)? This section describes popular scaling methods for forced-choice responses.

A classical approach, or measurement by "fiat"

Traditionally, forced-choice data has been treated in a similar way to rating scales. Points are awarded for preferring an item; and the points are added to the scale that the item is designed to measure. For instance, preferring an item from a pair may result in one point being added to that scale which is measured by the item:

	most true of me	*Score*
I am relaxed most of the time		0 (to Emotional Stability)
I start conversations	X	1 (to Extraversion)

In blocks of three, four or more items, inverted rank orders (or some linear function of these inverted rank orders) would be added to the respective scales that the items are designed to measure, so that the item ranked first would earn most points and the item ranked last would earn least points:

	most/least true of me	*rank order*	*score*
I am relaxed most of the time	least	3	0
I start conversations	most	1	2
I catch on to things quickly		2	1

If an incomplete ranking were obtained, the same logic would apply, with the item ranked first earning most points, the item ranked last earning least points, and the items not ranked earning an equal number of points in between:

	most/least true of me	*rank order*	*Score*
I am relaxed most of the time	least	4	0
I start conversations			1
I catch on to things quickly			1
I sympathize with others' feelings	most	1	2

For tasks in which participants are asked to distribute a fixed number of points between several items, these points would typically be awarded to the respective scales.

One common feature of all these scoring protocols is that the number of points awarded is quite arbitrary – it is not justified theoretically or empirically. Torgeson (1958) called this type of scaling **measurement by fiat**. Another common feature is that in all the above examples the total number of points awarded in the block is **constant** for all respondents. To illustrate, consider our previous example of a forced-choice pair, and another forced-choice pair measuring the same personality traits, with the following responses from respondent A:

Respondent A	*most true of me*	*score*
I am relaxed most of the time		0 (to Emot. Stability)
I start conversations	X	1 (to Extraversion)

Respondent A	*most true of me*	*score*
I rarely get irritated		0 (to Emot. Stability)
I make friends easily	X	1 (to Extraversion)

The responses here will result in 2 points being allotted to Extraversion and 0 points to Emotional Stability – 2 points in total. Now consider the following responses to the same item pairs (respondent B):

Respondent B	*most true of me*	*score*
I am relaxed most of the time	X	1 (to Emot. Stability)
I start conversations		0 (to Extraversion)

Respondent B	most true of me	score
I rarely get irritated	X	1 (to Emot. Stability)
I make friends easily		0 (to Extraversion)

These responses will result in 0 points being allotted to Extraversion and 2 points to Emotional Stability – again totaling 2 points.

An immediate implication is that, regardless of the choices made, every participant will receive the same total number of points on the test but that the points will be distributed differently between different scales. This type of data is called **ipsative** data. The name was coined by Cattell in 1944, from the Latin *ipse* (he, himself), reflecting the fact that any score obtained on an ipsative test is relative to self. Indeed, while respondents A and B obtained the same number of points, the points were allotted differently to the two scales. All we can conclude from these scores is that respondent A's score on Extraversion is higher than his score on Emotional Stability, and that the opposite is true for respondent B. We, however, cannot tell where respondents A and B stand in relation to each other on either of these scales – it is entirely possible, for example, that respondent B is just as high on Extraversion as respondent A, and he is higher on Emotional Stability still. There is simply no information in the assigned points in order to make such inferences.

To summarize, in ipsative data the number of points on any scale for an individual can only be interpreted in relation to the number of points on other scales, because the total number of points on all scales is the same for everyone. The self-referenced nature of ipsative scores means that scores are not interpersonally comparable. This is because a score on scale A is not scaled in relation to some absolute scale origin, but instead in relation to the individual's own mean. Unlike a **normative** measure, which allows individuals to have different test means, in an ipsative measure the mean is the same for everyone.

Ipsative data have been criticized for the lack of interpretability of individual differences, and other psychometric challenges that follow from this basic property. Clemans (1966) provided a full mathematical account of problems with using ipsative data (see also Dunlap & Cornwell, 1994). Other authors have illustrated how these challenges may manifest themselves in applications (e.g., Closs, 1996; Hicks, 1970; Johnson, Wood, & Blinkhorn, 1988; Meade, 2004; Tenopyr, 1988). In the following section, we discuss psychometric properties of ipsative data.

Psychometric properties of ipsative data

Ipsative scores are interpersonally incomparable   This is the most fundamental property of ipsative scores following directly from their definition. Because the same total number of points is allocated to everyone, it is impossible to achieve a high score on one scale without reducing scores on other scales. A high score received might not be a reflection of a high standing on a theoretical attribute in any normative sense (i.e., with reference to a population); instead, it might be simply an artifact of having low scores elsewhere on the test. Fundamentally, people with an identical relative ordering of attributes will obtain identical ipsative scores, regardless of their normative standing in relation to each other. Clearly, this can have serious implications for assessment decisions in applied settings.

Ipsative scores distort construct validity   Because the total test score on ipsative measures is the same for everyone, it has zero variance. Therefore, all elements of the scales' covariance matrix sum to zero (Clemans, 1966), and the average off-diagonal covariance is a negative value. In an ipsative test consisting of *k* scales with equal variances, the average correlation among the scales must be

$$\bar{\rho} = -1/(k-1). \tag{18.1}$$

That is, regardless of the expected relationships among the attributes measured by the test, their measured scales will correlate negatively on average. Clearly, when the true scores on the attributes correlate positively, the ipsative scores will distort these relationships.

Because elements of the ipsative variance-covariance matrix sum to zero, one of the eigenvalues must be zero and maximum likelihood factor analysis cannot be applied (Dunlap & Cornwell, 1994). Principal components analysis can be performed on ipsative scores; however, the resulting components are difficult to interpret as they typically consist of scales representing contrasting choices (Cornwell & Dunlap, 1994; Baron, 1996). Overall, ipsative data compromises the construct validity of forced-choice tests.

Ipsative scores distort criterion-related validity   As the variance of the total test score is zero, covariances of the ipsative scales with any external measure will sum to zero (Clemans, 1966; Hicks, 1970). Therefore, any positive covariances with the external variable have to be compensated by some spurious negative covariances, and vice versa (Johnson, Wood, & Blinkhorn, 1988). Such distortions to the covariance patterns will be larger when the scales are expected to covary with the criterion mostly positively (or negatively). Overall, ipsative data compromises the criterion-related validity of forced-choice tests.

Partially ipsative data

Having provided a brief summary of the psychometric properties of ipsative data, we show how varying item polarity and point assignment can yield data in which the individual total score on the test is only partially constrained. Consider our previous example of two forced-choice pairs. This time, the second item-pair is designed to indicate Extraversion and the negative end of Emotional Stability (i.e., Neuroticism). Here are possible responses from respondent A:

Respondent A	*most true of me*	*score*
I am relaxed most of the time		0 (to Emot. Stability)
I start conversations	X	1 (to Extraversion)

Respondent A	*most true of me*	*score*
I worry about things*	X	−1 (to Emot. Stability)
I feel at ease with people		0 (to Extraversion)

The item "I worry about things" indicates Neuroticism (the opposite end of emotional stability) and is **negatively keyed** (it is scored −1 if preferred in the comparison). The responses in this example will result in the allocation of 1 point to Extraversion and −1 point to Emotional Stability, 0 points in total.

Now consider the following responses to the same item pairs (respondent B):

Respondent B	most true of me	score
I am relaxed most of the time	X	1 (to Emot. Stability)
I start conversations		0 (to Extraversion)

Respondent B	most true of me	score
I worry about things*		0 (to Emot. Stability)
I feel at ease with people	X	1 (to Extraversion)

These responses will result in the allocation of 1 point to Extraversion and 1 point to Emotional stability, 2 points in total. The reader can see that respondents A and B obtain different numbers of points now. This is because the test contains both positively and negatively keyed items indicating the same attribute. Such tests will yield data that shows some variation in the total score. This variation is still constrained, because in both item pairs the items indicating Emotional Stability are scored relative to a baseline score obtained on the Extraversion items. The type of data derived from such tests is called **partially ipsative**. It is generally less problematic than fully ipsative data; however, its psychometric problems are not eliminated but merely reduced.

An Item Response Theory approach, or measurement by modelling

The general problem with measurement by fiat is that the scores assigned to items are not justified theoretically or empirically. Specifically, the classical approach to scoring of forced-choice items treats rankings (relative information) as if they were ratings (absolute information). Furthermore, scale scores are computed as the sum of item scores in both the forced-choice and the single-stimulus formats. These two formats, nevertheless, reflect very different response processes and assign very different meanings to item responses.

In the single-stimulus format, a respondent selects a rating option that represents the level of an attribute or behavior that is closest to that of his or her own. The response, therefore, can be directly referenced in relation to a criterion (e.g., the behavior is not demonstrated at all, demonstrated to a small extent, or to a large extent), and consequently to a scale origin. We make the same implicit assumption when assigning scores to forced-choice items using the classical approach, completely inconsistent with the fact that forced-choice responses represent items' relative positions (in that particular forced-choice block), not the absolute levels on the attributes. Consider the situation when a respondent gives the top rank to a particular item in a block. This choice does not reflect his/her degree of agreement with the item; it simply reflects that he/she agrees with it **more** than with the other items in the block. Thus, similar items indicating the same attribute might be ranked highest in one block and lowest in another, depending on the items they are contrasted against, resulting in item scores that are inconsistent with the implicit assumption of absolute scaling. Taking this reasoning further, we can see that the idea that adding relative positions together somehow will constitute a scale score that reflects an absolute attribute score is also illogical.

Another implicit assumption underlying the classical approach to scoring is that item responses are independent from each other, after they have been controlled for the attribute levels (local independence assumption). This assumption is clearly violated, because items within a block are **not assessed independently** but in relation to each other. Making forced choices creates mutual dependencies between responses to all items in the block.

To summarize, the classical method of assigning scores to forced-choice items does not correspond to the **meaning** of item responses. In other words, the implicit model underlying this scoring bears no relation to the psychological process used in comparative judgments (Meade, 2004). The consequences of this misrepresentation in the implicit scoring model are the problems of ipsative data (Brown & Maydeu-Olivares, 2013).

Can the situation be improved by adopting an approach that considers the meaning of preferential choices? It turns out that it can. By considering the response process to forced-choice items and devising a model to describe this process, model-based measurement may be inferred for forced-choice data. Mellenbergh (2011, p. 188) named this type of scaling **measurement by modelling**, in contrast to measurement by fiat. This approach is also known under the name of Item Response Theory (IRT).

Several item response models have been developed recently to infer measurement from forced-choice data. Four such approaches are briefly described in this chapter: the Thurstonian IRT model (Brown & Maydeu-Olivares, 2011a), the Zinnes–Griggs model for Unidimensional Pairwise Preferences (Zinnes & Griggs, 1974), the Multi-Unidimensional Pairwise-Preference (MUPP) model (Stark, Chernyshenko, & Drasgow, 2005), and the McCloy, Heggestad, and Reeve (2005) unfolding model for multidimensional ranking blocks. Each of these models has distinct objectives and assumes different forced-choice designs and different properties of items used. All models may be used for creating and scoring **new** forced-choice assessments. The Zinnes–Griggs model can also be applied to estimate item parameters in forced-choice item pairs where items measuring the same scale are compared (unidimensional items). The Thurstonian IRT model is currently the only one that can be readily applied to data collected with **existing** multidimensional forced-choice questionnaires, with the additional objectives of estimating item parameters and relationships between the latent attributes.

In what follows, we briefly describe these models using a common framework. Specifically, we distinguish two components of models for forced-choice data: (1) a model for the decision process leading to selection of items, and (2) a model for relationships between items and the underlying attributes they measure. Before we consider the logic of the IRT models, however, we need to introduce a suitable coding system for forced-choice responses.

Coding of forced-choice responses

The system described here is standard in the Thurstonian modelling literature (e.g., Maydeu-Olivares & Böckenholt, 2005). To begin, let us assume that full rankings are obtained. Full ranking of n items can be equivalently coded as $\tilde{n} = n(n-1)/2$ pairwise comparisons. If only two items $\{i, k\}$ are being ranked, there is only one comparison, the outcome of which can be coded as a binary variable:

$$y_{\{i,k\}} = \begin{cases} 1 & \text{if item } i \text{ is preferred over item } k \\ 0 & \text{if item } k \text{ is preferred over item } i \end{cases}. \quad (18.2)$$

If three items are being ranked, there are three pairwise comparisons – comparison between the first and second items, between the first and third items, and between the second and third items. Here is our earlier example ranking,

item		most/least true of me	rank order
A	I am relaxed most of the time	least	3
B	I start conversations	most	1
C	I catch on to things quickly		2

and its coding through three binary variables (binary outcomes of three pairwise comparisons),

$$\{A, B\} = 0 \quad \{A, C\} = 0 \quad \{B, C\} = 1.$$

The reader will notice that this binary coding contains exactly the same information as the ranking and that the original rank order can be obtained from the pairwise outcomes, and vice versa. The two coding systems are equivalent; however, the binary outcomes enable modelling of pairwise preferences using IRT, as we shall see.

Blocks of any size can be coded as pairwise comparisons. For blocks of four items (A, B, C, D), six pairwise comparisons are required:

$$\{A, B\} \ \{A, C\} \ \{A, D\} \ \{B, C\} \ \{B, D\} \ \{C, D\}.$$

For blocks of five, there will be 10 comparisons, and so on. When full rankings are obtained, every pairwise outcome will be known. When incomplete rankings are obtained, some outcomes will be unknown in which case they can be treated as missing data.

Thurstonian IRT model

The Thurstonian IRT model was introduced by Brown and Maydeu-Olivares (2011a) to enable analysis of data arising from forced-choice tests measuring multiple traits with ranking blocks of any size. The origins of this model reside within the structural equation modelling tradition. Specifically, Maydeu-Olivares (1999) proposed a method for analyzing the mean and covariance structure of paired comparisons conforming to any observed ranking pattern, as was originally suggested by Thurstone (1931) in one of his seminal papers on choice behavior. The method relates observed choices to the differences in psychological value that respondents place on stimuli. Methods using tetrachoric correlations of dichotomous choices are used to estimate these models.

Maydeu-Olivares and Böckenholt (2005) provided a full account of Thurstonian scaling methods as applied to single ranking tasks, including cases where a factorial structure may underlie choice behavior (Thurstonian factor models). Moving from a single ranking task to multiple tasks (forced-choice blocks making up a test), and reformulating Thurstonian factor models as IRT models so that respondents' scores on underlying dimension(s) could be estimated, Brown and Maydeu-Olivares (2011a) provided the first IRT model suitable for analyzing multidimensional forced-choice data. The model may be used for estimating item parameters, and estimating correlations between the latent attributes measured by the items. Once the model parameters have been estimated, individual attribute scores and their standard errors may be established.

The Thurstonian IRT model is applicable to forced-choice formats when items are ranked within blocks, either fully or partially. Ranking blocks may be of any size, for example, consisting of two items (item pairs), three items (triplets), four items (quads), and so on. Items in each block may indicate the same or different attributes, or any mixture of the two. The model assumes a monotonic relationship between any questionnaire item and the attribute(s) it is designed to measure; that is, the higher is the attribute score the higher is the item endorsement level for positively keyed items; the higher is the attribute score the lower is the item endorsement level for negatively keyed items (a **dominance** response process).

The remainder of this section gives a brief overview of the theory, implementation, and applications of Thurstonian IRT models.

Preference decision model Since responses to every forced-choice block are essentially rankings, suitable models for these data are models for ranking data. One of the oldest models for ranking data was proposed by Louis Thurstone (1927, 1931). In this model, preference judgments are assumed to arise from a comparison of **unobserved utilities** of each item. Utility is another name for the item's **psychological value** (Thurstone, 1929), described as "the affect that the object calls forth" (p. 160). For illustrative purposes, we can think of utility as the extent to which the behavior described in the item corresponds to the respondent's own behavior (Brown & Maydeu-Olivares, 2013). For any given item, Thurstone further assumed that its utility is normally distributed across individuals.

Thurstone argued that any preference judgment relies on comparison of the utility values attached by the respondent to the items in question. That is, for any pair of items $\{i, k\}$, the respondent will rank item i above item k if his/her utility for item i is higher:

$$\text{prefer item} \begin{cases} i & \text{if} \quad \text{utility}_i \geq \text{utility}_k \\ k & \text{if} \quad \text{utility}_i < \text{utility}_k \end{cases}. \tag{18.3}$$

Taking our first example, "I start conversations" was judged to be "very true" of the respondent, and "I am relaxed most of the time" to be "somewhat untrue" of him/her. These (single-stimulus) ratings reflected the respondent's utility judgments. When we asked the respondent which one of the two items was **most true** of him/her, the answer required a **comparison** of the utilities. In our example, the respondent preferred "I start conversations," presumably, because his/her utility for this item was greater.

Having adopted a convenient coding system that presents any ranking data as several pairwise comparisons with binary outcomes (preferred – not preferred), the responses to forced-choice blocks can be easily related to the utilities of items. The binary outcomes give us the link we need to Thurstone's law of comparative judgment, so that we can rewrite the decision rules 18.3, this time using differences of utilities

$$y_{\{i,k\}} = \begin{cases} 1 & \text{if } \text{utility}_i - \text{utility}_k \geq 0 \\ 0 & \text{if } \text{utility}_i - \text{utility}_k < 0 \end{cases}. \tag{18.4}$$

We can use these expressions to relate binary outcomes of pairwise comparisons within each ranking block to the underlying utilities.

Measurement model for attributes The next step in modelling forced-choice responses is postulating a model for relations between item utilities and the psychological attributes that the items are designed to measure. The Thurstonian IRT model assumes that the utilities are related to the attributes via a linear factor analysis model.

Let us assume that each item measures one attribute.[2] Then the utilities of items depend on the latent attributes as described by a standard linear factor analysis model:

$$\text{utility}_i = \text{mean}_i + \text{loading}_i \cdot \text{attribute}_a + \text{error}_i \tag{18.5}$$

In psychological assessment, the utility of items is not of interest. Instead, the focus is on measurement of attributes underlying these utilities. Therefore, the aim is to relate the observed pairwise preferences to the latent attributes directly. This is done by presenting the difference of two utilities as a function of the latent attributes,

$$\text{utility}_i - \text{utility}_k = (\text{mean}_i - \text{mean}_k) + (\text{loading}_i \cdot \text{attribute}_a - \text{loading}_k \cdot \text{attribute}_b)$$
$$+ (\text{error}_i - \text{error}_k). \tag{18.6}$$

Looking again at the decision rule 18.4, which describes preference for one item or the other depending on the item utilities, it becomes clear that we can relate the binary outcome to the psychological attributes using 18.6. If we further simplify this relationship by replacing the difference of means with a single threshold value

$$\text{threshold}_{\{i,k\}} = -(\text{mean}_i - \text{mean}_k), \tag{18.7}$$

the positive outcome of pairwise comparison $y_{\{i,k\}} = 1$ (item i is preferred) occurs when

$$-\text{threshold}_{\{i,k\}} + (\text{loading}_i \cdot \text{attribute}_a - \text{loading}_k \cdot \text{attribute}_b) + (\text{error}_i - \text{error}_k) \geq 0. \tag{18.8}$$

Since the attributes are continuous and the outcomes of pairwise comparisons are discrete, the application of Thurstone's model to forced-choice items results in an IRT

---

[2] This is certainly the aim in most forced-choice questionnaires. The Thurstonian IRT model can easily accommodate items measuring multiple attributes (see Brown and Maydeu-Olivares, 2012), but for simplicity of illustration here, we limit the number of measured attributes to one.

model. In the standard factor analysis model 18.5, the errors are assumed to be uncorrelated. Therefore, the error part of expression 18.8 has variance

$$\text{var}(\text{error}_{\{i,k\}}) = \text{var}(\text{error}_i - \text{error}_k) = \text{var}(\text{error}_i) + \text{var}(\text{error}_k), \quad (18.9)$$

and, finally, the conditional probability of preferring item i to item k as given by the cumulative standard normal function is:

$$P(y_{\{i,k\}} = 1) = \Phi\left(\frac{-\text{threshold}_{\{i,k\}} + \text{loading}_i \cdot \text{attribute}_a - \text{loading}_k \cdot \text{attribute}_b}{\sqrt{\text{var}(\text{error}_i) + \text{var}(\text{error}_k)}}\right). \quad (18.10)$$

This is a formulation of the Thurstonian IRT model for pairwise comparison between items measuring two different attributes.

The probability expression 18.10 is called the **item response function** and can be interpreted as follows. With an increase in attribute a and a decrease in attribute b, the probability of preferring item i to item k increases (when the items have positive factor loadings). This probability is further influenced by item properties: (1) factor loadings on the attributes that the items are designed to measure; (2) a threshold value governing the combination of the attributes where the items' utilities are equal; and (3) the error variances of the two items. Because two attributes are being measured, the item response function defines a surface, an example of which is presented in Figure 18.1, in which the probability of preferring one item to another is plotted against two latent attributes.

So far, we have assumed that two items measuring different attributes are compared. If items measuring the same attribute are being compared, the conditional probability of preferring item i to item k is given by the cumulative standard normal function

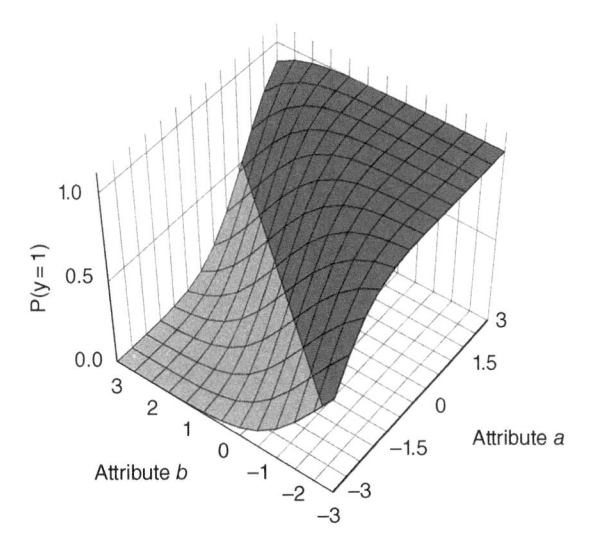

Figure 18.1 Example Thurstonian item response function for preferring an item measuring attribute a to an item measuring attribute b.

$$P\left(y_{\{i,k\}} = 1\right) = \Phi\left(\frac{-\text{threshold}_{\{i,k\}} + (\text{loading}_i - \text{loading}_k)\text{attribute}_a}{\sqrt{\text{var}(\text{error}_i) + \text{var}(\text{error}_k)}}\right). \quad (18.11)$$

One important feature of the one-dimensional model is that a comparison between two items measuring the same trait with similar factor loadings will result in a low pairwise factor loading, and the pairwise comparison will provide very little information on the latent attribute. Therefore, if one wants to present items measuring the same attribute in a forced-choice block, items with very different factor loadings should be used, for example an item with a positive factor loading could be compared to an item with a negative loading (Maydeu-Olivares & Brown, 2010).

The item response function in the one-dimensional case defines a curve, examples of which are presented in Figure 18.2, in which the probability of preferring one item to another is plotted against one latent attribute. Figure 18.2(a) illustrates the case in which two items with factor loadings of opposite sign yield a highly informative comparison; Figure 18.2(b) illustrates the case where two highly discriminating items yield an uninformative comparison.

Technical detail To enable parameter estimation, the above IRT model for pairwise preferences is embedded in a familiar structural equation modelling (SEM) framework. All pairwise comparisons and latent traits in the questionnaire are included, resulting in a single measurement model with binary outcomes (an IRT model). The following parameters are estimated: factor loadings and error variances for all items, thresholds for all pairwise comparisons, and correlations between the latent attributes.

When block size is $n = 2$ (item pairs), the model estimates one threshold, two factor loadings and one error variance per each pairwise comparison (error variances of individual items cannot be identified). In this case, the Thurstonian IRT model is simply the two-dimensional normal ogive IRT model.

When block size is $n = 3$ (triplets), $n = 4$ (quads) or greater, not all parameters are estimated freely for each pairwise comparison. The conditional probability expression 18.10 illustrates the item parameters estimated in this case. As many threshold values as there are **pairwise comparisons**, are estimated. As many factor loadings as there are **items** are estimated. Finally, as many error variances as there are **items** are estimated. That is, all pairwise comparisons involving the same item will have the same factor loading on the attribute measured by that item. For example, pairs $\{i, k\}$ and $\{i, q\}$ will have the same factor loading on the attribute measured by item i, loading$_i$. Similarly, error variances of individual items, for example var(error$_i$), are estimated. Furthermore, it follows from Equation 18.6 that errors of pairwise comparisons involving the same item will have a shared part, so that local dependencies exist among them:

$$\text{cov}\left(\text{error}_{\{i, k\}}, \text{error}_{\{i, q\}}\right) = \text{var}(\text{error}_i). \quad (18.12)$$

These special features when block size is $n \geq 3$ need to be specified in the measurement model; specifically, equality constraints need be placed on factor loadings and error variances relating to the same item since these values are estimated per item, not per pairwise comparison. In this case, the Thurstonian IRT model is an extension of the normal ogive model to items presented in forced-choice blocks. Practical

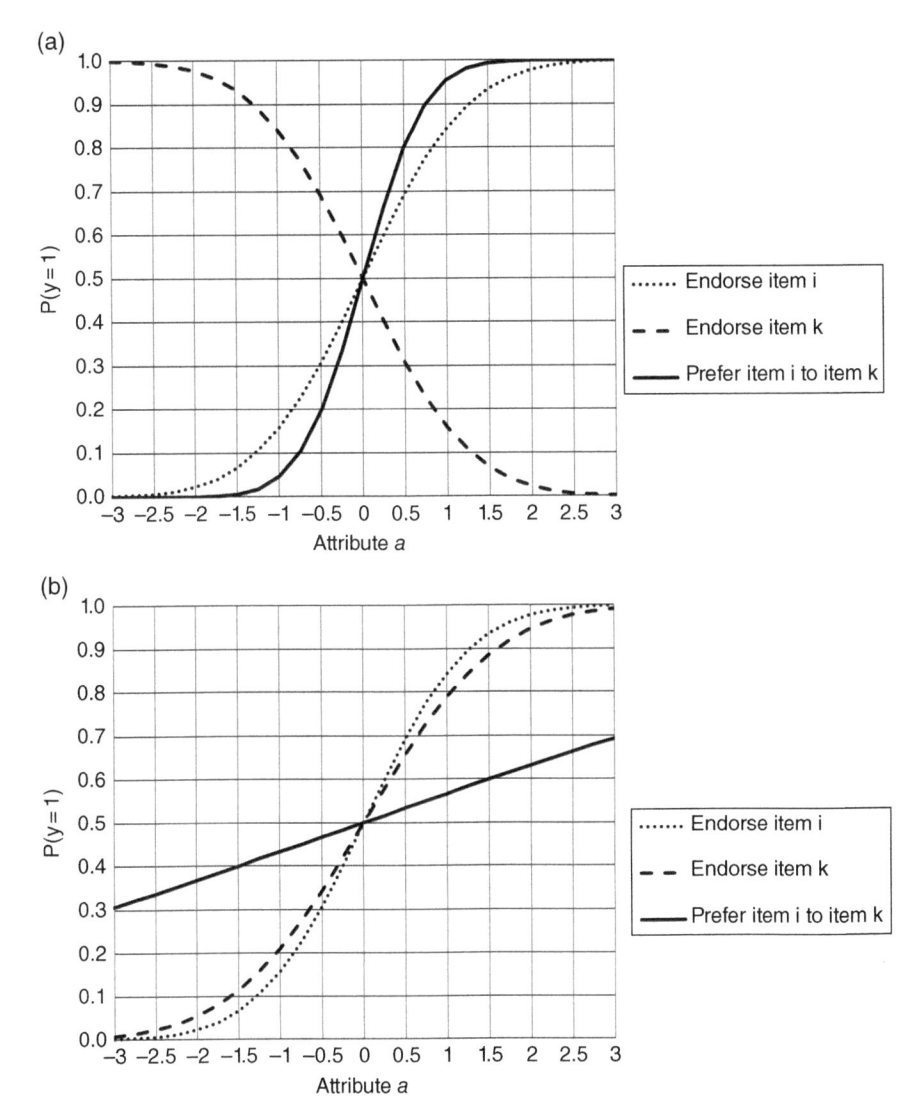

Figure 18.2 Example Thurstonian item response function for preferring an item measuring attribute a to an item measuring attribute b.
Note. The dotted and dashed lines illustrate the conditional probabilities of endorsing item i and k, respectively. The solid line illustrates the conditional probability of preferring item i to item k.

guidance on parameter and person score estimation in the case of forced-choice blocks of size 3 is given in the data analysis example in this chapter (see the data analysis example with the Forced-Choice Five Factor Markers).

Thurstonian IRT models can be estimated using any method but in typical applications, there are too many latent traits for maximum likelihood estimation to be feasible. The recommended alternative is to resort to limited information methods based on tetrachoric correlations. After the item parameters have been estimated, individual scores on latent attributes are estimated by the Maximum A Posteriori (MAP) method. The reader is referred to Brown and Maydeu-Olivares (2011a) for further technical detail.

These models can be estimated in MPlus (Muthén & Muthén, 1998–2012), which also performs estimation of attribute scores for individuals. The data analysis example in this chapter illustrates the workings of the Thurstonian modelling approach using MPlus.

Applications Applications of the Thurstonian IRT model so far have included reanalysis of existing forced-choice data and development of new forced-choice questionnaires. Reanalysis of existing forced-choice data is particularly interesting since it enables direct comparison between classical and model-based IRT scoring. Research using the Customer Contact Styles Questionnaire (CCSQ; SHL, 1997) demonstrates that even questionnaires with challenging features such as large block size and the use of incomplete rankings can be analyzed successfully. Furthermore, individual attribute scores estimated by the IRT method are free from the problems of ipsative data (Brown & Maydeu-Olivares, 2013).

Another example is the development of a short version of the Occupational Personality Questionnaire (OPQ32r; Brown, 2009), in which the questionnaire's redesign was informed by the use of item response modelling, and new IRT-based scoring was applied to produce individual attribute scores. This example illustrates how IRT modelling may be applied to reanalyze data from an existing assessment tool, and how to use this information to redevelop the tool, enhancing its strong features and transforming its scoring protocol.

For another example, a short forced-choice measure of the Five Factors of personality has been developed (Forced-Choice Five Factor Markers; Brown & Maydeu-Olivares, 2011b) using 60 items from the International Personality Item Pool (IPIP; Goldberg, 1992). The development of this measure was informed directly by simulation studies using IRT modelling. The data analysis example in this chapter uses data collected with this questionnaire.

An interesting application outside of tests that use explicit forced-choice formats is reported in a recent study by Lang, Zettler, Ewen, and Hulsheger (2012), who addressed the complexities in measuring implicit motives using the Operant Motive Test (OMT; Kuhl & Scheffer, 2002). The OMT asks respondents to generate stories in response to ambiguous pictures, assessing motives of power, affiliation, and achievement. Lang et al. argued that the notion of utility maximization, so central to Thurstone's account of choice behaviors, applies to implicit motives too. Only the strongest implicit motive is expressed in the narrated story, and therefore the observed responses must be modelled in relation to choices between different implicit (latent) motives. This research suggests a wider applicability of Thurstonian IRT modelling to psychological data than the authors of this model first envisaged, and we look forward to new developments in this area.

Zinnes–Griggs model for unidimensional pairwise preferences

Zinnes and Griggs (1974) introduced an IRT model describing preference judgments when choosing one of two items measuring the same attribute. This model originates from Coombs's (1950) "unfolding" scaling tradition for modelling preference data.

Preference decision model Coombs (1950) explained people's preferences for stimuli by their relative closeness to the position on the attribute that the stimuli represent. According to this model, when facing a choice between two stimuli, the person will prefer the stimulus closer to their own position on the attribute ("ideal point"). The ideal point is the person's location on the attribute of interest – the person's attribute score, and hence

$$\text{prefer item} \begin{cases} i & \text{if } |\text{attribute} - \text{location}_i| \leq |\text{attribute} - \text{location}_k| \\ k & \text{if } |\text{attribute} - \text{location}_i| > |\text{attribute} - \text{location}_k| \end{cases}. \quad (18.13)$$

For example, when choosing between statements measuring Extraversion, a respondent will choose a statement that represents a standing on the Extraversion attribute that is closest to their own. Any preferential rank ordering, therefore, can be thought of as an ordering of the stimuli's locations "folded" at the person's ideal point (conversely, the stimuli locations can be uncovered by "unfolding" the rank orders – hence the name of this decision model).

Zinnes and Griggs (1974) recognized the limitations of Coombs's deterministic model and modified it by talking about noisy "perceptions" of the locations of both the stimuli and the person's own ideal point at the time of comparison. Thus, Zinnes and Griggs considered three normally distributed random variables with expected values corresponding to the person's own ideal point, and the two items' locations.

Measurement model for attributes The preference decision model adopted here implicitly assumes an **ideal-point** response process for every item involved in the comparisons. The term "ideal point" was coined by Coombs (1950) based on the original work of Thurstone (1928), who described a process of responding to attitude items. Thurstone argued that the utility value for a statement such as "Fire arms should not belong in private hands" is the highest for individuals with this exact level of attitude toward "militarism," and reduces for persons with **both** higher and lower levels of this attitude. Coombs called this maximum preference point on the attitude continuum the individual's "ideal point," which is characteristic of each person.

Originally suggested for attitude items, it has recently been proposed that the ideal-point models can be applied more generally (Drasgow, et al., 2010a). Items in, say, the personality domain do not have to represent an extremely positive or negative standing on the attributes of interest. Items which represent intermediate or average positions can also be presented: For instance, "My attention to detail is about average." For such items, the linear factor analytic model is unlikely to represent the relationship between the item utility and the underlying construct (Conscientiousness) correctly, because the utility of this item is likely to peak around the average Conscientiousness score, and be lower for respondents with either high or low scores.

The latent tendency to endorse an item (utility in Thurstonian terms) in the Zinnes–Griggs probabilistic model is an inverse of the absolute difference between the person's attribute score and the item location, and their random errors,

$$\text{utility}_i = -|(\text{attribute} + \text{error}_a) - (\text{location}_i + \text{error}_i)|. \quad (18.14)$$

Because the absolute difference between the person's attribute and the item location is opposite to the person's utility for the item, Zinnes and Griggs called it **disutility**.

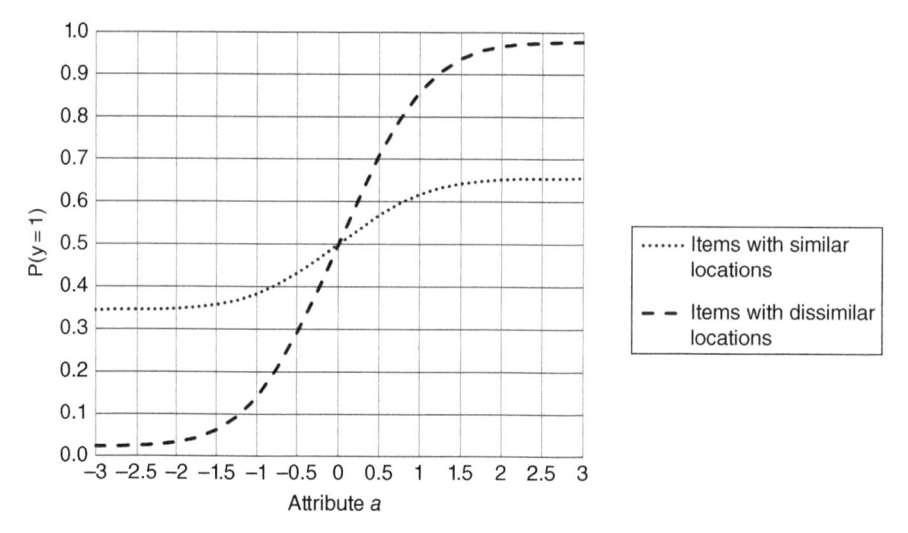

Figure 18.3 Example Zinnes–Griggs item response functions for preferring item i to item k; both items measure the same attribute a.
Note. The dotted line illustrates comparison between items with locations 0.2 and −0.2; the dashed line illustrates comparison between items with locations 1 and −1.

They showed that the probability of preferring one item to another conditional on the person's ideal point and the items' locations (all placed on the same attribute continuum) is a one-dimensional IRT model given by a linear combination of cumulative standard normal distribution functions:

$$P\left(y_{\{i,k\}} = 1\right) = 1 - \Phi\left(a_{\{i,k\}}\right) - \Phi\left(b_{\{i,k\}}\right) + 2\Phi\left(a_{\{i,k\}}\right)\Phi\left(b_{\{i,k\}}\right), \qquad (18.15)$$

where
$a_{\{i,k\}} = (2 \cdot \text{attribute} - \text{location}_i - \text{location}_k)/\sqrt{3}$
$b_{\{i,k\}} = \text{location}_i - \text{location}_k$

It can be seen that the conditional probability depends only on the person's score and the item locations. The model assumes that the items vary only in their locations on the underlying attribute continuum, thus all items are assumed to be **equally discriminating**. The item response function for a pairwise comparison can be plotted against the latent attribute, as illustrated in Figure 18.3. This figure shows that when items with similar locations are compared, the comparison yields a very "flat" function with a shallow slope; and when items with very dissimilar locations are compared, the comparison yields a function with a steep slope. Therefore, comparisons between items located closely on the same attribute are noninformative. This is a very similar feature to the one we observed when comparing items with similar factor loadings under the Thurstonian IRT model.

Technical detail Item parameters (locations) can be estimated by the marginal maximum likelihood (MML) procedure (Stark & Drasgow, 2002). Person parameters (attribute scores) can be estimated by either Expected A Posteriori (EAP) or MAP methods; EAP is recommended because it is a noniterative procedure and is fast and efficient for one-dimensional models.

Applications This straightforward unidimensional model has been applied recently in personality assessments in the workplace, with an added advantage of employing computerized adaptive algorithms. Borman et al. (2001) used it to measure job performance via a computerized adaptive test, and Schneider et al. (2007) used the model to build the NCAPS.

Multi-Unidimensional Pairwise-Preference (MUPP) model

The MUPP model was first introduced by Stark (2002) to enable scoring of forced-choice tests measuring multiple traits using item pairs (i.e., blocks of size 2). The model, further developed by Stark, Chernyshenko, and Drasgow (2005), adopts yet another approach to explaining preference judgments originally suggested by Andrich (1989). Andrich proposed that instead of devising an explicit multidimensional model for pairwise comparisons, the probability of preferring one item to another might be approximated by the joint probability of accepting one item and rejecting the other. These probabilities of acceptance and rejection are based on characteristics of each of the items involved (the items' IRT parameters) established through single-stimulus item trialling.

The MUPP model may be used to create new forced-choice tests by assembling pairs of items based on their single-stimulus IRT parameters, and to estimate individuals' scores on the latent attributes. However, the model does not allow estimating item parameters from the actual forced-choice data. Items in each pair may indicate the same or different attributes (hence the name multiunidimensional). The MUPP model assumes an ideal-point response process for the items involved in comparisons, and therefore it represents Coombs's unfolding tradition. The remainder of this section gives a brief overview of the theory, implementation, and applications of MUPP models.

Preference decision model Andrich (1989) constructed models for pairwise preferences from models for single-stimulus responses. His rationale was to consider the outcome $y_{\{i,k\}} = 1$ as a broad endorsement of item i and a nonendorsement of item k, $P(1, 0)$. Conversely, the outcome $y_{\{i,k\}} = 0$ corresponds to a nonendorsement of item i and an endorsement of item k, $P(0, 1)$. The other two possible evaluation outcomes, of either endorsing two items $(1, 1)$ or not endorsing ether $(0, 0)$ are not admissible in a forced-choice task. Then the conditional probability of preferring item i to item k is given by the joint probability of accepting one item and rejecting the other, divided by the total probability of the two admissible outcomes,

$$P\left(y_{\{i,k\}} = 1\right) = \frac{P_{ik}(1, 0)}{P_{ik}(1, 0) + P_{ik}(0, 1)}. \qquad (18.16)$$

Acceptances and rejections of individual items are assumed to be independent events, conditional only on the attributes the item measures, therefore

$$P_{\{i,k\}}(1) = \frac{P_i(1\,|\text{attribute}_a)P_k(0\,|\text{attribute}_b)}{P_i(1\,|\text{attribute}_a)P_k(0\,|\text{attribute}_b) + P_i(0\,|\text{attribute}_a)P_k(1\,|\text{attribute}_b)}. \tag{18.17}$$

The measurement model for attributes Once the probability of preferring one item to another has been established from the probabilities of endorsing and not endorsing the individual items, the latter can be easily described using any suitable unidimensional IRT models. Stark, et al. (2005) use ideal-point models to link individual items and the attributes they measure. Specifically, they advocate the use of a binary version of the Generalized Graded Unfolding Model or GGUM (Roberts, Donoghue, & Laughlin, 2000). Unlike the Zinnes–Griggs model, which assumes that all items are equally discriminating, the use of GGUM allows a much wider class of items to be used in pairwise comparisons – items measuring different attributes, having different discriminating power, different locations, and even different maximum probability of endorsement.

The two-dimensional item response function in Equation 18.17 in conjunction with the binary GGUM defines a surface. This is a more complex surface that that given in Figure 18.1 for the Thurstonian IRT model, because the ideal-point process of responding to individual items causes a "number of peaks and valleys" (Drasgow, Chernyshenko, & Stark, 2009; p. 74) in the response surface. If items measuring the same dimension are used, the MUPP gives a curve similar to those depicted in Figure 18.3.

Technical detail Person parameters (attribute scores) can be estimated by the Bayes modal method (Maximum A Posteriori, or MAP). Item parameters used in the unidimensional probability expressions (18.17) may be estimated using the freely available GGUM program (http://prdlab.gatech.edu/unfolding/freesoftware/) from data gathered in single-stimulus item trials. The item parameters and the correlations between latent attributes can only be estimated from single-stimulus data, not forced-choice data.

Applications To date, the MUPP model has been used to create new forced-choice questionnaires with items presented in pairs, and to estimate person attribute scores, after item parameters have been estimated from single-stimulus trials (e.g., Chernyshenko et al., 2009). Most recently, the MUPP model was used in the development of the TAPAS (Drasgow et al., 2010b), a comprehensive application taking advantage of computerized adaptive technology to select item pairs maximizing multidimensional information for person score estimation. The TAPAS is easily customizable to measure any of the 23 personality facets deemed important for predicting job performance in civil or military organizations.

McCloy–Heggestad–Reeve unfolding model for multidimensional ranking blocks

McCloy, Heggestad, and Reeve (2005) sketched a theoretical model for the process of responding to multidimensional forced-choice blocks compiled from ideal-point items, and used this model to create a system for item selection and scoring that would enable accurate estimation of latent attributes.

The preference decision model This approach also belongs to the family of Coombs's unfolding models. The model explains preferences for one item over another by the relative distances between the item locations and the respondent's attribute scores. This is an extension of Coombs's original one-dimensional model to the multidimensional case (Coombs, 1964; see also Bennett & Hayes, 1960). According to this model, a person will prefer an item to the extent that the person and the item are located nearer each other in multidimensional space than is true for another person and item located elsewhere in that space.

Measurement model for attributes Just as in the Zinnes–Griggs model, equally discriminating items with ideal-point response functions are used. However, items measuring different attributes may be compared, and forced-choice blocks can be comprised of more than two items. The use of equally discriminating items with ideal-point response functions is necessary for this model to yield forced-choice designs that are effective for accurate estimation of attribute scores. Once item parameters have been established, a questionnaire can be assembled from blocks of items with locations that vary across the attribute space.

Data Analysis Example with the Forced-Choice Five Factor Markers

This data analysis example is provided to illustrate how the Thurstonian IRT modelling approach can be used in practice for item parameter estimation and scoring individuals. Data for this example are available for download together with a questionnaire form and MPlus input files necessary to run the analyses from http://annabrown.name. In addition to the ready-made MPlus input files for this example, the reader can also download an Excel macro, which allows building MPlus syntax for a wide range of forced-choice designs using simple steps. The macro comes with a user guide providing step-by-step instructions.

Measure

We consider real participant data collected using the Forced-Choice Five Factor Markers questionnaire (Brown & Maydeu-Olivares, 2011b). Items for the questionnaire were drawn from the IPIP, more specifically from its subset of items measuring the Big Five factor markers (Goldberg, 1992). The forced-choice questionnaire consists of 60 items, which are presented in 20 triplets (blocks of 3), with all items within triplets measuring different attributes (so-called **multidimensional forced-choice**). Participants are asked to select one "most like me" item, and one "least like me" item from each block. The first triplet from this questionnaire was presented earlier in this chapter, together with example choices:

	most/least true of me
I am relaxed most of the time	Least
I start conversations	Most
I catch on to things quickly	

Each trait is measured with 12 items (8 positively keyed and 4 negatively keyed). The questionnaire "key" is given in Table 18.1.

Sample

Four-hundred-and-thirty-eight volunteers from the UK completed the questionnaire online in return for a feedback report. The sample was balanced in terms of gender (48.4% male); age ranged from 16 to 59 years, mean = 33.3, standard deviation = 10.37 years. This is the same sample described in Brown and Maydeu-Olivares (2011a).

Coding and describing data

The forced-choice design here is full ranking using 20 blocks of $n = 3$ items. Responses to each block are coded using $\tilde{n} = n(n-1)/2 = 3$ pairwise comparisons, making $20 \times 3 = 60$ pairwise comparisons in total. The outcome of each comparison is coded either 1 or 0 according to 18.2, therefore the data are binary.

The data file "FCFFMdata.dat" consists of 438 rows of data, one row per participant. Each row contains an identification number (ID), and 60 binary outcomes of pairwise comparisons. Here is an extract of MPlus syntax declaring our data file and variables:

```
DATA: FILE IS "FCFFMdata.dat";
VARIABLE:
 Names ARE ID
          i1i2 i1i3 i2i3   !first block
          i4i5 i4i6 i5i6   !second block
          ... {the rest of pairwise comparisons go here}
          i58i59 i58i60 i59i60;
 USEVARIABLES ARE i1i2-i59i60;  !ID is not used in analysis
 AUXILIARY IS ID; !Writes ID into file with estimated scores
 CATEGORICAL ARE ALL; !declaring all used variables categorical
```

Setting analysis options The Unweighted Least Squares estimator with robust standard errors (denoted ULSMV in MPlus) is used to estimate the model.[3] The parameterization with unstandardized thresholds and factor loadings used in the conditional

---

[3] Alternatively, the Diagonally Weighted Least Squares estimator with robust standard errors may be used (denoted WLSMV in MPlus).

Table 18.1 Estimated item parameters for the Forced-Choice Five Factor Markers example.

Blocks #	Items #	Attribute	Loading	var(error)	Pairwise comparisons #	threshold
1	1	N	−0.705	1.463	{1,2}	0.231
	2	E	1.108	0.242	{1,3}	1.287
	3	O	1.024	1	{2,3}	1.161
2	4	A	0.845	1.004	{4,5}	−0.327
	5	C	0.994	0.287	{4,6}	−1.237
	6	N	−0.804	1	{5,6}	−0.834
3	7	O	−0.476	0.052	{7,8}	0.203
	8	E	0.624	2.904	{7,9}	1.999
	9	A	0.822	1	{8,9}	2.102
4	10	C	0.734	1.083	{10,11}	0.415
	11	O	0.974	0.466	{10,12}	−2.155
	12	N	0.722	1	{11,12}	−2.507
5	13	A	0.552	1.249	{13,14}	−2.144
	14	N	1.194	3.157	{13,15}	−0.151
	15	E	1.243	1	{14,15}	1.813
6	16	O	0.903	0.92	{16,17}	−1.803
	17	E	−0.719	1.091	{16,18}	−2.514
	18	C	−0.720	1	{17,18}	−0.71
7	19	E	−1.251	2.711	{19,20}	−1.575
	20	N	1.864	4.828	{19,21}	2.378
	21	A	0.607	1	{20,21}	4.524
8	22	C	0.667	0.56	{22,23}	0.034
	23	O	0.665	0.287	{22,24}	−1.462
	24	E	−0.698	1	{23,24}	−1.505
9	25	O	1.235	4.803	{25,26}	−2.922
	26	N	1.379	2.276	{25,27}	−3.404
	27	A	−1.116	1	{26,27}	−0.499
10	28	C	−0.821	0.629	{28,29}	0.358
	29	N	0.636	0.675	{28,30}	1.636
	30	E	1.141	1	{29,30}	1.408
11	31	E	0.847	0.458	{31,32}	0.29
	32	A	0.676	0.42	{31,33}	0.165
	33	C	0.838	1	{32,33}	−0.249
12	34	N	−0.455	1.219	{34,35}	0.629
	35	A	0.570	0.79	{34,36}	−1.132
	36	O	−0.787	1	{35,36}	−1.887
13	37	E	−0.830	0.731	{37,38}	−0.673
	38	N	1.004	0.756	{37,39}	−0.598
	39	C	−0.985	1	{38,39}	−0.03
14	40	A	0.798	1.356	{40,41}	0.112
	41	C	1.114	1.134	{40,42}	0.301
	42	O	1.158	1	{41,42}	0.486
15	43	E	0.838	0.937	{43,44}	−0.178
	44	O	0.983	0.855	{43,45}	−2.307
	45	N	1.109	1	{44,45}	−2.424

(continued on p. 548)

Table 18.1 (*Continued*)

Blocks #	Items #	Attribute	Loading	var(error)	Pairwise comparisons #	threshold
16	46	C	1.202	2.074	{46,47}	−1.192
	47	N	−1.115	3.062	{46,48}	−3.287
	48	A	−0.417	1	{47,48}	−2.363
17	49	C	−0.830	2.558	{49,50}	2.644
	50	A	0.782	1.696	{49,51}	3.038
	51	O	0.878	1	{50,51}	0.775
18	52	A	−0.899	3.309	{52,53}	2.844
	53	E	0.956	3.941	{52,54}	−0.227
	54	O	−0.702	1	{53,54}	−2.758
19	55	O	−0.463	1.823	{55,56}	1.929
	56	C	0.801	1.036	{55,57}	−0.683
	57	N	0.701	1	{56,57}	−2.444
20	58	C	0.546	1.167	{58,59}	−1.992
	59	A	−0.339	0.315	{58,60}	−0.031
	60	E	1.052	1	{59,60}	2.027

Note. $N = 438$. N = Neuroticism, E = Extraversion, O = Openness, A = Agreeableness, C = Conscientiousness. Error variance of last item in each block is set to 1 for identification.

probability expression 18.10 is denoted "theta" in MPlus. Declaring these settings completes the ANALYSIS section.

```
ANALYSIS:
    ESTIMATOR = ulsmv;
    PARAMETERIZATION = theta;
```

It is important that the correct IRT parameterization (theta) be specified. Once the parameters have been estimated, they can be transformed using different parameterizations. For example, the results can be standardized with respect to the error variances of pairwise comparisons (their **error** variances are set to 1), to obtain the so-called **intercept/slope** IRT parameterization. This is done by dividing the threshold and the factor loadings of each pairwise comparison {i, k}, by the square root of its error variance, $\sqrt{var(error_{\{i, k\}})}$.

Alternatively, the results can be standardized with respect to the variances of pairwise comparisons (their **total** variances are set to 1). This is done by requesting the standardization with respect to observed variables, typing "OUTPUT: STDY;" in MPlus.

Model setup

The first part of MODEL command in MPlus describes the hypothesized factor structure of our questionnaire. Every latent attribute is defined "BY" its indicators, the pairwise comparisons. To provide a metric for the latent attributes, their variances are set to unity. For every pairwise comparison declared under an attribute, its factor loading will be estimated. We can provide starting values for this estimation depending on the item's position in the comparison and the keyed direction (whether it was designed to be a positive indicator of an attribute or a negative indicator). Remember that the first item in comparison retains the original sign of its factor loading, while the second has this sign reversed (refer to expression 18.10). To aid estimation, we can set the starting values to either 1 or −1 depending on the item's position and keying. Syntax will look as follows:

```
N   BY              !Neuroticism

    i1i2*-1 (L1)
    i1i3*-1 (L1)
    ... {the rest of pairwise comparisons involving items
measuring N}
;
E   BY              !Extraversion
    i1i2*-1 (L2_n)
    i2i3*1  (L2)
    ... {the rest of pairwise comparisons involving items
measuring E}
;
O   BY              !Openness
    i1i3*-1 (L3_n)
    i2i3*-1 (L3_n)
    ... {the rest of pairwise comparisons involving items
measuring O}
;
A   BY              !Agreeableness
    i4i5*1  (L4)
    i4i6*1  (L4)
    ... {the rest of pairwise comparisons involving items
measuring A}
;
C   BY              !Conscientiousness
    i4i5*-1 (L5_n)
    i5i6*1  (L5)
    ... {the rest of pairwise comparisons involving items
measuring C}
;
N-C@1;              ! variances for all factors are set to 1
```

Symbols in brackets inside the "BY" commands refer to the first special feature of forced-choice triplets. This special feature is that any two pairwise comparisons in each block involve the same item. For example, comparisons {1, 2} and {1, 3} both involve item 1. As explained in Thurstonian IRT model/Technical detail section, the factor loading of item 1, "loading$_1$," has to be the same in both comparisons. The way to tell MPlus to constrain both loadings to be the same is to give them the same parameter name (here, L1). When the item order in two comparisons is different, for instance, item 2 is last in comparison {1, 2} and first in comparison {2, 3}, the factor loadings are the same in magnitude but opposite in sign. Hence, we give the parameters different names (L2_n and L2), but constrain them the reverse of each other:

```
MODEL CONSTRAINT:
!factor loadings relating to the same item are equal in
absolute value
      L2_n = -L2;
      L5_n = -L5;
      ... {remaining constraints on factor loadings go here}
```

Similar considerations apply to error variance of pairwise comparisons involving the same item. First, according to 18.9, the error variance of any pairwise comparison {i, k} is the sum of two components – the error variance of item i and the error variance of item k. Second, according to 18.12, errors of pairwise comparisons involving the same item are not independent; instead, their covariance equals var(error$_i$). A fragment of MPlus syntax specifying these relationships for the first block is provided next:

```
! declare parameters for error variances of pairwise
comparisons
! and set their starting values
      i1i2*2 (e1e2);
      i1i3*2 (e1e3);
      i2i3*2 (e2e3);
      ... {remaining blocks go here}
! specify covariances between pairwise comparisons
involving the same item
! set parameters for error variances of items, and set their
starting values
      i1i2 WITH i1i3*1 (e1);
      i1i2 WITH i2i3*-1 (e2_n);
      i1i3 WITH i2i3*1 (e3);
      ... {remaining blocks go here}

MODEL CONSTRAINT:
! error variance of every pairwise comparison equals the sum
of item error variances
      e1e2 = e1 - e2_n;
      e1e3 = e1 + e3;
      e2e3 = -e2_n + e3;
      ... {remaining blocks go here}
```

It can be seen that only three unique parameters are estimated here: e1, e2_n, and e3. These are the error variances of the three items in the first triplet. The error variances of the pairwise comparisons are composites of these three parameters.

Finally, fixing the error variance of one item per block for identification (here, we arbitrarily fix the variance of the last item) completes the MODEL CONSTRAINT section:

```
MODEL CONSTRAINT:
! fix one error variance in each block for identification
      e3=1;    !first block
      e6=1;    !second block
      ...  {errors for remaining blocks go here}
      e60=1;
```

The above settings and syntax may seem complex and writing them out error prone. The good news is that the researcher does not have to do any syntax writing – it is automatically written by the Excel macro based on very basic information the researcher provides. For full detail, see the User Guide supplied with the macro.

Estimating attribute scores for individuals

Attribute scores for individuals in the sample can be estimated after the model parameters have been established. This is conveniently implemented in MPlus as an option within the estimation process, using the empirical Bayesian (MAP) estimator (Muthén, 1998–2004). The estimated scores can be saved in a separate file for further use:

```
SAVE: FILE IS 'FCFFMresults.dat';
      SAVE=FSCORES;
```

When estimating person attribute scores, the estimator makes a simplifying assumption that local independence holds. The use of this simplification for scoring individuals has little impact on the accuracy of the estimates (Maydeu-Olivares & Brown, 2010). Estimation of individual scores is very fast (scores for 438 individuals in this sample are estimated and saved in a few seconds).

Interpreting MPlus output

Estimation of our model takes little time (around a minute depending on the computer). Here we briefly discuss the most important features of MPlus output that are specific to Thurstonian IRT models.

The model estimation part of the output begins with two warnings. The first warning is "THE RESIDUAL COVARIANCE MATRIX (THETA) IS NOT POSITIVE DEFINITE. ... PROBLEM INVOLVING VARIABLE I2I3." This is normal and refers to the fact that by design, the residual covariance matrix in Thurstonian models is not of full rank (Maydeu-Olivares & Böckenholt, 2005). The second warning is "THE

MODEL CONTAINS A NON-ZERO CORRELATION BETWEEN DEPENDENT VARIABLES. SUCH CORRELATIONS ARE IGNORED IN THE COMPUTATION OF THE FACTOR SCORES." This warns the researcher that the local dependencies that we have specified for pairwise comparisons are ignored when estimating the attribute scores for individuals.

Next, goodness of fit statistics and indices are printed. The model yields a chi-square of 2,106.06 on 1,660 degrees of freedom; however, the degrees of freedom have to be adjusted since there is one redundancy in every block of three items (see Brown & Maydeu-Olivares, 2012). The fit indices including the degrees of freedom in their computation also need to be adjusted. Overall, there are 20 redundancies in the model, so that the correct $df = 1,640$, and the correct RMSEA = 0.025.

The rest of the output provides parameter estimates for our model. First, the factor loadings are printed. The reader can compare the below fragment of the output with the input instructions we provided for the factor structure, and confirm that the factor loadings we constrained to be equal are indeed equal in pairwise comparisons relating to the same item (may have opposite sign depending on the item's order in the pairwise comparison):

```
MODEL RESULTS

                                                              Two-Tailed
                      Estimate        S.E.      Est./S.E.     P-Value

  N         BY
    I1I2                -0.705       0.173       -4.086         0.000
    I1I3                -0.705       0.173       -4.086         0.000
 <...>
  E         BY
    I1I2                -1.108       0.192       -5.762         0.000
    I2I3                 1.108       0.192        5.762         0.000
 <...>
  O         BY
    I1I3                -1.024       0.202       -5.060         0.000
    I2I3                -1.024       0.202       -5.060         0.000
 <...>
  A         BY
    I4I5                 0.844       0.139        6.070         0.000
    I4I6                 0.844       0.139        6.070         0.000
 <...>
  C         BY
    I4I5                -0.994       0.139       -7.124         0.000
    I5I6                 0.994       0.139        7.124         0.000
 <...>
```

Some of the factor loadings are above 1. This is because these are **unstandardized** parameters, as defined by expression 18.10.

Next, the factor covariances are printed. Since we set the factor variances to 1, these are correlations between the latent attributes:

			Estimate	S.E.	Est./S.E.	Two-Tailed P-Value
E		WITH				
	N		-0.404	0.060	-6.693	0.000
O		WITH				
	N		-0.482	0.068	-7.068	0.000
	E		0.479	0.061	7.867	0.000
A		WITH				
	N		-0.403	0.075	-5.372	0.000
	E		0.413	0.068	6.100	0.000
	O		0.145	0.086	1.681	0.093
C		WITH				
	N		-0.299	0.073	-4.088	0.000
	E		0.232	0.072	3.205	0.001
	O		0.349	0.070	5.019	0.000
	A		0.307	0.076	4.044	0.000

Next, the estimated covariances between the errors of the pairwise comparisons are printed. The reader is reminded that these covariances equal to the error variance of the common item involved in both comparisons, as we specified, and hence the covariance between the error of comparison {1, 2} (referred to as I1I2 in MPlus) and {1, 3} (referred to as I1I3) is simply the error variance of item 1, var(error$_1$). A fragment next relates to the first block:

			Estimate	S.E.	Est./S.E.	Two-Tailed P-Value
I1I2		WITH				
	I1I3		1.463	0.517	2.831	0.005
	I2I3		-0.242	0.221	-1.098	0.272
I1I3		WITH				
	I2I3		1.000	0.000	Infinity	0.000

Because we fixed the error for the last item, item 3, to unity, no standard error was estimated for this parameter. The covariance between errors of {1, 2} and {2, 3} is negative since item 2 is first in comparison {2, 3} and last in comparison {1, 2}; however, the error variance of item 2 is of course positive, 0.242. The reader can compare the above output with the error variances of the pairwise comparisons printed further in the output:

	Estimate	S.E.	Est./S.E.	Two-Tailed P-Value
Residual Variances				
I1I2	1.705	0.619	2.754	0.006
I1I3	2.463	0.517	4.766	0.000
I2I3	1.242	0.221	5.628	0.000

It can be seen that the error variances of the pairwise comparisons are the sums of error variances of the two items involved in comparison, for instance 1.705 = 1.463 + 0.242. This is exactly how we specified the relationships between errors. Thus, it is clear that the only unique estimable parameters are the item errors – the errors of pairwise comparisons are simply their combinations.

Finally, the thresholds for each pairwise comparison are printed. The symbol $1 refers to the first and the only threshold, since the data are binary. Here are the thresholds for the first block.

	Estimate	S.E.	Est./S.E.	Two-Tailed P-Value
Thresholds				
I1I2$1	0.231	0.108	2.136	0.033
I1I3$1	1.287	0.192	6.706	0.000
I2I3$1	1.161	0.161	7.227	0.000

The estimated thresholds, factor loadings, and error variances for these data are given in Table 18.1. The estimated correlations between the five attributes are given in Table 18.2. They are provided so that the reader can practice finding the required parameters in MPlus outputs. For further practical guidance on model setup and identification for different forced-choice designs, including treatment of missing data in incomplete rankings, and example MPlus syntax, see Brown and Maydeu-Olivares (2012).

Table 18.2 Estimated latent attribute correlations for the Forced-Choice Five Factor Markers.

	N	E	O	A	C
Neuroticism (N)	1				
Extraversion (E)	−.404**	1			
Openness (O)	−.482**	.479**	1		
Agreeableness (A)	−.403**	.413**	.145	1	
Conscientiousness (C)	−.299**	.232*	.349**	.307**	1

Note. N = 438. * Correlation is significant at $p < .01$; ** correlation is significant at $p < .001$.

Recommendations for Creating Effective Forced-Choice Assessments

Recent methodological and technological advances have made item response modelling of forced-choice data possible, and new approaches to creating and scoring forced-choice tests have emerged. However, given that response processes involve comparisons between two or more items, and generally lead to multidimensional IRT models, test development using forced-choice formats is a more complex endeavor than when single-stimulus formats are used.

A number of factors affect forced-choice test design decisions. We have already discussed how the nature of preferential choice dictates rules for selecting items in one-dimensional comparisons. To yield informative comparisons, items with very different factor loadings must be used under factor analysis models, and items with very different locations should be used under ideal-point models. These are not limitations of particular response models – these are the limitations to comparative judgments in recovering absolute information. For instance, a small proportion (5–10%) of unidimensional item pairs have been recommended for use alongside multidimensional item pairs to identify the latent trait metric under the MUPP model (Drasgow, Chernyshenko, & Stark, 2009). Under Thurstonian IRT modelling, the latent attribute metric is generally identified without any unidimensional comparisons (Brown & Maydeu-Olivares, 2012), and therefore this model enables the use of purely multidimensional forced-choice formats.

Brown and Maydeu-Olivares (2011a) provide guidelines for constructing ordinal forced-choice questionnaires with common dominance items that are effective in measuring multiple attributes. They show that in questionnaires containing multidimensional comparisons only, the attribute scores can be estimated accurately if sufficient numbers of good quality items are used, and the following rules are met:

Keyed direction of items. When forced-choice tests involve comparisons between items keyed in the same direction, as well as items keyed in the opposite direction, accurate estimation of attribute scores can be achieved with any number of traits, and any level of trait correlations. However, when all comparisons are between items keyed in the same direction, the quality of measurement depends on the number of attributes assessed in the test.

Number of attributes. It is possible to estimate attribute scores accurately using only positively keyed items, when the number of traits assessed is large (20–30 or more) and the attributes are largely independent on average.

Correlations between traits. Given the same number of attributes, the lower the average correlation between them the more accurate the score estimation will be.

Block size. Given the same number of items available, combining them in larger blocks increases the level of information each item provides for latent attribute estimation. This is because the number of pairwise comparisons increases rapidly as the number of items in a block increases. However, increasing block size increases cognitive complexity and contributes to respondents' fatigue and random responding.

The reader interested in using a forced-choice format must remember that the format itself cannot correct for faults in item writing, and in some ways, makes these faults more apparent. In our experience, using negations in forced-choice formats is more problematic than in single-stimulus formats. Item length can also be a problem, particularly when four or more items are compared in one block. Adhering to good item writing practice (Brown & Maydeu-Olivares, 2010) and the previous general rules when designing a forced-choice questionnaire will increase its measurement quality.

To the authors' knowledge, all item response modelling of forced-choice questionnaires to date has been conducted with pairwise comparisons and ranking blocks. Pairwise comparisons using graded preferences, and compositional forced-choice formats are yet to be explored, therefore more research on forced-choice questionnaire design is needed.

Directions for Future Research and Concluding Remarks

Thanks to the recent developments in IRT-based analysis and scoring, forced-choice tests are enjoying a lot of attention from psychometricians, test developers, and test users alike. They are gaining popularity in personality assessments in the workplace, where concerns about response distortions are strong. We, however, would like to draw the reader's attention to applications that have been overlooked in the forced-choice literature, and where we believe the gains might be very important to the advancement of science.

In **cross-cultural research**, where culture-specific response sets present a challenge for comparability of scores (Johnson, Kulesa, Cho, & Shavitt, 2005; Van Herk, Poortinga, & Verhallen, 2004), the use of forced-choice formats are bound to be advantageous. A recent example of cross-cultural personality research using forced-choice tests is represented by a study of Bartram's (2013), which examined personality profiles across 31 cultures in relation to country-level cultural dimensions. Furthermore, measurement invariance of forced-choice tests can be formally tested; for example, constraining the thresholds, the factor loadings and the correlations between the latent attributes to be equal across two or more groups in the corresponding multi-group Thurstonian IRT model.

The use of forced-choice formats is likely to prove beneficial in **assessments of other individuals** (as in 360-degree feedback), **organizations** or **services** (as in satisfaction surveys). In these contexts, rater biases such as leniency/severity and the halo effects are notorious (e.g., Brown, Ford, Deighton, & Wolpert, 2012) and forced-choice formats are ideally placed to counter such biases and deliver more usable data. Historically, the psychometric assessment industry and test users have been more enthusiastic about the use of forced-choice assessments than academics have been. While the former groups have been excited by the advantages in overcoming common response biases and enhanced differentiation between stimuli, the latter group has been concerned about the psychometric properties of ipsative data, particularly its interpersonal incomparability. As we have shown in this article, academic concerns about the use of ipsative data are well founded. Therefore, we advocate the use of item response modelling with forced-choice data, which, in conjunction with good test development practices has the potential to overcome these problems, and consequently, forced-choice formats have the potential to compete with single-stimulus formats in applications.

References

Andrich, D. (1989). A probabilistic IRT model for unfolding preference data. *Applied Psychological Measurement, 13,* 193–216.

Baron, H. (1996). Strength and limitations of ipsative measurement. *Journal of Occupational and Organizational Psychology, 69,* 49–56.

Bartram, D. (2007). Increasing validity with forced-choice criterion measurement formats. *International Journal of Selection and Assessment, 15,* 263–272.

Bartram, D. (2013). Scalar Equivalence of OPQ32: Big Five Profiles of 31 Countries. *Journal of Cross-Cultural Psychology, 44,* 61–83.

Bennett, J. F., & Hays, W. L. (1960), Multidimensional unfolding: Determining the dimensionality of ranked preference data. *Psychometrika, 25*(1), 27–43.

Block, J. (1961). *The Q-sort method in personality assessment and psychiatric research.* Springfield, IL: Charles C. Thomas.

Block, J. (2008). *The Q-sort in character appraisal: Encoding subjective impressions of persons quantitatively.* Washington, DC: American Psychological Association.

Borman, W. C., Buck, D. E., Hanson, M. A., Motowidlo, S. J., Stark, S., & Drasgow, F. (2001). An examination of the comparative reliability, validity, and accuracy of performance ratings made using computerized adaptive rating scales. *Journal of Applied Psychology, 86*(5), 95–973.

Brown, A., Ford, T., Deighton, J., & Wolpert, M. M. (2012). Satisfaction in child and adolescent mental health services: Translating users' feedback into measurement. *Administration and Policy in Mental Health and Mental Health Services Research, 41,* 434–436.

Brown, A., & Maydeu-Olivares, A. (2010). Issues that should not be overlooked in the dominance versus ideal point controversy. *Industrial and Organizational Psychology, 3*(4), 489–493.

Brown, A., & Maydeu-Olivares, A. (2011a). Item response modeling of forced-choice questionnaires. *Educational and Psychological Measurement, 71,* 460–502.

Brown, A., & Maydeu-Olivares, A. (2011b). Forced-choice Five Factor markers. *PsycTESTS.* DOI: 10.1037/t05430-000

Brown, A., & Maydeu-Olivares, A. (2012). Fitting a Thurstonian IRT model to forced-choice data using MPlus. *Behavior Research Methods, 44,* 1135–1147.

Brown, A., & Maydeu-Olivares, A. (2013). How IRT can solve problems of ipsative data in forced-choice questionnaires. *Psychological Methods, 18*(1), 36–52.

Chan, W. (2003). Analyzing ipsative data in psychological research. *Behaviormetrika, 30,* 99–121.

Chernyshenko, O. S., Stark, S., Prewett, M. S., Gray, A. A., Stilson, F. R., & Tuttle, M. D. (2009). Normative scoring of multidimensional pairwise preference personality scales using IRT: Empirical comparisons with other formats. *Human Performance, 22,* 105–127. DOI: 10.1080/08959280902743303.

Cheung, M. W. L., & Chan, W. (2002). Reducing uniform response bias with ipsative measurement in multiple-group confirmatory factor analysis. *Structural Equation Modeling, 9,* 55–77.

Christiansen, N. D., Burns, G. N., & Montgomery, G. E. (2005). Reconsidering forced-choice item formats for applicant personality assessment. *Human Performance, 18*(3), 267–307.

Clemans, W. V. (1966). *An analytical and empirical examination of some properties of ipsative measures.* Psychometric Monograph No. 14. Richmond, VA: Psychometric Society. Retrieved from https://www.psychometricsociety.org/sites/default/files/pdf/MN14.pdf (accessed September 2017).

Closs, S. J. (1996). On the factoring and interpretation of ipsative data. *Journal of Occupational Psychology, 69,* 41–47.

Coombs, C. H. (1950). Psychological scaling without a unit of measurement. *Psychological Review, 57,* 145–158.

Coombs, C. H. (1964). *The theory of data.* New York: John Wiley & Sons, Inc.

Cornwell, J. M., & Dunlap, W. P. (1994). On the questionable soundness of factoring ipsative data: A response to Saville & Willson. *Journal of Occupational and Organizational Psychology, 67*(2), 89–100.

Cubiks. (2010). PAPI: Personality and Preference Inventory. Accessed July 1, 2016 from: www.cubiks.com/PRODUCTS/PERSONALITYASSESSMENTS/Pages/papi.aspx.

Drasgow, F., Chernyshenko, O. S., & Stark, S. (2009). Test theory and personality measurement. In J. N. Butcher (Ed.), *Oxford handbook of personality assessment* (pp. 59–80). London: Oxford University Press.

Drasgow, F., Chernyshenko, O. S., & Stark, S. (2010a). 75 years after Likert: Thurstone was right! *Industrial and Organizational Psychology: Perspectives on Science and Practice, 3,* 465–476.

Drasgow, F., Chernyshenko, O. S., & Stark, S. (2010b). *Tailored adaptive personality assessment system (TAPAS).* Urbana, IL: Drasgow Consulting Group.

Dunlap, W. P., & Cornwell, J. M. (1994). Factor analysis of ipsative measures. *Multivariate Behavioral Research, 29*(1), 115–126.

Feldman, M. J., & Corah, N. L. (1960). Social desirability and the forced choice method. *Journal of Consulting Psychology, 24*(6), 480–482.

Friedman, H. H., & Amoo, T. (1999). Rating the rating scales. *Journal of Marketing Management, 9*(3), 114–123.

Funder, D. C., Furr, M. R., & Colvin, C. R. (2000). The Riverside behavioral Q-sort: A tool for the description of social behavior. *Journal of Personality, 68*(3), 451–489.

Goldberg, L. R. (1992). The development of markers for the Big-Five factor structure. *Psychological Assessment, 4,* 26–42.

Gordon, L. V. (1976). *Survey of interpersonal values. Revised manual.* Chicago, IL: Science Research Associates.

Gordon, L. V. (1993). *Manual: Gordon personal profile-inventory.* San Antonio, TX: The Psychological Corporation.

Heggestad, E. D., Morrison, M., Reeve, C. L., & McCloy, R. A. (2006). Forced-choice assessments of personality for selection: Evaluating issues of normative assessment and faking resistance. *Journal of Applied Psychology, 91*(1), 9–24.

Hicks, L. E. (1970). Some properties of ipsative, normative, and forced-choice normative measures. *Psychological Bulletin, 74,* 167–184.

Jackson, D. N., Wroblewski, V. R., & Ashton, M. C. (2000). The impact of faking on employment tests: does forced choice offer a solution? *Human Performance, 13*(4), 371–388.

Johnson, T., Kulesa, P., Cho, Y. I., & Shavitt, S. (2005). The relation between culture and response styles evidence from 19 countries. *Journal of Cross-Cultural Psychology, 36*(2), 264–277.

Johnson, C. E., Wood, R., & Blinkhorn, S. F. (1988). Spuriouser and spuriouser: The use of ipsative personality tests. *Journal of Occupational Psychology, 61*(2), 153–162.

Kolb, A. Y., & Kolb, D. A. (2005). *The Kolb learning style inventory–version 3.1 2005 technical specifications.* Boston, MA: Hay Resource Direct.

Kuhl, J., & Scheffer, D. (2002). *Der operante Multi-Motiv-Test (OMT): Manual [The operant multi-motive-test (OMT): Manual].* Osnabrück, Germany: University of Osnabrück.

Kuncel, N. R., Goldberg, L. R., & Kiger, T. (2011). A plea for process in personality prevarication. *Human Performance, 24*(4), 373–378.

Lang, J. W. B., Zettler, I., Ewen, C., & Hülsheger, U. R. (2012). Implicit motives, explicit traits, and task and contextual performance at work. *Journal of Applied Psychology,* Advance online publication. DOI: 10.1037/a0029556.

Martin, B. A., Bowen, C. C., & Hunt, S. T. (2002). How effective are people at faking on personality questionnaires? *Personality and Individual Differences, 32*(2), 247–256.

Maydeu-Olivares, A. (1999). Thurstonian modeling of ranking data via mean and covariance structure analysis. *Psychometrika, 64*, 325–340.

Maydeu-Olivares, A., & Böckenholt, U. (2005). Structural equation modeling of paired-comparison and ranking data. *Psychological Methods, 10*, 285–304.

Maydeu-Olivares, A., & Böckenholt, U. (2008). Modeling subjective health outcomes: Top 10 reasons to use Thurstone's method. *Medical Care, 46*, 346–348.

Maydeu-Olivares, A., & Brown, A. (2010). Item response modeling of paired comparison and ranking data. *Multivariate Behavioral Research, 45*, 935–974.

McCloy, R. A., Heggestad, E. D., & Reeve, C. L. (2005). A silk purse from the sow's ear: Retrieving normative information from multidimensional forced-choice items. *Organizational Research Methods, 8*(2), 222–248.

Meade, A. W. (2004). Psychometric problems and issues involved with creating and using ipsative measures for selection. *Journal of Occupational and Organisational Psychology, 77*, 531–552.

Mellenbergh, G. J. (2011). *A conceptual introduction to psychometrics: Development, analysis and application of psychological and educational tests*. Eleven International Publishing.

Muthén, B. O. (1998–2004). *MPlus technical appendices*. Los Angeles, CA: Muthén & Muthén.

Muthén, L. K., & Muthén, B. O. (1998–2012). *MPlus user's guide* (7th ed.). Los Angeles, CA: Muthén & Muthén.

Roberts, J. S., Donoghue, J. R., & Laughlin, J. E. (2000). A general item response theory model for unfolding unidimensional polytomous responses. *Applied Psychological Measurement, 24*(1), 3–32.

Schneider, R. J., Ferstl, K. L., Houston, J. S., Borman, W. C., Bearden, R. M., & Lords, A. O. (2007). *Revision and expansion of Navy Computer Adaptive Personality Scales (NCAPS)*. Tampa, FL: Personnel decisions research Institute Inc.

Schwarz, N., Knäuper, B., Hippler, H. J., Noelle-Neumann, E., & Clark, L. (1991). Rating scales numeric values may change the meaning of scale labels. *Public Opinion Quarterly, 55*(4), 570–582.

SHL. (1997). *Customer Contact: Manual and User's Guide*. Surrey, UK: SHL Group.

SHL. (2006). *OPQ32 Technical Manual*. Surrey, UK: SHL Group.

Stark, S. (2002). *A new IRT approach to test construction and scoring designed to reduce the effects of faking in personality assessment* (Unpublished doctoral dissertation). Urbana-Champaign, IL: University of Illinois at Urbana-Champaign.

Stark, S., Chernyshenko, O. S., & Drasgow, F. (2005). An IRT approach to constructing and scoring pairwise preference items involving stimuli on different dimensions: The Multi-Unidimensional Pairwise-Preference Model. *Applied Psychological Measurement, 29*, 184–203.

Stark, S., & Drasgow, F. (2002). An EM approach to parameter estimation for the Zinnes and Griggs paired comparison IRT model. *Applied Psychological Measurement, 26*, 208–227.

Tenopyr, M. L. (1988). Artifactual reliability of forced-choice scales. *Journal of Applied Psychology, 73*, 749–751.

Thorndike, E. L. (1920). A constant error in psychological ratings. *Journal of Applied Psychology, 4*(1), 25–29.

Thurstone, L. L. (1927). A law of comparative judgment. *Psychological Review, 34*, 273–286.

Thurstone, L. L. (1929). The measurement of psychological value. In T. V. Smith & W. K. Wright (Eds.), *Essays in philosophy by seventeen doctors of philosophy of the University of Chicago* (pp. 157–174). Chicago: Open Court.

Thurstone, L. L. (1931). Rank order as a psychophysical method. *Journal of Experimental Psychology, 14*, 187–201.

Torgeson, W. S. (1958). *Theory and methods of scaling*. New York: John Wiley & Sons, Inc.

Van Herk, H., Poortinga, Y. H., & Verhallen, T. M. M. (2004). Response styles in rating scales evidence of method bias in data from six EU countries. *Journal of Cross-Cultural Psychology*, *35*(3), 346–360.

Vasilopoulos, N. L., Cucina, J. M., Dyomina, N. V., Morewitz, C. L., & Reilly, R. R. (2006). Forced-choice personality tests: A measure of personality and cognitive ability? *Human Performance*, *19*(3), 175–199.

Wagerman, S. A., & Funder, D. C. (2009). Personality psychology of situations. In P. J. Corr & G. Matthews (Eds.), *Cambridge handbook of personality psychology* (pp. 27–42). Cambridge: Cambridge University Press.

Zerbe, W. J., & Paulhus, D. L. (1987). Socially desirable responding in organizational behavior: A reconception. *Academy of Management Review*, *12*(2), 250–264.

Zinnes, J. L., & Griggs, R. A. (1974). Probabilistic, multidimensional unfolding analysis. *Psychometrika*, *39*(3), 327–350.

Code Appendix

Code 1 Mplus input file for Thurstonian IRT modelling of the Forced-Choice Five Factor Markers questionnaire.

```
TITLE:   FCFFM questionnaire analysis

DATA:    FILE IS FCFFMdata.dat;

VARIABLE:
Names ARE
ID
i1i2 i1i3 i2i3
i4i5 i4i6 i5i6
i7i8 i7i9 i8i9
i10i11 i10i12 i11i12
i13i14 i13i15 i14i15
i16i17 i16i18 i17i18
i19i20 i19i21 i20i21
i22i23 i22i24 i23i24
i25i26 i25i27 i26i27
i28i29 i28i30 i29i30
i31i32 i31i33 i32i33
i34i35 i34i36 i35i36
i37i38 i37i39 i38i39
i40i41 i40i42 i41i42
i43i44 i43i45 i44i45
i46i47 i46i48 i47i48
i49i50 i49i51 i50i51
i52i53 i52i54 i53i54
i55i56 i55i57 i56i57
i58i59 i58i60 i59i60;
```

```
AUXILIARY IS ID;
USEVARIABLES ARE i1i2-i59i60;
CATEGORICAL ARE ALL;

ANALYSIS:
ESTIMATOR = ulsmv;
PARAMETERIZATION = theta;

MODEL:

N  BY
i1i2*-1    (L1)
i1i3*-1    (L1)
i4i6*1     (L6_n)
i5i6*1     (L6_n)
i10i12*-1  (L12_n)
i11i12*-1  (L12_n)
i13i14*-1  (L14_n)
i14i15*1   (L14)
i19i20*-1  (L20_n)
i20i21*1   (L20)
i25i26*-1  (L26_n)
i26i27*1   (L26)
i28i29*-1  (L29_n)
i29i30*1   (L29)
i34i35*-1  (L34)
i34i36*-1  (L34)
i37i38*-1  (L38_n)
i38i39*1   (L38)
i43i45*-1  (L45_n)
i44i45*-1  (L45_n)
i46i47*1   (L47_n)
i47i48*-1  (L47)
i55i57*-1  (L57_n)
i56i57*-1  (L57_n);

E  BY
i1i2*-1    (L2_n)
i2i3*1     (L2)
i7i8*-1    (L8_n)
i8i9*1     (L8)
i13i15*-1  (L15_n)
i14i15*-1  (L15_n)
i16i17*1   (L17_n)
i17i18*-1  (L17)
i19i20*-1  (L19)
```

```
i19i21*-1   (L19)
i22i24*1    (L24_n)
i23i24*1    (L24_n)
i28i30*-1   (L30_n)
i29i30*-1   (L30_n)
i31i32*1    (L31)
i31i33*1    (L31)
i37i38*-1   (L37)
i37i39*-1   (L37)
i43i44*1    (L43)
i43i45*1    (L43)
i52i53*-1   (L53_n)
i53i54*1    (L53)
i58i60*-1   (L60_n)
i59i60*-1   (L60_n);

O BY
i1i3*-1     (L3_n)
i2i3*-1     (L3_n)
i7i8*-1     (L7)
i7i9*-1     (L7)
i10i11*-1   (L11_n)
i11i12*1    (L11)
i16i17*1    (L16)
i16i18*1    (L16)
i22i23*-1   (L23_n)
i23i24*1    (L23)
i25i26*1    (L25)
i25i27*1    (L25)
i34i36*1    (L36_n)
i35i36*1    (L36_n)
i40i42*-1   (L42_n)
i41i42*-1   (L42_n)
i43i44*-1   (L44_n)
i44i45*1    (L44)
i49i51*-1   (L51_n)
i50i51*-1   (L51_n)
i52i54*1    (L54_n)
i53i54*1    (L54_n)
i55i56*-1   (L55)
i55i57*-1   (L55);

A BY
i4i5*1      (L4)
i4i6*1      (L4)
i7i9*-1     (L9_n)
i8i9*-1     (L9_n)
```

```
i13i14*1    (L13)
i13i15*1    (L13)
i19i21*-1   (L21_n)
i20i21*-1   (L21_n)
i25i27*1    (L27_n)
i26i27*1    (L27_n)
i31i32*-1   (L32_n)
i32i33*1    (L32)
i34i35*-1   (L35_n)
i35i36*1    (L35)
i40i41*1    (L40)
i40i42*1    (L40)
i46i48*1    (L48_n)
i47i48*1    (L48_n)
i49i50*-1   (L50_n)
i50i51*1    (L50)
i52i53*-1   (L52)
i52i54*-1   (L52)
i58i59*1    (L59_n)
i59i60*-1   (L59);

C   BY
i4i5*-1     (L5_n)
i5i6*1      (L5)
i10i11*1    (L10)
i10i12*1    (L10)
i16i18*1    (L18_n)
i17i18*1    (L18_n)
i22i23*1    (L22)
i22i24*1    (L22)
i28i29*-1   (L28)
i28i30*-1   (L28)
i31i33*-1   (L33_n)
i32i33*-1   (L33_n)
i37i39*1    (L39_n)
i38i39*1    (L39_n)
i40i41*-1   (L41_n)
i41i42*1    (L41)
i46i47*1    (L46)
i46i48*1    (L46)
i49i50*-1   (L49)
i49i51*-1   (L49)
i55i56*-1   (L56_n)
i56i57*1    (L56)
i58i59*1    (L58)
i58i60*1    (L58);

! variances for all traits are set to 1
N-C@1;
```

```
! declare error variances of pairs and set their starting
values
i1i2*2   (e1e2);
i1i3*2   (e1e3);
i2i3*2   (e2e3);
i4i5*2   (e4e5);
i4i6*2   (e4e6);
i5i6*2   (e5e6);
i7i8*2   (e7e8);
i7i9*2   (e7e9);
i8i9*2   (e8e9);
i10i11*2 (e10e11);
i10i12*2 (e10e12);
i11i12*2 (e11e12);
i13i14*2 (e13e14);
i13i15*2 (e13e15);
i14i15*2 (e14e15);
i16i17*2 (e16e17);
i16i18*2 (e16e18);
i17i18*2 (e17e18);
i19i20*2 (e19e20);
i19i21*2 (e19e21);
i20i21*2 (e20e21);
i22i23*2 (e22e23);
i22i24*2 (e22e24);
i23i24*2 (e23e24);
i25i26*2 (e25e26);
i25i27*2 (e25e27);
i26i27*2 (e26e27);
i28i29*2 (e28e29);
i28i30*2 (e28e30);
i29i30*2 (e29e30);
i31i32*2 (e31e32);
i31i33*2 (e31e33);
i32i33*2 (e32e33);
i34i35*2 (e34e35);
i34i36*2 (e34e36);
i35i36*2 (e35e36);
i37i38*2 (e37e38);
i37i39*2 (e37e39);
i38i39*2 (e38e39);
i40i41*2 (e40e41);
i40i42*2 (e40e42);
i41i42*2 (e41e42);
i43i44*2 (e43e44);
i43i45*2 (e43e45);
i44i45*2 (e44e45);
```

```
i46i47*2 (e46e47);
i46i48*2 (e46e48);
i47i48*2 (e47e48);
i49i50*2 (e49e50);
i49i51*2 (e49e51);
i50i51*2 (e50e51);
i52i53*2 (e52e53);
i52i54*2 (e52e54);
i53i54*2 (e53e54);
i55i56*2 (e55e56);
i55i57*2 (e55e57);
i56i57*2 (e56e57);
i58i59*2 (e58e59);
i58i60*2 (e58e60);
i59i60*2 (e59e60);

! declare correlated error variances and set their
starting values
i1i2 WITH i1i3*1 (e1);
i1i2 WITH i2i3*-1 (e2_n);
i1i3 WITH i2i3*1 (e3);

i4i5 WITH i4i6*1 (e4);
i4i5 WITH i5i6*-1 (e5_n);
i4i6 WITH i5i6*1 (e6);

i7i8 WITH i7i9*1 (e7);
i7i8 WITH i8i9*-1 (e8_n);
i7i9 WITH i8i9*1 (e9);

i10i11 WITH i10i12*1 (e10);
i10i11 WITH i11i12*-1 (e11_n);
i10i12 WITH i11i12*1 (e12);

i13i14 WITH i13i15*1 (e13);
i13i14 WITH i14i15*-1 (e14_n);
i13i15 WITH i14i15*1 (e15);

i16i17 WITH i16i18*1 (e16);
i16i17 WITH i17i18*-1 (e17_n);
i16i18 WITH i17i18*1 (e18);

i19i20 WITH i19i21*1 (e19);
i19i20 WITH i20i21*-1 (e20_n);
i19i21 WITH i20i21*1 (e21);

i22i23 WITH i22i24*1 (e22);
```

```
i22i23 WITH i23i24*-1 (e23_n);
i22i24 WITH i23i24*1  (e24);

i25i26 WITH i25i27*1  (e25);
i25i26 WITH i26i27*-1 (e26_n);
i25i27 WITH i26i27*1  (e27);

i28i29 WITH i28i30*1  (e28);
i28i29 WITH i29i30*-1 (e29_n);
i28i30 WITH i29i30*1  (e30);

i31i32 WITH i31i33*1  (e31);
i31i32 WITH i32i33*-1 (e32_n);
i31i33 WITH i32i33*1  (e33);

i34i35 WITH i34i36*1  (e34);
i34i35 WITH i35i36*-1 (e35_n);
i34i36 WITH i35i36*1  (e36);

i37i38 WITH i37i39*1  (e37);
i37i38 WITH i38i39*-1 (e38_n);
i37i39 WITH i38i39*1  (e39);

i40i41 WITH i40i42*1  (e40);
i40i41 WITH i41i42*-1 (e41_n);
i40i42 WITH i41i42*1  (e42);

i43i44 WITH i43i45*1  (e43);
i43i44 WITH i44i45*-1 (e44_n);
i43i45 WITH i44i45*1  (e45);

i46i47 WITH i46i48*1  (e46);
i46i47 WITH i47i48*-1 (e47_n);
i46i48 WITH i47i48*1  (e48);

i49i50 WITH i49i51*1  (e49);
i49i50 WITH i50i51*-1 (e50_n);
i49i51 WITH i50i51*1  (e51);

i52i53 WITH i52i54*1  (e52);
i52i53 WITH i53i54*-1 (e53_n);
i52i54 WITH i53i54*1  (e54);

i55i56 WITH i55i57*1  (e55);
i55i56 WITH i56i57*-1 (e56_n);
i55i57 WITH i56i57*1  (e57);
```

```
i58i59 WITH i58i60*1 (e58);
i58i59 WITH i59i60*-1 (e59_n);
i58i60 WITH i59i60*1 (e60);

MODEL CONSTRAINT:

!factor loadings relating to the same item are equal in
absolute value
L2_n = -L2;
L5_n = -L5;
L8_n = -L8;
L11_n = -L11;
L14_n = -L14;
L17_n = -L17;
L20_n = -L20;
L23_n = -L23;
L26_n = -L26;
L29_n = -L29;
L32_n = -L32;
L35_n = -L35;
L38_n = -L38;
L41_n = -L41;
L44_n = -L44;
L47_n = -L47;
L50_n = -L50;
L53_n = -L53;
L56_n = -L56;
L59_n = -L59;

! pair's error variance is equal to sum of utility error
variances
e1e2 = e1 - e2_n;
e1e3 = e1 + e3;
e2e3 = -e2_n + e3;
e4e5 = e4 - e5_n;
e4e6 = e4 + e6;
e5e6 = -e5_n + e6;
e7e8 = e7 - e8_n;
e7e9 = e7 + e9;
e8e9 = -e8_n + e9;
e10e11 = e10 - e11_n;
e10e12 = e10 + e12;
e11e12 = -e11_n + e12;
e13e14 = e13 - e14_n;
e13e15 = e13 + e15;
e14e15 = -e14_n + e15;
e16e17 = e16 - e17_n;
e16e18 = e16 + e18;
```

```
e17e18 = -e17_n + e18;
e19e20 = e19 - e20_n;
e19e21 = e19 + e21;
e20e21 = -e20_n + e21;
e22e23 = e22 - e23_n;
e22e24 = e22 + e24;
e23e24 = -e23_n + e24;
e25e26 = e25 - e26_n;
e25e27 = e25 + e27;
e26e27 = -e26_n + e27;
e28e29 = e28 - e29_n;
e28e30 = e28 + e30;
e29e30 = -e29_n + e30;
e31e32 = e31 - e32_n;
e31e33 = e31 + e33;
e32e33 = -e32_n + e33;
e34e35 = e34 - e35_n;
e34e36 = e34 + e36;
e35e36 = -e35_n + e36;
e37e38 = e37 - e38_n;
e37e39 = e37 + e39;
e38e39 = -e38_n + e39;
e40e41 = e40 - e41_n;
e40e42 = e40 + e42;
e41e42 = -e41_n + e42;
e43e44 = e43 - e44_n;
e43e45 = e43 + e45;
e44e45 = -e44_n + e45;
e46e47 = e46 - e47_n;
e46e48 = e46 + e48;
e47e48 = -e47_n + e48;
e49e50 = e49 - e50_n;
e49e51 = e49 + e51;
e50e51 = -e50_n + e51;
e52e53 = e52 - e53_n;
e52e54 = e52 + e54;
e53e54 = -e53_n + e54;
e55e56 = e55 - e56_n;
e55e57 = e55 + e57;
e56e57 = -e56_n + e57;
e58e59 = e58 - e59_n;
e58e60 = e58 + e60;
e59e60 = -e59_n + e60;

! fix one error variance per block for identification
e3=1;
e6=1;
```

```
e9=1;
e12=1;
e15=1;
e18=1;
e21=1;
e24=1;
e27=1;
e30=1;
e33=1;
e36=1;
e39=1;
e42=1;
e45=1;
e48=1;
e51=1;
e54=1;
e57=1;
e60=1;

OUTPUT: STDY;

SAVE: FILE IS FCFFMresults.dat;
SAVE=FSCORES;
```

Part III
Scale Scoring

19
Scores, Scales, and Score Linking
Neil J. Dorans

In his tribute to the career of Paul Holland at the 75th anniversary meeting of the National Council on Measurement in Education that was held in San Francisco, Sinharay (2013) cited several of Holland's aphorisms. A favorite is:

> Few wish to assess others,
> Fewer still wish to be assessed,
> But everyone wants to see the scores.

Scores can have important consequences for some test takers. Test scores sometimes contribute to high-stakes decisions made in a number of settings. These settings include licensure for practicing in a profession, such as teaching or medicine, admissions to undergraduate or graduate school, and promotion from one grade to the next in school.

The chapter presumes that tests are composed of many questions or tasks. Tests covered by this discussion may include subjectively-scored components; for example, essays scored by human readers. Both the objective and subjective components should be governed by Ayer's (1936) principle of *empirical verification* as articulated in Dorans and Walker (2013). Empirical data should be used to verify the plausibility of empirical propositions posited by a model or framework. Specific predictions are made about observables, data are collected, and predictions are assessed.

Scores reported for a test used in high-stakes settings should offer reliable and nonredundant information. These scores should be interchangeable with scores that come from different editions of that test. The scores should be reported on properly maintained scales that are aligned with the purposes of the test. Steps need to be taken to ensure that these scores are properly interpreted and that they are used validly. All facets of a testing program should, whenever possible, be backed by empirical evidence of their relevance with respect to the intended purpose of the test. High reliability, interchangeability of scores from different test assessments, and validity are essential aspects of sound psychometric assessment. Empirical data are central to assessing reliability, equatability, and validity.

The Wiley Handbook of Psychometric Testing: A Multidisciplinary Reference on Survey, Scale and Test Development, First Edition. Edited by Paul Irwing, Tom Booth, and David J. Hughes.
© 2018 John Wiley & Sons Ltd. Published 2020 by John Wiley & Sons Ltd.

This chapter focuses on scores, the scales on which they are reported and the means by which scores are linked for testing programs that develop multiple forms of tests that are used in high-stakes assessments. In particular, it focuses on score interchangeability. Scoring, scale definition, and score linking are important to ensuring score interchangeability.

The first section (pages 574–578) deals with the prerequisites for scores, scales, and score linking, which includes what is meant by measurement, the importance of controlling for the influence of measurement conditions, and the critical need for well-defined content and statistical specifications. The second section (pages 578–581) discusses different types of scores, including item scores and different methods of combining information across items. The third section (pages 581–585) deals with scale definition, including those defined by groups of test takers, by content information and by scaling models. The fourth section (pages 585–588) is concerned with the most common data collection designs that are used to link test scores and ensure scale maintenance, including single group, equivalent groups, and anchor test designs. In the fifth section (pages 588–598), various methods and procedures for forming linking and equating functions between complete tests are described. Following that, the sixth section (pages 598–601) defines test score equating as a special case of the more general class of procedures called score linking or scale aligning. A brief final section concludes the chapter.

Prerequisites

Treatments of measurement vary in breadth, focus, and vintage. Treatises have been written on the foundations of measurement from an abstract, philosophical or mathematical perspective (Krantz, Luce, Suppes, & Tversky, 1971). Excellent introductions to measurement in education and psychology from an abstract perspective have existed for some time (e.g., Coombs, Dawes, & Tversky, 1970; Torgerson, 1958). I intend to consider measurement as it is conducted in the educational and psychological settings.

Measurement in practice

Abstract treatments of measurement are relevant for the world of physical measurements, where instrumentation is sophisticated and quite precise, and theories exist that use these measurements and relate them to other quantities via mathematical equations that fit the data quite well. Unfortunately, measurements in education lack precise measurement instrumentation. In addition, the linkage of observations derived from these instruments to constructs of interest is at best indirect.

The following *gedankenexperiment* should illustrate this point. Consider a tangible everyday example – the measurement of a person's size. By size, I mean a function of the volume of the continuous surface in three-dimensional space that defines a human's shape as well as the density of the person. With today's technology, measuring size of the body with computer images and other instrumentation may be straightforward.

Consider being limited to the use of primitive measures of physical size that result in 0/1 scores. For example, suppose we measure size by asking students to try on clothes of various sizes and then ask a panel of judges to note independently whether the clothes are too loose or too tight. A score of 1 is assigned to a student by a judge if the clothing item is too small; a 0 if it is too big. If students try on enough articles of clothing of sundry size, we will be able to order students from large to small simply by summing their clothes fit scores across articles of clothing and judges. We might even assign a common score to students who have the same 0/1 pattern with respect to a set of clothes and judges, and devise some rule for ordering these scores. We have engaged in a crude form of size measurement. With enough carefully selected clothing items, however, we should achieve a reproducible ordering of students.

Consider using height as a measure of size instead of the clothing fit score. Height is easy to measure, and these measures possess nice measurement properties. If individuals of the same height had the same shape and density, height would be an excellent approximation to size. But shape and density vary even when height is fixed. People with the same height have different sizes. Using height as a measure of size would lead to underrepresentation of the construct of interest, size in all its manifestations of shape and density.

We can see shape. We can see that the construct of size is not easily measured by a single number. We know that the clothing fit score is not a direct measure of size. We can see that height comes up short as a measure of size as well.

Compared to assessing an unobservable educational construct, however, measurement of size is straightforward, whether via sophisticated computer images, accurate measures of height, or judgments based on how well clothing fits. Maybe at some time in the future, we'll be able to measure the shape of academic achievement with comparable accuracy and fidelity. We are not there yet.

Where are we? We pose tasks to test takers and then score their responses according to some rubric. The rubric can be objectively applied to produce the same score, often a 0 (wrong) or 1 (right). Sometimes more costly scoring is used that involve expert judgments. With either type of data, we use either simple or complex models to score how people behave when faced with test questions.

Using height in place of size is analogous to using predictions based on restrictive psychometric models in place of empirical data. The Rasch model (Rasch, 1960) is favored by many who wish to achieve measurement rigor in the domain of educational measurement. This model makes restrictive assumptions about the data, which if met, lead to desirable measurement consequences. Unfortunately, simply applying the Rasch model to data does not yield scales with interval properties.[1] The model cannot imbue the data with measurement rigor that it does not possess. With the less visible constructs that populate the domain of educational assessment, it is harder to know how well the model fits the data. If we could see an educational construct as well as we could see size, we would know when our models fall short of describing the data.

In practice, score son educational tests derive their meaning from their practical usefulness, not from their formal measurement properties. These scores may possess predictive power, enabling them to predict with much efficiency, more complicated costly assessments from lower cost assessments. Their meaning may be derived from the manner in which the score scale is established, a focus of the section on scores (pages 578–581). The circumstances under which they are obtained circumscribe their meaning as well.

---

[1] If scores are on an interval scale, a difference between two scores means the same thing regardless of where the two scores are on the scale.

Measurement conditions

Since the late 1970s, psychometrics has applied increasingly sophisticated and restrictive models to data collected under less and less controlled conditions. This practice could be viewed as a consequence of a willingness to believe in numerical alchemy, fostered by readily available and inexpensive software. Another contributing factor may be the tendency to use computationally intensive models to generate simulated data that serves as a substitute for actual data. This practice may promote better understanding of the models, but less understanding of the data. Dorans (2012) noted that there is a tendency to fall prey to the substitution of simulations for reality – an example of what Kahneman (2011) called substitution bias.

Prior to the advent of superfast computational tools, sophisticated models could not be used because computation was arduous. Extrapolate Moore's Law backward. Eventually, you get to a point where a computer was no faster that a well-trained human. In fact, when the Educational Testing Service started in 1947, the computers were humans, and computational errors could lead to months of rework (Dorans, 2004b). Great care was given to thoughtful and careful data collection back then because mistakes were extremely costly in terms of time and human resources.

One of the most undesirable consequences of a substitution of simulated data for actual data is that data collection practices have become sloppier. During the mid-twentieth century, there was respect for the importance of *measurement conditions*. The first two editions of *Educational Measurement* had chapters dedicated to the nature of measurement that emphasized the importance of attending to measurement conditions.

Lorge (1951, p. 536) noted,

> In scientific observations, whether direct or indirect, the conditions for measurement are carefully specified in terms of time, place, and circumstance...The statement about observations, necessarily, must contain specification of condition.

Jones (1971, p. 338) cited the same point and added,

> In general, science demands a reproducibility of observations. Whenever conditions and methods are identical, the observations should be identical (within range of measurement error) unless the object underwent some changes during observation or subsequent to it. The development of apparatus as an aid to measurement has promoted commonality of perceptual judgments among observers and has enhanced opportunities for agreement and reproducibility.

Some measurement conditions are obvious, such as mode of administration, timing, whether the test is administered under standardized conditions. Language of administration, however, is often ignored as a condition of measurement. Comparisons of performance on tests administered in different languages employ sophisticated models with restrictive assumptions to deal with the inherent data collection complexities associated with comparisons across different languages. Assessments across different measurement conditions, such as different languages, are assessments relative to different frames of reference, which are likely to differ along multiple dimensions.

Consider the following *gedankenexperiment*. Identical triplets (T1, T2, T3), raised in the same environment, had always exhibited comparable mathematical proficiency throughout their school years. They had become multilingual, learning English and French in addition to their native Mandarin. T1 studies in China, T2 studies in England, and T3 in Vietnam. A few years later, they take part in an international assessment of university students. T1 earns a higher Math score than T2, who receives a higher math score than T3. Performance on a math test seems to be related to proficiency in the language of the test.

Had T1 gone to Vietnam while T3 stayed in China, would there be a reversal in their math proficiencies? Probably. Can we compare these proficiencies if the same person (and their very close siblings) obtains different scores on tests administered in different languages? Or must we require our interpretation of the meaning of these scores to be cognizant of the different frames of reference associated with the different languages of test administration? Dorans and Middleton (2012) addressed issues of comparability under divergent measurement conditions.

Test specifications

Kolen and Brennan (2004) listed common measurement characteristics and conditions as one of the necessary requirements of equating. Inequities in assessment may occur if the need for equivalent measurement conditions is ignored. Crude test specifications can also lead to poor measurement. Several steps, such as those indicated in the rest of this section, can be taken to ensure that common measurement conditions are achieved.

It is essential to identify the purpose(s) for the assessment. In defining the purpose(s) of the assessment, it is important to consider all plausible uses of the scores. For example, broad-range measures of developed verbal and quantitative abilities designed to predict performance during the first year of college are used for college admissions decisions. A test designed for one particular purpose, college admissions, is unlikely to serve another purpose as well as tests designed specifically for that second purpose; for example, placement tests that measure specific knowledge pertaining to the academic subject of interest. Scores from a test designed for college admissions, however, might be used for decisions regarding course placement even though the admissions test does not assess knowledge in the subject of the course. Professional standards maintain that tests that produce scores that are used for multiple purposes must be validated for each of those uses (AERA, APA, & NCME, 2014). Hence evidence must be provided to support the use of an admissions test of general verbal and quantitative proficiency for placement purposes. It is plausible that validity can be demonstrated for placement into quantitative courses; it is unlikely that evidence can be found to support placement in a foreign language course.

The *target population* is defined as the group for whom the test is designed. Members of the target population are a subset of the test-taking population, the people who actually take the test.

Having determined what the test is supposed to measure, why, and for whom, the next step is to convert these concepts into a concrete reality. The content domain needs to be clearly specified and linked to the purpose of the assessment and its intended use with the target population. Kane (2006) discussed how to link content to intended uses in a valid manner. The final product is a blueprint indicating the number of items of various item formats in each content subdomain that will appear on the test.

Innovations such as evidence-centered design (ECD) offer conceptual tools to help assessment designers in framing the content specifications of the test (Mislevy, Almond, & Lukas, 2003; Mislevy, Steinberg, & Almond, 2002). As more test makers discover how to incorporate ECD methods into their own production processes, these methods promise to gain even more widespread use (Snow et al., 2010). ECD approaches the construction of assessments in terms of evidentiary arguments, and the validity argument for the test becomes part of its formal development. ECD allows the test developer to (1) consider the skills to be measured, (2) identify the evidence that indicates that the skills are present, and (3) construct questions that reflect this evidence. The full ECD framework has several phases (Mislevy & Haertel, 2006; Mislevy, Steinberg, & Almond, 2002). Following this full framework ensures that all versions of the test follow the same test specifications.

Statistical specifications state the desired statistical properties of the test that should guide a test assembly process that ensures parallelism across multiple versions of the test.

The difficulty of a test question is a function of the percent of test takers who responded correctly to it (i.e., *p*-value). These *p*-values are influenced by the group of test takers who responded to the question. Ideally, the *p*-values should be estimated for the target population. At the very least, average test difficulty and some measure of spread of item difficulty around the average in the target population must be established. Where possible, the distribution of item difficulty (i.e., spread of item difficulty and shape of the item distribution) should also be specified. The shape of the distribution of item difficulty needs to reflect the intended uses of the test.

Item discrimination, expressed most simply as a correlation between the item and the total test score, is another statistic to consider. The more a question distinguishes test takers with high scores from those with low scores, the higher the correlation. Test questions with low or negative correlations should be avoided.

Item response theory (IRT) offers an array of tools for the assembly of tests, such as test information functions and conditional standard error curves. The foundations of IRT approaches can be found in Lord (1980). These procedures make strong assumptions about the data that may or may not be met. Violations of these assumptions, however, do not necessarily negate the utility of test assembly methods that are based on these assumptions. Recent research indicates that tests built to IRT specifications and tests built to specifications based on more classical item statistics (i.e., *p*-values and item-total correlations) tend to be of comparable quality (Davey & Hendrickson, 2010).

Scores

From a practical perspective, sound measurement requires well-defined content and statistical specifications, and careful control of measurement conditions. In this section, different types of scores are discussed including item scores and different methods of combining information across items.

Unit, item, and raw scores

Kolen (2006) made useful distinctions between *unit scores, item scores, raw scores,* and *scale scores.*

The *item score* refers to number assigned to performance on the item, task, or stimulus. It may be something as simple as a binary right/wrong score on a multiple-choice item or a function of multiple pieces of information. In the case of performance on a constructed-response item, for example, the item score might be the function of *unit scores*. For such an item, the unit scores may be ratings assigned by multiple raters, or the values associated with the components of an automated scoring engine (Williamson, Xi, & Bryer, 2012).

Kolen (2006) noted that item scores are considered to be operationally independent; for example, they refer to different tasks or stimuli. In contrast, the unit scores that contribute to an item score are operationally linked. The constructed-response task is an example of operationally linked units.

Any classification involves judgments. Consider the ubiquitous reading passage that has a set of items associated with it. Are the responses to the items best viewed as unit scores or as item scores? They refer to the same passage. Yet they are different questions. Kolen (2006) noted that this distinction between score and unit may matter for items that are scored by an IRT model that presumes that item performance is locally independent given knowledge of the ability being measured by all items on the test. If ability to answer questions pertaining to this passage relies on more than the ability underlying all items, the violations of local independence may invalidate the IRT scoring. Kolen (2006) discussed related issues with the rich data that can be gleaned from computer-based tests.

Typical item scores Binary item scoring, where items are either correct (1) or incorrect (0), is commonplace in testing. This scoring is used in settings where nonresponse is not an option, and nonresponses are treated as incorrect, which is a penalty for nonresponse. As a correction for random guessing, formula scoring (and associated instructions) was proposed (Thurstone, 1919). Formula scoring distinguishes between items that the test taker attempts but gets incorrect and items the test taker chooses to omit. It assigns a negative score to wrong, a zero to nonresponse, and a one to correct. The use of a negative number for incorrect (as opposed to zero) is referred to as a "penalty for guessing;" relative to the more severe rights-scoring approach, "credit for omission" is more apt. See Wendler and Walker (2006) for further discussion of issues associated with rights versus formula scoring.

Formula scoring can be viewed as an ordered response scoring method in which more credit is assigned to nonresponse than to wrong. Binary scoring is also ordered. Constructed-response scoring on a k-point scale, where increasingly higher scores are assigned to increasing higher levels of correctness or appropriateness of response, is another example of ordered scoring.

Typical raw scores The most common *raw score* is an equally-weighted sum of the item scores. For a test consisting of dichotomously scored items, the summed score is the number of items answered correctly. For other ordinally-scored items, it is the sum of the ordered item scores. For example, if a test is composed of scores on five constructed-response items, each of which is scored on a six-point scale (1–6), the sum score would range from 6 to 30. Equal weighting of items can be justified based on judgment. If the data follow a one-parameter logistic (1PL) IRT or Rasch model, the simple sum score also can be justified on theoretical grounds.

Sometimes the sum score is a function of differentially weighted item scores. Various procedures are used to choose the weights. If the two-parameter logistic (2PL) IRT model fits the data, theory suggests that the items should be weighted by the discrimination parameter. Weights that maximize the reliability of the raw score can be used. Another alternative is to select weights that optimize estimation of the composite true score (Haberman, 2011). Alternatively, proportional weights can be chosen subjectively so that each item reflects the desired relative contribution of the item to the raw score. This type of weighting is employed with the Advanced Placement® examination to weight items on the constructed-response portion of the test.

More complex scoring schemes exist as well. These procedures are associated with mathematical models such as IRT models. Kolen (2006) described both maximum likelihood and Bayesian approaches for different unidimensional IRT models. The restrictive assumptions made by the models underlying these elegant scoring procedures may not be met in practice, however, which may limit their practical utility.

Composite scores

Tests can be composed of items with different formats. For example, the Advanced Placement exams are composed of both multiple-choice items and constructed-response items. The multiple-choice item scores are summed via equal weighting to produce an MC score, while the constructed-response item scores are summed according to their importance with respect to test specifications to produce a weighted CR score. The acronym WCR is used in this chapter for this weighted CR score.

A common practice is to create a weighted sum of the MC score and the WCR score to create a composite. There are several ways to weight these components. One is based on perceived importance of the two components. Another is maximum reliability. These and other weighting schemes are described in Kolen (2006). Many of the methods that employ statistical criteria, however, produce weights that are population dependent; that is, they depend on statistics like variances and correlations that vary across populations. This dependency is not always noted.

Several caveats are relevant when considering weights for mixed format tests. While test developers may be fairly certain about how much weight to apply to each item format, they often weight formats in suboptimal ways. This probably occurs because they confuse the fallible measured attribute (test score) with the construct of interest, which has perfect reliability. For example, they may mistake a score on a mathematics test as a direct measure of the construct of interest, mathematics proficiency, instead of as an indirect fallible indicator of that proficiency.

The second mistake stems from an under appreciation of how measurement error can cloud the signal in data. It is well documented that, for a fixed amount of testing time, the reliability of scores associated with constructed-response items often is much lower than the reliability of scores associated with multiple-choice items (Thissen & Wainer, 2001). At times, the constructed-response reliability is so low that it is possible that the use of developer supplied weights will lead to a composite score that is less reliable than the multiple-choice score. In these settings, the weights based on maximizing reliability, or on an IRT model, might be quite different from those assigned by the test developer. Reliability is very important in high states settings. Discrepancies between psychometrically-based weights and those based on expert judgment should be resolved by improving reliability of the constructed-response scores or down-weighting their contribution to the composite score.

Keep the test taker in mind

The method used to score the test is an important psychometric consideration. It is essential in high-stakes settings, however, that test takers understand the scoring rules because knowledge of these rules could affect how they approach the test and how well they perform.

The simplest method for scoring a test is rights-scoring. The best way for a test taker to maximize the test score is to answer every item, even if the test taker must guess on some items. Random guessing adds noise to the measurement of knowledge or ability. As a correction for random guessing, formula scoring was proposed, making distinctions between nonresponse and wrong. It is hard, however, to craft instructions for test takers that will enable them to maximize their performance on formula-scored tests.

IRT offers an array of scoring methods that may use even more information in the data. An IRT score (based on a pattern score) uses information about the particular items that were answered to estimate a test taker's ability. Unfortunately, from the test taker's perspective, it is difficult to understand how this information contributes to a score. A possible exception may be 2PL scoring which weights items by item discrimination. Even here it is not clear what test takers would do with this information or what the unintended consequences would be of this knowledge.

Lord (1980, pp. 225–226) expressed reservations about the use of IRT models with tests administered under rights-scored instructions. "*In principle, item response theory can be applied to number-rights-scored tests only if they are unspeeded* [italics in original]." Lord was concerned that the random responding induced by speededness would lead to disruptive violations of the unidimensionality assumption. Despite Lord's concern, the use of IRT with rights-scored tests is ubiquitous. This use appears to be based on the presumption that IRT scoring is consonant with rights-scoring instructions, which is true only for the simplest IRT model. From the test taker's perspective, a test that is administered under rights-scoring instructions but then scored in a different manner (e.g., pattern-scored) may violate the rights of test takers to be informed about scoring criteria and general test-taking strategy (see Standard 8.2 of AERA, APA, & NCME, 2014).

Scale Definition

In the preceding section, different types of raw scores and their derivatives were described. Each of these scores was tied directly to a particular test form. In some high-stakes assessments settings, decisions are made on the basis of a single version or form of a test. There is no need to make comparisons of scores obtained from different versions of the test because there is only one version that matters. End of year assessments in school or admissions tests for university may be based on a single test form. In these settings, equating is unnecessary and scales are not essential. In many settings, however, it is essential to compare scores from different versions of a test. Score equating is essential for fairness purposes and scores need to be reported on a common scale.[2]

Scale scores are the most visible and widely used products of a testing program. The score scale provides the framework for the interpretation of scores. The choice of score

---

[2] Discussion of the mechanics of score equating appear in the fifth section (pages 588–598).

scale needs to be consonant with test specifications and test reliability and has implications for equating and validity, as well as for test interpretation. The utility of a score scale depends on how well it supports the inferences attached to its scores, and how well it facilitates meaningful interpretations and minimizes misinterpretations (Petersen, Kolen, & Hoover, 1989).

This section mentions different ways of setting score scales. For those seeking a more in-depth treatment of the topic, consult Kolen and Brennan (2004) and Kolen (2006) who provide a broad perspective on scale definition. Included in Kolen (2006) are sections on approaches for incorporating *normative information* (Dorans, 2002; McCall, 1939), *score precision* (Kolen, 1988; Kolen, Hansen, & Brennan, 1992) or *content information* (Zwick, Senturk, Wang, & Loomis, 2001) into score scales. In this section, these three alternative approaches are considered. Then I address the choice of scales for certification exams.

Incorporating normative information into score scores

One common means of imbuing scores with meaning is by using a target population or norms group to define the scale units of the score scale. The target population is the group for whom the test is designed. Members of the target population are a subset of the test-taking population, the people who actually take the test.

Statistical characteristics of the scale score distribution (mean, standard deviation, etc.) are set for the target population. The particular target population that is chosen for constructing a scale strongly influences the meaning of the resulting scale scores. The resulting scale scores derive their meaning from the target population. The SAT I tests were rescaled using a 1990 reference group of SAT test takers, in essence replacing a reference group that dated back to 1941 (Dorans, 2002). This rescaling was informed by guidelines that may pertain to other tests that base their score meaning on normative information.

What should a good normative scale look like? The scale should be well aligned with the intended uses of the scores. For a broad-range test for which high, middle, and low scores may be pertinent for some admissions decision, the well-aligned scale should possess several properties (Dorans, 2002).

1 First, the scores of the reference group used to define the scale should be *centered* near the midpoint of the scale.
2 Second, the distribution of aligned scores for the scale-defining reference group should be *unimodal*, and that mode should be near the midpoint of the scale.
3 Third, the distribution should be nearly *symmetric* about the average score.
4 Fourth, the shape of the distribution should follow a commonly *recognized form*, such as the bell-shaped normal curve.
5 Fifth, the *working range* of scores should extend enough beyond the *reported range* of scores to permit shifts in population away from the scale midpoint without stressing the endpoints of the scale.
6 Sixth, the number of scale units should not exceed the number of raw-score points, which is usually a simple function of the number of items. Otherwise, unjustified differentiation of test takers may occur.
7 Finally, a score scale should be viewed as *infrastructure* that is likely to require repair. Corrective action should be taken whenever average score distributions of current

populations move sufficiently far away from the midpoint, or when distributions move far enough away from one of the endpoints to jeopardize the integrity of the scale at that endpoint.

The rationale for these seven properties is articulated in Dorans (2002). The reasons for the first four properties are related. If we want to maximize the longevity of the scale, we center the score distributions at the center of the score scale. Given the symmetric or nearly symmetric nature of so many distributions of attributes, it seems logical to start with a symmetric distribution. The normal distribution is a unimodal symmetric distribution with a mathematically compact form that has known properties. The fifth property allows the distribution of scores to shift over time before the highest actual score is lower than the maximum reported score, or before the lowest actual score is higher than the minimum reported score. The sixth property is the fundamental *one item, one-scale-point* property. The seventh property recognizes that nothing lasts forever.

The purpose of a certification test is to determine whether a candidate, such as a teacher, knows enough about their subject area to warrant certification. Typically, less attention is given to the properties of scores scales used by these certification tests than is given to score scales that incorporate normative information into the scale. Threshold-focused thinking led Dorans, Liang, and Puhan (2010) to offer some guidelines for these types of tests. Instead of focusing on the target populations, these guidelines are centered about the thresholds used for certification of candidates.

For any type of scale, it is preferable to define the lowest scale score point above what may be expected under random guessing, an obvious point not always heeded.

Incorporating score precision into the score scale

The one-item, one-scale-point property cited in the preceding section is consistent with the recommendation that the number of scale score units should be large enough to preserve score precision in the raw scores, but small enough to ensure that users do not attach unjustified significance to small score differences. This recommendation has been made by authors dealing with score scale definition as far back as Flanagan (1951) in the first edition of *Educational Measurement* to Kolen (2006) in the fourth edition.

Determination of the number of score points depends also on the reliability (the ratio of true-score variance to observed-score variance) of the assessment. Reliability at the level of a given observed score is undefined, in a mathematical sense, because the observed-score variance (the denominator of the reliability variance ratio) is zero. Fortunately, the conditional error of measurement at each true-score level is a defined quantity as the variance of observed scores given true-score. To ensure equally precise measurement for all test takers, the conditional errors of measurement should be the same across scale score levels, but they are typically not. Test developers are encouraged by the profession to report conditional errors of measurement at various score levels when the errors of measurement vary (AERA, APA, & NCME, 2014).

Kolen (1988) suggested using a nonlinear transformation that stabilizes the magnitude of the conditional error of measurement for the resulting scale scores, in essence approximating a constant error of measurement. If the error of measurement were constant, a single constant error of measurement could be used when interpreting test scores. Kolen (1988) used an arcsine transformation suggested by Freeman and Tukey (1950) to stabilize the conditional standard errors of measurement for the transformed number-right scores. This approach has been used with a variety of models of the error variance of number correct scores based on binomial and compound binomial error test theory models (Jarjoura, 1985: Kolen, 1988; Kolen, Hansen, & Brennan, 1992; Wilcox, 1981) and in IRT models (Kolen, Zeng, & Hanson, 1996). These studies have shown that variance of measurement errors for resulting scaled scores are approximately constant under the arcsine transformation. Kolen (2006) described how the arcsine transformation approach can be used as part of a process that sets a score scale to achieve a particular constant error variance.

Incorporating content information into scales

It would nice if mastery of test content was directly related to proficiency as measured by a score on a scale. This desire has led to recommendations that content information be provided along score scales to aid in interpretation (Ebel, 1962). Over the decades, procedures for providing content meaning scale scores have been developed. Kolen (2006) sorted them into three types: *item mapping*, *scale anchoring*, and *standard setting*. Item mapping and scale anchoring both require empirical data, and are discussed here. See Hambleton and Pitoniak (2006) for a full treatment of standard setting, which may be used in the absence of empirical data.

Item mapping Zwick et al. (2001) reviewed and studied item mapping procedures that are used for identifying the set of items that are representatives of various scale score points. The notion of a *response probability* (RP) *level* is central to item mapping. The RP, which is provided by the test developer, is the probability of correct response given the scale score that is associated with mastery on a test item. The same RP level is typically used for all dichotomously scored items on the test. The outcome of an item mapping procedure is the specification of test questions that represent various scale score points.

Scale anchoring Scale anchoring builds upon the results of the item mapping process. Certain scale score points are chosen. These scale points may be spaced along the score scale in equal intervals. Sometimes the scale points correspond to percentiles, such as the 10th, 25th, 50th, 75th, and 90th, in some target population of test takers. Content or subject matter experts review the items that map near each of these scale points and posit statements about the skills possessed by test takers scoring at these points. Scale anchoring makes a strong assumption, in essence assuming that an ordering of item maps exists such that test takers know and are able to do all of the skills in the statements that are at or below a given score level.

Forsyth (1991) questioned whether the outcomes of methods for incorporating content information facilitate score interpretation, arguing that useful content-based information in terms of item mapping or scale anchoring may be unattainable unless content domains are well articulated. Forsyth conducted a detailed analysis of NAEP scale anchoring and item mapping results to buttress his skepticism about the usefulness of the approaches. In addition, it has been argued that the judges are given a difficult and confusing task and that the current process for setting NAEP achievement levels is overly subjective (Pellegrino, Jones, & Mitchell, 1999).

I share concerns expressed by Forsyth and others. The item mapping process is most plausible for tests that are composed of items with high discrimination. It would be preferable if all items would approximate the ideal item types associated with a deterministic item response model such as those suggested by Guttman (1941). Restricting the items chosen for mapping to only those that discriminate well between test takers who score above and below a scale score point might approximate this ideal. Unfortunately, few domains in educational measurement have items that reach this degree of discrimination.

Data Collection Designs

Once test specifications have been established and tests have constructed, it is necessary to equate scores from different test forms. In this section, I describe data collection designs that are used for this kind of linking. On pages 588–598, I describe procedures and methods that operate on the data to perform score equatings. On pages 598–601, I emphasize how score equating differs from other kinds of score linkings.

To obtain the clearest estimates of test form difficulty differences, all score equating methods must control for differential ability of the test taker groups employed in the linking process. The data collection procedures used for score equating strive to obtain equivalent groups, either directly or indirectly. Typically, two different, nonstrictly parallel tests are given to two different groups of test takers of unequal ability. Assuming that the samples are large enough to ignore sampling error, differences in the distributions of the resulting scores can be due to one or both of two factors. One factor is the relative difficulty of the two tests and the other is the relative ability of the two groups on these tests. Difference in ability of the groups is a confounding factor that needs to be eliminated before the equating process can adjust for differences in test difficulty.

There are two different approaches for addressing the separation of test difficulty and group ability differences. The first approach is to use a common population of test takers. The other approach is to use an anchor measure of the construct being assessed by tests X and Y.

When the same population of test takers takes both tests, we achieve direct control over differential test taker ability. In practice, it is more common to use two equivalent samples from a common population instead of identical test takers.

The second approach assumes that performance on a set of common items or an anchor test can quantify the ability differences between two distinct, but not necessarily equivalent, samples of test takers. The use of an anchor test allows for more flexible data collection designs than the use of a single population. The use of anchor tests comes with a cost. These designs employ procedures that make various assumptions that are not needed when the test takers taking the tests are from the same population. Different methods make different assumptions; see pages 588–598. When there are ability differences, the various statistical adjustments for these group differences in ability often produce different results.

All procedures that follow, including those for samples from a common population, makes a common set of assumptions. All samples are assumed to be random samples from their respective populations. In practice, this may be only an approximation. In addition, all test takers are assumed to have had the opportunity to answer all of the questions on one or both of the tests.

The amount of data collected has a substantial effect on the usefulness of the resulting equatings. Because it is desirable for the statistical uncertainty associated with test equating to be much smaller than the other sources of variation in test results, it is important that the results of test equating be based on samples that are large enough to insure this. This fact should always be kept in mind when selecting a data collection design.

The single group (SG) design

The SG design is the simplest data collection design. In the SG design, all test takers in a single sample from population **P** take both tests. The SG design can provide accurate equating results with relatively small sample sizes.

The *design table* notation defined in von Davier, Holland, and Thayer (2004), used earlier in Petersen et al. (1989) and in Braun and Holland (1982) helps visualize the process. The design table is a schematic representation of the "test takers by test" data matrix, with rows representing populations and samples and the columns representing the different tests, test sections, or test items involved. The design table for the SG design is illustrated in Table 19.1.

The SG design controls for differential group proficiency by having the same test takers take both tests. It has several major uses in the practice of scaling and equating. In using this design, however, it is necessary to assume that a test taker's score on the second test is unaffected by the fact that she or he has previously taken the first form.

To study whether order affects the results obtained with the SG design, the sample is sometimes randomly divided in half and in each half sample the two tests are taken in different orders – **X** first and then **Y** or **Y** first and then **X**. This is the counterbalanced (CB) data collection design. The CB design contains both the SG and equivalent groups designs, described below, within it.

The equivalent groups design (EG)

In most applied settings, there is not enough testing time for every test taker to take more than one test. In the EG design, two equivalent samples are taken from a common population **P**, one is tested with **X** and the other with **Y**. The EG design is often used for equating. The EG design avoids the issue of possible order effects that can arise in the SG design where each test taker takes both tests.

The design table for the EG design, Table 19.2, clearly shows the pattern of missing data (i.e., the blank cells).

Table 19.1 The design table for the SG design.

Population	Sample	X	Y
P	1	@	@

Note. The @ mark in the design table indicates that the sample for a given row takes the tests indicated in the column; otherwise the score data are not collected.

Table 19.2 The design table for the EG design.

Population	Sample	X	Y
P	1	@	
P	2		@

Sometimes test booklets are assigned randomly to groups, which is why this design is sometimes called the random groups design (Kolen & Brennan, 2004). A more common situation is to construct the two samples by "spiraling" the test booklets for the two tests. The booklets are alternated in the packaging process so that when the tests are distributed to test takers they are alternated, first **X**, then **Y** and then **X** again, and so on. Well-executed, spiraled samples are often more equivalent than random samples because they are approximately stratified random samples. The EG design is convenient to administer. While it does not require that the two tests have any items in common, this design can be used with items in common, which makes it an anchor test design (see next subsection). When samples sizes are large and tests forms are administered under secure conditions, the EG is the preferred data collection design.

Anchor test designs

In anchor test designs there are two populations, **P** and **Q**, with a sample of test takers from **P** taking test **X**, and a sample from **Q** taking test **Y**. In addition, both samples take an anchor test, **A**. von Davier et al. (2004) and Holland and Dorans (2006) called this the *nonequivalent groups with anchor test* (or NEAT) design. Kolen and Brennan (2004) and others referred to this as the *common-item nonequivalent groups design*. See Table 19.3.

The role of the anchor test is to quantify the differences in ability between samples from **P** and **Q** that affect their performance on the two tests to be equated, **X** and **Y**. The best kind of an anchor for equating is a test that measures the same construct that **X** and **Y** measure. The anchor **A** is usually, but not always, a shorter and less reliable test than the tests to be equated.

The relationship of **A** to **X** and **Y** can be of two different types. If **A** is a subset of items contained in both **X** and **Y**, then it is called an internal anchor test and scores on **A** are used in computing scores on the total tests. If **A** is a separately timed test that each test taker takes in addition to one or the other of the tests being equated, then it is called an external anchor test.

The anchor test design contains two SG designs within it. This structure underlies both anchor scaling (Holland & Dorans, 2006), and the chain equating methods; see pages 588–598. The anchor test design improves upon the flexibility of the EG design by allowing the two samples taking **X** and **Y** to be nonequivalent. It improves upon the SG design by not requiring test takers to take both **X** and **Y**.

While the use of anchor tests may appear to be a minor variation of the previous data collection designs, the use of common items rather than common test takers involves new assumptions that are not necessary in the use of SG, EG, and CB designs; see the fifth section. Some type of assumption is required in the NEAT design to make up for the fact that **X** is never observed for test takers in **Q** and **Y** is never observed

Table 19.3 The design table for the anchor test design.

Population	Sample	X	A	Y
P	1	@	@	
Q	2		@	@

for test takers in **P**. For this reason, there are several distinct methods of scaling and equating tests using the NEAT design. Each of these methods corresponds to making different untestable assumptions about the missing data.

The difference between the anchor test design and the SG, EG, and CB designs can be thought of as the difference between observational studies versus experimental designs (Rosenbaum, 1995). The SG design is a repeated measures design with a single group and two treatments, the EG design is a randomized comparison with two treatment groups, while the CB design is a repeated measures design with a single group and counterbalanced order of treatments. In contrast, the NEAT design is an observational study where there are two nonrandomized study groups that are possibly subject to varying amounts of self-selection. Liou, Cheng, and Li (2001) pointed out that the properly executed anchor test design produces missing data that are *missing at random* in the technical sense discussed in Little and Rubin (2002).

More extended discussions of data collection designs are given in Angoff (1971), Petersen et al. (1989), von Davier et al. (2004), Kolen and Brennan (2004), and Holland and Dorans (2006).

Procedures and Practices for Equating Scores

This section deals with the procedures and practices used to produce observed-score equating functions. I limit my discussion to observed-score equating methods that use the data collection designs described in the previous section. The focus is on observed-score equating because true scores are unobserved and consequently primarily of theoretical interest only. Even a platonic belief that observed scores are shadows of latent variables must face the reality that the observed score is all we can observe. Even sophisticated model-based scoring procedures produce manifest observed scores, not latent unobservable scores. Much of this section is an abridged version of the treatment provided by Holland and Dorans (2006), which should be consulted for more complete treatments of observed-score and true-score procedures.

First, preprocessing steps are described. Then observed-score procedures are described, first for the common population case, and then for the case where anchor tests are needed to adjust for population differences before the test scores can be properly equated. The section finishes with a consideration of common pitfalls that can make score equating challenging especially when the anchor test design is employed.

Data preprocessing practices

Having collected the data, several steps should be taken to improve the quality of the data prior to score equating. These data processing steps deal with sample selection, item screening, and continuizing and smoothing score distributions.

Sample selection Tests are designed with a target population in mind (defined as **T** throughout this section). For example, admissions tests are used to gather standardized information about candidates who plan to enter a college or university. The SAT excludes individuals who are not juniors or seniors in high school from its equating samples because they are not considered members of the target population. Consequently, junior high school students, for whom the test was not developed but who take the test, are not included in the equating sample. In addition, it is common practice to exclude individuals who may have taken the anchor test (whether internal or external) at an earlier administration. This is done to remove any potential influence of these individuals on the equating results. Test takers who perform well below chance expectation on the test are sometimes excluded; though many of these test takers may have already been excluded if they were not part of the target group. There is an issue as to whether nonnative speakers of the language in which the test is administered should also be excluded. One study by Liang, Dorans, and Sinharay (2009) suggested this may not be an issue as long as the proportion of nonnative speakers does not change markedly across administrations.

Statistical outlier analysis can be used to identify those test takers whose anchor test performance is substantially different from their performance on the operational test; that is, the scores are so different that both scores cannot be plausible indicators of the test taker's ability. Removing these test takers from the equating sample prevents their unusual performance from having an undue effect on the resulting equating function.

Checking that anchor items act like common items For both internal anchor (anchor items count toward the total score) and external anchor (items do not count toward the score) tests, the statistical properties of the common items should be evaluated to make sure they have not differentially changed from the one test administration to the other. Differential item functioning (DIF) methods compare the performance of the common items with the two test administrations treated as the reference and focal groups, and the total score on the common items as the matching criterion (see Holland & Wainer, 1993, especially Ch. 3). Simple plots of item difficulty values and other statistics may also be used to detect changes in items. Item difficulty estimates from old and new form samples should correlate in the high .90s.[3]

When English language tests are administered to samples from different countries with native languages and in which English is learned at different times and in different ways, common items may act uncommon. It is important to check whether or not the difficulties of the common items are ranked in the same way across the different countries. Correlations in the low .90s could signify problematic score equatings.

Internal common items are susceptible to context effects because they may be embedded within different sets of items in the two tests. Changes in widely held knowledge may also lead to changes in performance on anchor test items. For example, a hard question about a new law on a certification exam may become very easy once the law becomes part of the standard training curriculum. There are many examples of test questions getting old fast. Other issues with common items are discussed under best practices.

---

[3] Estimates of item difficulty, in contrast to person proficiency estimates which are sometimes based on responses to fewer than 30 test items, tend to be very stable because they are based on thousands of test takers. Correlations between item-difficulty estimates should approach 1.0 as the number of test takers gets larger and larger; correlations that fall below .90 approach shared variances of 80% or less, which suggest that the two groups of test takers are not ordering the difficulty of the items in the same way, and that the items are not as useful for linking as one thought.

The need to continuize the discrete distribution of scores Some notation will be used throughout the rest of this section. The *cumulative distribution function, cdf*, of the scores of test takers in the target population, **T**, on test **X** is denoted by $F_T(x)$, and it is defined as the proportion of test takers in **T** who score at or below x on test **X**. More formally, $F_T(x) = P\{\mathbf{X} \leq x | \mathbf{T}\}$, where $P\{.|\mathbf{T}\}$ denotes the population proportion or probability in **T**. Similarly, $G_T(y) = P\{\mathbf{Y} \leq y | \mathbf{T}\}$, is the cdf of **Y** over **T**. Cumulative distribution functions increase from 0 up to 1 as x (or y) moves from left to right along the horizontal axis in a two-way plot of test score by proportion of test takers. In this notation, x and y may be any real values, not necessarily just the possible scores on the two tests. For distributions of observed scores such as number-right scores, the cdfs are step functions that have points of increase only at each possible score (Kolen & Brennan, 2004).

The equipercentile function defined in a later subsection can depend on how the cumulative frequency distribution of **X** on **T**, $F_T(x)$, and **Y** on **T**, $G_T(y)$, are made continuous or "continuized." Test scores are typically integers, such as number-right scores or rounded formula scores. Because of this, the inverse function of $G_T(y)$, required in Equation 19.1 (see page 592) is not well-defined; that is, for many values of p, there is no score, y, for which $p = G_T(y)$. This is not due to the finite size of the samples, but rather to the discreteness of the test scores, which are typically integers. To get around this, there are three methods of "continuization" of $F_T(x)$ and $G_T(y)$ that are in current use. Holland and Dorans (2006) treated two of these methods, the linear interpolation and kernel smoothing methods, in detail. The linear equating function defined in Equation 19.3 (see page 593) can be thought of as a third continuization method.

There are two primary differences between the first two approaches to continuization. First, the use of linear interpolation results in an equipercentile function that is piecewise linear and continuous resulting in functions that have kinks that some prefer to post-smooth (Fairbank, 1987, Kolen & Brennan, 2004). In contrast, kernel continuization results in equipercentile functions that are differentiable everywhere and that do not need further postsmoothing. Second, the equipercentile functions obtained by linear interpolation always map the highest score on **X** into the highest score on **Y** and the same for the lowest scores (unlike the linear equating function). It is not clear why the highest score on an easier test should be mapped onto the highest score of a harder test or vice versa. For more discussion of this point, see Petersen et al. (1989), Kolen and Brennan (2004), and von Davier et al. (2004).

Presmoothing score distributions Irregularities in the score distributions can produce irregularities in the equipercentile equating function that do not generalize to other groups of test takers. Consequently, it is generally considered advisable to smooth the raw-score frequencies, the cdfs, or the equipercentile equating function itself (Holland & Thayer, 1987, 2000; Kolen & Jarjoura, 1987; Kolen & Brennan, 2004; von Davier et al., 2004). The purpose of this step is to eliminate some of the sampling variability present in the raw-score frequencies, in order to produce smoother cdfs for computation of the equipercentile function.

When presmoothing data, it is important to achieve a balance between a good representation of the original data and smoothness. Smoothness reduces sampling variability while a good representation of the data reduces the possibility of bias. The more parameters employed in the smoothing, the better the model will represent the original data, but the less smooth the fitted model becomes.

IRT observed-score equating was proposed by Lord (1980). Basically, it uses an IRT model to presmooth a number-right score distribution prior to equipercentile equating. Let **X** and **Y** denote number-right scores for two tests with dichotomous test items. Using IRT, the conditional distributions of **X** and **Y**, given the common latent ability, θ, may be estimated. This computation exploits the condition of local independence to compute $P\{\mathbf{X} = x|\theta\}$ and $P\{\mathbf{Y} = y|\theta\}$ as the probabilities of sums of independent but not identically distributed 0/1 variables. See Lord and Wingersky (1984) and Kolen and Brennan (2004) for a detailed example and additional references. The estimated density function for the ability distribution over **T**, $F_T(\theta)$, may be approximated in various ways, and these results combined via numerical integration. The resulting estimated probabilities, $P\{\mathbf{X} = x|\mathbf{T}\}$ and $P\{\mathbf{Y} = y|\mathbf{T}\}$, are IRT model-based estimates of the original raw-score sample proportions; that is, the proportion in the sample getting a score of x on **X**, or the proportion getting a score of y on **Y**. Thus, the estimates, $P\{\mathbf{X} = x|\mathbf{T}\}$ and $P\{\mathbf{Y} = y|\mathbf{T}\}$, may be regarded as a form of presmoothing of the two, unsmoothed sample score distributions. This is a use of an IRT model to presmooth the data, prior to continuization during equipercentile equating. Once the presmoothed estimated score probabilities are in hand, they may be continuized by either linear interpolation or Gaussian kernel smoothing and used to produce a version of the equipercentile function, $Equi_{YT}(x)$. See Holland and Dorans (2006) for a more complete discussion of this procedure.

IRT observed-score equating is seldom used in practice (see Kolen & Brennan, 2004). Compared to other presmoothing methods, it requires various judgments and assumptions, and is computationally burdensome. Furthermore, there is no guarantee that these presmoothed estimates of the score distributions will reproduce the types of score frequencies found in real data. For this reason, it is unlikely to be used except in research studies or very special situations with incomplete test data. For situations with data from complete tests, it is neither as efficient nor as flexible as the direct presmoothing of score frequencies using log linear models, as advocated by Holland and Thayer (2000), von Davier et al. (2004) and others.

Observed-score equating methods

Many procedures have been developed over the years for equating tests. Holland and Dorans (2006) considered three factors when attempting to develop taxonomy of equating methods:

1 common population versus common-item data collection designs,
2 observed-score versus true-score procedures, and
3 linear versus nonlinear methods.

Because equating is an empirical procedure, it requires a data collection design and a procedure for transforming scores on one test form to scores on another. Linear methods produce a linear function for mapping the scores from **X** to **Y**, while nonlinear methods allow the transformation to be curved. Observed-score procedures directly transform (or equate) the observed scores on **X** to those on **Y**. True-score methods are designed to transform the true scores on **X** to the true scores of **Y**. True-score methods employ a statistical model with a test taker's true score defined as their expected observed test score based on the chosen psychometric model. The psychometric models used to date are those of classical test theory and IRT. Holland and Hoskens (2003) show how these two psychometric models may be viewed as aspects of the same model.

Observed-score procedures for equating scores in a common population There are two data collection designs in the section on Data Collection Designs that make use of a common population of test takers: The SG and the EG designs. They all involve a single population, **P**, which is also the target population, **T**.

I use a definition of observed-score equating that applies to either linear or nonlinear procedures depending on whether additional assumptions are satisfied. This allows us to consider both linear and nonlinear observed-score equating methods from a single point of view.

The equipercentile equating function The equipercentile definition of *comparable* scores is that x (an **X**-score) and y (a **Y**-score) are *comparable* in **T** if $F_T(x) = G_T(y)$. This means that x and y have the same percentile in the target population, **T**. When the two cdfs are continuous and strictly increasing, the equation $F_T(x) = G_T(y)$ can always be satisfied and can be solved for y in terms of x. Solving for y leads to the **equipercentile function**, $Equi_{YT}(x)$, that links x to y on **T**, defined by:

$$y = Equi_{YT}(x) = G_T^{-1}(F_T(x)) \qquad (19.1)$$

In Equation 19.1, $y = G_T^{-1}(p)$ denotes the inverse function of $p = G_T(y)$. Note that with discrete data, this relationship does not hold because for most x-scores there is no y-score for which the two cumulative distributions, one for x and one for y are exactly equal. Hence, with most applications, steps are taken to make the data appear continuous, and different steps can yield different answers. Figures 35 to 38 of Moses and Holland (2007) illustrate the results produced by different methods of continuization; Figure 1 in Moses and Zhang (2001) demonstrate how well different continuization methods fit a discrete frequency distribution.

Note that the target population **T** is explicit in the definition of $Equi_{YT}(x)$ (Dorans & Holland, 2000; von Davier et al., 2004; Holland & Dorans, 2006). In general, there is nothing to prevent $Equi_{YT}(x)$ from varying with the choice of **T**. The equipercentile function is used for equating, and other kinds of linking. For equating, the influence of **T** is expected to be small or negligible and the scores are considered *equivalent* or interchangeable. In other kinds of linking, **T** can have a substantial effect and the scores can only be placed on *comparable* scales in **T**. Distinctions between equated and other typed of linked scores are discussed on pages 598–601.

If Equation 19.1 is satisfied, then $Equi_{YT}(x)$ will transform the distribution of x-scores **T** to a metric that has a distribution with the same shape as the distribution of y-scores **T**.

The linear equating function It is sometimes appropriate to assume that the two cdfs, $F_T(x)$ and $G_T(y)$, have the same shape and only differ in their means and standard deviations. To formalize the idea of a common shape, suppose that $F_T(x)$ and $G_T(y)$ both have the form,

$$F_T(x) = K[(x - \mu_{XT})/\sigma_{XT}] \text{ and } G_T(y) = K[(y - \mu_{YT})/\sigma_{YT}] \quad (19.2)$$

where K is a cdf with mean zero and standard deviation 1.

When Equation 19.2 holds, $F_T(x)$ and $G_T(y)$ both have the shape determined by K. In this case, it can be shown that the equipercentile function is the **linear function**, $Lin_{YT}(x)$, defined as

$$Lin_{YT}(x) = \mu_{YT} + (\sigma_{YT}/\sigma_{XT})(x - \mu_{XT}) \quad (19.3)$$

The linear function may also be derived as the transformation that gives the *x-scores* the same mean and standard deviation as the *y-scores* on **T**. Both of the linear and equipercentile functions satisfy the symmetry requirement for score equating noted on page 600. This means that $Lin_{XT}(y) = Lin_{YT}^{-1}(x)$, and $Equi_{XT}(y) = Equi_{YT}^{-1}(x)$, i.e., equating **Y** to **X** is the inverse of the function for equating **X** to **Y**. In general, the function, $Equi_{YT}(x)$, curves around the function, $Lin_{YT}(x)$.

The linear function requires estimates of the means and standard deviations of *x-scores* and *y-scores* over the target population, **T**. It is easy to obtain these estimates for the SG and EG designs described earlier on pages 586–587. See Angoff (1971) or Kolen and Brennan (2004) for details.

Procedures for equating scores on complete tests when using common items The anchor test design is widely used for equating scores because its use of common items to control for differential test taker ability gives it greater operational flexibility than the approaches using common test takers. Test takers need only take one test, and the samples need not be from a common population. However, this flexibility comes with a price. First of all, the target population is less clear-cut for the anchor test design (see the subsection on anchor test designs): there are two populations, **P** and **Q**, and either one could serve as the target population. In addition, the use of the anchor test design requires additional assumptions to allow for the missing data: **X** is never observed in **Q** and **Y** is never observed in **P**. I use the term *complete test* to indicate that everyone in **P** sees all items on **X** and that that everyone in **Q** sees all items on **Y**. Our use of the term *missing data* is restricted to data that are missing by design. The assumptions needed to make allowances for the missing data are not easily tested with the observed data, and they are often unstated. I will discuss two distinct sets of assumptions that may be used to justify the observed-score procedures that are commonly used with the NEAT design described on pages 587–588.

Braun and Holland (1982) proposed that the target population for the NEAT design, or what they called the *synthetic population*, be created by weighting **P** and **Q**. They denoted the synthetic population by $\mathbf{T} = w\mathbf{P} + (1-w)\mathbf{Q}$, by which they meant that the moments of **X** and **Y** on **T** are obtained by first computing them on **P** and **Q**, separately, and then averaging them with w and $(1-w)$ to get the distribution on **T**. There is considerable evidence that the choice of w has a relatively minor influence on equating results, for example, see von Davier et al. (2004). This insensitivity to w is an example of the population invariance requirement discussed on pages 600–601. The definition of the synthetic population forces the user to confront the need to create distributions (or moments) for $\mathbf{X}$ on $\mathbf{Q}$ and $\mathbf{Y}$ in $\mathbf{P}$, where there are no data. In order to do this, assumptions must be made about the missing data.

Equating methods used with the anchor test design can be classified into two major types, according to the way they use the information from the anchor. The first type of missing data assumption commonly employed is of the *post-stratification equating* (PSE) type; the second is of the *chain equating* (CE) type. Each of these types of assumptions asserts that an important distributional property that connects scores on $\mathbf{X}$ or $\mathbf{Y}$ to scores on the anchor test $\mathbf{A}$ is the same for any $\mathbf{T} = w\mathbf{P} + (1-w)\mathbf{Q}$, that is, is *population invariant*.

The PSE types of assumptions all have the form that the conditional distribution of $\mathbf{X}$ given $\mathbf{A}$ (or of $\mathbf{Y}$ given $\mathbf{A}$) is the same for any synthetic population, $\mathbf{T} = w\mathbf{P} + (1-w)\mathbf{Q}$. In this approach, we estimate, for each score on the anchor test, the distribution of scores on the new form and on the old form in $\mathbf{T}$. We then use these estimates for equating purposes as if they had actually been observed in $\mathbf{T}$. The PSE type of equating assumes that the relationship that generalizes from each equating sample to the target population is a conditional relationship. In terms of the missing data in the NEAT design, this means that conditional on the anchor test score, $\mathbf{A}$, the distribution of $\mathbf{X}$ in $\mathbf{Q}$ (where it is missing) is the same as in $\mathbf{P}$ (where it is not missing). In the special case of an EG design with anchor test, $\mathbf{P} = \mathbf{Q}$ and the PSE assumptions hold exactly. When $\mathbf{P}$ and $\mathbf{Q}$ are different, the PSE assumptions are not necessarily valid, but there are no data to contradict them.

The CE assumptions all have the form that a linking function from $\mathbf{X}$ to $\mathbf{A}$ (or from $\mathbf{Y}$ to $\mathbf{A}$) is the same for any synthetic population, $\mathbf{T} = w\mathbf{P} + (1-w)\mathbf{Q}$. In this approach, we link the scores on the new form to scores on the anchor and then link the scores on the anchor to the scores on the old form. The *chain* formed by these two *links* links the scores on the new form to those on the old form. The CE type of equating approach also assumes that the linking relationship that generalizes from each equating sample to the target population is an equating relationship. It is less clear for the CE assumptions than for the PSE assumptions what is implied about the missing data in the anchor test design (Kolen & Brennan, 2004, p. 146).

In the special case of an EG design with anchor test, $\mathbf{P} = \mathbf{Q}$ and the CE assumptions hold exactly. In this special situation, the corresponding methods based on either the PSE or the CE assumptions will produce identical results. When $\mathbf{P}$ and $\mathbf{Q}$ are different, the PSE assumptions and CE assumptions can result in equating functions that are different and there are no data to allow us to contradict or help us choose between either set of assumptions.

In addition to the PSE and CE types of procedures, classical test theory may be used to derive an additional linear observed-score procedure for the anchor test design, the Levine observed-score equating function, $Lev_{YT}(x)$ (Kolen & Brennan, 2004). $Lev_{YT}(x)$ may be derived from two population invariance assumptions that are different from those that we have considered so far and that are based on classical test theory. Holland and Dorans (2006) use the form of classical test theory discussed in Holland and Hoskens (2003) to derive the Levine observed-score equating function from these two assumptions. To formalize the intuition that $\mathbf{X}$, $\mathbf{Y}$, and $\mathbf{A}$ all measure the same construct, they assume their true scores are linearly related in a way that holds for all $\mathbf{T}$; that is, the three measures are congeneric.

When I started equating SAT tests over 30 years ago, available software was scant. Now there is much in the public domain. For example, Michael Kolen and his colleagues at the University of Iowa have provided software as part of the CASMA suite (https://education.uiowa.edu/centers/center-advanced-studies-measurement-and-assessment/computer-programs). The equating/linking programs are particularly relevant and available under various operating systems. Those interested who prefer R may want to consult http://cran.r-project.org/web/packages/equate/vignettes/equatevignette.pdf. Livingston (2004) has many practical examples for those who prefer to watch an equating transpire in a step by step fashion.

The widespread availability of software brings with it the potential for misuse. Just because a program produces output does not mean it produces something worthwhile. An understanding of the points raised in the balance of this chapter should help prevent the reader from common missteps.

Score equating pitfalls

Quality and similarity of tests to be equated, choice of data collection design, characteristics of anchor test in relation to the total tests, sample sizes and test taker characteristics, screening items and tests for outliers, and choice of analyses all involve best practices that contribute to a successful equating.

The ideal design, in theory and in terms of best practice, is a large sample EG design with an external anchor test. If the anchor test is administered last, only the anchor test can be affected by possible order effects. A comparison of the distributions of the anchor test in the two (equivalent) samples then allows differential order effects to be identified and if they are substantial, the anchor test can be ignored, leaving a simple EG design, where no order effects are possible. If the anchor test is internal to the two tests, then context or order (e.g., item location effects) may arise and need to be dealt with. In addition, the standard error of equating is smaller for anchor test designs.

Large representative motivated samples that result from a random assignment of test forms to test takers are not always attainable. Reliability is not always as high as desired. Anchor tests may not be very reliable, especially internal anchors with few items. Anchors, especially external anchors, are not always highly related to the tests being equated. Tests are not always appropriate for the group that takes them. These issues often arise when best design and data collection practices are not followed.

Sample size issues Unrepresentative or unmotivated samples undermine score equating. Special care should be taken to ensure that only members of the population of interest are included in the samples. If possible, the sample should be representative of the population as well.

Equating cannot be done effectively in small samples. The smaller the sample size, the more restricted is the class of stable equating methods. The SG design requires the smallest sample sizes, while the EG design requires the largest sample sizes to achieve the same level of accuracy, as measured by the standard error of equating (see Holland & Dorans, 2006; Lord, 1950). The anchor test designs require sample sizes somewhere in between those of the SG and EG designs; these requirements depend on how strongly correlated the anchor test is with the two tests to be equated and how similar the two populations are. Useful practical advice about sample size can be found toward the end of section 3.7 of Kolen and Brennan (2004).

Smoothing score distributions may be unnecessary in very large samples, and may work well enough in moderately-sized samples, but does not help much with very small samples, especially when it is not clear how representative the sample is of the intended population. The best practices solution to the small sample size problem may be to admit that equating is not possible for the time being. If the sample size suggested by consideration of standard errors is not achieved, raw scores could be reported with the caveat that they are not comparable to other scores, but that they could be made comparable when adequate data become available. This would protect testing organizations from challenges resulting from the use of either biased linking functions or unstable equating functions. To do otherwise might be problematic over the long term.

Anchor test design issues The anchor test design is often used because of the greater flexibility it provides. The role of the anchor test is to provide a common score that can be used to adjust for group ability differences before adjusting for test difficulty differences via equating. Scores from short anchor tests tend to have inadequate reliabilities, and consequently less than desirable correlations with the test scores. Low correlations may also result when the content of the anchor test differs from the test. Context effects can affect the comparability of anchor items. Anchors that are too hard or too easy for the target population produce skewed score distributions that are not helpful for equating.

Statistical procedures are needed to adjust for ability differences between groups when the anchor test design is used. Assumptions need to be made in order to make these adjustments. The assumptions may be flawed. In the anchor test case, it is particularly important to employ multiple models as each model rests on different sets of assumptions, which are described on pages 593–594. It is valuable to equate with several different models, including both linear and equipercentile models. Of course, there should be a principled selection from among equating methods. Equating is a means to an end. The end is a sound scaling function for the test form. Parsimony is factor to consider. As discussed on page 598 historical data are very relevant for assessing whether equating results are reasonable.

The equipercentile version of a particular method (say PSE) can be compared to the linear method version using the standard error of equating which describes sampling error, and the difference that matters (DTM), an effect size that can be used to assess whether differences in equating functions have practical significance or is an artifact of rounding. Holland and Dorans (2006) described the DTM, the standard error of equating and the standard error of the difference in equating or SEED. If the departures from linearity are less than the DTM and less than what would be expected due to sampling error, the linear model is often chosen on the grounds of parsimony because it was not sufficiently falsified by the data. Otherwise, the more general, less falsifiable, equipercentile model is selected.

With the anchor test design, the old and new form sample may perform very differently on the anchor test. Large ability differences on the anchor test tend to yield situations where equating is unsatisfactory unless the anchor score is highly related to both test scores to be equated. In this setting, different equating methods tend to give different answers unless the anchor test is strongly related to both the old and new tests. This divergence of results is indicative of a poor data collection design. The search for a single best model that could be employed universally would be unwise data analysis (Tukey, 1963).

Whether an equating test is an external anchor or an internal anchor also has an impact, as does the number of anchor tests and the type of score linking plan employed. For the observed-score equating methods, where the score on the anchor test plays an important role, it is often advised that the anchor test should be a "mini-version" of the two tests being equated (Angoff, 1971).

External anchors The phrase external anchor usually refers to items that are administered in a separately timed section and that do not count toward the test taker's score. One major advantage of external anchors is that they may serve multiple purposes, for example, equating, pretesting, and tryout of new item types. This is accomplished by spiraling versions of the test with different content in this *variable* section. This process also can be used to improve test security by limiting the exposure of the anchor test to a relatively small proportion of the total group tested.

For best practices, it is important to disguise the external anchor test so that it appears to be just another section of the test. This cannot always be achieved for tests that are composed of multiple distinct sections in which no one section contains all the item types. In these cases, the equating section is made to look like one of the sections, preferable the one with the most item types represented.

Internal anchors Items in an internal anchor test are part of the assessment and count toward each test taker's score. Internal anchor items are usually spread throughout the test. Because the items in an internal anchor test count toward the score, test takers are unlikely to skip them. For anchor items to be effective, they must maintain their statistical properties across the old and new forms.

Changes in the statistical properties, for example, difficulty, of items can occur with internal anchor tests due to context effects or security breaches. Context effects can occur when common items are administered in different locations (e.g., a common item in position 10 in one form appears in item 20 in the other form), or under different testing conditions (i.e., paper and pencil versus computer delivered), or when they are adjacent to different kinds of items in the two tests. These effects are well documented (Brennan, 1992; Harris & Gao, 2003; Leary & Dorans, 1985). Security breaches are an unfortunate reality for many testing programs, and due diligence is required to prevent them or to recognize them when they occur.

It is sound practice to exclude from the equating analysis any test takers whose anchor test performance is inconsistent with their total test performance, as well as items that exhibit shifts in difficulty that may be due to security breaches or context effects.

Lack of population invariance

One of the most basic requirements of score equating is that equating functions, to the extent possible, should be subpopulation invariant. These subpopulations should not be defined on the basis of the tests to be equated or the anchor test because the assumptions made by equating methods are sensitive to direct selection on the test or anchor.

One way to demonstrate that two tests are not equatable is to show that the equating functions used to link their scores are not invariant across different subpopulations of test takers. Lack of invariance in a linking function indicates that the differential difficulty of the two tests is not consistent across different groups. Note that subpopulation invariance is a matter of degree. In the situations where equating is usually performed, subpopulation invariance implies that the dependence of the equating function on the subpopulation used to compute it is small enough to be ignored.

Score Equity Assessment (SEA) focuses on whether or not test scores on different forms that are expected to be used interchangeably are in fact interchangeable across different subpopulations (Dorans & Liu, 2009; Liu & Dorans, 2013). It uses the subpopulation invariance of linking functions across important subgroups (e.g., gender groups) to assess the degree of score exchangeability. SEA focuses on invariance at the reported score level. It is a basic quality control tool that can be used to assess whether a test construction process is under control, as can checks on the consistency of raw-to-scale conversions across forms (Haberman, Guo, Liu, & Dorans, 2008).

Are the results reasonable?

An equating should be checked for its reasonableness. How do we determine reasonableness? We compare the raw-to-scale conversion for the new form to those that have been obtained in the past. Is the new form conversion an outlier? Is it consistent with other difficulty information that may be available for that form and other forms that have been administered in the past? Is the performance of the group taking the new form consistent with the performance of other groups that are expected to be similar to it? For example, in testing programs with large volumes and relatively stable populations, it is reasonable to expect that the new form sample will have a similar scale score distribution to that obtained at the same time the year before. If the test is used to certify mastery, then the pass rates should be relatively stable from year to year, though not necessarily across administrations within a year.

Score Linking: Prediction, Scale Aligning, Score Equating

The term equating is used too loosely, resulting in misinterpretations of score linking results. Several frameworks have been suggested for organizing the different types of links/uses that occur in practice. These can be found in Flanagan (1951), Angoff (1971), Mislevy (1992), Linn (1993), Feuer, Holland, Green, Bertenthal, and Hemphill (1999), and Dorans (2000, 2004a). Kolen (2004) and Kolen and Brennan (2004) contained reviews and syntheses of several frameworks.

Holland and Dorans (2006) provided their own framework that built on and clarified this prior work. They divided linking methods into three basic categories called *predicting, scale aligning,* and *equating*. It is important to distinguish between these categories because they are often seen as similar or identical when, in fact, they are not. The distinctions between different types of linkages are related to the similarities and differences between the tests as well as to the ways in which the linked scores are intended to be used and interpreted. The terms used for the various methods of score linking should have restricted meanings so that they may be used with precision. Understanding the distinctions among these categories can prevent violations of professional practice.

Predicting

Predicting, the oldest form of score linking, has been confused with equating from the earliest days of psychometrics. The goal of predicting is to minimize errors of prediction of a score on the dependent or criterion variable from information on other predictor variables. This goal guarantees an asymmetry between what is being predicted and what is used to make the prediction. This asymmetry prevents prediction from meeting one of the fundamental prerequisites of equating, the goal of which is to produce scores that can be used interchangeably. Holland and Dorans (2006) provided an introduction to prediction and the related procedure called projection for those who wish to explore these approaches and discuss their inappropriateness for score equating.

Scale aligning

The goal of scale aligning is to transform the scores from two different tests onto a common scale. Scaling procedures are about 100 years old. Scale aligning and score equating are often confused because the statistical procedures used for scale alignment can also be used to equate tests. As a consequence of this procedural identity, some view the distinction between equating and scale aligning (as well as distinctions among different types of scale aligning) as unnecessary because the numerical procedures used for scale aligning can also be used for score equating (Livingston, 2004; van der Linden, 2013). Dorans (2013) maintained that the distinctions made by Holland and Dorans (2006) framework and other frameworks refer to the meanings that can be legitimately attached to the outcomes of numerical operations, not to the operations themselves. For example, it is easy to align distributions of height and weight in a specified population, and assign them to a common scale: for example, largeness, such that a largeness unit of height is as far above the average height as a largeness unit of weight is above the average weight. That numerical alignment, however, does not mean that a largeness unit of height is equal in meaning to a largeness unit of weight.

Scale aligning has many subcategories, including activities such as *battery scaling* (Kolen, 2004), *anchor scaling* (Holland & Dorans, 2006), *vertical scaling* (Harris, 2007; Kolen & Brennan, 2004; Patz & Yao, 2007; Yen, 2007), *calibration* (Holland & Dorans, 2006), and *concordance* (Pommerich & Dorans, 2004). For a fuller treatment of distinctions among scale alignment, see Holland and Dorans (2006). For a description of procedures for vertical scaling or linking and a discussion of its limitations see Kolen (2006).

Score equating

Score equating, the focus of this chapter, is the strongest form of linking between the scores on two tests. Score equating may be viewed as a form of scale aligning in which very strong requirements are placed on the tests being linked. While impossible to achieve in practice, ideal equating can be approximated well with the type of sound equating practices promoted by Dorans, Moses, and Eignor (2011).

The goal of equating is to produce a linkage between scores on two test forms such that the scores from each test form can be used as if they had come from the same test. Among other things, the two tests must measure the same construct at almost the same level of difficulty, with the same degree of reliability and come from the same blueprint or specifications. Test assembly practices and measurement conditions that help ensure the achievement of equating requirements were described on pages 574–578.

What constitutes an equating? Score equating is the first step in a two-step process for putting scores on a new test onto an existing scale used for reporting. The first step in the process is the raw-to-raw equating – the computations of the function that links raw scores on a new form or edition of test **X** to those of an old form of test **Y**. The second step is the conversion of these equated raw scores from **X** to the reporting scale. In practice, there is a scaling function that maps the raw scores of **Y** to the reporting scale, call it $S = s(y)$. In the section on scale definition, I discussed how scales can be established. After the score equating step, the equating function, $y = e(x)$, is composed with $s(y)$ to put the raw scores of **X** onto the reporting scale. The composition function, $S = s(e(x))$, is called the scaling function for **X**.

All methods for linking test scores include: (1) two or more tests and rules for scoring them, such as those described on pages 578–585. (2) scores on these tests obtained by one or more samples of test takers, obtained via data collection methods as described on pages 585–588, and (3) one or more procedure for computing the transformation function, as described on pages 588–598. In addition, they all specify either an implicit or explicit population of test takers to which the test linking is to be applied. The thing that distinguishes test equating from other forms of linking is its goal. The goal of score equating is to allow the scores from both tests to be used interchangeably. Experience has shown that the two tests and the methods used to link them must satisfy very strong requirements to achieve it.

Five requirements for equated scores There are five requirements that are widely viewed as necessary for a linking to be an equating. Those requirements are:

1 *The Equal Construct Requirement*: The two tests should both be measures of the same construct (latent trait, skill, ability).
2 *The Equal Reliability Requirement*: The two tests should have the same reliability.
3 *The Symmetry Requirement*: The equating transformation for mapping the scores of **Y** to those of **X** should be the **inverse** of the equating transformation for mapping the scores of **X** to those of **Y**.
4 *The Equity Requirement*: It should be a matter of indifference to a test taker to be tested by either of the tests that have been equated.
5 *The Population Invariance Requirement*: The equating function used to link the scores of **X** and **Y** should be the same regardless of the choice of (sub)population from which it is derived.

Statements of these five requirements (or subsets) appear in a variety of earlier sources including Angoff (1971), Lord (1980), Petersen et al. (1989), Kolen and Brennan (2004), and Holland and Dorans (2006). These five requirements have value as criteria for evaluating whether or not two tests can be, or have been, successfully equated. In practice, requirements (1) and (2) mean that the tests need to be built to the same content and statistical specifications. Requirement (3) excludes the use of regression methods for test equating. Requirement (4) may be used to explain why both (1) and (2) are needed (Lord, 1980). If the two tests measure different constructs, test takers will prefer the one on which they believe they will score higher. Requirement (4) is, however, hard to evaluate empirically and its use is primarily theoretical (Lord, 1980; Hanson, 1991). Requirement (5) is easy to assess in practice and can be used to explain why requirements (1) and (2) are needed. Dorans and Holland (2000) used requirement (5), rather than requirement (4) to develop quantitative measures of equitability that indicate the degree to which equating functions depend on the subpopulations used to estimate them.

Holland and Dorans (2006) described how prediction fares with respect to these five criteria. Requirement (3) is obviously violated because the expected value of **Y** given **X** is not equal to the inverse of the expected value of **X** given **Y**. Prediction can be used in settings in which (1), (2), and (4) are violated, and there are settings where prediction makes use of the fact that (5) is violated, for example, when subgroup membership is used as a predictor.

Closing Comment

The following quote summarizes the motivation for this chapter.

> The comparability of measurements made in differing circumstances by different methods and investigators is a fundamental pre-condition for all of science. Psychological and educational measurement is no exception to this rule. Test equating techniques are those statistical and psychometric methods used to adjust scores obtained on different tests measuring the same construct so that they are comparable. (Dorans and Holland, 2000, p. 281)

In high-stakes settings, all test takers should be given an opportunity to maximize their performance under fair measurement conditions. Some aspects of fairness lie outside the locus of control of test developers, such as opportunity to learn, quality of teaching, and test-taker motivation. Some components, however, can and should be controlled by the test developer and test administrator. Multiple versions of a test should be as parallel as possible. Score reliability should be large enough to justify the trust that users place in the scores. Test instructions should be clear and widely accessible to prospective test takers. Scores across different versions of the test should be as equivalent as possible.

Scoring, scale definition, and score linking are important to ensuring interchangeability. This chapter focused on scores, the scales on which they are reported and the means by which scores are linked for testing programs that develop multiple forms of tests that are used in high-stakes assessments. The first section dealt with what is meant by measurement, the importance of controlling for the influence of measurement conditions, and the critical need for well-defined content and statistical specifications. Different types of scores were discussed in the second section. The third section addressed scale definition. The fourth section was concerned with the most common data collection designs in equating. In the fifth section, various methods and procedures for forming linking and equating functions between observed scores on complete tests were described. The section after that distinguished score equating from other forms of scale aligning, highlighting important differences in score interpretation that are needed to ensure proper score use.

References

American Educational Research Association, American Psychological Association, & National Council on Measurement in Education (2014). *Standards for educational and psychological testing*. Washington, DC: AERA.

Angoff, W. H. (1971). Scales, norms and equivalent scores. In R. L. Thorndike (Ed.), *Educational measurement* (2nd ed.) (pp. 508–600). Washington D.C.: American Council on Education.

Ayer, A. J. (1936). *Language, truth and logic*. London, England: Gollancz.

Braun, H. I., & Holland, P. W. (1982). Observed-score test equating: A mathematical analysis of some ETS equating procedures. In P. W. Holland and D. B. Rubin (Eds.), *Test equating* (pp. 9–49). New York: Academic.

Brennan, R. L. (1992). The context of context effects. *Applied Measurement in Education*, 5(3), 225–264.

Coombs, C. H., Dawes, R. M., & Tversky, A. (1970). *Mathematical psychology: An elementary introduction*. Englewood Cliffs, NJ: Prentice-Hall.

Davey, T., & Hendrickson, A. (2010, May). *Classical versus IRT statistical test specifications for building test forms*. Paper presented at the annual meeting of the National Council on Measurement in Education, Denver, CO. Retrieved August 21, 2010 from http://professionals.collegeboard.com/profdownload/pdf/Davey_Hendrickson_NC ME_2010_Test_specs.pdf (accessed September 2017).

Dorans, N. J. (2000). *Distinctions among classes of linkages* (College Board Research Note RN-11). New York: The College Board.

Dorans, N. J. (2002). Recentering and realigning the SAT score distributions: How and why. *Journal of Educational Measurement*, 39(1), 59–84.

Dorans, N. J. (Ed.). (2004a). Equating, concordance and expectation. *Applied Psychological Measurement*, 28, 227–246.

Dorans, N. J. (2004b). Profiles in research: Ledyard R Tucker. *Journal of Educational and Behavioral Statistics*, 29(1), 145–151.

Dorans, N. J. (2012). The contestant perspective on taking tests: Emanations from the statue within. *Educational Measurement: Issues and Practice*, 31(4), 20–37.

Dorans, N. J. (2013). On attempting to do what Lord said was impossible: Commentary on van der Linden's conceptual issues in observed-score equating. *Journal of Educational Measurement*, 50(3), 304–314.

Dorans, N. J., & Holland, P. J. (2000). Population invariance and the equitability of tests: Basic theory and the linear case. *Journal of Educational Measurement*, 37(4), 281–306.

Dorans, N.J., Liang, L. & Puhan, G. (2010). *Aligning scales of certification tests*. (ETS Research Report No. RR-10–07). Princeton, NJ: Educational Testing Service.

Dorans, N. J. & Liu, J. (2009). *Score equity assessment: Development of a prototype analysis using SAT Mathematics test data across several administrations* (ETS Research Report No. RR-09–08). Princeton, NJ: Educational Testing Service.

Dorans, N. J., & Middleton, K. (2012). Addressing the extreme assumptions of presumed linkings. *Journal of Educational Measurement*, 49(1), 1–18.

Dorans, N. J., Moses, T., & Eignor, D. E. (2011). Equating test scores: Towards best practices. In A. A. von Davier (Ed.), *Statistical models for scaling, equating and linking* (pp. 21–42). New York: Springer-Verlag.

Dorans, N. J., & Walker, M. E. (2013). Multiple test forms for large scale assessments: Making the real more ideal via empirically verified assessment. In K. F. Geisinger, B. A. Bracken, J. F. Carlson, J. C. Hansen, N. R. Kuncel, S. P. Reise, & M. C. Rodriguez (Eds.). *APA handbook of testing and assessment in psychology, Volume 3: Testing and assessment in school psychology and education*. (pp. 495–515) Washington, D.C.: American Psychological Association.

Ebel, R. L. (1962). Content standard test scores. *Educational & Psychological Measurement*, 22(1), 15–25.

Fairbank, B. A. (1987). The use of presmoothing and postsmoothing to increase the precision of equipercentile equating. *Applied Psychological Measurement, 11,* 245–262.

Feuer, M. J., Holland, P. W., Green, B. F., Bertenthal, M. W., & Hemphill, F. C. (Eds.). (1999). *Uncommon measures: Equivalence and linkage among educational tests* (Report of the Committee on Equivalency and Linkage of Educational Tests, National Research Council). Washington D.C.: National Academy Press.

Flanagan, J. C. (1951). Units, scores, and norms. In E. F. Lindquist (Ed.), *Educational measurement* (pp. 695–763). Washington DC: American Council on Education.

Forsyth, R. A. (1991). Do NAEP scales yield valid criterion-referenced interpretations? *Educational Measurement: Issues & Practice, 10*(3), 3–9, 16.

Freeman, M. F., & Tukey, J. W. (1950). Transformations related to the angular and square root. *Annals of Mathematical Statistics, 21,* 607–611.

Guttman, L. (1941) The quantification of a class of attributes: a theory and method of scale construction. In Social Science Research Council (U.S.). Committee on Social Adjustment. (1941). *The prediction of personal adjustment: A survey of logical problems and research techniques, with illustrative application to problems of vocational selection, school success, marriage, and crime.* New York: Social Science Research Council.

Haberman, S. (2011). Use of e-rater® in scoring of the TOEFL iBT® writing test.

Haberman, S. Guo, H., Liu, J., & Dorans, N. J. (2008). *Trend analysis in seasonal time series models. Consistency of SAT® reasoning score conversions* (ETS-RR-08-67). Princeton, NJ: Educational Testing Service.

Hambleton, R. K., & Pitoniak, M. J. (2006). Setting performance standards. In R. L. Brennan (Ed.), *Educational measurement* (4th ed.) (pp. 433–470). Westport, CT: American Council on Education/Praeger.

Hanson, B. A. (1991). A note on Levine's formula for equating unequally reliable tests using data from the common item nonequivalent groups design. *Journal of Educational Statistics, 16,* 93–100.

Harris, D. J. (2007). Practical issues in vertical scaling. In, N. J. Dorans, M. Pommerich, & P. W. Holland (Eds.), *Linking and aligning scores and scales* (pp. 233–251). New York: Springer-Verlag.

Harris, D. J., & Gao, X. (2003, April). *A conceptual synthesis of context effect.* In *Context effects: Implications for pretesting and CBT.* Symposium conducted at the 2003 annual meeting of the American Educational Research Association, Chicago, IL.

Holland, P. W., & Dorans, N. J. (2006). Linking and equating. In R. L. Brennan (Ed.), *Educational measurement* (4th ed.) (pp. 187–220). Westport, CT: American Council on Education/Prager.

Holland P. W., & Hoskens, M. (2003). Classical test theory as a first-order item response theory: application to true-score prediction from a possibly nonparallel test. *Psychometrika, 68,* 123–149.

Holland, P. W., & Thayer, D. T. (1987). *Notes on the use of log-linear model for fitting discrete probability distribution (ETS RR 87–31).* Princeton, NJ: Educational Testing Service.

Holland, P. W., & Thayer, D. T. (2000). Univariate and bivariate loglinear models for discrete test score distributions. *Journal of Educational and Behavioral Statistics, 25,* 133–183.

Holland, P. W., & Wainer, H. (1993). *Differential item functioning.* Hillsdale, NJ: Erlbaum.

Jarjoura, D. (1985). Tolerance intervals for true scores. *Journal of Educational Statistics, 10*(1), 1–17.

Jones, L. V. (1971). *The nature of measurement.* In E. F. Lindquist (Ed.), *Educational measurement* (pp. 335–355). Washington D.C.: American Council on Education.

Kahneman, D. (2011). *Thinking, fast and slow.* New York: Farrar, Strauss and Giroux.

Kane, M. T. (2006). Validation. In R. L. Brennan (Ed.), *Educational measurement* (4th ed.) (pp. 17–64). Westport, CT: American Council on Education/Prager.

Kolen, M. J. (1988). Defining score scales in relation to measurement error. *Journal of Educational Measurement, 25*(2), 97–110.

Kolen, M. J. (2004). Population invariance in equating and linking: Concept and history. *Journal of Educational Measurement, 41*, 3–14.

Kolen, M. J. (2006) Scaling and norming. In R. L. Brennan (Ed.), *Educational measurement* (4th ed.) (pp. 155–186). Westport, CT: American Council on Education/Prager.

Kolen, M. J., & Brennan, R. L. (2004). *Test equating, scaling, and linking: Methods and practices* (2nd ed.). New York: Springer.

Kolen, M. J., Hansen, B. A., & Brennan, R. L. (1992). Conditional standard errors of measurement for scaled scores. *Journal of Educational Measurement, 29*, 285–307.

Kolen, M. J., & Jarjoura, D. (1987). Analytic smoothing for equipercentile equating under the common item nonequivalent populations design. *Psychometrika, 52*, 43–59.

Kolen, M. J., Zeng, L., & Hanson, B. A. (1996). Conditional standard errors of measurement for scale scores using IRT. *Journal of Educational Measurement, 33*(2), 129–140.

Krantz, D. H., Luce, R. D., Suppes, P., & Tversky, A. (1971). *Foundations of measurement, Volume I: Additive and polynomial representations.* New York: Academic Press.

Leary, L. F., & Dorans, N. J. (1985). Implications for altering the context in which test items appear: An historical perspective on an immediate concern. *Review of Educational Research, 55*, 387–413

Liang, L., Dorans, N. J., & Sinharay, S. (2009). First language of examinees and its relationship to equating. *(ETS RR-09–05)*. Princeton, NJ: Educational Testing Service.

Linn, R. L. (1993). Linking results of distinct assessments. *Applied Measurement in Education, 6*, 83–102.

Liou, M., Cheng, P. E., & Li, M. Y. (2001). Estimating comparable scores using surrogate variables. *Applied Psychological Measurement, 25*, 197–207.

Little, R. J. A., & Rubin, D. B. (2002). *Statistical analysis with missing data* (2nd ed.). Hoboken NJ: John Wiley & Sons, Inc.

Liu, J., & Dorans, N. J. 2013). Assessing a critical aspect of construct continuity when test specifications change or test forms deviate from specifications. *Educational Measurement: Issues and Practice, 32*(1), 15–22.

Livingston, S. A. (2004). *Equating test scores (without IRT).* Princeton, NJ: Educational Testing Service.

Lord, F. M. (1950). *Notes on comparable scales for test scores* (ETS RB-50–48). Princeton, NJ: Educational Testing Service.

Lord, F. M. (1980). *Applications of item response theory to practical testing problems.* Hillsdale, NJ: Erlbaum.

Lord, F. M., & Wingersky, M. S. (1984). Comparison of IRT true-score and equipercentile observed-score equatings. *Applied Psychological Measurement, 8*, 453–461.

Lorge, I. (1951). The fundamental nature of measurement. In E. F. Lindquist (Ed.), *Educational measurement* (pp. 533–539). Washington D.C.: American Council on Education.

McCall, W. A. (1939). *Measurement.* New York, NY: Macmillan.

Mislevy, R. J. (1992). *Linking educational assessments: Concepts, issues, methods, and prospects.* Princeton, NJ: Educational Testing Service, Policy Information Center.

Mislevy, R. J., Almond, R. G., & Lukas, J. F. (2003). *A brief introduction to evidence-centered design* (Educational Testing Service Research Report RR-03–16). Princeton, NJ: Educational Testing Service.

Mislevy, R. J., & Haertel, G. D. (2006). Implications of evidence-centered design for educational testing. *Educational Measurement: Issues and Practice, 25*(4), 6–20.

Mislevy, R. J., Steinberg, L. S, & Almond, R. G. (2002). On the roles of task model variables in assessment design. In S. Irvine & P. Kyllonen (Eds.). *Generating items for cognitive tests: Theory and practice* (pp. 97–128). Hillsdale, NJ: Erlbaum.

Moses, T., & Holland, P. (2007). Kernel and traditional equipercentile equating with degrees of presmoothing (Educational Testing Service Research Report RR-07–15). Princeton, NJ: Educational Testing Service.

Moses, T., & Zhang, W. (2011). Standard errors of equating differences: Prior developments, extensions, and simulations. *Journal of Educational and Behavioral Statistics, 36,* 779–803.

Patz, R. J., & Yao, L. (2007). Methods and models for vertical scaling. In N. J. Dorans, M. Pommerich, & P. W. Holland (Eds.), *Linking and aligning scores and scales* (pp. 253–272). New York: Springer-Verlag.

Pellegrino, J. W., Jones, L. R., & Mitchell, K. J. (1999). *Grading the nation's report card: Evaluating NAEP and transforming the assessment of educational progress.* Washington, D.C.: National Academy Press.

Petersen, N. S., Kolen, M. J., & Hoover, H. D. (1989). Scaling, norming, and equating. In R. L. Linn (Ed.). *Educational measurement* (3rd ed.) (pp. 221–262). New York: Macmillan.

Pommerich, M., & Dorans, N. J. (Eds.). (2004). Concordance [Special issue]. *Applied Psychological Measurement, 28*(4).

Rasch, G. (1960/1980). *Probabilistic models for some intelligence and attainment tests.* (Copenhagen, Danish Institute for Educational Research), expanded ed. (1980) with foreword and afterword by B. D. Wright. Chicago: The University of Chicago Press.

Rosenbaum, P. R. (1995). *Observational studies.* New York: Springer-Verlag.

Sinharay, S. (2013, April). Contributions of Paul W. Holland. In *A look at our psychometric history: Contributions of Thurstone, Lindquist, Anastasi, Bock, Messick, and Holland.* Symposium conducted at the annual meeting of the National Council on Measurement in Education, San Francisco, CA.

Snow, E., Fulkerson, D., Feng, M., Nichols, P., Mislevy, R., & Haertel, G., (2010). *Leveraging evidence-centered design in large-scale test development.* (Large- Scale Assessment Technical Report 4). Menlo Park, CA: SRI International. Retrieved August 21, 2010 from http://ecd.sri.com/downloads/ECD_TR4_Leveraging_ECD_FL.pdf (accessed September 2017).

Thissen, D., & Wainer, H. (Eds.). (2001). *Test scoring.* Mahwah, NJ: Erlbaum.

Thurstone, L. L. (1919). A method for scoring tests. *Psychological Bulletin, 16,* 235–240.

Torgerson W. S. (1958) *Theory and methods of scaling.* New York: John Wiley & Sons, Inc.

Tukey, J. W. (1963). Mathematics 596 – An introduction to the frequency analysis of time series. In D. R. Brillinger (Ed.), *The collected works of John W. Tukey, Volume I: Time series, 1949–1964.* London: Chapman & Hall.

van der Linden, W. J. (2013). Conceptual issues in observed-score equating. *Journal of Educational Measurement, 50*(3), 249–285.

von Davier, A. A., Holland, P. W., & Thayer, D. T. (2004). *The kernel method of test equating.* New York: Springer.

Wendler, C., & Walker, M. E. (2006). Practical issues in designing and maintaining multiple test forms for large-scale programs. In S. M. Downing & T. M. Haladyna (Eds.). *Handbook of test development* (pp. 445–467). Mahwah, NJ: Lawrence Erlbaum.

Wilcox, R. R. (1981). A review of the beta-binomial model and its extensions. *Journal of Educational Statistics, 6*(1), 3–32.

Williamson, D. M., Xi, X., & Breyer, F. J. (2012). A framework for evaluation and use of automated scoring. *Educational Measurement: Issues and Practice, 31*(1), 2–13.

Yen, W. M. (2007). Vertical scaling and no child left behind. In N. J. Dorans, M. Pommerich, & P. W. Holland (Eds.), *Linking and aligning scores and scales* (pp. 273–283). New York: Springer-Verlag.

Zwick, R., Senturk, D., Wang, J., & Loomis, S. C. (2001). An investigation of alternative methods for item mapping in the National Assessment of Educational Progress. *Educational Measurement: Issues and Practice, 20*(2), 12–25.

20

Item Response Theory Approaches to Test Scoring and Evaluating the Score Accuracy

Anna Brown

The ultimate goal of psychological measurement is to produce a score by which people can be assessed and differentiated. Item Response Theory (IRT) views test items as a series of small experiments, "from which a measure is inferred" (van der Linden & Hambleton, 1997). In IRT, responses to test items serve as indicators of a person's standing on some underlying psychological construct or constructs, and devises special algorithms for determining that standing. The purpose of this chapter is to give an overview of IRT methods for inferring person's scores on the psychological constructs of interest, often referred to as **abilities**, **proficiencies**, or **traits** (we will call them **traits**).

To be useful in applications, the score must infer the person standing on the trait continuum accurately, and importantly, the precision level must be known for decision-making purposes. IRT has many advantages over Classical Test Theory (CTT) in estimating both the score and its precision. With IRT, we can control for properties of test items – such as difficulty or liability to guessing – making the score independent of these nuisance factors. With IRT, we can also drop unattainable assumptions of continuity for dichotomous test items (correct-incorrect, or yes-no), and of equal intervals in rating categories (e.g., 5-point scales with response options ranging from "strongly disagree" to "strongly agree"). Treating categorical item responses appropriately brings the test scores much closer to the interval level of measurement so that the standard statistics can be applied to them. With IRT, we can also drop an unattainable assumption that the precision of test scores is a single value that holds for a sample, and assess the measurement precision for each individual response pattern. In many testing contexts, knowing the measurement precision associated with a particular pattern (and score) enables better judgments about significance of difference between any two respondents, or any change occurring in scores, for instance in response to treatment, and so on (Reise & Haviland, 2005). At the same time, we often need to summarize the overall precision of measurement in a research sample, or in the population as a whole – and IRT provides methods for that too.

In this chapter, we attempt to make these methods more readily available to students and researchers by providing formulas for scoring and precision estimation suitable for most commonly used models – a single factor model, a correlated factor model, and a

---

The Wiley Handbook of Psychometric Testing: A Multidisciplinary Reference on Survey, Scale and Test Development, First Edition. Edited by Paul Irwing, Tom Booth, and David J. Hughes.
© 2018 John Wiley & Sons Ltd. Published 2020 by John Wiley & Sons Ltd.

bifactor model. All described methods are illustrated with a single data analysis example involving a short patient satisfaction measure, the Experience of Service Questionnaire (ESQ), completed by parents of children treated for mental health problems.

The Multidimensional Item Response Model

Psychometric tests often necessitate the capture of several related constructs. For example, several cognitive facets, which are correlated with each other, might be of interest. In mental health measures, we might be interested in capturing several distinct areas of functioning, which might also form an overall domain. To devise scoring methods suitable for all such measures, multidimensional factor models are recommended (Gibbons, Immekus, & Bock, 2007). In this section, we provide a brief overview of the core concepts of IRT and some general references necessary for this chapter. For a more detailed introduction, see Chapter 17.

Let $\theta = (\theta_1, \theta_2, \ldots, \theta_T)$ (pronounced "**theta**") be a set of T unobserved, or **latent** traits (we may also call them abilities, proficiencies, constructs or dimensions) measured by a psychometric test. In the simplest case $T = 1$, and we deal with a test measuring just one trait. Such models are generally referred to as **unidimensional** models (see Chapter 16). In all other cases, $T > 1$ and models are referred to as **multidimensional**. In both cases, the latent traits are assumed normally distributed, have mean zero and unit variance. In multidimensional models, latent traits may also be correlated, with their covariance matrix denoted Σ (pronounced "sigma").

Each test item is designed to measure one or more traits (usually one, but we will see that cases when an item contributes to measurement of two traits are quite common). An item elicits an internal response from a participant. To describe this internal item response, we use the notion of **response tendency**. The **unobserved** response tendency is most likely a complex process within individuals, which we cannot access or measure directly. Instead, we assess an **observed** item response u_i. Observed item responses are sometimes dichotomous ("yes" – "no," "agree" – "disagree"), and often polytomous ("never" – "sometimes" – "often" – "always"; or "strongly disagree" – "disagree" – "neutral" – "agree" – "strongly agree" etc.). From dichotomous responses, we do not know the exact extent of agreement with a statement; all we know is that the respondent picked "agree" out of two available response options. Although the polytomous options provide more opportunities to quantify the extent of agreement, the exact level of internal agreement (the response tendency) is not observed – only its categorization into one of response options is observed.

The observed response u_i relates to the unobserved response tendency u_i^* through a threshold process. There is one threshold when two response alternatives are used. When the response tendency is above the threshold, the keyed response $u_i = 1$ is given; and when the response tendency is below the threshold, the nonkeyed response $u_i = 0$ is given. In addition, we assume that the unobserved response tendency u_i^* is caused by one or more traits and can be described by a linear factor model of Spearman (the response tendency is a linear function of one or more thetas). For example, the tendency to solve a problem on a mathematics test increases as the mathematical ability increases; and if the solution achieved for this problem is enough to provide the answer (the response tendency is above the threshold), the correct response is given.

For ease of exposition, in what follows we give formulas for the dichotomous case, mentioning how to extend them to polytomous cases in passing. Polytomous models can be achieved by considering the probability of choosing (or otherwise) each response option, as is done in, for example, a graded response approach (Samejima, 1969), or a partial credit model (Masters & Wright, 1997). Not one but several thresholds are considered in this case ($k-1$ where k is the number of options), each representing a boundary between selecting one of the two adjacent response categories.

Dichotomous events such as passing/failing a test item are commonly described in terms of their probability, which directly depends on the response tendency – and consequently on the latent trait or traits. The probability of passing a mathematics item, for example, increases as the ability increases. This increase is not linear but s-shaped, with slow increases of the probability of passing at the extremes of ability scale, and more rapid increase in the range of the item threshold. A well-known function with the needed shape that is commonly used to describe the link between the probability and the response tendency is the cumulative standard normal distribution function (aka **normal ogive**).

With this, the **item response function** (IRF) for item i measuring T traits is given by

$$P_i = P(u_i = 1|\theta) = \Phi(-\tau_i + \beta_{i1}\theta_1 + \ldots + \beta_{iT}\theta_T), \quad (20.1)$$

where τ_i is the item **threshold**, and β_{ki} is the **slope** for k-th trait – describing how fast the probability of the keyed response changes with the unit change in trait k^1. $\Phi(x)$ denotes the cumulative standard normal distribution function evaluated at x. Without loss of generality, we use the normal-ogive (or **probabilistic**) link function here. Alternatively, the **logistic** link function $L(x) = 1/(1 + e^{-x})$ can be used (Reckase, 2009).

This general model allows items to measure any combination of T traits by having nonzero slopes on some traits and zero on others. Thus, we can easily accommodate the simplest situation when each test item indicates only one trait – the model possesses an **independent-clusters** structure (McDonald, 1999) – but the test overall may measure more than one trait.

Latent Trait Estimation

In IRT, the latent trait scores θ can be estimated by treating the model parameters (item threshold and slopes, and the correlations between traits) as if they were known. This is reasonable if model parameters have been accurately estimated. When the item and other model parameters are known, the IRF depends only on the latent traits, and the fundamental approach to estimating the trait scores is to search for values that maximize the likelihood of the observed pattern of responses $\mathbf{u} = (u_1, u_2, \ldots, u_m)$ to all m items in the test. To proceed with the estimation, we make an assumption of **local independence**, which states that in a subpopulation where the latent traits take fixed values (a subpopulation of people who have the same latent trait scores) the item responses are independent.

---

[1] This parameterization is convenient with multidimensional IRT models. With unidimensional models, an alternative IRT parameterization is often used, whereby the item *discrimination* a_i and *difficulty* b_i are defined so that $P_i = \Phi(a_i[\theta - b_i])$. Thus, the discrimination is equivalent to the slope, and the difficulty equals the threshold divided by the slope.

Given that the item responses are independent (conditional on the latent traits), it is easy to express the probability of the observed pattern as the product of probabilities of the responses to individual items. For items to which the keyed response ($u_i = 1$) was given, the probability P_i is given by (20.1). For items to which the nonkeyed response ($u_i = 0$) was given, the probability is $Q_i = 1 - P_i$. The **maximum likelihood** (ML) scores are found iteratively by searching for a set of trait scores θ that maximize the **likelihood function** – the product of the probabilities of all given responses:

$$l(u_1, u_2, \ldots, u_m | \theta) = \prod_{u_i = 1} P_i(\theta) \prod_{u_i = 0} (1 - P_i(\theta)). \quad (20.2)$$

ML scores only use information contained in the item responses, and therefore are philosophically uncontroversial (McDonald, 2011). They, however, are undefined for some response patterns, notably for "perfect" patterns when the respondent gave keyed responses to all items (for instance by answering "yes" or selecting the top rating category such as "strongly agree"). This situation is illustrated in Figure 20.1(a), where probabilities of observed responses to two test items conditional on the latent trait are shown, as well as the joint likelihood of these responses. In this case, the ML estimate does not exist because the joint likelihood increases infinitely when the latent trait score increases.[2] The score is also undefined when nonkeyed responses are given to all items (for instance by answering "no" or selecting "strongly disagree").

To avoid this indeterminacy and improve estimation efficiency, prior information about the trait score distribution may be used in addition to the observed item responses. The basis for incorporating this information is given by the Bayes theorem that, applied to the scoring problem, suggests that the probability of observing a particular ability level (theta score) given the observed response pattern is the product of two probabilities: the probability of observing the assumed ability, and the probability of observing the response pattern given the ability. More formally, in a Bayesian approach, the likelihood of trait scores θ given the observed response pattern (**posterior likelihood** l_P) is computed by multiplying: (1) the likelihood of the observed response pattern given the trait scores θ, and (2) the likelihood of the theta scores occurring in the population (**prior** distribution; usually multivariate standard normal). The former is, of course, the likelihood (20.2) used in ML estimation, and the latter is the normal density function ϕ, thus

$$l_P(\theta | u_1, u_2, \ldots, u_m) = \phi(\theta) \prod_{u_i = 1} P_i(\theta) \prod_{u_i = 0} (1 - P_i(\theta)). \quad (20.3)$$

An example posterior likelihood function is given in Figure 20.1(b), where IRF for two test items are shown together with the normal density function, and the joint likelihood is the product of all three functions. In this case, the ML estimate exists because the posterior likelihood function has a single peak. By adding information from the assumed multivariate normal distribution of scores, the problem of undefined trait scores for perfect patterns is overcome, that is, a score is always defined when the Bayesian estimation is used.

---

[2] This is true for all item response functions where the probability of a keyed response is monotonously increasing or decreasing, a so-called dominance response process.

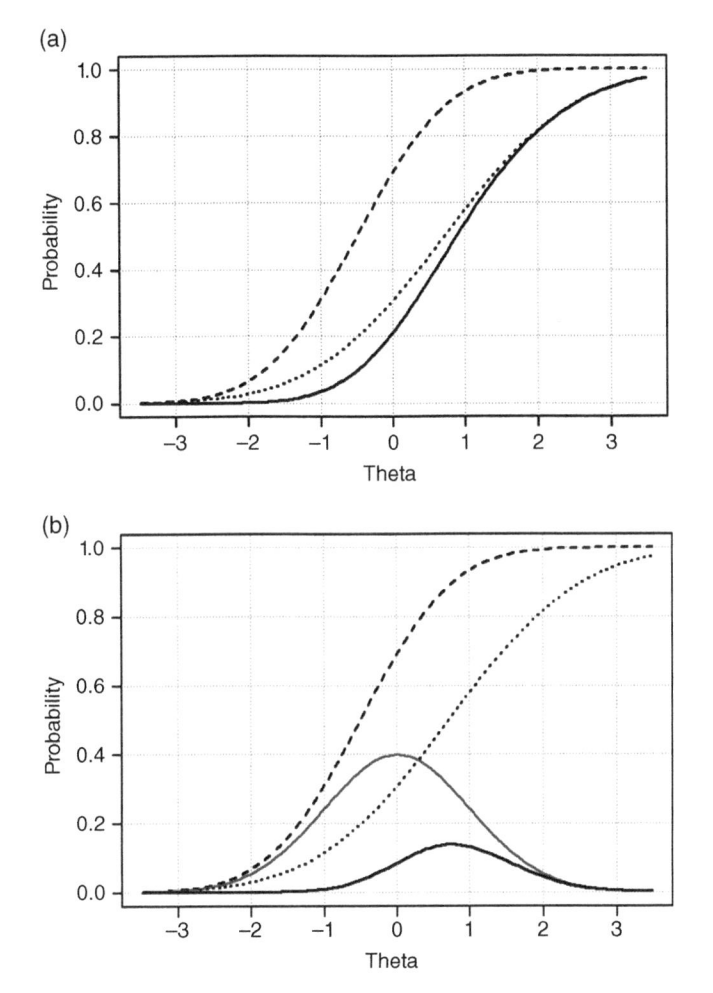

IRT Approaches to Test Scoring and Evaluating Score Accuracy

Figure 20.1 Example likelihood functions for two endorsed items (u1 = 1, u2 = 1) (a) Likelihood based on item responses only. (b) Likelihood based on item responses and population distribution (standard normal).
Note. The dashed line is the IRF for item 1; the dotted line is the IRF for item 2; the solid gray line is the normal density function; the solid black line in (a) is the total likelihood function, and in (b) it is the posterior likelihood function.

Two computational methods for test scoring using the Bayesian approach are (1) expected a posteriori (EAP) estimation, which computes the **mean** of the posterior distribution of the likelihood; and (2) maximum a posteriori (MAP) estimation, which computes **the mode** of the posterior distribution (Embretson & Reise, 2000). The EAP method is an excellent computational option for one-dimensional tests. The mean of the posterior likelihood is approximated taking "snapshots" of the continuous likelihood function at q points (**quadrature** points) selected along the latent trait continuum. Formula for computing the EAP scores for a single trait is given in Appendix A. In this formula, each quadrature point value θ_q is weighted by the value of the posterior likelihood function at that point, the weighted sum of all q points is computed, and then divided by the sum of weights. For this approximation of the mean value of the continuous distribution of the likelihood to be accurate, the choice of the quadrature points is important. The quadrature points are usually set at equal intervals, and a larger number of points would yield a more precise mean value. For a discussion regarding the number of points necessary for precise estimation, see Thissen and Orlando (2001).

The EAP score is easy to compute when only one dimension is involved. EAP estimation, however, becomes computationally demanding as the number of traits increases. This is because with two traits, one needs to sample q^2 quadrature points, for every combination of the theta values for trait 1 and trait 2. One needs to create a multidimensional grid of q^T points to compute an EAP score on T traits. Even with a small number of points on each trait continuum such as $q = 11$, the resulting number of points for two traits is manageable $q^2 = 121$; for five traits it is already $q^5 = 161,051$, and the number of points for 10 traits is almost 26 billion. Clearly, a less computationally demanding approach is needed in this case.

The MAP score corresponds to the mode of the posterior distribution. Finding a set of T trait scores that maximize the multidimensional posterior likelihood function requires iterative procedures using gradients. When $T = 1$ and only one trait is measured, this may be an unnecessary complication; however, in multidimensional models this estimation is much quicker than the EAP because it searches for the optimal set of theta values for all traits simultaneously and the number of iterations is not affected by the number of traits.

When an appropriate prior distribution is used, the Bayesian EAP and MAP approaches have been shown to achieve accurate estimates of the latent trait with fewer items than the ML method; however, they are known to shrink the latent trait distribution toward the population mean. In practice, this yields estimated scores with smaller variance than was assumed for the latent traits. The amount of shrinkage depends on several factors, including the test length, and can be quite substantial when the number of items in the test is small (Thissen & Orlando, 2001). Another concern with the use of Bayesian estimation methods is that when multivariate priors are used, correlated but conceptually distinct traits will influence each other's score estimates, or "borrow strength" from each other. Some authors, notably McDonald (2011, p. 535) argued against this inadvertent use of information on both philosophical and statistical grounds. Indeed, the fact that a person's ability in English may be judged by his/her results in mathematics may seem unjustified or even unfair. There are also measurement-related concerns with the use of multivariate priors, which we will discuss in due course.

Standard Error of Measurement, Test Information, and Reliability

The IRT scoring methods are only our best guess at estimating the true scores for people taking tests, and inevitably, all estimation methods are associated with a certain degree of error. The joint likelihood of the response pattern and the posterior likelihood functions describe probability values for a whole range of trait scores. These distributions are typically Gaussian in appearance and have a single peak (e.g., see Figure 20.1b). The mode (or the mean) of these distributions provides a limited summary of the likelihood function. The width or the spread of the likelihood, on the other hand, indicates the degree of uncertainty around the score estimation – the narrower the spread, the more confident we are that the true theta value is in close range of the estimated value. Responses that are less likely given the trait score, for instance an incorrect response to an easy question when ability is high, or a correct response to a difficult question when ability is low (so-called **aberrant** responses), will make the spread of likelihood values around the estimated theta wider. Responses that are in line with the estimated trait score will make the spread of likelihood values around the estimated theta narrower.

For approximately Gaussian distributions, the spread of the likelihood values is meaningfully described by the distribution's standard deviation. The standard deviation of the likelihood of the response pattern in ML estimation, or standard deviation of the posterior distribution in Bayesian estimation, therefore, is a measure of the **standard error** (SE) of measurement in IRT.

According to the estimation methods used, there are two main ways of computing the standard error of estimation. For the EAP estimator, it is natural to compute the standard deviation from the mean (which is the estimated EAP score) of the likelihood values taken at the quadrature points. Therefore, the standard error of the EAP estimator is based on direct evaluation of the standard deviation of the posterior distribution (the computational formula is given in Appendix A).

For the methods maximizing the mode of the likelihood function (ML and MAP), the variance of the likelihood function along the trait continuum θ is computed as the inverse of the **Fisher information** $\mathcal{I}$ (or simply **information**). The more information an item or a set of items provide for measuring latent traits, the more accurate the score estimation, and consequently, the smaller the standard error will be. For the **one-dimensional** case, the standard error of the estimated ML score $\hat{\theta}$ is

$$SE_{ML}(\hat{\theta}) = \frac{1}{\sqrt{\mathcal{I}(\hat{\theta})}}. \quad (20.4)$$

The standard error of the MAP score involves posterior information I_p (information provided by the test items together with the prior distribution) instead:

$$SE_{MAP}(\hat{\theta}) = \frac{1}{\sqrt{\mathcal{I}_P(\hat{\theta})}}. \quad (20.5)$$

In the **multidimensional** case, the standard error of the estimated ML score $\hat{\theta}_a$ involves computing the information in the direction of trait θ_a evaluated at the point-estimates $\hat{\boldsymbol{\theta}} = (\hat{\theta}_1, \hat{\theta}_2, \ldots, \hat{\theta}_T)$

$$SE^a(\hat{\boldsymbol{\theta}}) = \frac{1}{\sqrt{\mathcal{I}^a(\hat{\boldsymbol{\theta}})}}, \quad (20.6)$$

and the standard error of the MAP score $\hat{\theta}_a$ involves computing the posterior information in the direction of trait θ_a

$$SE^a_{MAP}(\hat{\boldsymbol{\theta}}) = \frac{1}{\sqrt{\mathcal{I}^a_P(\hat{\boldsymbol{\theta}})}}. \quad (20.7)$$

The following section shows how to compute the ML and the posterior information in both one-dimensional and multidimensional cases.

Item information function

When a test measures only **one trait**, the amount of information that item i provides toward measurement of the trait is given by the **item information function** (IIF)

$$\mathcal{I}_i(\theta) = \frac{[P_i'(\theta)]^2}{P_i(\theta)[1-P_i(\theta)]}, \qquad (20.8)$$

where $P_i'(\theta)$ denotes the first derivative of the IRF (McDonald, 1999). Because derivatives reflect the degree of change in the probability of the keyed response with change in the trait score, the item **slope** is at the heart of the information. At the theta value corresponding to steepest slope (in binary IRT models without guessing, this point corresponds to the item difficulty), the probability of keyed response in response to the change of theta changes faster than at any other point along the trait continuum. The item discriminates best around this theta value, or, in other words, provides most information for the trait estimation. Another theta value may correspond to a shallow slope, indicating little change in the probability of the keyed response in response to change in theta.

It can be seen that, unlike in classical psychometric test theory, the precision of measurement in IRT depends on the latent trait, and therefore on item responses. This means that persons with different item responses may potentially have scores estimated to different degrees of accuracy.

When we use the normal-ogive link, then the expression for IIF becomes

$$\mathcal{I}_i(\theta) = \frac{\beta_i^2 [\phi(-\tau_i + \beta_i\theta)]^2}{\Phi(-\tau_i + \beta_i\theta)[1-\Phi(-\tau_i + \beta_i\theta)]}, \qquad (20.9)$$

where $\Phi(x)$ denotes the cumulative standard normal distribution function; and $\phi(x)$ denotes the standard normal density function evaluated at x. The IIF is described by a curve conditional on the latent trait, and is sometimes called the **item information curve**.[3]

For items with graded response categories, the item information can be derived from category response curves as follows (Dodd, DeAyala, & Koch, 1995; Samejima, 1997):

$$\mathcal{I}_i(\theta) = \sum_{x=0}^{k} \frac{[P_{ix}'(\theta)]^2}{P_{ix}(\theta)}. \qquad (20.10)$$

---

[3] When we use the logistic link function $L(x)$, the information function amounts to

$$\mathcal{I}_i(\theta) = (D\beta_i)^2 L(-D\tau_i + D\beta_i\theta)[1-L(-D\tau_i + D\beta_i\theta)].$$

All formulae for item information involving the normal-ogive link function given further in this chapter can be adopted for the logistic link by using this expression. $D = 1.7$ is the scaling constant used with the normal ogive item parameters

When items contribute to measurement of **two or more latent traits**, the **direction** of information must be considered when computing the IIF (Ackerman, 2005; Reckase, 2009). Let **d** be a vector of angles $\mathbf{d} = (d_1, d_2, \ldots, d_T)$ to all T axes that defines the direction from a point $\boldsymbol{\theta}$ in the trait space. Then the information provided by item i in direction **d** is described by a surface

$$\mathcal{I}_i^{\mathbf{d}}(\boldsymbol{\theta}) = \frac{[\nabla_{\mathbf{d}} P_i(\boldsymbol{\theta})]^2}{P_i(\boldsymbol{\theta})[1 - P_i(\boldsymbol{\theta})]}, \quad (20.11)$$

where $\nabla_{\mathbf{d}} P_i(\boldsymbol{\theta})$ is the gradient in direction **d** given by (Reckase, 2009):

$$\nabla_{\mathbf{d}} P_i(\boldsymbol{\theta}) = \frac{\partial P_i(\boldsymbol{\theta})}{\partial \theta_1} \cos d_1 + \frac{\partial P_i(\boldsymbol{\theta})}{\partial \theta_2} \cos d_2 + \ldots + \frac{\partial P_i(\boldsymbol{\theta})}{\partial \theta_T} \cos d_T. \quad (20.12)$$

Test information function (TIF)

When local independence holds, the TIF for a trait can be computed as the sum of the IIFs contributing to measurement of the trait. In the **one-dimensional** case, the TIF is simply

$$\mathcal{I}(\theta) = \sum_{i=1}^{m} \mathcal{I}_i(\theta). \quad (20.13)$$

In the **multidimensional** case, the total information about trait θ_a is the sum of all IIFs in direction of that trait

$$\mathcal{I}^a(\boldsymbol{\theta}) = \sum_{i=1}^{m} \mathcal{I}_i^a(\boldsymbol{\theta}). \quad (20.14)$$

Note that some items might not contribute to measurement of the focus trait, as is the case with items forming an independent-clusters structure. Then, the item's slope on the trait is zero — and the information it contributes is also zero.

So far, we have only taken into account information provided by the item responses; that is, the ML information. However, when Bayesian estimation is used, prior information about distribution of the traits in the population will also contribute to the estimation of the latent trait. The total information from the item responses and the prior distribution is given by **posterior test information**, $\mathcal{I}_P$. For a **single trait**, a normally distributed prior with variance σ^2 adds $1/\sigma^2$ to the information uniformly across the latent trait continuum (Du Toit, 2003). Since we assumed the trait variance is unity, the posterior test information is

$$\mathcal{I}_P(\theta) = \mathcal{I}(\theta) + 1. \quad (20.15)$$

For **multiple traits**, the information given by the prior distribution is added to the multidimensional ML test information given in (20.14). Assuming the multivariate standard normal prior with correlation matrix Σ, the posterior test information is

$$\mathcal{I}_P^a(\boldsymbol{\theta}) = \mathcal{I}^a(\boldsymbol{\theta}) + \left[\Sigma^{-1}\right]_a, \quad (20.16)$$

where $\left[\Sigma^{-1}\right]_a$ is the ath diagonal element of the inverted trait correlation matrix, Σ^{-1} (e.g., Brown & Maydeu-Olivares, 2011). When all traits are uncorrelated, the term added to the ML test information in Equation (20.16) equals 1. When all the traits are correlated positively, the additional term is greater than 1 (and therefore the prior distribution contributes more information for the trait estimation).

Reliability

Reliability in CTT is defined as proportion of variance in the observed score due to the true score. This proportion is a single value within the sample on which the reliability is computed. Reliability is therefore sample-dependent, but independent of the test score in the classical account; it is the same for all people (and therefore test scores) within the same sample.

Information functions in IRT describe the precision of measurement provided by a test (and all its items) more completely than a single reliability coefficient. However, sometimes it is convenient in applications to summarize the information values into a single index. Such an index (rather than curves and surfaces) is more likely to appeal to, and be understood by, the test user, as it allows direct comparisons with CTT's reliability statistics. The reliability coefficient enables a quick evaluation of the test's overall measurement precision. Another important use for the reliability coefficient is predicting the relationship between the estimated and the true score, using

$$\text{corr}(\theta,\hat{\theta}) = \sqrt{\rho}. \qquad (20.17)$$

An appropriate index, **marginal reliability**, was suggested by Green, Bock, Humphreys, Linn, and Reckase (1984):

$$\rho = \frac{\text{var}[\theta] - \overline{SE^2}[\theta]}{\text{var}[\theta]} = 1 - \frac{\overline{SE^2}[\theta]}{\text{var}[\theta]}. \qquad (20.18)$$

This coefficient uses the classical definition of reliability as proportion of variance in the test score due to true score. The true score variance is computed as the test score variance minus error variance (squared standard error). The reliability increases as the standard error decreases; it approaches 1 as the standard error approaches 0.

There are two ways to compute the marginal reliability coefficient. **Theoretical reliability** (Du Toit, 2003) considers the theoretical distribution of the latent trait (which we assume standard normal), thus var[θ]=1, and formula (20.18) becomes

$$\rho = 1 - \overline{SE^2}[\theta], \qquad (20.19)$$

and the average squared standard error is the integral

$$\overline{SE^2}[\theta] = \int_{-\infty}^{\infty} SE^2(\theta)\phi(\theta)d\theta. \qquad (20.20)$$

The squared standard errors are computed for the theoretical distribution of the latent trait from the TIF using formula (20.4). In practice, the integral is approximated by evaluating the squared errors and the normal densities at multiple points taken at equal intervals along the trait continuum. The simple formula for theoretical reliability (20.19) allows connecting some established benchmarks for classical reliability with corresponding values of the IRT standard error and information. The reliability $\rho = .75$ corresponds to the squared standard error 0.25 ($SE = 0.5$), which in turn corresponds to information $I = 4$. The reliability $\rho = .90$ corresponds to the squared standard error 0.10 ($SE = 0.32$), which in turn corresponds to information $I = 10$.

An alternative approach to obtaining marginal reliability, **empirical reliability** (Du Toit, 2003), considers not a theoretical distribution of theta, but the estimated theta scores. For ML scores, formula (20.18) can still be applied. For shrunken Bayesian MAP and EAP scores, however, the true score variance is better approximated by the estimated score variance; and the observed variance is the sum of true and error variances:

$$\rho = \frac{\text{var}(\hat{\theta})}{\text{var}(\hat{\theta}) + SE^2(\hat{\theta})}. \tag{20.21}$$

Given a sample of N respondents, the trait variance is computed as the variance of the estimated theta score in the sample, and the average squared SE is computed by averaging the squared SEs of estimated theta scores $\hat{\theta}_j$ for each respondent j,

$$\overline{SE}^2[\hat{\theta}] = \frac{1}{N}\sum_{j=1}^{N} SE^2(\hat{\theta}_j). \tag{20.22}$$

The standard errors of person scores can be computed either using the standard deviation of the posterior likelihood (20.24) for the EAP score, or the inverse of Fisher information (20.5) for the ML or MAP score.

The empirical reliability is particularly quick and easy to compute when IRT software programs provide the standard errors for person scores as part of the scoring process. Since the observed score variance is known for the sample (it is simply the variance of the estimated scores), the empirical reliability can be easily computed. One simply needs to square the provided standard error values for all people, and compute the mean of the squared values to obtain the average error variance.

Applying IRT Scoring Methods and Estimating Measurement Accuracy in Practice

In this section, we show how person responses are scored and their standard errors are computed for a range of item response models popular in testing applications. Specifically, a unidimensional model, a correlated traits model, and a bifactor model are illustrated with a simple data analysis example.

Data example with the Experience of Service Questionnaire (ESQ)

Questionnaire To illustrate methods described in this chapter, we consider data from a short questionnaire measuring patient satisfaction in child healthcare. The ESQ was developed from focus groups with children and parents across the child health sector, identifying elements that are important for positive experience of care (Attride-Stirling, 2002). Here we consider the parent version of ESQ (given in Appendix B), which is intended for use with parents/carers of young children and adolescents.

The ESQ parent version includes 12 questions about the parent's experience of service that their child received. Questions also tap into parent-centered experiences, such as whether the parent felt that **he/she** was listened to, or **his/her** problems were addressed. The version uses affirmative statements; for example, "It was easy to talk to the people who have seen my child," and three response options ("certainly true" – "partly true" – "not true"). An appropriate coding of ESQ item responses is assigning consecutive integers to each response category, in accordance with the increasing level of agreement so that higher scores would represent higher levels of satisfaction. Since all questions indicate positive aspects of experiences, the appropriate coding would be **0** for the least favorable rating ("not true"), **1** for the intermediate rating ("partly true"), and **2** for the most favorable rating ("certainly true").

Sample Our example dataset comprises responses from $N = 716$ parents of children aged between 3 and 16 years (median age 11 years), who were treated for various mental health problems in one UK member service of Child and Adolescent Mental Health Services (CAMHS). This is part of a larger multiservice sample analyzed by Brown, Ford, Deighton, and Wolpert, (2012).

Item endorsement rates Distributions of responses to all ESQ items are highly skewed, with vast majority of responses falling within the category "certainly true," which represents most favorable ratings. For most items, approximately 70–80% of all parents choose the most favorable rating. Item 3 ("treated well") shows the highest endorsement (91% of parents/carers choose "certainly true"). The least endorsed item is that concerning appointment times (only around 59% of all parents chose "certainly true"). Considering whole response patterns rather than responses to individual items, 28.2% of parents endorse the top rating category for all items, and only 0.1% endorse the bottom rating category for all items.

Measured constructs In previous analyses conducted by Brown et al. (2012), the ESQ was shown to measure two highly correlated aspects of satisfaction, Satisfaction with Care and with Environment. We start by exploring the factor structure of these data by performing an exploratory factor analysis (EFA) with categorical variables in MPlus (Muthén & Muthén 1998–2012), using full information maximum likelihood (FIML) estimation. Samejima's (1969) graded response model is used by MPlus to model polytomous responses (Code Appendix, Code 1).

The first four eigenvalues for this analysis are 8.13, 1.23, 0.71, and 0.56. As the ratio of the first to the second eigenvalue is very large, a strong general factor is evident, together with one further factor. Goodness of fit of the exploratory two-factor solution is significantly better than the one-factor solution (likelihood ratio test reported by MPlus $\chi^2 = 128.6$, df = 11, $p < .001$).

An oblique rotation of two factors yields nearly ideal independent clusters, complying with the previously reported structure. The first factor is indicated by nine items: 1, 2, 3, 4, 5, 6, 7, 11, and 12. These items relate to satisfaction with **Care** including quality of communication, competence of medical staff, and consistency of care. The second factor is indicated by items 8, 9, and 10, which relate to satisfaction with **Environment** surrounding the treatment, such as appointment times, facilities, and location. Item

IRT Approaches to Test Scoring and Evaluating Score Accuracy

3 has a nontrivial cross-loading on this factor, suggesting that being "treated well" means good customer service in general as well as good medical help. As expected, the two aspects of satisfaction are moderately correlated at 0.60.

It has been argued that presence of a strong "halo" effect is evident in responses to the ESQ (Brown et al., 2012), because even theoretically unrelated aspects of service experience (i.e., appointment times, facilities, and location) correlate with each other and with care-related aspects. Global **affective satisfaction** has been suggested as the likely explanation of this halo effect, and an alternative model for item responses has been proposed whereby all item responses are underlain by the Affective Satisfaction factor, and in addition, care-related items are underlain by a specific Experience of Care factor.

To illustrate the process of estimating test scores and their precision using unidimensional and multidimensional IRT approaches, we consider three alternative conceptual measurement models for the ESQ.

The first model is a **unidimensional** model, in which one common factor (presumably satisfaction with service) explains all variation in the data (see Figure 20.2a) (Code Appendix, Code 2). This is the most basic IRT model, and is the crudest representation of these data. The unidimensional model assumes that the ESQ items are independent controlling for global satisfaction.

The second model is a **Correlated Traits** model, in which the two aspects of satisfaction, satisfaction with care and environment, are indicated by their respective items and correlate freely (Figure 20.2b) (Code Appendix, Code 3). This model is useful if the focus of measurement is to differentiate between the two domains of satisfaction.

The third model is a **bifactor** model, in which the care-related items indicate two factors – the general Affective Satisfaction factor and the specific Experience with Care factor (see Figure 20.2c) (Code Appendix, Code 4). The environment related items indicate the general factor only, assuming that there is no further common reason for co-variation between these items. The general factor accounts for the common variance shared by all items, and the specific factor is the "residual" dimension uncorrelated with the general factor, accounting for any remaining common variance specific to care-related experiences.

Scoring Under the Unidimensional IRT Model

We know that two factors underlie the ESQ data rather than one; however, for purposes of illustration we proceed as if the ESQ really did measure only one underlying trait, "satisfaction with service." This analysis will be later compared with other analyses using other, more suitable models. Assuming a one-dimensional structure when more than one factor is present would cause local dependencies between some ESQ items. When the local independence assumption does not hold, ML estimation might produce biased results. In addition, the standard errors might be biased because when local dependencies exist, the test information cannot be decomposed into the sum of IIFs.

Illustration: ESQ satisfaction scored by the unidimensional EAP method

We estimate item parameters according to the unidimensional model depicted in Figure 20.2a, using the ML estimator with the probabilistic link (LINK=PROBIT) in MPlus (Code Appendix, Code 2). Table 20.1 reports the loglikelihood with the

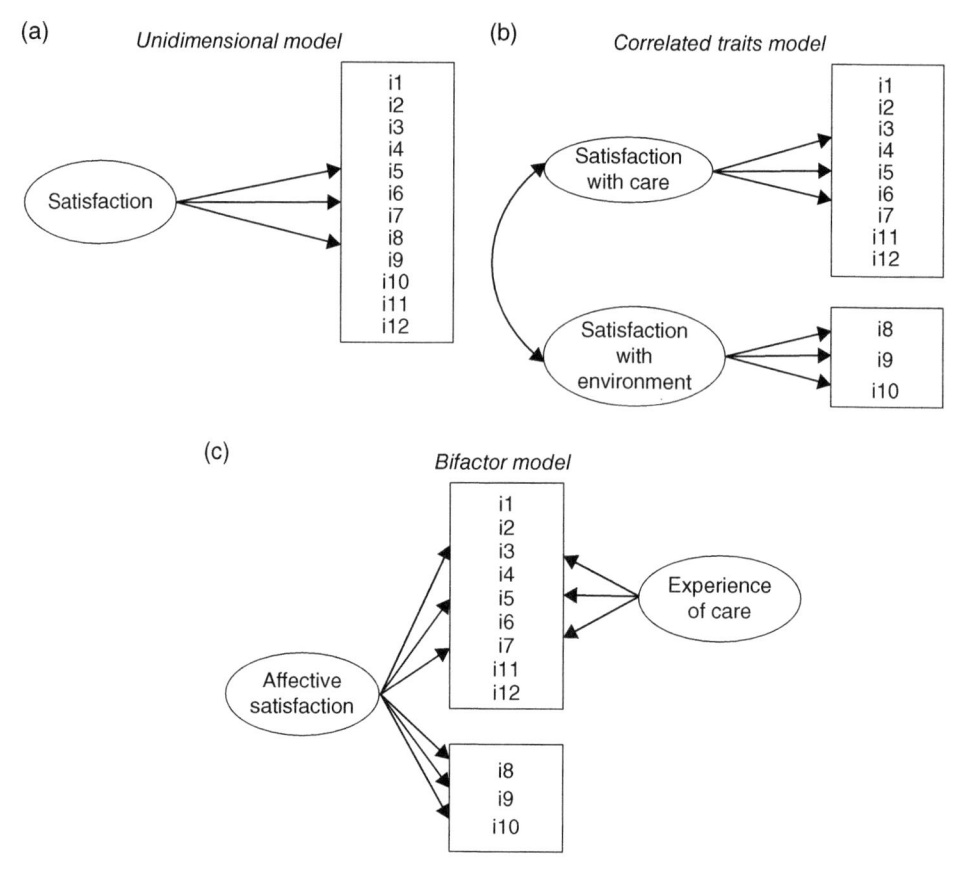

Figure 20.2 Three alternative models for the ESQ item responses.

Table 20.1 Goodness of fit for the three alternative ESQ models.

Model	Loglikelihood	Number of parameters	BIC
Unidimensional	−3989.27	36	8,215.18
Correlated traits	−3963.29	37	8,169.81
Bifactor	−3945.45	45	8,186.71

Note. BIC = Bayesian Information Criterion.

number of estimated parameters, and the Bayesian information criterion (BIC; Schwarz, 1978) for this and other models. These values, although not informative on their own, may be used for comparison of alternative models.

Table 20.2 gives the slopes for all 12 items; Table 20.3 gives the item thresholds. It can be seen that all the thresholds are large negative values, indicating high levels of endorsement ("easiness") of all items.

Next, we estimate the person satisfaction scores using the EAP method. The EAP scores range from −3.12 to 0.91 (mean = −0.002, SD = 0.88). The standard errors of the EAP scores range from 0.17 to 0.73. Figure 20.3 shows the standard errors

Table 20.2 Slopes for the three alternative ESQ models.

		Unidimensional	Correlated traits		Bifactor	
		Factor 1	Factor 1	Factor 2	Factor 1	Factor 2
Item		Satisfaction	Care	Environment	General	Specific
1	listened	2.04	2.04		1.57	1.39
2	easy to talk	1.54	1.54		1.37	0.98
3	treated well	1.77	1.76		2.23	1.19
4	taken seriously	2.29	2.30		1.48	1.72
5	know how to help	2.09	2.11		1.23	1.83
6	given explanation	1.60	1.61		0.98	1.28
7	working together	2.26	2.27		1.36	1.94
8	comfortable facilities	0.43		0.74	0.65	
9	convenient times	0.46		0.97	0.76	
10	convenient location	0.40		0.69	0.67	
11	recommend to a friend	2.55	2.53		1.75	1.85
12	good help overall	3.18	3.24		2.13	3.11

Note. All slopes are significant at the .001 level.

Table 20.3 Thresholds for the three alternative ESQ models.

		Unidimensional		Correlated traits		Bifactor	
Item		Thresh.1	Thresh.2	Thresh.1	Thresh.2	Thresh.1	Thresh.2
1	listened	−4.36	−2.17	−4.35	−2.16	−4.46	−2.22
2	easy to talk	−3.49	−1.88	−3.48	−1.87	−3.73	−1.99
3	treated well	−4.79	−2.73	−4.74	−2.71	−6.44	−3.66
4	taken seriously	−4.07	−2.21	−4.07	−2.21	−4.04	−2.19
5	know how to help	−3.07	−0.93	−3.08	−0.93	−3.20	−0.97
6	given explanation	−2.28	−0.78	−2.28	−0.77	−2.30	−0.78
7	working together	−3.61	−1.64	−3.60	−1.63	−3.72	−1.69
8	comfortable facilities	−2.36	−1.02	−2.69	−1.16	−2.58	−1.12
9	convenient times	−1.18	−0.25	−1.49	−0.31	−1.36	−0.29
10	convenient location	−1.56	−0.68	−1.76	−0.76	−1.75	−0.76
11	recommend to a friend	−3.90	−2.37	−3.86	−2.34	−3.89	−2.37
12	good help overall	−5.10	−2.29	−5.15	−2.30	−5.91	−2.66

plotted against the EAP trait scores for all parents in the sample. For the low end of satisfaction (scores ranging between −3.0 and 0.5), the precision of measurement is good, with the standard errors below 0.5. For the scores between approximately −2.5 and 0, the standard errors are 0.3 or below. We, however, know that the unidimensional model ignores the local dependencies between items (environment related items 8–10, as high residuals show). Ignoring local dependencies when they exist may lead to inflated estimates of test information (Thissen, Nelson, & Swygert, 2001), which in turn leads to deflated standard errors. Thus, the obtained standard errors are probably lower than they should be.

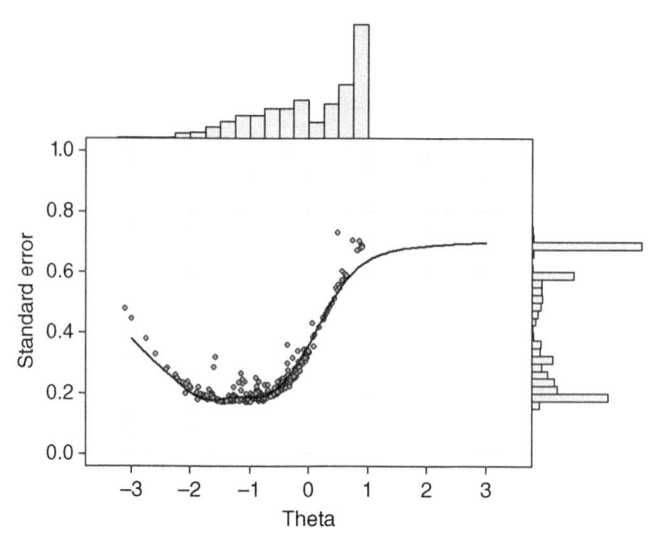

Figure 20.3 Standard Errors of the EAP Satisfaction scores under the unidimensional model.

We conclude that the scale discriminates well between parents with low to average levels of satisfaction, but lacks ability to differentiate between higher scores. The result is a profound "ceiling effect," whereby a very large group of parents (28.2%) who gave the top rating to all experiences, received the same score (see the histogram for theta score in Figure 20.3). The top estimated theta score has a large standard error, because the test items cannot differentiate between these respondents.

It can be also seen from Figure 20.3 that the vast majority of points on the graph can be approximated by a curve. This curve is the standard error function computed from the posterior TIF using formula (20.5). Because the item and TIFs depend on the theta but do not depend on the observed response pattern, the standard error function yields the same value for all respondents with the same estimated theta score. This is not true for the EAP-estimated standard errors, which depend not only on the estimated theta but also on the observed response pattern, as can be seen in formula (20.24). Therefore, some EAP standard errors on Figure 20.3 deviate somewhat from the smooth SE function. The standard errors are typically larger for those with aberrant response patterns – for instance, those parents who agreed with one item but disagreed with another, similar item. We compute empirical reliability of the EAP scores by averaging the squared standard errors of observed scores, which are produced and saved by MPlus for every respondent, and by obtaining the observed score variance from MPlus output. The squared values of standard errors average at .229, the variance of the observed score is .773, and the empirical reliability is therefore $\rho = 0.773/(0.773 + 0.229) = 0.77$.

To give some comparison with commonly used classical reliability statistics, we compute Cronbach's alpha, which is 0.90 for this scale (see Table 20.4 for comparison with other models). This example is a good illustration of pitfalls of using a single summary coefficient to describe the complexity of standard errors conditional on response patterns. We know that measurement accuracy is different in different ranges of the trait; the standard error functions describe that accuracy fully, while the reliability indices merely give an aggregated picture. When working with scales and measures that were developed without IRT, as the ESQ described here, it is common to find widely varying

Table 20.4 Reliability summary for the three alternative ESQ models.

Model and measured construct	Min SE	Max SE	Empirical reliability	Alpha*
Unidimensional				
Satisfaction with Service	0.17	0.73	.77	.90
Correlated traits				
Satisfaction with Care	0.17	0.73	.77	.93
Satisfaction with Environment	0.56	0.92	.55	.49
Bifactor				
Affective Satisfaction	0.46	0.86	.57	–
Experience of Care	0.43	0.88	.56	–

Note. Cronbach's alpha is calculated assuming that the item responses are continuous; it is not model-based and is given here for comparison only.

measurement precision levels for different values of the latent trait, which are difficult to summarize with any single index.

Scoring Under the Multidimensional IRT "Correlated Traits" Model

When every test item indicates one trait only (independent-clusters structure, as in Figure 20.2b), every trait may be considered separately for scoring purposes. Because each item response is conditional on one trait only, there is no difference between ML trait score estimation using a correlated traits model or using separate unidimensional models, if the item parameters in both estimations are identical (which might not be the case).

There is, however, a difference between the trait-by-trait estimation and the multivariate estimation when Bayesian estimators are used. In a correlated traits model, relationships between the latent traits will alter the multivariate normal distribution used as a prior. For example, when two traits are positively correlated, combination of trait scores ($\theta_1 = 1, \theta_2 = 1$) is more likely than combination ($\theta_1 = 1, \theta_2 = -1$). When the corresponding prior distribution is used in MAP or EAP estimation, one trait can "borrow strength" from related traits. The multivariate normal prior alters the posterior likelihood, and favors trait scores that are similar rather than different.

Multivariate priors add information and therefore enhance the measurement precision, which may be desired for shorter tests. However, their use has been criticized, notably by McDonald, who argued that they "corrupt measurement" in tests with independent clusters and correlated traits, because estimation is influenced by "indicators of conceptually distinct traits" (McDonald, 2011, pp. 531). Apart from philosophical concerns, the psychometric concern is that the multivariate prior makes errors of measurement correlated, even for independent clusters.

Illustration: ESQ satisfaction facets scored by the multidimensional EAP method

We estimate item parameters according to the correlated traits model (see Figure 20.2b), using the ML estimator (Code Appendix, Code 3). Loglikelihood and BIC values for this model are reported in Table 20.1. Because this model and the unidimensional models are nested, their relative goodness of fit can be compared using the likelihood ratio test. The difference between two loglikelihood values is multiplied by 2, and the resulting value (51.94) has a chi-square distribution with the degrees of freedom equal to the difference between the number of estimable parameters (37 − 36 = 1). As expected, the correlated trait model fits significantly better than the unidimensional model.

Table 20.2 gives the item slopes; Table 20.3 gives the item thresholds. The model-based correlation between Satisfaction with Care and Satisfaction with Environment is 0.59, which is very close to the correlation estimated in the exploratory factor model (0.60). The strong positive correlation ensures that the traits will "borrow strength" from each other when Bayesian estimation is used.

As the number of traits is small ($T = 2$) in this model, we can produce person scores using the EAP estimator easily. When more traits are measured, the MAP estimator would be more efficient. The EAP scores estimated using the correlated traits model range from −3.02 to 0.87 (mean = 0.003, SD = 0.87) for the Care facet; and they range from −2.84 to 0.86 (mean = 0.002, SD = 0.74) for the Environment facet. It can be seen that the standard deviations are much smaller than SD = 1 assumed for the latent trait. By assuming the standard multivariate prior, the EAP estimator shrank the scores for both scales. The shorter Environment scale is shrunken more severely.

The standard errors associated with all EAP-estimated trait scores in the sample are plotted in Figure 20.4. To compute the empirical reliability of the EAP scores, we use the squared standard errors of observed scores. For the Care scale, the standard errors range between 0.17 and 0.73. The squared values of standard errors average at 0.234, the variance of the observed score is 0.762, and the reliability is $\rho = 0.762/(0.762 + 0.234) = 0.77$. For comparison, Cronbach's alpha for the nine items forming the Care scale is impressive 0.93.

For the shorter Environment facet, the standard errors are much larger, ranging between 0.56 and 0.92. The squared values of standard errors average at 0.447, the variance of the observed score is only 0.553, and the reliability is $\rho = 0.553/(0.553 + 0.447) = 0.55$, unacceptable by any standards. For comparison, Cronbach's alpha for the three items forming the Environment scale is 0.49.

Scoring Under the Multidimensional IRT Bifactor Model

A bifactor model assumes that item responses are caused by **two factors** (hence the name, **bi**factor) – a general factor that influences all items, and one or more further specific factors – each influencing only a group of items. Specific factors are residuals left over after accounting for the general factor, and therefore represent specific, unique features common to a group of items that are not explained by the general factor. As all residuals, specific factors are assumed uncorrelated with the general factor and with each other.

Because any IRT bifactor model is a special case of the multidimensional IRT model given by (20.1), general formulas can be easily adopted to produce specialized IIFs for the bifactor model. These specialized formulas are given in Appendix C.

(a) Satisfaction with care

(b) Satisfaction with environment

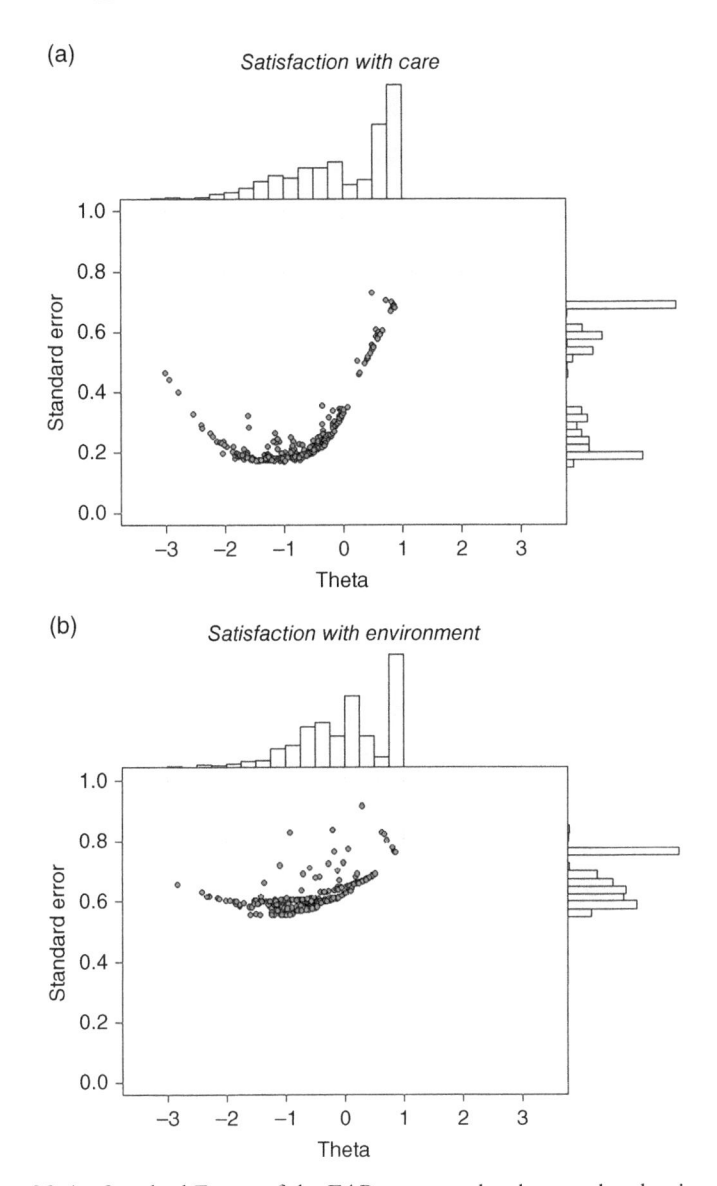

Figure 20.4 Standard Errors of the EAP scores under the correlated traits model.

Illustration: ESQ scored under the bifactor IRT model

Here we fit a bifactor model to the ESQ data (Code Appendix, Code 4). In the model illustrated in Figure 20.2(c), a common factor represents Affective Satisfaction influencing responses to all items. This factor explains all shared variance in the items describing the environment surrounding treatment (items 8–10); however, an additional specific factor is needed to capture the remaining shared variance in nine items describing care-related experiences. This specific factor cannot be thought of as "Satisfaction with Care" because it captures common features of care-related items once the overall satisfaction has been accounted for (Brown et al., 2012). Rather, the specific factor could be named "Experience of Care."

We test this model, again using the ML estimator. The model estimates 12 slopes for the general factor, and nine slopes for the specific factor. There are more estimable parameters in this model than in any other tested model, and not surprisingly, the loglikelihood reported in Table 20.1 is the largest. Because this model and the unidimensional models are nested, their relative goodness of fit can be compared using the likelihood ratio test. The resulting value ($\Delta\chi^2 = 87.64$), tested against the chi-square distribution with $45 - 36 = 9$ degrees of freedom is highly significant. Therefore, the bifactor model fits significantly better than the unidimensional model. Comparing the bifactor model to the rival "correlated traits" model using the Bayesian information criteria, however, reveal that the more parsimonious correlated traits model may be preferable (its BIC is the smallest of all alternative models).

Table 20.2 gives the item slopes; Table 20.3 gives the item thresholds for the bifactor model. Using these parameters, we estimate the general and specific factor scores by the EAP method. Alternatively, the MAP estimator could be used here. The EAP scores range from –2.97 to 0.85 (mean = 0.00, SD = 0.75) for the general factor Affective Satisfaction; and they range from –2.38 to 1.35 (mean = 0.00, SD = 0.75) for specific Experience with Care. It can be seen from the standard deviations (much smaller than the assumed standard deviation of 1 for the latent trait) that the EAP estimator shrank the scores for both factors severely.

Once the person EAP scores have been estimated together with their standard errors, we can plot them against each other for every person. Because the standard errors for both the general and the specific factors are conditional on **two** factor scores, 3D scatter plots are more suitable than the 2D scatters. Figure 20.5 shows plots of the standard errors fully conditioned on both the general and specific factor scores. It can be seen that the standard errors are highest for parents who experience high levels of affective satisfaction, as well as evaluate specific experiences with care highly. This means that the ESQ does not differentiate well between parents who are satisfied with the service they received. For moderate to low scores on either satisfaction or experience of care, the standard errors are lower, reaching the minimum of 0.46 for the general and 0.43 for the specific factors. For many parents, however, the scores are estimated with much lower precision than that.

To compute the empirical reliability of the EAP sample scores, we use the squared standard errors of estimated factor scores. For Affective Satisfaction, the standard errors range between 0.46 and 0.86. The squared values of standard errors average at 0.432, the variance of the observed score is only 0.570, and the empirical reliability is unacceptably low $\rho = 0.570/(0.570 + 0.432) = 0.57$. For Experience with Care, the standard errors range between 0.43 and 0.88. The squared values of standard errors average at 0.442, the variance of the observed score is only 0.557, and the empirical reliability is also very low $\rho = 0.557/(0.557 + 0.442) = 0.56$. The resulting empirical reliability likely misrepresents the measurement precision for most response patterns due to summarizing the conditional standard errors in IRT into a single coefficient.

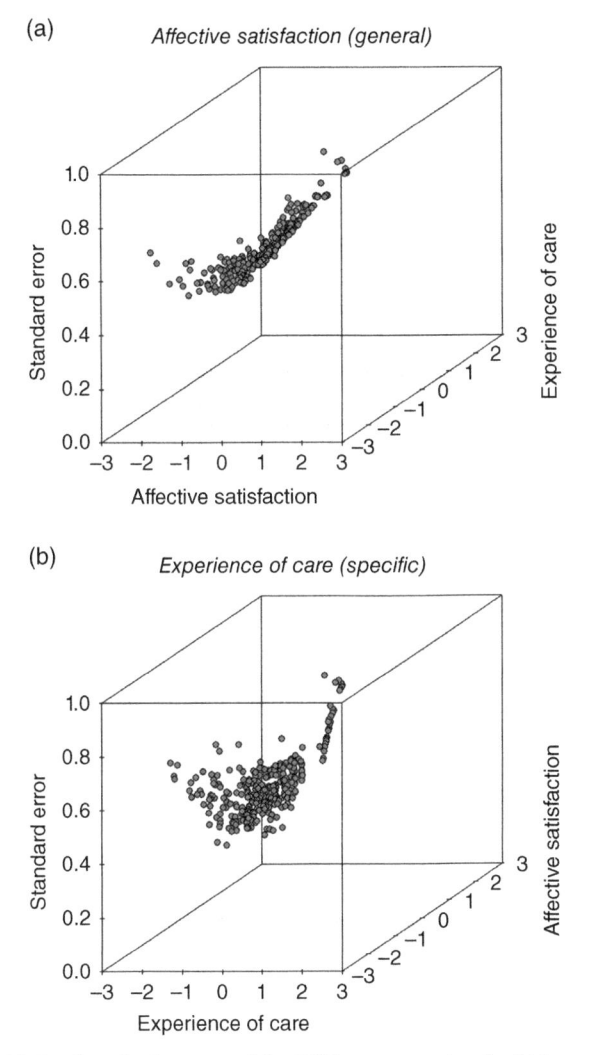

Figure 20.5 Standard errors of the EAP scores under the bifactor model.

Evaluation of the alternative scoring methods for ESQ data example

In this empirical example, we illustrated a range of measurement models that can be applied to the ESQ to produce scores on slightly different conceptual constructs (i.e., global satisfaction; facets of satisfaction; or affective satisfaction (halo) separated from specific aspects of care). We illustrated the EAP scoring under all these models using the same dataset. We concluded that the unidimensional model is deficient in that it does not reflect the two-factor structure that underlies these data. The other models, which address the multidimensional structure of the ESQ, fit the observed data significantly better.

Which model is the best to adopt when scoring the ESQ? Apart from the purpose of measurement, this depends on model properties, specifically: (1) what constructs the model measures; and (2) how accurately these constructs are measured.

Measured constructs in the three alternative models The unidimensional model assumes that the ESQ measures just one trait, which we tentatively named Satisfaction with Service. This scoring model would reflect the default approach to scoring the ESQ without investigating its factorial structure; the summated score would be the closest classical counterpart to the IRT score derived from this model. Does the measured construct actually represent Satisfaction with Service (i.e., overall satisfaction with all experiences)? Looking at correlations between this score and scores from the other models in Table 20.5, it becomes clear that the unidimensional model yields a common factor that is almost identical to Satisfaction with Care construct from the correlated traits model ($r = .999$). Thus, it appears that the construct measured by the unidimensional model is essentially Satisfaction with Care. Nine items contribute strongly to the measurement of this construct; the remaining three items provide almost no contribution – their weak positive loadings on the common factor merely reflect the overall halo effect.

Examining correlations between the scores estimated under the alternative models given in Table 20.5 further, it could be seen that Affective Satisfaction (general factor assessed by the bifactor model) is closest in meaning to Satisfaction with Environment from the correlated traits model ($r = .945$). This implies that these two constructs capture all nonspecific aspects of satisfaction – affect that colors parents' perceptions of their experiences. It also implies that Satisfaction with Environment construct probably has little to do with the environment surrounding treatment; rather, it captures aspects of satisfaction not related to Care.

Finally, Satisfaction with Care assessed by the correlated traits model is strongly related to the residual factor of the bifactor model – Experience of Care ($r = .858$). These constructs are, however, not the same. While Satisfaction with Care includes the affective element (hence its strong positive relationship with Satisfaction with Environment, $r = .756$), Experience of Care describes common features of care-related experiences controlling for the affective element of satisfaction.

Table 20.5 Correlations between ESQ global satisfaction scores estimated using the three alternative scoring models.

Model and measured construct	Correlated traits		Bifactor	
	S.Care	S.Env.	Aff.Sat.	Exp.Care
Unidimensional				
Satisfaction with Service	.999	.777	.814	.842
Correlated traits				
Satisfaction with Care		.756	.796	.858
Satisfaction with Environment			.945	.362
Bifactor				
Affective Satisfaction				.373
Experience of Care				

Note. S.Care = Satisfacion with Care; S.Env. = Satisfaction with Environment; Aff.Sat. = Affective Satisfaction; Exp.Care = Experience of Care.

Measurement precision provided by the three alternative scoring models The marginal reliability coefficients painted quite a mixed picture of measurement precision provided by the ESQ. Empirical reliabilities are mostly lower than Cronbach's alpha for the same scales, and sometimes are unacceptably low. Considering challenging features of this instrument – its profound ceiling effect and poor measurement accuracy at the top end of the latent trait – the marginal reliability does not reflect the measurement precision of individual trait scores. Indeed, looking at the range of standard errors for the Satisfaction with Care construct depicted in Figure 20.4, it can be seen that in the range from $\theta = -3$ to $\theta = 0$, the standard errors are small indeed. Many scores in this region have associated standard errors of around 0.2, and no scores have standard errors above 0.5. Using formula (20.19), the theoretical reliability corresponding to SE = 0.2 is .96; and the reliability corresponding to SE = 0.5 is .75. However, the above-average scoring half of the sample had large standard errors (between from about 0.5 to 0.73), corresponding to reliabilities from 0.75 to 0.47. The overall figure for the empirical reliability of 0.77 provides merely an aggregated picture. The aggregated picture would be more representative in applications where the standard error function is uniform, the estimated scores are distributed approximately normally.

Which Measurement Model to Choose?

Which model is the most suitable for a particular instrument should be a decision based on conceptual, statistical, and practical grounds. A particular measurement focus (e.g., whether the general factor or the facet factors are of interest) imposes practical requirements on the scoring model. Approaching the hypothesized model choice from the theoretical perspective governing the instrument's design, the ESQ used as an example in this chapter was constructed to measure one construct – satisfaction with service. The unidimensional model is clearly suitable from this point of view. However, this approach "masks" the near-zero contribution of Environment related items, and the real meaning of the measured construct, which is nearly identical to care-related satisfaction (Satisfaction with Care).

The correlated traits model, on the other hand, fits the data significantly better and enables measurement of two facets of satisfaction. The Satisfaction with Care scale representing care-related aspects of satisfaction is almost as reliable as the total scale. The Satisfaction with Environment scale representing nonspecific aspects of satisfaction is unreliable and is not useful for any practical purposes.

The bifactor model yields the best fit to these data, and enables measurement of two independent factors influencing item responses – Affective Satisfaction and Experience of Care. In our view, this model provides the most theoretically sound picture of these data. The model separates two sources of variance, and, unlike the other alternative models, provides an adequate explanation of strong dependencies between experiences that are theoretically unrelated for parents attending one service (i.e., facilities, location, appointment times). These dependencies are fully explained by the general halo or "affective overtones" factor, while care-specific experiences are explained by a separate factor. However, both constructs suffer from low accuracy of estimation for significant parts of the latent traits (specifically above-average satisfaction and experience of care). This makes the bifactor measurement model less useful for scoring the ESQ in practice.

Acknowledgments

The author is grateful to the CORC collaboration for providing data for the empirical example used in this chapter, and to the CAMHS Outcomes Research Consortium (CORC) central team researchers Jenna Bradley and Halina Flannery for preparing the data for analyses.

References

Ackerman, T. A. (2005). Multidimensional item response theory modeling. In A. Maydeu-Olivares & J. J. McArdle (Eds.), *Contemporary psychometrics* (pp. 3–26). Mahwah, NJ: Lawrence Erlbaum.

Attride-Stirling, J. (2002). *Development of methods to capture users' views of CAMHS in clinical governance reviews.* http://www.corc.uk.net/media/1215/chi_projectevaluationreport.pdf (accessed October 2, 2017).

Brown, A., Ford, T., Deighton, J., & Wolpert, M. (2012). Satisfaction in child and adolescent mental health services: Translating users' feedback into measurement. *Administration and Policy in Mental Health and Mental Health Services Research*, 1–13.

Brown, A., & Maydeu-Olivares, A. (2011). Item response modeling of forced-choice questionnaires. *Educational and Psychological Measurement*, 71(3), 460–502.

Dodd, B. G., De Ayala, R. J., & Koch, W. R. (1995). Computerized adaptive testing with polytomous items. *Applied Psychological Measurement*, 19(1), 5–22.

Du Toit, M. (2003). *IRT from Scientific Software International.* Chicago, IL: Scientific Software International.

Embretson, S. E., & Reise, S. P. (2000). *Item response theory.* Mahwah, NJ: Erlbaum Publishers.

Green, B. F., Bock, R. D., Humphreys, L. G., Linn, R. L., & Reckase, M. D. (1984). Technical guidelines for assessing computerized adaptive tests. *Journal of Educational Measurement*, 21(4), 347–360.

Gibbons, R. D., Immekus, J. C., & Bock, R. D. (2007). The added value of multidimensional IRT models. Didactic workbook. www.healthstats.org/articles/NCI_Didactic_Workbook.pdf (accessed October 2, 2017).

Masters, G. N., & Wright, B. D. (1997). The partial credit model. In W. J. van der Linden & R. Hambleton (Eds.), *Handbook of modern item response theory* (pp. 101–121). New York: Springer.

McDonald, R. P. (1999). *Test theory. A unified approach.* Mahwah, NJ: Lawrence Erlbaum.

McDonald, R. P. (2011). Measuring latent quantities. *Psychometrika*, 76, 511–536.

Muthén, L. K., & Muthén, B. O. (1998–2012). *MPlus user's guide* (7th ed.). Los Angeles, CA: Muthén & Muthén.

Reckase, M. (2009). *Multidimensional item response theory.* New York: Springer.

Reise, S., & Haviland, M. (2005). Item response theory and the measurement of clinical change. *Journal of Personality Assessment*, 84(3), 228–238.

Samejima, F. (1969). *Estimation of latent ability using a response pattern of graded scores* (Psychometric Monograph, No. 17). Richmond, VA: Psychometric Society. Accessed July 1 https://www.psychometricsociety.org/sites/default/files/pdf/MN17.pdf (accessed October 2, 2017).

Samejima, F. (1997). Graded response model. In W. J. van der Linden & R. Hambleton (Eds.), *Handbook of modern item response theory* (pp. 85–100). New York: Springer.

Schwarz, G. (1978). Estimating the dimension of a model. *Annals of Statistics*, 6, 461–464.

Thissen, D., Nelson, L., & Swygert, K. A. (2001). Item response theory applied to combinations of multiple-choice and constructed-response items – approximation methods for scale scores.

In D. Thissen & H. Wainer (Eds.), *Test scoring* (pp. 179–216). Mahwah, NJ: Lawrence Erlbaum.

Thissen, D., & Orlando, M. (2001). Item response theory for items scored in two categories. In D. Thissen & H. Wainer (Eds.), *Test scoring* (pp. 73–140). Mahwah, NJ: Lawrence Erlbaum.

van der Linden, W. J., & Hambleton, R. (1997). Item Response Theory: brief history, common models and extensions. In W. J. van der Linden & R. Hambleton (Eds.), *Handbook of modern item response theory* (pp. 1–28). New York: Springer.

Appendix A: Computation of EAP Scores and Their Standard Errors

The **EAP score** for one trait is computed as the ratio between the integral of the posterior function weighted by the latent trait θ, and the unweighted integral of the posterior function. The EAP scores are approximated using numerical integration of the posterior distribution along the latent trait continuum as follows:

$$\text{EAP}(u|\theta) \approx \frac{\sum_q l(u_1, u_2, \ldots, u_m | \theta_q) \phi(\theta_q) \theta_q d\theta_q}{\sum_q l(u_1, u_2, \ldots, u_m | \theta_q) \phi(\theta_q) d\theta_q}. \qquad (20.23)$$

In this expression, $l(u_1, u_2, \ldots, u_m | \theta_q)$ denotes the likelihood of the observed response pattern defined in (20.2), $\phi(x)$ is the standard normal density function evaluated at x (here, at each of the quadrature points); and $d\theta_q$ denotes the size of the interval between two adjacent quadrature points. The standard error of the EAP score is computed at the same quadrature points as follows:

$$\text{SE}_{EAP} \approx \sqrt{\frac{\sum_q l(u_1, u_2, \ldots, u_m | \theta_q) \phi(\theta_q) (\theta_q - \text{EAP})^2 d\theta_q}{\sum_q l(u_1, u_2, \ldots, u_m | \theta_q) \phi(\theta_q) d\theta_q}} \qquad (20.24)$$

Appendix B: Experience of Service Questionnaire (Parent Version)

Response options: *Certainly True – Partly True – Not True – (Don't know)*
("don't know" response option is considered missing data and is not scored).

1. I feel that the people who have seen my child listened to me
2. It was easy to talk to the people who have seen my child
3. I was treated well by the people who have seen my child
4. My views and worries were taken seriously
5. I feel the people here know how to help with the problem I came for
6. I have been given enough explanation about the help available here

7 I feel that the people who have seen my child are working together to help with the problem(s)
8 The facilities here are comfortable (e.g., waiting area)
9 The appointments are usually at a convenient time (e.g., don't interfere with work, school)
10 It is quite easy to get to the place where the appointments are
11 If a friend needed similar help, I would recommend that he or she come here
12 Overall, the help I have received here is good

Appendix C: IIF for a Bifactor Model

Here we give formulas necessary to compute the item and test information for the bifactor model. Let g be a **general factor** measured by a test, and $s_1, s_2, \ldots, s_T$ be T **specific factors**. The set of factors underlying item responses is therefore $\mathbf{g}^* = (g, s_1, s_2, \ldots, s_T)'$. The general factor and the specific factors are assumed uncorrelated with each other, and have zero means and unit variances so that their distribution is multivariate standard normal $\mathbf{g}^* \sim N_{T+1}(\mathbf{0}, \mathbf{I})$, where $\mathbf{I}$ denotes the identity covariance matrix. Under this model, the response to item i is influenced by two factors – the general factor g and one specific factor, say s_a

$$P_i(\mathbf{g}^*) = P(u_i = 1 | \mathbf{g}^*) = \Phi(-\tau_i + \beta_{0i} g + \beta_{ai} s_a), \qquad (20.25)$$

where, τ_i is the threshold, β_{0i} is the slope for the general factor g, and β_{ai} is the slope for the specific factor s_a.

Because the general factor and the specific factors in this model are orthogonal, the ML item information **about the general factor** g is computed substituting the gradient in Equation 20.11 with:

$$\nabla_g P_i(\mathbf{g}^*) = \frac{\partial P_i(\mathbf{g}^*)}{\partial g}. \qquad (20.26)$$

Now, the partial derivative with respect to g is

$$\frac{\partial P_i(\mathbf{g}^*)}{\partial g} = \beta_{0i} \phi(-\tau_i + \beta_{0i} g + \beta_{ai} s_a), \qquad (20.27)$$

where $\phi(z)$ is the normal density function evaluated at z (McDonald, 1999; p. 284). Thus, the IIF in direction of the general factor g is given by

$$\mathcal{I}_i^g(\mathbf{g}^*) = \frac{(\beta_{0i})^2 [\phi(-\tau_i + \beta_{0i} g + \beta_{ai} s_a)]^2}{\Phi(-\tau_i + \beta_{0i} g + \beta_{ai} s_a)[1 - \Phi(-\tau_i + \beta_{0i} g + \beta_{ai} s_a)]}. \qquad (20.28)$$

Note that the IIF for the bifactor model is fully conditioned on the general and the specific factors, therefore local independence holds and the IIFs are additive. The test information about the general factor g is the sum of all IIFs in the direction of g. This summation, however, will make the TIF for the general factor **conditional on all specific factors**, although each IIF is only conditional on **one** specific factor (in addition to the general factor).

When Bayesian estimation is used, the prior information must be added to the ML test information to compute the posterior test information. In bifactor models, the latent covariance matrix is the identity matrix, $\sum = I$, and the amount of information added by the multivariate normal prior is simply 1,

$$\mathcal{I}_P^g(\mathbf{g}^*) = \mathcal{I}^g(\mathbf{g}^*) + \left[\Sigma^{-1}\right]_g = \sum_i \mathcal{I}_i^g(\mathbf{g}^*) + 1. \qquad (20.29)$$

Code Appendix

Code 1 MPlus code for exploratory factor analysis of the Experience of Service Questionnaire – parent version.

```
TITLE: EFA analysis of CHI-ESQ Parent data

DATA: FILE IS CHI-ESQParentData.dat;

DEFINE:
!reverse score items
rESQP_01=3-ESQP_01;
rESQP_02=3-ESQP_02;
rESQP_03=3-ESQP_03;
rESQP_04=3-ESQP_04;
rESQP_05=3-ESQP_05;
rESQP_06=3-ESQP_06;
rESQP_07=3-ESQP_07;
rESQP_08=3-ESQP_08;
rESQP_09=3-ESQP_09;
rESQP_10=3-ESQP_10;
rESQP_11=3-ESQP_11;
rESQP_12=3-ESQP_12;

VARIABLE:
NAMES ARE
ESQP_01
ESQP_02
ESQP_03
ESQP_04
ESQP_05
ESQP_06
ESQP_07
ESQP_08
```

```
ESQP_09
ESQP_10
ESQP_11
ESQP_12;

MISSING ARE ESQP_01-ESQP_12 (4, 999);
USEVARIABLES ARE rESQP_01-rESQP_12;
CATEGORICAL ARE rESQP_01-rESQP_12;

ANALYSIS: TYPE = EFA 1 2;
ESTIMATOR=ML;

OUTPUT: RES; SAMPSTAT;
PLOT: TYPE=PLOT3;
```

Code 2 Scoring of unidimensional CFA model of the Experience of Service Questionnaire – parent version, using the EAP method.

```
TITLE: CFA analysis of CHI-ESQ Parent data - Unidimensional model

DATA: FILE IS CHI-ESQParentData.dat;

DEFINE:
!reverse score items
rESQP_01=3-ESQP_01;
rESQP_02=3-ESQP_02;
rESQP_03=3-ESQP_03;
rESQP_04=3-ESQP_04;
rESQP_05=3-ESQP_05;
rESQP_06=3-ESQP_06;
rESQP_07=3-ESQP_07;
rESQP_08=3-ESQP_08;
rESQP_09=3-ESQP_09;
rESQP_10=3-ESQP_10;
rESQP_11=3-ESQP_11;
rESQP_12=3-ESQP_12;

VARIABLE:
NAMES ARE

ESQP_01
ESQP_02
ESQP_03
ESQP_04
```

```
ESQP_05
ESQP_06
ESQP_07
ESQP_08
ESQP_09
ESQP_10
ESQP_11
ESQP_12;

MISSING ARE ESQP_01-ESQP_12 (4, 999);
USEVARIABLES ARE rESQP_01-rESQP_12;
CATEGORICAL ARE rESQP_01-rESQP_12;

ANALYSIS:
ESTIMATOR=ML; LINK=PROBIT;

MODEL:
SATISFACTION BY rESQP_01-rESQP_12*1;
SATISFACTION@1;

OUTPUT: RES;

PLOT: TYPE=PLOT3;
SAVEDATA:
FILE IS ResultsUnidimensional.dat;
SAVE=FSCORES;
```

Code 3 Scoring of multidimensional IRT "Correlated Traits" model of the Experience of Service Questionnaire – parent version, using the EAP method.

```
TITLE: CFA analysis of CHI-ESQ Parent data - Corr. traits model

DATA: FILE IS CHI-ESQParentData.dat;

DEFINE:
!reverse score items
rESQP_01=3-ESQP_01;
rESQP_02=3-ESQP_02;
rESQP_03=3-ESQP_03;
rESQP_04=3-ESQP_04;
rESQP_05=3-ESQP_05;
rESQP_06=3-ESQP_06;
rESQP_07=3-ESQP_07;
```

```
rESQP_08=3-ESQP_08;
rESQP_09=3-ESQP_09;
rESQP_10=3-ESQP_10;
rESQP_11=3-ESQP_11;
rESQP_12=3-ESQP_12;

VARIABLE:
NAMES ARE
ESQP_01
ESQP_02
ESQP_03
ESQP_04
ESQP_05
ESQP_06
ESQP_07
ESQP_08
ESQP_09
ESQP_10
ESQP_11
ESQP_12;

MISSING ARE ESQP_01-ESQP_12 (4, 999);
USEVARIABLES ARE rESQP_01-rESQP_12;
CATEGORICAL ARE rESQP_01-rESQP_12;

ANALYSIS:
ESTIMATOR=ML; LINK=PROBIT;

MODEL:

CARE BY rESQP_01-rESQP_07*1 rESQP_11-rESQP_12*1;
CARE@1;

ENVIR BY rESQP_08-rESQP_10*1;
ENVIR@1;

OUTPUT: RES;
PLOT: TYPE=PLOT3;
SAVEDATA:
FILE IS ResultsCorrTraits.dat; SAVE=FSCORES;
```

Code 4 Scoring of multidimensional IRT Bifactor model of the Experience of Service Questionnaire – parent version, using the EAP method.

```
TITLE: CFA analysis of CHI-ESQ Parent data - Bifactor model

DATA: FILE IS CHI-ESQParentData.dat;

DEFINE:
!reverse score items
rESQP_01=3-ESQP_01;
rESQP_02=3-ESQP_02;
rESQP_03=3-ESQP_03;
rESQP_04=3-ESQP_04;
rESQP_05=3-ESQP_05;
rESQP_06=3-ESQP_06;
rESQP_07=3-ESQP_07;
rESQP_08=3-ESQP_08;
rESQP_09=3-ESQP_09;
rESQP_10=3-ESQP_10;
rESQP_11=3-ESQP_11;
rESQP_12=3-ESQP_12;

VARIABLE:
NAMES ARE
ESQP_01
ESQP_02
ESQP_03
ESQP_04
ESQP_05
ESQP_06
ESQP_07
ESQP_08
ESQP_09
ESQP_10
ESQP_11
ESQP_12;

MISSING ARE ESQP_01-ESQP_12 (4, 999);
USEVARIABLES ARE rESQP_01-rESQP_12;
CATEGORICAL ARE rESQP_01-rESQP_12;

ANALYSIS:
ESTIMATOR=ML; LINK=PROBIT;
```

```
MODEL:

SATISFACTION BY rESQP_01-rESQP_12*;
SATISFACTION@1;

Exp_CARE BY rESQP_01-rESQP_07*1 rESQP_11-rESQP_12*1;
Exp_CARE@1;

SATISFACTION WITH Exp_CARE@0;

OUTPUT: RES;
PLOT: TYPE=PLOT3;
SAVEDATA:
FILE IS ResultsBifactor.dat;
SAVE=FSCORES;
```

21
IRT Linking and Equating
Won-Chan Lee and Guemin Lee

Introduction

This chapter presents an overview of item response theory (IRT) linking and equating procedures with various illustrative examples. The intent is to provide detailed information about how the procedures are implemented when working with real datasets.

In this chapter, the term "linking" refers to the process of placing IRT parameter estimates obtained based on data from different examinee populations on a common IRT-ability scale. By contrast, "equating" refers to a statistical process to adjust difficulty differences in test forms so that scores on the forms can be used interchangeably (Kolen & Brennan, 2014). If item parameter estimates from different test forms are on the same IRT scale, ability scores derived from those parameter estimates are comparable across different test forms and can be used interchangeably without any further transformations. Examinees will receive the same ability estimates regardless of the particular forms taken.

However, when number-correct scoring is used rather than IRT-ability scoring and the number-correct scores are associated with scale scores, additional "equating" procedures need to be conducted to achieve score comparability (Kolen & Brennan, 2014). Using item parameter estimates for the old and new forms that have been linked to be expressed on the same IRT scale, either IRT true-score or observed-score equating can be used to find equating relationships between the scores on the two forms. The process of scale linking is one of the prerequisites to equating.

The IRT linking and equating procedures are considered here in the context of the common-item nonequivalent groups design. In this data collection design, two groups of examinees that differ in ability are administered two forms of a test (a new form, Form N, and an old form, Form O) that have a set of items in common. This design is also referred to as a nonequivalent groups with anchor test design (NEAT; von Davier, Holland, & Thayer, 2004). Figure 21.1 depicts the common-item nonequivalent groups design. In this design, Form O and Form N have a set of common items (CI) and are given to two groups of examinees from different populations. The common items are administered to both groups and thus can serve as a link between the two forms/groups. It is often desired that the common items be representative of the total

---

The Wiley Handbook of Psychometric Testing: A Multidisciplinary Reference on Survey, Scale and Test Development, First Edition. Edited by Paul Irwing, Tom Booth, and David J. Hughes.
© 2018 John Wiley & Sons Ltd. Published 2020 by John Wiley & Sons Ltd.

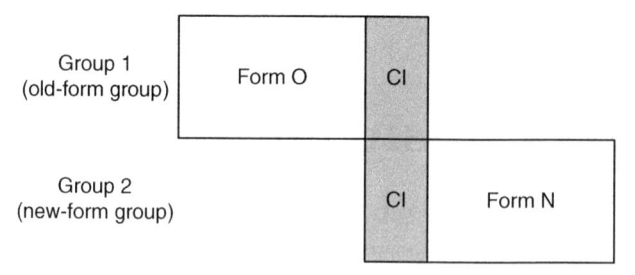

Figure 21.1 Data collection scheme for the common-item nonequivalent groups design.

test forms in content and statistical characteristics to link/equate the two forms adequately (Kolen & Brennan, 2014).

Beyond the common-item nonequivalent groups design, there are other data collection designs that are often considered in equating. The singlegroup design involves administering two forms to the same group of examinees, and thus the parameter estimates obtained from calibrating the old- and new-form data are on the same IRT-ability scale without the need for scale linking. Another popular design is called the random groups design, in which the two forms are given to two examinee groups that are randomly equivalent. Because the two examinee groups are assumed to come from the same population, separate calibration of the old- and new-form data will result in parameter estimates for the two forms that are on the same scale and further scale linking typically is not necessary. Thus, no scale linking is performed when equating is done with either the singlegroup design or the random groups design. In contrast, scale linking is almost always conducted on the data collected under the common-item nonequivalent groups design for subsequent IRT analyses such as differential item functioning, test scoring, and equating, which is the focus of this chapter.

This chapter consists of four sections. The IRT linking section provides an overview of three IRT linking methods with illustrative examples. The IRT equating section presents true-score and observed-score equating methods with examples. Some newly developed equating methods with multidimensional IRT frameworks are discussed in the third section, followed by concluding remarks.

IRT Linking

An IRT-ability scale (θ) is often viewed as an arbitrary scale because any linear transformation gives the same item response function (IRF), provided that the item parameters are also transformed in an analogous manner. Consider an IRF for the three-parameter logistic IRT model (Lord, 1980):

$$p(\theta|a_i, b_i, c_i) = c_i + \frac{1-c_i}{1+\exp[-1.7a_i(\theta-b_i)]}, \quad (21.1)$$

where a_i, b_i, and c_i are, respectively, the discrimination, difficulty, and guessing parameters for item i. Suppose θ is transformed as $\theta^* = S\theta + I$, where θ^* is a transformed ability and S and I are linear transformation coefficients. The IRF remains the same if the item parameters are also transformed as follows: $a_i^* = a_i/S$; $b_i^* = Sb_i + I$; and $c_i^* = c_i$. That is, $p(\theta|a_i, b_i, c_i) = p(\theta^*|a_i^*, b_i^*, c_i^*)$.

The arbitrariness of the origin and unit of the θ scale is referred to as scale indeterminacy (Baker & Kim, 2004; Kolen & Brennan, 2014). To deal with IRT scale indeterminacy, a common practice is to standardize the scale to have a mean of zero and a standard deviation (SD) of one, which hereafter is referred to as a "standard scale." Most IRT calibration programs commonly used in the field use the standard scale to define the underlying ability distribution when estimating item and ability parameters.

If data for Form N and Form O are obtained from two groups from the same population – that is, randomly equivalent groups – the item parameters for the two forms estimated from two separate calibrations are considered to be on the same ability scale. However, when the two groups are from different examinee populations, the item parameters for the two forms resulting from two separate calibrations will not be on the same scale due to the arbitrary use of the standard scale for each calibration. Many IRT applications, such as equating and creating an item pool, typically require that the item parameters for the two forms be on a common ability scale so that the item parameter estimates between the two administrations can be properly compared. Such comparability is achieved by linking using one of the linking methods discussed in this chapter.

The goal of IRT linking is to establish comparability for item and ability parameter estimates obtained based on data from sample groups that differ in ability. More specifically, the old-form group (Group 1 in Figure 21.1) serves here as a base scale on which the parameter estimates for Form N taken by the new-form group, as well as those for Form O, will be expressed. The parameter estimates for Form N will be linked to the Form O base scale through the common items included in both forms.

Although there do exist a variety of IRT linking methods, the three methods that are most frequently discussed in the literature and used widely in practice are presented in this chapter. The three methods are separate calibration, concurrent calibration, and fixed calibration. Each of these three methods are discussed in the following, followed by general comparisons between these methods.

Separate calibration

In separate calibration, Form O and Form N are calibrated separately, each based on the standard scale. Since the two groups taking the two forms are from different populations, item parameter estimates for the two forms will not be on the same scale. Two separate calibrations will result in two sets of parameter estimates for the common items, which are used to find the slope S and intercept I for a linear transformation. The estimated transformation coefficients are then applied to parameter estimates for both common and noncommon items in Form N on the new-form scale to transform them to the old-form base scale, as follows: $\hat{a}_i^* = \hat{a}_i/S$; $\hat{b}_i^* = S\hat{b}_i + I$; and $\hat{c}_i^* = \hat{c}_i$, where $\hat{a}_i, \hat{b}_i$, and $\hat{c}_i$ are parameter estimates for item i in Form N on the new-form scale, while $\hat{a}_i^*, \hat{b}_i^*$, and $\hat{c}_i^*$ are those expressed on the old-form scale after transformation. The discrimination and difficulty parameters for the graded response and generalized partial credit models are transformed in the same way – refer to Kim and Lee (2006) for more details about linking with polytomous IRT models.

The transformation coefficients need to be estimated as accurately as possible using the two sets of parameter estimates for the common items. Four scale transformation methods are often discussed in the literature (Kolen & Brennan, 2014). The first two methods, referred to as the moment methods, use the mean and SD of parameter estimates for the common items. The mean/mean method (Loyd & Hoover, 1980) uses the mean of the a-parameter estimates and the mean of the b-parameter estimates for the common items to estimate the slope S and intercept I as: $S = Mean(\hat{a}_N)/Mean(\hat{a}_O)$ and $I = Mean(\hat{b}_O) - S \cdot Mean(\hat{b}_N)$, where the subscripts N and O indicate the parameter estimates for the common items obtained based on the new-form and old-form data, respectively. Another moment method, the mean/sigma method (Marco, 1977), employs the mean and SD of the b-parameter estimates for the common items: $S = SD(\hat{b}_O)/SD(\hat{b}_N)$ and $I = Mean(\hat{b}_O) - S \cdot Mean(\hat{b}_N)$. In theory, the mean/mean and mean/sigma methods should produce the same results in terms of parameters, but tend to differ when estimates are used (Kolen & Brennan, 2014).

One of the criticisms of the two moment methods is that they do not consider all of the item parameter estimates simultaneously. The methods developed by Haebara (1980) and Stocking and Lord (1983), in contrast, use all item parameter estimates at the same time and tend to produce more accurate results than the two moment methods (Hanson & Béguin, 2002; Kim & Kolen, 2006; Kolen & Brennan, 2014). The Haebara and Stocking–Lord methods are called characteristic curve methods because they estimate the transformation coefficients using item characteristic curves or test characteristic curves, respectively. The Haebara method finds the transformation coefficients that minimize the sum of the squared differences between item characteristic curves for the common items in the two forms. In contrast, the Stocking–Lord method uses test characteristic curves in the minimization process. Kim and Lee (2006) extended the original moment and characteristic curve methods to more complex cases where a mixture of different IRT models is used, such as a mixed-format test consisting of both multiple-choice and constructed-response item types.

In sum, the separate calibration method can be viewed as a four-step procedure: (1) calibrate the old-form data to obtain parameter estimates for the items in Form O; (2) calibrate the new-form data to obtain parameter estimates for the items in Form N; (3) use the two sets of parameter estimates for the common items to estimate the linear scale transformation coefficients; and (4) apply the estimated scale transformation coefficients to all of the items in Form N to transform them to the old-form base scale.

Concurrent calibration

In contrast to separate calibration, which requires two separate calibrations and an additional scale transformation process, concurrent calibration involves only a single run of IRT estimation by combining the data for Form O and Form N. Then, calibration is conducted in such a way that one of the groups (e.g., the old-form group) is specified as a reference group to serve as the base scale, for which the mean and SD are fixed at 0 and 1. The mean and SD for the new-form group can differ from the base scale and are freely estimated relative to the standard base scale. Concurrent calibration produces only one set of parameter estimates for the common items. Following this single run of concurrent calibration, all of the parameter estimates for the items in both forms will be on the same base scale without requiring a further scale transformation process.

In order for concurrent calibration to work properly, multiple-group estimation needs to be employed, in which the old-form and new-form groups are specified to come from different populations and their means and SDs are allowed to differ. Another approach for calibrating the combined data concurrently, which produces biased parameter estimates and thus is not recommended in practice, is to use single-group estimation. Single-group concurrent calibration assumes that both groups are from the same population without specifying one of the groups as a reference group. Consequently, the parameter estimates for all items in both forms will be on the standard scale, a common scale. However, one problem with single-group calibration is that the unjustifiable use of a single population when, in fact, the two groups are from different populations, causes estimation error, which in turn introduces bias into the parameter estimates (Lee & Kim, 2011). The bias in the parameter estimates appears to come from the structure of the combined dataset, in which there are always missing data that appear in each of the two groups in a systematic way because of the existence of noncommon items in the two forms. When missing data do not occur at random, the parameter estimates tend to be biased (Finch, 2008; Mislevy & Wu, 1996). Therefore, it is almost always recommended that concurrent calibration be carried out with multiple-group estimation when data are collected based on the common-item nonequivalent groups design, and that IRT calibration software that has capability to perform multiple-group estimation be used, such as BILOG-MG (Zimowski, Muraki, Mislevy, & Bock, 2003), PARSCALE (Muraki & Bock, 2003), and flexMIRT (Cai, 2013).

Fixed calibration

Some of the essential elements of fixed calibration, for which the process is well-documented in Kim (2006a), are briefly discussed here. Readers may refer to Kim (2006a) for technical details. The fixed calibration method involves two steps. First, the data for the old form, Form O, are calibrated to obtain parameter estimates for the items in the old form, including the common items. Holding the common items fixed at the values obtained from the previous calibration using the old-form data, the data for the new form, Form N, are calibrated. Since the parameter estimates for the common items are already on the old-form base scale, the resulting parameter estimates for the noncommon items in the new form will be placed on the old-form base scale after calibration.

Although there are various ways of conducting fixed calibration, Kim (2006a) found that fixed calibration performs well only when a few specific technical requirements are met. When calibration is done employing marginal maximum likelihood estimation with Bock and Aitkin's (Bock & Aitkin, 1981) Expectation-Maximization (EM) algorithm as implemented in many IRT calibration programs, Kim (2006a) recommended that multiple EM cycles be used and that the prior ability distribution be updated after each EM cycle. The prior ability distribution typically is fixed to $N(0,1)$ during all EM iterations for single-group calibration. However, for fixed calibration with the parameter estimates for the common items held fixed, it is crucial to update the prior ability distribution multiple times based on the new-form data so that the parameter estimates for the noncommon items are gradually placed on the scale of the fixed common items during the EM cycles. Since the fixed common items are on the base standard scale, the updated prior distribution should **not** be rescaled to have a mean of zero and an SD of one. This standardization (i.e., rescaling) is a default setting for many IRT calibration programs, which will be discussed in greater detail in a later section.

Comparisons of three linking methods

There is rich literature that compares various IRT linking methods (Hanson & Béguin, 2002; Kang & Petersen, 2009; Kim, 2006a; Kim & Cohen, 1998; Kim & Kolen, 2006; Lee & Ban, 2010; Petersen, Cook, & Stocking, 1983), although there are not many studies that compare all three methods simultaneously. Relative performances of these linking methods reported in different studies seem to provide mixed conclusions. In general, concurrent calibration tends to be more accurate than separate calibration in conjunction with characteristic curve methods when the data fit the IRT model (Kolen & Brennan, 2014). However, when the data do not fit the IRT model (e.g., multidimensionality), separate calibration provides better results than concurrent calibration (Béguin & Hanson, 2001). The study by Kang and Petersen (2009) reported that the three linking methods perform similarly when fixed calibration has been conducted adequately.

Linking results for separate calibration provide useful diagnostic information when the two sets of parameter estimates for the common items obtained from two separate calibrations are compared to examine whether the common items behave similarly in two different administrations. For example, common items with two sets of parameter estimates that do not show a linear relationship in a bivariate scatter plot might be considered to be eliminated when estimating the scale transformation coefficients.

With the common-item nonequivalent groups design, it is usually the case that the data for the old form are obtained and calibrated at one time point, and the data for the new form are obtained at another time point. Concurrent calibration requires that both datasets be available at the time of calibration. Thus, if the old form was calibrated beforehand and item parameter estimates have already been obtained, concurrent calibration will result in a new set of item parameter estimates for the old form, and thus require a decision to be made regarding which set to retain for subsequent analyses, especially for the common items. Note that the parameter estimates for the common items from concurrent calibration based on the combined data would be more stable and accurate than those based on the old-form data due to the larger sample size.

Linking, either with separate calibration or fixed calibration, does not require data for the old form at the time of calibrating the new-form data. All that is needed is a set of parameter estimates for the common items obtained from calibration of the old form. Thus, the parameter estimates for the noncommon items in the old form are not altered. With respect to the common items, however, fixed calibration does not change the parameter estimates in the new-form calibration, while separate calibration will result in a set of parameter estimates, after transformation, which are different from those obtained from the old-form calibration.

Fixed calibration is particularly useful when the parameter estimates for pretest items need to be put on the scale of operational test items that have already been calibrated and placed on an existing scale in an item pool (Kim, 2006a). The parameter estimates for the operational items will be fixed when estimating the parameters for the pretest items to put them on the item-pool scale.

Illustrative examples

Two datasets from a large-scale testing program are used for illustrative purposes. The first example involves data for two forms (Form N and Form O) of a history test consisting of multiple-choice (MC) items only. The history test has 70 MC items on each

Table 21.1 Descriptive statistics for History.

	Old form	New form
Sample Size	3,500	3,334
# Items	70	70
# CI	23	23
Mean: Total, CI	42.50, 13.65	44.30, 13.63
SD: Total, CI	12.90, 4.44	12.90, 5.07
Correlation bet. Total and CI	.93	.94

Table 21.2 Descriptive statistics for Science.

	Old form	New form
Sample Size	3,500	3,592
# Items	80	80
# MC	75	75
# CR (Max score for each CR)	5 (10, 9, 10, 8, 8)	5 (10, 10, 9, 8, 8)
# MC CI	24	24
Score Range	0–120	0–121
Mean: Total, CI	58.31, 12.62	56.13, 12.27
SD: Total, CI	23.71, 5.20	25.66, 5.32
Correlation bet. Total and CI	.93	.93

form, and 23 items serve as common items between the two forms. The second example is based on data from a mixed-format science test containing both MC and constructed-response (CR) (open-ended) items. The science test has 75 MC items 5 CR items, with 24 MC items in the common-item set. Descriptive information for the two tests is provided in Tables 21.1 and 21.2.

Each of the three linking methods discussed in this chapter was applied to each of the two tests to link Form N to Form O (the base scale). Two different IRT calibration programs were used. For the MC history test, BILOG-MG (Zimowski et al., 2003) was used, and for the mixed-format science test, flexMIRT (Cai, 2013) was used. BILOG-MG can deal with MC items only (i.e., dichotomous models), while flexMIRT provides calibration options for most of the unidimensional and multidimensional models. Both programs have capabilities for all three linking methods, although some ad hoc procedures are needed for fixed calibration with BILOG-MG. The 3PL model was used to fit MC items and the graded response (GR) model was employed for CR items. Calibration procedures and results for the history test are discussed first, followed by those for the science test.

History test Separate calibration was conducted for both the old and new forms. Code 1 in the Code Appendix displays the BILOG-MG command file for calibration with the old form – the same command file was used for calibrating the new form, save for the file names. The parameter estimates for the common items on the two forms were used to find the linear transformation coefficients using each of the mean/mean, mean/sigma, Stocking–Lord, and Haebara methods. The computer program STUIRT (Kim & Kolen, 2004) was used for this purpose. Table 21.3 shows the linear transformation

Table 21.3 Estimated linear scale transformation coefficients for History.

Method	Slope	Intercept
Mean/Mean	1.0171	0.2917
Mean/Sigma	1.0006	0.2852
Haebara	1.0188	0.2836
Stocking–Lord	1.0388	0.2873

coefficients estimated based on the four transformation methods. The coefficients for the four methods appear to be very similar to each other, although using transformed parameter estimates based on different transformation methods might produce different results in subsequent analyses (e.g., equating). The Stocking–Lord method was used for further comparisons and analyses – note that this choice was not entirely arbitrary, as the characteristic curve methods typically are preferred over the moment methods, and the Stocking–Lord and Haebara methods usually perform very similarly (Hanson & Béguin, 2002; Kim & Kolen, 2006; Kolen & Brennan, 2014). The Stocking–Lord transformation coefficients were applied to all noncommon items in the new form to obtain new-form item parameter estimates expressed on the old-form scale.

Concurrent calibration was conducted first by combining the two datasets for the new and old forms into a single data file. Code 2 displays the structure of the combined dataset. The first four columns are examinee IDs and columns 6 and 7 represent the form and group identifiers, respectively. For the first 3,500 records, which are for the old form, the last 23 columns are responses to the common items in the old form, and for the following 3,334 records, which are for the new form, the first 23 columns (beginning with column 9) are responses to the common items in the new form. Concurrent calibration was conducted treating the old-form group as the reference group so that the resultant parameter estimates for the new-form items from this single run would be on the old-form scale. Code 3 provides the BILOG-MG command file for concurrent calibration.

Fixed calibration with BILOG-MG is much more complex than the other two methods, and a somewhat detailed explanation is provided here. BILOG-MG, by default, (1) uses $N(0,1)$ as a prior ability distribution, which is unchanged during the EM cycles; (2) updates the prior ability distribution (called a posterior distribution), after the final EM cycle, based on the item parameter estimates from the last iteration of the EM algorithm; and (3) produces a final set of item parameter estimates by rescaling them to have a mean of zero and an SD of one based on the posterior distribution (Kim & Lee, 2017). To properly place the parameter estimates for the noncommon items in the new form on the old-form base scale, rescaling (i.e., standardization) should **not** be performed. The NOADJUST keyword in BILOG-MG is used to prevent standardization of the parameter estimates.

When the prior ability distribution is not updated during the EM cycles as implemented in BILOG-MG, the fixed calibration method produces biased parameter estimates (Kang & Petersen, 2009; Kim, 2006a; Paek & Young, 2005). Kim (2006a, 2006b) suggested that the prior distribution be updated multiple times during the EM cycles so that the parameter estimates for the new-form noncommon items gradually become placed on the old-form scale. Instead of using a fixed $N(0,1)$ prior distribution, an ability distribution needs to be estimated in each iteration of the EM algorithm (called an empirical distribution), which in turn is used as the prior for the next EM cycle. If the

BILOG-MG keyword EMPIRICAL is invoked, empirical distributions are used instead of the fixed prior distribution. However, the EMPIRICAL keyword could not be used here for two reasons. First, the EMPIRICAL option overrides the NOADJUST option, which is necessary to suppress rescaling. Second, empirical distributions are standardized by default after each EM cycle when the EMPIRICAL option is used.

To account for this, an ad hoc procedure was employed with BILOG-MG as suggested by Kim (2006b). Fixed calibration was run multiple times to manually update the prior ability distribution. More specifically, the first fixed calibration was conducted using the NOADJUST option in the CALIB command to prevent standardization of the estimated posterior distribution (see Code Appendix, Code 4 for the BILOG-MG command file). The FIX option was specified in the TEST1 command to fix the parameter estimates for the common items (the first 23 items in the data) at the values stored in ItemParameter.PRM (see Code 5), and the parameters for the rest of the 47 noncommon items are freely estimated. The first record in ItemParameter.PRM in Code 5 indicates the number of common items that are fixed in calibration; these are followed by lines, each with an item number and a, b, and c-parameter estimates. In the second fixed calibration run, the unstandardized posterior distribution obtained from the first run was used as a fixed prior distribution for the second run by invoking the QUAD command to provide the quadrature points and weights, which were found in the Phase II output file of the first run. The second fixed calibration run produced another estimated posterior distribution, which was used as a fixed prior distribution for the third run, and so on. Code 6 in the Code Appendix shows the control card for the second fixed calibration run. This iterative process was stopped when the change in both the mean and SD of the estimated posterior distribution from those of the previous iteration was less than .001. Table 21.4 displays the means and SDs from iterations of fixed calibration. The iteration was stopped at the tenth iteration and the parameter estimates from the tenth iteration were adopted as the final set.

The performance of this ad hoc procedure for fixed calibration with BILOG-MG was found satisfactory compared to the separate and concurrent calibration methods (Kim, 2006b). Note that this ad hoc procedure is not necessary if a calibration program has a proper option to update the prior distribution during the EM cycles and to freely estimate the mean and SD for the empirical distributions – for example, PARSCALE (Muraki & Bock, 2003) and flexMIRT (Cai, 2013).

Table 21.5 presents the transformed parameter estimates for the 47 noncommon items in the new form using the three linking methods. The last two rows in the table are the means and SDs. It appears that the three linking methods produced somewhat

Table 21.4 Updated posterior distributions from iterative fixed calibration with BILOG-MG.

Iteration	Mean	SD
0	.0000	1.0000
1	.2322	1.0086
...	...	...
5	.2702	1.0353
6	.2695	1.0382
...	...	...
9	.2681	1.0431
10	.2671	1.0440

Table 21.5 Transformed parameter estimates for noncommon items in new form for History.

	Separate			Concurrent			Fixed		
	a	b	c	a	b	c	a	b	c
1	0.9145	−1.6464	0.2017	0.9650	−1.4090	0.3140	0.9425	−1.4711	0.3111
2	0.5988	0.6227	0.5000	0.6040	0.4860	0.5000	0.6206	0.4251	0.5000
3	0.8849	0.9652	0.1769	1.0160	0.9380	0.1840	0.9838	0.9517	0.1853
4	0.7371	−1.3742	0.1479	0.7770	−1.1820	0.2190	0.7505	−1.2682	0.2046
5	0.6139	1.0370	0.2025	0.7070	1.0210	0.2160	0.6860	1.0396	0.2181
6	1.2715	−0.6685	0.2519	1.3640	−0.5460	0.2790	1.3226	−0.5929	0.2780
7	0.9563	0.6955	0.1604	1.0940	0.7030	0.1690	1.0613	0.7071	0.1709
8	0.9845	0.1554	0.2080	1.1110	0.2310	0.2260	1.0748	0.2169	0.2271
9	0.6940	0.6363	0.1021	0.7840	0.6590	0.1160	0.7630	0.6655	0.1193
10	0.8256	0.3405	0.1654	0.9420	0.4020	0.1840	0.9078	0.3924	0.1844
11	0.8094	−0.3205	0.2201	0.9040	−0.1770	0.2560	0.8742	−0.2092	0.2556
12	0.4095	0.9421	0.1665	0.4470	0.9310	0.1740	0.4464	0.9764	0.1852
13	0.9458	−0.7368	0.1722	1.0110	−0.6070	0.2060	0.9831	−0.6474	0.2074
14	0.5049	0.1081	0.0806	0.5530	0.1840	0.0990	0.5351	0.1648	0.0985
15	0.4387	−1.4323	0.1674	0.4370	−1.4360	0.1630	0.4335	−1.4468	0.1716
16	0.3646	−2.5307	0.1959	0.3530	−2.6050	0.1980	0.3542	−2.5949	0.2053
17	0.5804	−0.9764	0.1281	0.5990	−0.8910	0.1450	0.5865	−0.9331	0.1448
18	0.9180	0.2110	0.2280	1.0370	0.2830	0.2450	1.0038	0.2720	0.2473
19	0.3446	0.6543	0.1341	0.3520	0.5440	0.1110	0.3516	0.6009	0.1261
20	1.0928	−1.5968	0.1265	1.0720	−1.5430	0.1640	1.0529	−1.5976	0.1645
21	0.4264	−0.8368	0.1183	0.4360	−0.8300	0.1090	0.4301	−0.8360	0.1176
22	1.0384	−1.2915	0.1248	1.0590	−1.1870	0.1650	1.0383	−1.2365	0.1664
23	0.7787	1.0210	0.0995	0.8880	0.9890	0.1070	0.8602	1.0033	0.1086
24	0.5574	1.8787	0.1987	0.6400	1.7410	0.2040	0.6347	1.7807	0.2085
25	0.5251	0.2684	0.1892	0.5770	0.3370	0.2070	0.5642	0.3405	0.2115
26	0.7960	−0.0168	0.0764	0.8680	0.0550	0.0910	0.8406	0.0352	0.0926
27	1.4180	0.2094	0.2622	1.5930	0.2700	0.2720	1.5388	0.2569	0.2741
28	1.0855	0.1264	0.0722	1.1980	0.1850	0.0830	1.1555	0.1687	0.0841
29	0.9218	0.3561	0.0765	1.0310	0.3980	0.0880	0.9921	0.3879	0.0880
30	0.8224	0.6465	0.1178	0.9350	0.6650	0.1300	0.9026	0.6674	0.1314
31	0.5020	1.2301	0.0846	0.5600	1.1810	0.0920	0.5485	1.2080	0.0960
32	0.9086	1.2840	0.2307	1.0520	1.2130	0.2350	1.0245	1.2363	0.2369
33	0.9366	−0.1683	0.2577	1.0540	−0.0420	0.2880	1.0160	−0.0729	0.2870
34	0.9351	0.3960	0.0670	1.0380	0.4290	0.0750	1.0015	0.4209	0.0761
35	0.7434	−0.2904	0.1076	0.8050	−0.1940	0.1280	0.7826	−0.2174	0.1311
36	0.5877	−0.0112	0.1037	0.6370	0.0630	0.1200	0.6201	0.0490	0.1224
37	0.5828	0.4901	0.1968	0.6530	0.5430	0.2150	0.6398	0.5543	0.2203
38	1.2285	0.1560	0.2673	1.3700	0.2190	0.2770	1.3117	0.2000	0.2774
39	0.7385	−0.1763	0.0620	0.8030	−0.0960	0.0770	0.7774	−0.1235	0.0770
40	0.7882	0.6095	0.2078	0.8960	0.6370	0.2210	0.8697	0.6428	0.2240
41	0.6274	−1.4992	0.1381	0.6390	−1.3840	0.1800	0.6210	−1.4732	0.1641
42	0.6413	1.7113	0.2781	0.7270	1.5890	0.2800	0.7289	1.6295	0.2865
43	1.0065	−0.6009	0.2286	1.0920	−0.4670	0.2610	1.0505	−0.5171	0.2575
44	0.9446	−0.1698	0.2535	1.0460	−0.0670	0.2740	1.0085	−0.0967	0.2738
45	0.9781	0.8649	0.3090	1.1230	0.8510	0.3150	1.0870	0.8623	0.3167
46	0.8233	0.3488	0.1159	0.9240	0.3970	0.1300	0.8949	0.3897	0.1313
47	0.6126	0.6847	0.1507	0.6750	0.6890	0.1580	0.6565	0.6956	0.1601
Mean	0.7839	0.0491	0.1730	0.8606	0.0887	0.1904	0.8368	0.0767	0.1920
SD	0.2437	0.9435	0.0807	0.2757	0.8982	0.0829	0.2625	0.9205	0.0822

Table 21.6 Transformed parameter estimates for common items in new form for History.

	Separate			Concurrent			Fixed		
	a	b	c	a	b	c	a	b	c
1	0.9766	−0.1362	0.2849	1.0340	0.0110	0.2880	0.8391	−0.0694	0.2378
2	0.6541	−0.6891	0.2228	0.7780	−0.3730	0.3270	0.7200	−0.5726	0.2782
3	0.3923	−0.7090	0.1992	0.4020	−0.6420	0.2380	0.3853	−0.9077	0.1969
4	0.7994	−1.4782	0.1319	0.8390	−1.1800	0.2570	0.8276	−1.2051	0.2449
5	0.8345	0.4647	0.1424	0.9130	0.4260	0.1500	0.8323	0.3144	0.1353
6	0.8028	0.8416	0.1430	1.0120	0.8650	0.1510	1.0078	0.9241	0.1493
7	0.6140	0.3474	0.1175	0.6960	0.3530	0.1370	0.6808	0.2749	0.1354
8	1.3950	−0.1087	0.1304	1.4780	−0.0430	0.1160	1.3240	−0.1096	0.0905
9	0.8682	1.8650	0.1908	1.0320	1.7070	0.2110	0.9247	1.8096	0.2222
10	0.6926	0.3387	0.1256	0.8950	0.6320	0.1960	0.8854	0.8085	0.2149
11	0.5309	−1.6452	0.1395	0.5520	−1.4680	0.1660	0.5651	−1.4551	0.1438
12	0.9100	−0.0096	0.1813	0.9430	0.0370	0.1960	0.8008	−0.0923	0.1636
13	0.5947	−2.0157	0.1728	0.5630	−2.0480	0.2200	0.5757	−2.0718	0.2020
14	0.6741	1.1795	0.1853	0.7730	1.1110	0.2090	0.7016	1.0935	0.2094
15	0.8385	−1.8616	0.1277	0.8510	−1.7700	0.1830	0.9344	−1.7120	0.1688
16	0.6791	0.4345	0.2511	0.8650	0.6050	0.2870	0.8227	0.6518	0.2788
17	0.4969	−0.0335	0.1078	0.5260	0.0010	0.1520	0.5305	−0.0320	0.1817
18	0.9389	1.5521	0.0866	1.1600	1.3720	0.0850	1.1718	1.3704	0.0850
19	0.9396	−0.3228	0.1986	0.8790	−0.3140	0.1980	0.7018	−0.5538	0.1291
20	0.6535	−0.2431	0.0944	0.6380	−0.2350	0.0770	0.5852	−0.2511	0.0777
21	0.6532	−0.5342	0.0912	0.7210	−0.3440	0.1050	0.7081	−0.3083	0.1024
22	0.5504	−0.4072	0.0803	0.5850	−0.4550	0.0640	0.6178	−0.4726	0.0854
23	1.0142	0.3712	0.1695	0.9280	0.2720	0.1510	0.7337	0.0639	0.1016
Mean	0.7610	−0.1217	0.1554	0.8288	−0.0643	0.1810	0.7772	−0.1088	0.1667
SD	0.2164	1.0106	0.0535	0.2321	0.9264	0.0680	0.2055	0.9520	0.0609

different results, in general, with the results for the concurrent and fixed calibration methods being more similar to each other than the separate calibration method. The similarity between the results for the fixed and concurrent calibration methods might be due to the fact that for these two methods, unlike separate calibration, linking is done while items are being calibrated without the need for an additional linking process. Table 21.6 displays the parameter estimates for the 23 common items in the new form obtained based on the three linking methods. Notice that the results for the separate and fixed calibration methods are more similar than those for the concurrent calibration method, which appears to be related to sample size. The parameter estimates for the common items with separate calibration and fixed calibration were based only on the new-form data and the old-form data, respectively, while those for concurrent calibration were based on the combined dataset with a larger sample size. Thus, it is generally expected that the concurrent calibration method will produce more accurate parameter estimates for the common items.

Science test In analyzing the data for the science mixed-format test, it is assumed that the data are unidimensional even with the existence of two different item types. If there is an evident format effect that violates the assumption of unidimensionality, linking two mixed-format test forms comprised of both MC and CR items through a common-item set consisting solely of MC items may not work properly. Previous research shows that adequate equating results may be obtained for mixed-format test forms with an MC common-item set, if the disattenuated correlation between the MC and CR scores is higher than .8 (Lee et al., 2012). Because the purpose of linking is to conduct IRT equating, as discussed later, the disattenuated correlation criterion of .8 is used here. The estimated disattenuated correlation between the MC and CR scores on the science test was .98 for both forms, which clearly suggests that there is no format effect and thus supports the use of the unidimensional models.

Different IRT calibration programs use different parameterizations of various IRT models. flexMIRT provides slope, intercept, and logit-guessing parameters in the logistic metric. The item parameter estimates from flexMIRT were transformed to make them comparable to the parameterization of item parameters employed in other computer software for linking and equating. The following transformation formulas were used: $a = a^* / 1.7$; $b = -c^* / a^*$; and $c = 1 / [1 + \exp(-\text{logit } g^*)]$, where a^*, c^*, and logit g^* are slope, intercept, and logit-guessing parameters from flexMIRT (Houts & Cai, 2013). The category difficulty parameters for the GR model were transformed in the same way.

Code 7 in the Code Appendix displays the flexMIRT command file for separate calibration with the old form. In the input data file, the first 51 columns are for non-common MC items, the next five for CR items, and the last 24 for MC common items. The 3PL and GR models were used for the MC and CR items, respectively. Some prior distributions were used, as specified in the < Constraints > section for the guessing and slope parameters to ensure convergence. The linear scale transformation coefficients were obtained using the four scale transformation methods based on the two sets of parameter estimates for the MC common items, with these coefficients then applied to all MC and CR items in the new form. The computer program STUIRT (Kim & Kolen, 2004) was used to obtain the scale transformation coefficients. Table 21.7 summarizes the results. The coefficients across the four methods were not substantially different, and the results for the Stocking–Lord method were used to transform the new-form parameter estimates for subsequent analyses.

Concurrent calibration with flexMIRT does not require the two datasets for the old and new forms to be combined in a single file. The two datasets were specified separately in the < Groups > section, as seen in Code 8. The mean and variance of the ability distribution for the new-form group were allowed to be freely estimated using the Free statement in the < Constraints > section. The mean and variance of the old-form group were fixed to the default standard scale, which served as the base scale. In addition, the parameter estimates for the common items were constrained to be equal for the two groups by the Equal statement in the < Constraints > section.

Table 21.7 Estimated linear scale transformation coefficients for Science.

Method	Slope	Intercept
Mean/Mean	1.0539	−0.1059
Mean/Sigma	1.0245	−0.0955
Haebara	1.0421	−0.0754
Stocking–Lord	1.0290	−0.0756

Table 21.8 Transformed parameter estimates for noncommon MC items in a new form for Science.

	\multicolumn{3}{c}{Noncommon MC items}								
	\multicolumn{3}{c}{Separate}	\multicolumn{3}{c}{Concurrent}	\multicolumn{3}{c}{Fixed}
	a	b	c	a	b	c	a	b	c
Mean	0.8907	0.3751	0.1859	0.8413	0.3941	0.1883	0.8800	0.3878	0.1927
SD	0.3009	0.8414	0.0664	0.2835	0.8936	0.0677	0.3002	0.8604	0.0693

	\multicolumn{3}{c}{Common MC items}								
	\multicolumn{3}{c}{Separate}	\multicolumn{3}{c}{Concurrent}	\multicolumn{3}{c}{Fixed}
	a	b	c	a	b	c	a	b	c
Mean	0.9585	0.2898	0.1638	0.9112	0.2800	0.1596	0.9358	0.2683	0.1600
SD	0.2962	0.7528	0.0825	0.3027	0.7927	0.0829	0.3280	0.7495	0.0689

The command file for fixed calibration with flexMIRT is provided in Code 9. As discussed earlier, fixed calibration using the new-form data involves fixing the parameter estimates for the common items at the values obtained from the old-form calibration. This was done using two statements in the < Constraints > section: The Fix and Value statements. The a-, b-, and c-parameter estimates for all 24 common items were supplied each after the Value statement. Because the prior ability distribution needs to be updated after each EM cycle and the ability distribution should not be standardized, EmpHist = yes in the < Groups > section and the Free statement in the < Constraints > section were selected.

Table 21.8 presents the means and SDs of the new-form parameter estimates for the noncommon MC items and common MC items transformed based on the three linking methods. These summary statistics show that the three linking methods produced different, but similar results. Table 21.9 displays the transformed parameter estimates for the five CR items. Again, the results tended to be similar across the three linking methods.

IRT Equating

One of the important psychometric practices related to the use of tests is "equating" to achieve score comparability over multiple forms of the same test (Kolen & Brennan, 2014). Raw scores (i.e., number-correct scores) typically are transformed to scale scores for reporting purposes. It is assumed here that the old form has an established score scale and a raw-to-scale-score conversion table is available. Equating can be viewed as a two-step process: (1) find the relationships between raw scores on the old form and raw scores on the new form, and (2) convert the equated new-form raw scores to scale scores using the old-form conversion table. Through this equating process, the score scale is maintained – that is, a scale score has the same meaning regardless of the test forms administered (Kolen & Brennan, 2014).

There are a number of traditional non-IRT equating methods that can be used for the common-item nonequivalent groups design (Angoff, 1971; Holland & Dorans, 2006;

Table 21.9 Transformed parameter estimates for CR items in a new form for Science.

Separate

	a	b_1	b_2	b_3	b_4	b_5	b_6	b_7	b_8	b_9	b_{10}
1	1.3697	-1.3784	-0.5320	-0.2611	0.0104	0.3548	0.5593	0.9799	1.5371	1.8841	2.4786
2	1.4986	-1.2066	-0.6983	-0.4232	-0.1240	0.1745	0.4364	0.7390	1.0428	1.3826	1.9315
3	1.4508	-1.5478	-1.0478	-0.6547	-0.3320	0.0181	0.3914	0.7771	1.2206	1.8378	
4	1.0833	-1.6417	-0.7251	-0.0159	0.6015	1.1172	1.6861	2.2233	2.9735		
5	1.3983	-1.3377	-0.8935	-0.4781	-0.0109	0.4146	0.8427	1.3419	1.9470	2.7013	

Concurrent

	a	b_1	b_2	b_3	b_4	b_5	b_6	b_7	b_8	b_9	b_{10}
1	1.2810	-1.4861	-0.5786	-0.289	0.0009	0.3682	0.5863	1.0345	1.6284	1.9986	2.6335
2	1.4021	-1.3012	-0.7562	-0.4619	-0.1421	0.1764	0.4554	0.7778	1.1012	1.4632	2.0486
3	1.3578	-1.6681	-1.1312	-0.7098	-0.3645	0.0094	0.4074	0.8183	1.2907	1.9487	
4	1.0132	-1.7687	-0.7859	-0.0276	0.6314	1.1814	1.7882	2.3617	3.1631		
5	1.3083	-1.442	-0.9656	-0.5209	-0.0217	0.4321	0.8881	1.4201	2.0654	2.8708	

Fixed

	a	b_1	b_2	b_3	b_4	b_5	b_6	b_7	b_8	b_9	b_{10}
1	1.3282	-1.4361	-0.5539	-0.2733	0.0072	0.3618	0.5719	1.0030	1.5717	1.9249	2.5298
2	1.4528	-1.2563	-0.7264	-0.4405	-0.1305	0.1775	0.4466	0.7569	1.0678	1.4154	1.9758
3	1.4082	-1.6147	-1.0916	-0.6820	-0.3465	0.0158	0.4000	0.7956	1.2497	1.8799	
4	1.0420	-1.7210	-0.7595	-0.0218	0.6169	1.1486	1.7338	2.2855	3.0553		
5	1.3546	-1.3939	-0.9304	-0.4985	-0.0147	0.4236	0.8632	1.3743	1.9906	2.7520	

Kolen & Brennan, 2014; von Davier et al., 2004). In this chapter, two IRT equating methods are discussed: the true-score and observed-score equating methods. IRT true-score equating is presented first, followed by observed-score equating.

True-score equating

In IRT true-score equating, true score on one form is considered to be equivalent to true score on the other form associated with a particular ability θ value. The test characteristic curves for two test forms, which define the relationships between ability θ and true scores, are used to determine equating relationships for raw scores. The true scores on Form N and Form O corresponding to a specific θ value are defined as:

$$\tau_N(\theta) = \sum_{i=1}^{K_N} p_i(\theta) \tag{21.2}$$

$$\tau_O(\theta) = \sum_{i=1}^{K_O} p_i(\theta), \tag{21.3}$$

where K_N and K_O are the number of items in Form N and Form O, respectively, and $p_i(\theta)$ is the probability of answering item i correctly. Using these equations, a particular θ can be transformed to a true-score estimate on each form.

As an example, consider a five-item test and that the 3PL item parameter estimates are available for Form N and Form O. Figure 21.2 shows test characteristic curves for the two forms. An examinee with a θ value of 0.5 has a true score of 3.4 on Form N, and a true score of 2.7 on Form O. Because the true scores on the two forms, 3.4 and 2.7, are related to the same ability level, the two true scores are considered to be equivalent.

Recall that the purpose of equating is to find an equivalent score on the old form that corresponds to a specific score on the new form. The actual IRT true-score equating starts with a raw score on the new form and involves the following two steps: (1) find a θ value corresponding to a specific raw score on the new form, and (2) determine a true score on the old form with the θ value obtained from step (1). The Newton–Raphson

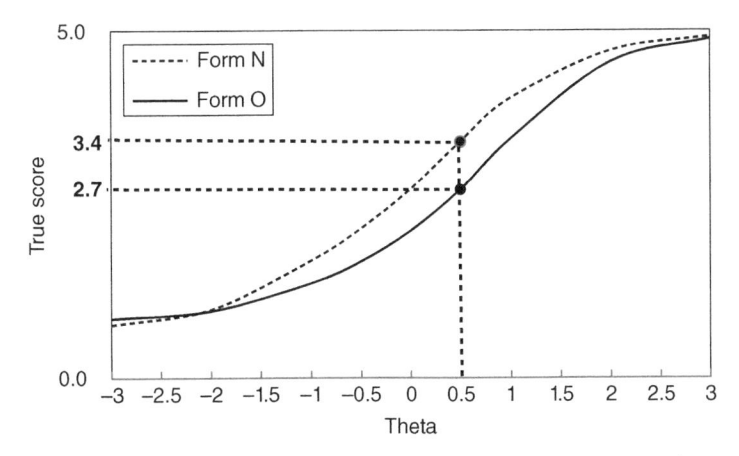

Figure 21.2 Test characteristics curves for Form N and Form O and equivalent true scores.

method is usually implemented in step (1) to find a θ value associated with a specified raw score (Cook & Eignor, 1991; Kolen & Brennan, 2014). The Newton–Raphson method finds the root of a nonlinear function, such as the relationship between θ and true score via an iteration process. These steps are repeated for all raw-score points in the new form to find their old-form equivalent scores.

The IRT true-score equating procedures are appropriate for equating true scores under the IRT framework. However, true scores of examinees are never known. Thus, in practice, the estimated true-score equating relationship is applied to observed scores, although there is no theoretical justification in doing so (Harris & Crouse, 1992; Lord & Wingersky, 1984). Note also that when the 3PL model is used, no true-score equivalents are defined at very low scores below the sum of the c-parameter estimates.

Observed-score equating

The IRT observed-score equating procedures utilize the processes of estimating observed-score distributions of raw scores for both the old and new forms using estimated item and ability parameters. Then, traditional equipercentile equating procedures are applied to the estimated observed-score distributions for finding equating relationships.

For dichotomous IRT models, a compound binomial distribution is used to compute the observed-score distribution given a θ value based on item parameter estimates. The conditional observed-score distributions are usually computed using a recursive formula such as the one proposed by Lord and Wingersky (1984). For polytomous IRT models, conditional observed-score distributions are produced by a compound multinomial model using the recursive algorithm described in Hanson (1994) and Thissen, Pommerich, Billeaud, and Williams (1995). The marginal observed-score distribution for examinees across all ability levels can be obtained by aggregating the conditional observed-score distributions over the entire range of ability levels as

$$f(x) = \int_{-\infty}^{\infty} f(x|\theta) g(\theta) d\theta. \qquad (21.4)$$

For computational simplicity, in practice the integration in Equation 21.4 is approximated by summation using a set of discrete quadrature points and weights.

Ability distributions for the two groups need to be estimated and placed on the same scale. The two estimated ability distributions expressed on the same scale are used to produce a synthetic population, for which the equating relationships are then determined. After the marginal observed-score distributions for Form N and Form O are obtained, the traditional equipercentile equating method is used to find equivalent scores between the two forms for the synthetic population.

Illustrative examples

The same two datasets used in the previous section on IRT linking are used in this section. All the parameter estimates for the two forms were already on the same scale (see previous section). Both IRT true-score and observed-score equating methods were conducted for each of three sets of parameter estimates obtained from the three different linking methods to examine the extent to which different linking methods affect equating results. The computer program POLYEQUATE (Kolen, 2004) was used to find equating relationships between the old-form and new-form scores for both IRT true- and observed-score equating procedures. The old form of the MC history test has a raw-to-scale-score conversion table where raw scores ranging from 0 to 70 are converted to unrounded scale scores ranging from 0 to 70. For the mixed-format science test, the conversion table for the old form has raw scores from 0 to 120 that are converted to unrounded scale scores of 0 to 70. Note that rounded scale scores are typically reported to examinees. However, for the purpose of equating, unrounded scale scores are usually used to improve the precision of equating results. The results for the history test are presented first, followed by the results for the science test.

History test Six input files were needed to operate the POLYEQUATE computer program, including a control card file, new- and old-form item parameter estimates, new- and old-form theta quadrature points and weights, and a raw-to-scale-score conversion table for the old form. Note that all of the item and ability parameter estimates were put on the same scale. The standard normal quadrature points and weights were used for both the old-form and new-form groups, but the quadrature points for the new-form groups were transformed to the old-form scale using the scale transformation coefficients obtained from the Stocking–Lord method. These quadrature distributions were used for all equatings.

Raw-score results for the IRT true-score and observed-score equating methods using the parameter estimates from the three linking methods are presented graphically in Figure 21.3. Differences between the new-form raw scores and the new-form equated scores are plotted in Figure 21.3. The comparison of the top panel and the bottom panel shows that the patterns are very similar between the true-score equating results and the observed-score equating results. Larger differences were found in the results for the three linking methods. In particular, the fixed linking method tended to produce equating results that were a little different from the other two methods. However, the differences were very small, all being less than one raw-score point, except for the true-score equating results at very low raw scores (i.e., lower than 12), where true scores could not be defined due to the guessing parameters.

Equating produced results for new-form unrounded scale scores. In Table 21.10, the results are summarized by equating methods and linking methods in terms of the first four moments of the equated unrounded scale-score distributions for the new form. Overall, the moments for the two equating methods and three linking methods were all similar. The two equating methods produced very similar unrounded scale scores with respect to the four moments. Unlike the raw-score results, among the three linking methods, concurrent calibration produced results that were slightly different from the other two linking methods.

The results for rounded scale scores need special attention as they are the scores that are reported to examinees. Table 21.11 reports rounded scale scores for the new form resulting from true-score equating based on the three linking methods. The highlighted cells indicate that there are differences in rounded scale scores among the three linking methods. Although the largest difference is only one scale-score point, this clearly suggests that different linking methods do influence equating results in reported scale scores. A similar pattern was found in the observed-score equating results, and thus not reported here. The results for the true-score and observed-score equating methods also showed some differences in rounded scale scores given a particular linking method, albeit less so than the comparison across different linking methods.

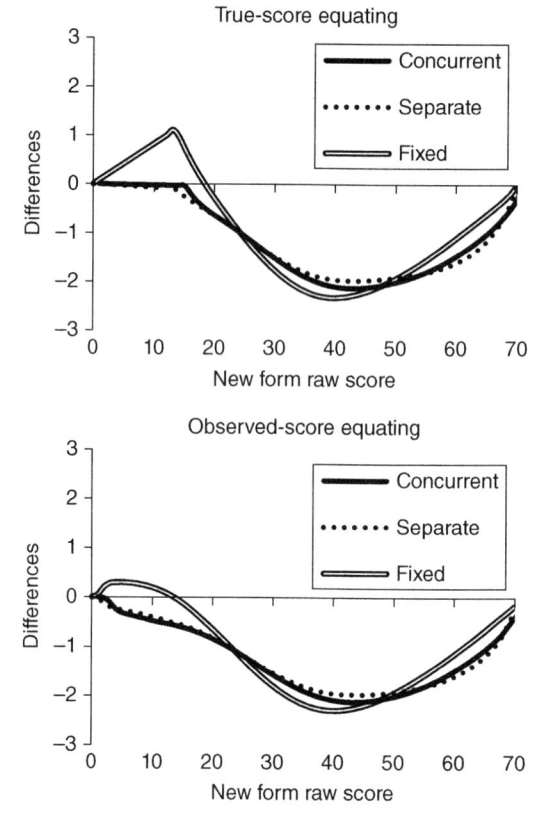

Figure 21.3 Raw-score results for IRT true- and observed-score equating based on three linking methods for History.

Table 21.10 First four moments of equated unrounded scale scores for History.

	\multicolumn{4}{c}{*True-score equating*}
	Mean	SD	Skewness	Kurtosis
Separate	45.7718	13.0552	−0.2827	2.2407
Concurrent	45.4152	13.4006	−0.2186	2.1310
Fixed	45.5087	13.1406	−0.2815	2.2522

	\multicolumn{4}{c}{*Observed-score equating*}
	Mean	SD	Skewness	Kurtosis
Separate	45.7982	13.0235	−0.2725	2.2284
Concurrent	45.4446	13.3700	−0.2057	2.1157
Fixed	45.5501	13.0897	−0.2583	2.2145

Science test The computer program POLYEQUATE (Kolen, 2004) was again used for the science test. The same procedures used for the history test forms were used for equating the science mixed-format test forms. Raw-score equating results are compared in Figure 21.4. As for the results for the history test, the true-score results displayed in the top panel and the observed-score results in the bottom panel appear to be very

Table 21.11 IRT true-score equating results for History (rounded scale scores).

Raw	Sep.	Conc.	Fixed	Raw	Sep.	Conc.	Fixed
0	0	0	0	36	38	38	38
1	1	1	1	37	39	39	39
2	2	2	2	38	40	40	40
3	3	3	3	39	41	41	41
4	4	4	4	40	42	42	42
5	5	5	5	41	43	43	43
6	6	6	6	42	44	44	44
7	7	7	6	43	45	45	45
8	8	8	7	44	46	46	46
9	9	9	8	45	47	47	47
10	10	10	9	46	48	48	48
11	11	11	10	47	49	49	49
12	12	12	11	48	50	50	50
13	13	13	12	49	51	51	51
14	14	14	13	50	52	52	52
15	15	15	14	51	53	53	53
16	16	16	16	52	54	54	54
17	17	17	17	53	55	55	55
18	18	19	18	54	56	56	56
19	20	20	19	55	57	57	57
20	21	21	20	56	58	58	57
21	22	22	21	57	59	59	58
22	23	23	23	58	60	60	59
23	24	24	24	59	61	60	60
24	25	25	25	60	62	61	61
25	26	26	26	61	63	62	62
26	27	27	27	62	63	63	63
27	28	28	28	63	64	64	64
28	29	29	30	64	65	65	65
29	30	31	31	65	66	66	66
30	31	32	32	66	67	67	67
31	33	33	33	67	68	68	67
32	34	34	34	68	69	68	68
33	35	35	35	69	69	69	69
34	36	36	36	70	70	70	70
35	37	37	37				

similar regardless of linking methods, except for the scores below the sum of the c-parameter (guessing) estimates. The three linking methods produced some differences along the score scale, with the results for separate calibration being most dissimilar. The largest difference observed was approximately one raw-score point.

The first four moments of unrounded scale scores are summarized in Table 21.12. Similar to the raw-score results, the moments produced by the two equating methods were similar for a given linking method, and the moments for separate calibration tended to be somewhat different from the other two linking methods. Finally, Table 21.13 displays rounded scale scores for the true-score equating method. There were quite a few raw-score points where the three linking methods showed a one scale-score point difference.

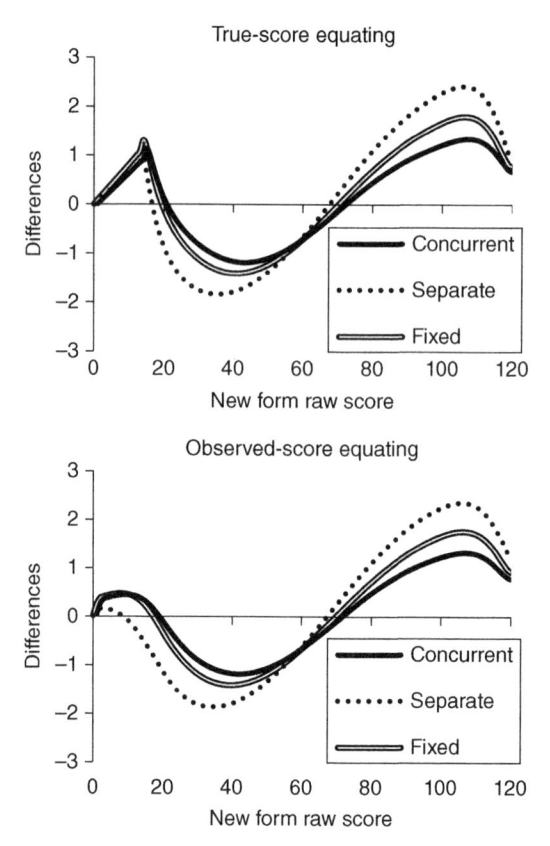

Figure 21.4 Raw-score results for IRT true- and observed-score equating based on three linking methods for Science.

Table 21.12 First four moments of equated unrounded scale scores for Science.

	True-score equating			
	Mean	*SD*	*Skewness*	*Kurtosis*
Separate	31.4592	12.5903	0.2166	2.8122
Concurrent	31.6119	14.8025	0.2510	2.5887
Fixed	31.5833	14.3270	0.2431	2.6389
	Observed-score equating			
	Mean	*SD*	*Skewness*	*Kurtosis*
Separate	31.5083	12.4906	0.2584	2.7656
Concurrent	31.6541	14.7111	0.2767	2.5740
Fixed	31.6331	14.2219	0.2749	2.6149

Multidimensional IRT Equating

Most of the discussion so far has focused on unidimensional IRT (UIRT) models in the context of linking and equating. UIRT models have been commonly used in practice and have proven to be useful under certain conditions. Sometimes, however, there is

Table 21.13 IRT true-score equating results for Science (rounded scale scores).

Raw	Sep.	Conc.	Fixed	Raw	Sep.	Conc.	Fixed	Raw	Sep.	Conc.	Fixed
0	0	0	0	41	25	25	25	82	43	44	44
1	0	0	0	42	26	25	25	83	44	44	44
2	0	0	0	43	26	26	26	84	44	45	45
3	0	0	0	44	27	26	26	85	45	45	45
4	0	0	0	45	27	27	27	86	45	46	46
5	0	0	0	46	28	27	27	87	46	46	46
6	0	0	0	47	28	28	28	88	46	47	47
7	0	0	0	48	28	28	28	89	47	47	47
8	0	0	0	49	29	29	29	90	47	48	48
9	0	0	0	50	29	29	29	91	48	48	48
10	0	0	0	51	30	30	30	92	48	49	49
11	0	0	0	52	30	30	30	93	49	50	49
12	0	0	0	53	31	31	31	94	50	50	50
13	0	0	0	54	31	31	31	95	50	51	50
14	1	1	1	55	31	31	31	96	51	51	51
15	4	4	3	56	32	32	32	97	51	52	52
16	7	6	6	57	32	32	32	98	52	52	52
17	9	8	8	58	33	33	33	99	52	53	53
18	10	9	9	59	33	33	33	100	53	54	53
19	11	10	10	60	34	34	34	101	54	54	54
20	12	11	11	61	34	34	34	102	54	55	55
21	13	12	12	62	35	35	35	103	55	56	55
22	14	13	13	63	35	35	35	104	56	56	56
23	15	14	14	64	35	35	35	105	56	57	57
24	15	15	15	65	36	36	36	106	57	58	57
25	16	16	16	66	36	36	36	107	58	58	58
26	17	16	16	67	37	37	37	108	58	59	59
27	18	17	17	68	37	37	37	109	59	60	59
28	18	18	18	69	38	38	38	110	60	61	60
29	19	18	18	70	38	38	38	111	61	62	61
30	19	19	19	71	38	39	39	112	62	63	62
31	20	19	20	72	39	39	39	113	63	63	63
32	21	20	20	73	39	40	39	114	64	65	64
33	21	21	21	74	40	40	40	115	65	66	66
34	22	21	21	75	40	40	40	116	67	68	67
35	22	22	22	76	41	41	41	117	68	69	69
36	23	22	22	77	41	41	41	118	69	70	69
37	23	23	23	78	42	42	42	119	70	70	70
38	24	23	23	79	42	42	42	120	70	70	70
39	24	24	24	80	43	43	43				
40	25	24	24	81	43	43	43				

a need for more complex IRT models to reflect the complexity of data structures. This such a need has led to the development of multidimensional IRT (MIRT) models to describe the interactions of latent traits and characteristics of test items (Reckase, 2009). Even though various MIRT models have been developed, their applications have been limited in practice.

Two simple MIRT models

Two relatively simple MIRT models that can be used to fit data from mixed-format tests with substantial format effects are considered here: simple structure MIRT (SS-MIRT) and bifactor MIRT (BF-MIRT) models. Both models have been increasingly applied and implemented as important statistical methods in psychological and educational measurement (Cai, Yang, & Hansen, 2011; Gibbons & Hedeker, 1992; Kolen, Wang, & Lee, 2012). Recently, IRT equating procedures based on the two models were proposed by Lee and Brossman (2012) and Lee and Lee (2016).

Equating with the two MIRT models is discussed using, as an example, a mixed-format test composed of MC and CR items. In the SS-MIRT model, two correlated dimensions (MC-related latent trait and CR-related latent trait) are considered and each item is assumed to be associated with only one latent trait. In contrast, the BF-MIRT model takes item-format effects into account by incorporating specific dimensions or factors (i.e., a specific factor for the MC-item format and another specific factor for the CR-item format) in addition to a general dimension. Figure 21.5 depicts the data structure for a test composed of mixed-format items where M and F represent MC and CR items, respectively; and θ_G, θ_M, and θ_F represent the general, MC-related, and CR-related factors, respectively.

Because a mixed-format test contains both MC and CR items, two different IRT models are needed for dichotomously and polytomously scored items. In this chapter, extensions of the classical two-parameter logistic UIRT model for MC items and Samejima's (1969, 1997) GR UIRT model for CR items are used for illustrative purposes (Cai et al., 2011).

Equating with MIRT models

Because MIRT models incorporate multiple latent traits (i.e., a vector of θs), it is generally necessary to conceptualize an "arbitrary" unidimensional latent trait to place test characteristic surfaces of two test forms on the same scale for true-score equating. Thus, a unidimensional approximation or reduction process is typically used to find equivalents with MIRT true-score equating. For this reason, Lee and Lee (2016) recommended use of observed-score equating rather than true-score equating.

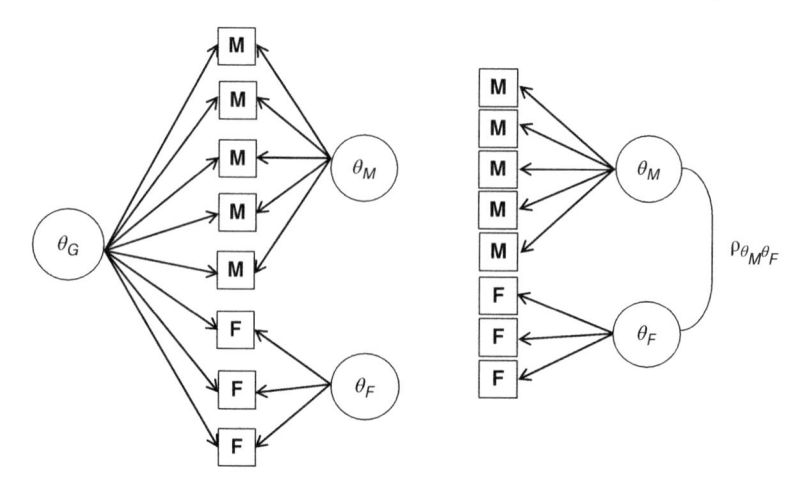

Figure 21.5 BF-MIRT and SS-MIRT models for a mixed-format test.

Few studies exist in the literature that investigate equating under a MIRT framework. Brossman and Lee (2013) may be the first study dealing with MIRT observed and true-score equating procedures with a multidimensional two-parameter logistic model. Recently, Lee and Brossman (2012) proposed observed-score equating procedures under the SS-MIRT framework for mixed-format tests. Lee and Lee (2016) suggested a BF-MIRT observed-score equating method and investigated its relative appropriateness compared to UIRT observed-score equating.

MIRT observed-score equating can be accomplished, in general, by using the following steps: (1) generate conditional observed-score distributions, (2) aggregate the conditional distributions to obtain marginal observed-score distributions, and (3) find equipercentile equating relationships. With the estimated item parameters for the SS-MIRT model, the conditional observed-score distribution is computed at each pair of θ_M (MC factor) and θ_F (CR factor) from a bivariate normal distribution with a correlation between the two latent traits. For the BF-MIRT model, the conditional observed-score distribution is computed at each combination of θ_G (general factor), θ_M (MC-specific factor), and θ_F (CR-specific factor) from a mutually uncorrelated trivariate normal distribution. For both models, extended versions of the recursive formulas by Lord and Wingersky (1984) for dichotomous items and Hanson (1994) and Thissen et al. (1995) for polytomous items are used.

A marginal observed-score distribution is obtained by aggregating conditional observed-score distributions using the following equations for the SS-MIRT and BF-MIRT models, respectively:

$$f(x) = \iint_{-\infty}^{\infty} f(x|\theta_M, \theta_F) g(\theta_M, \theta_F) d\theta_M d\theta_F, \quad (21.5)$$

$$f(x) = \iiint_{-\infty}^{\infty} f(x|\theta_G, \theta_M, \theta_F) g(\theta_G, \theta_M, \theta_F) d\theta_G d\theta_M d\theta_F. \quad (21.6)$$

Integration in these equations can be approximated by summation with a specified set of quadrature points and weights from density functions of a correlated bivariate normal distribution and an uncorrelated trivariate normal distribution for the SS-MIRT and BF-MIRT models, respectively. After the marginal observed-score distributions for both old and new forms are obtained, the traditional equipercentile equating method is applied to find the equating relationships.

An illustrative example

If data are collected using the random groups design, the SS-MIRT and BF-MIRT observed-score equating procedures can be readily conducted without any scale linking process (Brossman & Lee, 2013; Lee & Lee, 2016; Thompson, Nering, & Davey, 1997). The data used in this example were from a mixed-format literature test with the common-item nonequivalent groups design. In order to create a dataset for the random groups design, a single form of the literature test was split into two halves, which resulted in two short pseudo-forms (old and new) containing the same number of MC and CR items.

A sample of 3,000 examinees was selected randomly from a large pool of examinees who took the operational test form. Item responses for the 3,000 selected examinees to the pseudo-old-form items constituted one dataset for the old-form group, and item responses for a different random sample of 3,000 examinees to the pseudo-new-form items formed the dataset for the new-form group. Thus, these pseudo-form data represented a situation where two randomly equivalent groups of examinees were administered the pseudo-old and new forms. Table 21.14 presents descriptive statistics of the two pseudo-forms of the literature test used in this example.

The UIRT, SS-MIRT, and BF-MIRT observed-score equating procedures were conducted. For UIRT equating, item parameters of the two-parameter logistic model for MC items and the GR model for CR items were estimated using flexMIRT and UIRT observed-score equating relationships were found using POLYEQUATE (Kolen, 2004). For equating with the SS-MIRT and BF-MIRT models, item parameters were estimated using flexMIRT and the observed-score equating relationships were computed using a program developed by the senior author of this chapter.

Equating results for the UIRT, SS-MIRT, and BF-MIRT methods are displayed in Figure 21.6. Results for the three IRT models along with identity equating (i.e., no equating) are presented in this figure. Clearly, the equivalent scores for the three methods were very similar. The SS-MIRT method produced results that were a bit closer to the results for the UIRT method than the BF-MIRT method.

The differences among the three methods might be viewed as practically insignificant, in general. This conclusion can be interpreted as being indicative of very minor within-format residual dependence for the mixed-format test. Since the primary purpose of this example was to demonstrate the observed-score equating methods with the SS-MIRT and BF-MIRT models, the results reported here should not be over-generalized to

Table 21.14 Descriptive statistics for Literature pseudo-form datasets.

Form	No. of MC items	No. of CR items	Max. score point	No. of examinees	Mean	SD
New	18	2(5,5)	28	3,000	18.4	4.34
Old	18	2(5,5)	28	3,000	18.8	4.25

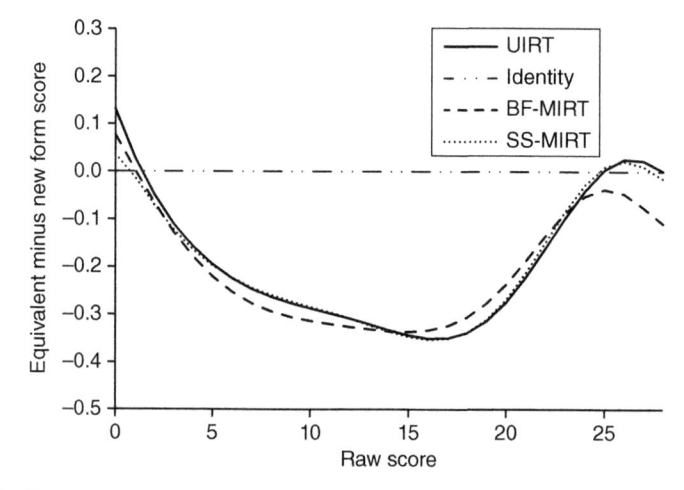

Figure 21.6 Equating results for UIRT, BF-MIRT, and SS-MIRT observed-score equating methods.

other mixed-format tests. For example, when it is suspected that there is a strong format effect indicated by a relatively large estimated disattenuated correlation, the MIRT alternatives might be preferred over UIRT models. The two MIRT models could also be used when a test is composed of testlets or content specifications contribute different dimensions. More research is needed to investigate the relationship between equating results and degree of multidimensionality.

Summary

In this chapter, we provide an overview of three IRT linking methods – separate, concurrent, and fixed calibration methods, under a UIRT framework, and demonstrate their performances using two real data examples that differ in composition of item formats. We also present somewhat detailed step-by-step processes of the linking methods by providing command files for two IRT calibration programs that are commonly used in the field. Although these linking methods have been frequently used in practice, there is little literature that compares these three methods together in a comprehensive study. In particular, a future research study would evaluate the relative performances of these methods when applied to mixed-format tests with varying compositions of item types in a common-item set.

We discuss two IRT equating methods and compare their results using the same two real datasets. In addition, the effects of use of different linking methods on equating are examined. Two MIRT models are considered in equating with mixed-format tests – simple structure and bifactor models. These relatively simple MIRT models could be useful when dealing with multidimensional test data in a confirmatory way. Linking and equating with these models may well deserve further research.

Acknowledgments

The authors are grateful to the RR student research group at the University of Iowa and graduate students at Yonsei University for their assistance in the data analysis and preparation of this manuscript.

References

Angoff, W. H. (1971). Scales, norms, and equivalent scores. In R. L. Thorndike (Ed.), *Educational measurement* (2nd ed.) (pp. 508–600). Washington, D.C.: American Council on Education.

Baker, F. B., & Kim, S.-H. (2004). *Item response theory: Parameter estimation techniques* (2nd ed.). New York: Marcel Dekker.

Béguin, A. A., & Hanson, B. A. (2001, April). *Effect of noncompensatory multidimensionality on separate and concurrent estimation in IRT observed score equating.* Paper presented at the Annual Meeting of the National Council on Measurement in Education, Seattle, WA.

Bock, R. D., & Aitkin, M. (1981). Marginal maximum likelihood estimation of item parameters: Application of an EM algorithm. *Psychometrika, 46,* 443–459.

Brossman, B. G., & Lee, W. (2013). Observed score and true score equating procedures for multidimensional item response theory. *Applied Psychological Measurement, 37,* 460–481.

Cai, L. (2013). *flexMIRT version 2: Flexible multilevel multidimensional item analysis and test scoring* [Computer software]. Chapel Hill, NC: Vector Psychometric Group.

Cai, L., Yang, J. S., & Hansen, M. (2011). Generalized full-information item bifactor analysis. *Psychological Methods, 16,* 221–248.

Cook, L. L., & Eignor, D. R. (1991). An NCME instructional module on IRT equating methods. *Educational Measurement: Issues and Practices, 10,* 37–45.

Finch, H. (2008). Estimation of item response theory parameters in the presence of missing data. *Journal of Educational Measurement, 45,* 225–245.

Gibbons, R. D., & Hedeker, D. R. (1992). Full-information item bifactor analysis. *Psychometrika, 57,* 423–436.

Haebara, T. (1980). Equating logistic ability scales by a weighted least squares method. *Japanese Psychological Research, 22,* 144–149.

Hanson, B. A. (1994). *An extension of the Lord–Wingersky algorithm to polytomous items.* Unpublished research note.

Hanson, B. A., & Béguin, A. A. (2002). Obtaining a common scale for item response theory item parameters using separate versus concurrent estimation in the common-item equating design. *Applied Psychological Measurement, 26,* 3–24.

Harris, D., J., & Crouse, T. D. (1993). A study of criteria used in equating. *Applied Measurement in Education, 6,* 195–240.

Holland, P. W., & Dorans, N. J. (2006). Linking and equating. In R. L. Brennan (Ed.), *Educational measurement* (4th ed.) (pp. 187–220). Westport, CT: American Council on Education and Praeger.

Houts, C. R., & Cai, L. (2013). *flexMIRT® user's manual version 2: Flexible multilevel multidimensional item analysis and test scoring.* Chapel Hill, NC: Vector Psychometric Group.

Kang, T., & Petersen, N. (2009). *Linking item parameters to a base scale* (ACT Research Report 2009-2). Iowa City, IA: ACT, Inc.

Kim, K. Y., & Lee, W. (2017). The impact of three factors on the recovery of item parameters for the three-parameter logistic model. *Applied Measurement in Education, 30,* 228–242.

Kim, S. (2006a). A comparative study of IRT fixed parameter calibration methods. *Journal of Education Measurement, 43,* 355–381.

Kim, S. (2006b). A study on IRT fixed parameter calibration methods using BILOG-MG. *Journal of Educational Evaluation, 19,* 323–342.

Kim, S.-H., & Cohen, A. S. (1998). A comparison of linking and concurrent calibration under item response theory. *Applied Psychological Measurement, 22,* 131–143.

Kim, S., & Kolen, M. J. (2004). *STUIRT* [Computer software]. Iowa City, IA: The Center for Advanced Studies in Measurement and Assessment, The University of Iowa. (Available from the web address: https://education.uiowa.edu/centers/center-advanced-studies-measurement-and-assessment/computer-programs)

Kim, S., & Kolen, M. J. (2006). Robustness of format effects of IRT linking methods for mixed format tests. *Applied Measurement in Education 19,* 357–381.

Kim, S., & Lee, W. (2006). An extension of four IRT linking methods for mixed-format tests. *Journal of Educational Measurement, 43,* 53–76.

Kolen, M. J. (2004). *POLYEQUATE* [Computer software]. Iowa City, IA: The Center for Advanced Studies in Measurement and Assessment, The University of Iowa. (Available from the web address: https://education.uiowa.edu/centers/center-advanced-studies-measurement-and-assessment/computer-programs).

Kolen, M. J., & Brennan, R. L. (2014). *Test equating, scaling, and linking: Methods and practices* (3rd ed.). New York, NY: Springer.

Kolen, M. J., Wang, T., & Lee, W. (2012). Conditional standard errors of measurement for composite scores using IRT. *International Journal of Testing, 12,* 1–20.

Lee, G., & Lee, W. (2016). Bi-factor MIRT observed-score equating for mixed-format tests. *Applied Measurement in Education, 29,* 224–241.

Lee, W., & Ban, J.-C. (2010). A comparison of IRT linking procedures. *Applied Measurement in Education, 23,* 23–48.

Lee, W., & Brossman, B. G. (2012). Observed score equating for mixed-format tests using a simple-structure multidimensional IRT framework. In M. J. Kolen, & W. Lee (Eds.), *Mixed-format tests: Psychometric properties with a primary focus on equating* (Vol. 2) (CASMA Monograph No. 2.2.) (pp. 115–142) Iowa City: Center for Advanced Studies in Measurement and Assessment, The University of Iowa. (Available on https://education.uiowa.edu/centers/center-advanced-studies-measurement-and-assessment/publications-and-data-files#mono)

Lee, W., He, Y., Hagge, S. L., Wang, W., & Kolen, M. J. (2012). Equating mixed-format tests using dichotomous common items. In M. J. Kolen, & W. Lee (Eds.), *Mixed-format tests: Psychometric properties with a primary focus on equating* (Vol. 2) (CASMA Monograph Number 2.2) (pp. 13–44). Iowa City, IA: Center for Advanced Studies in Measurement and Assessment, The University of Iowa. (Available on https://education.uiowa.edu/centers/center-advanced-studies-measurement-and-assessment/publications-and-data-files#mono)

Lee, W., & Kim, J. (2011, July). *Comparison of multiple-group and single-group calibration methods for linking*. Paper presented at the International Meeting of the Psychometric Society, The Hong Kong Institute of Education, Hong Kong.

Lord, F. M. (1980). *Applications of item response theory to practical testing problems*. Hillsdale, NJ: Erlbaum.

Lord, F. M., & Wingersky, M. S. (1984). Comparison of IRT true-score and equipercentile observed-score "equatings." *Applied Psychological Measurement, 8*, 452–461.

Loyd, B. H., & Hoover, H. D. (1980). Vertical equating using the Rasch model. *Journal of Educational Measurement, 17*, 179–193.

Marco, G. L. (1977). Item characteristic curve solutions to three intractable testing problems. *Journal of Educational Measurement, 14*, 139–160.

Mislevy, R. J., & Wu, P.-K. (1996). *Missing responses and IRT ability estimation: Omits, choice, time limits, and adaptive testing* (Research Report RR-96-30-ONR). Princeton, NJ: Educational Testing Service.

Muraki, E., & Bock, R. D. (2003). *PARSCALE 4: IRT item analysis and test scoring for rating scale data* [computer program]. Chicago, IL: Scientific Software.

Paek, I., & Young, M. J. (2005). Investigation of student growth recovery in a fixed-item linking procedure with a fixed-person prior distribution for mixed-format test data. *Applied Measurement in Education, 18*, 199–215.

Petersen, N. S., Cook, L. L., & Stocking, M. L. (1983). IRT versus conventional equating methods: A comparative study of scale stability. *Journal of Educational Statistics, 8*, 137–156.

Reckase, M. D. (2009). *Multidimensional item response theory*. New York, NY: Springer.

Samejima, F. (1969). *Estimation of latent ability using a response pattern of graded scores*. (Psychometrika Monograph No. 17) Richmond, VA: Psychometric Society.

Samejima, F. (1997). Graded response model. In W. J. van der Linden, & R. K. Hambleton (Eds.), *Handbook of modern item response theory* (pp. 85–100). New York: Springer-Verlag.

Stocking, M. L., & Lord, F. M. (1983). Developing a common metric in item response theory. *Applied Psychological Measurement, 7*, 201–210.

Thissen, D., Pommerich, M., Billeaud, K., & Williams, V. S. L. (1995). Item response theory for scores on tests including polytomous items with ordered responses. *Applied Psychological Measurement, 19*, 39–49.

Thompson, T., Nering, M., & Davey, T. (1997). *Multidimensional IRT scale linking*. Paper presented at the Annual Meeting of the Psychometric Society, Gatlinburg, TN.

von Davier, A. A., Holland, P. W., & Thayer, D. T. (2004). *The kernel method of test equating*. New York: Springer-Verlag.

Zimowski, M. F., Muraki, E., Mislevy, R. J., & Bock, R. D. (2003). *BILOG-MG 3 for Windows: Multiple-group IRT analysis and test maintenance for binary items* [Computer software]. Lincolnwood, IL: Scientific Software International, Inc.

Code Appendix

Code 1 BILOG-MG command file for separate calibration with history old form.

```
>COMMENTS
Separate calibration for History old form
>GLOBAL   DFNAME='History_old.DAT', NPARM=3, SAVE;
>SAVE     PARM='History_old.PAR';
>LENGTH   NITEM=70;
>INPUT    NTOTAL=70, SAMPLE=3500, NID=4;
>ITEMS    INAMES=(MC01(1)MC70);
>TEST1    TNAME='History_old', INUMBER=(1(1)70);
         (T1,4A1,T6,70A1)
>CALIB    CYCLES=100, NQPT=40, NEWTON=0, CRIT=0.001;
```

Code 2 History data for concurrent calibration with BILOG-MG.

```
0001  11  11101111111011111110111001111110101010101000111010100111101011001111111
0002  11  11101010111011111010001111111110110011100010000101010000101101010000000
...
3500  11  10101111111011111110111101111111111110111111111110111111111111111111011
0001  22  10001010000010000100000000000000000000101111101010000011100010011001100
0002  22  10110011010110110101010000001000101010100000011110010101001001110101110
...
3334  22  11000001001110000000110100000000110101010100000001001010000010100101110
```

Code 3 BILOG-MG command file for concurrent calibration for history.

```
>COMMENTS
Concurrent calibration for History
N=3500 for old form and N=3334 for new form
# common items = 23
Old    47 23       =  70
New       23 47    =  70
Total  47 23 47    = 117
>GLOBAL   DFNAME='History.DAT', NPARM=3,  SAVE;
>SAVE     PARM='History.PAR';
>LENGTH   NITEM=117;
>INPUT    NTOTAL=117, SAMPLE=6834, NALT=5, NID=4, NFORM=2, NGROUP=2;
>ITEMS
          ;
>TEST     TNAME='History', INUMBER=(1(1)117);
>FORM1    LENGTH=70, INUMBERS=(1(1)70);
>FORM2    LENGTH=70, INUMBERS=(48(1)117);
>GROUP1   GNAME='Old',  LENGTH=70,  INUMBERS=(1(1)70);
>GROUP2   GNAME='New',  LENGTH=70,  INUMBERS=(48(1)117);
          (T1,4A1,T6,I1,T7,I1,T9,70A1)
>CALIB    CYCLES=200, NQPT=40, NEWTON=0, CRIT=0.001, REF=1;
```

Code 4 First BILOG-MG command file for fixed calibration with history new form.

```
>COMMENTS
Fixed calibration for History
First Command File
>GLOBAL   DFNAME='History.DAT', PRNAME='ItemParameter.PRM',
          NPARM=3, SAVE;
>SAVE     PARM='History_First.PAR';
>LENGTH   NITEM=70;
>INPUT    NTOTAL=70, SAMPLE=3334, NID=4;
>ITEMS    INAMES=(MC01(1)MC70);
>TEST1    TNAME='History', INUMBER=(1(1)70), FIX=(1(0)23,
          0(0)47);
          (T1,4A1,T6,70A1)
>CALIB    CYCLES=100, NQPT=41, NEWTON=0, CRIT=0.001,
          NOADJUST;
```

Code 5 Fixed item parameter file from history old form (ItemParameter.PRM).

```
23
01   0.83911   -0.06944    0.23778
02   0.71998   -0.57261    0.27822
03   0.38532   -0.90767    0.19692
...
23   0.73374    0.06385    0.10158
```

Code 6 Second BILOG-MG command file for fixed calibration with history new form.

```
>COMMENTS
Fixed calibration for History
Second Command File
>GLOBAL   DFNAME='History.DAT', PRNAME='ItemParameter.
          PRM', NPARM=3, SAVE;
>SAVE     PARM='History_Second.PAR';
>LENGTH   NITEM=70;
>INPUT    NTOTAL=70, SAMPLE=3334, NID=4;
>ITEMS    INAMES=(MC01(1)MC70);
>TEST     TNAME='History', INUMBER=(1(1)70), FIX=(1(0)23,
          0(0)47);
          (T1,4A1,T6,70A1)
>CALIB    CYCLE=100, NQPT=41, NEWTON=0, IDIST=1, CRIT=0.001,
          NOADJUST;
>QUAD     POINTS=(
          -0.4000E+01 -0.3800E+01 -0.3600E+01 -0.3400E+01
          -0.3200E+01 -0.3000E+01 -0.2800E+01 -0.2600E+01
          -0.2400E+01 -0.2200E+01 -0.2000E+01 -0.1800E+01
          -0.1600E+01 -0.1400E+01 -0.1200E+01 -0.1000E+01
          -0.8000E+00 -0.6000E+00 -0.4000E+00 -0.2000E+00
           0.1277E-14  0.2000E+00  0.4000E+00  0.6000E+00
           0.8000E+00  0.1000E+01  0.1200E+01  0.1400E+01
           0.1600E+01  0.1800E+01  0.2000E+01  0.2200E+01
           0.2400E+01  0.2600E+01  0.2800E+01  0.3000E+01
           0.3200E+01  0.3400E+01  0.3600E+01  0.3800E+01
           0.4000E+01),
          WEIGHTS=(
           0.1088E-03 0.1977E-03 0.3375E-03 0.5448E-03
           0.8453E-03 0.1280E-02 0.1901E-02 0.2809E-02
           0.4096E-02 0.5881E-02 0.8214E-02 0.1123E-01
           0.1508E-01 0.1990E-01 0.2572E-01 0.3269E-01
           0.4087E-01 0.4985E-01 0.5884E-01 0.6690E-01
           0.7391E-01 0.8020E-01 0.8351E-01 0.8222E-01
           0.7632E-01 0.6652E-01 0.5486E-01 0.4289E-01
           0.3170E-01 0.2227E-01 0.1499E-01 0.9675E-02
           0.5976E-02 0.3528E-02 0.1991E-02 0.1078E-02
           0.5607E-03 0.2810E-03 0.1359E-03 0.6339E-04
           0.2841E-04);
>SCORE    NOPRINT;
```

Code 7   flexMIRT command file for separate calibration with science old form.

```
<Project>
  Title = "Separate calibration for Science old form";
  Description = "51 non-common MC, 5 CR, and 24 MC CI";

<Options>
  Mode = Calibration;
  SavePRM = Yes;

<Groups>
  %Old%
  File = "Science_old.DAT";
  Varnames = MC1-MC51, CR1-CR5, CI1-CI24;
  N = 3500;

  Ncats(MC1-MC51) = 2;
  Ncats(CR1) = 11;
  Ncats(CR2) = 10;
  Ncats(CR3) = 11;
  Ncats(CR4-CR5) = 9;
  Ncats(CI1-CI24) = 2;

  Model(MC1-MC51) = threePL;
  Model(CR1) = Graded(11);
  Model(CR2) = Graded(10);
  Model(CR3) = Graded(11);
  Model(CR4-CR5) = Graded(9);
  Model(CI1-CI24) = threePL;


<Constraints>
  Prior (MC1-MC51, CI1-CI24), Guessing: Beta(4.0, 16.0);
  Prior (MC1-MC51, CR1-CR5, CI1-CI24),
        Slope: logNormal(0, 0.5);
```

Code 8 flexMIRT command file for concurrent calibration for science.

```
<Project>
  Title = "Concurrent calibration for Science";
  Description = "2 forms, 51 non-common MC, 5 CR, and
                 24 MC CI";

<Options>
  Mode = Calibration;
  SavePRM = Yes;

<Groups>
  %Old%
  File = "Science_old.DAT";
  Varnames = MC1-MC51, CR1-CR5, CI1-CI24;
  N = 3500;

  Ncats(MC1-MC51) = 2;
  Ncats(CR1) = 11;
  Ncats(CR2) = 10;
  Ncats(CR3) = 11;
  Ncats(CR4-CR5) = 9;
  Ncats(CI1-CI24) = 2;

  Model(MC1-MC51) = threePL;
  Model(CR1) = Graded(11);
  Model(CR2) = Graded(10);
  Model(CR3) = Graded(11);
  Model(CR4-CR5) = Graded(9);

  Model(CI1-CI24) = threePL;

  EmpHist = Yes;

  %New%
  File = "Science_new.DAT";
  Varnames = MC1-MC51, CR1-CR5, CI1-CI24;
  N = 3592;

  Ncats(MC1-MC51) = 2;
  Ncats(CR1-CR2) = 11;
  Ncats(CR3) = 10;
  Ncats(CR4) = 9;
  Ncats(CR5) = 10;
  Ncats(CI1-CI24) = 2;
```

```
Model(MC1-MC51) = threePL;
Model(CR1-CR2) = Graded(11);
Model(CR3) = Graded(10);
Model(CR4) = Graded(9);
Model(CR5) = Graded(10);

Model(CI1-CI24) = threePL;

EmpHist = Yes;

<Constraints>
Prior Old, (MC1-MC51, CI1-CI24), Guessing: Beta(4.0, 16.0);
Prior New, (MC1-MC51, CI1-CI24), Guessing: Beta(4.0, 16.0);
Prior Old, (MC1-MC51, CR1-CR5, CI1-CI24),
           Slope: logNormal(0, 0.5);
Prior New, (MC1-MC51, CR1-CR5, CI1-CI24),
           Slope: logNormal(0, 0.5);

Free New, Mean(1);
Free New, Cov(1, 1);

Equal Old, (CI1-CI24), Guessing: New, (CI1-CI24), Guessing;
Equal Old, (CI1-CI24), Intercept: New, (CI1-CI24), Intercept;
Equal Old, (CI1-CI24), Slope: New, (CI1-CI24), Slope;
```

Code 9 flexMIRT command file for fixed calibration for science.

```
<Project>
  Title = "Fixed calibration for Science";
  Description = "51 non-common MC, 5 CR, and 24 MC CI";

<Options>
  Mode = Calibration;
  SavePRM = Yes;

<Groups>
  %New%
  File = "Science_new.DAT";
  Varnames = MC1-MC51, CR1-CR5, CI1-CI24;
  N = 3592;

  Ncats(MC1-MC51) = 2;
  Ncats(CR1-CR2) = 11;
  Ncats(CR3) = 10;
```

```
  Ncats(CR4) = 9;
  Ncats(CR5) = 10;
  Ncats(CI1-CI24) = 2;
  Model(MC1-MC51) = threePL;
  Model(CR1-CR2) = Graded(11);
  Model(CR3) = Graded(10);
  Model(CR4) = Graded(9);
  Model(CR5) = Graded(10);
  Model(CI1-CI24) = threePL;

  EmpHist = Yes;

<Constraints>
  Prior (MC1-MC51), Guessing: Beta(4.0, 16.0);
  Prior (MC1-MC51, CR1-CR5), Slope: logNormal(0, 0.5);

  Fix (CI1-CI24), Guessing;
  Value (CI1), Guessing, -0.6879958;
  ...
  Value (CI24), Guessing, -2.3508617;

  Fix (CI1-CI24), Intercept;
  Value (CI1), Intercept, -0.0519017;
  ...
  Value (CI24), Intercept, 0.1234690;

  Fix(CI1-CI24), Slope;
  Value (CI1), Slope, 0.9977019;
  ...
  Value (CI24), Slope, 0.7335777;

  Free Mean(1);
  Free Cov(1, 1);
```

Part IV
Evaluating Scales

22

Bifactor Modelling and the Evaluation of Scale Scores

Steven P. Reise, Wes Bonifay, and Mark G. Haviland

Hull, Lehn, and Tedlie (1991, p. 922) pointed out more than 20 years ago that, "Some of the most highly researched personality constructs in our field… are composed of multiple specific subcomponents." As such, Chen, West, and Sousa (2006, p. 189) noted recently that, "Researchers interested in assessing a construct often hypothesize that several highly related domains comprise the general construct of interest." In contemporary practice, to capture the richness of behavioral dispositions, psychological measures, typically, contain several items representing each of a trait construct's manifestations in phenotypically dissimilar domains.

Content complex measures, however, frequently are dimensionally ambiguous; in other words, the resulting item response data often are more or less consistent with an entire class of hierarchical models (e.g., unidimensional, second-order, correlated factors, and bifactor structural representations). In turn, this dimensionality quagmire creates confusion regarding how to score an instrument in clinical settings (e.g., global score only, subscales only, or both) or how to use it in research on prepathway predictors and postpathway external correlates.

One way to address the ambiguous dimensionality issue, and in turn, to empirically inform questions about scale scoring, is to apply a bifactor measurement model (Chen et al., 2006; Gustafsson & Åberg-Bengtsson, 2006; Reise, 2012; Reise, Bonifay, & Haviland, 2013; Reise, Moore, & Haviland, 2010) and to evaluate statistical indices derived from this model. Our primary goal in this chapter is to illustrate – with a real data example – a bifactor modelling approach for more broadly understanding an instrument's psychometric properties and their implications for its use.

After introducing the item response data used throughout this chapter, we begin by describing some preliminary analyses designed specifically to better understand sources of common variance, item content redundancy, and the degree to which the data depart from a unidimensional model. Next, we detail the application of both exploratory and confirmatory bifactor models as well as the important statistics that can be derived from these models. Our emphasis primarily will be on model-based reliability indices that inform scale scoring. Finally, we address the critical issues around the use of latent variable modelling to make judgments about how an instrument should be scored in both practice and research settings.

The Wiley Handbook of Psychometric Testing: A Multidisciplinary Reference on Survey, Scale and Test Development, First Edition. Edited by Paul Irwing, Tom Booth, and David J. Hughes.
© 2018 John Wiley & Sons Ltd. Published 2020 by John Wiley & Sons Ltd.

Real Data Example

To illustrate the central concepts, we describe the analysis of a real dataset throughout: item response data[1] from 500 nonclinical respondents to the 30-item, self-report Disgust Emotion Scale (DES; Walls & Kleinknecht, 1996). In theory, the 30 items can be partitioned into five content domains of six items each reflecting disgust reactions to: (1) **food that is rotten**, (2) **animals that are small**, (3) **injections and blood draws**, (4) **mutilation of the body and death**, and (5) **odors that are offensive**. Traditional psychometric testing (e.g., Olatunji, Sawchuk, de Jong, & Lohr, 2007) supports the theoretical five-factor structure; moreover, total and subscale scores relate as expected to another disgust measure as well as to measures of fear and obsessive compulsive symptoms. Code relating to this real data example can be found in the Code Appendix.

DES items are rated on a 0–4 scale ranging from "No disgust or repugnance at all" (0) to "Extreme disgust or repugnance" (4). Because so few individuals mark the highest response category, we collapsed Categories 3 and 4 for all analyses. Basic psychometric information and item content domain are provided in Table 22.1 (items are ordered by the proposed content domain). Standardized alpha for the global disgust score was .96 and for the domain-based subscales: .87 (rotten food), .92 (small animals), .94 (injections and blood), .89 (mutilation and death), and .91 (offensive odors). These results were obtained through analysis of raw data using the **psych** library **alpha** command (Revelle, 2013) available in the *R* software package (*R* Development Team, 2013).

Exploring Departures from Unidimensionality

The DES was designed to assess individual differences in disgust proneness (the "target" construct) as well as to allow for the reliable scoring of subscales, and it contains item content drawn from five domains of stimuli assumed to evoke disgust reactions (typically withdrawal/avoidance). Thus, even without examining DES scores, one reasonably can assume that the data will be multidimensional, at least, to some degree. Prior to employing either exploratory or confirmatory factor analytic methods (in this case, bifactor models) to evaluate multidimensionality, however, it is essential, first, to thoroughly understand the data structure, especially as it relates to item content.

In this section, we describe (and recommend) a series of analyses to better understand departures from unidimensionality and the magnitude of potential systematic sources of variance that may affect item responses and, thus, derived scale scores. These analyses are designed to: (1) better understand the sources of multidimensionality, (2) determine the degree to which the data may be consistent with a bifactor model (i.e., a general factor and multiple group factors corresponding to content domains), and (3) inform the ultimate determination of whether the content domains reflect mere nuisance variation or meaningful psychological variables.

---

[1] We thank Bunmi O. Olatunji, Ph.D., for providing this dataset, which is a subset of data from a much larger, multisample study of the structure of the Disgust Emotion Scale and its relationship to obsessive compulsive symptoms (Olatunji, Ebesutani, & Reise, 2015).

Table 22.1 Means, standard deviations, item-test correlations, and response frequencies for the DES items.

					\multicolumn{4}{c}{Response frequencies}
		M	SD	Item-test correlation	0	1	2	3
Animals	1. DES_5	.32	.63	.40	380	90	20	10
	2. DES_8	1.02	1.13	.54	220	135	55	90
	3. DES_13	.66	.83	.55	265	160	55	20
	4. DES_21	.84	.97	.62	235	150	70	45
	5. DES_26	1.51	1.07	.69	100	165	115	120
	6. DES_29	.94	1.05	.55	225	150	60	65
Foods	7. DES_1	1.07	.82	.56	120	255	95	30
	8. DES_6	1.38	.90	.53	70	240	115	75
	9. DES_12	1.90	.96	.66	40	140	150	170
	10. DES_16	1.02	.88	.64	150	225	85	35
	11. DES_20	1.12	.88	.60	120	245	90	45
	12. DES_24	1.54	.92	.66	55	205	145	90
Blood	13. DES_3	.97	1.08	.48	230	130	65	75
	14. DES_9	.85	1.01	.60	250	130	70	50
	15. DES_14	1.03	1.09	.58	210	145	65	80
	16. DES_19	.81	1.04	.59	265	120	55	60
	17. DES_23	1.31	1.10	.51	150	145	105	100
	18. DES_30	.64	.89	.57	290	130	50	30
Mutilation	19. DES_4	2.08	1.02	.53	50	85	135	230
	20. DES_10	2.01	1.01	.64	50	105	140	205
	21. DES_15	1.72	1.12	.53	100	110	125	165
	22. DES_18	1.78	1.10	.53	90	100	135	170
	23. DES_22	1.30	1.05	.60	140	150	130	80
	24. DES_27	1.77	1.00	.68	55	150	140	150
Odors	25. DES_2	1.49	.85	.61	50	225	155	70
	26. DES_7	2.13	.85	.64	10	115	170	205
	27. DES_11	2.32	.81	.66	10	75	155	255
	28. DES_17	1.76	.89	.62	30	185	165	125
	29. DES_25	1.68	.93	.61	45	180	160	115
	30. DES_28	1.68	.90	.67	35	205	145	115

Note. N = 500. Item-test correlations have been corrected for item overlap and scale reliability.

One fundamental analysis is the inspection of the polychoric correlation matrix, visually aided through shading or color coding. In Figure 22.1, we have ordered the items by assumed a priori content domain and then imposed a heat map where correlations of different magnitudes are represented by different shades of gray – higher correlations are darker, and lower correlations are lighter. Apparent in this representation is that the six items within each content domain are more highly correlated with each other than they are to items across domains. This is unsurprising and implies that multidimensional solutions ultimately will "fit" better, relative to a unidimensional model.

A second clear heat map finding is that some items do not appear to belong to their intended content domain. This is evident by the relatively lighter shades for the

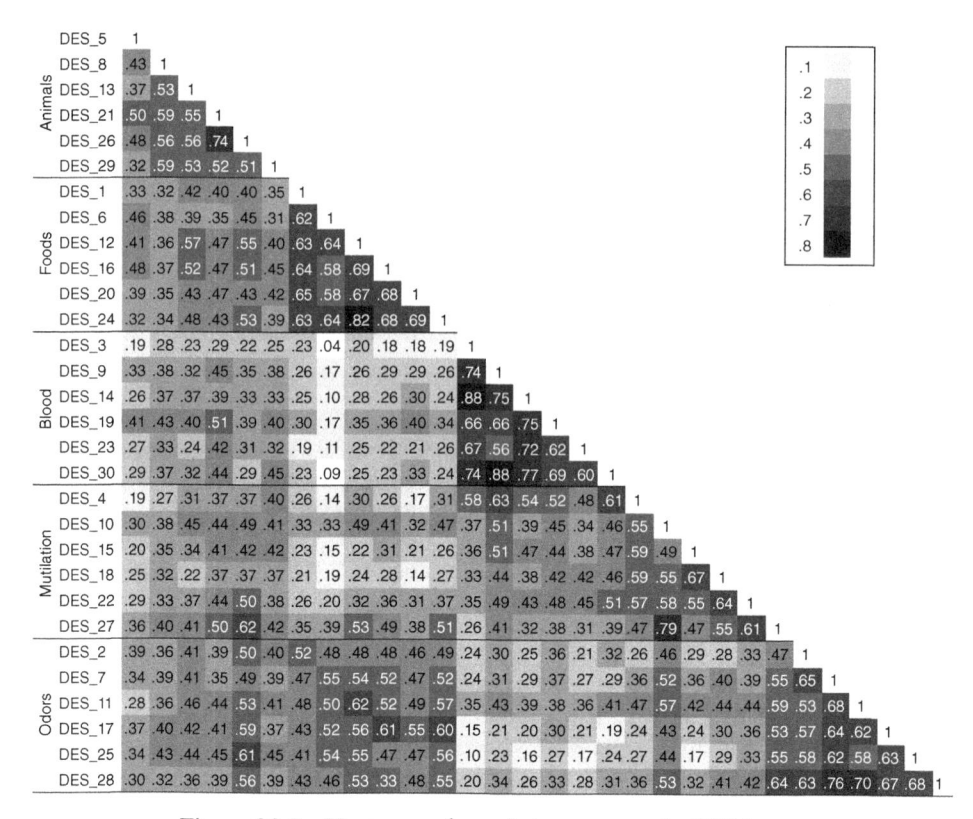

Figure 22.1 Heat map of correlations among the DES items.

correlations. Item 1 (DES_5; "An alley cat"), for example, does not cohere as strongly as the other **small animal** items. This item would not be expected to be a good marker of a specific small animal disgust dimension in either a correlated-factors or bifactor model. Other items, such as Item 13 (DES_3; **Having blood drawn from your arm**) appear highly related to other **injections and blood** items but not to items outside that domain. We, thus, would expect this item to be a good marker of a specific dimension but not a good marker of a general disgust construct.[2]

A third potentially important observation is that if one inspects the correlations across the content domains, it is apparent that "injection and blood" and "mutilation and death" domains tend to go together relative to either domain's relation to "small animals," "rotten food," or "offensive odors." This pattern suggests testing a much more complicated hierarchical structure, such as a two-tier model (Cai, 2010; two [possibly] correlated general dimensions with subdomains nested within each). Such a model, however, is well beyond the present scope.

---

[2] Zinbarg, Revelle, Yovel, & Li (2007) stated, "…covariances among items loading on different group factors are pure reflections of general factor saturation, whereas covariances among items loading on the same group factor reflect a mixture of general factor saturation and group factor saturation." In the present context, the term "subdomain" can be substituted for group factor and the term "target construct" (*Disgust*) substituted for general factor, without loss of meaning.

Before detailing the next method, we must make one final point. It is clear from the heat map that some of the highest correlated item pairs simply are the same question asked twice (and there are several in the DES). We have dubbed this common scale construction practice as the cheating (inflating internal consistency reliability) by repeating (asking the same item twice – a content doublet) phenomenon, which in turn leads to what Cattell (1978) called "bloated specifics" (nuisance dimensions that arise due to shared content when data are factor analyzed).

Content doublets are not an unusual occurrence in personality or psychopathology measures, and the practice has its roots in the demand for obtaining high alpha values. Simply put, when one attempts to write multiple items to represent a conceptually narrow construct (so that item inter-correlations are large, and, thus, alpha is high, and scoring subscales can be justified as "reliable"), it becomes clear that the diversity of trait manifestations is limited and, thus, it is extremely challenging to write items that are not merely repeats of the same stimuli over and over.

A second and complimentary analysis is hierarchical clustering (Revelle, 1979) using the *iCLUST* routine (all defaults) implemented in the *psych* library (Revelle, 2013) of R. Revelle noted (1979, p. 71) that, "Hierarchical clustering procedures are most appropriate when the variables to be clustered have some hierarchical structure (i.e., a general factor, several common factors, and then several specific factors)." This procedure, thus, is well suited for the DES and should be highly informative in determining whether the items join together into content-based subscales as expected by theory.

In Figure 22.1, this clustering is shown, asking for five clusters, based on the DES polychoric correlations. The *Cs* in the circles represent the order of cluster joining (e.g., Cluster 1 joined Items DES_12 and DES_24). Shown within each cluster circle are the alpha coefficient, Revelle's beta (smallest split-half reliability coefficient), and the number of items within the cluster. Clusters are merged whenever the resulting combined cluster provides increased alpha and beta coefficients. The numbers above the lines linking the clusters are correlations.

iCLUST graphs provide a wealth of information. Most important, they reveal whether the a priori content domains are consistent with the empirical data. Here the answer is an overwhelming yes, but with a caveat. That caveat is that DES_10 (The *mutilated body of a dog that had been run over by car*) and DES_27 (A *decaying animal on the road*) join together in the fourth cluster, but this cluster never ultimately merges with the other four items from this domain. Instead, the algorithm formed two larger clusters of *rotten food* and *offensive odors* items and then joined them in Cluster 24.

Returning to the content redundancy issue raised above, it also is interesting to observe that Clusters 1 through 9 reveal that there are many very highly correlated item pairs (as learned from the heat map) and that these sets form highly internally consistent subscales. Cluster 1, for example, contains items with spoiled meat content, Cluster 2 contains snake/spider content, and Cluster 3 contains blood content (merely a "vial" versus a "bottle" of blood).

One of the conundrums caused by these content repeats, beyond the complexities they create for determining dimensionality prior to factor analysis, and for ultimately determining whether a factor represents a real psychological phenomena or a "bloated specific," is that it is not clear how the inclusion of additional items within a content domain improves the quality of measurement (in terms of alpha) beyond some of those two item clusters. Cluster 1, for example, has an alpha of .90, and the six-item Cluster 18 has an alpha of .92, an increase of .02 for a tripling of scale length. Again, such results are not surprising. When the conceptual scope of disgust is fragmented into a very specific class of stimuli, the ability to gain unique information through multiple items is greatly diminished.

Another problem caused by these highly inter-related content doublets is that very likely they will cause severe violations of local independence (i.e., correlated residuals) even if the DES data are "essentially unidimensional" – most of the **common** variance is attributable to a single general factor, or, summed scores reflect mostly a single general factor. In turn, these local independence violations will make the measure look superior in terms of measuring a single construct (disgust) than it really is (by inflating the average correlation and, thus, coefficient alpha) if one relies on conventional psychometric analyses. To more formally evaluate the extent to which this is true in the DES, and to indirectly assess the degree to which a multidimensional (bifactor) model will be required to account for the covariances among DES items, we suggest a third analysis.

In contrast to the first two analyses, this one requires fitting a formal parametric latent variable model to the data. We recommend the fitting of a unidimensional item response theory (IRT) model and inspecting local dependence violation indices. We estimated a unidimensional graded response model (Samejima, 1997) using the **mirt** (Chalmers, 2013) library available in R. We then requested residual statistics. Note that the point here is not to report on or evaluate the IRT model parameters or the "fit" of the unidimensional IRT model, for neither would be helpful at this point in ultimately understanding the latent structure of DES responses or in the scoring of general or domain specific DES scales.

In Table 22.2 are shown local dependence (residual dependencies after accounting for a single latent variable) statistics (for details, see Chen & Thissen, 2007). These basically are Z-values of the residuals after fitting a unidimensional model. Although statistical tests could be performed, the convention in IRT analysis simply is to look for large positive values, with the larger values (>10) indicating rather severe violations of unidimensionality. Clearly, within each domain, there are many very large and positive values that, in turn, tell us that the multidimensionality caused by the content domains simply cannot be ignored as trivial. That is, the multidimensionality is sizable and potentially consequential and, thus, needs to be modelled in some way to more clearly understand how well the DES reflects a single construct of disgust proneness that is independent of its distinct components and vice versa. In what follows, we suggest a bifactor approach to addressing this issue.

What is a Bifactor Model and How is it Useful?

The idea that psychological assessment data can (or should) be modelled through a bifactor structure has its origin in the early writings of Holzinger (1939) and Holzinger and Swineford (1937, 1939). A bifactor measurement model specifies that the **common** variance among item responses can be partitioned into one general factor and two or more group factors where all factors are orthogonal. In these pioneering days of factor analysis, the bifactor model was viewed as an alternative to the correlated-factors model, which "hides" a general factor in the matrix of factor intercorrelations. The bifactor measurement structure now is understood to be a "parent" model in the sense that,

Table 22.2 Chen–Thissen (1997) standardized local dependence values for each subscale.

	Animals				Foods			
DES_5					DES_1			
DES_8	6.23				DES_6	68.21		
DES_13	10.30	12.81			DES_12	41.33	39.65	
DES_21	13.69	35.55	14.68		DES_16	34.12	23.70	33.90
DES_26	6.62	15.92	16.75	51.08	DES_20	46.35	30.65	37.45	52.35
DES_29	−16.94	55.58	15.28	25.93	16.04	DES_24	22.75	46.56	88.04	43.12	45.74

	Blood				Mutilation			
DES_3					DES_4			
DES_9	143.36				DES_10	22.10		
DES_14	319.09	133.16			DES_15	48.96	15.90	
DES_19	68.98	50.66	101.49		DES_18	54.60	28.94	89.51
DES_23	98.45	56.38	111.44	50.12	DES_22	35.93	23.20	31.98	59.84
DES_30	121.80	239.01	113.03	68.08	50.59	DES_27	12.24	70.88	8.92	24.36	20.59

	Odors				
DES_2					
DES_7	19.19				
DES_11	−26.06	18.57			
DES_17	15.21	13.60	12.53		
DES_25	18.58	15.64	9.50	20.38	
DES_28	18.52	47.09	27.84	31.20	37.33

second-order and unidimensional measurement structures are nested within a bifactor (Rindskopf & Rose, 1988; Yung, Thissen, & McLeod, 1999).

The classic example of a bifactor model application is a battery of cognitive tests where the common variance is partitioned into a general factor related to all indicators (thought to represent general intelligence – G) and a set of orthogonal groups factors related only to subsets of items (thought to represent specific abilities beyond G). Gustafsson and Balke (1993) provide an excellent example, but by no means should bifactor modelling be considered limited to the analyses of the structure of cognitive abilities (see, e.g., Chen et al., 2006; Reise, 2012; Thomas, 2012; Zinbarg, Barlow, & Brown, 1997).

Three common misunderstandings (or myths) of bifactor measurement models are that: (1) they are confirmatory only, (2) they cannot accommodate cross loadings (when items load on the general and more than one group factor), and (3) the group factors are required to be orthogonal to each other. The first myth clearly will be debunked as we demonstrate several methods for conducting an exploratory bifactor analysis of the DES. The second myth simply is ill-informed; the only requirement for interpreting a group factor is that there be at least three items loading solely on the general and the group factor (Zinbarg et al., 2007). Once this basic requirement is met, other items that load on a specific group factor may have cross loadings on other group factors. The third myth has been dismissed by Jennrich and Bentler (2012) who described an exploratory bifactor model where all group factors are orthogonal to the general (for identification), but the group factors are allowed to be correlated.[3]

A bifactor structure is a viable measurement model whenever an instrument has been designed to scale individuals along a single global construct but also contains multiple sets of content homogeneous items (and those subsets are correlated). Because such data rarely will meet strict unidimensionality assumptions, the obvious alternative multidimensional models are second-order, correlated-factors, and bifactor. The bifactor has the conceptual advantage over the correlated-factors model in that the latter provides no easy mechanism for understanding the common variance running among the items (importantly, the target construct the instrument primarily was designed to measure!)

The bifactor and second-order models view the common dimension quite differently. The general factor in a second-order model "causes" variation on a set of primary factors (and, thus, its designation as a "higher-order" model), which in turn, "cause" variation on the items. That is, there are no direct relations between the general factor and the items in a second-order measurement model (see Chen et al., 2006; Yung et al., 1999). In contrast, in a bifactor model, the general and the group factors both have direct effects on the items, and, thus, are on equal conceptual footing and "compete" to explain item response variance.

This is the mechanism that promotes the bifactor model's utility in: (1) understanding what portion of an item's variance is due to the general and group factors (Chen, et al., 2012; Simms, Gros, Watson, & O'Hara, 2008), (2) exploring the effect of forcing multidimensional data into a misspecified unidimensional model (Reise, Morizot, & Hays, 2007; Reise et al., 2013), and most relevant here, (3) better understanding

---

[3] By no means does this imply that estimating bifactor models with correlated group factors is not complicated or that solutions are readily interpretable; they are not.

the interpretability and feasibility of global and subscale scores (Reise, Bonifay, & Haviland, 2013; Reise, Moore, & Haviland, 2010).

To realize these objectives, however, we first must fit some data to a bifactor model. We begin with exploratory bifactor modelling, and there are, at least, four viable options:

1 The Schmid–Leiman (SL; Schmid & Leiman, 1957) orthogonalization,
2 The Jennrich–Bentler (JB; Jennrich & Bentler, 2011) analytic rotation,
3 Target rotations to a bifactor structure (Reise, Moore, & Maydeu-Olivares, 2011) and,
4 Bayesian exploratory structural equation modelling (Muthén & Asparouhov, 2012).

Space does not allow for an extended description and comparison of each of these procedures and, thus, we will limit ourselves here to the demonstration of the first two only. Historically, the SL has been the only available exploratory approach, and its strengths and limits, generally, are well understood. The JB, on the other hand, was introduced recently and, thus, has received less research attention. We chose to illustrate application of the JB because it simply is another analytic rotation (based on a bifactor, not simple structure criteria) – a procedure familiar to any researcher who has conducted a factor analysis.

In Table 22.3 are displayed the results of a SL orthogonalization with one general and five group factors. This model was estimated using the *psych* (Revelle, 2013) library **omega** command in *R*. The SL is not a direct analytic rotation to bifactor structure, rather it is a multistage, orthogonalized model. Our first step was to estimate a (smoothed) polychoric correlation matrix, and then based on theory and our preliminary *iCLUST* analyses, five factors were extracted using maximum likelihood,[4] and then rotated using Oblimin (the default in *psych*). This five correlated-factors model then was transformed to a second-order model by factor analyzing (i.e., extracting one factor) the correlations among the five primary factors. Finally, the second-order solution was transformed, via the SL, into a bifactor representation.

The second type of exploratory bifactor model applied here is the orthogonal version of the JB (Jennrich & Bentler, 2011). The JB is a direct analytic rotation method as opposed to the two-tier SL described before and is available in MPlus (Muthén & Muthén, 2012) and EQS (Bentler & Wu, 2012). In this application, we report the EQS results. To maintain closer comparability with the SL results, here we read in the smoothed polychoric correlation matrix used in the SL analysis and then specified maximum likelihood estimation with BF (bifactor) rotation to implement the JB.

The SL solution in Table 22.3 shows that all items have salient loadings on the general factor with Item 5 (DES_26; *sewer rat*), Item 9 (DES_12; *hamburger turned green*), Item 12 (DES_24; *rotting steak*), Item 24 (DES_27; *smell of feces*), Item 27 (DES_11; *smell of vomit*), and Item 30 (DES_28; *smell of urine*) having loadings around .70. Generally speaking, items from the *rotten foods* and *offensive odors* domains tend to load the highest on the general, which is not a surprising finding given the previous *iCLUST* results.

---

[4] We note that some researchers would prefer a least squares type extraction in this context. We tend to favor maximum likelihood for technical reasons, which, too, are beyond the present scope.

Table 22.3 Schmid–Leiman rotated factor loadings.

Item	General	Grp 1	Grp 2	Grp 3	Grp 4	Grp 5	h^2	u^2	p^2
1. DES_5	.47	**.36**	.10	.07	−.04	.03	.38	.62	.59
2. DES_8	.52	**.50**	−.03	.12	−.02	.07	.54	.46	.50
3. DES_13	.58	**.33**	.20	.06	.03	−.01	.50	.50	.67
4. DES_21	.61	**.57**	.06	.07	.09	−.03	.73	.27	.51
5. DES_26	.69	**.46**	.03	−.06	.12	.15	.72	.28	.66
6. DES_29	.54	**.36**	.05	.07	.13	.03	.46	.54	.64
7. DES_1	.59	.00	**.45**	.09	−.06	.02	.56	.44	.61
8. DES_6	.60	.05	**.38**	−.10	−.07	.13	.59	.41	.61
9. DES_12	.71	.00	**.55**	.00	.05	.00	.80	.20	.63
10. DES_16	.67	.09	**.42**	−.02	.04	.03	.64	.36	.70
11. DES_20	.63	.08	**.46**	.10	−.13	.02	.65	.35	.61
12. DES_24	.70	−.05	**.56**	−.04	.10	.00	.79	.21	.62
13. DES_3	.34	−.09	.00	**.88**	−.04	.02	.86	.14	.14
14. DES_9	.47	.06	−.02	**.65**	.15	.02	.74	.26	.29
15. DES_14	.43	.03	.02	**.85**	−.04	.00	.88	.12	.21
16. DES_19	.50	.16	.05	**.59**	.03	.00	.66	.34	.39
17. DES_23	.39	.07	.00	**.60**	.06	.01	.55	.45	.28
18. DES_30	.45	.07	−.03	**.67**	.13	.01	.75	.25	.26
19. DES_4	.46	−.05	.04	**.32**	**.47**	.00	.62	.38	.34
20. DES_10	.62	.01	.09	.04	**.49**	.12	.65	.35	.60
21. DES_15	.44	.11	.00	.11	**.53**	−.05	.55	.45	.35
22. DES_18	.46	.02	−.03	.03	**.63**	.04	.63	.37	.34
23. DES_22	.53	.09	.05	.06	**.54**	.00	.61	.39	.46
24. DES_27	.68	.09	.07	−.09	**.46**	.19	.70	.30	.66
25. DES_2	.63	.09	.03	.09	−.07	**.39**	.55	.45	.72
26. DES_7	.69	−.04	.03	.08	.02	**.49**	.72	.28	.66
27. DES_11	.71	−.06	.14	.14	.15	**.31**	.66	.34	.75
28. DES_17	.67	.10	.12	−.04	−.02	**.37**	.63	.37	.72
29. DES_25	.66	.18	.02	−.08	−.03	**.41**	.65	.35	.68
30. DES_28	.71	−.03	−.01	.02	.09	**.53**	.79	.21	.63
Eigenvalue	10.15	1.31	1.47	3.31	1.81	1.18			

Note. All loadings > .30 in bold. h^2 = communalities; u^2 = uniquenesses; p^2 = percentage of common variance that can be attributed to the general factor.

Each item also loads primarily on a single group factor, with the exception of Item 19 (DES_4; *observing an amputation operation*), which loads above .30 on *injections and blood* and *mutilation and death* group factors. Observe that most items have higher loadings on the general factor than the group factor. This is evident from the p^2 values on the far right, which is the percentage of an item's common variance attributable to the general factor – above .50 means the item's common variance derives mostly from the general factor. The exception occurs in the *injections and blood* domain where Item 13 (DES_3; *blood drawn from arm*) and Item 15 (DES_24; *receiving an injection in the arm*), for example, have much higher loadings on their group factor than the general.

The JB rotation in Table 22.4 provides mostly similar results to the SL with three exceptions. First, the JB rotation has a slightly stronger general factor and, thus, every item loads higher on the general factor and has a higher p^2 value in the JB as opposed to the SL. Interestingly, notice that there is little difference in communality (h^2) between

Table 22.4 Jennrich–Bentler rotated factor loadings.

Item	General	Grp 1	Grp 2	Grp 3	Grp 4	Grp 5	h^2	u^2	p^2
1. DES_5	.50	.29	.12	−.01	−.10	−.06	.37	.63	.69
2. DES_8	.58	.44	.00	.05	−.06	−.03	.52	.48	.63
3. DES_13	.59	.31	.34	.02	−.02	−.04	.50	.50	.62
4. DES_21	.68	.50	.04	.02	.00	−.15	.74	.26	.63
5. DES_26	.70	.48	.09	−.10	.08	.13	.77	.23	.64
6. DES_29	.64	.22	.00	−.02	−.01	−.12	.47	.53	.87
7. DES_1	.53	.00	.53	−.01	−.08	.04	.57	.43	.49
8. DES_6	.52	.05	.49	−.21	−.11	.15	.59	.41	.46
9. DES_12	.65	.02	.60	−.08	−.01	.04	.79	.21	.53
10. DES_16	.62	.10	.50	−.09	.01	.06	.65	.35	.59
11. DES_20	.62	.00	.50	−.05	−.23	−.06	.69	.31	.55
12. DES_24	.64	−.03	.60	−.11	.03	.03	.78	.22	.52
13. DES_3	.45	−.06	−.04	.80	.03	.03	.85	.15	.24
14. DES_9	.68	−.11	−.19	.51	.02	−.18	.81	.19	.58
15. DES_14	.53	.06	−.01	.80	.02	.00	.92	.08	.30
16. DES_19	.61	.12	.02	.52	.02	−.06	.66	.34	.56
17. DES_23	.47	.10	−.02	.57	.11	.02	.57	.43	.39
18. DES_30	.73	−.21	−.28	.50	−.09	−.30	1.00	.00	.53
19. DES_4	.59	−.09	−.10	.32	.39	−.04	.61	.39	.56
20. DES_10	.70	−.04	.02	.03	.39	.09	.64	.36	.75
21. DES_15	.54	.09	−.10	.19	.47	−.06	.56	.44	.51
22. DES_18	.57	−.03	−.16	.09	.53	.01	.64	.36	.51
23. DES_22	.64	.04	−.08	.10	.42	−.06	.61	.39	.67
24. DES_27	.74	.04	.02	−.11	.34	.15	.70	.30	.78
25. DES_2	.65	.00	.10	−.10	−.14	.30	.56	.44	.77
26. DES_7	.68	−.07	.14	−.08	.01	.48	.72	.28	.64
27. DES_11	.73	−.08	.18	.02	.10	.30	.66	.34	.79
28. DES_17	.64	.09	.24	−.17	−.05	.36	.63	.37	.64
29. DES_25	.68	.09	.10	−.26	−.13	.32	.66	.34	.69
30. DES_28	.73	−.09	.07	−.16	.02	.48	.79	.21	.66
Eigenvalues	11.72	1.06	2.10	2.77	1.26	1.13			

Note. All loadings > .30 in bold. h^2 = communalities; u^2 = uniquenesses; p^2 = percentage of common variance that can be attributed to the general factor.

the SL and JB solutions, suggesting the common variance is the same, only partitioned (i.e., rotated) differently. Second, the JB solution includes more salient (>.20) cross loadings (e.g., DES_17 *smell of city dump* loads .24 on *rotten foods*), and some of the salient cross loadings are negative (e.g., DES_25, DES_30). Finally, a Heywood case occurred for DES_30 (*a small vial of your blood*), that is, its communality went to 1.0 and error variance to 0.

Which exploratory solution is more accurate or "better?" In theory, the JB analytic rotation should be the more accurate because it is a direct rotation, rather than an orthogonalization, and because the SL solution entails a set of "hidden" proportionality constraints that can distort parameter estimates (Yung et al., 1999). On the other hand, the JB has not been thoroughly evaluated, and we do not yet fully understand its strengths and limits under different conditions. Because we cannot choose one or

Table 22.5 Confirmatory factor analysis.

Item	General	Grp 1	Grp 2	Grp 3	Grp 4	Grp 5	h^2	u^2	p^2
1. DES_5	.48	.31					.33	.67	.71
2. DES_8	.54	.53					.56	.44	.51
3. DES_13	.61	.33					.48	.52	.77
4. DES_21	.65	.53					.70	.30	.60
5. DES_26	.76	.35					.70	.30	.83
6. DES_29	.57	.37					.46	.54	.70
7. DES_1	.53		.55				.59	.41	.48
8. DES_6	.57		.49				.56	.44	.58
9. DES_12	.72		.48				.75	.25	.69
10. DES_16	.67		.44				.64	.36	.70
11. DES_20	.60		.54				.65	.35	.55
12. DES_24	.70		.52				.76	.24	.64
13. DES_3	.33			.86			.84	.16	.13
14. DES_9	.50			.69			.72	.28	.34
15. DES_14	.42			.84			.89	.11	.20
16. DES_19	.53			.61			.64	.36	.43
17. DES_23	.40			.62			.55	.45	.29
18. DES_30	.47			.71			.73	.27	.30
19. DES_4	.50				.53		.53	.47	.47
20. DES_10	.74				.30		.64	.36	.86
21. DES_15	.47				.61		.59	.41	.37
22. DES_18	.69				.69		.73	.27	.50
23. DES_22	.61				.48		.60	.40	.62
24. DES_27	.80				.22		.70	.30	.93
25. DES_2	.63					.36	.53	.47	.75
26. DES_7	.67					.53	.73	.27	.62
27. DES_11	.72					.31	.62	.38	.84
28. DES_17	.69					.34	.59	.41	.80
29. DES_25	.70					.33	.59	.41	.82
30. DES_28	.74					.48	.77	.23	.70
Eigenvalue	11.22	1.03	1.53	3.18	1.50	.96			

Note. h^2 = communalities; u^2 = uniquenesses; p^2 = percentage of common variance that can be attributed to the general factor.

the other as "best" or "better," next we present the results from both to illustrate how different exploratory algorithms can provide different results.

Finally, in Table 22.5 we report the results of a confirmatory factor analysis (CFA) that specified all items freely load on the general factor and only one of five group factors. That is, any group factor cross loadings identified in the exploratory analyses were ignored by fixing the loading to 0 in the confirmatory analysis. The CFA was performed in EQS based on raw data and employing **robust** maximum likelihood estimation to obtain more appropriate fit indices for ordinal data. This bifactor model CFA yielded the following robust fit statistics: Satorra–Bentler chi-square = 900 (df = 375), RMSEA = .053, CFI = .985, and SRMSR = .084. These values would all be deemed "acceptable" by conventional standards (Hu & Bentler, 1999).

For comparison, a five correlated-factors model yielded: Satorra–Bentler chi-square = 1,017 (df = 395), RMSEA = 0.056, CFI = 0.982, and SRMSR = 0.070; a second-order model with one second-order factor and five primary factors yielded: Satorra–Bentler chi-square = 1,291 (df = 400), RMSEA = 0.067, CFI = 0.888, and SRMSR = 0.076; and a unidimensional model yielded: Satorra–Bentler chi-square = 5,076 (df = 405), RMSEA = 0.152, CFI = 0.863, and SRMSR = 0.131. Clearly, although the multidimensional models can be differentiated statistically, in practical terms, essentially they are equivalent in accounting for the observed correlations. In the next section, we consider the use of these bifactor results in evaluating scale scoring.

Model-Based Reliability and the Bifactor Model

The psychometric literature bemoaning the misunderstandings, limits, and abuses of coefficient alpha (Cronbach, 1951) to judge the precision of unit-weighted composite measurements is substantial (e.g., Revelle & Zinbarg, 2009; Schmitt, 1996; Sijtsma, 2009). Among the main concerns are, first, alpha is based on an essentially tau-equivalent measurement model, and its interpretation as a lower bound estimate of the reliability (estimator of true score over observed score variance) depends critically on the data being unidimensional, such that true score variation reflects individual differences on a single construct – "a single latent true variable" (Graham, 2006, p. 931; ten Berge & Sočan, 2004). When the data are multidimensional, alpha is affected by all sources of systematic variation (sources of common and specific item variance), and it can over- or under-estimate the reliability of a multidimensional composite. Moreover, when data are multidimensional, it is not entirely clear what the proper interpretation of "true score" variation is because the true score itself also is a weighted composite of multiple latent dimensions.

Second, it has been well documented that researchers treat alpha as a content homogeneity index, and in turn, confuse alpha as a unidimensionality indicator (Miller, 1995). Nevertheless, generally it is known that alpha is a poor indicator of the degree to which test scores reflect a single construct (Schmitt, 1996). For example, alpha can be high even when the data are highly multidimensional with zero correlation among the dimensions (Cortina, 1993). Also, it is easy to demonstrate that alpha can be low even when the data are perfectly unidimensional.

These concerns are not new. Revelle (1979, p. 62), writing over 30 years ago, summarizes, "…in the case of a 'lumpy test' (one with several large group factors) alpha overestimates the general factor saturation of the test and underestimates the total common factor saturation." "Lumpy" means that a test, such as the DES, may measure a single common dimension (note that all the items are positively and at least moderately correlated) but has clear multidimensionality caused by clusters of items with highly similar content (see heat map).

Given these concerns, it is clear that in judging the viability of scoring global scales or subscales, alternative approaches to estimating reliability are needed. In this regard, it is interesting to note that, "Cronbach (1951) viewed reliability, including internal consistency measures, as the proportion of test variance that was attributable to group and general factors. Specific item variance, or uniqueness, was considered error." (Schmitt, 1996, p. 350). Consistent with this quote, in the following, we consider a (factor) model-based (Bentler, 2009; Miller, 1995; Raykov, 1997, 2004; Raykov & Stout, 2003) approach to examining reliability, which is more informative regarding the scoring of general scales and, possibly, domain-based subscales.

A Bifactor Model Alternative to Alpha

In this section, we use the exploratory and confirmatory bifactor results reported previously to study: (1) the degree to which reliable variance on a global sum score reflects reliable variation due to a single latent variable and (2) the degree to which unit-weighted subscale scores reflect reliable variation that is independent from the general dimension. Our presentation will be nontechnical, and throughout we will assume that analyses are based on correlations, the variances of all latent factors are 1.0, and all factor loadings are standardized.

Readers interested in more detailed research on this topic are directed to Zinbarg, Revelle, Yovel, and Li's (2005) comprehensive evaluation of model-based reliability estimators using the bifactor model as a foundation. Also recommended are Brunner and Süb (2005) who describe statistical approaches to differentiating between "composite" reliability (reliability due to all systematic factors) and "construct" reliability (reliability due to a single factor), and Lucke (2005) who reviews coefficients alpha and omega when tests contain content heterogeneity. Finally, Gustafsson and Åberg-Bengtsson (2006): (1) review the history of the tension between researchers wanting to assess one construct but needing to include heterogeneous item content, (2) describe hierarchical (bifactor) approaches to analyzing psychometric data, and (3) provide examples of how highly multidimensional achievement tests can result in test scores that predominantly reflect a single construct.

In the common factor model, an item's variance is partitioned into that due to common factors and error, paralleling the classical test theory partitioning of test scores into orthogonal true and error components. Expanding this basic model in bifactor model terms, an item's variance can be partitioned into that due to a general factor (G), a group factor (GR), a specific (S) factor that contains reliable variance unique to a particular item, and error (E), as shown in Equation 22.1.

$$X = G + GR + S + E \qquad (22.1)$$

In Equation 22.1, all terms are uncorrelated and errors are normally distributed. In most applications of the common factor model, S cannot be estimated and, thus, is combined with E. This leaves us with (latent) true score variation equaling $G + GR$ and error variation equaling $S + E$. In factor analytic terms, the percent of variance attributable to the common factors is called "communality" (h^2) and is found by squaring loadings and adding across the orthogonal common factors (general and group in this case). The error variance (uniqueness or u^2) is simply $1 - h^2$.

Equation 22.1 provides a nice framework for estimating various types of reliabilities depending on what a researcher considers true score variance and error. In practice, researchers typically sum unit-weighted item responses to form either a global scale score (summing across all items) or a subscale score (summing across only items within a content domain or group factor in this case). The (observed score) variance in this case easily is derivable through the variance sum law; it equals the sum of the covariance or correlation matrix. Note, here we are using correlation matrices and, thus, the total variance represents the variance of observed scores after standardizing each item before summing.

Table 22.6 Omega total and omega hierarchical for the general disgust factor and each subscale.

	Schmid–Leiman		Jennrich–Bentler		CFA	
	ωS	ωHS	ωS	ωHS	ωS	ωHS
Disgust	.97	.76	.97	.89	.97	.85
Animals	.87	.32	.88	.24	.87	.27
Foods	.92	.32	.92	.41	.92	.36
Blood	.94	.68	.96	.51	.94	.68
Mutilation	.90	.44	.90	.28	.92	.33
Odors	.92	.25	.92	.21	.91	.22

One model-based alternative to alpha is coefficient omega (ω; McDonald, 1999; see also Lucke, 2005), which can be defined as:

$$\omega = \frac{\left(\Sigma\lambda_{gen}\right)^2 + \left(\Sigma\lambda_{grp}\right)^2}{\left(\Sigma\lambda_{gen}\right)^2 + \left(\Sigma\lambda_{grp}\right)^2 + \Sigma(1-h^2)} = \frac{\left(\Sigma\lambda_{gen}\right)^2 + \left(\Sigma\lambda_{grp}\right)^2}{\Sigma R} \quad (22.2)$$

Omega considers both general and group sources of common variance as "true" score variance and estimates the reliability of a multidimensional composite. The numerator is the sum of the factor loadings on the general factor, squared, plus the sum of the factor loadings on each group factor, squared. The denominator is the reliable variance plus error variance, which is equal to the total variance of test scores. When Equation 22.2 is computed using all the items, we refer to it as ω, and when it is calculated based on using only subscale items, we refer to is as ωS.

Like alpha, when the data are multidimensional, as they are here, ω reflects the reliability of global unit-weighted scores viewed as a multidimensional composite. Also like alpha, ω will increase as the number of items increases. An important difference between omega and alpha is that the former is based on the congeneric measurement model, and the latter is based on the more restrictive essentially tau-equivalent model.

Table 22.6 displays the estimated ω and ωS values for each of the SL, JB, and CFA solutions. Because these values differ minimally across the solutions, we limit our comments to the CFA results where ω and ωS values were .97 (*disgust*), .87 (*small animals*), .92 (*rotten food*), .94 (*injections and blood*), .92 (*mutilation and death*), and .91 (*offensive odors*). Thus, when viewed through the lens of omega (or alpha), the (multidimensional) composite total scale and the subscale scores must be considered highly reliable (judged by internal consistency).

Omega statistics are valuable psychometric tools, but more important to the present research are omega hierarchical (ωH), and what we call here, omega hierarchical subscale (ωHS). ωH is the percent of unit-weighted total score variance due to a single latent factor. This can be estimated by Equation 22.3:

$$\omega_h = \frac{\left(\Sigma\lambda_{gen}\right)^2}{\left(\Sigma\lambda_{gen}\right)^2 + \left(\Sigma\lambda_{grp}\right)^2 + \Sigma(1-h^2)} = \frac{\left(\Sigma\lambda_{gen}\right)^2}{\Sigma R} \quad (22.3)$$

(Zinbarg, Barlow, & Brown, 1997; Zinbarg et al., 2005). Notice here that the numerator is the variance of total scores attributable to a single general factor, and the denominator is the total score variance. In the DES data, this value is .85. Given that ω was .97, this value implies that 12% (97% – 85%) of the reliable variance on the global DES scores is due to secondary dimensions (i.e., true score variation on the subdomains), 85% is due to a general latent variable (assumed to reflect true score differences in disgust), and 3% is random error. If one considers group factor variation to be more appropriately treated as nuisance or error, then the error variance is 15%, not 3% as implied by ω.

For each subscale, we also can consider how much reliable variance is due to the systematic variance that is independent of the general factor. This is shown in Equation 22.4 where the calculations are performed solely for items within a content domain, and the correlation matrix (R) is the correlation matrix among subscale items, such that its sum reflects the variance of subscale scores.

$$\omega_{hs} = \frac{\left(\Sigma\lambda_{grp}\right)^2}{\left(\Sigma\lambda_{gen}\right)^2 + \left(\Sigma\lambda_{grp}\right)^2 + \Sigma(1-h^2)} = \frac{\left(\Sigma\lambda_{gen}\right)^2}{\Sigma R} \qquad (22.4)$$

In the DES data, based on the CFA solution, ωHS are .27 (*small animals*), .36 (*rotten foods*), .68 (*injections and blood*), .33 (*mutilation and death*), and .22 (*offensive odors*). Recall that ω values were .87, .92, .94, .92, and .91 for these five subscales, respectively. Clearly, when one examines omega, it appears that the subscales are highly internally consistent and, thus, provide reliable scores. That is an accurate view, but only if one views the domain scores as a composite of reliable variance due to disgust and reliable variance due to some specific aspect of disgust.

On the other hand, if a researcher were to ask, what is the reliability of subscale scores due to a specific construct (i.e., domain true score variance), with the possible exception of the *injections and blood* subscale, that answer would be the less impressive ωHS values shown previously. Clearly, to the extent that DES subscales are believed to be reliable (when judged by alpha or omega), this is "precision" mostly borrowed from the reliability of general disgust.

Unit-Weighted Scoring in the Presence of Multidimensionality

When measurement scales yield data with a hierarchical structure, such as the general and group factors evident in the DES, this creates a conundrum for researchers seeking to understand the relations between the target construct (disgust), domain-based constructs, and external variables (see Chen et al., 2012). The obvious roots of the conundrum are: (1) the confounded variance among global and subscale scores, and (2) without the computation of indices such as omega hierarchical, the ambiguity of what sources of variance influence the global scores and to what degree.[5] A secondary concern with data such as the DES is how to properly correct observed

---

[5] Interestingly, omega hierarchical implies that the degree to which a unit-weighted composite score reflects a single general construct changes depending on what items are administered; or equivalently, what is measured is item dependent. This is one reason why item response theory models, which form the basis of computerized adaptive testing, require a strict unidimensional assumption, such that estimation of an individual's position on a latent variable is not item dependent.

correlations for attenuation. As we demonstrate next, when global and subscale scores are used in the same analysis, often there is no satisfying solution to the problem.

To demonstrate these concerns, we conducted two simulations. In the first, we generated item response data for 10,000 cases based on the bifactor model parameters in Table 22.5 – the confirmatory solution. This large sample was used to mimic population results. Item response data were simulated for a five-item criterion measure. The criterion variable was generated to have an alpha reliability of around .80. This was accomplished by specifying the loadings for the five indictor items to be .65. The data were simulated such that the true population correlation between the general factor and the criterion was .50, and the true correlation between each group factor and the criterion was zero.

After generating data, we then simply unit-weighted scored the item responses for the global scale and each subscale. Coefficient alpha for the global score was .95 and .79 for the criterion variable in the simulated data; omega hierarchical was .83 for the global score. The observed correlation between the global summed score and the criterion summed score was .40, a severe underestimation. This underestimation can be corrected, not through alpha, but by knowing coefficient ωh. Specifically, the general-to-criterion correlation corrected for attenuation using alpha is:

$$\frac{.40}{\sqrt{(.95)(.79)}} = .46$$

but using ωh, the corrected correlation is more accurate:

$$\frac{.40}{\sqrt{(.83)(.79)}} = .49$$

The observed subscale-to-criterion correlations were .35, .32, .22, .33, and .36, respectively, all wildly inflated from their true value of zero due to the contamination with the general factor. Unfortunately, there are no corrections for attenuation that can fix this problem. The only solution is to attempt various partialling, such as partialling out the global score from the *small animals* score, and then correlating the residuals with the criterion. Chen et al. (2012) refer to these partialling schemes as "residual regression" methods, which have their limits.

In simulation #2 we generated N = 10,000 item responses from the same confirmatory bifactor model for the DES as simulation #1, but now both a general factor and the third group factor (*injections and blood*) are correlated with the five-item criterion .50. As in simulation #1, we calculated global, subscale, and criterion scores by simple unit weighting. Coefficient alpha for the global score was .95 and .79 for the criterion variable in the simulated data; omega hierarchical was .83 for the global score.

In simulation #2, the observed correlations with the criterion were .50, .34, .32, .59, .34, and .36, for global and subscale summed scores, respectively. Notice that the general-to-criterion correlation no longer is underestimated (because it is biased positively), but when corrected for attenuation using the observed ωh value of .83 and the criterion reliability of .79, the disattenuated correlation equals,

$$\frac{.50}{\sqrt{(.83)(.79)}} = .62$$

a substantial overestimate of the true relation. The subscale-to-criterion correlation of .59 also is positively biased, and when corrected for attenuation by the observed ωHS value of .66 and criterion alpha of .79, the disattenuated subscale-to-criterion correlation equals,

$$\frac{.59}{\sqrt{(.66)(.79)}} = .82$$

a substantial overestimation.

The moral of these simulations is simple; it is difficult to use unit-weighted composite scores and correlation analyses (with or without correcting for attenuation) to test theories when the data have a hierarchical structure. When researchers are interested in identifying correlates of subscale constructs independent of the general construct, or differential correlations for subscale constructs, one attractive alternative approach for working around the problems inherent in raw score analysis is to specify a bifactor model and use structural equation modelling (SEM), a topic we consider next.

Structural Equation Modelling (SEM) and Bifactor Models

In this section, we consider several issues that arise in using the DES (and like measures) in SEM research. An advantage of SEM is that it allows the modelling of both general and group factors and corrects for errors of measurement (Chen et al., 2006). Here we consider two questions. We begin by asking whether the bifactor model is accurate in achieving its goal in allowing researchers to investigate the unique contributions of general and subdomain relations with external variables. Although we provide two demonstrations using simulated data, we acknowledge that the topic of parameter recovery is very complex once one starts considering nonnormality, missing data patterns, and complex model-misspecifications inherent in real data.

In the previous section, we generated two simulated data sets. In the first, there was a true correlation between a general factor and a criterion of .50 and zero relations between each group factor and the criterion. In the second, we retained the .50 true correlation between the general and criterion but added a .50 true correlation between a single group factor and the criterion. To analyze these simulated data, we used EQS software (Bentler & Wu, 2012) to fit SEM models specifying a bifactor structure for the simulated DES items, with five items freely loading on the criterion latent variable, and all paths from the general and group factors to the criterion latent variable freely estimated.

In the first simulated data set, the estimated path between the general and criterion was .49, and all group to criterion paths were estimated to be near zero. In the second simulated data set, the estimated path between the general factor and criterion was .49, and the path between the group and criterion was .50. All other paths between the group factor and criterion were estimated to be near zero. These results illustrate that in a correctly specified model, and with a large sample size, SEM can correctly estimate the true relations among latent variables when the construct of interest has a bifactor structure. Next, we consider the more realistic case of model misspecification.

We now ask the second question, what if a researcher only is interested in *disgust* and wishes to employ a unidimensional measurement model? There are several issues involved, such as how the model should be specified (all 30 items versus parcels) and to what degree would model misspecification bias the resulting parameter estimates? This latter issue can be restated as, "What are the consequences of forcing multidimensional data into a unidimensional measurement model?"

When researchers are interested in studying the disattenuated (i.e., controlling for measurement error) interrelations among a network of constructs, SEM is the appropriate analytic tool, as argued by numerous scholars. As with all latent variable modelling, SEM requires the latent variable to properly reflect variation on a single construct. Stated differently, SEM assumes that the latent variable indicators reflect a single common latent variable (Little, Cunningham, Shahar, & Widaman, 2002).

This is a strict assumption, and violating unidimensionality can have severe consequences. That is, treating multidimensional data as if it were unidimensional is a form of model misspecification that can lead to biased parameter estimates (i.e., loadings too high, error estimates too low), and more importantly, the biased parameter estimates lead to biased estimates of the relationships among latent variables by either under or overcorrecting for reliability. In effect, such bias can defeat the primary advantage of SEM; namely, to accurately gauge the true relations among constructs represented as latent variables.

We first consider the case where there is only a relation between the general factor and the criterion – group factors merely are a nuisance, not of any substantive interest, and not related to the criterion. If only *disgust* is represented in the measurement model by having a single latent variable indicated by all 30 items, the model obviously is misspecified. The loadings on the single factor likely are going to be too high, and, thus, reliability is overestimated, and consequently, there will be an underestimation of the correction for attenuation.

But does this misspecification matter? At the very least, it is debatable. Reise, Scheines, Widaman, and Haviland (2012), for example, argued that when the explained common variance (ECV; percentage of common variance that is due to the general factor) is high, and the percentage of uncontaminated correlations (PUC; the percentage of correlations that reflect general factor variance only[6]) is high, the consequences of forcing multidimensional data into a unidimensional measurement model are modest. In other words, as the data become more unidimensional, and the percent of correlations affected by the general factor increases, bias in model parameters should decrease.

In the DES data, judging by the CFA model parameters, the ECV is 58% and the PUC is 83%. The former is relatively low, meaning that only slightly over half the common variance is general factor variance. The PUC value, however, is high and, thus, we expect very little parameter bias when these multidimensional data are forced into a unidimensional measurement model.

Indeed, in the present example, in the unidimensional only model, the path coefficient estimate from the general factor to criterion was .47, versus a value of .49 in the correctly specified model reported previously – a small difference. In fact, when we formed five parcels of six items each on the basis of the subdomains, and then defined

---

[6] Again, as noted, correlations among items within a content domain reflect both general and group factor variance, whereas correlations between items from different content domains reflect general factor variance only.

a single latent variable by these five parcels, our path estimate was .49, even closer to the true value. These results illustrate what happens when only the general factor is related to the criterion. Now we consider what occurs when both the general and group factors are related to the criterion.

The results of simulation #2 reflect a more severe misspecification – ignoring variance from a subdomain that is related to the criterion. When we specified a 30-item measurement model for *disgust*, the general factor to criterion path estimate was .53, an overestimate. Although this inaccuracy from the true value of .50 is not large, it does illustrate an important occurrence; namely, when there are unspecified or unmodelled relations (i.e., group factors related to the outcome beyond the general factor), general factor to criterion relations will be overestimated due to the collapsing of common variance from multiple sources in the unidimensional model. The collapsing of items into parcels does not help in this regard; in fact, the general factor defined by five parcels and the criterion had an estimated path of .54. In short, parcelling makes the problem worse when we collapse a multidimensional space into a unidimensional space, when those secondary dimensions are meaningfully related to the criterion.

Discussion

The analytic tools for making more informed decisions regarding the sources of common variance affecting global and subscale scores are readily available but seldom employed in applied research. The main goal of this chapter was to raise awareness of these psychometric tools through their application. In this section, we review our methodology and findings and raise conceptual caveats and technical issues that require further research. We conclude by summarizing conceptual issues relevant to the construction and psychometric analysis of content heterogeneous psychological measures.

Review of DES analyses

The DES was designed to assess individual differences in disgust and includes multiple items (6 items each) to represent five content domains of disgust reaction: *small animals, rotten foods, injections and blood, mutilation and death,* and *offensive odors*. Like many instruments of this type, multiple domains of item content are included to capture a broad range of trait manifestation and to afford the possibility of examining both global and domain scores. This latter "capability" often is thought important by researchers who believe that specific "aspects" of a trait construct may be influenced by different developmental pathways or may be related differentially to some external criteria (for details, see Chen et al., 2012; Smith, McCarthy, & Zapolski, 2009).

In approaching the psychometric analysis of these types of multicomponent, content diverse measures, we believe that it is critical to design a methodology to assist us in better understanding several important issues. Among them are: (1) to what degree do the items all cohere and, thus, suggest they all are markers of a single common latent variable? (2) to what degree are the item intercorrelations consistent with the proposed content domain structure? (3) to what degree are the items within domains merely content repeats? And (4) what is the magnitude of the residual variation after controlling for a general factor underlying the common variance? In the following section, we review and comment on the three preliminary analyses designed to answer these questions as best we can.

Preliminary analyses

First, from the heat map analysis of the polychoric correlation matrix (Figure 22.1), we gained visual and empirical evidence that the DES items appear to cluster together more tightly within content domains than they do across content domains. We also identified several items that may not be performing as well as the other items (DES_5, *An alley cat*) and items that are so highly correlated that they may reflect content doublets. This is valuable information, especially in terms of justifying our decision to fit a bifactor measurement model.

We noted previously that correlations among items within a domain reflect the operation of both a general factor and a group factor, whereas correlations among items across domains purely must be a function of a general factor. Thus, the overall shading of the heat map informs about the overall communality (darker implies more common variance to be explained), the shading within the between domains areas informs on the strength of a general factor (darker implies stronger), and the shading within domain areas, relative to the across, informs on the potential strength of group factors (the darker the within area relative to the between area, the stronger the group factors).

Second, the hierarchical clustering (*iCLUST*, Figure 22.2) provided us with an empirical map of the content similarity or conceptual equivalence of the items and the degree to which the item clusters are consistent with the a priori theory. Overall, DES items conformed well to the a priori domains. We also discerned that items joining together early appeared to be content doublets and resulted in small item clusters with high internal consistency. In fact, within a content domain, after small clusters were formed, no appreciable gains in internal consistency were made when more items were joined to form a larger cluster. We will consider content redundancy further in the final section.

In our third preliminary analysis, we fit a unidimensional IRT model and then within each content domain, evaluated a statistic that indexes the degree to which the items are **not** locally independent (i.e., "correlated residuals" in factor analytic terminology) after controlling for a single latent variable (Table 22.2). These analyses showed that even after controlling for a single common dimension, the size of the residuals was substantial. Such findings suggest that the residuals need to be accounted for in some way to correctly identify the general *disgust* latent dimension. Stated differently, this residual analysis served to justify the ultimate application of a bifactor model.

Fitting bifactor models

We next introduced exploratory and confirmatory bifactor modelling as a foundational structural representation for understanding sources of common variance in a multicomponent instrument such as the DES. Beyond partitioning the common variance into general and group components, these models provide the basis for computing useful indices such as the ECV (representing degree of unidimensionality), the PUC (a structural index that represents robustness of the general factor; Reise et al., 2013), and most important, the omega and omega hierarchical reliability indices (see also, Zinbarg, et al., 2005).

In the present investigation, we illustrated two applications of exploratory bifactor modelling, the SL (Schmid & Leiman, 1957) and JB (Jennrich & Bentler, 2011), as well as a maximum likelihood confirmatory bifactor model. Although the parameter

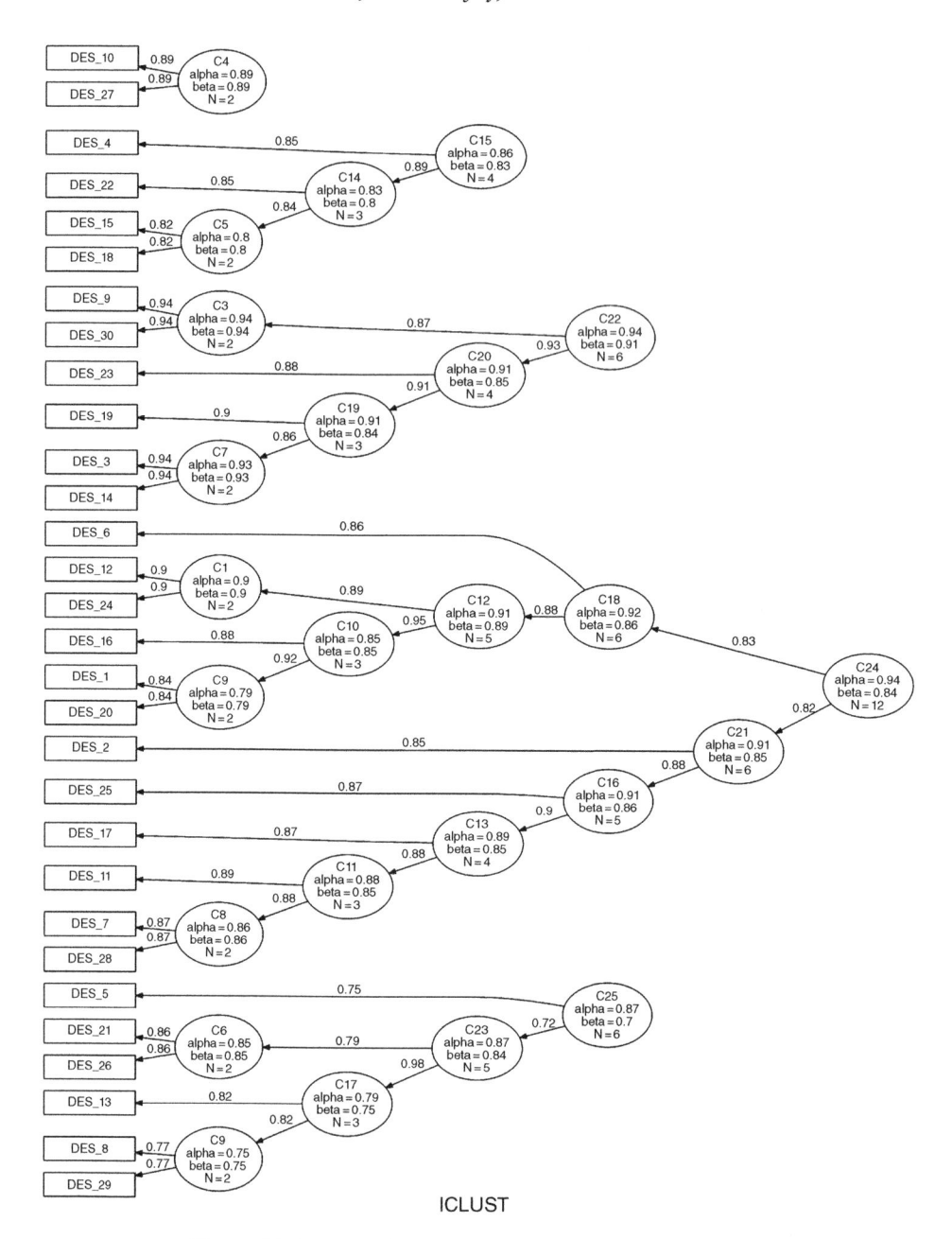

Figure 22.2 Item clusters derived from iCLUST algorithm.

estimates were quite similar across the three methods, and the data fit the confirmatory model well, there are three issues that require further comment.

First, for many reasons, it is important for us to warn that bifactor modelling will not always be as straightforward as in the present application due to potential problems and complications arising in model identification, estimation, and establishing fit. For example, a technical problem we encountered is that the *psych* package (Revelle, 2013), EQS

(Bentler & Wu, 2012), and MPlus (Muthén & Muthén, 2012), did not yield exactly the same results for the JB bifactor rotation. In fact, with MPlus bi-Quartimin rotation, the fifth group factor (*offensive odors*) collapsed into the general factor, leaving only four group factors. We, thus, strongly suggest examining any type of bifactor analysis using different software packages and experimenting with different estimation methods, as well as rotation methods for the correlated-factor solution, which forms the basis of the SL orthogonalization.

A second applied bifactor modelling issue is the relative merits of exploratory versus confirmatory modelling. The main issue is, what is the better analysis on which to base the omega and omega hierarchical statistics? We are well aware that some researchers suggest that if you have an a priori theory (or previous data analysis), one must go straight to confirmatory modelling. In contrast to this commonly held view, we argue that it is better to identify potential problems prior to fitting a confirmatory model than it is to fit a confirmatory model, find problems in fit, and try to diagnose (and "fix") them (see Browne, 2001).

The exploratory bifactor models provide a lot of useful information: (1) identifying items that are not loading as expected, (2) discovering that hypothesized group factors, in fact, do not form a distinct group factor, and (3) identifying whether items cross-load on group factors (which ultimately may bias the parameters in a confirmatory model if items are restricted to load on a single group factor). Most important, the exploratory bifactor models better reflect the sources of variance that are operating in the data and are affecting summed scores; forcing a parameter to zero in a CFA and finding acceptable fit, does not magically make those small model violations (e.g., cross loadings) go away. Thus, in this sense, the exploratory models, arguably, are the better foundation for computing omega and omega hierarchical statistics.

On the other hand, when the restricted confirmatory model fits the data well, one could argue that the noisiness of the exploratory solutions (e.g., the nonzero cross loadings or small negative loadings) are just that – unreplicable noise that should not be modelled. For this reason, the confirmatory model parameters, arguably, are the better ones to use for the computation of omega and omega hierarchical. Indeed, that is exactly what we reported in the present study (although method did not really matter – see Table 22.6). We note that the Bayesian exploratory SEM (Muthén & Asparouhov, 2012) may be a superior choice to CFA because it does not force small cross loadings to be absolutely zero.

A third important issue to raise is that we have not emphasized model testing or model comparison in this chapter. The reason for these omissions is that we view the bifactor model as a psychometric tool for understanding sources of common variance and as a foundation for computing specific types of reliability indices to inform the scoring of an instrument. That said, we note that unidimensional and second-order models each are nested within the bifactor model, and, thus, model comparison tests could be performed. We see little ultimate value in such fit competitions, however, given that relative model fit does not indicate relative model validity.

The overall fit of the bifactor model to the sample covariances/correlations also can be examined as customary; however, there is little research on the performance of fit indices under a bifactor model, and in our experience, if the data are consistent with a correlated-factors model, they will be more or less consistent with second-order and bifactor models as well. Observe that in the present data, the SRMR values were essentially the same for correlated-factors, second-order, and bifactor models, suggesting that the sample correlation matrix was reproduced well by any of these models. Note, too, that the unidimensional model would be deemed a "poor fit" or "unacceptable" by any CFA benchmarks, but yet, our conclusion was that DES global scores are highly interpretable as reflecting mostly a single dimension.

Model-based reliability estimation

The three estimated bifactor models formed the basis for the computation of model-based reliability coefficients. Although much research has been extended to this topic, and several approaches exist and controversies remain, our interest was omega and omega hierarchical (McDonald, 1999). The former is of value in estimating the percent of reliable variance of a unit-weighted multidimensional composite. The latter is useful for estimating the percent of reliable variance in a unit-weighted composite due to a single latent variable.

In this regard, our findings were clear that in applied settings, researchers confidently can form unit-weighted DES global scores with the knowledge that the overwhelming majority of variance can be attributable to variation on a common latent variable, *disgust*. This result may be surprising to some, given the highly multidimensional nature of DES responses (e.g., ECV = .58), but it is the inevitable result of having many items (30) all related to the same latent variable (*disgust*) and fewer items (6) related to each group factor. Generally speaking, assuming that all items are influenced by the general factor, the influence of a general factor on unit-weighted summed scores increases as a function of the square of the number of items on a measure (Gustafsson & Åberg-Bengtsson, 2006).

The unit-weighted scoring and interpretation of domain-based subscales, in our judgment, is questionable. Although omega indices for subscales were high, our omega hierarchical subscale indices indicted that the reliable variation attributable to distinct content domains is modest, at best, and a substantial proportion of reliable subscale variance is due to the general factor. We will elaborate on our concerns with subscale scoring in the last section of this chapter. For now, to better understand these results, consider that the group factors in a bifactor model are "residualized" factors – what remains after removing the general factor.

As a consequence, it often is challenging to create a subscale that will appear highly reliable after controlling for the general factor (as defined by omega hierarchical subscale). The only way for a residualized (group factor) variance to be highly reliable is for it to contain many items with high inter-correlations and relatively low correlations with items from other content domains. The only content domain that matches these criteria is *injections and blood*, and observe that in the present investigation, it has the highest omega hierarchical subscale value of the five domains.

The DES in applied settings

In our final result section, we considered the applied consequences of using the DES in research, either using unit weighting of global and subscales (typical practice) or in the context of SEM research (see also Olatunji, Enesutani, & Reise, 2014). As we noted, we have little concern with the practice of scoring the DES global scale and correlating these scores with other variables. Our one caution would be that researchers recognize alpha is neither an appropriate index in judging whether the scores reflect a single construct nor of any use in correcting for attenuation. Omega hierarchical is the better choice in terms of communicating the reliability of the DES global score as a reflection of *disgust* and for use in corrections for attenuation.

Our results showed that substantial interpretation problems occur when researchers use both global scores and subscale scores in the same analysis and then attempt to meaningfully interpret this common variance **mishmash**. At the very least, the global scores should be residualized out of subscale scores prior to correlating subscales with criteria. If researchers are willing to go to the trouble of doing that, however, they might just as well use SEM, which, in a sense, automates the process.

In applying SEM to model the DES, there are at least three viable options for specifying the measurement model. The first and most ideal for theory testing is to specify a bifactor measurement model including a general factor and five group factors. On the other hand, this option is potentially the most technically difficult because the bifactor model can be challenging to estimate, especially with small sample sizes. The bifactor model also is a highly parameterized model, and some of the group factors may not replicate well or be statistically well identified due to the relatively smaller loadings on some group factors (e.g., *offensive odors*).

Second and third options for specifying a measurement model for the DES are to collapse it into a unidimensional model, using either all 30-items as a marker of *disgust* or forming parcels based on the content domains, and using a five-indicator measurement model. In our simulated data demonstrations, we showed that if only the general factor is important in predicting the criterion, we could collapse the measurement model into a unidimensional space (using either 30 items or 5 parcels) with little bias in important parameter estimates. On the other hand, if a domain also has a relation with the criterion, and a unidimensional model fit, the path between the general factor and criterion will be biased positively, especially when parcels are used instead of items.

Conclusion: Assessing Hierarchical Trait Constructs

In closing this chapter, we would like to add commentary regarding the (hierarchical) nature of psychological traits and the measurement of constructs at different levels of conceptual breath; that is, global scores reflecting general broadband constructs with phenotypically diverse manifestations, and subscale scores reflecting conceptually narrow constructs with limited, phenotypically similar manifestations. To place our commentary in context, we first consider quotes from two luminaries in the field of personality and personality assessment.

First, we ask, what is a psychological trait, such as disgust? Tellegen (1991) favored "…defining a *trait* as an inferred relatively enduring organismic (psychological, psychobiological) *structure* underlying an extended family of behavioral dispositions" (p. 13, italics in original). Allport (1963, p. 28) defines personality as "the dynamic organization within the individual of those psychophysical systems that determine his characteristic behavior and thought." He further refines the concept of a trait as (p. 347), "a neuropsychic structure having the capacity to render many stimuli functionally equivalent, and to initiate and guide consistent (meaningfully equivalent) forms of adaptive and expressive behavior."

Particularly noteworthy in Tellegen's quote is, "extended family of behavioral dispositions," which means to us that a psychological trait worthy of empirical investigation should be more than an explanation of the covariance among responses to phenotypically nearly equivalent stimuli (e.g., *rat in my kitchen, rat in my bedroom, rat running across my bathroom floor, rat crawling out of a sewer*, and so forth). Traits are explanatory units that are only required if there are content diverse manifestations, and, thus, valid trait measures demand heterogeneous item content. For this reason, we believe multidimensional factor solutions should be the goal of scale construction (rather than seeking strict unidimensionality).

In Allport's quotes, similarly, we agree that psychological traits are "determinative" – they determine how a phenotypically dissimilar stimuli or situational contexts are perceived, and responded to, such that a mouse or rat, the sight of blood or mutilated bodies, odors emitted by vomit or feces, or moldy cheese, all are rendered psychologically equivalent, and forge the same emotional/behavioral reaction, because there is an underlying trait (psychobiological structure) of disgust. For some individuals, it is challenging to react to these diverse stimuli in an objective, mature, or adaptive manner, whereas for others, these stimuli do not represent a threat to their equilibration.

To us, it is individual differences in this broad trait of disgust that renders diverse stimuli functionally equivalent and that should be the primary concern in scale development and more broadly, psychological research. A strength of the DES is that it yields item response data that are multidimensional, but at the same time yields global scores that primarily reflect a single latent variable. Even given the well-known limits of self-report instruments (e.g., response sets), the DES appears to provide an excellent foundation for further research examining the possible dozens of psychological, developmental, and biological mechanisms and processes that result in individual differences in disgust or that result from these individual differences.

On the other hand, we remain cautious/skeptical of the value of exceptionally narrow constructs, representing them as subscale scores, and interpreting research findings based on such scoring. Beyond the confounded variance problems we noted previously, primarily, we do not view the DES domains as being "components of disgust," "facets of disgust," "aspects of disgust," "ingredients of disgust," or any other commonly used tag to name domains of trait manifestation; we believe those terms wrongly define the construct of disgust as a composite variable emerging from its components[7] (see Bollen & Lennox, 1991, on the difference between emergent and latent variables). Instead, we view the stimuli within the content domains as diverse manifestations of an underlying disgust personality trait.[8] Accordingly, we view the domain variation more as nuisance variation emerging from repeated item content and that needs to be controlled in the measurement of *disgust* (e.g., by using SEM) and not as distinct substantively meaningful and interpretable traits.

There is no doubt that many researchers would disagree with our viewpoint and point out the value of very narrow constructs and the scoring of subscales for research

---

[7] As if the trait were a puzzle and the content domains pieces.

[8] If disgust were viewed as the outcome of its "aspects" or "components," as in an emergent measurement model, then it would be appropriate to criticize the measure for not including potentially important components, such as sexual behaviors, moral transgressions, and contaminations. On the other hand, if disgust is viewed as following a latent variable measurement model, the issue of forming a "census" of components is rendered irrelevant, because the construct is not defined by its indicators!

purposes. Beyond theoretical hypothesis testing arguments, empirical arguments justifying scoring subscales (or modelling group factors in SEM) most certainly would be based on demonstrations of differential correlates. Such demonstrations, however, would not necessarily persuade us of the value of scoring subscales.

There are two main reasons underlying our cautious approach to subscale scoring. First, for any two subscales and a criterion variable, there inevitably are many sources of variance (fear, phobia, anxiety sensitivity, histrionic personality, emotional instability, and so forth) that we remain unaware of because we have not included measures of them in our analyses. These hidden sources of variance always are possible explanations for differential subscale correlates, and such findings do not require researchers to recognize different "aspects of" *disgust* as representing meaningful or valid distinctions.

Third, and most important, our results show that, paradoxically, with the exception of *injections and blood draws*, adding items to the content domains would make them worse indicators of their respective constructs, not better. Notice that for four of the five domains, p^2 values are above .50 for most items (e.g., Table 22.5), meaning that items are relatively better measures of the general factor than a group factor. As a consequence, adding more of the same types of items to a domain would increase the influence of the general factor relative to the group factor on the unit-weighted subscale score. This subscale invalidating fact – the measure becomes less valid as items increase – would be completely missed if researchers attended only to indices such as alpha or omega.

Ultimately, however, we do not see the solution to the global versus subscale debate (or "clumpers" versus "splitters") as being resolvable under the present, nomological network-based, paradigm for establishing construct validity. What is needed, perhaps, is a much stronger program of validation of the kind outlined by Borsboom, Mellenbergh, and van Heerden (2004), where the psychology moves beyond dubbing constructs as "valid" because a covariance matrix can be "fit" by a confirmatory factor model, or a score correlates with other scores that it theoretically should, and toward a real understanding of the psychobiological underpinnings that *cause* the variation we represent as latent variables in our measurement models. Only then can we be on solid ground in arguing, for example, whether *small animal disgust* truly is a psychobiological trait worth measuring and researching or merely one of many domains upon which the general disgust trait can manifest in some individuals.

References

Allport, G. W. (1963). *Pattern and growth of personality*. New York: Holt, Rinehart, & Winston.

Bentler, P. M. (2009). Alpha, dimension-free, and model-based internal consistency reliability. *Psychometrika, 74*, 137–143.

Bentler, P. M., & Wu, E. J. C. (2012). *EQS 6 for Windows user's guide*. Encino, CA: Multivariate Software.

Bollen, K., & Lennox, R. (1991). Conventional wisdom on measurement: A structural equation perspective. *Psychological Bulletin, 110*, 305–314.

Borsboom, D., Mellenbergh, G. J., & van Heerden, J. (2004). The concept of validity. *Psychological Review, 111*, 1061–1071.

Browne, M. W. (2001). An overview of analytic rotation in exploratory factor analysis. *Multivariate Behavioral Research, 36*, 111–150.

Brunner, M., & Süb, H. M. (2005). Analyzing the reliability of multidimensional measures: An example from intelligence research. *Educational and Psychological Measurement, 65*, 220–240.

Cai, L. (2010). A two-tier full information item factor analysis model with applications. *Psychometrika, 75*, 581–612.

Cattell, R. B. (1978). *Scientific use of factor analysis in behavioral and life sciences.* New York: Plenum Press.

Chalmers, P. (2013). MIRT; Multidimensional item response theory Package for the R Environment. *Journal of Statistical Software, 48*, 1–29. www.jstatsoft.org/v48/i06/

Chen, W. H., & Thissen, D. (1997). Local dependence indexes for item pairs using item response theory. *Journal of Educational and Behavioral Statistics, 22*, 265–289.

Chen, F. F., Hayes, A., Carver, C. S., Laurenceau, J., & Zhang, Z. (2012). Modeling general and specific variance in multifaceted constructs: A comparison of the bifactor model to other approaches. *Journal of Personality, 80*, 219–251.

Chen, F. F., West, S. G., & Sousa, K. H. (2006). A comparison of bifactor and second-order models of quality of life. *Multivariate Behavioral Research, 41*, 189–225.

Cortina, J. M. (1993). What is coefficient alpha? An examination of theory and application. *Journal of Applied Psychology, 78*, 98–104.

Cronbach, L. J. (1951). Coefficient alpha and the internal structure of tests. *Psychometrika, 12*, 1–16.

Graham, J. M. (2006). Congeneric and (essentially) tau-equivalent estimates of score reliability. *Educational and Psychological Measurement, 66*, 930–944.

Gustafsson, J., & Åberg-Bengtsson, L. (2006). Unidimensionality and interpretability of psychological instruments. In S. Embretson (Ed.) *New directions in measuring psychological constructs with model-based approaches.* Washington, D.C.: American Psychological Association.

Gustafsson J., & Balke, G. (1993). General and specific abilities as predictors of school achievement. *Multivariate Behavioral Research, 28*, 407–434.

Holzinger, K. J. (1939). Relationships between three multiple orthogonal factors and four bifactors. *Journal of Educational Psychology, 30*, 513–519.

Holzinger, K. J., & Swineford, F. (1937). The bi-factor method. *Psychometrika, 2*, 41–54.

Holzinger, K., & Swineford, F. (1939). A study in factor analysis: The stability of a bi- factor solution. *Supplementary Educational Monographs*, no. 48. Chicago, IL: University of Chicago Press

Hu, L. & Bentler, P. M. (1999). Cutoff criteria for fit indexes in covariance structure analysis: Conventional criteria versus new alternatives. *Structural Equation Modeling: A Multidisciplinary Journal, 6*, 1–55.

Hull, J. G., Lehn, D. A., & Tedlie, J. C. (1991). A general approach to testing multifaceted personality constructs. *Journal of Personality and Social Psychology, 61*, 932–945.

Jennrich, R. I., & Bentler, P. M. (2011). Exploratory bi-factor analysis. *Psychometrika, 76*, 537–549.

Jennrich, R. I., & Bentler, P. M. (2012). Exploratory bi-factor analysis: The oblique case. *Psychometrika, 77*, 442–454.

Little, T. D., Cunningham, W. A., Shahar, G., & Widaman, K. F. (2002). To parcel or not to parcel: Exploring the question, weighing the merits. *Structural Equation Modeling, 9*, 151–173.

Lucke, J. F. (2005). The α and the ω of congeneric test theory: An extension of reliability and internal consistency to heterogeneous tests. *Applied Psychological Measurement, 29*, 65–81.

McDonald, R. P. (1999). *Test theory: A unified treatment.* Mahwah, NJ: Erlbaum.

Miller, M. B. (1995). Coefficient alpha: A basic introduction from the perspectives of classical test theory and structural equation modeling. *Structural Equation Modelling, 2*, 255–273.

Muthén, B., & Asparouhov, T. (2012). Bayesian structural equation modeling: A more flexible representation of substantive theory. *Psychological Methods, 17*, 313.

Muthén, L. K., and Muthén, B. O. (2012). *MPlus user's guide* (6th ed.). Los Angeles, CA: Muthén & Muthén.

Olatunji, B. O., Ebesutani, C., & Reise, S. P. (2015). *A bifactor model of disgust proneness: Examination of the Disgust Emotion Scale.* Assessment, 22, 248–262.

Olatunji, B. O., Sawchuk, C. N., de Jong, P. J., & Lohr, J. M. (2007). Disgust sensitivity and anxiety disorder symptoms: Psychometric properties of the Disgust Emotion Scale. *Journal of Psychopathology and Behavioral Assessment, 29,* 115–124.

R Development Core Team (2013). *R: A language and environment for statistical computing. R Foundation for Statistical Computing,* Vienna, Austria. ISBN 3-900051-07-0, URL: www.R-project.org

Raykov, T. (1997). Estimation of composite reliability for congeneric measures. *Applied Psychological Measurement, 23,* 173–184.

Raykov, T. (2004). Point and interval estimation of reliability for multiple-component measuring instruments via linear restraint covariance structure modeling. *Structural Equation Modeling, 11,* 343–356.

Raykov, T., & Stout, P. E. (2003). Reliability of scales with general structure: Point and interval estimation using a structural equation modeling approach. *Structural Equation Modeling, 9,* 195–212.

Reise, S. P. (2012). The rediscovery of bifactor measurement models. *Multivariate Behavioral Research, 47,* 667–696.

Reise, S. P., Bonifay, W. E., & Haviland, M. G. (2013). Scoring and modeling psychological measures in the presence of multidimensionality. *Journal of Personality Assessment, 95,* 129–140.

Reise, S. P., Moore, T. M., & Haviland, M. G. (2010). Bifactor models and rotations: Exploring the extent to which multidimensional data yield univocal scale scores. *Journal of Personality Assessment, 92,* 544–559.

Reise, S. P., Moore, T. M., & Maydeu-Olivares, A. (2011). Targeted bifactor rotations and assessing the impact of model violations on the parameters of unidimensional and bifactor models. *Educational and Psychological Measurement, 71,* 684–711.

Reise, S. P., Morizot, J., & Hays, R. D. (2007). The role of the bifactor model in resolving dimensionality issues in health outcomes measures. *Quality of Life Research, 16,* 19–31.

Reise, S. P., Scheines, R., Widaman, K. F., & Haviland, M. G. (2013). Multidimensionality and structural coefficient bias in structural equation modeling: A bifactor perspective. *Educational and Psychological Measurement, 73,* 5–26.

Revelle, W. (1979). Hierarchical cluster analysis and the internal structure of tests. *Multivariate Behavioral Research, 14,* 57–74.

Revelle, W. (2013). *psych: Procedures for personality and psychological research,* Evanston, Illinois: Northwestern University, http://CRAN.R-project.org/package=psych Version = 1.3.10

Revelle, W., & Zinbarg, R. E. (2009). Coefficients alpha, beta, omega and the glb: Comments on Sijtsma. *Psychometrika, 74,* 145–154.

Rindskopf, D., & Rose, T. (1988). Some theory and applications of confirmatory and second-order factor analysis. *Multivariate Behavioral Research, 23,* 51–67.

Samejima, F. (1997). Graded response model. In W. J. van der Linden, & R. Hambleton (Eds.), *Handbook of modern item response theory* (pp. 85–100). New York: Springer.

Schmitt, N. (1996). Uses and abuses of coefficient alpha. *Psychological Assessment, 8,* 350–353.

Schmid, J., & Leiman, J. (1957). The development of hierarchical factor solutions. *Psychometrika, 22,* 53–61.

Sijtsma, K. (2009). On the use, the misuse, and the very limited usefulness of Cronbach's alpha. *Psychometrika, 74,* 107–120.

Simms, L. J., Gros, D. F., Watson, D., & O'Hara, M. W. (2008). Parsing the general and specific components of depression and anxiety with bifactor modeling. *Depression and Anxiety, 25,* E34–E46.

Smith, G. T., McCarthy, D. M., & Zapolski, T. C. B. (2009). On the value of homogeneous constructs for construct validation, theory testing, and the description of psychopathology. *Psychological Assessment, 21,* 272–284.

Tellegen, A. (1991). Personality traits: Issues of definition, evidence, and assessment. In D. Cicchetti, & W. Grove (Eds.), *Thinking clearly about psychology: Essays in honor of Paul E. Meehl* (pp. 10–35). Minneapolis MN: University of Minnesota Press.

ten Berge, J. M. F., & Sočan, G. (2004). The greatest lower bound to the reliability of a test and the hypothesis of unidimensionality. *Psychometrika, 69*, 613–625.

Thomas, M. L. (2012). Rewards of bridging the divide between measurement and clinical theory: Demonstration of a bifactor model for the Brief Symptom Inventory. *Psychological Assessment, 24*, 101–113.

Walls, M. M., & Kleinknecht, R. A. (1996, April). *Disgust factors as predictors of blood injury fear and fainting*. Paper presented at the Annual Meeting of the Western Psychological Association, San Jose, CA.

Yung, Y., Thissen, D., & McLeod, L. D. (1999). On the relationship between the higher-order factor model and the hierarchical factor model. *Psychometrika, 64*, 113–128.

Zinbarg, R. E., Barlow, D. H., & Brown, T. A. (1997). Hierarchical structure and general factor saturation of the anxiety sensitivity index: Evidence and implications. *Psychological Assessment, 9*, 277–284.

Zinbarg, R. E., Revelle, W., Yovel, I., & Li, W. (2005). Cronbach's α, Revelle's β, and McDonald's ω_h: Their relations with each other and two alternate conceptualizations of reliability. *Psychometrika, 70*, 1–11.

Zinbarg, R. E., Revelle, W., Yovel, I., & Li, W. (2007). Estimating ω_h for structures containing two group factors: Perils and prospects. *Applied Psychological Measurement, 31*, 135–157.

Code Appendix

Code 1   R code for bifactor modelling and the evaluation of scale scores.

```
# read in the data file and call it des
des < - read.table("c:/foldername/datafilename.dat")

#Table 1: Means, standard deviations, item-test correlations,
#and response frequencies for the DES items
library(psych)
describe(des)    #M & SD
table1 < - cbind(describe(des)$mean,
                describe(des)$sd,
                alpha(des)$item$r.cor,
                alpha(des)$resp*500)

#Table 2: Chen-Thissen (1997) standardized local dependence
#values for each subscale
library(mirt)
des_mod < - mirt(des,1)
LD < - residuals(des_mod)
table2a < - LD[1:6,1:6]
table2b < - LD[7:12,7:12]
table2c < - LD[13:18,13:18]
table2d < - LD[19:24,19:24]
table2e < - LD[25:30,25:30]
```

```
#Table 3: Schmid-Leiman rotated factor loadings
R < - polychoric(des,smooth = TRUE)$rho
main < - omega(R,5, fm = "ml", n.obs = 500)
SL < - main$schmid$sl #loadings, communalities, uniquenesses
eigen < - colSums(SL^2) #eigenvalues
table3 < - rbind(SL,eigen)

#Tables 4 & 5 produced by EQS

#Table 6: Omega total and omega hierarchical for the
general disgust
#factor and each subscale found on bottom of omega
command output

#Figure 1: Heat map of correlations among the DES items
round(R,2)    # R is polychoric matrix
#Shading was done in Excel

#Figure 2: Item clusters derived from the iCLUST algorithm
iclust(R,5)
```

23

Reliability

William Revelle and David M. Condon

Introduction

All measures reflect an unknown mixture of interesting signal and uninteresting or irrelevant noise. Separating signal from noise is the primary challenge of measurement and is the fundamental goal of all approaches to reliability theory. What makes this challenge particularly difficult is that what is signal to some is noise to others. In climate science, short term variations in weather mask long term trends in climate. In oceanography, variations in waves mask tidal effects; waves and tides in turn mask long term changes in sea level. Within psychology, stable individual differences in affective traits contaminate state measures of momentary affective states; acquiescence and extreme response tendencies contaminate trait measures; moment to moment or day to day fluctuations in alertness or motivation affect measures of ability. All of these examples may be considered as problems of reliability: separating signal from noise. They also demonstrate that the classification of signal depends on what is deemed relevant. For indeed, meteorologists care about the daily weather, climate scientists about long term trends in climate; similarly, emotion researchers care about one's current emotion, personality researchers care about stable consistencies and long term trends.

Whether recording the time spent walking to work or the number of questions answered on an exam, people differ. They differ not only from each other, but from measure to measure. Thus, one of us walks to work in 16 minutes one day, but 15.5 minutes the next, and 16.5 on the third day. We can say that his mean time is 16 minutes with a standard deviation of 0.5 minutes. When asked how long it takes him to get to work, we should say that our best estimate is 16 minutes but we would expect to observe anything between 15 and 17 minutes. We tend to emphasize his central tendency (16 minutes) and consider the variation in his walking rate as irrelevant noise. The expected score across multiple replications that minimizes squared deviations is just the arithmetic average score. In the "classical test theory" as originally developed by Spearman (1904), the expected score across an infinite number of replications is known as the *true score*. True score defined this way should not be confused with *Platonic Truth*, for if there is any systematic bias in the observations, then the mean score will show this bias (Lord & Novick, 1968).

The Wiley Handbook of Psychometric Testing: A Multidisciplinary Reference on Survey, Scale and Test Development, First Edition. Edited by Paul Irwing, Tom Booth, and David J. Hughes.
© 2018 John Wiley & Sons Ltd. Published 2020 by John Wiley & Sons Ltd.

By defining true score, θ, as the expected observed score, $\theta = \mathcal{E}(x)$, and error as the deviation of an observed score from this expectation, $\epsilon = x - \mathcal{E}(x)$, error is independent of observed score for it will have an expected value of 0 for all values of true score. That is, for raw scores, X, and deviation scores $x = X - \bar{X}$, the scores for an individual may be expressed as

$$X_i = \Theta_i + E_i \Leftrightarrow x_i = \theta_i + \epsilon_i, \tag{23.1}$$

and because across individuals the covariance of true and error score, $\sigma_{\theta\epsilon} = 0$,

$$\sigma_x^2 = \sigma_\theta^2 + \sigma_\epsilon^2 + 2\sigma_{\theta\epsilon} = \sigma_\theta^2 + \sigma_\epsilon^2. \tag{23.2}$$

Just as we can decompose the observed scores into two components, so can we decompose the observed score variance into the variance of the expected (true) scores and the variance of error scores.

Furthermore, because observed scores are the sum of expected scores and error scores, the covariance of observed score with the expected score is just σ_θ^2, and the correlation of true scores with observed scores will be

$$\rho_{\theta x} = \frac{\sigma_{\theta x}}{\sigma_\theta \sigma_x} = \frac{\sigma_\theta^2}{\sigma_\theta \sigma_x} = \frac{\sigma_\theta}{\sigma_x}. \tag{23.3}$$

This means that the squared correlation of true scores with observed scores (which is the amount of variance shared between observed and true scores) is the ratio of their respective variances:

$$\rho_{\theta x}^2 = \frac{\sigma_\theta^2}{\sigma_x^2}. \tag{23.4}$$

The *reliability* of a test is defined as this squared correlation of true score with observed score, or as the ratio of true to observed variances. Expressing this in engineering terms of the ratio of signal, S, in a test to noise, N (Brennan & Kane, 1977; Cronbach & Gleser, 1964):

$$\frac{S}{N} = \frac{\rho_{\theta x}^2}{1 - \rho_{\theta x}^2}. \tag{23.5}$$

Finally, from regression, the true deviation score predicted from the observed score is just

$$\hat{\theta} = \beta_{\theta x} x = \frac{\sigma_\theta^2}{\sigma_x^2} x = \rho_{\theta x}^2 x. \tag{23.6}$$

That is, the estimated true deviation score is just the observed deviation score times the test reliability. The estimated true score will be the mean of the raw scores plus this estimated true score:

$$\hat{\Theta} = \bar{X} + \beta_{\theta x} x = \bar{X} + \frac{\sigma_\theta^2}{\sigma_x^2} x = \bar{X} + \rho_{\theta x}^2 x.$$

Reliability and validity

Although the validity of a test reflects the content of the items and the particular criterion of interest, it is important to note that a test cannot correlate with *any* criterion, y, more than it can correlate with the latent variable that it measures, θ. That is, $r_{xy} \leq \rho_{\theta x}$. This logically is the upper bound of the validity of a test, and thus validity must be less than or equal to the square root of the reliability: $r_{xy} \leq \rho_{\theta x} = \sqrt{\rho_{\theta x}^2}$.

Using Reliability

There are three primary reasons to be concerned about a measure's reliability. The first is that the relationship between any two constructs will be *attenuated* by the level of reliability of each measure: two constructs can indeed be highly related at a latent level, but if the measures are not very reliable, the observed correlation will be reduced. The second reason that understanding reliability is so important is the problem of *regression to the mean*. Failing to understand how reliability affects the relationship between observed scores and their expected values plagues economists, sports fanatics, and military training officers. The final reason to examine reliability is to estimate the true score given an observed score, and to establish confidence intervals around this estimate based upon the *standard error* of the observed scores.

Correction for attenuation

The original development of reliability theory was to estimate the correlation of latent variables in terms of observed correlations "corrected" for their reliability (Spearman, 1904). Measures of "mental character" showed almost the same correlations (.52) between pairs of brothers as did various physical characteristics (.52), but when the mental character correlations were corrected for their reliability, they were shown to be much more related (.81; Spearman, 1904).

The logic of correcting for attenuation is straightforward. For even if observed scores are contaminated by error, the errors are independent of the true scores, and the covariance between the observed scores of two different measures, x and y, just reflects the covariance of their true scores. Consider two observed variables, x and y, which are imperfect measures of two latent traits, θ and ψ:

$$x = \theta + \epsilon \qquad y = \psi + \zeta,$$

with variances

$$\sigma_x^2 = \sigma_\theta^2 + \sigma_\epsilon^2 \qquad \sigma_y^2 = \sigma_\psi^2 + \sigma_\zeta^2,$$

reliabilities

$$\rho_{\theta x}^2 = \frac{\sigma_\theta^2}{\sigma_x^2} \qquad \rho_{\psi y}^2 = \frac{\sigma_\psi^2}{\sigma_y^2},$$

and covariance

$$\sigma_{xy} = \sigma_{(\theta+\epsilon)(\psi+\zeta)} = \sigma_{\theta\psi} + \underline{\sigma_{\theta\zeta} + \sigma_{\psi\epsilon} + \sigma_{\epsilon\zeta}} = \sigma_{\theta\psi}.$$

Then the correlation between the two latent variables may be expressed in terms of the observed correlation and the two reliabilities:

$$\rho_{\theta\psi} = \frac{\sigma_{\theta\psi}}{\sigma_\theta \sigma_\psi} = \frac{\sigma_{xy}}{\sqrt{\rho_{\theta x}^2 \sigma_x^2 \rho_{\psi y}^2 \sigma_y^2}} = \frac{r_{xy}}{\sqrt{\rho_{\theta x}^2 \rho_{\psi y}^2}}.$$

That is, the correlation between the true parts of any two tests will the ratio of their observed correlation to the square root of their respective reliabilities. This *correction for attenuation* is perhaps the most important use of reliability theory, for it allows for an estimate of the true correlation between two constructs when the constructs are perfectly measured, without error. It does require, however, that we find the reliability of the separate tests.

The concept that observed covariances reflect true covariances is the basis for structural equation modeling, in which relationships between observed scores are expressed in terms of relationships between latent scores and the reliability of the measurement of the latent variables. By correcting for unreliability in this way we are able to determine the underlying latent relationships without the distraction of measurement error.

Regression to the mean

First considered by Galton (1886, 1889) as he was developing the correlation coefficient, reversion to mediocrity was the observation that the offspring of tall parents tended to be shorter, just as those of short parents tended to be taller. Although originally interpreted as of interest only to geneticists, the concept of *regression to the mean* is a classic problem of reliability theory that is unfortunately not as well recognized as it should be (Stigler, 1986, 1997). Whenever groups are selected on the basis of being extreme on an observed variable, the scores on a retest will be closer to the mean than they were originally. Classic examples include the tendency of companies with award-winning CEOs to become less successful than comparable companies whose CEOs do not win the award (Malmendier & Tate, 2009), for flight instructors to think that rewarding good pilots is counterproductive because they get worse on their next flight (Kahneman & Tversky, 1973), for athletes who make the cover of *Sports Illustrated* to do less well following the publication (Gilovich, 1991), for training programs for disadvantaged children to help their students (Campbell & Kenny, 1999), and for the breeding success of birds to improve following prior failures (Kelly & Price, 2005). Indeed, the effect of regression to mean artifacts on the market value of baseball players was the subject of the popular book and movie, *Moneyball* (Lewis, 2004). A critical review of various examples of regression artifacts in chronobiology has the the impressive title "How to show that unicorn milk is a chronobiotic," and provides thoughtful simulated examples (Atkinson, Waterhouse, Reilly, & Edwards, 2001). Regression effects should be controlled for when trying to separate placebo from treatment effects in behavioral and drug intervention studies (Davis, 2002).

So, if it is so well known, what is it? If observed score is imperfectly correlated with true score (Equation 23.3) then it is also correlated with error because

$$\sigma_x^2 = \sigma_\theta^2 + \sigma_\epsilon^2,$$

$$\sigma_{\epsilon x} = \sigma_{\epsilon(\theta+\epsilon)} = \cancel{\sigma_{\epsilon\theta}} + \sigma_\epsilon^2 = \sigma_\epsilon^2,$$

and thus

$$\rho_{\epsilon x} = \frac{\sigma_{\epsilon x}}{\sqrt{\sigma_\epsilon^2 \sigma_x^2}} = \frac{\sigma_\epsilon^2}{\sqrt{\sigma_\epsilon^2 \sigma_x^2}} = \frac{\sigma_\epsilon}{\sigma_x}. \qquad (23.7)$$

That is, individuals with extreme observed scores might well have extreme true scores, but are most likely to also have extreme error scores. From Equation 23.6 we see that for any observed score, the expected true score is regressed toward the mean with a slope of $\rho_{x\theta}^2$.

In the case of pilot trainees, if the reliability of flying skill is .5, with a mean score of 50 and a standard deviation of 20, the top 10% of the fliers will have an average score of 75.6 on their first trial but will regress 12.8 points (the reliability value × their deviation score) toward the mean or have a score of 62.8 on the second trial. The bottom 10%, on the other hand, will have scores far below the mean, with an average of 24.4, but improve 12.8 points on their second flight to 37.2. Flight instructors seeing this result will falsely believe that punishing those who do badly leads to improvement, perhaps due to heightened effort, while rewarding those who do well leads to a decrease in effort (Kahneman & Tversky, 1973). Similarly, because the mean batting average in baseball is $\approx .260$ with a standard deviation of $\approx .0275$ and has a year to year reliability of $\approx .38$, those who have a batting average of 3σ or .083 above the average in one year (.343 instead of .260) are expected to be just $1.1\sigma \approx .031$ above the average, or .291, in the succeeding year (Schall & Smith, 2000). That is, a spectacular year is most likely followed by a return, not to the overall average, but rather to the player's average.

Standard error of observed score

Given an observation for one person of x_i, what is our best estimate of that person's true score, and what is the standard deviation of that estimate? The estimate of true score was found before (Equation 23.6), and is just $\hat{\theta}_i = \rho_{\theta x}^2 x_i$. Since the variance of the error scores is the unreliability times the observed score variance, $(1-\rho_{\theta x}^2)\sigma_x^2$, the standard deviation of our estimated true score will be

$$\sigma_\epsilon = \sigma_x \sqrt{1-\rho_{\theta x}^2}. \qquad (23.8)$$

This means that the 95% confidence interval of a true score will be

$$\rho_{\theta x}^2 x_i \pm 1.96 \sigma_x \sqrt{1-\rho_{\theta x}^2}. \qquad (23.9)$$

Note that this confidence interval is symmetric around the regressed score. Thus, for our flight instructor example with a reliability of .5 and a standard deviation of 20, a pilot with an observed score of 70 will have an estimated true score of $60 \pm 1.96 \times 20 \times \sqrt{1-.50} = 32$ to 88, and our baseball player who was batting .343 had a 95% confidence interval of $.291 \pm 1.96 \times .0275 \times \sqrt{1-.38} = .249$ to .333! Given this amount of expected variation, it is not surprising that so many baseball aficionados develop superstitious explanations for baseball success; stellar performance one year is not very predictive of performance in the subsequent year.

True Score Theory

Estimating reliability using parallel tests

Unfortunately, all of the analyses discussed so far are of no use unless we have some way of estimating σ_θ^2 and σ_ϵ^2. With one test, it is obviously impossible to find a unique decomposition into true scores and error scores.

Spearman's basic insight was to recognize that if there are two (or more) observed measures (x and x') that have true scores in common but independent error scores with equal variances, then the correlation of these two measures is a direct estimate of σ_θ^2 (Spearman, 1904). For if both x and x' are measures of θ, and both have equal amounts of independent error,

$$\sigma_e^2 = \sigma_{e'}^2,$$

then

$$r_{xx'} = \frac{\sigma_{\theta x} \sigma_{\theta x'}}{\sigma_x \sigma_{x'}} = \frac{\sigma_{\theta x}^2}{\sigma_x \sigma_{x'}}. \tag{23.10}$$

But since both x and x' are thought to be measures of the same latent variable, and their error variances are equal, then $\sigma_x = \sigma_{x'}$ and $\sigma_{\theta x} = \sigma_{\theta x'} = \sigma_\theta$, and thus the correlation of two parallel tests is the squared correlation of the observed score with the true score:

$$r_{xx'} = \frac{\sigma_{\theta x}^2}{\sigma_x^2} = \frac{\sigma_\theta^2}{\sigma_x^2} = \rho_{x\theta}^2, \tag{23.11}$$

which is defined as the reliability of the test. Reliability is the correlation between two *parallel tests* or measures of the same construct; it is the ratio of the amount of true variance in a test to the total variance of the test, and is the square of the correlation between either measure and the true score.

Estimating reliability using τ equivalent measures

The previous derivation requires the assumption that the two measures of the latent (unobserved) trait are exactly equally good and that they have equal error variances. These are very strong assumptions, for "unlike the correlation coefficient, which is

Table 23.1 Observed correlations and modeled parameters when estimating the parameters of parallel, τ equivalent, and congeneric tests. To solve for two parallel tests (lines 1–2) requires the assumption of equal true ($\lambda_1\sigma_\theta = \lambda_2\sigma_\theta$) and error ($\epsilon_1^2 = \epsilon_2^2$) variances. To solve the six equations for three τ equivalent tests (lines 1–3) we can relax this assumption, but require the assumption of equal error variances. Congeneric measures (four or more tests) can be solved with no further assumptions.

Variable	Test$_1$	Test$_2$	Test$_3$	Test$_4$
Test$_1$	$\sigma_{x_1}^2 = \lambda_1\sigma_\theta^2 + \epsilon_1^2$			
Test$_2$	$\sigma_{x_1 x_2} = \lambda_1\sigma_\theta\lambda_2\sigma_\theta$	$\sigma_{x_2}^2 = \lambda_2\sigma_\theta^2 + \epsilon_2^2$		
Test$_3$	$\sigma_{x_1 x_3} = \lambda_1\sigma_\theta\lambda_3\sigma_\theta$	$\sigma_{x_2 x_3} = \lambda_2\sigma_\theta\lambda_3\sigma_\theta$	$\sigma_{x_3}^2 = \lambda_3\sigma_\theta^2 + \epsilon_3^2$	
Test$_4$	$\sigma_{x_1 x_4} = \lambda_1\sigma_\theta\lambda_4\sigma_\theta$	$\sigma_{x_2 x_4} = \lambda_2\sigma_\theta\lambda_4\sigma_\theta$	$\sigma_{x_3 x_4} = \lambda_3\sigma_\theta\lambda_4\sigma_\theta$	$\sigma_{x_4}^2 = \lambda_4\sigma_\theta^2 + \epsilon_4^2$

merely an observed fact, the reliability coefficient has embodied in it a belief or point of view of the investigator" (Kelley, 1942, p. 75). Kelley, of course, was commenting upon the assumption of parallelism as well as the assumption that the test means the same thing as when it is given again. With the assumption of parallelism it is possible to solve the three equations (two for variances and one for the covariance) shown in the first two rows of Table 23.1 for the three unknowns (σ_θ^2, σ_ϵ^2, and λ_1). A relaxation of the exact parallelism assumption is to assume that the covariances of observed scores with true scores are equal ($\lambda_1 = \lambda_2 = \lambda_3$), but that the error variances are unequal (Table 23.1, lines 1–3). With this assumption of equal covariances with true score (known as *tau equivalence*) we have six equations (one for each correlation between the three tests, and one for each variance) and five unknowns (σ_θ^2, $\lambda_1 = \lambda_2 = \lambda_3$, and the three error variances, ϵ_1^2, ϵ_2^2, ϵ_1^2), and we can solve using simple algebra.

Estimating reliability using congeneric measures

If there are at least four tests, it is possible to solve for the unknown parameters (covariances with true score, true score variance, error score variances) without any further assumptions other than that all of the tests are imperfect measures of the same underlying construct (Table 23.1). In terms of factor analysis, the *congeneric* model merely assumes that all measures load on one common factor. Indeed, with four or more measures of the same construct it is possible to evaluate how well each measure reflects the construct, λ_i, and the amount of error variance in each measure, $r_{x_i\theta}^2 = \dfrac{\lambda_i^2}{\sigma_{x_i}^2}$.

Reliability Over What?

The previous paragraphs discuss reliability in terms of the correlations between two or more measures. What is unstated is when or where these measures are given, as well as the meaning of alternative measures. Reliability estimates can be found based upon variations in the overall test, variations over time, variation over items in a test, and variability associated with who is giving the test. Each of these alternatives has a different

Table 23.2 Reliability is the ability to generalize about individual differences across alternative sources of variation. Generalizations within a domain of items use internal consistency estimates. If the items are not necessarily internally consistent, reliability can be estimated based upon the worst split half, β, the average split (corrected for test length), or the best split, λ_4. Reliability across forms or across time is just the Pearson correlation. Reliability across raters depends upon the particular rating design and is one of the family of intraclass correlations. Functions in R may be used to find all of these coefficients. Except for cor, all functions are in the *psych* package.

Generalization over	Type of reliability	R function	Name
Unspecified	Parallel tests	cor(xx')	r_{xx}
	Tau equivalent tests	cov(xx') and fa	r_{xx}
	Congeneric tests	cov(xx') and fa	r_{xx}
Forms	Alternative form	cor(x,y)	r_{xx}
Time	Test–retest	cor($time_1\, time_2$)	r_{xx}
Split halves	Random split half	splitHalf	r_{xx}
	Worst split half	iclust or splitHalf	β
	Best split half	splitHalf	λ_4
Items	Internal consistency		
	General factor (g)	omega or omegaSem	ω_h
	Average	alpha or scoreItems	α
	smc	alpha or scoreItems	λ_6
	All common (h^2)	omega or omegaSem	ω_t
Raters	Single rater	ICC	ICC_2, ICC_2, ICC_3
	Average rater	ICC	$ICC_{1k}, ICC_{2k}, ICC_{3k}$

meaning, and sometimes a number of different estimates. In the abstract case of parallel tests or congeneric measurement, the domain of generalization (time, form, items) is not specified. It is possible, however, to organize reliability coefficients in terms of a simple taxonomy (Table 23.2). Each of these alternatives is discussed in more detail in the subsequent sections.

Reliability over alternate forms

Perhaps the easiest two to understand, because they are just raw correlations, are the reliability of *alternate forms* and the reliability of tests over time (*test–retest*). *Alternative form reliability* is just the correlation between two tests measuring the same construct, both measures of which are thought to measure the construct equally well. Such tests might be the same items presented in a different order to avoid cheating on an exam, or made up different items with similar but not identical content (e.g., 2 + 4 = ? and 4 + 2 = ?). Ideally, to be practically useful, such equivalent forms should have equal means and equal variances. Although the intuitive expectation might be that two such tests would correlate perfectly, they won't, for all of the reasons previously discussed. Indeed, the correlation between two such alternate forms gives us an estimate of the amount of variance that each test shares with the latent construct being measured. If we have three or more alternate forms, then their correlations may be treated as if they were τ equivalent or congeneric measures, and we can use factor analysis to find each test's covariance (λ_i) with the latent factor, the square of which will be the reliability.

The construction of such alternate forms can be done formulaically by randomizing items from one form to prepare a second or third form, or by creating quasi-matching pairs of items across forms ("The capital of Brazil is ?" and "Brasilia is the capital of ?"). To control for subtle differences in difficulty, multiple groups of items can be matched across forms (e.g., $4 \times 9 = ?$ and $3 \times 7 = ?$ might be easier than $9 \times 4 = ?$ and $7 \times 3 = ?$, so form A could have $4 \times 9 = ?$ and $7 \times 3 = ?$ while form B could have $9 \times 4 = ?$ and $3 \times 7 = ?$).

With the ability to computer-generate large sets of equivalently difficult ability items (e.g., Condon & Revelle, 2014; Embretson, 1998; Leon & Revelle, 1985), the construction of alternate forms becomes amazingly straightforward. The typical use of such alternate forms of measurement is to enable equivalent tests to be given to different groups over time without worrying about the particular test items being disclosed by earlier test takers to later test takers.

Stability over time

The second type of reliability (*test–retest*) that is a correlation between two forms is the correlation of the same test given at two different occasions. Unlike the correlations between alternate forms, which should be high, the expected test–retest correlation depends upon the construct being measured. A fundamental question in measuring any construct is its stability over time. Some measures should be stable over time; others should not. Traits such as ability, extraversion, or the propensity to experience positive affect are thought to be relatively consistent across time and space. Although there might be changes in mean scores over time, rank orders of people on these tests should be relatively stable.

There is, however, at least one serious difficulty with test retest measures:

> The retest coefficient on the same form gives, in general, estimates that are too high, because of material remembered on the second application of the test. This memory factor cannot be eliminated by increasing the length of time between the two applications, because of variable growth in the function tested within the population of individuals. These difficulties are so serious that the method is rarely used. (Kuder & Richardson, 1937, p. 151)

In addition, test–retest measurement of many constructs (e.g., state measures of positive or negative emotion) are not expected to show any consistency over time. Indeed, the very concept of a state is that it is not consistent over time. Perhaps the earliest discussion of dispositions or propensities (traits) and states may be found in Cicero's *Tusculan Disputations* in 45 BCE (Cicero, 1877; Eysenck, 1983). Among later but still early work distinguishing between states and traits, perhaps Allport and Odbert (1936) is the most influential. More recently, Fleeson (2001) conceived of traits as density distributions of states, and Revelle (1986) as the rate of change of achieving a state. The state–trait distinction is used in longitudinal studies by the state–trait–occasion model (Cole, Martin & Steiger, 2005), which explicitly decomposes measures over time into their state and trait components.

When examining the correlates of a putative stable trait measured at one time with a subsequent measure of another trait predicted by the first, the natural question is to what extent is the trait measure at time 1 the same as if it were measured at the later time. Consider the case of intelligence at age 11 predicting subsequent risk for mortality (Deary, Whiteman, Starr, Whalley, & Fox, 2004). How stable is the measure taken at age 11? Correlations of .66 and .54 with performance on the identical exam 68 years and 79 years later (Deary, Pattie, & Starr, 2013; Gow et al., 2011) suggest that the test is remarkably stable. These correlations are even higher when corrected for restriction of range of those taking the retest (there was differential attrition associated with IQ).

The stability of intelligence measures across 68–79 years is in marked contrast to the much lower (but non-zero) correlations of affect over a few years. That positive state affect among high school students is related .34 to positive state affect three years later suggests that the measure reflects not just a state component, but rather a reliable trait component as well (Kendall, 2013).

Split half reliability: the reliability of composites

For his dissertation research at the University of London, William Brown (1910) examined the correlations of a number of simple cognitive tasks (e.g., crossing out e's and r's from jumbled French text, adding up single digits in groups of ten) given two weeks apart. For each task, he measured the test–retest reliability by correlating the two time periods and then formed a composite based upon the average of the two scores. He then wanted to know the reliability of these composites so that he could correct the correlations with other composites for their reliability. That is, given a two-test composite, X, with a reliability for each test, ρ, what would the composite correlate with a similar (but unmeasured) composite, X'?

Consider X and X', both made up of two subtests. The reliability of X is just its correlation with X' and can be thought of in terms of the variance–covariance matrix, $\Sigma_{XX'}$:

$$\Sigma_{XX'} = \begin{pmatrix} V_x & \vdots & C_{xx'} \\ \cdots & \cdots & \cdots \\ C_{xx'} & \vdots & V_{x'} \end{pmatrix}; \quad (23.12)$$

letting $V_x = 1 V_x 1'$ and $C_{XX'} = 1 C_{XX'} 1'$, where 1 is a a column vector of 1s and 1' is its transpose, the correlation between the two tests will be

$$\rho_{xx'} = \frac{C_{xx'}}{\sqrt{V_x V_{x'}}}.$$

But the variance of a test is simply the sum of the true covariances and the error variances, and we can break up each test into two subtests (X_1 and X_2) and their respective variances and covariances. The structure of the two tests seen in Equation 23.12 becomes

$$\Sigma_{XX'} = \begin{pmatrix} V_{x_1} & \vdots & C_{x_1 x_2} & C_{x_1 x_1'} & \vdots & C_{x_1 x_2'} \\ \dots & & \dots & \dots & & \dots \\ C_{x_1 x_2} & \vdots & V_{x_2} & C_{x_2 x_1'} & \vdots & C_{x_2 x_1'} \\ \hline C_{x_1 x_1'} & \vdots & C_{x_2 x_1'} & V_{x_1'} & \vdots & C_{x_1' x_2'} \\ C_{x_1 x_2'} & \vdots & C_{x_2 x_2'} & C_{x_1' x_2'} & \vdots & V_{x_2'} \end{pmatrix}. \qquad (23.13)$$

Because the splits are done at random and the second test is parallel with the first test, the expected covariances between splits are all equal to the true score variance of one split (V_{t_1}), and the variance of a split is the sum of true score and error variances:

$$\Sigma_{XX'} = \begin{pmatrix} V_{t_1} + V_{e_1} & \vdots & V_{t_1} & V_{t_1} & \vdots & V_{t_1} \\ \dots & & \dots & \dots & & \dots \\ V_{t_1} & \vdots & V_{t_1} + V_{e_1} & V_{t_1} & \vdots & V_{t_1} \\ \hline V_{t_1} & \vdots & V_{t_1} & V_{t_1'} + V_{e_1'} & \vdots & V_{t_1'} \\ V_{t_1} & \vdots & V_{t_1} & V_{t_1'} & \vdots & V_{t_1'} + V_{e_1'} \end{pmatrix}.$$

The correlation between a test made up of two halves with intercorrelation ($r_1 = V_{t_1}/V_{x_1}$) with another such test is

$$r_{xx'} = \frac{4 V_{t_1}}{\sqrt{(4 V_{t_1} + 2 V_{e_1})(4 V_{t_1} + 2 V_{e_1})}} = \frac{4 V_{t_1}}{2 V_{t_1} + 2 V_{x_1}} = \frac{4 r_1}{2 r_1 + 2},$$

and thus

$$r_{xx'} = \frac{2 r_1}{1 + r_1}. \qquad (23.14)$$

Equation 23.14 is known as the *split half* estimate of reliability. It is important to note that the split half reliability is not the correlation between the two halves, but rather is adjusted upward by Equation 23.14.

In the more general case where the two splits do not have equal variance ($V_{x_1} \neq V_{x_2}$), Equation 23.14 becomes a little more complicated and may be expressed in terms of the total test variance as well as the covariance between the two subtests, or in terms of the subtest variances and correlations (J. Flanagan as cited in Rulon, 1939):

$$r_{xx'} = \frac{4 C_{x_1 x_2}}{V_x} = \frac{4 C_{x_1 x_2}}{2 C_{x_1 x_2} + V_{x_1} + V_{x_2}} = \frac{4 r_{x_1 x_2} s_{x_1} s_{x_2}}{2 C_{x_1 x_2} + V_{x_1} + V_{x_2}} = \frac{4 r_{x_1 x_2} s_{x_1} s_{x_2}}{2 r_{x_1 x_2} s_{x_1} \sigma_{x_2} + s_{x_1}^2 + s_{x_2}^2}. \qquad (23.15)$$

Because the total variance $V_{x_1+x_2} = V_{x_1} + V_{x_2} + 2C_{x_1 x_2}$, and the variance of the differences is $V_{x_1-x_2} = V_{x_1} + V_{x_2} - 2C_{x_1 x_2}$, then $C_{x_1 x_2} = \dfrac{V_{x_1} + V_{x_2} - V_{x_1-x_2}}{2}$, and we can express reliability as a function of the variances of differences scores between the splits and the variances of the two splits:

$$r_{xx'} = \frac{4C_{x_1 x_2}}{V_x} = \frac{2(V_{x_1} + V_{x_2} - V_{x_1-x_2})}{V_{x_1} + V_{x_2} + 2C_{x_1 x_2}} = \frac{2(V_{x_1} + V_{x_2} - V_{x_1-x_2})}{V_{x_1} + V_{x_2} + V_{x_1} + V_{x_2} - V_{x_1-x_2}} = \frac{V_{x_1} + V_{x_2} - V_{x_1-x_2}}{V_{x_1} + V_{x_2} - \dfrac{V_{x_1-x_2}}{2}}.$$

(23.16)

When calculating correlations was tedious compared to finding variances, Equation 23.16 was a particularly useful formula because it just required finding variances of the two halves as well as the variance of their differences. It is still useful, for it expresses reliability in terms of test variances and recognizes that unreliability is associated with the variances of the difference scores (perfect reliability implies that $V_{x_1-x_2} = 0$).

But how to decide how to split a test? Brown compared the scores at time one with those at time two and then formed a composite of the tests taken at both times. But estimating reliability based upon stability over time implies no change in the underlying construct over time. This is reasonable if measuring speed of processing, but is a very problematic assumption if measuring something more complicated:

> ...the reliability coefficient has embodied in it a belief or point of view of the investigator. Consider the score resulting from the item, "Prove the Pythagorean theorem." One teacher asserts that this is a unique demand and that there is no other theorem in geometry that can be paired with it as a similar measure. It cannot be paired with itself if there is any memory, conscious or subconscious, of the first attempt at proof at the time the second attempt is made, for then the mental processes are clearly different in the two cases. The writer suggests that anyone doubting this general principle take, say, a contemporary-affairs test and then retake it a day later. He will undoubtedly note that he works much faster and the depth and breadth of his thinking is much less—he simply is not doing the same sort of thing as before. (Kelley, 1942, pp. 75–76)

The alternative to estimating composite reliability by repeating the measure to get two splits is to split the test items from one administration. Thus, it is possible to consider splits such as the odd versus even items of a test. This would reflect differences in speed of taking a test in a different manner than would splitting a test into a first and second part (Brown, 1910). Unfortunately, the number of ways to split an n-item test into two is an explosion of possible combinations $\binom{n}{n/2} = \dfrac{n!}{2(n/2)!^2}$.

A 16-item test has 6,435 possible 8-item splits, and a 20-item test has 92,378 10-item splits. Most of these possible splits will yield slightly different split half estimates. Consider all possible splits of the 16 cognitive ability items in the ability data set included in the *psych* package (Revelle, 2017) in R (R Core Team, 2017). The split half reliabilities found from Equation 23.15 range from .73 to .87, with an average of .83 (Figure 23.1).

Split half reliabilities of a test with 16 ability items

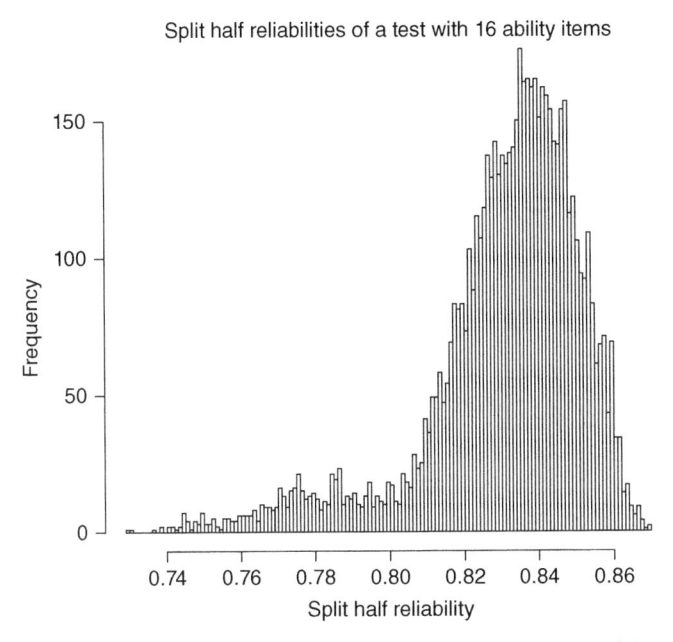

Figure 23.1 There are 6,435 possible 8-item splits of the 16 ability items of the ability data set. Of these, the maximum split half reliability is .87, the minimum is .73, and the average is .83. All possible splits were found using the splitHalf function.

Internal consistency estimates of reliability

The generalization of Equation 23.14 to predict the reliability of a composite made up of n tests with average intercorrelation of $\bar{r}_{ij}$ was developed by both (Brown, 1910) and (Spearman, 1910), and has become known as the *Spearman–Brown prophecy formula*:

$$r_{xx} = \frac{n\bar{r}_{ij}}{1+(n-1)\bar{r}_{ij}}. \tag{23.17}$$

Expressed in terms of the average covariance, $\bar{c}_i$, the unstandardized reliability is

$$r_{xx} = \frac{n\bar{c}_{ij}}{1+(n-1)\bar{c}_{ij}}. \tag{23.18}$$

That is, the reliability of a composite of n tests (or items) increases as a function of the number of items and the average intercorrelation or covariance of the tests (items). By combining items, each of which is a mixture of signal and noise, the ratio of signal to noise (S/N) increases linearly with the number of items and the resulting composite is a purer measure of signal (Cronbach & Gleser, 1964). If we think of every item as a very weak thread (the amount of signal is small compared to the noise), we can make a very strong rope by binding many threads together (Equation 23.17).

Considering how people differ from item to item and from trial to trial, Guttman (1945) defined reliability as variation over trials:

> Using this definition, no assumptions of zero means for errors or zero correlations are needed to prove that the total variance of the test is the sum of the error variance and

the variance of expected scores; this relationship between variances is an algebraic identity. Therefore, the reliability coefficient is defined without assumptions of independence as the complement of the ratio of error variance to total variance. (Guttman, 1945, p. 257)

That is,

$$r_{xx} = \frac{\sigma_x^2 - \sigma_e^2}{\sigma_x^2} = 1 - \frac{\sigma_e^2}{\sigma_x^2}. \tag{23.19}$$

KR-20, λ_3, and α as indicators of internal consistency

Although originally developed to predict the reliability of a composite where the reliability of the subtests is found from their test–retest correlation, the Spearman–Brown methodology was quickly applied to estimating reliability based upon the internal structure of a particular test. Because of the difficulty of finding the average between-item correlation or covariance in Equations 23.17 or 23.18, reliability was expressed in terms of the total test variance, V_x, and a function of the item variances, $V\,x_i$. For dichotomous items with a probability of being correct, p, or being wrong, q, $V_{x_i} = p_i q_i$ (Kuder & Richardson, 1937). This approach was subsequently generalized to polytomous and continuous items by Guttman (1945) and by Cronbach (1951).

The approach to find σ_e^2 for dichotomous items taken by Kuder and Richardson (1937) was to recognize that for an n-item test, the average covariance between items estimates the reliable variance of each item, and the error variance for each item will therefore be

$$\sigma_{e_i}^2 = \sigma_{x_i}^2 - \overline{\sigma_{ij}} = \sigma_{x_i}^2 - \frac{\sigma_x^2 - \Sigma \sigma_{x_i}^2}{n(n-1)} = p_i q_i - \frac{\sigma_x^2 - \Sigma p_i q_i}{n(n-1)},$$

and thus

$$r_{xx} = \frac{\sigma_x^2 - \sigma_e^2}{\sigma_x^2} = \frac{\sigma_x^2 - \Sigma \left(p_i q_i - \frac{\sigma_x^2 - \Sigma p_i q_i}{n(n-1)} \right)}{\sigma_x^2},$$

or

$$r_{xx} = \frac{\sigma_x^2 - \Sigma(p_i q_i)}{\sigma_x^2} \frac{n}{n-1}. \tag{23.20}$$

In their derivation in terms of the total item variance and the sum of the (dichotomous) item variances, Equation 23.20 was the 20th equation in Kuder and Richardson (1937) and is thus is known as the Kuder–Richardson (20), KR-20, or KR_{20} formula for reliability. Generalizing this to the polytomous or continuous item case, it is known either as α (Cronbach, 1951) or as λ_3 (Guttman, 1945):

$$r_{xx} = \alpha = \lambda_3 = \frac{\sigma_x^2 - \Sigma \sigma_{x_i}^2}{\sigma_x^2} \cdot \frac{n}{n-1}. \tag{23.21}$$

Guttman (1945) considered six different ways to estimate reliability from the pattern of item correlations. His λ_3 coefficient used the average inter-item covariance as an estimate of the reliable variance for each item. He also suggested an alternative, λ_6, which is to use the amount of an item's variance which is predictable by all of the other variables. That is, to find the *squared multiple correlation* or *smc* of the item with all the other items and then find the shared variance as $V_{s_i} = smc_i V_{x_i}$,

$$\lambda_6 = \frac{V_x - \Sigma V_{x_i} + \Sigma V_{s_i}}{V_x}. \tag{23.22}$$

Guttman (1945) also considered the maximum split half reliability (λ_4). Both λ_4 and λ_6 are obviously more complicated to find than λ_3 or α. To find λ_4 requires finding the maximum among many possible splits, and λ_6 requires taking the inverse of the correlation matrix to find the *smc*. But with modern computational power, it is easy to find λ_6 using the `alpha,scoreItems`, or `splitHalf` functions in the *psych* package. It is a little more tedious to find λ_4, but this can be done by comparing all possible splits for up to 16 items or by sampling thousands of times for larger data sets using the `splitHalf` function.

Consider the 16 ability items with the range of split half correlations as shown in Figure 23.1. Using the `splitHalf` function we find that the range of possible splits is from .73 to .87 with an average of .83, α = .83, λ_6 = .84, and a maximum (λ_4) of .87.

Standard error of alpha

There are at least two ways to find the standard error of the estimated α. One is through bootstrapping, the other is through normal theory. Consider the variability in values of α for the 16 ability items for 1,525 subjects found in the `ability` data set. Using the `alpha` function to bootstrap by randomly resampling the data (with replacement) 10,000 times yields a distribution of alpha that ranges from .802 to .848 with a mean value of .829 (Figure 23.2). Compare this to the observed value of .829.

Using the assumption of multivariate normality, Duhachek and Iacobucci (2004) showed that the standard error of α, ASE, is a function of the covariance matrix of the items, V, the number of items, n, and the sample size, N. Defining Q as

$$Q = \frac{2n^2}{(n-1)^2 (1'V1)^3} \left[1'V1 \left(trV^2 + tr^2V \right) - 2trV \left(1'V^2 1 \right) \right], \tag{23.23}$$

where tr is the trace of a matrix (the sum of the diagonal of a matrix), and **1** is a row vector of 1 s, then the standard error of α is

$$ASE = \sqrt{\frac{Q}{n}} \tag{23.24}$$

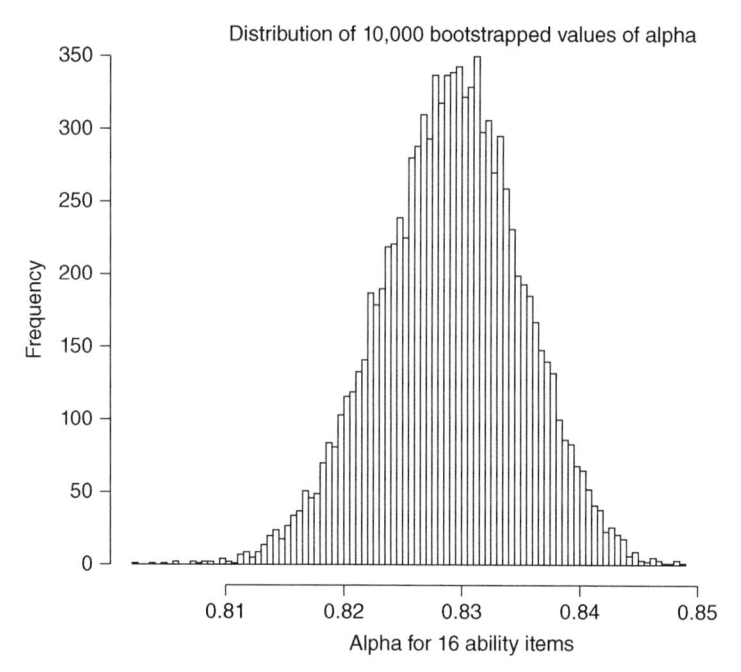

[Figure: Distribution of 10,000 bootstrapped values of alpha — histogram of Alpha for 16 ability items, ranging approximately from 0.81 to 0.85]

Figure 23.2 The value of α for the `ability` data set varies across 10,000 bootstrapped resamplings from .80 to .85. For the 1,525 subjects in the 16-item `ability` data set, the 95% confidence interval using normal theory is from 0.8167 to 0.8418, which is very similar to the empirical bootstrapped estimates of 0.8168 to 0.8405.

and the resulting 95% confidence interval is

$$\alpha \pm 1.96\sqrt{\frac{Q}{n}}. \qquad (23.25)$$

These confidence intervals are reported in the `alpha` function. For the 1,525 subjects in the 16-item `ability` data set, the 95% confidence interval using normal theory is from 0.8167 to 0.8418, which is very similar to the empirical bootstrapped estimates of 0.8166 to 0.8403.

Reliability and item analysis

The α reliability of a scale is a function of the number of items in the scale as well as the average inter-item correlation in the scale (Equations 23.17–23.21). Thus, even if the items do not correlate very highly, the reliability of the total scale can be increased by merely adding items. Consider scales ranging in length from 1 to 100 items with average inter-item correlations of .01, .05, .1, .2, .3, and .4 (left-hand panel of Figure 23.3). An α of .9 may be achieved by using 14 highly correlated items ($\bar{r} = .4$), while to achieve this same level of reliability it would take 21 items with a somewhat lower inter-correlation

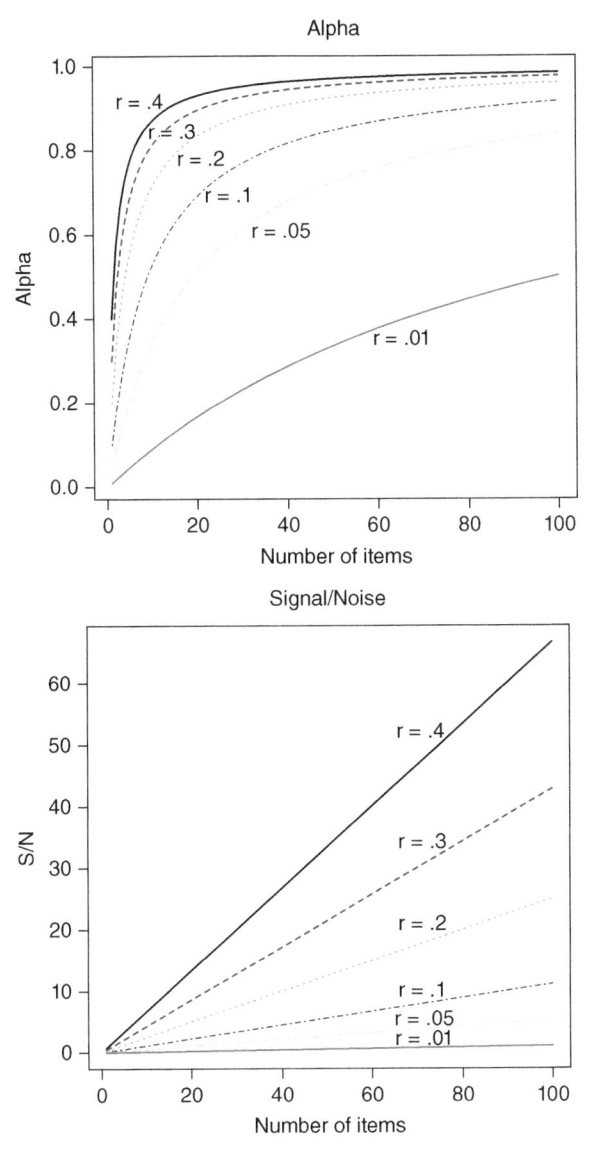

Figure 23.3 α or λ_3 reliability is an increasing function of the number of items and the inter-item correlation. Just six highly correlated items ($r = .4$) are needed to achieve an $\alpha = .8$. which requires 16 items with more typical correlations ($r = .2$). Even with barely related items (e.g., $r = .05$), an α of .8 may be achieved with 76 items. α values of .90 require 14, 21, 36, and 81 for intercorrelations of .4, .3, .2, and .1 respectively. Although α is a decelerating function of the number of items, the relationship between signal/noise ratio and both the inter-item correlations and the number of items is linear.

($\bar{r} = .3$) or 36 with an even lower value ($\bar{r} = .2$). For reference purposes, the average correlation of the 16 ability items in the ability data set have an $\bar{r} = .23$ while the five item scales measuring "Big 5" constructs in the bfi data set have average rs ranging from .23 (for openness/intellect) to .46 (for emotional stability).

The ratio of reliable variance to unreliable variance is known as the signal/noise ratio and is just $\frac{S}{N} = \frac{\rho^2}{1-\rho^2}$, which, for the same assumptions as for α, will be

$$\frac{S}{N} = \frac{n\bar{r}}{1-\bar{r}}. \tag{23.26}$$

That is, the S/N ratio increases linearly with the number of items as well as with the average intercorrelation. By thinking in terms of this ratio, the benefits of increased reliability due to increasing the number of items is seen not to be negatively accelerated as it appears when thinking just in reliability units (Equation 23.21). Indeed, while the S/N ratio is linear with the number of items, it is an accelerating function of the conventional measures of reliability. That is, while the S/N = 1 for a test with a reliability of .5, it is 2 for a test with a reliability of .66, 3 for .75, and 4 for .8; it is 9 for a test with a reliability of .9 and 19 for a reliability of .95 (right-hand panel of Figure 23.3). Depending upon whether the test is norm referenced (comparing two individuals) or domain referenced (comparing an individual to a criterion), there are several different S/N ratios to consider, but all follow this same general form (Brennan & Kane, 1977).

It is not unusual when creating a set of items thought to measure one construct to have some items that do not really belong. This is, of course, an opportunity to use *factor analysis* to explore the structure of the data. If just a few items are suspect, it is possible to find α and λ_6 for all the subsets found by dropping out one item. That is, if an item doesn't really fit, the α and λ_6 values of a scale without that item will actually be higher (Table 23.3). In the example, five items measuring Agreeableness and one measuring Conscientiousness were scored using the alpha function. Although the α and λ_6 values for all six items were .66 and .65 respectively, if item C1 is dropped, the values become .70 and .68. For all other single items, dropping the item leads to a decrease in α and λ_6 either because it reduces the average r (items A2–A5) or because the test length is less (items A1–A5). Note that the alpha function recognizes that one item (A1) needs to be reverse scored. If it were not reverse scored, the overall α value would be .44. This reverse scoring is done by finding the sign of the loading of each item on the first principal component of the item set and then reverse scoring those with a negative loading.

If internal consistency were the only goal when creating a test, clearly reproducing the same item many times will lead to an extraordinary reliability. (It will not be one because given the same item repeatedly, some people will in fact change their answers.) But this kind of *tautological consistency* is meaningless and should be avoided. Items should have similar domain content, but not identical content.

Reliability of scales formed from dichotomous or polytomous variables

Whether using true/false items to assess ability or four- to six-level polytomous (Likert-like) items to assess interests, attitudes, or temperament, the inter-item correlations are reduced from what would be observed with continuous measures. The *tetrachoric* and *polychoric* correlation coefficients are estimates of what the relationship would be between two bivariate, normally distributed items if they had not been dichotomized (tetrachoric) or trichotomized, tetrachotomized, pentachotomized. or otherwise broken into discrete but ordered categories (Pearson, 1901). The use of tetrachoric

Table 23.3 Item analysis of five Agreeableness items and one Conscientiousness item from the bfi data set using the `alpha` function. Note that one item is automatically reversed. Without reverse scoring item A1, $\alpha = .44$ and $\lambda_6 = .52$. The items are: A1: "Am indifferent to the feelings of others." A2: "Inquire about others' well-being." A3: "Know how to comfort others." A4: "Love children." A5: "Make people feel at ease." C1: "Am exacting in my work." The item statistics include the number of subjects who answered the item, the raw correlation (inflated by item overlap), a correlation that corrects for scale unreliability and item overlap, the correlation with the scale without that item, the mean and standard deviation for each item. Examining the effect of dropping one item at a time or of looking at the correlations of the item with the scale, item C1 does not belong to this set of items.

```
> alpha(bfi[1:6])
Reliability analysis
Call:   alpha(x  =  bfi[1:6])

    raw_alpha  std.alpha  G6(smc)  average_r   ase   mean    sd
       0.66       0.66      0.65     0.25     0.014   4.6    0.8

 lower  alpha   upper       95% confidence boundaries
  0.63   0.66   0.68

Reliability if an item is dropped:
     raw_alpha  std.alpha  G6(smc)  average_r  alpha se
A1-     0.66       0.66      0.64      0.28      0.015
A2      0.56       0.56      0.55      0.20      0.018
A3      0.55       0.55      0.53      0.20      0.018
A4      0.61       0.62      0.61      0.24      0.016
A5      0.58       0.58      0.56      0.22      0.017
C1      0.70       0.71      0.68      0.33      0.014

Item statistics
        n     r   r.cor   r.drop   mean   sd
A1-  2784  0.52   0.35     0.27    4.6   1.4
A2   2773  0.72   0.67     0.55    4.8   1.2
A3   2774  0.74   0.71     0.57    4.6   1.3
A4   2781  0.61   0.48     0.39    4.7   1.5
A5   2784  0.69   0.61     0.49    4.6   1.3
C1   2779  0.37   0.13     0.11    4.5   1.2

Non  missing  response  frequency  for   each  item
            1     2     3     4     5     6   miss
A1      0.33  0.29  0.14  0.12  0.08  0.03  0.01
A2      0.02  0.05  0.05  0.20  0.37  0.31  0.01
A3      0.03  0.06  0.07  0.20  0.36  0.27  0.01
A4      0.05  0.08  0.07  0.16  0.24  0.41  0.01
A5      0.02  0.07  0.09  0.22  0.35  0.25  0.01
C1      0.03  0.06  0.10  0.24  0.37  0.21  0.01
```

correlations to model what would be the case if the data were in fact bivariate normal had they not been dichotomized is not without critics. The most notable was Yule (1912), who suggested that some phenomena (vaccinated / not vaccinated, alive vs. dead) were truly dichotomous, while Pearson and Heron (1913) defended the use of his tetrachoric correlation.

Some have proposed that one should use tetrachoric or polychoric correlations when finding the reliability of categorical scales (Gadermann, Guhn, & Zumbo, 2012; Zumbo, Gadermann, & Zeisser, 2007). We disagree. The Zumbo et al. (2007) procedure estimates the correlation between unobserved continuous scores and true scores rather than the correlation of the observed scores (formed by dichotomizing the unobserved continuous scores) with the latent true score. Reliability is the squared correlation between observed score and true score, not an unobserved score with true score. With a simple simulation it is easy to see that the use of ϕ or Pearson's r provides reliability estimates that closely match the squared correlation of observed and latent, but that using the tetrachoric or polychoric correlation inflates the reliability estimate.

Partially following the simulation of Zumbo et al. (2007), we simulated 14 items for 10,000 participants using the `sim.congeneric` function. For each participant, a normally distributed latent score was used to generate a probability of response. This latent score was then used to generate 14 different scores broken into 1 of n categories, where n ranged from 2 to 7. All items were set to have the same difficulty. The item factor loadings were varied to produce three different sets of data with different levels of reliability (Table 23.4). Several conclusions can be drawn from this simulation: (1) With the same underlying distribution, inter-item r and thus α or λ_3 increase as the number of response categories increases. (2) The correlation of observed scores with the latent scores also increases as more categories are used. (3) If we are concerned with how well our test scores correlate with the latent scores from which they were generated, the squared correlation of observed scores based upon either simply summing the items or by doing an item response theory based scoring (not shown) is almost exactly the same as the α found using the raw correlations. This is indeed what we would expect given Equations 23.17–23.21. This is not the case when we use the tetrachoric or polychoric correlations. The suggestion that we should use "ordinal α" seems incorrect.

Domain sampling theory and structural measures of reliability

A great deal of space has been devoted to finding λ_3 or α. This is not because we recommend the routine use of either, for we don't. They are important to discuss both for historical reasons and because so many applied researchers use them. It would seem that one cannot publish a paper without reporting "Cronbach's α." This is unfortunate, for as we (Revelle, 1979; Revelle & Zinbarg, 2009) and many others (e.g., Bentler, 2009; Green & Yang, 2009; Lucke, 2005; Schmitt, 1996; Sijtsma, 2009), including Cronbach and Shavelson (2004), have discussed, α is neither a measure of how well a test measures one thing (Revelle, 1979; Revelle & Zinbarg, 2009; Zinbarg, Revelle, Yovel, & Li, 2005), nor the greatest lower bound for reliability (Bentler, 2009).

The basic problem is that α assesses neither the reliability of a test nor the internal consistency of a test, *unless* the test items all represent just one factor. This is generally not the case. When we think about a test made up of specific items thought to measure a

Table 23.4 The average inter-item correlation, and thus α varies as a function of the number of categories in a scale as well as the discrimination parameter (factor loadings) of the items. α based upon the raw correlations more closely approximates the squared correlation of the observed scores with the latent score, ρ_{oo}^2, than does the α based upon the polychoric correlations. The ratio of alpha to the squared correlation is shown for both the raw, α/ρ^2, and the polychoric based α, $\alpha_{\text{poly}}/\rho^2$. Simulated data using the sim.congeneric function.

Simulated results for 10,000 cases

Factor loading	Number of categories	$\bar{r}$	α	ρ_{oo}	ρ_{oo}^2	$\bar{r}_{\text{poly}}$	α_{poly}	$\rho_{p\theta}$	$\rho_{p\theta}^2$	α/ρ^2	$\alpha_{\text{poly}}/\rho^2$
.33	2	0.06	0.48	0.69	0.47	0.10	0.60	0.65	0.43	1.02	1.41
	3	0.07	0.53	0.73	0.53	0.10	0.61	0.71	0.51	1.00	1.20
	4	0.08	0.56	0.75	0.56	0.10	0.60	0.74	0.54	0.99	1.12
	5	0.09	0.58	0.76	0.59	0.10	0.61	0.75	0.57	0.99	1.08
	6	0.09	0.58	0.76	0.58	0.10	0.60	0.76	0.58	1.00	1.03
	7	0.09	0.59	0.77	0.59	0.10	0.61	0.76	0.57	1.00	1.06
.47	2	0.14	0.69	0.83	0.69	0.22	0.80	0.83	0.69	1.00	1.16
	3	0.16	0.73	0.85	0.73	0.22	0.80	0.85	0.73	1.00	1.10
	4	0.18	0.76	0.87	0.77	0.22	0.80	0.87	0.76	0.99	1.04
	5	0.19	0.77	0.88	0.77	0.22	0.80	0.88	0.77	0.99	1.03
	6	0.20	0.78	0.88	0.78	0.22	0.80	0.88	0.78	1.00	1.02
	7	0.21	0.79	0.89	0.79	0.22	0.80	0.89	0.79	1.00	1.01
.63	2	0.26	0.83	0.90	0.80	0.39	0.90	0.90	0.81	1.03	1.12
	3	0.29	0.85	0.92	0.85	0.39	0.90	0.91	0.84	1.00	1.08
	4	0.33	0.87	0.93	0.87	0.39	0.90	0.93	0.87	1.00	1.04
	5	0.35	0.88	0.94	0.88	0.39	0.90	0.94	0.88	1.00	1.02
	6	0.36	0.89	0.94	0.89	0.39	0.90	0.94	0.89	1.00	1.01
	7	0.37	0.89	0.94	0.89	0.39	0.90	0.94	0.89	1.00	1.01

construct, we are concerned not so much with those particular items as we are with how those items represent the larger (perhaps infinite) set of possible items that reflect that construct. Thus, extraversion is not just responding with strong agreement to an item asking about enjoying lively parties, but it also reflects a preference for talking to people rather than reading books, to seeking out exciting situations, to taking charge, and many, many more affective, behavioral, cognitive, and goal-directed items (Wilt & Revelle, 2009). Nor is general intelligence just the ability to do spatial rotation problems, to do number or word series, or the ability to do a matrix reasoning task (Gottfredson, 1997). Items will correlate with each other not just because they share a common core or *general factor*, but also because they represent some subgroups of items which share some common affective, behavioral, or cognitive content, i.e., *group factors*. Tests made up of such items will correlate with other tests to the extent they both represent the general core that all items share, but also to the extent that specific group factors match across tests.

By a general factor, we mean a factor on which most if not all of the items have a substantial loading. It is analogous to the general 2.7 K background radiation in radio astronomy used as evidence for the "Big Bang." That is, it pervades all items (Revelle & Wilt, 2013). Group factors, on the other hand, represent item clusters where only some or a few items share some common variance in addition to that shared with the general factor. These group factors represent systematic content (e.g., party-going behavior vs. talkativeness in measures of extraversion, spatial and verbal content in measures of ability) over and above what is represented by the general factor. Typically, when we assign a name to a scale we are implicitly assuming that a substantial portion of that scale does in fact reflect one thing: the general factor.

Reliability is both the ratio of true score variance to observed variance and the correlation of a test with a test *just like it* (Equation 23.11). But what does it mean to be a test just like another test? If we are concerned with a test made up of a set of items sampled from a domain, then the other test should also represent samples from that same domain. If we are interested in what is common to all the items in the domain, we are interested in the general factor saturation of the test. If we are interested in a test that shares general as well as group factors with another test, then we are concerned with the total reliability of the test.

Seven measures of internal consistency: α, λ_3, λ_6, β, ω_g, ω_t, and λ_4

This distinction between general, group, and total variance in a test, and the resulting correlations with similar tests, has led to at least seven different coefficients of internal consistency. These are: α (Cronbach, 1951), Equation 23.21, and its equivalent, λ_3 (Guttman, 1945), Equation 23.21, which are estimates based upon the average inter-item covariance; λ_6, an estimate based upon the squared multiple correlations of the items (Equation 23.22); β, defined as the worst split half reliability (Revelle, 1979); ω_g (McDonald, 1999; Revelle & Zinbarg, 2009; Zinbarg et al., 2005), the amount of general factor saturation; ω_t, the total reliable variance estimated by a factor model; and λ_4, the greatest split half reliability.

As an example of the use of these coefficients, consider the 16 ability items discussed earlier (Figure 23.1). We have already shown that this set has $\alpha = \lambda_3 = .83$ with a $\lambda_6 = .84$ and a $\lambda_4 = .87$. To find the other coefficients requires either cluster analysis for β or factor analysis for the two ω coefficients. A parallel analysis of random data (Horn, 1965) suggests that two principal components or four factors should be extracted. When four factors are found, the resulting structure may be seen in the left-hand panel of Figure 23.4. But these factors are moderately correlated, and when the matrix of factor correlations is in turn factored, the hierarchical structure may be seen in the right-hand panel of Figure 23.4.

Although hierarchical, higher-level, or bifactor models of ability have been known for years (Holzinger & Swineford, 1937, 1939; Schmid & Leiman, 1957), it is only relatively recently that these models have been considered when addressing the reliability of a test (McDonald, 1999; Revelle & Zinbarg, 2009; Zinbarg et al., 2005). Rather than consider the reliable variance of a test as reflecting just one factor, **F**, with correlations modeled as $\mathbf{R} = \mathbf{FF}' + \mathbf{U}^2$ and reliability as

$$\rho_{xx} = \frac{\mathbf{1FF'1'}}{\mathbf{1FF'1'} + \text{tr}(\mathbf{U}^2)}, \qquad (23.27)$$

the hierarchical approach decomposes test variance into that due to a *general factor*, **g**, and a number of independent *group factors*, **G**$_i$, with a correlation matrix of

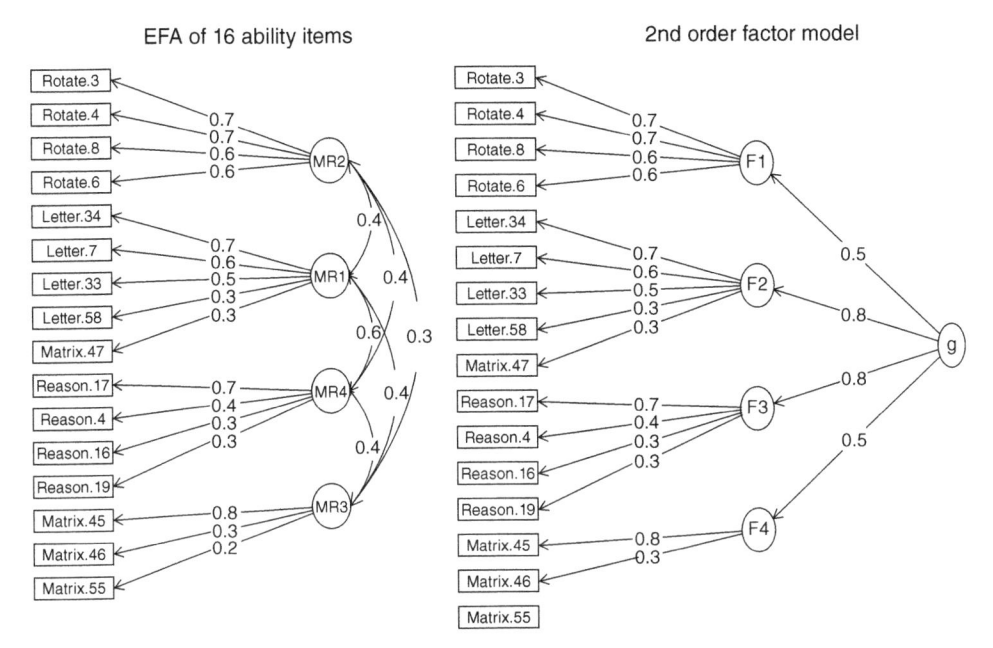

Figure 23.4 An exploratory factor analysis of 16 ability items shows four moderately correlated factors (left panel). When these in turn are factored, a second-order general factor is shown to account for much of the variance of the items (right panel and Table 23.5).

$\mathbf{R} = (\mathbf{g} + \mathbf{G})(\mathbf{g} + \mathbf{G})' + \mathbf{U}^2$. This representation leads to two different measures of reliability ω_g and ω_t, where

$$\omega_g = \frac{1gg'1'}{1gg'1' + 1\mathbf{GG}'1' + \mathrm{tr}(\mathbf{U}^2)} = \frac{(1g1')^2}{1\mathbf{R}1'} \tag{23.28}$$

and

$$\omega_t = \frac{1gg'1' + 1\mathbf{GG}'1'}{1gg'1' + 1\mathbf{GG}'1' + \mathrm{tr}(\mathbf{U}^2)} = \frac{1gg'1' + 1\mathbf{GG}'1'}{1\mathbf{R}1'}. \tag{23.29}$$

ω_g represents that percentage of the variance of a test which is due to the general factor that is common to all of the items in the test, while ω_t is the total amount of reliable variance in the test. When ω_g is estimated using a Schmid and Leiman (1957) transformation or by using a higher-order model, it is also known (Revelle & Zinbarg, 2009; Zinbarg et al., 2005) as ω_h, for $\omega_{\text{hierarchical}}$, to reflect that it represents a hierarchical model. To make the terminology even more confusing, (McDonald, 1999, Equations 6.20a and 6.20b), who introduced ω, used Equations 23.28 and 23.29 to define ω without distinguishing between these as two very different models.

The approach of Schmid and Leiman (1957) is to extract a number of factors, **F**, rotate them obliquely, and then extract one, general, factor, g_h, from the resulting factor intercorrelation matrix. The loadings of the original variables on this higher-order factor are found by the product $g = g'_h F$. That is, the g loadings are fully mediated by the lower-order factors (Gignac, 2007). The original loadings in **F** are then residualized by $\mathbf{F}^* = \mathbf{F} - g_h \mathbf{F}$. This results in the model

$$\mathbf{R} = (\mathbf{g} + \mathbf{F}^*)(\mathbf{g}' + \mathbf{F}^{*'}) + \mathbf{U}^2,$$

where **F**∗ represents the residualized group factors and **g** the matrix of factor coefficients of the original variables. Then ω_g and ω_t are found by Equations 23.28 and 23.29. This approach is implemented in the omega function in the *psych* package. The solution for the 16 ability items is shown in Table 23.5, where $\omega_h = 0.65$ and $\omega_t = 0.86$.

Alternatively, an $\omega_{g_{bi}}$ from a *bifactor* solution (Holzinger & Swineford, 1937, 1939) may be found directly by using a confirmatory factor model where **g** loads on all variables and the **G** matrix has a cluster structure such that items load on one, and only one, of multiple groups. This approach is implemented in the omegaSem function in the *psych* package and makes use of the *sem* package (Fox, Nie, & Byrnes, 2013) to do the confirmatory fit.

Unfortunately, these two approaches do not always agree. ω_{g_h} as found with the Schmid and Leiman (1957) transformation using omega is .65, while ω_{gbi} found with the omegaSem function is .75. The reason for the difference is that that the bifactor sem solution tends to find the general factor as almost equivalent to the first group factor found with the hierarchical solution. The two approaches differ most obviously in the case of a very small to no general factor (see "When α goes wrong" below).

Another approach to finding the general factor reliability is through the use of hierarchical cluster analysis with the ICLUST algorithm (Revelle, 1979), which is

Table 23.5 An analysis of the hierarchical structure of 16 ability items shows a general factor and four lower-level factors. $\omega_h = 0.65$, $\alpha(\lambda_3) = 0.83$, $\lambda_{6^*} = 0.84$, $\omega_t = 0.86$.

Variable	g	F1*	F2*	F3*	F4*	h2	u2	p2
An omega analysis table from the psych package in R								
reason.4	0.50			0.27		0.34	0.66	0.73
reason.16	0.42			0.21		0.23	0.77	0.76
reason.17	0.55			0.47		0.52	0.48	0.57
reason.19	0.44			0.21		0.25	0.75	0.77
letter.7	0.52		0.35			0.39	0.61	0.69
letter.33	0.46		0.30			0.31	0.69	0.70
letter.34	0.54		0.38			0.43	0.57	0.67
letter.58	0.47		0.20			0.28	0.72	0.78
matrix.45	0.40				0.66	0.59	0.41	0.27
matrix.46	0.40				0.26	0.24	0.76	0.65
matrix.47	0.42		0.15			0.23	0.77	0.79
matrix.55	0.28				0.14		0.88	0.65
rotate.3	0.36	0.61				0.50	0.50	0.26
rotate.4	0.41	0.61				0.54	0.46	0.31
rotate.6	0.40	0.49				0.41	0.59	0.39
rotate.8	0.32	0.53				0.40	0.60	0.26
SS loadings	3.04	1.32	0.46	0.42	0.55			

implemented in the *psych* package as `iclust`. This approach is very simple: (1) Find the overall correlation matrix; (2) combine the two most similar items into a new (composite) item; (3) find the correlation of this new item with the remaining items; (4) repeat steps 2 and 3 until the worst split half correlation, β, fails to increase. β for a cluster is found by the correlation between the two lower-level parts of the cluster (corrected by Equation 23.15). Because the only variance that the two worst splits share will be general variance, β is an estimate of the general factor saturation. β found by `iclust` will usually, but not always, agree with the estimated ω_{gbi} found by the omega function.

When α goes wrong: the misuse of α

α is frequently reported without any evidence for scale homogeneity. The assumption is made that if a test has a medium to high value of α it must automatically measure one thing. This is, unfortunately, not correct, for α is just a measure of the average inter-item correlation and the number of items. It does not measure homogeneity. We have shown how a 12-item scale with average correlations of .3 (and thus α = .84) can represent one general factor in which all the items correlate at .3, two correlated but distinct groups with within-group correlations .42 or .54 but between-group correlations of .2 or .1 respectively, or even two unrelated sets with within-group correlations of .66 and between-group correlations of 0 (Revelle & Wilt, 2013).

Consider 10 items from the Big Five Inventory (BFI), five of which measure *emotional stability* and five of which measure *intellect* or *openness*. These 10 items are included as part of the `bfi` data set in the *psych* package. Their correlations are shown in Table 23.6. Using the `alpha` function on these items yields α = .70 with an average intercorrelation of .18 (Table 23.7). This is not particularly impressive, but is not

Table 23.6 The correlation matrix of the 10 BFI items suggests two different clusters of content. Note that three items (O1, O3, O4) have been reverse keyed. The items have been rearranged to show the structure more clearly. See also the heat map (Figure 23.5). The items are N1: Get angry easily. N2: Get irritated easily. N3: Have frequent mood swings. N4: Often feel blue. N5: Panic easily. O1: Am full of ideas. O2: Avoid difficult reading material. O3: Carry the conversation to a higher level. O4: Spend time reflecting on things. O5: Will not probe deeply into a subject. The average correlation within the N set of items is .47, and is .24 within the O set. However, the average inter-item correlation between the two sets is just .035.

```
lowerCor(reverse.code(keys = c("O1","O3","O4"), bfi[16:25]))
```

Variable	N1	N2	N3	N4	N5	O1-	O3-	O5	O2	O4-
N1	1.00									
N2	0.71	1.00								
N3	0.56	0.55	1.00							
N4	0.40	0.39	0.52	1.00						
N5	0.38	0.35	0.43	0.40	1.00					
O1-	0.05	0.05	0.03	0.05	0.12	1.00				
O3-	0.05	0.03	0.03	0.06	0.08	0.40	1.00			
O5	0.11	0.04	0.06	0.04	0.14	0.24	0.31	1.00		
O2	0.13	0.13	0.11	0.08	0.20	0.21	0.26	0.32	1.00	
O4-	−0.08	−0.13	−0.18	−0.21	−0.11	0.18	0.19	0.18	0.07	1.00

Table 23.7 Using `alpha` and `splitHalf` functions to examine the structure of 10 items from the Big Five Inventory. Although $\alpha = .7$ might be thought of as satisfactory, the worst split half reliability of .14 suggests that making one scale out of these 10 items is probably a mistake. In fact, the items were chose to represent two relatively independent scales of five items each.

```
This input
> alpha(bfi[16:25],keys = c("O1","O3","O4"))
> splitHalf(bfi[16:25],keys = c("O1","O3","O4"))
produces this output

Reliability analysis
Call: alpha(x = bfi[16:25], keys = c("O1", "O3", "O4"))
  raw_alpha std.alpha G6(smc) average_r   ase mean   sd
       0.7      0.68    0.73       0.18 0.011  2.8 0.75
 lower alpha upper     95% confidence boundaries
  0.68  0.7 0.72

 Reliability if an item is dropped:
     raw_alpha std.alpha G6(smc) average_r alpha se
 N1       0.64      0.62    0.67      0.16    0.013
 N2       0.64      0.63    0.67      0.16    0.013
 N3       0.64      0.63    0.68      0.16    0.013
 N4       0.66      0.65    0.70      0.17    0.012
 N5       0.65      0.64    0.70      0.17    0.012
 O1-      0.69      0.67    0.72      0.18    0.011
 O2       0.68      0.66    0.72      0.18    0.012
 O3-      0.69      0.66    0.71      0.18    0.011
 O4-      0.73      0.72    0.76      0.22    0.010
 O5       0.69      0.66    0.72      0.18    0.011

 Item statistics
         n    r  r.cor r.drop  mean  sd
 N1  2778 0.65 0.6574  0.550   2.9 1.6
 N2  2779 0.61 0.6121  0.510   3.5 1.5
 N3  2789 0.61 0.5916  0.508   3.2 1.6
 N4  2764 0.54 0.4766  0.412   3.2 1.6
 N5  2771 0.58 0.5148  0.456   3.0 1.6
 O1- 2778 0.46 0.3486  0.256   2.2 1.1
 O2  2800 0.49 0.3862  0.305   2.7 1.6
 O3- 2772 0.48 0.3789  0.270   2.6 1.2
 O4- 2786 0.18 0.0086 -0.045   2.1 1.2
 O5  2780 0.48 0.3751  0.284   2.5 1.3

Split half reliabilities
Call:   splitHalf(r = bfi[16:25], keys = c("O1", "O3", "O4"))
Maximum split half reliability   (lambda 4) = 0.78
Guttman lambda 6                            = 0.73
Average split half reliability              = 0.68
Guttman lambda 3 (alpha)                    = 0.68
Minimum split half reliability   (beta)     = 0.14
```

Ten items from the bfi data set

	N1	N2	N3	N4	N5	O1−	O3−	O5	O2	O4−
N1	1	0.71	0.56	0.4	0.38	0.05	0.05	0.11	0.13	−0.08
N2	0.71	1	0.55	0.39	0.35	0.05	0.03	0.04	0.13	−0.13
N3	0.56	0.55	1	0.52	0.43	0.03	0.03	0.06	0.11	−0.18
N4	0.4	0.39	0.52	1	0.4	0.05	0.06	0.04	0.08	−0.21
N5	0.38	0.35	0.43	0.4	1	0.12	0.08	0.14	0.2	−0.11
O1−	0.05	0.05	0.03	0.05	0.12	1	0.4	0.24	0.21	0.18
O3−	0.05	0.03	0.03	0.06	0.08	0.4	1	0.31	0.26	0.19
O5	0.11	0.04	0.06	0.04	0.14	0.24	0.31	1	0.32	0.18
O2	0.13	0.13	0.11	0.08	0.2	0.21	0.26	0.32	1	0.07
O4−	−0.08	−0.13	−0.18	−0.21	−0.11	0.18	0.19	0.18	0.07	1

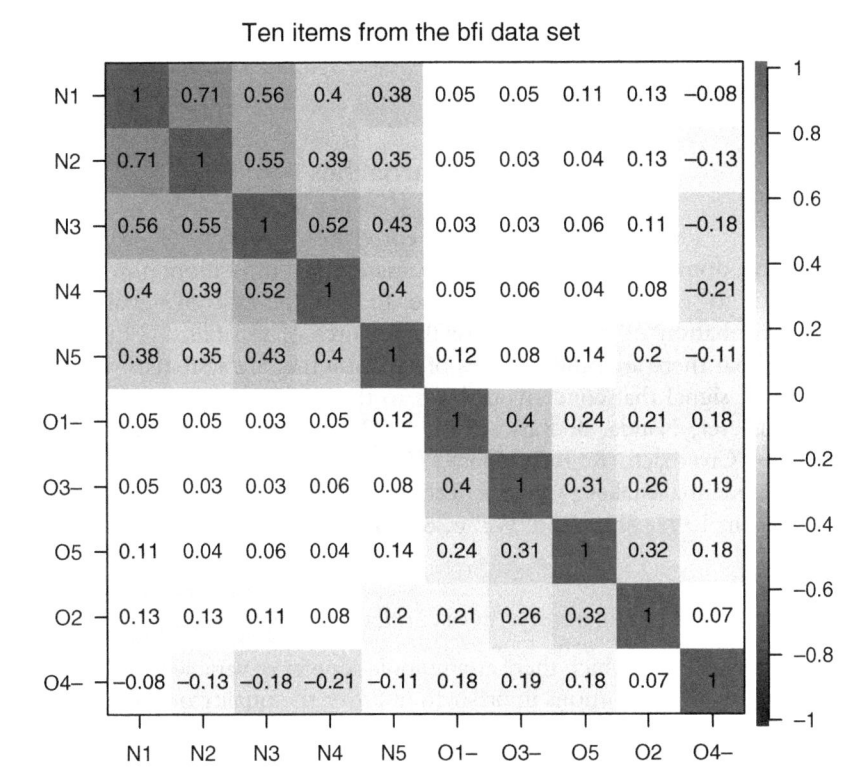

Figure 23.5 The ten items from the bfi data set represent five from the Neuroticism scale and five from the Openness/Intellect scale. Although the overall $\alpha = .70$ is marginally acceptable for a ten-item inventory, in fact two subsets correlate at .07 with α values of .81 and .61 respectively. The two-factor structure is easily identifiable by showing the correlations in a "heat map" where the darker the color, the higher the correlation. Plotted with the cor.plot function.

atypical of personality items and meets an arbitrary standard of an "adequate" α. When we examine this result more closely, however, we see that α is not very informative. For ease of demonstration, we reverse code the three items (O1, O3, and O4) that are flagged by the alpha function as needing to be reverse keyed, and then plot the resulting correlation matrix using a "heat map" plot from the cor.plot function (Figure 23.5). When this is done we see that we have two sub-scales (as expected), one measuring (Lack of) Emotional Stability or Neuroticism, the other measuring Openness/Intellect. The two sub-scales have α reliabilities separately of .81 and .61, but only correlate at .07 for a split half reliability of the entire 10 items of .14 ($=2 \times .07/(1 + .07)$). Indeed, although the average correlation within the N scale is .47 and within the O scale is .24, the average inter-item correlation between the two parts is .035. Expressed in terms of *factor analysis* this is an example of where a test has two large *group factors* but a not very large *general factor*. Indeed, $\omega_h = .17$ and $\omega_t = .76$. The value of $\beta = .14$ found by iclust agrees exactly with the worst split found by splitHalf.

This was obviously a case with two factors that should not be combined into one construct even though the α reliability was adequate. How often this happens in published studies is hard to know, but unless evidence is provided that the test is indeed homogeneous, one should treat studies that just report α with great skepticism. If the scale is indeed unifactorial then α is quite adequate, but this needs to be shown rather than assumed.

Other approaches

Reliability is typically considered to be the correlation between two equivalent tests sampled from a domain of items. It is also a variance decomposition: how much of test variance is due to signal, how much to noise. Indeed, the ratio of signal to noise is a simple transformation of the conventional measures of reliability (Equation 23.5). Recognizing that there are other sources of variation that are systematic but not associated with the signal that concerns us leads to the concept of *generalizability theory* (Cronbach, Gleser, Nanda, & Rajaratnam, 1972; Cronbach, Rajaratnam, & Gleser, 1963; Gleser, Cronbach, & Rajaratnam, 1965; Rajaratnam, Cronbach, & Gleser, 1965), which essentially takes a variance decomposition approach to the problem of reliability (Brennan, 1997; Shavelson, Webb, & Rowley, 1989).

Generalizability theory: reliability over facets

When doing any study in which there are multiple sources of variance, it is important to know their relative contributions in order to improve the quality of the measurement. For example, if student performance is nested within teachers who are nested within schools, and the tests are given at different times, then all of these terms and their interactions are potential sources of variance in academic performance. If we want to track changes due to an intervention and correct for errors in reliability, we need to know what are the relevant sources of variance in performance. Should we increase the number of students per classroom, the number of classrooms, or the number of schools? Similarly, if clinicians rate patients on various symptoms, then we want to know the variance associated with patients, that with symptoms, that with clinicians, as well as the interactions of each. Is it better to use more clinicians or better to have them each rate more symptoms? The procedure as discussed by Cronbach et al. (1972) is first to do an analysis of variance in the *generalizability (G) study* to estimate all of the variance components, then determine which variance components are relevant for the application in the *decision (D) study* in which one is trying to use the measure (Cronbach et al., 1972). Similarly, the components of variance associated with parts of a test can be analyzed in terms of the generalizability of the entire test.

Consider the data shown in the top of Table 23.8, which has been adapted from Gleser et al. (1965). Twelve patients were rated on six symptoms by two clinicians in a G study. Clearly the patients differ in their total scores (ranging from 13 to 44), and the symptoms differ in their severity (ratings ranging from 9 to 35). The two clinicians seem to agree fairly highly with each other. The ANOVA table (bottom section of Table 23.8) suggests that there are meaningful interactions of people by items and judges by items. The analysis of variance approach to the measurement of reliability focuses on the relevant facets in an experimental design and decomposes these facets in terms of their contribution to the total variance. The application to the D study uses knowledge gained in the original G study to consider the sources of variance relevant to the particular inference. Examining the components of variance, we can see that people

Reliability 737

Table 23.8 An example of a generalization study, adapted from Gleser et al. (1965). Twelve patients are rated by two clinicians on six symptoms with a severity ranging from 0 to 6. A simple ANOVA provides the sums of squares (not shown) and the mean squares. From these, it is possible to estimate the respective variance components to be used in the decision study.

The raw data

	Item 1		Item 2		Item 3		Item 4		Item 5		Item 6		
Patient	C1	C2	C1	C2	C1	C2	C1	C2	C1	C2	C1	C2	Total
1	0	0	2	1	2	0	2	1	1	1	1	2	13
2	0	0	2	1	2	0	1	2	2	1	2	1	14
3	0	0	1	1	3	3	2	1	2	1	1	2	17
4	2	0	2	1	2	2	2	1	2	1	4	1	20
5	0	0	1	2	2	0	2	3	3	3	3	3	22
6	2	0	2	1	2	0	4	1	3	3	3	1	22
7	0	1	3	1	3	1	3	4	2	2	2	3	25
8	0	0	0	1	4	3	3	4	2	3	3	3	26
9	1	2	2	1	3	6	1	3	2	3	2	1	27
10	0	1	2	4	3	3	2	2	3	5	3	1	29
11	3	4	2	2	3	2	4	5	3	3	5	5	41
12	1	1	2	4	4	4	3	3	4	6	6	6	44
Total	9	9	21	20	33	24	29	30	29	32	35	29	300

With associated estimated components of variance

Source	df		MS		Estimated variance components	
Persons	$n-1$	11	MS_p	7.65	$\hat{V}_p = \dfrac{MS_p - MS_{pi} - MS_{pj} + MS_r}{km}$	.419
Items	$k-1$	5	MS_i	12.93	$\hat{V}_i = \dfrac{MS_i - MS_{ij} - MS_{pi} + MS_r}{nm}$	.471
Judges	$m-1$	1	MS_j	1.00	$\hat{V}_j = \dfrac{MS_j - MS_{ij} - MS_{pj} + MS_r}{nk}$	-0.14*
Persons: Items	$(n-1)(m-1)$	55	MS_{pi}	1.48	$\hat{V}_{pi} = \dfrac{MS_{pi} - MS_r}{k}$	.427
Persons: Judges	$(n-1)(k-1)$	11	MS_{pj}	1.77	$\hat{V}_{pj} = \dfrac{MS_{pi} - MS_r}{m}$	.192
Items: Judges	$(k-1)(m-1)$	5	MS_{ij}	0.87	$\hat{V}_{ij} = \dfrac{MS_{pi} - MS_r}{n}$	.021
Persons: Items: Judges	$(n-1)(k-1)(m-1)$	55	MS_r	0.62	$\hat{V}_{e_{pij}} = MS_r$	.621

*Negative variance estimates are typically replaced with 0.

differ a great deal ($\hat{V}_p = .42$), but that there is also a great deal of variance associated with the various symptoms being examined ($\hat{V}_i = .47$). There is negligible variance associated with the mean level of the raters (judges), although there is some degree of interaction between the raters and the patients. There is substantial variation left over in the residual ($\hat{V}_{e_{pij}} = .62$). If the decision study is concerned with generalizing to the universe of judges but for the same six symptoms, then the ratio of the expected universe score variance (that due to individuals and that due to the interaction of individuals with items) to the expected observed score variance (which includes all terms involving individuals) is $\frac{.419 + .427/6}{.419 + .427/6 + .192/2 + .621/12} = .768$. On the other hand, if the generalization is to any pair of judges and any set of six items, the ratio will be $\frac{.419}{.419 + .427/6 + .192/2 + .621/12} = .657$.

A special case of generalizability theory: intraclass correlations and the reliability of ratings

The components of variance approach associated with *generalizability theory* is particularly appropriate when considering the reliability of multiple raters or judges. By forming appropriate ratios of variances, various *intraclass correlation coefficients* (ICC) may be found (Shrout & Fleiss, 1979). The term *intraclass* is used because judges are seen as indistinguishable members of a "class." That is, there is no logical way of distinguishing them.

For example, six subjects are given some scores by four different judges (Table 23.9). The judges differ in their mean leniency and in their range. Values of six different ICC coefficients, their probability of occurring, and confidence intervals for the estimates are reported by the ICC function in the *psych* package. ICC reports the variance between subjects (MS_b), the variance within subjects (MS_w), the variances due to the judges (MS_j), and the variance due to the interaction of judge by subject (MS_e). The variance within subjects is based upon the pooled SS_j and the SS_e. The reliability estimates from this *generalizability analysis* will depend upon how the scores from the judges are to be used in the *decision analysis*.

If one wants to know how well the scores of a particular rater will match those of another particular rater, then the appropriate ICC is that of a single rater (ICC_{11}). If, however, raters are selected at random from a population of raters, the measure of similarity of scores will be ICC_{21}. Both of these measures reflect the fact that raters can differ in their means. If these effects are removed by considering deviations from each judge's average rating, then the agreement between two fixed raters will be ICC_{31}. The effect of pooling raters is seen in the ICC_{1k}, ICC_{2k}, and ICC_{3k} coefficients, which benefit in the same way as the Spearman–Brown formula predicts an increase in reliability by pooling items.

Reliability of composites

A common problem is to assess the reliability of a set of tests that are thought to measure one construct. In this case, it is possible to assess the reliability of each test, to examine their intercorrelations, and to estimate the reliability of the overall composite score. This problem is conceptually identical to the estimation of a general factor and group factor contributions to overall reliability (see Equations 23.28 and 23.29). Consider two tests X_1 and X_2 with reliabilities $r_{x_1 x_1}$ and $r_{x_2 x_2}$, and correlation $c_{x_1 x_2}$. We want to find the correlation of this composite with another composite of similar subtests and similar covariances. Unlike the assumption we made of parallel tests (Equation 23.13), here we assume that the covariances between the subtests are not the same as the true variance

Table 23.9 The intraclass correlation coefficient (ICC) measures the correlation between multiple observers when the observations are all of the same class. It is a special case of generalizability theory. The ICC is found by doing an analysis of variance to identify the effects due to subjects, judges, and their interaction. These are combined to form the appropriate ICC. There are at least six different ICCs, depending upon the type of generalization that is to be made. The data and formulae are adapted from Shrout and Fleiss (1979). The analysis was done with the ICC function.

Six subjects and four raters...					...produces the following analysis of variance table				
Subject	J1	J2	J3	J4	Total	Source	Df	SS	MS	Label
S1	1	3	2	6	12	Subjects	5	56.21	11.24	MS_b
S2	1	2	6	7	16	Within subjects	18	112.75	6.26	MS_w
S3	2	4	7	6	19	Judges	3	97.46	32.49	MS_j
S4	2	5	8	9	24	Residuals	15	15.29	1.02	MS_e
S5	4	6	8	8	26					
S6	5	6	9	10	30					
Total	15	26	40	46	127	Number of subjects (n) = 6, number of raters (k) = 4				

The ANOVA can then be used to find six different ICCs

Variable	Type	Formula	ICC	F	df1	df2	p
Single raters absolute	ICC_{11}	$\dfrac{MS_b - MS_w}{MS_b + (k-1)MS_w}$	0.17	1.79	5	18	0.16
Single random raters	ICC_{21}	$\dfrac{MS_b - MS_e}{MS_b + (k-1)MS_e + k(MS_j - MS_e)/n}$	0.29	11.03	5	15	0.00
Single fixed raters	ICC_{31}	$\dfrac{MS_b - MS_e}{MS_b + (k-1)MS_e}$	0.71	11.03	5	15	0.00
Average raters absolute	ICC_{1k}	$\dfrac{MS_b - MS_w}{MS_b}$	0.44	1.79	5	18	0.16
Average random raters	ICC_{2k}	$\dfrac{MS_b - MS_e}{MS_b + (MS_j - MS_e)/n}$	0.62	11.03	5	15	0.00
Average fixed raters	ICC_{3k}	$\dfrac{MS_b - MS_e}{MS_b}$	0.91	11.03	5	15	0.00

within each subtest, but we do assume that the variances and covariances for the alternate form will match those of the original two subtests:

$$\left(\begin{array}{cc:cc} \mathbf{V}_{x_1} & \mathbf{C}_{x_1 x_2} & \rho_{x_1 x_1'} \mathbf{V}_{x_1} & \mathbf{C}_{x_1 x_2'} \\ \hdashline \mathbf{C}_{x_1 x_2} & \mathbf{V}_{x_2} & \mathbf{C}_{x_2 x_1'} & \rho_{x_2 x_2'} \mathbf{V}_{x_2} \\ \hline \rho_{x_1 x_1'} \mathbf{V}_{x_1} & \mathbf{C}_{x_2 x_1'} & \mathbf{V}_{x_1'} & \mathbf{C}_{x_1' x_2'} \\ \mathbf{C}_{x_1 x_2'} & \rho_{x_2 x_2'} \mathbf{V}_{x_2} & \mathbf{C}_{x_1' x_2'} & \mathbf{V}_{x_2'} \end{array} \right). \qquad (23.30)$$

For simplicity, we consider the standardized solution expressed in correlations rather than in variances and covariances. Then the correlation between two such tests, and thus the reliability of the composite test, will be

$$r_{(x_1+x_2)(x_1+x_2)} = \frac{r_{x_1 x_1} + r_{x_2 x_2} + 2 r_{x_1 x_2}}{2(1 + r_{x_1 x_2})}. \qquad (23.31)$$

In the case that the reliabilities of the two subtests match their intercorrelation, this is identical to Equation 23.14. It is perhaps useful to note that a composite made up of two reliable but unrelated subtests will have a reliability of the average of the two subtests, even though there is no common factor to the two subtests! For example, a composite of six items of German speaking ability with six items measuring knowledge of sailboat racing, with α reliabilities for the two subtests of .8 and intercorrelation of 0, will still be expected to correlate at .8 (have a reliability of .8) with another 12-item composite of six parallel German and six parallel sailing items. The pooled α reliability of such a test will be $\alpha = .68$, even though $\omega_g = 0$.

Reliability of difference scores

A related problem is the reliability of a difference score. Replacing the $C_{x_1 x_2}$ in Equation 23.30 with $-C_{x_1 x_2}$ leads to a change in sign of the corrections in Equation 23.31, and we find that the reliability of a difference score is an inverse function of the correlation between the two tests:

$$r_{(x_1-x_2)(x_1-x_2)} = \frac{r_{x_1 x_1} + r_{x_2 x_2} - 2 r_{x_1 x_2}}{2(1 - r_{x_1 x_2})}. \qquad (23.32)$$

That is, as the correlation between the two tests tends toward their reliabilities, the reliability of the difference tends toward 0. This is particularly a problem when one wants to interpret differential deficits in cognitive processing by finding the difference, for example, between verbal and spatial abilities, each of which is reliably measured, but which are also highly correlated. Consider the case where $r_{vv} = .9$, $r_{ss} = .9$, and $r_{vs} = .6$. Then while the composite $V + S$ measure has a reliability of $r_{(v+s)(v+s)} = \frac{.9 + .9 + 2 \times .6}{2(1 + .6)} = \frac{3.0}{3.2} = .9375$, the reliability of the difference $V - S$ is $r_{(v-s)(v-s)} = \frac{.9 + .9 - 2 \times .6}{2(1 - .6)} = \frac{.6}{.8} = .75$. But if $r_{vs} = .8$, the reliability of the composite will increase only slightly ($r_{(v+s)(v+s)} = .94$), but the reliability of the difference scores decreases considerably ($r_{(v-s)(v-s)} = .5$).

Conclusion

All signals are contaminated by noise. The effect of such contamination is to attenuate latent relationships and to raise the threat of regression artifacts. Perhaps because psychological measures are so threatened with lack of reliability, psychologists have spent more than a century trying to understand the challenges of reliability theory (Traub, 1997). Even as IRT approaches become more prevalent (Bock, 1997; Embretson & Hershberger, 1999; Wright, 1997), the study of reliability is a worthwhile enterprise, for even today there remains confusion about the ways of estimating and correcting for reliability.

References

Allport, G. W., & Odbert, H. S. (1936). Trait-names: A psycho-lexical study. *Psychological Monographs, 47* (211).

Atkinson, G., Waterhouse, J., Reilly, T., & Edwards, B. (2001). How to show that unicorn milk is a chronobiotic: The regression-to-the-mean statistical artifact. *Chronobiology International: The Journal of Biological & Medical Rhythm Research, 18* (6), 1041–1053.

Bentler, P. (2009). Alpha, dimension-free, and model-based internal consistency reliability. *Psychometrika, 74* (1), 137–143. doi: 10.1007/s11336-008-9100-1

Bock, R. D. (1997). A brief history of item theory response. *Educational Measurement: Issues and Practice, 16* (4), 21–33. doi: 10.1111/j.1745-3992.1997.tb00605.x

Brennan, R. L. (1997). A perspective on the history of Generability theory. *Educational Measurement: Issues and Practice, 16* (4), 14–20. doi: 10.1111/j.1745-3992.1997 .tb00604.x

Brennan, R. L., & Kane, M. T. (1977). Signal/noise ratios for domain referenced tests. *Psychometrika, 42* (4), 609–625.

Brown, W. (1910). Some experimental results in the correlation of mental abilities. *British Journal of Psychology, 3* (3), 296–322.

Campbell, D. T., & Kenny, D. (1999). *A primer on regression artifacts.* New York, NY: Guilford Press.

Cicero, M. T. (1877). *Tusculan disputations* (translated by C. D. Yonge, Ed.). New York, NY: Harper & Brothers (Originally published c.45BCE).

Cole, D. A., Martin, N. C., & Steiger, J. H. (2005). Empirical and conceptual problems with longitudinal trait-state models: Introducing a trait-state-occasion model. *Psychological Methods, 10* (1), 3–20.

Condon, D. M., & Revelle, W. (2014). The International Cognitive Ability Resource: Development and initial validation of a public-domain measure. *Intelligence, 43,* 52–64. doi: 10.1016/j.intell.2014.01.004

Cronbach, L. J. (1951). Coefficient alpha and the internal structure of tests. *Psychometrika, 16,* 297–334. doi: 10.1007/BF02310555

Cronbach, L. J., & Gleser, G. C. (1964). The signal/noise ratio in the comparison of reliability coefficients. *Educational and Psychological Measurement, 24* (3), 467–480.

Cronbach, L. J., Gleser, G. C., Nanda, H., & Rajaratnam, N. (1972). *The dependability of behavioral measurements: Theory of generalizability for scores and profiles.* New York, NY: J. Wiley & Sons.

Cronbach, L. J., Rajaratnam, N., & Gleser, G. C. (1963). Theory of generalizability: A liberalization of reliability theory. *British Journal of Statistical Psychology, 41,* 137–163.

Cronbach, L. J., & Shavelson, R. J. (2004). My current thoughts on coefficient alpha and successor procedures. *Educational and Psychological Measurement, 64* (3), 391–418.

Davis, C. E. (2002). Regression to the mean or placebo effect? In H. A. Guess (Ed.), *The science of the placebo: Toward an interdisciplinary research agenda* (pp. 158–166). London, UK: BMJ Books.

Deary, I. J., Pattie, A., & Starr, J. M. (2013). The stability of intelligence from age 11 to age 90 years: The Lothian Birth Cohort of 1921. *Psychological Science, 24* (12), 2361–2368. doi: 10.1177/0956797613486487

Deary, I. J., Whiteman, M., Starr, J., Whalley, L., & Fox, H. (2004). The impact of childhood intelligence on later life: Following up the Scottish mental surveys of 1932 and 1947. *Journal of Personality and Social Psychology, 86,* 130–147.

Duhachek, A., & Iacobucci, D. (2004). Alpha's standard error (ASE): An accurate and precise confidence interval estimate. *Journal of Applied Psychology, 89* (5), 792–808.

Embretson, S. E. (1998). A cognitive design system approach to generating valid tests: Application to abstract reasoning. *Psychological Methods, 3* (3), 380–396. doi: 10.1037/1082-989X.3.3.380

Embretson, S. E., & Hershberger, S. L. (1999). *The new rules of measurement: What every psychologist and educator should know.* Mahwah, NJ: L. Erlbaum Associates.

Eysenck, H. J. (1983). Cicero and the state-trait theory of anxiety: Another case of delayed recognition. *American Psychologist, 38* (1), 114–115. doi: 10.1037/0003-066X.38.1.114

Fleeson, W. (2001). Toward a structure- and process-integrated view of personality: Traits as density distributions of states. *Journal of Personality and Social Psychology, 80* (6), 1011–1027.

Fox, J., Nie, Z., & Byrnes, J. (2013). sem: Structural equation models [Computer software manual]. Retrieved from http://CRAN.R-project.org/package=sem (R package version 3.1-3).

Gadermann, A. M., Guhn, M., & Zumbo, B. D. (2012). Estimating ordinal reliability for Likert-type and ordinal item response data: A conceptual, empirical, and practical guide. *Practical Assessment, Research & Evaluation, 17* (3), 1–13.

Galton, F. (1886). Regression towards mediocrity in hereditary stature. *Journal of the Anthropological Institute of Great Britain and Ireland, 15,* 246–263.

Galton, F. (1889). *Natural inheritance.* London, UK: Macmillan.

Gignac, G. E. (2007). Multi-factor modeling in individual differences research: Some recommendations and suggestions. *Personality and Individual Differences, 42* (1), 37–48.

Gilovich, T. (1991). *How we know what isn't so.* New York, NY: Free Press.

Gleser, G., Cronbach, L., & Rajaratnam, N. (1965). Generalizability of scores influenced by multiple sources of variance. *Psychometrika, 30* (4), 395–418. doi:10.1007/BF02289531

Goldberg, L. R. (1999). A broad-bandwidth, public domain, personality inventory measuring the lower-level facets of several five-factor models. In I. Mervielde, I. Deary, F. De Fruyt, & F. Ostendorf (Eds.), *Personality psychology in Europe* (Vol. 7, pp. 7–28). Tilburg, The Netherlands: Tilburg University Press.

Gottfredson, L. S. (1997). Why *g* matters: The complexity of everyday life. *Intelligence, 24* (1), 79–132. doi: 10.1016/S0160-2896(97)90014-3

Gow, A. J., Johnson, W., Pattie, A., Brett, C. E., Roberts, B., Starr, J. M., & Deary, I. J. (2011). Stability and change in intelligence from age 11 to ages 70, 79, and 87: The Lothian Birth Cohorts of 1921 and 1936. *Psychology and Aging, 26* (1), 232–240.

Green, S., & Yang, Y. (2009). Commentary on coefficient alpha: A cautionary tale. *Psychometrika, 74* (1), 121–135. doi: 10.1007/s11336-008-9098-4

Guttman, L. (1945). A basis for analyzing test-retest reliability. *Psychometrika, 10* (4), 255–282. doi: 10.1007/BF02288892

Holzinger, K., & Swineford, F. (1937). The bi-factor method. *Psychometrika, 2* (1), 41–54. doi: 10.1007/BF02287965

Holzinger, K., & Swineford, F. (1939). *A study in factor analysis: The stability of a bi-factor solution* (No. 48). Chicago, IL: Department of Education, University of Chicago.

Horn, J. (1965). A rationale and test for the number of factors in factor analysis. *Psychometrika, 30* (2), 179–185. doi: 10.1007/BF02289447

Kahneman, D., & Tversky, A. (1973). On the psychology of prediction. *Psychological Review, 80* (4), 237–251.

Kelley, T. L. (1942). The reliability coefficient. *Psychometrika, 7* (2), 75–83.

Kelly, C., & Price, T. D. (2005). Correcting for regression to the mean in behavior and ecology. *The American Naturalist, 166* (6), 700–707. doi: 10.1086/497402

Kendall, A. D. (2013). *Depressive and anxiety disorders: Results from a 10-wave latent trait-state modeling study* (Unpublished master's thesis). Northwestern University.

Kuder, G., & Richardson, M. (1937). The theory of the estimation of test reliability. *Psychometrika, 2* (3), 151–160. doi: 10.1007/BF02288391

Leon, M. R., & Revelle, W. (1985). Effects of anxiety on analogical reasoning: A test of three theoretical models. *Journal of Personality and Social Psychology, 49* (5), 1302–1315. doi: 10.1037//0022-3514.49.5.1302

Lewis, M. (2004). *Moneyball:* The art of winning an unfair game. New York, NY: WW Norton & Company.

Lord, F. M., & Novick, M. R. (1968). *Statistical theories of mental test scores.* Reading, MA: Addison-Wesley Publishing Co.

Lucke, J. F. (2005). The α and the ω of congeneric test theory: An extension of reliability and internal consistency to heterogeneous tests. *Applied Psychological Measurement, 29* (1), 65–81.

Malmendier, U., & Tate, G. (2009). Superstar CEOs. *The Quarterly Journal of Economics, 124* (4), 1593–1638.

McDonald, R. P. (1999). *Test theory: A unified treatment.* Mahwah, NJ: L. Erlbaum Associates.

Pearson, K. (1901). On lines and planes of closest fit to systems of points in space. *The London, Edinburgh and Dublin Philosophical Magazine and Journal, 6* (2), 559–572.

Pearson, K., & Heron, D. (1913). On theories of association. *Biometrika, 9* (1/2), 159–315.

R Core Team. (2017). R: A language and environment for statistical computing [Computer software manual]. Vienna, Austria. Retrieved from http://www.R-project.org/

Rajaratnam, N., Cronbach, L., & Gleser, G. (1965). Generalizability of stratified-parallel tests. *Psychometrika, 30* (1), 39–56. doi: 10.1007/BF02289746

Revelle, W. (1979). Hierarchical cluster-analysis and the internal structure of tests. *Multivariate Behavioral Research, 14* (1), 57–74. doi: 10.1207/s15327906mbr1401_4

Revelle, W. (1986). Motivation and efficiency of cognitive performance. In D. R. Brown & J. Veroff (Eds.), *Frontiers of motivational psychology: Essays in honor of J. W. Atkinson* (pp. 105–131). New York, NY: Springer.

Revelle, W. (2017, August). psych: Procedures for personality and psychological research [Computer software manual]. Retrieved from https://CRAN.R-project.org/package=psych (R package version 1.7.8).

Revelle, W., & Wilt, J. (2013). The general factor of personality: A general critique. *Journal of Research in Personality, 47* (5), 493–504. doi: 10.1016/j.jrp.2013.04.012

Revelle, W., & Zinbarg, R. E. (2009). Coefficients alpha, beta, omega and the glb: Comments on Sijtsma. *Psychometrika, 74* (1), 145–154. doi: 10.1007/s11336-008-9102-z

Rulon, P. J. (1939). A simplified procedure for determining the reliability of a test by split-halves. *Harvard Educational Review, 9,* 99–103.

Schall, T., & Smith, G. (2000). Do baseball players regress toward the mean? *The American Statistician, 54* (4), 231–235. doi: 10.1080/00031305.2000.10474553

Schmid, J. J., & Leiman, J. M. (1957). The development of hierarchical factor solutions. *Psychometrika, 22* (1), 83–90.

Schmitt, N. (1996). Uses and abuses of coefficient alpha. *Psychological Assessment, 8* (4), 350–353.

Shavelson, R. J., Webb, N. M., & Rowley, G. L. (1989). Generalizability theory. *American Psychologist, 44* (6), 922–932.

Shrout, P. E., & Fleiss, J. L. (1979). Intraclass correlations: Uses in assessing rater reliability. *Psychological Bulletin, 86* (2), 420–428.

Sijtsma, K. (2009). On the use, the misuse, and the very limited usefulness of Cronbach's alpha. *Psychometrika, 74* (1), 107–120. doi: 10.1007/s11336-008-9101-0

Spearman, C. (1904). The proof and measurement of association between two things. *The American Journal of Psychology, 15* (1), 72–101. doi: 10.2307/1412159

Spearman, C. (1910). Correlation calculated from faulty data. *British Journal of Psychology, 3* (3), 271–295.

Stigler, S. M. (1986). *The history of statistics:* The measurement of uncertainty before 1900. Cambridge, MA: Belknap Press of Harvard University Press.

Stigler, S. M. (1997). Regression towards the mean, historically considered. Statistical Methods in Medical Research, *6* (2), 103–114.

Traub, R. E. (1997). Classical test theory in historical perspective. *Educational Measurement: Issues and Practice, 16* (4), 8–14. doi: 10.1111/j.1745-3992.1997.tb00603.x

Wilt, J., & Revelle, W. (2009). Extraversion. In M. R. Leary & R. H. Hoyle (Eds.), *Handbook of individual differences in social behavior* (pp. 27–45). New York, NY: Guilford Press.

Wright, B. D. (1997). A history of social science measurement. *Educational Measurement: Issues and Practice, 16* (4), 33–45. doi: 10.1111/j.1745-3992.1997.tb00606.x

Yule, G. U. (1912). *On the methods of measuring association between two attributes.* Journal of the Royal Statistical Society, LXXV, 579–652.

Zinbarg, R. E., Revelle, W., Yovel, I., & Li, W. (2005). Cronbach's α, Revelle's β, and McDonald's ωH: Their relations with each other and two alternative conceptualizations of reliability. *Psychometrika, 70* (1), 123–133. doi: 10.1007/s11336-003-0974-7

Zumbo, B. D., Gadermann, A.M., & Zeisser, C. (2007). Ordinal versions of coefficients alpha and theta for Likert rating scales. *Journal of Modern Applied Statistical Methods, 6,* 21–29.

Appendix

R functions called

The examples in this chapter made use of various functions and data sets in the *psych* package (Revelle, 2017) in the R statistical system (R Core Team, 2017). The particular functions used were:

alpha   A function to find α and λ_6 as well as total scores for a set of items.

scoreItems   A function to find α and λ_6 as well as total scores for multiple scales.

splitHalf   A function to find all possible split half reliabilities for 16 or fewer items or to sample >10,000 possible splits for more than 16 items. This includes the lowest β and highest λ_4 splits.

fa   A function for exploratory factor analysis using maximum likelihood, minimal residual, or principal axis factor extraction and a large number of orthogonal and oblique rotations.

Omega   A function to find ω_{gh} and ω_t for an item set using exploratory factor analysis.

omegaSem   A function to find ω_{gbi} and ω_t for an item set using confirmatory factor analysis.

ICC   A function to find intraclass correlation coefficients.

A number of functions that are convenient for analysis

fa.diagram   Graphically show a factor analysis structure.
cor.plot   Show a heat map of correlations.
lowerCor   Find and display the lower off-diagonal correlation matrix.
reverse.code   Reverse code specified items.

Data sets used for demonstrations

bfi   Twenty-five items measuring Extraversions, Agreeableness, Conscientiousness, Emotional Stability, and Openness/Intellect. Adapted from the International Personality Item Pool (Goldberg, 1999) and administered as part of the Synthetic Aperture Personality Assessment (SAPA) project. Number of observations = 2,800.

ability Sixteen ability items given as part of the SAPA project. See Condon and Revelle (2014) for details on this and other open source measures of ability. Number of observations = 1,525.

Sample R code for basic reliability calculations

In order to use the *psych* package functions, it is necessary to install the package. This needs to be done only once, but it is recommended to get the latest version from CRAN at least every six months as R and the *psych* package get updated. Then, for each new session of R, it is necessary to make the *psych* package active by issuing the library command. The following examples use two built-in data sets: bfi, which includes 25 items taken from the International Personality Item Pool and used as part of the sapa-project.org online personality assessment (Condon & Revelle, 2014), and a set of 16 ability items also collected as part of sapa-project.org. More detail may be found in the package vignette "An overview of the psych package," which is included when downloading the package. For all functions, if more help is needed, consult the help menu for that function by ?function (e.g., ?alpha).

More extensive examples are found in the *psych* package vignette, as well as various tutorials at the Personality Project: http://personality-project.org/r.

```
install.packages(list(c("GPArotation","mvtnorm","MASS") #do this once
library(psych) #do this every time R is started
```

Once the package is installed, a data set to be analyzed may be read into R using the read.file command, or just read into a text editor/spreadsheet and copied into the clipboard. The data may be then be pasted into R using the read.clipboard command. In the listing below, the # symbol denotes a comment and the > symbol an R command.

```
#first copy the data to the clipboard then
> my.data <- read.clipboard()
 #or, if copying from a spreadsheet
> my.data <- read.clipboard.tab()
#or, use a built in data set such as ability
> my.data <- ability
#then, to see if the data have been entered correctly,
#find out the dimensions of the data set and some descriptive
statistics.
> dim(my.data)
> describe(my.data)

> dim(my.data)
1525 16
> describe(my.data)
```

```
           var  n    mean sd   median trimmed mad min max range skew  kurtosis se
reason.4     1  1442 0.68 0.47 1      0.72    0   0   1   1     -0.75 -1.44    0.01
reason.16    2  1463 0.73 0.45 1      0.78    0   0   1   1     -1.02 -0.96    0.01
reason.17    3  1440 0.74 0.44 1      0.80    0   0   1   1     -1.08 -0.84    0.01
reason.19    4  1456 0.64 0.48 1      0.68    0   0   1   1     -0.60 -1.64    0.01
letter.7     5  1441 0.63 0.48 1      0.67    0   0   1   1     -0.56 -1.69    0.01
letter.33    6  1438 0.61 0.49 1      0.63    0   0   1   1     -0.43 -1.82    0.01
letter.34    7  1455 0.64 0.48 1      0.68    0   0   1   1     -0.59 -1.65    0.01
letter.58    8  1438 0.47 0.50 0      0.46    0   0   1   1      0.12 -1.99    0.01
matrix.45    9  1458 0.55 0.50 1      0.56    0   0   1   1     -0.20 -1.96    0.01
matrix.46   10  1470 0.57 0.50 1      0.59    0   0   1   1     -0.28 -1.92    0.01
matrix.47   11  1465 0.64 0.48 1      0.67    0   0   1   1     -0.57 -1.67    0.01
matrix.55   12  1459 0.39 0.49 0      0.36    0   0   1   1      0.45 -1.80    0.01
rotate.3    13  1456 0.20 0.40 0      0.13    0   0   1   1      1.48  0.19    0.01
rotate.4    14  1460 0.22 0.42 0      0.15    0   0   1   1      1.34 -0.21    0.01
rotate.6    15  1456 0.31 0.46 0      0.27    0   0   1   1      0.80 -1.35    0.01
rotate.8    16  1460 0.19 0.39 0      0.12    0   0   1   1      1.55  0.41    0.01
```

Find the α and λ_6 estimates of reliability for this data set.

```
> alpha(ability)

Reliability analysis
Call: alpha(x = ability)
  raw_alpha std.alpha G6(smc) average_r ase  mean sd
    0.83      0.83     0.84    0.23   0.0086 0.51 0.25

 lower alpha upper    95% confidence boundaries
 0.81  0.83  0.85

Reliability if an item is dropped:
           raw_alpha std.alpha G6(smc) average_r alpha se
reason.4      0.82     0.82     0.82    0.23    0.0093
reason.16     0.82     0.82     0.83    0.24    0.0091
reason.17     0.82     0.82     0.82    0.23    0.0093
reason.19     0.82     0.82     0.83    0.24    0.0091
letter.7      0.82     0.82     0.82    0.23    0.0092
letter.33     0.82     0.82     0.83    0.24    0.0092
letter.34     0.82     0.82     0.82    0.23    0.0093
letter.58     0.82     0.82     0.82    0.23    0.0092
matrix.45     0.82     0.83     0.83    0.24    0.0090
matrix.46     0.82     0.82     0.83    0.24    0.0091
matrix.47     0.82     0.82     0.83    0.24    0.0091
matrix.55     0.83     0.83     0.83    0.24    0.0089
rotate.3      0.82     0.82     0.82    0.23    0.0092
rotate.4      0.82     0.82     0.82    0.23    0.0092
rotate.6      0.82     0.82     0.82    0.23    0.0092
rotate.8      0.82     0.82     0.83    0.24    0.0091

Item statistics
             n     r   r.cor  r.drop mean  sd
reason.4    1442  0.58  0.54   0.50  0.68 0.47
```

```
reason.16 1463 0.50  0.44       0.41 0.73 0.45
reason.17 1440 0.57 0.54 0.49 0.74 0.44
reason.19 1456 0.52 0.47 0.43 0.64 0.48
letter.7  1441 0.56 0.52 0.48 0.63 0.48
letter.33 1438 0.53 0.48 0.44 0.61 0.49
letter.34 1455 0.57 0.53 0.49 0.64 0.48
letter.58 1438 0.57 0.52 0.48 0.47 0.50
matrix.45 1458 0.48 0.42 0.38 0.55 0.50
matrix.46 1470 0.49 0.43 0.40 0.57 0.50
matrix.47 1465 0.52 0.47 0.43 0.64 0.48
matrix.55 1459 0.42 0.35 0.32 0.39 0.49
rotate.3  1456 0.54 0.51 0.44 0.20 0.40
rotate.4  1460 0.58 0.56 0.48 0.22 0.42
rotate.6  1456 0.56 0.53 0.46 0.31 0.46
rotate.8  1460 0.51 0.47 0.41 0.19 0.39

Non missing response frequency for each item
             0    1 miss
reason.4   0.32 0.68 0.05
reason.16  0.27 0.73 0.04
reason.17  0.26 0.74 0.06
reason.19  0.36 0.64 0.05
letter.7   0.37 0.63 0.06
letter.33  0.39 0.61 0.06
letter.34  0.36 0.64 0.05
letter.58  0.53 0.47 0.06
matrix.45  0.45 0.55 0.04
matrix.46  0.43 0.57 0.04
matrix.47  0.36 0.64 0.04
matrix.55  0.61 0.39 0.04
rotate.3   0.80 0.20 0.05
rotate.4   0.78 0.22 0.04
rotate.6   0.69 0.31 0.05
rotate.8   0.81 0.19 0.04
```

Find the ω estimates of reliability. Specify that you want to try a four-factor solution.

```
> omega(ability,4)

Omega
Call: omega(m = ability, nfactors = 4)
Alpha:                0.83
G.6:                  0.84
Omega Hierarchical:   0.65
Omega H asymptotic:   0.76
Omega Total 0.86

Schmid Leiman Factor loadings greater than 0.2
              g    F1*   F2*   F3*   F4*  h2     u2   p2
reason.4   0.50                   0.27        0.34 0.66 0.73
reason.16  0.42                   0.21        0.23 0.77 0.76
```

```
reason.17 0.55            0.47        0.52 0.48 0.57
reason.19 0.44            0.21        0.25 0.75 0.77
letter.7  0.52      0.35              0.39 0.61 0.69
letter.33 0.46      0.30              0.31 0.69 0.70
letter.34 0.54      0.38              0.43 0.57 0.67
letter.58 0.47      0.20              0.28 0.72 0.78
matrix.45 0.40                  0.66  0.59 0.41 0.27
matrix.46 0.40                  0.26  0.24 0.76 0.65
matrix.47 0.42                        0.23 0.77 0.79
matrix.55 0.28                        0.12 0.88 0.65
rotate.3  0.36 0.61                   0.50 0.50 0.26
rotate.4  0.41 0.61                   0.54 0.46 0.31
rotate.6  0.40 0.49                   0.41 0.59 0.39
rotate.8  0.32 0.53                   0.40 0.60 0.26

With eigenvalues of:
   g    F1*   F2*   F3*  F4*
 3.04  1.32  0.46  0.42 0.55

general/max 2.3 max/min = 3.17
mean percent general = 0.58 with sd = 0.2 and cv of 0.35
Explained Common Variance of the general factor = 0.53
```

The degrees of freedom are 62 and the fit is 0.05
The number of observations was 1525 with Chi Square = 70.19 with prob < 0.22
The root mean square of the residuals is 0.01
The df corrected root mean square of the residuals is 0.03
RMSEA index = 0.01 and the 90% confidence intervals are NA 0.019
BIC = -384.25

Compare this with the adequacy of just a general factor and no group factors
The degrees of freedom for just the general factor are 104 and the fit is 0.78
The number of observations was 1525 with Chi Square = 1186.18 with prob < 5e-183
The root mean square of the residuals is 0.09
The df corrected root mean square of the residuals is 0.13

RMSEA index = 0.083 and the 90 % confidence intervals are 0.078 0.087
BIC = 423.88

Measures of factor score adequacy

```
                                         g    F1*  F2*  F3*  F4*
Correlation of scores with factors      0.83 0.80 0.53 0.56 0.71
Multiple R square of scores with factors 0.69 0.64 0.28 0.32 0.50
```

```
Minimum correlation of factor score
estimates                               0.37 0.28 -0.45 -0.36 0.00

Total, General and Subset omega for each subset
                                          g   F1*   F2*   F3*  F4*
Omega total for total scores and subscales
                                        0.86 0.77 0.69 0.64 0.53
Omega general for total scores and subscales
                                        0.65 0.23 0.52 0.47 0.27
Omega group for total scores and subscales
                                        0.13 0.53 0.17 0.17 0.26
```

24

Psychometric Validity: Establishing the Accuracy and Appropriateness of Psychometric Measures

David J. Hughes

"The problem of validity is that of whether a test really measures what it purports to measure." (Kelley, 1927, p. 14)

"The essential question of test validity is how well a test does the job it is employed to do. The same test may be used for several different purposes, and its validity may be high for one, moderate for another and low for a third" (Cureton, 1951, p. 621)

Validity is "an integrated evaluative judgment of the degree to which empirical evidence and theoretical rationales support the adequacy and appropriateness of inferences and actions based on test scores or other modes of assessment." (Messick, 1989, p. 13)

"A test is valid for measuring an attribute if (a) the attribute exists and (b) variations in the attribute causally produce variation in the measurement outcomes." (Borsboom, Mellenbergh, & van Heerden, 2004, p. 1061)

"At its essence, validity means that the information yielded by a test is appropriate, meaningful, and useful for decision making – the purpose of mental measurement." (Osterlind, 2010, p. 89)

Validity is widely acknowledged to be "the most fundamental consideration" in the development of psychometric measures (American Educational Research Association [AERA], American Psychological Association [APA], and National Council on Measurement in Education [NCME], 2014, p. 11). The psychometrician's principal goal is to develop valid measures and no self-respecting researcher or practitioner would knowingly use an invalid test – or would they? The answer to that question will vary, perhaps substantially, according to who is answering it and how they choose to define validity. As the quotes above demonstrate, there are a surprising number of conceptualizations of validity, some not even closely analogous. The variety of meanings associated with the word validity means that many see it as a complicated and daunting concept while reading that a measure (or an inference based upon a measure) is "valid" is somewhat meaningless unless accompanied by an explicit definition. Despite the

---

The Wiley Handbook of Psychometric Testing: A Multidisciplinary Reference on Survey, Scale and Test Development, First Edition. Edited by Paul Irwing, Tom Booth, and David J. Hughes.
© 2018 John Wiley & Sons Ltd. Published 2020 by John Wiley & Sons Ltd.

conceptual mêlée surrounding validity, it remains the ultimate aim of psychometric test development and thus, validity remains a central tenet of this *Handbook of Psychometric Testing*.

Much of the current debate in the validity literature concerns discussions of epistemology or ontology, truth absolute, or otherwise, the existence of constructs, the role of belief true or justified, and a number of other philosophical debates (Borsboom et al., 2004; Hood, 2009; Kane, 2006, 2016; Markus & Borsboom, 2013). Equally, validity theorists have been grouped as traditionalists, liberals, conservatives, ultra-conservatives; as expanders, unifiers, partitioners; as realists, anti-realists, constructivists, and pragmatists (e.g., Hood, 2009; Markus & Borsboom, 2013; Newton & Shaw, 2016). The focus of this chapter, however, is to explore the contribution of validity theory in answering two essential psychometric questions:

1 Am I measuring what I want to measure?
2 Is my measure useful?

The remainder of this chapter is broken down into five main sections. First, I will consider why we need the concept of validity and why it is so important for psychometricians. Second, I review the evolution of the concept of validity focusing on seminal works throughout the last century. Third, I consider the surprisingly tumultuous state of validity theory and practice within the twenty-first century. Fourth, I consider suggestions for advancing validity theory and provide my own model designed to improve the theoretical clarity and practical utility of validity theory. Finally, I provide practical guidance regarding what forms of "validity evidence" there are, which of the questions each form of evidence can help us answer, and what tools are available to generate such evidence.

Why Do We Need Validity?

Develop a theory, design a measure, collect data using the measure, test the theory, and if the theory is supported, then use your measure to make decisions based on the theory. In my view, this is science. The same broad approach applies whether examining gravity (or gravitational waves) through to the design of a spaceship, or whether examining cognitive ability through to placing a student within a particular school class. There are three main elements here: theory, measurement, and decisions. Theory and measurement are the core aspects of any science, social or otherwise, and if we want to use our theories and measures, we must also consider our decision-making processes. As Cone and Foster (1991) note, "measurement provides the foundation for all other scientific pursuits" with "developments in all areas of science follow[ing] discoveries of appropriate measurement techniques" (p. 653). Psychometrics are measures, their development does indeed contribute to theory development (see Booth & Murray, Chapter 29), and they are often used to make important real-world decisions (e.g., who to hire; Hughes & Batey, 2017). Validity is the word commonly assigned to describe evaluations of psychometric measurement and decisions made based on this measurement. Primary within this arena are two questions: are you measuring what you think you are measuring? If so, are your measures useful for decision making?

Establishing what a psychometric measures, it turns out, is a rather difficult task. Most measurement is directed toward constructs that we cannot directly observe, such as attitudes, mental health, knowledge, executive functions, personality traits, political preferences, culture, cognitive biases, and motives. In circumstances when we cannot directly access the construct of interest, we must observe theoretically relevant behaviors and infer from these observations the existence and nature of the underlying construct (c. f., Borsboom, Mellenbergh, & van Heerden, 2003). Let us look at an example: an affluent person gives money to a homeless person they pass on the street; clearly, this is a marker of empathy-driven generosity. Alternatively, our focal person might consider the homeless an irritant, but nevertheless give money to the homeless person in order to demonstrate empathetic generosity to their newly acquired romantic partner, who is walking beside them. After all, the monetary cost is trivial but the reputational reward could be substantial. Both explanations for this behavior are plausible, but which is right? Is the giving driven by the construct of empathy or the construct of Machiavellianism? In the realm of psychometrics, this problem would manifest in the query: what does the questionnaire item "I give money to the homeless" really measure (if anything at all)? It is important that we can answer this question before we can make decisions based on our measure (questionnaire item) to guide theoretical developments or practical decisions (Cizek, 2016; Kane, 2016; Sireci, 2016).

A simple example such as this highlights the real difficulty associated with psychological measurement through behavioral observation; namely, it rests on assumptions concerning things and processes we cannot see. Our measures provide us with some information or data, but it is not the information or data that we really want (Zumbo, 2007). In the example here, the data we want pertains to the degree to which our focal person is empathetic or Machiavellian, the data we have is a count of how often that person gives to the homeless. One can see immediately a genuine gap between the knowledge that we want and the knowledge that we have. Validity refers to the evaluation of the relationship between the knowledge we want (the nature of the construct) and the knowledge we have (the measured behavior) and the judgments regarding whether or not this relationship justifies the use of a measure for decision making.

The Evolving Notion of Validity

Papers as early as 1884 readily use the word validity within article titles and abstracts, suggesting that the word was in common use. However, none of these early papers defined validity. The context of the use suggested that validity referred either to the accuracy of a measure (i.e., does the measure, measure the construct of interest) or the appropriateness of a measure (i.e., is the measure useful) for some form of decision making (e.g., Kiernan, 1884; Germann, 1899). The absence of a clear definition within these early articles perhaps explains why Buckingham's 1921 article, which used the word validity to describe the property that a test measures what it purports to measure, is the most the widely cited origin of the concept of validity.

Since 1921, the concept of validity has been a contentious subject of debate and has evolved a great deal. Numerous highly regarded scholars have proposed a number of revisions and expansions of the validity domain (for detailed historical developments see Kane, 2001; Newton & Shaw, 2013, 2014). From 1921–1950 validity was predominantly assessed by matching the content of psychometric measures with theory and by examining predictive capabilities (e.g., Buckingham, 1921; Cureton, 1950; Guilford, 1946; Kelley, 1927). From the mid-1950s to the mid-1980s, and notably following Cronbach and Meehl's (1955) seminal work outlining "construct validity," validity became a much broader concept concerned with the examination of a constructs' nomological net. Construct validity dominated (eventually subsuming the notions of content and prediction as branches within the nomological net) until Messick's (1989) proposal of the unified model of validity, which retained all of construct validity but added the examination of the consequences of psychometric use. The extent of these revisions and expansions are such that arguably the most authoritative source on psychometric testing today (Hubley & Zumbo, 2011; Kane, 2013, 2016; Newton, 2012; Newton & Shaw, 2013, 2014; Sireci, 2016; Zumbo 2007, 2009), the *Standards for Educational and Psychological Testing* (AERA, APA, NCME, 1999, 2014), defines validity very differently from Buckingham (1921). The *Standards* draws heavily on Messick's (1989) unified model and states that,

> Validity refers to the degree to which evidence and theory support the interpretations of test scores for proposed uses of tests. Validity is, therefore, the most fundamental consideration in developing tests and evaluating tests. The process of validation involves accumulating relevant evidence to provide a sound scientific basis for the proposed score interpretations. It is the interpretations of test scores for proposed uses that are evaluated, not the test itself. (AERA, APA, NCME, 2014, p. 11)

There is one rather notable departure from the early definitions of validity. In this definition, validity is not a question of whether a psychometric measures what it purports to, but rather is concerned with the interpretations of psychometric scores and the decisions that one makes based on those interpretations. Validity is not a property of a measure but of an interpretation and thus one validates not a psychometric but an interpretation of a psychometric score (Kane, 2006). The "consensus position" (Newton & Shaw, 2013, p. 13) espoused within the *Standards* (2014) makes several additional points regarding the nature of validity, namely:

- Validity is not an all or nothing property, it is a matter of degree; the use of two tests can be somewhat valid in both cases but one can be more valid than the other.
- Validity does not exist as distinct types; rather, validity is the single overall judgment of the adequacy of a test interpretation or use. Thus, one should not speak of X validity or Y validity. Validity is a single evaluative judgment.
- While validity is a single entity, there are five forms of validity evidence: content, response processes (e.g., cognitive processes during item responding), relations with other variables (e.g., convergent, discriminant, concurrent, and predictive validity evidence), internal structure (e.g., factor structure), and evidence based on consequences (i.e., whether test use is fair and unbiased).
- Validation is an on-going process in which various sources of validity evidence are accumulated to build an argument in favor of the validity of the intended interpretation and use of the test.

The view of validity put forward by the *Standards* (AERA, APA, NCME, 1999, 2014) encompasses much of the previous 100 years of validity debate. Central to this notion of validity are the five different sources of evidence required to demonstrate validity.

The first element of evidence relates to the content of a psychometric measure and suggests that psychometric measures should contain exclusively content relevant to the construct at hand and that the content should be representative of the whole construct domain. This is very similar to original validity arguments made by Buckingham (1921) who, working within the domain of cognitive ability, argued that measures of intelligence should cover general learning ability across domains rather than learning of a narrow topic that is overly sensitive to the recency with which the learning had taken place (Buckingham, 1921). Simply, if a psychometric is designed to measure X, it should contain representative coverage of X.

Evidence relating to response processes is perhaps one of the most sophisticated elements of validity (Borsboom et al., 2004; Cronbach & Meehl, 1955; Embretson, 1984, 1993, 1998, 2016) and is often ignored in practice (Borsboom et al., 2004). Briefly, if a psychometric is designed to measure a construct (e.g., school knowledge) then responding to the items of the psychometric should require the use of the construct (e.g., retrieval of school knowledge). It follows that the examination of these item responses is vital for establishing what is measured.

Evidence regarding relations with other variables represents the vast majority of previous validity debate and encapsulates criterion associations and a large proportion of construct validity (Cronbach & Meehl, 1955). Relations between psychometric measures and criterion variables have always been seen as important with many early validity discussions focusing heavily on predictive capabilities (Buckingham, 1921; Cureton, 1950, 1951; Guilford, 1942, 1946). The simple suggestion is that if, for example, intelligence drives learning then a measure of the rate at which learning occurs or of scholastic achievement should constitute a measure of intelligence (Buckingham, 1921). Thus, a positive correlation between a measure of intelligence and educational attainment would provide validity evidence (Cureton, 1950; 1951; Guilford, 1942, 1946). In addition to criterion relations, Cronbach and Meehl's (1955) conception of construct validity implied that a psychometric measure can, in part, be defined by its relationship with other measures or observables. In other words, we should be able to predict, using theory, how a construct will relate to other things. If our measure of that construct does indeed relate as predicted, then we can be confident that we are measuring the target construct. These predicted relations were termed a system of laws or nomological net. In practice, the nomological net is often assessed via convergent validity evidence (i.e., correlations between multiple measures of the same construct are high) and discriminant validity evidence (i.e., that there are small correlations between measures designed to assess different constructs; Campbell & Fiske, 1959). However, Cronbach and Meehl (1955) presented four additional methods to examine construct validity: the previously discussed response processes, known group differences (e.g., a depression measure should differentiate between those who have been diagnosed with depression and those who have not), item correlations and internal structure (e.g., factor structure), and changes over time (e.g., development or stability).

Evidence relating to the internal structure of a measure concerns the relationship between items and represents a separate branch of validity evidence according to the *Standards*. If 10 items are expected to measure the same construct then they should be correlated and load onto a single factor (e.g., Spearman, 1904). If the items are hypothesized to measure four subcomponents of one higher-order factor then all items should be correlated, but there should be four distinguishable factors and modelling a higher-order factor should be possible.

Evidence concerning consequences regards the suggestion that we must consider the intended and unintended effects of test use when deciding whether or how a psychometric test should be used (e.g., Cronbach, 1988; Hubley & Zumbo, 2011; Messick, 1989; Zumbo, 2007, 2009). In essence, consequences consider fairness and represent the major contribution of Messick (1989) to validity theory. The idea that the social consequences of psychometric use constitutes a branch of validity is quite a step from the scientific (or statistical) forms of validity evidence previously endorsed; indeed, it is inherently political. Even those who introduced consequences into the validity domain noted that they do not sit neatly within a unified validity model (e.g., Cronbach, 1988, p. 6). Ultimately, however, validity theorists concluded that given the status of validity as the key concern in psychometric development and the importance of consequences that the two should remain unified (Messick, 1989; Newton & Shaw, 2016; Shepard, 2016; Zumbo & Hubley, 2016).

Nevertheless, shoehorning consequences under the label of validity remains controversial today. As the editors of a recent special issue focused on validity noted, "the controversy over consequences still looms largest" (Newton & Baird, 2016, p. 174). The most common line of argument put forward by critics of the Messick-inspired validity model is to depart from unification and split validity into: construct validity and consequences (Lees-Haley, 1996), or construct representation and nomothetic span (Embretson, 1983), or internal and external validity (Lissitz & Samuelson, 2007), or validity and intended use (Cizek, 2016), or validity and quality (Borsboom et al., 2004). However, these suggestions are often rebuffed with authors arguing that little is gained by a theoretical or conceptual split, that the validity of a test (or test score interpretation) is inextricably linked to its use and thus consequences, that a split would diminish the focus on consequences, or that a split would confuse researchers and practitioners (e.g., Kane, 2016; Moss, 1998, 2016; Shepard, 2016; Sireci, 2007, 2016; Zumbo & Hubley, 2016).

Evolving Notion of Validity: Consensus, What Consensus?

So, the current "consensus position" (Newton & Shaw, 2013, p. 13) regarding validity, endorsed by major educational and psychological bodies (AERA, APA, & NCME, 1999, 2014) and numerous validity scholars (Hubley & Zumbo, 2011; Kane, 2016; Newton, 2012; Newton & Shaw, 2013; Shepard, 2016; Sireci, 2016; Zumbo & Hubley, 2016) states that validity pertains to interpretations not tests, is a single evaluative judgment based on five sources of evidence, is a matter of degree, and is a continuous process. If this view represents a genuine consensus then one would expect it to be reflected in psychometric practice, especially given that the 1999 and 2014 *Standards* are largely consistent regarding their validity guidelines, giving psychometricians more than 15 years to familiarize themselves with and adopt the recommendations. Thus, it is surprising to note that two reviews conducted by Cizek and colleagues (2008, 2010) revealed that surprisingly few psychometric investigations follow these recommendations. Cizek, Rosenberg, and Koons (2008) found that just 2.5% of articles reviewed take a unitary perspective (i.e., that validity is a single evaluative judgment), that only 9.5% cite the *Standards* or Messick (1989), and that numerous authors refer to validity as a characteristic of a psychometric tool, with only 24.7% referring to validity as a property of score interpretations. Further, Cizek et al. (2008, 2010) noted that hardly any papers examined response processes and consequences.

These observations suggest (at least) two possibilities; either researchers are ignorant of the *Standards'* recommendations, or there may not be a consensus after all. A closer inspection of the validity literature suggests the latter (e.g., Borsboom et al., 2004, 2007, 2009; Cizek, 2012, 2016; Lees-Haley, 1996; Lissitz & Samuelson, 2007; Mehrens, 1997; Popham, 1997; Scriven, 2002; Shadish, Cook, & Campbell, 2002; Wiley, 1991). Discontent with the consensus position covers two fundamental issues. First, to what does validity refer? Researchers do not agree on whether psychometrics, interpretations of scores, or uses of psychometrics should be validated. Second, which pieces of evidence should be considered validity evidence? Over time, the *Standards'* definition of validity has come to encapsulate every important test-related issue within a unified validity model, and as a result, validity has become a complex and cumbersome concept. Some would argue that as validity now covers everything it means nothing, and no longer provides a useful framework to highlight the critical features of high-quality measurement (Borsboom et al., 2004; Mehrens, 1997; Wiley, 1991). There is no dispute regarding the importance of the different types of validity evidence, but many have questioned whether all these types of evidence should be considered under the "validity" banner (c.f., Borsboom et al., 2004; Cizek, 2012, 2016; Lees-Haley, 1996; Lissitz & Samuelson, 2007; Popham, 1997; Scriven, 2002; Shadish et al., 2002).

The turn of the twenty-first century saw Borsboom and colleagues (2004) make a compelling critique of the "consensus position" on both counts and in doing so, argue for a return to the 1920s version of validity:

> Validity is not complex, faceted, or dependent on nomological networks and social consequences of testing. It is a very basic concept and was correctly formulated, for instance, by Kelley (1927, p. 14) when he stated that a test is valid if it measures what it purports to measure ... a test is valid for measuring an attribute if and only if (a) the attribute exists and (b) variations in the attribute causally produce variations in the outcomes of the measurement procedure. (Borsboom et al., 2004, p. 1061)

Borsboom et al. (2004) put forward a very simple view of validity. Validity is not about interpretations or intended uses but is a property of tests, and a test is valid if the construct you are trying to measure exists (in a realist sense) and causes the measured behavior/response. In other words, completing an intelligence test should require the use of intelligence, and thus differences in test responses between persons would be the result of differences in intelligence. The simplicity of Borsboom et al.'s view is a virtue and provides clear guidance for establishing validity through a single question: does the construct of interest cause the observed/measured behavior/response? If so, the test is valid.

From a validity evidence perspective, Borsboom et al.'s (2004) view sees validity limited to evidencing the response process and in making this point they deliver hefty critiques regarding the role of the other elements of the nomological network. Put simply, they argue that while a nomological network is useful for theory building, knowing that your measure correlates with other measures does not help identify what your measure actually measures:

> it is farfetched to presume that such a network implicitly defines the attributes in question.... It is even more contrived to presume that the validity of a measurement procedure derives, in any sense, from the relation between the measured attribute and other attributes. (Borsboom et al., 2004, p. 1064)

This critique is undoubtedly strong.[1] Observing a positive correlation between a measure labeled intelligence and educational achievement actually tells you nothing about what is actually measured. What makes a measure of intelligence so, is that responding to the test requires the use of intelligence, what makes a test of high school history knowledge so, is that answering the questions requires the use of knowledge gained during high school history class. This point seems indisputable.

In keeping with the impassioned and often antagonistic nature of the validity debate (Newton & Shaw, 2016), numerous authors have, in turn, critiqued Borsboom's view and similar views espoused by others (e.g., Cizek, 2012, 2016; Lissitz & Samuelson, 2007; Scriven, 2002; Shadish et al., 2002). One counter argument states that validity cannot be a measurement-based property of tests as measurement is conditional (i.e., a measure performs differently with different groups; Newton, 2012). This is true; any given measure is unlikely to operate equivalently across all populations or contexts. However, this is an empirical question ripe for empirical examination and not a point that warrants the abandonment of the notion that a psychometric test can be validated. All that is needed to negate this concern is a simple specification of the population or context of interest (as is the norm, e.g., child, or adult intelligence tests).

A second counter argument asserts that a test cannot be validated independently of an interpretation of a test score (e.g., Hubley & Zumbo, 2011; Kane, 2013, 2016; Newton, 2012; Sireci, 2007; 2016; Zumbo, 2007, 2009). For example, Kane states that it would be difficult to validate a test without a label, and a label requires an interpretation. This seems an odd concern. If a psychometric measure is designed to measure construct X, then the label would be "measure of X." This seems uncontroversial and if the interpretation is limited to "the psychometric measures the target construct" then a critique based on interpretations is weak. It is true that any scientific endeavor cannot be separated from values and the labeling process can be particularly value-laden (divergent thinking vs scatter-brained, conscientious vs. boring, emotionally stable vs. cold). Nevertheless, one can still evaluate whether the psychometric measures what it purports to measure. Simply, if you can show that construct X causes variation in responses to "measure of X" then this is concrete evidence that the measure of X, measures X within the given population (Borsboom et al., 2004).

---

[1] Whilst I agree with the notion that convergent and discriminant validity cannot tell us whether our measure accurately captures the target construct, it is worth noting that Borsboom et al. (2004) critique a caricature of the nomological net that is probably the predominant interpretation in current practice. However, convergent and discriminant evidence are only a small proportion of the nomological net as proposed by Cronbach & Meehl (1955). If one were to establish evidence based on all of Cronbach and Meehl's (1955) sources of evidence (which include response processes), one would have a strong evidence base to assess whether the target construct drives variation in the measured behavior.

Third, validity theorists have argued that a psychometric cannot be validated unless one considers the purpose for which it will be used (Hubley & Zumbo, 2011; Kane, 2016; Sireci, 2007, 2016). For example, Sireci (2007) cannot imagine convening a committee of experts to evaluate a test without telling them the purpose for which the test is to be used. This argument is premised on the mistaken assumption that measurement informed decisions but not measurement per se represent a purpose. However, if the purpose of the test is to measure a construct (as Borsboom et al. suggest), then all the experts need to know is the theory surrounding the nature of that construct. If the construct to be assessed is sixth-grade mathematical knowledge (Sireci's example), then it is quite clear that the test should contain questions representative of knowledge delivered during sixth-grade mathematics education. What the test scores will subsequently be used for (e.g., training, awarding high school diplomas, college entry) is a separate point to that of whether or not the test accurately captures mastery of sixth-grade mathematics knowledge.

Fourth, Kane (2013, 2016) has argued that Borsboom and colleague's view is reductionist and would see many important elements of psychometric evaluation currently considered as indicators of validity evidence (e.g., predictive validity evidence) omitted from the definition of validity. Borsboom et al. (2004) counter this point within their original thesis by stating explicitly that they believe validity is already too large, and that as the unified model encompasses every test-related concern, it is essentially meaningless. Those who oppose segmenting the different forms of validity evidence are often most concerned that such a split would see psychometric developers ignore social consequences (e.g., Kane, 2016; Messick, 1989; Sireci, 2007, 2016). This is a noble concern, but one that is neither scientifically relevant nor empirically supported. First, we should not define the concept of validity based on political concerns. If including evidence regarding psychometric measurement and evidence regarding the use of a psychometric for a given purpose represent separate concerns then we should not artificially combine them. Second, the *Standards* state explicitly that the responsibility for evaluating the social consequences of the primary intended use of a psychometric is to be evidenced by the developer, but that subsequent uses require the user to evaluate the consequences (AERA, APA, & NCME, 1999, 2014). Third, as evidenced by the two reviews conducted by Cizek and colleagues (2008, 2010), social consequences are already largely ignored. Current evidence would suggest that sacrificing a clear and logically coherent definition of validity in order to protect consideration of consequences does not work.

Sadly, as an observer of this debate, I concur with Newton and Shaw (2016), who have suggested that the style of academic discourse within the validity field promotes the taking of sides that generates a false dichotomy that is not conducive to progress (Newton & Shaw, 2016). Given that validity is "the most fundamental consideration" in the development and use of psychometric measures (AERA, APA, NCME, 2014, p. 11) that gives rise to numerous practical implications (i.e., guidance for test developers), it would be beneficial if we could generate a definition that was useful. How we define the term "validity" is not simply an academic or semantic debate but one that sets the standards for what evidence is required before proclaiming our measure, our measure interpretation, or measure use is **valid**.

In summary, there are two notable areas of disagreement. First, to what should validity apply? Some argue that validity is a property of a test (Borsboom et al., 2004), some that validity refers to interpretations of test meaning (e.g., Cizek, 2012, 2016), some that validity refers to test interpretation and test use arguments (Kane, 2006, 2016), and others that validity refers to test use as without a use a test is meaningless (e.g., Sireci, 2016). Second, which pieces of evidence constitute validity evidence? Borsboom et al. (2004) say validity lives and dies by evidence that test completion elicits use of the target variable while others see validity as established by demonstrating good psychometric properties (e.g., Lissitz & Samuelson, 2007). Cizek (2016) believes all elements of test evidence except consequences should be considered validity, while others believe all test evidence including consequences should be considered validity evidence (e.g., Zumbo, 2007). Yet still, others suggest that validity is situation specific and that demonstrating validity in one instance to one audience is not synonymous with demonstrating validity in another instance to another audience (Kane, 2013, 2016). Thus, the current "consensus position" is actually anything but a consensus (c.f., Hood, 2009; Markus, 2016; Newton & Shaw, 2013, 2016). The differences in definition and content are not trivial; they represent radically different approaches to validity. The result is a validity concept (AERA, APA, NCME, 2014) that is among the most contested concepts I have come across (c.f. Newton & Shaw, 2016). Not only this, but the *Standards'* definition is so complex and imprecise that it promotes numerous misunderstandings (Newton, 2012; Newton, & Shaw, 2013) that lead to diverse and often substandard validation practices (Cizek, 2008, 2010), and acts as a barrier to successful communication in science and practice (Cizek, 2016; Koretz, 2016). It is possible that these problems stem from the inability of psychometricians and those who use our tools to fully appreciate validity theory, it is also possible that the unified model is simply incoherent and untenable (Borsboom et al., 2004; Cizek, 2016; Popham, 1997).

Evolving Notion of Validity: A Way Forward?

So, what are we to do in defining the construct of validity, and importantly for this chapter, making useful recommendations for evaluating psychometric validity? Newton and Shaw (2016), having grappled with these issues for longer than most, suggest three possible options for progress.

First, continue the academic debate until we arrive at a logical conclusion regarding the validity construct. Newton and Shaw suggest that while this is possible, it seems highly unlikely. I agree. As we have discussed, theorists are at loggerheads and base their arguments on differing assumptions. A review of 20 papers published – during the writing of this chapter – in a recent special issue concerning validity in *Assessment in Education: Principles, Policy & Practice* further demonstrates the distance between theorists, and the vigor with which they defend their own corner (e.g., Borsboom & Wijsen, 2016; Cizek, 2016; Kane, 2016; Shepard, 2016; Sireci, 2016; Zumbo & Hubley, 2016).

Second, Newton and Shaw suggest we could mold validity into a family resemblance concept so that it has a nontechnical meaning that approximates "good." Using this approach would require only a limited change to the research lexicon and allow the term validity (read good) to be applied to any element of testing: a valid item, a valid selection program, convergent validity, predictive validity, which is how it is currently used within academia and industry (Cizek et al., 2008, 2010; Newton & Shaw, 2013). This option might change the debate regarding validity, but it does not address the two core controversies: whether a test can be valid and which bits of testing belong in a single model.

Third, Newton and Shaw suggest that we can retire the word validity without any undue consequences:

> ...given the omnipresent reality of imprecise and ambiguous usage, and the fact that even testing specialists use the word in quite different ways, it is hard to see how anything conceptually fundamental could be lost if the word were to be retired. (p. 190)

I agree. Validity is used in so many different ways that removing it would not pose a serious problem. We will explore this controversial claim next. However, simply removing the term validity will not move the current debate forward. A change in lexicon is needed, but so too is a theoretically driven change in conceptualization.

Here, I would like to propose another solution drawing upon the second and third of Newton and Shaw's suggestions and the work of Cizek (2012, 2016) and Borsboom et al. (2004). I suggest that we can drop the term validity altogether. However, if this seems too radical a proposition, then we can continue to use the word "validity" as a family resemblance construct. In doing so, we strip the term validity from having any precise technical definition and thus need other words that can fill this void. We will come to this shortly. However, before we can address the semantic debate, we must focus on the core scientific question: what types of evidence should count toward validity? One extreme is that validity should be evidenced by demonstrating that the measure accurately captures its intended target (e.g., Borsboom et al., 2004, 2009). The other extreme is that validity should be comprised of all information regarding test development and test use (e.g., Messick, 1989; Zumbo & Hubley, 2016). Thus, the major problem we must solve is whether it is logical to use a single model and label to refer to all elements of psychometric measure evaluation. My view, simply, is **no**, it is not logical. To make this argument, and provide a practically useful and theoretically meaningful split in the validity domain, I return to the two questions posed at the outset of this chapter:

1. Am I measuring what I want to measure?
2. Is my measure useful?

These two questions guide measure development, refinement, and use. Establishing whether a measure accurately captures its intended target is a very different beast to establishing whether it is appropriate to use a measure in any given scenario. Let us look at an example using IQ tests:

1. Does my IQ test measure intelligence?
2. Is my IQ test useful for employee selection/guiding the design of educational programs?

Hopefully, it is clear to all readers that the information and evidence necessary to address question one is different from that needed to answer question two. In Borsboom et al.'s (2004) terms, question one requires evidence that completing the test requires the use of one's intelligence and that the test captures that variation accurately.

The second question(s) requires a great deal more evidence and we must consider whether the test predicts job or school performance, whether the prediction offered holds across groups, what cut-off scores should represent "success," whether it is ethical to segregate children based on intelligence, and so on. As Cizek (2016, p. 215) puts it,

> a diverse array of empirical and logical rationales confirms that [test score interpretation and test score use] require distinct sources of evidence bearing on differing purposes and that a single synthesis of evidence on both inference and use is not possible.

I could not agree more. Establishing that a psychometric accurately measures intelligence has only a minor bearing on whether it is deemed appropriate as a selection tool. Equally, evidence that a test predicts job performance might indicate its appropriateness for use in selection but it does not give any indication of whether that test measures intelligence. The evidence needed to answer question one differs markedly from the evidence required to address question two and no matter how strong the evidence in relation to either issue, it is not enough to answer the other.

I am not the first author to point out that validity evidence would be better suited to a two-component model. However, my approach has two major differences. First, the divide is driven by the pragmatic need to address the two fundamental questions of test evaluation (as opposed to an attempt to remove consequences from validity) and the theoretical argument that these two endeavors cannot meaningfully be combined. Second, I am not precious about the word validity. In contrast, previous discussions along similar lines have made impassioned pleas that validity pertains to question one calling evidence relating to the other question utility, consequences, quality, or some other label for "good" or "useful" (Borsboom et al., 2004; Cizek, 2016; Lees-Haley, 1996; Lissitz & Samuelson, 2007). Rather than take this antagonistic approach – perhaps inspired by the lexical tradition held dearly by my native world of personality research – I turned to the dictionary to identify two words that match the two fundamental questions, which I believe can serve us well and move us forward. Here are some definitions taken directly from the Oxford English Dictionary Online:

- **Accuracy** (n.d.): The closeness of a measurement, calculation, or specification to the correct value. Contrasted with **precision** (the degree of refinement of the measurement, etc.)
- **Appropriate** (n.d.): Suitable or proper in the circumstances
- **Validity** (n.d.): Well-founded on fact, or established on sound principles, and thoroughly applicable to the case or circumstances; soundness and strength (of argument, proof, authority, etc.)

Question one, refers to whether your psychometric measures what it purports to – or in other words, whether your measure is **accurate**.[2] It is important to note that in the dictionary (and scientific discourse more broadly) accuracy is contrasted with precision which

---

[2] The terminology of measurement within psychology is hotly contested and the phrase "correct value" is likely to annoy some (Markus & Borsboom, 2013). However, taking a realist approach (Borsboom et al., 2004) that abilities, traits, attitudes, and knowledge exist and drive item responses then standard psychometric techniques could justifiably be labeled as measures seeking to arrive at the "correct value" (Markus & Borsboom, 2012). After all, this is the fundamental principle of psychometrics (*psycho* = mental, *metric* = measurement).

is essentially reliability (see Revelle & Condon, Chapter 23). Note also that the concept of accuracy as defined here aligns to the use of the term validity when it was first embraced in psychological science. Perhaps Buckingham (1921) simply chose the wrong word. Question two, refers to whether or not a measure should be used – or in other words, how **appropriate** it is to use your psychometric for a given purpose in a given situation.

Using the terminology suggested here we can say that the goal of psychometric development is to generate a psychometric that **accurately** measures the intended construct, as **precisely** as possible, and that uses of the psychometric are **appropriate** for the given purpose, population, and context. A psychometric should be accurate, precise, and appropriate or in current terminology, a psychometric (or psychometric score interpretation) should be valid, reliable, and valid. The ambiguity of validity is inherent in its inability to differentiate between these two markedly different aims. The validity label does not serve us well and we should drop it.

Two questions, two steps

Establishing the accuracy and appropriateness of psychometric measures are both equally noble pursuits; neither one is necessarily more interesting or worthwhile. They do, however, concern different elements within the life span of a psychometric. Accuracy is likely to be most relevant during initial conceptualization and development whereas appropriateness concerns the later use of a psychometric for theory building or decision making. As implied by the previous sentence, I see accuracy and appropriateness forming a two-step approach to psychometric evaluation.

The first-step is to ascertain whether your psychometric accurately measures what it purports to. If we cannot say with confidence what our psychometric is measuring then I would suggest that use of the psychometric for theory testing or decision making is inappropriate. Thus, establishing a measure's accuracy is a fundamental base for all other psychometric activities, and is a necessary but not sufficient condition for establishing the appropriateness of a particular psychometric use (e.g., Cizek, 2016, Kane, 2013, 2016; Sireci, 2016). Some might disagree and suggest that if a psychometric predicts an outcome then its use is appropriate. I disagree. The atheoretical use of a psychometric which measures an unknown source is unwise, unethical, and possibly illegal (i.e., in the case of employee selection). Once we have some degree of confidence that our psychometric accurately measures what it purports to, then we can assess the appropriateness of its use for a particular purpose, within a particular population, within a particular context. So how do we establish psychometric accuracy and appropriateness? The answers to these questions draw heavily on the hundred years of discussion of validity summarized earlier in the chapter. There has been a great deal of work regarding the assessment of different elements of psychometric measures and much of it is useful here.

Establishing the Accuracy and Appropriateness of Psychometric Measures

"Validity evidence" comes in many forms. Indeed, Newton and Shaw (2013) listed 151 types of validity evidence (or "types of validity" as they are commonly referred to) that they identified within the literature. Given the definitional maze that is validity, it is not surprising that researchers have invented ever more types of validity evidence. After all, if validity encapsulates all things that can be "good" about a psychometric (or interpretations and uses) then why not demonstrate its goodness in myriad ways, especially as judgments of psychometric quality tend to be related to the quantity not quality of validity evidence present (Cizek et al., 2008). As a result, navigating the various forms of validity evidence can be succinct and useful validity evidence checklists are scarce. The one exception is perhaps the *Standards* (1999, 2014) but even this tends to shy away from providing precise definitions and practical guidance. This, I believe, is unhelpful for those wishing to design and evaluate psychometrics. Thus, based on two separate reviews, I have constructed succinct and user-friendly checklists of types of evidence that can be used to establish the accuracy and appropriateness of psychometric measures.

The first review conducted for this chapter examined introductory textbooks, "validity" chapters, and whole "validity" books and was focused on understanding how types of 'validity evidence' are generally defined (AERA, APA, NCME, 1974, 1985, 1999, 2014; Carmines & Zeller, 1979; Carver & Scheier, 2003; Cooper, 2002; Hubley & Zumbo, 2013; Kline, 2000; Larsen, Buss, & Wismeijer, 2013; Markus & Borsboom, 2013; Osterlind, 2010; Smith, 2011; Woods & West, 2010). The second review examined all newly developed scales published in two highly regarded psychometrics journals, *Psychological Assessment* and *Assessment*, between April 2015 and June 2016. I use the data gathered from these two reviews to provide a list of the major forms of "validity evidence" with clear and distinct definitions. The second review is useful in presenting a snapshot of current "validation" practices. The user-friendly checklists are displayed in Tables 24.1 and 24.2, and contain definitions of evidence types, methods that are particularly useful for generating each type of evidence, and also the percentage of papers introducing new psychometrics that report each type of evidence.

Accuracy

Accuracy is defined as the closeness of a measurement to the correct value and is contrasted with precision or reliability (the degree of refinement of the measurement). In psychometric terms, a measure is accurate when it measures what it purports to measure or perhaps more specifically, when variations in the target construct are clearly represented by variations in item responses (c.f., Borsboom et al., 2004). Previous models that have separated validity into two components have tended to include the majority of types of validity evidence under question one (e.g., Cizek, 2016), including criterion associations and correlations with other variables that are central to the classic construct validity model (Cronbach & Meehl, 1955). However, I agree with Borsboom et al. (2004, 2009), who say that while correlations between psychometric measures are interesting and can be informative, they do not tell us anything about what is actually measured. Thus, in establishing psychometric accuracy, I will focus only on evidence that relates directly to determining the nature of the measurement, namely, response processes, content representativeness, and content structure. Table 24.1 provides an overview of the most useful forms of evidence for establishing psychometric accuracy.

Table 24.1 Evidence for establishing psychometric accuracy: labels, definitions, methods, and prevalence of current use.

Type of evidence	Definition	Example methods	% used
Content	The degree to which the content (i.e., items, tasks) of a psychometric measure comprehensively captures the target construct	Matching content to standardized descriptions (i.e., curriculum lists or diagnostic criteria) Matching content to theory using expert ratings	55
Response processes	The mechanism by which the target construct causes item responses	Cognitive mapping Think-aloud protocols	0
Structural	The degree to which the relationships among psychometric content (items, tasks) reflect the theoretical framework	Exploratory factor analysis Confirmatory factor analysis	90
Stability across groups	The degree to which the content, structure, and response processes remains stable across groups	Differential Item Functioning Invariance measurement	35

Response Processes

The gold standard for estimating accuracy lies in the investigation of response processes. Psychometrics are designed to measure unobservable constructs (e.g., abilities, attitudes, traits, knowledge), and the core underlying assumption of psychometrics is that variation in the construct is reflected in item responses (Cronbach & Meehl, 1955). Thus, whenever a psychometric measure is to be interpreted as a measure of a construct, we should be most interested in understanding the mechanisms through which the item responses come about (Borsboom et al., 2004, 2009; Embretson, 1983, 1994). Accuracy here then, concerns the match between the psychological processes hypothesized to be under investigation and the processes that respondents actually engage in or draw upon when responding to items.

To examine response processes, one must first identify the processes, decisions, strategies, and knowledge stores involved in generating item responses. Recall the "item" proposed at the beginning of this chapter, "I give money to the homeless." If this item is designed to measure empathy-driven generosity, then one might hypothesize that the respondent would engage in a number of processes (see Karabenick et al., 2007, figure 1 for a formalized and generic information-processing model of item responses):

1 Read and interpret the item.
2 Recall from memory seeing a homeless person (perhaps how they felt when considering how the homeless person must feel living outside, vulnerable to the weather, and financially unsupported).
3 Have an emotional reaction to this sequence of thoughts.
4 If the emotional reaction is negative (i.e., sadness), decide to give money because it will alleviate some of the homeless persons' pain and perhaps reduce personal

feelings of guilt. If the emotional reaction is neutral or positive then it is unlikely that the person will respond to give money.
5 Read and interpret the response options.
6 Select a response option that is congruent with their thoughts and feelings. In this instance, the stronger the emotional reaction, the more extreme the response on the rating scale.

One could examine the processes the respondent actually engages to clearly examine whether the item responses measure empathy-driven generosity. If, however, a respondent has a neutral emotional reaction, but notes the social esteem one gets from giving to the homeless and then endorses the item strongly, we can conclude that this item might be accurately measuring empathy for some respondents but not for others (instead measuring Machiavellianism). One could then change the item to, "would you give to a homeless person even if no one ever knew about it?" Hopefully, responses to this item would give a more accurate reflection of empathy-driven generosity.

I can imagine some test developers thinking "this seems like a lot of work" – and they would be correct. Identifying response processes, especially for attitudinal measures is not easy but it is worthwhile work. Many psychometrics are designed to assess complex behaviors and in such cases, the response processes are unlikely to be unidimensional in the purest sense. However, many items have been shown to conform to criteria supporting unidimensionality and provide accurate and precise measurement of only one construct. If however, the construct you wish to measure cannot be measured with unidimensional items then an examination of response processes will uncover this and help in the accurate modelling of item-level data (e.g., Booth & Hughes, 2014). Nevertheless, a focus on response processes allows us to derive firm conclusions regarding the accuracy of our psychometric measures and accurate psychometric measures are essential. Using inaccurate psychometric measures can stifle theory and lead to precarious real-world consequences. The benefits of understanding response processes have the potential to improve measurement accuracy but also theory development and decision making. If we understand how a child solves a mathematics problem, we can improve teaching; if we can understand how Warren Buffet makes investment decisions, we can test this and select better investors. Whatever your intended use for a psychometric, establishing that it accurately captures the response process you are interested in is paramount. It is therefore disappointing to see that not one of the twenty papers reviewed for this chapter assessed the processes elicited during item response (see Table 24.1).

There are a number of different methods for evaluating response processes. For example, cognitive design systems are very useful for evaluating the accuracy of decision-making or problem-solving items (e.g., Embretson, 1994, 1998, 2016). Cognitive design systems posit a theory of item response processes, build a series of hypotheses regarding these processes, and then test them. In many respects, cognitive models reflect good quality theory testing. In very simple terms, if we posit that compared to item X, item Y requires a greater use of construct A, then there should be a greater number of correct responses to item X than item Y. This kind of modelling allows one to develop expected item response patterns and then examine whether or not these response patterns are met. Embretson (1998, 1999, 2010, 2016), Embretson and Gorin (2001), Jansen and van der Maas (1997), and Mislevy and Verhelst (1990) provide useful empirical examples of how cognitive models of item responses can be evaluated.

Another method of investigating item response processes is to use think-aloud protocols (Ericsson & Simon, 1980, 1993, 1998). Think-aloud protocols require participants to say whatever comes into their mind as they respond to an item (what they are thinking, recalling, feeling, etc.). This technique can give researchers an understanding of the cognitive processes undertaken and would be useful for the hypothetical example concerning empathy-driven generosity/Machiavellianism described before. Researchers should train respondents in the think-aloud technique and provide clear guidance regarding the type of information they are looking for. Think-aloud protocols can either be conducted concurrently (as the participant responds) or retrospectively (upon completion of the response). Both have merits and weaknesses as concurrent protocols allow for more spontaneous and potentially accurate insights but increase cognitive demand on participants, whereas retrospective protocols (sometimes termed cognitive interviews) do not interfere with item responses but, like all retrospective analyses, are subject to forgetting and bias, and cannot detect dynamic real-time changes in response processes. Some practical examples of the think-aloud process can be found in Ericsson and Simon (1998), Darker and French (2009), Durning et al. (2013), Vandevelde, van Keer, Schellings and van Hout-Wolters (2015), with van Someren, Barnard, and Sandberg (1994) providing a comprehensive practical guide to think-aloud protocols.

Although think-aloud protocols and similar cognitive interview techniques are valuable, there remain numerous questions regarding the optimal approach to their implementation (e.g., Presser et al., 2004). For example, there are questions concerning which constructs are suitable for cognitive probing, the optimal number of probes, the merits of concurrent or retrospective probing, whether the think-aloud distorts the true respondent process, and how to amalgamate, analyze, and interpret the results. Nevertheless, despite slow methodological progress in this area (driven largely by test developers' reluctance to carry out appropriate studies), understanding response processes is vital and is to be encouraged whenever applicable.

Content

Content evidence ("content validity") is well known and widely discussed within the psychometric literature (Nunnally & Bernstein, 1994; Haynes, Richard, & Kubany, 1995). Evidencing accurate content involves demonstrating a match between the content theorized to be related to the construct and the actual content of the psychometric. So, if psychopathy is theorized to consist of four main content dimensions then items should represent those four dimensions. Within our review, content evidence was one of the most widely reported with 55% of articles explicitly examining the accuracy of the psychometric content of items.

All examinations of content accuracy are inherently theoretical. The first and most important step in assessing content accuracy is to define the domain and the facets of the target construct (Nunnally & Bernstein, 1994). A poorly defined construct, based on a weak theoretical footing will, almost certainly, lack content accuracy. In many fields, there are authoritative sources that provide a "gold standard" construct definition that can be used to guide content development and evaluation (e.g., the APA's

Diagnostic and Statistical Manual of Mental Disorders). However, relying solely on a single widely accepted model is not always suitable and certainly should not be done blindly. Even well-established models deserve thorough examination and it is not uncommon to find dominant construct definitions wanting (see Irwing & Hughes, Chapter 1). Once one has carefully defined the construct domain, content must be generated that is likely to elicit appropriate response processes. In order to generate such content, one can conduct expert and general population sampling to identify relevant content (Haynes et al., 1995; Irwing & Hughes, Chapter 1). The generated content should then be assessed using formalized rating procedures whereby multiple experts rate the quality of the content based on its relevance, representativeness, specificity, and clarity (see, Nunnally & Bernstein, 1994; Lynn, 1986; Stewart, Lynn, & Mishel, 2005). Content deemed to be content accurate based on theoretical examination can then be examined empirically for evidence that the content does indeed elicit the expected response processes across all facets of the construct.

There are two major threats to content accuracy, namely, construct-irrelevance and construct under-representation (Messick, 1989). If a psychometric is designed to measure psychopathy but contains items pertaining to intelligence, we say the psychometric has construct-irrelevant content, whereas if the psychometric only measures three out of four psychopathy factors then we say that we have construct under-representation.

Content-based evidence provides one of the most compelling demonstrations of the failings of the unified model of validity (AERA, APA, NCME, 2014). There are two common goals when reviewing psychometric content, one is to optimize accuracy (i.e., full content representation) and the other is to optimize predictive properties while reducing adverse impact (or negative social consequences). These two aims of psychometric test construction are not convergent. For example, a truly accurate measure of personality would require the measurement of many facets, taking respondents a long time. In contrast, the most appropriate way to use personality for prediction (e.g., employee selection) involves measuring only relevant facets (e.g., Hughes & Batey, 2017). If, however, we accept that these two lines of enquiry are distinct we can say clearly that one should first build a fully accurate measure of personality (with many facets, regardless of their predictive capabilities) and then, when using personality for prediction, compile a measure with only the most appropriate facets (Hughes & Batey, 2017).

Structure

Closely related to content evidence is evidence relating to how that content is structured. Evidence of an accurate structure involves the demonstration of a match between the theorized content structure and the actual content structure. Using the psychopathy example from before, if we hypothesize four factors of psychopathy then we should be able to identify those factors within our item responses, but we should also be able to model the general, higher-order psychopathy factor (see Tokarev, Phillips, Hughes & Irwing, 2017, for such an example). Structural evidence is most commonly amassed using forms of factor analysis, including exploratory and confirmatory factor analysis (see Cai & Moustaki, Chapter 9; Jennrich, Chapter 10; Mulaik, Chapter 8; Timmerman, Lorenzo-Seva, & Cuelemans, Chapter 11) and more recently, exploratory structural equation modelling (Asparouhov & Muthén, 2009; Booth & Hughes, 2014). Each of these techniques is popular within current psychometric practice

(Table 24.1) and is discussed in excellent fashion within this *Handbook of Psychometric Testing* and elsewhere, so I will not discuss them further.

It is also important to establish whether or not the structure you have identified holds across different groups. In general, response process, content, and structure should be examined across all populations of relevance (e.g., across ability levels, ages, national groups). Two tools are of particular value when examining structural stability across groups. First, invariance analysis (Millsap & Kim, Chapter 26) can examine whether the number of factors is stable across groups (configural invariance), whether the factor loadings are of the same magnitude (metric invariance), whether the intercepts are stable (scalar invariance), and whether the unique factor variances are stable (strict invariance, though Little [2013] provides compelling arguments as to why this is not an appropriate criterion for measurement equivalence). Thirty-five percent of articles in our review reported some form of invariance analyses. Second, differential item functioning (Drasgow, Nye, Stark, & Chernyshenko, Chapter 27) identifies items for which members of different subgroups with identical total test scores show differing response patterns and thus can identify potentially biased items.

Appropriateness

Whereas there are currently a limited number of methods for establishing the accuracy of a psychometric measure, there are many potential methods for establishing appropriateness. A psychometric can be used for many different purposes across many different contexts and for each a unique set of evidence could be required to demonstrate appropriateness (Kane, 2006, 2013, 2016). Broadly speaking, there are two main classifications of use: theory testing and decision making. Theory testing captures the majority of research activities (does X correlate with Y, how does X interact with Y to produce Z, etc.), while decision-making refers to applied use (e.g., selecting or training employees, diagnosing mental health problems, placing students within ability-based classes). In keeping with currently accepted nomenclature, I will discuss evidence concerning three main categories, namely, evidence based on relationships with other variables, evidence relating to consequences and fairness (e.g., AERA, APA, NCME, 2009, 2014; Cronbach & Meehl, 1955; Messick, 1989), and evidence relating to feasibility concerns (e.g., Cizek, 2016). Table 24.2 provides a summary of the most common forms of evidence that can be used to establish psychometric appropriateness.

Relationships with other variables

Perhaps the most common use of psychometrics is as a predictor of a criterion. Criterion association evidence comes in two major forms: concurrent and predictive. Concurrent criterion associations are essentially cross-sectional with both the predictor and criterion measured at roughly the same time. Sixty percent of articles reviewed reported concurrent criterion associations. In contrast, predictive criterion associations are time-lagged. The predictor is measured at time one and the criterion at some later point in time. Predictive criterion associations are more powerful for all the reasons longitudinal research is superior to cross-sectional (Menard, 2002). Of articles reviewed, only 10% reported predictive criterion relations though many who presented concurrent relations claimed that they were predictive. In addition to simple models with a single predictor and a single criterion, it is also advisable to demonstrate that a measure offers incremental prediction beyond other established predictors (see Smith, Fischer, & Fister, 2003, for an accessible treatment of how to consider incremental prediction during measure development). Such models use multiple predictors and focus on the additional variance explained by the focal measure, thus allowing for more concrete claims regarding the appropriateness of a measure. For example, if we wanted to predict job performance it would be of great value to know that our newly developed measure predicted even when modelled alongside well-known predictors such as intelligence and conscientiousness. In such a situation, we could then say confidently that using our measure during selection is appropriate. As displayed in Table 24.2, criterion relationships are commonly reported within new scale development papers but, overwhelmingly, these associations are concurrent. Common methods include various regression models, structural equation models, and tests of known group differences (e.g., those diagnosed with a mental disorder and those who are healthy).

Table 24.2 Evidence for establishing psychometric appropriateness: labels, definitions, methods, and prevalence of current use.

Type of evidence	Definition	Example methods	% used
Convergent	The relationship between psychometric measures of a construct and other measures of the same construct.	Correlations	75
Discriminant	The relationship between test scores and scores on measures assessing different constructs.	Correlations Confirmatory factor analysis (CFA)	85
Predictive	The ability to longitudinally predict criterion scores based on test scores.	Time-lagged or longitudinal regression models Time-lagged or longitudinal structural equation models (SEM)	10
Concurrent	Cross-sectional prediction with both predictor and criterion data collected at the same time.	Regression models SEM	60
Incremental	Improvements in prediction of a criterion variable added by a particular test over and above other measures.	Regression models SEM	20
Known groups	The extent to which a psychometric measure correctly discriminates between those known to be low and those know to be high in a construct.	T-tests ANOVA Latent mean differences (mean structures analysis)	10
Consequences	The intended and unintended consequences of test use.	Differential item functioning Invariance analysis Estimates of adverse impact False-positive and false-negative rates	0
Feasibility	The practical concerns related to psychometric use.	Cost Time Respondent reactions	0

Convergent and discriminant evidence were first introduced by Campbell and Fiske (1959). Convergent evidence is "represented in the agreement between two attempts to measure the same trait through maximally different methods" (Campbell & Fiske, 1959, p. 83) though the same traits measured using the same method can be considered a weak form of convergent evidence. As we can see in Table 24.2, convergent evidence is commonly reported within new scale development papers but in the overwhelming majority of cases the construct is measured using the same method (i.e., two self-report measures of Narcissism). The review of new scales also revealed that convergent evidence is often claimed when the methods used are the same (i.e., two self-report questionnaires) or simply when a psychometric correlates with other measures that theoretically it should (i.e., intelligence and school performance), and often Campbell and Fiske (1959) were cited as the justification for these analyses. However, this is not convergent validity as proposed by Campbell and Fiske (1959). In fact, it is not entirely clear what "type" of evidence this is, if any. Although often described as "nomological validity" or "construct validity," evidencing positive correlations between two measures is perhaps best viewed as a test of theory, not a specific form of validity evidence (Cronbach & Meehl, 1955).

Discriminant evidence (frequently mislabeled as divergent evidence in the literature) is the degree to which measures of theoretically distinct constructs are empirically unrelated to one another. Discriminant evidence is particularly important for showing that a new measure is actually new and preventing construct proliferation (e.g., Le, Schmidt, Harter, & Lauver, 2010; Reeve & Basalik, 2014; Shaffer, DeGeest, & Li, 2016). Construct proliferation occurs either when researchers propose multiple scales that claim to measure the same underlying construct but actually do not (Jingle Fallacy) or when ostensibly new constructs are proposed that are theoretically and/or empirically indistinguishable from existing constructs (Jangle Fallacy, Kelley, 1927; Ziegler, Booth, & Bensch, 2013). Construct proliferation impedes the creation of cumulative knowledge and hinders the development of parsimonious theories (Le et al., 2010). Discriminant evidence is designed for this purpose (Bagozzi, Yi, & Phillips, 1991; Campbell & Fiske, 1959) and is critical in establishing whether a new measure is appropriate for theory building and testing (Harter & Schmidt, 2008). Discriminant evidence can be garnered through the use of the multitrait-multimethod approach (Campbell & Fiske; 1959; see Koch, Eid, & Lochner, Chapter 25) and via confirmatory factor analysis (Bagozzi et al., 1991; Fornell & Larcker, 1981; Voorhees, Brady, Calantone, & Ramirez, 2016). Shaffer et al. (2016) recently presented a practical guide to conducting more rigorous investigations of discriminant properties of measures by taking into account measure reliability. They also make the very important point that researchers should select a reasonably broad number of measures of theoretically similar constructs (e.g., happiness and joy rather than happiness and fear) when investigating the discriminant properties of a measure. Failing to do so provides a weak examination of discriminant properties (Shaffer et al., 2016).

Consequences and fairness

Consistent controversy arises when the consequences of psychometric use are argued to be a component of validity (c.f., Cizek, 2016; Newton & Shaw, 2016; Sireci, 2016; Zumbo & Hubley, 2016). I cannot imagine the same degree of controversy if we say that examining the consequences of psychometric use is a core component of establishing whether that use is appropriate. By explicating the difference between accuracy and appropriateness, consequences become more obviously relevant within appropriateness and clearly irrelevant to questions of accuracy. When producing a new psychometric or trying to sell one, researchers or test publishers can currently make a convoluted, lengthy, and convincing "validity argument" while ignoring consequences completely. Indeed, the review conducted specifically for this chapter showed that not a single publication considered potential social consequences (see Table 24.2). However, if psychometric publications had to make two specific evidence-based statements regarding accuracy and appropriateness, it would be much more difficult to hide the lack of consideration of consequences. Any appropriateness statement would be clearly incomplete without an assessment of possible biases and their consequences. Ironically, this is contrary to the commonly raised concern that changes to the current validity consensus (AERA, APA, NCME, 2014) would see consequences ignored (Kane, 2013, 2016; Sireci, 2007, 2016).

Consequences are undoubtedly important and psychometric users must always examine whether or not their intended use will have adverse effects on any particular group (Cronbach, 1988; Messick, 1989; see Reckase, 1998 for practical recommendations). Group differences can be assessed using techniques such as multigroup confirmatory factor analysis (Koch et al., Chapter 25), invariance analysis (Millsap & Kim, Chapter 26), and differential item functioning (Drasgow, et al., Chapter 27). Equally, if psychometrics are used to choose people for jobs or educational opportunities, careful examination of success rates are also important. It is important here to restate that not all group differences are due to bias, they might be due to naturally occurring group differences (e.g., height or conscientiousness between males and females). Whether the use of a psychometric that has known group differences – and thus will adversely impact one group – is appropriate, is a difficult decision to make and one for which generic guidance is difficult to give.

Feasibility

Finally, when deciding whether the use of a psychometric is appropriate for a given purpose within a given context we often have to consider more than predictive capabilities and biases. We also have to address practical considerations including monetary cost, time cost, respondent reactions, and administration procedures. Organizational researchers and employee selection practitioners have considered these elements for a long time (e.g., Hough, Oswald, & Ployhart, 2001; Hughes & Batey, 2017) and in his recent paper, Cizek (2016) noted that educational program evaluation models could also provide a framework to guide considerations of feasibility (e.g., Patton, 2008; Shadish, Cook, & Leviton, 1991).

Conclusion

Adopted by psychometricians in the 1920s, validity has been the subject of continuous debate and revision but always retained its status as the most fundamental consideration in test development. Unfortunately, the current unified validity model (AERA, APA, NCME, 2014) is so complicated and convoluted that it baffles researchers, practitioners, and even validity theorists (Cizek et al., 2008, 2010; Markus & Borsboom, 2013; Newton & Shaw, 2013, 2016). Much of the theoretical confusion and practical difficulty stems from tensions that arise when trying to shoehorn considerations of a measure's accuracy, reliability, factor structure, predictive capability, test scoring, test administration, social consequences, and more into a single unified model (Borsboom et al., 2004; Cizek, 2012, 2016; Koretz, 2016; Newton & Shaw, 2016). Many of these sources of "validity evidence" are not just difficult to combine, they are sometimes diametrically opposed and cannot be meaningfully represented within a unified model. This fact has led numerous authors to call for substantial revisions to validity theory (e.g., Borsboom, et al., 2004, 2009; Cizek, 2012, 2016; Koretz, 2016; Lissitz & Samuelson, 2007; Newton, 2012; Newton & Shaw, 2013, 2016; Popham, 1997). I agree with the major premise of these critiques and hope that the introduction of the accuracy and appropriateness model of psychometric evaluation goes some way to providing the theoretical advance required.

The accuracy and appropriateness model has a number of notable advantages over the unified model (AERA, APA, NCME, 2014; Messick, 1989). First, the model answers calls for a coherent partition of the different types of validity evidence according to the two major questions in psychometric evaluation (Cizek, 2016), namely, what do psychometrics measure and are they useful? This reconfiguration addresses the logical inconsistencies associated with the unified model (Borsboom et al., 2004; Cizek, 2016; Popham, 1997) and means that each of the major forms of validity evidence espoused in validity models throughout history now sits in a sensible place alongside other forms of validity evidence that help address the same question.

Second, structuring the two main questions and associated sources of validity evidence into a two-step process provides psychometric developers and users with a clear and coherent model to follow in practice. This theoretically coherent and conceptually simple model leaves little question regarding which types of evidence are needed to establish accuracy and appropriateness and thus has the potential to improve psychometric development and use (Cizek, 2016; Koretz, 2016).

Third, the model allows us to drop the emotive word validity (Newton & Shaw, 2016) and in doing so move past the adversarial and antagonistic semantic debate that has distracted theorists for decades (Hood, 2009; Markus, 2016; Newton & Shaw, 2016). In turn, we can refocus our attention on the scientific and ethical questions that really form the core of psychometric evaluations. Those who might be skeptical of this, are encouraged to revisit the sections of this chapter which outline methods for establishing accuracy and appropriateness. These sections were written without the use of the word validity except when in reference to previous work, demonstrating that test evaluation can be discussed without our prized and poorly defined label.

Fourth, the labels accuracy and appropriateness address calls to provide simple yet precise terminologies that allow us to communicate whether or not a psychometric measures what it claims to (Borsboom, 2012) and whether or not a specific test use is justified (Cizek, 2016; Koretz, 2016). The precision and simplicity of these terms make it easy to communicate within and across research domains, and across the research-practice divide.

Fifth, the importance of consequences can be stated without invoking the theoretical and logical critiques promoted by the inadequacies of the unified model. Numerous authors have correctly emphasized the importance of test consequences (Kane, 2016; Sireci, 2016; Zumbo & Hubley, 2016) and simultaneously argued that changes to the unified model would see them ignored. However, as we have discussed, consequences are already ignored (see Cizek, et al., 2008, 2010, and this chapter's review).

Currently, psychometric developers are able to hide a lack of consideration for consequences by presenting a myriad of other forms of validity evidence (Cizek et al., 2008, 2010). However, if psychometricians were to adhere to the model espoused here, they would need to present two explicit bodies of evidence, one concerning accuracy and a second concerning appropriateness. It is inconceivable that consideration of consequences could be omitted from a discussion of whether or not it is appropriate to use a psychometric for a specific real-world purpose.

This chapter set out to provide psychometric researchers and practitioners with a guide for "validating" measures. I believe the current chapter has achieved its aims by stating clearly that psychometric validity is concerned with establishing the **accuracy** and **appropriateness** of measures. I hope that the theoretical discussion and practical guidelines provided will serve as a stimulus for further theoretical clarification and prove useful for those developing and using psychometric measures. Perhaps the key practical take-home messages for those who develop, evaluate, and use psychometrics are as follows. The accuracy of a psychometric can be established through examination of: participant response processes, psychometric content, and the structure of psychometric content. Whether it is appropriate to use a psychometric for a given purpose can be established through examination of: the relationship between psychometric scores and other variables, the potential or actual consequences of psychometric use, and the practical feasibility of psychometric use.

References

Accuracy. (n.d.): In Oxford English Dictionary Online. Retrieved from www.oed.com

American Educational Research Association, American Psychological Association, & National Council on Measurement in Education. (1974). *Standards for educational and psychological testing* (2nd ed.). Washington, D.C.: American Educational Research Association.

American Educational Research Association, American Psychological Association, & National Council on Measurement in Education. (1985). *Standards for educational and psychological testing* (3rd ed.). Washington, D.C.: American Educational Research Association.

American Educational Research Association, American Psychological Association, & National Council on Measurement in Education. (1999). *Standards for educational and psychological testing* (4th ed.). Washington, D.C.: American Educational Research Association.

American Educational Research Association, American Psychological Association, National Council on Measurement in Education. (2014). *Standards for educational and psychological testing* (5th ed.). Washington, D.C.: American Educational Research Association.

Appropriate. (n.d.): In Oxford English Dictionary Online. Retrieved from www.oed.com

Asparouhov, T., & Muthén, B. (2009). Exploratory structural equation modeling. *Structural Equation Modeling: A Multidisciplinary Journal, 16*(3), 397–438.

Bagozzi, R. P., Yi, Y., & Phillips, L. W. (1991). Assessing construct validity in organizational research. *Administrative Science Quarterly, 36*(3), 421–458.

Booth, T., & Hughes, D. J. (2014). Exploratory structural equation modeling of personality data. *Assessment, 21*(3), 260–271.

Borsboom, D. (2012). Whose consensus is it anyway? Scientific versus legalistic conceptions of validity. *Measurement: Interdisciplinary Research and Perspectives, 10*(1–2), 38–41.

Borsboom, D., & Mellenbergh, G. J. (2007). Test validity in cognitive assessment. In J. P. Leighton, & M. J. Gierl (Eds.), *Cognitive diagnostic assessment for education* (pp. 85–115). Cambridge: Cambridge University Press.

Borsboom, D., & Wijsen, L. D. (2016). Frankenstein's validity monster: The value of keeping politics and science separated. *Assessment in Education: Principles, Policy & Practice, 23* (2), 281–283.
Borsboom, D., Cramer, A. O., Kievit, R. A., Scholten, A. Z., & Franic, S. (2009). The end of construct validity. In R. W. Lissitz (Ed.), *The concept of validity: Revisions, new directions, and applications* (pp. 135–170). Charlotte, NC: Information Age Publishing.
Borsboom, D., Mellenbergh, G. J., & van Heerden, J. (2004). The concept of validity. *Psychological Review, 111*, 1061–1071.
Borsboom, D., Mellenbergh, G. J., & van Heerden, J. (2003). The theoretical status of latent variables. *Psychological Review, 110*, 203–219.
Buckingham, B. R. (1921). Intelligence and its measurement: A symposium – XIV. *Journal of Educational Psychology, 12*(5), 271–275.
Campbell, D. T., & Fiske, D. W. (1959). Convergent and discriminant validation by the multi-trait-multimethod matrix. *Psychological Bulletin, 56*(2), 81–105.
Carmines, E. G., & Zeller, R. A. (1979). *Reliability and validity assessment.* Beverly Hills, CA: Sage.
Carver, C. S., & Scheier, M. F. (2003). *Perspectives on personality* (5th ed.). Boston: Allyn & Bacon.
Cizek, G. J. (2012). Defining and distinguishing validity: Interpretations of score meaning and justifications of test use. *Psychological Methods, 17*(1), 31–43.
Cizek, G. J. (2016). Validating test score meaning and defending test score use: different aims, different methods. *Assessment in Education: Principles, Policy & Practice, 23*(2), 212–225.
Cizek, G. J., Bowen, D., & Church, K. (2010). Sources of validity evidence for educational and psychological tests: A follow-up study. *Educational and Psychological Measurement, 70*(5), 732–743.
Cizek, G. J., Rosenberg, S. L., & Koons, H. H. (2008). Sources of validity evidence for educational and psychological tests. *Educational and Psychological Measurement, 68*(3), 397–412.
Cone, J. D., & Foster, S. L. (1991). Training in measurement: Always the bridesmaid. *American Psychologist, 46*(6), 653–654.
Cooper, C. (2002). *Individual differences* (2nd ed.). London: Arnold.
Cronbach, L. J. (1988). Internal consistency of tests: Analyses old and new. *Psychometrika, 53*(1), 63–70.
Cronbach, L. J., & Meehl, P. E. (1955). Construct validity in psychological tests. *Psychological Bulletin, 52*(4), 281–302.
Cureton, E. E. (1950). Validity, reliability and baloney. *Educational and Psychological Measurement, 10*, 94–96.
Cureton, E. E. (1951). Validity. In E. F. Lindquist (Ed.), *Educational measurement.* Washington, D.C.: American Council on Education.
Darker, C. D., & French, D. P. (2009). What sense do people make of a theory of planned behaviour questionnaire? A think-aloud study. *Journal of Health Psychology, 14*(7), 861–871.
Durning, S. J., Artino Jr, A. R., Beckman, T. J., van der Vleuten, C., Holmboe, E., & Schuwirth, L. (2013). Does the think-aloud protocol reflect thinking? Exploring functional neuroimaging differences with thinking (answering multiple choice questions) versus thinking aloud. *Medical Teacher, 35*, 720–726.
Embretson, S. (1984). A general latent trait model for response processes. *Psychometrika, 49*(2), 175–186.
Embretson, S. (1994). Applications of cognitive design systems to test development. In C. R. Reynolds (Ed.), *Cognitive assessment* (pp. 107–135). New York: Springer.
Embretson, S. E. (1998). A cognitive design system approach to generating valid tests: Application to abstract reasoning. *Psychological Methods, 3*(3), 380–396.
Embretson, S. E. (2010). Cognitive design systems: A structural modeling approach applied to developing a spatial ability test. In S. E. Embretson (Ed.), *Measuring psychological constructs: Advances in model-based approaches* (pp. 247–273). Washington, D.C.: American Psychological Association.

Embretson, S. E. (1983). Construct validity: Construct representation versus nomothetic span. *Psychological Bulletin, 93*(1), 179–197.

Embretson, S. E. (1999). Generating items during testing: Psychometric issues and models. *Psychometrika, 64*(4), 407–433.

Embretson, S. E. (1993). Psychometric models for learning and cognitive processes. In N. Fredericksen, R. J. Mislevy, & I. I. Bejar (Eds.), *Test theory for a new generation of tests* (pp. 125–150). Hillsdale, NJ: Erlbaum.

Embretson, S. E. (2016). Understanding examinees' responses to items: Implications for measurement. *Educational Measurement: Issues and Practice, 35*(3), 6–22.

Embretson, S. E., & Gorin, J. (2001). Improving construct validity with cognitive psychology principles. *Journal of Educational Measurement, 38*(4), 343–368.

Ericsson, K. A., & Simon, H. A. (1980). Verbal reports as data. *Psychological Review, 87*(3), 215–251.

Ericsson, K. A., & Simon, H. A. (1993). *Protocol analysis*, revised ed. Cambridge, MA: MIT Press.

Ericsson, K. A., & Simon, H. A. (1998). How to study thinking in everyday life: Contrasting think-aloud protocols with descriptions and explanations of thinking. *Mind, Culture, and Activity, 5*(3), 178–186.

Fornell, C., & Larcker, D. R. (1981). Evaluating structural equation models with unobservable variables and measurement error, *Journal of Marketing Research, 18*, 39–50.

Germann, G. B. (1899). On the invalidity of the aesthesiometric method as a measure of mental fatigue. *Psychological Review, 6*(6), 599–605.

Guilford, J. P. (1942). *Fundamental statistics in psychology and education*. New York, NY: McGraw-Hill.

Guilford, J. P. (1946). New standards for test evaluation. *Educational and Psychological Measurement, 6*(4), 427–438.

Harter, J. K., & Schmidt, F. L. (2008). Conceptual versus empirical distinctions among constructs: Implications for discriminant validity. *Industrial and Organizational Psychology, 1*(1), 36–39.

Haynes, S. N., Richard, D., & Kubany, E. S. (1995). Content validity in psychological assessment: A functional approach to concepts and methods. *Psychological Assessment, 7*(3), 238–247.

Hood, S. B. (2009). Validity in psychological testing and scientific realism. *Theory & Psychology, 19*(4), 451–473.

Hough, L. M., Oswald, F. L., & Ployhart, R. E. (2001). Determinants, detection and amelioration of adverse impact in personnel selection procedures: Issues, evidence and lessons learned. *International Journal of Selection and Assessment, 9*(1–2), 152–194.

Hubley, A. M., & Zumbo, B. D. (2011). Validity and the consequences of test interpretation and use. *Social Indicators Research, 103*, 219–230.

Hubley, A. M., & Zumbo, B. D. (2013). Psychometric characteristics of assessment procedures: An overview. In K. F. Geisinger, B. A. Bracken, J. F. Carlson, J.-I. C. Hansen, N. R. Kuncel, S. P. Reise, et al. (Eds.), *APA handbook of testing and assessment in psychology* (Vol. 1) (pp. 3–19). Washington, DC: American Psychological Association Press.

Hughes, D. J., & Batey, M. (2017). Using personality questionnaires for selection. In H. Goldstein, E. Pulakos, J. Passmore, & C. Semedo (Eds.), *The Wiley Blackwell handbook of the psychology of recruitment, selection & retention* (pp. 151–180). Chichester, UK: Wiley-Blackwell.

Jansen, B. R., & van der Maas, H. L. (1997). Statistical test of the rule assessment methodology by latent class analysis. *Developmental Review, 17*(3), 321–357.

Kane, M. T. (2001). Current concerns in validity theory. *Journal of Educational Measurement, 38*(4), 319–342.

Kane, M. T. (2006). Validation. In R. L. Brennan (Ed.), *Educational measurement* (4th ed.) (pp. 17–64). Westport, CT: American Council on Education and Praeger.

Kane, M. T. (2013). Validating the interpretations and uses of test scores. *Journal of Educational Measurement, 50*(1), 1–73.
Kane, M. T. (2016). Explicating validity. *Assessment in Education: Principles, Policy & Practice, 23*(2), 198–211.
Karabenick, S. A., Woolley, M. E., Friedel, J. M., Ammon, B. V., Blazevski, J., Bonney, C. R., et al. (2007). Cognitive processing of self-report items in educational research: Do they think what we mean? *Educational Psychologist, 42*, 139–151.
Kelley, T. L. (1927). *Interpretation of educational measurements*. New York: World Books.
Kiernan, J. G. (1884). Feigned insanity: An enquiry into the validity of the reasons for recent diagnoses of this kind. *Journal of Nervous and Mental Disease, 11*(2), 177–184.
Kline, P. (2000). *The handbook of psychological testing* (2nd ed.). London, United Kingdom: Routledge.
Koretz, D. (2016). Making the term "validity" useful. *Assessment in Education: Principles, Policy & Practice, 23*(2), 290–292.
Larsen, R. J., Buss, D. M., Wismeijer, A., & Song, J. (2013). *Personality psychology*. Maidenhead: McGraw-Hill Higher Education.
Le, H., Schmidt, F. L., Harter, J. K., & Lauver, K. J. (2010). The problem of empirical redundancy of constructs in organizational research: An empirical investigation. *Organizational Behavior and Human Decision Processes, 112*(2), 112–125.
Lees-Haley, P. R. (1996). Alice in Validityland, or the dangerous consequences of consequential validity. *American Psychologist, 51*(9), 981–983.
Lissitz, R. W., & Samuelson, K. (2007). A suggested change in terminology and emphasis regarding validity and education. *Educational Researcher, 36*(8), 437–448.
Little, T. D. (2013). *Longitudinal structural equation modeling*. New York, NY: Guilford Press.
Lynn, M. R. (1986). Determination and quantification of content validity. *Nursing Research, 35*(6), 382–386.
Markus, K. A. (2016). Validity bites: comments and rejoinders. *Assessment in Education: Principles, Policy & Practice, 23*(2), 312–315.
Markus, K. A., & Borsboom, D. (2012). The cat came back: evaluating arguments against psychological measurement. *Theory and Psychology, 22*, 452–466.
Markus, K. A., & Borsboom, D. (2013). *Frontiers of test validity theory: Measurement, causation, and meaning*. New York, NY: Routledge.
Mehrens, W. A. (1997). The consequences of consequential validity. *Educational Measurement: Issues and Practice, 16*(2), 16–18.
Menard, S. W. (2002). *Longitudinal research* (2nd ed.). Thousand Oaks, CA: Sage Publications.
Messick, S. (1989). Validity. In R. L. Linn (Ed.), *Educational measurement* (3rd ed.) (pp. 13–103). Washington, D.C.: The American Council on Education & The National Council on Measurement in Education.
Mislevy, R. J., & Verhelst, N. (1990). Modeling item responses when different subjects employ different solution strategies. *Psychometrika, 55*(2), 195–215.
Moss, P. A. (1998). The role of consequences in validity theory. *Educational Measurement: Issues and Practice, 17*(2), 6–12.
Moss, P. A. (2016). Shifting the focus of validity for test use. *Assessment in Education: Principles, Policy & Practice, 23*(2), 236–251.
Newton, P. E. (2012). Clarifying the consensus definition of validity. *Measurement: Interdisciplinary Research and Perspectives, 10*(1–2), 1–29.
Newton, P. E., & Baird, J.-A. (2016). The great validity debate. *Assessment in Education: Principles, Policy & Practice, 23*(2), 173–177.
Newton, P. E., & Shaw, S. D. (2013). Standards for talking and thinking about validity. *Psychological Methods, 18*(3), 301–319.
Newton, P., & Shaw, S. (2014). *Validity in educational and psychological assessment*. London: Sage.

Newton, P. E., & Shaw, S. D. (2016). Disagreement over the best way to use the word "validity" and options for reaching consensus. *Assessment in Education: Principles, Policy & Practice, 23* (2), 178–197.

Nunnally, J. C., & Bernstein, I. H. (1994). *Psychometric theory* (3rd ed.). New York: McGraw-Hill.

Osterlind, S. J. (2010). *Modern measurement: Theory, principles, and applications of mental appraisal* (2nd ed.). Boston, MA: Pearson Education.

Patton, M. Q. (2008). *Utilization-focused evaluation.* Thousand Oaks: Sage.

Popham, W. J. (1997). Consequential validity: Right concern-wrong concept. *Educational Measurement: Issues and Practice, 16*(2), 9–13.

Presser, S., Rothgep, J., Couper, M., Lessler, J., Martin, E., Martin, J., & Singer, E. (Eds.) (2004). *Methods for testing and evaluating survey questionnaires.* New York, NJ: John Wiley & Sons, Inc.

Reckase, M. D. (1998). Consequential validity from the test developer's perspective. *Educational Measurement: Issues and Practice, 17*(2), 13–16.

Reeve, C. L., & Basalik, D. (2014). Is health literacy an example of construct proliferation? A conceptual and empirical evaluation of its redundancy with general cognitive ability. *Intelligence, 44*, 93–102.

Scriven, M. (2002). Assessing six assumptions in assessment. In H. I. Braun, D. N. Jackson, & D. E. Wiley (Eds.) *The role of constructs in psychological and educational measurement.* Mahwah, NJ: Lawrence Erlbaum.

Shadish, W. R., Cook, T. D., & Campbell, D. T. (2002). *Experimental and quasi-experimental designs for generalized causal inference.* Boston, MA: Houghton Mifflin.

Shadish, W. R., Cook, T. D., & Leviton, L. C. (1991). *Foundations of program evaluation: Theories of practice.* Newbury Park: Sage.

Shaffer, J. A., DeGeest, D., & Li, A. (2016). Tackling the problem of construct proliferation a guide to assessing the discriminant validity of conceptually related constructs. *Organizational Research Methods, 19*(1), 80–110.

Shepard, L. A. (2016). Evaluating test validity: reprise and progress. *Assessment in Education: Principles, Policy & Practice, 23*(2), 268–280.

Sireci, S. G. (2007). On validity theory and test validation. *Educational Researcher, 36*(8), 477–481.

Sireci, S. G. (2016). On the validity of useless tests. *Assessment in Education: Principles, Policy & Practice, 23*(2), 226–235.

Smith, G. T., Fischer, S., & Fister, S. M. (2003). Incremental validity principles in test construction. *Psychological Assessment, 15*(4), 467–477.

Smith, M. (2011). *Fundamentals of management* (2nd ed.). Maidenhead: McGraw-Hill Higher Education.

Spearman, C. (1904). The proof and measurement of association between two things. *The American Journal of Psychology, 15*(1), 72–101.

Stewart, J. L., Lynn, M. R., & Mishel, M. H. (2005). Evaluating content validity for children's self-report instruments using children as content experts. *Nursing Research, 54*(6), 414–418.

Tokarev, A., Phillips, A. R., Hughes, D. J., & Irwing, P. (2017). Leader dark traits, workplace bullying, and employee depression: Exploring mediation and the role of the dark core. *Journal of Abnormal Psychology, 126*(7), 911–920.

van Someren, M. W., Barnard, Y. F., & Sandberg, J. A. (1994). *The think aloud method: a practical approach to modelling cognitive processes.* London: Academic Press.

Vandevelde, S., van Keer, H., Schellings, G., & van Hout-Wolters, B. (2015). Using think-aloud protocol analysis to gain in-depth insights into upper primary school children's self-regulated learning. *Learning and Individual Differences, 43*, 11–30.

Voorhees, C. M., Brady, M. K., Calantone, R., & Ramirez, E. (2016). Discriminant validity testing in marketing: an analysis, causes for concern, and proposed remedies. *Journal of the Academy of Marketing Science, 44*(1), 119–134.

Wiley, D. E. (1991). Test validity and invalidity reconsidered. In R. E. Snow, & D. E. Wiley (Eds.), *Improving inquiry in social science: A volume in honor of Lee J. Cronbach*. Hillsdale, NJ: Erlbaum.

Woods, S. A., & West, M. A. (2010). *The psychology of work and organizations*. Andover: South-Western Cengage Learning.

Ziegler, M., Booth, T., & Bensch, D. (2013). Getting entangled in the nomological net. *European Journal of Psychological Assessment, 29*, 157–161.

Zumbo, B. D. (2007). Three generations of DIF analyses: Considering where it has been, where it is now, and where it is going. *Language Assessment Quarterly, 4*(2), 223–233.

Zumbo, B. D. (2009). Validity as contextualized and pragmatic explanation, and its implications for validation practice. In R. W. Lissitz (Ed.), *The concept of validity: Revisions, new directions, and applications* (pp. 65–82). Charlotte, NC: Information Age Publishing.

Zumbo, B. D., & Hubley, A. M. (2016). Bringing consequences and side effects of testing and assessment to the foreground. *Assessment in Education: Principles, Policy & Practice, 23*(2), 299–303.

25

Multitrait-Multimethod-Analysis: The Psychometric Foundation of CFA-MTMM Models

Tobias Koch, Michael Eid, and Katharina Lochner

Introduction to the "Classical" MTMM Analysis

One of the most fundamental questions in social and behavioral sciences is the question of the adequacy and appropriateness of inferences, psychological decisions, and/or actions based on test scores. According to Messick (1980, 1989, 1995) as well as most authors of the standards on educational and psychological testing (e.g., APA, AERA, & NCME, 1999) this issue refers to the concept of validity.[1] Invalid and/or inaccurate measurements may lead to inaccurate psychological judgments (e.g., wrong diagnoses), wrong or suboptimal practical decisions (e.g., treatments), or biased estimates of treatment effects (see Courvoisier, Nussbeck, Eid, Geiser, & Cole, 2008). Hence, many researchers are especially interested in scrutinizing the validity of their measures (e.g., tests). The multitrait-multimethod (MTMM) approach originally developed by Campbell and Fiske (1959) represents one of the most common ways to investigate the validity of a given measure. As David Kenny (1995) states "The MTMM matrix represents one of the most important discoveries in the social and behavioral sciences. It is as important an invention in the behavioral science field as the microscope is in biology and the telescope is in astronomy" (p. 123). Moreover, the seminal article by Campbell and Fiske (1959) has been cited over 5,000 times and is known to be one of the most influential articles in psychology (Sternberg, 1992).

But what is the basic idea of MTMM analysis? Simply speaking, the basic idea of MTMM analysis is that theoretically **related** test scores measuring the same or similar traits should also be empirically associated with each other (i.e., show high positive correlations), whereas theoretically **unrelated** test scores measuring different (theoretically unrelated) constructs should also be empirically unrelated with each other (i.e., show low or insignificant correlations). The first statement refers to the degree of **convergent validity** among the measures; the second statement refers to the degree of **discriminant**

---

[1] Note that there is an on-going philosophical discourse on whether or not validity should be defined as a property of a given test (e.g., Borsboom, Mellenbergh, & van Heerden, 2004) or as the adequacy of the interpretation of test scores (e.g., Messick, 1980, 1989, 1995).

	Traits	Method 1			Method 2		
		Trait 1	Trait 2	Trait 3	Trait 1	Trait 2	Trait 3
Method 1	Trait 1	(.90)					
	Trait 2	.10	(.90)				
	Trait 3	.10	.10	(.90)			
Method 2	Trait 1	**.50**	.12	.12	(.80)		
	Trait 2	.14	**.50**	.12	.20	(.80)	
	Trait 3	.14	.14	**.50**	.20	.20	(.80)

Figure 25.1 Multitrait-multimethod correlation matrix for two traits and two methods. *Note:* The figure was adopted from Eid (2010). The correlations are artificial. The reliabilities are in parentheses. Heterotrait-monomethod correlations are enclosed by a solid line. Heterotrait-heteromethod correlations are enclosed by a broken line. Monotrait-heteromethod correlations are given in a bold font.

validity. Campbell and Fiske (1959) suggested analyzing the convergent and discriminant validity among measures by using multitrait-multimethod correlation matrices. Moreover, Campbell and Fiske (1959) recommended researchers to employ multiple (at least two) methods for the assessment of multiple (at least two) constructs. In the simplest case, a (2 methods × 2 traits) multitrait-multimethod design can be studied. It is important to note that Campbell and Fiske (1959) conceived each test score to be affected by trait as well as method (or measurement) influences. Hence, each test score corresponds to a trait-method unit (TMU) according to Campbell's and Fiske's conceptualization of MTMM correlation matrices.

The MTMM correlation matrix (see Figure 25.1) consists of four correlation blocks: (1) the monotrait-monomethod block, (2) the monotrait-heteromethod block, (3) the heterotrait-monomethod block, and (4) the heterotrait-heteromethod block. The monotrait-monomethod block contains the correlations between the same traits measured by the same method. However, in order to take account of measurement errors usually the reliability coefficients are presented in this block. The monotrait-heteromethod block refers to correlations between the same traits measured by different methods. These correlations indicate the degree of convergent validity. That is, to what extent different methods converge in their assessment of a particular trait. Therefore, higher correlations in the monotrait-heteromethod block indicate higher levels of convergent validity. The heterotrait-monomethod block includes correlations between different traits measured by the same method. These correlations indicate whether or not a particular method is sensitive to differences in the traits. Hence, these correlations can be interpreted as the discriminant validity of the measures. High correlations in the heterotrait-monomethod block indicate low discriminant validity. Finally, the heterotrait-heteromethod block contains correlations of different traits measured by different methods. These correlations can be also interpreted as discriminant validity. Campbell and Fiske (1959, pp. 82–83) proposed four different criteria (rules) for the evaluation of MTMM correlation matrices (see also Eid, 2010, pp. 851–852):

1 The correlations in the monotrait-heteromethod block should be statistically significant and large. This property refers to the convergent validity among the measures.

2. The correlations in the heterotrait-heteromethod block should be smaller or equal to the correlations in the heterotrait-monomethod block. This property concerns the discriminant validity of the measures.
3. The correlations in the heterotrait-monomethod block should be smaller than the correlations in the monotrait-heteromethod block. This property also refers to the discriminant validity of the measures.
4. The pattern of the trait intercorrelations in all heterotrait triangles should be similar for the mono- as well as the heteromethod blocks. This property also refers to the discriminant validity of the measures.

Despite the fact that these criteria (rules) are easy to apply in practice, they are limited in several ways (see also Eid, 2010).

First of all, it is difficult to apply the previously mentioned criteria, if the correlations in the MTMM matrix are based on manifest test scores instead of true-score variables, given that they may be distorted due to the influence of measurement error (Eid, 2010). Second, there is no statistical test for the fulfillment of specific MTMM criteria. Third, given that in the classical MTMM analysis there are no measurement models for trait and/or method effects, it is not feasible to decompose the total variance of the manifest test scores into different variance components such as trait-, method-, and/or measurement error variance. Fourth, it is not possible to include other external variables in the validation process in order to explain trait or method effects.

Nowadays, MTMM measurement designs are frequently analyzed with confirmatory factor models (CFA-MTMM models). For an overview of CFA-MTMM models see Dumenci (2000), Eid, Lischetzke, and Nussbeck (2006), as well as Shrout and Fiske (1995). CFA-MTMM models have many advantages. For example, CFA-MTMM models allow (1) separating unsystematic measurement error variance from systematic trait or method influences, (2) relating latent trait or method variables to other external variables in order to explain trait or method effects, and (3) testing specific assumptions with regard to the measurement model (Dumenci, 2000; Eid et al., 2006). Besides that, alternative MTMM approaches such as variance component models (Browne, 1984; Dudgeon, 1994; Millsap 1995a, 1995b; Wothke, 1995; Wothke & Browne, 1990) or multiplicative correlation models (Wothke & Browne, 1990) have been proposed.

However, in the present work we will only focus on CFA-MTMM models. One of the first significant developments in the field of CFA-MTMM models was provided by Keith Widaman (1985). Widaman presented a taxonomy of CFA models for multitrait-multimethod data with (t) traits and (m) methods. In total, Widaman (1985) proposed 16 different CFA models for all possible combinations of four trait structures (i.e., no trait factor, general trait factor, t orthogonal trait factors, t oblique trait factors) and four method structures (i.e., no method factor, general method factor, m orthogonal method factors, m oblique method factors).

One of the simplest CFA-MTMM models of this taxonomy is the CT-model (see Figure 25.2A) that just assumes correlated trait factors, but no method factors. In the Correlated Trait-Correlated Uniqueness (CT-CU, see Figure 25.2B) model (Kenny, 1976; Marsh, 1989; Marsh & Bailey, 1991) there are t correlated trait factors, no method factors, but correlated error variables (unique factors). The correlations between the trait factors in the CT-CU model reflect the degree of discriminant validity. That means, to what extent one method (e.g., self-reports) can differentiate between different constructs (e.g., empathy or aggression). High correlations indicate a lack

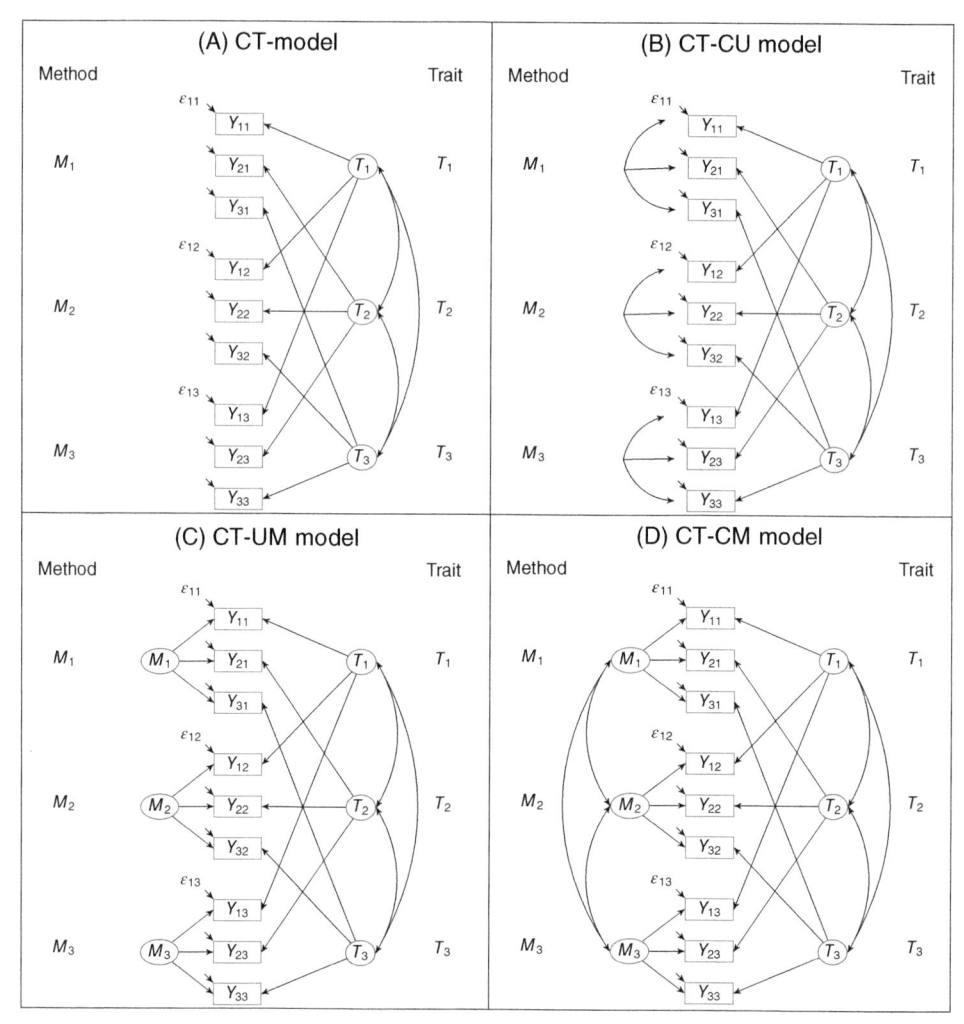

Figure 25.2 Single-indicator CFA-MTMM models. (A) Correlated Trait (CT) model; (B) Correlated Trait-Correlated Uniqueness (CT-CU) model; (C) Correlated Trait-Uncorrelated Method (CT-UM) model; and (D) Correlated Trait-Correlated Method (CT-CM) model Y_{jk} = observed variable, j = trait, k = method. T_j = trait factor. M_k = method factor. ε_{jk} = measurement error. Factor loadings are not depicted for reasons of simplicity.

of discriminant validity. Since there are no method factors in the CT-CU model, the method effects are confounded with measurement error as well as indicator-specific effects (see Geiser, 2008). Furthermore, the CT-CU model becomes more complex as the number of traits and methods increase, given that more correlations among the unique factors have to be estimated (see Geiser, 2008 as well as Lance, Noble, & Scullen, 2002 for a detailed critique). In the Correlated Trait-Correlated Method (CT-CM, see Figure 25.2D) model (Marsh & Grayson, 1995; Widaman, 1985), the method effects are directly modelled (instead of indirectly represented by correlations among residual variables). Hence, in the CT-CM models as many traits and method factors are modelled as there are traits and methods in the given measurement design.

The trait factors are allowed to correlate with each other as are the method factors. However, correlations between trait and method factors are not permissible. The advantage of the CT-CM model is that it allows for the decomposition of observed variance into trait, method, and error variance. The Correlated Trait-Uncorrelated Method (CT-UM, see Figure 25.2C) model is a more restrictive variant of the CT-CM model and implies that the method effects do not generalize across different methods (Eid et al., 2006, Geiser, 2008).

With regard to these "traditional" CFA-MTMM models, the meaning of the trait and method factors often remains unclear. This is due to the fact that in traditional CFA-MTMM analysis it is just assumed that trait and method factors exist. However, in order to properly interpret trait and method effects, it is important to clarify what the latent factors mean. Recent developments in stochastic measurement theory (see Steyer, 1989; Zimmerman, 1975) have provided an approach to define the factors of MTMM models in terms of **random variables** in a well-defined random experiment. As a consequence of this definition, the existence as well as the meaning of the latent factors is clarified. Many different models for different purposes and data structures can be defined in this way. However, not all of the traditional CFA-MTMM models that have been proposed in the past can be construed in this way. In the present work, we will focus on CFA-MTMM models that can be clearly defined on the basis of stochastic measurement theory. Moreover, we will discuss the meaning of other CFA-MTMM models from the perspective of stochastic measurement theory and show why the definition of CFA-MTMM models in terms of stochastic measurement theory is superior to the traditional definition of CFA-MTMM models.

In the next section, we will show how different MTMM models can be described by a specific random experiment, how observed and latent variables can be **constructively** defined within these random experiments, and how MTMM models can be derived straightforwardly. The current chapter is structured as follows: First, we will familiarize the reader with two important concepts of measurement theory (i.e., the random experiment and constructively defined latent variables) by revisiting the basic concepts of classical test theory (CTT). Second, we will show how the type of method (i.e., structurally different method, interchangeable method or a combination of both methods) used in the MTMM measurement design can guide the model selection process. More specifically, we will show that different types of methods imply different random experiments and thereby different data structures and different MTMM models for different types of methods. Moreover, we will compare common CFA-MTMM models (i.e., CT-CM CT-UM, CT-C(M-1), latent means, and latent differences models) in terms of their underlying random experiments. We will thereby show that the CFA-MTMM models following the M-1 modelling approach (i.e., CT-C(M-1), the latent means, and latent differences models) are superior to CFA-MTMM models following the M modelling approach (i.e., the CT-CM and the CT-UM model) in cases of MTMM measurement designs with structurally different methods. Third, we will discuss CFA-MTMM models for measurement designs with interchangeable methods. In the case of measurement designs with interchangeable methods, it is shown how to constructively define a multilevel CFA-MTMM model or a classical (single-level) CFA-MTMM model. Fourth, we will present a CFA-MTMM model that combines structurally different and interchangeable methods. All models presented in this chapter will be illustrated with empirical applications. Finally, we will show how some of the CFA-MTMM models presented here can be extended to longitudinal MTMM measurement designs.

The Psychometric Foundation of CFA-MTMM Models

CFA models of classical test theory (CTT)

Latent variables, such as true scores or error variables, can be considered as random variables. Random variables are always defined in terms of a random experiment that maps onto a set of possible outcomes. In order to fully understand the meaning of the latent variables the set of possible outcomes has to be specified and it has to be shown how the variables can be defined in terms of the set of possible outcomes. Latent variable models (e.g., CFA-MTMM models) that cannot be constructively defined based on the set of possible outcomes are tenuous, at best, since in consequence the meaning of such latent variables remains ambiguous. One of the simplest latent variable models is a one factor model (see Figure 25.3C), which can also be linked to CTT; Bollen, 1989; Jöreskog, 1969, 1971; Lord & Novick, 1968; Steyer, 1989; Steyer & Eid, 2001).

In CTT, the random experiment is the Cartesian cross-product of two sets (see Steyer, 1989; Steyer & Eid, 2001):

$$\Omega = \Omega_U \times \Omega_M, \tag{25.1}$$

where Ω is the set of possible outcomes, Ω_U is the set of possible observational units u (e.g., targets), Ω_M is the set of possible observations (e.g., a response on a Likert scale). Note that the set of possible outcomes Ω_M may contain more than a single outcome from a single item or test, e.g. the set of possible values of the first six items in a questionnaire Hence, $\Omega_M = \Omega_{M_1} \times \ldots \times \Omega_M I$, with i = {1, ..., I}. The Cartesian product operator is denoted by $\times$. The random experiment which corresponds to CTT implies that first a person u (e.g., Larry) is randomly drawn out of a set of possible observational units Ω_U, and then a possible value m (e.g., 4) out of a set of possible values Ω_M is observed. Thus, for the simplest case, a possible outcome ω might be given by:

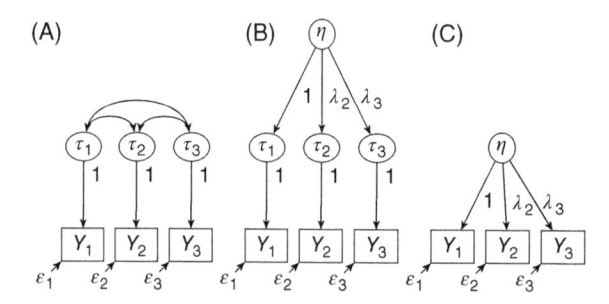

Figure 25.3 Definition of a common factor model. (A) Correlated true-score model; (B) Reparameterizing model A by assuming τ-congeneric true-score variables and defining a common factor η; and (C) Rearranging model A and B to be consistent with the classical path diagram for a common factor model. Y_i = observed variable, i = indicator, η = common latent factor, ε_i = measurement error, λ_i = factor loading. The first factor loading has to be set to a positive real number (here: 1) for identification reasons. All models are data equivalent.

$\omega = \{Larry, 4\}$. That is, Larry achieved a score of 4 on a single test or a single item. In frequency-based probability theory, it is assumed that the experiment can be repeated an infinite number of times under the same conditions.

Furthermore, two mappings are required for defining the latent variables. First, the mapping $p_U : \Omega \to \Omega_U$, which maps the possible outcomes to the set of observational units. Second, the mapping $Y_i : \Omega \to \mathbb{R}$, which maps the possible outcomes to the real numbers. With respect to these mappings, the true-score and the measurement error variables for each item i can be **constructively** defined. For example, the true-score variable τ_i is defined as the conditional expectation of Y_i given the person-variable (p_U), that is $\tau_i = E(Y_i | p_U)$. The measurement error variable ε_i is defined as difference between the observed variable Y_i and the true-score variable τ_i, hence $\varepsilon_i = Y_i - E(Y_i | p_U)$.

One may ask, why are these formal definitions important? The answer is: Once we set up the random experiment and constructively define the random variables in the probability space, we can derive important properties of the latent variables.[2] For example, with regard to the definitions of the true-score and measurement error variables previously, we are able to logically derive the following properties:

$$Cov(\tau_i, \varepsilon_i) = 0, \tag{25.2}$$

$$Y_i = \tau_i + \varepsilon_i, \tag{25.3}$$

$$Var(Y_i) = Var(\tau_i) + Var(\varepsilon_i), \tag{25.4}$$

$$E(\varepsilon_i) = 0. \tag{25.5}$$

The properties are sometimes called axioms of CTT (e.g., Embretson, 1991; Novick, 1966). However, in contrast to the axiomatic definition of CTT, it can be shown that the properties (Equations 25.2–25.5) are direct consequences of the definition of the latent variables and thus are always true in terms of stochastic measurement theory (see Steyer, 1989, Steyer & Eid, 2001, Zimmerman, 1975). In order to estimate parameters of the model shown previously, one additional assumption has to be imposed in CTT. This assumption refers to the associations between different measurement error variables, $Cov(\varepsilon_i, \varepsilon_j) = 0$, for $i \neq j$. Additional assumptions may also be introduced with regard to the latent true-score variables τ_i and τ_j pertaining to different indictors i and j (e.g., items, tests) or with regard to the variance of different latent measurement error variables i and j:

$$\tau_i = \tau_j, \tag{25.6}$$

$$\tau_i = \tau_j + \alpha_{ij}, \tag{25.7}$$

$$\tau_i = \alpha_{ij} + \lambda_{ij} \tau_j, \tag{25.8}$$

The first assumption implies that all latent true-score variables τ_i and τ_j are identical (i.e., perfectly correlated with each other). If the assumption holds, one can replace the latent true-score variables τ_i by a common latent variable η. Note that the index i for the item is not needed in Equation 25.9 (given that Equation 25.6 holds) and is

---

[2] For a detailed description of stochastic measurement theory see also Steyer & Eid (2001).

therefore dropped. Consequently, the general measurement equation for the model (of τ-equivalent variables) can be written as follows:

$$Y_i = \eta + \varepsilon_i. \tag{25.9}$$

Due to the additive decomposition (see Equations 25.2 and 25.9), the reliability coefficient can be defined by:

$$Rel(Y_i) = \frac{Var(\eta)}{Var(\eta) + Var(\varepsilon_i)} = \frac{Var(\eta)}{Var(Y_i)}. \tag{25.10}$$

The model of *τ-equivalent* variables (see Equation 25.9) assumes that the latent true-score variables τ_i and τ_j are equivalent (see Equation 25.6). An even more restrictive variant of this model of *τ-equivalent* variables is obtained by additionally assuming that the variances of the latent measurement error variables $Var(\varepsilon_i)$ are equivalent:

$$Var(\varepsilon_i) = Var(\varepsilon_j). \tag{25.11}$$

This more restrictive model is called the *τ-parallel* variable model. The τ-parallel variable model implies that the latent true scores variables τ_i and τ_j are equivalent (Equation 25.6) and that the reliabilities of the observed variables Y_i and Y_j are equivalent (see Equation 25.10 and 25.11). The second assumption (Equation 25.7) states that the latent true-score variables τ_i and τ_j are **essentially** τ-equivalent, and only differ by an additive constant α_{ij}. The constant α_{ij} is defined as the difference between the true-score variables τ_i and τ_j and is usually referred to as the difficulty parameter. The general measurement equation of this model (of **essentially** τ-equivalent variables) can be expressed as follows:

$$Y_i = \alpha_i + \eta + \varepsilon_i. \tag{25.12}$$

Again, if, additionally, the measurement error variances are assumed to be equivalent (Equation 25.11), this model can be called the **essentially** τ-parallel variable model. The least restrictive variant of CTT measurement models is the model with τ-**congeneric** variables (see Figure 25.3B and C), also known as the "common factor model" (e.g., Bollen, 1989; Jöreskog, 1969, 1971). In the common factor model the latent true-score variables τ_i and τ_j are positive linear transformations of each other (see Equation 25.8). Hence, the general equation of this model (of τ-congeneric variables) is given by:

$$Y_i = \alpha_i + \lambda_i \eta + \varepsilon_i. \tag{25.13}$$

It is important to note that the implications of these assumptions (see Equation 25.2–25.8 and 25.11) can be empirically tested and the parameters of the model can be estimated by CFA. In Figure 25.3 (A to C), it is illustrated how the "common" factor model (with *τ-congeneric* variables) can be defined in three steps. In the next section, it will be shown how MTMM models can be defined in a similar way.

CFA models for different MTMM measurement designs

Following a similar logic, CFA-MTMM models can be constructively defined. However, it is crucial to consider the differences between structurally different and interchangeable methods first. The reason for this is that measurement designs with different types of methods imply different random experiments, and thereby they have different implications for the definition of latent trait and latent method variables (see, e.g., Eid, et al., 2008; Kenny, 1995). In general, MTMM measurement designs can either incorporate (1) structurally different methods, (2) interchangeable methods, or (3) a combination of both types of methods (see Eid et al., 2008). Structurally different methods are methods that stem from **different** method (rater) populations. For example, leaders' self-reports are different from reports by supervisors or colleagues because the ratings stem from different rater distributions. The same applies to ratings by someone's partner versus ratings by their friends. Moreover, these methods may have little in common, given that these methods (raters) may have different perspectives on the target's behavior. Consequently, these methods cannot be easily replaced by one another. Structurally different methods are also often fixed for each target (see Figure 25.4A). For example, the ratings of the significant others (e.g., **the** partner or **the** best friend) are considered as being fixed[3] for each person. In contrast, interchangeable methods are methods that stem out of a unique method (rater) distribution. For example, consider multiple colleague ratings for leadership quality. In other words, interchangeable methods (e.g., colleagues) are not fixed for a particular target (e.g., leader), but rather randomly drawn out of a common target-specific rater population (see Figure 25.4B). From a conceptual point of view, interchangeable methods correspond to random factors in analysis of variance, whereas the structurally different methods are similar to fixed factors in analysis of variance (see Eid et al., 2008; Hays, 1994). In the case of random factors, the different factorial groups are considered as randomly chosen from a population (e.g., some colleagues out of all the colleagues a leader has), and the researcher aims to estimate the mean and the variance of the factor. In contrast, the fixed effect model aims at analyzing the specific effects of different groups that are not randomly chosen and to contrast them (e.g., the leader's self-rating).

In many cases, MTMM measurement designs consist of a combination of structurally different and interchangeable methods. For example, in 360-degree feedback designs (see, e.g., Ghorpade, 2000; Mahlke, et al., 2015), multiple sources (e.g., employees' self-reports, supervisor reports, and colleague reports) for the evaluation of the work performance of a particular target (e.g., employee) are collected (see Figure 25.4C).

In the following sections, we will present appropriate MTMM models for (1) structurally different methods, (2) interchangeable methods, and (3) the combination of both. We will define **trait** and **method factors** in detail and discuss the concept of method bias for each model. Moreover, we will illustrate each model with an empirical application. In contrast to the traditional MTMM matrix that considers one indicator for each trait-method combination we will focus on multiple-indicator models. Only a few multiple-indicator models for MTMM data exist (Eid, Lischetzke, Nussbeck, & Trierweiler, 2003; Marsh, 1993; Marsh & Hocevar, 1988), but they have strong

---

[3] Note that the distinction between structurally different and interchangeable methods is based on theoretical as well as substantive considerations. For detailed guidelines for choosing a reference method see Geiser et al. (2008).

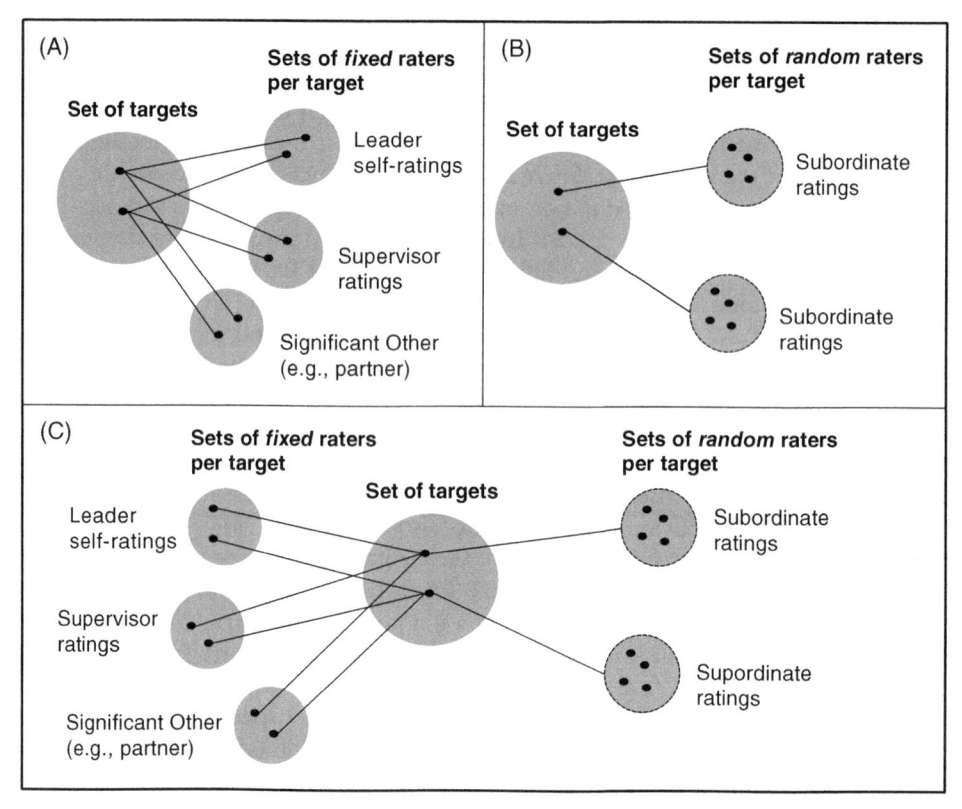

Figure 25.4 Illustration of the sampling procedures for MTMM measurement designs for different types of methods. (A) Sampling procedure for MTMM measurement designs with structurally different (fixed) methods; (B) Sampling procedure for MTMM measurement designs with interchangeable (random) methods; and (C) Sampling procedure for MTMM measurement designs with a combination of structurally different and interchangeable (random) methods. Straight lines that connect the black dots (targets and rater) directly indicate that the rater is fixed for a particular target. Straight lines that connect the black dots with gray circles indicate that the rater in the set of possible raters can be randomly chosen for each target.

advantages over single-indicator models (Eid et al., 2006). They provide a general method for separating measurement error from trait-specific method influences, and they allow for a statistical test of the hypothesis that method effects are trait specific. For simplicity, we will only use two indicators for each TMU. We chose two indicators for several reasons. First, models with two indicators are the simplest extension of single-indicator models. Second, in MTMM analyses, there are often only very few indicators available for one trait-method combination. Third, in order to separate measurement error from method-specific influences two indicators are sufficient. Fourth, without loss of generality all models can easily be extended to more than two indicators. Moreover, we will compare different MTMM models that have been proposed in the literature (e.g., the CT-CM model, the CT-UM model, the CT-C(M-1) model, the latent means model, and the latent difference model) and discuss the advantages and disadvantages of these models. For simplicity, we will refer to raters as methods (Kenny, 1995), but the models proposed in this work can be easily transferred to other types of methods.

Finally, we illustrate how the CFA-MTMM models for structurally different methods, interchangeable methods, and a combination of both methods can be extended to longitudinal MTMM measurement designs.

Defining CFA-MTMM models for structurally different methods

Again, the starting point for the definition of appropriate CFA-MTMM models for structurally different methods is the random experiment. The random experiment for MTMM measurement designs with three structurally different methods (e.g., method 1 = leaders' self-ratings, method 2 = supervisor ratings, method 3 = best friend or partner ratings) is given by:

$$\Omega = \Omega_T \times \Omega_{ij1} \times \Omega_{ij2} \times \Omega_{ij3}. \qquad (25.14)$$

According to Equation 25.14, the set of possible outcomes Ω is the Cartesian product of the set of possible targets Ω_T and the set of possible values (Ω_{ijk}, ratings) with respect to indicator i of trait j given by rater (method) k. Note that in case of structurally different raters, there is no set of possible raters because the raters are **not** randomly chosen, but **fixed** for each target. If, for example, three structurally different raters (k = 1, 2, 3) and only one indicator i of one trait j are considered, it is sufficient to consider a set Ω_{ijk} of possible outcomes that contains the possible ratings of rater k with respect to indicator i of trait j. In this case, the possible outcome is ω = (Larry, self-rating, supervisor rating, partner rating) [e.g., (Larry, 4, 3, 5)]. It is worth noting that the random experiment for MTMM measurement design with structurally different raters is similar to the random experiment of the CTT described before. Similar to the random experiment of CTT, two mappings are required for defining latent true-score variables with regard to the MTMM measurement design.

First, the mapping of the set of possible outcomes into the set of possible targets that is given by:

$$p_T : \Omega \to \Omega_T \qquad (25.15)$$

Second the mapping of the possible outcomes of the ratings in the set of real numbers can be expressed by:

$$\Upsilon_{tijk} : \Omega \to \mathbb{R} \qquad (25.16)$$

The values of this random variable Υ_{tijk} are the observed values of the ith indicator of the jth trait of target subject t rated by rater k. The true-score variables are defined as the conditional expectations of Υ_{tijk} given the target-variable $p_T : \tau_{tijk} = E(\Upsilon_{tijk}| p_T)$. Figure 25.5(A) shows the basic CFA-MTMM measurement model with correlated true-score variables. Similar to the models of CTT (see Figure 25.3 parts A–C), the basic CFA-MTMM measurement model assumes τ-*congeneric* true-score variables for each TMU (see Figure 25.5 parts A–C). In other words, it is assumed that the true-score variables pertaining to the same construct and method (rater), but different indicators are positive linear transformations of each other. Hence, the indicator-specific true-score variables were replaced by common true-score variables, similar as shown before

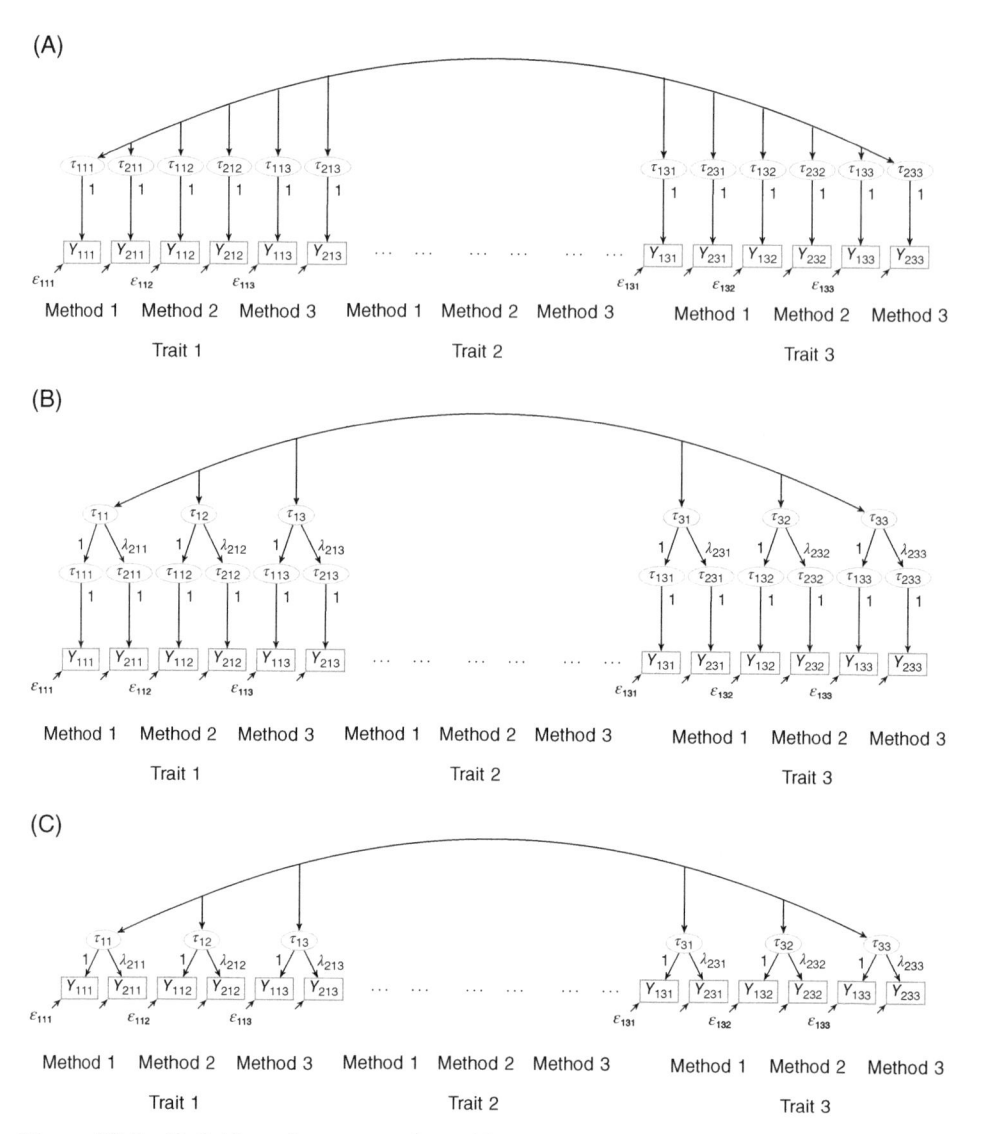

Figure 25.5 Definition of a common factor TMU model for two indicators, three traits, and three methods. (A) Model with correlated indicator-specific latent true-score variables; (B) Reparameterizing model A by assuming τ-*congeneric* true-score variables and defining a common true-score factor τ_{jk} for each TMU; and (C) Rearranging model A and B to be consistent with the classical path diagram for a common factor TMU model. Y_{ijk} = observed variable, i = indicator, j = trait, k = method, τ_{jk} = common factor for each TMU, ε_{ijk} = measurement error, λ_{ijk} = factor loading. All models are data equivalent and in line with the basic idea of MTMM matrices by Campbell and Fiske (1959).

for CTT measurement models (Figure 25.4C). For simplicity, we omitted the index for the target t in the subsequent figures, given that all raters are fixed for each target. Instead, we only used three indices in the path diagrams of the single-level CFA models: i for indicator, j for construct (trait), and k for method (rater).

The main advantage of the common factor TMU model (see Figure 25.5C) is that systematic influences (i.e., true variance) can be separated from unsystematic influences (i.e., measurement error variance). Therefore, researchers are able to estimate the reliability of their measures and investigate the correlations among the latent variables. Moreover, the common factor TMU model is fully in line with the original idea of the MTMM matrix by Campbell and Fiske (1959). However, with regard to the common factor TMU model it is not feasible to separate construct from method effects. More precisely, the common true-score variables in the common factor TMU model contain both construct as well as method-specific influences.

In fixed factor ANOVA models, researchers often use different coding schemes in order to examine the effect of a factor level. For example, in fixed factor ANOVA there are at least two ways to analyze the effect of a factor level: A factor level can be contrasted with another factor level, and a factor level can be compared with the mean (or another linear combination) of all levels. Researchers usually choose between these different (contrast or effect) coding schemes according to their substantive theory and specific hypotheses. In this section, we will show how method effects for structurally different (fixed) methods can be defined in a similar way. Specifically, we will argue that the different definitions of method effects in CFA-MTMM models (i.e., the CT-C(M-1) model, the latent difference model, and the latent means models) are similar to the differences of coding schemes in analysis of variance (see also Geiser et al., 2012).

Before we present the different models for a classical MTMM structure, we will first discuss three different ways to define trait and method factors for only one trait and three methods. We will then extend the measurement models for a single trait to the analysis of three traits and three methods. We will describe two kinds of method factors that are based on the idea of contrasting two methods: First, a latent regression model and, second, a latent difference model. A third possibility is based on the definition of a trait factor as the mean of the true-score variables of all methods. In this case, the deviation of the true-score variable for one method from the mean of all methods is considered as the method variable.

Latent regression/CT-C(M-1) models

In latent regression models such as the Correlated-Trait-Correlated-(Method-1) Model [CT-C(M-1) model; see Eid, 2000; Eid et al., 2003, 2008] one method is taken as the comparison standard (reference method, e.g., leader's self-report). The true-score variable of a nonreference method (e.g., supervisor rating) is regressed on the true-score variable (belonging to the same indicator) of the reference method (e.g., leader's self-report). These linear latent regressions can be formally described by:

$$E(\tau_{tij2}|\tau_{tij1}) = \alpha_{\tau ij2} + \lambda_{\tau ij2}\tau_{tij1} \quad (1^{st} \text{nonreference method}) \quad (25.17)$$

$$E(\tau_{tij3}|\tau_{tij1}) = \alpha_{\tau ij3} + \lambda_{\tau ij3}\tau_{tij1} \quad (2^{nd} \text{nonreference method}) \quad (25.18)$$

The residuals of these latent regressions represent method-specific effects that are unique to a nonreference method (e.g., supervisor ratings) and are not shared with the reference method (e.g., leaders' self-reports). Hence, the residuals of the linear latent regressions (see Equations 25.17 and 25.18) can be defined as latent method variables:

$$M_{tij2} = \tau_{tij2} - E(\tau_{tij2}|\tau_{tij1}) \quad (1^{st}\text{nonreference method}) \quad (25.19)$$

$$M_{tij3} = \tau_{tij3} - E(\tau_{tij3}|\tau_{tij1}) \quad (2^{nd}\text{nonreference method}) \quad (25.20)$$

The method variables M_{tij2} of the supervisor ratings (see Equation 25.19) represent the deviation of the error-free supervisor ratings from the value of these ratings that are predicted by the leaders' self-ratings. Similarly, the method variables M_{tij3} of the significant other ratings (see Equation 25.20) reflect the "true" ratings of a significant other ratings that is not shared with the self-reports. Moreover, because one method is taken as reference method, there are only M-1 method variables (where M = total number of methods). Due to the fact that the latent method variables are defined as latent residuals with respect to the reference method (see Equations 25.19 and 25.20), the general properties of residual variables apply as well:

$$E(M_{tijk}) = 0 \quad (25.21)$$

$$\text{Cov}(M_{tijk}, \tau_{tij1}) = \text{Cov}(M_{tijk}, \varepsilon_{tijk}) = \text{Cov}(\tau_{tij1}, \varepsilon_{tijk}) = 0. \quad (25.22)$$

According to Equations 25.21 and 25.22 the expected values of the method residual variables are always zero. Moreover, the method variables are not correlated with their regressors (i.e., the reference method true-score variables, τ_{tij1}). In order to estimate the CT-C(M-1) model described here, it is necessary to impose two additional assumptions. The first assumption concerns the **homogeneity of the latent method variables**. For each method M_{tijk} pertaining to the same trait j and same method k, but different indicator i and i', it is assumed that the latent method variables M_{tijk} and $M_{ti'jk}$ are positive linear functions of a single method factor M_{tjk} and a congeneric measurement structure:

$$M_{tijk} = \lambda_{Mijk} M_{tjk} \quad (25.23)$$

Note that the method factors are different for different traits. That means that the method bias is trait specific (see Figure 25.7A). The steps for defining a CT-C(M-1) model for two indicators, one trait, and three methods are illustrated in Figure 25.6(A–D). The method factors can be correlated across traits, reflecting the degree of the generalizability of method effects. A model with one general (trait-unspecific) method factor indicating the perfect generalizability of method effects is a special case of this more general model. The second assumption concerns the **uncorrelatedness of error variables**. That means, we assume that all error variables are uncorrelated with each other. For two indicators and three traits, these two assumptions taken together, imply the factor model depicted in Figure 25.7(A). This measurement model assumes indicator-specific trait variables. If the indicator-specific trait variables are unidimensional, a model with one latent trait variable and a congeneric measurement structure can be defined instead.

Due to the definition of the latent variables (see previously), the general measurement equation of the CT-C(M-1) model can be expressed as follows:

$$Y_{tij1} = \tau_{tij1} + \varepsilon_{tij1} \quad (\text{reference method}) \quad (25.24)$$

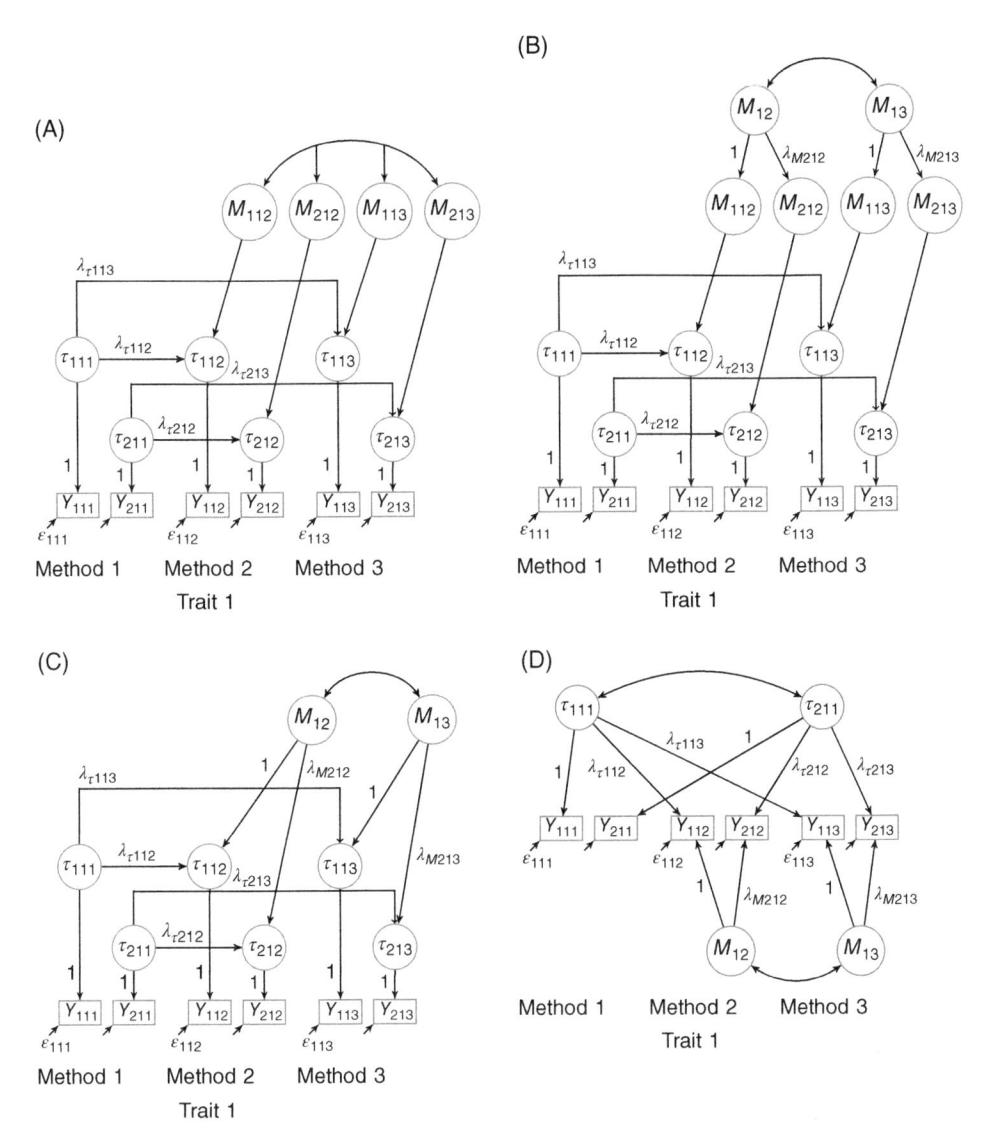

Figure 25.6 Definition of a CT-C(M-1) model for two indicators, one trait, and three methods. (A) Reparameterizing the correlated true-score model by assuming latent linear regressions among the latent true-score variables; (B) Reparameterizing model A by assuming a τ-congeneric structure of the latent method variables M_{ijk}; (C) Rearranging model B by defining common latent method factors M_{jk}; and (D) Rearranging model C to be consistent with the typical representation of the CT-C(M-1) model. Y_{ijk} = observed variable, i = indicator, j = trait, k = method, τ_{ijk} = indicator-specific true-score variables, ε_{ijk} = measurement error, $\lambda_{\tau ijk}$ = regression weights (factor loadings) of the true-score variables, λ_{Mijk} = factor loadings of the method variables, M_{ijk} = indicator-specific latent method variables. M_{jk} = indicator-unspecific latent method variables (i.e., method factors). All models are data equivalent.

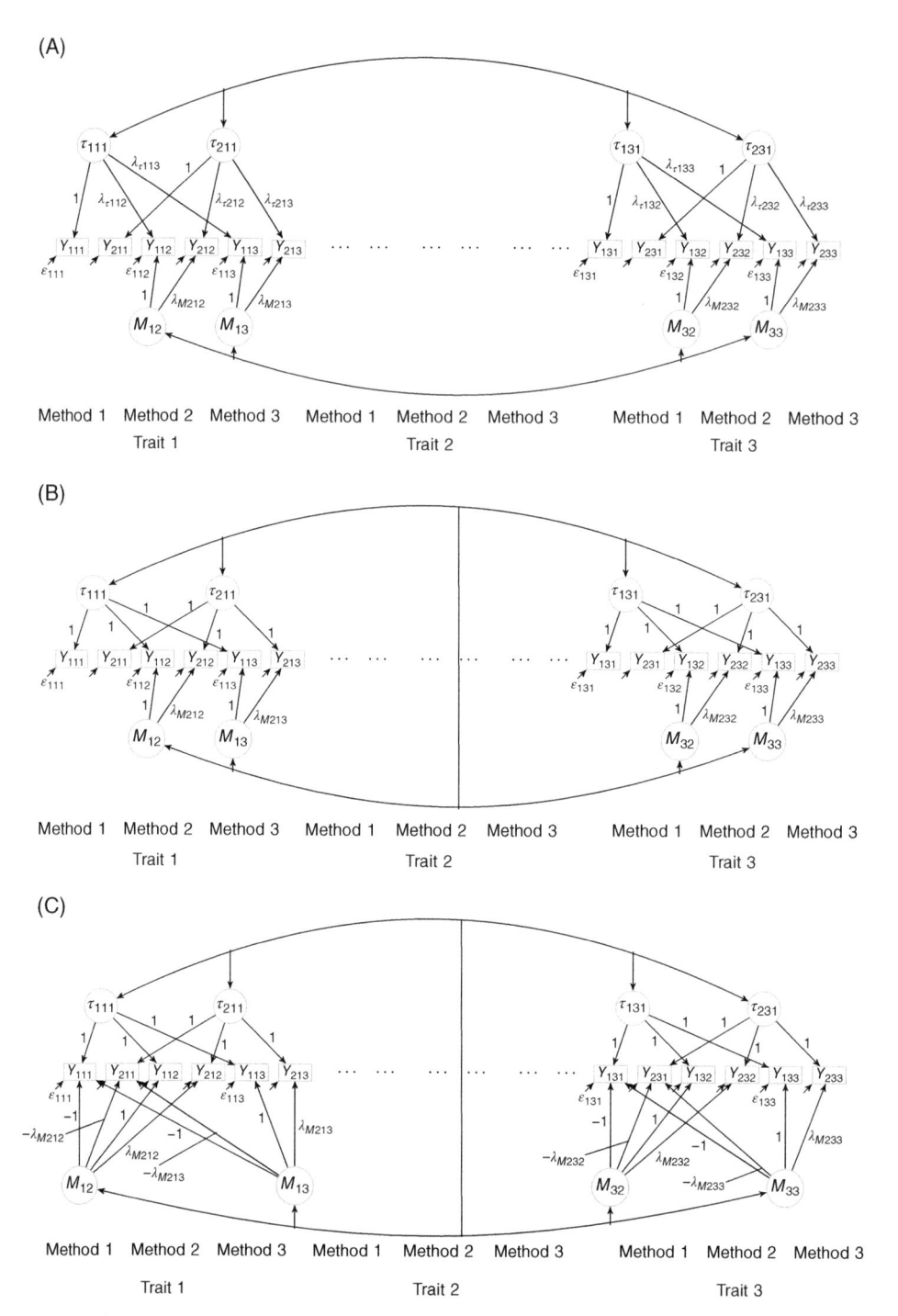

Figure 25.7 Multiple-indicator CFA-MTMM models for two indicators, three traits, and three structurally different methods. (A) Multiple-indicator CT-C(M-1) model; (B) Multiple-indicator latent difference model; and (C) Multiple-indicator latent means model. Y_{ijk} = observed variable, i = indicator, j = trait, k = method, T_{ijk} = indicator-specific trait variables representing the indicator-specific trait factor, ε_{ijk} = measurement error, λ_{Tijk} = factor loadings of the trait variables, λ_{Mijk} = factor loadings of the method variables, M_{jk} = method factors. All models imply specifying M-1 (instead of M) method factors.

$$Y_{tij2} = \alpha_{\tau ij2} + \lambda_{\tau ij2}\tau_{tij1} + \lambda_{Mij2}M_{tj2} + \varepsilon_{tij2} \quad (1^{st}\text{nonreference method}) \quad (25.25)$$

$$Y_{tij3} = \alpha_{\tau ij3} + \lambda_{\tau ij3}\tau_{tij1} + \lambda_{Mij3}M_{tj3} + \varepsilon_{tij3} \quad (2^{nd}\text{nonreference method}) \quad (25.26)$$

Note that the additive decompositions here follow directly, given that the latent method variables M_{tjk} as well as the measurement error variables ε_{tijk} are defined as residuals with respect to the reference-method true scores τ_{tij1}. Hence, the variance of an observed variable can be also additively decomposed into several variance components: For example, coefficients of consistency and method specificity can be defined (see Table 25.1).

The **consistency coefficient** represents the amount of true variance of a nonreference method that is explained by the true-score variable of the nonreference method (see Eid, 2000). The **method specificity coefficient** indicates the amount of true variance of a nonreference method that is specific to a reference method (see Eid, 2000). The coefficients of consistency and method specificity can be also defined based on the amount of **observed** variance of a nonreference method indicator. However, defining the coefficients based on the amount of observed variance makes it difficult to compare these coefficients when the observed indicators (e.g., item or test halves) differ in their reliabilities. This is not the case, if the coefficients are standardized with regard to the **true** variance of the observed indicators.

In sum, CT-C(M-1) models can be defined in three steps. First, choose a reference (standard or comparison) method. According to Geiser, Eid, and Nussbeck (2008) the choice of the reference method should be strongly guided by theoretical considerations as well as substantive research questions. Second, define general (common or indicator-specific) trait variables and M-1 method factors. Third, impose additional constraints with regard to (1) the uncorrelatedness of measurement errors, (2) the uncorrelatedness of method variables with trait variables of the same TMU, and (3) the homogeneity of trait and/or method variables. Moreover, if one puts specific restrictions on the parameters of the model, the model is data equivalent to the common factor TMU model (see Geiser et al., 2008; Geiser, Eid, West, Lischetzke, & Nussbeck, 2012).

Latent difference models

Latent difference models represent a second way to contrast methods. These have been developed for longitudinal research (Steyer, Partchev, & Shanahan, 2000) but can be adapted to multimethod research (see Lischetzke, Eid, & Nussbeck, 2002; Pohl, Steyer, & Kraus, 2008). This modelling approach also requires that one method serves as a reference method. However, the latent method variables are not defined as residuals with respect to the reference method true-score variables. Instead the latent method variables are defined as latent difference variables of true-score variables pertaining to different methods. Specifically, the latent difference variable represents the deviation of the true-score variable of the nonreference method (τ_{tijk}) from the true-score variable of the reference method (τ_{tij1}) $M_{tijk} = \tau_{tijk} - \tau_{tij1}$. A positive value of this variable means that the value of the nonreference method (e.g., supervisor rating) is higher than the value of the reference method (e.g., self-rating). A value of 0 indicates that there are no method-specific effects (the error-free supervisor and self-ratings are the same) whereas a negative value indicates an underestimation of the trait by the nonreference method with respect to the reference method (the supervisor assigns a lower value than

Table 25.1 Definition of the three models for structurally different raters.

	CT-C(M−1) model	Latent difference model	Latent means model
Definition of trait factors	True-score variables of the indicators of the reference method ($k=1$) τ_{tij1}	True-score variables of the indicators of the reference method ($k=1$) τ_{tij1}	Means of the true-score variables of different methods k ($k=1,\ldots,K$) $$T_{tij} = \frac{1}{K}\sum_{k=1}^{K}\tau_{tijk}$$
Definition of method-specific variables (method effects, method bias)	for $k \neq 1$: $M_{tijk} = \tau_{tijk} - (\alpha_{\tau tjk} + \lambda_{\tau tijk}\tau_{tij1})$	for $k \neq 1$: $M_{tijk} = \tau_{tijk} - \tau_{tij1}$	$$M_{tijk} = \tau_{tijk} - \frac{1}{K}\sum_{k=1}^{K}\tau_{tijk}$$
Definition of method factors	$M_{tijk} = \lambda_{Mijk}M_{tjk}$	$M_{tijk} = \alpha_{Mijk} + \lambda_{Mijk}M_{tjk}$	for $k \neq 1$: $M_{tijk} = \alpha_{Mijk} + \lambda_{Mijk}M_{tjk}$
Means of method factors	have to be 0	can be estimated	can be estimated
Correlation between method factors	allowed	allowed	allowed
Correlation between trait and method factors	allowed only for trait and method factors that belong to different traits	allowed	allowed
Complete equations	a. for the indicators of the reference method ($k=1$) $Y_{tij1} = \tau_{tij1} + \varepsilon_{tij1}$ b. for the indicators of the nonreference method ($k \neq 1$) $Y_{tijk} = \alpha_{\tau tjk} + \lambda_{\tau tijk}\tau_{tij1} + \lambda_{Mijk}M_{tjk} + \varepsilon_{tijk}$	a. for the indicators of the reference method ($k=1$) $Y_{tij1} = \tau_{tij1} + \varepsilon_{tij1}$ b. for the indicators of the nonreference method ($k \neq 1$) $Y_{tijk} = \tau_{tij1} + \alpha_{Mijk} + \lambda_{Mijk}M_{tjk} + \varepsilon_{tijk}$	a. For the indicators of the reference method ($k=1$) $Y_{tij1} = T_{tij} + \sum_{k \neq 1}M_{tijk} + \varepsilon_{tij1}$ b. for the indicators of the nonreference method ($k \neq 1$) $Y_{tijk} = T_{tij} + \alpha_{Mijk} + \lambda_{Mijk}M_{tjk} + \varepsilon_{tijk}$

Identifying restrictions	One loading for each method factor or the variance of each method factor has to be fixed to a value larger than 0.	For each method factor (a) one intercept has to be fixed, and (b) one loading or the factor variance has to be fixed to a value larger than 0.	For each method factor (a) one intercept has to be fixed, and (b) one loading or the factor variance has to be fixed to a value larger than 0. The intercept belonging to an indicator of the reference method ($k=1$) is a linear combination of the intercepts of this indicator measured by the other methods. This restriction has also to be implemented by linear constraints.
Variance components	Consistency $$CO(\tau_{tijk}) = \frac{\lambda_{tijk}^2 Var(\tau_{tij1})}{Var(\tau_{tijk})}$$ Method specificity $$MS(\tau_{tijk}) = \frac{\lambda_{Mijk}^2 Var(M_{tjk})}{Var(\tau_{tijk})}$$	none	none

the self-rating of the leader). The least restrictive model of this class of models (model with indicator-specific traits) is depicted in Figure 25.7(B).

As in the other MTMM models presented so far, it is assumed that each indicator has its own trait variable, but that the difference variables (method variables) are unidimensional. Hence, there is a common method factor for all indicators belonging to the same method and the same trait. The formal definition of the model is presented in Table 25.1. If the indicator-specific trait variables are unidimensional, a model with one latent trait variable and a congeneric measurement structure can be defined. Because of the definition of the method variables, the method factors and the trait factors can be correlated.

Latent means models

The latent regression and difference models contrast two methods. As a consequence, the "common" latent trait variables in these models are the true-score variables of the standard method. That means that a common trait factor is not a measure of a trait that is corrected for method effects. Instead, it is totally confounded with the standard method. In some applications, it might be preferable to have a common trait variable representing the mean of different methods. This aggregation principle is widely applied in psychology (Epstein, 1983, 1986; Steyer & Schmitt, 1990). The basic idea of aggregating latent variables is to get rid of specific influences that are due, for example, to methods. One hopes to get a trait value that is more representative of the person and less affected by the measurement method. A latent (indicator-specific) trait variable can be defined as the mean of the true-score variables of the different methods (Pohl & Steyer, 2010). For three methods, the latent trait variable for the first indicator of trait j, for example, is defined as

$$T_{t1j} = (1/3)(\tau_{t1j1} + \tau_{t1j2} + \tau_{t1j3}). \qquad (25.27)$$

A reasonable (indicator-specific) method variable M_{tijk} would be the deviation of the true-score variable of a method k from the trait variable (the mean of the different true scores). For the first indicator, the method variable is defined as:

$$M_{t1jk} = \tau_{t1jk} - T_{t1jk}. \qquad (25.28)$$

For defining a multimethod measurement model on the basis of this approach, it is sufficient to consider only two method factors although we have three methods. The reason for this reduction is that if we know the deviation of two true-score variables from the mean, we also know the deviation of the third true-score variable from the mean. That means that the deviation of the third true-score variable contains redundant information. This describes the same situation that we know from analysis of variance since the definition of method factors presented is perfectly in line with the **effect coding** scheme in analysis of variance. This results in a model with only two method factors for each indicator. A latent means model is depicted in Figure 25.7(C). To be consistent with the CT-C(M-1) model and the latent difference model presented in the last sections, we define the method variables for the second and third method. As in all other models presented so far, we assume that the method variables belonging to the same model are unidimensional. The formal definition of the model is given in Table 25.1. Modelling approaches with a common one-dimensional trait factor can also be defined in a similar manner as in the other models.

Conceptual similarities and differences between the three approaches

Figure 25.7(A–C) reveals several similarities between the three modelling approaches. There are only two method factors although there are three methods considered. For designs with M methods, only M-1 methods are modelled. This differs from other classical CFA models such as the CT-CM (Marsh, 1989) or the CT-UM model (Kenny, 1976), where each method (rater) has its own method factor. In all models, the error variables have to be uncorrelated with the latent variables because the error variables are residuals with respect to the true-score variables and the latent variables are functions of true-score variables.

In the CT-C(M-1) model and the latent difference model the trait factors have the same meaning. They are the true-score variables of the reference method. The trait factor has a different meaning in the latent means model in which the trait factor is the mean of the true-score variables of the different methods. The meanings of the method factors differ between the three approaches. In all three approaches, the method factors are linear functions of the method variables. Therefore, their meaning depends on the meaning of the method variables. In the CT-C(M-1) model the method variable represents the deviations of the true-score variables of a nonreference method from the expected value given the true-score variable of the reference method. A method bias indicates, for example, that the true supervisor rating is higher or lower than the average supervisor rating one expects for a given true self-rating of a particular leader. That means that even if the true supervisor rating equals the true self-rating, there could be a method effect if the regression coefficient differs from one, and the intercept differs from 0. If, for example, the true supervisor rating is 1, the true self-rating of the leader is 1, but the expected (average) supervisor rating for all self-ratings with a true score of 1 is 0.8, there is a method effect – although the true self-rating and supervisor rating are identical. This is not the case in the latent difference model. In this model, a method effect indicates the difference between the true scores of the self-ratings and supervisor ratings and there is no method effect if the true self and the true supervisor ratings do not differ. In the latent means model, the method effects indicate the deviation of a true rating from the mean of all true ratings. As a consequence of their definition the method factors are uncorrelated with the trait factors only in the CT-C(M-1) model. Only in this model, a decomposition of the variance into a component of convergent validity (consistency) and method specificity is possible. Moreover, only with regard to this model it is possible to study "pure" (i.e., free of trait influences) method effects. In the two other approaches method effects are related to trait differences and cannot be separated. For a more detailed comparison of the CT-C(M-1) and the latent difference model see Geiser et al. (2012).

Applications of MTMM Models for Structurally Different Raters

Description of the study

The three modelling approaches described previously will be applied to the same data set in order to illustrate their different theoretical focuses. The data are taken from a cross-sectional 360-degree feedback process that was conducted in a large German bank. Three-hundred-and-sixty-degree feedback assessments make use of multiple informant

Table 25.2 Content of the items used in the analysis.

Construct (trait)	Item	Content
captivating speaking skills	item 1	Puts own arguments forward in a way that others can follow and buy into them.
	item 2	Comes across as positive and authentic.
	item 3	Wins over and enthuses others for own plans and ideas.
	item 4	Explains the advantages of change initiatives convincingly even to critical audiences.
general leadership skills	item 1	Delegates tasks in a way that draws upon the individual strengths of own direct reports.
	item 2	Gives own team members the latitude to tackle tasks in a self-reliant and responsible way.
	item 3	Establishes measurable objectives which serve to motivate own direct reports.
	item 4	Supports the development of employees in own area of responsibility.
	item 5	Ensures roles, goals, and responsibilities are clearly defined.
	item 6	Regularly provides own direct reports with open and respectful feedback on their performance.

Note. The (translated) items were construed by *cut-e* Group (Hamburg). The items were parceled into two test halves for each construct (trait).

ratings (e.g., self-ratings, supervisor ratings, direct reports, colleagues reports, etc.) in order to evaluate the behavior of a particular target person (e.g., employee or leader). Moreover, 360-degree feedback processes can be implemented at different hierarchical levels in the organization. For the subsequent model applications, we used a subset of the original data. The subset consists of 309 leaders (all from the second highest level in the hierarchy) rated by their corresponding supervisors as well as by multiple subordinates (i.e., with on average 4.22 direct reports for each leader). With regard to the following applications of the CFA-MTMM models for structurally different raters, we will only use the self-ratings and the ratings of the supervisors. Hence, in these analyses we do **not** include the multiple ratings of the subordinates. Later in this chapter, we propose a CFA-MTMM model that enables researchers to directly model a varying number of subordinate ratings per target and contrast the common view of the subordinate ratings against the leaders' self-reports. For this application, two dimensions of leadership quality (traits) were selected: **captivating speaking skills** measured by four items and **general leadership skills** measured by six items. Each item was measured using a five-point response scale (1 – not at all true, 5 – totally true). The items and their content is presented in Table 25.2.

In order to create two continuous indicators for each TMU, we split each scale mentioned here into two subscales (parcels). That is, for each scale, two parcels were compiled using half of the items for one parcel and the remaining items for the second parcel. Parcel-scores were constructed by computing the mean of the respective items. For the first construct, **captivating speaking skills**, the following items were combined: item 1 and item 3 (parcel 1); item 2 and item 4 (parcel 2). With regard to the second

Table 25.3 Goodness of fit coefficients for the common factor TMU model for speaking and leadership skills.

Models	χ^2	df	p	CFI	RMSEA	χ^2_{dif}	df_{dif}	p_{dif}
Model 1	15.57	14	.34	1.00	.02	–	–	–
Model 2	19.15	18	.38	1.00	.01	3.64	4	.46
Model 3	**30.24**	**22**	**.11**	**.99**	**.04**	**10.62**	**4**	**.03**
Model 4	117.85	26	<.001	.92	.11	84.17	4	<.001

Note. Model 1 = common factor TMU model with *essentially τ-congeneric* variables per TMU. Model 2 = common factor TMU model with *essentially τ-equivalent* variables per TMU. Model 3 = common factor TMU model with *essentially τ-parallel* variables per TMU. Model 4 = general CFA-MTMM-TMU model with *τ-parallel* variables per TMU. Model 3 (bold) was chosen for further analysis. All models were estimated using the robust maximum likelihood estimator implemented in MPlus. The χ^2-difference testing was done by using the Satorra-Bentler Scaled Chi-Square formula (see Muthén & Muthén, 1998–2012).

construct **general leadership skills** the following items were combined: item 1, item 5, and item 6 (parcel 1); item 2, item 3, and item 4 (parcel 2).

All models were estimated using the robust maximum likelihood (MLR) estimator implemented in MPlus 7.0 (Muthén & Muthén, 1998–2012). Missing data was handled by using full maximum likelihood (FIML) estimation. The coverage rate of present data was relatively high (above 92%), indicating low rate of missingness.

Testing the fit of the models

The common factor TMU model with a *τ-congeneric* factor structure for each TMU (see Table 25.3 Model 1, Code Appendix, Code 1a, and Figure 25.5B–C) fit the data extremely well, $\chi^2(14) = 15.57$, $p = .34$, CFI = 1.00, RMSEA = .02. Given that this general CFA-MTMM model fit the data well, we subsequently imposed further equality restrictions with regard to the factor loadings (Model 2; Code Appendix Code 1b), the measurement error variables (Model 3; Code Appendix Code 1c) and the intercepts of the observed variables (Model 4; Code Appendix Code 1d). The overall fit statistics as well as the results of the χ^2-difference tests are given in Table 25.3.

According to the results in Table 25.3, the common factor TMU model with equal factor loadings and equal measurement error variances per TMU (Model 3) fit the data well, $\chi^2(22) = 30.24$, $p = .11$, CFI 0 = .99, RMSEA = .04. The χ^2-difference test was marginally significant in comparison to the less restrictive version of this model with essential τ-equivalent variables (Model 2), $\chi^2_{dif}(4) = 10.62$, $p = .03$. However, given that the overall model fit was good, we chose this model for further analyses. It is important to note that the three modelling approaches described previously (i.e., the CT-C(*M*-1) model, the latent differences model, and the latent means model) are just reparametrizations of the common factor TMU model and therefore fit the data equally well (see Model 3 in Table 25.3). Hence, the three different models described in the following section show identical model fit.

CT-C(*M*-1) model

See Figure 25.7a, Code Appendix Code 2a. The consistency, method-specificity, and reliability coefficients are reported in Table 25.4. The results show that the reliabilities

Table 25.4 Coefficients of reliability, consistency and method specificity of the MTMM models for structurally different rater with one common trait variable per construct.

	CT-C(M-1)			Latent difference	Latent means
Indicator	Reliability	Consistency	Method specificity	Reliability	Reliability
captivating speaking skills					
Y_{111}	.73	.73 (1.00)	–	.73	.73
Y_{211}	.73	.73 (1.00)	–	.73	.73
Y_{112}	.68	.06 (.08)	.62 (.92)	.68	.68
Y_{212}	.68	.06 (.08)	.62 (.92)	.68	.68
general leadership skills					
Y_{121}	.74	.74 (1.00)	–	.74	.74
Y_{221}	.74	.74 (1.00)	–	.74	.74
Y_{122}	.73	.11 (.15)	.62 (.85)	.73	.73
Y_{222}	.73	.11 (.15)	.62 (.85)	.73	.73

Note. The coefficients in parentheses represent the "true" consistency and "true" method specificity coefficients.

Table 25.5 Means, variances (diagonal), and correlations (subdiagonal) of the trait and method factors in the CT-C(M-1) model, the latent difference model, and the latent means model.

	CT-C(M-1)				Latent difference				Latent means			
	1	2	3	4	1	2	3	4	1	2	3	4
1 T_1	.20				.20				.14			
2 T_2	.84*	.17			.84*	.17			.76*	.13		
3 M_1		–.04	.20		–.56*	–.50*	.30		.06	–.03	.07	
4 M_2	–.08		.76*	.17	–.49*	–.51*	.84*	.23	.02	.08	.84*	.06
Means	2.43*	2.39*	–	–	2.43*	2.39*	0.00	–0.09*	2.43*	2.35*	0.00	–0.04*

Note. * $p < .05$; T_j = trait factor; M_j = trait-specific method factor. Variances of the latent variables are given in the diagonal.

are generally high (between .68 and .74). The method specificities are much higher (.62) than the consistencies (between .06 and .11) indicating a low convergent validity between the leaders' self-ratings and supervisor ratings. Nevertheless, the convergent validity between the leaders' self-ratings and supervisor ratings was higher with regard to the construct **general leadership skills** than to the construct **captivating speaking skills**. That means that leaders and supervisors share more of a common view with regard to the evaluation of **general leadership skills**.

The absolute value of the correlation between the traits is rather high ($r = .84$) indicating low discriminant validity (see Table 25.5). The correlations between the same method factors (supervisors) belonging to the different traits are large as well ($r = .76$). This indicates that supervisors tend to generalize across different traits. In other words, supervisors who tend to over- or underestimate a particular leader's speaking skills also tend to over- or underestimate the leadership skills for the particular person. Correlations between latent trait variables and latent method variables belonging to different constructs j and j' are, in general, permissible in the CT-C(M-1) model. In the empirical application, these correlations are rather low and nonsignificant ($r = -.04$ and $r = -.08$). However, significant correlations would indicate that method effects of one construct are associated with trait effects of another construct (e.g., the deviation of the supervisor leadership ratings from the self-rated leadership quality might be associated with the level of self-rated speaking skills).

Latent difference model

See Figure 25.7b, Code Appendix, Code 2b. The estimated reliabilities (Table 25.4) are identical to the reliabilities estimated in the CT-C(M-1) model. Also. the correlations (Table 25.5) between the trait factors are identical ($r = .84$) because they are the common true-score variables of the reference method in the two models. In the latent difference model, however, the means of the method factors can differ from 0. The mean value of a method factor indicates the general bias of this method for the trait under consideration. For the supervisor rating, the means of the latent method factors do differ significantly from zero with respect to the general leadership skills ($E(M_2) = -0.09$, $p < .05$), but not with regard to the captivating speaking skills ($E(M_1) = 0.00$, $p = .95$). The latent mean of the method factor is negative, which means that, in general, the supervisors underestimate the leadership skills compared to the self-reports of the leaders. The correlations between the latent trait factors and the latent method (difference) factors are all negative and relatively high (range: $r = -.49$ and $r = -.56$; see Table 25.5). For example, the trait factor regarding the first construct (i.e., captivating speaking skills) is negatively correlated with the supervisor method factor for the same construct. This indicates that leaders who tend to rate themselves high with regard to their speaking skills are generally underestimated by the corresponding supervisor. Similarly, high self-rated leadership skills are associated with an underestimation of leadership skills by the supervisor. It is worth noting, that the method effects in the latent difference model are confounded with trait effects. That means, it is not possible to study pure method effects in the latent difference model, given that the trait and method factor can be correlated in this model.

Latent means model

See Figure 25.7(C), Code Appendix Code 2c. The reliabilities for the indicators in the latent means model are depicted in Table 25.4. They do not differ from the parameters for the two other models. The means and correlations of the latent variables in the latent means model are presented in Table 25.5. The means of the latent trait factors reflect that the speaking and leadership skills of the leaders were rated by all methods (i.e., that is self-ratings and supervisor ratings). The mean of the first method factor shows that supervisors do not significantly differ from the overall average (of all ratings). However, the mean of the second method factor does significantly differ from zero, indicating that supervisors tend to underestimate the overall average leadership skills of the leaders. The correlations of the method factors belonging to the same trait as well as their correlations with the trait factors are difficult to interpret because they are not independent from each other. Moreover, the correlations between the trait and method factors pertaining to the same or different constructs are not significant (see Table 25.5), and therefore not of empirical relevance.

Choice of a model

Which of the three models should be selected for an application? The answer to this question depends on the aim of the study and the methods considered. One major decision concerns the question whether one wants to contrast nonreference methods against a reference method or whether one wants to define a trait as the mean of all measures applied. This decision strongly depends on whether a trait defined as the mean of structurally different ratings is meaningful or not. Consider the following example of leaders' self-ratings, supervisor ratings, and the ratings of significant others (e.g., partners). If the target person (e.g., the leader) thinks that she or he is a relatively average leader but the supervisor and the significant other (e.g., best friend) have a fundamentally different perspective and perceive the leadership quality of the given target as below average and/or above average, it is questionable whether the mean of these ratings would be a reasonable trait measure. The mean value would reflect a mixture of all ratings, even though these ratings differ fundamentally from one another. In this case, it would be more reasonable to contrast the self-rating with the supervisor and the rating of the best friend in order to explain this difference (method effect) and to find out why the supervisor and the best friend differ from the self-rated leadership quality. Hence, the first decision one has to make is to decide whether a trait as mean value is meaningful or not. If one wants to contrast methods one has to decide whether the CT-C(M-1) or the latent difference model should be applied. If one wants to have "pure" method effects which are not related to trait differences, and if one wants to estimate the degree of method specificity, the CT-C(M-1) model should be preferred. For example, if one wants to explain why supervisor ratings differ from leaders' self-ratings and if one wants to analyze pure method effects of the supervisor ratings that are not shared with the leader her- or himself, the CT-C(M-1) model can be applied. Moreover, the method variables can be related to other variables in order to explain method effects. If the aim, however, is to consider the differences between self and supervisor ratings then the latent difference model is preferable. In this model, however, the method factor can also share some variance with the trait factor, and the degree of method specificity cannot be quantified.

Geiser et al. (2012) discuss two further advantages of the CT-C(M-1) model over the two other models. First, the CT-C(M-1) model offers the estimation of variance components indicating the degree of convergent validity versus method specificity. Second, because the model is a regression type model, it is not necessary that the three types of raters use the same scales. If the raters use different scales, the interpretation of a difference score and a mean score might be difficult. In this case, the CT-C(M-1) model seems to be more appropriate because the regression of nonreference method indicators on the trait variable is not affected by scaling differences (see Geiser et al., 2012). Moreover, the method factors defined as residuals allow for a clearer interpretation than the method factors defined as difference variables or as deviations from a mean. The latter are very difficult to interpret when the methods are structurally quite different and consist of very different scales (e.g., self-reports, implicit measures, physiological measures). However, as Pohl et al. (2008) showed the latent difference model can be used for the analysis of individual causal effects, if other potential causes can be ruled out (see also Geiser et al., 2012).

M versus *M*-1 modelling approaches for structurally different methods

In the previous section, we focused on MTMM measurement designs with structurally different methods. Structurally different methods are methods that stem out of different method (rater) populations. Given that these raters may fundamentally differ in their perspectives on the targets' behavior, researchers may be particularly interested in comparing these different perspectives with one another and may want to scrutinize why these perspectives differ by including different explanatory background variables. Moreover, structurally different methods (raters) are fixed (i.e., determined beforehand) for each target, similarly to fixed factors in the analysis of variance (see Eid et al., 2008). We discussed three different CFA-MTMM models that can be properly defined with regard to the random experiment of measurement designs with structurally different methods. Specifically, we showed that the latent variables of the CT-C(M-1), the latent difference, and the latent mean model can be constructively defined with regard to the random experiment. Therefore, the latent variables of these models have a clear psychometric meaning. Moreover, we showed that all models are data equivalent to the common factor TMU model. Hence, the three models discussed before are in line with the basic conceptualization of the MTMM correlation matrix of Campbell and Fiske (1959). The three models have in common that one method factor less is specified than there are methods in the actual measurement design. We argued that the *M*-1 modelling approach is similar to different coding schemes in fixed factor ANOVA. Coding schemes such as effect or contrast coding are widely accepted in psychology and statistics, given that they enable researchers to study the effects of specific factor levels.

In contrast to that, the CT-CM model (see Figure 25.2D; Marsh & Grayson, 1995; Widaman, 1985) requires specifying *M*, instead of *M*-1 method factors. In the CT-CM model, it is assumed that the trait and method factors exist and have a clear meaning. However, it is not possible to constructively define the CT-CM model on the basis of stochastic theory using random experiments as outlined previously. Moreover, with regard to the analogy of different coding schemes in fixed factor ANOVA, the CT-CM model is similar to using as many contrasts or dummy variables as there are factor levels in the design. As a consequence of this, the CT-CM model is highly overfactorized and overfits the data in comparison to the *M*-1 models or the common factor TMU model (see Geiser, Koch, & Eid, 2014). This overfactorization of the CT-CM model (caused by specifying more method factors than needed) leads to problems of model identification, convergence, improper solutions, and interpretation difficulties of resulting parameter estimates (Eid, 2000; Grayson & Marsh, 1995; Kenny & Kashy, 1992; Marsh, 1989). Moreover, the CT-CM model is not globally identified (Grayson & Marsh, 1994), whereas the CT-C(M-1) model is (see Eid, 2000). For example, it was not possible to estimate the CT-CM model for our example data due to identification problems. These methodological as well as conceptual problems of the CT-CM model are well-known (e.g., Marsh, 1989; Marsh & Bailey, 1991). They arise given that the random experiment for MTMM measurement designs with structurally different methods requires researchers to consider that the methods are fixed and **not** randomly drawn out of a common set of equivalent methods. Hence, in cases of fixed or structurally different methods (raters), it is not reasonable to assume a common trait factor that reflects the common view of all measures. Instead, it is sensible to specify M-1 method factors as in fixed factor ANOVAs.

Nevertheless, in cases of interchangeable (random) methods, it is possible to properly define CFA-MTMM models with M (instead of M-1) method factors as we will show in the next section. However, even with regard to these models, method factors belonging to same traits are uncorrelated with each other as a consequence of the definition of the latent variables in the model. In the next section, we address the formal definition of CFA-MTMM models for interchangeable methods (raters). The first model is similar to the CT-UM model and therefore incorporates M (instead of M-1) uncorrelated method factors for each trait. The second model implies a multilevel structure and therefore defines trait and method effects in a different way than the previous models.

Defining CFA-MTMM models for interchangeable methods

In the following section, it is shown how CFA-MTMM models for measurement designs with interchangeable methods (raters) can be constructively defined. Again, interchangeable raters are raters that are assumed to be randomly sampled out of a unique rater distribution (see Eid et al., 2008). Consider, for example, multiple colleagues' ratings for the evaluation of the leadership quality of their corresponding supervisors. In order to properly define CFA-MTMM models for interchangeable raters, we once again set up the random experiment for this particular MTMM measurement design. To define the random experiment three sets of possible outcomes are needed: Ω_T is the set of targets, Ω_R is the set of raters, Ω_{ij} is the set of possible outcomes that contains the possible values of the ratings of indicator i of trait j, for example the values of a rating scale. Again, note that Ω_{ij} can incorporate all possible values of I observed indicators for J traits: $\Omega_{ij} = \Omega_{11} \times \ldots \times \Omega_{ij}$, with i = {1, ..., I} and j = {1, ..., J}. Hence, the set Ω of possible outcomes of this random experiment is

$$\Omega = \Omega_T \times \Omega_R \times \Omega_{ij} \quad (25.29)$$

That means, for example, that a target t (e.g., Larry) has been chosen from the set of targets Ω_T, a rater r (e.g., Linda) from the set of raters Ω_R, and the ratings o (e.g., 4, 2, 3, 4) have been observed measuring trait j (e.g., leadership skills) with items 1 to 4. In this case, the possible outcome is $\omega = (t, r, o) = $ (Larry, Linda, 4, 2, 3, 4).

Then, the following three variables that can be defined on the set of possible outcomes are of importance for defining the variables of the model. The variable

$$p_T : \Omega \to \Omega_T \quad (25.30)$$

maps the set of possible outcomes onto the set of targets. A value of the variable p_T is a single chosen target. The variable

$$p_R : \Omega \to \Omega_R \quad (25.31)$$

maps the set of possible outcomes onto the set of raters. A value of the variable p_R is a single chosen rater. The random variable

$$Y_{trij}: \Omega \to \mathbb{R} \qquad (25.32)$$

maps the possible outcomes of the ratings onto the set of real numbers. The values of this variable are the observed values of indicator i of the jth trait of target t rated by rater r. Note that we replaced the index k by r in Equation 25.32. This was done for two reasons. First, the index k was used to differentiate between **structurally different methods** (e.g., self-reports, supervisors' reports, and significant other reports). In the case of structurally different methods (raters) it was sensible to choose a reference method (e.g., the first method, $k = 1$) in order to contrast the remaining methods against this reference method (e.g., nonreference methods, $k \neq 1$). However, with regard to interchangeable raters (e.g., multiple colleagues' ratings) it is often difficult to choose a reference method, given that all raters have more or less the same access to the behavior of the target (e.g., the leader). Moreover, the random experiment previously (Equation 25.29) clarifies that measurement designs with interchangeable methods imply a multistage sampling procedure. First, a target t is randomly sampled from a set of possible targets T. Second, a rater r is randomly sampled out of a possible set of raters R for that target t and then the observed values of indicator i of the jth trait are recorded. In order to represent this multistage sampling procedure, we changed the subscripts as indicated before.

The variables Y_{trij} are the starting point for defining a multi-indicator CFA-MTMM model. Each observed variable Y_{trij} is decomposed into a true-score variable τ_{trij} and an error variable ε_{trij}:

$$Y_{trij} = \tau_{trij} + \varepsilon_{trij} \qquad (25.33)$$

with

$$\tau_{trij} = E(Y_{trij}|p_T, p_R) \qquad (25.34)$$

$$\varepsilon_{trij} = Y_{trij} - E(Y_{trij}|p_T, p_R) \qquad (25.35)$$

and $E(\cdot|p_T, p_R)$ denoting the conditional expectation (regression). A value of the true-score variable is the "true" rating of the ith indicator of the jth trait that we expect for a rater r rating target t. An error value is the deviation of an observed rating of this rater r and target t from the expected value for this target-rater combination. This is the classical definition of the true-score variables transferred to this data situation. This definition of the true-score variable is based on the idea that each single rating is affected by measurement error.

Based on this true-score variable we define a **latent (indicator-specific) trait variable** T_{trij} as the conditional expectation of the true-score variable τ_{trij} given the targets:

$$T_{trij} = E(\tau_{trij}|p_T) = E[E(Y_{trij}|p_T, p_R)|p_T] = E(Y_{trij}|p_T) \qquad (25.36)$$

That means that a value of this trait variable is the "true" value of the ith indicator of the jth trait we expect for a target t over all possible raters. Whereas the **true score** is the expected value of the observed variable for a specific rater-target combination (i.e., the expected rating of Linda for Larry's leadership skills), the **trait value** is the expected value of the true-score variables for a target t across all possible raters (Larry's leadership skills). The trait value is therefore not only free of measurement error but also free of rater-specific influences. In case of a random selection of multiple targets t and multiple raters r for each target (i.e., multilevel structure of raters nested within targets), a value of T_{trij} is similar to the true average of all ratings for a particular target t. Hence, the index denoting the rater r is not needed and can therefore be dropped (i.e., T_{tij}).

The deviation of the true-score variable from the trait variable defines the **latent (indicator- and trait-specific) method variable** M_{trij}:

$$M_{trij} = \tau_{trij} - T_{tij}. \qquad (25.37)$$

A value of this method variable, the method effect, is the deviation of the true-score of one rater (for target t) from the expected value of all possible raters (for target t). It can also be considered as a value of the **method bias** because it represents the over- or underestimation of a trait value by a particular rater r. This is Linda's deviation from the general rating for Larry's leadership skills.

Consequently, an observed variable Y_{trij} can be decomposed in the following way:

$$Y_{trij} = \tau_{trij} + \varepsilon_{trij} = T_{tij} + M_{trij} + \varepsilon_{trij}. \qquad (25.38)$$

That means that an observed rating depends on (1) the trait of the target, (2) the rater-specific effect (bias), and (3) measurement error. Because the method variables and the error variables are residuals, the variables T_{tij}, M_{trij}, and ε_{trij} have to be uncorrelated. Moreover, in case of a multilevel structure of multiple raters nested within targets, it is assumed that the method variables M_{trij} and the error variables ε_{trij} characterizing the responses of the different raters (level-1 units) are independent and identically distributed. In fact, this assumption means that method effects are independent across raters. If r and r' indicate two different raters, the equation $Cov(M_{trij}, M_{tr'ij}) = 0$ holds for all pairs of raters (for all $r \neq r'$). However, as each observed variable is decomposed into three components, an MTMM model like this would not be identified. Some restrictions must be made to define identified MTMM models. Moreover, several indicators have to be considered to separate measurement error from true scores appropriately, and several traits have to be considered in order to analyze discriminant validity.

Defining MTMM models for interchangeable raters

In order to define a very general MTMM model for interchangeable raters we make two assumptions. The **first** assumption concerns the **homogeneity of method variables**. We assume that all indicators i and i' (e.g., items, scales, parcels, test halves) that are supposed to measure the same trait (e.g., leadership skills) are affected by the same method (rater) bias. That means, that we assume that all method variables M_{trij}

belonging to the same trait j but to different indicators i and i' are linear functions of a single method factor M_{trj} and have a congeneric measurement structure:

$$M_{trij} = \lambda_{Mij} M_{trj} \tag{25.39}$$

The method factors, however, are different for different traits. That means that the method bias is trait specific (see Figures 25.8, 25.9, and 25.10). The method factors, however, can be correlated across traits, reflecting the degree of the generalizability of method effects. The **second** assumption concerns the **uncorrelatedness of error variables** that means we assume that all error variables are uncorrelated with each other. Consequently, the measurement equation can be written as follows:

$$Y_{trij} = T_{tij} + \lambda_{Mij} M_{trj} + \varepsilon_{trij}. \tag{25.40}$$

As indicated here, the model (see Equation 25.40) can be either specified as a multilevel CFA-MTMM model (see Eid et al., 2008) or as a "classical" single-level CFA-MTMM model (see also Nussbeck, Eid, Geiser, Courvoisier, & Lischetzke, 2009). The single-level CFA-MTMM model can be used in cases of few (and equally numbered) raters per target. Consider, for example, that each leader is rated by only three colleagues. The multilevel CFA-MTMM model is especially useful when each target (e.g., leader) is rated by a varying number of raters. However, the single-level CFA-MTMM model enables researchers to directly test equality restrictions on specific model

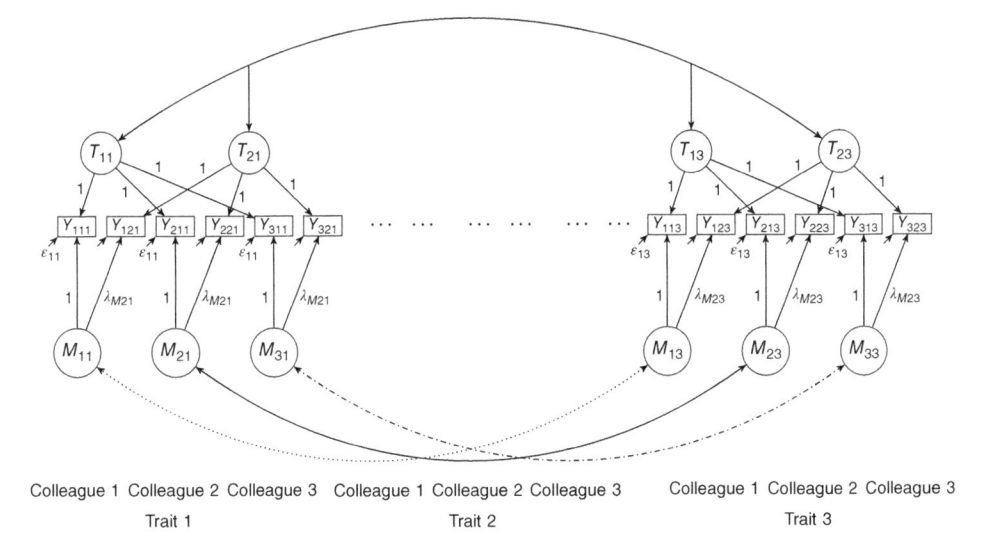

Figure 25.8 Model for interchangeable raters as classical multiple-indicator CFA model with indicator-specific trait variables. Y_{rij} = observed variables; T_{ij} = latent trait variables; M_{rj} = method factors; $\varepsilon_{rij} = \varepsilon_{r'ij} = \varepsilon_{ij}$ error variables. For simplicity reasons, the indices indicating the targets (t) have been omitted. r = method (rater), i = indicator, j = trait. The model is similar to a multiple-indicator CT-UM model or a multiconstruct latent state-trait model.

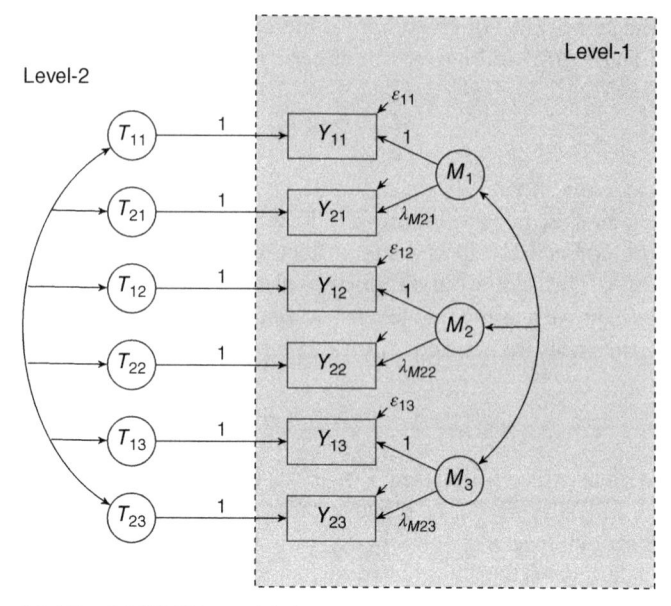

Figure 25.9 Multilevel MTMM model for interchangeable raters. For simplicity reasons, the indices indicating the targets (t) and the raters (r) have been omitted. Y_{ij} = observed variables, T_{ij} = latent trait variables, M_j = method factors, ε_{ij} = measurement error variables, i = indicator, j = trait.

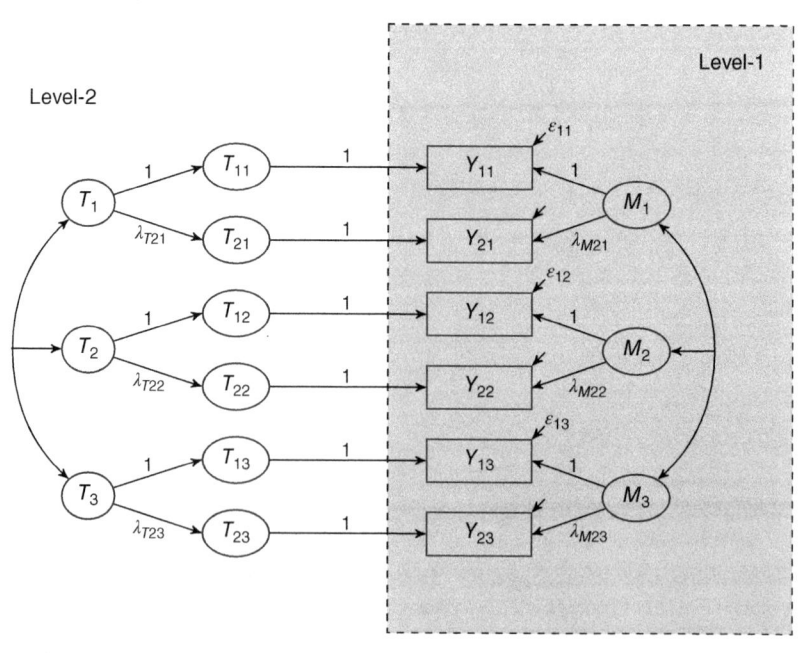

Figure 25.10 A multilevel MTMM-CFA model for interchangeable raters and with homogeneous trait variables. For simplicity reasons, the indices indicating the targets (t) and the raters (r) have been omitted. Y_{ij} = observed variables. T_{ij} = latent trait variables. M_j = method factors. ε_{ij} = measurement error variables, i = indicator, j = trait.

parameters, which are not testable in the multilevel CFA-MTMM model (see Nussbeck et al., 2009). The single-level model for two indicators, three traits, and three methods (here: colleagues' ratings) is depicted in Figure 25.8. The measurement equation for this classical CFA model assuming three colleagues' ratings per target ($r = 1, 2, 3$) can be derived from Equation 25.40:

$$Y_{t1ij} = T_{tij} + \lambda_{Mij} M_{t1j} + \varepsilon_{t1ij} \qquad (25.41)$$

$$Y_{t2ij} = T_{tij} + \lambda_{Mij} M_{t2j} + \varepsilon_{t2ij}, \qquad (25.42)$$

$$Y_{t3ij} = T_{tij} + \lambda_{Mij} M_{t3j} + \varepsilon_{t3ij}. \qquad (25.43)$$

In the multilevel model in Figure 25.9, a level-1 method factor represents the deviations of the different colleagues' ratings from the trait value of a target. In the classical CFA-MTMM model in Figure 25.8, there is now a method factor (and also an observed variable) for each rater. This is only possible because the number of colleagues' ratings is assumed to be equal for all targets. As in the multilevel model (Figure 25.9), it is assumed that the rater variables are independent and identically distributed. This assumption has two consequences for the classical CFA-MTMM model: (1) The method factors are uncorrelated between the three raters (because the rater variables are independent), and (2) all the variances (of the method factors and the error variables), loading parameters and mean values are constrained to be equal across the three raters (the variables are identically distributed for the three raters). Because of these restrictions, the models in Figures 25.8 and 25.9 do not differ in the number of estimated parameters. Moreover, consistency, method specificity, and reliability coefficients can be defined and estimated in the same way with both versions of the model.

The variance of the true-score variable that is due to trait differences is the **consistency coefficient**:

$$CO(\tau_{trij}) = \frac{Var(T_{tij})}{Var(\tau_{trij})}. \qquad (25.44)$$

The variance of the true-score variable that is determined by the method factor is the **method specificity** coefficient:

$$MS(\tau_{trij}) = \frac{\lambda_{Mij}^2 Var(M_{trj})}{Var(\tau_{trij})}. \qquad (25.45)$$

High **convergent validity** is indicated by a large consistency coefficient, whereas a high method specificity coefficient shows that the convergent validity is small, but method influences (interrater differences) are strong. Both coefficients add up to 1.

The **reliability**

$$Rel(Y_{trij}) = \frac{Var(T_{tij}) + \lambda_{Mij}^2 Var(M_{trj})}{Var(Y_{trij})}, \qquad (25.46)$$

indicates the proportion of the variance of an observed variable that is due to (true) trait- and method-specific differences. The degree of **discriminant validity** is assessed by the correlations of the latent trait variables belonging to different traits (e.g., T_{11} and T_{22})

Model with common trait factors

The model defined so far allows indicator-specific trait variables. A more restrictive model with homogeneous trait variables can easily be defined by assuming that the trait variables belonging to the same trait are one-dimensional with respect to a congeneric measurement structure:

$$T_{tij} = \alpha_{Tij} + \lambda_{Tij} T_{tj} \quad (25.47)$$

The correlations of the common trait variables T_{tj} indicate the degree of discriminant validity. Because the trait factors T_{tj} are linear functions of the trait variables T_{tij}, they have to be uncorrelated with the method M_{trij} and the error ε_{trij} variables. The multilevel CFA model with common trait factors is depicted in Figure 25.10. The consistency coefficient for this model is then defined by:

$$CO(\tau_{trij}) = \frac{\lambda_{Tij}^2 Var(T_{tj})}{Var(\tau_{trij})}. \quad (25.48)$$

Applications of MTMM models for interchangeable raters

With regard to the application of the ML-CFA model for interchangeable raters, we used the direct reports ($N = 1{,}303$) from the 360-degree feedback dataset described before. Again, we focused on the psychometric properties of the two scales: **captivating speaking skills** and **general leadership skills**. To separate measurement error from method-specific influences, the items were grouped into two test halves. Again, the means of the responses of the two items belonging to each test half were taken as observed indicators for the models. Given that the number of raters (colleagues' ratings) differed across targets (leaders), we directly applied the multilevel CFA-MTMM models depicted in Figures 25.9 and 25.10. In our application, the number of colleagues' ratings per leader varied between 1 and 13 (average = 4.22 ratings per target). In cases of a small and balanced number of raters per target (e.g., three colleagues' ratings), it is also possible to use the classical CFA-MTMM model depicted in Figure 25.8.

With respect to the multilevel CFA-MTMM approach, we modelled the direct reports on the within-level and the leaders on the between-level, using the *type = twolevel* option in MPlus. Moreover, the robust maximum likelihood (MLR) estimator that is recommended for this kind of analysis was applied (Muthén & Muthén, 1998–2012). We tested different ML-CFA models against one another by imposing restrictions on model parameters. The least restrictive model in Figure 25.9 has been already defined in Equation 25.40:

$$Y_{trij} = T_{tij} + \lambda_{Mij} M_{trj} + \varepsilon_{trij} \quad (25.40 \text{ repeated})$$

The model here (Equation 25.40) is a general ML-CFA model with indicator-specific trait variables (on level-2) and τ-congeneric method variables (on level-1). According to Equation 25.40, this model does not contain any intercepts. Hence, all intercepts are fixed to 0 in this model. The mean values of the indicator-specific trait variables are then identified on level-2. They equal the mean values of the observed variables Y_{trij} (because the mean values of the method factors and the error variables are 0 and have to be fixed). In the factor model for level-2 (left part of Figure 25.9), the factor loadings of the observed variables on their trait factor have to be fixed to 1, and the level-2 residuals of the general multilevel factor model have to be fixed to 0. The covariances of the indicator-specific trait variables (T_{trij}), representing discriminant validity, are not restricted in any way. The level-1 factor model equals the structure of the method factors in Figure 25.9. In the level-1 factor model all residuals are estimated. The variances of these residuals are the measurement error variances. This model with indicator-specific trait variables and τ-congeneric method variables fitted the data well, $\chi^2(1) = 2.22$, $p = .14$, CFI = 1.00, RMSEA = .03 (see Table 25.6). The means of the indicator-specific trait variables vary between 2.20 and 2.44 (see Table 25.7) and show that the mean speaking as well as mean leadership skills are in general lower than the center of the scale (2.50). The level-2 variances of the indicator-specific trait variables differ from 0, indicating that individual differences between leaders exist. The two indicator-specific trait variables belonging to the same trait are highly correlated (between $r = .93$ and $r = .94$). Hence, the two indicators are very homogeneous. Correlations between trait variables belonging to different traits are large as well ($r = .69$ to $r = .78$), suggesting relatively low discriminant validity. The loadings of the indicators belonging to the same method factor (level-1 factors) are similar, indicating that both indicators belonging to the same method factor deviate in the same manner from their corresponding trait. In the next step, we restricted the factor loadings belonging to the same construct j, but different indicators i and i' to be equal, $\lambda_{Mij} = \lambda_{Mi'j}$, for $i \neq i'$. That is, we assumed τ-equivalent method variables. This more restrictive model (see Model 2) fit the data also well, $\chi^2(3) = 6.54$, $p = .09$, CFI = 1.00, RMSEA = .03. The results of a χ^2-difference test showed that this more restrictive model did not fit the data significantly worse than the less restrictive model with τ-congeneric method variables, $\chi^2(2) = 4.31$, $p = .12$. According to the results of this model, the variances of the measurement errors pertaining to the leadership parcels were similar [i.e., var(ε_{12}) = .104 and var(ε_{22}) = .124]. Hence, we restricted the measurement error variance pertaining to these variables to be equal in the next step. Again, this more restrictive ML-CFA model (see Model 3) fit the data well, $\chi^2(4) = 8.55$, $p = .07$, CFI = 1.00, RMSEA = .03. According to the results of a χ^2-difference test, this more restrictive model fitted data not significantly worse than the less restrictive model (Model 2). In Model 4, we additionally constrained the measurement errors of the speaking skills items to be equal. However, in comparison to Model 3, this model fitted the data significantly worse, $\chi^2_{dif}(1) = 12.34$, $p < .001$. In Model 5, we assumed item-homogenous latent trait factors, instead of item-specific latent trait factors. However, this model did not fit the data well according to the overall χ^2-model fit. Moreover, according to the information criteria (sample adjusted BIC) Model 3 fitted the data better than Model 5. Consequently, Model 3 was chosen for the further analysis (see Code Appendix Code 3c).

The results of Model 3 are given in Table 25.7. Table 25.7 shows that the unstandardized trait and method factor loadings are set equal. Moreover, the reliability coefficients of the two leadership scales are equivalent due to the model restrictions

Table 25.6 Goodness of fit coefficients for the multilevel CFA model with indicator-specific trait variables on level-2.

Models	χ^2	df	p	CFI	RMSEA	AIC	BIC	s.a. BIC	χ^2_{dif}	df_{dif}	p_{dif}
Model 1	2.22	1	.14	1.00	.03	8,130.63	8,249.59	8,176.53	–	–	–
Model 2	6.54	3	.09	1.00	.03	8,131.55	8,240.17	8,173.46	4.31	2	.12
Model 3	**8.55**	**4**	**.07**	**1.00**	**.03**	**8,131.92**	**8,235.37**	**8,171.84**	**2.02**	**1**	**.16**
Model 4	19.22	5	<.05	1.00	.05	8,141.26	8,239.54	8,179.18	12.34	1	<.001
Model 5	48.86	9	<.001	.99	.06	8,152.39	8,229.98	8,182.33	–	–	–

Notes. s.a. BIC = Sample Size adjusted BIC. The fit values of selected model are given in bold font.

Table 25.7 Unstandardized means, loading parameters, and variance components of the multilevel MTMM model for interchangeable raters with indicator-specific trait factors for model 3.

Indicator	Latent means $E(T_{ij})$	Trait factor loading λ_{Tij}	Method factor loading λ_{Mij}	Consistency $CO(\tau_{trij})$	Method specificity $MS(\tau_{trij})$	Reliability $Rel(Y_{trij})$
Captivating Speaking Skills						
Y_{tr11}	2.32	1.00	1.00	.21	.79	.87 (.84)
Y_{tr21}	2.20	1.00	1.00	.25	.75	.82 (.77)
General Leadership Skills						
Y_{tr12}	2.44	1.00	1.00	.20	.80	.80 (.77)
Y_{tr22}	2.27	1.00	1.00	.17	.83	.80 (.77)

Notes. In parentheses are the level-1 reliability coefficients.

explained previously. The reliability coefficients are calculated according to Equation 25.46. However, it is also possible to define a level-1 reliability coefficient:

$$Rel_{level-1}(Y_{trij}) = \frac{\lambda^2_{Mij} Var(M_{trij})}{\lambda^2_{Mij} Var(M_{trij}) + Var(\varepsilon_{trij})}. \tag{25.49}$$

According to Equation 25.49, the level-1 reliability coefficient is defined as proportion of level-1 observed variance that is determined by "true" rater-specific influences. This reliability coefficient is directly reported in MPlus and is given in the parentheses in Table 25.7. Moreover, coefficients of "true" consistency and method specificity (as defined in Equations 25.44 and 25.45) are also provided in Table 26.7. The "true" consistency coefficient can be interpreted as convergent validity of the true ratings of the direct reports, that is, how "true-score" variance is shared by different subordinates belonging to the same leader. According to the results, 17–25% of variance of the "true" subordinates' ratings is shared with all other subordinates. The "true" method-specificity coefficient represents the amount of heterogeneity among the "true" subordinates' ratings. According to the results, the amount of heterogeneity among the subordinates is rather high, varying between 79 and 83%.

Table 25.8 contains the variances and correlations between the item-specific latent trait variables and the latent method variables. The results show that the item-specific latent trait variables pertaining to the same construct j, but different indicators i and i' are highly correlated. The correlations between trait variables belonging to different traits are large as well ($r = .70$ to $r = .81$). Again, these correlations indicate low discriminant validity. The method variables on level-1 also correlate highly ($r = .83$), reflecting high generalizability of method effects across constructs.

Links to other models

In the form of the classical confirmatory factor analysis model, the model for interchangeable raters is an extension of the random analysis of variance model for MTMM data (Dumenci, 2000) to a model with multiple indicators. Like the random coefficient

Table 25.8 Variances (diagonal), and correlations (subdiagonal) of the trait and method factors in the multilevel CFA model for interchangeable raters for model 3.

	1	2	3	4	5	6
T_{11}	.11					
T_{21}	.94*	.13				
T_{12}	.81*	.70*	.09			
T_{22}	.72*	.71*	.93*	.08		
M_1	–	–	–	–	.40	
M_2	–	–	–	–	.83*	.38

Notes. * $p < .05$.

model, the model for interchangeable raters proposed here assumes that an observed variable is decomposed into a trait and a method factor as well as an error variable, and that the method variables are uncorrelated. However, the multiple indicators for each TMU make it possible to formulate a much less restrictive model: First, in our model, the method factors are trait specific. In Dumenci's (2000) model, however, there is only one general method factor for each method. The empirical analyses have shown that the assumption of trait-unspecific general method factors is often too restrictive. Moreover, our modelling approach allows item-specific traits in contrast to the general traits of the model of Dumenci (2000) and Millsap (1995b). In our application, item-specific traits were necessary. The single-level CFA-MTMM model (see Figure 25.8) is also similar to the CT-UM model (see Figure 25.8; Kenny, 1976), where method factors belonging to the same trait must be uncorrelated with each other, but can be correlated with each other across different traits. Hence, for a small number of interchangeable raters per target, it is possible to constructively define a single-level CFA-MTMM model that uses M (instead of M-1) method factors. Nussbeck et al. (2009) showed how this model can also be extended to MTMM measurement designs with students' self-reports (target) and two peer-reports (per target).

In contrast, the multilevel CFA-MTMM model (see Figure 25.9) is a special case of a multilevel model of confirmatory factor analysis (Hox, 2002; Muthén, 1994; Muthén & Khoo, 1998; Muthén & Muthén, 2000). It differs from the general model in the way the latent variables are defined. In contrast to the general multilevel factor model, it is not just assumed that trait and method factors exist but they are constructively defined on the basis of a random experiment. This approach leads to clear implications for the inclusion of latent residuals on level-2 that have to be zero, which is quite unusual but theoretically justified. Hence, this approach helps to avoid conceptual specification errors that might result in estimation problems.

CFA-MTMM models for a combination of both methods

So far, we have examined two distinct groups of methods: structurally different raters who differ with respect to several qualities from each other and interchangeable raters who are considered randomly selected methods. In this section, we will show how the two approaches can be integrated. We will not discuss the approaches in detail, because the models are a combination of the modelling approaches for each class of methods that have been extensively discussed in the previous sections. Instead, we will illustrate the combination of the two modelling approaches with respect to an empirical example. For the application of the model we once again used the 360-degree feedback data set. As stated before, the direct reports have been considered as interchangeable (i.e., randomly selected) ratings, and the convergent and discriminant validity of the ratings was modelled with a **multilevel** structural equation model. In contrast, the ratings of the leaders and supervisors have been considered as structurally different (i.e., fixed) methods and the convergent and discriminant validity was scrutinized by **traditional** (single-level) structural equation models. More specifically, we provided three different CFA-MTMM models (i.e., CT-C(M-1) model, latent difference model, latent means model) for contrasting different raters' perspectives against each other or against an overall mean. We will now show how these different measurement models (for structurally different and interchangeable methods) can be linked. For simplicity reasons, we will only use the CT-C(M-1) modelling approach. However, the other two approaches (i.e., latent difference models, and latent mean models) can be applied in a similar fashion. The CFA-MTMM model for the combination of structurally different and interchangeable methods is an extension of the multilevel model presented in Figure 25.10. For simplicity, we will only refer to the model of one trait factor (see Figure 25.11). The model can be defined in three steps. In the first step, the measurement models for interchangeable and structurally different methods are combined (see Figure 25.11A). In this model, all true-score variables on level-2 are freely estimated and allowed to correlate with each other. Again, we omitted the indices r for rater and t for target with respect to the observed variables in the path diagram (see Figure 25.11A) and labeled both layers for the measurement levels (i.e., level-1 = rater- and target-specific level and level-2 = target-specific level). Similar to the models for structurally different methods, the index k was used in order to differentiate between the different methods (i.e., $k = 1$ = self-reports, $k = 2$ = supervisor reports, and $k = 3$ = direct reports). Therefore, each observed variable Y_{ijk} pertaining to item i, construct j, and method k is either measured on level-1 (in case of the direct reports) or level-2 (in case of the self- or supervisor reports). It is important to note that the true-score variables on level-2 reflect the "true" (measurement-error free) ratings of a target's behavior or ability by a specific method (e.g., self-reports, supervisor reports, or direct reports). Therefore, these latent scores capture trait as well as method-specific influences.

In case of the direct reports, the true-score variables on level-2 represent the "common" view on the targets behavior or ability shared by all subordinates belonging to that target. The method variables on level-1 reflect the deviation of a particular subordinate rating from the "common" of all subordinates belonging to a particular leader. Given that these variables represent the unique view of a particular subordinate on the leader's behavior or ability, these method variables are named **unique** method variables. In the second step, the different true-score variables on level-2 are regressed on each other, following the CT-C(M-1) modelling approach (see Figure 25.11B). The CT-C(M-1) modelling approach requires to select a reference (standard) method and to regress the true scores of the nonreference methods on the true scores of the reference method (Eid, 2000; Eid et al., 2003, 2008). In the application, we used the leaders' self-reports as reference method ($k = 1$), given that we were particularly interested in the over- or underestimation of leadership quality by the corresponding supervisors and subordinates. Subsequently, the supervisor ratings ($k = 2$) as well as the ratings of the direct reports ($k = 3$) were chosen as nonreference methods. In order to contrast the different perspectives against each other, the true scores of the reference method (i.e., self-report, $k = 1$) were used as predictors for the true scores of the nonreference methods (see Figure 25.11B). With regard to these latent regressions, it is possible to separate trait

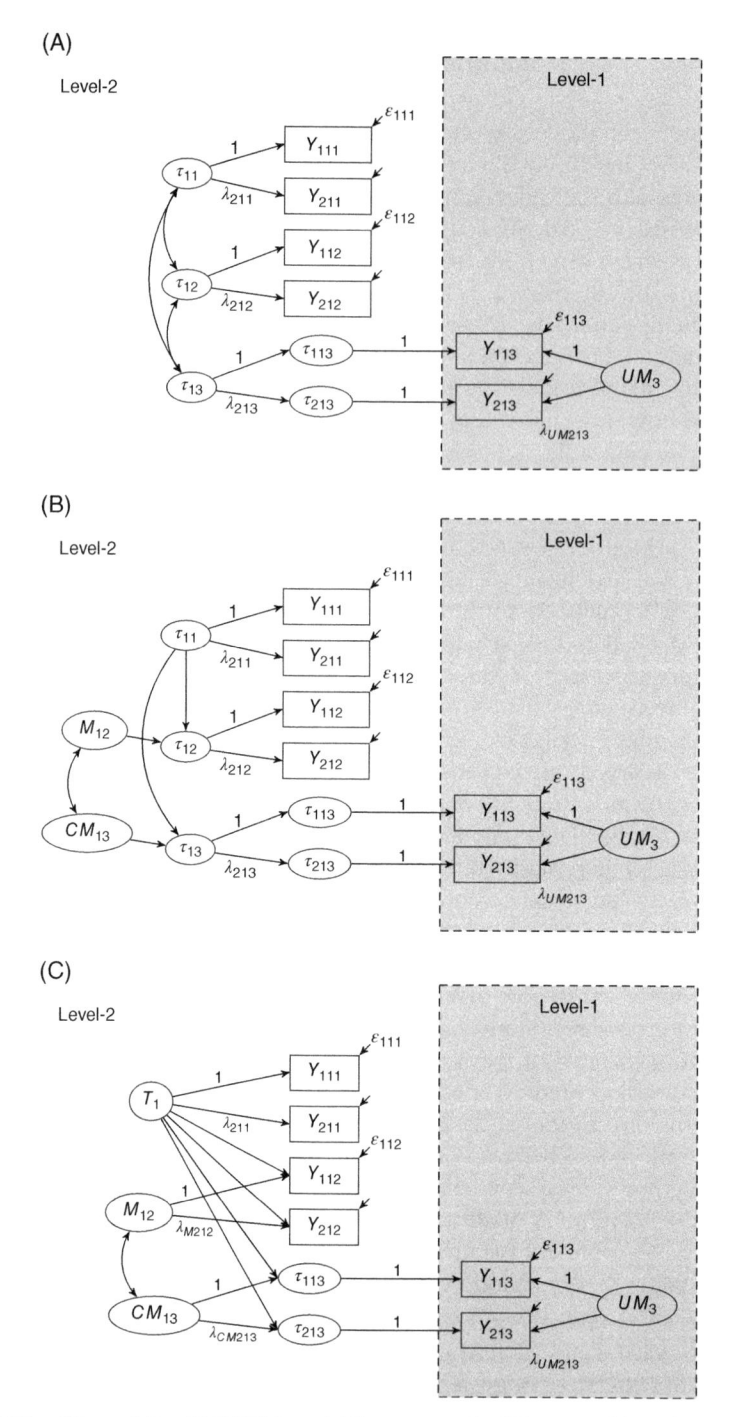

Figure 25.11 The multilevel MTMM model for structurally different and interchangeable raters. For simplicity reasons, the indices indicating the targets (t) and the interchangeable raters (r) have been omitted. (A) Combination of the measurement models for structurally different and interchangeable methods. Assumption of homogeneous trait (true-score) variables and correlated trait variables on level-2. (B) CT-C(M-1) structure predicting the trait variables of the supervisor and direct reports (τ_{12} and τ_{13}) by the trait variable of the self-report (τ_{11}). In addition, the correlations of the residuals M_{jk} and CM_{jk} are shown in this figure. (C) Rearranging model B to be consistent with the typical representation of the Multilevel-CT-C(M-1). Assumption of homogeneous trait (true-score) and homogeneous method variables. Y_{ijk} = observed variables, T_{jk} = latent trait variables, M_{jk} = method factors, CM_{jk} = common method factors, UM_{jk} = unique method factors, ε_{ijk} = measurement error variables, i = indicator, j = trait, k = method.

from method-specific effects of the nonreference true scores. The residuals of these latent regressions are defined as latent method variables. Note that two different method variables can be defined on level-2 (i.e., target-level). The method variable M_{jk} represents the deviation of the true supervisor ratings from the predicted supervisor ratings by the self-report of the leader. Positive values on this method variable indicate that the supervisor overestimates the self-reported leadership quality of a particular leader. Negative values represent an underestimate, by the supervisor, of self-reported leadership quality. The method variable CM_{jk} refers to the over- or underestimation of the self-reported leadership quality by "all" subordinates belonging to a particular leader. In other words, these method variables represent the "common" view of the subordinates that is **not** shared with the leader, but shared by all other subordinates of that leader. Given that the method variables are defined as latent residuals variables, they have an expectation of zero and are uncorrelated with the true-score variables of the reference method (i.e., the trait factor). However, correlations between the two method variables are permissible. Positive correlations indicate that both methods (supervisors and subordinates) share a similar view on the target. That is, for example, the overestimation of the self-reported leadership quality by a supervisor might be associated with the overestimation of the self-reported leadership quality by the subordinates. In the third step, homogeneity assumptions for the trait as well as the method factors are introduced. In Figure 25.11(C) the model with homogeneous trait and method variables is depicted.

We extended this model to two traits and fitted it to the data (see Code Appendix, Code 4). Again, we assumed τ-equivalent trait and method variables as well as equal error variance for general leadership skills as in the models before. The model fits the data acceptably well, $\chi^2(54) = 93.95$, $p < .001$, CFI = 1.00, RMSEA = .02. Table 25.9 summarizes the results of the ML-CT-(M-1) model with regard to the unstandardized intercepts, trait, and method factor loadings, as well as the coefficients of consistency, method specificity, and reliability. The unstandardized factor loadings were set to 1, assuming equal trait as well as equal method factor loadings for the indicators i and i' belonging to the same construct j, and the same method k. The intercepts vary between 2.19 and 2.43 for the first construct (captivating speaking skills) and between 2.26 and 2.44 for the second construct (general leadership skills). Given that the intercepts are always close to the center of the scale (2.5), the two constructs are rated as being average or little below average. The true consistency coefficients indicate the degree of true convergent validity among the different rater groups. For the first method (self-reports), the true consistency coefficient is 1, because no method effects are modelled for the reference method in the CT-C(M-1) framework. The reliability coefficients for the reference method indicators vary between .74 and .78, showing acceptable reliability coefficients for the self-report measures. For the nonreference methods (i.e., supervisor reports and direct reports) the true consistency coefficients are notably lower, varying between 11 and 17% for the supervisor reports and between 5 and 7% for the direct reports. The method specificity coefficients are always greater than the consistency coefficients, indicating substantial method effects. The method specificities for the supervisor reports vary between 83 and 89%. For the direct reports, two method specificity coefficients can be calculated: the unique method specificity coefficients (UMS) and the common method specificity coefficient (CMS). The unique method specificity coefficient reflects the proportion of true interindividual differences of the subordinate ratings that can neither be explained by true interindividual differences of the leaders' self-reports, nor explained by true "common" differences of all subordinates. Hence, this coefficient represents the amount of unique (rater-specific)

Table 25.9 Unstandardized means, loading parameters, and variance components of the multilevel MTMM model for structurally different and interchangeable raters with indicator-specific trait factors.

Indicator	Intercepts α_{ijk}	Trait factor loading λ_{Tijk}	(Common) Method factor loading $\lambda_{Mij2}/\lambda_{CMij3}$	Unique method factor loading λ_{UMij3}	Consistency $CO(\tau_{ijk})$	(Common) Method specificity $MS(\tau_{ij2})/CMS(\tau_{ij3})$	Unique method specificity $UMS(\tau_{ij3})$	Reliability $Rel(Y_{ijk})$
Captivating Speaking Skills								
Self (Leaders)								
Y_{111}	2.42	1.00			1.00	—	—	.74
Y_{211}	2.31	1.00			1.00	—	—	.77
Supervisors								
Y_{112}	2.43	0.37	1.00	1.00	.11	.89	—	.70
Y_{212}	2.28	0.37	1.00	1.00	.13	.87	—	.70
Direct report								
Y_{113}	2.31	0.40	1.00	1.00	.06	.20	.74	.87
Y_{213}	2.19	0.40	1.00	1.00	.07	.19	.74	.81
General Leadership Skills								
Self (Leaders)								
Y_{121}	2.39	1.00			1.00	—	—	.78
Y_{221}	2.28	0.95			1.00	—	—	.76
Supervisors								
Y_{122}	2.31	0.43	1.00	1.00	.17	.83	—	.74
Y_{222}	2.26	0.43	1.00	1.00	.15	.85	—	.74
Direct reports								
Y_{133}	0.44	0.38	1.00	1.00	.06	.15	.79	.80
Y_{223}	2.27	0.38	1.00	1.00	.05	.15	.80	.80

Notes. i = indicator; j = trait (construct); k = method.

influences. The common method specificity coefficient represents the proportion of true interindividual differences of the subordinate ratings that cannot be explained by true interindividual differences of the leaders' self-reports, but that is common to all subordinates. Hence, this coefficient reflects the amount of "common" rater influences. This coefficient can also be interpreted as degree of true convergent validity of the interchangeable raters. The common method specificity coefficients are always lower than the unique method specificity coefficients (see Table 25.9), varying between 15 and 20%. This indicates that the rater agreement among the subordinates is rather low. Given that two method factors can be defined with regard to the subordinates' ratings, it is possible to calculate the total amount of method specificity by simply by adding up the unique and the common method specificity coefficient (i.e., UMS + CMS). In the application, the total method specificity coefficient varied between 93 and 95%, indicating a large amount of rater influences. Moreover, the consistency coefficient and the common method specificity coefficient could be also added up (i.e., CO + CMS). The sum of both coefficients can be interpreted as degree of total convergent validity of the subordinates, given that this coefficient reflects the amount of true variance of the subordinates' ratings that is due to target-specific influences. In the application, the total convergent validity coefficient varies between 20 and 26%. Finally, it is possible to calculate a level-2 consistency coefficient by dividing the consistency coefficient (CO) by the total consistency coefficient (CO + CMS). This consistency coefficient represents the true convergent validity of the self-reports and subordinates' ratings that is corrected for rater-specific as well as measurement error effects and is only based on the **common**, not the individual true subordinates' ratings. In the application, this coefficient varies between 23 and 29%, which refers to correlation coefficients between the latent variables of .48 to .54. The coefficients described previously can be also used for comparing the degree of true convergent validity among the different measures. For example, for the individual subordinates' ratings, the true consistency coefficient is rather low (between 5 and 7%). One could therefore conclude that the supervisors agree more strongly with the self-ratings than with the subordinate ratings and that direct reports are not really valuable for the evaluation of leadership quality. However (with regard to the true level-2 consistency coefficients), supervisors have in fact less in common with the self-ratings than the group of subordinates of that leader. Moreover, it might be interesting to include further manifest or latent covariates in order to explain the different method effects on the different measurement levels. For example, variables such as gender, age, job experiments, commitment, and other personality variables could be used for the investigation of the method effects.

Researchers can also study the degree of discriminant validity and the generalization of method effects by analyzing the correlations among the latent variables. According to Table 25.10, the correlations between latent method variables pertaining to the same nonreference method k, but different constructs j and j' are high, varying between .74 and .84. These correlations indicate to what degree the nonreference methods (supervisors or direct reports) generalize across different constructs. High positive correlations show that the nonreference methods (i.e., supervisors or direct reports) deviate from the leaders self-rated speaking skills in a similar way as they deviate from the leaders self-rated leadership skills. The correlations between the latent method variables that belong to different nonreference methods k and k', but to the same constructs j can be interpreted as generalization of methods effects across different methods. For example, the correlation between M_{22} and CM_{23} is .37 showing that supervisors and subordinates in general over- or underestimate the self-reported leadership quality in

Table 25.10 Variances (diagonal), and correlations (subdiagonal) of the trait and method factors in the multilevel model for structurally different and interchangeable raters.

	1	2	3	4	5	6	7	8	9	10
T_{11}	.19									
T_{21}	.95*	.22								
T_{12}	.87*	.75*	.19							
T_{22}	.82*	.76*	.96*	.17						
M_{12}	–	–	–	–	.21					
M_{22}	–	–	–	–	.74*	.17				
CM_{13}	–	–	–	–	.29*	.30*	.10			
CM_{23}	–	–	–	–	.23*	.37*	.77*	.07		
UM_{13}	–	–	–	–	–	–	–	–	.40	
UM_{23}	–	–	–	–	–	–	–	–	.84*	.37

Notes. * $p < .05$.

a similar way. Similarly, supervisors and subordinates in general over- or underestimate the self-report speaking skills in a similar way ($r = .29$). The correlations between latent method variables belonging to different nonreference methods k and k' as well as different constructs j and j' represent the generalization of method effects across constructs as well as across different methods. These correlation coefficients between the indicator-specific trait factors are rather small ($r = .23$ and $r = .30$). These latent correlations can be interpreted in a similar way as discussed before.

Discussion

In this chapter, we focused on different CFA-MTMM models that can be **constructively** defined for different sets of possible outcomes (i.e., different random experiments). More specifically, we discussed three CFA-MTMM models for measurement designs with structurally different methods (i.e., the CT-C(M-1), the latent difference, and the latent means model) and two CFA-MTMM models for measurement designs with interchangeable methods (a ML-CFA-MTMM model and a CT-UM model for interchangeable methods). Additionally, we showed how structurally different and interchangeable methods can be combined and analyzed simultaneously by using a multilevel CT-C(M-1) model (see also Eid et al., 2008). Moreover, we highlighted the advantages of defining CFA-MTMM models based on the set of possible outcomes (i.e., the random experiment) in contrast to the "traditional" approach which is often data-driven and highly arbitrary (see Eid et al., 2008). Defining CFA-MTMM models based on the set of possible outcomes requires researchers to consider the type of method that is used in the study beforehand. This has several important implications.

First, different types of methods imply different random experiments, and therefore different types of data structures. As shown in this chapter, measurement designs with interchangeable methods (raters) imply a multistage (multilevel) sampling procedure, given that the interchangeable methods are randomly chosen from a unique method distribution (e.g., raters nested in targets), whereas in measurement designs with structurally different methods, these methods are often conceptualized as being fixed for a particular target.

Second, different types of methods that imply different random experiments offer different definitions of trait and method factors. As shown in this chapter, it is sensible to specify M-1 (instead of M) method factors for measurement designs with fixed (i.e., structurally different) methods, similar to fixed factors in ANOVA. As a consequence, it is possible to contrast different methods against one another or against an overall mean. The M-1 modelling approach for measurement designs with structurally different methods is similar to using different coding schemes in fixed factor ANOVA (see Geiser et al., 2012) and allows different interpretations of trait as well as method effects. This becomes especially crucial when explaining different method effects by including other covariates or calculating variance coefficients. In contrast, CFA-MTMM models that cannot be constructively defined based on the set of possible outcomes (e.g., the CT-CM model) often assume that the method factors exist and have a clear interpretation. However, building CFA-MTMM models on this relatively weak psychometric foundation can lead to problems of identification and convergence, improper solutions, and interpretation difficulties of resulting parameter estimates. As shown in this chapter, only in the case of measurement designs with interchangeable methods (e.g., raters), is it possible to constructively derive a CFA-MTMM model which incorporates M method factors. However, this classical CFA model implies uncorrelated method factors that belong to the same trait and therefore is similar to the traditional CT-UM model. Hence, CFA-MTMM models that can be constructively defined on the set of possible outcomes (i.e., the random experiment) enable researchers to clarify what the latent factors mean.

Third, CFA-MTMM models that can be constructively defined on the set of possible outcomes adapt the concepts of a **test theory of minimal assumptions** proposed by Zimmerman (1975) that has also been successfully applied to models of CTT (Steyer, 1989). Thereby, it is possible to derive important properties of the latent variables (e.g., uncorrelateness of trait and method variables) and show that variance coefficients (e.g., consistency, method specificity, reliability) are meaningful. Most importantly, constructively defined CFA-MTMM models are in line with the basic idea of MTMM analysis proposed by Campbell and Fiske (1959) and do not overfactorize the basic measurement model with true-score variables for each TMU. By discussing these advantages of constructively defined CFA-MTMM models in this chapter, we strongly encourage researchers to adopt a (more) theory-driven approach when selecting an appropriate MTMM model. One of the most important guidelines for choosing an appropriate model is the type of method considered. We have discussed three types of methods: (1) interchangeable methods, (2) structurally different methods, and (3) mixed methods consisting of interchangeable and structurally different methods. In order to find an appropriate model, a researcher must investigate what methods are used in the study (or what random experiment/data structure is implied by the measurement design), and how the method effects should be conceptualized.

If the study contains **interchangeable** methods a multilevel modelling and a classical CFA modelling strategy can be chosen. The latter can only be applied when the number of raters does not differ between targets and is rather small. The multilevel strategy is more flexible as it allows different numbers of methods (raters) for different targets. If the study contains **structurally different methods**, several modelling strategies can be considered. If the aim is to estimate **pure** method effects that are not related to trait factors, a CT-C(M-1) **model** should be chosen. If one wants to obtain method factors that represent the differences between different methods, a **latent difference model** would be the model of choice. If the traits should be defined as aggregated (mean) variables, a **latent means model** should be chosen. Each model has its own properties that should correspond to the research question under consideration. If the study contains **interchangeable and structurally different methods** the modelling strategies for interchangeable and structurally different raters can easily be combined. Finally, there is not **one** single model that is optimal for all types of MTMM measurement designs. Instead the model has to be chosen with regard to theoretical reasons and the purpose of the MTMM study.

Outlook: Longitudinal CFA-MTMM models

In the final part of this chapter, we want to briefly discuss some of the recent developments of longitudinal CFA-MTMM models. Longitudinal CFA-MTMM models possess many advantages. For example, researchers are able to investigate the true (i.e., measurement error-free) stability and change of constructs as well as method effects pertaining to different measurement levels (e.g., rater and target-level). That means, researchers are able to analyze whether or not a given construct (e.g., leadership skills) has changed over time and whether or not different method effects (e.g., common or unique rater effects) have changed over time. Furthermore, researchers can scrutinize the convergent and discriminant validity of their measures at each occasion of measurement as well as across different occasions of measurement. Hence, it is possible to investigate to what extent different methods converge in their assessment of change. This refers to the concept of **convergent validity of change** that might be particularly interesting in intervention studies. Moreover, it is possible to include external covariates (e.g., gender, age, job experience, personality characteristic, etc.) in order to explain the interindividual differences in "true" change of constructs and/or method effects. Most importantly, longitudinal studies are more informative than cross-sectional measurement designs and enable researchers to test important assumptions, such as measurement invariance or the existence of item-specific effects (see Geiser, 2008). Similar to cross-sectional MTMM measurement designs, longitudinal MTMM (also called multitrait-multimethod-multioccasion; MTMM-MO) measurement designs make it necessary to consider the set of possible outcomes (i.e., the random experiment).

The main difference between cross-sectional and longitudinal MTMM measurement designs is that different methods or a combination of different methods is not only examined at **one** single measurement occasion, but on **multiple** measurement occasions. Hence, similar to latent state-trait theory (see Steyer, Ferring & Schmitt, 1992; Steyer & Schmitt, 1990; Steyer, Schmitt, & Eid, 1999), where persons are assessed **in** a situation, in MTMM-MO measurement designs, different methods (e.g., raters) are assessed **in** a method-(rater)-specific situation. Besides, researchers can decide whether they want to study **variability** processes or processes of **change** (see Eid, 1995). Variability processes imply that there is a trait-like attribute which is invariant (stable) across measurement occasions as well as that there are occasion-specific deviations (fluctuations) from this time-invariant trait. In contrast, processes of change imply that the attribute under consideration does not remain invariant across time, but rather changes. For example, growth or developmental process are usually considered as change processes. For longitudinal MTMM measurement designs with **structurally different** methods, readers should consult Courvoisier (2006) as well as Geiser (2008). Courvoisier (2006) proposed a multimethod latent state-trait (MM-LST) model that combines latent state-trait (LST) theory with the CT-C(M-1) modelling framework for structurally different methods. This model is especially useful for studying variability in structurally different methods (e.g., teacher, parent, and students' self-ratings). For example, the MM-LST model allows study of convergent and discriminant validity at the trait- and occasion-specific level. For an illustrative application of this model see Courvoisier et al. (2008). Researchers that are rather interested in studying change processes in longitudinal MTMM measurement designs with structurally different methods can apply the Correlated-State-Correlated-Method-Minus-One [CS-C(M-1)] change model by Geiser (2008). Using this model, it is possible to examine the convergent validity of change among structurally different methods. Moreover, it is possible to investigate the true change of method effects as well as the existence of indicator-specific effects. The CS-C(M-1) change model has been applied in developmental psychology (see Geiser et al., 2010) as well as in intervention studies (see Crayen, Geiser, Scheithauer, & Eid, 2011). So far, no such models have been proposed for longitudinal MTMM measurement designs with **interchangeable methods**. Recent studies have shown how CFA models can be constructively defined for longitudinal MTMM measurement designs including structurally different and interchangeable methods (Holtmann, Koch, Bohn, & Eid, 2017; Koch, 2013; Koch, Schultze, Eid, & Geiser, 2014; Koch, Schultze, Holtmann, Geiser, & Eid, 2017). A main advantage of these models is that they can be constructively defined on the basis of stochastic measurement theory (Steyer, 1989; Steyer & Eid, 2001; Zimmerman, 1975). Therefore, the latent factors in these models have a clear psychometric meaning. As we explained in this chapter, it is extremely important to clarify what latent factors mean. Finally, alternative longitudinal CFA-MTMM models that do not explicitly follow this approach have been also proposed (see e.g., Burns & Haynes, 2006; Burns, Walsh, & Gomez, 2003; Cole & Maxwell, 2003; Grimm, Pianta, & Konold, 2009).

References

American Educational Research Association, American Psychological Association & National Council of Measurement in Education (1999). *Standards for educational and psychological testing*. Washington: American Educational Research Association.

Bollen, K. A. (1989). *Structural equations with latent variables*. New York: Wiley.

Borsboom, D., Mellenbergh, G. J., & van Heerden, J. (2004). The concept of validity. *Psychological Review, 111*, 1061–1071. doi: 10.1037/0033-295X.111.4.1061

Browne, M. W. (1984). The decomposition of multitrait-multimethod matrices. *British Journal of Mathematical and Statistical Psychology, 37*, 1–21. doi: 10.1111/j.2044-8317.1984.tb00785.x

Burns, G. L., & Haynes, S. N. (2006). Clinical psychology: construct validation with multiple sources of information and multiple settings. In M. Eid & E. Diener (Eds.), *Handbook of multimethod measurement in psychology* (pp. 401–418). Washington, DC: American Psychological Association.

Burns, G. L., Walsh, J. A., & Gomez, R. (2003). Convergent and discriminant validity of trait and source effects in ADHD-inattention and hyperactivity/impulsivity measures across a 3-month Interval. *Journal of Abnormal Child Psychology: An Official Publication of the International Society for Research in Child and Adolescent Psychopathology, 31*, 529–541. doi: 10.1023/A:1025453132269

Campbell, D. T., & Fiske, D. W. (1959). Convergent and discriminant validation by the multitrait-multimethod matrix. *Psychological Bulletin, 56*, 81–105.

Cole, D. A., & Maxwell, S. E. (2003). Testing mediational models with longitudinal data: Questions and tips in the use of structural equation modeling. *Journal of Abnormal Psychology*, 112, 558–577. doi: 10.1037/0021-843X.112.4.558

Courvoisier, D. S. (2006). *Unfolding the constituents of psychological scores: Development and application of mixture and multitrait-multimethod LST models.* (doctoral dissertation). University of Geneva, Switzerland.

Courvoisier, D. S., Nussbeck, F. W., Eid, M., Geiser, C., & Cole, D. A. (2008). Analyzing the convergent and discriminant validity of states and traits: Development and applications of multimethod latent state-trait models. *Psychological Assessment*, 20, 270–280. doi: 10.1037/a0012812

Crayen, C., Geiser, C., Scheithauer, H., & Eid, M. (2011). Evaluating interventions with multimethod data: a structural equation modeling approach. *Structural Equation Modeling: A Multidisciplinary Journal*, 18, 497–524. doi: 10.1080/10705511.2011.607068

Dudgeon, P. (1994). A reparameterization of the restricted factor analysis model for multitrait-multimethod matrices. *British Journal of Mathematical and Statistical Psychology*, 47, 283–308. doi: 10.1111/j.2044-8317.1994.tb01038.x

Dumenci, L. (2000). Multitrait-multimethod analysis. In S. D. Brown & H. E. A. Tinsley (Eds.), *Handbook of applied multivariate statistics and mathematical modeling* (pp. 583–611). San Diego, CA: Academic Press.

Eid, M. (1995). Modelle der Messung von Personen in Situationen *[Models for measuring persons in situations]*. Weinheim: Psychologie Verlags Union.

Eid, M. (2000). A multitrait-multimethod model with minimal assumptions. *Psychometrika*, 65, 241–261.

Eid, M. (2010). Multitrait-multimethod-matrix. In N. Salkind (Ed.), Encyclopedia of research design *(Vol. 1)* (pp. 850–855). Thousand Oaks: Sage.

Eid, M., & Diener, E. (2006). Introduction: The need for multimethod measurement in psychology. In M. Eid & E. Diener (Eds.), *Handbook of multimethod measurement in psychology* (pp. 3–9). Washington, D.C.: American Psychological Association.

Eid, M., Lischetzke, T., & Nussbeck, F. W. (2006). Structural equation models for multitrait-multimethod data. In M. Eid & E. Diener (Eds.), *Handbook of multimethod measurement in psychology* (pp. 283–299). Washington, D.C.: American Psychological Association.

Eid, M., Lischetzke, T., Nussbeck, F. W., & Trierweiler, L. I. (2003). Separating trait effects from trait-specific method effects in multitrait-multimethod models: A multiple-indicator CT-C (M-1) model. *Psychological Methods*, 8, 38–60. doi: 10.1037/1082-989X.8.1.38

Eid, M., Nussbeck, F. W., Geiser, C., Cole, D. A., Gollwitzer, M., & Lischetzke, T. (2008). Structural equation modeling of multitrait-multimethod data: Different models for different types of methods. *Psychological Methods*, 13, 230–253. doi: 10.1037/a0013219

Embretson, S. E. (1991). The new rules of measurement. *Psychological Assessment*, 8, 341–349. doi: 10.1037/1040-3590.8.4.341

Epstein, S. (1983). Aggregation and beyond: Some basic issues on the prediction of behavior. *Journal of Personality*, 51, 360–392. doi: 10.1111/j.1467-6494.1983.tb00338.x

Epstein, S. (1986). Does aggregation produce spuriously high estimates of behavior stability? *Journal of Personality and Social Psychology*, 50, 1199–1210. doi: 10.1037//0022-3514.50.6.1199

Ghorpade, J. (2000). Managing five paradoxes of 360-degree feedback. *Academy of Management Perspectives*, 14, 140–150. doi: 10.5465/AME.2000.2909846

Geiser, C. (2008). *Structural equation modeling of multitrait-multimethod-multioccasion data.* (doctoral dissertation). Freie Universität Berlin, Germany.

Geiser, C., Eid, M., & Nussbeck, F. W. (2008). On the meaning of the latent variables in the CTC(M-1) model: A comment on Maydeu-Olivares and Coffman (2006). *Psychological Methods*, 13, 49–57. doi: 10.1037/1082-989X.13.1.49

Geiser, C., Eid, M., Nussbeck, F. W., Courvoisier, D. S., & Cole, D. A. (2010). Analyzing true change in longitudinal multitrait-multimethod studies: Application of a multimethod change model to depression and anxiety in children. *Developmental Psychology*, 46, 29–45. doi: 10.1037/a0017888

Geiser, C., Eid, M., West, S. G., Lischetzke, T., & Nussbeck, F. W. (2012). A comparison of method effects in two confirmatory factor models for structurally different methods. *Structural Equation Modeling: A Multidisciplinary Journal, 19*, 409–436. doi: 10.1080/10705511.2012.687658

Geiser, C., Koch, T., & Eid, M. (2014). Data-generating mechanisms versus constructively-defined latent variables in multitrait-multimethod analysis: A comment on Castro-Schilo, Widaman, & Grimm. *Structural Equation Modeling: A Multidisciplinary Journal, 21*, 509–203. doi: 10.1080/10705511.2014.919816

Grimm, K. J., Pianta, R. C., & Konold, T. (2009). Longitudinal multitrait-multimethod models for developmental research. *Multivariate Behavioral Research, 44*, 233–258. doi: 10.1080/00273170902794230

Hays, W. L. (1994). *Statistics* (5th ed.). Orlando, FL: Harcourt Brace College Publishers.

Holtmann, J., Koch, T., Bohn, J, & Eid, M. (2017). Bayesian analysis of longitudinal multitrait-multimethod data with ordinal response variables. *British Journal of Mathematical and Statistical Psychology, 70*, 42–80. doi: 10.1111/bmsp.12081

Hox, J. J. (2002). *Multilevel analysis techniques and applications*. Mahwah, NJ: Lawrence Erlbaum Associates.

Jöreskog, K. G. (1969). A general approach to confirmatory factor analysis. *Psychometrika, 34*, 183–202.

Jöreskog, K. G. (1971). Statistical analysis of sets of congeneric tests. *Psychometrika, 36*, 109–133.

Kenny, D. A. (1976). An empirical application of confirmatory factor analysis to the multitrait-multimethod matrix. *Journal of Experimental Social Psychology, 12*, 247–252. doi: 10.1016/0022-1031(76)90055-X

Kenny, D. A. (1995). The multitrait-multimethod matrix: Design, analysis, and conceptual issues. In S. T. Fiske & P. E. Shrout (Eds.), *Personality research, methods, and theory: A festschrift honoring Donald W. Fiske* (pp. 111–124). Hillsdale, NJ: Lawrence Erlbaum Associates.

Kenny, D. A., & Kashy, D. A. (1992). Analysis of the multitrait-multimethod matrix by confirmatory factor analysis. *Psychological Bulletin, 112*, 165–172.

Koch, T. (2013). *Multilevel structural equation modeling of multitrait-multimethod-multioccasion data*. (doctoral dissertation). Freie Universität Berlin, Germany.

Koch T., Schultze M., Eid M., & Geiser C. (2014). A longitudinal multilevel CFA-MTMM model for interchangeable and structurally different methods. *Frontiers in Psychology, 5*, 311. doi: 10.3389/fpsyg.2014.00311

Koch, T., Schultze, M., Holtmann, J., Geiser, C., & Eid, M. (2017). A multimethod latent state-trait model for structurally different and interchangeable methods. *Psychometrika, 82*, 17–47. doi: 10.1007/s11336-016-9541-x

Lance, C. E., Noble, C. L., & Scullen, S. E. (2002). A critique of the correlated trait-correlated method and correlated uniqueness models for multitrait-multimethod data. *Psychological Methods, 7*, 228–244. doi: 10.1037//1082-989X.7.2.228

Lischetzke, T., Eid, M., & Nussbeck, F. W. (2002, September). Unterschiedliche Definitionen von Methodeneffekten in MTMM Modellen und ihre Implikationen für die Analyse der Validität [Different definitions of method effects in MTMM models and their implications for validity analysis]. Paper presented at the 43rd meeting of the German Psychological Association, Berlin, Germany.

Lord, F. M., & Novick, M. R. (1968). *Statistical theories of mental test scores*. Reading, MA: Addison-Wesley.

Mahlke, J., Schultze, M., Koch, T., Eid, M., Eckert, R., & Brodbeck, F. C. (2015). A multilevel CFA–MTMM approach for multisource feedback instruments: presentation and application of a new statistical model. *Structural Equation Modeling: A Multidisciplinary Journal, 23*, 91–110. doi: 10.1080/10705511.2014.990153

Marsh, H. W. (1989). Confirmatory factor analysis of multitrait-multimethod data: Many problems and a few solutions. *Applied Psychological Measurement, 13*, 335–361. doi: 10.1177/014662168901300402

Marsh, H. W. (1993). Multitrait-multimethod analyses: Inferring each trait-method combination with multiple indicators. *Applied Measurement in Education*, 6, 49–81. doi: 10.1207/s15324818ame0601_4

Marsh, H. W., & Bailey, M. (1991). Confirmatory factor analyses of multitrait-multimethod data: A comparison of alternative models. *Applied Psychological Measurement*, 15, 47–70. doi: 10.1177/014662169101500106

Marsh, H. W., & Grayson, D. (1995). Latent variable models of multitrait-multimethod data. In R. H. Hoyle (Ed.), *Structural equation modeling: Concepts, issues, and applications* (pp. 177–198). Thousand Oaks: Sage.

Marsh, H. W., & Hocevar, D. (1988). A new, more powerful approach to multitrait-multimethod analyses: Application of second-order confirmatory factor analysis. *Journal of Applied Psychology*, 73, 107–117. doi: 10.1037/0021-9010.73.1.107

Messick, S. (1980). Test validity and the ethics of assessment. *American Psychologist*, 35, 1012–1027. doi: 10.1037//0003-066X.35.11.1012

Messick, S. (1989). Validity. In R. L. Linn (Ed.), *Educational measurement* (3rd ed.) (pp. 13–103). New York: Macmillan Publishing Co.

Messick, S. (1995). Validity of psychological assessment: Validation of inferences from persons' responses and performances as scientific inquiry into score meaning. *American Psychologist*, 50, 741–749. doi: 10.1037/0003-066X.50.9.741

Millsap, R. E. (1995a). Measurement invariance, predictive invariance, and the duality paradox. *Multivariate Behavioral Research*, 30, 577–605. doi: 10.1207/s15327906mbr3004_6

Millsap, R. E. (1995b). The statistical analysis of method effects in multitrait-multimethod data: A review. In P. E. Shrout & S. T. Fiske (Eds.), *Personality research, methods, and theory: A festschrift honoring Donald W. Fiske* (pp. 99–109). Hillsdale, NJ: Lawrence Erlbaum Associates.

Muthén, B. O. (1994). Multilevel covariance structure analysis. *Sociological Methods and Research*, 22, 376–398 doi: 10.1177/0049124194022003006.

Muthén, B. O., & Khoo, S. T. (1998). Longitudinal studies of achievement growth using latent variable modeling. *Learning and Individual Differences*, 10, 73–101.doi: 10.1016/S1041-6080(99)80135-6

Muthén, B. O., & Muthén, L. K. (2000). Integrating person-centered and variable-centered analyses: Growth mixture modeling with latent trajectory classes. *Alcoholism: Clinical and Experimental Research*, 24, 882–891. doi: 10.1111/j.1530-0277.2000.tb02070.x

Muthén, L. K., & Muthén, B. O. (1998–2012). *MPlus user's guide*. (7th ed.) Los Angeles, CA: Muthén & Muthén.

Novick, M. R. (1966). The axioms and principal results of classical test theory. *Journal of Mathematical Psychology*, 3, 1–18. doi: 10.1016/0022-2496(66)90002-2

Nussbeck, F. W., Eid, M., Geiser, C., Courvoisier, D. S., & Lischetzke, T. (2009). CTC(M-1) Model for different types of raters. *Methodology*, 5, 88–98. doi: 10.5167/uzh-19988

Pohl, S., & Steyer, R. (2010). Modeling common traits and method effects in multitrait–multimethod analysis. *Multivariate Behavioral Research*, 45, 45–72.doi: 10.1080/00273170903504729

Pohl, S., Steyer, R., & Kraus, K. (2008). Modelling method effects as individual causal effects. *Journal of the Royal Statistical Society Series A*, 171, 41–63.doi: 10.1111/j.1467-985X.2007.00517.x

Shrout, P. E., & Fiske, S. T. (Eds.). (1995). *Personality research, methods, and theory: A festschrift honoring Donald W. Fiske*. Hillsdale, NJ: Lawrence Erlbaum Associates.

Sternberg, R. J. (1992). Psychological Bulletin's top 10 "hit parade." *Psychological Bulletin*, 112, 387–388.

Steyer, R. (1989). Models of classical psychometric test theory as stochastic measurement models: Representation, uniqueness, meaningfulness, identifiability, and testability. *Methodika*, 3, 25–60.

Steyer, R., & Eid, M. (2001). Messen und Testen *[Measurement and testing]*. Berlin: Springer.

Steyer, R., Ferring, D., & Schmitt, M. J. (1992). States and traits in psychological assessment. *European Journal of Psychological Assessment*, 8, 79–98.

Steyer, R., Partchev, I., & Shanahan, M. J. (2000). Modeling true intraindividual change in structural equation models: The case of poverty and children's psychosocial adjustment. In T. D. Little, K. U. Schnabel, & J. Baumert (Eds.), *Modeling longitudinal and multilevel data: Practical issues, applied approaches, and specific examples* (pp. 109–126). Mahwah, NJ: Lawrence Erlbaum.

Steyer, R., & Schmitt, M. (1990). The effects of aggregation across and within occasions on consistency, specificity, and reliability. *Methodika, 4,* 58–94.

Steyer, R., Schmitt, M., & Eid, M. (1999). Latent state-trait theory and research in personality and individual differences. *European Journal of Personality, 13,* 389–408. doi: 10.1002/(SICI)1099-0984(199909/10)13:53.0.CO;2-A

Widaman, K.-F. (1985). Hierarchically nested covariance structure models for multitrait-multimethod data. *Applied Psychological Measurement, 9,* 1–26.

Wothke, W. (1995). Covariance components analysis of the multitrait-multimethod matrix. In P. E. E. A. Shrout (Ed.), *Personality research, methods, and theory: A festschrift honoring Donald W. Fiske* (pp. 125–144). Hillsdale, NJ: Lawrence Erlbaum Associates.

Wothke W., & Browne, M. W. (1990). The direct product model for the MTMM matrix parameterized as a second order factor analysis model. *Psychometrika, 55,* 255–262.

Zimmerman, D. W. (1975). Two concepts of "true-score" in test theory. *Psychological Reports, 36,* 795–805. doi: 10.2466/pr0.1975.36.3.795

Code Appendix

MPlus example using 360-degree feedback from self- and supervisor ratings of captivating speaking and general leadership skills.

Code 1 Common factor TMU models.

(a) Essential tau-congeneric.

```
Title: Single Level Latent TMU-Model
       Tau-congeneric variables

Data: File = cuteL1.dat;

! Yijk = observed variable (indicator)
! i = indicator (1,2)
! j = construct (1,3)
! k = method (1,2)

Variable:
        names = id Y111 Y211 Y112 Y212
                Y131 Y231 Y132 Y232;

        usevar = Y111 Y211 Y112 Y212
                 Y131 Y231 Y132 Y232;

        missing = all(-99);

Analysis:
    Type = General;
    estimator = MLR;
```

```
Model:

TMU11 by Y111
         Y211;
TMU12 by Y112
         Y212;
TMU31 by Y131
         Y231;
TMU32 by Y132
         Y232;

Output: stdyx Tech4 modindices residual;
```

(b) Essential tau-equivalent.
```
Title: Single Level Latent TMU-Model
       Essential tau-equivalent variables

Data: File = cuteL1.dat;

! Yijk = observed variable (indicator)
! i = indicator (1,2)
! j = construct (1,3)
! k = method (1,2)

Variable:
        names = id Y111 Y211 Y112 Y212
                   Y131 Y231 Y132 Y232;

        usevar =   Y111 Y211 Y112 Y212
                   Y131 Y231 Y132 Y232;

        missing = all(-99); ! Missing value flag

Analysis:
    Type = General;
    estimator = MLR;

Model:

TMU11 by Y111     ! per default factor loading is set to 1
         Y211@1;  ! fix factor loading to 1
TMU12 by Y112     ! per default factor loading is set to 1
         Y212@1;  ! fix factor loading to 1
TMU31 by Y131     ! per default factor loading is set to 1
         Y231@1;  ! fix factor loading to 1
TMU32 by Y132     ! per default factor loading is set to 1
         Y232@1;  ! fix factor loading to 1

Output: stdyx Tech4 modindices residual;
```

(c) Essential tau-parallel.
```
Title: Single Level Latent TMU-Model
       Essential tau-parallel variables

Data: File=cuteL1.dat;
! Yijk = observed variable (indicator)
! i = indicator (1,2)
! j = construct (1,3)
! k = method (1,2)

Variable:
        names=id Y111 Y211 Y112 Y212
                 Y131 Y231 Y132 Y232;

        usevar =
                Y111 Y211 Y112 Y212
                Y131 Y231 Y132 Y232;

        missing=all(-99);! Missing value flag

Analysis:
    Type = General;
    estimator = MLR;

Model:

TMU11 by Y111 Y211@1; ! per default factor loading is set to 1
TMU12 by Y112 Y212@1; ! per default factor loading is set to 1
TMU31 by Y131 Y231@1; ! per default factor loading is set to 1
TMU32 by Y132 Y232@1; ! per default factor loading is set to 1

Y111 Y211 (eps1); ! set residuals (epsilons) equal
Y112 Y212 (eps2); ! set residuals (epsilons) equal
Y131 Y231 (eps3); ! set residuals (epsilons) equal
Y132 Y232 (eps4); ! set residuals (epsilons) equal

Output: stdyx Tech4 modindices residual;
```

(d) Tau-parallel.
```
Title: Single Level Latent TMU-Model
       Essential tau-parallel variables

Data: File=cuteL1.dat;

! Yijk = observed variable (indicator)
! i = indicator (1,2)
! j = construct (1,3)
! k = method (1,2)
```

```
Variable:
        names=id Y111 Y211 Y112 Y212
                 Y131 Y231 Y132 Y232;

        usevar=
                 Y111 Y211 Y112 Y212
                 Y131 Y231 Y132 Y232;

        missing=all(-99);! Missing value flag

Analysis:
   Type=General;
   estimator=MLR;

Model:

TMU11 by Y111 Y211@1;! per default factor loading is set to 1
TMU12 by Y112 Y212@1;! per default factor loading is set to 1
TMU31 by Y131 Y231@1;! per default factor loading is set to 1
TMU32 by Y132 Y232@1;! per default factor loading is set to 1

Y111 Y211 (eps1);! set residuals (epsilons) equal
Y112 Y212 (eps2);! set residuals (epsilons) equal
Y131 Y231 (eps3);! set residuals (epsilons) equal
Y132 Y232 (eps4);! set residuals (epsilons) equal

[Y111 Y211] (alp1); ! set intercepts (alphas) equal
[Y112 Y212] (alp2); ! set intercepts (alphas) equal
[Y131 Y231] (alp3); ! set intercepts (alphas) equal
[Y132 Y232] (alp4); ! set intercepts (alphas) equal

Output: stdyx Tech4 modindices residual;
```

Code 2 CFA-MTMM models for structurally different methods.

(a) CTC(M-1) Model.
```
Title: CTC(M-1) Model

Data: File = cuteL1.dat;
! Yijk = observed variable (indicator)
! i = indicator (1,2)
! j = construct (1,3)
! k = method (1,2)
```

```
Variable:
      names=id    Y111 Y211 Y112 Y212
                  Y131 Y231 Y132 Y232;

      usevar=Y111 Y211 Y112 Y212
             Y131 Y231 Y132 Y232
             ;

      missing=all(-99);
Analysis:
   Type = General;
   estimator = MLR;
Model:
! Captivating speaking skills
! Trait Factor
! Equal factor loading parameters for each method
T11 by Y111@1    ! Reference method indicators
       Y211@1
       Y112 (lam1) ! Non-Reference method indicator
       Y212 (lam1);

! Method Factor
M1 by Y112@1 Y212@1;

T11 M1 (T11 M1); ! Label Variances

! Impermissible Correlation fixed to 0
T11 with M1@0;

! General leadership skills
! Trait Factor
! Equal factor loading parameters for each method
T13 by Y131@1
       Y231@1
       Y132 (lam2)
       Y232 (lam2);

! Method Factor
M3 by Y132@1 Y232@1;

T13 M3 (T13 M3); ! Label Variances

! Impermissible Correlation fixed to 0
T13 with M3@0;

! Equal Residual Variances
  Y111 Y211 (eps1);
  Y112 Y212 (eps2);
  Y131 Y231 (eps3);
  Y132 Y232 (eps4);
```

```
! Mean Structure
[Y111@0 Y131@0];
[T11 T13];

Model Constraint:
! Model Constraints are used
! to compute the variance coefficients

! Observed Variance
NEW(Var11 Var12 Var31 Var32);
Var11 = T11 + eps1;
Var12 = lam1**2*T11+ M1+ eps2;
Var31 = T13+ eps3;
Var32 = lam2**2*T13+ M3+ eps4;

! Consistency / Reliability
NEW(Con11 Con12 Con31 Con32);
Con11 = T11/Var11;
Con12 = (lam1**2*T11)/Var12;
Con31 = T13/Var31;
Con32 = (lam2**2*T13)/Var32;

! Method Specificity
NEW(Msp12 Msp32);
Msp12 = (M1)/Var12;
Msp32 = (M3)/Var32;

! Reliability
NEW(Rel12 Rel32);
Rel12 = Con12 + Msp12;
Rel32 = Con32 + Msp32;

Output: stdyx Tech4 modindices residual;
```

(b) Latent Difference Model.

```
Title: Latent Difference Model

Data: File=cuteL1.dat;

Variable:
        names=id Y111 Y211 Y112 Y212
                 Y131 Y231 Y132 Y232;
        usevar =
                 Y111 Y211 Y112 Y212
                 Y131 Y231 Y132 Y232;

        missing = all(-99);

Analysis:
    Type = General;
    estimator = MLR;
```

```
Model:
! Captivating speaking skills
! Measurement Model
T11 by Y111 Y211@1;
T21 by Y112 Y212@1;

! Latent Difference Method Factor
M1 by Y112@0;

! Perfect Regression
! Tautological decomposition
T21 on T11@1 M1@1;
T21@0;

! General leadership skills
! Measurement Models
T12 by Y131 Y231@1;
T22 by Y132 Y232@1;

! Latent Difference Method Factor
M2 by Y112@0;

! Perfect Regression
! Tautological decomposition
T22 on T12@1 M2@1;
T22@0;

! Zero-Correlations
T21 with T12-T22@0 M2@0;
T22 with T11-T21@0 M1@0;

! Equal Residual Variances
Y111 Y211 (eps1);
Y112 Y212 (eps2);
Y131 Y231 (eps3);
Y132 Y232 (eps4);

! Mean Structure
[Y111@0 Y112@0 Y131@0 Y132@0];
[T11 M1 T12 M2];

Output: stdyx Tech4 modindices residual;
```

(c) Latent Means Model.
```
Title: Latent Means Model
Data: File=cuteL1.dat;
Variable:
```

```
            names=id Y111 Y211 Y112 Y212
                    Y131 Y231 Y132 Y232;
            usevar =
                    Y111 Y211 Y112 Y212
                    Y131 Y231 Y132 Y232;
            missing=all(-99);
Analysis:
    Type=General;
    estimator=MLR;
Model:
! Captivating speaking skills
! Overal Trait-Factor
T1 by Y111@1 Y211@1 Y112@1 Y212@1;

! Latent Method Factor
! factor loading restrictions
M1 by Y111@-1
      Y211@-1
      Y112@1
      Y212@1;

! General leadership skills
! Overal Trait-Factor
T2 by Y131@1 Y231@1 Y132@1 Y232@1;

! Latent Method Factor
! factor loading restrictions
M2 by Y131@-1
      Y231@-1
      Y132@1
      Y232@1 ;

! Equal Residual Variances
Y111 Y211 (eps1);
Y112 Y212 (eps2);
Y131 Y231 (eps3);
Y132 Y232 (eps4);

! Mean Structure
[Y111@0 Y131@0 Y112@0 Y132@0];
[T1 M1 T2 M2];
Output: stdyx Tech4 modindices residual;
```

Code 3 ML-CFA models for interchangeable methods (see Table 25.6).

(a) Model 1 (tau-congeneric method variables).

```
Title: Model 1 Table 25.6

Data: File=cuteL2.dat;

Variable:
   names=id Y111 Y211 Y112 Y212 Y113 Y213
            Y131 Y231 Y132 Y232 Y133 Y233 ;

   cluster=id;

   usevar=  Y113 Y213
            Y133 Y233;

   missing = all(-99);

Analysis:
    Type = Twolevel;
    Estimator = MLR;

Model:

%within%
! Level-1 Method Factors
M1 by Y113@1 Y213;
M3 by Y133@1 Y233;

%between%
! Level-2 Trait Factors
! Indicator-Specific Trait Factors
T11 by Y113@1;
T21 by Y213@1;
T13 by Y133@1;
T23 by Y233@1;

! Fix all error variables to zero
Y113-Y213@0;
Y133-Y233@0;

! Fix all intercepts to zero
[Y113-Y213@0];
[Y133-Y233@0];

[T11-T21];
[T13-T23];

Output: Tech4 residual stdyx modindices;
```

(b) Model 2 (essential tau-equivalent method variables).
```
Title: Model 2 Table 25.6

Data: File = cuteL2.dat;

Variable:
   names=id Y111 Y211 Y112 Y212 Y113 Y213
            Y131 Y231 Y132 Y232 Y133 Y233 ;

   cluster=id;

   usevar=  Y113 Y213
            Y133 Y233;

   missing=all(-99);

Analysis:
    Type=Twolevel;
    Estimator = MLR;

Model:

%within%
! Level-1 Method Factors
M1 by Y113@1 Y213@1;
M3 by Y133@1 Y233@1;

%between%
! Level-2 Trait Factors
! Indicator-Specific Factors
T11 by Y113@1;
T21 by Y213@1;
T13 by Y133@1;
T23 by Y233@1;

! Fix all error variables to zero
Y113-Y213@0;
Y133-Y233@0;

! Fix all intercepts to zero
[Y113-Y213@0];
[Y133-Y233@0];

[T11-T21];
[T13-T23];


Output: Tech4 residual stdyx modindices;
```

(c) Model 3 (essential tau-parallel method variables of leadership skills).
```
Title: Model 3 Table 25.6

Data: File=cuteL2.dat;

Variable:
   names=id Y111 Y211 Y112 Y212 Y113 Y213
            Y131 Y231 Y132 Y232 Y133 Y233 ;

   cluster=id;

   usevar=  Y113 Y213
            Y133 Y233;

   missing = all(-99);

Analysis:
    Type=Twolevel;
    Estimator=MLR;

Model:

%within%
! Level-1 Method Factors
M1 by Y113@1 Y213@1;
M3 by Y133@1 Y233@1;

Y133 Y233 (eps1);

%between%
! Level-2 Trait Factors
! Indicator-Specific Factors
T11 by Y113@1;
T21 by Y213@1;
T13 by Y133@1;
T23 by Y233@1;

! Fix all error variables to zero
Y113-Y213@0;
Y133-Y233@0;

! Fix all intercepts to zero
[Y113-Y213@0];
[Y133-Y233@0];

[T11-T21];
[T13-T23];


Output: Tech4 residual stdyx modindices;
```

(d) Model 4 (essential tau-parallel method variables for both constructs).
```
Title: Model 4 Table 25.6

Data: File=cuteL2.dat;

Variable:
   names = id Y111 Y211 Y112 Y212 Y113 Y213
              Y131 Y231 Y132 Y232 Y133 Y233 ;

   cluster = id;

   usevar=  Y113 Y213
            Y133 Y233;

   missing=all(-99);

Analysis:
    Type=Twolevel;
    Estimator=MLR;

Model:

%within%
! Level-1 Method Factors
M1 by Y113@1 Y213@1;
M3 by Y133@1 Y233@1;

Y133 Y233 (eps1);
Y113 Y213 (eps2);

%between%
! Level-2 Trait Factors
! Indicator-Specific Factors
T11 by Y113@1;
T21 by Y213@1;
T13 by Y133@1;
T23 by Y233@1;

! Fix all error variables to zero
Y113-Y213@0;
Y133-Y233@0;

! Fix all intercepts to zero
[Y113-Y213@0];
[Y133-Y233@0];

[T11-T21];
[T13-T23];


Output: Tech4 residual stdyx modindices;
```

(e) Model 5 (Model 3 with homogeneous trait factors).
```
Title: Model 5 Table 25.6

Data: File=cuteL2.dat;

Variable:
   names=id Y111 Y211 Y112 Y212 Y113 Y213
            Y131 Y231 Y132 Y232 Y133 Y233 ;

   cluster=id;

   usevar=  Y113 Y213
            Y133 Y233;

   missing=all(-99);

Analysis:
     Type=Twolevel;
     Estimator=MLR;

Model:

%within%
! Level-1 Method Factors
M1 by Y113@1 Y213@1;
M3 by Y133@1 Y233@1;

Y133 Y233 (eps1);

%between%
! Level-2 Trait Factors
! Indicator-Specific Factors
T11 by Y113@1;
T21 by Y213@1;
T13 by Y133@1;
T23 by Y233@1;

! Common Trait Factors
T1 by T11@1 T21;
T3 by T13@1 T23;

! Fix all error variables to zero
T11-T21@0;
T13-T23@0;

! Fix all error variables to zero
Y113-Y213@0;
Y133-Y233@0;
```

```
! Fix all intercepts to zero
[Y113-Y213@0];
[Y133-Y233@0];

! Fix all intercepts to zero
[T11-T21];
[T13-T23];

Output: Tech4 residual stdyx modindices;
```

Code 4 ML-CTC(M-1) model for a combination of structurally different and interchangeable methods for two traits.

```
Title: ML-CTC(M-1) for a combination of structurally
different and interchangeable methods with two
indicators, two constructs, two structurally different
methods and one set of
interchangeable methods

Data: File=cuteL2.dat;

Variable:
   names= id Y111 Y211 Y112 Y212 Y113 Y213
             Y131 Y231 Y132 Y232 Y133 Y233 ;

   cluster=id;

   Between=
            Y111 Y211 Y112 Y212
            Y131 Y231 Y132 Y232;

   usevar=  Y111 Y211
            Y112 Y212
            Y113 Y213
            Y131 Y231
            Y132 Y232
            Y133 Y233;

   missing = all(-99);

Analysis:
   Type = Twolevel;
   Estimator = MLR;
```

```
Model:

%within%
! Unique Method Factors
! Equal Factor Loading Parameters
UM1 by Y113@1 Y213@1;
UM3 by Y133@1 Y233@1;

! Equal Error Variance
! Leadership Skills
Y133 Y233 (eps1);

%between%
! Captivating Speaking Skills
! Indicator-Specific Trait Factors
! Equal Factor Loading For Each Method
T11  by Y111@1
        Y112 (lam21)
        Y113 (lam31);
T21  by Y211@1
        Y212 (lam21)
        Y213 (lam31);

! Method Factor for the structural different method
! Equal Factor Loadings
M21 by Y112@1
        Y212@1;

! Common Method Factor for the interchangeable method
! Equal Factor Loadings
CM31 by Y113@1
        Y213@1;

! General Leadership Skills
! Indicator-Specific Trait Factors
! Equal Factor Loading For Each Method
T13  by Y131@1
        Y132 (lam22)
        Y133 (lam32);
T23  by Y231@1
        Y232 (lam22)
        Y233 (lam32)
        ;
! Method Factor for the structural different method
! Equal Factor Loadings
M23 by Y132@1 Y232@1;
```

```
! Common Method Factor for the interchangeable method
! Equal Factor Loadings
CM33 by Y133@1 Y233@1;

! Correlation between Trait and Method Factors
! Are fixed to zero
T11-T21 with M21-CM31@0 M23-CM33@0;
T13-T23 with M21-CM31@0 M23-CM33@0;

! Equal Residual Variances
! Restrictions are NOT neccessary
Y131 Y231 (eps2);
Y132 Y232 (eps3);
Y111 Y211 (eps4);
Y112 Y212 (eps5);

! Fix Residual Variances
! of the interchangeable methods
! to zero
Y113@0 Y213@0;
Y133@0 Y233@0;

Output: Tech4 residual stdyx modindices;
```

Part V
Modelling Groups

26

Factorial Invariance Across Multiple Populations in Discrete and Continuous Data

Roger E. Millsap and Hanjoe Kim

In psychology, a measurement model describes the relationship between scores on a measuring instrument and scores on the latent variable that the instrument was designed to measure. Here the "latent variable" plays the role of the construct: It is what we believe the instrument is measuring. The relationship between scores on the instrument and scores on the latent variable is ordinarily conceived as probabilistic. There is uncertainty in measurement. Measurement invariance concerns the stability or invariance in this relationship across diverse measurement conditions. For example, is the relationship between the measuring instrument and the latent variable the same for individuals from different populations?

A simple example will help illustrate this invariance concept. Suppose that the "instrument" is an algebra problem designed to measure understanding of the quadratic formula, with the problem being posed as a story problem in English. Now consider two students whose understanding of the quadratic formulas is the same, but whose understanding of English varies greatly. Student A is a native speaker of English, and student B is a native Spanish speaker, with only a modest understanding of English. Both students attempt to solve the item. If the item truly measures understanding of the quadratic formula, and if the item is measurement invariant in relation to language, we expect that students A and B have the same chance of passing the item. Their understanding of the quadratic formula is identical, and so if the item is invariant, we expect them to have the same chance of passing. Under the circumstances, however, this is not a reasonable expectation. A more realistic view is that measurement invariance does not hold for this item in relation to language, because some English skills are needed to solve the item. The lack of invariance in this item only becomes apparent once we encounter populations that lack the needed English skills.

The notion of measurement invariance is defined broadly to include all types of measurement "instruments" (item-level scores, whole test scores) and a variety of possible latent variable models (common factor models, models from item response theory) (Meredith, 1993). It is also defined to be stringent in specifying that the entire probability distribution for each measured variable under study is invariant. In other words, all of the conditional response probabilities for the various possible responses are invariant for each measured variable. Suppose that we have p measured variables with scores in a p × 1 vector **X**, which could be p item scores or a battery of p test scores. We will also assume that we have K populations or groups of individuals to be compared. We let V denote the variable that defines the groups. Finally, we assume there are r latent variables, with scores in an r × 1 vector **W** that are targeted by the measured variables **X**. We assume r < p, but we need not require r = 1 because there may be more than one latent variable targeted by the measured variables. Let P(**X** = x | **W**, V) denote the conditional probability that **X** has the value x, given scores on **W**, and groups defined by V. Then measurement invariance holds for **X** in relation to **W** and V if and only if

$$P(\mathbf{X}|\mathbf{W}, V) = P(\mathbf{X}|\mathbf{W}) \qquad (26.1)$$

for all **X**, **W**, and V (Mellenbergh, 1989; Meredith & Millsap, 1992), where P(A|B) denotes the conditional probability of A given B. The exact statement of this probability will depend on the nature of (**X**, **W**, V). This definition says that the probability of scoring any particular value on **X** is independent of V, once the latent variables in **W** are considered. In other words, while there may be group differences on **X**, these differences arise through differences on **W**, and no other sources of group differences affect the measures in **X**. If measurement invariance fails, there are group differences on **X** that are due to some influence apart from **W**. The definition does not identify what those influences might be.

To make the definition of measurement invariance practical, we need a measurement model for the relations between **X** and **W**. Here we will consider the common factor model, which is one of the oldest and still widely used measurement models. Under a common factor model for continuous **X** with r common factors **W**, we have

$$\mathbf{X} = \boldsymbol{\tau} + \boldsymbol{\Lambda}\mathbf{W} + \mathbf{u} \qquad (26.2)$$

where $\boldsymbol{\tau}$ is a p × 1 vector of measurement intercept parameters, $\boldsymbol{\Lambda}$ is a p × r matrix of factor loadings, and **u** is a p × 1 vector of unique factor scores. In a multiple-group context, we can expand the expression in Equation 26.2 to permit model parameters and scores to vary across groups

$$\mathbf{X}_k = \boldsymbol{\tau}_k + \boldsymbol{\Lambda}_k \mathbf{W}_k + \mathbf{u}_k \qquad (26.3)$$

for k = 1, 2,..., K. This model has implications for the structure of both the means and the covariance matrix for the measured variables. Under standard assumptions,

$$E(\mathbf{X}_k) = \boldsymbol{\mu}_k = \boldsymbol{\tau}_k + \boldsymbol{\Lambda}_k \boldsymbol{\kappa}_k \qquad (26.4)$$

$$\mathrm{Cov}(\mathbf{X}_k) = \boldsymbol{\Sigma}_k = \boldsymbol{\Lambda}_k \boldsymbol{\Phi}_k \boldsymbol{\Lambda}_k' + \boldsymbol{\Theta}_k \qquad (26.5)$$

where the mean vector and covariance matrix for **W** are $\boldsymbol{\kappa}_k$ and $\boldsymbol{\Phi}_k$ respectively, and $\boldsymbol{\Theta}_k$ is the covariance matrix (diagonal) for the unique factor scores. If we condition on **W**, the parameters that determine measurement invariance become clearer:

$$E(X_k|W_k) = \tau_k + \Lambda_k W_k \qquad (26.6)$$

$$\text{Cov}(X_k|W_k) = \Theta_k \qquad (26.7)$$

If measurement invariance is to hold, the parameters $(\tau_k, \Lambda_k, \Theta_k)$ must have the same values across groups, and we can drop the subscripts: $(\tau_k, \Lambda_k, \Theta_k) = (\tau, \Lambda, \Theta)$. When all of these parameters are invariant across groups, we say that **strict factorial invariance** holds for X. Technically, strict factorial invariance is a weaker condition than measurement invariance in Equation 26.1 because factorial invariance only involves the means and covariance matrices in each group, rather than the full probability distributions. This distinction is often ignored because multivariate normality is assumed by many factor estimation methods, and under multivariate normality, strict factorial invariance does imply measurement invariance in Equation 26.1. Even if normality does not hold, strict factorial invariance meets many practical needs in applications that focus mainly on mean or covariance structure.

Factorial invariance has a long history, with the earliest work questioning whether invariance in factor structure is even possible (Thomson, 1939; Thurstone, 1947). Computational methods for actually investigating factorial invariance were limited, employing rotational methods. Real progress was made following Jöreskog's (1971) work on confirmatory factor analysis (CFA) in multiple populations and Sörbom's (1974) extension to mean structures. For the first time it became possible to test for group differences in measurement intercepts and unique factor covariance structure in addition to factor loadings. Subsequent developments led to invariance modelling for discrete measures and to robust test statistics (Bartholomew, 1983, 1984, 1987; Browne, 1984; Muthén, 1978, 1984; Muthén & Christoffersson, 1981; Satorra & Bentler, 1994).

Aside from the technical aspects of studies of factorial invariance, several conceptual issues should be addressed before proceeding with any such study. First, tests of factorial invariance are model-based: we assume that a factor model adequately describes the data for a fixed number of factors. A common mistake in studying invariance is to rush into tests of invariance prior to knowing (1) whether a common factor model describes the measures in each group considered separately, and (2) the features of the model itself: the number of factors and the pattern of loadings. For example, if no firm idea about the number of factors exists for the measures being studied (at least with respect to the more familiar groups), a study of factorial invariance would be premature. Second, tests of factorial invariance generally require at least one measured variable per factor to be invariant across groups. We must have at least some invariant measures in order to detect bias in the rest of the measures. This requirement implies that some planning is needed to include some invariant measures along with the rest of the measures. Procedures do exist for helping to locate which measures might be invariant as a preliminary step (Woods, 2009), but previous research with the measures should also be used to help identify invariant measures. Third, the nature of the response scales for the measured variables X should be considered before deciding on a factor model. If the number of possible scale points for a given variable X_j is small (less than four), the factor model for discrete or ordered-categorical variables should be considered. Use of this model can avoid problems that may arise when a discrete variable is approximated by a continuous one. If X_j contains more than six possible values, the traditional common factor model for continuous measures may provide a good approximation. Both of these models are described next.

The Factor Model for Continuous Measures

The most widely used factor model in studies of invariance is the common factor model for continuous measures **X**. The analysis ordinarily employs a CFA in multiple groups defined by V. The groups are viewed as independent, with each individual belonging to only one group. The analysis typically proceeds as a nested series of model fit evaluations, with each successive model representing a more highly constrained, invariant model. Four such models are usually considered.

Configural invariance

In the beginning, the model stipulates that (1) the number of factors r is identical across groups, and (2) the locations of any zero elements in Λ_k are identical across groups. This second restriction is only meaningful if r > 1. The restriction serves to ensure that the same measured variables load on each factor across groups. **Configural invariance** (Thurstone, 1947) means that the factors are defined by the same indicators across groups. No invariance restrictions on the parameter values for the parameters (τ_k, Λ_k, Θ_k) are imposed, apart from those needed to identify the model.

Identification constraints are needed for the factor model within each group. The topic of identification in factor analysis has generated a large literature (see Hayashi & Marcoulides, 2006, for a review), and we will not provide a thorough review here. Multiple-group CFA provides new opportunities for identification using invariance constraints. In specifying configural invariance, at least two identification issues must be resolved: (1) the indeterminacy in the scales for the loadings and factor variances, and (2) the indeterminacy in the locations for the measurement intercepts and factor means. More identification issues arise if the factor structure permits more than one nonzero loading per measured variable. The first issue is usually resolved by either fixing one loading per factor to one, or fixing the variance for each factor to one. In the multiple-group CFA, we would not adopt the last option in each group because doing so would make the factor variances identical across groups. Those variances are ordinarily permitted to vary over groups, as the variability in the common factors is subject to selection influences (Meredith, 1964). The method of choice is usually to require one loading per factor to be fixed to one. For multiple groups, we would pick the same measured variable in each group for this purpose. A variation on this option, available only in the multiple-group case, is to fix all of the factor variances to one in a single group only, and then simply require invariance for one loading per factor. The value of the invariant loading is not fixed in advance.

The indeterminacy in the measurement intercepts and factor means can also be resolved in at least three ways. One approach is to fix the factor means to zero in all groups. This approach is not useful in invariance studies, however, because the factor means are generally believed to vary across groups, and like the factor variances, are affected by selection (Meredith, 1964). A second approach is to leave the factor means unconstrained and instead fix r of the p measurement intercepts to zero in each group. The same intercepts are usually chosen for this purpose across groups. The third option is to fix the factor means to zero in one group only, and then constrain r of the p measurement intercepts to invariance without specifying any fixed value for the intercepts.

All of the this advice concerning identification has assumed that the factor structure in the configural model limited each indicator to loading on a single factor, with no restrictions on the factor covariance matrix. This restriction is fairly common in CFA, and leads to great simplifications in conditions for identification. Not all applications will meet these requirements, however. A good example of a more complex factor structure is the bifactor model, which is becoming more widely used (Gibbons & Hedeker, 1992; Reise, Morizot, & Hays, 2007). In the general case in which each indicator loads on multiple factors, additional constraints are needed to identify the factor loadings and other parameters. This topic is complex, and it becomes useful to distinguish constraints needed for rotational uniqueness of the loadings and those needed for global identification of the factor model (Bollen & Jöreskog, 1985). Millsap (2011) addresses the uniqueness issue in the invariance case.

One weakness in these identification schemes is that some model parameters are required to be invariant a priori. This fact explains why it was stated earlier that at least one indicator per factor should be known to be invariant prior to investigating invariance in the full set. The potential pitfalls in ignoring this advice have been widely discussed (Johnson, Meade, & DuVernet, 2009; Little, Slegers, & Card, 2006; Rensvold & Cheung, 2001; Yoon & Millsap, 2007). If no indicators can be taken as meeting conditions for invariance a priori, various statistical approaches have been proposed for identifying indicators that can serve as reference variables for identification purposes (Rensvold & Cheung, 2001; Woods, 2009). All of these methods operate with the data at hand to try to identify indicators that are free of bias and that can serve as reference variables. This problem is not unique to studies of factorial invariance; similar problems arise in approaches that use item response theory (Glas & Verhelst, 1995).

If the configural model does not fit, there are three possibilities: (1) the pattern of zero loadings varies across groups, (2) the number of factors varies across groups, or (3) the common factor model itself does not fit in one or more groups. Which of these possibilities might apply in a given case can be investigated, but further investigation of invariance will likely cease. At this point, the investigation becomes one of finding the proper model in one or more groups, and the analyses may be viewed as exploratory.

Metric invariance

Metric invariance (Horn & McArdle, 1992; Thurstone, 1947) is said to hold for X when configural invariance holds, and we also have invariant factor loadings

$$\Lambda_k = \Lambda \quad (26.8)$$

for all $k = 1, 2, \ldots, K$. Identification constraints used for the factor loadings in the configural model will be maintained under metric invariance. The identification constraints for the mean structure are also maintained. If we think of the factor model as specifying a regression for each measured variable on the common factor(s), metric invariance means that in these regressions, the same regression weights are used in all groups. The invariance of these weights helps establish that the factors have a common interpretation across groups, although metric invariance alone does not fully anchor the meaning of the factors. If the groups are to be compared on their means on X_k, metric invariance is needed to justify the claim that the mean differences are solely due to the common factors. Metric invariance alone is not enough, however, as group differences in measurement intercepts can also affect the mean differences.

If measurement invariance is rejected, further analyses may be pursued to locate which loadings vary across groups. Depending on the number of variables p, searches of this type can require multiple hypothesis tests, with the problem of error-rate inflation becoming a concern. Methods for controlling inflation using false discovery rate procedures have been proposed (Benjamini & Hochberg, 1995; Raykov, Marcoulides, & Millsap, 2012; Steinberg, 2001). Another concern is how such a search should be conducted. For example, should one begin with fully invariant loadings and sequentially relax constraints, or start from an unconstrained solution and sequentially add invariance constraints? The answer will depend in part on how many loadings are invariant. If most loadings are invariant, the strategy of sequentially removing constraints would be more efficient in general (Meade & Lautenschlager, 2004; Yoon & Millsap, 2007; see Stark, Chernyshenko, & Drasgow, 2006, for a different view). Also, the sizes of the communalities for the measured variables are an influence to consider. Higher communalities will produce more accurate searches.

The search for loadings that vary across groups will eventually lead to a model that includes a mixture of invariant and varying loadings, representing partial metric invariance (Byrne, Shavelson, & Muthén, 1989). The implications of partial metric invariance for whether the indicators can be said to measure the same factors across groups are hard to describe in the abstract. If four of seven indicators for a factor load differently across groups, is the same factor being measured in all groups? Do the indicators themselves have the same interpretations across groups? The answer will depend on how the loading differences are explained, and this explanation turns on the specifics of the variables involved. Simple rules of thumb based on the number of indicators that lack invariance do not seem adequate.

Strong or scalar invariance

Once the metric invariance question is settled, the next stage examines the measurement intercepts for invariance. We now add invariance restrictions on the intercepts to the metric invariance model

$$\tau_k = \tau \tag{26.9}$$

for k = 1,2,…,K. All of the identification constraints used under metric invariance are maintained here. The metric invariance model, when combined with the restrictions in Equation 26.9, becomes the model for **strong factorial invariance** or **scalar invariance** (Meredith, 1993; Steenkamp & Baumgartner, 1998). If full metric invariance was retained, all intercepts are constrained to invariance under the strong invariance model. If partial metric invariance holds, only the intercepts for indicators with invariant loadings are restricted under strong invariance. The logic of this distinction is that if loadings are truly varying across groups, it is mathematically unlikely that intercepts would be invariant. Partial metric invariance implies partial scalar invariance.

If both the loadings and the intercepts are invariant for an indicator, we can state that any group differences in the means on the indicator are due to influences that operate through the common factors. In this sense, we can interpret mean differences on the indicator as indicating differences on the targeted latent variable, rather than bias in the indicator. Scalar invariance is highly useful when group differences in means are of interest. Metric invariance alone is not sufficient to ensure that comparisons of means across groups are not confounded with bias in the indicators.

Rejection of scalar invariance might be followed by further analyses devoted to finding intercepts that vary across groups. This investigation encounters the same problems faced by the analogous investigation after rejection of metric invariance. Type I error rates can again be controlled using false discovery rate procedures. The best method for deciding which intercepts may vary across groups is again unclear, especially in the absence of theory that would guide the choice. Once a decision has been made about which intercepts lack invariance, the resulting model will be one of partial strong invariance. We again must address the question of when the number of varying intercepts is too large to believe that any scale created from the indicators will measure the targeted latent variable in the same way across groups. One advantage of the scalar case, however, is that it is relatively easy to evaluate what portion of the scale mean difference across groups is due to the varying intercepts. We return to this issue next.

Strict invariance

As a final step following the evaluation of scalar invariance, invariance in the unique factor variances is examined. The invariance restriction on the unique factor variances is

$$\Theta_k = \Theta \tag{26.10}$$

for all $k = 1,2,\ldots,K$. The model that combines scalar invariance with invariance in the unique factor variances is said to exhibit **strict factorial invariance** (Meredith, 1993). In understanding this form of invariance, it is helpful to recall the definition of the unique factor variance. The classical view of unique factor scores is that they combine two components: measurement error and specific factors (Lord & Novick, 1968). Measurement error is viewed as random, unrelated to other variables. The specific factor is the portion of the true score for the measured variable that is unrelated to the other p-1 measured variables in the set being factor analyzed. Hence the specific factor represents unique influences on the measured variable that are not shared with the other measured variables. A specific factor in an item might be created through some idiosyncratic wording of the item stem that influences responses to the item. If such effects operate differently across groups, we might expect group differences in unique factor variances. Group differences in unique factor variances could also arise from group differences in reliabilities of the measured variables.

Invariance in the factor loadings and the unique factor variances implies that any group differences in the covariance structure for the measured variables are due solely to influences that operate through the common factors. For example, any group difference in the correlation between a pair of variables must be due to group differences in the factor variances (or covariances, for $r > 1$). Invariance in the factor loadings alone is not enough to ensure that group differences in correlations are only due to the common factors. For this reason, strict invariance does add something to the interpretation of correlations across groups. On the other hand, it is sometimes argued that strict invariance is not required if group differences in means are the focus. We support this view generally, but there will be exceptions; see DeShon, (2004) and Lubke & Dolan (2003) for good discussions of this issue.

Effect size

If invariance constraints for a given indicator are rejected at one or more of the three stages (metric, scalar, strict), interest usually shifts to evaluating the size of the group difference and deciding whether the violation of invariance matters. A statistically significant difference need not be large in practical terms, and it may not have meaningful consequences. We therefore need to have some method for evaluating violations of invariance for meaningfulness, starting with measures of effect size that can be understood. Here we focus on violations of metric and scalar invariance, as effect size measures for violation of strict invariance have not been used.

Effect size measures for group difference in measurement intercepts are not difficult to develop because the intercept parameters are essentially means. We will assume that metric invariance holds. We can express the group difference in indicator means as a function of two influences in the factor model. For groups 1 and 2, we have

$$\mu_{j1} - \mu_{j2} = (\tau_{j1} - \tau_{j2}) + \lambda_j(\kappa_1 - \kappa_2) \quad (26.11)$$

where (μ_{j1}, μ_{j2}) are the indicator means for the jth indicator, (τ_{j1}, τ_{j2}) are the measurement intercepts, (κ_1, κ_2) are the factor mean vectors (if r > 1), and λ_j is the jth row of the factor loading matrix. The equation shows the partitioning of the indicator mean difference into two portions. One portion $(\tau_{j1} - \tau_{j2})$ is the measurement intercept difference, which is nonzero in violation of scalar invariance. The second portion is a function of the difference in common factor mean vectors $(\kappa_1 - \kappa_2)$. Under this partitioning, a possible measure of effect size would be the proportion of the indicator group mean difference that is due to the intercept difference:

$$\Delta_j = \frac{\tau_{j1} - \tau_{j2}}{\mu_{j1} - \mu_{j2}} \quad (26.12)$$

To be useful, we assume that $\Delta_j > 0$. If $\Delta_j < 0$, the signs of the two differences in the ratio are in conflict, and it will be difficult to interpret the ratio. There are no established rules for interpreting Δ_j, but if $\Delta_j > .50$, it can be argued that the violation of invariance is large enough to strongly interfere with conclusions about group differences on the indicator.

Effect size measures for the factor loading differences are more difficult to develop, in part because the loadings affect both the mean and the covariance structures. Simulation studies in invariance methods often use fixed differences in loading values to represent small, medium, and large effects. A disadvantage of this approach is that there is no clear justification for considering these particular fixed values apart from convention. A different approach, but one that is more complicated, is to regard the loading difference as an interaction: the effect of the common factor on the indicator varies by group. Another way of describing this interaction is to say that the group difference on the indicator varies as a function of the common factor. If multiple common factors are involved, this view of the loading difference becomes complex quickly. For the case of only a single factor however, it becomes possible to explore how the group difference varies as a function of the single factor.

Within each group, the factor model specifies a linear regression for the indicator scores on the common factor scores. If metric invariance fails for the indicator, the groups being compared have regression lines with different slopes (factor loadings) and intercepts (measurement intercepts). The expected difference in indicator scores across groups, given the factor score, is

$$E(X_{j1} - X_{j2}|W) = (\tau_{j1} - \tau_{j2}) + (\lambda_{j1} - \lambda_{j2})W = \tau_d + \lambda_d W \qquad (26.13)$$

This expression relates the size of the expected group difference on the indicator to the factor score, using a linear function. The configural model can provide estimates of the group specific loadings and measurement intercepts, and these estimates in turn yield estimates of τ_d and λ_d. If we can specify a difference $(X_{j1} - X_{j2})$ that in meaningful in practical terms, we can then find the range of W scores that would produce a meaningful expected difference in Equation 26.13. At that point, we can consider whether anyone in our populations is likely to have values of W in the range needed. We can base this judgment on the estimated factor means (κ_1, κ_2) and factor variances (φ_1, φ_2), along with the standard normality assumptions.

An example

To illustrate factorial invariance tests using continuous variables, data from the Early Steps Multisite Study (Dishion, Shaw, Connell, Gardner, Weaver, & Wilson, 2008; Shaw, Connell, Dishion, Wilson, & Gardner, 2009) are used. A total of 731 families were recruited and about half (n = 367) of the families were randomly assigned to participate in the Family-Check-Up (FCU) program. More details of the Early Steps study are described in Dishion et al. (2008). In this example, the coder impression data collected at age 2 are used (Child and Family Center, 2003). Families were given short tasks (e.g., meal preparation with child) and the parent-child interaction was observed. Later, the coders were asked to give their impressions about the family on nine-point rating scales for 51 items. Among the 51 items, seven items were related to proactive parenting, six of which are used in the analyses below (item 30 was dropped due to a low communality in preliminary analyses). See Table 26.1 for the items. There were six completely missing cases among the 731 observations and therefore, a total of 725 observations were analyzed in this example, apart from some further missing item scores for a small number of cases. There were 359 girls and 366 boys. The descriptive statistics by gender are shown in Table 26.2.

All analyses reported here were done using Mplus Version 7.1 (Muthén & Muthén, 1998–2012). For this continuous case, maximum likelihood estimation was used, with

Table 26.1 Proactive parenting items.

1	Does the parent use directives that seem specific and clear to the child?
2	Is the parent appropriately contingent in responding to positive or compliant child behavior?
3	Does the parent communicate to the child in plain, simple, and clear terms?
4	Does the parent give understandable, age appropriate reasons for behavior change?
5	Does the parent seem to be mindful of the child's behavior, whereabouts, activities, and feelings?
6	Does the parent use verbal structuring to make the task manageable?
7	Does the parent actively engage in care giving, including dressing, feeding, and managing the day to day demands and needs of the child?

Note. All items have a 1–9 rating scale.

Table 26.2 Proactive parenting example: Sample covariance matrix and means by gender.

Girls\Boys	item 2	item 10	item 13	item 14	item 18	item 21	item 30
item 2	1.014\\1.305	0.829	0.912	0.871	0.845	1.101	0.427
item 10	0.484	1.434\\1.754	0.952	1.053	1.061	1.377	0.597
item 13	0.712	0.678	1.179\\1.615	1.088	1.134	1.189	0.538
item 14	0.664	0.673	0.881	1.778\\1.929	1.208	1.467	0.637
item 18	0.637	0.790	0.863	0.885	1.401\\1.720	1.441	0.678
item 21	0.758	0.891	0.819	0.898	0.855	2.632\\3.113	0.725
item 30	0.511	0.679	0.563	0.549	0.715	0.575	1.839\\1.684
Means	7.150\\6.962	6.891\\6.815	7.189\\7.066	6.733\\6.623	6.986\\6.904	5.794\\5.855	6.950\\6.877

Note. The values on the left and lower triangular represent statistics for the girl sample and the values on the right and upper triangular represent statistics for the boy sample.

full information maximum likelihood (FIML) adjustment for missing data. Global fit of each model was assessed using the chi-square test statistic and three approximate fit indices: the root mean square error of approximation (RMSEA; Browne & Cudeck, 1993; Steiger & Lind, 1980), the comparative fit index (CFI; Bentler & Bonett, 1980), and the standardized root mean square residual (SRMR). Values of the RMSEA ≤ .05 are considered as indicative of good fit, with values between .05 and .08 indicating fair fit (Browne & Cudeck, 1993). For the CFI, values of the CFI ≥ .95 are considered indicative of good fit (Hu & Bentler, 1995). For the SRMR, values of the SRMR ≤ .05 are considered indicative of good fit (Hu & Bentler, 1995). All of these cutpoints are rules of thumb at best, and have been criticized (Barrett, 2007; Marsh, Hau, & Wen, 2004). We will not explore these fit assessment controversies here. We also considered local fit information in assessing fit, relying on residuals, normalized residuals, and modification indices produced by Mplus.

We began the analyses with the configural model that specified a single common factor for the six items (Code Appendix, Code 1). Item 2 was chosen to have invariant loadings and measurement intercepts. The factor variance in the female group was fixed to 1.0, with the factor variance in the male group being free. Similarly, the factor mean in the female group was fixed to zero, while the factor mean in the male group was free. Collectively, these constraints are sufficient to identify the model in both groups. The fit of this model was fair, but not great: $\chi^2(18) = 55.455$, RMSEA = .076, CFI = .98, SRMR = .024. The local fit information did not reveal any source of misfit that was decisive, with all normalized residuals less than one, aside from one residual that was 1.47. All modification indices were less than 10, apart from one index that was 11.66. We decided to retain the configural model and proceed without further modifications.

Table 26.3 Proactive parenting example: Unstandardized factor loading and intercept estimates under strict invariance.

Item	Loading	Intercept
2	.717	7.103
10	.806	6.900
13	.895	7.182
14	.931	6.731
18	.931	6.998
21	1.049	5.893

The next model introduced invariance constraints on all factor loadings, while retaining all other constraints from the configural model. This model represents metric invariance (Code Appendix, Code 2). The fit of this model was not substantially affected by the additional constraints: $\chi^2(23) = 61.493$, RMSEA = .068, CFI = .98, SRMR = .048. A direct comparison between this model and the configural model shows that the metric invariance model fits no worse than the configural model: difference of χ^2 (5) = 6.038. We therefore retained the metric invariance model in preference to the configural model.

Next, the invariance constraints on the measurement intercepts were added to the metric invariance model, creating a scalar invariance model (Code Appendix, Code 3). All constraints used in the metric invariance model were included here. The scalar invariance model showed little loss of fit in relation to the previous metric invariance model: $\chi^2(28) = 69.459$, RMSEA = .064, CFI = .98, SRMR = .043. Direct comparison of the scalar invariance model to the metric invariance model showed no significant loss of fit: difference of χ^2 (5) = 7.966. It therefore appears that both the factor loadings and the measurement intercepts can be taken as invariant across gender.

Finally, invariance constraints on the unique factor variances were added to the scalar invariance model, retaining all other constraints from the latter model. This new model represents strict factorial invariance (Code Appendix, Code 4). Some loss of fit was noted in this model in relation to the scalar invariance model: $\chi^2(34) = 92.246$, RMSEA = .069, CFI = .97, SRMR = .064. The direct comparison between the strict and scalar invariance models showed significant loss of fit: difference of χ^2 (6) = 22.787. Modification indices pointed to the unique factor variance for item 13 as a contributor to the lack of fit, but the release of the invariance constraint on this parameter would not fully resolve the loss of fit. We decided to go back to the scalar invariance model as the final model to retain.

Table 26.3 gives the unstandardized, invariant factor loading, and intercept estimates common to the two groups. The results for the scalar invariance model showed that the parents of the male children had the lower factor mean (−.115), but the gender difference in means did not reach significance.

The Factor Model for Discrete Measures

The traditional common factor model does not formally recognize that the response scale for an item is often discrete with relatively few possible values. In the extreme case, an item might be scored as a binary variable (e.g., pass/fail). A substantial literature exists on the pitfalls in modelling such variables using linear latent variable models (Babakus, Ferguson, & Jöreskog, 1987; Bernstein & Teng, 1989; Carroll, 1945, 1983; McDonald & Ahlawat, 1974; Olsson, 1979; Rigdon & Ferguson, 1991). Modifications to the traditional factor model to handle discrete response scales are now available (Bartholomew, 1983, 1984, 1987; Bock & Aitkin, 1981; Browne & Arminger, 1995; Christoffersson, 1975; Jöreskog, 1993; Maydeu-Olivares, 2005; Mislevy, 1986; Muthén, 1978, 1984; Wirth & Edwards, 2007) and have been applied to the multiple-group case for invariance studies (Browne & Arminger, 1995; Lee, Poon, & Bentler, 1989; Millsap & Tein, 2004; Muthén & Christoffersson, 1981; Poon, Lee, Afifi, & Bentler, 1990). We will not provide a full description of the multiple-group discrete factor model here, but we will describe the most commonly used structure.

When should this discrete model be used in preference to the traditional linear factor model? No exact answer to this question is possible because it depends to some extent on the distributions of the item responses. A seven-point response scale may effectively become a four-point scale if no respondents use three of the seven response categories. Studies have examined the performance of the linear model in discrete data (Babakus et al., 1987; Bernstein & Teng, 1989; Olsson, 1979; Rigdon & Ferguson, 1991). We can conclude from these studies that binary or three-point items should be modelled using the discrete model, and response scales with seven or more scale points can be modelled with the traditional linear factor model without great distortion. Lubke and Muthén (2004) argue that even with the larger number of scale points, distortions can occur under the linear model that would prove to be important, and so caution is advised. Response scales in the four to six-point range are in a gray area; the choice is not as clear here. The conservative choice would be to use the discrete model in such cases, particularly if adequate sample sizes per group are available.

To describe the discrete model, we now assume that the jth measured variable X_{jk} can have the values $(0, 1, \ldots, C)$ where C is a positive integer, so that X_{jk} effectively has $C + 1$ possible values. The binary case is $C = 1$. In the discrete factor model, the measured variable X_{jk} is assumed to depend on the values of a latent continuous response variate X_{jk}^* that determines X_{jk} via a threshold:

$$X_{jk} = m \text{ if } v_{km} \leq X_{jk}^* < v_{k(m+1)} \qquad (26.14)$$

where $m = 0, 1, \ldots, C$ and $\{v_{k1}, \ldots, v_{kC}\}$ are the latent threshold parameters unique to variable X_{jk}. These thresholds are fixed. The variate X_{jk}^* is random and is modelled by the factor model

$$\mathbf{X}_k^* = \boldsymbol{\tau}_k + \boldsymbol{\Lambda}_k \mathbf{W}_k + \mathbf{u}_k \qquad (26.15)$$

where the factor model parameters are interpreted as in the linear case, and $\mathbf{X}_k^*$ is a p × 1 vector of the X_{jk}^* for $j = 1, 2, \ldots, p$. The measurement intercept parameters $\boldsymbol{\tau}_k$ may or may not be included in the model, depending on the software implementation. Researchers who use the discrete factor model, particularly in the multiple-group case, should be aware that software programs vary in their specifications of this model (Millsap & Tein, 2004). Our description will follow the Mplus specification of the model (Muthén & Muthén, 1998–2012), which eliminates the measurement intercepts from the model.

The typical assumptions for the discrete case are that $\mathbf{X}_k^*$ has a multivariate normal distribution

$$\mathbf{X}_k^* \sim MVN(\boldsymbol{\mu}_k^*, \boldsymbol{\Sigma}_k^*) \qquad (26.16)$$

with

$$\boldsymbol{\mu}_k^* = \boldsymbol{\Lambda}_k \boldsymbol{\kappa}_k \quad \boldsymbol{\Sigma}_k^* = \boldsymbol{\Lambda}_k \boldsymbol{\Phi}_k \boldsymbol{\Lambda}_k' + \boldsymbol{\Theta}_k \qquad (26.17)$$

The assumptions regarding the distribution of the factor scores ($\mathbf{W}_k$, $\mathbf{u}_k$) parallel those in the traditional factor model. The distributional assumptions on $\mathbf{X}_k^*$ have more importance in the discrete case in one sense: nonnormality in $\mathbf{X}_k^*$ undercuts the motivation for studying factorial invariance of $\mathbf{X}_k^*$, since in that case $(\boldsymbol{\mu}_k^*, \boldsymbol{\Sigma}_k^*)$ do not fully determine the distribution of $\mathbf{X}_k$, the measured variable. The parameters of interest for studies of factorial invariance are the thresholds $\{\boldsymbol{\nu}_1, \boldsymbol{\nu}_2, ..., \boldsymbol{\nu}_K\}$, and the loadings and unique factor covariance matrices $\{\boldsymbol{\Lambda}_1, \boldsymbol{\Theta}_1, \boldsymbol{\Lambda}_2, \boldsymbol{\Theta}_2, ..., \boldsymbol{\Lambda}_K, \boldsymbol{\Theta}_K\}$. Note that $\boldsymbol{\nu}_k$ is a p × C matrix of parameters, with jth row being the C thresholds for the jth measured variable. The factor means $\boldsymbol{\kappa}_k$ and the factor covariance matrices $\boldsymbol{\Phi}_k$ are not relevant to the invariance question, but may be of interest for other reasons.

Identification

An immediate problem facing invariance studies under the discrete model is that the model is not identified without further constraints, and the required constraints have not always been clearly described in the literature. Here we follow the specification of Millsap and Tein (2004) for the Mplus implementation. Given that $\mathbf{X}_k^*$ is itself latent, the parameters $\boldsymbol{\mu}_k^*$ and $\boldsymbol{\Sigma}_k^*$ are not identified because the thresholds can be adjusted for any linear transformation of $\mathbf{X}_k^*$. To help resolve this problem, we will fix $\boldsymbol{\kappa}_k = \mathbf{0}$ for one group (denoted the reference group), resulting in $\boldsymbol{\mu}_k^* = \mathbf{0}$ in the reference group. The factor means in the other groups are free. We also fix the diagonal elements of $\boldsymbol{\Sigma}_k^*$ to one in the reference group: $diag(\boldsymbol{\Sigma}_k^*) = \mathbf{I}$ for this group. Under this constraint, the matrix $\boldsymbol{\Sigma}_k^*$ can be directly estimated in the reference group by the sample polychoric (for C > 1) or tetrachoric (for C = 1) correlation matrix.

The remaining identification constraints will vary depending on (1) whether the measured variables are binary, and (2) whether the measured variables load on more than one factor. Here we assume that each measured variable loads on only one factor, although there may be more than one factor when the entire set of variables is considered. For the polytomous case of C > 1, the additional constraints for identification are: (1) fix $\boldsymbol{\Theta}_k = \mathbf{I}$ in the reference group only, (2) fix one loading per factor to one for each factor, in each group, (3) constrain one threshold to invariance across groups for each measured variable, and (4) select a second threshold for an additional r measured variables to constrain to invariance. The r measured variables are usually selected to be the same as the r variables whose loadings were fixed to one. These constraints have been shown to be sufficient to identify the model. When using Mplus (Muthén & Muthén, 1998–2012), the theta parameterization is chosen for the discrete model, which brings the unique factor variances into the model as parameters that can be constrained.

In the binary case ($C = 1$), the constraints in point (4) cannot be implemented because only one threshold parameter exists per measured variable. The constraints in point (3) force all of the thresholds to be invariant in the binary case. We can replace the constraints in (4) with an alternative set: fix r unique factor variance elements in Θ_k to ones. This constraint means that r of the unique variances are invariant and fixed to one. The choice of which set of r unique variances to fix is again usually selected to match the r variables whose loadings were fixed to one.

The above "invariant thresholds" formulation for the binary case is one choice, but there is an alternative formulation that may be useful in some cases. This alternative releases most of the constraints on the thresholds, and goes with the following constraints: (1) fix $\Theta_k = I$ in all groups, (2) fix one loading per factor to one for each factor, in each group, and (3) for the r variables whose loadings were fixed to one, constrain their thresholds to invariance. This alternative identification permits thresholds for p-r variables to vary across groups, while constraining the unique variances to invariance. We will return to this alternative method of identification next.

Model evaluation

The process of model evaluation and the sequence of such evaluations in the discrete case differ from that of the continuous case. New parameters are present (thresholds) and some parameters in the continuous model are dropped (measurement intercepts). The first model of interest in both the polytomous and binary cases is a configural invariance model that retains only enough invariance constraints to identify the model. These identification constraints were described above for both the polytomous and binary cases. For the binary case, some judgment may be needed to decide whether to fully constrain the thresholds or the unique variances. Either alternative will yield the same fit for the configural model, but may produce different results at later stages when more constraints are added. Failure of the configural model could have a number of possible explanations, each of which could be investigated. If only one factor was specified ($r = 1$), the possibility of additional factors can be investigated. If multiple factors were specified and the model fit is poor, the pattern of loadings may be misspecified, or additional factors may be needed. In all of these cases, the factor structure has been misunderstood. Further invariance analyses may be premature.

If the configural model fits well, the next model to be tested places invariance constraints on all factor loadings, leading to metric invariance, as in Equation 26.8. This model is testable in both the polytomous and binary cases. In the binary case, the addition of constraints on the loadings to the preexisting invariance constraints on the thresholds may lead to lack of fit for specific items where the proportions endorsing an item vary widely across groups. The varying proportions did not create lack of fit in the configural model because the loadings could also vary to compensate. If partial metric invariance is to be pursued, a choice will exist here between releasing constraints on the thresholds, or on the loadings. The process of releasing constraints to improve the fit faces the same issues that arose in the continuous case. Multiple tests of model fit will again be required, raising issues of error-rate inflation. Error rates can be controlled using the same methods used in the continuous case. Questions of strategy also must be resolved: Is it better to release constraints from a fully constrained model, or add constraints to the configural model? Again there does not appear to be one correct answer that applies in all applications. If few violations of invariance are anticipated, the logical course is to release constraints from the metric invariance model.

The next and final model to be tested will either constrain all of the unique factor variances to invariance, or will constrain all of the thresholds to invariance. The choice here depends on which set of constraints were used in the configural model. If the thresholds were fully constrained in the configural model, the new constraints to be introduced are those in Equation 26.10. Given that $\Theta_k = \mathbf{I}$ for the one group in the configural model, the new constraints imply $\Theta_k = \mathbf{I}$ for all k. If the unique variances were fully constrained in the configural model, the new constraints to be introduced are on the thresholds

$$\nu_k = \nu \qquad (26.18)$$

for all k. In either case of constraints in Equations 26.10 or 26.18, the addition of the constraints implies strict factorial invariance for $\mathbf{X}_k^*$, and hence for $\mathbf{X}_k$.

If strict invariance does not fit, a search can again begin to determine which parameters may vary across groups from among those constrained in Equations 26.10 or 26.18. Any search of this type will face the same problems discussed earlier at the metric invariance stage.

Effect sizes

At the time of writing, there appears to be no literature on effect size measures for violations of invariance in the discrete factor model. Unlike the factor model for continuous measures, there are no simple mathematical expressions for the means and covariance structure of the measured variables $\mathbf{X}_k$ in terms of the parameters of the discrete factor model. For example, in the continuous case, we can express the means on the measured variables $\mathbf{X}_k$ as a simple function of the measurement intercepts, loadings, and factor means (see Equation 26.4). No such expression is possible in the discrete case because the means of the measured variables involve integral expressions in normal probabilities. In the binary case with one factor, it is possible to apply measures of effect size used in item response theory to the discrete factor model. Area measures of item-level bias can be applied, for example (Raju, 1988). In the polytomous case with one factor, no simple area measures are available even in item response theory. Once the factor model is extended to permit loadings on multiple factors, the proper measure of effect size is unclear. The topic of effect size measurement in the discrete factor model needs further research.

An example

To illustrate invariance tests with discrete data, the home visitor's ratings from the Early Steps study are used. During the home visit, the visitors filled in 26 binary yes-no questions (originally from Bradley, Corwyn, McAdoo, & Garcia-Coll, 2001) based on their observations. More details about the Early Steps home visit can be found in Dishion et al. (2008). Among the 26 items, 14 items measuring parent responsivity/involvement and five items measuring noncoerciveness were used for this example (Child and Family Center, 2003). The items are shown in Table 26.4. There was one

Table 26.4 Home visitor rating items.

1. Parent spontaneously vocalized to the child at least twice.
2. Parent responds verbally to child's vocalizations or verbalizations.
3. Parent tells child name of object or person during visit.
4. Parent's speech is distinct, clear, and audible.
5. Parent initiates verbal interchanges with visitor.
6. Parent converses freely and easily.
7. Parent permits child to engage in "messy" play.
8. Parent spontaneously praises child at least twice.
9. Parent's voice conveys positive feelings toward child.
10. Parent caresses or kisses child at least once.
11. Parent responds positively to praise of child offered by lead examiner.
12. Parent keeps child in visual range, looks often.
13. Parent talks to child while doing household work.
14. Parent structures child's play periods.
15. Parent does not shout at child.
16. Parent does not express overt annoyance with or hostility to child.
17. Parent neither slaps nor spanks child during visit.
18. Parent does not scold or criticize child during visit.
19. Parent does not interfere or restrict child more than 3 times.

Note. All items are binary (0 = "no," 1 = "yes").

completely missing case, leaving a total of 730 observations used for this example. Among the 730 observations, 364 observations were from families with girls and 366 observations were from families with boys. Frequency counts and percentages by the child's gender are shown in Table 26.5. Gender will again serve as the grouping variable for the invariance analyses.

All analyses were again conducted using Mplus Version 7.1 (Muthén & Muthén, 1998–2012). The estimation method was weighted least-square (WLSMV) with mean and variance adjustments. For global fit evaluation, we again used the chi-square fit test and two indices of approximate fit, the RMSEA, and the CFI. Given that direct differences of chi-squares between nested models are not interpretable under WLSMV, we used the DIFFTEST procedure in Mplus to conduct comparative tests of fit for nested models. For local fit information, we relied on modification indices and unstandardized residuals.

The first model examined was the configural invariance model in which each item is constrained to load on one factor (Code Appendix, Code 5). Items 2–7, 9–12, 20, and 21 were specified to load on the Responsivity factor, and items 13–17 were specified to load on the Acceptance (noncoerciveness) factor. Items 8 and 22 were dropped from the analysis after initial analyses showed that they both had very low communalities (<.15). Loadings for items 3 and 13 were fixed to one on their respective factors in each group. Factor means were fixed to zero in the female group, but were free in the male group. Factor covariance matrices were free in both groups. All thresholds were invariant. The unique factor variances were fixed to one for females. For males, the unique factor variances for items 3 and 13 were fixed to one, while all others were free. Finally, this model and all subsequent models were fit using the Mplus theta parameterization.

The global fit statistics for this model indicated some lack of fit, but the model provides a good approximation: $\chi^2(236) = 439.103$, RMSEA = .049, CFI = .933. Modification indices showed evidence that items 10 and 16 would have nonzero loadings on

Table 26.5 Home visitor example: Item response counts and percentages by gender.

Item	Category	Girls Percentage	Girls Count	Boys Percentage	Boys Count
2	0	0.030	11	0.027	10
	1	0.970	353	0.973	355
3	0	0.033	12	0.033	12
	1	0.967	352	0.967	354
4	0	0.099	36	0.167	61
	1	0.901	326	0.833	305
5	0	0.041	15	0.049	18
	1	0.959	349	0.951	348
6	0	0.137	50	0.178	65
	1	0.863	314	0.822	300
7	0	0.099	36	0.124	45
	1	0.901	327	0.876	317
9	0	0.229	83	0.262	95
	1	0.771	280	0.738	268
10	0	0.088	32	0.112	41
	1	0.912	332	0.888	325
11	0	0.378	137	0.385	139
	1	0.622	225	0.615	222
12	0	0.246	86	0.293	103
	1	0.754	263	0.707	248
13	0	0.135	49	0.194	71
	1	0.865	315	0.806	295
14	0	0.149	54	0.208	76
	1	0.851	309	0.792	290
15	0	0.030	11	0.049	18
	1	0.970	351	0.951	346
16	0	0.273	99	0.310	113
	1	0.727	264	0.690	251
17	0	0.424	154	0.482	176
	1	0.576	209	0.518	189
20	0	0.212	77	0.240	88
	1	0.788	287	0.760	278
21	0	0.149	54	0.189	69
	1	0.851	308	0.811	296

both factors in each group. We decided to retain the loadings for these items as originally conceived (item 10 on Responsivity only, and item 16 on Acceptance only), given no theory that would justify the additional loadings.

The next model examined was the metric invariance model in which all factor loadings are invariant (Code Appendix, Code 6). The global fit indices did not change a great deal with the addition of these constraints: $\chi^2(251) = 445.718$, RMSEA = .046, CFI = .936. The DIFFTEST procedure was used to provide a comparison between the configural and metric invariance models. The test showed no significant difference: $\chi^2(15) = 14.441$, $p = .4924$. Examination of the modification indices showed no substantial changes from the configural model. The item with the largest loading difference by gender was item 10 (.549 for females, .733 for males). This item's content

Table 26.6 Home visitor example: Unstandardized factor loading and threshold estimates under strict invariance.

Factor	Item	Loading	Threshold
1	2	0.816	−3.686
	3	1.000*	−4.18
	4	0.409	−1.292
	5	0.341	−2.092
	6	0.862	−2.115
	7	1.028	−2.902
	9	0.547	−1.11
	10	0.727	−2.348
	11	0.378	−0.447
	12	0.413	−1.036
	20	0.406	−1.036
	21	0.469	−1.384
2	13	1.000*	−2.439
	14	1.336	−2.976
	15	0.514	−2.616
	16	0.65	−1.099
	17	0.279	−0.226

* Fixed for identification.

sets it apart from the other Responsivity items. An examination of a model that would free this item to permit different loadings by gender revealed a significant difference by DIFFTEST: $\chi^2(1) = 4.224$, $p = .0399$. It is also possible, however, that our initial decision to force this item to load only on the Responsivity factor has influenced this result. The two factors are significantly correlated for males, but not for females. Theory suggests that the omission of factors can lead to apparent violations of invariance when none are present in the multiple-factor model (Camilli, 1992; Millsap, 2011). We decided to retain the invariance constraint on the loadings for item 10.

The final model imposed strict invariance by fixing all unique variances in both groups to ones (Code Appendix, Code 7). The global fit indices did not change substantially under these new constraints: $\chi^2(266) = 457.821$, RMSEA = .044, CFI = .937. The DIFFTEST procedure showed no significant change in fit in relation to the metric invariance model: $\chi^2(15) = 21.629$, $p = .1179$. Modification indices did not change substantially from the metric invariance model. These results suggest that the items can be taken as meeting strict factorial invariance in relation to gender, under the two-factor model. Table 26.6 presents the threshold and factor loading estimates common to the two groups. The two factors were not significantly correlated in the female group ($r = .089$, $p = .240$) but were significantly correlated in the male group ($r = .217$, $p = .007$). The factor means were lower in the male group (−.395 for Responsivity, −.655 for Acceptance) but were not significantly different across groups for either factor.

Discussion

Concerns about measurement invariance are really concerns about validity in measurement: do our items, tests, and questionnaires really measure what we intend them to measure? Studies of measurement invariance provide one way of answering this question. If an item really measures its intended construct, all systematic influences on item scores should operate through that construct. There should be no "back door" routes through which other variables influence item scores directly, circumventing the intended construct. Hence if we look at a group of males and females who are identical on the intended construct, there should be no relation between gender and the item scores in that homogeneous group. In essence, this is the logic of the measurement invariance argument.

Factorial invariance is a limited form of measurement invariance, evaluated within the assumptions of the factor analysis model. This model focuses on the mean and covariance structures for continuous measures. For discrete measures, the model includes the full probability structure, and is closer to a model for full measurement invariance. In either case, real applications of CFA in studies of factorial invariance face practical problems that must be resolved, as discussed earlier. First, some knowledge of the factor structure is needed before the investigation can begin. At least some measures must be regarded as having invariant properties (i.e., invariant loadings and intercepts) before the remaining measures can be examined. Second, the process of finding which measures violate invariance is affected by the difficulties facing any complex model respecification. Multiple model fit evaluations are needed, a process that becomes risky as the number of measures increases. Third, once violations of invariance are found, the translation of these violations into measures of effect size is not always clear. In some cases, no practical measures of effect size yet exist. More broadly, what is the impact of violations of factorial invariance on various uses for the measures? The presence of a few biased items in a long test may have minimal practical impact on most uses of the test scores (Stark et al., 2004). On the other hand, violations of factorial invariance may undermine the validity of a test when used for selection purposes, depending on the nature of the violation (Millsap & Kwok, 2004).

Factor analysis has several advantages as a tool for investigating invariance. The model can specify multiple common factors and is not limited to the unidimensional case. It can be used for either continuous or discrete measures. We now have software that can efficiently estimate parameters even in fairly large models, providing an array of fit measures. Extensions or alternatives to the factor model are useful to consider, however, and we now review some of these alternatives.

Continuous grouping variables

In some applications, we may want to consider how the relationship between observed measures X and the targeted latent variable W varies as a function of a grouping variable V that is continuous in scale. For example, suppose that V is age. We could divide age into intervals and apply a conventional multiple-group analysis, but this ignores the fact that the relationship between X and W varies continuously as a function of age. Also, any grouping on age will use arbitrary boundaries for the intervals. Methods are now available for retaining age as a continuous scale, and examining invariance as a continuous function of age (Merkle & Zeileis, 2013). These methods could greatly expand the scope of invariance investigations to include potential continuous moderators of invariance. One potentially interesting application would be in the use of "validity scales" as moderators of invariance in clinical measurement.

Invariance with many groups

Suppose the number of groups being studied becomes very large, as in a study of invariance in an employee survey for a multinational corporation across many countries. The conventional CFA approach as described here is now cumbersome because the simultaneous analysis in many groups is difficult, and is likely to reject strict invariance even with small violations. Alternatives to this conventional approach are now available (De Jong, Steenkamp, & Fox, 2007; Verhagen & Fox, 2012). These methods use Bayesian modelling, representing violations of invariance as variance in the relevant model parameters. The analysis uses the data to update estimates of these variances, allowing investigators to evaluate whether the variability is sufficiently large to warrant concern. The latest version of Mplus incorporates some aspects of this Bayesian approach.

Item response theory

The single-factor model for discrete measures can be viewed as a graded response model (Samejima, 1969; Takane & de Leeuw, 1987) within the broad class of item response theory (IRT) models. The multiple-factor model can be viewed as a compensatory model within the class of multidimensional IRT (MIRT) models (Reckase, 2009). IRT contains a wider variety of model types than is found in factor analysis, and can accommodate phenomena that cannot be easily modelled within the factor model (e.g., guessing behavior in multiple choice tests). Historical distinctions between the factor analysis model and IRT models are becoming less important, given that both modelling traditions are subsumed within a general latent variable framework (McDonald, 1999). For example, the program IRTPRO (Cai, du Toit, & Thissen, 2011) includes MIRT modelling features that are essentially CFA procedures. Furthermore, methods for examining item-level violations of invariance in IRT are well established, although some of the same challenges encountered in factorial invariance studies are also found in IRT invariance studies.

Longitudinal data

The methods for studying factorial invariance described here have assumed that invariance over independent groups is the focus. A different set of invariance issues arise in longitudinal data in which the same measures are given to a single group of individuals repeatedly. For example, a developmental study may administer the same set of personality measures over waves of measurement from the early teenage years to young adulthood. Participants are expected to show changes over time, but are changes in observed scores a reflection of true change, or do they reflect changes in factor structure? Studies of longitudinal factorial invariance attempt to answer these questions. Procedures for longitudinal factorial invariance share some features with the multiple-group methods, but also have some unique features (Bieber & Meredith, 1986; Corballis & Traub, 1970; Little, 2013; Millsap & Cham, 2012; Tisak & Meredith, 1989; Widaman, Ferrer, & Conger, 2010). For example, while we expect common factors to correlate across waves, we must usually allow for autocorrelations among unique factors in these models. Further complications arise if different versions of some measures are used across waves, as is common in longer developmental studies.

As shown in this brief survey, researchers who need to investigate invariance in measurement now have a rich set of methodological tools to apply in such studies. We hope that the information and examples provided here will help researchers gain a realistic understanding of the strengths and weaknesses in these methods.

Acknowledgments

The examples described in this chapter were supported by Grant 5 R01 DA16110 from the National Institutes of Health to the second author.

References

Babakus, E., Ferguson, C. E., & Jöreskog, K. G. (1987). The sensitivity of confirmatory maximum likelihood factor analysis to violations of measurement scale and distributional assumptions. *Journal of Marketing Research*, 24, 222–228.

Bartholomew, D. J. (1983). Latent variable models for ordered-categorical data. *Journal of Econometrics*, 22, 229–243.

Bartholomew, D. J. (1984). Scaling binary data using a factor model. *Journal of the Royal Statistical Society, Series B*, 46, 120–123.

Bartholomew, D. J. (1987). *Latent variable models and factor analysis.* London: Charles Griffin & Company.

Barrett, P. (2007). Structural equation modeling: Adjudging model fit. *Personality and Individual Differences*, 42, 812–824.

Benjamini, Y., & Hochberg, Y. (1995). Controlling the false discovery rate: A practical and powerful approach to multiple testing. *Journal of the Royal Statistical Society, Series B*, 57, 289–300.

Bentler, P. M., & Bonett, D. G. (1980). Significance tests and goodness-of-fit in the analysis of covariance structures. *Psychological Bulletin*, 88, 588–606.

Bernstein, I. H., & Teng, G. (1989). Factoring items and factoring scales are different: Spurious evidence of multidimensionality due to item categorization. *Psychological Bulletin*, 105, 467–477.

Bieber, S. L., & Meredith, W. (1986). Transformation to achieve longitudinally stationary factor pattern matrix. *Psychometrika*, 51, 535–547.

Bock, R. D., & Aitkin, M. (1981). Marginal maximum likelihood estimation of item parameters: An application of the EM algorithm. *Psychometrika*, 46, 443–449.

Bollen, K. A., & Jöreskog, K.G. (1985). Uniqueness does not imply identification. *Sociological Methods and Research*, 14, 155–163.

Bradley, R. H., Corwyn, R. F., McAdoo, H. P., & Garcia-Coll, C. (2001). The home environments of children in the United States part I: Variations by age, ethnicity, and poverty status. *Child Development*, 72(6), 1844–1867.

Browne, M. W. (1984). Asymptotically distribution free methods in the analysis of covariance structures. *British Journal of Mathematical and Statistical Psychology*, 37, 62–83.

Browne, M. W., & Arminger, G. (1995). Specification and estimation of mean and covariance structure models. In G. Arminger, C. C. Clogg, & M. E. Sobel (Eds.), *Handbook of statistical modeling for the social and behavioral sciences* (pp. 185–249). New York: Plenum.

Browne, M. W., & Cudeck, R. (1993). Alternative ways of assessing model fit. In K. A. Bollen & J. S. Long (Eds.), *Testing structural equation models* (pp. 136–162). Newbury Park, CA: Sage.

Byrne, B. M., Shavelson, R. J., & Muthén, B. (1989). Testing for equivalence of factor covariance and mean structures: The issue of partial measurement invariance. *Psychological Bulletin, 105*, 456–466.

Cai, L., du Toit, S. H. C., & Thissen, D. (2011). *IRTPRO: Flexible, multidimensional, multiple categorical IRT modeling.* Chicago: SSI International.

Camilli, G. (1992). A conceptual analysis of differential item functioning in terms of a multidimensional item response model. *Applied Psychological Measurement, 16*, 129–147.

Carroll, J. B. (1945). The effect of difficulty and chance success on correlations between items and between tests. *Psychometrika, 26*, 347–372.

Carroll, J. B. (1983). The difficulty of a test and its factor composition revisited. In H. Wainer & S Messick (Eds.), *Principles of modern psychological measurement.* Hillsdale, NJ: Erlbaum.

Child and Family Center (2003). *Early Steps Coder Impressions (ESCOIMP).* Available from the Child and Family Center, 195 W 12th Ave, Eugene, OR, 97401.

Christoffersson, A. (1975). Factor analysis of dichotomized variables. *Psychometrika, 40*, 5–32.

Corballis, M. C., & Traub, R. E. (1970). Longitudinal factor analysis. *Psychometrika, 35*, 79–95.

De Jong, M. G., Steenkamp, J. E. M., & Fox, J. P. (2007). Relaxing measurement invariance in cross-national consumer research using a hierarchical IRT model. *Journal of Consumer Research, 34*, 260–278.

DeShon, R. P. (2004). Measures are not invariant across groups without error variance homogeneity. *Psychology Science, 46*, 137–149.

Dishion, T. J., Shaw, D., Connell, A., Gardner, F., Weaver, C., & Wilson, M. (2008). The family check-up with high-risk indigent families: preventing problem behavior by increasing parents' positive behavior support in early childhood. *Child Development, 79*(5), 1395–1414.

Gibbons, R. D., & Hedeker, D. R. (1992). Full-information item bifactor analysis. *Psychometrika, 57*, 423–436.

Glas, C. A. W., & Verhelst, N. D. (1995). Testing the Rasch model. In G. H. Fischer & I. W. Molenaar (Eds.), *Rasch models: Foundations, recent developments, and applications.* (pp. 69–95). New York: Springer.

Hayashi, K. & Marcoulides, G. A. (2006). Examining identification issues in factor analysis. *Structural Equation Modeling, 13*, 631–645.

Horn, J. L., & McArdle, J. J. (1992). A practical guide to measurement invariance in research on aging. *Experimental Aging Research, 18*, 117–144.

Hu, L., & Bentler, P. M. (1995). Evaluating model fit. In R. H. Hoyle (Ed.), *Structural equation modeling: Concepts, issues, and applications* (pp. 76–99). Thousand Oaks, CA: Sage.

Johnson, E. C., Meade, A. W., & DuVernet, A. M. (2009). The role of referent indicators in tests of measurement invariance. *Structural Equation Modeling, 16*, 642–657.

Jöreskog, K. G. (1971). Simultaneous factor analysis in several populations. *Psychometrika, 36*, 409–426.

Jöreskog, K. G. (1993). Latent variable modeling with ordinal variables. In K. Haagen, D. J. Bartholomew, & M. Deistler (Eds.), *Statistical modeling and latent variables* (pp. 163–171). Amsterdam: North-Holland.

Lee, S. Y., Poon, W. Y., & Bentler, P. M. (1989). Simultaneous analysis of multivariate polytomous variates in several groups. *Psychometrika, 54*, 63–73.

Little, T. D. (2013). *Longitudinal structural equation modeling.* New York: Guilford.

Little, T. D., Slegers, D. W., & Card, N. A. (2006). A non-arbitrary method of identifying and scaling latent variables in SEM and MACS models. *Structural Equation Modeling, 13*, 59–72.

Lord, F. M., & Novick, M. E. (1968). *Statistical theories of mental test scores.* Reading: Addison-Wesley.

Lubke, G. H., & Dolan, C. V. (2003). Can unequal residual variances across groups mask differences in residual means in the common factor model? *Structural Equation Modeling, 10,* 175–192.

Lubke, G. H., & Muthén, B. O. (2004). Applying multi-group confirmatory factor models for continuous outcomes to Likert scale data complicates meaningful group comparisons. *Structural Equation Modeling, 11,* 514–534.

Marsh, H. W., Hau, K. T., & Wen, Z. (2004). In search of Golden Rules: Comment on hypothesis-testing approaches to setting cutoff values for fit indexes and dangers in overgeneralizing Hu and Bentler's (1999) findings. *Structural Equation Modeling, 11,* 320–341.

Maydeu-Olivares, A. (2005). Linear item response theory, nonlinear item response theory, and factor analysis: A unified framework. In A. Maydeu-Olivares & J. J. McArdle (Eds.), *Contemporary Psychometrics* (pp. 73–100). Mahwah, NJ: Lawrence Erlbaum.

McDonald, R. P. (1999). *Test theory: A unified treatment.* Mahwah, NJ: Lawrence Erlbaum.

McDonald, R. P., & Ahlawat, K. S. (1974). Difficulty factors in binary data. *British Journal of Mathematical and Statistical Psychology, 27,* 82–99.

Meade, A. W., & Lautenschlager, G. J. (2004). A Monte-Carlo study of confirmatory factor analytic tests of measurement invariance. *Structural Equation Modeling, 11,* 60–72.

Mellenbergh, G. J. (1989). Item bias and item response theory. *International Journal of Educational Research, 13,* 127–143.

Meredith, W. (1964). Notes on factorial invariance. *Psychometrika, 29,* 177–185.

Meredith, W. (1993). Measurement invariance, factor analysis, and factorial invariance. *Psychometrika, 58,* 525–543.

Meredith, W., & Millsap, R. E. (1992). On the misuse of manifest variables in the detection of measurement bias. *Psychometrika, 57,* 289–311.

Merkle, E. C., & Zeileis, A. (2013). Tests of measurement invariance without subgroups: A generalization of classical methods. *Psychometrika, 78,* 59–82.

Millsap, R. E. (2011). *Statistical approaches to measurement invariance.* New York: Routledge.

Millsap, R. E., & Cham, H. (2012). Investigating factorial invariance in longitudinal data. In B. Laursen, T. D. Little, & N. A. Card (Eds.), *Handbook of developmental research methods* (pp. 109–126). New York: Guilford.

Millsap, R. E., & Kwok, O. M. (2004). Evaluating the impact of partial factorial invariance on selection in two populations. *Psychological Methods, 9,* 93–115.

Millsap, R. E., & Tein, J. Y. (2004). Assessing factorial invariance in ordered-categorical measures. *Multivariate Behavioral Research, 39,* 479–515.

Mislevy, R. J. (1986). Recent developments in the factor analysis of categorical variables. *Journal of Educational Statistics, 11,* 3–31.

Muthén, B. O. (1978). Contributions to factor analysis of dichotomized variables. *Psychometrika, 43,* 551–560.

Muthén, B. O. (1984). A general structural equation model with dichotomous, ordered categorical and continuous latent variable indicators. *Psychometrika, 49,* 115–132.

Muthén, B. O., & Christoffersson, A. (1981). Simultaneous factor analysis of dichotomous variables in several groups. *Psychometrika, 46,* 407–419.

Muthén, L., & Muthén, B. O. (1998–2012). *Mplus user's guide* (7th ed.). Los Angeles, CA: Muthén & Muthén.

Olsson, U. (1979). Maximum likelihood estimation of the polychoric correlation coefficient. *Psychometrika, 44,* 443–460.

Poon, W. Y., Lee, S. Y., Afifi, A. A., & Bentler, P. M. (1990). Analysis of multivariate polytomous variates in several groups via the partition maximum likelihood approach. *Computational Statistics and Data Analysis, 10,* 17–27.

Raju, N. S. (1988). The area between two item characteristic curves. *Psychometrika, 56,* 365–379.

Raykov, T., Marcoulides, G. A., & Millsap, R. E. (2012). Factorial invariance in multiple populations: A multiple testing procedure. *Educational and Psychological Measurement, 73,* 713–727.

Reckase, M. D. (2009). *Multidimensional item response theory.* New York: Springer.

Reise, S. G., Morizot, J., & Hays, R. D. (2007). The role of the bifactor model in resolving dimensionality issues in health outcomes measures. *Quality of Life Research, 16,* 19–31.

Rensvold, R. B., & Cheung, G. W. (2001). Testing for metric invariance using structural equation models: Solving the standardization problem. In C. A. Schriesheim & L. L. Neider (Eds.), *Research in management* (Vol. 1) (pp. 25–50). Greenwich, CN: Information Age Publishing.

Rigdon, E. E., & Ferguson, C. E. (1991). The performance of the polychoric correlation coefficient and selected fitting functions in confirmatory factor analysis with ordinal data. *Journal of Marketing Research, 28,* 491–497.

Samejima, F. (1969). Estimation of ability using a response pattern of graded scores. *Psychometrika Monograph,* No. 17.

Satorra, A., & Bentler, P. M. (1994). Corrections to test statistics and standard errors on covariance structure analysis. In A. von Eye & C. C. Clogg (Eds.), *Latent variables analysis* (pp. 399–419). Thousand Oaks, CA: Sage.

Shaw, D. S., Connell, A., Dishion, T. J., Wilson, M. N., & Gardner, F. (2009). Improvements in maternal depression as a mediator of intervention effects on early childhood problem behavior. *Development and Psychopathology, 21,* 417–439.

Sörbom, D. (1974). A general method for studying differences in factor means and factor structure between groups. *British Journal of Mathematical and Statistical Psychology, 27,* 229–239.

Stark, S., Chernyshenko, O. S., & Drasgow, F. (2004). Examining the effects of differential item functioning and differential test functioning on selection decisions: When are statistically significant effects practically important? *Journal of Applied Psychology, 89,* 497–508.

Steenkamp, J. E. M., & Baumgartner, H. (1998). Assessing measurement invariance in cross-national consumer research. *Journal of Consumer Research, 25,* 78–90.

Steiger, J. H., & Lind, J. M. (1980). *Statistically based tests for the number of common factors.* Paper presented at the annual meeting of the Psychometric Society, Iowa City, IA.

Steinberg, L. (2001). The consequences of pairing questions: Context effects in personality measurement. *Journal of Personality and Social Psychology, 81,* 332–342.

Takane, Y., & de Leeuw, J. (1987). On the relationship between item response theory and factor analysis of discretized variables. *Psychometrika, 52,* 393–408.

Thomson, G. H. (1939). *The factorial analysis of human ability.* London: University of London Press.

Thurstone, L. L. (1947). *Multiple factor analysis.* Chicago: University of Chicago Press.

Tisak, J., & Meredith, W. (1989). Exploratory longitudinal factor analysis in multiple populations. *Psychometrika, 54,* 261–281.

Verhagen, A. J., & Fox, J. P. (2012). Bayesian tests of measurement invariance. *British Journal of Mathematical and Statistical Psychology,* doi: 10.1111/j.2044-8317.2012.02059.x.

Widaman, K. F., Ferrer, E., & Conger, R. D. (2010). Factorial invariance within longitudinal structural equation models: Measuring the same construct across time. *Child Development Perspectives, 4,* 10–18.

Wirth, R. J., & Edwards, M. C. (2007). Item factor analysis: Current approaches and future directions. *Psychological Methods, 12,* 58–79

Woods, C. M. (2009). Empirical selection of anchors for tests of differential item functioning. *Applied Psychological Measurement, 33,* 42–57.

Yoon, M., & Millsap, R. E. (2007). Detecting violations of factorial invariance using data-based specification searches: A Monte Carlo study. *Structural Equation Modeling, 14,* 435–463.

Code Appendix

Mplus code for factorial invariance tests for continuous variables, using proactive parenting data.

Code 1 Code for testing configural invariance.

```
TITLE:
CFA of the proactive parenting;
Items 2,10,13,14,18 & 21

DATA:
FILE IS continuous_data_example.csv;

VARIABLE:
NAMES ARE family tcgen W922P01 W922P02 W922P03
    W922P04  W922P05    W922P06    W922P07    W922P08
    W922P09  W922P10    W922P11    W922P12    W922P13
    W922P14  W922P15    W922P16    W922P17    W922P18
    W922P19  W922P20    W922P21    W922P22    W922P23
    W922P24  W922P25    W922P26    W922P27    W922P28
    W922P29  W922P30    W922P31    W922P32    W922P33;

MISSING ARE *;

USEVARIABLES ARE W922P02 W922P10
    W922P13 W922P14    W922P18
    W922P21;

GROUPING = tcgen (1=female 2=male);

ANALYSIS:
ESTIMATOR = ML;

MODEL:
proact BY W922P02  W922P10
    W922P13  W922P14  W922P18
    W922P21;

MODEL female:
proact BY W922P02* (l1)
    W922P10 W922P13 W922P14
    W922P18 W922P21;
[W922P10 W922P13 W922P14
 W922P18 W922P21];
```

```
    [W922P02] (tau);
    [proact@0];
    proact@1;

    MODEL male:
    proact BY W922P02* (l1)
        W922P10 W922P13 W922P14
        W922P18 W922P21;
    [W922P10 W922P13 W922P14
     W922P18 W922P21];
    [W922P02](tau);
    [proact];
    proact*;

    OUTPUT: TECH1; STDYX; SAMPSTAT; RESIDUAL; MODINDICES;
```

Code 2 Code for testing metric invariance.

```
TITLE:
CFA of the proactive parenting;
Items 2,10,13,14,18 & 21

DATA:
FILE IS continuous_data_example.csv;

VARIABLE:
NAMES ARE family tcgen W922P01 W922P02 W922P03
    W922P04  W922P05 W922P06    W922P07    W922P08
        W922P09  W922P10    W922P11    W922P12    W922P13
        W922P14  W922P15    W922P16    W922P17    W922P18
        W922P19  W922P20    W922P21    W922P22    W922P23
        W922P24  W922P25    W922P26    W922P27    W922P28
        W922P29  W922P30    W922P31    W922P32    W922P33;

MISSING ARE *;

USEVARIABLES ARE W922P02 W922P10
    W922P13  W922P14   W922P18
    W922P21;

GROUPING = tcgen (1=female 2=male);


ANALYSIS:
ESTIMATOR = ML;
```

```
MODEL:
proact BY W922P02 W922P10
    W922P13  W922P14  W922P18
    W922P21;

MODEL female:
proact BY W922P02* W922P10 W922P13 (l1-l3)
    W922P14 W922P18 W922P21 (l4-l6);
[W922P10 W922P13 W922P14
 W922P18 W922P21];
[W922P02] (tau);
[proact@0];
proact@1;

MODEL male:
proact BY W922P02* W922P10 W922P13 (l1-l3)
    W922P14 W922P18 W922P21 (l4-l6);
[W922P10 W922P13 W922P14
 W922P18 W922P21];
[W922P02] (tau);
[proact];
proact*;

OUTPUT:
TECH1; STDYX; SAMPSTAT; RESIDUAL; MODINDICES;
```

Code 3   Code for testing scalar invariance.

```
TITLE:
CFA of the proactive parenting;
Items 2,10,13,14,18 & 21

DATA:
FILE IS continuous_data_example.csv;

VARIABLE:
NAMES ARE family tcgen W922P01 W922P02 W922P03
    W922P04   W922P05     W922P06     W922P07    W922P08
    W922P09   W922P10     W922P11     W922P12    W922P13
    W922P14   W922P15     W922P16     W922P17    W922P18
    W922P19   W922P20     W922P21     W922P22    W922P23
    W922P24   W922P25     W922P26     W922P27    W922P28
    W922P29   W922P30     W922P31     W922P32    W922P33;
```

```
MISSING ARE *;

USEVARIABLES ARE W922P02 W922P10
    W922P13 W922P14    W922P18
    W922P21;

GROUPING = tcgen (1=female 2=male);


ANALYSIS:
ESTIMATOR = ML;


MODEL:
proact BY W922P02 W922P10
    W922P13 W922P14    W922P18
    W922P21;

MODEL female:
proact BY W922P02* W922P10 W922P13 (l1-l3)
    W922P14 W922P18 W922P21 (l4-l6);
[W922P10 W922P13 W922P14] (I2-I4);
[W922P18 W922P21] (I5-I6);
[W922P02] (tau);
[proact@0];
proact@1;

MODEL male:
proact BY W922P02* W922P10 W922P13 (l1-l3)
    W922P14    W922P18 W922P21 (l4-l6);
[W922P10 W922P13 W922P14] (I2-I4);
[W922P18 W922P21] (I5-I6);
[W922P02] (tau);
[proact];
proact*;

OUTPUT:
TECH1; STDYX; SAMPSTAT; RESIDUAL; MODINDICES;
```

Code 4 Code for testing strict invariance.

```
TITLE:
CFA of the proactive parenting;
Items 2,10,13,14,18 & 21

DATA:
FILE IS continuous_data_example.csv;

VARIABLE:
NAMES ARE family tcgen W922P01 W922P02 W922P03
    W922P04   W922P05     W922P06       W922P07      W922P08
    W922P09   W922P10     W922P11       W922P12      W922P13
    W922P14   W922P15     W922P16       W922P17      W922P18
    W922P19   W922P20     W922P21       W922P22      W922P23
    W922P24   W922P25     W922P26       W922P27      W922P28
    W922P29   W922P30     W922P31       W922P32      W922P33;

MISSING ARE *;

USEVARIABLES ARE W922P02 W922P10
    W922P13  W922P14    W922P18
    W922P21;

GROUPING = tcgen (1=female 2=male);


ANALYSIS:
ESTIMATOR = ML;


MODEL:
proact BY W922P02 W922P10
    W922P13  W922P14  W922P18
    W922P21;

MODEL female:
proact BY W922P02* W922P10 W922P13 (l1-l3)
    W922P14 W922P18 W922P21 (l4-l6);
[W922P10 W922P13 W922P14] (I2-I4);
[W922P18 W922P21] (I5-I6);
[W922P02] (tau);
[proact@0];
proact@1;
W922P02 W922P10 W922P13 (u1-u3)
W922P14 W922P18 W922P21 (u4-u6);
```

```
MODEL male:
proact BY W922P02* W922P10 W922P13 (l1-l3)
    W922P14      W922P18 W922P21 (l4-l6);
[W922P10 W922P13 W922P14] (I2-I4);
[W922P18 W922P21] (I5-I6);
[W922P02] (tau);
[proact];
proact*;
W922P02 W922P10 W922P13 (u1-u3)
W922P14 W922P18 W922P21 (u4-u6);
OUTPUT:
TECH1; STDYX; SAMPSTAT; RESIDUAL; MODINDICES;
```

Mplus code for invariance testing with discrete data, using home visitor's ratings.

Code 5 Code for testing configural invariance.

```
TITLE:
CFA of home visitor;
Two-factor model

DATA:
FILE IS discrete_data_example.csv;

VARIABLE:
NAMES ARE FAMILY tcgen
    WIH202   WIH203      WIH204      WIH205
    WIH206   WIH207      WIH208      WIH209      WIH210
    WIH211   WIH212      WIH213      WIH214      WIH215
    WIH216   WIH217      WIH220      WIH221      WIH222;

MISSING ARE *;

USEVARIABLES ARE WIH202   WIH203      WIH204      WIH205
    WIH206   WIH207      WIH209      WIH210
    WIH211   WIH212      WIH213      WIH214      WIH215
    WIH216   WIH217      WIH220      WIH221      ;

CATEGORICAL ARE WIH202    WIH203      WIH204      WIH205
    WIH206   WIH207      WIH209      WIH210
    WIH211   WIH212      WIH213      WIH214      WIH215
    WIH216   WIH217      WIH220      WIH221      ;

GROUPING IS tcgen (1=female 2=male);
```

```
ANALYSIS:
ESTIMATOR = WLSMV;
PARAMETERIZATION = THETA;

MODEL:
response BY WIH202*    WIH203@1    WIH204    WIH205
    WIH206  WIH207    WIH209    WIH210
    WIH211  WIH212  WIH220    WIH221      ;
accept BY WIH213@1 WIH214 WIH215 WIH216 WIH217;

MODEL female:
response BY WIH202*
    WIH203@1
    WIH204  WIH205
    WIH206  WIH207    WIH209    WIH210
    WIH211  WIH212  WIH220    WIH221      ;
accept BY WIH213@1
          WIH214
            WIH215 WIH216 WIH217 ;
[WIH202$1 WIH203$1 WIH204$1 WIH205$1] (thrs2-thrs5);
[WIH206$1 WIH207$1 WIH209$1 WIH210$1] (thrs6 thrs7 thrs9
thrs10);
[WIH211$1 WIH212$1 WIH213$1  WIH220$1 WIH221$1] (thrs11-
thrs13 thrs20 thrs21);
[WIH214$1 WIH215$1 WIH216$1 WIH217$1] (thrs14-thrs17);
[response@0 accept@0];
    WIH202@1      WIH204@1      WIH205@1
    WIH206@1      WIH207@1      WIH209@1      WIH210@1
    WIH211@1      WIH212@1      WIH220@1      WIH221@1
    WIH214@1 WIH215@1 WIH216@1 WIH217@1 ;
WIH203@1 WIH213@1 ;


MODEL male:
response BY WIH202*
    WIH203@1
    WIH204      WIH205
    WIH206      WIH207     WIH209     WIH210
    WIH211      WIH212  WIH220    WIH221      ;
accept BY WIH213@1
          WIH214
            WIH215 WIH216 WIH217 ;
[WIH202$1 WIH203$1 WIH204$1 WIH205$1] (thrs2-thrs5);
[WIH206$1 WIH207$1 WIH209$1 WIH210$1] (thrs6 thrs7
thrs9 thrs10);
[WIH211$1 WIH212$1 WIH213$1 WIH220$1 WIH221$1]
(thrs11-thrs13 thrs20 thrs21);
[WIH214$1 WIH215$1 WIH216$1 WIH217$1] (thrs14-thrs17);
```

```
   [response accept];
      WIH202   WIH204      WIH205
      WIH206   WIH207      WIH209       WIH210
      WIH211   WIH212   WIH220       WIH221
      WIH214 WIH215 WIH216 WIH217 ;
   WIH203@1 WIH213@1 ;



   OUTPUT:
   TECH1; STDYX; RESIDUAL; MODINDICES;
```

Code 6   Code for testing metric invariance.

```
TITLE:
CFA of home visitor;
Two-factor model

DATA:
FILE IS discrete_data_example.csv;

VARIABLE:
NAMES ARE FAMILY tcgen
   WIH202   WIH203         WIH204         WIH205
   WIH206   WIH207         WIH208         WIH209         WIH210
   WIH211   WIH212         WIH213         WIH214         WIH215
   WIH216   WIH217         WIH220         WIH221         WIH222;

MISSING ARE *;

USEVARIABLES ARE WIH202   WIH203         WIH204         WIH205
   WIH206   WIH207         WIH209         WIH210
   WIH211   WIH212         WIH213         WIH214         WIH215
   WIH216   WIH217         WIH220         WIH221         ;

CATEGORICAL ARE WIH202   WIH203         WIH204         WIH205
   WIH206   WIH207         WIH209         WIH210
   WIH211   WIH212         WIH213         WIH214         WIH215
   WIH216   WIH217         WIH220         WIH221         ;

GROUPING IS tcgen (1=female 2=male);


ANALYSIS:
ESTIMATOR = WLSMV;
PARAMETERIZATION = THETA;
DIFFTEST = configural.dat;
```

```
MODEL:
response BY WIH202*
   WIH203@1 WIH204    WIH205
     WIH206  WIH207    WIH209    WIH210
    WIH211  WIH212 WIH220    WIH221;
accept BY WIH213@1
          WIH214 WIH215 WIH216 WIH217;

MODEL female:
response BY WIH202* (l2)
   WIH203@1 WIH204    WIH205 (l3-l5)
     WIH206  WIH207    WIH209    WIH210 (l6-l7 l9-l10)
    WIH211  WIH212 WIH220    WIH221    (l11-l12 l20-l21);
accept BY WIH213@1
          WIH214 WIH215 WIH216 WIH217 (l14-l17);
[WIH202$1 WIH203$1 WIH204$1 WIH205$1] (thrs2-thrs5);
[WIH206$1 WIH207$1 WIH209$1 WIH210$1] (thrs6 thrs7 thrs9
thrs10);
[WIH211$1 WIH212$1 WIH213$1 WIH220$1 WIH221$1] (thrs11-
thrs13 thrs20 thrs21);
[WIH214$1 WIH215$1 WIH216$1 WIH217$1] (thrs14-thrs17);
[response@0 accept@0];
    WIH202@1      WIH204@1      WIH205@1
    WIH206@1      WIH207@1      WIH209@1      WIH210@1
    WIH211@1      WIH212@1      WIH220@1      WIH221@1
    WIH214@1 WIH215@1 WIH216@1 WIH217@1 ;
WIH203@1 WIH213@1 ;


MODEL male:
response BY WIH202* (l2)
   WIH203@1    WIH204    WIH205 (l3-l5)
     WIH206     WIH207    WIH209    WIH210 (l6-l7 l9-l10)
    WIH211     WIH212 WIH220  WIH221    (l11-l12 l20-l21);
accept BY WIH213@1
          WIH214 WIH215 WIH216 WIH217 (l14-l17);
[WIH202$1 WIH203$1 WIH204$1 WIH205$1] (thrs2-thrs5);
[WIH206$1 WIH207$1 WIH209$1 WIH210$1] (thrs6 thrs7 thrs9
thrs10);
[WIH211$1 WIH212$1 WIH213$1 WIH220$1 WIH221$1] (thrs11-
thrs13 thrs20 thrs21);
[WIH214$1 WIH215$1 WIH216$1 WIH217$1] (thrs14-thrs17);
[response accept];
     WIH202       WIH204      WIH205
     WIH206       WIH207      WIH209     WIH210
     WIH211      WIH212  WIH220     WIH221
     WIH214      WIH215 WIH216 WIH217 ;
WIH203@1 WIH213@1 ;
```

```
OUTPUT:
TECH1; STDYX; RESIDUAL; MODINDICES;

SAVEDATA:
DIFFTEST IS metric.dat;
```

Code 7 Code for testing strict invariance.

```
TITLE:
CFA of home visitor;
Two-factor model

DATA:
FILE IS discrete_data_example.csv;

VARIABLE:
NAMES ARE FAMILY tcgen
    WIH202     WIH203     WIH204     WIH205
    WIH206     WIH207     WIH208     WIH209     WIH210
    WIH211     WIH212     WIH213     WIH214     WIH215
    WIH216     WIH217     WIH220     WIH221     WIH222;

MISSING ARE *;

USEVARIABLES ARE WIH202     WIH203     WIH204     WIH205
    WIH206     WIH207     WIH209     WIH210
    WIH211     WIH212     WIH213     WIH214     WIH215
    WIH216     WIH217     WIH220     WIH221     ;

CATEGORICAL ARE WIH202     WIH203     WIH204     WIH205
    WIH206     WIH207     WIH209     WIH210
    WIH211     WIH212     WIH213     WIH214     WIH215
    WIH216     WIH217     WIH220     WIH221     ;

GROUPING IS tcgen (1=female 2=male);

ANALYSIS:
ESTIMATOR = WLSMV;
PARAMETERIZATION = THETA;
DIFFTEST = metric.dat;

MODEL:
response BY WIH202*
```

```
   WIH203@1      WIH204       WIH205
   WIH206        WIH207       WIH209       WIH210
   WIH211        WIH212  WIH220    WIH221;
accept BY WIH213@1
          WIH214 WIH215 WIH216 WIH217;

MODEL female:
response BY WIH202* (l2)
   WIH203@1      WIH204       WIH205  (l3-l5)
   WIH206        WIH207       WIH209       WIH210 (l6-l7 l9-l10)
   WIH211        WIH212  WIH220    WIH221   (l11-l12 l20-l21);
accept BY WIH213@1
          WIH214 WIH215 WIH216 WIH217 (l14-l17);
[WIH202$1 WIH203$1 WIH204$1 WIH205$1] (thrs2-thrs5);
[WIH206$1 WIH207$1 WIH209$1 WIH210$1] (thrs6 thrs7 thrs9
thrs10);
[WIH211$1 WIH212$1 WIH213$1 WIH220$1 WIH221$1] (thrs11-
thrs13 thrs20 thrs21);
[WIH214$1 WIH215$1 WIH216$1 WIH217$1] (thrs14-thrs17);
[response@0 accept@0];
    WIH202@1       WIH204@1       WIH205@1
    WIH206@1       WIH207@1       WIH209@1       WIH210@1
    WIH211@1       WIH212@1  WIH220@1       WIH221@1
    WIH214@1  WIH215@1  WIH216@1  WIH217@1 ;
WIH203@1  WIH213@1 ;


MODEL male:
response BY WIH202* (l2)
   WIH203@1      WIH204       WIH205  (l3-l5)
   WIH206        WIH207       WIH209       WIH210 (l6-l7 l9-l10)
   WIH211        WIH212  WIH220    WIH221   (l11-l12 l20-
l21);
accept BY WIH213@1
          WIH214 WIH215 WIH216 WIH217 (l14-l17);
[WIH202$1 WIH203$1 WIH204$1 WIH205$1] (thrs2-thrs5);
[WIH206$1 WIH207$1 WIH209$1 WIH210$1] (thrs6 thrs7 thrs9
thrs10);
[WIH211$1 WIH212$1 WIH213$1 WIH220$1 WIH221$1] (thrs11-
thrs13 thrs20 thrs21);
[WIH214$1 WIH215$1 WIH216$1 WIH217$1] (thrs14-thrs17);
[response accept];
    WIH202@1       WIH204@1       WIH205@1
    WIH206@1       WIH207@1       WIH209@1       WIH210@1
    WIH211@1       WIH212@1  WIH220@1       WIH221@1
    WIH214@1  WIH215@1  WIH216@1  WIH217@1 ;
WIH203@1  WIH213@1 ;
```

```
OUTPUT:
TECH1; STDYX; RESIDUAL; MODINDICES;

SAVEDATA:
DIFFTEST IS strict.dat;
```

27

Differential Item and Test Functioning

Fritz Drasgow, Christopher D. Nye, Stephen Stark, and Oleksandr S. Chernyshenko

Fairness requires that every test taker has an unimpeded opportunity to demonstrate his or her proficiency on the construct assessed by a test (AERA, APA, & NCME, 2014). If this condition is not satisfied, a test may disadvantage members of one group and thereby advantage members of other groups. The original approach to studying this issue examined the relation of a test to some important criterion measure. More than six decades ago Lloyd Humphreys wrote "it is important not only to determine whether standard errors of measurement are equal, but also whether the same score has the same meaning in the groups being compared, i.e., whether the regression lines are identical or merely parallel" (Humphreys, 1952, p. 134). Along the same lines, the Cleary definition of test bias states

> A test is biased for members of a subgroup of the population if, in the prediction of a criterion for which the test was designed, consistent nonzero errors of prediction are made for members of the subgroup. In other words, the test is biased if the criterion score predicted from the common regression lines is consistently too high or too low for members of the subgroup. With this definition of bias, there may be a connotation of "unfair," particularly if the use of the test produces a prediction that is too low. (Cleary, 1968, p. 115)

A second approach to the study of fairness is directed explicitly at the test:

> Equivalent measurement is obtained when the relations between observed test scores and the latent attribute measured by the test are identical across subpopulations. In particular, individuals with equal standings on the latent trait, say verbal aptitude, but sampled from different subpopulations, say male and female, should have the same expected observed score. (Drasgow, 1984, p. 134)

Items that fail to provide equivalent measurement are said to exhibit **differential item functioning** (DIF) and a lack of measurement equivalence at the test level is termed **differential test functioning** (DTF).

In this chapter, we focus on DIF and DTF. Interestingly research has focused principally on DIF, even though important decisions are rarely, if ever, made on the basis of individual test items. Although test scores are used for many important purposes, DTF has received far less attention. Raju, van der Linden, and Fleer's (1995) differential functioning of items and tests (DFIT) method is a notable exception.

It is important to realize that mean differences in item or test scores across groups do not imply DIF or DTF. Ordinarily there is no reason to believe that the distributions of the trait assessed by a test are identical across subgroups. In fact, interests, educational opportunities, and life experiences probably differ for groups formed on the basis of anything except random assignment and, because these factors often affect test performance, we should **expect** mean differences in scores.

The sine qua non of methods for investigating DIF and DTF is the examination of the difference in a **conditional** relation: Given a specific level of the trait assessed by a test, is there any difference in item or test performance across groups? In this chapter, we describe two general approaches to examining this conditional relation. The first is confirmatory factor analysis (CFA). This method assumes that the regression of an item on the latent trait assessed by a test is **linear**. In contrast, item response theory, the second approach, assumes that the regression of an item on the latent trait is **nonlinear**.

The CFA approach has its roots in the study of factorial invariance (e.g., Meredith, 1964a, 1964b). Historically, factors were extracted via exploratory methods, rotated to achieve maximal congruence, and then some index of the similarity of factor loading matrices was computed. In 1971, Karl Jöreskog placed empirical examination of factorial invariance on a rigorous statistical foundation with his "simultaneous factor analysis in several populations" or SIFASP. Here, CFA is used to freely estimate factor loading matrices in each group and then a factor loading matrix that is constrained to be identical across groups is estimated. The decrement in fit resulting from the constraints can be used to index the nonequivalence of measurement across groups. Recently, Jöreskog's SIFASP has been relabeled as "multiple group factor analysis".

A seminal contribution to the IRT study of DIF was Frederic Lord's (1980) chapter on what was then called "item bias." Lord proposed estimating the IRT item parameters of an item separately in each group, placing the estimates on a common scale, and then performing a multivariate test of the equality of item parameters. This approach has subsequently come to be known as "Lord's χ^2".

When analyzing large samples of test takers from two or more groups, researchers have repeatedly found many items to exhibit statistically significant DIF (e.g., Drasgow, 1987). Close examination of such items rarely provides insights into **why** DIF occurred. Are the differences truly nugatory and significant only due to overwhelming statistical power? To address this concern, measures of effect size have been developed recently.

The next section of this chapter describes Thissen, Steinberg, and Wainer's (1993) likelihood ratio approach to the IRT study of DIF. In addition, effect size indices are described for DIF and DTF. Then two CFA approaches to DIF are described. The first is the traditional approach that examines configural, metric, and scalar factorial invariance and the second is Stark, Chernyshenko, and Drasgow's (2006a) simultaneous method. Again, an effect size index is described for CFA DIF. Then an example of the study of DIF with IRT and CFA is presented. The final section of this chapter contains some comments on the advantages and disadvantages of the various methods.

The IRT Approach to the Study of Measurement Equivalence

Detecting DIF using the likelihood ratio method

The likelihood ratio (LR) method (Thissen, 1991; Thissen, Steinberg, & Wainer, 1988; Thissen et al., 1993) is a general approach for detecting DIF in either CFA or IRT contexts. In the literature, there are two widely used implementations. The first and, perhaps, most popular is to form a baseline model by constraining all items to have equal parameters across the studied groups (Thissen, 1991). Augmented models are then formed to sequentially test for DIF by freeing parameters for one item at a time while keeping the parameters for the other items constrained. In each case, if the change in chi-square relative to the baseline model exceeds a critical chi-square with degrees of freedom equal to the difference in model parameters, then the studied item is flagged as DIF. The second approach to performing the LR test is to form a baseline model in which all items are free to vary across studied groups, except for one or more referent items needed to identify the metric. Then, compact models are formed in which parameters for each additional item, one at a time, are constrained while the others remain free, and the changes in goodness of fit relative to the baseline are compared with a critical chi-square to detect DIF.

Although, at first glance, the differences between these two implementations may seem minute, Type I error rates can differ dramatically when large proportions of DIF items are present. For example, in some simulation conditions Stark et al. (2006a) found Type I error rates as high as .93 using the first implementation, which they referred to as the **constrained-baseline** method. In contrast, the second implementation, which they referred to as the **free-baseline** method, yielded Type I error rates close to the nominal level in nearly all conditions. Thus, the free-baseline implementation is recommended whenever one or more unbiased referent items can be identified.

The key question, of course, is how to identify one or more unbiased referents in practice. Several authors have suggested performing the LR test in two stages (Lopez-Rivas, Stark, & Chernyshenko, 2009; Stark et al., 2006a; Thissen et al., 1988; Wang & Yeh, 2003). In the first stage, the constrained-baseline method is used, which is prone to Type I errors when DIF items are present. Items that are not flagged as DIF in stage 1 are then used as referents for free-baseline LR tests in stage two. In fact, Meade and Wright (2012) compared several strategies for choosing an unbiased referent group and found that this two-stage strategy provided the best power while maintaining nominal Type I error rates.

IRT effect size

As described previously, the traditional methods of identifying DIF using IRT are primarily based on χ^2 significance statistics. Although these methods are commonly used, it is widely known that chi-square tests are sensitive to sample size and this limitation has been demonstrated empirically in previous research (e.g., Stark et al., 2006a). In the broader psychological literature, significance tests have been criticized for the limited information that they provide about empirical comparisons (Cohen, 1990; Kirk, 1996; Schmidt, 1996). Consequently, effect size indices have been recommended as supplements to significance tests because they can provide important additional information about research findings (e.g., Cohen, 1988). Although some effect size indices have been proposed for IRT DIF studies (see Gierl, Gotzmann, & Boughton, 2004), these measures are not generally in a standardized metric and, therefore, may not have a consistent interpretation across studies. Until recently, standardized effect sizes were not available for IRT approaches to detecting measurement bias.

Nye (2011) suggested an IRT effect size for DIF. For item i, $P_{iF}(\theta)$ is the probability of a positive or correct response and θ is the individual's standing on the latent trait. Here, the probability is computed using item parameters estimated from the focal group. Conceptually, DIF occurs when there are differences between this probability and the corresponding probability computed from the reference group item parameters and denoted by $P_{iR}(\theta)$ (assuming the item parameters from the two groups have been placed on the same metric). As such, the effect size of DIF on item i is

$$d_{DIF} = \frac{1}{SD_{iP}} \sqrt{\int [P_{iR}(\theta) - P_{iF}(\theta)]^2 f_F(\theta) d\theta}$$

where $f_F(\theta)$ is the assumed normal distribution of the latent trait in the focal group with the mean and variance estimated from the transformed $\hat{\theta}$ distribution and SD_{iP} is a pooled estimate of the standard deviation on item i. Dividing by the pooled SD places d_{DIF} on a standardized scale like Cohen (1988) and Glass's (1976) effect size measures.

In 2004, Stark, Chernyshenko, and Drasgow suggested that an index of overall DTF could be defined as the contribution that bias makes to observed score differences. The basis for this measure is the test characteristic curve (TCC), which gives the expected total test or scale score for individuals with standing θ on the latent trait and is computed as

$$TCC = \sum_{i=1}^{n} P_i(\theta)$$

for a measure composed of n items. Then Stark et al. (2004) defined an effect size for DTF as

$$d_{DTF} = \frac{1}{SD_F} \int [TCC_R(\theta) - TCC_F(\theta)] f_F(\theta) d\theta.$$

Here, the magnitude of the effect is operationalized as the differences between the TCCs in the reference (TCC_R) and focal (TCC_F) groups. This operationalization is similar to the definition of DTF proposed by Raju et al. (1995). These differences are averaged across the latent trait distribution $f_F(\theta)$ in the focal group and the result is divided by the observed standard deviation (SD_F) of the test in this group. Again, dividing by SD_F puts this effect size in a standardized metric (see Cohen, 1988; Glass, 1976).

It is important to note that the numerator of Stark et al.'s (2004) equation is in raw score points. Thus, this value, which Stark et al. labeled DTFR, represents the effects of bias on the mean of the scale. DTFR can be used to determine how much of the observed differences between the reference and focal groups can be attributed to bias (see later text for an example). This information may be particularly useful for understanding the effects of DTF on high-stakes decisions (e.g., educational or employment-related) and on the conclusions drawn from empirical research. Although it would be ideal to have $d_{DTF} = 0$, in practice values less than Cohen's (1988) "small" effect size of .20 might be regarded as tolerable and larger values seen as requiring remediation.

The CFA Approach to the Study of Measurement Equivalence

Detecting DIF using CFA

In the CFA literature, a sequential procedure has often been used to examine measurement invariance. In the first step, **configural invariance** is examined. This term is used for multidimensional factor analysis models to describe the situation where the same number of factors is found for all groups and, moreover, each observed variable has a nonzero loading on the same factor for all groups. This latter condition means that the same pattern of fixed (at zero) and free factor loadings is appropriate for all groups. To determine whether configural invariance holds, the overall χ^2 goodness of fit can be tested for significance. However, this statistic is sensitive to sample size and trivial violations of the assumptions of the CFA model. Consequently, researchers have developed a variety of overall goodness of fit measures such as the standardized root mean squared residual (SRMSR), the Tucker–Lewis index (TLI; Tucker & Lewis, 1973), and the root mean squared error of approximation (RMSEA; Browne & Cudeck, 1993) to evaluate fit. Although simple rules of thumb are often cited (e.g., RMSEA should be .08 or smaller) for these fit statistics, they are nonetheless affected by sample size, model complexity, and the degree to which the distributions of the manifest variables depart from the assumed multivariate normality (Nye & Drasgow, 2011a). Thus, care is needed in evaluating fit.

If configural invariance holds to a reasonable degree, the next step in the traditional CFA procedure examines **metric invariance**. Here the equivalence of factor loading matrices across groups is examined. Because the metric invariance model is a nested submodel of the configural invariance model, the difference in χ^2 values follows a chi-square distribution with degrees of freedom (df) equal to the difference in df of the two models when metric invariance (and all model assumptions) holds. Again, this significance test is susceptible to problems due to sample size and trivial model misspecifications, so researchers ordinarily examine the change in goodness of fit statistics to decide whether to conclude that metric invariance holds.

The third and final step in the traditional CFA approach to measurement equivalence examines **scalar invariance**. Here Sörbom's (1974) mean and covariance structure (MACS) analysis is used. As suggested by its name, the MACS analysis models both the means and covariances of the observed variables. Here, for group g,

$$x_g = \tau_g + \Lambda_g \xi_g + \delta_g,$$

where x_g is a vector containing the manifest variables, τ_g is the vector of intercepts of the regressions of the manifest variables on the latent factor ξ_g, and δ_g is the vector of measurement errors. Whereas metric invariance tests the equality of factor loading matrices across groups g and g' (i.e., $\Lambda_g = \Lambda_{g'}$), scalar invariance tests the equality of both intercepts and factor loadings (i.e., $\tau_g = \tau_{g'}$ and $\Lambda_g = \Lambda_{g'}$).

To make the CFA analysis more directly comparable to the IRT approach, Stark et al. (2006) devised the LR approach previously described. For the free-baseline approach, this method frees intercept parameters τ_i^g and $\tau_i^{g'}$, and factor loadings λ_i^g and $\lambda_i^{g'}$, one item at a time and examines the decrease in the χ^2 value.

CFA effect sizes

Similar to the IRT methods for identifying DIF, the CFA approach relies on chi-square tests and empirically derived rules of thumb for identifying nonequivalence. Again, the information that these criteria can provide about the magnitude of the effect is limited because the results are confounded with other factors (e.g., sample size). Building on the IRT effect size proposed by Stark et al. (2004), Nye and Drasgow (2011b) derived several effect sizes for CFA analyses of measurement equivalence to address these issues.

A standardized effect size for MACS analyses can be defined as

$$d_{MACS} = \frac{1}{SD_{iP}}\sqrt{\int (\hat{X}_{iR} - \hat{X}_{iF}|\xi)^2 f_F(\xi) d\xi}$$

where $\hat{X}_{iR}$ and $\hat{X}_{iF}$ are the mean predicted scores to item i in the reference and focal groups, respectively. These predicted scores are based on the CFA model and the squared differences between them are evaluated at each level of the latent trait (ξ) and averaged (i.e., integrated) over the distribution of this trait in the focal group. The square root of these differences is then divided by the pooled standard deviation of the item (SD_{iP}).

Although similar to the d_{IRT} effect size, there is an important difference between these measures. Note that d_{MACS} uses the squared differences between predicted responses. As such, bias in opposite directions at different points on the latent trait scale will not cancel out and **any** differences between groups will influence the effect size. However, the unsquared differences can also be used if the effect size of compensatory DIF is of interest.

d_{IRT} and d_{MACS} are calculated at the item level. Understanding the effects of nonequivalence at the item level is important for test development and for identifying items and content that may be problematic. However, decisions in educational and employment settings are made on the basis of total test scores. Consequently, Nye and Drasgow (2011b) also proposed a second index for calculating overall DTF. This index is defined as

$$\Delta Mean(X_S) = \sum_{1}^{n} \int (\hat{X}_{iR} - \hat{X}_{iF}|\xi) f_F(\xi) d\xi.$$

Here, differences at the item level are summed over all n items. In addition, the unsquared differences between the predicted scores in the reference and focal group are used because bias in opposite directions can cancel out at the scale level and limit the influence of DIF on the mean. As a result, this index describes the effect of measurement bias on the mean of the scale and is analogous to the DTFR effect size proposed by Stark et al. (2004). Using an empirical example, Nye and Drasgow found that $\Delta Mean$ accounted for between 18 and 126% of the observed mean differences between the reference and focal groups on a measure of personality. Note that in some cases, bias accounted for more than 100% of the observed mean differences. This occurs when the effects of bias reverse the sign of the mean difference. For example, Nye and Drasgow found that a U.S. sample had a significantly higher observed mean on an Extraversion scale than a sample of Greek respondents. However, calculating $\Delta Mean$ showed that the effects of bias were larger than this observed difference. Therefore, after removing the effects of bias, the Greek sample actually had a higher true mean level of Extraversion. These results suggest that bias can influence the conclusions that are drawn from a study. Although not originally part of the effect size proposed by Nye and Drasgow, this value could also be divided by the pooled standard deviation to put it in a standardized metric. The resulting effect size would be analogous to Stark et al.'s d_{DTF} index.

Empirical Example of IRT and CFA DIF Analyses

To illustrate the LR approaches to DIF and effect size analysis for IRT and CFA, we analyzed data from a large sample of individuals who completed a 10-item Traditionalism scale (Chernyshenko, 2002), which measures the rule following and respect for authority aspects of the Big Five factor Conscientiousness (Roberts, Chernyshenko, Stark, & Goldberg, 2005). The items are shown in Table 27.1. Because research has found differences in Traditionalism scores across age groups, we wanted to examine the extent to which these differences might have resulted from DIF. To address this question, we formed two comparison samples (N = 750 each) that differed in age by at least 20 years. The first sample consisting of 15–20-year-olds was designated the focal group. The second sample consisting of adults age 40 and above was designated as the reference group.

To prepare for the DIF analyses, we reverse-scored negatively worded items and verified that the data were sufficiently unidimensional for analysis assuming a single latent trait (Drasgow & Parsons, 1983). Next, we conducted constrained-baseline IRT LR tests, based on Samejima's (1969) Graded Response model, using the MULTILOG computer program (Thissen, 1991). Figure 27.1 shows MULTILOG syntax files for the constrained-baseline model in which all parameters were constrained across groups, and one augmented model that tested for DIF on Item 1 by allowing parameters for that item to vary across groups.

Table 27.1 Items from Chernyshenko's (2002) Traditionalism scale.

Item No.	Item Content
1	I have the highest respect for authorities and assist them whenever I can.
2	People respect authority more than they should.
3	Even if I knew how to get around the rules without breaking them, I would not do it.
4	I believe that people should be allowed to take drugs, as long as it doesn't affect others.
5	I support long-established rules and traditions.
6	People who resist authority should be severely punished.
7	When I was in school, I used to break rules quite regularly.
8	In my opinion, all laws should be strictly enforced.
9	In my opinion, censorship slows down progress.
10	When working with others I am the one who makes sure that rules are observed.

```
Constrained baseline model for SGR 10-item, 4-option IRT LR Test
>PROBLEM RANDOM,
    INDIVIDUAL,
    DATA = 'focref1.DAT',
    NITEMS = 20,
    NGROUPS = 2,
    NEXAMINEES = 1500,
    NCHARS = 5;
>TEST ALL,
    GRADED,
    NC = (4(0)20);
>EQUAL AJ IT=(1,2,3,4,5,6,7,8,9,10) WI=(11,12,13,14,15,16,17,18,19,20);
>EQUAL BK=(1,2,3) IT=(1,2,3,4,5,6,7,8,9,10)
WI=(11,12,13,14,15,16,17,18,19,20);
>EST NC=300;
>END ;
4
1234
11111111111111111111
22222222222222222222
33333333333333333333
44444444444444444444
(5A1,1x,I1,1x,20A1)


****************************************************
Augmented model to test for DIF on item 1
>PROBLEM RANDOM,
    INDIVIDUAL,
    DATA = 'focref1.DAT',
    NITEMS = 20,
    NGROUPS = 2,
    NEXAMINEES = 1500,
    NCHARS = 5;
>TEST ALL,
    GRADED,
    NC = (4(0)20);
>EQUAL AJ IT=(2,3,4,5,6,7,8,9,10) WI=(12,13,14,15,16,17,18,19,20);
>EQUAL BK=(1,2,3) IT=(2,3,4,5,6,7,8,9,10) WI=(12,13,14,15,16,17,18,19,20);
>EST NC=300;
>END ;
4
1234
11111111111111111111
22222222222222222222
33333333333333333333
44444444444444444444
(5A1,1x,I1,1x,20A1)
```

Figure 27.1 Examples of MULTILOG syntax files for constrained-baseline IRT LR tests.

The results of these analyses are presented in Table 27.2, columns 2 through 5. Column 2 shows the G^2 values provided by MULTILOG for the constrained-baseline model and the 10 augmented comparison models. Column 3 shows the difference in G^2 values, which is distributed approximately as a chi-square with 4 degrees of freedom because there are four parameters estimated per item (one discrimination parameter and three location

```
Free-baseline model for SGR 10-item, 4-option IRT LR with items 1, 4, 8, and 9 as
referents
    >PROBLEM RANDOM,
        INDIVIDUAL,
        DATA = 'focref1.DAT',
        NITEMS = 20,
        NGROUPS = 2,
        NEXAMINEES = 1500,
        NCHARS = 5;
    >TEST ALL,
        GRADED,
        NC = (4(0)20);
    >EQUAL AJ IT=(1,4,8,9) WI=(11,14,18,19);
    >EQUAL BK=(1,2,3) IT=(1,4,8,9) WI=(11,14,18,19);
    >EST NC=300;
    >END ;
4
1234
11111111111111111111
22222222222222222222
33333333333333333333
44444444444444444444
(5A1,1x,I1,1x,20A1)
*********************************************
Compact model to test for DIF on item 2
>PROBLEM RANDOM,
        INDIVIDUAL,
        DATA = 'focref1.DAT',
        NITEMS = 20,
        NGROUPS = 2,
        NEXAMINEES = 1500,
        NCHARS = 5;
    >TEST ALL,
        GRADED,
        NC = (4(0)20);
    >EQUAL AJ IT=(1,4,8,9,2) WI=(11,14,18,19,12);
    >EQUAL BK=(1,2,3) IT=(1,4,8,9,2) WI=(11,14,18,19,12);
    >EST NC=300;
    >END ;
4
1234
11111111111111111111
22222222222222222222
33333333333333333333
44444444444444444444
(5A1,1x,I1,1x,20A1)
```

Figure 27.2 Examples of MULTILOG syntax files for free-baseline IRT LR tests.

parameters). Column 4 shows the *p*-values for the statistical tests comparing the observed G^2 differences to a critical chi-square of 9.49 corresponding to an area of .05 in the upper tail. As can be seen, 6 of the 10 Traditionalism items were flagged as DIF in this comparison. Consequently, we chose the four unflagged items (1, 4, 8, and 9) as referents for the subsequent IRT and CFA analyses using the free-baseline approach.

Figure 27.2 shows MULTILOG syntax files for the free-baseline model, in which parameters for all non-referent items were free to vary across groups, and the compact model that tested for DIF on Item 2 by constraining its parameters. Figure 27.3 shows the corresponding LISREL syntax for MACS analysis via linear CFA. The full DIF results are presented in Table 27.2. Note that the critical chi-square value for the

```
! Free-baseline model with items 1, 4, 8, and 9 as referents
GROUP 1: BASELINE_rep1
DA NG=2 NI=10 NO=750
LA
*
v1 v2 v3 v4 v5 v6 v7 v8 v9 v10
RA=foc1_CFA.dat FO RE
(4X,10F1.0)
MO NX=10 NK=1 TX = FR LX = FR KA = FR TD=DI
LK
F1
FI LX (1, 1)
VA 1 LX (1, 1)
OU TV SC ND=2
GROUP 2: reference
DA NO=750
LA
*
v1 v2 v3 v4 v5 v6 v7 v8 v9 v10
RA=ref1_CFA.dat FO RE
(4X,10F1.0)
MO LX=FR TX=FR KA=FI TD=DI
EQ TX (1,1) TX (1)
EQ LX (1, 4, 1) LX (4, 1)
EQ TX (1,4) TX (4)
EQ LX (1, 8, 1) LX (8, 1)
EQ TX (1,8) TX (8)
EQ LX (1, 9, 1) LX (9, 1)
EQ TX (1,9) TX (9)
FI LX (1,1)
VA 1 LX (1,1)
OU GF=Free_FIT.txt

! Compact model to test for DIF on item 2
GROUP 1: CONSTRAIN2_rep1
DA NG=2 NI=10 NO=750
LA
*
v1 v2 v3 v4 v5 v6 v7 v8 v9 v10
RA=foc1_CFA.dat FO RE
(4X,10F1.0)
MO NX=10 NK=1 TX = FR LX = FR KA = FR TD=DI
LK
F1
FI LX (1, 1)
VA 1 LX (1, 1)
OU TV SC ND=2
GROUP 2: reference
DA NO=750
LA
*
v1 v2 v3 v4 v5 v6 v7 v8 v9 v10
RA=ref1_CFA.dat FO RE
(4X,10F1.0)
MO LX=FR TX=FR KA=FI TD=DI
EQ LX (1,2, 1) LX (2, 1)
EQ TX (1,2) TX (2)
EQ TX (1,1) TX (1)
EQ LX (1, 4, 1) LX (4, 1)
EQ TX (1,4) TX (4)
EQ LX (1, 8, 1) LX (8, 1)
EQ TX (1,8) TX (8)
EQ LX (1, 9, 1) LX (9, 1)
EQ TX (1,9) TX (9)
FI LX (1,1)
VA 1 LX (1,1)
OU GF=Free_FIT.txt
```

Figure 27.3 Examples of LISREL syntax files for free-baseline CFA LR tests.

free-baseline IRT analysis was the same as in the constrained-baseline IRT analysis. In both cases, MULTILOG was used to model item responses with four categories; thus, a discrimination parameter and three location parameters were estimated for each item. Therefore, the observed chi-square value was compared to a critical chi-square value based on four degrees of freedom (9.49). However, because the MACS analysis was performed using the linear CFA model, only two parameters were estimated per item (one loading and one intercept). Thus, the observed chi-square differences were compared to the critical chi-square based on two degrees of freedom (5.99).

As can be seen in Table 27.2, the free-baseline IRT and CFA LR tests yielded the same results, except for Item 2, which showed no DIF in the CFA MACS analysis. Inspection of the MULTILOG focal (F) and reference (R) group parameters for Item 2 revealed differences in both the discrimination and thresholds ($a_F = 1.41$, $b_{1F} = -2.32$, $b_{2F} = -0.44$, $b_{3F} = 1.18$; $a_R = 1.12$, $b_{1R} = -2.68$, $b_{2R} = -0.73$, $b_{3R} = 1.44$). In contrast, the CFA MACS analysis revealed a difference in loadings (.86 vs. .73) but no difference in intercepts (2.78 vs. 2.79).

Example of IRT and CFA Effect Sizes

We next calculated Stark et al.'s (2004) d_{DTF} effect size statistics for the free and constrained-baseline analyses of the Traditionalism scale using a C++ program developed by Seybert[1] (2011). Here, the effect size was .001 for the free-baseline analysis and –.03 for the constrained-baseline analysis, suggesting that the DIF identified in the Traditionalism scale cancels out at the scale level and has virtually no effect on the scale mean. Table 27.2 also shows the item-level effect sizes for both the IRT and CFA analyses. As shown, the CFA effect sizes were all .24 and below, which is generally considered a small effect. In addition, items 2, 5, and 10 all had negligible effect sizes (.06). Thus, DIF does not appear to have a substantial effect on the differences between these groups at the item level. However, the IRT effect sizes suggested slightly larger effects. The effect sizes for items 3 and 6 were .34 and .41 in the free-baseline condition. Nevertheless, the effect sizes for the remaining items were still below .15.

It is important to note that the effects of DIF/DTF on observed differences between groups can be quantified using the indices described previously. The observed difference between the reference and focal groups examined here was 1.74 ($t = 8.67$, $p < .05$), meaning that individuals age 40 and older (i.e., the reference group) scored significantly higher on the Traditionalism scale than individuals between the ages of 15 and 20. However, this difference may be misleading when there is DIF in the measure.

Stark et al. (2004) noted that observed differences are a function of both bias and impact such that

$$\text{Observed Differences} = \text{Bias} + \text{Impact}$$

Here, the DIF identified is a form of bias and impact refers to true mean differences between groups. Therefore, observed differences can be enhanced or reduced by the effects of DIF in the measure. For this reason, it is important to calculate the effects of bias on observed mean differences and these effects are quantified by the DTFR measure

---

[1] Readers interested in obtaining a copy of the software may contact Jacob Seybert: seybertjm@gmail.com.

Table 27.2 Results from invariance analyses.

	IRT LR Constrained-Baseline					IRT LR Free-Baseline					CFA LR Free-Baseline				
	G^2	Difference	p	DIF	d_{DIF}	G^2	Difference	P	DIF	d_{DIF}	χ^2	Difference	p	DIF	d_{MACS}
Baseline	14132.7					13926.5[a]					291.81[a]				
Item 1	14127.2	5.5	.24	no	.07										
Item 2	14120.5	12.2	.02	yes	.08	13937.4	10.9	.03	yes	.12	295.74	3.93	.14	no	.06
Item 3	14068.9	63.8	.00	yes	.29	13975.9	49.4	.00	yes	.34	344.53	52.72	.00	yes	.24
Item 4	14128.1	4.6	.33	no	.08	[a]					[a]				
Item 5	14116.8	15.9	.00	yes	.03	13941.5	15.0	.00	yes	.07	298.97	7.16	.03	yes	.06
Item 6	14027.9	104.3	.00	yes	.49	14010.8	84.3	.00	yes	.41	340.56	48.75	.00	yes	.22
Item 7	14122.8	9.9	.04	yes	.17	13937.4	10.9	.03	yes	.13	316.20	24.39	.00	yes	.23
Item 8	14127.7	5.0	.29	no	.14	[a]					[a]				
Item 9	14129.0	3.7	.45	no	.01	[a]									
Item 10	14118.8	13.9	.01	yes	.12	13939.9	13.4	.01	yes	.09	309.28	17.47	.00	yes	.06

Note. [a] Referent item used to link metrics.

described by Stark et al. (2004) and the $\Delta Mean$ index proposed by Nye and Drasgow (2011b). For the Traditionalism scale, DTFR was .00 in the free-baseline condition suggesting that the DIF identified using the LR approach cancels out and has no effect on the mean of the scale. In contrast, DTFR was −.15 in the constrained-baseline condition, indicating that the focal group was slightly favored by DIF in the measure. However, again, the effect was negligible and does not substantially affect the mean of the scale. For the CFA analyses, $\Delta Mean = -.04$, suggesting that DIF in the measure enhanced the mean in the younger sample to a very small degree. Consistent with DTFR values, the magnitude of the effect is negligible and indicates that nonequivalence in the measure would have very little influence on the conclusions drawn from the observed differences.

Discussion

In principle, the IRT approach to DIF and DTF should be preferred for discrete item responses, whether dichotomously scored or polytomously scored. The CFA approach assumes that the manifest variables are distributed as multivariate normal, so at first blush this approach would not be the method of choice for item-level data. However, polytomously scored items can have distributions that are approximately normal and it is surprising how quickly the normality assumption is reasonably satisfied (Drasgow & Dorans, 1982). In Stark et al.'s (2006b) comparison of the IRT and CFA approaches to identifying DIF, IRT had a small superiority in terms of power for dichotomously scored data, but CFA was clearly superior for polytomously scored data with five response options. Moreover, the CFA approach can be easily extended to multidimensional latent traits, whereas IRT has been largely restricted to unidimensional models. In addition, software for CFA is more widely available and is, perhaps, easier to use.

An important consideration is that CFA is a dominance model: CFA assumes a linear relation between the latent trait and response variables. Thus, higher levels of the latent trait lead us to expect higher scores on the manifest variables. In contrast, ideal point models assume nonmonotonic relations so that it is possible for individuals with intermediate trait values to have the highest expected scores. The idea underlying ideal point models is that individuals will endorse items that closely describe themselves, so that the probability of endorsement is inversely related to $|\theta - b_i|$ where b_i is a parameter indexing an item's location on the latent trait continuum. For example, the item "My social skills are about average" is unlikely to be endorsed by individuals very high or low in sociability, but is likely to be endorsed by individuals with intermediate trait values. A growing body of research has found ideal point models to be more appropriate for the measurement of personality (Stark et al., 2006b), attitudes (Roberts, Laughlin, & Wedell, 1999), vocational interests (Tay, Drasgow, Rounds & Williams, 2009) and other non-cognitive traits (Drasgow, Chernyshenko, & Stark, 2010). While this chapter has focused on DIF and DTF methods for dominance models, extending these approaches to ideal point models is an important area for future research.

References

American Educational Research Association, American Psychological Association, & National Council on Measurement in Education, (2014). *Standards for educational and psychological testing*. Washington, DC: American Educational Research Association.

Browne, M. W., & Cudeck, R. (1993). Alternative ways of assessing model fit. In K. A. Bollen & J. S. Long (Eds.), *Testing structural equations models* (pp. 136–162). Newbury Park, CA: Sage.

Chernyshenko, O. S. (2002). *Applications of ideal point approaches to scale construction and scoring in personality measurement: The development of a six-faceted measure of conscientiousness* (Unpublished doctoral dissertation). University of Illinois at Urbana-Champaign.

Cleary, T. A. (1968). Test bias: Prediction of grades of Negro and White students in integrated colleges. *Journal of Educational Measurement, 5*, 115–124.

Cohen, J. (1988). *Statistical power analysis for the behavioral sciences* (2nd ed.). Hillsdale, NJ: Erlbaum

Cohen, J. (1990). Things I have learned (so far). *American Psychologist, 45*, 1304–1312.

Drasgow, F. (1984). Scrutinizing psychological tests: Measurement equivalence and equivalent relations with external variables are the central issues. *Psychological Bulletin, 95*, 134–135.

Drasgow, F. (1987). A study of the measurement bias of two standardized psychological tests. *Journal of Applied Psychology, 72*, 19–29.

Drasgow, F., Chernyshenko, O. S., & Stark, S. (2010). 75 years after Likert: Thurstone was right! *Industrial and Organizational Psychology: Perspectives on Science and Practice, 3*, 465–476.

Drasgow, F., & Dorans, N. J. (1982). Robustness of estimators of the squared multiple correlation and squared cross-validity coefficient to violations of multivariate normality. *Applied Psychological Measurement, 6*, 185–200.

Drasgow, F., & Parsons, C. K. (1983). Application of unidimensional item response theory models to multidimensional data. *Applied Psychological Measurement, 7*, 189–199.

Gierl, M. J., Gotzmann, A., & Boughton, K. A. (2004). Performance of SIBTEST when the number of DIF items is large. *Applied Measurement in Education, 17*, 241–264.

Glass, G. V. (1976). Primary, secondary, and meta-analysis of research. *Educational Researcher, 5*, 3–8.

Humphreys, L. G. (1952). Individual differences. In C. P. Stone & D. Taylor (Eds.), *Annual Review of Psychology, 3*, 131–150.

Jöreskog, K. G. (1971). Simultaneous factor analysis in several populations. *Psychometrika, 36*, 409–426.

Kirk, R. E. (1996). Practical significance: A concept whose time has come. *Educational and Psychological Measurement, 56*, 746–759.

Lopez-Rivas, G. E., Stark, S., & Chernyshenko, O. S. (2009). The effects of referent item parameters on differential item functioning detection using the free baseline likelihood ratio test. *Applied Psychological Measurement, 33*, 251–265.

Lord, F. M. (1980). *Applications of item response theory to practical testing problems*. Hillsdale, NJ: Lawrence Erlbaum.

Meade, A. W., & Wright, N. A. (2012). Solving the measurement invariance anchor item problem in item response theory. *Journal of Applied Psychology, 97*, 1016–1031.

Meredith, W. (1964a). Rotation to achieve factorial invariance. *Psychometrika, 19*, 187–206.

Meredith, W. (1964b). Notes on factorial invariance. *Psychometrika, 19*, 177–185.

Nye, C. D. (2011). *The development and evaluation of effect size measures for CFA and IRT studies of measurement equivalence* (Doctoral Dissertation). University of Illinois at Urbana-Champaign.

Nye, C. D., & Drasgow, F. (2011a). Assessing goodness of fit: Simple rules of thumb simply don't work. *Organizational Research Methods, 14*, 548–570.

Nye, C. D., & Drasgow, F. (2011b). Effect size indices for analyses of measurement equivalence: Understanding the practical importance of differences between groups. *Journal of Applied Psychology, 96*, 966–980.

Raju, N. S., van der Linden, W. J., & Fleer, P. F. (1995). IRT-based internal measures of differential functioning of items and tests. *Applied Psychological Measurement, 19*, 353–368.

Roberts, B., Chernyshenko, O. S., Stark, S., & Goldberg, L. (2005). The construct of conscientiousness: The convergence between lexical models and scales drawn from six major personality questionnaires. *Personnel Psychology, 58*, 103–139.

Roberts, J. S., Laughlin, J. E., & Wedell, D. H. (1999). Validity issues in the Likert and Thurstone approaches to attitude measurement. *Educational and Psychological Measurement, 59*, 211–233.

Samejima, F. (1969). Estimation of latent ability using a response pattern of graded scores. *Psychometrika Monograph*, No. 17.

Schmidt, F. L. (1996). Statistical significance testing and cumulative knowledge in psychology: Implications for training of researchers. *Psychological Methods, 1*, 115–129.

Seybert, J. M. (2011). *DTFR-Poly: A computer program for calculating DTFR effect sizes for polytomous IRT models*. Unpublished manuscript. University of South Florida.

Sörbom, D. (1974). A general method for studying differences in factor means and factor structure between groups. *British Journal of Mathematical and Statistical Psychology, 27*, 229–239.

Stark, S., Chernyshenko, O. S., & Drasgow, F. (2004). Examining the effects of differential item (functioning and differential) test functioning on selection decisions: When are statistically significant effects practically important? *Journal of Applied Psychology, 89*, 497–508.

Stark, S., Chernyshenko, O. S., & Drasgow, F. (2006a). Detecting differential item functioning with confirmatory factor analysis and item response theory: Toward a unified strategy. *Journal of Applied Psychology, 91*, 1292–1306.

Stark, S., Chernyshenko, O. S., Drasgow, F., & Williams, B. (2006b). Investigating the appropriateness of an ideal point response process for personality data. *Journal of Applied Psychology, 91*, 25–39.

Tay, L., Drasgow, F., Rounds, J., & Williams, B. A. (2009). Fitting measurement models to vocational interest data: Are dominance models ideal? *Journal of Applied Psychology, 94*, 1287–1304.

Thissen, D. (1991). *MULTILOG user's guide: Multiple, categorical item analysis and test scoring using item response theory*. Mooresville, IN: Scientific Software International.

Thissen, D., Steinberg, L., & Wainer, H. (1988). Use of item response theory in the study of group differences in trace lines. In H. Wainer & H. Braun (Eds.), *Test validity* (pp. 147–169). Hillsdale, NJ: Erlbaum.

Thissen, D., Steinberg, L., & Wainer, H. (1993). Detection of differential item functioning using the parameters of item response models. In P. W. Holland & H. Wainer (Eds.), *Differential item functioning* (pp. 67–113). Hillsdale, NJ: Lawrence Erlbaum.

Tucker, L. R., & Lewis, C. (1973). A reliability coefficient for maximum likelihood factor analysis. *Psychometrika, 38*, 1–10.

Wang, W. C., & Yeh, Y. L. (2003). Effects of anchor item methods on differential item functioning detection with the likelihood ratio test. *Applied Psychological Measurement, 27*, 479–498.

Part VI
Applications

28

Psychometric Methods in Political Science

Christopher Hare and Keith T. Poole

Introduction

In political science, psychometric methods have been integrated with the spatial (geometric) voting model to measure latent quantities (e.g., ideology) from political choice and judgment behavior. The spatial voting model posits that individuals' preferences can be represented in abstract, geometric (usually Euclidean) space and that individuals will choose the alternative or stimulus closest to them (Downs, 1957; Enelow & Hinich, 1984). Psychometric methods can be used to recover the locations of the individuals and/or stimuli in the latent space using **preferential** or **perceptual** choice data. The two types of data may be indicators of the same construct even though they originate from different data-generating processes (Coombs, 1964). For instance, the ideological positions of a set of candidates may be measured with survey respondents' placements of the candidates on a left-right scale (perceptual data) or candidates' voting records on a series of legislative proposals (preferential data).[1] In this chapter, we review several different methods that have been developed for the analysis of each type of data in political science.

Psychometrics has contributed to the field of political science by showing that the key theoretical assumptions of the spatial voting model – that political preferences can be represented in geometric space and that political actors accurately perceive the distance between themselves and rival stimuli and choose accordingly – perform well under empirical scrutiny. An impressive regularity from psychometric analyses of political preferential and perceptual data is that the recovered choice spaces are low-dimensional, rarely consisting of more than two dimensions and virtually never more than three (Poole, 2005). That is, only one or two fundamental dimensions are usually sufficient to model legislative voting across hundreds of roll call votes (Poole & Rosenthal, 1997) or citizens' policy attitudes (Hare & Poole, 2012; Treier & Hillygus, 2009) and feeling thermometer rankings of candidates and parties (Bakker & Poole, 2013; Jacoby & Armstrong, 2014; Weisberg & Rusk, 1970). Moreover, citizens are also adept in

---

[1] In the United States Congress, recorded votes are referred to as "roll call" votes. We use the term "roll call voting" to refer to legislative voting in general throughout this chapter.

The Wiley Handbook of Psychometric Testing: A Multidisciplinary Reference on Survey, Scale and Test Development, First Edition. Edited by Paul Irwing, Tom Booth, and David J. Hughes.
© 2018 John Wiley & Sons Ltd. Published 2020 by John Wiley & Sons Ltd.

perceiving the latent ideological positions of public officials, a finding we demonstrate in this chapter.

These latent dimensions are understood as **ideological** dimensions because they bundle or **constrain** a complex array of political preferences together as a belief system (Converse, 1964; Hinich & Munger, 1994). Advocacy for social welfare programs is bundled with opposition to military action in left-wing ideologies, while aversion to tax increases is bundled with support for abortion restrictions in right-wing ideologies. Converse (1964) emphasized that these ideological configurations need not be strictly logical, they can also arise from psychological or social sources. However, ideologies are not incoherent assemblages of policy positions: adherents must perceive that they encompass a fundamental vision of the "good society" (Hinich & Munger, 1994).

The application of psychometrics to political science has been so successful because of the ideological structure of political actors' perceptions and preferences. This ideological structure manifests itself in political choice and judgment behavior, and hence spatial "maps" of the latent space can be recovered and analyzed using psychometric techniques. First, however, the regularity of low-dimensional political choice spaces deserves some theoretical explanation: on such a dizzying array of issues, why are only a few dimensions necessary to explain individuals' political attitudes and choices? To address this question, we consider the primary sources of ideological constraint within the framework of the Basic Space theory developed by Hinich, Ordeshook, and their colleagues. We then proceed to an exposition of the scaling methods that have been developed and utilized in political science for the analysis of preferential and perceptual choice data.[2]

The Basic Space Theory

> One of the curious things about political opinions is how often the same people line up on opposite sides of different issues. These issues may have no intrinsic connection with each other. They may range from military spending to drug laws to monetary policy to education. Yet the same familiar faces can be found glaring at each other from opposite sides of the political fence, again and again. It happens too often to be coincidence and is too uncontrolled to be a plot. (Sowell, 2007, p. 3)

The two-space or Basic Space theory of ideology was developed by Melvin J. Hinich, Peter C. Ordeshook, and their colleagues (Cahoon, Hinich, & Ordeshook, 1976; Enelow and Hinich, 1984; Hinich and Munger, 1994, 1997; Hinich & Pollard, 1981; Ordeshook, 1976). It is of interest to us here because it provides a theoretical explanation for the results obtained from empirical scaling methods with a geometric interpretation of Converse's (1964) notion of ideological constraint.

The first work on the theory came with Cahoon, Hinich, and Ordeshook's (1976) use of a metric multidimensional scaling (MDS) procedure based on Torgerson

---

[2] Many of these scaling procedures are available as functions in the popular open-source program **R**. Our book *Analyzing Spatial Models of Choice and Judgment with R* (with David A. Armstrong, II., Ryan Bakker, Royce Carroll, and Howard Rosenthal) provides detailed instruction on how to use these procedures in **R**.

(1958) and Schönemann (1970) to scale citizens' feeling thermometer rankings of 1968 presidential candidates and sociopolitical groups (e.g., the "military," "Vietnam war protestors," and "liberals"). What they found was that the diverse set of thermometer rankings overlaid with each other on one of two latent dimensions (left-right ideology and partisanship), echoing earlier results from Weisberg and Rusk (1970) and Rusk and Weisberg (1972). Voters did choose candidates closest to them in the choice space, as predicted by the spatial model, but the structure of the recovered space was different than what they expected. Namely, the space consisted not of a comprehensive set of orthogonal, ordered issue dimensions, but rather of a greatly reduced set of abstract dimensions.

This result led Cahoon et al. (1976) to reconsider the standard spatial voting model in which the issues are confined to separate dimensions and each individual is assumed to have an ideal point (i.e., a most preferred location) on, and single-peaked preferences over, each issue dimension (e.g., Davis & Hinich, 1966). The Basic Space theory states that this is but one of **two** spaces: the complex issue or **action** space, and the low-dimensional **basic** space that is recovered by scaling procedures. The presence of constraint – the bundling of issues into a compact platform or program (Converse, 1964) – allows for the linear mapping of one space to the other. If individuals have highly structured (constrained) belief systems, then the action space reduces to the basic space. Hence, the Basic Space theory is a geometric model of Converse's notion of ideological constraint.

For instance, suppose that one group of voters or legislators favors an increase in defense spending, tighter immigration restrictions, and harsher penalties for illegal drug use, and another group takes the opposite position on all three issues. In this case, only a single (**basic**) dimension is needed to explain attitudinal variation between the two groups. The basic dimensions are often referred to as **ideological** dimensions because they organize a diverse set of issue positions under an ideological rubric: "an internally consistent set of propositions that makes both proscriptive and prescriptive demands on human behavior" (Hinich & Munger, 1994, p. 11).

Technically stated, let n represent the number of individuals (voters or legislators), let m represent the number of issue dimensions, and s the number of basic or ideological dimensions. According to the Basic Space theory, the relationship between the action and basic spaces can be summarized with the simple algebraic expression:

$$X = YW \tag{28.1}$$

where X is the n by m matrix of individuals' positions on the issue dimensions, Y is the n by s matrix of individual positions in the basic space, and W is an s by m matrix of linear mappings. That is, W maps the basic or ideological space onto the action space.

The Basic Space theory posits that political competition takes place in the latent, low-dimensional ideological space because this is the space that structures individuals' choice and judgment behavior. The understanding that voters and legislators operate in ideological space is consistent with results from psychology on how individuals make similarities judgments. Specifically, the Shepard–Nosofsky–Ennis model of stimulus comparison states that individuals compare two stored **exemplars** (representative models) in abstract space and, when asked to rate the similarity of the two objects, report the distance between them (Ennis, 1988; Nosofsky, 1986, 1992; Shepard, 1986, 1987). Their findings persuasively demonstrate that simple geometric models structure individuals' similarities and preferential choice judgments. Gärdenfors (2000) has also presented a compelling case that spatial conceptualization is a natural way for humans to process and organize many different types of information. Why else would diagrams be so useful in such a variety of situations (Larkin & Simon, 1987), and, specifically to our point, spatial metaphors ("left," "right," and "center") be so prevalent in politics?

These findings are relevant to the spatial voting model because the notion of **preference** used in economics and political science can be reduced to psychologists' notion of **similarity**. For example, suppose a voter has an ideal standard (or ideal **point** in political science) labeled X. To decide between Candidate A and Candidate B, the voter compares the similarity between X and A to the similarity between X and B. The voter will prefer Candidate A if the similarity between X and A is greater than X and B, and Candidate B if the reverse is true. Hence, spatial voting can be thought of as a form of similarities judgment.

The use of simple geometric models to make similarities judgments also stems from limits on human cognitive processing and storage abilities (Miller, 1956; Simon, 1985). In political science, ideologies and ideological labels are understood in the Basic Space theory as economical devices that reduce the complexity of the political world so that parties and candidates can communicate their broad policy agendas to voters and voters can hold them accountable. The idea that ideology could serve as a means to reduce information costs was originally posed by Downs (1957) in his seminal work *An Economic Theory of Democracy*. This view has also been articulated by Conover and Feldman (1989) and Popkin (1994), who demonstrate that voters can overcome low information to infer candidates' policy positions by connecting bits of information – cues, signals, and symbols – to recognized patterns from past experiences. For instance, voters may use only a few known (likely salient) policy positions of the candidates to locate their position in ideological space (e.g., a voter who knows only that Senator Edward Kennedy favors a national health insurance plan can safely place him on the left end of the ideological spectrum) (Hinich & Pollard, 1981, p. 328).

These types of heuristics are not foolproof (Tversky & Kahneman, 1974), but they are generally considered to be effective ways for citizens to grapple with a complex political world (Lupia & McCubbins, 1998). In addition, this process is aided by a polarized political environment where the parties are tightly and visibly constrained to their respective policy agendas (Levendusky, 2010). Campaigns also seem to play an important role in influencing the mapping functions between the two spaces; that is, how voters infer specific policy stances from ideological labels (Enelow & Hinich, 1984) and which issues are salient (Vavreck, 2009). Finally, the use of ideological labels is no doubt aided by their durability, since party platforms and elected officials themselves occupy remarkably stable ideological positions over time (Gerring, 1998; Poole, 2007).

From a psychological perspective, then, the direct use of the complex action space – with a separate dimension for each issue – for political decision-making tasks seems quite implausible. A reduced political choice space consisting of a small number of ideological dimensions is at least desirable, if not necessary, given the nature of human cognition: its practical limits and its propensity for geometric organization and pattern recognition. This goes a long way in explaining the success of the spatial model of choice in its empirical applications and the consistent recovery of only a few latent ideological dimensions from political choice data.

However, what are the specific mechanisms of ideological constraint? That is, how do issues become bundled into ideological "packages"? As Jost, Federico, and Napier

(2009) discuss, political scientists and psychologists have tended to differ in their emphasis of top-down and bottom-up processes, respectively, in addressing this question. Political scientists have most frequently emphasized the role of political elites – parties, interest groups, and elected officials – in assembling ideological programs and providing competing "menus" of policy positions to the mass public (Converse, 1964; Sniderman & Bullock, 2004). In this view, citizens learn about the content of ideologies ("what goes with what," in Converse's words) based on elite behavior. According to Carmines and Stimson's (1989) influential theory of issue evolution, parties – especially losing or challenger parties – have powerful incentives to adopt and promote positions on new or latent issues in order to attract support (see also De Vries and Hobolt, 2012). Over time, it makes more and more sense that this issue position goes with other elements of a party's ideological platform. Indeed, the fact that the left or right position on a given issue can change (sometimes dramatically, as in the case of abortion in the 1970s (Stimson, 2004, pp. 58–60) illustrates the important role of elite political actors in the mapping process between the action and basic spaces.

Nonetheless, it seems unlikely that the regular folding of both economic and social/cultural issues into the left-right spectrum in a variety of political systems (Benoit & Laver, 2006; Poole & Rosenthal, 2007) could be entirely an artifact of elite manipulation. It is not immediately clear why support for traditional moral values and opposition to large social welfare programs should go together, but the fact that they so frequently do suggests there may be an underlying connection. Accordingly, psychologists (although also a growing number of political scientists) tend to view ideological constraint as stemming from manifold psychological sources: value orientations, personality traits, and motivational needs (Gerber et al., 2010; Goren, 2013; Jost et al., 2009). For example, it has been shown that openness to change promotes a left-wing political orientation, while heightened needs for order and certainty exert a rightward effect (Gerber et al., 2010; Jost, Glaser, Kruglanski, & Sulloway, 2003). The influence of some value orientations is mostly limited to attitudes in relevant policy contexts; for instance, religious orthodoxy has important effects on social/cultural issue attitudes but only weak effects for economic issues (Layman & Green, 2006). But theoretical (Sowell, 2007) and empirical (Barker & Tinnick, 2006; Hare, 2013) work has concluded that some values serve to promote consistent attitudes across the economic, social, and/or foreign policy domains.

The Basic Space theory and the phenomenon of ideological constraint provide important insight into the relevance of scaling results in political science. Namely, the data itself (for instance, a matrix of roll call votes in which legislators vote on multiple issues) can be understood as the complex action space. The recovered basic spaces are best understood as providing spatial maps of political competition: how individuals collectively perceive the choice space and make decisions between competing alternatives (which candidate to support, how to vote on a bill, etc.). It is important to emphasize that these spatial maps aren't just interesting or visually appealing, but are accurate representations of how legislators and voters think and make decisions. In other words, they are simplified models of the political process that nonetheless possess considerable explanatory power. Scaling or ideal point estimation procedures, then, are intimately connected to the field of psychometrics since both assume that latent dimensions of individual attributes (intelligence or ideology, for example) can be recovered through revealed measures of these attribute (test items or roll call votes).

Basic Space scaling

The Basic Space scaling procedure was developed by Poole (1998) and can be used to analyze both preferential and perceptual data organized as rectangular matrices. The model is built directly upon the Basic Space theory. Recall from Equation 28.1 that the Basic Space theory states that the observed n by m issue (action) space is a product of the n by s matrix of individual ideal points in the s-dimensional basic space and an s by m matrix of linear mappings. That is, if ideological constraint is present and individuals have structured belief systems (Converse, 1964), individual ideal points lie on a low-dimensional hyperplane through the complex action space. This low-dimensional hyperplane represents the ideological (basic) space that is recovered with the Basic Space procedure.

In the Basic Space scaling model, let x_{ij} be the ith individual's $(i = 1, ..., n)$ reported position on the jth issue $(j = 1, ..., m)$ and let X_0 be the n by m matrix of observed data where the 0 subscript indicates that elements are missing from the matrix — not all individuals report their positions on all issues. Let Ψ_{ik} be the ith individual's position on the kth $(k = 1, ..., s)$ basic dimension. The model estimated is:

$$X_0 = [\Psi W' + J_n c']_0 + E_0 \qquad (28.2)$$

where Ψ is the n by s matrix of coordinates of the individuals on the basic dimensions, W is an m by s matrix of weights, c is a vector of constants of length m, J_n is an n length vector of ones, and E_0 if a n by m matrix of error terms. W and c map the individuals from the basic space onto the issue dimensions.

Our primary quantities of interest from Basic Space scaling are Ψ and W. Ψ provides the estimated positions of the individuals in the recovered s-dimensional space. W is analogous to a set of factor loadings from factor analysis in that they both provide information about how strongly each of the m items is related to the s latent dimension(s). However, the Basic Space scaling method differs from factor analysis in that the rectangular matrix of observed data X_0 is analyzed directly, rather than through a transformed correlation or covariance matrix as is the case with factor analytic methods. This approach is more consistent with the spatial (geometric) model of choice, since individual preferences and perceptions across a range of alternatives are modelled directly. Some information in the choice data (specifically, the means and variances of the variables) is also lost when collapsed to a correlation matrix (Jackman, 2001, p. 230).

The Basic Space scaling procedure has been implemented in two functions — **blackbox()** and **blackbox_transpose()** — available in the **R** package **basicspace** (Poole et al., 2013). The **blackbox()** function is used to analyze rectangular matrices of preferential choice data (e.g., survey respondents' policy preferences) in which the individuals are on the rows and the issues are on the columns. The **blackbox_transpose()** function is used to transpose and analyze rectangular matrices of preferential or perceptual choice data (e.g., feeling thermometers or left-right placements of political parties) so that the stimuli are on the rows and the individuals are on the columns. In both cases, fit statistics (R^2) can be used to assess how well a latent basic dimension explains variation in attitudes toward a particular issue or stimulus. In addition, the W_k terms are analogous to factor loadings in factor analysis in that they indicate how strongly a particular issue loads onto the kth basic dimension.

Preferential Data

Procedures for the analysis of preferential choice data in political science are built on either Clyde Coombs' (1950, 1952, 1958, 1964) unfolding model or the cumulative scaling model. The unfolding model assumes the existence of two scales. The I scale represents an individual's preference ordering of alternatives and can be **unfolded** around the individual's ideal point to produce the J scale. The recovered J scale represents the locations of both the individuals and stimuli as points on a common evaluative dimension. For example, Figure 28.1 illustrates how the I scale for an individual with preference order ABC (that is, who prefers choice A to choice B, and choice B to choice C) is unfolded onto a common J scale. The intersection of the J and I scales marks this particular individual's ideal point, which is closest to choice A and furthest from choice C. As will be discussed, various criteria are used to unfold the I scales (the individual preference orderings) to recover the latent J scales; for instance, to maximize the likelihood of the observed choices (NOMINATE) or minimize the number of classification errors (Optimal Classification).

The unfolding model is easiest to conceptualize in unidimensional terms, but can easily be extended to cases in which multiple dimensions or J scales are needed to represent the preference orderings. Unfolding in s dimensions is accomplished by constructing a series of $s-1$ dimensional hyperplanes dividing each pair of stimuli alternatives (Coombs, 1964, Ch. 7). For example, unfolding three stimuli (A, B, and C) in two dimensions requires three hyperplanes (lines) in the latent space that divide A and B, A and C, and B and C. This produces a "Coombs mesh" with 3! (6) regions for each of the possible preference orderings (ABC, ACB, BAC, etc.). Finally, the unfolding model is consistent with the assumption of the standard spatial voting model that individuals possess single-peaked and symmetric utility functions over common latent dimensions (Coombs, 1964, pp. 193–195). Whether or not a specific functional form is specified for the utility function and the error term depends on whether the unfolding procedure is parametric or nonparametric.

Methods of cumulative scaling model the probability of a given response (e.g., the correct answer on a test item or a Yea vote on a bill) as a monotonically increasing or decreasing function over values of the latent attribute. Above some threshold individuals are predicted to answer correctly/vote Yea and below some threshold they are

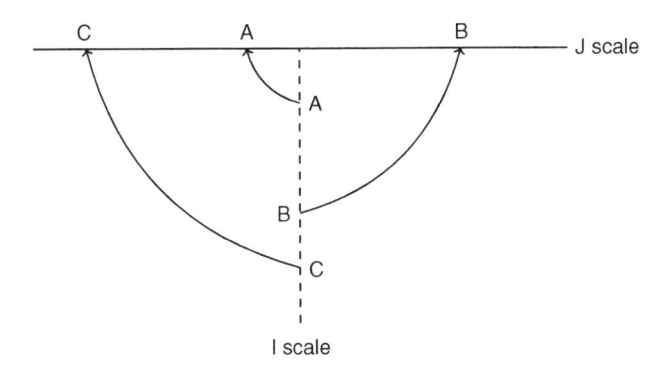

Figure 28.1 Unfolding in a single dimension.

predicted to answer incorrectly/vote Nay. Cumulative scaling methods, particularly Item Response Theory (IRT) models, have been especially prominent in social sciences in general and psychometrics in particular. Scalogram analysis or Guttman scaling (Guttman 1944, 1950) is simply a nonparametric form of the IRT model.

Interestingly, these two very different models are observationally equivalent in the context of political choice data (Poole, 2005; Weisberg, 1968). In the unfolding model, there are multiple outcomes for each policy alternative, and individuals choose the option closest to their ideal point. In one dimension, this forms a perfect scalogram (Weisberg, 1968). Hence, Guttman scaling methods and their IRT descendants can be and have been (e.g., Clinton, Jackman, & Rivers, 2004; Treier & Hillygus, 2009) used to analyze choice data (e.g., legislative roll call voting or public opinion survey responses) in political science.

The fields of political science and psychometrics have been the most intertwined in the development of scaling methods designed for the analysis of binary choice data (in which individuals vote Yea or Nay) like the kind routinely encountered in legislative and judicial settings. These types of procedures measure latent quantities (i.e., the position of legislators and policy alternatives in latent ideological space) based on the assumption that roll call votes are the product of the distance between legislators' ideal points and competing policy proposals. We next cover three of the most influential ideal point estimation methods in political science: Poole and Rosenthal's (1997) NOMINATE procedure, methods based on the IRT model (Clinton et al., 2004), and Poole's (2000) Optimal Classification algorithm.

Poole and Rosenthal's NOMINATE method

NOMINATE (an acronym for **Nomin**al **T**hree-Step **E**stimation) is a parametric unfolding method that is the product of a decades-long collaboration between political scientists Keith T. Poole and Howard Rosenthal (Poole & Rosenthal, 1985, 1991, 1997, 2007). NOMINATE recovers the locations of legislator ideal points and policy alternatives in latent ideological space from binary roll call data using alternating estimation methods developed in psychometrics (Chang & Carroll, 1969; Carroll & Chang, 1970; Takane, Young, & de Leeuw, 1977; Young, de Leeuw, & Takane, 1976). The application of the NOMINATE method to substantive questions has revealed numerous insights about American politics; for instance, that congressional roll call voting has been highly structured by no more than two underlying dimensions (one representing left-right conflict and the other representing regional or cross-cutting cleavages such as civil rights) and that the parties in Congress have moved apart from one another over recent decades. NOMINATE has also been used outside of the U.S. to study voting in the European Parliament (Hix, Noury, & Roland, 2006) and the United Nations (Voeten, 2000).

In the NOMINATE model, each legislator's utility function over the policy alternatives is treated as having a **deterministic** and a **stochastic** component. The deterministic component is based directly upon the spatial theory of choice: legislators and the roll call alternatives are treated as occupying positions in a common latent space and a legislator's roll call vote is a function of the relative distance between her ideal point and the two outcomes. An illustration of deterministic utility in a single dimension is provided in Figure 28.2. In this example, a legislator with an ideal point at 0 on an abstract policy

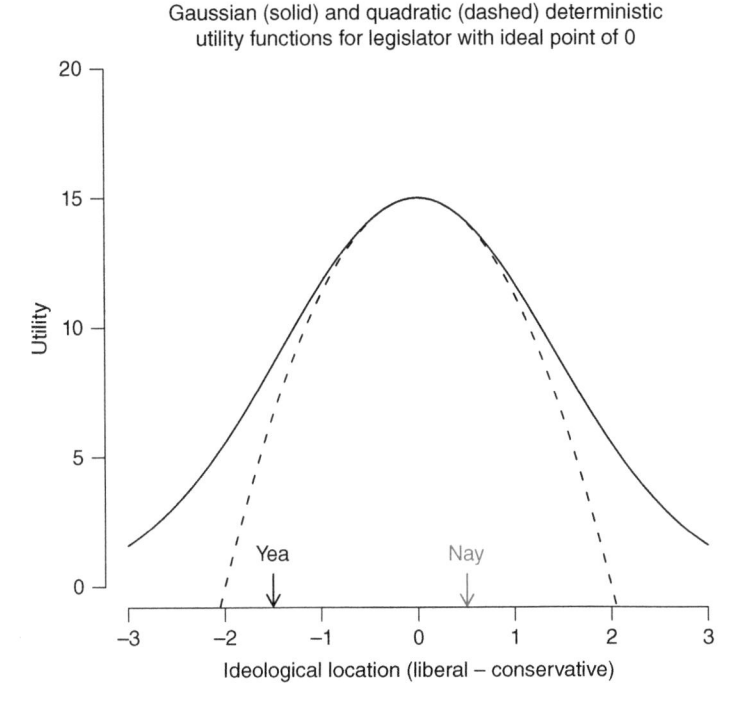

Figure 28.2 Deterministic utility over a single policy dimension.

dimension is faced with two alternatives on a roll call vote: Yea (with a corresponding location of −1.5) and Nay (located at 0.5).

The functional form of the deterministic utility functions specifies how utility decreases as the policy moves away from the legislator's ideal point. Two standard utility functions are shown in Figure 28.2: The normal (Gaussian) function (the solid line) and the quadratic function (the dashed line). The major difference between the two preference functions lies in how they treat policy alternatives that are distant from a legislator's ideal point. The normal function posits that a legislator will become increasingly indifferent between two alternatives as they move away from her ideal point, while the quadratic function indicates just the reverse: that the drop-off in utility accelerates as the alternatives become more distant.[3] In the NOMINATE model, the deterministic utility function is normal, while the IRT model uses the quadratic function to model the deterministic component of legislators' utility. In both cases, a legislator with an ideal point of 0 in Figure 28.2 would most prefer a policy at her ideal point, but will accrue more utility by voting Nay than Yea.

---

[3] Use of the normal (Gaussian) distribution is consistent with findings from psychology that individuals use an exponential response function when judging the level of similarity between stimuli (Shepard, 1987). According to these results, perceived similarities are an exponential function of the actual similarity between two objects. That is, as two stimuli become more (objectively) dissimilar, the perceived dissimilarity between the two objects increases exponentially. When perceptual error is added, the expected value of the response function approximates the Gaussian form (Ennis, 1988; Nosofsky, 1986).

Accordingly, the deterministic component would predict a Nay vote in this case. However, the second component of utility – the stochastic component – is based on the random utility model developed in economics (McFadden, 1976) and introduces random shocks to the utility function. NOMINATE (specifically, the DW-NOMINATE procedure) uses the normal distribution to model the stochastic component or error term (ε_{ij}). The normal distribution is preferable because it guarantees that the ε_{ij} are a random sample from a known distribution (i.e., they are independent and identically distributed (iid) errors) and that their distributions are symmetric and unimodal (Poole, 2005, p. 98). Spatial voting errors (i.e., casting a vote inconsistent with the deterministic utility component) become less likely as the relative distances between a legislator's ideal point and the Yea and Nay alternatives increase. For example, in Figure 28.2, an error is more likely if the Yea and Nay alternatives are at –1.5 and 0.5, respectively, than at –3 and 0.5.

In the NOMINATE model, let U_{ijy} be the utility accrued from a Yea vote by the ith legislator ($i = 1, ..., n$) on the jth roll call vote ($j = 1, ..., q$). U_{ijy} is the sum of a deterministic and stochastic component, that is:

$$U_{ijy} = u_{ijy} + \varepsilon_{ijy} \qquad (28.3)$$

where u_{ijy} is the deterministic component and ε_{ijy} is the stochastic (random) component or error term. To allow for the estimation of multiple dimensions, let k represent the number of dimensions ($k = 1, ..., s$). The squared distance of the ith legislator (X_{ik}) to the Yea outcome for roll call j on the kth dimension (O_{jky}) is:

$$d_{ijky}^2 = (X_{ik} - O_{jky})^2 \qquad (28.4)$$

When using the normal (Gaussian) function to model the deterministic component of utility, legislator i's utility from Equation 28.4 is:

$$U_{ijy} = u_{ijy} + \varepsilon_{ijy} = \beta e^{\left(-\frac{1}{2}\sum_{k=1}^{s} w_k d_{ijky}^2\right)} + \varepsilon_{ijy} \qquad (28.5)$$

The deterministic component of Equation 28.5 (d_{ijky}^2, which is equal to $(X_{ik} - O_{jky})^2$) means that legislator utility declines as the distance between the legislator's ideal point and the policy alternative increases. But, when multiple dimensions are estimated, it may not be realistic to assume that legislators are equally sensitive to deviations from their ideal points across different dimensions. The w_k term in Equation 28.5 represents salience weights ($w_k > 0$) that allow dimensions to vary in importance and the indifference curves of the utility function to be ellipses rather than circles.

In Equation 28.5, β is a constant term of little substantive interest. Because there is no natural metric, β adjusts for the overall noise level and is proportional to the variance of the error distribution. If the stochastic portion of the utility function is normally distributed with common variance, β is proportional to $\frac{1}{\sigma^2}$, where

$$\varepsilon \sim N(0, \sigma^2) \qquad (28.6)$$

Hence the probability that legislator i votes Yea on the jth roll call is:

$$P_{ijy} = P(U_{ijy} > U_{ijn})$$
$$= P(\varepsilon_{ijn} - \varepsilon_{ijy} < u_{ijy} - u_{ijn})$$
$$= \Phi(u_{ijy} - u_{ijn}) \qquad (28.7)$$
$$= \Phi\left[\beta\left(e^{\left(-\frac{1}{2}\sum_{k=1}^{s} w_k d_{ijky}^2\right)} - e^{\left(-\frac{1}{2}\sum_{k=1}^{s} w_k d_{ijkn}^2\right)}\right)\right]$$

where Φ is the standard normal cumulative density function, restricting probabilities to be between 0 and 1. The greater the difference in utility between the roll call outcomes, the higher the probability of choosing the closer policy alternative.

Let Y be the $p \times q$ matrix of observed roll call choices (y_{ij}). Given Y, NOMINATE estimates the combination of parameters for legislator ideal points and roll call outcomes that maximizes the joint probability of the observed data (choices). The likelihood function is computed over the legislators and roll calls:

$$L(u_{ijy} - u_{ijn}|Y) = \prod_{i=1}^{n}\prod_{j=1}^{q}\prod_{\tau=1}^{2} P_{ij\tau}^{C_{ij\tau}} \qquad (28.8)$$

which is the product of individual vote probabilities over the n legislators, q roll call votes, and 2 (Yea and Nay) choices. where τ is the index for Yea and Nay, $P_{ij\tau}$ is the probability of voting for choice τ as given by Equation 28.7, and $C_{ij\tau} = 1$ if the legislator's actual choice is τ, and 0 otherwise.

The likelihood function to be optimized is a continuous distribution over the $ps + 2qs + s$ hyperplane, where s is the number of estimated dimensions. ps is the number of legislator ideal points (X_{ik}), $2qs$ is the number of roll call parameters (the locations of the Yea and Nay alternatives O_{jky} and O_{jkn}), and s is the number of the β and $w_2, ..., w_s$ terms. For a hypothetical legislative session with 100 legislators and 500 roll calls estimated in two dimensions, this amounts to finding the maximum of a 2,202-dimensional hyperplane. This is a nontrivial optimization problem that NOMINATE solves using high-quality starting values for the legislator parameters and an alternating maximum likelihood procedure. Starting values for the legislator ideal points are calculated from the agreement score matrix (which is like a correlation matrix but shows the proportion of roll call votes that legislators vote in agreement with each other) and provisional values for the scaling constants β and w are assigned.

With these starting values, the three-step iterative estimation algorithm begins. First, holding the legislator ideal points and the β and w terms fixed, NOMINATE finds the values for the roll call parameters that maximize the likelihood function (the BHHH hill-climbing procedure (Berndt, Hall, Hall, & Hausman, 1974) is used in all three steps to optimize the objective function). Then, the likelihood function is maximized over the β and w terms while holding fixed the legislator ideal points and roll call parameters. Finally, the roll call parameters and the β and w terms are held fixed while searching for the values of the legislator ideal points that maximize the likelihood function. The process is repeated until convergence.

To illustrate the DW-NOMINATE procedure, we plot the 98th (1983–1985) U.S. Senate's vote to table a U.S.-Soviet nuclear freeze amendment from Senator Ted Kennedy (D-MA) in Figure 28.3. The first (x-axis) latent dimension represents liberal-conservative ideology, and the second (y-axis) dimension taps into regional differences within the parties (particularly between the Southern and Northern wings of the Democratic Party). The solid line running through the middle of the space is the cutting line. The cutting line (or plane in more than two dimensions) is equidistant from the Yea and Nay alternatives, and hence it divides the predicted Yea votes from the predicted Nay votes. Voting errors that are close to the cutting line are considered less serious since a legislator whose ideal point is directly on the cutting line will accrue the same deterministic utility from the Yea and Nay alternatives and will be indifferent between the two choices.

The cutting line in Figure 28.3 is nearly vertical, meaning that this vote primarily divides Senators along the liberal-conservative dimension. Most Republican Senators vote Yea and most Democratic Senators vote Nay, but the spatial (geometric) model of choice offers an improvement on simple party-line model by capturing ideological differences within the parties: classifying liberal Republicans as Nay votes and conservative Democrats as Yea votes. Accordingly, DW-NOMINATE produces only three classification errors (isolated in the right panel of Figure 28.3), all of which are very close to the cutting line. Indeed, the PRE (proportional reduction in error) statistic – which measures the improvement in classification beyond the baseline of predicting that all cases are in the modal category – is a very high 0.92. Figure 28.3 illustrates why spatial "maps" are so useful in understanding and conveying the latent structure underlying political competition.

One of the species of NOMINATE procedures – W-NOMINATE – has been implemented in the **wnominate** package in **R** (Poole, Lewis, Lo, & Carroll, 2011). W-NOMINATE uses the deterministic utility function provided in Equation 28.5 that allows different salience weights on the estimated dimensions. The errors in the W-NOMINATE are assumed to follow a logit distribution. Finally, W-NOMINATE constrains the legislators and roll call midpoints to lie within an s-dimensional hypersphere of radius one (in other words, between −1 and 1 in the one-dimensional model and within the unit circle in the two-dimensional model). W-NOMINATE is a static procedure that is meant to be applied to one or possibly a few legislative sessions, but it is very computationally efficient and its results are highly correlated with those from other NOMINATE procedures.

Item Response Theory (IRT) models

Scholars in the field of psychometrics are no doubt already familiar with the IRT model and the subject has been covered extensively throughout this volume. In this section, we focus on the extension of the two-parameter Bayesian IRT model to the analysis of binary and ordinal choice data in political science. This effort has been spearheaded in a series of works by Simon Jackman (Clinton et al., 2004; Jackman 2000, 2001; Treier & Jackman, 2008) and Andrew Martin and Kevin Quinn (Martin & Quinn, 2002; Quinn 2004) and use of the Bayesian IRT model in political science has been facilitated by the development of the **R** packages **pscl** (Jackman, 2011) and **MCMCpack** (Martin, Quinn, & Park, 2011).

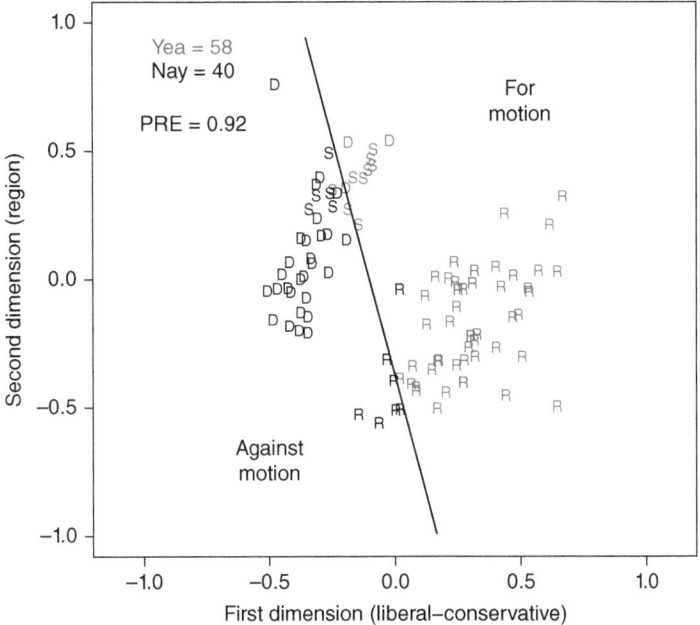

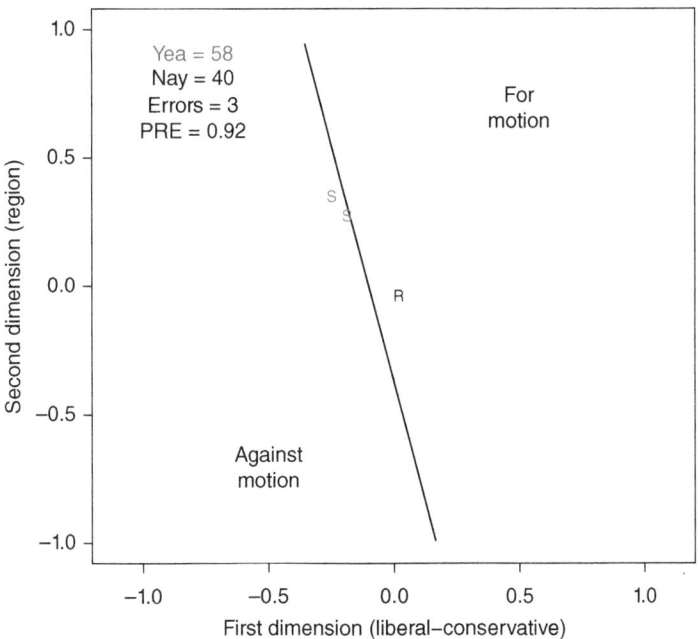

Figure 28.3 DW-NOMINATE scaling of U.S. Senate roll call vote.

The IRT model was developed to measure a latent individual attribute such as mental ability from observed indicators such as test items. This model has been extended to political science by substituting latent ability with political ideology, test subjects with legislators, and test items with roll call votes. The discrimination parameter indicates how well a roll call vote classifies individuals based on ideology, and can thus be interpreted in the same manner as the factor loading of an item in factor analysis. In political science, the quantity of interest is usually the individual parameters (the legislator ideal points) rather than the item parameters as in psychometric testing (Clinton et al., 2004, p. 356).

Since IRT models involve the estimation of the ability, difficulty, and (in the two-parameter model) discrimination parameters, Bayesian methods are attractive because they allow for the simultaneous estimation of the parameters. More specifically, the Gibbs sampler offers an efficient means of analyzing high-dimensional posterior densities, like those regularly produced from legislative roll call data. The Gibbs sampler breaks down the high-dimensional posterior density into a series of more tractable components and samples from the conditional densities for each component, improving the approximation to the posterior density at each iteration (Jackman, 2009, pp. 214–221).

In the Clinton–Jackman–Rivers (CJR) model, x_i is the legislator ideology score (ideal point), α_j is the roll call difficulty parameter and β_j is the roll call discrimination parameter. As before, let i index legislators, ($i = 1, \ldots, n$) and j index roll calls ($j = 1, \ldots, q$). The CJR model uses the quadratic function to model legislators' utility function. Hence, in a single dimension, legislator i's utility for the Yea outcome on the jth roll call is:

$$U_{ijy} = u_{ijy} + \varepsilon_{ijy} = -(x_i - O_{jy})^2 + \varepsilon_{ijy} \tag{28.9}$$

As with NOMINATE, the CJR model assumes that errors are normally distributed. Assuming quadratic utility and normally distributed errors, the probability that legislator i votes Yea on the jth roll call is:

$$\begin{aligned} P_{ijy} &= P(U_{ijy} > U_{ijn}) \\ &= P(\varepsilon_{ijn} - \varepsilon_{ijy} < u_{ijy} - u_{ijn}) \\ &= P(\varepsilon_{ijn} - \varepsilon_{ijy} < \|x_i - O_{jn}\|^2 - \|x_i - O_j\|^2 \\ &= P(\varepsilon_{ijn} - \varepsilon_{ijy} < 2(O_{jy} - O_{jn})'x_i + O'_{jn}O_{jn} - O'_{jy}O_{jy} \\ &= \Phi(\beta'_j x_i - \alpha_j) \end{aligned} \tag{28.10}$$

The midpoint on the jth roll call is equal to $\frac{\alpha_j}{\beta_j}$, which represents the point at which legislators are equally distant from and hence indifferent between the two outcomes. Equation 28.10 yields the likelihood function:

$$L(B, \alpha, X | Y) = \prod_{i=1}^{n} \prod_{j=1}^{q} (P_{ijy})^{y_{ij}} (1 - P_{ijy})^{1 - y_{ij}} \tag{28.11}$$

which, as in Equation 28.8, is the product of individual vote probabilities over the n legislators and q roll call votes. In Equation 28.12, B is a $q \times s$ matrix of β_j values, α

is a q length vector of α_j values, and X is a $n \times s$ (Clinton et al., 2004; Jackman, 2001). Priors (usually vague normal) are assigned for the unknown parameters B, α, and X. This yields the posterior distribution:

$$\pi(B,\alpha,X|\Upsilon) \propto p(B,\alpha,X) \times L(B,\alpha,X|\Upsilon) \qquad (28.12)$$

which is then analyzed with MCMC simulation methods to produce estimates of the quantities of interest. One advantage of the Bayesian approach is that uncertainty estimates can be easily obtained by summarizing the posterior distributions of the parameters (although the parametric bootstrap can be used to estimate standard errors for estimates from "frequentist" methods like NOMINATE: Lewis & Poole, 2004).

Despite its relatively recent introduction to political science, the Bayesian IRT model has produced a surge of interest in the field. The method has been used to study legislative voting (Clinton & Meirowitz, 2001, 2003), judicial behavior (Martin & Quinn, 2002), the measurement of democracy across nations (Treier & Jackman, 2008), ideology in the mass public (Treier & Hillygus, 2009), spatial voting in the American electorate (Jessee, 2009), and legislative representation of constituent preferences (Bafumi & Herron, 2010).

As the IRT model continues to expand in political science, two issues concerning its application in multidimensional cases will need to be addressed. First, when a single item difficulty parameter (α_j) is estimated for each roll call in a multidimensional IRT model, then this is implicitly a **compensatory** (as opposed to a **noncompensatory**) model (Bolt & Lall, 2003). That is, scores on each of the dimensions are interchangeable in influencing the probability of observing a given response (e.g., a Yea vote) rather than independent as in the noncompensatory model (Reckase, 1985, 2010). For example, if separate dimensions are estimated for economic and social policy preferences, a high (conservative) score on the economic dimension can offset or compensate a low (liberal) score on the social dimension. This may or may not be the appropriate model given the nature of the application, and more attention to the distinction between compensatory and noncompensatory models is needed in political science.

The second challenge concerns identification in the general multidimensional IRT model, and in this case, it may be political scientists (see Bakker and Poole, 2013; Rivers, 2003) who are able to contribute to psychometrics. A solution remains unidentified so long as multiple configurations of the parameters are equally valid. In a single dimension, identification can be easily achieved with a normalization constraint: requiring that the estimated ideal points have mean 0 and variance 1 (Clinton et al., 2004). In multiple dimensions, identification requires constraints on some of the subject and/or item parameters; for example, setting some legislator ideal points to fixed locations or restricting some roll calls to discriminate only on a single dimension. However, **over**-identification arises when two or more points are fixed and the distances between them are no longer elastic (that is, the distances are constrained to equal some fixed amount) (Bakker & Poole, 2013). Hence, the uncertainty about the true distances between the fixed points propagates to other inter-point distances in the solution.

The Bakker–Poole (2013) solution to identification (in the context of Bayesian metric MDS) is to "freeze" the posterior distributions of the legislators in certain quadrants. In two dimensions, this is achieved by setting one point at the origin and the first or second dimension coordinate of another point at 0. At the end of each iteration of the MCMC procedure (in this case, slice sampling), the sign of the draws from the

Optimal Classification

Optimal Classification (OC) is a nonparametric unfolding method developed by Poole (2000) and available in the **R** package **oc** (Poole, Lewis, Lo, & Carroll, 2012). OC is nonparametric in that it does not make parametric assumptions about the functional form of the error process or legislators' utility functions other than that they are single-peaked and symmetric. As an unfolding procedure, OC uses binary choice data to recover the locations of both legislators and policy alternatives in latent space. The algorithm has been applied in psychometric contexts outside of political science; for instance, linguistic studies (Croft & Poole, 2008).

Unlike the parametric methods discussed previously, OC is not designed to estimate the parameters that maximize the joint likelihood of the observed legislative choice data. The goal of OC is to estimate the configuration of legislator ideal points and roll call cutting planes (which divide predicted Yea votes from predicted Nay votes) that maximizes the correct classification of the choices themselves. Equivalently stated, OC seeks to **minimize** the number of classification errors, meaning that no error is treated as more or less severe than others.

The OC procedure is executed in three steps. First, a starting configuration of the legislator coordinates is generated through an eigenvalue/eigenvector decomposition of the double-centered agreement score matrix.[4] Second, from this configuration, the cutting plane procedure uses an iterative process to position cutting planes on each roll call vote in such a manner that the number of classification errors is minimized. The configuration of all cutting planes is also known as a **Coombs mesh** (Coombs, 1964). An example of a Coombs mesh is shown in Figure 28.4, which was generated by plotting the cutting lines from 100 random roll call votes from the 98th U.S. Senate.

As can be seen in Figure 28.4, the cutting lines intersect to form a large number of **polytopes**: bounded regions in the latent space that correspond to patterns of Yea/Nay choices. For example, a triangular polytope formed by the intersection of three cutting planes may be on the Yea side of the first roll call vote and the Nay side of the second and third votes. A legislator who voted *YNN* could be placed in this polytope with no classification errors. Indeed, in the final step of the OC routine, the legislator procedure then locates the polytope for each legislator which maximizes correct classification. For example, the *R* token near the middle of Figure 28.4 denotes the polytope in which OC places Senator Alfonse D'Amato (R-NY). This polytope minimizes Senator D'Amato's total number of voting errors.

The difference between parametric (NOMINATE and IRT) and nonparametric (OC) methods for the analysis of preferential choice data can be understood as a trade-off between making strong parametric assumptions about the data and precise estimation of the parameters. In a single dimension, the OC result is identified only up to a rank order and in two dimensions legislators are identified only to a polytope, although this is sufficient for the recovery of metric-level information (Peress, 2012).

---

[4] A matrix is double-centered by subtracting the row and column means from, adding the grand mean to, and multiplying by −0.5 each entry of the matrix.

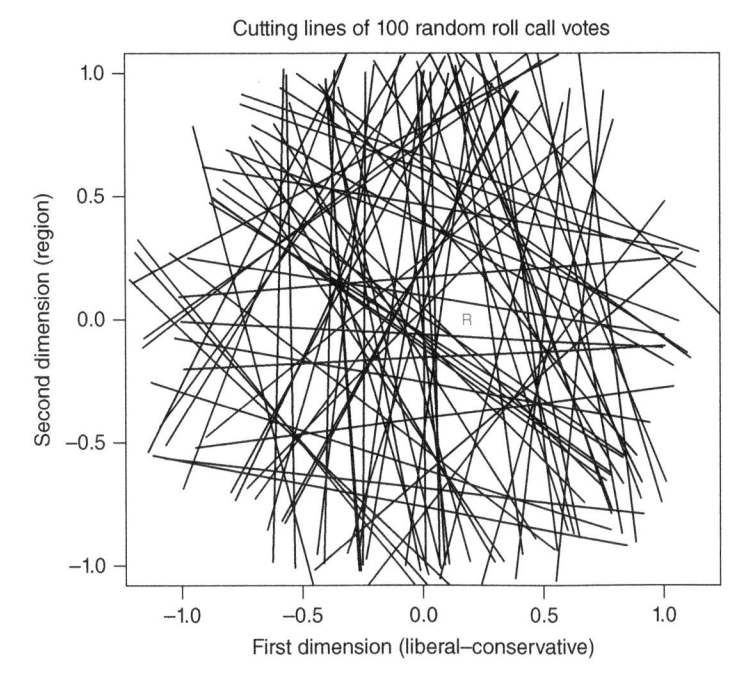

Figure 28.4 Coombs mesh from optimal classification scaling of the 98th U.S. Senate.

This means that in Figure 28.4, Senator D'Amato could be anywhere inside the specified polytope, but by default OC places him in the center. However, parametric assumptions (e.g., the assumption that errors are iid) can be quite costly, and in these cases OC provides a more accurate picture of preferential choice behavior (Rosenthal and Voeten, 2004). However, in many cases the results from parametric and nonparametric methods are virtually identical (Poole & Rosenthal, 2001).

Perceptual Data

Perceptual data is collected by asking individuals (usually public opinion survey respondents or experts) to evaluate the positions of stimuli on abstract policy dimensions. For example, the Chapel Hill Expert Survey (CHES) asks political experts to place European national parties on an eleven-point left-right ideological scale (Bakker et al., 2012). This type of data is of great interest to political scientists because they allow us to test the basic tenets of spatial voting theory and to assess democratic accountability. For instance, do citizens accurately perceive the policy positions of their elected representatives, and if so, do they hold them accountable for drifting from their own preferences?

However, the greatest challenge in interpreting perceptual data is that of interpersonal incomparability or differential item functioning (DIF). In political science, DIF and DIF-correction mechanisms have been detailed by Henry Brady (Brady, 1985, 1990) and more recently by Gary King and colleagues (King, Murray, Salomon, & Tandon, 2004). DIF arises when individuals interpret the meaning of the response categories on a scale differently. Personal biases are a frequent source of DIF. For instance, a radical leftist may place a left-of-center party near the middle of an ideological scale, while a very right-wing respondent may place the same party on the extreme leftward end of the scale.

Various procedures have been developed to correct for DIF and recover the true locations of individuals and stimuli from perceptual data. In this section, we focus our attention on the Aldrich–McKelvey scaling method (Aldrich & McKelvey, 1977), which has been the workhorse DIF-correction procedure in political science since its development in the late 1970s.[5] The fundamental insight of Aldrich and McKelvey (1977) is that respondents distort their reported placements in estimable ways based on differences in their ratings of common stimuli. Suppose that the true positions of Party A and Party B are 2 and 5, respectively, on a seven-point scale. If Respondent 1 places Party A at 1 and Party B at 4, then it is clear that we should shift all of Respondent 1's placements (including her own self-placement) to the right one unit. The stimuli are often real parties or candidates, but may be fictional vignettes (especially if there is are no stimuli that are familiar to all of the respondents) (Bakker, Jolly, Polk, & Poole, 2014).

We next provide an exposition of the original Aldrich–McKelvey scaling model and a Bayesian means of estimating the model developed by Armstrong et al. (2014).

Aldrich–McKelvey scaling

The Aldrich–McKelvey (A-M) scaling model proceeds as follows. Let z_{ij} be the perceived location of stimulus j ($j = 1, ..., q$) by individual i ($i = 1, ..., n$). The A–M model assumes that the individual reports a noisy linear transformation of the true location of stimulus $j(z_j)$; that is

$$\alpha_i + \beta_i z_j = z_{ij} + u_j \qquad (28.13)$$

where u_{ij} satisfies the usual Gauss–Markov assumptions of zero mean, homoscedasticity, and independence (Aldrich & McKelvey, 1977, p. 113). To illustrate the intuition behind Equation 28.13, assume that the true position of Party L on a ten-point, left-right or liberal-conservative is 3 (making it a left-wing party). Let Party R, a right-wing party, occupy the position of 7 on the scale. According to Equation 28.13, individuals' placements of these parties can be distorted in one (or both) of two ways: they can shift the placements too far to the left or right (for example, a very left-wing individual may view party L as insufficiently left-wing and party R as extremely right-wing, and her placements of the two parties might be 5 and 9, respectively) or they can stretch or flip the true positions of the stimuli. The first type of distortion is captured by the α_i term and the second type is captured by the b_i term. When individuals flip the space (for example, placing party L to the right of party R), b_i will be negative. Hence, the sign on the b_i values is a useful way to screen respondents by level of political information (i.e., whether they correctly perceive the ordering of stimuli along an issue scale) (Palfrey & Poole, 1987).

---

[5] Alternative methods to diagnose and treat DIF using "anchoring vignettes" have been developed by King et al. (2004) and Wand (2013) and are available in the **R** package **anchors** (Wand et al., 2011). Note that the B-scale detailed in Wand (2013) is equivalent to a nonparametric form of Aldrich–McKelvey scaling.

Let $\hat{z}_j$ be the estimated location of stimulus j and let $\hat{\alpha}_i$ and $\hat{\beta}_i$ be the estimates of α_i and β_i; define

$$\hat{\alpha}_i + \hat{\beta}_i \hat{z}_j - z_{ij} = e_{ij} \tag{28.14}$$

Hence, by estimating the perceptual distortion parameters α_i (the intercept or shift term) and β_i (the weight or stretch term) for each individual, we can recover the z_j: the "true" (DIF-corrected) locations of the stimuli and individuals. Of course, there remains the practical issue of how the perceptual distortion parameters are to be estimated. The original A-M scaling procedure solved the problem with an elegant approach that worked around computing limitations in the 1970s by using Lagrangian multipliers to minimize the loss function (Aldrich & McKelvey, 1977, pp. 111–113). Hence, the original A–M procedure is a maximum likelihood estimation (MLE) method.

Advances in computing power have made Bayesian (Markov chain Monte Carlo (MCMC)-based) estimation of the A-M model tractable, and the Bayesian approach (BAM, for Bayesian Aldrich–McKelvey scaling) offers two major advantages (see Armstrong et al., 2014). First, it is straightforward to directly assess uncertainty in the BAM estimates because inferences are made directly from the marginal posterior densities of the parameters. Second, BAM allows for the inclusion of individuals with missing responses. The degree of "missingnesss" is simply transmitted as greater uncertainty for the individual distortion parameters.

The BAM scaling procedure is a variation of the Bayesian factor model (Jackman, 2009, pp. 438–444). In the standard factor model, the latent variable or factor is indexed by individual and the factor loadings are held constant across all observations. The BAM scaling model, however, reverses this indexing. That is, the factor loadings (α_i and b_i) are allowed to vary across individuals while the latent variable ($\hat{z}_j$) is held constant:

$$z_{ij} \sim N\left(\mu_{ij}, \tau_{ij}\right) \tag{28.15}$$

$$\mu_{ij} = \alpha_i + \beta_i z_j \tag{28.16}$$

$$\tau_{ij} = \tau_i \tau_j \tag{28.17}$$

BAM scaling can be executed with MCMC simulation programs such as WinBUGS (Lunn et al., 2000) or JAGS (Plummer, 2003).[6] Next, we use BAM scaling to analyze perceptual data from the 2010 Cooperative Congressional Election Study (CCES) (Ansolabehere, 2012), which surveyed 55,400 respondents. In one series of questions, respondents were asked to rate the ideological positions of their states' U.S. Senators and major party Senatorial candidates on a seven-point liberal-conservative scale. We combine these data with respondents' placements of themselves and four national (and hence, common) stimuli – President Barack Obama, the Democratic and Republican parties, and the Tea Party movement—on the same ideological scale. We run the

---

[6] Code available at: http://voteview.com/BAM.asp. The maximum likelihood Aldrich–McKelvey scaling method is available in the **aldmck()** function in the **basicspace** package in **R** (Poole et al., 2013).

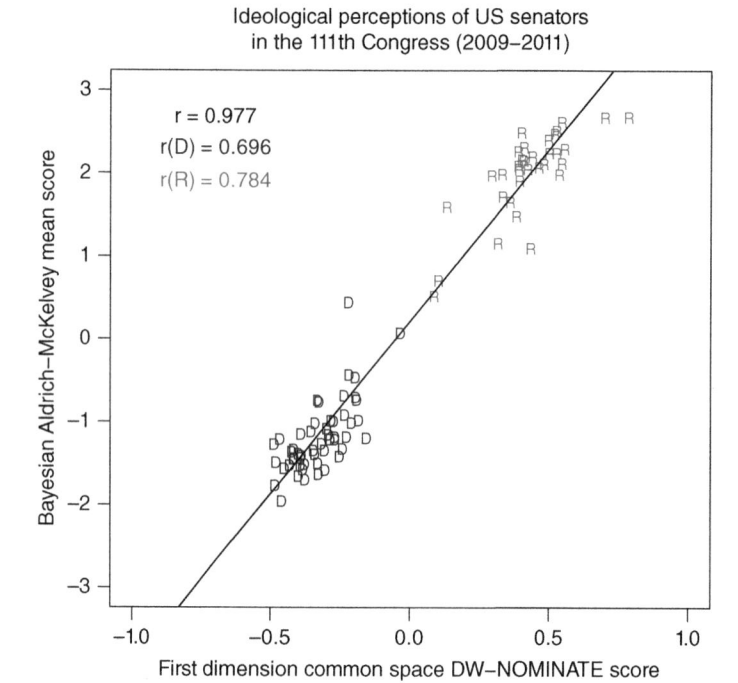

Figure 28.5 Citizens' perceptions of the ideological positions of U.S. Senators.

BAM scaling procedure using a burn-in period of 10,000 iterations and two chains of 2,500 iterations thinned by 5.

The means of the samples are used as the point estimates of z_j: the DIF-corrected estimate of citizens' ideological perceptions of the political stimuli. In Figure 28.5, we plot incumbent Senators' first (liberal-conservative) dimension Common Space DW-NOMINATE score with the BAM estimates. It is immediately clear that popular perceptions of Senators' locations on the liberal-conservative spectrum are strongly correlated with their ideological positions as measured by their roll call voting record (see also Jacobsmeier, 2013). The Pearson correlation between the two for Senators in the 111th Congress is 0.977, although this figure is biased upwards given the distinction between the two parties. A more demanding test involves whether citizens are able to ideologically differentiate between Senators of the same party. The intra-party correlations between the DW-NOMINATE and BAM scores suggest that they are, with Democrats correlated at 0.696 (Kendall's $\tau = 0.494$) and Republicans are correlated at 0.784 ($\tau = 0.582$). Indeed, in 21 of 26 states in which both Senators were of the same party and included in the CCES's ideological placement section, the BAM and DW-NOMINATE scores have the same ideological ordering.

Consistent with the Basic Space theory, these results suggest that citizens are capable of piecing together limited amounts of political information to develop accurate, spatially organized ideological profiles of elected officials (see also Jacoby & Armstrong, 2014). These bits of information used to infer ideological locations may include legislators' roll call votes or positions on salient issues (Ansolabehere & Jones, 2010; Nyhan et al., 2012), campaign rhetoric (Franklin, 1991), or other heuristic devices such as personal affect (Brady & Sniderman, 1985). Nyhan et al.'s (2012) results are especially important on this point: they find that voters' ideological perceptions of incumbent members of Congress mediate the effect of visible congressional roll call votes on incumbent vote shares. These finding mesh with the Basic Space theory's prediction that competition will occur in the basic (ideological) space. Indeed, the basic space (the liberal-conservative dimension) appears to structure the behavior of both elected officials in Congress and evaluations of them by their constituents.

Concluding Thoughts

We conclude by discussing some promising future directions for research at the intersection of psychometrics and political science. The first involves the accurate representation of political actors' preferences over the abstract policy space. Utility functions – quadratic or normal (Gaussian) – are usually simply assumed, with occasional theoretical debate about which functional form best approximates individual preferences across policy alternatives. Carroll et al. (2013), however, develop a method (α-NOMINATE) that addresses this question by estimating a parameter (α) that shapes the utility function to fit the observed choice data (see also Carroll et al. (2014) for the **anominate** package in **R**). They find that in a diverse set of legislative and judicial contexts, the value of the α parameter strongly points toward the Gaussian function. This result fits well with psychological findings concerning the exponential response function discussed earlier. We think this is a good illustration of just how rich political choice data can be. Consequently, these types of models need not be limited to producing ideal point estimates, but can also uncover ever-deeper insights into the nature of political actors' decision-making processes.

The second area in which further work is needed involves the mapping process between the basic and action spaces. For instance, how realistic is the assumption (implicit in Equation 28.1) that all individuals project their issue positions onto their ideal points on the basic dimensions in the same manner? That is, is the mapping process between the two spaces homogenous across individuals? This issue has been addressed in part in the field of legislative studies by examining the role of selective party pressure in legislators' roll call voting behavior (McCarty, Poole, & Rosenthal, 2001). However, public opinion offers another arena where these sorts of question abound. Here, we suspect that differences in political information levels could have a mediating influence on the mapping process. Because public opinion data contains such rich variation across individuals and across time (i.e., political contexts), it also offers an opportunity to parse out the relative influence of elite and individual-level (e.g., core values and beliefs) factors as sources of constraint.

Finally, the methods discussed in this chapter have most frequently been applied to legislative roll call data, but their utility is certainly not limited to this particular political arena. Other types of political choice data can be analyzed using the basic spatial model presented here. For example, Bonica (2014) treats campaign contributions as choices and uses this data to simultaneously estimate the ideological positions of hundreds of thousands of individual donors, political organizations, and candidates. Numerous insights into public opinion have also been revealed by analyzing survey data with these types of scaling methods (see, e.g., Hare and Poole, 2012; Jacoby, 1994, 1995; Treier &

Hillygus, 2009). There are also exciting opportunities to apply spatial models to "big data"; for example, measuring the ideological locations of social network users (Barberá, 2012). All of these and more are promising frontiers for expanding the use of psychometric-based techniques in political science.

References

Aldrich, J. H., & McKelvey, R. D. (1977). A method of scaling with applications to the 1968 and 1972 presidential elections. *American Political Science Review*, 71(1), 111–130.

Ansolabehere, S. (2012). *Cooperative Congressional Election Study, 2010: Common Content*. Harvard University, Cambridge, MA. Release 2: August 10, 2012.

Ansolabehere, S., & Jones, P. E. (2010). Constituents' responses to congressional roll-call voting. *American Journal of Political Science*, 54(3), 583–597.

Armstrong, D., Bakker, R., Carroll, R. A., Hare, C., & Poole, K. T. (2014). Using Bayesian Aldrich–McKelvey scaling to study citizens' ideological preferences and perceptions. *American Journal of Political Science*, 59(30), 759–774.

Bafumi, J., & Herron, M. C. (2010). Leapfrog representation and extremism: A study of American voters and their members in Congress. *American Political Science Review*, 104(3), 519–542.

Bakker, R., Jolly, S., Polk, J., & Poole, K. T. (2014). The European common space: Extending the use of anchoring vignettes. *Journal of Politics*, 76(4), 1089–1101.

Bakker, R., & Poole, K. T. (2013). Bayesian metric multidimensional scaling. *Political Analysis*, 21(1), 125–140.

Bakker, R., de Vries, C., Edwards, E., Hooghe, L., Jolly, S., Marks, G., Polk, J., Rovny, J., Steenbergen, M., & Vachudova, M. A. (2012). Measuring party positions in Europe: The Chapel Hill expert survey trend file, 1999–2010. *Party Politics*, 21(1), 143–152, http://doi.org/10.1177/1354068812462931.

Barberá, P. (2012). *Birds of the same feather tweet together: Bayesian ideal point estimation using Twitter data*. Presented at the Annual Meeting of the American Political Science Association, New Orleans, LA.

Barker, D. C., & Tinnick, J. D. I. (2006). Competing visions of parental roles and ideological constraint. *American Political Science Review*, 100(2), 249–263.

Benoit, K., & Laver, M. (2006). *Party policy in modern democracies*. London: Routledge.

Berndt, E., Hall, B. H., Hall, R. E., & Hausman, J. (1974). Estimation and inference in nonlinear structural models. *Annals of Economic and Social Measurement*, 3/4, 653–666.

Bolt, D. M., & Lall, V. F. (2003). Estimation of compensatory and noncompensatory multidimensional item response models using Markov chain Monte Carlo. *Applied Psychological Measurement*, 27(6), 395–414.

Bonica, A. (2014). Mapping the ideological marketplace. *American Journal of Political Science*, 58(2), 367–386.

Brady, H. E. (1985). The perils of survey research: Inter-personally incomparable responses. *Political Methodology*, 11(3-4), 269–291.

Brady, H. E. (1990). Dimensional analysis of ranking data. *American Journal of Political Science*, 34(4), 1017–1048.

Brady, H. E., & Sniderman, P. M. (1985). Attitude attribution: A group basis for political reasoning. *American Political Science Review*, 79(4), 1061–1078.

Cahoon, L. S., Hinich, M. J., & Ordeshook, P. C. (1976). A multidimensional statistical procedure for spatial analysis. Manuscript, Carnegie-Mellon University.

Carmines, E. G., & Stimson, J. A. (1989). *Issue evolution: Race and the transformation of American politics*. Princeton, NJ: Princeton University Press.

Carroll, J. D., & Chang, J.-J. (1970). Analysis of individual differences in multidimensional scaling via an n-way generalization of "Eckart–Young" decomposition. *Psychometrika*, 35(3), 283–319.

Carroll, R., Hare, C., Lewis, J., Lo, J., Poole, K., & Rosenthal, H. (2014). *alpha-NOMINATE: Ideal Point Estimator*. R package version 0.4.

Carroll, R., Lewis, J. B., Lo, J., Poole, K. T., & Rosenthal, H. (2013). The structure of utility in spatial models of voting. *American Journal of Political Science*, 57(4), 1008–1028.

Chang, J. J., & Carroll, J. D. (1969). How to use MDPREF, a computer program for multidimensional analysis of preference data. In *Multidimensional scaling program package of Bell Laboratories*. Murray Hill, NJ: Bell Laboratories.

Clinton, J., Jackman, S., & Rivers, D. (2004). The statistical analysis of roll call data. *American Political Science Review*, 98(2), 355–370.

Clinton, J. D., & Meirowitz, A. (2001). Agenda constrained legislator ideal points and the spatial voting model. *Political Analysis*, 9(3), 242–259.

Clinton, J. D., & Meirowitz, A. (2003). Integrating voting theory and roll call analysis: A framework. *Political Analysis*, 11(4), 381–396.

Conover, P. J., & Feldman, S. (1989). Candidate perception in an ambiguous world: Campaigns, cues, and inference processes. *American Journal of Political Science*, 33(4), 912–940.

Converse, P. E. (1964). The nature of belief systems in mass publics. In Apter, D. E. (Ed.), *Ideology and discontent* (pp. 206–261). New York: Free Press.

Coombs, C. H. (1950). Psychological scaling without a unit of measurement. *Psychological Review*, 57(3), 145–158.

Coombs, C. H. (1952). A theory of psychological scaling. In *Engineering research bulletin number 34*. Ann Arbor: University of Michigan Press.

Coombs, C. H. (1958). On the use of inconsistency of preferences in psychological measurement. *Journal of Experimental Psychology*, 55(1), 1–7.

Coombs, C. H. (1964). *A theory of data*. New York: John Wiley & Sons, Inc.

Croft, W., & Poole, K. T. (2008). Inferring universals from grammatical variation: Multidimensional scaling for typological analysis. *Theoretical Linguistics*, 34(1), 1–37.

Davis, O. A., & Hinich, M. J. (1966). A mathematical model of policy formation in a democratic society. In Bernd, J. (Ed.), *Mathematical applications in political science* (Vol. II) (pp. 175–208). Dallas, TX: SMU Press.

De Vries, C. E., & Hobolt, S. B. (2012). When dimensions collide: The electoral success of issue entrepreneurs. *European Union Politics*, 13(2), 246–268.

Downs, A. (1957). *An economic theory of democracy*. New York: Harper and Row.

Enelow, J. M., & Hinich, M. J. (1984). *The spatial theory of voting*. New York: Cambridge University Press.

Ennis, D. M. (1988). Confusable and discriminable stimuli: Comment on Nosofsky (1986) and Shepard (1986). *Journal of Experimental Psychology: General*, 117(4), 408–411.

Franklin, C. H. (1991). Eschewing obfuscation? Campaigns and the perception of U.S. Senate incumbents. *American Political Science Review*, 85(4), 1193–1214.

Gärdenfors, P. (2000). *Conceptual spaces: The geometry of thought*. Cambridge, MA: MIT Press.

Gerber, A. S., Huber, G. A., Doherty, D., Dowling, C. M., & Ha, S. E. (2010). Personality and political attitudes: Relationships across issue domains and political contexts. *American Political Science Review*, 104(1), 111–133.

Gerring, J. (1998). *Party ideologies in America, 1828–1996*. Cambridge: Cambridge University Press.

Goren, P. (2013). *On voter competence*. New York: Oxford University Press.

Guttman, L. L. (1944). A basis for scaling qualitative data. *American Sociological Review*, 9, 139–150.

Guttman, L. L. (1950). The basis for scalogram analysis. In *Measurement and prediction: The American soldier* (Vol. IV). New York: John Wiley & Sons, Inc.

Hare, C. (2013). *Polarization and the ideological mapping of core values and beliefs.* Presented at the Annual Meeting of the Midwest Political Science Association, Chicago, IL.

Hare, C. and Poole, K. T. (2012). *Using Optimal Classification to analyze public opinion data.* Presented at the Annual Meeting of the Midwest Political Science Association, Chicago, IL.

Hinich, M. J., & Munger, M. C. (1994). *Ideology and the theory of political choice.* Ann Arbor: University of Michigan Press.

Hinich, M. J., & Munger, M. C. (1997). *Analytical politics.* Cambridge: Cambridge University Press.

Hinich, M. J., & Pollard, W. (1981). A new approach to the spatial theory of electoral competition. *American Journal of Political Science*, 25(2), 323–341.

Hix, S., Noury, A., & Roland, G. (2006). Dimensions of politics in the European Parliament. *American Journal of Political Science*, 50(2), 494–520.

Jackman, S. (2000). Estimation and inference are missing data problems: Unifying social science statistics via Bayesian simulation. *Political Analysis*, 8(4), 307–332.

Jackman, S. (2001). Multidimensional analysis of roll call data via Bayesian simulation: Identification, estimation, inference, and model checking. *Political Analysis*, 9(3), 227–241.

Jackman, S. (2009). *Bayesian analysis for the social sciences.* New York: John Wiley & Sons, Inc.

Jackman, S. (2011). *pscl: Political science computational laboratory, Stanford University.* R package version 1.04.1.

Jacobsmeier, M. L. (2013). Religion and perceptions of candidates' ideologies in United States House elections. *Politics and Religion*, 6(2), 342–372.

Jacoby, W. G. (1994). Public attitudes toward government spending. *American Journal of Political Science*, 38(2), 336–361.

Jacoby, W. G. (1995). The structure of ideological thinking in the American electorate. *American Journal of Political Science*, 39(2), 314–335.

Jacoby, W. G., & Armstrong II., D. A. (2014). Bootstrap confidence regions for multidimensional scaling solutions. *American Journal of Political Science*, 58(1), 264–278.

Jessee, S. A. (2009). Spatial voting in the 2004 presidential election. *American Political Science Review*, 103(1), 59–81.

Jost, J. T., Federico, C. M., & Napier, J. L. (2009). Political ideology: Its structure, functions, and elective affinities. *Annual Review of Psychology*, 60(1), 307–337.

Jost, J. T., Glaser, J., Kruglanski, A. W., & Sulloway, F. J. (2003). Political conservatism as motivated social cognition. *Psychological Bulletin*, 129(3), 339–375.

King, G., Murray, C. J., Salomon, J. A., & Tandon, A. (2004). Enhancing the validity and cross-cultural comparability of measurement in survey research. *American Political Science Review*, 98(1), 191–207.

Larkin, J. H., & Simon, H. A. (1987). Why a diagram is (sometimes) worth ten thousand words. *Cognitive Science*, 11(1), 65–100.

Layman, G. C., & Green, J. C. (2006). Wars and rumours of wars: The contexts of cultural conflict in American political behaviour. *British Journal of Political Science*, 36(1), 61–89.

Levendusky, M. (2010). Clearer cues, more consistent voters: A benefit of elite polarization. *Political Behavior*, 32(1), 111–131.

Lewis, J. B., & Poole, K. T. (2004). Measuring bias and uncertainty in ideal point estimates via the parametric bootstrap. *Political Analysis*, 12(2), 105–127.

Lunn, D. J., Thomas, A., Best, N., & Spiegelhalter, D. (2000). WinBUGS – A Bayesian modelling framework: concepts, structure, and extensibility. *Statistics and Computing*, 10(4), 325–337.

Lupia, A., & McCubbins, M. D. (1998). *The democratic dilemma: Can citizens learn what they need to know?* Cambridge: Cambridge University Press.

Martin, A. D., & Quinn, K. M. (2002). Dynamic ideal point estimation via Markov chain Monte Carlo for the U.S. Supreme Court, 1953–1999. *Political Analysis*, 10(2), 134–153.

Martin, A. D., Quinn, K. M., & Park, J. H. (2011). MCMCpack: Markov chain Monte Carlo in R. *Journal of Statistical Software*, 42(9), 1–21.

McCarty, N., Poole, K. T., & Rosenthal, H. (2001). The hunt for party discipline in Congress. *American Political Science Review*, 95(3), 673–687.

McFadden, D. L. (1976). Quantal choice analysis: A survey. *Annals of Economic and Social Measurement*, 5(4), 363–390.

Miller, G. A. (1956). The magical number seven, plus or minus two: Some limits on our capacity for processing information. *Psychological Review*, 63(2), 81–97.

Nosofsky, R. M. (1986). Attention, similarity, and the identification-categorization relationship. *Journal of Experimental Psychology: General*, 115(1), 39–57.

Nosofsky, R. M. (1992). Similarity scaling and cognitive process models. *Annual Review of Psychology*, 43, 25–53.

Nyhan, B., McGhee, E., Sides, J., Masket, S., & Greene, S. (2012). One vote out of step? The effects of salient roll call votes in the 2010 election. *American Politics Research*, 40(5), 844–879.

Ordeshook, P. C. (1976). The spatial theory of elections: A review and a critique. In Budge, I., Crewe, I., & Farlie, D. J. (Eds.)., *Party identification and beyond: Representations of voting and party competition* (pp. 285–313). New York: John Wiley & Sons, Inc.

Palfrey, T. R., & Poole, K. T. (1987). The relationship between information, ideology, and voting behavior. *American Journal of Political Science*, 31(3), 511–530.

Peress, M. (2012). Identification of a semiparametric item response model. *Psychometrika*, 77(2), 223–243.

Plummer, M. (2003). JAGS: A program for analysis of Bayesian graphical models using Gibbs Sampling. In Hornik, K., Leisch, F., & Zeileis, A. (Eds.), *Proceedings of the 3rd International Workshop on Distributed Statistical Computing*, Vienna, Austria.

Poole, K. T. (1998). Recovering a basic space from a set of issue scales. *American Journal of Political Science*, 42(3), 954–993.

Poole, K. T. (2000). Nonparametric unfolding of binary choice data. *Political Analysis*, 8(3), 211–237.

Poole, K. T. (2005). *Spatial models of parliamentary voting*. New York: Cambridge University Press.

Poole, K. T. (2007). Changing minds? Not in Congress! *Public Choice*, 131(3/4), 435–451.

Poole, K., Lewis, J., Lo, J., & Carroll, R. (2011). Scaling roll call votes with wnominate in R. *Journal of Statistical Software*, 42(14), 1–21.

Poole, K., Lewis, J., Lo, J., & Carroll, R. (2012). oc: OC roll call analysis software. R package version 0.93.

Poole, K. T., & Rosenthal, H. (1985). A spatial model for legislative roll call analysis. *American Journal of Political Science*, 29(2), 357–384.

Poole, K. T., & Rosenthal, H. (1991). Patterns of congressional voting. *American Journal of Political Science*, 35(1), 228–278.

Poole, K. T., & Rosenthal, H. (1997). *Congress: A political-economic history of roll call voting*. New York: Oxford University Press.

Poole, K. T., & Rosenthal, H. (2007). *Ideology and congress*. New Brunswick, NJ: Transaction.

Poole, K., Rosenthal, H., Lewis, J., Lo, J., & Carroll, R. (2013). basicspace: A package to recover a basic space from issue scales. R package version 0.07.

Popkin, S. L. (1994). *The reasoning voter: Communication and persuasion in presidential campaigns* (2nd ed.). Chicago, IL: University of Chicago Press.

Quinn, K. M. (2004). Bayesian factor analysis for mixed ordinal and continuous responses. *Political Analysis, 12*(4), 338–353.

Reckase, M. D. (1985). The difficulty of test items that measure more than one ability. *Applied Psychological Measurement, 9*(4), 401–412.

Reckase, M. D. (2010). A linear logistic multidimensional model for dichotomous item response data. In van der Linden, W. J. & Hambleton, R. K. (Eds.), *Handbook of modern item response theory* (pp. 271–286). New York: Springer.

Rivers, D. (2003). Identification of multidimensional spatial voting models. Manuscript, Stanford University.

Rosenthal, H., & Voeten, E. (2004). Analyzing roll calls with perfect spatial voting: France 1946–1958. *American Journal of Political Science, 48*(3), 620–632.

Rusk, J. G., & Weisberg, H. F. (1972). Perceptions of presidential candidates: Implications for electoral change. *Midwest Journal of Political Science, 16*(3), 388–410.

Schönemann, P. (1970). On metric multidimensional unfolding. *Psychometrika, 35*(3), 349–366.

Shepard, R. N. (1986). Discrimination and generalization in identification and classification: Comment on Nosofsky. *Journal of Experimental Psychology: General, 115*(1), 58–61.

Shepard, R. N. (1987). Toward a universal law of generalization for psychological science. *Science, 237*(4820), 1317–1323.

Simon, H. A. (1985). Human nature in politics: The dialogue of psychology with political science. *American Political Science Review, 79*(2), 293–304.

Sniderman, P. M., & Bullock, J. (2004). A consistency theory of public opinion and political choice: The hypothesis of menu dependence. In Saris, W. E. & Sniderman, P. M. (Eds.), *Studies in public opinion: Attitudes, nonattitudes, measurement error, and change* (pp. 337–357). Princeton, NJ: Princeton University Press.

Sowell, T. (2007). *A conflict of visions: Ideological origins of political struggles* (rev. ed.). New York: Basic Books.

Stimson, J. A. (2004). *Tides of consent: How public opinion shapes American Politics*. Cambridge: Cambridge University Press.

Takane, Y., Young, F., & de Leeuw, J. (1977). Nonmetric individual differences multidimensional scaling: An alternating least squares method with optimal scaling features. *Psychometrika, 42*(1), 7–67.

Torgerson, W. S. (1958). *Theory and methods of scaling*. New York: John Wiley & Sons, Inc.

Treier, S., & Hillygus, D. S. (2009). The nature of political ideology in the contemporary electorate. *Public Opinion Quarterly, 73*(4), 679–703.

Treier, S., & Jackman, S. (2008). Democracy as a latent variable. *American Journal of Political Science, 52*(1), 201–217.

Tversky, A., & Kahneman, D. (1974). Judgment under uncertainty: Heuristics and biases. *Science, 185*(4157), 1124–1131.

Vavreck, L. (2009). *The message matters: The economy and presidential campaigns*. Princeton, NJ: Princeton University Press.

Voeten, E. (2000). Clashes in the assembly. *International Organization, 54*(2), 185–215.

Wand, J. (2013). Credible comparisons using interpersonally incomparable data: Nonparametric scales with anchoring vignettes. *American Journal of Political Science, 57*(1), 249–262.

Wand, J., King, G., & Lau, O. (2011). Anchors: Software for anchoring vignette data. *Journal of Statistical Software, 42*(3), 1–25.

Weisberg, H. F. (1968). *Dimensional analysis of legislative roll calls* (Doctoral dissertation). University of Michigan.

Weisberg, H. F., & Rusk, J. G. (1970). Dimensions of candidate evaluation. *American Political Science Review, 64*(4), 1167–1185.

Young, F., de Leeuw, J., & Takane, Y. (1976). Regression with qualitative and quantitative variables: An alternating least squares method with optimal scaling features. *Psychometrika, 41*(4), 505–529.

Code Appendix

Code 1 R code for chapter examples.

```
library(pscl)
library(wnominate)
library(oc)
#
#
#  Utility functions
#
norm.util <- function(x){ return(15*exp(-0.25*(0-x)^2))}
quad.util <- function(x){ return(15+15*(-0.25*(0-x)^2))}

plot(c(-3,3),c(0,20),type="n",bty="n",
     main="Gaussian (solid) and Quadratic (dashed)
     Deterministic\nUtility
     Functions for Legislator with Ideal Point of 0",
xlab="Ideological Location (Liberal - Conservative)",
ylab="Utility",cex.lab=1.2)
lines(seq(-3,3,0.01), norm.util(seq(-3,3,0.01)),lwd=2,
lty=1)
lines(seq(-3,3,0.01), quad.util(seq(-3,3,0.01)),lwd=2,
lty=2)
arrows(-1.5,0.5,-1.5,-0.75,length=0.1,lwd=2,
col="gray20")
text(-1.5,1.0,"Yea",font=2,col="gray20")
arrows(0.5,0.5,0.5,-0.75,length=0.1,lwd=2,col="gray60")
text(0.5,1.0,"Nay",font=2,col="gray60")
#
#
#  Optimal Classification
#
hr89 <- readKH("c:/Dropbox/Files/Research/
Psychometrics_PoliticalScience/sen98kh.ord",
        dtl=NULL,
        yea=c(1,2,3),
        nay=c(4,5,6),
        missing=c(7,8,9),
        notInLegis=0,
        desc="90th House Roll Call Data",
        debug=FALSE)
#
result <- oc(hr89, dims=2, minvotes=20, lop=0.005,
polarity=c(1,3))
#
```

```
ws <- result$rollcalls[,8]
N1 <- result$rollcalls[,6]
N2 <- result$rollcalls[,7]
oc1 <- result$legislators$coord1D
oc2 <- result$legislators$coord2D
#
xws <- ws*N1
yws <- ws*N2
N1W <- N1
N2W <- N2
#
plot(oc1,oc2,type="n",asp=1,main="",
     xlab="",
     ylab="",
     xlim=c(-1.0,1.0),ylim=c(-1.0,1.0),font=2,cex=1.2)
# Main title
mtext("Coombs Mesh Created from Cutting Lines of\n100
Roll Calls in the 89th US Senate",
      side=3,line=1.50,cex=1.2,font=2)

# x-axis title
mtext("First Dimension (Liberal - Conservative)",side=1,
line=3.25,cex=1.2)

# y-axis title
mtext("Second Dimension (Region)",side=2,line=2.5,cex=1.2)
#
#rcsamp <- sample(1:nrow(result$rollcalls), 100, replace=F)
rcsamp <-   c(227, 654, 513, 338, 103, 413, 537, 355, 474, 100,
              621, 71, 152, 286, 94, 402, 505, 82, 76, 514,
              297, 143, 151, 477, 602, 582, 287, 392, 597, 566,
              47, 652, 313, 87, 376, 42,91, 131, 460, 54, 631,
              366, 280, 588, 250, 33, 341, 214, 492, 302, 308,
              630, 519, 322,24, 74, 478, 67, 657, 465, 324, 476,
              488, 148, 614, 373, 605, 486, 593, 330, 351,
              219, 352,
              453, 259, 288, 553, 592, 661, 424, 641, 333,
              660, 418,
              283, 636, 52, 379, 589, 583, 303, 335, 199,
              656, 662,
              533, 464, 421, 31, 383)

#
for (i in 1:length(rcsamp)){
arrows(xws[rcsamp[i]], yws[rcsamp[i]], xws[rcsamp[i]]
+N2W[rcsamp[i]],
    yws[rcsamp[i]]-N1W[rcsamp[i]], length=0.0, lwd=2,
    col="black")
```

```
    arrows(xws[rcsamp[i]], yws[rcsamp[i]], xws[rcsamp[i]]-
    N2W[rcsamp[i]],
        yws[rcsamp[i]]+N1W[rcsamp[i]], length=0.0, lwd=2,
        col="black")
}
#
text(result$legislators["DAMATO (R NY)","coord1D"],
     result$legislators["DAMATO (R NY)","coord2D"],"R",
     col="red",font=2)
#
#
```

29

How Factor Analysis Has Shaped Personality Trait Psychology

Tom Booth and Aja L. Murray

Introduction

"Traits are 'lost causes'; their existence requires, rather than provides, a scientific explanation." (Wiggins, 1973, cited in Pervin, 1994, p. 109)

For centuries, people have been fascinated by the characters of man; asking what it is that makes people moral or immoral, kind or mean, active or languid? In the parlance of current day psychology, such discussions are concerned with traits; specifically, personality traits. The definitions and nature of traits have been much debated (Pervin, 1994), but in crude terms can be characterized as "…relatively enduring patterns of thoughts, feelings and actions" (McCrae & Costa, 2008).

Despite a turbulent early history (in particular the association of the early ideas of genetic heredity of characteristics of individuals with the atrocities of World War II) and subsequent theoretical critiques (most famously that of Mischel, 1968), personality trait psychology has shown an overall upward trajectory of popularity. In this chapter, we argue that two key events contributed to the rapid expansion in popularity of the trait perspective and were instrumental in shaping how personality researchers think about traits to this day. These events were the introduction by Charles Spearman of the single common factor model (1904), and later the extension of this model to multiple factors by Thurstone (1931). From the outset, trait psychology made use of the factor model, most notably in the works of individuals such as Raymond Cattell, who was a pioneer of both factor analytic methodologies (e.g., the scree test for the number of factors problem, 1966; and the use of item parcels, 1974) and the study of personality structure and personality trait theory (e.g., the development of the 16 Personality Factor Questionnaire (16PF), 1943a, 1943b, 1945; see Revelle, 2009 for discussion).

Using Gigerenzer's (1991) "tools-to-theories" framework, we will trace: the development of the currently-dominant descriptive model in contemporary personality trait research, the Five-Factor Model (FFM), its continual interactions with factor analysis, and the later development of Five Factor Theory (FFT). We begin with brief a description of the history and development of the FFM, and the key aspects of tools-to-theories heuristic. We then highlight the ways in which factor analysis-to-personality trait psychology may represent a specific example of this heuristic. We focus specifically on the role of variable selection and data prestructuring, rotational indeterminacy, the number of factors problem, and simple structure, in influencing the development of personality trait models and theory.

The Five-Factor Model

The FFM is frequently cited as being the consensus descriptive model of personality trait structure (Allen & DeYoung, 2015). In its current form, it comprises five broad domains, each of which subsume six narrow facets, namely Neuroticism (subsuming Anxiety, Angry Hostility, Depression, Self-Consciousness, Impulsiveness, & Vulnerability); Extraversion (Warmth, Gregariousness, Assertiveness, Activity, Excitement Seeking, & Positive Emotions); Openness to Experience (Fantasy, Aesthetics, Feelings, Actions, Ideas, & Values); Agreeableness (Trust, Straightforwardness, Altruism, Compliance, Modesty, & Tender-Mindedness); and Conscientiousness (Competence, Order, Dutifulness, Achievement Striving, Self-Discipline, & Deliberation). The FFM traits are commonly measured using the NEO-PI-R Personality Inventory, which is now in its fourth edition.

Two distinct (but related) tracks of research evidence converged on the notion of five broad personality domains: the lexical and the psychometric. The lexical hypothesis holds that all concepts that are important to human beings are encoded into natural language in the form of single words (John & Srivastava, 1999). Thus, those who subscribe to this position argue that meaningful understanding of personality concepts can be identified by grouping trait adjectives from large pools of words. This line of research in the English language began with Allport and Odbert's (1936) classic study of 17,953 adjectives, which replicated a similar study in German by Klages (1926). Further lexical work continued by Norman (1963, 1967) and Goldberg (1981, 1990, 1993). Allport and Odbert's study was also influential in the early work of Cattell, who, using factor analytic methodology, sought to find congruence between personality characteristics located in behavioral ratings of adjectives, questionnaire items, and objective tests. In more recent times, work on the structure of personality from a lexical tradition has largely focused on the universality of adjective factor structures in different languages (e.g. Saucier, 2009; Saucier, et al., 2014).

The psychometric FFM was primarily developed over a period of 15 years from the mid-1970s by Paul T. Costa Jr and Robert R. McCrae (see Costa & McCrae, 2008). The primary focus in the early studies of personality was to identify a set of personality trait dimensions that could be used to study changes of personality with age. To this end, Costa and McCrae (1976) began by cluster analyzing Cattell's 16PF, identifying three consistent clusters, which were labeled Neuroticism (N), Extraversion (E), and Openness (O). These three constructs formed the basis of the NEO model. Two constructs, Neuroticism and Extraversion, were argued to be similar to those identified by Eysenck in his PEN model, while Openness was somewhat novel. In a series of follow-up studies (see for example Costa & McCrae, 1978; McCrae & Costa, 1980), the nature of Openness was defined and six finer grained facet scales per domain were constructed. Collectively these scales comprised the original NEO inventory.

In the mid-1980s, the lexical and psychometric threads united in a series of studies in which Costa and McCrae considered the overlap in the constructs assessed by the lexical five factors, and their own NEO inventory (e.g., Costa & McCrae, 1985; McCrae & Costa, 1987). The outcome of these studies, in short, was that N, E, and O were similar across the lexical and psychometric approaches, and that Agreeableness (A) and Conscientiousness (C) should be included in the psychometric taxonomies.

Following this, a series of studies were published exploring whether five factors could be located in joint factor analyses of a variety of scales each alongside a NEO measure. These included the Eysenck Personality Inventory (EPI) (McCrae & Costa, 1985); the Multiphasic Personality Inventory (MMPI) (Costa, Zonderman, McCrae, & Williams, 1985; Costa, Busch, Zonderman, & McCrae, 1986); the California Q-Set (McCrae, Costa, & Busch, 1986); Wiggin's Circumplex Model (McCrae & Costa, 1989), and the Adjective Check List (Piedmont, McCrae, & Costa, 1991). The overall conclusion drawn from this collection of studies was that factor solutions were quite consistent in identifying five factors of similar content (Costa & McCrae, 2008), and after the addition of facet scales for A and C (Costa, McCrae, & Dye, 1991), the full NEO-PI-R questionnaire was born (Costa & McCrae, 1992a).

Thus, the FFM was, in large part, derived from the application of factor analytic methods to data from questionnaire measures in a variety of data sets. The same is true of the foundational studies of the lexical five factors, only in this instance the variables for analysis were not questionnaire items, but ratings on pools of single adjectives. This observation forms the basis of one of the most serious criticisms leveled at the FFM, namely, the lack of an a priori theoretical basis (Block, 1995, 2000, 2010; McAdams, 1992; Pervin, 1994). However, and perhaps more interestingly, it also makes the FFM a strong candidate for an instance of a tools-to-theories heuristic.

The Tools-to-Theories Heuristic

Gigerenzer and Sturm (2007) describe the tools-to-theories heuristic as being about the practice of scientists, and the way in which they apply analytic and physical tools in empirical study. The main principles of the heuristic were set out in a series of chapters and articles in the early 1990s (Gigerenzer, 1991, 1992);

> My thesis is twofold: (1) *Discovery*: New scientific tools suggest new theoretical metaphors and concepts, once they are entrenched in a scientist's practice. (2) *Acceptance*: Once proposed by an individual scientist (or group), the new theoretical metaphors and concepts are more likely to be accepted by the scientific community if the members of the community are also familiar with the tools. (Gigerenzer, 1992, p. 332)

Tools, in this context can take a variety of forms: they may be analytic, in the form of statistical procedure conducted on data; they may be analytic but not require actual data, such as procedures for theoretical evaluation; or they may be physical measurement instruments that produce data. However, what they have in common is that they serve as "tools of justification" (Gigerenzer, 1992) for a given theory. In particular,

Gigerenzer (e.g., 1991) focuses on the way in which social scientists embraced new tools of statistical inference to develop cognitive theories of the mind. It is argued that these discoveries were not discoveries driven by eureka moments of genius, or through the availability of new data, but through the availability of a new tool in the form of inference, which provided a metaphor for the way in which the mind may work.

Many factors can influence familiarity and thus acceptance of a given tool, such as technological or physical boundaries, to the application of tools or the institutionalization of tools in a given context. However, for familiarity with a given tool within a field to develop, general uptake is essential. It is through mainstream applications of the tools that acceptance comes to pass. Importantly, sophisticated understanding of the tools by all users is not essential, merely a practical familiarity (Gigerenzer & Sturm, 2007).

Interrelation of tools, data, and theories

The potential interactions between tools, data, and theories are presented in Figure 29.1. Panel A represents the common view of the relation, namely that scientific tools produce data that can be used to support or refute a given theoretical idea. This process is objective, with the data under study produced in a theory-neutral manner.

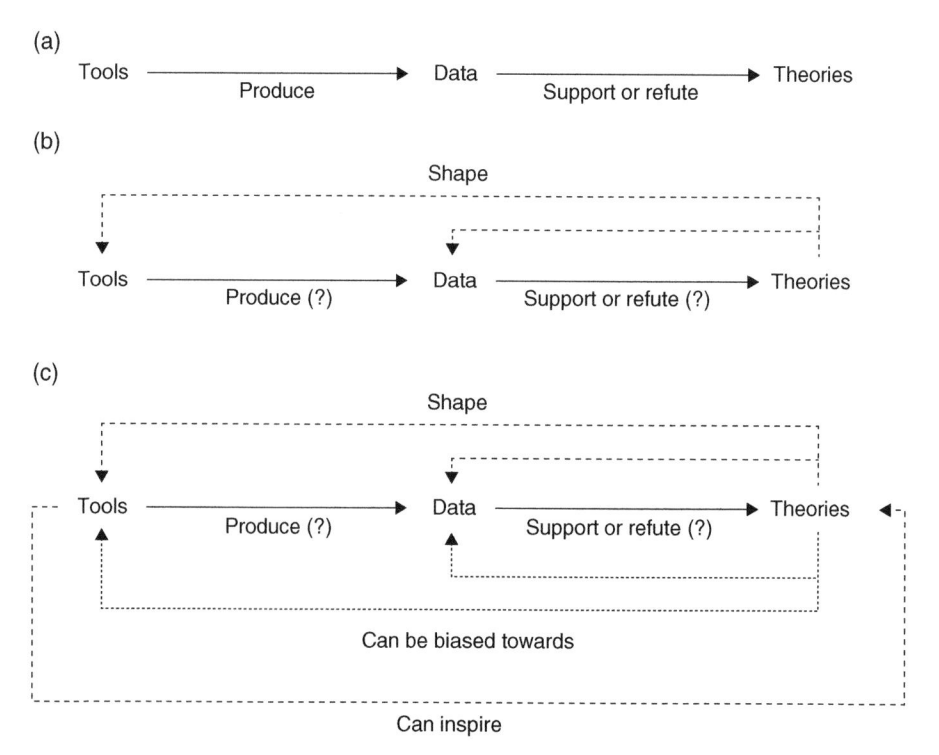

Figure 29.1 Possible interactions between tools, data, and theories. Reproduced with permission from Gigerenzer and Sturm (2007), Figure 14.1–3, pp. 313–314.

In panel B, the dashed lines denote the way in which both tools and data become theory-laden, potentially compromising their ability to support or refute theories in an objective way. Finally, in panel C, the dotted arrows introduce the idea of reciprocal relations between tools, data, and theories. Here, tools can be an inspiration for theory and the potential for theory to drive data, and data to drive tool development, use and so on is seen. Gigerenzer (1992, p. 13) has argued that while the influence of tools on theory generation may not be immediately obvious, the "birthmarks" of tools may be visible in theories. That is, inherent features of the tools themselves, or their practical use, might become embedded in the theories.

FFM as an Example of Tools-to-Theories

In this section, we consider the major components of the tools-to-theories heuristic in relation to the history of personality trait psychology and the FFM. From the definition of tools provided by Gigerenzer (discussed above), we can define two main interrelated tools in the history of the FFM, namely, the questionnaires designed to measure personality traits and the factor analytic method used as the statistical tool to analyze the data generated from their administration. We focus primarily on the latter. This is not to diminish the importance of the inventories used in personality research as influential tools; however, we suggest that these tools are only seen in the abundance and form we see in modern psychology as a result of the more foundational tool of factor analysis.

Specifically, we focus on: the **discovery** of factor analytic methods and its connection to the concept of the latent trait; the **acceptance** of factor analysis as the tool for the study of personality traits; the **birthmarks** of the factor model on personality trait psychology; and finally, we will review these elements in light of the potential interactions depicted in Figure 29.1.

Discovery

The rudiments of trait psychology had begun to emerge at the turn of the twentieth century. Interest in the qualities that differentiate individuals' thoughts, feelings, and behavior, and the extent to which such qualities may be heritable across generations were topics of vigorous scientific debate. However, it was not until the advent of factor analysis, and the associated notion of the latent variable, that researchers had a quantitative way to conceive of these traits.

The factor model can be traced to Spearman (1904; see Borsboom, 2005 for a comprehensive account). Spearman was the first to present the common factor model on the basis of observed correlations, with the model later extended by Thurstone to multiple factors (Thurstone, 1947). Later that century Jöreskog (1967) provided the framework for the confirmatory factor model and developments in both traditions have continued since. Spearman's initial focus was not so much the method of factor analysis, but on whether there exists some general ability factor that underlies both sensory discrimination and cognitive test performance (Bartholomew, 2007). The insight was that through consideration of the patterns of observed correlation, we might in some way gain access to this general ability. As Bartholomew (2007, p. 9, quoting Spearman, 1904, p. 272) states; "Whenever branches of intellectual activity are at all dissimilar, then their correlations with one another appear wholly due to their being all variants wholly saturated with some common fundamental function…". Thus, from the outset, factor analysis was tightly intertwined with the concept of underlying "functions" – what we would now refer to as traits – which manifest in observed data.

But how should we conceive of the functions (factors) from Spearman's model? Borsboom (2005, see also 2008) argues that there was no explicit theory of latent variables at the outset. However, latent variable theory cannot be entirely philosophically neutral for its application carries an implicit realist ontological assumption, that is, the latent construct is a common cause, existing separately from any specific set of variables used in empirical studies. It is easy to see this implicit theory in the application of factor analysis within the field of personality psychology. For example, the very notion that we should be able to recover the same five factors from a host of different inventories (i.e., the standard structure of studies in support of the FFM across the late 1980s and early 1990s discussed before) suggests an implicit idea of a common cause separate from any individual set of variables.

The advent of the factor model and the associated concept of the latent variable allowed psychologists, in some sense, to quantify unmeasured hypothesized causes. This development, we argue, paved the way for the rapid growth and development of trait psychology generally and personality trait psychology specifically. In this sense, factor analysis opened the floodgates for a research field which up to this point lacked appropriate tools.

Acceptance

It takes only a cursory glimpse at the field of personality psychology, and individual difference psychology more broadly, to appreciate the extensive uptake of factor analytic methodology. It is no exaggeration to suggest factor analysis is **the** method of the field. For illustration, Figure 29.2 plots the results of a PubMed search for the term "factor analysis" in the title or abstract of articles and "Psychology" (upper panel) or "Personality" (lower panel) in any field, from 1943 (the year of Cattell's first publication on his factor model) to 2014 (last complete year of data given publication lag at the time of writing; for R code see Code Appendix). As is clear from Figure 29.2, there has been a huge upsurge in the reference to factor analysis in the published literature, and although the plot does not directly show use, only reference, it is reasonable to infer that use would follow a similar trend.

This rise in the use of factor analysis as an analytic tool has, unsurprisingly, coincided with the availability of computing hardware and software. As Gigerenzer and Sturm (2007) document, through the 1960s and 1970s there was a steady rise in the use of mainframe computers in academic research, which was supplanted during the 1980s by the meteoric rise in micro computing. The introduction of personal computing made analytic software more readily accessible. In 1984, SPSS became one of the first statistical software tools to be available on individual computers as opposed to mainframes, and it was not long before other software packages followed suit. Nowadays, nearly all major statistical programs (e.g., SAS, SPSS, STATA, and R) include factor analysis.

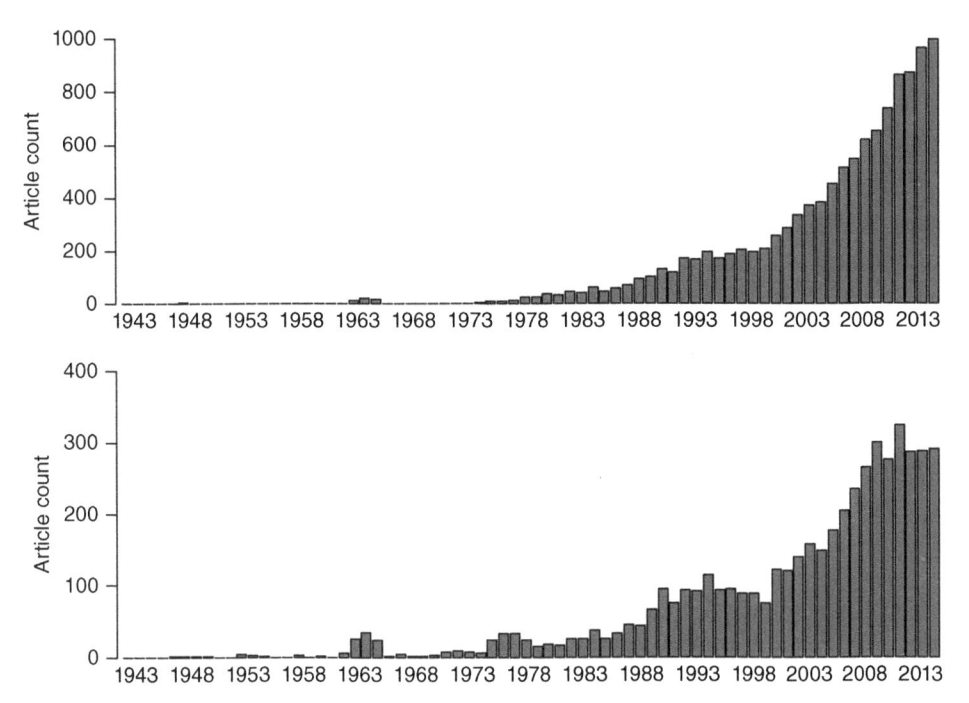

Figure 29.2 Reference to factor analysis in journals including psychology (upper) and personality (lower) in their title between 1943 and 2014 from the PubMed database.

In the early days of applied factor analysis, when hand calculation was required, the pool of those able to use the tool was select and even in the early days of computing the widespread acceptance and uptake was limited by the ability to program early computers. However, with the proliferation of computing power and easy to use programs, factor analysis became a widely accessible tool even for those without in-depth statistical or mathematical knowledge. The requirement for in-depth understanding was reduced further by the development of many rules of thumb prescribing certain analytic strategies to generically apply across research studies. In the field of personality, this was exemplified in what became labeled the "little jiffy" approach. The "little jiffy" involves conducting a principal components analysis with the orthogonal varimax rotation and deciding on the number of factors based on the Kaiser Criterion (initial eigenvalues greater than 1; Kaiser, 1970). There have been a large number of published critiques of this procedure (see Preacher & MacCallum, 2003 for extended discussion), and we will not repeat these here.[1]

In sum, while there has been growth in the application of factor analysis to the field of personality, Figure 29.2 indicates that the period of rapid expansion in the acceptance and application of factor analysis as a tool in personality research came in the early 1980s, and has been on a rapid rise since. This period also saw the expansion of personal computing, readily accessible software, analytic shortcuts, and the FFM.

---

[1] For general critiques of the applications of factor analysis in applied research see, for example, Fabrigar, Wegener, MacCallum, & Strahan (1999).

Birthmarks of FA in personality trait psychology

In the following section, we examine the birthmarks of factor analysis in the field of personality psychology. Specifically, we focus on: (1) data prestructuring and resultant solutions, (2) the number of factors problem, and (3) rotational indeterminacy.

Data prestructuring and the FFM Data prestructuring refers to the idea that any factor analytic solution is inexorably linked to the initial input variables, and that the choice of these input variables is subjective. In an ideal factor-analytic study – at least in terms of the kinds of conclusions most factor analytic studies are intended to draw – one would have access to the entire domain of possible items representing a construct of interest, and assessed in the population of interest. However, in any practical sense, we are always sampling from these domains – either sampling people from populations, items from the hypothetical pool or both (Type 1, Type 2, & Type 1–2, respectively, Lord, 1955). The general problem of data prestructuring within factor analytic studies concerns the constraints placed on the location of factor solutions by the manner in which we choose to sample from these domains. We will focus specifically here on item sampling.

To make it more concrete, suppose we start with a large pool of items representative of the entire domain of interest and we want to select some smaller subset for practical purposes. This is a problem common to those who wish to create short form questionnaires from longer inventories. There are many examples in the field of personality, such as the, NEO-FFI (Costa & McCrae, 1992a), BFI (John, Donahue, & Kentle, 1991) and TIPI (Gosling, Rentfrow, & Swann, 2003). All of which are commonly used short form measures of the five broad personality domains of the FFM that were derived from item selection procedures applied to longer questionnaires (i.e., already preselected item pools). But how do we choose which items to sample?

Though there are a number of ways to approach this problem, one common method is to simply take a subset of items which load most highly on a factor from the broader inventory. This approach can be supplemented with considerations about lower order structures (e.g., equal sampling across items from facets in the case of the FFM), but the essence remains the same; take the best items for a given number of factors. Given this targeted reduction in items, it becomes increasingly unlikely that an analysis based on the resulting short form will result in anything other than the number of factors in the original instruments being retained.

To demonstrate these effects, consider the following brief simulation. A true population factor model was created to contain seven factors derived from 140 items in a sample of 100,000. Items were simulated to have primary loadings ranging from 0.40 to 0.80 and cross loadings that ranged from 0.20 to 0.50. From this initial sample of 100,000, four random subsamples were selected without replacement (n = 1,000, 700, 500, and 300). Next, in order to demonstrate the sequential strengthening of solutions through data preselection, an "incorrect" number of factors (5) were extracted from the first random sample of 1,000. To evaluate the properties of the solution, Table 29.1 contains the first 10 eigenvalues, as well as the number of factors suggested by parallel analysis, the minimum average partial test, and sample size adjusted BIC. The total variance explained by the solution is also given.

The sample of 1,000 (study 1) represents the original solution from which we are going to preselect our items. The samples of 700 (hypothetical study 2), 500 (hypothetical study 3), and 300 (hypothetical study 4) are then selected at random from the

Table 29.1 Factor analysis results for simulation study on data prestructuring.

	First 10 Eigenvalues										MAP	PA	saBIC	Total Variance Explained
	1	2	3	4	5	6	7	8	9	10				
Study 1 (N = 1,000)	10.88	3.61	3.47	3.21	3.21	2.98	2.74	1.52	1.51	1.47	7	7	7	14%
Study 2 (N = 700)	5.24	2.44	2.35	2.32	1.41	1.23	1.21	1.17	1.08	1.06	5	5	5	21%
Study 3 (N = 500)	3.93	1.87	1.78	1.66	1.51	1.07	1.05	1.01	0.98	0.96	1	5	5	22%
Study 4 (N = 300)	3.14	1.61	1.53	1.40	1.34	1.00	0.96	0.96	0.85	0.84	1	5	5	26%

Note. MAP = Minimum Average Partial; PA = Parallel Analysis; saBIC = sample size adjusted Bayesian Information Criterion; Variance explained taken from a forced five factor solution.

original 100,000. These samples represent a quite typical observation that once an inventory or item pool is considered reasonable, analyses are conducted on smaller data sets. Across these samples, we sequentially reduce the number of items used. For study 2, we retained the 10 highest loading items for each factor from study 1. For study 3, we retain the six highest loading items for each factor from study 2. For study 4, we retain the four highest loading items for each factor from study 3. In each study, we retain five factors. Here we select five as an arbitrary number which differs from the population model that generated the data. Collectively this represents a series of chronological studies of random samples from the population where items are sequentially and increasingly prestructured toward an incorrect factor solution in that population.

Table 29.1 shows the results of this simulation. What is obvious is that, over the course of the studies, the support for the incorrect number of factors in the population gets stronger. If we try to recover the true population number of factors from the data in study 4, evidence for the additional factors is weak. In essence, our true model is now lost unless we resample our domain again. And if our new solutions begin to define our domain (i.e., they become the model or theory of this domain), we may never think we have strong reason to do so.

So then, is data prestructuring evident in the history of the FFM? The answer is yes. A number of papers commonly cited as seminal with respect to the emergence of the FFM were replication attempts of the factor structures proposed by Cattell. John, Angleitner, and Ostendorf (1988, p. 177) diagrammatically show the interconnections between Cattell's reduction of Allport and Odbert (1936) and the replication studies of Fiske (1949), Tupes and Christal (1961), Norman (1963), and Borgatta (1964). More precisely, Cattell's reductions generated 35 (in later works this is reported variably as between 42 and 45 trait clusters). Across studies, Cattell argued variably that these clusters were best represented by 11, 12, and eventually settling on 16 factors.

Fiske (1949), in one of the first replications of Cattell's work, selected 22 of Cattell's clusters in his analysis. While at this stage the selection of variables was not directly focused toward the five-factor model, the reduction in the number of variables analyzed inevitably predisposed a solution with fewer factors. Fiske identified five factors from this analysis that were argued to align to five of those identified by Cattell. However, with respect to a direct prestructuring targeted toward a five-factor solution, perhaps the most critical study is that of Tupes and Christal (1961).

Tupes and Christal (1961) re-analyzed both Fiske and Cattell's matrices, and analyzed four data sets of their own that used a slightly reduced set of 30 of Cattell's clusters. Using a Procrustes rotation procedure, these authors argued for five recurrent factors across each of the correlation matrices produced from these data sets. Later, Norman (1963) and Borgatta (1964) both selected only the highest four loading clusters from Tupes and Christal (1961) for each of the five factors identified. Subsequently, both authors claim support for the five-factor solution of Tupes and Christal. While all of these studies predate the modern FFM, all have been cited as historical support for five recurrent broad factors of human personality. Yet, due to the nature of the prestructuring of the variable sets, in particular the latter studies of Norman and Borgatta, we suggest here that identifying anything other than five factors was unlikely.

In and of itself, there is no significant problem with an analytic approach with preselection, if the aim is to produce a set of variables which map to a particular structure of interest. The importance comes in how we evaluate the findings from the resultant factor analyses. Such findings do not provide evidence of the "truth" of the factors identified, only that our selection of variables has led to reasonable measurement of those factors we targeted in our item selection.

In contrast to the questionnaire approach to personality structure, lexical studies have, by and large, retained an emphasis on identifying a wide range of trait adjectives from each lexicon analyzed. Interestingly, a number of recent large-scale analyses have reported that, when such pools of variables are analyzed, there is no recurrent five factor-solution (Saucier et al., 2014). Indeed, the only solution that shows any degree of replicability is a simple two factor model.

In sum, when variable sets show preselection, at best we are providing evidence for the quality of our item selection to assess a prespecified model – we are not providing any evidence for the veracity of the traits themselves.

Number of factors problem A highly related issue to data prestructuring within factor analysis is that of deciding on the number of factors to extract from a given correlation matrix. Empirically, this is the most important decision made in the context of a factor analytic study. In the simulation here, a world was created with seven factors, and as such, we can in some sense discuss the "correct" and "incorrect" number of factors to retain. However, there is no such luxury in the world beyond simulation studies. The notion of a "correct" number of factors is not, by and large, the best way to consider the problem. Instead, we are concerned with selecting the optimal number of factors from any given set of variables (Preacher, Zhang, Kim, & Mels, 2013).

In the context of personality trait research, the question as to the appropriate number of factors to retain has become conflated with a debate as to what number of factors constitutes the correct number of basic traits. This debate is typified by the exchange in the early 1990s between Costa and McCrae, Eysenck, and Zuckerman (Costa & McCrae, 1992b, 1992c; Eysenck, 1991, 1992; Zuckerman, 1992). Central to the arguments within these papers was the presentation of a large number of criteria as to what constitutes a basic personality trait. The consistency of factor analytic results was a prominent criterion, particularly for Costa and McCrae. Indeed, this debate has been so central to the history of personality trait psychology that Pervin (1994) argues that progress in trait theory can be equated to consensus on the number of factors. While Pervin was writing over 20 years ago, the fundamental issue of the importance of the number of factors decision for the identification of the basic units on which personality models and theory are based remains.

For example, perhaps the primary competing model to the FFM is the six-factor HEXACO model, operationalized in the HEXACO Personality Inventory (HEXACO-PI: Lee & Ashton, 2004). The six factors of the HEXACO model are Honesty-Humility, Emotionality, Extraversion, Agreeableness, Conscientiousness, and Openness to Experience. Early work suggesting that six, not five factors may be a better representation of the broad domain of normal range human personality came from studies using the Jackson Personality Inventory (JPI; Jackson, 1970, 1994) and the Personality Research Form (PRF; Jackson, 1967, 1984). Later work from the lexical tradition (discussed above) has also provided some support for this notion (e.g., Saucier, 2009). In a long series of studies, Ashton and Lee (e.g., Ashton & Lee, 2001) have provided theoretical justification for their retained six factors.

In the context of the present discussion, we argue that such debates on the very nature of the basic units of human personality boil down to a largely unsolvable problem in the context of the factor model – namely, the optimal number of factors to extract. Debate arises when researchers select different input sets, and find a different number of factors are required to "account for" the data. In doing so, new traits (factors) are added, or old traits (factors) are removed from personality models with often post hoc theoretical rationales provided to justify the new trait.

Rotational indeterminacy Rotational indeterminacy concerns the fact that for a given factor solution, it is possible to rotate or transform the relations between items to reproduce the variance-covariance matrix in an infinite number of ways (Mulaik, 2005, p. 174). Thurstone (1947) proposed a solution to this problem, that of "simple structure." In essence, Thurstone's solution involved assuming that a given set of items is linearly related to only a subset of common factors. Therefore, if we can transform a given solution to locate this subset, then a "true" structure will emerge in which items will load only on their given subset. A further consequence of this is that any given sub-sample of items related to the same factor may be used to consistently identify said factor.

The consistency in the identification of the five factors of the FFM is held up as a marker of its power and utility as a descriptive model of personality. However, an important debate which stems directly from this issue concerns just how consistent these factors are. While supporters of the FFM will argue that variants across samples and item sets are near identical, critics point out that while many studies have located five factors, it is not entirely clear that these are the same five factors in each study (Hayes, 1994). For example, we may expect that if the factors identified by different inventories across studies are indeed the same five factors, that we would see high correlations between scores on say Extraversion, across measures and studies. That is, we would see strong evidence for convergent validity. Pace and Brannick (2010) investigated this very issue using data gathered from studies which had reported the correlations between two or more personality measures as well as reliability information for these scales. Meta-analyses were conducted on correlations between scales measuring each of the five broad factors of the FFM, with separate estimates for all scales, and for scales specifically designed to measure the FFM. All analyses were corrected for sampling error only. Table 29.2 summarizes their findings.

Pace and Brannick's (2010) results show that scales that share the same name and purport to measure the same construct, share mean convergent validity estimates indicating less than half of the variability in trait scores is shared. Clearly, there is considerable divergence in the nature of the five factor constructs across inventories.

A second, and perhaps more direct, example of the issue of rotational indeterminacy comes from the discussion of competing models of the structure of normal range human personality. We return again to the HEXACO model discussed previously. While a number of factors share labels across the FFM and HEXACO, arguments are made that these are **rotational variants** of one another. For example, the variant of Extraversion within the HEXACO model is defined by sociability and liveliness, rather than aspects of bravery and toughness; the variant of Agreeableness is defined by gentleness and patience with the addition of anger and temper, traditionally viewed as part of the negative pole of Neuroticism within the FFM; and the variant of Openness to Experience is defined by intellect, imagination, and unconventionality (Ashton, Lee, & Goldberg,

Table 29.2 Summary of the findings from Pace and Brannick (2010).

	All inventories			FFM specific inventories		
	K	N	Convergent validity	K	N	Convergent validity
Neuroticism	33	7,717	0.51	8	1,489	0.68
Extraversion	103	28,521	0.56	9	2,449	0.61
Openness to Experience	25	4,750	0.45	9	1,519	0.48
Agreeableness	35	6,320	0.47	10	2,930	0.61
Conscientiousness	55	9,868	0.43	10	2,573	0.63

2004). That such debates have been so central to personality trait theory is a marker of the influence that factor analysis has had on the framing of theoretical questions surrounding them.

Five-Factor Theory (FFT)

Here, we have argued based on a set of **birthmarks** evident in the debates and empirical evidence within personality trait psychology, that the use of factor analysis within personality trait psychology can be viewed as an example of a tools-to-theories heuristic. Others may of course argue that these examples are not strong support for our conclusion. However, there is perhaps a somewhat more direct sign of such a relation, specifically, the rationale for the FFT. FFT was explicitly discussed as "… an effort to construct such a theory that is consistent with the current knowledge about personality." (McCrae & Costa, 1999). In their chapter, McCrae and Costa go on to discuss the flurry of evidence supporting this acquired knowledge, which is, by and large, based on the results of factor analytic studies supporting five factors, and subsequent applied studies using these five factors. In short, the "theory" was a direct result of the empirical results from the tools.

Interplay Between Tools, Theories, and Data in Personality Trait Psychology

It is clear that the method of factor analysis was inspired by theory, the theory of general ability. It has been noted that Spearman's statistical innovation played second fiddle in the 1904 paper to the theoretical notion of general ability, with only a small amount of the original paper recognizable as a modern factor analysis (Bartholomew, 2007). The tool became a way to operationalize this theory. The resultant connection between the trait approach, latent variables, and factor analysis meant that in subsequent applications the broad theoretical ideas became implicit and, as has been argued by Borsboom (2008), became laden with specific philosophical conclusions. In adopting Spearman's factor analytic method, Cattell, for example (who happened to be a student of Spearman), was drawing on this same notion of using observed association to probe underlying cause. As we move forward in time and the applications of factor analysis increase, the interplay of tools and data can be seen to manifest in theoretical issues rooted in data prestructuring, the number of factors question, and rotational indeterminacy.

An interesting question to ask is, what would personality trait psychology have looked like, if factor analysis had not been the tool of choice? In the context of cognitive ability this has been discussed in reference to Thompson's bonds model (see Bartholomew, Deary, & Lawn, 2009). In brief, the bonds model provided an explanation for observed patterns of correlations without the need for a latent common cause variable. More Further, Van der Maas et. al., (2006) provided a detailed exposition of another alternative causal structure that could underlie the same pattern of observed correlation, a dynamic model of reciprocal causation. Would trait psychology have developed if tools based on these theories had been preferred?

Again, current trait psychology provides us with an interesting case. Over the past 10 years there has been increasing interest in the network perspective with respect to psychopathology (Borsboom & Cramer, 2013) and normal range human personality (Cramer et al., 2012). This approach does not require or insist upon a latent variable, but instead, posits a network of interrelating symptoms or behaviors. The network approach itself has been made viable by progress in three areas. First, the availability of high-powered personal computing has allowed for advances in statistical procedures and estimation. Second, new tools for data collection, such as experience sampling, have enabled detailed longitudinal measurement of key variables. Indeed, experience sampling, a tool for in-depth momentary data collection, has been influential in and of itself, being a focal element of recent ideas such as Whole Trait Theory (Fleeson & Jayawickreme, 2015). Finally, conceptual advances driven, in part, by proposed deficiencies of the factor model in answering the questions of interest within the field. In terms of shaping thinking regarding the nature of traits, while factor analysis encourages theorizing on common causes, network analysis encourages theorizing on local interactions between more specific behaviors, thoughts, and feelings (e.g., Murray, Eisner, & Ribeuad, 2016). For example, the concept of centrality, crudely the most important or connected nodes within the network, might encourage theorizing on which behaviors and so on are particularly critical in influencing an individual's broader pattern of behavior. Similarly, network analysis is likely to foster individual difference theories related not only to behavior, thought, and feeling **levels**, but also in the patterns of their interaction within a person.

Summary

In the current chapter, we have provided a reflection on our field, through the lens of the tools-to-theories heuristic. Such a lens can be powerful as it serves to highlight how the statistical tools at a researcher's disposal can shape the theoretical models that develop within research fields, and as such, how the fallibilities of those methods become embedded within the evidence for those theories. As Gigerenzer (1991) puts it; "In those cases where the tools-to-theories heuristic operates, this means taking a long hard look at the tools – and the statistical tools of psychologists are overdue for such a skeptical inspection." (p. 16).

In closing a volume on advanced statistical methodologies for psychometric data analysis, this message of careful skeptical reflection appears apt.

References

Allen, T. A., & DeYoung, C. G. (2015). Personality neuroscience and the five factor model. In T. A. Widiger (Ed.). *Oxford handbook of the five factor model.* New York: Oxford University Press.

Allport, G. W., & Odbert, H. S. (1936). Trait-names: A psycho-lexical study. *Psychological Monographs, 47,* (1, Whole No. 211).

Ashton, M. C., & Lee, K. (2001). A theoretical basis for the major dimensions of personality. *European Journal of Personality, 15,* 327–353.

Ashton, M. C., Lee, K., & Goldberg, L. R. (2004). A hierarchical analysis of 1,710 English personality-descriptive adjectives. *Journal of Personality and Social Psychology, 87,* 707–721.

Bartholomew, D. J. (2007). The three faces of factor analysis. In R. Cudek & R. C. MacCallum (Eds.). *Factor analysis at 100: Historical developments and future directions.* London: Lawrence Erlbaum Associates.

Bartholomew, D. J., Deary, I. J., & Lawn, M. (2009). A new lease of life for Thomson's bonds model of intelligence. *Psychological Review, 116,* 567–579.

Block, J. (1995). A contrarian view of the five-factor approach to personality description. *Psychological Bulletin, 117,* 187–215.

Block, J. (2001). Millennial contrarianism: The five-factor approach to personality description 5 years later. *Journal of Research in Personality, 35,* 98–107.

Block, J. (2010). The five-factor framing of personality and beyond: Some ruminations. *Psychological Inquiry, 21,* 2–25.

Borgatta, E. F. (1964). The structure of personality characteristics. *Behavioral Science, 9,* 8–17.

Borsboom, D. (2005). *Measuring the mind: Conceptual issues in contemporary psychometrics.* Cambridge: Cambridge University Press.

Borsboom, D. (2008). Latent variable theory. *Measurement: Interdisciplinary Research and Perspectives, 6,* 25–53.

Borsboom, D., & Cramer, A. O. (2013). Network analysis: an integrative approach to the structure of psychopathology. *Annual Review of Clinical Psychology, 9,* 91–121.

Cattell, R. B. (1943a). The description of personality: I. Foundations of trait measurement. *Psychological Review, 50,* 559–594.

Cattell, R. B. (1943b). The description of personality: Basic traits resolved into clusters. *Journal of Abnormal and Social Psychology, 38,* 476–506.

Cattell, R. B. (1945). The description of personality: principles and findings in a factor analysis. *American Journal of Psychology, 58,* 69–90.

Cattell, R. B. (1966). The scree test for the number of factors. *Multivariate Behavioral Research, 1,* 245–276.

Cattell, R. B. (1974). Radial parcel factoring-vs-item factoring in defining personality structure in questionnaires: Theory and experimental checks. *Australian Journal of Psychology, 26,* 103–119.

Costa, P. T., Busch, C. M., Zonderman, A. B., & McCrae, R. R. (1986). Correlations of MMPI factor scales with measures of the Five Factor Model of personality. *Journal of Personality Assessment, 50,* 640–650.

Costa, P. T., & McCrae, R. R. (1976). Age differences in personality structure: A cluster analytic approach. *Journal of Gerontology, 31,* 564–570.

Costa P. T., & McCrae, R. R. (1978). Objective personality assessment. In M. Storandt, I. Siegler, & M. F. Elias (Eds.). *The clinical psychology of aging.* New York: Plenum.

Costa. P. T., & McCrae, R. R. (1992a). *Revised NEO personality inventory (NEO-PI-R) and NEO Five-Factor Inventory (NEO-FFI) professional manual.* Odessa, FL: Psychological Assessment Resources.

Costa, P. T., & McCrae, R. R. (1992b). Four ways five factors are basic. *Personality and Individual Differences, 13,* 653–665.

Costa, P. T., & McCrae, R. R. (1992c). Reply to Eysenck. *Personality and Individual Differences, 13*, 861–865.

Costa, P. T., & McCrae, R. R. (2008). The revised NEO Personality Inventory (neo-pi-r). *In The SAGE handbook of personality theory and assessment, 2*, 179–198.

Costa. P. T., Jr., McCrae, R. R., & Dye. D. A. (1991). Facet scales for Agreeableness and Conscientiousness: A revision of the NEO Personality Inventory. *Personality and Individual Differences, 12*, 887–898.

Costa, P. T., Zonderman, A. B., McCrae, R. R., & Williams, R. B. (1985). Content and comprehensiveness in the MMPI: An item factor analysis in a normal adult sample. *Journal of Personality and Social Psychology, 48*, 925–933.

Cramer, A. O., Sluis, S., Noordhof, A., Wichers, M., Geschwind, N., Aggen, S. H., ... & Borsboom, D. (2012). Dimensions of normal personality as networks in search of equilibrium: You can't like parties if you don't like people. *European Journal of Personality, 26*, 414–431.

Eysenck, H. J. (1991). Dimensions of personality: 16, 5 or 3? – Criteria for a taxonomic paradigm. *Personality and Individual Differences, 12*, 773–790.

Eysenck, H. J. (1992). Four ways five factors are not basic. *Personality and Individual Differences, 13*, 667–673

Fabrigar, L. R., Wegener, D. T., MacCallum, R. C., & Strahan, E. J. (1999). Evaluating the use of exploratory factor analysis in psychological research. *Psychological Methods, 4*, 272–299.

Fiske, D. W. (1949). Consistency of the factorial structures of personality ratings from different sources. *Journal of Abnormal and Social Psychology, 44*, 329–344.

Fleeson, W., & Jayawickreme, E. (2015). Whole trait theory. *Journal of Research in Personality, 56*, 82–92.

Gigerenzer, G. (1991). From tools to theories: A heuristic of discovery in cognitive psychology. *Psychological Review, 98*, 254–267.

Gigerenzer, G. (1992). Discovery in cognitive psychology: New tools inspire new theories. *Science in Context, 5*, 329–350.

Gigerenzer, G., & Sturm, T. (2007). Tools=Theories=Data? On some circular dynamics in cognitive science. In M. G. Ash & T. Sturm (Eds.). *Psychology's territories: Historical and contemporary perspectives from different disciplines.* Mahwah: NJ: Lawrence Erlbaum.

Goldberg, L. R. (1981). Unconfounding situational attributions from uncertain, neutral, and ambiguous ones: A psychometric analysis of descriptions of oneself and various types of others. *Journal of Personality and Social Psychology, 41*, 517–552.

Goldberg, L. R. (1990). An alternative "Description of personality": The Big-Five factor structure. *Journal of Personality and Social Psychology, 59*, 1216–1229.

Goldberg, L. R. (1993). The structure of phenotypic personality traits. *American Psychologist, 48*, 26–34.

Gosling, S. D., Rentfrow, P. J., & Swann, W. B. (2003). A very brief measure of the Big-Five personality domains. *Journal of Research in Personality, 37*, 504–528.

Hayes, N. (1994). *Foundations of psychology.* London: Routledge.

Jackson, D. N. (1967). *Personality research form manual.* Goshen, NY: Research Psychologist Press.

Jackson, D. N. (1970). A sequential system for personality scale construction. In C. D. Speilberger (Ed.). *Current topics in clinical and community psychology* (Vol. 2). New York: Academic Press.

Jackson, D. N. (1984). *Personality research form manual.* Port Huron, MI: Research Psychologists Press.

Jackson, D. N. (1994). *Jackson personality inventory-revised manual.* Port Huron, MI: Research Psychologists Press.

John, O. P., Angleitner, A., & Ostendorf, F. (1988). The lexical approach to personality: A historical review of trait taxonomic research. *European Journal of Personality, 2*, 171–203.

John, O. P., Donahue, E. M., & Kentle, R. L. (1991). *The Big Five Inventory – versions 4a and 54.* Berkeley, CA: University of California, Berkeley, Institute of Personality and Social Research.

John, O. P., & Srivastava, S. (1999). The Big-Five trait taxonomy: History, measurement, and theoretical perspectives. In L. Pervin & O. P. John (Eds.). *Handbook of personality: Theory and Research* (2nd ed.) (pp. 139–153). The Guilford Press: New York.

Jöreskog, K. G. (1967). A general approach to confirmatory maximum likelihood factor analysis. *ETS Research Bulletin Series, 2,* 183–202.

Kaiser, H. F. (1970). A second generation Little Jiffy. *Psychometrika, 35,* 401–415

Klages, L. (1926). *The science of character* (Trans. 1932). London: Allen & Unwin.

Lee, K., & Ashton, M. C. (2004). Psychometric properties of the HEXACO Personality Inventory. *Multivariate Behavioral Research, 39,* 329–358.

Lord, F. M. (1955). Sampling fluctuations resulting from the sampling of test items. *Psychometrika, 20,* 1–22.

McAdams, D. P. (1992). The five-factor model in personality: A critical appraisal. *Journal of Personality, 60,* 329–361.

McCrae, R. R., & Costa, P. T. (1980). Openness to experience and ego level in Loevinger's sentence completion test: Dispositional contributions to developmental models of personality. *Journal of Personality and Social Psychology, 39,* 1179–1190.

McCrae, R. R., & Costa, P. T. (1985). Comparison of EPI and psychoticism scales with measures of the Five-Factor Model of personality. *Personality and Individual Differences, 6,* 587–597.

McCrae, R. R., & Costa, P. T. (1987). Validation of the five-factor model of personality across instruments and observers. *Journal of Personality and Social Psychology, 52,* 81–90.

McCrae, R. R., & Costa, P. T. (1989). The structure of interpersonal traits: Wiggin's circumplex and the Five Factor Model. *Journal of Personality and Social Psychology, 56,* 586–595.

McCrae, R. R., & Costa P. T. (1999). A Five-Factor Theory of personality. In L. A. Pervin & O. P. John (Eds.). *Handbook of personality: Theory and research* (2nd ed.) (pp. 139–153). The Guilford Press: New York.

McCrae, R. R., & Costa, P. T. (2008). Empirical and theoretical status of the five-factor model of personality traits. *The SAGE handbook of personality theory and assessment, 1,* 273–294.

McCrae. R. R., Costa, P. T., & Busch, C. M. (1986). Evaluating comprehensiveness in personality systems: The California Q-Set and the five-factor model. *Journal of Personality, 54,* 430–446.

Mischel, W. (1968). *Personality and assessment.* New York: John Wiley & Sons, Inc.

Mulaik, S. (2005). Looking back on the indeterminacy controversies in factor analysis. In A. Maydeu-Olivares, and J. J. McCardle (Eds.), *Contemporary psychometrics.* Mahwah: NJ: Lawrence Erlbaum.

Murray, A. L., Eisner, M., & Ribeaud, D. (2016). The development of the general factor of psychopathology "p factor" through childhood and adolescence. *Journal of Abnormal Child Psychology, 44*(8), 1573–1586.

Norman, W. T. (1963). Toward an adequate taxonomy of personality attributes: Replicated factor structure in peer nomination personality ratings. *The Journal of Abnormal and Social Psychology, 66,* 574–583.

Norman, W. T. (1967). *2800 personality trait descriptors: Normative operating characteristics for a University population.* Ann Arbor: University of Michigan, Department of Psychology.

Pace, V. L., & Brannick, M. T. (2010). How similar are personality scales of the "same" construct? A meta-analytic investigation. *Personality and Individual Differences, 49,* 669–676.

Pervin, L. A. (1994). A critical analysis of current trait theory. *Psychological Inquiry, 2,* 103–113.

Piedmont, R. L., McCrae, R. R., & Costa, P. T. (1991). Adjective check list scales and the five-factor model. *Journal of Personality and Social Psychology, 60,* 630–637.

Preacher, K. J., & MacCallum, R. C. (2003). Repairing Tom Swift's electric factor analysis machine. *Understanding Statistics, 2,* 13–43.

Preacher, K. J., Zhang, G., Kim, C., & Mels, G. (2013). Choosing the optimal number of factors in exploratory factor analysis: A model selection perspective. *Multivariate Behavioral Research, 48*, 28–56.

Revelle, W. (2009). Personality structure and measurement: The contributions of Raymond Cattell. *British Journal of Psychology, 100*, 253–257.

Saucier, G. (2009). Recurrent personality dimensions in inclusive lexical studies: Indications for a Big Six structure. *Journal of Personality, 77*, 1577–1614.

Saucier, G., Thalmayer, A. G., Payne, D. L., Carlson, R., Sanogo, L., Ole-Kotikash, L., ... & Szirmák, Z. (2014). A basic bivariate structure of personality attributes evident across nine languages. *Journal of Personality, 82*, 1–14.

Spearman, C. (1904). General intelligence, objectively determined and measured. *American Journal of Psychology, 15*, 201–293.

Thurstone, L. L. (1931). Multiple factor analysis. *Psychological Review, 38*, 406–427.

Thurstone, L. L. (1947). *Multiple factor analysis.* Chicago: University of Chicago Press.

Tupes, E. C., & Christal, R. E. (1961). *Recurrent personality factors based on trait ratings. Technical Report ASD-TR-61-97.* Personnel Laboratory, Aeronautical Systems Division, Air Force Systems Command, United States Air Force.

Van der Maas, H. L., Dolan, C. V., Grasman, R. P., Wicherts, J. M., Huizenga, H. M., & Raijmakers, M. E. (2006). A dynamical model of general intelligence: the positive manifold of intelligence by mutualism. *Psychological Review, 113*, 842–861.

Zuckerman, M. (1992). What is a basic factor and which factors are basic? Turtles all the way down? *Personality and Individual Differences, 13*, 675–681.

Code Appendix

Code 1 Example R code for production of Figure 29.2.

Note that text following # is author annotation.

```
## Required packages
library(RISmed)

# There is a warning on when large searches are conducted using these
# functions. Limit large jobs to either weekends or between 9:00 PM and
# 5:00 AM Eastern time during weekdays. Failure to comply with this policy
# may result in an IP address being blocked from accessing NCBI.

# Set up an empty array to read results into
tally <- array()

# For loop which searches by increments of a year(x) from 1943 to 2015
# and saves the count of articles found.
```

```
x <- 1
for (i in 1943:2015){
  Sys.sleep(1)
  r <- EUtilsSummary("psychology[journal] factor analysis",
                    type='esearch',
                    db='pubmed',mindate=i, maxdate=i)
  tally[x] <- QueryCount(r)
  x <- x + 1
}


# Assigns labels which are the years.
names(tally) <- 1943:2015

# produce a barplot of the counts per year
barplot(tally, las=2, ylim=c(0,600),
        main="Number of PubMed articles containing retrotransposon")
```

30

Network Psychometrics

Sacha Epskamp, Gunter Maris, Lourens J. Waldorp, and Denny Borsboom

Introduction

"In fact, statistical field theory may have even more to offer. It always struck me that there appears to be a close connection between the basic expressions underlying item-response theory and the solutions of elementary lattice fields in statistical physics. For instance, there is almost a one-to-one formal correspondence of the solution of the Ising model (a lattice with nearest neighbor interaction between binary-valued sites; e.g., Kindermann & Snell (1980), Chapter 1) and the Rasch model Fischer (1974). (Molenaar, 2003, p. 82)"

In recent years, network models have been proposed as an alternative way of looking at psychometric problems Van der Maas et al. (2006); Cramer, Waldorp, van der Maas& Borsboom (2010); Borsboom & Cramer (2013). In these models, psychometric item responses are conceived of as proxies for variables that directly interact with each other. For example, the symptoms of depression (such as loss of energy, sleep problems, and low self-esteem) are traditionally thought of as being determined by a common latent variable (depression, or the liability to become depressed; Aggen, Neale, and Kendler (2005)). In network models, these symptoms are instead hypothesized to form networks of mutually reinforcing variables (e.g., sleep problems may lead to loss of energy, which may lead to low self-esteem, which may cause rumination that in turn may reinforce sleep problems). On the face of it, such network models offer an entirely different conceptualization of why psychometric variables cluster in the way that they do. However, it has also been suggested in the literature that latent variables may somehow correspond to sets of tightly intertwined observables (e.g., see the Appendix of Van der Maas et al. (2006)), and as the above quote shows, (Molenaar, 2003) already suspected that network models in physics are closely connected to psychometric models with latent variables.

In the current chapter, we aim to make this connection explicit. As we will show, a particular class of latent variable models (namely, multidimensional item response theory models) yields exactly the same probability distribution over the observed variables as a particular class of network models (namely, Ising models). In the current

---

The Wiley Handbook of Psychometric Testing: A Multidisciplinary Reference on Survey, Scale and Test Development, First Edition. Edited by Paul Irwing, Tom Booth, and David J. Hughes.
© 2018 John Wiley & Sons Ltd. Published 2020 by John Wiley & Sons Ltd.

chapter, we exploit the consequences of this equivalence. We will first introduce the general class of models used in network analysis called Markov random fields. Specifically, we will discuss the Markov random field for binary data called the *Ising model*, which originated from statistical physics but has since been used in many fields of science. We will show how the Ising model relates to psychometrical practice, with a focus on the equivalence between the Ising model and multidimensional item response theory. We will demonstrate how the Ising model can be estimated, and finally we will discuss the conceptual implications of this equivalence.

Notation

Throughout this chapter we will denote random variables with capital letters and possible realizations with lower-case letters; vectors will be represented with bold-faced letters. For parameters, we will use bold-faced capital letters to indicate matrices instead of vectors, whereas for random variables we will use bold-faced capital letters to indicate a random vector. Roman letters will be used to denote observable variables and parameters (such as the number of nodes), and Greek letters will be used to denote unobservable variables and parameters that need to be estimated.

In this chapter we will mainly model the random vector $\boldsymbol{X}^\top = [X_1 \, X_2 \ldots X_P]$ containing P binary variables that take the values 1 (e.g., correct, true, or yes) and -1 (e.g., incorrect, false, or no). We will denote a realization, or *state*, of $\boldsymbol{X}$ with $\boldsymbol{x}^\top = [x_1 \, x_2 \ldots x_p]$. Let N be the number of observations and $n(\boldsymbol{x})$ the number of observations that have response pattern $\boldsymbol{x}$. Furthermore, let i denote the subscript of a random variable and j the subscript of a different random variable ($j \neq i$). Thus, X_i is the ith random variable and x_i its realization. The superscript $-(\ldots)$ will indicate that elements are removed from a vector; for example, $\boldsymbol{X}^{-(i)}$ indicates the random vector $\boldsymbol{X}$ without X_i: $\boldsymbol{X}^{-(i)} = [X_1, \ldots, X_{i-1}, X_{i+1}, \ldots X_P]$, and $\boldsymbol{x}^{-(i)}$ indicates its realization. Similarly, $\boldsymbol{X}^{-(i,j)}$ indicates $\boldsymbol{X}$ without X_i and X_j and $\boldsymbol{x}^{-(i,j)}$ its realization. An overview of all notations used in this chapter can be seen in Appendix.

Markov Random Fields

A network, also called a graph, can be encoded as a set G consisting of two sets: V, which contains the nodes in the network, and E, which contains the edges that connect these nodes. For example, the graph in Figure 30.1 contains three nodes, $V = \{1, 2, 3\}$, which are connected by two edges, $E = \{(1, 2), (2, 3)\}$. We will use this type of network to represent a *pairwise Markov random field* (PMRF; Lauritzen (1996); Murphy (2012)), in which nodes represent observed random variables[1] and edges represent (conditional) association between two nodes. More importantly, the absence of an edge represents the Markov property that two nodes are conditionally independent given all other nodes in the network:

$$X_i \amalg X_j \mid \boldsymbol{X}^{-(i,j)} = \boldsymbol{x}^{-(i,j)} \Leftrightarrow (i,j) \notin E. \tag{30.1}$$

---

[1] Throughout this chapter, nodes in a network designate variables, hence the terms are used interchangeably.

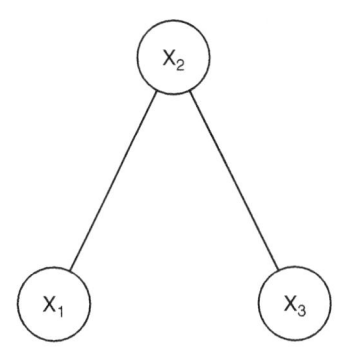

Figure 30.1 Example of a PMRF of three nodes, X_1, X_2, and X_3, connected by two edges, one between X_1 and X_2 and one between X_2 and X_3.

Thus, a PMRF encodes the independence structure of the system of nodes. In the case of Figure 30.1, X_1 and X_3 are independent given that we know $X_2 = x_2$. This could be due to several reasons: there might be a causal path from X_1 to X_3 or vice versa, X_2 might be the common cause of X_1 and X_3, unobserved variables might cause the dependencies between X_1 and X_2 and X_2 and X_3, or the edges in the network might indicate actual pairwise interactions between X_1 and X_2 and X_2 and X_3.

Of particular interest to psychometrics are models in which the presence of latent common causes induces associations among the observed variables. If such a common cause model holds, we cannot condition on any observed variable to completely remove the association between two nodes Pearl (2000). Thus, if an unobserved variable acts as a common cause to some of the observed variables, we should find a fully connected clique in the PMRF that describes the associations among these nodes. The network in Figure 30.1, for example, cannot represent associations between three nodes that are subject to the influence of a latent common cause; if that were the case, it would be impossible to obtain conditional independence between X_1 and X_3 by conditioning on X_2.

Parameterizing Markov random fields

A PMRF can be parameterized as a product of strictly positive potential functions $\phi(x)$ Murphy (2012):

$$\Pr(X = x) = \frac{1}{Z} \prod_i \phi_i(x_i) \prod_{<ij>} \phi_{ij}(x_i, x_j), \qquad (30.2)$$

in which $\prod_i$ takes the product over all nodes, $i = 1, 2, \ldots, P$, $\prod_{<ij>}$ takes the product over all distinct pairs of nodes i and j ($j > i$), and Z is a normalizing constant such that the probability function sums to unity over all possible patterns of observations in the sample space:

$$Z = \sum_x \prod_i \phi_i(x_i) \prod_{<ij>} \phi_{ij}(x_i, x_j).$$

Here, $\sum_x$ takes the sum over all possible realizations of X. All $\phi(x)$ functions result in positive real numbers, which encode the *potentials*: the preference for the relevant part of X to be in some state. The $\phi_i(x_i)$ functions encode the node potentials of the network: the preference of node X_i to be in state x_i, regardless of the state of the other nodes in the network. Thus, $\phi_i(x_i)$ maps the potential for X_i to take the value x_i regardless of the rest of the network. If $\phi_i(x_i) = 0$, for instance, then X_i will never take the value x_i, $\phi_i(x_i) = 1$ indicates that there is no preference for X_i to take any particular value, and $\phi_i(x_i) = \infty$ indicates that the system always prefers X_i to take the value x_i. The $\phi_{ij}(x_i, x_j)$ functions encode the pairwise potentials of the network: the preference of nodes X_i and X_j to both be in states x_i and x_j. As $\phi_{ij}(x_i, x_j)$ grows higher we would expect to observe $X_j = x_j$ whenever $X_i = x_i$. Note that the potential functions are not identified; we can multiply both $\phi_i(x_i)$ or $\phi_{ij}(x_i, x_j)$ with some constant for all possible outcomes of x_i, in which case this constant becomes a constant multiplier to Equation 30.2 and is canceled out in the normalizing constant Z. A typical identification constraint on the potential functions is to set the marginal geometric means of all outcomes equal to 1; over all possible outcomes of each argument, the logarithm of each potential function should sum to 0:

$$\sum_{x_i} \ln \phi_i(x_i) = \sum_{x_i} \ln \phi_{ij}(x_i, x_j) = \sum_{x_j} \ln \phi_{ij}(x_i, x_j) = 0 \quad \forall x_i, x_j, \qquad (30.3)$$

in which $\sum_{x_i}$ denotes the sum over all possible realizations for X_i, and $\sum_{x_j}$ denotes the sum over all possible realizations of X_j.

We assume that every node has a potential function $\phi_i(x_i)$ and nodes only have a relevant pairwise potential function $\phi_{ij}(x_i, x_j)$ when they are connected by an edge; thus, two unconnected nodes have a constant pairwise potential function which, due to the identification above, is equal to 1 for all possible realizations of X_i and X_j:

$$\phi_{ij}(x_i, x_j) = 1 \quad \forall x_i, x_j \Leftrightarrow (i,j) \notin E. \qquad (30.4)$$

From Equation 30.2 it follows that the distribution of X marginalized over X_k and X_l, that is, the marginal distribution of $X^{-(k,l)}$ (the random vector X without elements X_k and X_l), has the following form:

$$\Pr\left(X^{-(k,l)} = x^{-(k,l)}\right) = \sum_{x_k, x_l} \Pr(X = x)$$

$$= \frac{1}{Z} \prod_{i \notin \{k,l\}} \phi_i(x_i) \prod_{<ij \notin \{k,l\}>} \phi_{ij}(x_i, x_j)$$

$$\sum_{x_k, x_l} \left(\phi_k(x_k) \phi_l(x_l) \phi_{kl}(x_k, x_l) \prod_{i \notin \{k,l\}} \phi_{ik}(x_i, x_k) \phi_{il}(x_i, x_l) \right), \qquad (30.5)$$

in which $\prod_{i \notin \{k,l\}}$ takes the product over all nodes except node k and l and $\prod_{<ij \notin \{k,l\}>}$ takes the product over all unique pairs of nodes that do not involve k and l. The expression in Equation 30.5 has two important consequences. First, Equation 30.5 does not have the form of Equation 30.2; a PMRF is *not* a PMRF under marginalization. Second, by dividing Equation 30.2 by Equation 30.5, an expression can be obtained for the conditional distribution of $\{X_k, X_l\}$ given that we know $\boldsymbol{X}^{-(k,l)} = \boldsymbol{x}^{-(k,l)}$:

$$\Pr\left(X_k, X_l \mid \boldsymbol{X}^{-(k,l)} = \boldsymbol{x}^{-(k,l)}\right) = \frac{\Pr(\boldsymbol{X} = \boldsymbol{x})}{\Pr\left(\boldsymbol{X}^{-(k,l)} = \boldsymbol{x}^{-(k,l)}\right)}$$

$$= \frac{\phi_k^*(x_k)\,\phi_l^*(x_l)\,\phi_{kl}(x_k, x_l)}{\sum_{x_k, x_l} \phi_k^*(x_k)\,\phi_l^*(x_l)\,\phi_{kl}(x_k, x_l)}, \qquad (30.6)$$

in which $\phi_k^*(x_k) = \phi_k(x_k) \prod_{i \notin \{k,l\}} \phi_{ik}(x_i, x_k)$ and $\phi_l^*(x_l) = \phi_l(x_l) \prod_{i \notin \{k,l\}} \phi_{il}(x_i, x_l)$. Now, Equation 30.6 *does* have the same form as Equation 30.2; a PMRF *is* a PMRF under conditioning. Furthermore, if there is no edge between nodes k and l, $\phi_{kl}(x_k, x_l) = 1$ according to Equation 30.4, in which case Equation 30.6 reduces to a product of two independent functions of x_k and x_l which renders X_k and X_l independent; thus proving the Markov property in Equation 30.1.

The Ising model

The node potential functions $\phi_i(x_i)$ can map a unique potential for every possible realization of X_i, and the pairwise potential functions $\phi_{ij}(x_i, x_j)$ can likewise map unique potentials to every possible pair of outcomes for X_i and X_j. When the data are binary, only two realizations are possible for x_i, while four realizations are possible for the pair x_i and x_j. Under the constraint that the log potential functions should sum to 0 over all marginals, this means that in the binary case each potential function has one degree of freedom. If we let all X's take the values 1 and -1, there exists a conveniently log-linear model representation for the potential functions:

$$\ln \phi_i(x_i) = \tau_i x_i,$$
$$\ln \phi_{ij}(x_i, x_j) = \omega_{ij} x_i x_j.$$

The parameters τ_i and ω_{ij} are real numbers. In the case that $x_i = 1$ and $x_j = 1$, it can be seen that these parameters form an identity link with the logarithm of the potential functions:

$$\tau_i = \ln \phi_i(1),$$
$$\omega_{ij} = \ln \phi_{ij}(1,1).$$

These parameters are centered around 0 and have intuitive interpretations. The τ_i parameters can be interpreted as *threshold parameters*. If $\tau_i = 0$ the model does not prefer to be in one state or the other, and if τ_i is higher (lower) the model prefers node X_i to be in state 1 (-1). The ω_{ij} parameters are the *network parameters* and denote the pairwise interaction between nodes X_i and X_j; if $\omega_{ij} = 0$ there is no edge between nodes X_i and X_j.

$$\omega_{ij} \begin{cases} = 0 & \text{if } (i,j) \notin E, \\ \in \mathbb{R} & \text{if } (i,j) \in E. \end{cases} \quad (30.7)$$

The higher (lower) ω_{ij} becomes, the more nodes X_i and X_j prefer to be in the same (different) state. Implementing these potential functions in Equation 30.2 gives the following distribution for X:

$$\Pr(X = x) = \frac{1}{Z}\exp\left(\sum_i \tau_i x_i + \sum_{<ij>} \omega_{ij} x_i x_j\right)$$

$$Z = \sum_x \exp\left(\sum_i \tau_i x_i + \sum_{<ij>} \omega_{ij} x_i x_j\right), \quad (30.8)$$

which is known as the Ising model Ising (1925).

For example, consider the PMRF in Figure 30.1. In this network there are three nodes (X_1, X_2, and X_3), and two edges (between X_1 and X_2, and between X_2 and X_3). Suppose these three nodes are binary, and take the values 1 and −1. We can then model this PMRF as an Ising model with three threshold parameters, τ_1, τ_2, and τ_3, and two network parameters, ω_{12} and ω_{23}. Suppose we set all threshold parameters to $\tau_1 = \tau_2 = \tau_3 = -0.1$, which indicates that all nodes have a general preference to be in the state −1. Furthermore we can set the two network parameters to $\omega_{12} = \omega_{23} = 0.5$. Thus, X_1 and X_2 prefer to be in the same state, and X_2 and X_3 prefer to be in the same state as well. Due to these interactions, X_1 and X_3 become associated; these nodes also prefer to be in the same state, even though they are independent once we condition on X_2. We can then compute the nonnormalized potentials $\exp\left(\sum_i \tau_i x_i + \sum_{<ij>} \omega_{ij} x_i x_j\right)$ for all possible outcomes of X, and finally divide that value by the sum over all nonnormalized potentials to compute the probabilities of each possible outcome. For instance, for the state $X_1 = -1$, $X_2 = 1$, and $X_3 = -1$, we can compute the potential as $\exp(-0.1 + 0.1 + -0.1 + -0.5 + -0.5) \approx 0.332$. Computing all these potentials and summing them leads to the normalizing constant of $Z \approx 10.443$, which can then be used to compute the probabilities of each state. These values can be seen in Table 30.1.

Table 30.1 Probability of all states from the network in Figure 30.1.

x_1	x_2	x_3	Potential	Probability
−1	−1	−1	3.6693	.3514
1	−1	−1	1.1052	.1058
−1	1	−1	0.4066	.0389
1	1	−1	0.9048	.0866
−1	−1	1	1.1052	.1058
1	−1	1	0.3329	.0319
−1	1	1	0.9048	.0866
1	1	1	2.0138	.1928

Not surprisingly, the probability $Pr(X_1 = -1, X_2 = -1, X_3 = -1)$ is the most probable state in Table 30.1, due to the the threshold parameters being all negative. Furthermore, the probability $P(X_1 = 1, X_2 = 1, X_3 = 1)$ has the second highest probability in Table 30.1; if one node is put into state 1 then all nodes prefer to be in that state due to the network structure.

The Ising model was introduced in statistical physics, to explain the phenomenon of magnetism. To this end, the model was originally defined on a field of particles connected on a lattice. We will give a short introduction on this application in physics because it exemplifies an important aspect of the Ising model; namely, that the interactions between nodes can lead to synchronized behavior of the system as a whole (e.g., spontaneous magnetization). To explain how this works, note that a magnet, such as a common household magnet or the arrow in a compass, has two poles: a north pole and a south pole. Figure 30.2 shows the effect of pushing two such magnets together: the north pole of one magnet attracts to the south pole of another magnet and vice versa, and the same poles on both magnets repulse each other. This is due to the general tendency of magnets to align, called *ferromagnetism*. Exactly the same process causes the arrow of a compass to align with the magnetic field of the Earth itself, causing it to point north. Any material which is ferromagnetic, such as a plate of iron, consists of particles that behave in the same way as magnets; they have a north and south pole and lie in some direction. Suppose the particles can only lie in two directions: the north pole can be up or the south pole can be up. Figure 30.3a shows a simple two-dimensional representation of a possible state for a field of 4 × 4 particles. We can encode each particle as a random variable, X_i, which can take the values − 1 (south pole is up) and 1 (north pole is up). Furthermore, we can assume that the probability of X_i being in state x_i only depends on the direct neighbors (north, south east and west) of particle i. With this assumption in place, the system in Figure 30.3a can be represented as a PMRF on a lattice, as in Figure 30.3b.

A certain amount of energy is required for a system of particles to be in some state, such as in Figure 30.2. For example, in Figure 30.3b the node X_7 is in the state − 1 (south pole up). Its neighbors X_3 and X_{11} are both in the same state and thus aligned, which reduces the stress on the system and thus reduces the energy function. The other

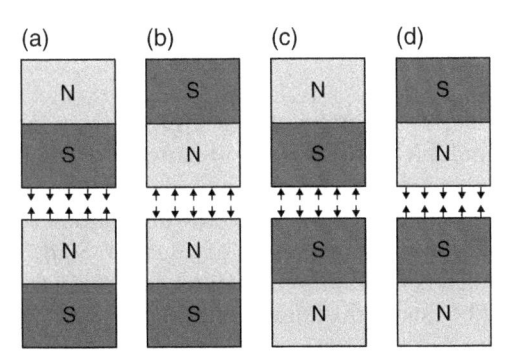

Figure 30.2 Example of the effect of holding two magnets with a north and south pole close to each other. The arrows indicate the direction the magnets want to move; the same poles, as in (b) and (c), repulse each other and opposite poles, as in (a) and (d), attract each other.

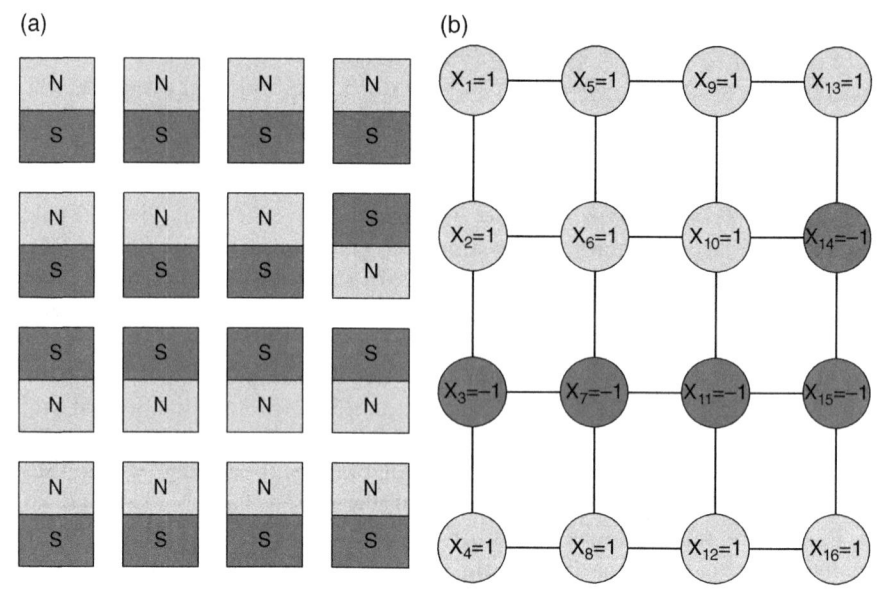

Figure 30.3 A field of particles (a) can be represented by a network shaped as a lattice, as in (b). Here, + 1 indicates that the north pole is aligned upwards and − 1 indicates that the south pole is aligned upwards. The lattice in (b) adheres to a PMRF in that the probability of a particle (node) being in some state is only dependent on the state of its direct neighbors.

neighbors of X_7, X_6 and X_8, are in the opposite state to X_7, and thus are not aligned, which increases the stress on the system. The total energy configuration can be summarized in the *Hamiltonian* function:

$$H(x) = -\sum_{i} \tau_i x_i - \sum_{<i,j>} \omega_{ij} x_i x_j,$$

which is used in the Gibbs distribution Murphy (2012) to model the probability of X being in some state x:

$$\Pr(X = x) = \frac{\exp(-\beta H(x))}{Z}. \qquad (30.9)$$

The parameter β indicates the inverse temperature of the system, which is not identifiable since we can multiply β with some constant and divide all τ and ω parameters with that same constant to obtain the same probability. Thus, it can be set arbitrarily to $\beta = 1$. Furthermore, the minus signs in the Gibbs distribution and Hamiltonian cancel out, leading to the Ising model as expressed in Equation 30.8.

The threshold parameters τ_i indicate the natural deposition for particle i to point up or down, which could be due to the influence of an external magnetic field not part of the system of nodes in X. For example, suppose we model a single compass; there is only one node, and thus the Hamiltonian reduces to $-\tau x$. Let $X = 1$ indicate that the compass points north and $X = -1$ indicate that the compass points south. Then, τ should be positive as the compass has a natural tendency to point north due to the presence of the Earth's magnetic field. As such, the τ parameters are also called external fields. The network parameter ω_{ij} indicates the interaction between two particles; its sign indicates if particles i and j tend to be in the same state (positive; ferromagnetic) or in different states (negative; anti-ferromagnetic). The absolute value, $|\omega_{ij}|$, indicates the strength of the interaction. For any two nonneighboring particles ω_{ij} will be 0; for neighboring particles, the stronger ω_{ij}, the stronger the interaction between the two. Because the closer magnets, and thus particles, are moved together, the stronger the magnetic force, we can interpret $|\omega_{ij}|$ as a measure for *closeness* between two nodes.

While the inverse temperature β is not identifiable in the sense of parameter estimation, it is an important element in the Ising model; in physics the temperature can be manipulated whereas the ferromagnetic strength or distance between particles cannot. The inverse temperature plays a crucial part in the *entropy* of Equation 30.9 Wainwright & Jordan (2008):

$$\text{Entropy}(X) = \mathbb{E}[-\ln\Pr(X = x)]$$
$$= -\beta\mathbb{E}\left[-\ln\frac{\exp(-H(x))}{Z^*}\right], \quad (30.10)$$

in which Z^* is the rescaled normalizing constant without inverse temperature β. The expectation $\mathbb{E}\left[-\ln\frac{\exp(-H(x))}{Z^*}\right]$ can be recognized as the entropy of the Ising model as defined in Equation 30.8. Thus, the inverse temperature β directly scales the entropy of the Ising model. As β shrinks to 0, the system is "heated up" and all states become equally likely, causing a high level of entropy. If β is subsequently increased, then the probability function becomes concentrated on a smaller number of states, and the entropy shrinks to eventually only allow the state in which all particles are aligned. The possibility that all particles become aligned is called *spontaneous magnetization* Kac (1966); Lin (1992); when all particles are aligned (all X are either 1 or –1) the entire field of particles becomes magnetized, which is how iron can be turned into a permanent magnet. We take this behavior as a particularly important aspect of the Ising model; behavior on the microscopic level (interactions between neighboring particles) can cause noticeable behavior on the macroscopic level (the creation of a permanent magnet).

In our view, psychological variables may behave in the same way. For example, interactions between components of a system (e.g., symptoms of depression) can cause synchronized effects for the system as a whole (e.g., depression as a disorder). Do note that, in setting up such analogies, we need to interpret the concepts of closeness and neighborhood less literally than in the physical sense. Concepts such as "sleep deprivation" and "fatigue" can be said to be close to each other, in that they mutually influence each other; sleep deprivation can lead to fatigue, and in turn fatigue can lead to a disrupted sleeping rhythm. The neighborhood of these symptoms can then be defined as the symptoms that frequently co-occur with sleep deprivation and fatigue, which can be seen in a network as a cluster of connected nodes. As in the Ising model, the states of these nodes will tend to be the same if the connections between these nodes are positive. This leads to the interpretation that a latent trait, such as depression, can be seen as a cluster of connected nodes (Borsboom, Cramer, Schmittmann, Epskamp & Waldorp, 2011).

In the next section, we will prove that there is a clear relationship between network modeling and latent variable modeling; indeed, clusters in a network can cause data to behave as if they were generated by a latent variable model.

The Ising Model in Psychometrics

In this section, we show that the Ising model is equivalent to, or closely related to, prominent modeling techniques in psychometrics. We will first discuss the relationship between the Ising model and log-linear analysis and logistic regressions, and next show that the Ising model can be equivalent to item response theory (IRT) models which dominate psychometrics. In addition, we highlight relevant earlier work on the relationship between IRT and the Ising model.

To begin, we can gain further insight into the Ising model by looking at the conditional distribution of X_i given that we know the value of the remaining nodes ($X^{(-i)} = x^{(-i)}$):

$$\Pr\left(X_i \mid X^{(-i)} = x^{(-i)}\right) = \frac{\Pr(X = x)}{\Pr\left(X^{(-i)} = x^{(-i)}\right)}$$

$$= \frac{\Pr(X = x)}{\sum_{x_i} \Pr\left(X_i = x_i, X^{(-i)} = x^{(-i)}\right)} \quad (30.11)$$

$$= \frac{\exp\left(x_i \left(\tau_i + \sum_j \omega_{ij} x_j\right)\right)}{\sum_{x_i} \exp\left(x_i \left(\tau_i + \sum_j \omega_{ij} x_j\right)\right)},$$

in which $\sum_{x_i}$ takes the sum over both possible outcomes of x_i. We can recognize this expression as a *logistic regression* model Agresti (1990). Thus, the Ising model can be seen as the joint distribution of response and predictor variables, where each variable is predicted by all the other nodes in the network. The Ising model therefore forms a predictive network in which the neighbors of each node, the set of connected nodes, represent the variables that predict the outcome of the node of interest.

Note that the definition of Markov random fields in Equation 30.2 can be extended to include higher-order interaction terms:

$$\Pr(X = x) = \frac{1}{Z} \prod_i \phi_i(x_i) \prod_{<ij>} \phi_{ij}(x_i, x_j) \prod_{<ijk>} \phi_{ijk}(x_i, x_j, x_k) \cdots,$$

all the way up to the Pth order interaction term, in which case the model becomes saturated. Specifying $\nu_{...}(\ldots) = \ln \phi_{...}(\ldots)$ for all potential functions, we obtain a log-linear model:

$$\Pr(X = x) = \frac{1}{Z} \exp\left(\sum_i \nu_i(x_i) + \sum_{<ij>} \nu_{ij}(x_i, x_j) + \sum_{<ijk>} \nu_{ijk}(x_i, x_j, x_k) + \cdots\right).$$

Let $n(\mathbf{x})$ be the number of respondents with response pattern $\mathbf{x}$ from a sample of N respondents. Then, we may model the expected frequency $n(\mathbf{x})$ as follows:

$$\mathbb{E}[n(\mathbf{x})] = N\Pr(X = \mathbf{x})$$

$$= \exp\left(\nu + \sum_{i} \nu_i(x_i) + \sum_{<ij>} \nu_{ij}(x_i, x_j) + \sum_{<ijk>} \nu_{ijk}(x_i, x_j, x_k) + \cdots\right), \quad (30.12)$$

in which $\nu = \ln N - \ln Z$. The model in Equation 30.12 has been used extensively in log-linear analysis Agresti (1990); Wickens (1989).[2] In log-linear analysis, the same constraints are typically used as in Equation 30.3; all ν functions should sum to 0 over all margins. Thus, if at most second-order interaction terms are included in the log-linear model, it is equivalent to the Ising model and can be represented exactly as in Equation 30.8. The Ising model, when represented as a log-linear model with at most second-order interactions, has been used in various ways. (Agresti, 1990) and (Wickens, 1989) call the model the *homogeneous association* model. Because it does not include three-way or higher-order interactions, the association between X_i and X_j—the odds ratio—is constant for any configuration of $X^{-(i,\,j)}$. Also, (Cox, 1972) and (Cox & Wermuth, 1994) used the same model, but termed it the *quadratic exponential binary distribution*, which has since often been used in biometrics and statistics (e.g., Fitzmaurice, Laird & Rotnitzky (1993); Zhao & Prentice (1990)). Interestingly, none of these authors mention the Ising model.

The relation between the Ising model and item response theory

In this section we will show that the Ising model is closely related to the modeling framework of IRT, which is of central importance to psychometrics. In fact, we will show that the Ising model is equivalent to a special case of the multivariate two-parameter logistic model (MIRT). However, instead of being hypothesized common causes of the item responses, in our representation the latent variables in the model are *generated* by cliques in the network.

In IRT, the responses on a set of binary variables X are assumed to be determined by a set of M ($M \leq P$) latent variables $\mathbf{\Theta}^\top = [\Theta_1 \, \Theta_2 \, \ldots \, \Theta_M]$. These latent variables are often termed *abilities*, which betrays the roots of the model in educational testing. In IRT, the probability of obtaining a realization x_i on the variable X_i—often called *items*—is modeled through item response functions, which model the probability of obtaining one of the two possible responses (typically, scored 1 for correct responses and 0 for incorrect responses) as a function of θ. For instance, in the (Rasch, 1960) model, also called the one-parameter logistic model (1PL), only one latent trait is assumed ($M = 1$ and $\mathbf{\Theta} = \Theta$) and the conditional probability of a response given the latent trait takes the form of a simple logistic function:

$$\Pr(X_i = x_i \mid \Theta = \theta)_{1\text{PL}} = \frac{\exp(x_i \alpha(\theta - \delta_i))}{\sum_{x_i} \exp(x_i \alpha(\theta - \delta_i))},$$

---

[2] Both Agresti and Wickens used λ rather than ν to denote the log potentials, which we changed in this chapter to avoid confusion with eigenvalues and the LASSO tuning parameter.

in which δ_i acts as a *difficulty parameter* and α is a common *discrimination* parameter for all items. A typical generalization of the 1PL is the (Birnbaum, 1968) model, often called the two-parameter logistic model (2PL), in which the discrimination is allowed to vary between items:

$$\Pr(X_i = x_i \mid \Theta = \theta)_{2\text{PL}} = \frac{\exp(x_i \alpha_i (\theta - \delta_i))}{\sum_{x_i} \exp(x_i \alpha_i (\theta - \delta_i))}.$$

The 2PL reduces to the 1PL if all discrimination parameters are equal: $\alpha_1 = \alpha_2 = \cdots = \alpha$. Generalizing the 2PL model to more than one latent variable ($M > 1$) leads to the 2PL multidimensional IRT model (MIRT; Reckase (2009)):

$$\Pr(X_i = x_i \mid \Theta = \theta)_{\text{MIRT}} = \frac{\exp(x_i (\alpha_i^\top \theta - \delta_i))}{\sum_{x_i} \exp(x_i (\alpha_i^\top \theta - \delta_i))}, \tag{30.13}$$

in which θ is a vector of length M that contains the realization of Θ, while α_i is a vector of length M that contains the discrimination of item i on every latent trait in the multidimensional space. The MIRT model reduces to the 2PL model if α_i equals zero in all but one of its elements.

Because IRT assumes local independence—the items are independent of each other after conditioning on the latent traits—the joint conditional probability of $X = x$ can be written as the product of the conditional probabilities of each item:

$$\Pr(X = x \mid \Theta = \theta) = \prod_i \Pr(X_i = x_i \mid \Theta = \theta). \tag{30.14}$$

The marginal probability, and thus the likelihood, of the 2PL MIRT model can be obtained by integrating over the distribution $f(\theta)$ of Θ:

$$\Pr(X = x) = \int_{-\infty}^{\infty} f(\theta) \Pr(X = x \mid \Theta = \theta) \, d\theta, \tag{30.15}$$

in which the integral is over all M latent variables. For typical distributions of Θ, such as a multivariate Gaussian distribution, this likelihood does not have a closed-form solution. Furthermore, as M grows it becomes hard to numerically approximate Equation 30.15. However, if the distribution of Θ is chosen such that it is conditionally Gaussian—the posterior distribution of Θ given that we observed $X = x$ takes a Gaussian form—we *can* obtain a closed-form solution for Equation 30.15. Furthermore, this closed-form solution is, in fact, the Ising model as presented in Equation 30.8.

As also shown by Marsman, M., Maris, G., Bechger, T., and Glas, C. (2015) and in more detail in Appendix, after reparameterizing $\tau_i = -\delta_i$ and $-2\sqrt{\lambda_j/2}\, q_{ij} = a_{ij}$, in which q_{ij} is the ith element of the jth eigenvector of Ω (with an arbitrary diagonal chosen such that Ω is positive definite), the Ising model is equivalent to a MIRT model in which the posterior distribution of the latent traits is equal to the product of univariate normal distributions with equal variance:

$$\Theta_j \mid X = x \sim N\left(\pm \frac{1}{2}\sum_i a_{ij} x_i, \sqrt{\frac{1}{2}}\right).$$

The mean of these univariate posterior distributions for Θ_j is equal to the weighted sumscore $\pm \frac{1}{2} \sum_i a_{ij} x_i$. Finally, since

$$f(\pmb{\theta}) = \sum_{\mathbf{x}} f(\pmb{\theta} \mid \pmb{X} = \pmb{x}) \Pr(\pmb{X} = \pmb{x}),$$

we can see that the marginal distribution of $\pmb{\Theta}$ in (30.15) is a *mixture of multivariate Gaussian distributions with homogenous variance-covariance*, with the mixing probability equal to the marginal probability of observing each response pattern.

Whenever $a_{ij} = 0$ for all i and some dimension j—i.e., none of the items discriminate on the latent trait—we can see that the marginal distribution of Θ_j becomes a Gaussian distribution with mean 0 and standard deviation $\sqrt{1/2}$. This corresponds to complete randomness; all states are equally probable given the latent trait. When discrimination parameters diverge from 0, the probability function becomes concentrated on particular response patterns. For example, in the case X_1 when designates the response variable for a very easy item, while X_2 is the response variable for a very hard item, the state in which the first item is answered correctly and the second incorrectly becomes less likely. This corresponds to a decrease in entropy and, as can be seen in (30.10), is related to the *temperature* of the system. The lower the temperature, the more the system prefers to be in states in which all items are answered correctly or incorrectly. When this happens, the distribution of Θ_j diverges from a Gaussian distribution and becomes a bimodal distribution with two peaks, centered around the weighted sumscores that correspond to situations in which all items are answered correctly or incorrectly. If the entropy is relatively high, $f(\Theta_j)$ can be well approximated by a Gaussian distribution, whereas if the entropy is (extremely) low a mixture of two Gaussian distributions best approximates $f(\Theta_j)$.

For example, consider again the network structure of Figure 30.1. When we parameterized all threshold functions $\tau_1 = \tau_2 = \tau_3 = -0.1$ and all network parameters $\omega_{12} = \omega_{23} = 0.5$ we obtained the probability distribution as specified in Table 30.1. We can form the matrix Ω first with zeros on the diagonal:

$$\begin{bmatrix} 0 & 0.5 & 0 \\ 0.5 & 0 & 0.5 \\ 0 & 0.5 & 0 \end{bmatrix},$$

which is not positive semi-definite. Subtracting the lowest eigenvalue (-0.707) from the diagonal gives us a positive semi-definite Ω matrix:

$$\Omega = \begin{bmatrix} 0.707 & 0.5 & 0 \\ 0.5 & 0.707 & 0.5 \\ 0 & 0.5 & 0.707 \end{bmatrix}.$$

Its eigenvalue decomposition is as follows:

$$Q = \begin{bmatrix} 0.500 & 0.707 & 0.500 \\ 0.707 & 0.000 & -0.707 \\ 0.500 & -0.707 & 0.500 \end{bmatrix},$$

$$\lambda = [1.414 \quad 0.707 \quad 0.000].$$

Using the transformations $\tau_i = -\delta_i$ and $-2\sqrt{\lambda_j/2}q_{ij} = \alpha_{ij}$ (arbitrarily using the negative root) defined above, we can then form the equivalent MIRT model with discrimination parameters A and difficulty parameters δ:

$$\delta = [0.1\ \ 0.1\ \ 0.1],$$

$$A = \begin{bmatrix} 0.841 & 0.841 & 0 \\ 1.189 & 0 & 0 \\ 0.841 & -0.841 & 0 \end{bmatrix}.$$

Thus, the model in Figure 30.1 is equivalent to a model with two latent traits: one defining the general coherence between all three nodes, and one defining the contrast between the first and the third node. The distributions of all three latent traits can be seen in Figure 30.4. In Table 30.1, we see that the probability is the highest for the two states in which all three nodes take the same value. This is reflected in the distribution of the first latent trait in Figure 30.4a: because all discrimination parameters relating to this trait are positive, the weighted sumscores of $X_1 = X_2 = X_3 = -1$ and $X_1 = X_2 = X_3 = 1$ are dominant and cause a small bimodality in the distribution. For the second trait, Figure 30.4b shows an approximately normal distribution, because this trait acts as a contrast and cancels out the preference for all variables to be in the same state. Finally, the third latent trait is nonexistent, since all of its discrimination parameters equal 0; Figure 30.4c simply shows a Gaussian distribution with standard deviation $\sqrt{1/2}$.

This proof serves to demonstrate that the Ising model is equivalent to a MIRT model with a posterior Gaussian distribution on the latent traits; the discrimination parameter column vector α_j—the item discrimination parameters on the jth dimension—is directly related to the jth eigenvector of the Ising model graph structure Ω, scaled by its jth eigenvector. Thus, the latent dimensions are orthogonal, and the rank of Ω directly corresponds to the number of latent dimensions. In the case of a Rasch model, the rank of Ω should be 1 and all ω_{ij} should have exactly the same value, corresponding to the common discrimination parameter; for the unidimensional Birnbaum model the rank of Ω is still 1, but now the the ω_{ij} parameters can vary between items, corresponding to differences in item discrimination.

The use of a posterior Gaussian distribution to obtain a closed-form solution for Equation 30.15 is itself not new in the psychometric literature, although it has not previously been linked to the Ising model and the literature related to it. (Olkin & Tate, 1961) already proposed to model binary variables jointly with

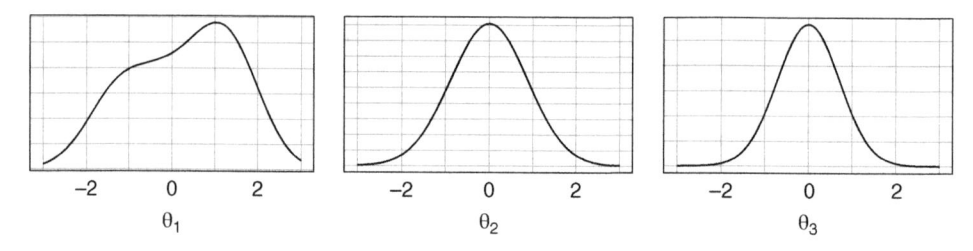

Figure 30.4 The distributions of the three latent traits in the equivalent MIRT model to the Ising model from Figure 30.1.

conditional Gaussian distributed continuous variables. Furthermore, (Holland, 1990) used the "Dutch identity" to show that a representation equivalent to an Ising model could be used to characterize the marginal distribution of an extended Rasch model Cressie & Holland (1983). Based on these results, Anderson and colleagues proposed an IRT modeling framework using log-multiplicative association models and assuming conditional Gaussian latents Anderson & Vermunt (2000); Anderson & Yu (2007); this approach has been implemented in the R package "plRasch" Anderson, Li & Vermunt (2007); Li & Hong (2014).

With our proof we furthermore show that the clique factorization of the network structure *generated* a latent trait with a functional distribution through a mathematical trick. Thus, the network perspective and common cause perspective could be interpreted as two different explanations of the same phenomena: cliques of correlated observed variables. In the next section, we show how the Ising model can be estimated.

Estimating the Ising Model

We can use Equation 30.8 to obtain the log-likelihood function of a realization x:

$$\mathcal{L}(\tau,\Omega;x) = \ln \Pr(X = x) = \sum_{i} \tau_i x_i + \sum_{<ij>} \omega_{ij} x_i x_j - \ln Z. \qquad (30.16)$$

Note that the constant Z is only constant with regard to x (as it sums over all possible realizations) and is *not* a constant with regard to the τ and ω parameters; Z is often called the *partition function* because it is a function of the parameters. Thus, when sampling from the Ising distribution Z does not need to be evaluated, but it *does* need to be evaluated when maximizing the likelihood function. Estimating the Ising model is notoriously hard because the partition function Z is often not tractable to compute Kolaczyk (2009). As can be seen in Equation 30.8, Z requires a sum over all possible configurations of x; computing Z requires summing over 2^k terms, which quickly becomes intractably large as k grows. Thus, maximum likelihood estimation of the Ising model is only possible for trivially small data sets (e.g., $k < 10$). For larger data sets, different techniques are required to estimate the parameters of the Ising model. Markov samplers can be used to estimate the Ising model by either approximating Z Dryden et al. (2003); Green & Richardson (2002); Sebastiani & Sørbye (2002) or circumventing Z entirely via sampling auxiliary variables (Møller, Pettitt, Reeves & Berthelsen, 2006); Murray (2007); Murray, Ghahramani & MacKay (2006). Such sampling algorithms can, however, still be computationally costly.

Because the Ising model is equivalent to the homogeneous association model in log-linear analysis Agresti (1990), the methods used in log-linear analysis can also be used to estimate the Ising model. For example, the iterative proportional fitting algorithm Haberman (1972), which is implemented in the `loglin` function in the statistical programming language R R Core Team (2014), can be used to estimate the parameters of the Ising model. Furthermore, log-linear analysis can be used for model selection in the Ising model by setting certain parameters to zero. Alternatively, while the full likelihood in Equation 30.8 is hard to compute, the conditional likelihood for each node in Equation 30.11 is very easy and does not include an intractable normalizing constant;

the conditional likelihood for each node corresponds to a multiple logistic regression Agresti (1990):

$$\mathcal{L}_i(\tau, \Omega; x) = x_i\left(\tau_i + \sum_j \omega_{ij} x_j\right) - \sum_{x_i} \exp\left(x_i\left(\tau_i + \sum_j \omega_{ij} x_j\right)\right).$$

Here, the subscript i indicates that the likelihood function is based on the conditional probability for node i given the other nodes. Instead of optimizing the full likelihood of Equation 30.8, the pseudolikelihood (PL; Besag (1975)) can be optimized instead. The pseudolikelihood approximates the likelihood with the product of univariate conditional likelihoods in Equation 30.11:

$$\ln \text{PL} = \sum_{i=1}^{k} \mathcal{L}_i(\tau, \Omega; x).$$

Finally, disjoint pseudolikelihood estimation can be used. In this approach, each conditional likelihood is optimized separately (Liu & Ihler, 2012). This routine corresponds to repeatedly performing a multiple logistic regression in which one node is the response variable and all other nodes are the predictors; by predicting x_i from $x^{(-i)}$, estimates can be obtained for Ω_i and τ_i. After estimating a multiple logistic regression for each node on all remaining nodes, a single estimate is obtained for every τ_i and two estimates are obtained for every ω_{ij}—the latter can be averaged to obtain an estimate of the relevant network parameter. Many statistical programs, such as the R function glm, can be used to perform logistic regressions. Estimation of the Ising model via log-linear modeling, maximal pseudolikelihood, and repeated multiple logistic regressions have been implemented in the EstimateIsing function in the R package IsingSampler Epskamp (2014b).

While the above-mentioned methods of estimating the Ising model are tractable, they all require a considerable amount of data to obtain reliable estimates. For example, in log-linear analysis, cells in the 2^P contingency table that are zero—which will occur often if $N < 2^P$—can cause parameter estimates to grow to ∞ Agresti (1990), and in logistic regression, predictors with low variance (e.g., a very hard item) can substantively increase standard errors Whittaker (1990). To estimate the Ising model, P thresholds and $P(P-1)/2$ network parameters have to be estimated, while in standard log-linear approaches, rules of thumb suggest that the sample size needs to be three times higher than the number of parameters to obtain reliable estimates. In psychometrics, the number of data points is often far too limited for this requirement to hold. To estimate parameters of graphical models with limited numbers of observations, therefore, regularization methods have been proposed (Friedman, Hastie & Tibshirani, 2008); (Meinshausen & Bühlmann, 2006).

When regularization is applied, a penalized version of the (pseudo)likelihood is optimized. The most common regularization method is ℓ_1 regularization—commonly known as the least absolute shrinkage and selection operator (LASSO; Tibshirani (1996))—in which the sum of absolute parameter values is penalized to be under some value. (Ravikumar et al., 2010) employed ℓ_1-regularized logistic regression to estimate the structure of the Ising model via disjoint maximum pseudolikelihood estimation.

For each node i the following expression is maximized (Friedman, Hastie & Tibshirani, 2010):

$$\max_{\tau_i,\omega_i} [\mathcal{L}_i(\tau,\Omega;x) - \lambda \text{Pen}(\omega_i)], \qquad (30.17)$$

where Ω_i is the ith row (or column due to symmetry) of Ω, and $\text{Pen}(\omega_i)$ denotes the penalty function, which is defined in the LASSO as follows:

$$\text{Pen}_{\ell_1}(\omega_i) = ||\omega_i||_1 = \sum_{j=1, j \neq i}^{k} |\omega_{ij}|.$$

The λ in Equation 30.17 is the regularization tuning parameter. The problem above is equivalent to the constrained optimization problem:

$$\max_{\tau_i,\omega_i} [\mathcal{L}_i(\tau,\Omega;x)] \text{ subject to } ||\omega_i||_1 < C,$$

in which C is a constant that has a one-to-one monotonic decreasing relationship with λ (Lee, Abbeel & Ng et al., 2006). If $\lambda = 0$, C will equal the sum of absolute values of the maximum likelihood solution; increasing λ will cause C to be smaller, which forces the estimates of Ω_i to shrink. Because the penalization uses absolute values, this causes parameter estimates to shrink to exactly zero. Thus, with moderately high values for λ a sparse solution to the logistic regression problem is obtained in which many coefficients equal zero; the LASSO results in simple predictive models including only a few predictors.

Ravikumar et al., (2010) used LASSO to estimate the neighborhood—the connected nodes—of each node, resulting in an unweighted graph structure. In this approach, an edge is selected in the model if either ω_{ij} or ω_{ji} is nonzero (the OR rule) or if both are nonzero (the AND rule). To obtain estimates for the weights, ω_{ij} and ω_{ji} can again be averaged. The λ parameter is typically specified such that an optimal solution is obtained, which is commonly done through cross-validation or, more recently, by optimizing the extended Bayesian information criterion (EBIC; Chen & Chen, 2008); Foygel & Drton (2010, 2014); van Borkulo et al. (2014).

In K-fold cross-validation, the data is subdivided into K (usually $K = 10$) blocks. For each of these blocks a model is fitted using only the remaining $K - 1$ blocks of data, which are subsequently used to construct a prediction model for the block of interest. For a suitable range of λ values, the predictive accuracy of this model can be computed, and subsequently the λ under which the data were best predicted is chosen. If the sample size is relatively low, the predictive accuracy is typically much better for $\lambda > 0$ than it is at the maximum likelihood solution of $\lambda = 0$; it is preferred to regularize to avoid overfitting.

Alternatively, an information criterion can be used to directly penalize the likelihood for the number of parameters. The EBIC (Chen & Chen 2008) augments the Bayesian information criterion (BIC) with a hyperparameter γ to additionally penalize the large space of possible models (networks):

$$\text{EBIC} = -2\mathcal{L}_i(\tau,\Omega;x) + |\omega_i|\ln(N) + 2\gamma|\omega_i|\ln(k-1),$$

in which $|\boldsymbol{\omega}_i|$ is the number of nonzero parameters in $\boldsymbol{\Omega}_i$. Setting $\gamma = 0.25$ works well for the Ising model (Foygel & Drton, 2014). An optimal λ can be chosen either for the entire Ising model, which improves parameter estimation, or for each node separately in disjoint pseudolikelihood estimation, which improves neighborhood selection. While K-fold cross-validation does not require the computation of the intractable likelihood function, EBIC does. Thus, when using EBIC estimation λ need be chosen per node. We have implemented ℓ_1-regularized disjoint pseudolikelihood estimation of the Ising model using EBIC to select a tuning parameter per node in the R package *IsingFit* (van Borkulo & Epskamp, 2014); van Borkulo et al., 2014), which uses *glmnet* for optimization (Friedman, Hastie & Tibshirani, 2010).

The LASSO works well in estimating sparse network structures for the Ising model, and can be used in combination with cross-validation or an information criterion to arrive at an interpretable model. However, it does so under the assumption that the true model in the population is sparse. So what if reality is not sparse, and we would not expect many missing edges in the network? As discussed earlier in this chapter, the absence of edges indicates conditional independence between nodes; if all nodes are caused by an unobserved cause, we would not expect missing edges in the network but rather a low-rank network structure. In such cases, ℓ_2 regularization—also called ridge regression—can be used, which uses a quadratic penalty function:

$$\text{Pen}_{\ell_2}(\boldsymbol{\omega}_i) = ||\boldsymbol{\omega}_i||_2 = \sum_{j=1, j! = i}^{k} \omega_{ij}^2.$$

With this penalty, parameters will not shrink to exactly zero but more or less smooth out; when two predictors are highly correlated the LASSO might pick only one, where ridge regression will average out the effect of both predictors. (Zou & Hastie, 2005) proposed a compromise between both penalty functions in the *elastic net*, which uses another tuning parameter, α, to mix between ℓ_1 and ℓ_2 regularization:

$$\text{Pen}_{\text{ElasticNet}}(\boldsymbol{\omega}_i) = \sum_{j=1, j! = i}^{k} \frac{1}{2}(1-\alpha)\omega_{ij}^2 + \alpha|\omega_{ij}|.$$

If $\alpha = 1$, the elastic net reduces to the LASSO penalty, and if $\alpha = 0$ the elastic net reduces to the ridge penalty. When $\alpha > 0$, exact zeros can still be obtained in the solution, and sparsity increases both with λ and α. Since moving towards ℓ_2 regularization reduces sparsity, selection of the tuning parameters using EBIC is less suited in the elastic net. Cross-validation, however, is still capable of sketching the predictive accuracy for different values of both α and λ. Again, the R package *glmnet* (Friedman, Hastie & Tibshirani, 2010) can be used for estimating parameters using the elastic net. We have implemented a procedure to compute the Ising model for a range of λ and α values and obtain the predictive accuracy in the R package *elasticIsing* (Epskamp, 2014a).

One issue that is currently debated is the inference of regularized parameters. Since the distribution of LASSO parameters is not well behaved (Bühlmann & van de Geer, 2011; Bühlmann, 2013), (Meinshausen, Meier & Bühlmann, 2009) developed the idea of using repeated sample splitting, where in the first sample the sparse set of variables are selected, followed by multiple comparison corrected *p*-values in the second sample.

Another interesting idea is to remove the bias introduced by regularization, upon which "standard" procedures can be used (van de Geer, Bühlmann & Ritov, 2013). As a result, the asymptotic distribution of the so-called de-sparsified LASSO parameters are asymptotically normal, with the true parameter as mean and efficient variance (i.e., achieves the Cramér–Rao bound). Standard techniques are then applied, and even confidence intervals with good coverage are obtained. The limitations here are (a) the sparsity level, which has to be $\leq \sqrt{n/\ln(P)}$, and (b) the "beta-min" assumption, which imposes a lower bound on the value of the smallest obtainable coefficient (Bühlmann & van de Geer, 2011).

Finally, we can use the equivalence between MIRT and the Ising model to estimate a low-rank approximation of the Ising model. MIRT software, such as the R package *mirt* Chalmers (2012), can be used for this purpose. More recently, Marsman, M., et.al., (2015) have used the equivalence also presented in this chapter as a method for estimating alow-rank Ising model using full-data-information estimation. A good approximation of the Ising model can be obtained if the true Ising model is indeed low rank, which can be checked by looking at the eigenvalue decomposition of the elastic net approximation or by sequentially estimating the first eigenvectors through adding more latent factors in the MIRT analysis or estimating sequentially higher rank networks using the methodology of Marsman, M., et.al., (2015).

Example analysis

To illustrate the methods described in this chapter we have simulated two datasets, both with 500 measurements on 10 dichotomous scored items. The first dataset, dataset A, was simulated according to a multidimensional Rasch model, in which the first five items are determined by the first factor and the last five items by the second factor. Factor levels were sampled from a multivariate normal distribution with unit variance and a correlation of 0.5, while item difficulties were sampled from a standard normal distribution. The second dataset, dataset B, was sampled from a sparse network structure according to a Boltzmann machine. A scale-free network was simulated using the Barabasi game algorithm (Barabási & Albert, 1999) in the R package *igraph* (Csardi & Nepusz, 2006) and a random connection probability of 5%. The edge weights where subsequently sampled from a uniform distribution between 0.75 and 1 (in line with the conception that most items in psychometrics relate positively with each other), and thresholds were sampled from a uniform distribution between − 3 and − 1. To simulate the responses the R package *IsingSampler* was used. The datasets were analyzed using the *elasticIsing* package in R (Epskamp, 2014a); 10-fold cross-validation was used to estimate the predictive accuracy of the tuning parameters λ and α on a grid of 100 logarithmically spaced λ values between 0.001 and 1, and 100 α values equally spaced between 0 and 1.

Figure 30.5 shows the results of the analyses. The left panels show the results for dataset A and the right panels show the results for dataset B. The top panels show the negative mean-squared prediction error for different values of λ and α. In both datasets, regularized models perform better than unregularized models. The plateaus on the right of the graphs show the performance of the independence graph in which all network parameters are set to zero. Dataset A obtained a maximum accuracy

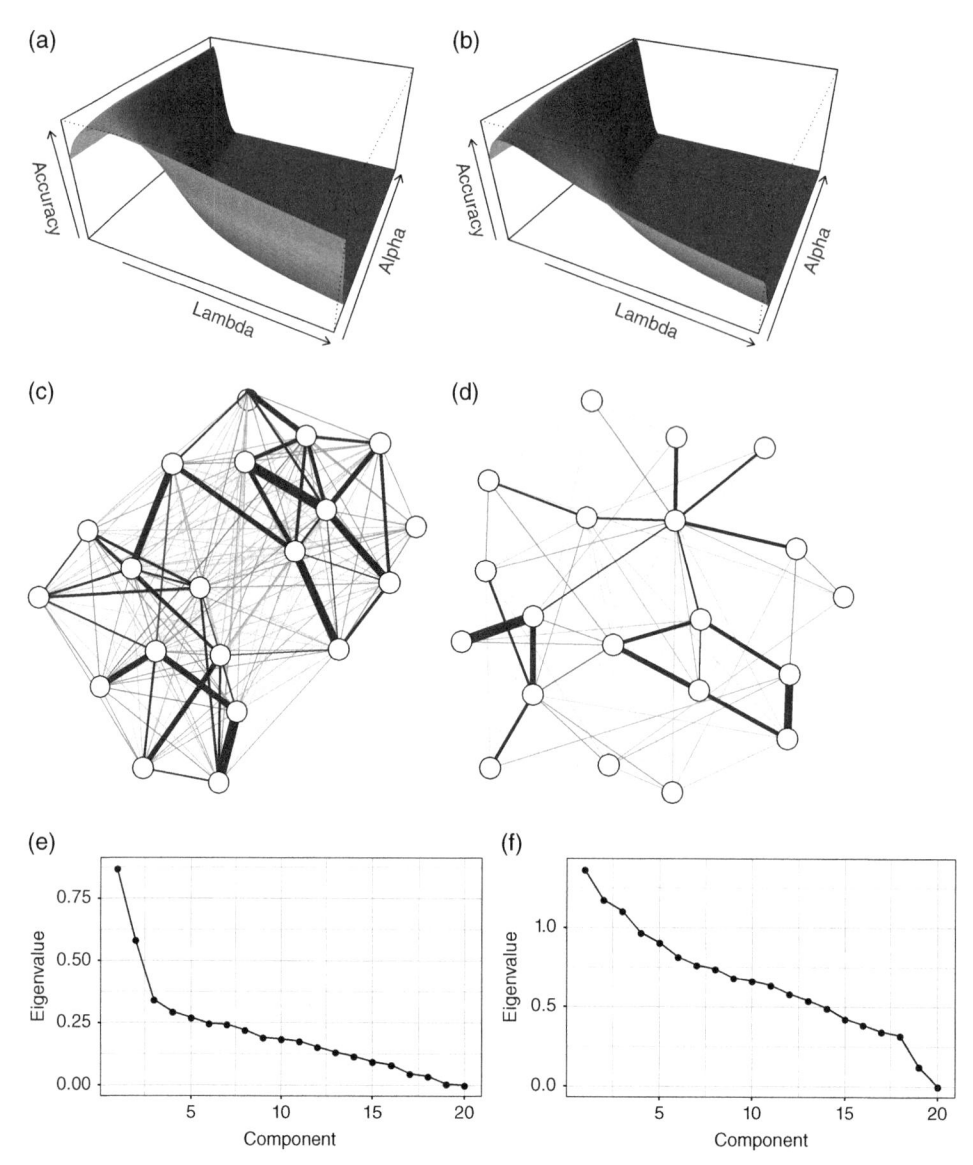

Figure 30.5 Analysis results of two simulated datasets. The left panels show results based on a dataset simulated according to a two-factor MIRT model, while the right panels show results based on a dataset simulated with a sparse scale-free network. Panels (a) and (b) show the predictive accuracy under different elastic net tuning parameters λ and α, panels (c) and (d) the estimated optimal graph structures, and panels (e) and (f) the eigenvalues of these graphs.

at $\alpha = 0$ and $\lambda = 0.201$; thus, in dataset A ℓ_2 regularization is preferred over ℓ_1 regularization, which is to be expected since the data was simulated under a model in which none of the edge weights should equal zero. In dataset B, a maximum was obtained at $\alpha = 0.960$ and $\lambda = 0.017$, indicating that in dataset B regularization close to ℓ_1 is preferred. The middle panels show visualizations of the obtained best-performing networks made with the *qgraph* package (Epskamp, Cramer, Waldorp, Schmittmann & Borsboom, 2012); green edges represent positive weights, red edges negative weights, and the wider and more saturated an edge the stronger the absolute weight. It can be seen that dataset A portrays two clusters while dataset B portrays a sparse structure. Finally, the bottom panels show the eigenvalues of both graphs; dataset A clearly indicates two dominant components, whereas dataset B does not indicate any dominant component.

These results show that the estimation techniques perform adequately, as expected. As discussed earlier in this chapter, the eigenvalue decomposition directly corresponds to the number of latent variables present if the common cause model is true, as is the case in dataset A. Furthermore, if the common cause model is true, the resulting graph should not be sparse but low rank, as is the case in the results on dataset A.

The Interpretation of Latent Variables in Psychometric Models

Since Spearman's (1904) conception of general intelligence as the common determinant of observed differences in cognitive test scores, latent variables have played a central role in psychometric models. The theoretical status of the latent variable in psychometric models has been controversial and the topic of heated debates in various subfields of psychology, like those concerned with the study of intelligence (e.g., Jensen, 1998) and personality (McCrae & Costa, 2008). The pivotal issue in these debates is whether latent variables posited in statistical models have referents outside of the model; that is, the central question is whether latent variables like g in intelligence or "extraversion" in personality research refer to a property of individuals that exists independently of the model-fitting exercise of the researcher Borsboom, Mellenbergh & Van Heerden (2003); (Cramer, Waldorp, van der Maas & Borsboom, 2010); Van der Maas et al. (2006). If they do have such independent existence, then the model formulation appears to dictate a causal relation between latent and observed variables, in which the former cause the latter; after all, the latent variable has all the formal properties of a common cause because it screens off the correlation between the item responses (a property termed *local independence* in the psychometric literature; Borsboom (2005); Reichenbach, 1991). The condition of *vanishing tetrads* that Spearman (1904) introduced as a model test for the veracity of the common factor model is currently seen as one of the hallmark conditions of the common cause model (Bollen & Lennox, 1991).

This would suggest that the latent variable model is intimately intertwined with a so-called reflective measurement model interpretation (Edwards & Bagozzi, 2000); (Howell, Breivik & Wilcox, 2007), also known as an effect indicators model (Bollen & Lennox, 1991), in which the measured attribute is represented as the cause of the test scores. This conceptualization is in keeping with causal accounts of measurement and validity (Borsboom, Mellenbergh & Van Heerden (2003); Markus & Borsboom, 2013), and indeed seems to fit the intuition of researchers in fields where psychometric models dominate, like personality. For example, McCrae & Costa (2008) note that they assume that extraversion causes party-going behavior, and as such this trait determines the answer to the question "Do you often go to parties?" in a causal fashion. (Jensen,

1998) offers similar ideas on the relation between intelligence and the *g* factor. Also, in clinical psychology, (Reise and Waller, 2009, p. 26) note that "to model item responses to a clinical instrument [with IRT], a researcher must first assume that the item covariation is caused by a continuous latent variable."

However, not all researchers are convinced that a causal interpretation of the relation between latent and observed variable makes sense. For instance, McDonald (2003) notes that the interpretation is somewhat vacuous as long as no substantive theoretical or empirical identification of the latent variable can be given; a similar point is made by Borsboom & Cramer, 2013. That is, as long as the sole evidence for the existence of a latent variable lies in the structure of the data to which it is fitted, the latent variable appears to have a merely statistical meaning and to grant such a statistical entity substantive meaning appears to be tantamount to over-interpreting the model. Thus, the common cause interpretation of latent variables at best enjoys mixed support.

A second interpretation of latent variables that has been put forward in the literature is one in which latent variables do not figure as common causes of the item responses, but as so-called behavior domains. Behavior domains are sets of behaviors relevant to substantive concepts like intelligence, extraversion, or cognitive ability (McDonald, 2003; Mulaik & McDonald, 1978). For instance, one can think of the behavior domain of addition as being defined through the set of all test items of the form $x + y = \ldots$ The actual items in a test are considered to be a sample from that domain. A latent variable can then be conceptualized as a so-called *tail measure* defined on the behavior domain (Ellis & Junker, 1997). One can intuitively think of this as the total test score of a person on the infinite set of items included in the behavior domain. Ellis & Junker (1997) have shown that, if the item responses included in the domain satisfy the properties of monotonicity, positive association, and vanishing conditional independence, the latent variable can indeed be defined as a tail measure. The relation between the item responses and the latent variable is, in this case, not sensibly construed as causal, because the item responses are a part of the behavior domain; this violates the requirement, made in virtually all theories of causality, that cause and effect should be separate entities (Markus & Borsboom, 2013). Rather, the relation between item responses and latent variable is conceptualized as a sampling relation, which means the inference from indicators to latent variable is not a species of causal inference, but of statistical generalization.

Although in some contexts the behavior domain interpretation does seem plausible, it has several theoretical shortcomings of its own. Most importantly, the model interpretation appears to beg the important explanatory question of why we observe statistical associations between item responses. For instance, the Ellis & Junker (1997) manifest conditions specify that the items included in a behavior domain should look exactly as if they were generated by a common cause; in essence, the only sets of items that would qualify as behavior domains are infinite sets of items that would fit a unidimensional IRT model perfectly. The question of why such sets would fit a unidimensional model is thus left open in this interpretation. A second problem is that the model specifies infinite behavior domains (measures on finite domains cannot be interpreted as latent variables because the axioms of Ellis & Junker will not be not satisfied in this case). In many applications, however, it is quite hard to come up with more than a few dozen of items before one starts repeating oneself (e.g., think of psychopathology symptoms or attitude items), and if one does come up with larger sets of items the unidimensionality requirement is typically violated. Even in applications that would seem to naturally suit the behavior domain interpretation, like the addition ability example given earlier, this is no trivial issue. Thus, the very property that buys the behavior domain interpretation its theoretical force (i.e., the construction of latent variables as tail measures on an infinite set of items that satisfies a unidimensional IRT model) is its substantive Achilles heel.

Thus, the common cause interpretation of the latent variable model seems too make assumptions about the causal background of test scores that appear overly ambitious given the current scientific understanding of test scores. The behavior domain interpretation is much less demanding, but appears to be of limited use in situations where only a limited number of items is of interest, and in addition offers no explanatory guidance with respect to answering the question of why items hang together as they do. The network model may offer a way out of this theoretical conundrum because it specifies a third way of looking at latent variables, as explained in this chapter. As Van der Maas et al., (2006) showed, data generated under a network model could explain the positive manifold often found in intelligence research, which is often described as the g factor or general intelligence; the g factor emerged from a densely connected network even though it was not "real." This idea suggests the interpretation of latent variables as functions defined as cliques in a network of interacting components Borsboom, Cramer, Schmittmann, Epskamp & Waldorp (2011); Cramer, Waldorp, van der Maas& Borsboom (2010, 2012). As we have shown in this chapter, this relation between networks and latent variables is quite general: given simple models of the interaction between variables, as encoded in the Ising model, one expects data that conform to psychometric models with latent variables. The theoretical importance of this result is that (a) it allows for a model interpretation that invokes no common cause of the item responses as in the reflective model interpretation, but (b) does not require assumptions about infinite behavior domains either.

Thus, network approaches can offer a theoretical middle ground between causal and sampling interpretations of psychometric models. In a network, there clearly is nothing that corresponds to a causally effective latent variable, as posited in the reflective measurement model interpretation (Bollen & Lennox, 1991; Edwards & Bagozzi, 2000). The network model thus evades the problematic assignment of causal force to latent variables like the g factor and extraversion. These arise out of the network structure as epiphenomena; to treat them as causes of item responses involves an unjustified reification. On the other hand, however, the latent variable model as it arises out of a network structure does not require the antecedent identification of an infinite set of response behaviors as hypothesized to exist in behavior domain theory. Networks are typically finite structures that involve a limited number of nodes engaged in a limited number of interactions. Each clique in the network structure will generate one latent variable with entirely transparent theoretical properties and an analytically tractable distribution function. Of course, for a full interpretation of the Ising model analogous to that in physics, one has to be prepared to assume that the connections between nodes in the network signify actual interactions (i.e., they are not merely correlations); that is, connections between nodes are explicitly not spurious as they are in the reflective latent variable model, in which the causal effect of the latent variable produces the correlations between item responses. But if this assumption is granted, the theoretical status of the ensuing latent variable is transparent and may in many contexts be less problematic than the current concepts in terms of reflective measurement models and behavior domains.

Naturally, even though the Ising and IRT models have statistically equivalent representations, the interpretations of the model in terms of common causes and networks is not equivalent. That is, there is a substantial difference between the causal implications of a reflective latent variable model and of an Ising model. However, because for a given dataset the models are equivalent, distinguishing network models from common cause models requires the addition of (quasi-)experimental designs into the model. For example, suppose that in reality an Ising model holds for a set of variables; say we consider the depression symptoms "insomnia" and "feelings of worthlessness." The model implies that, if we were to causally intervene on the system by reducing or increasing insomnia, a change in feelings of worthlessness should ensue. In the latent variable model, in which the association between feelings of worthlessness and insomnia is entirely due to the common influence of a latent variable, an experimental intervention that changes insomnia will not be propagated through the system. In this case, the intervention variable will be associated only with insomnia, which means that the items will turn out to violate measurement invariance with respect to the intervention variable (Mellenbergh, 1989; Meredith, 1993). Thus, interventions on individual nodes in the system can propagate to other nodes in a network model, but not in a latent variable model. This is a testable implication in cases where one has experimental interventions that plausibly target a single node in the system. Fried, Nesse, Zivin, Guille & Sen (2014) have identified a number of factors in depression that appear to work in this way.

Note that a similar argument does not necessarily work with variables that are causal consequences of the observed variables. Both in a latent variable model and in a network model, individual observed variables may have distinct outgoing effects, i.e., affect unique sets of external variables. Thus, insomnia may directly cause bags under the eyes, while feelings of worthlessness do not, without violating assumptions of either model. In the network model, this is because the outgoing effects of nodes do not play a role in the network if they do not feed back into the nodes that form the network. In the reflective model, this is because the model only speaks on the question of where the systematic variance in indicator variables comes from (i.e., this is produced by a latent variable), but not on what that systematic variance causes. As an example, one may measure the temperature of water by either putting a thermometer into the water, or by testing whether one can boil an egg in it. Both the thermometer reading and the boiled egg are plausibly construed as effects of the temperature in the water (the common cause latent variable in the system). However, only the boiled egg has the outgoing effect of satisfying one's appetite.

In addition to experimental interventions on the elements of the system, a network model rather than a latent variable model allows one to deduce what would happen upon changing the connectivity of the system. In a reflective latent variable model, the associations between variables are a function of the effect of the latent variable and the amount of noise present in the individual variables. Thus, the only ways to change the correlation between items is by changing the effect of the latent variable (e.g., by restricting the variance in the latent variable so as to produce restriction of range effects in the observables) or by increasing noise in the observed variables (e.g., by increasing variability in the conditions under which the measurements are taken). Thus, in a standard reflective latent variable model, the connection between observed variables is purely a correlation, and one can only change it indirectly through the variables that have proper causal roles in the system (i.e., latent variables and error variables).

However, in a network model, the associations between observed variables are not spurious; they are real, causally potent pathways, and thus externally forced changes in connection strengths can be envisioned. Such changes will affect the behavior of the system in a way that can be predicted from the model structure. For example, it is well known that increasing the connectivity of an Ising model can change its behavior from being linear (in which the total number of active nodes grows proportionally to the strength of external perturbations of the system) to being highly nonlinear. Under a situation of high connectivity, an Ising network features tipping points: in this situation, very small perturbations can have catastrophic effects. To give an example, a weakly connected network of depression symptoms could only be made depressed by strong external effects (e.g., the death of a spouse), whereas a strongly connected network could tumble into a depression through small perturbations (e.g., an annoying phone call from one's mother-in-law). Such a vulnerable network will also feature very specific behavior; for instance, when the network is approaching a transition, it will send out early warning signals like increased autocorrelation in a time series (Scheffer et al., 2009). Recent investigations suggest that such signals are indeed present in time series of individuals close to a transition (van de Leemput et al., 2014). Latent variable models have no such consequences.

Thus, there are at least three ways in which network models and reflective latent variable models can be distinguished: through experimental manipulations of individual nodes, through experimental manipulations of connections in the network, and through investigation of the behavior of systems under highly frequent measurements that allow one to study the dynamics of the system in time series. Of course, a final and direct refutation of the network model would occur if one could empirically identify a latent variable (e.g., if one could show that the latent variable in a model for depression items was in fact identical with a property of the system that could be independently identified—say, serotonin shortage in the brain). However, such identifications of abstract psychometric latent variables with empirically identifiable common causes do not appear forthcoming. Arguably, then, psychometrics may do better to bet on network explanations of association patterns between psychometric variables than to hope for the empirical identification of latent common causes.

Discussion

The correspondence between the Ising model and the MIRT model offers novel interpretations of long-standing psychometric models, but also opens a gateway through which the psychometric can be connected to the physics literature. Although we have only begun to explore the possibilities that this connection may offer, the results are surprising and, in our view, offer a fresh perspective on the problems and challenges of psychometrics. In the current chapter, we have illustrated how network models could be useful in the conceptualization of psychometric data. The bridge between network models and latent variables offers research opportunities that range from model estimation to the philosophical analysis of measurement in psychology, and may very well alter our view of the foundations on which psychometric models should be built.

As we have shown, network models may yield probability distributions that are exactly equivalent to those of IRT models. This means that latent variables can receive a novel interpretation: in addition to an interpretation of latent variables as common causes of the item responses (Bollen & Lennox, 1991; Edwards & Bagozzi, 2000), or as behavior domains from which the responses are a sample (Ellis & Junker, 1997); McDonald

(2003), we can now also conceive of latent variables as mathematical abstractions that are defined on cliques of variables in a network. The extension of psychometric work to network modeling fits current developments in substantive psychology, in which network models have often been motivated by critiques of the latent variable paradigm. This has, for instance, happened in the context of intelligence research Van der Maas et al. (2006), clinical psychology (Borsboom & Cramer, 2013; Cramer, Waldorp, van der Maas& Borsboom, 2010), and personality (Costantini et al., 2014; Cramer et al., 2012). It should be noted that, in view of the equivalence between latent variable models and network models proven here, even though these critiques may impinge on the common cause interpretation of latent variable models, they do not directly apply to latent variable models themselves. Latent variable models may in fact fit psychometric data well *because* these data result from a network of interacting components. In such a case, the latent variable should be thought of as a convenient fiction, but the latent variable model may nevertheless be useful; for instance, as we have argued in the current chapter, the MIRT model can be profitably used to estimate the parameters of a (low-rank) network. Of course, the reverse holds as well: certain network structures may fit the data because cliques of connected network components result from unobserved common causes in the data. An important question is under what circumstances the equivalence between the MIRT model and the Ising model breaks down, i.e., which experimental manipulations or extended datasets could be used to decide between a common cause versus a network interpretation of the data. In the current paper, we have offered some suggestions for further work in this direction, which we think offers considerable opportunities for psychometric progress.

As psychometrics starts to deal with network models, we think the Ising model offers a canonical form for network psychometrics, because it deals with binary data and is equivalent to well-known models from IRT. The Ising model has several intuitive interpretations: as a model for interacting components, as an association model with at most pairwise interactions, and as the joint distribution of response and predictor variables in a logistic regression. In particular, the analogy between networks of psychometric variables (e.g., psychopathology symptoms such as depressed mood, fatigue, and concentration loss) and networks of interacting particles (e.g., as in the magnetization examples) offers suggestive possibilities for the construction of novel theoretical accounts of the relation between constructs (e.g., depression) and observables as modeled in psychometrics (e.g., symptomatology). In the current chapter, we only focused on the Ising model for binary data, but of course the work we have ignited here invites extensions in various other directions. For example, for polymotous data, the generalized Potts model could be used, although it should be noted that this model does require the response options to be discrete values that are shared over all variables, which may not suit typical psychometric applications. Another popular type of PMRF is the Gaussian random field GRF; (Lauritzen, 1996)), which has exactly the same form as the model in Equation 1 except that now x is continuous and assumed to follow a multivariate Gaussian density. This model is considerably appealing as it has a tractable normalizing constant rather than the intractable partition function of the Ising model. The inverse of the covariance matrix—the precision matrix—can be standardized as a partial correlation matrix and directly corresponds to the Ω matrix of the Ising model. Furthermore, where the Ising model reduces to a series of logistic regressions for each node, the GRF reduces to a multiple linear regression for each node. Also in the GRF, it can easily be proven that the rank of the (partial) correlation matrix—cliques in the network—

corresponds to the latent dimensionality if the common cause model is true (Chandrasekaran, Parrilo & Willsky, 2012). A great body of literature exists on estimating and fitting GRFs even when the number of observations is limited versus the number of nodes Friedman, Hastie & Tibshirani (2008); Foygel & Drton (2010); Meinshausen & Bühlmann (2006). Furthermore, promising methods are now available for the estimation of a GRF even in non-Gaussian data, provided the data are continuous (Liu, Han, Yuan, Lafferty & Wasserman, 2012; H. Liu, Lafferty & Wasserman, 2009).

Proof of equivalence between the Ising model and MIRT

To prove the equivalence between the Ising model and MIRT, we first need to rewrite the Ising Model in matrix form:

$$p(X = x) = \frac{1}{Z}\exp\left(\tau^\top x + \frac{1}{2}x^\top \Omega x\right), \quad (30.18)$$

in which Ω is a $P \times P$ matrix containing network parameters ω_{ij} as its elements, which corresponds in graph theory to the adjacency or weights matrix. Note that, in this representation, the diagonal values of Ω are used. However, since x_i can only be -1 or 1, $x_i^2 = 1$ for any combination, and the diagonal values are cancelled out in the normalizing constant Z. Thus, arbitrary values can be used in the diagonal of Ω. Since Ω is a real and symmetrical matrix, we can take the usual eigenvalue decomposition:

$$\Omega = Q\Lambda Q^\top,$$

in which Λ is a diagonal matrix containing eigenvalues $\lambda_1, \lambda_2, \ldots, \lambda_P$ on its diagonal, and Q is an orthonormal matrix containing eigenvectors $q_1, q_2, \ldots, q_P$ as its columns. Inserting the eigenvalue decomposition into (1) gives:

$$p(X = x) = \frac{1}{Z}\exp\left(\sum_i \tau_i x_i\right)\prod_j \exp\left(\frac{\lambda_j}{2}\left(\sum_i q_{ij} x_i\right)^2\right). \quad (30.19)$$

Due to the unidentified and arbitrary diagonal of Ω we can force Ω to be positive semi-definite—requiring all eigenvalues to be nonnegative—by shifting the eigenvalues with some constant c:

$$\Omega + cI = Q(\Lambda + cI)Q^\top.$$

Following the work of (Kac, 1966), we can use the the following identity:

$$e^{y^2} = \int_{-\infty}^{\infty} \frac{e^{-2ct-t^2}}{\sqrt{\pi}}dt,$$

with $y = \sqrt{\frac{\lambda_j}{2}\left(\sum_i q_{ij}x_i\right)^2}$ and $t = \theta_j$ to rewrite (2) as follows:

$$p(X = x) = \frac{1}{Z}\int_{-\infty}^{\infty} \frac{\exp\left(\sum_j - \theta_j^2\right)}{\sqrt{\pi^P}} \prod_i \exp\left(x_i\left(\tau_i + \sum_j -2\sqrt{\frac{\lambda_j}{2}}q_{ij}\theta_j\right)\right) d\theta.$$

Reparameterizing $\tau_i = -\delta_i$ and $-2\sqrt{\frac{\lambda_j}{2}}q_{ij} = \alpha_{ij}$ we obtain:

$$p(X = x) = \int_{-\infty}^{\infty} \frac{1}{Z} \frac{\exp\left(\sum_j - \theta_j^2\right)}{\sqrt{\pi^P}} \prod_i \exp(x_i(\boldsymbol{\alpha}_i^\top \boldsymbol{\theta} - \delta_i)) d\theta. \tag{30.20}$$

The same transformations can be used to obtain a different expression for Z:

$$Z = \int_{-\infty}^{\infty} \frac{\exp\left(\sum_j - \theta_j^2\right)}{\sqrt{\pi^P}} \sum_x \prod_i \exp(x_i(\boldsymbol{\alpha}_i^\top \boldsymbol{\theta} - \delta_i)) d\theta$$

$$= \int_{-\infty}^{\infty} \frac{\exp\left(\sum_j - \theta_j^2\right)}{\sqrt{\pi^P}} \prod_i \sum_{x_i} \exp(x_i(\boldsymbol{\alpha}_i^\top \boldsymbol{\theta} - \delta_i)) d\theta. \tag{30.21}$$

Finally, inserting (4) into (3), multiplying by $\dfrac{\prod_i \sum_{x_i} \exp(x_i(\boldsymbol{\alpha}_i^\top \boldsymbol{\theta} - \delta_i))}{\prod_i \sum_{x_i} \exp(x_i(\boldsymbol{\alpha}_i^\top \boldsymbol{\theta} - \delta_i))}$, and rearranging gives:

$$p(X = x) = \int_{-\infty}^{\infty} \frac{\dfrac{\exp\left(\sum_j - \theta_j^2\right)}{\sqrt{\pi^P}} \prod_i \sum_{x_i} \exp(x_i(\boldsymbol{\alpha}_i^\top \boldsymbol{\theta} - \delta_i))}{\int_{-\infty}^{\infty} \dfrac{\exp\left(\sum_j - \theta_j^2\right)}{\sqrt{\pi^P}} \prod_i \sum_{x_i} \exp(x_i(\boldsymbol{\alpha}_i^\top \boldsymbol{\theta} - \delta_i)) d\theta}$$
$$\cdot \prod_i \frac{\exp(x_i(\boldsymbol{\alpha}_i^\top \boldsymbol{\theta} - \delta_i))}{\sum_{x_i} \exp(x_i(\boldsymbol{\alpha}_i^\top \boldsymbol{\theta} - \delta_i))} d\theta. \tag{30.22}$$

The first part of the integral on the right-hand side of (5) corresponds to a distribution that sums to 1 for a P-dimensional random vector $\boldsymbol{\Theta}$:

$$f(\boldsymbol{\theta}) \propto \frac{\exp\left(\sum_j - \theta_j^2\right)}{\sqrt{\pi^P}} \prod_i \sum_{x_i} \exp(x_i(\boldsymbol{\alpha}_i^\top \boldsymbol{\theta} - \delta_i)),$$

and the second part corresponds to the two-parameter logistic MIRT probability of the response vector as in (30.13):

$$P(X = x \mid \Theta = \theta) = \prod_i \frac{\exp(x_i(\alpha_i^\top \theta - \delta_i))}{\sum_{x_i} \exp(x_i(\alpha_i^\top \theta - \delta_i))}.$$

We can look further at this distribution by using Bayes' rule to examine the conditional distribution of θ given $X = x$:

$$f(\theta \mid X = x) \propto \Pr(X = x \mid \Theta = \theta) f(\theta)$$
$$\propto \exp(x^\top A\theta - \theta^\top \theta)$$
$$\propto \exp\left(-\frac{1}{2}\left(\theta - \frac{1}{2}A^\top x\right)^\top 2I\left(\theta - \frac{1}{2}A^\top x\right)\right)$$

and see that the posterior distribution of Θ is a multivariate Gaussian distribution:

$$\Theta \mid X = x \sim N_P\left(\pm \frac{1}{2}A^\top x, \sqrt{\frac{1}{2}}I\right), \tag{30.23}$$

in which A is a matrix containing the discrimination parameters α_i as its rows and $\pm$ indicates that columns a_j could be multiplied by -1 because either the positive and negative root can be used in $\sqrt{\frac{\lambda_j}{2}}$, simply indicating whether the items overall are positively or negatively influenced by the latent trait θ. Additionally, since the variance-covariance matrix of θ equals zero in all nondiagonal elements, θ is orthogonal. Thus, the multivariate density can be decomposed as the product of univariate densities:

$$\Theta_j \mid X = x \sim N\left(\pm \frac{1}{2}\sum_i a_{ij} x_i, \sqrt{\frac{1}{2}}\right).$$

Glossary of Notation

Symbol	Dimension	Description
$\{\ldots\}$		Set of distinct values.
(a, b)		Interval between a and b.
P	$\mathbb{N}$	Number of variables.
N	$\mathbb{N}$	Number of observations.
X	$\{-1,1\}^P$	Random vector of binary variables.
x	$\{-1,1\}^P$	A possible realization of X.
$n(x)$	$\mathbb{N}$	Number of observations with response pattern x.
$i, j, k,$ and l	$\{1,2,\ldots,P\}, j \neq i$	Subscripts of random variables.

$\boldsymbol{X}^{-(i)}$	$\{-1,1\}^{P-1}$	Random vector of binary variables without X_i.
$\boldsymbol{x}^{-(i)}$	$\{-1,1\}^{P-1}$	A possible realization of $\boldsymbol{X}^{-(i)}$.
$\boldsymbol{X}^{-(i,j)}$	$\{-1,1\}^{P-2}$	Random vector of binary variables without X_i and X_j.
$\boldsymbol{x}^{-(i,j)}$	$\{-1,1\}^{P-2}$	A possible realization of $\boldsymbol{X}^{-(i,j)}$.
$\Pr(\ldots)$	$\to (0,1)$	Probability function.
$\phi_i(x_i)$	$\{-1,1\} \to \mathbb{R}_{>0}$	Node potential function.
$\phi_i(x_i, x_j)$	$\{-1,1\}^2 \to \mathbb{R}_{>0}$	Pairwise potential function.
τ_i	$\mathbb{R}$	Threshold parameter for node X_i in the Ising model. Defined as $\tau_i = \ln \phi_i(1)$.
$\boldsymbol{\tau}$	$\mathbb{R}^P$	Vector of threshold parameters, containing τ_i as its ith element.
ω_{ij}	$\mathbb{R}$	Network parameter between nodes X_i and X_j in the Ising model. Defined as $\omega_{ij} = \ln \phi_{ij}(1,1)$.
$\boldsymbol{\Omega}$	$\mathbb{R}^{P \times P}$ and symmetrical	Matrix of network parameters, containing ω_{ij} as its ijth element.
$\boldsymbol{\Omega}_i$	$\mathbb{R}^P$	The ith row or column of $\boldsymbol{\Omega}$.
$\text{Pen}(\boldsymbol{\omega}_i)$	$\mathbb{R}^P \to \mathbb{R}$	Penalization function of $\boldsymbol{\Omega}_i$.
β	$\mathbb{R}_{>0}$	Inverse temperature in the Ising model.
$H(\boldsymbol{x})$	$\{-1,1\}^P \to \mathbb{R}$	Hamiltonian function denoting the energy of state $\boldsymbol{x}$ in the Ising model.
$\nu_{\ldots}(\ldots)$	$\to \mathbb{R}$	The log potential functions, used in log-linear analysis.
M	$\mathbb{N}$	The number of latent factors.
$\boldsymbol{\Theta}$	$\mathbb{R}^M$	Random vector of continuous latent variables.
$\boldsymbol{\theta}$	$\mathbb{R}^M$	Realization of $\boldsymbol{\Theta}$.
$\mathcal{L}(\boldsymbol{\tau}, \boldsymbol{\Omega}; \boldsymbol{x})$	$\to \mathbb{R}$	Likelihood function based on $\Pr(\boldsymbol{X} = \boldsymbol{x})$.
$\mathcal{L}_i(\boldsymbol{\tau}, \boldsymbol{\Omega}; \boldsymbol{x})$	$\to \mathbb{R}$	Likelihood function based on $\Pr\left(X_i = x_i \mid \boldsymbol{X}^{-(i)} = \boldsymbol{x}^{-(i)}\right)$.
λ	$\mathbb{R}_{>0}$	LASSO tuning parameter.
α	$(0,1)$	Elastic net tuning parameter.

References

Aggen, S. H., Neale, M. C., & Kendler, K. S. (2005). DSM criteria for major depression: evaluating symptom patterns using latent-trait item response models. *Psychological Medicine*, 35(04), 475–487.

Agresti, A. (1990). *Categorical data analysis*. New York, NY: John Wiley & Sons Inc.

Anderson, C. J., Li, Z., & Vermunt, J. (2007). Estimation of models in the Rasch family for polytomous items and multiple latent variables. *Journal of Statistical Software*, 20(6), 1–36.

Anderson, C. J. & Vermunt, J. K. (2000). Log-multiplicative association models as latent variable models for nominal and/or ordinal data. *Sociological Methodology*, 30(1), 81–121.

Anderson, C. J. & Yu, H.-T. (2007). Log-multiplicative association models as item response models. *Psychometrika*, 72(1), 5–23.

Barabási, A.-L. & Albert, R. (1999). Emergence of scaling in random networks. *Science*, 286 (5439), 509–512.

Besag, J. (1975). Statistical analysis of non-lattice data. *The Statistician, 24*, 179–195.
Birnbaum, A. (1968). Some latent trait models and their use in inferring an examinee's ability. F. Lord& M. Novick (Eds.), *Statistical theories of mental test scores.* Reading, MA: Addison-Wesley.
Bollen, K. & Lennox, R. (1991). Conventional wisdom on measurement: A structural equation perspective. *Psychological Bulletin, 110*(2), 305–314.
Borsboom, D. (2005). *Measuring the mind: Conceptual issues in contemporary psychometrics.* Cambridge, UK: Cambridge University Press.
Borsboom, D. & Cramer, A. O. J. (2013). Network analysis: an integrative approach to the structure of psychopathology. *Annual Review of Clinical Psychology, 9*, 91–121.
Borsboom, D., Cramer, A. O. J., Schmittmann, V. D., Epskamp, S., & Waldorp, L. J. (2011). The small world of psychopathology. *PloS ONE, 6*(11), e27407.
Borsboom, D., Mellenbergh, G. J., & Van Heerden, J. (2003). The theoretical status of latent variables. *Psychological Review, 110*(2), 203–219.
Bühlmann, P. (2013). Statistical significance in high-dimensional linear models. *Bernoulli, 19*(4), 1212–1242.
Bühlmann, P. & van de Geer, S. (2011). *Statistics for high-dimensional data: Methods, theory and applications.* New York, NY: Springer.
Chalmers, R. P. (2012). MIRT: A multidimensional item response theory package for the R environment. *Journal of Statistical Software, 48*(6), 1–29.
Chandrasekaran, V., Parrilo, P. A., & Willsky, A. S. (2012). Latent variable graphical model selection via convex optimization (with discussion). *The Annals of Statistics, 40*(4), 1935–1967.
Chen, J.& Chen, Z. (2008). Extended Bayesian information criteria for model selection with large model spaces. *Biometrika, 95*(3), 759–771.
Costantini, G., Epskamp, S., Borsboom, D., Perugini, M., Mõttus, R., Waldorp, L. J., & Cramer, A. O. (2015). State of the aRt personality research: A tutorial on network analysis of personality data in R. *Journal of Research in Personality, 54*, 13–29.
Cox, D. R. (1972). The analysis of multivariate binary data. *Applied Statistics, 21*, 113–120.
Cox, D. R. & Wermuth, N. (1994). A note on the quadratic exponential binary distribution. *Biometrika, 81*(2), 403–408.
Cramer, A. O. J., Sluis, S., Noordhof, A., Wichers, M., Geschwind, N., Aggen, S. H.,... Borsboom, D. (2012). Dimensions of normal personality as networks in search of equilibrium: You can't like parties if you don't like people. *European Journal of Personality, 26* (4), 414–431.
Cramer, A. O. J., Waldorp, L. J., van der Maas, H. L. J., & Borsboom, D. (2010). Comorbidity: a network perspective. *Behavioral and Brain Sciences, 33*(2–3), 137–150.
Cressie, N. & Holland, P. W. (1983). Characterizing the manifest probabilities of latent trait models. *Psychometrika, 48*(1), 129–141.
Csardi, G. & Nepusz, T. (2006). The igraph software package for complex network research. *InterJournal, Complex Systems, 1695.* http://igraph.org
Dryden, I. L., Scarr, M. R., & Taylor, C. C. (2003). Bayesian texture segmentation of weed and crop images using reversible jump Markov chain Monte Carlo methods. *Journal of the Royal Statistical Society: Series C (Applied Statistics), 52*(1), 31–50.
Edwards, J. R. & Bagozzi, R. P. (2000). On the nature and direction of relationships between constructs and measures. *Psychological Methods, 5*(2), 155–174.
Ellis, J. L. & Junker, B. W. (1997). Tail-measurability in monotone latent variable models. *Psychometrika, 62*(4), 495–523.
Epskamp, S. (2014a). *elasticIsing: Ising network estimation using elastic net and k-fold cross-validation.* R package version 0.1. Retrieved from https://github.com/SachaEpskamp/elasticIsing
Epskamp, S. (2014b). *IsingSampler: Sampling methods and distribution functions for the Ising model.* R package version 0.1.1. Retrieved from https://github.com/SachaEpskamp/IsingSampler

Epskamp, S., Cramer, A. O. J., Waldorp, L. J., Schmittmann, V. D., & Borsboom, D. (2012). qgraph: Network visualizations of relationships in psychometric data. *Journal of Statistical Software*, 48, 41–18.

Fischer, G. H. (1974). *Einführung in die theorie psychologischer tests: Grundlagen und anwendungen.* Bern, CH: Huber.

Fitzmaurice, G. M., Laird, N. M., & Rotnitzky, A. G. (1993). Regression models for discrete longitudinal responses. *Statistical Science*, 8, 284–299.

Foygel, R. & Drton, M. (2010). Extended Bayesian information criteria for Gaussian graphical models. *Advances in Neural Information Processing Systems*, 23, 2020–2028.

Foygel, R.& Drton, M. (2014). High-dimensional Ising model selection with Bayesian information criteria. *arXiv preprint arXiv:1403.3374.* doi:10.1214/154957804100000000

Fried, E. I., Nesse, R. M., Zivin, K., Guille, C., & Sen, S. (2014). Depression is more than the sum score of its parts: individual DSM symptoms have different risk factors. *Psychological Medicine*, 1–10, 2067–2076.

Friedman, J. H., Hastie, T., & Tibshirani, R. (2008). Sparse inverse covariance estimation with the graphical LASSO. *Biostatistics*, 9(3), 432–441.

Friedman, J. H., Hastie, T., & Tibshirani, R. (2010). Regularization paths for generalized linear models via coordinate descent. *Journal of Statistical Software*, 33(1), 1–22.

Green, P. J. & Richardson, S. (2002). Hidden Markov models and disease mapping. *Journal of the American Statistical Association*, 97(460), 1055–1070.

Haberman, S. J. (1972). Log-linear fit for contingency tables—algorithm AS51. *Applied Statistics*, 21, 218–225.

Holland, P. W. (1990). The Dutch Identity: A new tool for the study of item response models. *Psychometrika*, 55(1), 5–18.

Howell, R. D., Breivik, E., & Wilcox, J. B. (2007). Reconsidering formative measurement. *Psychological Methods*, 12, 2205–218.

Ising, E. (1925). Beitrag zur theorie des ferromagnetismus. *Zeitschrift für Physik A Hadrons and Nuclei*, 31(1), 253–258.

Jensen, A. R. (1998). *The g factor: The science of mental ability*. Westport, CT: Praeger.

Kac, M. (1966). *Mathematical mechanism of phase transition*. New York, NY: Gordon & Breach.

Kindermann, R. & Snell, J. L. (1980). *Markov random fields and their applications*. Providence, RI: American Mathematical Society.

Kolaczyk, E. D. (2009). *Statistical analysis of network data*. New York, NY: Springer.

Lauritzen, S. L. (1996). *Graphical models*. Oxford, UK: Clarendon Press.

Lee, S.-I., Lee, H., Abbeel, P., & Ng, A. Y. (2006). Efficient ℓ_1 regularized logistic regression. In *Proceedings of the national conference on artificial intelligence* (Vol. 21, 1, P. 401). Cambridge, MA: AAAI Press.

Li, Z. & Hong, F. (2014). *plRasch: Log linear by linear association models and Rasch family models by pseudolikelihood estimation*. R package version 1.0. Retrieved from http://CRAN.R-project.org/package=plRasch

Lin, K.-Y. (1992). Spontaneous magnetization of the Ising model. *Chinese Journal of Physics*, 30(3), 287–319.

Liu, H., Han, F., Yuan, M., Lafferty, J. D., & Wasserman, L. (2012). High-dimensional semiparametric Gaussian copula graphical models. *The Annals of Statistics*, 40(4), 2293–2326.

Liu, H., Lafferty, J. D., & Wasserman, L. (2009). The nonparanormal: Semiparametric estimation of high dimensional undirected graphs. *The Journal of Machine Learning Research*, 10, 2295–2328.

Liu, Q. & Ihler, A. (2012). Distributed parameter estimation via pseudo-likelihood. *Proceedings of the International Conference on Machine Learning (ICML)*.

Markus, K. A. & Borsboom, D. (2013). Reflective measurement models, behavior domains, and common causes. *New Ideas in Psychology*, 31(1), 54–64.

Marsman, M., Maris, G., Bechger, T., and Glas, C. (2015). Bayesian inference for low-rank ising networks. *Scientific reports*, 5(9050), 1–7.

McCrae, R. R. & Costa, P. T. (2008). Empirical and theoretical status of the five-factor model of personality traits. In G. J. Boyle, G. Matthews & D. H. Saklofske (Eds.), *The SAGE Handbook of Personality Theory and Assessment* (Vol. 1, pp. 273–294). Los Angeles, CA: SAGE.

McDonald, R. P. (2003). Behavior domains in theory and in practice. *Alberta Journal of Educational Research*, 49, 212–230.

Meinshausen, N. & Bühlmann, P. (2006). High-dimensional graphs and variable selection with the LASSO. *The Annals of Statistics*, 34(3), 1436–1462.

Meinshausen, N., Meier, L., & Bühlmann, P. (2009). P-values for high-dimensional regression. *Journal of the American Statistical Association*, 104(488), 1671–1681.

Mellenbergh, G. J. (1989). Item bias and item response theory. *International Journal of Educational Research*, 13(2), 127–143.

Meredith, W. (1993). Measurement invariance, factor analysis and factorial invariance. *Psychometrika*, 58(4), 525–543.

Molenaar, P. C. (2003). State space techniques in structural equation modeling. Retrieved from http://statistics.ucla.edu/preprints/uclastat-preprint-2011:14

Møller, J., Pettitt, A. N., Reeves, R., & Berthelsen, K. K. (2006). An efficient Markov chain Monte Carlo method for distributions with intractable normalising constants. *Biometrika*, 93(2), 451–458.

Mulaik, S. A. & McDonald, R. P. (1978). The effect of additional variables on factor indeterminacy in models with a single common factor. *Psychometrika*, 43(2), 177–192.

Murphy, K. P. (2012). *Machine learning: a probabilistic perspective*. Cambridge, MA: MIT Press.

Murray, I. (2007). *Advances in Markov chain Monte Carlo methods* (Doctoral dissertation, Gatsby Computational Neuroscience Unit, University College London).

Murray, I., Ghahramani, Z., & MacKay, D. J. C. (2006). MCMC for doubly-intractable distributions. *Uncertainty in Artificial Intelligence (UAI)* (pp. 359–366). Arlington, VA: AUAI Press.

Olkin, I. & Tate, R. F. (1961). Multivariate correlation models with mixed discrete and continuous variables. *The Annals of Mathematical Statistics*, 32, 448–465.

Pearl, J. (2000).*Causality: models, reasoning and inference* Cambridge, UK: Cambridge University Press.

R Core Team. (2014). *R: A Language and Environment for Statistical Computing*. R Foundation for Statistical Computing. Vienna, Austria. Retrieved from http://www.R-project.org/

Rasch, G. (1960). *Probabilistic models for some intelligence and attainment tests*. Copenhagen, Denmark Danish Institute for Educational Research.

Ravikumar, P., Wainwright, M. J., & Lafferty, J. D. (2010). High-dimensional Ising model selection using ℓ_1-regularized logistic regression. *The Annals of Statistics*, 38(3), 1287–1319.

Reckase, M. D. (2009). *Multidimensional item response theory*. New York, NY:Springer.

Reichenbach, H. (1991). *The direction of time*. Berkeley, CAUniversity of California Press.

Reise, S. P. & Waller, N. G. (2009). Item response theory and clinical measurement. *Annual Review of Clinical Psychology*, 5, 27–48.

Scheffer, M., Bascompte, J., Brock, W. A., Brovkin, V., Carpenter, S. R., Dakos, V.,... Sugihara, G. (2009). Early-warning signals for critical transitions. *Nature*, 461(7260), 53–59.

Sebastiani, G. & Sørbye, S. H. (2002). A Bayesian method for multispectral image data classification. *Journal of Nonparametric Statistics*, 14(1-2)169–180.

Spearman, C. (1904). "General Intelligence," Objectively Determined and Measured. *The American Journal of Psychology*, 15(2), 201–292.

Tibshirani, R. (1996). Regression shrinkage and selection via the LASSO. *Journal of the Royal Statistical Society. Series B (Methodological)*, 58, 267–288.

van Borkulo, C. D., Borsboom, D., Epskamp, S., Blanken, T. F., Boschloo, L., Schoevers, R. A., & Waldorp, L. J. (2014). A new method for constructing networks from binary data. *Scientific Reports*, 4(5918), 1–10.

van Borkulo, C. D. & Epskamp, S. (2014). *IsingFit: Fitting Ising models using the eLasso method*. R package version 0.2.0. Retrieved from http://CRAN.R-project.org/package=IsingFit

van de Geer, S., Bühlmann, P., & Ritov, Y. (2013). On asymptotically optimal confidence regions and tests for high-dimensional models. *arXiv preprint arXiv:1303.0518.*

van de Leemput, I. A., Wichers, M., Cramer, A. O. J., Borsboom, D., Tuerlinckx, F., Kuppens, P.,... Scheffer, M. (2014). Critical slowing down as early warning for the onset and termination of depression. *PNAS, 111*(1), 87–92.

Van der Maas, H. L. J., Dolan, C. V., Grasman, R. P. P. P., Wicherts, J. M., Huizenga, H. M., & Raijmakers, M. E. J. (2006). A dynamical model of general intelligence: the positive manifold of intelligence by mutualism. *Psychological Review, 113*(4), 842.

Wainwright, M. J. & Jordan, M. I. (2008). Graphical models, exponential families, and variational inference. *Foundations and Trends® in Machine Learning, 1*(1–2), 1–305.

Whittaker, J. (1990). *Graphical models in applied multivariate statistics.* Chichester, UK: John Wiley & Sons.

Wickens, T. D. (1989). *Multiway contingency tables analysis for the social sciences.* Hillsdale, NJ: Lawrence Erlbaum.

Zhao, L. P. & Prentice, R. L. (1990). Correlated binary regression using a quadratic exponential model. *Biometrika, 77*(3), 642–648.

Zou, H. & Hastie, T. (2005). Regularization and variable selection via the elastic net. *Journal of the Royal Statistical Society: Series B (Statistical Methodology), 67*(2), 301–320.

Index

Page references to Figures are followed by the letter 'f' in italics, while references to Tables are followed by the letter 't'. References to Notes contain the letter 'n', followed by the number of the note.

abduction, 242
Abedi, J., 12
aberrant responses, 613
ability, 4, 9, 12, 17, 75, 655
　versus achievement, 10
　cognitive/intellectual, 3, 5, 7–9, 19, 21, 24, 28, 188, 944, 974
　distribution, 58, 59, 66, 423
　　prior, 643, 646, 647, 650, 651
　general, 937, 938, 945
　group differences, 585, 596, 609
　history testing, 655
　IRT linking and equating, 639, 641, 643, 646, 647, 650, 651, 653, 654, 661
　latent, 63, 591, 916
　learning, 755
　mathematical/numerical, 2, 5, 447n2, 608
　multitrait-multimethod models, 819
　network psychometrics, 979
　posterior-based measurement of student proficiency, 501–507
　reading, 447
　reliability issues, 709, 717, 720, 721*f*, 723–726, 724*f*, 729, 730, 732, 740, 745
　scores and scoring, 579, 581, 585, 587, 589, 591, 593, 596, 610, 612, 622

　spatial, 76, 89, 188
　of test taker, 581, 585, 589, 593
　UIRT (unidimensional item response theory), 417, 421, 425
　validity considerations, 752, 755, 769
　verbal, 188, 215, 332
Absolmin solution, 235
Abstract Reasoning Test, 81*f*, 84, 86, 89, 90, 91, 92
academic performance, 211, 575, 736
accuracy in parameter estimation *see* AIPE (accuracy in parameter estimation)
accuracy of psychometric tests, 19, 763, 764, 765*t*
　see also AIPE (accuracy in parameter estimation), confirmatory power models
　content, 767–768
　response processes, 765–767
　structure, 768–769
Achenbach, T. M., 418
achievement, 76, 90, 153, 165, 167, 211, 217, 348
　mathematical, 77, 78*t*, 80, 86
　scoring, 575, 585, 600
　tests, 9, 10, 17, 56, 75, 86, 87, 253, 690
　validity considerations, 755, 758

The Wiley Handbook of Psychometric Testing: A Multidisciplinary Reference on Survey, Scale and Test Development, First Edition. Edited by Paul Irwing, Tom Booth, and David J. Hughes.
© 2018 John Wiley & Sons Ltd. Published 2020 by John Wiley & Sons Ltd.

ADF (asymptotic distribution-free) fit function, 259
Adler, N. E., 198
Advanced Placement exams, 580
Agresti, A., 962, 963, 967, 968
AIC (Akaike's information criterion), 504, 506
AIPE (accuracy in parameter estimation), confirmatory power models
  see also sample size planning, confirmatory factor models
  goal, 115
  model parameters in bifactor model, 130–131
  planning sample size, 116
  population model parameters of interest, 125–126
  population model RMSEA, 119–121
AISP (automated item selection algorithm), 430–431
Aitkin, I., 496
Aitkin, M., 256, 459, 496, 643
Akaike's information criterion (AIC), 504, 506
Albert, J. H., 496
Aldrich–McKelvey scaling, 920–923
alexithymia, 357–358
algorithmic item generation, 22–23, 76–77
Allport, G. W., 702, 717, 934
American Psychological Association Task Force on Statistical Inference, 144
analytic ability, 217
analytic methods (rotation), 285–288
  see also rotation
  analytic oblique algorithms, 288–290
  bifactor criteria, 286–287
  direct methods, 288
  early, 287–288
  geomin criterion, 160, 163, 285–286, 292, 293
  gradient projection algorithms, 234, 284f, 289–290
  pairwise algorithms, 288–289, 290
  quartic criteria, 285, 288
  reference structure, 287–288
analytic oblique rotation algorithms, 288–290
analytical dimension reduction, 267–268
anchor test, data collection, 587–588
  checking that anchor items act like common items, 589
  design issues, 596–597
  external and internal anchors, 597

Anderson, C. J., 967
Anderson, T. W., 295
Andrich, D., 543
Angoff, W. H., 588, 600
ANOVA (analysis of variance), 825
anxiety, 308, 340
appropriateness, 19–20, 24, 25, 28, 763, 769, 772
aptitude testing, 9, 75, 87, 216, 224
Archer, C. O., 295
Armed Services Vocational Aptitude Test (ASVAB) see ASVAB (Armed Services Vocational Aptitude Test)
Armstrong II, D. A., 410
ASVAB (Armed Services Vocational Aptitude Test), 75, 356
  Assembling Objects subtest, 82f, 83, 88–89
asymptotic distribution free theory, 348
asymptotic distribution, rotated loadings, 297–298
  see also rotation; standard errors, rotated loadings
  initial loadings, using, 295–296
asymptotic distribution-free (ADF) fit function, 259
Athletic Competence of Harter's Self Perception Profile for Children, 420
attenuation, correction for, 711–712
automated item selection algorithm (AISP), 430–431
automatic item generation
  see also item generation
  construct definition, 10
  defining, 77
  examples, 76
  explanatory models for structures, 85–86
  modeling psychometric properties, 84–86
  prediction models for item variants, 84–85
  research basis for, 83–86
    modeling psychometric properties, 84–86
    relevance to item generation, 83–84
  response processes, 85
auxiliary variables, 155, 162
axioms (mathematical assumptions), in CTT, 49–51, 787
Ayer, A. J., 573

badness-of-fit measures, 394
  see also goodness-of-fit (GOF)
Baker, F. B., 422
Bakker, R., 410, 917–918

Index

Balanced Incomplete Block (BIB), 166
Bartholomew, D. J., 256, 264, 267, 937
Basic Space Theory, 904–908
Bauer, D. J., 348
Bauldry, S., 195
Bayes' theorem, 497
Bayesian estimation, 66, 69, 149, 299
  Bayesian scale construction (BSC), 511–514, 969
    Dutch intelligence scale construction, 513–514
    item selection, 511–513
  hyperparameters, 497, 502, 504, 505t, 506, 970
  item response models using latent variables, 498–501
  latent trait estimation, 612
  Markov chain Monte Carlo (MCMC) algorithm, 497, 498, 502, 503
  methods, 496–498
  multistage sampling design, 507–511
  nonnormality, latent trait modeling, 355
  parameter estimation, 500–501
  PISA study, 509
  posterior distribution, 497–498
  posterior-based measurement of student proficiency, 501–507
  prior specification of Bayesian IRT models, 499–500
  psychometric scaling, 495–521
  simulation techniques, 495–496, 502, 503–507, 514
  socioeconomic status (SES), 510
  student clustering, 507–511
  test information function (TIF), 615
  unidimensional item response theory (UIRT), 423, 425
Bayesian information criterion (BIC), 355, 504, 506
Behavioral Risk Factor Surveillance System (BRFSS), 96
Béland, S., 426
Bentler, P. M., 16, 201, 286, 287, 298
Bermond–Vorst alexithymia questionnaire, 357–358
Bernaads, C. A., 234
bias
  measurement, 96, 888, 890
  nonresponse, 96
  personal, 919–920
  selection, 96
  test, 885

BIB (Balanced Incomplete Block), 166
BIC (Bayesian information criterion), 355, 504, 506
bifactor criteria, rotation, 286–287
bifactor modeling and evaluation of scale scores, 677–707
  see also bifactor models
  assessing hierarchical trait constructs, 701–703
  bifactor model alternative to alpha, 690–692
  confirmatory factor analysis (CFA), 688
  defining bifactor model, usefulness of, 682, 684–689
  Disgust Emotion Scale (DES), 678, 681, 682, 693, 694, 696
  fitting bifactor models, 697–700
  model-based reliability 689, 700
  preliminary analyses, 697
  R Code, 706–707
  real data example, 678
  structural equation models and bifactor models, 694–696
  unidimensionality, departures from, 678–682, 683t
  unit-weighted scoring in the presence of multidimensionality, 692–694
bifactor models, 325–346
  see also bifactor modeling and evaluation of scale scores; well-being
  advantages, 332–333
  AIPE for model parameters in, 130–131
  analytical dimension reduction, 267–268
  applications, 335–342
  bifactor rotations, 335
  canonical, , 341
  comparing with second-order models, 128–130, 327–331
  confirmatory, 327–333
  conventional alternative models, 331–332
  convergent and discriminant validity of constructs, testing, 340
  correlated-factor model, 331–332
  and elaborated or generalized simple structure, 455
  exploratory bifactor model analysis, 333–335
  first-order factors, 329–330, 331, 333
  fitting, 697–700
  full-information item bifactor analysis, 326n1
  general factors, 327–328

bifactor models (*cont'd*)
  group factors, 327–328
  higher-order factors, 326, 328, 329, 330
    in IRT, 326n1
  item information function (IIF) for,
    632–633
  latent variable models, 267–268, 270–271
  limitations, 341–342
  and model-based reliability, 689
  multidimensional IRT bifactor model,
    scoring under, 624–629
  multidimensional item response theory,
    454–455
  multifaceted constructs, test and
    measurement of, 336–338
    bifactor model approach, 337–338
    individual score approach, 337
    total score approach, 336–337
  one-factor models, 331
  in psychometric test development, 325–326
  residual variance, 328
  Schmid–Leiman transformations, 218, 326,
    330–331, 334, 685
  simulation techniques, 693, 694, 696
  and structural equation modeling, 694–696
  target rotations, 334–335
  well-being, 339–340
Big Five factors/personality traits, 220,
  308, 540
BILOG-MG command file, 646, 647
binary item scoring, 579
biquartimin criterion, rotation, 287
Birnbaum, A., 413
Bock, D., 264, 267
Bock, R. D., 256, 418, 425, 451, 452, 643
  Bock–Aitkin EM algorithm, 459
Böckenholt, U., 535
Bodner, T. E., 195
Bollen, K. A., 18, 194–195, 201, 202, 261
Bolt, D. D., 432
Bolt, D. M., 449, 452, 455
Booth, T., 24
bootstrap tests, 194–195
Borenstein, M., 8
Borg, I., 410
Borman, W. C., 543
Borsboom, D., 202, 703, 757, 758, 759, 764
Box–Cox procedures, 22, 26
Bradburn, N. M., 338
Bradlow, E. T., 65, 455, 496
Brannick, M. T., 944
Braun, H. I., 593

Braun, R. L., 586
Brennan, R. L., 63, 577, 582, 588, 600
BRFSS (Behavioral Risk Factor Surveillance
  System), 96
British empiricism, 214
broad versus narrow spectrum tests, 3
Broers, N., 76–77
Brossman, B. G., 661
Brown, A., 12, 13–14, 534, 535, 546, 555
Brown, T. A., 113
Brown, W., 720
Browne, M. W., 259, 261, 286, 288–289,
  290, 291
Buckingham, B. R., 754, 755, 763
Burt, C., 215, 216, 219

CA (conditional association), 430
CA (correspondence analysis), 408–409
CAF (common part accounted for), 315
Cahoon, L. S., 905
Cai, L., 270, 271, 452, 455
calibration
  concurrent, 642–643, 646
  fixed, 643, 646
  separate, 641–642, 645, 657
California Adult Q-Set test, 525
Camilli, G., 505, 506
Campbell, D. T., 20, 771, 781, 782
Campbell, J. P., 18
canonical correlation analysis, 201
Carpenter, P. A., 10, 81, 82n2
Carroll, J. B., 24, 59, 218, 287, 288
Carroll, J. D., 410
Carver, L. S., 336
CAT (computerized adaptive testing), 17, 22,
  141, 435
  Bayesian estimation, 511, 512, 514
  item generation, 75, 77, 89
categorical variables, 149, 153–154, 158
category response function (CRF), 418,
  422*f*
Cattell, R. B., 216–217, 218, 220, 229, 310,
  530, 933
Catten–Horn–Carroll (CHC) model, 5, 218
causal and effect indicators, factor loading,
  188, 198
causal indicators, 187–207
  canonical correlation analysis, 201
  CFA (confirmatory factor analysis), 193
  conceptual criteria for choosing approach,
    191–193
  conceptual unity, 189

confirmatory tetrad analysis (CTA), 194, 195
construct definition and item generation, 198
content validity checks, 199
defining, 187–190
determining when indicators should be viewed as, 190–197
disturbance terms, 189, 190
and effect indicators/effect indicator models, 187, 188, 190, 192t
indicator weight determination, 201–202
iso-strain example, 191, 197
JCQ (Job Contents Questionnaire), 191
local independence, 188
mediation tests, 196–197
multiple indicator multiple cause (MIMIC) models, 200–201
research, use in, 199–202
scale development with, 197–199
socioeconomic status (SES), 187, 197, 198
statistical criteria for choosing causal indicators approach, 193–197
traditional definitions, issues with, 190
CCSQ (Customer Contact Styles Questionnaire), 525, 540
CDMS (classical multidimensional scaling), 378
CEFA (comprehensive exploratory factor analysis), 289
Centers for Disease Control and Prevention, Behavioral Risk Factor Surveillance Survey, 102
centroid method, 215
CES (coefficient of equivalence and stability), 18
CFA (common factor analysis) *see* common factor analysis
CFA (confirmatory factor analysis), 242–247, 851
see also CFA–MTMM models; exploratory factor analysis (EFA); factor analysis; sample size planning, confirmatory factor models
bifactor analysis, 286
bifactor modeling and evaluation of scale scores, 688
causal indicators, 193–194
confirmatory bifactor models, 327–333
confirmatory item factor analysis, 454–455
confirmatory versus exploratory research, 242–243
and CTT, 54, 55
effect size, 890–891, 895, 896t, 897
estimates, 115
importance in psychometrics, 113
of JCQ, 195–196
MAT test battery, 25
maximum likelihood (ML) estimation, 149
measurement equivalence, study of, 889–891
ML-CFA models for interchangeable methods, 839–844
model equations, 243–245
model fit, 16
models for different MTMM measurement designs, 789–791
models of classical test theory, 786–788
MPlus eight-factor, using WLSMV estimator, 40
one-factor models, 117
rotation, 296
scale construction, 13, 14, 15
second-order models, 117
structural equation models, 113
tests of fit, 245–247
CFA–MTMM models, 781–846
see also CFA (confirmatory factor analysis); MTMM (multitrait-multimethod) models
applications of MTMM models for structurally different raters, 801–824
"classical" MTMM analysis, 781–785
for a combination of both methods, 818–819, 820f, 821, 822t, 823–824
common factor TMU models, 792, 793, 831–834
conceptual similarities and differences between approaches, 801
Correlated-Trait-Correlated-(Method-1) Model (CT-C(M-1)), 793–800, 798–799t, 803–805
defining for interchangeable methods, 808–810
defining for structurally different methods, 791–793
latent difference models, 797, 800, 805
latent means model, 800, 805–806
latent regression, 793–797, 798–799t
links to other models, 817–818
longitudinal, 826–827
psychometric foundation, 786–801
structurally different models, 834–838
CFI (comparative fit index), 16, 116

CFMs (common factor models)
  see also common factor analysis
  and component analysis, 241, 242
  exploratory common factor analysis, 227, 228, 231, 238
  exploratory factor analysis (EFA), 214, 241, 242
  intellect, multiple factors of, 216
  minimum average partial (MAP), 310
  multiple factor analysis, 221, 223
  number of factors problem, 306
  problem-solving, 248, 249
  structural equation modeling, 312–316
  test development, 14–15
  TMU models, 793, 831–834
CFs (common factors)
  see also CFMs (common factor models); common factor analysis
  bifactor models, 681, 690
  cluster sampling, 100
  confirmatory factor analysis (CFA), 245
  exploratory factor analysis (EFA), 212, 214
  factorial homogeneity, 248
  illustration of an exploratory common factor analysis, 224, 225, 227–234, 238, 239
  and intelligence, 215, 216, 217, 218
  invariance, 852–855
  latent variable models (categorical), 254
  longitudinal data, 868
  multiple common factors, 856, 867
  multiple factor analysis, 221, 223
  nonlinearity issue, 249
  number of factors problem, 306, 307, 309, 310, 311, 318t
  orthogonality, 690
  rotation, 280
  rotational indeterminacy, 944
  simple structure, 233
CF-varimax criterion, rotation, 285, 291, 292–293
chain equating (CE), 594
chained equations (fully conditional specification) imputation, 151, 152, 153–154
Chang, H. H., 512–513
Chapel Hill Expert Survey (CHES), 919
CHC theory, 218
Chen, F. F., 28, 299–300, 301, 302, 677, 693
Chen, W. H., 63, 426
Cheng, P. E., 588
Chernyshenko, O. S., 435, 543, 888, 891t
Chib, S., 496

chi-square tests, 121
  categorical variables, 259, 261, 273
  causal indicators, 195–196
  chi-square difference test, 313
  factor analysis, 214, 231, 245, 247, 248
  number of factors problem, 312, 313, 315, 316, 317
Chiu, T. W., 505, 506
Christoffersson, A., 445
Cicero, 717
Cizek, G. J., 756, 757, 759, 760
classical multidimensional scaling (CDMS), 378, 406, 408, 409
classical test theory see CTT (classical test theory)
Cleary, T. A., 885
Clemans, W. V., 530
Clinton–Jackman–Rivers (CJR) model, 916
cluster analysis, 405, 681
cluster sampling, 99–100
  survey weights, 101–102
CML see composite maximum likelihood estimation (CML); conditional maximum likelihood estimation (CML)
coefficient of equivalence and stability (CES), 18
cognitive ability 188, 944, 974
  test development, 3, 5, 7–9, 19, 21, 24, 28
cognitive complexity theory, 81
cognitive design system approach, item generation, 77, 80–82
  development of item structures and databases, 88–89
cognitive interviews, 13
Cohen, J., 115, 169
Collins, L. M., 143
color vision theory, 215, 219
common factor analysis, 211–251
  see also CFMs (common factor models); exploratory factor analysis (EFA); factor analysis; number of factors problem
  CFA for ordinal variables (CFA-ord), 306
  common and unique factors, 212
  communalities, estimating, 225, 227, 229
  versus component analysis, 240–242
  conditions for, 224–225
  illustration of an exploratory common factor analysis, 223–225, 226t, 227–242
  number of factors problem, 306
  single common factor of intellectual tasks, 211–213, 221

standard for exploratory factor analysis, 224–225
total variance, 223
common factor models *see* CFMs (common factor models)
common factor space, 232
common items (CI) in equating, 639
common part accounted for (CAF), 315
common pathway model, 196
comparative fit index (CFI), 16, 315
comparative judgment, law of, 536
component analysis
  see also PCA (principal components analysis)
  versus common factor analysis, 240–242
composite maximum likelihood estimation (CML), 261–263
composites, 189
  reliability of, 718–720, 721*f*, 738, 737*t*, 740
comprehensive exploratory factor analysis (CEFA) software, 289
computerized testing, 103, 106, 295, 317
  computerized adaptive testing (CAT) *see* CAT (computerized adaptive testing)
  factor analysis, 216, 218, 224, 227, 231, 232, 233, 234, 244
  factorial invariance, 851
  high-level language, 22
  IRT equating, 654–655, 656, 657
  IRT linking, 645
  IRTPRO software, 420, 425
  item generation, 77, 90, 92
  item response theory (IRT), 268
  latent variable models, 258, 260, 271–272
  MBESS (software package), 117, 122
  multidimensional scaling software, 409
  propensity score matching, 108–109
  structural equation models (SEMs), 333
  test development, 10, 22
  WinBUGS software package, 497, 503–507, 510, 514
conceptual parallelism, 188
conceptual variables, 188
concurrent calibration, 642–643, 646
concurrent criterion associations, 769
conditional association (CA), 430
conditional maximum likelihood estimation (CML), 423–424
Cone, J. D., 752
configural invariance, 852–853
  code for testing, 873–874, 878–880

confirmatory factor analysis (CFA) *see* CFA (confirmatory factor analysis)
confusions data, 387
congeneric measures, 715
Conijn, J. M., 427
consistency coefficient, 813
consistency measures, internal, 18
constrained maximum likelihood methods, 296–297
construct definition, 5, 10, 198
content doublets, 681
content validity checks, causal indicators, 199
continuous measures, factor model for, 852–859
  configural invariance, 852–853
  effect size, 856–857
  metric invariance, 853–854
  scalar invariance, 854–855
  strict invariance, 855
continuous variables, 245, 254, 258–259
  continuous grouping variables, 867
convenience samples, 96
convergent evidence/validity, 771, 781–782, 813
Converse, P. E., 904, 905
Coombs, C. H., 523, 540, 541, 543, 545, 909
Correlated Trait-Correlated Uniqueness (CT-CU), 783, 786
Correlated Trait-Uncorrelated Method (CT-UM), 784, 787, 801
correlated-factor model, 331–332
Correlated-Trait-Correlated-(Method-1) Model (CT-C(M-1)), 793–797, 798–799*t*, 803–805
correlation coefficients, 50, 116, 227, 240, 387, 823, 824
  reliability, 712, 714–715, 726
correlation matrix
  factor analysis, 211, 212*t*, 213, 214, 216, 224, 227, 229, 230, 231, 238, 239, 242, 244, 245
  latent variable models, 254, 255, 260–261
  missing data handling methods, 144, 158
  multitrait-multimethod models, 782–783
  number of factors problem, 309, 311
  polychoric, 679
  raw, 229
  reduced, 229
  rotation, 291, 299
  sample size planning, confirmatory factor models, 119*t*, 123, 129
  weighted, 229

correlation weights, 202
correlational analysis
  see also correlation coefficients; correlation matrix
  canonical, 201
  intraclass correlations and reliability, 738
  Pearson correlation, 52, 58, 59, 312
  point-biserial correlation, 58–59, 66
  polychoric correlations, 259, 260, 317
  tetrachoric correlations, 259, 260
  weights, 202
correspondence analysis (CA), 408–409
Costa, P. T., 933, 934
counterbalanced (CB) data collection design, 586
Courvoisier, D. S., 826, 827
covariance matrix, 150, 151, 978
Cox, D. R., 262
Cox, M. A. A., 410
Cox, T. F., 410
Crawford–Ferguson criterion, rotation, 285, 293
CRF (category response function), 418, 422f
Cronbach, L. J., 52, 53, 55–56, 62, 448, 754, 755
Cronbach's alpha, 17, 52, 622
cross-cultural research, 556
cross-sequential design, 167
crystallized intelligence, 217–218
CTA (confirmatory tetrad analysis), 194
  of JCQ, 195–196
CT-CU (Correlated Trait-Correlated Uniqueness), 783, 786
CTT (classical test theory), 49–59, 785
  assumptions, mathematical, 49–51, 787
  biserial correlation, 59
  CFA models, 786–788
  compared to IRT, 64, 65, 66, 68, 69, 413, 414, 436, 607
  compared to STT, 59, 60
  congeneric forms, 50–51
  dichotomous items, 53, 54, 55, 58, 59
  error variance, 50, 51, 53–58, 787
  estimation of reliability and the SEM, 51–57
  internal consistency measures, 51, 52
  item and test information, 68
  item discrimination, 58–59
  item level indices, 58–59
  linearity/nonlinearity, 55
  parallel measurements, 50, 52–53, 55, 56
  Pearson correlation, 52, 58, 59
  permissible replications, 56–57
  Platonic true score, 49
  point-biserial correlation, 58–59
  reliability, 50, 51–58, 67
  standard error of measurement (SEM), 50, 51–58
  and STT, 59, 60, 69
  subdividing of test, 52–55
  tetrachoric correlation, 59
  true score, 49, 709
CT-UM (Correlated Trait-Uncorrelated Method), 784, 787, 801
Cudeck, R., 288–289, 290, 295
cumulative sum statistics, 427
Cureton, E. E., 291
Current Population Survey (CPS), 109, 110
Customer Contact Styles Questionnaire (CCSQ), 525, 540

data
  analysis examples, 159–165
  artificial, 139, 140
  augmented, 503
  coding of, 12
  confusions, 387
  Coombs' theory, 523
  data collection designs, 585–588
  data sets used for demonstrations, 744–745
  item-level, 15
  longitudinal, 167–168
  missing see missing data handling methods
  multidimensional scaling, 376, 378, 379, 385, 386–388, 387
  partially ipsative, 531–532
  perceptual data, 919–923
  preferential data, 909–919
  preprocessing practices, 588–591
  prestructuring, 940, 941t, 942–943
  real see real data
data collection designs, 585–588
  anchor test, 587–588
  equivalent groups (EG), 586–587, 594
  notation (design table), 586
  single-group (SG), 586
De Boeck, P., 352, 448, 500
debriefings, 12
decision analysis, 738
deduction, 242, 243
Dehejia, R. H., 109, 110
demonstrations, data sets used for, 744–745
dendogram (tree diagram), 405, 406f
depression, 308, 340

DES *see* Disgust Emotion Scale (DES)
DES (Disgust Emotion Scale), 678, 681–694, 695
  in applied settings, 700–701
  review of analyses, 696
DETECT procedure, 431, 432, 435
DFIT (differential functioning of items and tests), 886
diagonally weighted least squares (DWLS), 16, 261
Diamantopoulos, A., 199, 201, 202
dichotomous items, 53, 54, 55, 58
Diener, E., 325, 338
DIF (differential item functioning), 885
  anchor designs, 589
  constrained-baseline method, 887
  detecting using CFA, 889–890
  detecting using the likelihood ratio method, 887
  empirical example of IRT and CFA analyses, 891–893, 892*f*, 895, 894*f*
  free-baseline method, 887
  multidimensional item response theory, 458
  Type I error rates, 887
difference scores, reliability of, 740
difference that matters (DTM), 596
differential functioning of items and tests (DFIT), 886
differential item functioning *see* DIF (differential item functioning)
differential test functioning (DTF), 885, 886
dimensionality
  see also multidimensional scaling; number of factors problem; unidimensionality
  assessment methods, 309
  exploratory factor modeling, 306–324
  in item response theory, 63
  meaning, 307–308
  nonparametric IRT, 430–432
  unidimensionality, 63, 64
Direct Oblimin method, 234, 235
discrete measures, factor model for, 859–866
  effect size, 863
  identification, 861–862
  model evaluation, 862–863
discriminant evidence/validity, 771, 782
Disgust Emotion Scale (DES) *see* DES (Disgust Emotion Scale)
distortion, ipsative scores, 531
disutility, 541
DMM (double monotonicity model), 428–430, 434

Dolan, C. V., 348–349, 352, 359
domain mapping, 10
  systematic, 6–7
domain sampling theory and structural reliability measures, 728–736
  measures of internal consistency, 730–733
  misuse of alpha, 732*t*, 733, 735–736
Dorans, N. J., 573, 576, 577, 583, 587, 588, 589, 591, 594, 599, 600, 601
double monotonicity model (DMM), 428–430, 434
Downing, S. M., 10
Downs, A., 906
Drasgow, F., 20, 21, 435, 543, 888, 890–891
DTF (differential test functioning), 885, 886
DTM (difference that matters), 596
Duhachek, A., 723
Dumenci, L., 418, 818

EAP (expected-a-posterior) estimation, 67, 543
  Experience of Service Questionnaire (ESQ)
    satisfaction scored by multidimensional method, 623–624
    satisfaction scored by unidimensional method, 619–623
    scoring of "correlated traits" model, 635–636
    scoring of multidimensional IRT bifactor model, 637–638
    scoring of unidimensional CFA model, 634–635
  latent trait estimation, 611, 612
  UIRT (unidimensional item response theory), 424
ECD (evidence-centered design), 578
Educational Testing Service, 576
EFA (exploratory factor analysis), 279
  see also common factor analysis; factor analysis
  common use of, 295
  comprehensive exploratory factor analysis software, 289
  conditions for, 224–225
  exploratory bifactor model analysis, 333–335
  exploratory bifactor rotation, 302
  exploratory item factor analysis, 453
  factor scores and indeterminacy, 238–239
  factorial invariance, 239–240
  fit assessment, 213–214

EFA (exploratory factor analysis) (cont'd)
  illustration of an exploratory common factor analysis, 223–225, 226t, 227–242
  interpretation, 214–215
  missing data handling methods, 159, 160, 162, 163
  numbers of factors, 229–231
  orthogonal, 286
  rotation, 160t, 280–281
  simple structure rotation, 231–235, 236–237t, 238
  single common factor of intellectual tasks, 211–213
  standard for, 224–225
  starting point, 294–295
effect indicators/ indicator models, 187, 188, 198
  see also causal indicators
  and causal indicators, 190, 192t, 194, 196
  scales, 198
effect size
  see also CFA (confirmatory factor analysis); sample size planning, confirmatory factor models
  AIPE (accuracy in parameter estimation)
    for model parameters in bifactor model, 130–131
    for population model parameters of interest, 125–126
    for population model RMSEA, 119–121
  confidence intervals, 115
  confirmatory factor analysis (CFA), 890–891
    example, 895, 896t, 897
  continuous measures, 856–857
  discrete measures, 863
  empirical demonstrations of sample size planning, 117–131
  existence of an effect, 115
  item response theory (IRT), 887–889
    example, 895, 896t, 897
  magnitude of an effect, 115
  omnibus or targeted, 116
  power analysis
    comparing a bifactor model and a second-order factor model, 128–130
    for population model parameters of interest, 121–125
    for population model RMSEA, 118–119
    SEM, statistical theories for, 124–125

RMSEA (root mean square error of approximation)
  AIPE for, 119–121
  power analysis for, 118–119
  sample size planning, 8, 114–131
  scaling, 116
  scope, 116
  standardized or unstandardized, 116
EG (equivalent groups) design, data collection, 586–587, 594, 595
Egberink, I. J. L., 430
Eid, M., 20, 333
eigenvalues/eigenvalue matrix
  exploratory common factor analysis, 227–230
  multidimensional scaling, 379, 383t, 384f, 386n3
  number of factors problem, 309–312
eigenvectors/eigenvector matrix
  common factor analysis, 227, 228, 229
  multidimensional scaling, 379, 383t
Eignor, D. E., 600
Ellis, J. L., 974
E–M (expectation-maximization) algorithm, 149, 264, 268, 269, 272, 273, 643
Embretson, S. E., 10, 14, 22, 418, 446
empirical information matrix, 265–266
empirical reliability, 617
empirical verification principle, 573
EPQ-R (Eysenck Personality Questionnaire), 447, 454, 458–462
  see also MIRT (multidimensional item response theory)
  eight-factor confirmatory MIRT model, 478–490
  IRTPRO Code
    for the eight-factor confirmatory MIRT model of the EPQ, 478–490
    for the three-factor confirmatory MIRT of the EPQ, 474–478
    for the three-factor EFA model of the EPQ, 471–474
    for unidimensional 2PL model of the EPQ, 469–471
  three-dimensional exploratory item factor analysis, 459–460, 463–464
  three-factor confirmatory MIRT of, 474–478
  three-factor EFA model, 471–474
  unidimensional 2PL model, 469–471
  unidimensional model, 459–462

EQSIRT, 446
equating of scores, 598, 599–601
   see also scores/scoring
   anchor test design issues, 596–597
   in a common population, 592
   on complete tests, using common items, 593–595
   description, 600
   equipercentile equating function, 592
   external anchors, 597
   goal of equating, 600
   internal anchors, 597
   linear equating function, 592–593
   observed-score equating methods, 591–595
   pitfalls, 595–597
   procedures and practices for, 588–598
   requirements, 600–601
   sample size issues, 595–596
equivalence coefficients, 18
equivalent groups (EG) design, data collection, 586–587, 594, 595
error variance, 122, 133, 223
   absolute, 57, 62–63, 63
   classical test theory (CTT), 50, 51, 53–58, 787
   forced-choice response formats, 550, 551
   generalizability theory, 62–63
   item response theory (IRT), 67
   strong true-score theory (STT), 59, 60
   test development, 17, 21
errors
   see also error variance; RMSEA (root mean square error of approximation), confirmatory factor models; standard error of measurement (SEM); standard errors, rotated loadings
   correlated, 53n3
   nonsampling, 96
   random/random response, 17, 57
   relative, 62
   sampling, 8, 96, 97, 242, 295
   specific, 17
   standard, 96
   systematic, 57
   transient, 17
   Type I error rates, 887
European Social Survey, 3
Evers, A., 436
evidence-centered design (ECD), 578
expectation–maximization (E–M) algorithm, 149, 264, 268, 269, 272, 273, 643

expected-a-posterior (EAP) estimation *see* EAP (expected-a-posterior) estimation
Experience of Service Questionnaire (ESQ), 617–619
   alternative scoring methods, evaluation, 627–629
   bifactor IRT model, scored under, 625–627
   choice of measurement model, 629
   item endorsement rates, 618
   measured constructs, 618–619
   sample, 618
   satisfaction scored by multidimensional EAP method, 623–624
   satisfaction scored by unidimensional EAP method, 619–623, 621*t*
   scoring of "correlated traits" model, 635–636
   scoring of multidimensional IRT bifactor model, 637–638
   scoring of unidimensional CFA model, 634–635
experts, utilizing, 11, 12
exploratory bifactor rotation, 301–302
exploratory factor analysis (EFA) *see* EFA (exploratory factor analysis)
exploratory item factor analysis, 453, 459–460, 463–464*t*
extant sources, using, 11
extraversion, 219, 325
Eysenck, H. J., 219
Eysenck Personality Questionnaire (EPQ-R) *see* EPQ-R (Eysenck Personality Questionnaire)

Fabrigar, L. R., 315
facet analysis, 76–77, 218
   reliability, 736–738
factor analysis, 197
   see also factor analysis; factor loading; number of factors problem
   Big Five Factors (of personality), 220, 308, 540
   Big Three factors (of meaning), 220–221
   chi-square tests, 214, 231, 245, 247, 248
   common factor analysis *see* common factor analysis
   common variance, 223
   and compensatory MIRT models, 452–453
   versus component analysis, 240–242
   and computers, 216, 218, 224, 227, 231, 232, 233, 234, 244

factor analysis (*cont'd*)
  confirmatory *see* CFA (confirmatory factor analysis)
  exploratory, 211–215
    illustration, 223–225, 226t, 227–242
  facet analysis, 76–77, 218
  factor extraction, 227
  factor loading, 213, 217, 221, 223, 231, 232, 245, 248
  factorial heterogeneity or homogeneity issue, 248
  first-order factors, 216, 217, 218, 235, 329–330, 331, 332
  general factors, 218, 219, 327, 729
  group factors, 327, 341, 729–730
  higher-order factors, 216, 218, 232, 235, 326, 329, 330, 731–732, 755
  intellect, multiple factors of, 215–218
  linear model, 272, 273, 536, 541, 608, 860
    nonnormality, latent trait modeling, 347, 348, 350–354, 356, 359, 360
  maximum likelihood (ML) estimations, 227
  MIRT, as item factor analysis, 452–455
  multiple, 221, 223
  nonlinearity issue, 248–249
  normal distribution, 347–348
  one-factor models, 117, 331
  orthogonal factors, 218
  parallel analysis (PA), 230
  personality, 219–221, 222t
  personality trait psychology, 940, 941t, 942–943
  problems, 6, 248–249
  rotational indeterminacy, 216
  ruler method, 229–230
  scale construction, 14–15
  and Second World War, 216
  second-order factors, 5, 8, 128–130, 216, 218, 332, 341
    comparing a bifactor model and a second-order factor model, 128–130, 327–331
  starting point, 294
  third-order factors, 216
  traditional, 455
  two-factor model, 212
  unique variance, 223
factor indeterminacy, 238–239
factor loading
  bifactor models, 328, 330, 331, 332, 334, 340–341
  causal and effect indicators, 188, 198
  common factor analysis, 213, 217, 221, 223, 231, 232, 245, 248
  forced-choice response formats, 548
  latent trait modeling, nonnormality in, 348–351, 354, 355, 356–359
  latent variable models, 254, 255, 256
  level-dependent, 348, 349, 351, 354, 355, 359, 360
  MAT test battery, 27–28t
  number of factors, assessing, 318
  quadratic, 351, 354
  rotation, 279, 287, 297, 303
  sample size planning, confirmatory factor models, 122, 124, 127, 128–129, 130, 131
  unique, 221, 231, 245
factor score indeterminacy, 15, 238–239
factor simplicity, 308
  see also simple structure rotation
factor-pattern loading *see* factor loading
fairness
  MAT test battery, 28–30
  psychometric validity, 771–772
  and test bias, 885
  validation, 20
feasibility, 772
Feldt, L. S., 53, 54
FFM (Five Factor Model), personality, 5, 6, 7, 8, 932–933
  acceptance, 938–939
  data prestructuring, 940, 941t, 942–943
  discovery, 937–938
  tools-to-theories heuristic, 937–945
field pretests, item review, 12
FIML (full information maximum likelihood), 149, 256, 261, 263–267, 446, 858
first-order factors, 216, 217, 218, 235
  bifactor models, 329–330, 331, 332, 333
Fisher, R. A., 216
Fisher information/Fisher information matrix, 265, 266, 513, 613
Fiske, D. W., 20, 771, 781, 783
Five Factor Model (FFM), personality *see* FFM (Five Factor Model), personality
fixed calibration, 643, 646
Fleer, P. F., 886
Fletcher–Power algorithm, 258–259
flexMIRT command file, 272, 643, 645, 647, 650, 651, 670–673
Flugel, J., 338
fluid intelligence, 217

Forced-Choice Five Factor Markers
  Questionnaire, 539, 547–548t,
  551–554
 attribute scores, estimating, 551
 coding and describing data, 546, 548
 measure, 545–546, 547–548t
 model setup, 551–554
 sample, 546
forced-choice response formats
 advantages of using for questionnaire items,
  526–528
 applications, 540
 block size, 555
 coding of responses, 533–534
 correlations between traits, 555
 cross-cultural research, 556
 data analysis example (Forced-Choice Five
  Factor Markers questionnaire), 539,
  545–554, 547–548t
  attribute scores, estimating, 551
  coding and describing data, 546, 548
  measure, 545–546, 547–548t
  model setup, 548–551
  MPlus output, 551–554
  sample, 546
 defining, 523–526
 effective assessments, recommendations,
  555–556
 future research, 556
 intercept/slope IRT parameterization, 548
 IR approach or measurement by modeling,
  532–533
 keyed direction of items, 555
 modeling, 523–569
 multidimensional forced-choice, 545
 number of attributes, 555
 ordinal forced-choice formats,
  524–525, 527
 Q-sort ranking, 525, 527
 scaling of, 528–545
  applications, 540, 543, 544
  attributes, measurement models for,
   536–538, 541–542, 544, 545
  classical approach, 528–530
  ipsative scores as interpersonally
   incomparable, 530–531
  ipsative scores distorting construct
   validity, 531
  ipsative scores distorting criterion-related
   validity, 531
  ipsative data, psychometric properties,
   530–531

McCloy–Heggestad–Reeve unfolding
  model, 533, 545
 measurement by fiat, 529, 533
 multi-unidimensional pairwise-preference
  (MUPP) model, 533, 543–544
 partially ipsative data, 531–532
 preference decision models, 535–536,
  541, 543–544, 545
 technical detail, 538–540, 543, 544
 Thurstonian IRT model, 534–540,
  545, 549
 Zinnes–Griggs model, 540–543, 542f
Forero, C. G., 261
Forsyth, R. A., 584, 585
Foster, S. L., 752
Fox, J. P., 496, 500
Freeman, M. F., 584
Friedman, J. H., 968
Fu, J., 455
full information maximum likelihood (FIML)
  estimation, 149, 256, 261, 263–267,
  446, 858

g theory see generalizability theory (g theory)
Galton, F., 211, 712
Gärdenfors, P., 906
Gauss–Hermite quadrature, 265
Gaussian distribution, 911, 912, 964,
  966, 967
 multivariate, 964, 965
Gaussian random field, 978
G-coefficient, 62, 63
Gelman, A., 163, 496, 498
General Component Latent Trait Model
  (GLTM), 446
General Health Questionnaire, 196
general intelligence
 bifactor models, 332, 333, 338
 concept, 973
 exploratory factor analysis (EFA), 212, 214
 multiple factors of the intellect,
  215–218
 nonnormality, latent trait modeling, 347,
  357, 359
generalizability theory (g theory), 57,
  62–63, 69
 reliability, 736–738
Generalized Graded Unfolding Model
  (GGUM), 544
generalized least squares (GLS), 256, 258,
  259, 260–261
generalized partial credit model, 421

general-specific factor models *see* bifactor models
genome wide association studies, 348
geomin criterion, rotation, 285–286, 292, 293, 318
  missing data handling methods, 160, 163
GGUM (Generalized Graded Unfolding Model), 544
Ghiselli, E. E., 18
Gibbons, R. D., 270–271, 454–455, 455, 456
Gierl, M. J., 79, 80
Gifford, J. A., 496
Gigerenzer, G., 933, 935, 936, 938, 946
Gilks, W. R., 498
Girshick, M. A., 295
Glas, C. A. W., 426, 496, 500
GLS (generalized least squares), 256, 258, 259, 260–261
GLTM (General Component Latent Trait Model), 446
GMAT (Graduate Management Admission Test), 30, 31, 32
Godambe (sandwich) information matrix, 263
goodness-of-fit (GOF)
  see also badness-of-fit measures
  asymptotic, 456
  latent variable models, 259, 263
  multidimensional item response theory, 456–458
  nested model comparisons, 458
  number of factors problem, 312, 313, 314–315
  overall fit assessment, 456–457
  piecewise fit assessment, 458
  source of model misfit, 457–458
Gordon's Personal Profile Inventory (GPP-I), 525
GP (gradient projection algorithms), 234, 284f, 289–290, 290
GPP-I (Gordon's Personal Profile Inventory), 525
graded response models (GRMs), 33, 421–422, 451
gradient projection (GP) algorithms, 234, 235, 284f, 289–290
Graduate Management Admission Test (GMAT), 30, 31, 32
Graduate Record Examination (GRE), 75
Graham, J. W., 156, 157, 166, 167, 168
graphs/graphical methods, 106, 282, 283f, 283t, 376
GRE (Graduate Record Examination), 75

Greenacre, M. J., 410
Griffith, D., 225
Griggs, R. A., 540, 541
GRMs (graded response models), 33, 421–422, 451
Groenen, P., 410
group factors, 327–328, 341, 729–730
grouping of items, 6–7
Groves, R. M., 13
Gu, M. G., 269
guessing parameters, 64
  Bayesian estimation, 505, 506
  IRT linking and equating, 640, 655
  logit-guessing, 650
  UIRT (unidimensional item response theory), 415, 417
Guildford, J. P., 216
Gustafsson, J., 333
Guttman, L., 10, 52, 217, 218, 229, 239, 721–722, 723

Haebara, T., 642, 645
Haladyna, T. H., 10
Hambleton, R. K., 418, 422, 498
Hansen, M., 455
Hanson, B. A., 661
Harman, H. H., 287
Hastie, T., 968
Hedeker, D., 454–455, 455, 456
Heggestad, E. D., 545
Hessen, D. J., 353
Hessian matrix, 265
heteroscedasticity, nonnormality in latent trait modeling, 349, 351, 353–354, 358
HEXACO Personality Inventory, 943, 944
hierarchical clustering, 681
higher-order factors, 216, 218, 232, 235, 731–732, 755
  bifactor models, 326, 329, 330, 341–342
Hinich, M. J., 904
history of testing, 6
history test
  IRT equating, 655
  IRT linking, 645–647, 648–649t, 649
Hively, W., 76
Hofacker, C., 348
Holland, P. W., 573, 586, 587, 588, 591, 592, 593, 594, 599, 600, 601
Holzinger, K. J., 327, 334, 682
Horn, J., 217, 218
Horn's parallel analysis (Horn's PA), 311, 312, 315

Horvitz–Thompson type estimator, 105
Hoskens, M., 448
Howe, W. G., 227
Hu, L.-T., 16
Hughes, D. J., 18, 19, 21
Hull, J. G., 336, 677
Hull method, 315–316, 318
Hull-CAF, 315
Hull-CFI, 315, 318, 319f
Humphreys, L. G., 311, 885
Hunter, J. E., 8, 17, 18, 33
hyperplanes, 232–233

Iacobucci, D., 723
i*CLUST* algorithm
   and bifactor modeling, 681, 685, 697, 698f
   reliability, 732, 733, 735
ideal point models, 435
IIF (item information function), 614–615
   for a bifactor model, 632–633
IIO (invariant item ordering), 429, 430, 434
IJK (infinitesimal jackknife), 298, 299
Ilgen, D. R., 311
image analysis, 228, 240
implicit imputation, 147
imputation
   see also missing data handling methods
   chained equations, 151, 152, 153–154
   versus direct estimation, 156–159
   implicit, 147
   between-imputation (thinning interval), 152, 163
   latent categorical variable, 153–154
   and maximum likelihood, 156
   multiple *see* multiple imputation, missing data handling
   phase, 150–153
   process, 147
   single, 144
   stochastic, 270
   within-imputation variance, 154
incomplete data *see* missing data handling methods
independent pathway mode, versus common pathway model (in behavior genetics), 196
induction, 242
inductive generalizations, 214
inferential methods, 311
infinitesimal jackknife (IJK), 298, 299
information
   content, incorporating into scales, 584–585
   external, embedding of, 402–405
   Fisher information/Fisher information matrix, 265, 266, 513
   full information maximum likelihood (FIML) estimation, 149, 256, 261, 263–267, 446, 858
   full-information item bifactor analysis, 326
   Godambe (sandwich) information matrix, 263
   item and test, in IRT, 67–69
   Kullback–Leibler information, 513
   limited information estimation methods, 256, 260–263
   normative, incorporating into scores, 582–583
informax criterion, rotation, 287, 291
intellect/intelligence
   see also general intelligence
   crystallized intelligence, 217–218
   Dutch intelligence scale construction, 513–514
   faceted theory of intelligence, 218
   factor analytic theory, 217
   fluid intelligence, 217
   hierarchical theory, 215
   intelligence subtest scores, 356–357
   multiple factors of, 215–218
   and personality, 219
   single common factor of intellectual tasks, 211–213, 221
   verbal ability, 188, 215, 332
internal consistency, 160, 730–733
   classical test theory (CTT), 51, 52
   domain sampling theory and structural reliability measures, 730–733
   KR-20, λ_3, and α as indicators of, 722–723
   reliability estimates, 721–722
   test development, 17, 18
interview techniques, 767
intraclass correlations and reliability, 738
invariance, 849–884
   configural, 852–853, 873–874, 878–880
   exploratory common factor analysis, 239–240
   factor model for continuous measures, 852–859
   factor model for discrete measures, 859–866
   factorial, 239–240, 849–884
   with many groups, 868
   MAT test battery, 20, 28
   measurement, 333

invariance (cont'd)
  metric, 853–854, 874–875, 880–882
  MPlus program, 42–43
  population, lack of, 597–598
  rotation, 239
  simulation techniques, 856
  strict, 855, 877–878, 882–884
  strong or scalar, 854–855, 875–876
invariant item ordering (IIO), 429, 430, 434
IPLM (one-parameter logistic model), 255, 414, 416f, 422–424
ipsative data
  defining, 530
  partially ipsative, 531–532
  psychometric properties, 530–531
  scores distorting construct validity, 531
  scores distorting criterion-related validity, 531
  scores interpersonally incomparable, 530–531
IRF (item response function), 414, 415, 417, 537, 609
IRT (item response theory), 63–69
  applying scoring methods and estimating measurement accuracy, 617–619
  assumptions
    correct dimensionality, 63
    form of model correctly specified, 64
    local independence, 63
  automatic item generation, 85
  Bayesian estimation, 509–511
    IRT models, prior specification of, 499–500
  bifactor models, 326
  categorical variables, analysis, 254, 255–256
  and causal indicators, 197
  compared to CTT, 64, 65, 66, 68, 69, 413, 414, 436, 607
  compared to STT, 67
  computer packages, 268
  dichotomous models, 64
  discrete measures, factor model for, 868
  effect size, 887–889, 895, 896t, 897
  equating see IRT equating
  and Ising model, 961–965
  item and test information, 67–69
  item generation, 85
  as item-level theory, 63
  latent traits, 63
  likelihood function, 66–67
  linking see IRT linking
  MAT test battery, 32–34

  measurement equivalence, study of, 887–889
  missing data handling methods, 149
  models, 64–66
  multidimensional see MIRT (multidimensional item response theory)
  multilevel, 496, 509–511
  nonparametric, 427–434
  one-parameter logistic model, 255, 414
  phase response probability, 65
  plausible values, 509–511
  point-biserial correlation, 58–59, 66
  political science, psychometric analysis, 914, 916–918
  Rasch model, 65, 414, 415
  scale construction, 13, 14
  scoring, 21
  steepness of IRF, 415–416
  test specifications, 578
  three-parameter logistic (3PL) model, 64–65, 505, 506
  Thurstonian model see Thurstonian IRT model
  time difficulty parameter, 255
  two-parameter logistic (2PL) model, 65, 85, 255, 580
  unidimensional see UIRT (unidimensional item response theory)
IRT approaches to test scoring, 607–638
  applying scoring methods and estimating measurement accuracy, 617–619
  choice of measurement model, 629
  expected-a-posterior (EAP) estimation, 611
  ESQ satisfaction scored by multidimensional method, 623–624
  ESQ satisfaction scored by unidimensional method, 619–623
  Experience of Service Questionnaire (ESQ), 617–619
  computation of scores, 631
  evaluation of the alternative scoring methods for data sample, 627–629
  item endorsement rates, 618
  measured constructs, 618–619, 628
  MPlus code, EFA, 633–634
  parent version, 631–632, 634–635
  sample, 618, 627–629
  scored under bifactor IRT model, 625–627
  scoring of unidimensional CFA model (parent model), 634–635

standard errors, 631
item information function (IIF), 614–615, 632–633
latent trait estimation, 609–612
maximum-a-posteriori (MAP) estimation, 611
multidimensional IRT model, 608–609
reliability, 616–617
scoring under the multidimensional IRT bifactor model, 624–629
scoring under the multidimensional IRT "correlated traits" model, 623–624, 635–636
scoring under unidimensional IRT model, 619–620, 621t, 622–623
standard error of measurement (SEM), 613–614
test information function (TIF), 615–616
IRT equating, 639, 651, 653–657, 658f, 659t
history test, 655
illustrative examples, 654–657
multidimensional, 658–660
observed score, 654
science test, 656–657, 658t
true score, 653–654
IRT linking, 639, 640–651
comparisons of linking methods, 644
concurrent calibration, 642–643, 646
fixed calibration, 643, 646
history test, 645–647, 648–649t, 649
illustrative examples, 644–651
science test, 649–651, 652t
separate calibration, 641–642, 645
IRTPRO software
eight-factor confirmatory MIRT model, 478–490
item response theory (IRT), 868
multidimensional item response theory, 446, 459
three-factor confirmatory MIRT, 474–478
three-factor EFA model, 471–474
UIRT (unidimensional item response theory), 421, 425, 427
unidimensional 2PL model, 469–471
Irwing, P., 219
Ising model, 957–962
estimating, 967–971
and IRT, 963–967
proof of equivalence between the Ising model and MIRT, 979–981
in psychometrics, 962–963
iso-strain construct, 191, 197

ISRF (item-step response function), 421, 428, 429f
item bifactor model, 267
item development, 10–13
item review, 12–13
piloting of test, 12, 13
item discrimination, in CTT, 58
item generation, 75–94
Abstract Reasoning Test, 81f, 84, 86, 89, 90, 91, 92
advantages, 76, 77
algorithmic, 22–23, 76–77
approaches, 77–83
cognitive design system, 77, 80–82, 88–89
item model, 77–79, 86, 87–88
norm-referenced tests, 90
other structures, 82–83
standards-based tests, 90–91
template, 77, 79–80, 88–89
automatic see automatic item generation
causal indicators, 198
components, 76
computerized adaptive testing (CAT), 75, 77, 89
and construct definition, 198
empirical tryout, 75, 83, 92
facet analysis, 76–77
"on-the-fly," 90
generated items on tests, using, 91–92
item content valuation, 89–90
item form, 76
item psychometric properties, 91
item structures and databases, development, 87–91
matrix problems, 81, 82
nature of, 76–83
research stages, 86–92
theoretical/conceptual framework, development, 86–87
traditional, limitations of, 75–76
item information function (IIF) see IIF (item information function)
item level indices, in CTT, 58–59
item mapping, 584
item model approach
development of item structures and databases, 87–88
development of theoretical/conceptual framework, 86
generation of items, 77–79
structural variants, 87

item parameters estimation, 422–424
item response function (IRF), 414, 415, 417, 537, 609
item response theory *see* IRT (item response theory)
item review, 12–13
item scores, 578, 579
item structures and databases, development
  see also item generation
  abstract structures, 89
  cognitive design system and template approaches, 88–89
  high-stakes tests, 90, 91
  item content valuation, 89–90
  item model approach, 87–88
  norm-referenced tests, 90
  standards-based tests, 90–91
item-step response function (ISRF), 421, 428, 429f

Jackman, S., 914
Jackson, P. H., 496
Jacoby, W. G., 410
JCQ (Job Contents Questionnaire)
  CTA (Confirmatory Tetrad Analysis) and CFA of, 195–196
  description, 191
  indicators, 193, 194
  mediation test on, 196–197
Jennrich, R. I., 234–235, 282, 286, 288, 289, 290, 295, 296, 298, 299
Jennrich–Butler analytic rotation, 685, 686–687
JML (joint maximum likelihood estimation), 422
Job Contents Questionnaire *see* JCQ (Job Contents Questionnaire)
Johnson, T. R., 195, 449, 452
Johnson curves, 350
joint imputation methods *see* multiple imputation, missing data handling
joint maximum likelihood estimation (JML), 422
Jones, L. V., 576
Jöreskog, K. G., 15, 254, 261, 295, 348, 454, 851, 886
Juniper, E. F., 199
Junker, B. W., 432, 434, 496, 974
Just, M. A., 10, 81

Kahneman, D., 576
Kaiser, H., 229, 234, 308

Kaiser criterion, 309–310, 939
Kam, C. M., 143
Kane, M. T., 577, 759
Karasek, R. A., 191
Katsikatsou, M., 261–262, 263
Kelley, K., 13, 114, 115, 116, 121
Kenny, D., 113, 781
kernal smoothing technique, 433
KernSmoothIRT package, 432–433
Kim, D., 63
Kim, H., 20, 21
Kim, S., 642
Kim, S. H., 422
King, G., 919
Koch, T., 20
Kolaczyk, E. D., 967
Kolb Learning Style Inventory, 525
Kolen, M. J., 577, 578, 579, 580, 582, 583–584, 588, 595, 600
Kong, F. H., 269
Koons, H. H., 756, 757
Kruskal, J. B., 394, 410
Kruskal's Stress, 392, 394
Kuder, G., 722
Kuhn, J. T., 426
Kullback–Leibler information, 513
Kuncel, N. R., 32
kurtosis, 26

Lagrange multiplier (LM), 426, 458
Lai, H., 79, 80
Lai, K., 13, 121
Lalonde, R., 109
Lang, J. W. B., 540
LASSO (least absolute shrinkage and selection operator), 968, 969, 970
  de-sparsified parameters, 971
latent difference models, 797, 800, 805
latent means model, 800, 805–806
latent regression, 202, 793–797, 798–799t
latent trait modeling *see* nonnormality, latent trait modeling
latent variable models, 109, 149, 253–277
  see also variables
  analytical dimension reduction, 267–268
  applications, 270–273
  Bayesian item response models using, 498–501
  categorical responses, 253–259
  categorical variables, estimation methods in, 253–277
  composite likelihood estimation, 261–263

discrete latent variables, 253
estimation methods
    with categorical items, 260–270
    limited information, 256, 260–263
    overview of, 256–258
    review, for continuous variables, 258–259
expectation–maximization (E–M) algorithm, 149, 264, 268, 269, 272, 273
exploratory factor analysis (EFA), 212
full-information maximum likelihood estimation, 263–267
HYBRID model, 253
imputation, 153–154
item response theory approach, 254, 255–256
latent class model, 253
limited-information estimation methods, 260–263
Metropolis–Hastings Robbins–Munro (MH–RM), 264, 268–270
MIMIC models, 200
network psychometrics, 975, 977
Newton–Raphson (N–R) maximization algorithm, 264–265, 268, 269, 273, 653–654
psychometric models, interpretation of latent variables in, 973–977
as tail measures, 974
underlying variable (UV) approach, 254–255, 260
Law of Diminishing Returns, 347, 349
Lawley, D. N., 295, 296
least squares estimates, 258
    diagonally weighted least squares (DWLS), 16, 261
    full weighted least squares, 261
    generalized least squares (GLS), 256, 258, 259, 260–261
    unweighted least squares (ULS), 256, 258, 259, 261
    weighted least squares (WLS), 256, 258
Lee, G., 661
Lee, W., 642, 661
Lehn, D. A., 677
Leiman, J. M., 455
Lemeshow, S., 97
Levy, P. S., 97
Lewis, C., 496
lexical hypothesis, Five Factor Model, 7
Li, M. Y., 588

Li, Y., 455
Liang, L., 583, 589
Ligtvoet, R., 434
likelihood function, 66–67, 257
likelihood ratio tests (LRTs), 313–314, 425, 887
Likert, R., 10
Likert scale, 9n1, 11, 435, 449
    UIRT (unidimensional item response theory), 419, 435
limited information estimation methods, categorical items, 256, 260–263
    three-stage methods, 260–261
Lin, H. Y., 496
linearity
    factor analysis, 272, 273, 536, 541, 608, 860
        nonnormality, latent trait modeling, 347, 348, 350–354, 356, 359, 360
    linear logistic test model (LLTM), 85, 87, 88t, 89
    linear regression, 109, 150, 153, 211
Liou, M., 588
LISREL software program, 258, 260, 271, 894f
Little, R. J. A., 588
Liu, J., 262
Liu, Y., 458
LLTM (linear logistic test model), 85, 87, 88t, 89
LM (Lagrange multiplier), 426, 458
local dependence, 447–449, 682
local independence, 63, 188
Lochner, K., 20
log likelihood, 145–147, 263
logistic regression models, 105, 153
longitudinal data
    designs for, 167–168
    discrete measures, factor model for, 868–869
Lord, F. M., 56, 60, 62, 413, 434, 445, 578, 581, 591, 600, 645, 886
Lorenzo-Seva, U., 310
Lorge, I., 576
LRTs (likelihood ratio tests), 313–314
Lu, B., 109

McCloy, R. A., 545
McCloy–Heggestad–Reeve unfolding model, 533, 545
McCrae, R. R., 933, 934
McDonald, R. P., 54, 238, 445, 623

McDonald's Omega, 17, 26, 41–42
McKeon, J. J., 287
MACS (mean and covariance structure) analysis, 889
Magis, D., 426
Mahalanobis distance, 108, 146
Mair, P., 201
manifest monotonicity (MM), 432
MAP (minimum average partial), 310–312
MAP (modal-a-posterior) estimate, 67, 69, 540
MAR (missing at random) mechanism, 141, 143, 155, 156, 157, 161, 168
Marcoulides, G. A., 49n1
Mardia, K. V., 348
marginal maximum likelihood (MML), 33, 67, 263, 422, 423, 497, 643
Markov chain Monte Carlo (MCMC) algorithm *see* MCMC (Markov chain Monte Carlo) algorithm
Markov random fields, 954–955
  parameterizing, 955–957
Markus, K. A., 190, 202
Martin, A., 914
MAT (test battery for managerial position recruitment), 4
  see also test development
  appropriateness, 24, 25, 28
  Business, Personality, Motivation and Leadership Scale, 25
    definition and sample items, 26t
    and fairness, 28–30
    reliability and scale characteristics, 26
    standardized factor loadings, 27–28t
  Business Numeracy scale, 32
  demographic characteristics of norm sample, 24, 25t
  description, 23
  Global MBA program, sample of applicants to, 24, 32
  invariance testing, 28, 29t
  language standard, 29–30
  Leadership scale, illustrative IRT analysis, 32–34
  omissions, 34
  predictive validity evidence, 30–32
  reliability and scale characteristics, 26, 28
  Technical Manual, 23–34
    example analyses, 24–28
matrix problems, 81, 82
matrix sampling designs, 165–166, 168
Matteucci, M., 513, 514

maximum likelihood (ML) estimation
  asymptotic properties, benefits of, 257
  categorical variables, 256, 257
  common factor analysis, 227
  composite maximum likelihood estimation (CML), 261–263
  conditional maximum likelihood estimation (CML), 422–423
  constrained methods, rotated loadings, 296–297
  direct estimation, 159–160
    versus imputation, 156–159
  distribution for population data, 145
  full information, 149, 256, 261, 263–267
  implicit imputation, 147
  and imputation, 156
  item response theory (IRT), 66–67
  joint maximum likelihood estimation (JML), 422
  likelihood function, 66–67, 257
  log likelihood, 145–147, 263
  marginal maximum likelihood, 33, 67, 263, 422, 424, 497, 643
  missing data handling methods, 139, 144–149, 148f, 155, 158, 159–164, 169, 170
  ML-CFA models for interchangeable methods, 839–844
  ML-CTC(M-1) model, 841–843
  multidimensional item response theory, 458
  normal distribution function, 145–146, 147
  robust maximum likelihood (RML), 261
  rotation, 292
  scale construction, 15–16
  simple structure rotation, 231
  two-stage, 159
  UIRT (unidimensional item response theory), 423
Maximum Posterior Weighted Kullback–Leibler Information criterion, 512–513
Maxwell, A. E., 295
Maxwell, S. E., 115, 116
Maydeu-Olivares, A., 261, 457, 534, 535, 546, 555
MBESS (software package), 117, 122
MBTI personality test, 7
MCAR (missing completely at random) mechanism, 140, 141, 143, 155, 158, 160, 162, 168
MCH-FS (Montreal Children's Hospital Feeding Scale), 316–320

MCMC (Markov chain Monte Carlo)
    algorithm, 152, 163, 264, 295, 299,
        424, 456, 917, 921
    Bayesian estimation, 497, 498, 502, 503
    political science, psychometric analysis,
        917–918
MDPREF (multidimensional analysis of
    preferences), 408
MDS (multidimensional scaling), 375–412
    asymmetric (ASYMSCAL), 408
    classical (CMDS), 378, 406, 408, 409
    cluster analysis, 405
    confusions data, 387
    data, 376, 378, 379, 385, 386–388, 387
    data reduction, 376
    dendogram (tree diagram), 405, 406f
    development of methodology, 410
    disparities, 392, 394
    dissimilarities, 377, 378, 381, 385–386,
        388, 389, 393f, 394
        profile dissimilarities, 386–387
    embedding of external information,
        402–405
    general Euclidean model (GEMSCAL),
        407, 408, 409
    general formulation, 376–378
    geometric model, 375
    input data, 376, 378, 379, 385
    interpretation strategies, 401–405, 406f
    Kruskal's Stress, 392, 394
    metric, 378–401, 383t, 384f, 405, 406f
    Mokken scaling, 388n5
    monotonic functions, 387, 389
    nonmetric, 378, 388–398, 390t, 391f,
        393f, 395f, 396f, 406f
    political psychology, 398–399, 400t,
        401, 405
    proximities, 375, 376, 377
    replicated MDS (RMDS), 406, 407
    Shepard diagram, 385, 392, 393f,
        395f, 396f
    software, 409
    square matrix, 377n1
    strengths, 376
    substantive examples
        metric multidimensional scaling,
            381–386, 382t, 384f
        nonmetric multidimensional scaling,
            398–399, 400t, 401
    terminology, 375
    unfolding model, 408
    variety of models, 406–409

weighted (WMDS), 407–408
Meade, A. W., 887
mean and covariance structure (MACS)
    analysis, 889
measurement, practical issues, 574–575
measurement bias, 96, 888, 890
measurement conditions, 576–577
measurement equivalence, study of
    CFA approach to, 889–891
    IRT approach to, 887–889
measurement instruments, 305, 316, 328,
    413, 935
measurement invariance, 159, 333, 851, 854,
    866–867, 889, 935, 976
    depression scale, 160, 164
measurement models, 158, 619, 850, 975
    for attributes, 536–538, 541–542, 544
    Bayesian estimation, 495, 496
    bifactor models, 684, 703
    causal indicators, 197, 199–200
    choice of, 629
    classical test theory, 788, 791, 792
    item response approach, or measurement by
        modeling, 532–533
    multitrait-multimethod models, 782–785,
        793, 819, 820f
mediation tests, 196–197
Medicaid, US, 103
Meehl, P. E., 754, 755
Meijer, E., 351
Meijer, R. R., 426, 427, 430
Mellenbergh, G. J., 533, 703
mental health-related impairment (MHI),
    104
Messick, S., 754, 756, 781
meta-analysis, 8–9
    limits, 9
method specificity coefficient, 813
metric invariance, 853–854
    code for testing, 874–875, 880–882
metric multidimensional scaling,
    378–401, 380t
    Basic Space Theory, 904
    caveat, 405, 406f
    data for, 386–388
    dissimilarities, 378, 381, 385–386
    driving distances, American cities, 380t,
        381, 382t
    Shepard diagram, 385
    substantive example (map construction),
        381–386, 382t, 384f
    two-dimensional solution, 381

Metropolis–Hastings Robbins–Munro (MH–RM) algorithm, 264, 268–270, 456
Meyer, P., 63
MHI (mental health-related impairment), 104
MHM (monotone homogeneity model), 428
MH–RM (Metropolis–Hastings Robbins–Munro) algorithm, 264, 268–270, 456
Micceri, T., 348
Middleton, K., 577
Mignani, S., 514
military tests, 76, 216
  see also ASVAB (Armed Services Vocational Aptitude Test)
Millsap, R. E., 20, 21, 28, 818
MIMIC (multiple indicator multiple cause) models
  causal indicators, 195, 200–201
  missing data handling methods, 156, 157f
minimum average partial (MAP) see MAP (minimum average partial)
MIRT (multidimensional item response theory), 445–493, 608–609
  bifactor models, 454–455
  compensatory and noncompensatory models, 446–447
  compensatory models and factor analysis, 452–453
  components, 446–447
  confirmatory item factor analysis, 454–455
  constructs at different levels of generality
    complete modeling, 449
    planned versus unintentional factor structure, 447–448
    response sets, 448–449
    between-versus within-item multidimensionality, 447
  dichotomous, 449–451
  eight-dimensional confirmatory model, 462
  elaborated or generalized simple structure and bifactor models, 455
  equating with MIRT models, 660–661
  exploratory item factor analysis, 453, 463–464t
  Eysenck Personality Questionnaire (EPQ-R) see EPQ-R (Eysenck Personality Questionnaire), 458–462
  factors and local dependence, 447–449
  future directions, 462–465
  goodness of fit, 456–458
  graded response model (GRM), 451
  Ising model, 963, 979–981
  as item factor analysis, 452–455
  models, 449–452
  network psychometrics, 975, 977
  nominal responses, models for, 451–452
  parameter estimation, 456
  polytomous, 451–452
  R Code examples, 490–493
  simple structure models, 454, 660
  subtasks, 446–447
  three-dimensional confirmatory model, 460–462, 463–464t
  two simple models, 660
  2PL MIRT model, 449–451
MIs (modification indices), 196–197
Mislevy, R. J., 83, 149, 496, 513
missing at random see MAR (missing at random) mechanism
missing completely at random see MCAR (missing completely at random) mechanism
missing data handling methods, 139–185
  artificial data set, using, 139, 140
  categorical variables, 149
  common nature of missing data in psychometric research, 139, 170
  data analysis examples, 159–165
  deletion method, 144
  direct estimation versus imputation, 156–159
  illustrative computer simulation, 142–143
  inclusive strategy, 155–156
  longitudinal data, designs for, 167–168
  MAR (missing at random) mechanism, 141, 143, 155, 156, 157, 161, 168
  matrix sampling designs, 165–166
  maximum likelihood (ML) estimations, 139, 144–149, 148f, 155, 158, 159–162, 159–164, 169, 170
  MCAR (missing completely at random) mechanism, 140, 141, 143, 155, 158, 160, 162, 168
  missing data mechanisms, 141–142
  multiple imputation, 139, 150–154, 162–165, 170
  NMAR (not missing at random) mechanism, 142, 143, 155, 156, 157
  older methods, 144
  planned missing data designs, 165–168
  power in, 168–170
  reliability, 143
  simulation techniques, 142–143, 144, 152, 153, 163, 167, 169

single imputation method, 144
three-form design, 166–167
ML *see* maximum likelihood (ML) estimations
MLTM (Multicomponent Latent Trait Model), 446
MM (manifest monotonicity), 432
MML (marginal maximum likelihood), 33, 67, 263, 423, 424, 497, 643
MNRM (multidimensional nominal response model), 452
modal-a-posterior (MAP) estimate, 67, 69, 424, 540
modification indices (MIs), 196–197
Mokken, R. J., 348, 428
Mokken scaling, 388n5, 431
Molenaar, D., 348–349, 352, 354, 358, 359, 430, 434
monotone homogeneity model (MHM), 428
monotonicity, 248
  checking, 432–434
  double monotonicity model (DMM), 428–430, 434
  manifest, 432
  monotone homogeneity model (MHM), 428
  multidimensional scaling, 387, 389
Monro, S., 269
Monte Carlo algorithm, 16, 25–26, 269, 273, 335
  see also simulation techniques
  Markov chain *see* MCMC (Markov chain Monte Carlo) algorithm
Montreal Children's Hospital Feeding Scale (MCH-FS), 316–320
Mooijaart, A., 351
Mooney, J. A., 448
Moore's Law, 576
Morrison, K. M., 10
Moses, T., 592, 600
Moustaki, I., 261, 264, 267
MPlus program
  ESEM procedure, 317
  Forced-Choice Five Factor Markers Questionnaire, 551–554
  forced-choice response formats, 546, 549, 551
  invariance testing, 42–43
  latent variable models, 271
  missing data handling methods, 143, 158, 159, 162, 163
  MPlus 7, 159

MPlus EFA program (maximum likelihood), 174
MPlus EFA program (multiple imputation), 179
MPlus imputation phase program (multiple imputation), 179
MPlus multiple group CFA with auxiliary variables (maximum likelihood), 178
MPlus multiple group CFA with constrained parameters, 184–185
MPlus multiple group CFA with constrained parameters (maximum likelihood), 177–178
MPlus multiple group CFA with unconstrained parameters (maximum likelihood), 177
MPlus multiple group CFA with unconstrained parameters (multiple imputation), 183–184
MPlus multiple group imputation phase program (multiple imputation), 182–183
MPlus two-stage reliability analysis and pooling program (multiple imputation), 180–181
MPlus two-stage reliability analysis (maximum likelihood), 174–176
number of factors problem, 317
power simulation with three-form design (maximum likelihood), 185
test development, 17, 21, 25, 26, 40, 42–43
WLSMV estimator, 40, 158, 160, 164, 864
Mroch, A. A., 432
MTMM (multitrait-multimethod) models, 20
  see also CFA–MTMM models
  applications for interchangeable raters, 814–815, 816t
  applications for structurally different raters, 801–824
  assumptions, 810
  blocks, 782
  CFA models for different measurement designs, 789–791
  choice of model, 806–807
  classical analysis, 781–785
  Correlated-Trait-Correlated-(Method-1) Model (CT-C(M-1)), 803–805
  correlation matrix, 782–783
  defining for interchangeable raters, 810–811, 811f, 812f, 813–814
  description of study, 801–803
  homogeneity of method variables, 810

MTMM (multitrait-multimethod) models (cont'd)
  M versus M-1 modeling approaches for structurally different methods, 807–808
  testing fit of the models, 803
Mulaik, S. A., 220, 222t, 225, 227, 235, 240, 291, 341
Multicomponent Latent Trait Model (MLTM), 446
multidimensional IRT equating, 658, 659
  equating with MIRT models, 660–661
  illustrative example, 661–663
  two simple models, 660
multidimensional item response theory *see* MIRT (multidimensional item response theory)
multidimensional nominal response model (MNRM), 452
multidimensional scaling *see* MDS (multidimensional scaling); metric multidimensional scaling; nonmetric multidimensional scaling
multidimensionality
  see also multidimensional IRT equating; multidimensional scaling; unidimensionality
  multidimensional item response theory *see* MIRT (multidimensional item response theory)
  unit-weighted scoring in the presence of, 692–694
multiple factor analysis, 221, 223
multiple imputation, missing data handling, 139, 150–154, 158, 162–165, 170
  analysis and pooling phases, 154
  categorical variables, 153–154, 158
  chained equations (fully conditional specification) approach, 151, 152, 153–154
  covariance matrix, 150, 151
  imputation phase, 150–153
  I-step, 150, 151
  multivariate normal variables, 150, 153
  P-step, 150, 151
  updated mean vector, 150, 151
multiple indicator multiple cause (MIMIC) models *see* MIMIC (multiple indicator multiple cause) models
multitrait-multimethod models *see* MTMM (multitrait-multimethod) models
multi-unidimensional pairwise-preference (MUPP) model, 533, 543–544

MUPP (multi-unidimensional pairwise-preference) model, 533, 543–544
Muthen, B., 348, 445
Mx codes, 356, 364–373

NAEP scales, 584, 585
National Council on Measurement in Education, 573
National Health Interview Survey, 102, 103
National Supported Work (NSW), 109, 110
Navy Computerized Adaptive Personality Scales (NCAPS), 524
NCAPS (Navy Computerized Adaptive Personality Scales), 524
NEAT (Nonequivalent groups with Anchor Test) design, 587, 588, 593
NEO-PIR test, 5, 7
Nering, M. L., 418
nested models *see* bifactor models
network psychometrics, 953–984
  example analyses, 971, 972f, 973
  Ising model, 957–962
    estimating, 967–971
    and IRT, 963–967
    proof of equivalence between the Ising model and MIRT, 979–981
    in psychometrics, 962–963
  Markov random fields, 954–955
  notation, 954
  parameterizing Markov random fields, 955–957
  psychometric models, interpretation of latent variables in, 973–977
neuroticism, 219–220
Newton, P., 759, 760, 761, 763
Newton–Raphson (N–R) maximization algorithm, 264–265, 268, 269, 273, 653–654
NIRT (nonparametric IRT), 427–434
  dimensionality, 430–432
  double monotonicity model (DMM), 428–430, 434
  monotone homogeneity model (MHM), 428
NMAR (not missing at random) mechanism, 142, 143, 155, 156, 157
nodes, graphs, 106, 107
nominal response model (NRM) *see* NRM (nominal response model)
NOMINATE method (Poole and Rosenthal), 910–914, 915f
nonlinearity, common factor analysis, 248–249

nonmetric multidimensional scaling, 378, 388–398, 390t, 391f, 393f, 395f, 396f
  substantive example, 398–399, 400t, 401
nonnormality, latent trait modeling, 347–373
  see also latent trait modeling; nonnormality
  benefits of testing, 359
  distribution of trait, 350–351
  estimation, 609–612
  examples, 356–358
  factor loading, 348–351, 355, 356–359
    level-dependent, 348, 349, 351, 354, 355, 359, 360
  factor model and existing approaches to test for sources of, 349–351
  future research, 360
  heteroscedasticity, 349, 351, 353–354, 358, 359
  identification, 354–355
  inconsistency in trait estimates, 359
  intelligence subtest scores, 356–357
  Law of Diminishing Returns, 347, 349
  model selection, 355–359
  Mx codes, 356, 364–373
  nonnormal factor distribution, 352
  nonparametric models, 348
  parametric models, 348, 351, 355
  self-reported affective analyzing item scores, 357–358
  skewed distribution, 349, 352, 357
  unified approach to test for, 352–359
nonparametric IRT see NIRT (nonparametric IRT)
nonprobability sampling, 96, 97
nonresponse bias, 96
nonsampling errors, 96
normal distribution
  central limit theorem, 348
  factor analysis, 347–348
  maximum likelihood (ML) estimations, 145–146, 147
norm-referenced tests, item content evaluation, 90
not missing at random see NMAR (not missing at random) mechanism
notation, 954
Novick, M. R., 56, 60, 62, 445, 496
N–R (Newton–Raphson) maximization algorithm, 264–265, 268, 269, 273, 653–654
NRM (nominal response model)
  multidimensional item response theory, 451–452

UIRT (unidimensional item response theory), 418–420, 435
NSW (National Supported Work), 109, 110
number of factors problem, 305–324
  see also CFMs (common factor models); common factor analysis; factor analysis
  assessment of the number of factors in empirical practice, 316–320
  categorizing criteria to indicate number of factors, 306–307
  criterion matching the hypothesized structure, importance, 305–306
  dimensionality, 307–309
  goodness of fit measures, 312, 313, 314–315
  Hull method, 315–316, 318
  Kaiser criterion, 309–310, 939
  likelihood ratio tests (LRTs), 313–314
  minimum average partial (MAP), 310–312
  personality trait psychology, 941–942
  scree test, 310
  simulation techniques, 310, 312, 313, 315–316
  statistical test versus major factors criteria, 307
  structural equation models (SEMs), selection methods in, 312–316
Nussbeck, F. W., 818
Nye, C. D., 888, 890–891

oblique rotation, 281, 334
  analytic oblique rotation algorithms, 288–290
  CF-Quartimax, 453, 459
  comparing with orthogonal, 300
observational studies, 104–105
observed score
  classical test theory (CTT), 49
  equating methods, 591–595
  equating scores on complete tests when using common items, 593–595
  equipercentile equating function, 592
  linear equating function, 592–593
  procedures for equating scores in a common population, 592
  standard error, 713–714
  and true score, 708
Occupational Personality Questionnaire (OPQ), 525, 540
Odbert, H. S., 717, 934
O'Dell, L. L., 295
Oh, I.-S., 32
Oh, M.-S., 410

Ohio Medicaid Assessment Survey (OMAS), 103–104
omnibus effect size, 115–116
OMT (Operant Motive Test), 540
one-parameter logistic model (IPLM), 255, 414, 416f, 423–424
Operant Motive Test (OMT), 540
OPQ (Occupational Personality Questionnaire), 525, 540
Optimal Classification (OC), 918–919
Ordeshook, P. C., 904
orthogonality, 234, 286, 3277, 332, 341
  orthogonal rotation, 279, 281, 300, 685
  orthogonal transformation matrices, 235
Osgood, C. E., 220
Ostini, R., 418
Owen, R. J., 512, 513

Pace, V. L., 944
Page, S. H., 76
pairwise algorithms, rotation
  closed-form, for quartic criteria, 288
  general line search algorithms, 288–289, 290
pairwise Markov random field (PMRF), 954, 955, 956, 957, 978
pairwise maximum likelihood (PML) estimation, 261–262, 263
PA–MRFA, 311–312, 318
Panel Study of Income Dynamics (PSID), 109
PAPI (Personality and Preference Inventory), 525
parallel analyses
  Horn's parallel analysis (Horn's PA), 311, 312, 315
  PA–MRFA/other variants, 311–312, 318
parallel measurements, 50, 53
parameter estimation
  see also AIPE (accuracy in parameter estimation), confirmatory power models
  Bayesian, 500–501
  latent trait modeling, 355
  multidimensional item response theory, 456
partial credit model (PCM), 420–421
Patterson, H. L., 76
Patz, R. J., 496
PCA (principal components analysis)
  causal indicators, 202
  and factor analysis, 240, 242
  number of factors problem, 306, 307, 309
  scale construction, 14, 15
PCM (partial credit model), 420–421
PCs (principal components), 309
Pearson, K., 211
Pearson correlation, 52, 58, 59, 312, 424
Peirce, C. S., 242
perceptual data, 919–923
Personality and Preference Inventory (PAPI), 525
personality/personality trait psychology, 933–951
  see also EPQ-R (Eysenck Personality Questionnaire); personality
  abnormal psychology, 5
  bifactor models, 325–326
  Big Five factors/personality traits, 220, 308, 540
  birthmarks of factor analysis in, 940, 941t, 942–943
  common factor analysis, 219–221, 222t
  example R Code, 950–951
  Five Factor Model (FFM) see Five Factor Model (FFM), personality, 934–935
  forced-choice response formats, 527
  and intelligence, 219
  interplay between tools, theories and data, 945–946
  lexical similarity between trait scales, 219
  number of factors problem, 943–944
  predictive validity, 8
  reliability, 18
  simulation techniques, 940, 941t, 943
  16PF (personality inventory), 220
  tests, 8, 220
  tools-to-theories heuristic, 933, 935–937
  traits, 219
Petersen, N. S., 586, 588, 600
Petter, S., 199
Pitoniak, M. J., 584
PIV (polychoric instrumental variable estimator), 261
planar rotations, 234
plausible values, Bayesian estimation, 509–511
PML (pairwise maximum likelihood) estimation, 261–262, 263
PMRF (pairwise Markov random field), 954, 955, 956, 957, 978
point-biserial correlation, 58–59, 66
political science, psychometric analysis, 903–931

Aldrich–McKelvey scaling, 920–923
Basic Space Theory, 904–908
IRT models, 914, 916–918
NOMINATE method (Poole and Rosenthal), 910–914, 915f
Optimal Classification (OC), 918–919
perceptual data, 919–923
preferential data, 909–919
polychoric instrumental variable estimator (PIV), 261
POLYEQUATE program, 654–655, 656
polytomous variables, 245
Poole, K. T., 410, 910–914, 915f, 917–918
post-stratification equating, 594
power analysis
  comparing a bifactor model and a second-order factor model, 128–130
  population model parameter of interest, 121–125
  for population model RMSEA, 118–119
  SEM, statistical theories for, 124–125
Preacher, K. J., 114, 299
precision matrix, 978
predictive criterion associations, 769
predictive validity evidence, 30–32
preference decision models, 535–536, 541, 543–544, 545
preferential data, 909–919
  NOMINATE method (Poole and Rosenthal), 910–914, 915f
Presser, S., 13
Preston, K., 419
primary sampling units (PSUs), 99
principal axis factoring, 315
principal components analysis see PCA (principal components analysis)
principles of psychometric testing, 3
probability sampling
  cluster sampling, 99–100, 101–102
  designs for, 97–104
  versus nonprobability sampling, 96
  simple random sampling (SRS), 97–98, 99, 100
  standard errors, 96
  stratified sampling, 98–99, 101
  survey weights, 101
proficiency, posterior-based measurement of, 501–507
  WinBUGS, simulation study using, 497, 503–507, 510, 514
propensity score matching (PSM), 109

see also survey sampling
bipartite/nonbipartite matching, 106, 108
design, 108–110
example (reevaluation of a job training program), 109–110
full matching, 108
Mahalanobis distance, 108
matching structure and algorithm, 106–107
observational studies, 104–105
one-to-k matching, 108
one-to-one matching, 108, 109
optimal matching, 106, 107
propensity score distance, 108
software, 108–109
variable matching, 108
PSID (Panel Study of Income Dynamics), 109
PSM see propensity score matching (PSM)
PSMATCH2 (propensity score matching software), 108–109
psychological well-being (PWB), versus subjective well-being (SWB), 338–340
psychometric validity, 751–777
see also validation
accuracy, 19, 763–769, 765t
appropriateness, 19–20, 24, 25, 28, 763, 769, 772
consensus issues, 756–760
consequences and fairness, 771–772
content, 767–768
decision making, 769
evolving notion of validity, 753–763
feasibility, 772
future steps, 760–763
need for, 752–753
relationships with other variables, 769–771
response processes, 765–767
structure, 768–769
theory testing, 769
psychopathy, 767, 768
psychoticism, 219, 220
Puhan, G., 583

Q-sort ranking, 525, 527
Quality of Life (QoL), 270, 271
Quartetti, D. A., 341
quartic criteria, rotation, 285, 288
quartimax rotation, comparing with varimax, 300–301
quartimin rotation, 285, 291, 292
quasi-homogeneous variables, 216

questionnaires
   see also EPQ-R (Eysenck Personality Questionnaire)
   Experience of Service Questionnaire (ESQ) *see* Experience of Service Questionnaire (ESQ)
   Forced-Choice Five Factor Markers Questionnaire, 539, 551–554
      attribute scores, estimating, 551
      coding and describing data, 546, 548
      measure, 545–546, 547–548*t*
      model setup, 551–554
      sample, 546
   forced-choice response formats, 526–528
   Job Contents Questionnaire (JCQ)
      CTA and CFA of, 195–196
      indicators, 193, 194
      mediation test on, 196–197
   multidimensional item response theory, 448
Quinn, K., 914

Rabe-Hesketh, S., 264
Rabinowitz, G. B., 387
Raftery, A. E., 410
Rai, A., 199
Raîche, G., 426
Raju, N. S., 886, 888
raking, 102
Ramsay, J. O., 410
random digit dialing (RDD) telephone survey, 102–104
random response errors, 17, 18, 57
randomized controlled experiments, 13, 104
Ranger, J., 426
Rasch model, 65, 414, 415, 421, 434
   network psychometrics, 969
   and scoring, 575, 579
Rausch, J. R., 115
Ravikumar, P., 968
raw scores, 21–22, 578, 651, 655
   typical, 579–580
Raykov, T., 49n1
real data
   bifactor modeling and evaluation of scale scores, 678
   rotation, 299–302
Reckase, M. D., 450
Reeve, C. L., 545
regression analysis, 89, 105, 109
   latent regression *see* latent regression
   least squares estimates *see* least squares estimates

linear regression, 109, 150, 153, 211
logistic regression, 105, 153
multidimensional scaling, 402
regression to the mean, 712–713
simple regression, 116
Reid, N., 262
Reise, S. P., 14, 418, 695
relative error, 62
reliability, 616–617, 707–749
   see also internal consistency
   attenuation, correction for, 711–712
   bifactor modeling and evaluation of scale scores, 689, 700
   classical test theory (CTT), 50, 51–58, 67
   of composites, 718–720, 721*f*, 738, 737*t*, 740
   congeneric measures, using, 715
   correlation coefficients, 712, 714–715, 726
   data sets used for demonstrations, 744–745
   of difference scores, 740
   empirical, 617
   generalizability theory, 736–738
   generic, 56
   IRT (item response theory), 67
   and item analysis, 724–728, 725*t*
   MAT test battery, 26, 28
   missing data handling methods, 143
   model-based, and bifactor model, 689
   over alternate forms, 716–717
   parallel tests, using, 714
   R functions, 744
   of ratings, and intraclass correlations, 738
   regression to the mean, 712–713
   sample R code for basic calculations, 745–749
   of scales formed from dichotomous or polytomous variables, 726, 728
   split half, 718–720, 721*f*
   stability over time, 717–718
   standard error of alpha, 723–724
   standard error of observed score, 713–714
   structural measures of and domain sampling theory, 728–736
   test development, 17–18
   theoretical, 616
   using, 711–714
   and validity, 711
   τ equivalent measures, using, 714–715
replicated MDS (RMDS), 406, 407
response probability (RP), 584
response processes, 19, 85, 765–767
response sets, 448–449

Revelle, W., 689
Revised NEO Personality Inventory (NEO-PI-R), 325
Richardson, M., 722
Richardson, S., 498
rights-scoring, 581
Rijmen, F., 455
Rindskopf, D., 341
Riverside Behavioral Q-sort, 525
Riverside Situational Q-sort, 525
RML (robust maximum likelihood), 261
RMSEA (root mean square error of approximation)
   see also sample size planning, confirmatory factor models
   AIPE for population model RMSEA, 119–121
   effect size, 116
   goodness of fit, 314
   latent variable models, 272
   MAT test battery, 25, 29, 31
   power analysis for population model RMSEA, 118–119
   sample size planning, confirmatory factor models, 116, 118–121
   scale construction, 16
Robbins, H., 269
robust maximum likelihood (RML), 261
robust WLS (robust weighted least squares), 312, 317
root mean square error of approximation *see* RMSEA (root mean square error of approximation)
Rose, T., 341
Rosenberg, S. L., 756, 757
Rosenthal, H., 910–914, 915*f*
Roskam, E., 76–77
rotation, 279–304
   analytic methods, 285–288, 288–290
      early, 287–288
   bifactor criteria, 286–287, 335
   biquartimin criterion, 287
   CF-varimax criterion, 285, 291, 292–293
   choice of method, 290–294
   closed-form pairwise algorithms, 288
   comparisons, 300–301
   Crawford–Ferguson criterion, 285, 293
   criteria, 285–287
   direct methods, 288
   EFA (exploratory factor analysis), 160*t*, 279, 280–281
   exploratory bifactor, 301–302
   general pairwise line search algorithms, 288–289, 290
   geomin criterion, 160, 163, 285–286, 292, 293, 318
   gradient projection (GP) algorithms, 234, 284*f*, 289–290
   graphical methods, 233, 282, 283*f*, 283*t*
   infinitesimal jackknife (IJK), 298, 299
   infomax criterion, 287, 291
   invariance, 239
   Jennrich–Butler analytic rotation, 685, 686–687
   less linear methods, 299
   minimum entropy criterion, 287
   oblique, 232, 281, 288–290, 300, 334, 453
   orthogonal, 279, 281, 300, 685
   planar rotations, 234
   problem-solving, 281–282
   pseudo-value methods, 298–299
   quartic criteria, 285, 288
   quartimax and varimax, comparing, 300–301
   quartimin, 285, 291, 292
   real data, examples using, 299–302
   reference structure and early analytic methods, 287–288
   simple structure *see* simple structure rotation
   sorted absolute loading (SAL) plots, 282
   standard errors for rotated loadings, 295–299
   target rotations, 334–335
   26-variable box problem (Thurstone), 282, 283*t*, 284*f*, 291
   unrotated factor matrix, 231, 232
   varimax method, 234, 238, 287, 300–301
rotational indeterminacy, 216
   personality trait psychology, 942–943
Rubin, D. B., 139, 141, 143, 154, 163, 588
Rubin, H., 295
Ruehlman, L. S., 140
rule-inferring ability, 217
Rulon, P. J., 719
Rulon's formula, 52
Rushton, J. P., 219
Ryff, C. D., 325

SAL (sorted absolute loading) plots, 282
Samejima, F., 445
Samejima's Graded Response model, 33

sample size planning, confirmatory factor
    models, 113–138
  see also AIPE (accuracy in parameter
    estimation), confirmatory power
    models; CFA (confirmatory factor
    analysis); effect size, sample size
    planning; RMSEA (root mean square
    error of approximation)
  empirical demonstrations, 117–131
  factor loading, 122, 124, 127, 128–129,
    130, 131
  importance of, 114
  as neglected aspect in research, 113–114
  null hypothesis, 115, 118, 121
  R Code, 132–138
  two-by-two conceptualization, 116, 117t
samples/sampling
  bias, 96
  cluster, 99–100, 101–102
  convenience samples, 96
  matrix sampling designs, 165–166, 168
  multistage sampling design, 507–511
  nonprobability, 96, 97
  piloting of test, 13
  population representative, 21
  primary sampling units (PSUs), 99
  probability see probability sampling
  selection of sample, 589
  strata in, 99, 100, 102, 103, 104, 105
  stratified, 98–99, 101
  survey sampling see survey sampling
  systematic, 97–98
sampling errors, 8, 96, 97, 242, 295
Sampson, P. F., 234, 288, 289
Saris, W. E., 124
Sass, D. A., 291, 292, 293
SAT (Scholastic Assessment Test), 75
Satorra, A., 124, 261, 298
Satorra–Saris method, sample size planning,
    122–125
scalar invariance, 854–855
  code for testing, 875–876
scale construction
  see also scales/scaling
  Bayesian scale construction (BSC),
    511–514
  bifactor models, 340–341
  confirmatory factor analysis (CFA), 13,
    14, 15
  Dutch intelligence scale construction,
    513–514
  factor analysis, 14–15

item response theory (IRT), 13, 14
maximum likelihood (ML)
  estimation, 15–16
multidimensional item response theory, 455
principal components analysis, 14, 15
test development, 13–17
scales/scaling
  see also multidimensional scaling; scale
    construction; scores/scoring
  Basic Space Theory, 908
  causal indicators, scale development with,
    197–199
  CFA (confirmatory factor analysis), 13,
    14, 15
  content information, incorporating,
    584–585
  defining, 581–585
  forced-choice response formats see forced-
    choice response formats; forced-choice
    response formats
  item response theory (IRT), 13, 14
  MAT test battery, 26, 28
  normative information, incorporating into
    scores, 582–583
  purpose of scales, 305
  refinement, 198–199
  scale anchoring, 584–585
  scales formed from dichotomous or
    polytomous variables, 726, 728
  score precision, incorporating into scale,
    583–584
  similarity, 3
  single scale versus test battery, 3
  test development, 13–17
Schafer, J. L., 143, 150, 153
Schmid, J., 455
Schmid–Leiman transformation, 218, 326,
    330–331, 334, 685, 731, 732
  see also bifactor models
Schmidt, F. L., 8, 17, 18, 33
Schmidt, T. A., 292, 293
Schmitt, T., A., 291, 292, 293
Schneider, R. J., 543
Scholastic Assessment Test (SAT), 75
Schönemann, P., 905
science test
  IRT equating, 656–657, 658t
  IRT linking, 649–651, 652t
Score Equity Assessment (SEA), 598
scores/scoring
  see also scales/scaling
  aligning, 598, 599

anchor items, checking that acting like common items, 589
anchor test design issues, 596–597
applying IRT scoring methods/estimating measurement accuracy, 617–619
bifactor modeling and evaluation of scale scores, 677–707
choice of system, 22
classical test theory (CTT), 49, 58
composite scores, 580
data collection designs, 585–588
data preprocessing practices, 588–591
discrete distribution, continuizing, 590
equating of scores, 598, 599–601
  in a common population, 592
  on complete tests, using common items, 593–595
  description, 600
  equipercentile equating function, 592
  goal of equating, 600
  linear equating function, 592–593
  observed-score equating methods, 591–595
  pitfalls, 595–597
  procedures and practices for, 588–598
  requirements, 600–601
external anchors, 597
factor scores, 15, 22, 238–239
individual score approach, 336n4, 337
internal anchors, 597
ipsative scores, 530–531
IRT scoring methods, applying, 617–619
item scores, 578, 579
measurement conditions, 576–577
measurement in practice, 574–575
multidimensional IRT "correlated traits" model, scoring under, 623–624, 635–636
normative information, incorporating into, 582–583
population invariance, lack of, 597–598
prediction, 598, 599
prerequisites, 574–578
presmoothing score distributions, 590–591
procedures and practices for equating, 588–598
raw scores, 21–22, 578, 651, 655, 657
results, whether reasonable, 598
sample size issues, 595–596
score precision, incorporating into scale, 583–584

self-reported affective analyzing item scores, 357–358
standardized scores, 22
test development, 21–22
test specifications, 577–578
test taker, 581
total score approach, 336, 337
typical item scores, 579
typical raw scores, 579–580
unidimensional EAP method, ESQ satisfaction scored by, 619–623, 621t
unidimensional IRT model, 424, 619–620, 621t, 622–623
  ESQ satisfaction, 619–623, 621t
unit scores, 578, 692–694
weighted schemes, 21
scree point, 229
scree test, 310, 315
scree-plot, 310
second-order factors, 5, 8, 216, 218, 332, 341
  comparing a bifactor model and a second-order factor model, 128–130, 327–331
  uses of second-order models, 328
selection bias, 96
Self Perception Profile for Children (SPPC), 419–420
SEM *see* standard error of measurement (SEM); structural equation model (SEM)
separate calibration, 641–642, 645, 657
SES *see* socioeconomic status (SES)
Shaffer, J. A., 771
Shapiro, S. S., 348, 349
Shavelson, R. J., 63
Shaw, S., 759, 760, 76, 763
Sheehan, K. M., 83
Shell, P., 10, 81
Shepard, R. N., 410
Shepard diagram, 385, 392, 393f, 395f, 396f
Shepard–Nosofsky–Ennis model, 905
Shoemaker, D. M., 165
SIFASP (simultaneous factor analysis in several populations), 886
Siguaw, J. A., 199
Sijtsma, K., 426, 430–431, 434
Silvey, S., 296
Simms, L. J., 340
simple random sampling (SRS), 97–98, 99, 100

simple structure rotation, 216, 231–235,
236–237t, 238, 241, 281, 282
  see also common factor analysis; exploratory factor analysis (EFA); factor analysis; rotation
  factor-pattern matrix, 234, 235, 236–237t
  hyperplanes, 232–233
  new methods, 235
  oblique simple structure, 232
  reference structure matrix, 233
  varimax method, 234, 238
simulation techniques
  see also computerized testing
  Bayesian estimation, 495–496, 502, 503–507, 514
  bifactor models, 341, 693, 694, 696
  comparative studies, 310, 313, 315–316
  and computers, 142–143, 169
  differential item and test functioning, 887
  factorial invariance, 856
  fairness measurement, 28
  latent trait modeling, 349
  latent variable models, 262
  MCMC programs, 917, 921
  and measurement conditions, 576
  minimum average partial (MAP), 310
  missing data handling methods, 142–143, 144, 152, 153, 163, 167, 169
  Monte Carlo algorithm, 16, 26, 335
  number of factors problem, 310, 312, 313, 315–316
  parallel analysis (PA), 312
  personality trait psychology, 940, 941t, 943
  reliability, 728
  test development, 16, 25, 26
  WinBUGS, study using, 497, 503–507, 510, 514
single imputation method, 144
single scale versus test battery, 3
single-group (SG) design, data collection, 586
single-stimulus format, 523
Sinharay, S., 589
Sireci, S. G., 759
SIV (Survey of Interpersonal Values), 525
16PF (personality inventory), 220
Skrondal, A., 264
Smits, I. A. M., 354
Snijders, T. A. B., 426
Social Inhibition (SI) Scale, 417
Society for Multivariate Experimental Psychology (SMEP), 225

socioeconomic status (SES)
  Bayesian estimation, 510
  and causal indicators, 187, 197, 198
Sörbom, D., 851, 889
sorted absolute loading (SAL) plots, 282
Sousa, K. H., 299–300, 301, 302, 677
spatial voting model, 903
Spearman, C., 211–215, 217, 332, 347, 349, 707, 714, 937, 945, 973
Spearman–Brown prophecy formula, 52, 57
specifications, test, 22–23
Spiegelhalter, D., 498
spontaneous magentization, 959
SPPC (Self Perception Profile for Children), 419–420
SRMR (standardized root mean square residual), 16, 314–315, 317, 699
SRS (simple random sampling), 97–98, 99, 100
stability coefficients, 17
standard error of measurement (SEM), 613
  CTT (classical test theory), 50, 51, 53, 57, 58, 69
  generalizability theory, 62, 69
  IRT (item response theory), 67, 68
  item response theory (IRT), 67, 69
  strong true-score theory (STT), 60
standard errors
  see also standard error of measurement (SEM); standard errors, rotated loadings
  of alpha, 723–724
  maximum likelihood (ML) estimation, 159
  observed score, 713–714
  probability sampling, 96
standard errors, rotated loadings, 279, 295–299
  asymptotic distribution, 297–298
  of initial loadings, using, 295–296
  constrained maximum likelihood methods, 296–297
  historical note, 295
standard setting, 584
standardized root mean square residual (SRMR), 16, 314–315, 317, 699
Standards for Educational and Psychological Testing (AERA), 4
standards-based tests, item content evaluation, 90–91
Stark, S., 435, 543, 887, 888, 890
STATA, xvi, 26, 104, 109, 409
  test development, 22, 26

state–trait–occasion model, 717
statistical specifications, 578
Stegeman, A., 354
Steinberg, L., 448
stepwise forward procedure, LRTs, 313–314
stochastic imputation/approximation, 270
Stocking, M. L., 642, 645
Stout, W., 432
Straat, J. H., 430–431
stratified sampling, 98–99, 101
Straub, D., 199
strict invariance, 855
  code for testing, 877–878, 882–884
strong true-score theory (STT) *see* STT (strong true-score theory)
structural equation models (SEMs), xv, 258, 260
  and bifactor models, 694–696
  CFMs as special case, 312–316
  confirmatory factor models, 113, 124–125, 243
  latent variable models, 271
  missing data handling methods, 149
  selection methods, 312–316
  software, 333
  statistical theories for power analysis, 124–125
  test development, 14, 20, 30
STT (strong true-score theory), 59–61
  assumptions, 59
  beta distribution, 60–61
  binomial distribution, 61
  and CTT, 59, 60, 69
  dichotomous items, 59
  and generalizability theory, 62
  and IRT, 67
  as item-level theory, 59
  two-parameter beta distribution, 60–61
STUIRT program, 645, 650
Sturm, T., 936
Suárez-Falcón, J. C., 426
subjective well-being (SWB)
  bifactor model, 325, 326f
  versus psychological well-being (PWB), 338–340
Suci, G. J., 220
Survey of Interpersonal Values (SIV), 525
survey sampling, 95–104
  see also probability sampling; propensity score matching
  cluster sampling, 99–100, 101–102
  element, 96

good quality samples, 95–96
nonresponse, 102
Ohio Medicaid Assessment Survey (OMAS), 103–104
population, 96
probability and nonprobability samples, 96
propensity scoring, 95
random digit dialing (RDD) telephone survey, 102–104
sampling frame, 96
sampling unit, 96
simple random sampling (SRS), 97–98, 99, 100
stratified sampling, 98–99, 101
survey weights, 101–104
terminologies, 95–97, 99
Swaminathan, H., 496
Swineford, S., 327, 334, 682
synthetic population, 593
systematic domain mapping, 6–7
systematic error, 57
systematic sampling, 97–98

Tailored Adaptive Personality Assessment System (TAPAS), 524, 544
Takane, Y., 410
Tannenbaum, P. H., 220
Tanner, M. A., 502
TAPAS (Tailored Adaptive Personality Assessment System), 524, 544
targeted effect size, 115–116
TCC (test characteristic curve), 888
team size, 3–4
Tedlie, J. C., 677
telephone survey, RDD, 102–104
Tellegen, A., 701–702
template approach, item generation, 79–80, 88–89
Tendeiro, J. N., 426–427
test administration, 10
test characteristic curve (TCC), 888
test development, 3–47
  see also MAT (test battery for managerial position recruitment)
  bifactor models in, 325–326
  broad versus narrow spectrum tests, 3
  construct definition, 5, 10
  definition of test, 3
  empirical advances, 6
  implementation and testing, 23–24
  item development, 10–13
  item review, 12–13

test development (cont'd)
  length of process, 77
  meta-analysis, 8–9
  motivations for, 5–6
  piloting of test, 12, 13
  planning, 9–10
  practical (market) need, 6, 7–8
  publications of relevance to, 4
  reliability, 17–18
  scale construction, 13–17
  scale similarity, 3
  scoring and norming, 21–22
  single scale versus test battery, 3
  specifications, 22–23
  stages, 4
  systematic domain mapping, 6–7
  team size, 3–4
  theoretical advancements, 6
  validation, 18–21
test information function (TIF), 615–616
TestGraf program, 434
testlet response model, 455
test-retest design, 717
  CTT (classical test theory), 51–52
  generalizability theory, 62
  test development, 17, 34
TetradSEM, 195
Thayer, D. T., 586, 591
Theunissen, T. J. J. M., 512
think-aloud protocols, 767
Thissen, D., 63, 426, 447, 448, 449, 452, 661
Thissen-Roe, A., 447, 449
Thorndike, R. L., 57
three-form design, missing data handling, 166–167
three-parameter logistic (3PL) model, in IRT, 64–65, 505, 506
three-parameter model (3PLM), 415, 417, 425, 434
Thurstone, L. L., 10, 15, 215–217, 224–225, 228, 232–234, 239, 241, 281, 282, 284, 287, 291, 534, 535, 536, 933
Thurstonian IRT model, 534–540, 545
  applications, 540
  measurement model for attributes, 536–538
  pairwise comparisons, 538
  preference decision model, 535–536
  technical detail, 538–540
Tibshirani, R., 968
Timmerman, M. E., 354
Ting, K.-F., 194–195
Titterington, D. M., 269

TLI (Tucker–Lewis index), 16, 116, 272
tools-to-theories heuristic, 934, 935–937
  FFM as an example, 937–945
  interrelation of tools, data and theories, 936–937
topic definition, 11
Torgerson, W. S., 379, 410, 529, 904–905
total score approach, 336, 337
total variance, common factor model, 223
Treiblmaier, H., 201
true score
  classical test theory (CTT), 49, 707
  item response theory equating, 653–654
  and observed score, 708
  theory, 714–715
Tsutakawa, R. K., 496
Tucker–Lewis Index (TLI), 16, 116, 272
Tukey, J. W., 584
Turner, N. E., 230
Turner, S., 80
26-variable box problem (Thurstone), 282, 283t, 284f, 291
2PL MIRT model, 449–451
two-parameter Birnbaum model (2PLM), 415, 423, 434
two-parameter logistic (2PL) model, 65, 85, 255, 580

UIRT (unidimensional item response theory), 63, 64, 413–443
  assumptions and basic ideas, 414–415, 416f, 417–418
  checking monotonicity and invariant item ordering, 432–434
  dichotomous parametric item response models, 414–418
  generalized partial credit model, 421
  graded response model, 421–422
  ideal point models, 435
  item parameters estimation, 422–424
  model data fit, 424–427
    item and model fit, 424–426
    misfit, 427
    person fit, 426–427
  model selection, 434–435
  nominal response model (NRM), 418–420, 435
  nonparametric IRT, 427–434
    dimensionality, 430–432
    double monotonicity model (DMM), 428–430, 434
    monotone homogeneity model (MHM), 428

one-parameter logistic model (IPLM), 414, 416f, 423–424
partial credit model (PCM), 420–421
polytomous models, 418–422
Rasch model, 414, 415, 421, 434
scoring under, 619–620, 621t, 622–623
standard models, 413
test scoring and information, 424
three-parameter model (3PLM), 415, 417, 423, 434
two-parameter Birnbaum model (2PLM), 415, 423, 434
ULS (unweighted least squares), 256, 258, 259, 261, 312
ULSMV (unweighted least squares with robust standard errors), 546
underlying variable (UV) approach, 254–255, 260
unidimensional item response theory *see* UIRT (unidimensional item response theory)
unidimensional pairwise preferences, 533, 540–543
unidimensionality (UD)
  see also dimensionality; multidimensionality; UIRT (unidimensional item response theory); unidimensional item response testing
  assumption of, 414
  departures from, 678–682, 683t
  multi-unidimensional pairwise-preference (MUPP) model, 533, 543–544
  Zinnes–Griggs model (unidimensional pairwise preferences), 540–543, 542f, 544, 545
unit scores, 578
univariate log-likelihoods, 262
unweighted least squares (ULS), 256, 258, 259, 261, 312
unweighted least squares with robust standard errors (ULSMV), 546
UV (underlying variable) approach, 254–255, 260

validation
  see also psychometric validity
  appropriateness of using test for a given purpose, 19–20
  convergent validity, 20, 34
  criterion relations, 20
  CTT (classical test theory), 58
  divergent validity, 20
  feasibility, 21
  ipsative scores distorting construct validity, 531
  ipsative scores distorting criterion-related validity, 531
  relations with related and unrelated constructs, 20
  response processes, 19
  test content and structure, 19
  test development, 18–21
  unitary models, 19
validity evidence, 763, 764
Van Abswoude, A. A. H., 432
Van der Ark, L. A., 430–431, 432
Van der Linden, W. J., 418, 422, 498, 500, 511, 512, 886
Van der Maas, H. I., 359
Van der Sluis, S., 359
Van Heerden, J., 703
Van Krimpen-Stoop, E. M. L. A., 426
variance, common factor model, 223
varimax rotation, 234, 238, 287
  comparing with quartimax, 300–301
Varin, C., 261
Veldkamp, B. P., 513, 514
verbal ability, 188, 215, 332
Verhelst, N. D., 348–349
Vidoni, P., 261
Von Davier, A. A., 586, 587, 588, 593

Wahba, S., 109, 110
Wainer, H., 65, 455, 496
Wald test, 355
Walker, M. E., 573, 579
Wanders, R. B. K., 427
Wang, X., 65, 455, 496
Webb, E., 219
Webb, N. M., 63
weighted least squares (WLS), 256, 258, 312, 313
weighted multidimensional scaling (WMDS), 407–408
well-being
  bifactor modeling of, 339–340
  eudemonic tradition, 338
  hedonic theories, 338
  psychological well-being (PWB), versus subjective well-being (SWB), 338–340
  theories of, 338–339
Wendler, C., 579
West, S. G., 299–300, 301, 302, 677
Wexler, N., 295
Widaman, K., 190, 242, 783
Wilks, M. B., 348, 349

WinBUGS software package, 497, 503–507, 510, 514
Wingersky, M., 83, 591
WLS (weighted least squares), 256, 258, 312, 313
WMDS (weighted multidimensional scaling), 407–408
Wong, W. H., 502
Woodcock–Johnson IV battery of cognitive tests, 3, 5, 7
working memory load, 81, 82, 86, 89
Wright, N. A., 887

XML programming code, 82–83

Yang, J. S., 455
Yang-Wallentin, F., 261

Yates, A., 285–286
Yen, W. M., 425–426
Ying, Z., 512–513
Yule, G. U., 211
Yung, Y.-F., 331
Yun-Tein, J., 28

Zedeck, S., 18
Zhang, G., 299
Zhang, J., 432
Zimmerman, D. W., 825
Zinbarg, R. E., 690
Zinnes, J. L., 540, 541
Zinnes–Griggs model (unidimensional pairwise preferences), 540–543, 542f, 544, 545
Zwick, R., 584
Zwinderman, A. H., 513